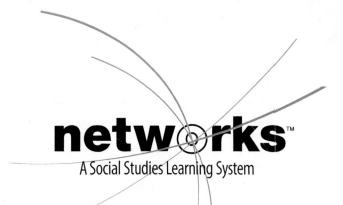

networks™
A Social Studies Learning System

Teacher Edition

INDIANA
DISCOVERING
WORLD
GEOGRAPHY
Western Hemisphere

Richard G. Boehm, Ph. D.

Mc
Graw
Hill
Education

About the Cover: Bolivian girl dressed for annual carnival; Nevado Sajama, an extinct volcano and Bolivia's highest peak

Front cover: ©Peter Langer/Design Pics/Corbis; Jack Goldfarb/Getty Images; Dominic Cram/Getty Images; ©Ocean/Corbis; peter zelei/Getty Images; (bkgd)Grant Dixon/Lonely Planet Images/Getty Images.

Back cover: Nash Photos/Getty Images; John Coletti/Getty Images; altrendo travel/Getty Images; ©Jeff Henry/Corbis; Design Pics/Don Hammond; Grant Dixon/Lonely Planet Images/Getty Images.

Understanding By Design® is a registered trademark of the Association for Supervision and Curriculum Development ("ASCD").

National Council for the Social Studies (NCSS), National Curriculum Standards for Social Studies: A Framework for Teaching, Learning, and Assessment (Silver Spring, MD: NCSS, 2010). See www.socialstudies.org/standards.

Heffron, Susan Gallagher and Roger M. Downs, eds. Geography for Life: National Geography Standards, Second Edition, Copyright 2012. National Council for Geographic Education, 1145 17th Street NW, Rm. 7620, Washington, D.C., 20036.

www.mheonline.com

Send all inquiries to:
McGraw-Hill Education
8787 Orion Place
Columbus, OH 43240

Teacher Edition
ISBN: 978-0-02-136077-2
MHID: 0-02-136077-4

Student Edition
ISBN: 978-0-02-136073-4
MHID: 0-02-136073-1

Printed in the United States of America.

2 3 4 5 6 7 MER 18 17 16 15

SENIOR AUTHOR

Richard G. Boehm, Ph.D., was one of the original authors of *Geography for Life: National Geography Standards,* which outlined what students should know and be able to do in geography. He was also one of the authors of the *Guidelines for Geographic Education*, in which the Five Themes of Geography were first articulated. Dr. Boehm has received many honors, including "Distinguished Geography Educator" by the National Geographic Society (1990), the "George J. Miller Award" from the National Council for Geographic Education (NCGE) for distinguished service to geographic education (1991), "Gilbert Grosvenor Honors" in geographic education from the Association of American Geographers (2002), and the NCGE's "Distinguished Mentor Award" (2010). He served as president of the NCGE, has twice won the Journal of Geography award for best article, and also received the NCGE's "Distinguished Teaching Achievement." Presently, Dr. Boehm holds the Jesse H. Jones Distinguished Chair in Geographic Education at Texas State University in San Marcos, Texas, where he serves as director of The Gilbert M. Grosvenor Center for Geographic Education. His most current project includes the production of the video-based professional development series, *Geography: Teaching With the Stars*. Available programs may be viewed at www.geoteach.org.

CONTRIBUTING AUTHORS

Jay McTighe has published articles in a number of leading educational journals and has coauthored 10 books, including the best-selling *Understanding by Design* series with Grant Wiggins. McTighe also has an extensive background in professional development and is a featured speaker at national, state, and district conferences and workshops. He received his undergraduate degree from the College of William and Mary, earned a master's degree from the University of Maryland, and completed post-graduate studies at the Johns Hopkins University.

Dinah Zike, M.Ed., is an award-winning author, educator, and inventor recognized for designing three-dimensional, hands-on manipulatives and graphic organizers known as Foldables®. Foldables are used nationally and internationally by parents, teachers, and other professionals in the education field. Zike has developed more than 150 supplemental educational books and materials. Her two latest books, *Notebook Foldables®* and *Foldables®, Notebook Foldables®, & VKVs® for Spelling and Vocabulary 4th–12th* were each awarded *Learning Magazine's* Teachers' Choice Award for 2011. In 2004 Zike was honored with the CESI Science Advocacy Award. She received her M.Ed. from Texas A&M, College Station, Texas.

ACADEMIC CONSULTANTS

William H. Berentsen, Ph.D.
Professor of Geography and European Studies
University of Connecticut
Storrs, Connecticut

David Berger, Ph.D.
Ruth and I. Lewis Gordon Professor of Jewish History
Dean, Bernard Revel Graduate School
Yeshiva University
New York, New York

R. Denise Blanchard, Ph.D.
Professor of Geography
Texas State University–San Marcos
San Marcos, Texas

Brian W. Blouet, Ph.D.
Huby Professor of Geography and International Education
The College of William and Mary
Williamsburg, Virginia

Olwyn M. Blouet, Ph.D.
Professor of History
Virginia State University
Petersburg, Virginia

Maria A. Caffrey, Ph.D.
Lecturer, Department of Geography
University of Tennessee
Knoxville, Tennessee

So-Min Cheong, Ph.D.
Associate Professor of Geography
University of Kansas
Lawrence, Kansas

Alasdair Drysdale, Ph.D.
Professor of Geography
University of New Hampshire
Durham, New Hampshire

Rosana Ferreira, Ph.D.
Assistant Professor of Geography and Atmospheric Science
East Carolina University
Greenville, North Carolina

Eric J. Fournier, Ph.D.
Associate Professor of Geography
Samford University,
Birmingham, Alabama

Matthew Fry, Ph.D.
Assistant Professor of Geography
University of North Texas
Denton, Texas

Douglas W. Gamble, Ph.D.
Professor of Geography
University of North Carolina
Wilmington, North Carolina

Gregory Gaston, Ph.D.
Professor of Geography
University of North Alabama
Florence, Alabama

Jeffrey J. Gordon, Ph.D.
Associate Professor of Geography
Bowling Green State University
Bowling Green, Ohio

Alyson L. Greiner, Ph.D.
Associate Professor of Geography
Oklahoma State University
Stillwater, Oklahoma

William J. Gribb, Ph.D.
Associate Professor of Geography
University of Wyoming
Laramie, Wyoming

Joseph J. Hobbs, Ph.D.
Professor of Geography
University of Missouri
Columbia, Missouri

Ezekiel Kalipeni, Ph.D.
Professor of Geography and Geography Information Science
University of Illinois
Urbana, Illinois

Pradyumna P. Karan, Ph.D.
Research Professor of Geography
University of Kentucky
Lexington, Kentucky

Christopher Laingen, Ph.D.
Assistant Professor of Geography
Eastern Illinois University
Charleston, Illinois

Jeffrey Lash, Ph.D.
Associate Professor of Geography
University of Houston–Clear Lake
Houston, Texas

Jerry T. Mitchell, Ph.D.
Research Professor of Geography
University of South Carolina
Columbia, South Carolina

Thomas R. Paradise, Ph.D.
Professor, Department of Geosciences and the King Fahd Center for Middle East Studies
University of Arkansas
Fayetteville, Arkansas

David Rutherford, Ph.D.
Assistant Professor of Public Policy and Geography
Executive Director, Mississippi Geographic Alliance
University of Mississippi
University, Mississippi

Dmitrii Sidorov, Ph.D.
Professor of Geography
California State University
Long Beach, California

Amanda G. Smith, Ph.D.
Professor of Education
University of North Alabama
Florence, Alabama

Jeffrey S. Ueland, Ph.D.
Associate Professor of Geography
Bemidji State University
Bemidji, Minnesota

Fahui Wang, Ph.D.
Professor of Geography
Louisiana State University
Baton Rouge, Louisiana

TEACHER REVIEWERS

Precious Steele Boyle, Ph.D.
Cypress Middle School
Memphis, TN

Jason E. Albrecht
Moscow Middle School
Moscow, ID

Jim Hauf
Berkeley Middle School
Berkeley, MO

Elaine M. Schuttinger
Trinity Catholic School
Columbus, OH

Mark Stahl
Longfellow Middle School
Norman, OK

Mollie Shanahan MacAdams
Southern Middle School
Lothian, MD

Sara Burkemper
Parkway West Middle Schools
Chesterfield, MO

Alicia Lewis
Mountain Brook Junior High School
Birmingham, AL

Steven E. Douglas
Northwest Jackson Middle School
Ridgeland, MS

LaShonda Grier
Richmond County Public Schools
Martinez, GA

Samuel Doughty
Spirit of Knowledge Charter School
Worcester, MA

CONTENTS

UNIT ONE

Prisma/SuperStock

Carsten Peter/National Geographic/
Getty Images

CONTENTS

©Hugh Sitton/Corbis

UNIT TWO

©Christopher Morris/VII/Corbis

Just One Film/The Image Bank/
Getty Image

Michelle Gilders Canada West/Alamy

©Sergio Pitamitz/Robert Harding World Imagery/Corbis

UNIT THREE

Silvia Izquierdo/AP Images

CONTENTS

UNIT FOUR

Christophe Boisvieux/age fotostock

CHAPTER 12

Dmitry Kostyukov/AFP/Getty Images

CHAPTER 13

FEATURES

Indiana CONNECTION

GLOBAL CONNECTIONS

What Do You Think?

Thinking Like a Geographer

MAPS

CHARTS, GRAPHS, DIAGRAMS, AND INFOGRAPHICS

Videos

Every lesson has a video to help you learn more about your world!

 ## Infographics

Chapter 2
Lesson 3 Fresh and Salt Water in the World

Chapter 9
Lesson 2 Important Crops: Tropical North

 ## Interactive Charts/Graphs

Chapter 2
Lesson 1 Rain Shadow; Climate Zones

Chapter 3
Lesson 1 Understanding Population
Lesson 3 Economic Questions

Chapter 5
Lesson 3 Hispanic Population Growth

 ## Animations

Chapter 1
Lesson 1 The Earth; Regions of Earth
Lesson 2 Elements of a Globe

Chapter 2
Lesson 1 Earth's Daily Rotation; Earth's Layers; Seasons on Earth
Lesson 3 How the Water Cycle Works

Chapter 3
Global Connections: Social Media

Chapter 4
Lesson 2 Down the Mississippi

Chapter 5
Lesson 1 Chinooks

Chapter 7
Lesson 1 Waterways as Political Boundaries
Global Connections: NAFTA

Chapter 8
Global Connections: The Rain Forest and Resources

Chapter 12
Lesson 1 How the Alps Formed
Global Connections: A Budget Game

 ## Slide Shows

Chapter 1
Lesson 1 Spatial Effect; Places Change Over Time
Lesson 2 Special Purpose Maps; History of Mapmaking

Chapter 2
Lesson 1 Effects of Climate Change
Lesson 2 Human Impact on Earth

Chapter 3
Lesson 1 Different Places in the World

Chapter 4
Lesson 1 Agriculture East of the Mississippi
Lesson 2 Early Settlements; Immigrate/Emigrate

Chapter 5
Lesson 1 Bodies of Water: West of the Mississippi; How the Hoover Dam Works
Lesson 3 NAFTA; Economic Terms: Private and Public Sector

Chapter 6
Lesson 2 The First Peoples in Canada

Chapter 8
Lesson 1 Landforms of Brazil
Lesson 2 Brazil's Natural Products
Lesson 3 Brazilian Culture

Chapter 9
Lesson 1 Mining Emeralds
Lesson 3 What Is Carnival?

Chapter 10
Lesson 1 Landforms: Andean Region
Lesson 3 Traditional and Modern Lifestyles

Chapter 11
Lesson 1 Agriculture in Western Europe
Lesson 2 World War II

Chapter 12
Lesson 2 The Renaissance
Lesson 3 Recreation in Northern and Southern Europe

Jochen Schlenker/Photographer's Choice/Getty Images

Interactive Maps

Interactive Images

Games

Chapter 1
Lesson 1 True or False
Lesson 2 Concentration; Map Legends

Chapter 2
Lesson 1 Fill in the Blank
Lesson 2 Tic-Tac-Toe
Lesson 3 Columns

Chapter 3
Lesson 1 Crossword
Lesson 2 Identification
Lesson 3 Flashcard; Economic Systems; Bartering and Trade

Chapter 4
Lesson 1 Concentration
Lesson 2 Identification
Lesson 3 Columns

Chapter 5
Lesson 1 Climate Vocabulary; Flashcard
Lesson 2 Tic-Tac-Toe
Lesson 3 Fill in the Blank

Chapter 6
Lesson 1 Columns
Lesson 2 True or False
Lesson 3 Crossword

Chapter 7
Lesson 1 Columns
Lesson 2 Flashcard
Lesson 3 Tic-Tac-Toe

Chapter 8
Lesson 1 Crossword
Lesson 2 Fill in the Blank
Lesson 3 True or False

Chapter 9
Lesson 1 Concentration
Lesson 2 Identification
Lesson 3 Tic-Tac-Toe

Chapter 10
Lesson 1 Crossword
Lesson 2 Columns

Chapter 11
Lesson 1 Concentration
Lesson 2 Flashcard
Lesson 3 Identification

Chapter 12
Lesson 1 Columns
Lesson 2 Fill in the Blank
Lesson 3 Crossword

Chapter 13
Lesson 1 Columns
Lesson 2 Tic-Tac-Toe
Lesson 3 Concentration

▼ Presentation Resources

INTERACTIVE WHITEBOARD ACTIVITIES

Unit 1
The World Video Montage
Drag-and-Drop Physical Geography Game of the World
Interactive World Maps

Chapter 1 Time Line and Map of the World
Lesson 1 Drag-and-Drop Vocabulary Game
Chart of the Six Essential Elements
Animation of Relative Location
Spatial Effect
Lesson 2 Forms of Technology Graphic Organizer
Map Legends

Chapter 2
Lesson 1 World Climates Map
Chart of How Temperature and Precipitation Affect Biomes
Lesson 2 Architecture for Earthquakes Slide Show
Lesson 3 Physical Geography of Earth Map
Population of Earth Map
Uses of Water for Recreation vs. Livelihood Graphic Organizer

Chapter 3
Lesson 1 Population Changes Slide Show
Population Density Map
Why Do People Move? Graphic Organizer
Lesson 2 Elements of Culture Graphic Organizer
Chart of the Major World Religions
Chart of Different Types of Government
Lesson 3 Drag-and-Drop Economic Systems Game
Types of Economic Activities and Sectors Interactive Image
GDP Around the World Graph
Bartering and Trade Game

Unit 2
North America Video Montage
Drag-and-Drop Physical Geography Game of North America
Interactive Maps of North America

Chapter 4 Time Line and Map of United States: East of the Mississippi
Lesson 1 Region Map of East Coast of U.S.
The Gulf Coast Region Interactive Image
Animation of How the Great Lakes Were Formed
The Atlantic Coast Fall Line Map
Lesson 2 Early History of the Eastern United States Time Line
Colonial Expansion Map
Lesson 3 Where People Live Graphic Organizer
Eastern United States Population Map
Economic Growth Chart

Chapter 5 Time Line and Map of United States: West of the Mississippi
Lesson 1 Physical Geography of the Western United States Map
Climates of the Western United States Map
Landforms of the Western United States Graphic Organizer
Drag-and-Drop Resources of the West Game
Lesson 2 Missions and Pueblos Interactive Images
Time Line of Notable Events of the Western United States
Westward Expansion Map
Resources of the Western United States Map
Lesson 3 Major Cities in the Western United States Population Map
Drag-and-Drop Major Cities Game
Population Change Lecture Slides
History of Drought and Irrigation Slide Show
Drag-and-Drop Renewable vs. Nonrenewable Resources Game
Graph of Industries in the Western United States

Chapter 6 Time Line and Map of Canada
Lesson 1 Physical Geography of Canada Map
Drag-and-Drop Comparing Landforms Game
Lesson 2 Government Policies and Native Groups Lecture Slides
People in Canada Graphic Organizer
Drag-and-Drop Comparing U.S. and Canadian History Game
Lesson 3 Population of Canada Map
Resources of Canada Map
VIA Train Route Across Canada Map
Drag-and-Drop Canada Compared to the U.S. and the UK Game

Chapter 7 Time Line and Map of Mexico, Central America, and the Caribbean Islands
Lesson 1 Landforms and Waterways of Mexico, Central America, and the Caribbean Islands Graphic Organizer
Mexico, Central America, and the Caribbean Islands Climate Map
Mexico, Central America, and the Caribbean Islands Physical Geography Map
Lesson 2 Lake Farming: Then and Now Images
The Colonization of Central America Map
The Panama Canal: Before and After Map
The Columbian Exchange Map
Lesson 3 Central American Culture Slide Show

Unit 3
South America Video Montage
Drag-and-Drop Physical Geography Game of South America
Interactive Maps of South America

Chapter 8 Time Line and Map of Brazil
Lesson 1 Animation Showing Elements of a Globe
Climates of Brazil Map
The Amazon River Image
Regional Resources Graphic Organizer
Chart of How Coffee is Made

Worksheets

These printable worksheets are available for every lesson, chapter, or unit.
- Guided Reading Activities
- Physical Geography Activity
- Cultural Geography Activity
- Chapter Summaries (available in English and Spanish)
- Reading Essential and Study Guide Workbook and Answer Key

These printable assessment worksheets are available for every unit or chapter and can be edited on eAssessment.
- What Do You Know? Background Knowledge Assessment
- Vocabulary Builder Academic and Content Vocabulary Assessment
- Physical Location GeoQuiz
- Political Location GeoQuiz
- City Location GeoQuiz

These printable worksheets are for point-of-use instruction.

Unit 1
Environmental Case Study: Maintaining Fresh Water Sources
Geolab Activity: Desalinating Water

Chapter 1
Lesson 1 Geography Skills Activity: Understanding Lines on a Map
Lesson 2 Technology Skills Activity: Using Geospatial Technology

Chapter 2
Lesson 1 Geography and History Activity: Participating in the Global Warming Debate
Geography Skills Activity: Reading a Thematic Map of Wind and Ocean Currents

Chapter 3
Lesson 1 Writing Skills Activity: Investigating Population Movement
Lesson 2 Critical Thinking Skills Activity: Comparing and Contrasting Changes in Government Through History
Lesson 3 Geography and Economics Activity: Understanding both the Pros and Cons of Free Market Trade

Unit 2
Environmental Case Study: Practicing Conservation and Sustainability

Chapter 4
Lesson 1 Writing Skills Activity: Immigrating to America
Lesson 3 Primary Source Reading Skills Activity: Learning About America's National Parks
Geography Skills Activity: Mapping Native American Removal
Technology Skills Activity: Evaluating a Website

Chapter 5
Lesson 3 Geography and Economics Activity: Taking a Closer Look at NAFTA
Critical Thinking Skills Activity: Following the Rise of Silicon Valley

Chapter 6
Lesson 1 Geography Skills Activity: Using an Elevation Chart to Understand How the St. Lawrence Seaway Changed Trade and the Landscape

Chapter 7
Lesson 1 Critical Thinking Skills Activity: Mapping the Ring of Fire
Lesson 2 Geography and History Activity: Building the Panama Canal
Geography Skills Activity: Using an Informational Map to Understand the Columbian Exchange

Unit 3
Environmental Case Study: Exploring Alternative Energy
Writing Skills Activity: Choosing Between Pro and Con

Chapter 8
Lesson 1 Geography Skills Activity: Reading a Bar Graph About Deforestation
Lesson 2 Primary Source Reading Skills Activity: Understanding the Jesuits' Position on Slavery
Lesson 3 Geography and Economics Activity: Building the Transamazonica Highway
Critical Thinking Skills Activity: Learning How Brazil Became a Leader in the Production and Use of Alternative Fuels

Chapter 9
Lesson 1 Geography and History Activity: Learning More About Devil's Island
Lesson 3 Primary Source Reading Activity: Understanding Why Hugo Chavez is Popular In Venezuela
Technology Skills Activity: Finding an International Pen Pal

Chapter 10
Lesson 2 Primary Source Reading Skills Activity: Learning How Juan and Eva Peron Impacted The People of Argentina
Lesson 3 Critical Thinking Skills Activity: Predicting Consequences and the Contribution of Salmon Farming on a Local Economy

Unit 4
Environmental Case Study: Monitoring Land Use
Writing Skills Activity: Writing a Rebuttal to the Author's Argument
Reading Skills Activity: Understanding How an Aging Population Affects Communities

Chapter 11
Lesson 1 Technology Skills Activity: Researching the Internet for Information on the Bronze Age
Lesson 3 Geography and Economics Activity: Understanding How the Banking Crisis Affected the European Union

Chapter 12
Lesson 1 Geography Skills Activity: Reading a Circle Graph On Tourism in the Mediterranean

Chapter 13
Lesson 1 Geography and History Activity: Discussing the Balkan Peninsula and What Balkanization Means
Lesson 3 Critical Thinking Skills Activity: Recognizing Bias and Understanding Its Effect on Conflict in Serbia and Eastern Europe

Developed in partnership with EdTechTeacher, these chapter projects can be used with or without the use of technology in an individual or collaborative setting.

Chapter 1 Create Map from School to Home
Create Digital Travel Brochure

Chapter 2 Build Large Wall Map of the Earth
Design Physical Features Map of the Earth Using Online
   Map-Making Program

Chapter 3 Assemble Present-Day Time Capsule
Create Family Scrapbook Using Online Ancestry Resources

Chapter 4 Prepare Regional Travel Brochure
Design Interactive Regional Poster

Chapter 5 Write Fictional Travel Journal
Publish Online Activity Flashcards

Chapter 6 Build Large Wall Puzzle of Canada
Write Digital Essay about Life in Canada

Chapter 7 Assemble News Clippings on Large Regional Wall Map
Create Virtual Interactive Tour Using Multimedia Web Sites

Chapter 8 Write and Illustrate Graphic Novel
Compose Story about Brazil Using Online Photos, Videos, or Art

Chapter 9 Design Poster Boards of Indigenous Group Cultures
Build Web Pages for Countries of the Tropical North

Chapter 10 Assemble Photo Collage
Produce and Upload Online Historical Video

Chapter 11 Write and Illustrate Fictional Travel Journal
Create Online Travel Scrapbook

Chapter 12 Write and Illustrate Children's Picture Book
Build Annotated Online Maps

Chapter 13 Write and Perform Historical Event Skits
Record Fictional Interviews as Podcasts

These case studies develop student awareness of major global issues. Every project can be extended with ePals®, which allows your students to collaborate with schools around the world.

Unit 1 Maintenance of Fresh Water Sources

Unit 2 Conservation and Sustainability

Unit 3 Finding and Using Alternative Energy Sources

Unit 4 Land Use

Planning the Unit

Understanding By Design®

All Networks programs have been created using the approach developed by Jay McTighe, coauthor of *Understanding By Design®*.

- The main goal is to focus on the desired results before planning each unit's instruction.
- The Unit Planner lists the Enduring Understandings and the Essential Questions that students will learn and use as they study the chapters in the unit.
- Identifying the Predictable Misunderstandings will help you anticipate misconceptions students might have as they read the chapters.
- Information in the Unit Planners is expanded upon in the Chapter Planners.

Differentiated Instruction

Activities are designed to meet the needs of:

BL Beyond Level

AL Approaching Level

ELL English Language Learners

In addition, activities are designed to address a range of *learning styles*.

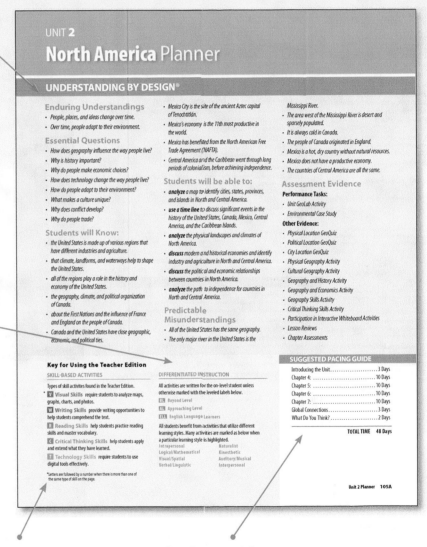

UNIT **2**

North America Planner

UNDERSTANDING BY DESIGN®

Enduring Understandings
- *People, places, and ideas change over time.*
- *Over time, people adapt to their environment.*

Essential Questions
- *How does geography influence the way people live?*
- *Why is history important?*
- *Why do people make economic choices?*
- *How does technology change the way people live?*
- *How do people adapt to their environment?*
- *What makes a culture unique?*
- *Why does conflict develop?*
- *Why do people trade?*

Students will Know:
- *the United States is made up of various regions that have different industries and agriculture.*
- *that climate, landforms, and waterways help to shape the United States.*
- *all of the regions play a role in the history and economy of the United States.*
- *the geography, climate, and political organization of Canada.*
- *about the First Nations and the influence of France and England on the people of Canada.*
- *Canada and the United States have close geographic, economic, and political ties.*

- *Mexico City is the site of the ancient Aztec capital of Tenochtitlán.*
- *Mexico's economy is the 11th most productive in the world.*
- *Mexico has benefited from the North American Free Trade Agreement (NAFTA).*
- *Central America and the Caribbean went through long periods of colonialism, before achieving independence.*

Students will be able to:
- **analyze** *a map to identify cities, states, provinces, and islands in North and Central America.*
- **use a time line** *to discuss significant events in the history of the United States, Canada, Mexico, Central America, and the Caribbean Islands.*
- **analyze** *the physical landscapes and climates of North America.*
- **discuss** *modern and historical economies and identify industry and agriculture in North and Central America.*
- **discuss** *the political and economic relationships between countries in North America.*
- **analyze** *the path to independence for countries in North and Central America.*

Predictable Misunderstandings
- *All of the United States has the same geography.*
- *The only major river in the United States is the*

Mississippi River.
- *The area west of the Mississippi River is desert and sparsely populated.*
- *It is always cold in Canada.*
- *The people of Canada originated in England.*
- *Mexico is a hot, dry country without natural resources.*
- *Mexico does not have a productive economy.*
- *The countries of Central America are all the same.*

Assessment Evidence
Performance Tasks:
- *Unit GeoLab Activity*
- *Environmental Case Study*
Other Evidence:
- *Physical Location GeoQuiz*
- *Political Location GeoQuiz*
- *City Location GeoQuiz*
- *Physical Geography Activity*
- *Cultural Geography Activity*
- *Geography and History Activity*
- *Geography and Economics Activity*
- *Geography Skills Activity*
- *Critical Thinking Skills Activity*
- *Participation in Interactive Whiteboard Activities*
- *Lesson Reviews*
- *Chapter Assessments*

SUGGESTED PACING GUIDE

Introducing the Unit	3 Days
Chapter 4:	10 Days
Chapter 5:	10 Days
Chapter 6:	10 Days
Chapter 7:	10 Days
Global Connections	3 Days
What Do You Think?	2 Days
TOTAL TIME	**48 Days**

Key for Using the Teacher Edition

SKILL-BASED ACTIVITIES

Types of skill activities found in the Teacher Edition.
* **V** Visual Skills require students to analyze maps, graphs, charts, and photos.
W Writing Skills provide writing opportunities to help students comprehend the text.
R Reading Skills help students practice reading skills and master vocabulary.
C Critical Thinking Skills help students apply and extend what they have learned.
T Technology Skills require students to use digital tools effectively.

*Letters are followed by a number when there is more than one of the same type of skill on the page.

DIFFERENTIATED INSTRUCTION

All activities are written for the on-level student unless otherwise marked with the leveled labels below.
BL Beyond Level
AL Approaching Level
ELL English Language Learners

All students benefit from activities that utilize different learning styles. Many activities are marked as below when a particular learning style is highlighted.
Intrapersonal   Naturalist
Logical/Mathematical   Kinesthetic
Visual/Spatial   Auditory/Musical
Verbal/Linguistic   Interpersonal

Unit 2 Planner 105A

Skill-Based Activities

Print-based and digital activities throughout the unit are designed to teach a range of skills, including:

C Critical Thinking Skills

V Visual Skills

R Reading Skills

T Technology Skills

W Writing Skills

Pacing Guide

Suggestions are provided on how to pace the unit's content based on your state's curriculum and number of school days.

Planning the Unit (continued)

Unit Opener Planner
The Unit Opener Planner provides a menu of the print and digital resources available to teach the Unit Opener. These activities are organized by skill type, level, and learning style.

Introduce the Unit
Every unit has activities that introduce students to the region. The activities may include discussion questions or brief cooperative learning activities to help students make connections to the unit content.

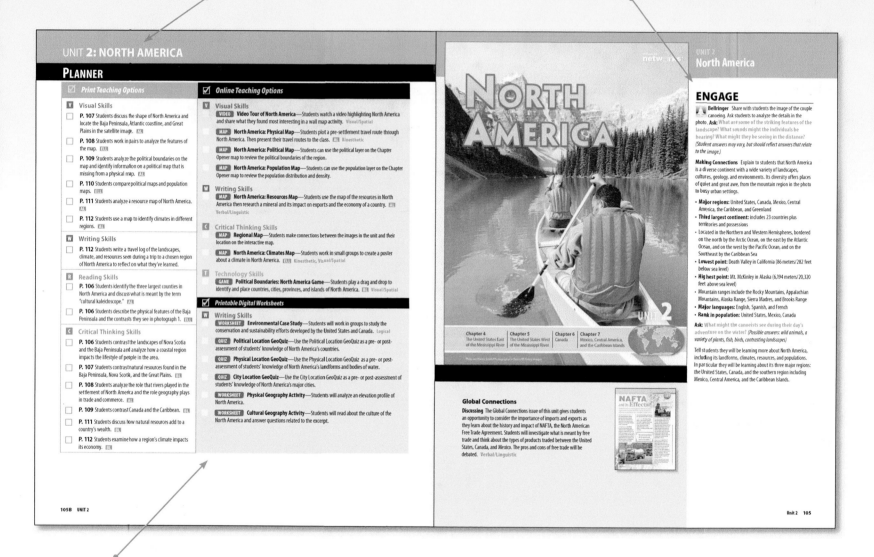

Online Teaching Activities
Digital assets and activities are cited here throughout the Teacher Edition to help you teach unit, chapter, and lesson content.

Teaching activities are provided for every digital asset in the Teacher Edition.

Digital assets include:

- interactive maps
- photos
- animations
- slide shows
- whiteboard activities
- lesson videos
- worksheets

networks

Don't forget! You can customize all your Lesson Plans online.

Planning the Chapter

Understanding By Design®
Like the Unit Planner, the Chapter Planner focuses on *Understanding By Design®* principles, including learning expectations, student misconceptions, and assessment options.

Standards
Each Chapter Planner identifies the Indiana Academic Standards that are covered in the chapter.

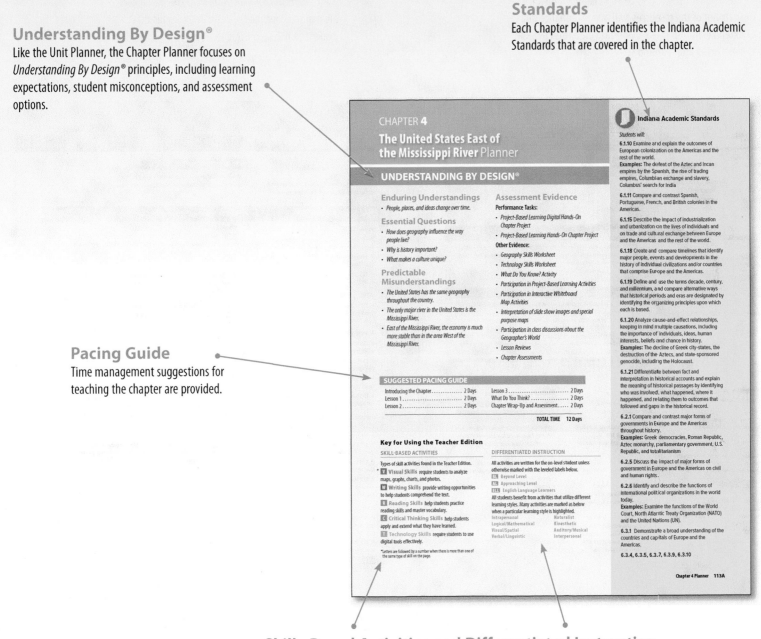

Pacing Guide
Time management suggestions for teaching the chapter are provided.

Skills-Based Activities and Differentiated Instruction
Print-based and digital activities throughout the chapter and lessons are designed to teach a range of skills, including:

C Critical Thinking Skills

V Visual Skills

R Reading Skills

T Technology Skills

W Writing Skills

Planning the Chapter (continued)

Planners

The Chapter Opener and Lesson Planners provide a snapshot of the resources available to enhance and extend learning. The activities are organized by skill type, level, and learning style.

Student Objectives

Using *Understanding By Design*® as the framework, the planners outline the content and skills that students will be expected to know.

CHAPTER 4: THE UNITED STATES EAST OF THE MISSISSIPPI RIVER

CHAPTER OPENER PLANNER

Students will know:
- the United States east of the Mississippi River is made up of various regions.
- the regions of this area have different industries and agriculture.
- climate, landforms, and waterways help to shape the region.
- there are many major cities in this region of the United States.
- the history of this region in the United States is complex and involves diverse groups of people.

Students will be able to:
- *identify* the cities and states east of the Mississippi River using a map.
- *use a time line* to discuss significant events in the history of the United States east of the Mississippi River.

☑ **Print Teaching Options**

W Writing Skills
- ☐ **P. 115** Students write a paragraph describing a social, environmental, or economic effect.

V Visual Skills
- ☐ **P. 114** Students use a political map to identify the eastern region of the United States.
- ☐ **P. 115** Students use a time line to answer questions about major events between 1620 and 2014.

☑ **Online Teaching Options**
- ☐ **MAP** Reading a Map—Students identify aspects and locations of the region on a map.
- ☐ **TIME LINE** Reading a Time Line and Map—Students learn about where historical events occurred in the eastern United States.
- ☐ **MAP** Interactive World Atlas—Students use the interactive world atlas to identify the region and describe its terrain.

☑ **Printable Digital Worksheets**
- ☐ **WORKSHEET** Geography Skills: Mapping the Trail of Tears—Students use the worksheet to map the forced migration of Native Americans.
- ☐ **WORKSHEET** Writing Skills: Immigrating to America—Students use the worksheet to construct a short essay about immigrating to America
- ☐ **WORKSHEET** Primary Source Reading Skills: National Parks—Students use the information on the worksheet as a guide to research the law that gave presidents power over the park system the first national park.
- ☐ **WORKSHEET** Technology Skills: Evaluating a Website—Students use the worksheet as a guide to evaluate a Web site.

Project-Based Learning

Hands-On

Making a Travel Brochure
Students will create travel brochures highlighting one of the regions east of the Mississippi River. After learning about the physical features, history, and culture of the different subregions, students should identify information to highlight in their brochures. Brochures might include photographs, maps, and fun facts that try to entice travelers to visit places east of the Mississippi. Have students then present their brochures to the class.

Digital Hands-On

Making an Interactive Poster
Students will create an online, interactive poster highlighting one of the subregions east of the Mississippi River. After learning about subregions' physical features, histories, and cultures, students will identify fun facts and other information to highlight in their posters. Students can use state tourist Web sites for photos and videos to add to their posters. Have students then present their posters to the class.

edtechteacher 21st Century Learning

Print Resources

ANCILLARY RESOURCES
These ancillaries are available for every chapter and lesson
- Reading Essentials and Study Guide Workbook
- Chapter Tests and Lesson Quizzes Blackline Masters

PRINTABLE DIGITAL WORKSHEETS
These printable digital worksheets are available for every *chapter* and *lesson!*
- Hands-On Chapter Projects
- What Do You Know? Activities
- Chapter Summaries (English and Spanish)
- Vocabulary Builder Activities
- Quizzes and Tests (English and Spanish)
- Reading Essentials and Study Guide (English and Spanish)
- Guided Reading Activities

More Media Resources

SUGGESTED VIDEOS **MOVIES**
NOTE: Be sure to preview videos to ensure they are age-appropriate.
- American Experience: We Shall Remain (76 min.)
- Nature Parks: Acadia New England (45 min.)
- Sacred Sites and Mound Builders (82 min.)

SUGGESTED READING
- *The Breaker Boys*, by Pat Hughes
- *We've Got a Job: The 1963 Birmingham Children's March*, by Cynthia Levinson
- *Chasing the Nightbird*, by Krista Russell

113B

LESSON 1 PLANNER

PHYSICAL FEATURES

Students will know:
- the United States east of the Mississippi is made up of various regions.
- the regions of this area have different industries and agriculture.
- climate, landforms, and waterways help to shape the region.

Students will be able to:
- *describe* the different regions that make up the United State east of the Mississippi.
- *identify* industries and agriculture in each region.
- *describe* the physical landscape of the United States east of the Mississippi.

☑ **Print Teaching Options**

V Visual Skills
- ☐ **P. 117** Students locate bodies of water on the subregions map of the United States.
- ☐ **P. 119** Students identify the route of a ship transporting goods from Chicago to London might take.
- ☐ **P. 121** Students locate where the Allegheny and Monongahela rivers combine in western Pennsylvania.

W Writing Skills
- ☐ **P. 120** Students write paragraphs explaining the benefits and disadvantages of a natural and a man-made boundary.

R Reading Skills
- ☐ **P. 116** Students describe how subregions are similar to and different from regions.
- ☐ **P. 117** Students identify subregions based on their characteristics.
- ☐ **P. 118** Students make connections to remember the names of the Great Lakes by using a mnemonic device.
- ☐ **P. 123** Students summarize information about mineral and energy resources in the eastern United States.

C Critical Thinking Skills
- ☐ **P. 117** Students trace the route farmers on the east coast of Mexico and farmers in southern Illinois use for trade.
- ☐ **P. 119** Students infer how the Mississippi River affects the lifestyle of Americans.
- ☐ **P. 120** Students compare and contrast the benefits and disadvantages of the Mississippi River.
- ☐ **P. 122** Students infer what the younger Rocky Mountains look like compared to the worn-down Appalachian Mountains.

T Technology Skills
- ☐ **P. 118** Students create a visual presentation to show the harmful effects of the 2010 oil spill in the Gulf of Mexico.
- ☐ **P. 122** Student groups give presentations comparing and contrasting two subregion climates in Eastern United States.

☑ **Online Teaching Options**

V Visual Skills
- **MAP** Regions: The Eastern United States—Students review the different physical features for each subregion using the regional layer of the Chapter Opener map. Visual/Spatial
- **IMAGE** The Gulf Coast Region—Students evaluate the interactive image of the Gulf Coast and discuss the importance of the coast on the local economy. Visual/Spatial, Verbal/Linguistic
- **VIDEO** The Mississippi River—Students use the video to trace the path of the Mississippi River and discuss the river's importance to the economy, transportation, and lifestyles of the people living along its banks. Visual Spatial, Verbal/Linguistic
- **MAP** The Fall Line—Students discuss the features of a fall line along the Atlantic coast, then use the map to answer questions. Visual/Spatial, Verbal/Linguistic
- **IMAGE** 360 View: Appalachia—Students use the 360 view of the Appalachian Mountains to further discuss the landscape.
- **SLIDE SHOW** Agriculture East of the Mississippi River—For more on this ahead—use the slide show about agriculture to discuss the important crops grown in this region.

W Writing Skills
- **VIDEO** Extreme Heat in Urban Areas—Students watch a video about the extreme temperatures in Eastern United States. Then write three questions they have about this region. Visual/Spatial, Verbal/Linguistic

R Reading Skills
- **MAP** Political: The Eastern United States—political layer of the Chapter Opener map to further explain the ideas of a subregion, connecting to the definitions in the text.
- **MAP** Resources: Eastern United States—Students use the resources layer on the Chapter Opener map to extend the connection to the descriptions in the text.

C Critical Thinking Skills
- **ANIMATION** How the Great Lakes Formed—Students use the animation to discuss the creation of the landscape and waterways in the area. Then explain in their own words how glaciers formed the Great Lakes. Visual/Spatial, Verbal/Linguistic
- **MAP** Physical Geography and Climate: The Eastern United States—Students compare and contrast the physical features and climate conditions in different subregions. Visual/Spatial, Verbal/Linguistic

T Technology Skills
- **DIAGRAM** Comparing Glaciers to Modern Landscapes—Students use the diagram to make comparisons of glacier size to modern landmarks to reveal depth and extent of glacier
- **ONLINE SELF-CHECK QUIZ** Lesson 1—Students receive instant feedback on their mastery of lesson content

Chapter 4 Planner 113C

Project-Based Learning
Cumulative projects bring the subject to life for the student and help you assess your students' level of understanding. The program includes Hands-On Projects, as well as Digital Hands-On Projects.

Print Resources
Every chapter includes printable worksheets, including tests, quizzes, and materials to build vocabulary and improve reading comprehension.

Make It Relevant
Enrich and extend the content with videos and books.

Print and Digital Options
Each planner has two columns listing print-based activities and online digital options, including printable digital worksheets.

Don't forget! You can customize all your Lesson Plans online.

Using the Wraparound Resources and Activities

STUDENT EDITION PAGES AND WRAPAROUND ACTIVITIES

The entire Student Edition appears in the Teacher Edition. Activities and recommended resources appear in the side and bottom margins of the Teacher Edition, at point of use.

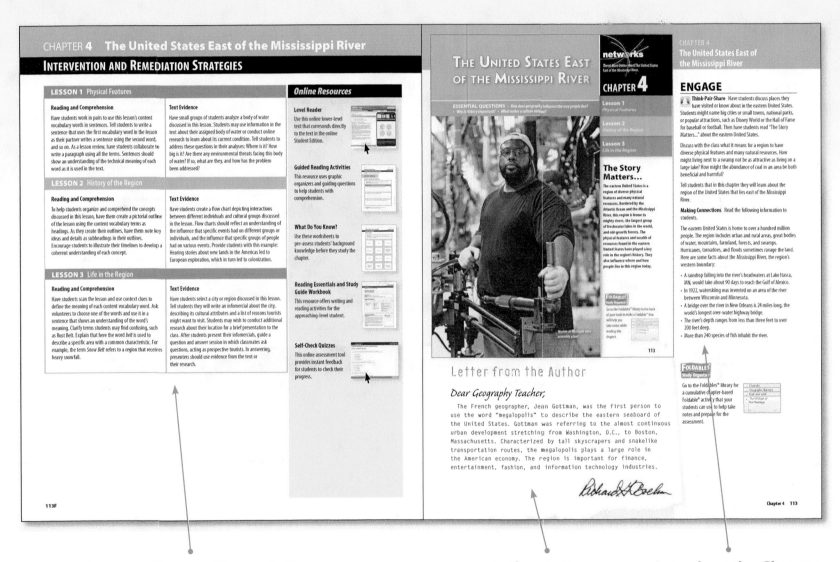

Intervention and Remediation
Each Chapter Planner concludes with intervention and remediation strategies for every lesson, as well as Online Resources that can be used to help students understand the content.

Author Letter
Each chapter begins with the author's perspective about key concepts found in the chapter.

Introduce the Chapter
Each chapter begins with activities to engage students' interest in the chapter's content.

Using the Wraparound Resources and Activities (continued)

Step Into the Place/Step Into the Time

These two pages of the Chapter Opener are designed to help students locate the region in the world that they will learn about, along with important historical events that took place in that region.

The Teacher Edition contains activities and discussion questions for these features.

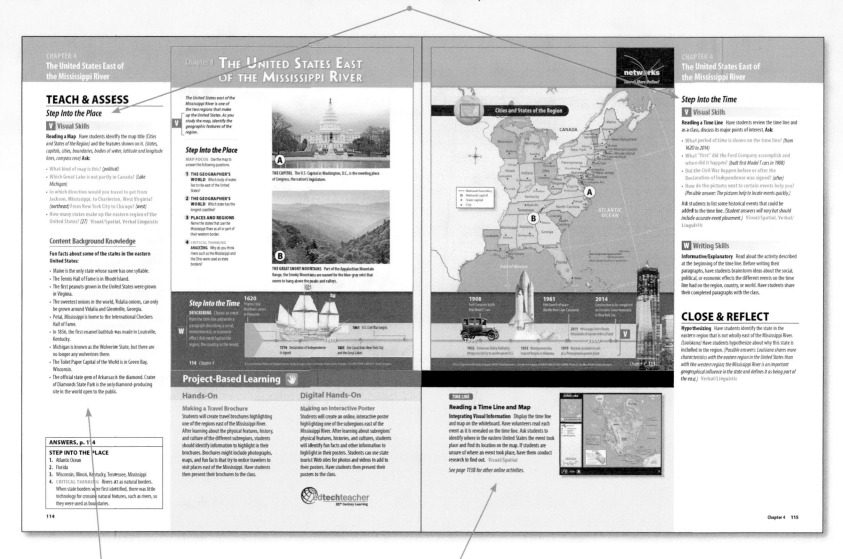

Print-Based Activities

Activities in the margins correspond to the text in the Student Edition. These activities are coded to indicate their level and the learning style they support.

Online Digital Activities

Online digital activities for the lesson appear at the bottom of each page. The gray icon indicates the type of activity available in the online Teacher Center. Activities include interactive whiteboard activities, animations, videos, interactive maps, images, and worksheets. Activities can be projected or used on your classroom whiteboard. Worksheets can be edited and printed, or assigned online, depending on student access to technology.

![networks - Don't forget! You can customize all your Lesson Plans online.]

ENGAGE
Every lesson begins with an Engage activity designed to motivate students and focus their attention on the lesson topic.

Guiding Questions
Guiding Questions in the Student Edition point out key knowledge that students need to acquire to be able to answer the chapter's Essential Questions.

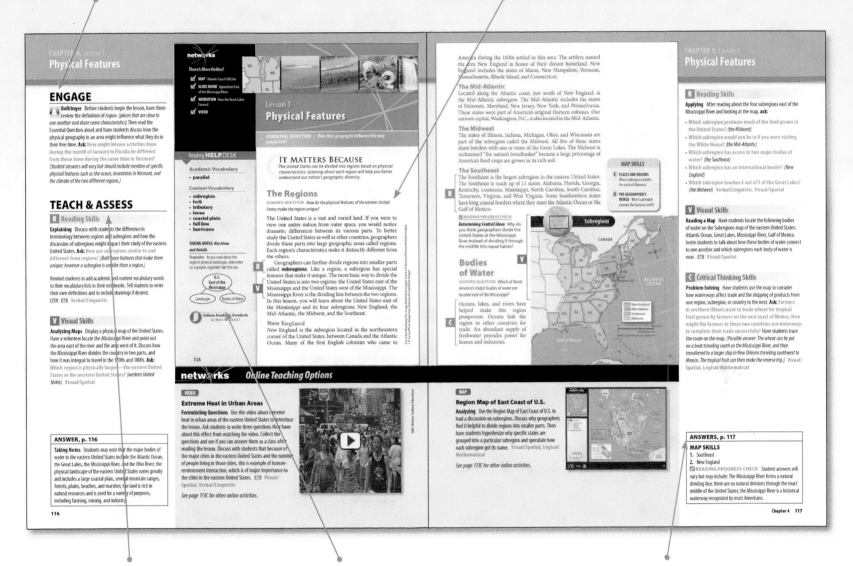

TEACH & ASSESS
Teach & Assess is the core of the lesson. It contains activities, lecture notes, background information, and discussion questions to teach the lesson.

Reading Help Desk
- Academic Vocabulary
- Content Vocabulary
- Note-Taking Activity and Graphic Organizer

Answers
Answers to questions and activities in the Student Edition appear in the bottom corner of the Teacher Edition pages.

Using the Wraparound Resources and Activities *(continued)*

Brackets

Brackets on the Student Edition page correspond to teaching strategies and activities in the Teacher Edition. As you teach the lesson, the brackets show you where to use these activities and strategies.

Reading Progress Check

A Reading Progress Check appears at the end of each topic in the Student Edition to help gauge student reading comprehension.

Letters

The letters on the reduced Student Edition page identify the type of activity. See the key on the first planning page of each chapter to learn about the different types of activities.

CLOSE & REFLECT

Each lesson ends with activities designed to help students link the content to the lesson's Guiding Questions and the chapter's Essential Questions.

Don't forget! You can customize all your Lesson Plans online.

Special Features

Global Connections

Global Connections are provided for each unit. Each Global Connections feature focuses on an event or a topic that affects the world community.

The online Global Connections includes numerous interactive digital assets to enrich your teaching. Digital assets include:

- animations
- photos
- maps, charts, and diagrams
- videos
- worksheets
- whiteboard activities

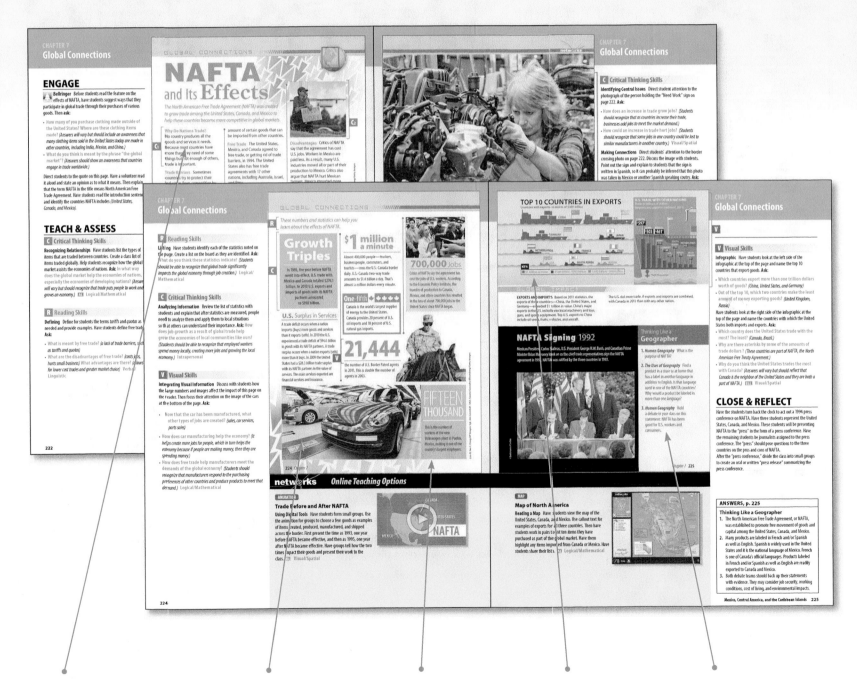

Background information is provided to help students understand the event or topic.

Dynamic photos enrich the study of the content.

Fun and interesting statistics and facts are listed in a magazine-like format.

Maps, graphs, charts, and diagrams are engaging and student-friendly.

Questions assess students' understanding of the information in the feature.

Special Features *(continued)*

What Do You Think?

Each unit includes a What Do You Think? feature. Students are asked to analyze different points of view on current world issues and events.

Background information is provided to help students understand why there are opposing viewpoints about the issue or event.

Two primary sources present opposing points of view.

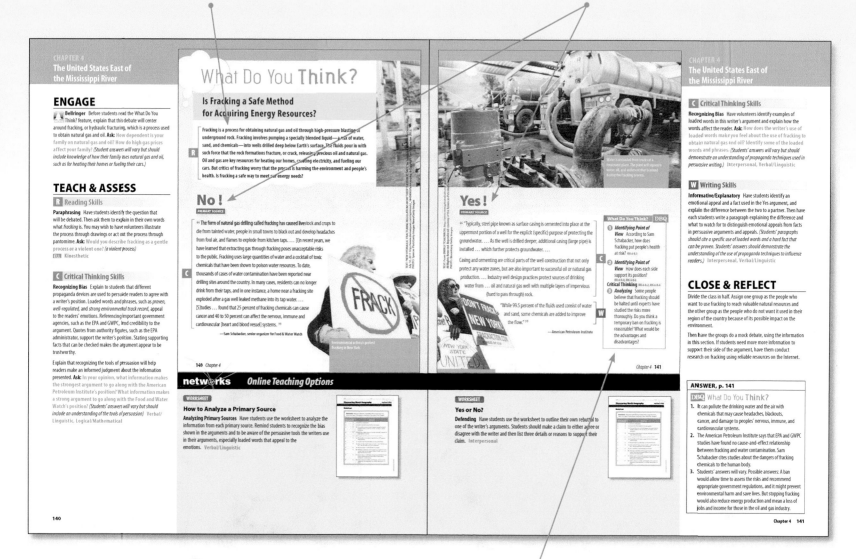

Questions assess students' understanding of both points of view and ask students to make comparisons between the arguments.

Activities and Assessment

Chapter Assessment

Each chapter ends with a chapter assessment that includes the following:

- Foldables® Writing Activity
- 21st Century Skills Activity
- Thinking Like a Geographer Activity
- Geography Activity
- Review the Guiding Questions
  Standardized Test Practice
- Document-Based Questions and Writing
  Activities

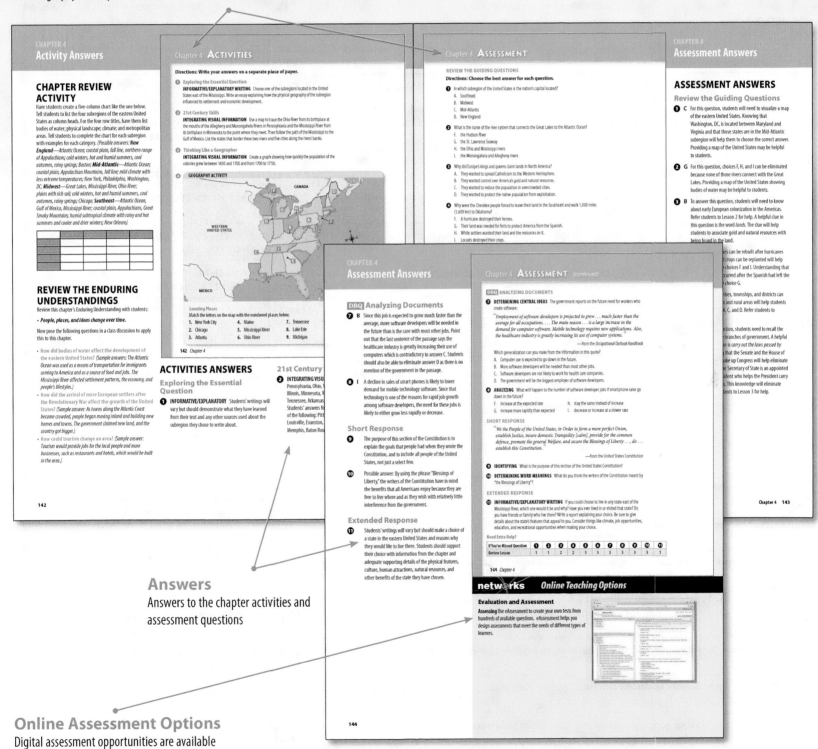

Answers
Answers to the chapter activities and assessment questions

Online Assessment Options
Digital assessment opportunities are available for every chapter.

The revised standards continue to be focused on ten themes, like the original standards. They represent a way of categorizing knowledge about the human experience, and they constitute the organizing strands that should thread through a social studies program.

Theme and Learning Expectation	Student Edition Chapter/Lesson
1. CULTURE	
1. "Culture" refers to the socially transmitted behaviors, beliefs, values, traditions, institutions, and ways of living together for a group of people	Ch 3 L2; Ch 4 L2; Ch 5 L2; Ch 6 L2; Ch 7 L3; Ch 8 L3; Ch 9 L3; Ch 10 L3; Ch 11 L3; Ch 12 L3; Ch 13 L3
2. Concepts such as beliefs, values, mores, institutions, cohesion, diversity, accommodation, adaption, assimilation, and dissonance	Ch 3 L2; Ch 4 L2; Ch 5 L2; Ch 6 L3; Ch 7 L3; Ch 8 L3; Ch 9 L3; Ch 10 L3; Ch 11 L3; Ch 12 L2, L3; Ch 13 L2, L3
3. How culture influences the ways in which human groups solve the problems of daily living	Ch 3 L2; Ch 4 L2; Ch 5 L2, L3; Ch 6 L3; Ch 7 L3; Ch 8 L3; Ch 9 L3; Ch 10 L3; Ch 11 L3; Ch 12 L3; Ch 13 L3
4. That the beliefs, values, and behaviors of a culture form an integrated system that helps shape the activities and ways of life that define a culture	Ch 3 L2; Ch 4 L2; Ch 5 L2, L3; Ch 6 L3; Ch 7 L3; Ch 8 L3; Ch 9 L3; Ch 10 L3; Ch 11 L3; Ch 12 L3; Ch 13 L3
5. How individuals learn the elements of their culture through interactions with others, and how individuals learn of other cultures through communication and study	Ch 1 L1; Ch 3 L2, GC; Ch 11 L3; Ch 12 L3; Ch 13 L3
6. That culture may change in response to changing needs, concerns, social, political, and geographic conditions	Ch 3 L1, L2, GC; Ch 6 L3; Ch 7 L3; Ch 8 L2, L3; Ch 10 WDYT; Ch 12 L2, L3; Ch 13 L2, L3
7. How people from different cultures develop different values and ways of interpreting experience	Ch 3 L2; Ch 6 L3; Ch 7 L3; Ch 8 L3; Ch 9 L3; Ch 10 L3; Ch 11 L2, L3; Ch 12 L2, L3; Ch 13 L3
8. That language, behaviors, and beliefs of different cultures can both contribute to and pose barriers to cross-cultural understanding	Ch 3 L1, L2; Ch 6 L3; Ch 8 L2, L3; Ch 11 L3; Ch 12 L3; Ch 13 L2, L3
2. TIME, CONTINUITY, AND CHANGE	
1. The study of the past provides a representation of the history of communities, nations, and the world	Ch 4 L2; Ch 5 L2; Ch 6 L2; Ch 7 L2; Ch 8 L2; Ch 9 L2; Ch 10 L2; Ch 11 L2; Ch 12 L2; Ch 13 L2
2. Concepts such as: chronology, causality, change, conflict, complexity, multiple perspectives, primary and secondary sources, and cause and effect	Ch 1 CO, WDYT; Ch 4 CO, L2, L3, WDYT; Ch 5 CO, L2, L3; Ch 6 CO, L2, L3; Ch 7 CO, L2, L3; Ch 8 CO, L2, L3; Ch 9 CO, L2, L3; Ch 10 CO, L2, L3, WDYT; Ch 11 CO, L2, L3, WDYT; Ch 12 CO, L2, L3; Ch 13 CO, L2, L3
3. That learning about the past requires the interpretation of sources, and that using varied sources provides the potential for a more balanced interpretive record of the past	Ch 4 WDYT; Ch 5 L2; Ch 10 L2, WDYT; Ch 11 L2, WDYT
4. That historical interpretations of the same event may differ on the basis of such factors as conflicting evidence from varied sources, national or cultural perspectives, and the point of view of the researcher	Ch 1 WDYT; Ch 4 WDYT; Ch 10 WDYT; Ch 11 WDYT
5. Key historical periods and patterns of change within and across cultures (e.g., the rise and fall of ancient civilizations, the development of technology, the rise of modern nation-states, and the establishment and breakdown of colonial systems)	Ch 4 L2, L3; Ch 5 L2; Ch 6 L2; Ch 7 L2; Ch 8 L2; Ch 9 L2; Ch 10 L2; Ch 11 L2; Ch 12 L2; Ch 13 L2
6. The origins and influences of social, cultural, political, and economic systems	Ch 3 L3, GC; Ch 4 L2, L3; Ch 5 L2; Ch 6 L2, L3; Ch 7 L2, L3, GC; Ch 8 L2, L3; Ch 9 L2; Ch 10 L2, L3; Ch 11 L2, L3; Ch 12 L2, L3; Ch 13 L2, L3
7. The contributions of key persons, groups, and events from the past and their influence on the present	Ch 4 L2, L3; Ch 5 L2; Ch 6 L2; Ch 7 L2; Ch 8 L2; Ch 9 L2; Ch 10 L2; Ch 11 L2; Ch 12 L2; Ch 13 L2
8. The history of democratic ideals and principles, and how they are represented in documents, artifacts and symbols	Ch 3 L2; Ch 4 L3; Ch 6 L2; Ch 7 L2; Ch 9 L2; Ch 11 L2
9. The influences of social, geographic, economic, and cultural factors on the history of local areas, states, nations, and the world	Ch 3 L2, L3, GC; Ch 4 L2; Ch 5 L2; Ch 6 L2, L3; Ch 7 L2; Ch 8 L2; Ch 9 L2; Ch 10 L2; Ch 11 L2; Ch 12 L2; Ch 13 L2

Note: CO=Chapter Opener; WDYT=What Do You Think?; GC=Global Connections

Theme and Learning Expectation	Student Edition Chapter/Lesson
3. PEOPLE, PLACES, AND ENVIRONMENTS	
1. The theme of people, places, and environments involves the study of the relationships between human populations in different locations and geographic phenomena such as climate, vegetation, and natural resources	**Ch 1** L1; **Ch 2** L1; **Ch 3** L3; **Ch 4** L2, WDYT; **Ch 5** L2; **Ch 6** L1, L3; **Ch 7** L1, L2, L3; **Ch 8** L1, L2, L3, GC; **Ch 9** L1, L3; **Ch 10** L1, L3; **Ch 11** L1, L3; **Ch 12** L1, L3; **Ch 13** L1, L3
2. Concepts such as: location, region, place, migration, as well as human and physical systems	**Ch 1** L1; **Ch 2** L1, L2; **Ch 3** L1, L2; **Ch 4** L1, L2; **Ch 5** L1, L2, L3; **Ch 6** L1, L2, L3; **Ch 7** L1, L2; **Ch 8** L1, L3; **Ch 9** L1, L2, L3; **Ch 10** L1, L3; **Ch 11** L1, L2, L3; **Ch 12** L1, L2, L3; **Ch 13** L1, L2, L3
3. Past and present changes in physical systems, such as seasons, climate, and weather, and the water cycle, in both national and global contexts	**Ch 1** L2; **Ch 2** L1, L3; **Ch 3** L1; **Ch 5** L3; **Ch 6** L3
4. The roles of different kinds of population centers in a region or nation	**Ch 4** L3; **Ch 5** L3; **Ch 6** L3; **Ch 7** L3; **Ch 8** L3; **Ch 9** L3; **Ch 10** L3; **Ch 11** L3; **Ch 12** L3; **Ch 13** L3
5. The concept of regions identifies links between people in different locations according to specific criteria (e.g., physical, economic, social, cultural, or religious)	**Ch 1** L1; **Ch 3** L2; **Ch 4** L2, L3; **Ch 5** L2, L3; **Ch 6** L2, L3; **Ch 7** L3, GC; **Ch 8** L3; **Ch 9** L3; **Ch 10** L3; **Ch 11** WDYT; **Ch 12** L2, L3; **Ch 13** L1, L2
6. Patterns of demographic and political change, and cultural diffusion in the past and present (e.g., changing national boundaries, migration, and settlement, and the diffusion of and changes in customs and ideas)	**Ch 3** L1; L2; **Ch 4** L2; **Ch 5** L2; **Ch 6** L2, L3; **Ch 7** L2, L3; **Ch 9** L2, L3; **Ch 10** L2, L3, WDYT; **Ch 12** L3, GC; **Ch 13** L2, L3
7. Human modifications of the environment	**Ch 1** L1; **Ch 2** L1, L2; **Ch 3** L1, L3; **Ch 4** L2, L3, WDYT; **Ch 5** L2, L3; **Ch 6** L1, L2, L3; **Ch 7** L1, L3; **Ch8** GC; **Ch 9** L3; **Ch 10** L3; **Ch 11** L2, L3; **Ch 12** L3; **Ch 13** L1, L3
8. Factors that contribute to cooperation and conflict among peoples of the nation and world, including language, religion, and political beliefs	**Ch 3** L2, L3; **Ch 4** L2, L3; **Ch 6** L2, L3; **Ch 7** L2, L3; **Ch 9** L2, L3; **Ch 10** L2; **Ch 11** L2, L3, WDYT; **Ch 12** L2, L3; **Ch 13** L2, L3
9. The use of a variety of maps, globes, graphic representations, and geospatial technologies to help investigate the relationships among people, places, and environments	**Ch 1** CO, L2, WDYT; **Ch 2** CO; **Ch 3** CO; **Ch 4** CO; **Ch 5** CO; **Ch 6** CO, L1; **Ch 7** CO, L1, L2; **Ch 8** CO; **Ch 9** CO, L1, L2; **Ch 10** CO, L1, L2, L3; **Ch 11** CO, L1, L2, L3; **Ch 12** CO, L2, GC; **Ch 13** CO, L1, L2, L3
4. INDIVIDUAL DEVELOPMENT AND IDENTITY	
1. The study of individual development and identity helps us know that individuals change physically, cognitively, and emotionally over time	**Ch 3** L2, GC; Ch 11, L3; **Ch 12** L3, GC
2. Concepts such as: development, change, personality, learning, individual, family, groups, motivation, and perception	**Ch 3** L2; **Ch 4** L3; **Ch 5** L3; **Ch 6** L2, L3; **Ch 7** L3; **Ch 8** L3; **Ch 9** L3; **Ch 10** L3; **Ch 11** L3; **Ch 12** L3; **Ch 13** L3
3. How factors such as physical endowment, interests, capabilities, learning, motivation, personality, perception, and beliefs influence individual development and identity	**Ch 3** L2; **Ch 5** L3; **Ch 10** L3; **Ch 11** L2, L3; **Ch 12** L2, L3; **Ch 13** L3
4. How personal, social, cultural, and environmental factors contribute to the development and the growth of personal identity	**Ch 3** L2; **Ch 4** L2; **Ch 6** L3; **Ch 7** L3; **Ch 9** L3; **Ch 10** L3; **Ch 11** L3; **Ch 12** L3; **Ch 13** L3
5. That individuals' choices influence identity and development	**Ch 3** L1, L2 GC; **Ch 4** L2; **Ch 5** L3; **Ch 6** L3; **Ch 7** L3; **Ch 10** L3, WDYT; **Ch 11** L3; **Ch 12** L3; **Ch 13** L3
6. That perceptions are interpretations of information about individuals and events, and can be influenced by bias and stereotypes	**Ch 4** L3; **Ch 5** L2; **Ch 6** L2, L3; **Ch 7** L2; **Ch 9** L2; **Ch 11** L2; **Ch 12** L2
5. INDIVIDUALS, GROUPS, AND INSTITUTIONS	
1. This theme helps us know how individuals are members of groups and institutions, and influence and shape those groups and institutions	**Ch 1** L1; **Ch 3** L2, GC; **Ch 4** L2, L3; **Ch 5** L3; **Ch 6** L3; **Ch 7** L3; **Ch 8** L3; **Ch 9** L3; **Ch 10** L2, L3; **Ch 11** L2, L3; **Ch 12** L3; **Ch 13** L2, L3
2. Concepts such as: mores, norms, status, role, socialization, ethnocentrism, cultural diffusion, competition, cooperation, conflict, race, ethnicity, and gender	**Ch 3** L1, L2; **Ch 4** L3; **Ch 5** L3; **Ch 6** L3; **Ch 7** L3; **Ch 8** L3; **Ch 9** L3; **Ch 10** L3, GC; **Ch 11** L3, WDYT; **Ch 12** L2, L3, GC; **Ch 13** L3
3. Institutions are created to respond to changing individual and group needs	**Ch 3** L2, L3; **Ch 4** L3; **Ch 5** L3; **Ch 7** WDYT; **Ch 8** L3; **Ch 9** L3; **Ch 10** L3; **Ch 11** L3, WDYT; **Ch 12** L3
4. That ways in which young people are socialized include similarities as well as differences across cultures	**Ch 3** L2, GC; **Ch 8** L3; **Ch 11** L3; **Ch 12** L3; **Ch 13** L3

Theme and Learning Expectation	Student Edition Chapter/Lesson
5. That groups and institutions change over time	**Ch 3** L2, L3, GC; **Ch 4** L3; **Ch 5** L2; **Ch 6** L2; **Ch 7** L2, GC; **Ch 8** L3; **Ch 10** L2, L3, WDYT; **Ch 11** L2, L3, WDYT; **Ch 12** L2, L3, GC; **Ch 13** L2, L3
6. That cultural diffusion occurs when groups migrate	**Ch 3** L1, L2; **Ch 7** L3; **Ch 8** L3; **Ch 9** L3; **Ch 10** L3; **Ch 11** L2, L3; **Ch 12** L2, L3; **Ch 13** L2, L3
7. That institutions may promote or undermine social conformity	**Ch 3** L1, L2; **Ch 4** L3; **Ch 5** L3; **Ch 6** L2; **Ch 7** GC; **Ch 8** L3; **Ch 9** L3; **Ch 11** L3; **Ch 12** L3
8. That when two or more groups with differing norms and beliefs interact, accommodation or conflict may result	**Ch 3** L2; **Ch 4** L2; **Ch 5** L2; **Ch 6** L2; **Ch 7** L2, WDYT; **Ch 9** L2, L3; **Ch 10** L3, GC; **Ch 11** L3, WDYT; **Ch 12** L3; **Ch 13** L2, L3
9. That groups and institutions influence culture in a variety of ways	**Ch 3** L2, GC; **Ch 8** L3; **Ch 9** L2; **Ch 10** L3, GC; **Ch 11** L3; **Ch 12** L2, L3; **Ch 13** L2, L3

6. POWER, AUTHORITY, AND GOVERNANCE

Theme and Learning Expectation	Student Edition Chapter/Lesson
1. Rights are guaranteed in the U.S. Constitution, the supreme law of the land	**Ch 3** L2; **Ch 4** L3
2. Fundamental ideas that are the foundation of American constitutional democracy (including those of the U.S. Constitution, popular sovereignty, the rule of law, separation of powers, checks and balances, minority rights, the separation of church and state, and Federalism)	**Ch 3** L2; **Ch 4** L3
3. Fundamental values of constitutional democracy (e.g., the common good, liberty, justice, equality, and individual dignity)	**Ch 3** L2; **Ch 4** L3; **Ch 8** L2; **Ch 9** L2, L3; **Ch 10** L2; **Ch 11** L3
4. The ideologies and structures of political systems that differ from those of the United States	**Ch 3** L2; **Ch 6** L2; **Ch 7** L2; **Ch 8** L2; **Ch 9** L3; **Ch 10** L2; **Ch 11** L2, L3; **Ch 12** L3; **Ch 13** L2, L3
5. The ways in which governments meet the needs and wants of citizens, manage conflict, and establish order and security	**Ch 3** L2; **Ch 4** L3; **Ch 5** L3; **Ch 6** L2, L3; **Ch 7** L2, L3; **Ch 8** L3; **Ch 9** L3; **Ch 10** L3; **Ch 11** WDYT; **Ch 12** L3; **Ch 13** L2, L3

7. PRODUCTION, DISTRIBUTION, AND CONSUMPTION

Theme and Learning Expectation	Student Edition Chapter/Lesson
1. Individuals, government, and society experience scarcity because human wants and needs exceed what can be produced from available resources	**Ch 3** L3; **Ch 7** L3; **Ch 9** L3; **Ch 10** L2; **Ch 13** L2, L3
2. How choices involve trading off the expected value of one opportunity gained against the expected value of the best alternative	**Ch 3** L3
3. The economic choices that people make have both present and future consequences	**Ch 3** L3; **Ch 4** L3; **Ch 5** L3; **Ch 6** L3; **Ch 7** L3; **Ch 8** L3; **Ch 9** L3; **Ch 10** L3; **Ch 11** L3; **Ch 12** L3; **Ch 13** L3
4. Economic incentives affect people's behavior and may be regulated by rules or laws	**Ch 3** L3; **Ch 4** WDYT; **Ch 5** L3; **Ch 6** L3; **Ch 7** L3, WDYT; **Ch 9** L3; **Ch 11** WDYT; **Ch 12** L3; **Ch 13** L2, L3
5. That banks and other financial institutions channel funds from savers to borrowers and investors	**Ch 7** L3; **Ch 10** L2; **Ch 11** L3; **Ch 12** L3
6. The economic gains that result from specialization and exchange as well as the trade-offs	**Ch 3** L3; **Ch 4** L2; **Ch 5** L3; **Ch 6** L3; **Ch 7** L3 GC; **Ch 8** L3; **Ch 9** L2, L3; **Ch 10** L3; **Ch 11** L3, WDYT
7. How markets bring buyers and sellers together to exchange goods and services	**Ch 3** L3; **Ch 5** L3; **Ch 6** L3; **Ch 7** L3, WDYT; **Ch 8** L3; **Ch 9** L3; **Ch 10** L3; **Ch 11** L3, WDYT; **Ch 12** L3
8. How goods and services are allocated in a market economy through the influence of prices on decisions about production and consumption	**Ch 3** L3; **Ch 9** L3; **Ch 12** L3; **Ch 13** L3
9. How the overall levels of income, employment, and prices are determined by the interaction of households, firms, and the government	**Ch 3** L2, L3; **Ch 5** L3; **Ch 6** L3; **Ch 7** L3; **Ch 9** L2, L3; **Ch 10** L3; **Ch 12** L3; **Ch 13** L3

8. SCIENCE, TECHNOLOGY, AND SOCIETY

Theme and Learning Expectation	Student Edition Chapter/Lesson
1. Science is a result of empirical study of the natural world, and technology is the application of knowledge to accomplish tasks	**Ch 1** L2, WDYT; **Ch 4** L2; **Ch 5** L3; **Ch 6** L1, L2, L3; **Ch 10** L2, L3; **Ch 11** L2; **Ch 12** L1
2. Society often turns to science and technology to solve problems	**Ch 1** L2, WDYT; **Ch 4** L2, WDYT; **Ch 5** L3; **Ch 6** L1, L2, L3; **Ch 8** L3; **Ch 10** L2; **Ch 12** L1; **Ch 13** L1, L2, L3
3. Our lives today are media and technology dependent	**Ch 1** WDYT; **Ch 3** GC; **Ch 4** L2, L3; **Ch 12** L3; **Ch 13** L3

Theme and Learning Expectation	Student Edition Chapter/Lesson
4. Science and technology have had both positive and negative impacts upon individuals, societies, and the environment in the past and present	Ch 1 WDYT; Ch 2 L1; Ch 3 L3; Ch 4 L3, WDYT; Ch 5 L3; Ch 6 L1, L2, L3; Ch 7 L3; Ch 8 L3; Ch 10 L3; Ch 11 L2; Ch 12 L1, L2; Ch 13 L1, L3
5. Science and technology have changed peoples' perceptions of the social and natural world, as well as their relationship to the land, economy and trade, their concept of security, and their major daily activities	Ch 1 L2, WDYT; Ch 3 L1, L3, GC; Ch 4 L2; Ch 5 L3; Ch 6 L1, L2; Ch 8 L3; Ch 10 L3; Ch 11 L2; Ch 12 L2, Ch 13 L2, L3
6. Values, beliefs, and attitudes that have been influenced by new scientific and technological knowledge (e.g., invention of the printing press, conceptions of the universe, applications of atomic energy, and genetic discoveries)	Ch 1 WDYT; Ch 3 GC; Ch 4 L3, WDYT; Ch 7 L3; Ch 8 L3; Ch 12 L2
7. How media are created and received depends upon cultural contexts	Ch 1 WDYT; Ch 3 GC; Ch 6 L3; Ch 13 L3
8. Science and technology sometimes create ethical issues that test our standards and values	Ch 1 L WDYT; Ch 3 GC; Ch 4 L3, WDYT; Ch 10 WDYT; Ch 12 L2
9. The need for laws and policies to govern scientific and technological applications	Ch 6 L3; Ch 7 L3; Ch 8 L3; Ch 10 L3
10. That there are gaps in access to science and technology around the world	Ch 8 L3; Ch 9 L2; Ch 10 L3

9. GLOBAL CONNECTIONS

1. Global connections have existed in the past and increased rapidly in current times	Ch 1 WDYT; Ch 3 L1, L2, GC; Ch 5 L3; Ch 6 L3; Ch 7 L3, WDYT; Ch 8 L3; Ch 9 L3; Ch 10 WDYT; Ch 11 WDYT; Ch 12 L2, L3; Ch 13 L2, L3
2. Global factors such as cultural, economic, and political connections are changing the places in which people live (e.g., through trade, migration, increased travel, and communication)	Ch 3 L1, GC; Ch 4 L2; Ch 5 L3; Ch 6 L2, L3; Ch 7 L3, WDYT; Ch 8 L3, GC; Ch 9 L3; Ch 10 L2, L3, WDYT; Ch 11 L3, WDYT; Ch 12 L3; Ch 13 L2, L3
3. Spatial relationships that relate to ongoing global issues (e.g., pollution, poverty, disease, and conflict) affect the health and well-being of Earth and its inhabitants	Ch 1 L1; Ch 2 L1, L3; Ch 3 L1; Ch 4 WDYT; Ch 7 L3; Ch 8 GC; Ch 10 L3; Ch 13 L3
4. Global problems and possibilities are not generally caused or developed by any one nation	Ch 5 L3; Ch 6 L3; Ch 7 L3, WDYT; Ch 8 L3; Ch 9 L3; Ch 10 WDYT; Ch 11 L2, L3, WDYT; Ch 12 L2, L3; Ch 13 L2, L3
5. Global connections may make cultures more alike or increase their sense of distinctiveness	Ch 3 L2, GC; Ch 6 L3; Ch 7 L3, WDYT; Ch 8 GC; Ch 10 L3, WDYT; Ch 11 L3, WDYT; Ch 12 L3; Ch 13 L3
6. Universal human rights cut across cultures but are not necessarily understood in the same way in all cultures	Ch 3 L2; Ch 6 L2, L3; Ch 7 L2; Ch 13 L3

10. CIVIC IDEALS AND PRACTICES

1. The theme of civic ideals and practices helps us to learn about and know how to work for the betterment of society	Ch 3 L2; Ch 7 L3; Ch 8 L2; Ch 10 L2; Ch 11 L2; Ch 12 L3; Ch 13 L3
2. Concepts and ideals such as: individual dignity, liberty, justice, equality, individual rights, responsibility, majority and minority rights, and civil dissent	Ch 3 L2; Ch 4 L3; Ch 6 L1, L3; Ch 7 L2; Ch 9 L3; Ch 10 L2; Ch 11 L2
3. Key practices involving the rights and responsibilities of citizenship and the exercise of citizenship (e.g., respecting the rule of law and due process, voting, serving on a jury, researching issues, making informed judgments, expressing views on issues, and collaborating with others to take civic action)	Ch 3 L2; Ch 6 L3; Ch 7 L2; Ch 8 L2; Ch 9 L3; Ch 10 L2; Ch 12 L3
4. The common good, and the rule of law	Ch 3 L2; Ch 4 L3; Ch 6 L3; Ch 7 L2, L3; Ch 8 L2, L3; Ch 9 L2, L3; Ch 11 L3, WDYT; Ch 12 L2
5. Key documents and excerpts from key sources that define and support democratic ideals and practices (e.g., the U.S. Declaration of Independence, the U.S. Constitution, the Gettysburg Address, the Letter from Birmingham Jail; and international documents such as the Declaration of the Rights of Man, and the Universal Declaration of the Rights of Children)	Ch 3 L2; Ch 4 L3
6. The origins and function of major institutions and practices developed to support democratic ideals and practices	Ch 3 L2; Ch 4 L2, L3; Ch 6 L2; Ch 7 L2; Ch 9 L2; Ch 11 L2, WDYT
7. Key past and present issues involving democratic ideals and practices, as well as the perspectives of various stakeholders in proposing possible solutions to these issues	Ch 3 L2; Ch 4 L2, L3; Ch 6 L3; Ch 7 L2; Ch 8 L2; Ch 9 L2, L3; Ch 11 L2, L3; Ch 13 L2
8. The importance of becoming informed in order to make positive civic contributions	Ch 1 WDYT; Ch 4 WDYT; Ch 6 L3; Ch 7 WDYT; Ch 8 L3; Ch 11 WDYT

The second edition of *Geography For Life,* as in the first edition, ensures that the National Geography Standards continue to challenge students and address the most important and enduring ideas in geography. The second edition of *Geography For Life* also incorporates new ideas about geography, the learning process, and additional skills that transcend disciplinary boundaries.

The goal of the National Geography Standards is to help students become geographically informed through knowledge and mastery of factual knowledge, mental maps and geographic tools, and ways of thinking.

The Six Essential Elements and Related National Geography Standards	Student Edition Chapter/Lesson
Essential Element: The World in Spatial Terms	
Geography Standard 1 **How to use maps and other geographic representations, geospatial technologies, and spatial thinking to understand and communicate information** The geographically informed person must use maps and other geographic representations, geospatial technologies, and spatial thinking to acquire, understand, and communicate information.	**Ch 1** CO, L1, L2, WDYT; **Ch 2** CO; **Ch 3** CO, GC; **Ch 4** CO; **Ch 5** CO; **Ch 6** CO, L1; **Ch 7** CO, L1, L2; **Ch 8** CO, L1, L2, GC; **Ch 9** CO, L1, L2; **Ch 10** CO, L1, L2, L3; **Ch 11** CO, L1, L2, L3; **Ch 12** CO, L2, GC; **Ch 13** CO, L1, L2, L3
Geography Standard 2 **How to use mental maps to organize information about people, places, and environments in a spatial context** A geographically informed person must mentally organize spatial information about people, places, and environments and must be able to call upon and use this information in appropriate contexts.	**Ch 1** CO, L1, L2, WDYT, ACT; **Ch 2** CO, L1, ACT; **Ch 3** CO, GC; **Ch 4** CO, L1, ACT; **Ch 5** CO, L1, ACT; **Ch 6** CO, L1, ACT; **Ch 7** CO, L1, ACT; **Ch 8** CO, L1, L2, GC; **Ch 9** CO, L1, L2, ACT; **Ch 10** CO, L1, L2, L3, ACT; **Ch 11** CO, L1, L2, L3, ACT; **Ch 12** CO, L2, GC, ACT; **Ch 13** CO, L1, L2, L3, ACT
Geography Standard 3 **How to analyze the spatial organization of people, places, and environments on Earth's surface** The geographically informed person must understand that physical and human phenomena are distributed across Earth's surface and see meaning in their arrangements across space.	**Ch 1** CO, L1, L2, WDYT; **Ch 2** CO, L2, L3; **Ch 3** CO, L1, L2; **Ch 4** CO, L1; **Ch 5** CO, L1; **Ch 6** CO, L1; **Ch 7** CO, L1, L2; **Ch 8** CO, L1; **Ch 9** CO, L1, L3; **Ch 10** CO, L1, L2, L3; **Ch 11** CO, L1, L2, L3; **Ch 12** CO, L1, L2; **Ch 13** CO, L1, L3
Essential Element: Places and Regions	
Geography Standard 4 **The physical and human characteristics of places** The geographically informed person must understand the genesis, evolution, and meaning of places. Places are locations having distinctive features that give them meaning and character that differs from other locations.	**Ch 1** L1, WDYT; **Ch 2** L1, L2, L3; **Ch 3** L1, L2; **Ch 4** L1, L3; **Ch 5** L1, L3; **Ch 6** L1, L3; **Ch 7** L1, L3; **Ch 8** L1, L3; **Ch 9** L1, L3; **Ch 10** L1, L3; **Ch 11** L1, L3; **Ch 12** L1, L3; **Ch 13** L1, L3
Geography Standard 5 **That people create regions to interpret Earth's complexity** The geographically informed person must understand the origins and functions of regions. Regions are human creations used to manage and interpret the complexity of Earth's surface. They help us understand and organize the arrangements of people, places, and environments.	**Ch 1** L1; **Ch 3**, L1, L2; **Ch 4** CO, L1; **Ch 5** CO, L1; **Ch 6** CO, L1, L3; **Ch 7** CO, L1, L3; **Ch 8** CO, L1; **Ch 9** CO, L1, L3; **Ch 10** CO, L1; **Ch 11** CO, L1, L3; **Ch 12** CO, L1; **Ch 13** CO, L1, L3
Geography Standard 6 **How culture and experience influence people's perceptions of places and regions** The geographically informed person must understand that our own culture and life experiences shape the way we perceive places and regions. Perceptions are the basis for understanding a place's location, extent, characteristics, and significance. Throughout our lives, culture and experience shape our worldviews, which in turn influence our perceptions of places and regions.	**Ch 1** L1; **Ch 3** L2; **Ch 4** L2, L3; **Ch 5** L2; **Ch 6** L1, L3; **Ch 7** L3; **Ch 8** L2, L3; **Ch 9** L2, L3; **Ch 10** L3; **Ch 11** L3; **Ch 12** L3; **Ch 13** L2, L3
Essential Element: Physical Systems	
Geography Standard 7 **The physical processes that shape the patterns of Earth's surface** The geographically informed person must understand that physical systems create, maintain, and modify the features that constitute Earth's surface. The physical environment provides the essential background for all human activity on Earth.	**Ch 2** L1, L2, L3; **Ch 4** L1, L2; **Ch 5** L1; **Ch 6** L1; **Ch 7** L1; **Ch 10** L1; **Ch 11** L1; **Ch 12** L1; **Ch 13** L1
Geography Standard 8 **The characteristics and spatial distribution of ecosystems and biomes on Earth's surface** The geographically informed person must understand that Earth's surface is home to multiple biophysical communities. All elements of the environment, including the human, are part of many different but nested ecosystems that comprise different biomes.	**Ch 1** L1; **Ch 2** L1, L3; **Ch 4** L1; **Ch 5** L1; **Ch 6** L1; **Ch 7** L1; **Ch 8** L1, GC; **Ch 9** L1; **Ch 10** L1; **Ch 11** L1; **Ch 12** L1; **Ch 13** L1

Note: CO=Chapter Opener; WDYT=What Do You Think?; GC=Global Connections; ACT=Chapter Activities

The Six Essential Elements and Related National Geography Standards	Student Edition Chapter/Lesson
Essential Element: Human Systems	
Geography Standard 9 **The characteristics, distribution, and migration of human populations on Earth's surface** The geographically informed person must understand that the growth, spatial distribution, and movements of people on Earth's surface are driving forces behind not only human events but also physical events. Human population is a dynamic force in reshaping the planet.	**Ch 1** L1; **Ch 3** L1, L2; **Ch 4** L2, L3; **Ch 5** L2; **Ch 6** L2, L3; **Ch 7** L3; **Ch 8** L2; **Ch 10** L3; **Ch 11** L2, L3; **Ch 12** L3, GC; **Ch 13** L2, L3
Geography Standard 10 **The characteristics, distribution, and complexity of Earth's cultural mosaics** The geographically informed person must understand that culture is an intricate and complex idea. As the learned behavior of people, culture shapes each group's way of life and its own view of itself and other groups.	**Ch 3** L1, L2, GC; **Ch 4** L2; **Ch 5** L2, L3; **Ch 6** L2, L3; **Ch 7** L3; **Ch 8** L2, L3; **Ch 10** L3, WDYT; **Ch 11** L3; **Ch 12** L2, L3; **Ch 13** L2, L3
Geography Standard 11 **The patterns and networks of economic interdependence on Earth's surface** The geographically informed person must understand the spatial organization of the economic, transportation, and communication systems that support networks of trade in raw materials, manufactured goods, capital (human and monetary), ideas, and services.	**Ch 1** L1; **Ch 3** L3; **Ch 5** L3; **Ch 6** L3; **Ch 7** L3, WDYT; **Ch 8** L3; **Ch 9** L3; **Ch 10** L3; **Ch 11** L3, WDYT; **Ch 12** L3; **Ch 13** L2, L3
Geography Standard 12 **The processes, patterns, and functions of human settlement** The geographically informed person must understand the varying forms of human settlements in terms of their size, composition, location, arrangement, organization, function, and history.	**Ch 1** L1; **Ch 3** L1, L2; **Ch 4** L2, L3; **Ch 5** L2, L3; **Ch 6** L2, L3; **Ch 7** L2, L3; **Ch 8** L2, L3; **Ch 9** L2, L3; **Ch 10** L3; **Ch 11** L2, L3; **Ch 12** L2, L3; **Ch 13** L2, L3
Geography Standard 13 **How the forces of cooperation and conflict among people influence the division and control of Earth's surface** The geographically informed person must understand how and why different groups of people have divided, organized, and unified areas of Earth's surface. Competing for control of areas of Earth's surface, large and small, is a universal trait among societies and has resulted in both productive cooperation and destructive conflict between groups.	**Ch 3** L1, L3; **Ch 4** L2; **Ch 5** L2; **Ch 6** L2, L3; **Ch 7** L2, L3, GC; **Ch 8** L2; **Ch 9** L2; **Ch 11** L2, L3, WDYT; **Ch 12** L2, L3; **Ch 13** L2, L3
Essential Element: Environment and Society	
Geography Standard 14 **How human actions modify the physical environment** The geographically informed person must understand the human imprint on the physical environment. Many of the important issues facing modern society are the result of human modifications of the physical environment. Some of these modifications are intended and positive; others unintended and negative. These changes have political, economic, and social implications at all scales, from global to local.	**Ch 1** L1; **Ch 2** L1, L2; **Ch 3** L1, L3; **Ch 4** L2, WDYT; **Ch 5** L1, L2, L3; **Ch 6** L1, L2, L3; **Ch 7** L2, L3; **Ch 8** L1, L3, GC; **Ch 9** L2, L3; **Ch 10** L2, L3; **Ch 11** L1, L2, L3; **Ch 12** L2, L3; **Ch 13** L3
Geography Standard 15 **How physical systems affect human systems** The geographically informed person must understand how humans are able to live in various physical settings and the role the physical features of those settings play in shaping human activity.	**Ch 2** L1; **Ch 4** L2, WDYT; **Ch 5** L2, L3; **Ch 6** L2, L3; **Ch 7** L1; **Ch 8** L1, L2, L3, GC; **Ch 9** L3; **Ch 10** L3; **Ch 11** L1, L3; **Ch 12** L1, L3; **Ch 13** L1, L2, L3
Geography Standard 16 **The changes that occur in the meaning, use, distribution, and importance of resources** The geographically informed person must understand that a "resource" is a cultural concept. A resource is any physical material constituting part of Earth that people need and value. The uses and values of resources change from culture to culture and from time to time.	**Ch 1** L1; **Ch 3** L3; **Ch 4** WDYT; **Ch 5** L2, L3; **Ch 6** L2, L3; **Ch 7** L3; **Ch 8** L2, L3, GC; **Ch 9** L1, L3; **Ch 10** L1, L3, WDYT; **Ch 11** L2; **Ch 12** L3; **Ch 13** L2, L3
Essential Element: The Uses of Geography	
Geography Standard 17 **How to apply geography to interpret the past** The geographically informed person must understand the importance of bringing spatial and ecological perspectives of geography to bear on the events of history, and vice versa, and the value of learning about the geographies of the past.	**Ch 1** L1; **Ch 4** L2; **Ch 5** L2; **Ch 6** L2; **Ch 7** L2; **Ch 8** L2; **Ch 9** L2; **Ch 10** L2; **Ch 11** L2; **Ch 12** L2; **Ch 13** L2
Geography Standard 18 **How to apply geography to interpret the present and plan for the future** The geographically informed person must understand that the study of geography is critical to understanding the world, now and in the future, and is not simply an exercise for its own sake. Geography is valuable for comprehending current events and planning for the future in geographically-appropriate and sustainable ways.	**Ch 1** L2; **Ch 3** L1, L2, L3; **Ch 4** L3; **Ch 5** L3; **Ch 6** L3; **Ch 7** L3; **Ch 8** L3; **Ch 9** L3; **Ch 10** L3; **Ch 11** L3; **Ch 12** L3; **Ch 13** L3

USING FOLDABLES® IN THE CLASSROOM

by Rhonda Meyer Vivian, Ph.D., and Nancy F. Wisker, M.A.

Graphic Organizers

Current research shows that graphic organizers are powerful teaching and learning tools. Most of us are familiar with common graphic organizers such as diagrams, maps, outlines, and charts, all of which are two-dimensional. Foldables® are three-dimensional, interactive graphic organizers that were created more than 30 years ago by educator Dinah Zike.

Graphic organizers are visual representations combining line, shape, space, and symbols to convey facts and concepts or to organize information. Graphic organizers, when designed and used appropriately:

- Speed up communication
- Help organize information
- Are easy-to-understand
- Show complex relationships
- Clarify concepts with few words
- Convey ideas and understanding
- Assess comprehension

Graphic organizers help students organize information in a visual manner. This is a profound concept, especially as the number of non-native English-speaking students increases. A student is able to use graphic organizers to clarify concepts or to convey ideas and understandings with fewer words.

Graphic organizers also make complex relationships or concepts easier to understand, particularly for visual learners. Foldables take that process to the next level, most notably, for tactile/kinesthetic learners.

When to Use Graphic Organizers

Graphic organizers may be used at any point during instruction, but just as with any other instructional strategy, they are most successful when they are built into the instructional plan, rather than presented as an "extra" activity.

Graphic organizers may work better than outline notes in helping students discover or understand relationships between concepts. Foldables help teach students how to take notes by visually and kinesthetically chunking information into sections.

Foldables may be used as an alternative form of assessment in the classroom. Because the Foldable has readily identifiable sections, a teacher can quickly see gaps in student knowledge.

Reading, Writing, and Social Studies

Graphic organizers have been shown to be highly effective in literacy development. In numerous studies, graphic organizers help improve the development of literacy skills—including oral, written, and comprehension.

Graphic organizers have been found to help students organize information from expository social studies texts and comprehend content area reading. They also help students develop critical thinking skills and help transfer these skills to new situations and content areas.

Students With Special Needs

Graphic organizers may help English language learners improve higher-order thinking skills.

Because of their visual organization, graphic organizers seem to be quite beneficial for use with learning disabled students. They appear to help students understand content area material, to organize information, and to retain and recall content.

Conclusions

Graphic organizers may lead to improved student performance, whether measured by classroom-based observation, textbook assessments, or standardized assessments, when compared with more traditional forms of instruction.

When students construct their own graphic organizers, as they do with Foldables, they are active participants in their learning.

Our goal as educators is to help students glean important information and understand key concepts and to be able to relate these concepts or apply them to real-world situations. Graphic organizers help support and develop students' note-taking skills, summarizing skills, reading comprehension, and vocabulary development, which leads to better understanding and application of social studies content.

Foldables® are found in every chapter of *Discovering World Geography* so that students can take notes and organize the chapter information.

Dinah Zike is an award-winning author, educator, educational consultant, and inventor, known internationally for graphic organizers known as Foldables®. Based outside of San Antonio, Texas, Zike is a frequent keynote speaker and conducts seminars for over 50,000 teachers and parents annually.

Rhonda Meyer Vivian, Ph.D., is CEO of Dinah-Might Adventures, LP, and Nancy F. Wisker, M.A., is Director of Math and Science for Dinah-Might Adventures, L.P.

btw
McGraw-Hill's Current Events Web Site

The **btw** current events Web site was created specifically for students. It provides up-to-date coverage of important national and world news, along with contests, polls, and activities.

Each news story has activities and questions to extend the content and provide skills practice, including:
- Tips on how to use **btw** articles in your social studies classroom
- Ideas for using social media and other technology resources
- 21st Century Skill options

Use **btw** as a bellringer activity, to activate critical thinking, or to engage students in high-interest projects.

Engaging, student-friendly content guides readers through the major events that affect our nation and our world. **Top Stories** examine everything from unrest in Libya to the newest shows on television.

You Decide asks students to take a stand after they analyze different points of view on issues around the United States and the world.

Election Central takes a closer look at upcoming elections with information about party platforms, candidates, and important issues.

Real people **Profiles** provide first-person accounts of events, such as what it is like to be a soldier in Iraq or to testify in front of Congress.

Be an Active Citizen! helps students learn more about the government, courts, and economy to help them become informed citizens.

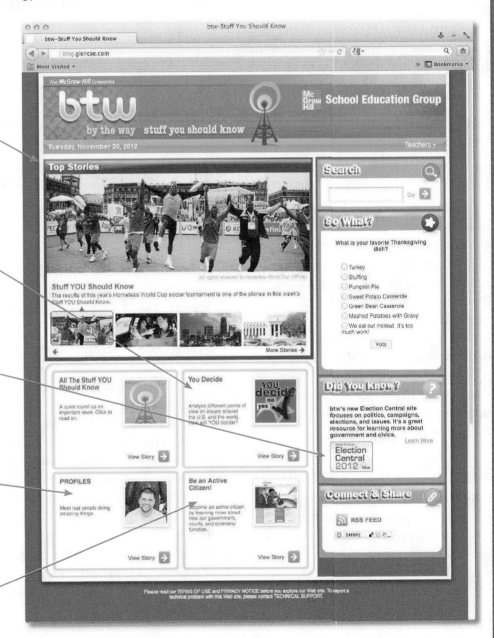

Visit the **btw** Current Events Web site at **blog.glencoe.com**.

ePals GlobalCommunity

Stockbyte/Punchstock

ePals®, a global community of more than one million K-12 classrooms in 200 countries and territories, provides teachers with the opportunity to facilitate safe, authentic, and dynamic exchanges with other classrooms. McGraw-Hill Education, The Smithsonian Institution, International Baccalaureate, and leading educators around the globe have partnered with ePals® to help make learning dynamic for students, improve academic achievement, and meet multiple Common Core standards.

What Is Global Collaboration?

Global collaboration leverages the power of social media to connect classrooms around the world for real-life lessons and projects in virtual study groups, in and out of school. Students can safely work together on ePals® using familiar social media tools to collaborate on research, discussions, and multimedia projects. By connecting with peers in other parts of the world, students can discover people, places, and cultures far beyond the classroom.

Why Collaboration Is Crucial

Research shows that collaborative learning has a positive effect on student achievement. Collaborative, project-based experiences inspire students with real-world problems and bring lessons to life with dynamic, participatory learning. Students

are more motivated and try harder because they're communicating with a real person, for a real purpose. ePals®collaboration benefits students and educators in a variety of ways:

- Facilitates classroom-led delivery of Common Core-aligned, project-based learning experiences, including Writing 6 and Writing 7

- Demonstrates student knowledge by publishing written projects to share ideas and receive feedback from an international audience

- Develops core academic, college and career skills such as critical thinking, problem solving, communication and global awareness

Connect Globally

On ePals®, teachers can browse hundreds of thousands of classroom profiles and projects by location, age range, language, and subject matter, to find collaboration partners. Classrooms then partner in virtual project workspaces for digital collaboration around tailored projects, activities, and content. Each project workspace enables roundtable classroom collaboration and includes a suite of safe social media tools (private to that workspace and controlled by the teacher), including blogs, wikis, forums, and media galleries. ePals® also provides safe student email accounts for one-on-one student exchanges.

ePals® is specifically designed for safe K-12 communication and collaboration, compliant with the Children's Online Privacy Protection Act (COPPA), Family Educational Rights and Privacy Act (FERPA) and Children's Internet Protection Act (CIPA). A team of ePals® educators moderates all classroom profiles and projects to maintain a robust education community safe for K-12 students.

Tips for Collaborating Globally on ePals®

Pair Students With Global Peers: Pair students within a project workspace with peers from other countries to accomplish specific goals, such as completing joint-inquiry projects.

Host Online Discussions: Host dynamic discussions between students by posting forum topics for students to build on one another's ideas and learn to express their own thoughts clearly and persuasively.

Share Student Work: Have students publish their work and ideas to the project group using media galleries and encourage peer review.

Create Collaborative Content: Use wikis to have student groups author joint content, such as digital presentations and multimedia research reports.

To get started, visit ePals® at www.epals.com/learningcenter

UNDERSTANDING BY DESIGN®

by Jay McTighe

Understanding by Design® (UbD®) offers a planning framework to guide curriculum, assessment, and instruction. Its two key ideas are contained in the title: 1) focus on teaching and assessing for understanding and transfer, and 2) design curriculum "backward" from those ends.
UbD is based on seven key tenets:

1. UbD is a way of thinking purposefully about curricular planning, not a rigid program or prescriptive recipe.

2. A primary goal of UbD is developing and deepening student understanding: the ability to make meaning of learning via "big ideas" and transfer learning.

3. Understanding is revealed when students autonomously make sense of and transfer their learning through authentic performance. Six facets of understanding—the capacity to explain, interpret, apply, shift perspective, empathize, and self assess—serve as indicators of understanding.

4. Effective curriculum is planned "backward" from long-term desired results though a three-stage design process (Desired Results, Evidence, Learning Plan). This process helps to avoid the twin problems of "textbook coverage" and "activity-oriented" teaching in which no clear priorities and purposes are apparent.

5. Teachers are coaches of understanding, not mere purveyors of content or activity. They focus on ensuring learning, not just teaching (and assuming that what was taught was learned); they always aim and check for successful meaning making and transfer by the learner.

6. Regular reviews of units and curriculum against design standards enhance curricular quality and effectiveness.

7. UbD reflects a continuous improvement approach to achievement. The results of our designs —student performance—inform needed adjustments in curriculum as well as instruction.

Three Stages of Backward Design

In UbD, we propose a 3-stage "backward design" process for curriculum planning. The concept of planning "backward" from desired results is not new. In 1949 Ralph Tyler described this approach as an effective process for focusing instruction. More recently, Stephen Covey, in the best selling book, *Seven Habits of Highly Effective People*, reports that effective people in various fields are goal-oriented and plan with the end in mind. Although not a new idea, we have found that the deliberate use of backward design for planning curriculum units and courses results in more clearly defined goals, more appropriate assessments, more tightly aligned lessons, and more purposeful teaching.

Backward planning asks educators to consider the following three stages:

Stage 1 – Identify Desired Results

What should students know, understand, and be able to do? What content is worthy of understanding? What "enduring" understandings are desired? What essential questions will be explored?

In the first stage of backward design we consider our goals, examine established Content Standards (national, state, province, district), and review curriculum expectations. Since there is typically more "content" than can reasonably be addressed within the available time, teachers must make choices. This first stage in the design process calls for setting priorities.

More specifically, Stage 1 of UbD asks teachers to identify the "big ideas" that we want students to come to understand, and then to identify or craft companion essential questions. Big ideas reflect transferable concepts, principles and processes that are key to understanding the topic or subject. Essential questions present open-ended, thought-provoking inquiries that are explored over time.

More specific knowledge and skill objectives, linked to the targeted Content Standards and Understandings, are also identified in Stage 1. An important point in UbD is to recognize that factual knowledge and skills are not taught for their own sake, but as a means to larger ends. Ultimately, teaching should equip learners to be able to use or transfer their learning; i.e., meaningful performance with content. This is the "end" we always want to keep in mind.

professional development

Stage 2 – Determine Acceptable Evidence

How will we know if students have achieved the desired results? What will we accept as evidence of student understanding and proficiency? How will we evaluate student performance?

Backward design encourages teachers and curriculum planners to first "think like an assessor" before designing specific units and lessons. The assessment evidence we need reflects the desired results identified in Stage 1. Thus, we consider in advance the assessment evidence needed to document and validate that the targeted learning has been achieved. Doing so invariably sharpens and focuses teaching.

In Stage 2, we distinguish between two broad types of assessment—Performance Tasks and Other Evidence. The performance tasks ask students to apply their learning to a new and authentic situation as means of assessing their understanding. In UbD, we have identified six facets of understanding for assessment purposes[1]. When someone truly understands, they:

- Can **explain** concepts, principles and processes; i.e., put it in their own words, teach it to others, justify their answers, show their reasoning.

- Can **interpret**; i.e., make sense of data, text, and experience through images, analogies, stories, and models.

- Can apply; i.e., effectively use and adapt what they know in new and complex contexts.

- Demonstrate **perspective**; i.e., can see the big picture and recognize different points of view.

- Display **empathy**; i.e., perceive sensitively and "walk in someone else's shoes."

- Have **self-knowledge**; i.e., show metacognition, use productive habits of mind, and reflect on the meaning of their learning and experience.

These six facets do not present a theory of how people come to understand something. Instead, the facets are intended to serve as indicators of how understanding is revealed, and thus provide guidance as to the kinds of assessments we need to determine the extent of student understanding. Here are two notes regarding assessing understanding through the facets:

1) All six facets of understanding need not be used all of the time in assessment. In social studies, Empathy and Perspective may be added when appropriate.

2) Performance Tasks based on one or more facets are not intended for use in daily lessons. Rather, these tasks should be seen as culminating performances for a unit of study.

In addition to Performance Tasks, Stage 2 includes Other Evidence, such as traditional quizzes, tests, observations, and work samples to round out the assessment picture to

Examples of Essential Questions in Social Studies	
Understandings or Big Ideas	**Essential Questions**
History involves interpretation, and different people may interpret the same events differently.	*Whose "story" is this? How do we know what <u>really</u> happened in the past?*
The geography, climate, and natural resources of a region influence the culture, economy, and lifestyle of its inhabitants.	*How does <u>where</u> we live influence <u>how</u> we live?*
History often repeats itself. Recognizing the patterns of the past can help us better understand the present and prepare for the future.	*Why study the past? What does the past have to do with today?*
Governments can change based on the changing needs of their people, the society, and the world.	*What makes an effective government? Why do/should governments change?*

[1] Wiggins, G. and McTighe, J. and (1998, 2005). *Understanding By Design.* Alexandria, VA: The Association for Supervision and Curriculum Development.

UNDERSTANDING BY DESIGN®
(continued)

determine what students know and can do. A key idea in backward design has to do with alignment. In other words, are we assessing everything that we are trying to achieve (in Stage 1) or only those things that are easiest to test and grade? Is anything important slipping through the cracks because it is not being assessed? Checking the alignment between Stages 1 and 2 helps insure that *all* important goals are appropriately assessed.

Stage 3 – Plan Learning Experiences and Instruction

How will we support learners in coming to an understanding of important ideas and processes? How will we prepare them to autonomously transfer their learning? What enabling knowledge and skills will students need in order to perform effectively and achieve desired results? What activities, sequence, and resources are best suited to accomplish our goals?

In Stage 3 of backward design, teachers now plan the most appropriate learning activities to help students acquire important knowledge and skills, come to understand important ideas and processes, and transfer their learning in meaningful ways. When developing a plan for learning, we propose that teachers consider a set of instructional principles, embedded in the acronym W.H.E.R.E.T.O. These design elements provide the armature or blueprint for instructional planning in Stage 3 in support of our goals of understanding and transfer.

Each of the W.H.E.R.E.T.O. elements is presented in the form of questions to consider.

> **W** = *How will I help learners know – What they will be learning? Why this is worth learning? What evidence will show their learning? How will their performance be evaluated?*

Learners of all ages are more likely to put forth effort and meet with success when they understand the learning goals and see them as meaningful and personally relevant. The "W" in W.H.E.R.E.T.O. reminds teachers to clearly communicate the goals and help students see their relevance. In addition, learners need to know the concomitant performance expectations and assessments through which they will demonstrate their learning so that they have clear learning targets and the basis for monitoring their progress toward them.

> **H** = *How will I hook and engage the learners?*

There is wisdom in the old adage: "Before you try to teach them, you've got to get their attention." The best teachers have always recognized the value of "hooking" learners through introductory activities that "itch" the mind and engage the heart in the learning process, and we encourage teachers to deliberately plan ways of hooking their learners to the topics they teach. Examples of effective hooks include provocative essential questions, counter-intuitive phenomena, controversial issues, authentic problems and challenges, emotional encounters, and humor. One must be mindful, of course, of not just coming up with interesting introductory activities that have no carry-over value. The intent is to match the hook with the content

and the experiences of the learners—by design—as a means of drawing them into a productive learning experience.

> **E** = *How will I equip students to master identified standards and succeed with the transfer performances? What learning experiences will help develop and deepen understanding of important ideas?*

Understanding cannot be simply transferred like a load of freight from one mind to another. Coming to understand requires active intellectual engagement on the part of the learner. Therefore, instead of merely covering the content, effective educators "uncover" the most enduring ideas and processes in ways that engage students in constructing meaning for themselves. To this end, teachers select an appropriate balance of constructivist learning experiences, structured activities, and direct instruction for helping students acquire the desired knowledge, skill, and understanding. While there is certainly a place for direct instruction and modeling, teaching for understanding asks teachers to engage learners in making meaning through active inquiry.

> **R** = *How will I encourage the learners to rethink previous learning? How will I encourage on-going revision and refinement?*

Few learners develop a complete understanding of abstract ideas on the first encounter. Indeed, the phrase "coming to understand" is suggestive of a process. Over time, learners develop and deepen their understanding by thinking and re-thinking, by examining ideas from a different point of view, from examining underlying assumptions, by receiving feedback and revising. Just as the quality of

writing benefits from the iterative process of drafting and revising, so to do understandings become more mature. The "R" in W.H.E.R.E.T.O. encourages teachers to explicitly include such opportunities.

> **E** = *How will I promote students' self-evaluation and reflection?*

Capable and independent learners are distinguished by their capacity to set goals, self-assess their progress, and adjust as needed. Yet, one of the most frequently overlooked aspects of the instructional process involves helping students to develop the metacognitive skills of self-evaluation, self-regulation, and reflection. The second "E" of WHERETO reminds teachers to build in time and expectations for students to regularly self-assess, reflect on the meaning of their learning, and set goals for future performance.

> **T** = *How will I tailor the learning experiences to the nature of the learners I serve? How might I differentiate instruction to respond to the varied needs of students?*

"One size fits all teaching" is rarely optimal. Learners differ significantly in terms of their prior knowledge and skill levels, their interests, talents, and preferred ways of learning. Accordingly, the most effective teachers get to know their students and tailor their teaching and learning experiences to connect to them. A variety of strategies may be employed to differentiate *content* (e.g., how subject matter is presented), *process* (e.g., how students work), and *product* (e.g., how learners demonstrate their learning). The logic of backward design offers a cautionary note here: the Content Standards and Understandings should *not* be differentiated (except for students with Indi-

vidualized Education Plans—I.E.P.s). In other words, differentiate means keeping the end in mind for all.

> **O** = *How will I organize the learning experiences for maximum engagement and effectiveness? What sequence will be optimal given the understanding and transfer goals?*

When the primary educational goals involve helping students acquire basic knowledge and skills, teachers may be comfortable "covering" the content by telling and modeling.

However, when we include understanding and transfer as desired results, educators are encouraged to give careful attention to how the content is organized and sequenced. Just as effective story tellers and filmmakers often don't begin in the "beginning," teachers can consider alternatives to sequential content coverage. For example, methods such as the Case Method, Problem or Project-Based Learning, and Socratic Seminars immerse students in challenging situations, even before they may have acquired all of the "basics." They actively engage students in trying to make meaning and apply their learning in demanding circumstances without single "correct" answers.

Conclusion

Many teachers who are introduced to the backward design process have observed that while the process makes sense in theory, it often feels awkward in use. This is to be expected since the principles and practices of UbD often challenge conventional planning and teaching habits. However, with some practice, educators find that backward design becomes not only more comfortable, but a way of thinking. The resources found in this program support teaching and assessing for understanding and transfer.

WHY TEACH WITH TECHNOLOGY?

by Tom Daccord and Justin Reich, EdTechTeacher

✓ **Technology is transforming the practice of historians and should transform history classrooms as well.** While printed documents, books, maps, and artwork constitute the bulk of the historical record before 1900, the history of the last century is also captured in sound and video recording and in Web sites and other Internet resources. Today's students need to learn how to analyze and build arguments using these multimedia records as well as traditional primary sources.

✓ **So many of the sources that helped historians and history teachers fall in love with the discipline are now available online.** In recent decades, universities, libraries, archives, and other institutions have scanned and uploaded many vast treasure troves of historical sources. The Internet-connected classroom increasingly has access to the world's historical record, giving students a chance to develop critical thinking skills as well as learning historical narratives.

✓ **Whoever is doing most of the talking or most of the typing is doing most of the learning, and the more people listening the better.** Technology allows us to transfer the responsibility for learning from teachers to students, and to put students in the driver's seat of their own learning. Students who are actively engaged in creating and presenting their understandings of history are learning more than students passively listening. Technology also allows students to publish their work to broader audiences of peers, parents, and even the entire Internet-connected world. Students find the opportunities challenging, exciting, and engaging.

✓ **The more ways students have to engage with content, the more likely they are to remember and understand that content.** The Internet can provide students and teachers with access to text documents, images, sounds and songs, video, simulations, and games. The more different ways students engage with historical content, the more likely they are to make meaning of that material.

✓ **Students live in a technology-rich world, and classrooms should prepare students for that world.** When students spend most of their waking hours connected to a worldwide, online network of people, resources, and opportunities, they experience dissonance and disappointment in entering a "powered-down" school. Many students will leave school to go on to workplaces completely transformed by technology, and teachers have a responsibility to prepare students for these environments.

Integrating Technology Effectively

Ben Shneiderman, in his book *Leonardo's Laptop*, lays out a four-part framework for teaching with technology: Collect-Relate-Create-Donate. This framework is a helpful blueprint for designing projects and learning experiences with technology.

Collect Students should begin a project by collecting the resources necessary to produce a meaningful presentation of their understanding. In some cases, students might collect these resources through textbook reading and teacher lecture, but students should also collect resources from

For More Information

Visit the EdTechTeacher Web sites for more links, tutorials, and other resources.

Teaching With Technology

In addition to the many other online resources in this program, EdTech Teacher has created digital project-based learning activities for every chapter. These can be used independently or with the print chapter-based hands-on activities. These cumulative projects bring geography to life and reveal student understanding through performance assessment. The digital hands-on projects integrate technology with instruction. Students use software and the Internet to create projects that are fun and challenging.

professional development

online collections, school library Web sites, and online searches.

Relate Technology greatly facilitates the process of students working together socially. The ability to collaborate is essential to the workplace and civic sphere of the future. In creating technology projects, students should have the chance to work together, or at least comment on each other's work, using blogs, wikis, podcasts, and other collaborative publishing tools.

Create Using multimedia publishing tools, students should have the opportunity to design presentations and performances of their historical understanding. They should make historical arguments in linear text, as well as through images, audio and video recordings, and multimedia presentations.

Donate Finally, students should create work not just for their teachers, but for broader audiences. Students who have a chance to share their work with their peers, their families, their community, and the Internet-connected world find that opportunity rewarding. Today's students experience very few barriers to expression in their networked lives, and they crave these opportunities in schools.

Guidelines for Successful Technology Projects

1) **Plan for problems.** Things can go wrong when working with technology, and learning how to deal with these challenges is essential for students, and for their teachers. As you start using technology in the classroom, try to have an extra teacher, aide, student-teacher, or IT staff member in the room with you to help troubleshoot problems. When things do go wrong, stay calm, and ask your students to help you resolve challenges and make the most of class time. Always have a back up, "pencil and paper" activity prepared in case there are problems with computers or networks. Over time, teachers who practice teaching with technology experience fewer and fewer of these problems, but they can be very challenging the first time you experience them!

2) **Practice from multiple perspectives.** Whenever you develop a technology project, try to do everything that students will do from a student's perspective. If you create a blog or wiki with a teacher account, create a student account to test the technology.

3) **Adapt to your local technology resources, but don't let those resources keep you from using technology.** Some schools have excellent and ample technology resources—labs and laptop carts—that make completing technology projects straightforward. Other schools have fewer resources, but virtually every student can get access to a networked computer in school, at the library or at home, especially if you give them a few nights to do so. Many technology activities are described as if you could complete them in a few class periods, but if resources are limited, you might consider spreading the activity out over a few days or weeks to give students the chance to get online.

4) **Plan with a partner.** Going it alone can be scary. If possible, have another teacher in your department or on your team, design and pilot technology projects with you to help solve the challenges that crop up whenever trying out new pedagogies.

5) **It's harder, then it gets easier.** Learning new teaching strategies is always hard. With technology, however, once you get past the initial learning curve there are all sorts of ways technology can make teaching more efficient and simultaneously make learning more meaningful for students.

Learn More about Teaching Geography with Technology

EdTechTeacher has several Web sites designed to help social studies and geography teachers learn more about teaching with technology. The Best of History Web Sites (www.besthistorysites.net) is the Internet's authoritative directory of social studies-related resources, Web sites, games, simulations, lesson plans, and activities. Teaching History with Technology (www.thwt.org) has a series of white papers, tutorials, and guides for enriching teaching strategies (lecturing, discussion, presentations, assessments, and so forth) with educational technology. EdTechTeacher (www. edtechteacher.org) has additional teaching resources and information about learning opportunities such as free webinars and other professional development workshops.

Tom Daccord and Justin Reich are co-Directors of EdTechTeacher. Together they authored Best Ideas for Teaching With Technology: A Practical Guide for Teachers by Teachers.

BACKGROUND KNOWLEDGE:
THE KEY TO UNDERSTANDING
by Doug Fisher, Ph.D., and Nancy Frey, Ph.D.

Mention background knowledge and most middle school educators will tell you that it is an essential component of history and social studies learning. They will discuss the importance of activating it in their students and building it when there are gaps. Yet most will also confess to being unsure of how to accomplish this in a systematic way beyond asking some questions about prior experiences. As for the gaps, how can anyone find the time to build it when there is so much new information to be covered?

The answer is to integrate background knowledge activation, building, and assessment into the heart of the lesson, not just as bookends to new learning. The reasons for this are pretty striking. Background knowledge directly influences a learner's ability to understand new information and act upon it (RAND Reading Study Group, 2002). In addition, background knowledge is demonstrated through the use of academic vocabulary and academic language, an important measure of content learning (Cromley & Azevedo, 2007). Finally, students with strong background knowledge about a topic process text better, especially in their ability to monitor and correct comprehension difficulties (Cakir, 2008).

Cultivating Background Knowledge

The key to understanding new information is to link it to what is already known. A feature of initial learning is that we aren't very good at doing so. Our efforts to focus on what is unfamiliar temporarily blind us to what we already know. It is helpful to have well-placed reminders about what is already known, because it assists us in marshalling the familiar in order to understand the new.

When we ask questions of students about prior experiences, or invite them to engage in a quickwrite about a previously taught topic, we are activating their background knowledge. More importantly, we are providing the signposts they need to direct them to the most salient information they will need to learn the new material. For example, a study of Ancient Rome doesn't merely begin with the legendary founding of a great city by two boys raised by wolves. It also requires knowledge of the influence of ancient Greek civilization on Rome's governance, military, art, and culture. It is easy, however, for students to temporarily forget everything they have learned about Greece in their effort to assimilate new information. Well-placed questions, writing opportunities, and graphic organizers can remind them of what they have previously learned.

Another means for cultivating background knowledge is to assess what students know (or think they know) about a topic. This shouldn't be a quiz of isolated facts, but instead should focus on the anticipated misconceptions that a learner is likely to hold about a new topic. For instance, it is easy for students to confuse what they have learned about Greek mythology when learning about Roman gods and goddesses. Those terms (gods and goddesses) alone suggest that for Romans this was at the heart of their religious beliefs. But Roman mythology differs from Greek mythology. For Greeks, mythology formed the heart of religion. For Romans, the gods and goddesses made for good stories, but weren't necessarily worshipped. Posing questions that are designed to surface misconceptions such as this help to rectify incorrect perceptions before they are ingrained.

Assessing Background Knowledge

Despite the efforts of caring educators, families, and communities, students come to us with gaps in their background knowledge. This can be due to a variety of causes, including frequent moves, second language acquisition, lack of experience with a topic, or difficulty with the content itself. Students at the middle school level face the additional well-documented challenges of transitioning from elementary school, where one teacher made connections for them to background knowledge, to a middle school schedule with many teachers and content areas. These changes require them to make more of their own connections across subjects.

In addition, a middle school schedule leaves us with less time across the day to get to know our students and the background knowledge they possess. It is useful to have formative assessment embedded into lessons in order to gauge where gaps might exist.

Activities that draw on core background knowledge necessary for deep understanding of new information provide these opportunities. Lessons that invite students to construct graphic organizers using both new knowledge and background knowledge give us such a window. A well-placed question invites students to consider what they already know.

If and when students have difficulty with activities like this, the teacher can pause to supply missing background knowledge. This may be done through direct explanation, by drawing their attention to features in the text, and even to returning to a previous chapter to revisit information. These need not be seen as delays, but rather as time well spent to solidify foundational knowledge.

Building Background Knowledge

Effective middle school educators take a proactive stance to building background knowledge by creating opportunities to do so. They conduct read alouds and shared readings of text and provide visual information to build students' mental image banks. Texts and images related to necessary background knowledge are especially useful in history and social studies, where students are required to understand and use primary source documents. A challenge is that many of these are hard for students to make sense of on their own, as they often use archaic language and represent ideas that are not contemporary to adoles-

cent lives. Texts and images carefully selected with middle school students in mind can build their background knowledge of the people and times being studied, and help them more fully appreciate the influences one culture has upon another. For example, illustrations of Greek and Roman architecture invite comparison. Maps of the ancient world highlight why empires fought over land.

Student background knowledge is also built through deeper understanding of the academic vocabulary and language that lies at the heart of history and social studies. By using a think aloud technique, teachers build

their students' background knowledge about the derivation of the term, as well as the way they approach an unfamiliar word. This ensures that students will recall the term more precisely while also equipping them with a problem-solving strategy to apply to other new words.

Conclusion

McGraw-Hill **networks** learning system offers middle school educators the tools needed to activate, assess, and build student background knowledge by infusing approaches like this into the lesson design. The habit of mind of drawing on what one already knows and seeking information to fill in knowledge gaps begins with educators like you who show students how this is done.

Doug Fisher, Ph.D., and Nancy Frey, Ph.D., are professors in the School of Teacher Education at San Diego State University.

Cakir, O. (2008). The effect of textual differences on children's processing strategies. *Reading Improvement, 45*(2), 69-83.

Cromley, J. G., & Azevedo, R. (2007). Testing and refining the direct and inferential mediation model of reading comprehension. *Journal of Educational Psychology, 99*(2), 311-325.

RAND *Reading Study Group. (2002). Reading for understanding: Toward an R&D program in reading comprehension.* Office of Educational Research and Improvement. Santa Monica, CA: RAND.

COLLEGE AND CAREER READINESS

Why Is College & Career Readiness Crucial?

- Only 70% of American students receive a high school diploma.
- Of that 70% of high school graduates, 53% of those who make it to college require remedial help.
- Over 90% of new jobs that will be available to students in the 21st century will require some postsecondary education.
- Most employers today cannot compete successfully without a workforce that has solid academic skills.
- The average difference in salary between someone with a high school degree and someone with postsecondary credentials can be $1 million over their lifetimes.

What Is College & Career Readiness?

Students are college and career ready when they have the level of preparation needed to academically, socially, and cognitively complete a postsecondary course of study without remediation. Students are prepared when they can enter the workforce at a level at which they are in line for promotion and career enhancement.

The ultimate goal of the college and career readiness initiative is to maintain America's competitive edge in the global economy of today. The workforce of the 21st century is an increasingly global, knowledge-based economy that demands the ability to:

- Think critically
- Solve problems
- Create and innovate
- Communicate
- Collaborate
- Learn new skills
- Use ICT (information and communications technology)

Explain College & Career Readiness to Students

One of the first steps you should take is to provide students with a framework that will help them see the relevancy of what they do in school. The three principal elements of College and Career Readiness (CCR) are:

- an understanding of core academic skills and the ability to apply them in educational and employment settings
- familiarity with skills valued by a broad range of employers such as communication, critical thinking, and responsibility
- mastery of the technologies and skill sets associated with a career pathway

Once students have been exposed to these elements, it is critical for them to see how they relate to their own plans for continuing education and career choice. Mention that CCR is more than just a personal issue, and it affects the country and our quality of life.

Most students—as well as many adults—consider work to be an obligation that they must perform in order to have money. Earning a salary is, of course, a central benefit of working, but so is the sense of satisfaction that comes from doing a job well. Moreover, every job contributes to the quality of life in our communities and our nation. Being prepared to pursue an education or get a job after high school is the hallmark of a good citizen.

Recognize That All Careers Are Important

Without question, the greatest challenge faced by educators, parents, and the public is recognizing that all jobs are important. When you discuss careers, be generous with your reflections and encourage your students to do the same. Be sure to mention the enormous variety of opportunities available to them in diverse fields. The more that students can recognize the

Mark Scott/Getty Images

rich possibilities of whatever career they pursue, the more likely they will be to enjoy success and personal satisfaction.

Students typically have a relatively narrow perspective on the careers and jobs available to them. As part of the discussion of careers, broaden this perspective by reviewing some opportunities that your students might not be aware of. An interesting place to start is in the high profile industries of sports and entertainment.

Many students dream of being celebrities and have no idea about how unlikely this is. What they don't realize is that for every professional athlete, singer, or movie star, there are a hundred or more fascinating careers including sports trainers, writers, administrative assistants, drivers, and a seemingly endless list of other jobs. Not surprisingly, students usually respond positively when they learn that just in case they are not the next superstar in sports or entertainment, there are other opportunities that will allow them to achieve their dream in a slightly different way.

Students can explore careers in many ways; one way is by reviewing the 16 career clusters. Career clusters are groups of similar occupations and industries. They were developed by the U.S. Department of Education as a way to organize career planning. Students can visit the Career Center at http://ccr.mcgraw-hill.com/ to begin their explorations.

Make It Clear That There Are Various Paths To Success

A surprisingly small percentage of adults reach their careers through a direct and well-planned strategy. Familiarizing students with the various paths to success provides them with a realistic view of what life is like after high school and college. It may also give them an anchor in their own lives in the future when they find that they are wandering, which most of them will inevitably do.

Divergence from a direct path to a career is almost inevitable, and in many cases, is a desirable and enriching experience. Helping students to recognize this will make their future challenges seem less intimidating.

Have students investigate and discuss the career paths of people they know personally and by reputation, including celebrities. This discussion will promote engagement while showing the twists and turns that usually lead to success. Be sure to include some common but less-known paths, like the college benefits associated with military service or the arrangements nurses might make with a hospital to exchange tuition payments for a commitment of several years.

Make College & Career Readiness a regular part of interactive classroom discussions.

Unlike many other school subjects, a critical aspect of College & Career Readiness is its focus is on the future of each student, not the content of a course. Perhaps the best way to have students recognize this is to be sure that the time you spend discussing students' future pathways is truly interactive, with at least as much commentary from students as there is from you or other adult participants.

Because students are more willing to participate in discussions that have personal meaning to them, consider using these questions as starting points. These are "self-mentoring" questions that will help students clarify their thinking.

- What is something you really want to do in the next 10 years?
- How do you plan to get there?
- What is your back-up plan?
- What is something that you have done that made you proud?
- In which postsecondary courses do you think you would do best? Why do you think this?
- Imagine that you are going into the military. This choice involves activities that are hard physically and mentally. How would you handle these challenges?
- When you can't make up your mind about something important, what do you do?

Have students explore college and career readiness on their own at http://ccr.mcgraw-hill.com/

MEETING THE DIVERSE NEEDS OF OUR STUDENTS

by Douglas Fisher, Ph.D.

Today's classroom contains students from a variety of backgrounds with a variety of learning styles, strengths, and challenges. As teachers we are facing the challenge of helping students reach their educational potential. With careful planning, you can address the needs of all students in the social studies classroom. The basis for this planning is universal access. When classrooms are planned with universal access in mind, fewer students require specific accommodations.

What Is a Universal Access Design for Learning?

Universal design was first conceived in architectural studies when business people, engineers, and architects began making considerations for physical access to buildings. The idea was to plan the environment in advance to ensure that everyone had access.

As a result, the environment would not have to be changed later for people with physical disabilities, people pushing strollers, workers who had injuries, or others for whom the environment would be difficult to negotiate. The Center for Universal Design at www.design.ncsu.edu/cud defines Universal Design as:

The design of products and environments to be usable by all people, to the greatest extent possible, without the need for adaptation or specialized design.

Universal Design and Access in Education

Researchers, teachers, and parents in education have expanded the development of built-in adaptations and inclusive accommodations from architectural space to the educational experience, especially in the area of curriculum.

In 1998, the National Center to Improve the Tools of Educators (NCITE), with the partnership of the Center for Applied Special Technology (CAST), proposed an expanded definition of universal design focused on education: *In terms of learning, universal design means the design of instructional materials and activities that allows the learning goals to be achievable by individuals with wide differences in their abilities to see, hear, speak, move, read, write, understand English, attend, organize, engage, and remember.*

How Does Universal Design Work in Education?

Universal design and access, as they apply to education and schooling, suggest the following:

✔ **Inclusive Classroom Participation**
Curriculum should be designed with all students and their needs in mind. The McGraw-Hill social studies print and online texts and materials were designed with a wide range of students in mind. For example, understanding that English learners and students who struggle with reading would be using this text, vocabulary is specifically taught and reinforced. Similarly, the teacher-support materials provide multiple instructional points to be used depending on the needs of the students in the class. Further, the text is written such that essential questions and guiding questions are identified for all learners.

✔ **Maximum Text Readability**
In universally designed classrooms that provide access for all students, texts use direct language, clear noun-verb agreements, and clear construct-based wording. In addition to these factors, the McGraw-Hill social

professional development

studies texts use embedded definitions for difficult terms, provide for specific instruction in reading skills, use a number of visual representations, and include note-taking guides.

✔ **Adaptable and Accommodating**
The content in this textbook can be easily translated, read aloud, or otherwise changed to meet the needs of students in the classroom. The lesson and end-of-chapter activities and assessments provide students with multiple ways of demonstrating their content knowledge while also ensuring that they have practice with thinking in terms of multiple-choice questions. Critical thinking and analysis skills are also practiced.

How Is Differentiated Instruction the Key to Universal Access?

To differentiate instruction, teachers must acknowledge student differences in background knowledge and current reading, writing, and English language skills. They must also consider student learning styles and preferences, interests, and needs, and react accordingly. There are a number of general guidelines for differentiating instruction in the classroom to reach all students, including:

✔ **Link Assessment With Instruction**
Assessments should occur before, during, and after instruction to ensure that the curriculum is aligned with what students do and do not know. Using assessments in this way allows you to plan instruction for whole groups, small groups, and individual stu-

dents. Backward planning, where you establish the assessment before you begin instruction, is also important.

✔ **Clarify Key Concepts and Generalizations**
Students need to know what is essential and how this information can be used in their future learning. In addition, students need to develop a sense of the big ideas—ideas that transcend time and place.

✔ **Emphasize Critical and Creative Thinking**
The content, process, and products used or assigned in the classroom should require that students think about what they are learning. While some students may require support, additional motivation, varied tasks, materials, or equipment, the overall focus on critical and creative thinking allows for all students to participate in the lesson.

✔ **Include Teacher- and Student-Selected Tasks**
A differentiated classroom includes both teacher- and student-selected activities and tasks. At some points in the lesson or day, the teacher must provide instruction and assign learning activities. In other parts of the lesson, students should be provided choices in how they engage with the content. This balance increases motivation, engagement, and learning.

How Do I Support Individual Students?

The vast majority of students will thrive in a classroom based on universal access and differentiated instruction. However, wise teachers recognize that no single option will work for all students and that there may be students who require unique systems of support to be successful.

Classroom Activity

Display a map of imperialism in Africa around 1914. Discuss with students the map's general information and have them list each country under the European power that controlled it.

To differentiate this activity:

- Have students imagine they are living in the early 1900s. Have them write a letter to a British newspaper about colonial rule in Africa.
- Have students record the number of African countries under European rule. Have them take the data and create a bar graph that shows which European powers were the most active colonizers at the time.
- Have students compose a song or poem about European rule in Africa, from an African's point of view.
- Have students choose a country of modern Africa to research. Have them write a three-page paper discussing how that country was affected by colonialism and how it has changed since the days of European rule.

MEETING THE DIVERSE NEEDS OF OUR STUDENTS
(continued)

Tips For Instruction

The following tips for instruction can support your efforts to help all students reach their maximum potential.

✓ Survey students to discover their individual differences. Use interest inventories of their unique talents so you can encourage contributions in the classroom.

✓ Be a model for respecting others. Adolescents crave social acceptance. The student with learning differences is especially sensitive to correction and criticism, particularly when it comes from a teacher. Your behavior will set the tone for how students treat one another.

✓ Expand opportunities for success. Provide a variety of instructional activities that reinforce skills and concepts.

✓ Establish measurable objectives and decide how you can best help students who meet them.

✓ Celebrate successes and make note of and praise "work in progress."

✓ Keep it simple. Point out problem areas if doing so can help a student effect change. Avoid overwhelming students with too many goals at one time.

✓ Assign cooperative group projects that challenge all students to contribute to solving a problem or creating a product.

How Do I Reach Students With Learning Disabilities?

✓ Provide support and structure. Clearly specify rules, assignments, and responsibilities.

✓ Practice skills frequently. Use games and drills to help maintain student interest.

✓ Incorporate many modalities into the learning process. Provide opportunities to say, hear, write, read, and act out important concepts and information.

✓ Link new skills and concepts to those already mastered.

✓ If possible, allow students to record answers on audio.

✓ Allow extra time to complete assessments and assignments.

✓ Let students demonstrate proficiency with alternative presentations, including oral reports, role plays, art projects, and musical presentations.

✓ Provide outlines, notes, or recordings of lecture material.

✓ Pair students with peer helpers, and provide class time for pair interaction.

How Do I Reach Students With Behavioral Challenges?

✓ Provide a structured environment with clear-cut schedules, rules, seat assignments, and safety procedures.

✓ Reinforce appropriate behavior and model it for students.

✓ Cue distracted students back to the task through verbal signals and teacher proximity.

✓ Set goals that can be achieved in the short term. Work for long-term improvement in the big areas.

How Do I Reach Students With Physical Challenges?

✓ Openly discuss with the student any uncertainties you have about when to offer aid.

✓ Ask parents or therapists and students what special devices or procedures are needed and whether any special safety precautions need to be taken.

✓ Welcome students with physical challenges into all activities, including field trips, special events, and projects.

✓ Provide information to assist class members and adults in their understanding of support needed.

How Do I Reach Students with Visual Impairments?

✓ Facilitate independence. Modify assignments as needed.

✓ Teach classmates how and when to serve as visual guides.

✓ Limit unnecessary noise in the classroom if it distracts the student with visual impairments.

✓ Provide tactile models whenever possible.

Comstock/Corbis

professional
development

✔ Foster a spirit of inclusion. Describe people and events as they occur in the classroom. Remind classmates that the student with visual impairments cannot interpret gestures and other forms of nonverbal communication.

✔ Provide recorded lectures and reading assignments for use outside the classroom.

✔ Team the student with a sighted peer for written work.

How Do I Reach Students With Hearing Impairments?

✔ Seat students where they can see your lip movements easily and where they can avoid any visual distractions.

✔ Avoid standing with your back to the window or light source.

✔ Use an overhead projector so you can maintain eye contact while writing information for students.

✔ Seat students where they can see speakers.

✔ Write all assignments on the board, or hand out written instructions.

✔ If the student has a manual interpreter, allow both student and interpreter to select the most favorable seating arrangements.

✔ Teach students to look directly at each other when they speak.

How Do I Reach English Learners?

✔ Remember, students' ability to speak English does not reflect their academic abilities.

✔ Try to incorporate the students' cultural experience into your instruction. The help of a bilingual aide may be effective.

✔ Avoid any references in your instruction that could be construed as cultural stereotypes.

✔ Preteach important vocabulary and concepts.

✔ Encourage students to preview text before they begin reading, noting headings.

✔ Remind students not to ignore graphic organizers, photographs, and maps since there is much information in these visuals.

✔ Use memorabilia and photographs whenever possible to build background knowledge and understanding. An example of this would be coins in a foreign currency or a raw cotton ball to reinforce its importance in history.

How Do I Reach Gifted Students?

✔ Make arrangements for students to take selected subjects early and to work on independent projects.

✔ Ask "what if" questions to develop high-level thinking skills. Establish an environment safe for risk taking in your classroom.

✔ Emphasize concepts, theories, ideas, relationships, and generalizations about the content.

✔ Promote interest in the past by inviting students to make connections to the present.

✔ Let students express themselves in alternate ways such as creative writing, acting, debates, simulations, drawing, or music.

✔ Provide students with a catalog of helpful resources, listing such things as agencies that provide free and inexpensive materials, appropriate community services and programs, and community experts who might be called upon to speak to your students.

✔ Assign extension projects that allow students to solve real-life problems related to their communities.

Classroom Activity

Students respond eagerly to a subject when they can relate it to their own experiences. With the growing number of students who come from other world regions, explaining geography through a global theme (such as volcanoes) can give them a worldwide as well as a regional perspective. To develop this awareness, display a large world map. Have students use the library or the Internet to research the latitude and longitude of 15 major volcanoes around the world. Ask them to mark these locations on the map and answer the following questions:

- What patterns do you see in volcanic activity?
- What causes volcanic activity?
- Where in the world are volcanoes most active?

As a follow-up, suggest students use the Internet to find legends about the origins of some of the world's volcanoes. Encourage students to share what they find with the class.

ACADEMIC VOCABULARY
How Can I Help My Students Learn Academic Vocabulary?

What Is Academic English?

Academic English is the language used in academics, business, and courts of law. It is the type of English used in textbooks, and contains linguistic features associated with academic disciplines like social studies. Proficiency in reading and using academic English is especially related to long-term success in all parts of life.

By reinforcing academic English, teachers can help learners to access authentic, academic texts—not simplified texts that dummy down the content. In this way, they can provide information that will help build their students' background knowledge rapidly.

What Is Academic Vocabulary?

Academic vocabulary is based on academic English. By the time children have completed elementary school, they must have acquired the knowledge needed to understand academic vocabulary. How many words should they acquire to be able to access their texts? A basic 2,000-word vocabulary of high-frequency words makes up 87% of the vocabulary of academic texts. Eight hundred other academic words comprise an additional 8% of the words. Three percent of the remaining words are technical words. The remaining 2% are low-frequency words. There may be as many as 123,000 low-frequency words in academic texts.

Why Should Students Learn Academic Vocabulary?

English learners who have a basic 2,000-word vocabulary are ready to acquire most general words found in their texts.

Knowledge of academic words and general words can significantly boost a student's comprehension level of academic texts. Students who learn and practice these words before they graduate from high school are more likely to master academic material with increased

professional development

confidence and speed. They waste less time and effort in guessing words or consulting dictionaries than those who only know the basic 2,000 words that characterize general conversation.

How Do I Include Academic Vocabulary and Academic English in My Teaching?

Teachers can provide students with academic vocabulary and help students understand the academic English of their text.

To develop academic English, learners must have already acquired basic proficiency in everyday English.

Academic English should be taught within contexts that make sense. In terms of instruction, teaching academic English includes providing students with access to core curriculum—in this case social studies.

Academic English arises in part from social practices in which academic English is used. The acquisition of academic vocabulary and grammar is necessary to advance the development of academic English.

Tips for Teaching Academic Vocabulary

✔ **Expose Students to Academic Vocabulary** You do not need to call attention to words students are learning because they will acquire them subconsciously.

✔ **Do Not Correct Students' Mistakes When Using the Vocabulary Words** All vocabulary understanding and spelling errors will disappear once the student reads more.

✔ **Help Students Decode the Words Themselves** Once they learn the alphabet, they should be able to decode words. Decoding each word they don't recognize will help them more than trying to focus on sentence structure. Once they can recognize the words, they can read "authentic" texts.

✔ **Do Not Ignore the English Learner in This Process** They can learn academic vocabulary before they are completely fluent in oral English.

✔ **Helping Students Build Academic Vocabulary Leads to Broader Learning** Students who have mastered the basic academic vocabulary are ready to acquire words from the rest of the groups. To help determine which words are in the 2,000-word basic group, refer to *West's General Service List of English Words,* 1953. The list is designed to serve as a guide for teachers and as a checklist and goal list for students.

Guidelines for Teaching Academic Vocabulary

1. Direct and planned instruction
2. Models—that have increasingly difficult language
3. Attention to form—pointing out linguistic features of words

Classroom Activity

Writing About Modern America

Give students a brief writing assignment. Ask them to write a short essay about one of the topics listed below in the left column. Have students use as many of the academic vocabulary words in the right column as they can in their essay. When completed, ask student volunteers to share their writing. Note what academic vocabulary words they use.

Topic	Academic Vocabulary
The challenges of reducing poverty in America	sufficient minimum medical income
Recent technological advances	innovate technology media potential data transmit

Indiana Academic Standards for *Discovering World Geography, Western Hemisphere* ©2016

STANDARDS	PAGE REFERENCES

Peoples, Places and Cultures in Europe and the Americas

Students in sixth grade compare the history, geography, government, economic systems, current issues, and cultures of the Western World with an emphasis on: (1) Europe, (2) North America, (3) South America, (4) Central America, (5) and the Caribbean region. Instructional programs for sixth grade students include experiences which foster the passage from concrete examples to abstract reasoning, concepts, ideas, and generalizations. Opportunities to develop skills include the use of a variety of resources and activities. Students should acquire positive attitudes regarding active participation, cooperation, responsibility, open-mindedness, and respect for others. The Indiana's K–8 academic standards for social studies are organized around four content areas. The content area standards and the types of learning experiences they provide to students in Grade 6 are described below. On the pages that follow, age-appropriate concepts are listed for each standard. Skills for thinking, inquiry and participation are integrated throughout.

Standard 1 History

Students explore the key historic movements, events and figures that contributed to the development of modern Europe and America from early civilizations through modern times by examining religious institutions, trade and cultural interactions, political institutions, and technological developments.

Historical Knowledge

Early and Classical Civilizations: 1900 B.C. /B.C.E to 700 A.D. /C.E.

6.1.1 Summarize the rise, decline, and cultural achievements of ancient civilizations in Europe and Mesoamerica. **Examples:** Greek, Roman, Mayan, Inca, and Aztec civilizations	**Student Edition:** 210–211, 342–343, 372–374 *Guiding Question* 372 *Map Skills* 373 *Reading Progress Check* 212, 374 *Thinking Like A Geographer* 343 **Teacher Edition:** **CTS** 211, 342; **E** 210; **RS** 343; **TS** 373, 374; **VS** 210, 343, 373; **WS** 373
6.1.2 Describe and compare the beliefs, the spread and the influence of religions throughout Europe and Mesoamerica. **Examples:** Judaism, Christianity, Islam and native practices in Mesoamerica and Europe	**Student Edition:** 343, 374 **Teacher Edition:** **RS** 374; **VS** 343

Medieval Period: 400 A.D./C.E.–1500 A.D./C.E.

6.1.3 Explain the continuation and contributions of the Eastern Roman Empire after the fall of the Western Roman Empire. **Examples:** Influence of the spread of Christianity in Russia and Eastern Europe	**Student Edition:** 342–343, 373–374 *Map Skills* 373 **Teacher Edition:** **E** 342; **RS** 342, 374

STANDARDS	PAGE REFERENCES
6.1.4 Identify and explain the development and organization of political, cultural, social and economic systems in Europe and the Americas. **Examples:** Feudal system, manorial system, rise of kingdoms and empires, and religious institutions	**Student Edition:** 342–345, 374–376 *Guiding Question* 342, 375 *Reading Progress Check* 376 *Think Again?* 376 *Thinking Like A Geographer* 343, 374 **Teacher Edition:** **CTS** 342, 344, 345, 375, 376; **RS** 342, 343, 374; **SS** 375; **TS** 375
6.1.5 Analyze the diverse points of view and interests of those involved in the Crusades and give examples of the changes brought about by the Crusades. **Examples:** Increased contact between European and non-European peoples, impact on Jews and Muslims in Europe and the Middle East, changes in technology, and centralization of political and military power	**Student Edition:** 343–344 **Teacher Edition:** **CTS** 344; **VS** 343
6.1.6 Identify trade routes and discuss their impact on the rise of cultural centers and trade cities in Europe and Mesoamerica **Examples:** Florence, Genoa, Venice, Naples, Tenochtitlan, Machu Pichu and Teotihuacan	**Student Edition:** 210–211, 252, 280, 308, 375–376 **Teacher Edition:** **CTS** 376; **RS** 210; **VS** 376
6.1.7 Describe how the Black Death, along with economic, environmental and social factors led to the decline of medieval society	**Student Edition:** 343–345 *Infographic* 344 **Teacher Edition:** **CS** 344; **I** 344; **RS** 343; **TS** 345
6.1.8 Compare the diverse perspectives, ideas, interests and people that brought about the Renaissance in Europe. **Examples:** Ideas: the importance of the individual, scientific inquiry based on observation and experimentation, interest in Greek and Roman thought, and new approaches in the fine arts and literature; People: Leonardo da Vinci, Michelangelo, Nicholas Copernicus, William Shakespeare and Galileo Galilei	**Student Edition:** 375, 381, 417 *Guiding Question* 375 **Teacher Edition:** **CTS** 375; **RS** 381; **TS** 375, 381
6.1.9 Analyze the interconnections of people, places and events in the economic, scientific and cultural exchanges of the European Renaissance that led to the Scientific Revolution, voyages of discovery and imperial conquest.	**Student Edition:** 375–376, 381 *Guiding Question* 375 **Teacher Edition:** **CTS** 375, 376; **RS** 381; **TS** 375, 381; **VS** 376

STANDARDS	PAGE REFERENCES
Early Modern Era: 1500 to 1800	
6.1.10 Examine and explain the outcomes of European colonization on the Americas and the rest of the world. **Examples:** The defeat of the Aztec and Incan empires by the Spanish, the rise of trading empires, Columbian exchange and slavery, Columbus' search for India	**Student Edition:** 125–128, 157–163, 211–215, 250–252 *Critical Thinking* 126, 128, 162 *Guiding Question* 158, 250 *Map Skills* 159, 252 *Photograph* 162 *Reading Progress Check* 127, 163, 212, 213 *Thinking Like A Geographer* 158 **Teacher Edition:** **CR** 163; **CTS** 126, 162, 213, 250, 251; **RS** 126, 127, 128, 157, 212, 251, 252; **TS** 159, 211; **VS** 159, 252; **WS** 160, 212
6.1.11 Compare and contrast Spanish, Portuguese, French, and British colonies in the Americas.	**Student Edition:** 125–127, 157–158, 185–186, 211–212 *Critical Thinking* 126 *Photograph* 126 *Reading Progress Check* 127, 158, 212 **Teacher Edition:** **CBK** 126, 127; **CTS** 125, 126; **MAP** 127; **RS** 126, 127, 157, 185; **TS** 211
6.1.12 Describe the Reformations and their effects on European and American society. **Examples:** Missionary activities, the rise of Calvinism and Lutheranism, Henry VIII's break with Parliament and the Catholic Church, the principle of separation of church and state, Papal reform, and the Council of Trent	**Student Edition:** 345, 376 **Teacher Edition:** **CTS** 376; **TL** 345; **WS** 345
6.1.13 Explain the origin and spread of scientific, political, and social ideals associated with the Age of Enlightenment/Age of Reason. **Examples:** The American and French Revolutions and the spread of democratic ideals, the Scientific Revolution, and the influence on world religions resulting in the assimilation of religious groups.	**Student Edition:** 345–346 **Teacher Edition:** **CBK** 346; **CTS** 345; **LS** 346; **RS** 346
6.1.14 Describe the origins, developments and innovations of the Industrial Revolution and explain the impact these changes brought about. **Examples:** Steam engine, factory system, urbanization, changing role of women and child labor	**Student Edition:** 346–347 *Critical Thinking* 347 *Paining* 347 **Teacher Edition:** **RS** 346; **TS** 347

STANDARDS	PAGE REFERENCES
Modern Era: 1700 to the present	
6.1.15 Describe the impact of industrialization and urbanization on the lives of individuals and on trade and cultural exchange between Europe and the Americas and the rest of the world.	**Student Edition:** 80–81, 130, 347 *Guiding Question* 346 *Photograph* 80–81 *Reading Progress Check* 81 **Teacher Edition:** **RS** 81,130; **TS** 80, 347; **VS** 80
6.1.16 Identify individuals, beliefs and events that represent various political ideologies during the nineteenth and twentieth century's and explain their significance. **Examples:** Liberalism, conservatism, nationalism, socialism, communism, fascism and popular sovereignty	**Student Edition:** 86–87, 406 *Reading Progress Check* 87 **Teacher Edition:** **CBK** 87; **CTS** 87; **RS** 87, 406; **WS** 406
6.1.17 Discuss the benefits and challenges related to the development of a highly technological society. **Examples:** Atomic energy, computers and environmental change	**Student Edition:** 30–31, 89, 170–171 *Global Connections* 90–91 *What Do You Think?* 34–35, 318–319 **Teacher Edition:** **CR** 171; **CTS** 90, 171; **E** 90; **TS** 89; **VS** 170; **W** 30; **WS** 31, 171
Chronological Thinking, Historical Comprehension, Analysis and Interpretation, Research	
6.1.18 Create and compare timelines that identify major people, events and developments in the history of individual civilizations and/or countries that comprise Europe and the Americas.	**Student Edition:** *Step Into the Time* 16–17, 70–71, 114–115, 146–147, 176–177, 200–201, 238–239, 272–273, 332–333 **Teacher Edition:** **CTS** 177; **TL** 71, 115, 147, 273; **VS** 17, 71, 115, 147, 177, 201, 273, 333; **WS** 115, 147, 201, 239, 273; **VS** 252
6.1.19 Define and use the terms decade, century, and millennium, and compare alternative ways that historical periods and eras are designated by identifying the organizing principles upon which each is based.	**Student Edition:** *Step Into the Time* 16–17, 70–71, 114–115, 146–147, 176–177, 200–201, 238–239, 272–273, 332–333 **Teacher Edition:** **CTS** 177; **TL** 71, 115, 147, 273, 345; **VS** 17, 71, 115, 147, 177, 201, 252, 273, 333; **WS** 115, 147, 201, 239, 273
6.1.20 Analyze cause-and-effect relationships, keeping in mind multiple causations, including the importance of individuals, ideas, human interests, beliefs and chance in history. **Examples:** The decline of Greek city-states, the destruction of the Aztecs, and state-sponsored genocide, including the Holocaust.	**Student Edition:** 88–89 *Global Connections* 222–225 *What Do You Think?* 34–35, 140–141, 318–319, 358–359 **Teacher Edition:** **A** 224; **G** 250; **SS** 88, 348; **TL** 345; **TS** 89, 417

STANDARDS	PAGE REFERENCES
6.1.21 Differentiate between fact and interpretation in historical accounts and explain the meaning of historical passages by identifying who was involved, what happened, where it happened, and relating them to outcomes that followed and gaps in the historical record.	**Student Edition:** *What Do You Think?* 140–141, 318–319, 358–359 **Teacher Edition:** **CR** 319, 359; **CTS** 140, 319, 358, 359; **WS** 359
6.1.22 Form research questions and use a variety of information resources to obtain, evaluate and present data on people, cultures and developments in Europe and the Americas. **Examples:** Collect data and create maps, graphs or spreadsheets showing the impact of immigration patterns in Canada, the Chernobyl nuclear disaster on Russia and access to health care in the European Union (EU).	**Student Edition:** *Global Connections* 222–225 **Teacher Edition:** **A** 224; **CTS** 224; **TS** 131, 224, 251, 341, 351; **W** 130; **WS** 345
6.1.23 Identify issues related to an historical event in Europe or the Americas and give basic arguments for and against that issue utilizing the perspectives, interests and values of those involved. **Examples:** The role of women in different time periods, decline of ancient civilizations, and attitudes toward human rights	**Student Edition:** 405–409 *Map Skills* 408 *Reading Progress Check* 407 **Teacher Edition:** **CR** 409; **CTS** 405, 407; **MAP** 405, 407; **TS** 407; **VS** 408

Standard 2 Civics and Government

Students compare and contrast forms of government in different historical periods with contemporary political structures of Europe and the Americas and examine the rights and responsibilities of individuals in different political systems.

Foundations of Government

6.2.1 Compare and contrast major forms of governments in Europe and the Americas throughout history. **Examples:** Greek democracies, Roman Republic, Aztec monarchy, parliamentary government, U.S. Republic, and totalitarianism	**Student Edition:** 86–87, 136–137 *Critical Thinking* 87 *Guiding Question* 86 *Lesson 2 Review* 89 #3 *Reading Progress Check* 87 **Teacher Edition:** **CBK** 87, 136; **CTS** 87, 136; **RS** 87; **WS** 86
6.2.2 Explain how elements of Greek direct democracy and Roman representative democracy are present in modern systems of government.	This objective may be met using the following references combined with classroom discussion about the origins of government philosophy. **Student Edition:** 86–87, 373 **Teacher Edition:** **CBK** 87

STANDARDS	PAGE REFERENCES
6.2.3 Examine key ideas of Magna Carta (1215), the Petition of Right (1628), and the English Bill of Rights (1689) as documents to place limits on the English monarchy and how they have affected the shaping of other governments.	**Student Edition:** 345, 346 *Reading Progress Check* 346 **Teacher Edition:** **CBK** 346; **RS** 346
6.2.4 Define the term nation-state and describe the rise of nation-states headed by monarchs in Europe from 1500 to 1700.	This objective may be met using the following references combined with classroom discussion. **Student Edition:** 86–87, 344, 345 **Teacher Edition:** **CBK** 87

Functions of Government

6.2.5 Discuss the impact of major forms of government in Europe and the Americas on civil and human rights.	**Student Edition:** 87, 137, 215, 220, 310–311, 408–409 *Reading Progress Check* 87 **Teacher Edition:** **CBK** 310; **CR** 409; **CTS** 87, 137, 215, 220; **RS** 311, 409; **TS** 137; **VS** 311
6.2.6 Identify and describe the functions of international political organizations in the world today. **Examples:** Examine the functions of the World Court, North Atlantic Treaty Organization (NATO) and the United Nations (UN).	**Student Edition:** 133, 193, 407 **Teacher Edition:** **CBK** 193; **TS** 407

Roles of Citizens

6.2.7 Define and compare citizenship and the citizen's role throughout history in Europe and the Americas. **Examples:** Compare methods of voting; participation in voluntary organizations of civil society; and participation in the government in Great Britain, Russia, Brazil, Mexico and Canada.	**Student Edition:** 85, 87, 255, 408–409, 411 *Guiding Question* 86 *Photograph* 254 **Teacher Edition:** **CR** 409; **LS** 254; **RS** 87, 409

Standard 3 Geography

Students identify the characteristics of climate regions in Europe and the Americas and describe major physical features, countries and cities of Europe and the Western Hemisphere.

The World in Spatial Terms

6.3.1 Demonstrate a broad understanding of the countries and capitals of Europe and the Americas.	**Student Edition:** *Map* 6–7, 12–13, 109, 115, 201, 336, 395 *Thinking Like a Geographer* 136 **Teacher Edition:** **CTS** 109; **G** 109; **TS** 336; **VS** 109

STANDARDS	PAGE REFERENCES
6.3.2 Use latitude and longitude to locate the capital cities of Europe and the Americas and describe the uses of locational technology, such as Global Positioning Systems (GPS) to distinguish absolute and relative location and to describe Earth's surfaces.	**Student Edition:** 20–21, 30–33 *Critical Thinking* 32 *Guiding Question* 30 *Photograph* 32 *Reading Progress Check* 33 *Think Again?* 31 **Teacher Edition:** **CBK** 31; **CTS** 30; **RS** 31, 32; **TS** 32; **WS** 31

Places and Regions

STANDARDS	PAGE REFERENCES
6.3.3 Describe and compare major physical characteristics of regions in Europe and the Americas. **Examples:** Mountain ranges, rivers, deserts, etc.	**Student Edition:** 18–25, 49–51, 58–65, 108–112, 232–236, 326–330 *Guiding Question* 49 *Lesson 1 Review* 25 #4 *Reading Progress Check* 51 *Step Into the Place* 40–41 **Teacher Edition:** **CR** 112; **CTS** 50, 233, 235, 330; **RS** 22; **TS** 49; **VS** 22, 49, 50, 59, 109, 110, 111, 112, 236, 330; **WS** 329
6.3.4 Describe and compare major cultural characteristics of regions in Europe and the Western Hemisphere. **Examples:** Language, religion, recreation, clothing, diet, music/dance, family structure, and traditions	**Student Edition:** 82–86, 88–89, 138–139, 217, 219, 221, 259–260, 288–290, 314–315, 352–353, 380–382, 412–415 *Chart Skills* 84, 354 *Critical Thinking* 83, 139, 314, 381 *Graph Skills* 138 *Guiding Question* 82, 88, 288, 314 *Lesson 2 Review* 89 #5 *Photograph* 289 *Reading Progress Check* 89, 221, 315 *Think Again* 217 *Think Like A Geographer* 380 **Teacher Edition:** **CBK** 84, 414; **CR** 89, 139; **CTS** 83, 85, 221, 413; **RS** 84, 259, 352, 381, 382; **TS** 83, 84, 221, 260, 353, 382, 414; **VS** 83, 217, 259, 314, 413; **WS** 415

Physical Systems

STANDARDS	PAGE REFERENCES
6.3.5 Give examples and describe the formation of important river deltas, mountains and bodies of water in Europe and the Americas. **Examples:** Volga River, Canadian Rockies, Sierra Madre Mountains and Lochs in Scotland	**Student Edition:** 61–62, 117–121, 149–152, 180, 182–183, 202–205, 240, 397–398 *Guiding Question* 182 *Photograph* 182, 205, 241, 398 *Reading Progress Check* 152, 183 **Teacher Edition:** **A** 119; **CBK** 118, 119, 120, 151, 205, 398; **CTS** 60, 117; **I** 60, 241; **RS** 149, 204; **VS** 117, 149, 151, 398

STANDARDS	PAGE REFERENCES
6.3.6 Explain how ocean currents and winds influence climate differences on Europe and the Americas.	**Student Edition:** 47–48 *Diagram Skills* 48 *Map Skills* 47 **Teacher Edition:** **CTS** 47; **RS** 48; **VS** 47, 48; **WS** 48
6.3.7 Locate and describe the climate regions of Europe and the Americas and explain how and why they differ. **Examples:** Gulf Stream and North Atlantic Current	**Student Edition:** 46–51, 122, 153–154, 205–206, 208, 243–245, 338–339, 369–370, 399 *Critical Thinking* 51 *Graph Skills* 206 *Guiding Question* 46, 243, 338, 369 *Map Skills* 12–13 *Photograph* 50, 154 *Reading Progress Check* 49, 51, 339 **Teacher Edition:** **CTS** 47, 49; **MAP** 46, 206, 339; **RS** 244, 339; **TS** 49, 154; **VS** 50, 206, 369; **WS** 339
6.3.8 Identify major biomes of Europe and the Americas and explain how these are influenced by climate. **Examples:** Rainforests, tundra, woodlands, and deserts	**Student Edition:** 50, 181, 241, 243, 369 **Teacher Edition:** **CBK** 181; **CTS** 50, 243; **RS** 243; **V** 50, 181, 240

Human Systems

STANDARDS	PAGE REFERENCES
6.3.9 Identify current patterns of population distribution and growth in Europe and the Americas using a variety of geographic representations such as maps, charts, graphs, and satellite images and aerial photography. Evaluate different push and pull factors that trigger migrations **Examples:** Rural and urban areas; immigration	**Student Edition:** 77–79, 130–131, 357 *Critical Thinking* 79 *Guiding Question* 77 *Think Again* 78 **Teacher Edition:** **CTS** 78; **RS** 77, 78, 79; **VS** 79, 130; **WS** 79, 357
6.3.10 Explain the ways cultural diffusion, invention, and innovation change culture.	**Student Edition:** 82–86, 88–89, 138–139, 217, 219, 221, 259–260, 288–290, 314–315, 352–353, 380–382, 412–415 *Chart Skills* 84, 354 *Critical Thinking* 83, 139, 314, 381 *Graph Skills* 138 *Guiding Question* 82, 88, 288, 314 *Lesson 2 Review* 89 #5 *Photograph* 289 *Reading Progress Check* 89, 221, 315 *Think Again* 217 *Think Like A Geographer* 380 **Teacher Edition:** **CBK** 84, 414; **CR** 89, 139; **CTS** 83, 85, 221, 413; **RS** 84, 259, 352, 381, 382; **TS** 83, 84, 221, 260, 353, 382, 414; **VS** 83, 217, 259, 314, 413; **WS** 415

STANDARDS	PAGE REFERENCES
6.3.11 Define the terms anthropology and archeology and explain how these fields contribute to our understanding of societies in the present and the past.	**Student Edition:** 25, 210 **Teacher Edition:** **E** 210

Environment and Society

STANDARDS	PAGE REFERENCES
6.3.12 Compare the distribution and evaluate the importance of natural resources such as natural gas, oil, forests, uranium, minerals, coal, seafood and water in Europe and the Americas.	**Student Edition:** 61–64, 94–95, 182–183, 206, 240, 245–247, 277–279, 340–341, 370–371, 400–401 *Critical Thinking* 62 *Guiding Question* 245, 277 *Infographic* 278 *Photograph* 62, 182 *Reading Progress Check* 63, 247, 341, 371 **Teacher Edition:** **CBK** 206; **CR** 341; **CTS** 61, 245, 278, 370, 400; **RS** 95, 247; **TS** 370, 401; **VS** 94, 246, 278; **WS** 246
6.3.13 Explain the impact of humans on the physical environment in Europe and the Americas.	**Student Edition:** 57, 65, 74 *Global Connections* 264–267 *Photograph* 65, 74 *Reading Progress Check* 57, 75 *What Do You Think?* 140–141 **Teacher Edition:** **CR** 57, 65; **CTS** 140, 141, 264; **RS** 57, 264; **TS** 74; **VS** 74; **WS** 57
6.3.14 Explain and give examples of how nature has impacted the physical environment and human populations in specific areas of Europe and the Americas. **Examples:** Hurricanes, earthquakes, floods and drought	**Student Edition:** 72–81, 167–169, 195 *Critical Thinking* 74 *Reading Progress Check* 75, 169 *What Do You Think?* 140–141 **Teacher Edition:** **CR** 81, 141; **CTS** 73, 80, 140, 169; **RS** 168; **TS** 74; **VS** 74, 167, 195; **WS** 168

Standard 4 Economics

Students examine the influence of physical and cultural factors upon the economic systems of countries in Europe and the Americas.

STANDARDS	PAGE REFERENCES
6.4.1 Give examples of how trade related to key developments in the history of Europe and the Americas. **Examples:** The growth of trading towns and cities in medieval Europe led to money economies, competition to expand world trade led to European voyages of trade and exploration, and Mayan trade in Mesoamerica led to colonization and the diffusion of art.	**Student Edition:** 99–101, 219, 252, 290, 350–351 *Global Connections* 222–225 *Graph Skills* 99, 253 *Guiding Question* 99 *Reading Progress Check* 101 **Teacher Edition:** **CR** 101, 225; **CTS** 219, 222, 223, 224; **E** 222; **RS** 222, 224; **TS** 351; **VS** 100, 350, 351

STANDARDS	PAGE REFERENCES
6.4.2 Analyze how countries of Europe and the Americas have been influenced by trade in different historical periods. **Examples:** Increased production and consumption and lower prices	**Student Edition:** 94–101 *Diagram Skills* 98 *Global Connections* 222–225 *Graph Skills* 99 *Infographic* 95 *Lesson 3 Review* 101 #1, #5 *Reading Progress Check* 101 **Teacher Edition:** **CR** 101, 225; **CTS** 95, 99, 101, 222, 223, 224; **RS** 95, 96, 99, 222, 224; **TS** 101; **VS** 95, 98, 99, 100
6.4.3 Explain why international trade requires a system for exchanging currency between various countries.	**Student Edition:** 101, 290 *What Do You Think?* 358–359 **Teacher Edition:** **CR** 359**RS** 358; **TS** 101; **WS** 290
6.4.4 Describe how different economic systems (traditional, command, market and mixed) in Europe and the Americas answer the basic economic questions on what to produce, how to produce and for whom to produce.	**Student Edition:** 96–99 *Diagram Skills* 98 *Guiding Question* 96 *Photograph* 97 *Reading Progress Check* 99 **Teacher Edition:** **D** 98; **TS** 96; **VS** 96, 97, 98; **WS** 98
6.4.5 Compare the standard of living of various countries of Europe and the Americas today using Gross Domestic Product (GDP) per capita as an indicator.	**Student Edition:** 98 *Graph Skills* 99 **Teacher Edition:** **G** 99; **VS** 99
6.4.6 Analyze current economic issues in the countries of Europe or the Americas using a variety of information resources. **Examples:** Use information sources such as digital newspapers, the Internet and podcasts to examine changes in energy prices and consumption, exchange rates and currency values.	**Student Edition:** 290–291, 410, 416–417 *What Do You Think?* 358–359 **Teacher Edition:** **CR** 291; **CTS** 410; **GO** 290; **WS** 290, 291

STANDARDS	PAGE REFERENCES
6.4.7 Identify economic connections between the local community and the countries of Europe or the Americas and identify job skills needed to be successful in the workplace.	The following references may be used to connect community and job availability based on local resources when combined with classroom discussion. **Student Edition:** 61–64, 94–95, 182–183, 206, 240, 245–247, 277–279, 340–341, 356, 370–371, 400–401, 416–417 *Critical Thinking* 62 *Guiding Question* 245, 277 *Infographic* 278 *Photograph* 62, 182 *Reading Progress Check* 63, 247, 341, 371 **Teacher Edition:** **CBK** 206; **CR** 341; **CTS** 61, 245, 278, 370, 400; **GO** 416; **RS** 95, 247, 356; **TS** 370, 401, 416; **VS** 94, 246, 278; **WS** 246
6.4.8 Identify ways that societies deal with helpful and harmful externalities (spillovers*) in Europe or the Americas. **Examples:** Government support of public education and governments taxing or regulating pollution * **externality (spillover):** the impact of an activity (positive or negative) on the well-being of a third party	This objective may be met by using the following references combined with classroom discussion. **Student Edition:** 290–291, 410, 416–417 *What Do You Think?* 358–359 **Teacher Edition:** **CR** 291, 359; **CTS** 410; **GO** 290; **RS** 358; **WS** 290, 291
6.4.9 Explain how saving and investing help increase productivity and economic growth and compare and contrast individual saving and investing options. **Examples:** Savings accounts, certificates of deposit and stocks	This objective may be met by using the following references combined with classroom discussion. **Student Edition:** 94–96 *Guiding Question* 84 *Infographic* 95 **Teacher Edition:** **RS** 96

REFERENCE ATLAS

ATLAS KEY

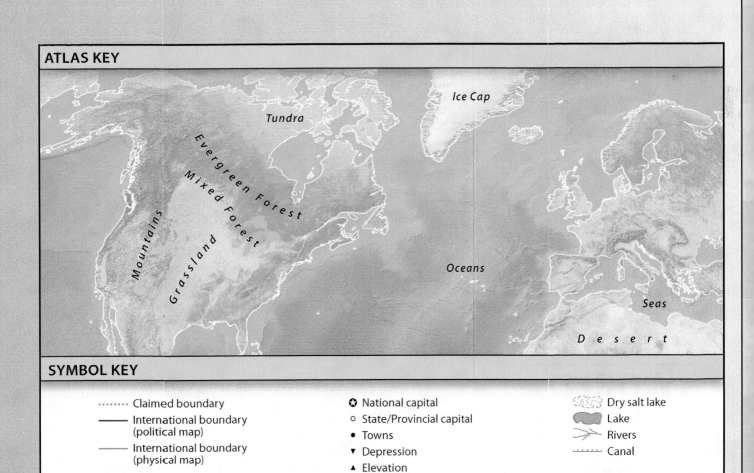

Ice Cap

Tundra

Evergreen Forest

Mixed Forest

Mountains

Grassland

Oceans

Seas

Desert

SYMBOL KEY

.... Claimed boundary

——— International boundary (political map)

——— International boundary (physical map)

✪ National capital
○ State/Provincial capital
● Towns
▼ Depression
▲ Elevation

Dry salt lake
Lake
Rivers
Canal

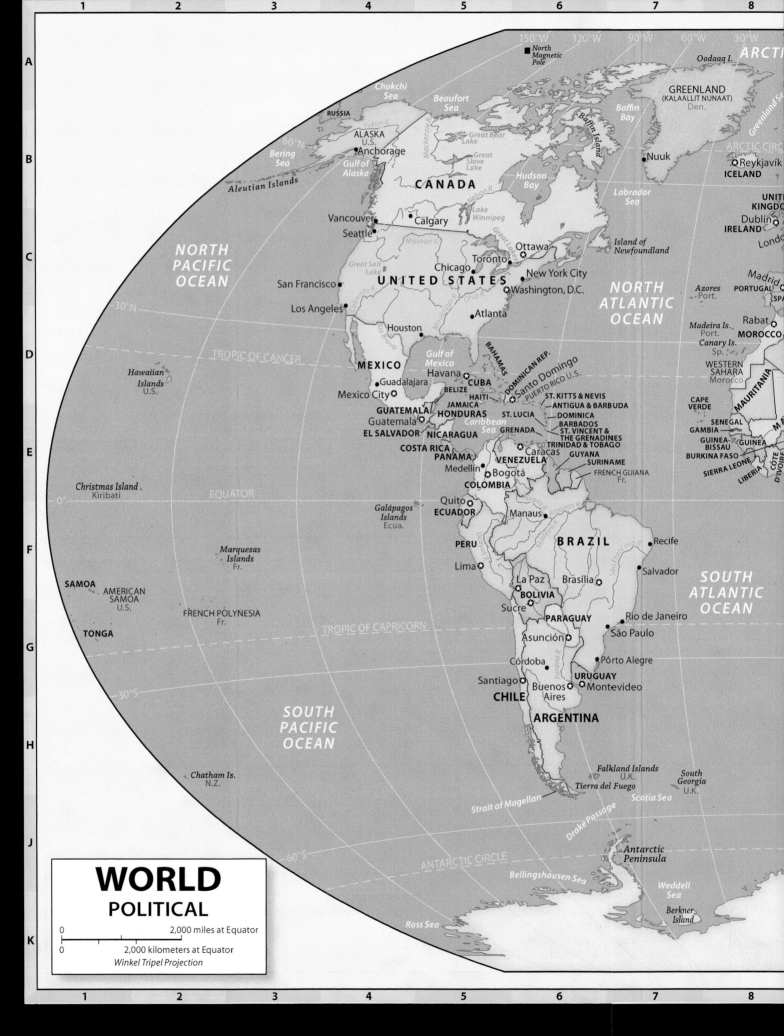

WORLD
POLITICAL

0 — 2,000 miles at Equator
0 — 2,000 kilometers at Equator
Winkel Tripel Projection

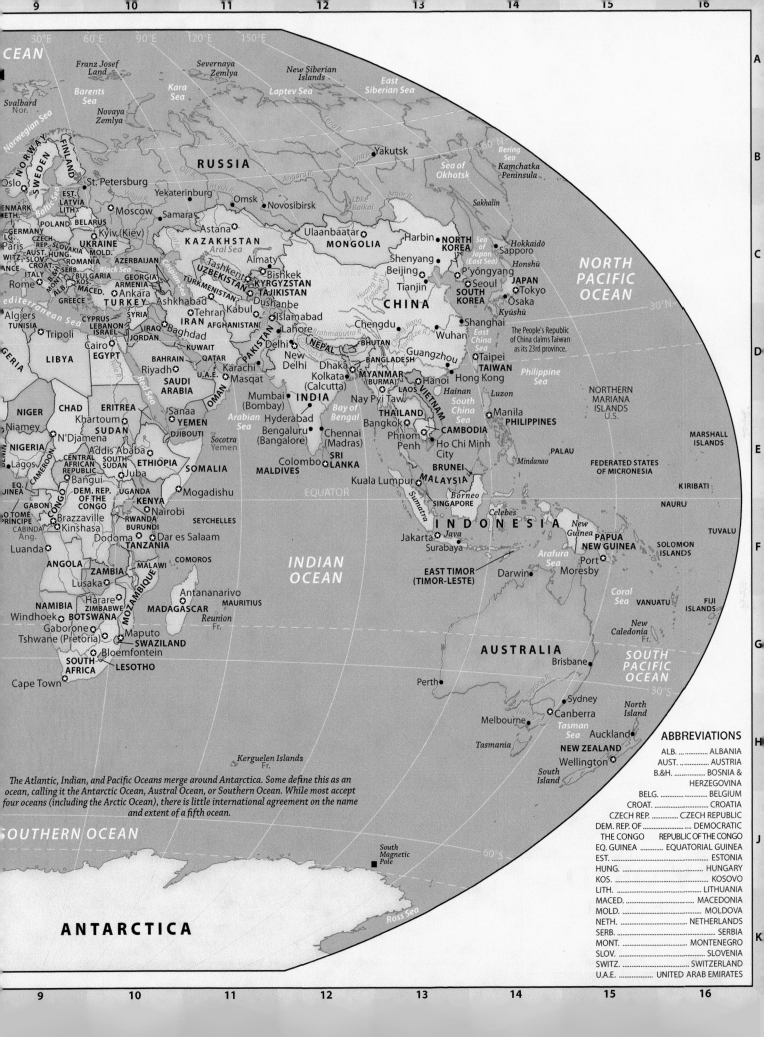

ABBREVIATIONS

ALB. .... ALBANIA
AUST. .... AUSTRIA
B.&H. .... BOSNIA &
                    HERZEGOVINA
BELG. .... BELGIUM
CROAT. .... CROATIA
CZECH REP. .... CZECH REPUBLIC
DEM. REP. OF .... DEMOCRATIC
THE CONGO   REPUBLIC OF THE CONGO
EQ. GUINEA .... EQUATORIAL GUINEA
EST. .... ESTONIA
HUNG. .... HUNGARY
KOS. .... KOSOVO
LITH. .... LITHUANIA
MACED. .... MACEDONIA
MOLD. .... MOLDOVA
NETH. .... NETHERLANDS
SERB. .... SERBIA
MONT. .... MONTENEGRO
SLOV. .... SLOVENIA
SWITZ. .... SWITZERLAND
U.A.E. .... UNITED ARAB EMIRATES

The Atlantic, Indian, and Pacific Oceans merge around Antarctica. Some define this as an ocean, calling it the Antarctic Ocean, Austral Ocean, or Southern Ocean. While most accept four oceans (including the Arctic Ocean), there is little international agreement on the name and extent of a fifth ocean.

The People's Republic of China claims Taiwan as its 23rd province.

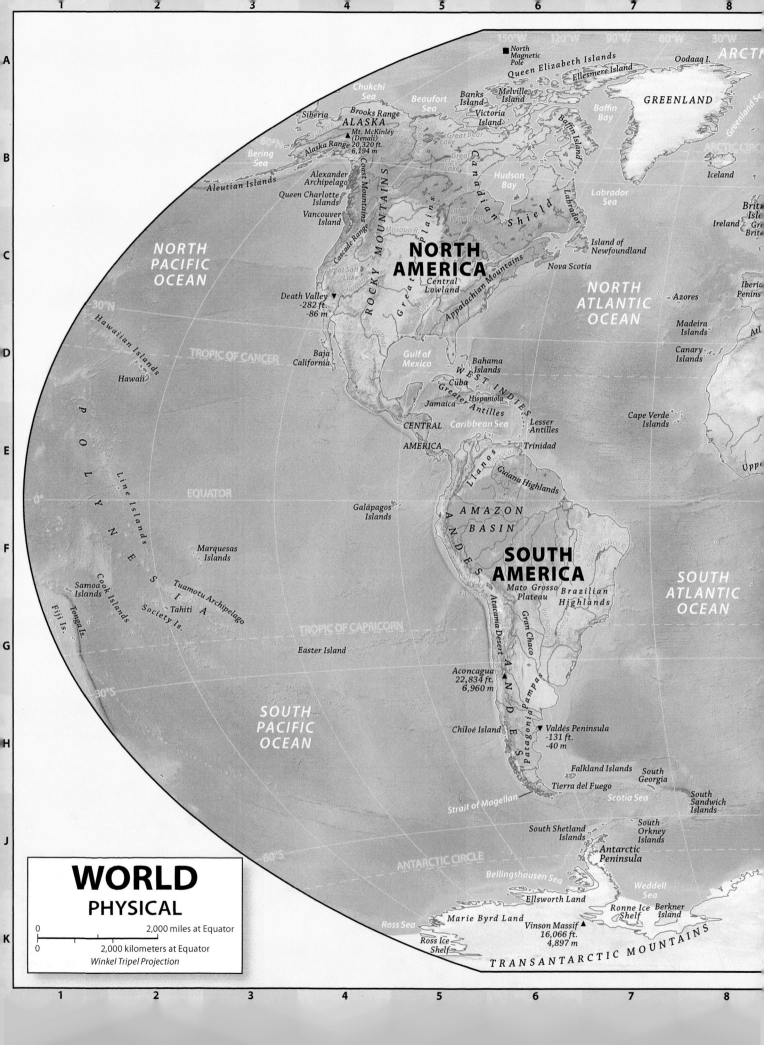

WORLD
PHYSICAL

0 —————————— 2,000 miles at Equator
0 —————————— 2,000 kilometers at Equator
Winkel Tripel Projection

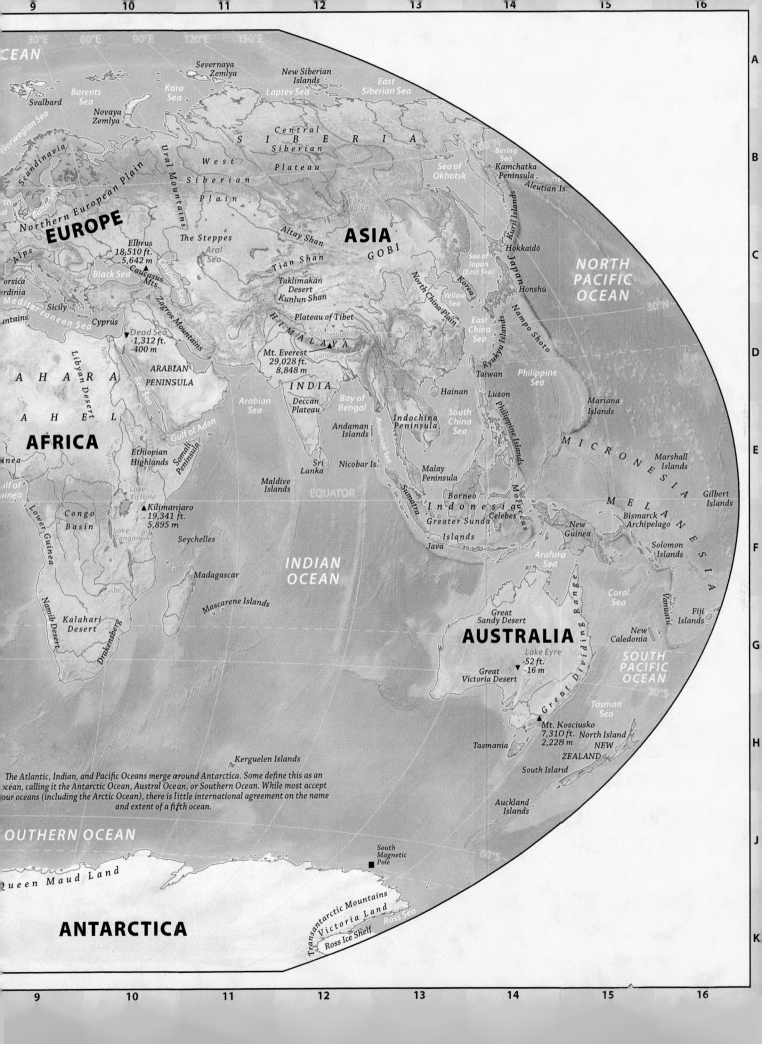

9 **10** **11** **12** **13** **14** **15** **16**

30°E 60°E 90°E 120°E 150°E

OCEAN

A

Svalbard

Barents Sea

Novaya Zemlya

Severnaya Zemlya

New Siberian Islands

Laptev Sea

East Siberian Sea

Bering Sea

Kamchatka Peninsula

Aleutian Is.

Norwegian Sea

Scandinavia

Kara Sea

B

Central Siberian Plateau

West Siberian Plain

S I B E R I A

Sea of Okhotsk

Kuril Islands

Ural Mountains

Lake Baikal

Hokkaidō

NORTH PACIFIC OCEAN

C

Alps

EUROPE

Elbrus 18,510 ft. 5,642 m

Caucasus Mts.

Black Sea

The Steppes

Aral Sea

Altay Shan

ASIA

GOBI

Japan

Honshū

Sea of Japan (East Sea)

Nampo Shoto

30°N

Corsica Sardinia

Sicily

Mediterranean Sea

Cyprus

Zagros Mountains

Caspian Sea

Tian Shan

Taklimakan Desert

Kunlun Shan

H I M A L A Y A

Plateau of Tibet

Brahmaputra

Korea

Yellow Sea

North China Plain

East China Sea

Ryukyu Islands

D

Dead Sea -1,312 ft. -400 m

ARABIAN PENINSULA

Red Sea

Mt. Everest 29,028 ft. 8,848 m

Ganges

I N D I A

Taiwan

Philippine Sea

Mariana Islands

S A H A R A

Libyan Desert

Nile R.

S A H E L

Arabian Sea

Deccan Plateau

Bay of Bengal

Hainan

Luzon

Philippine Islands

South China Sea

E

AFRICA

Gulf of Aden

Ethiopian Highlands

Somali Peninsula

White Nile

Blue Nile

Andaman Islands

Andaman Sea

Indochina Peninsula

Nicobar Is.

Malay Peninsula

M I C R O N E S I A

Marshall Islands

Guinea

Gulf of Guinea

Sri Lanka

Maldive Islands

EQUATOR

Sumatra

Borneo

Moluccas

Celebes

New Guinea

Bismarck Archipelago

M E L A N E S I A

Gilbert Islands

F

Congo Basin

Lower Guinea

Congo

Lake Victoria

Kilimanjaro 19,341 ft. 5,895 m

Lake Tanganyika

Seychelles

I n d o n e s i a

Greater Sunda Islands

Java

Solomon Islands

INDIAN OCEAN

Madagascar

Zambezi

Arafura Sea

Vanuatu

G

Namib Desert

Kalahari Desert

Drakensberg

Mascarene Islands

Great Sandy Desert

Great Victoria Desert

AUSTRALIA

Lake Eyre -52 ft. -16 m

Great Dividing Range

Coral Sea

New Caledonia

Fiji Islands

SOUTH PACIFIC OCEAN

30°S

Murray

Darling

Mt. Kosciusko 7,310 ft. 2,228 m

Tasman Sea

North Island

NEW ZEALAND

H

Tasmania

South Island

Kerguelen Islands

The Atlantic, Indian, and Pacific Oceans merge around Antarctica. Some define this as an ocean, calling it the Antarctic Ocean, Austral Ocean, or Southern Ocean. While most accept four oceans (including the Arctic Ocean), there is little international agreement on the name and extent of a fifth ocean.

Auckland Islands

SOUTHERN OCEAN

J

60°S

South Magnetic Pole

Queen Maud Land

ANTARCTICA

Transantarctic Mountains

Victoria Land

Ross Ice Shelf

Ross Sea

K

9 **10** **11** **12** **13** **14** **15** **16**

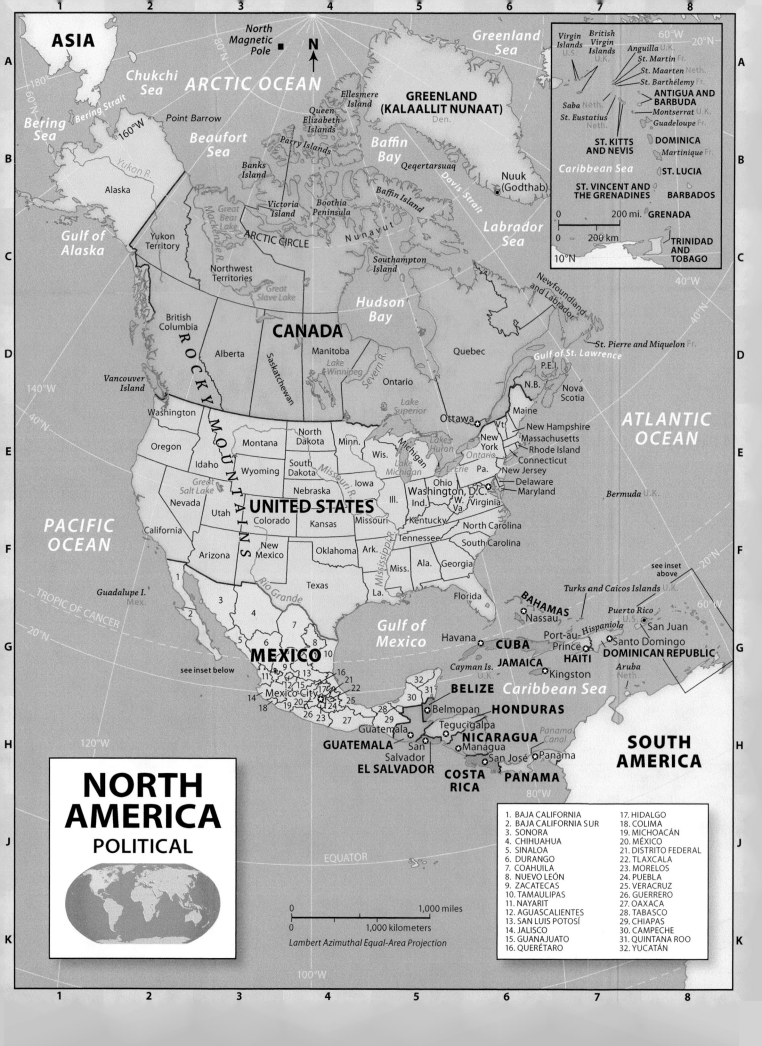

NORTH AMERICA
POLITICAL

Column grid labels: 1 2 3 4 5 6 7 8
Row labels: A B C D E F G H J K

ASIA

ARCTIC OCEAN

North Magnetic Pole

N

Chukchi Sea

Bering Strait

Point Barrow

Beaufort Sea

Bering Sea

Alaska

Gulf of Alaska

Yukon R.

160°W

Greenland Sea

GREENLAND (KALAALLIT NUNAAT) Den.

Ellesmere Island

Queen Elizabeth Islands

Parry Islands

Banks Island

Victoria Island

Boothia Peninsula

Baffin Bay

Baffin Island

Qeqertarsuaq

Nuuk (Godthab)

Davis Strait

Labrador Sea

ARCTIC CIRCLE

Great Bear Lake

Mackenzie R.

Yukon Territory

Northwest Territories

Great Slave Lake

Nunavut

Southampton Island

Hudson Bay

Newfoundland and Labrador

St. Pierre and Miquelon Fr.

British Columbia

Alberta

Saskatchewan

Manitoba

Lake Winnipeg

Severn R.

Ontario

Quebec

CANADA

Gulf of St. Lawrence

P.E.I.

N.B.

Nova Scotia

Vancouver Island

ROCKY MOUNTAINS

140°W

40°N

Washington

Oregon

Idaho

Montana

Wyoming

North Dakota

South Dakota

Nebraska

Minn.

Iowa

Wis.

Lake Superior

Lake Michigan

Michigan

Lakes Huron

Lake Ontario

Lake Erie

Ottawa

Maine

Vt.

N.H.

New Hampshire

Massachusetts

Rhode Island

Connecticut

New York

Pa.

New Jersey

Delaware

Maryland

W. Va.

Ohio

Ind.

Ill.

Missouri

Kentucky

Virginia

Washington, D.C.

ATLANTIC OCEAN

PACIFIC OCEAN

Nevada

Utah

California

Great Salt Lake

Colorado

Kansas

UNITED STATES

Arizona

New Mexico

Oklahoma

Ark.

Tennessee

North Carolina

South Carolina

Georgia

Ala.

Miss.

La.

Texas

Mississippi R.

Missouri R.

Rio Grande

Bermuda U.K.

1

Guadalupe I. Mex.

2

3

4

5

6

7

8

9

10

11

12 15

13

14

16 17

18

19 20

21

22

23 24

25

26

27

28

29

30

31

32

Mexico City

MEXICO

see inset below

TROPIC OF CANCER

120°W

20°N

Florida

Gulf of Mexico

Havana

CUBA

Cayman Is. U.K.

JAMAICA

Kingston

BAHAMAS

Nassau

Turks and Caicos Islands U.K.

see inset above

Puerto Rico U.S.

San Juan

Hispaniola

Port-au-Prince

HAITI

Santo Domingo

DOMINICAN REPUBLIC

Aruba Neth.

Caribbean Sea

BELIZE

Belmopan

GUATEMALA

Guatemala

San Salvador

EL SALVADOR

HONDURAS

Tegucigalpa

NICARAGUA

Managua

COSTA RICA

San José

PANAMA

Panama

Panama Canal

SOUTH AMERICA

80°W

EQUATOR

100°W

0 — 1,000 miles

0 — 1,000 kilometers

Lambert Azimuthal Equal-Area Projection

Inset (Caribbean):

Virgin Islands U.S.

British Virgin Islands U.K.

Anguilla U.K.

St. Martin Fr.

St. Maarten Neth.

St. Barthélemy Fr.

Saba Neth.

St. Eustatius Neth.

ANTIGUA AND BARBUDA

Montserrat U.K.

Guadeloupe Fr.

ST. KITTS AND NEVIS

DOMINICA

Martinique Fr.

Caribbean Sea

ST. LUCIA

ST. VINCENT AND THE GRENADINES

BARBADOS

GRENADA

TRINIDAD AND TOBAGO

0 — 200 mi.

0 — 200 km

10°N

60°W

20°N

40°W

Legend:
1. BAJA CALIFORNIA
2. BAJA CALIFORNIA SUR
3. SONORA
4. CHIHUAHUA
5. SINALOA
6. DURANGO
7. COAHUILA
8. NUEVO LEÓN
9. ZACATECAS
10. TAMAULIPAS
11. NAYARIT
12. AGUASCALIENTES
13. SAN LUIS POTOSÍ
14. JALISCO
15. GUANAJUATO
16. QUERÉTARO
17. HIDALGO
18. COLIMA
19. MICHOACÁN
20. MÉXICO
21. DISTRITO FEDERAL
22. TLAXCALA
23. MORELOS
24. PUEBLA
25. VERACRUZ
26. GUERRERO
27. OAXACA
28. TABASCO
29. CHIAPAS
30. CAMPECHE
31. QUINTANA ROO
32. YUCATÁN

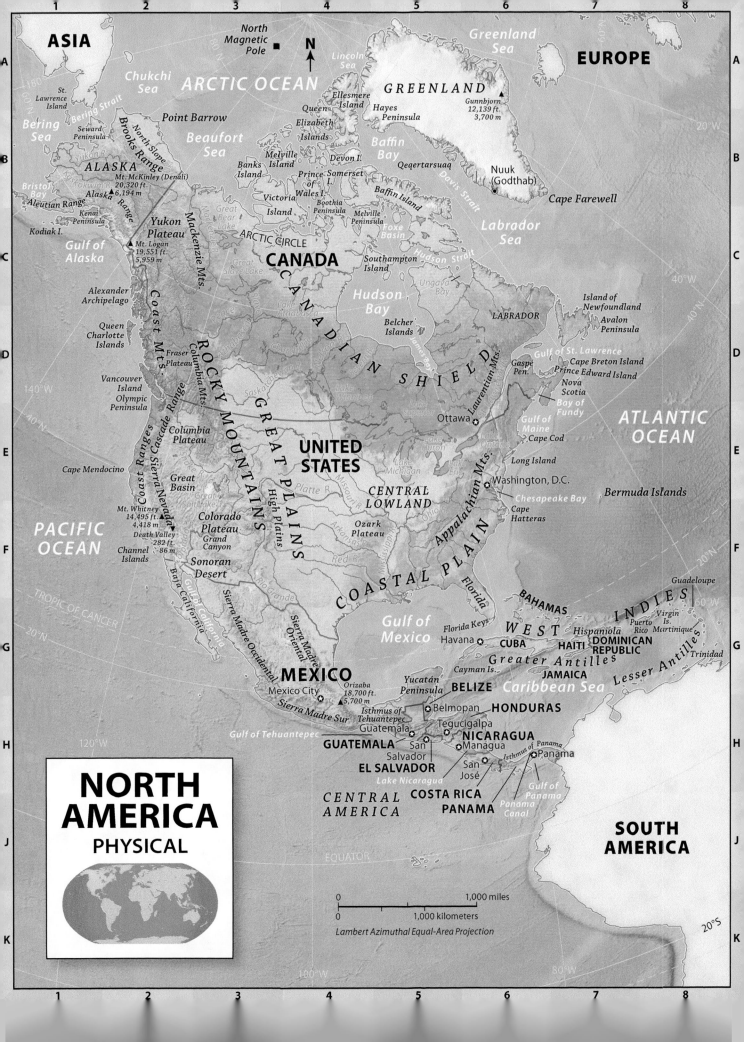

NORTH AMERICA
PHYSICAL

Lambert Azimuthal Equal-Area Projection

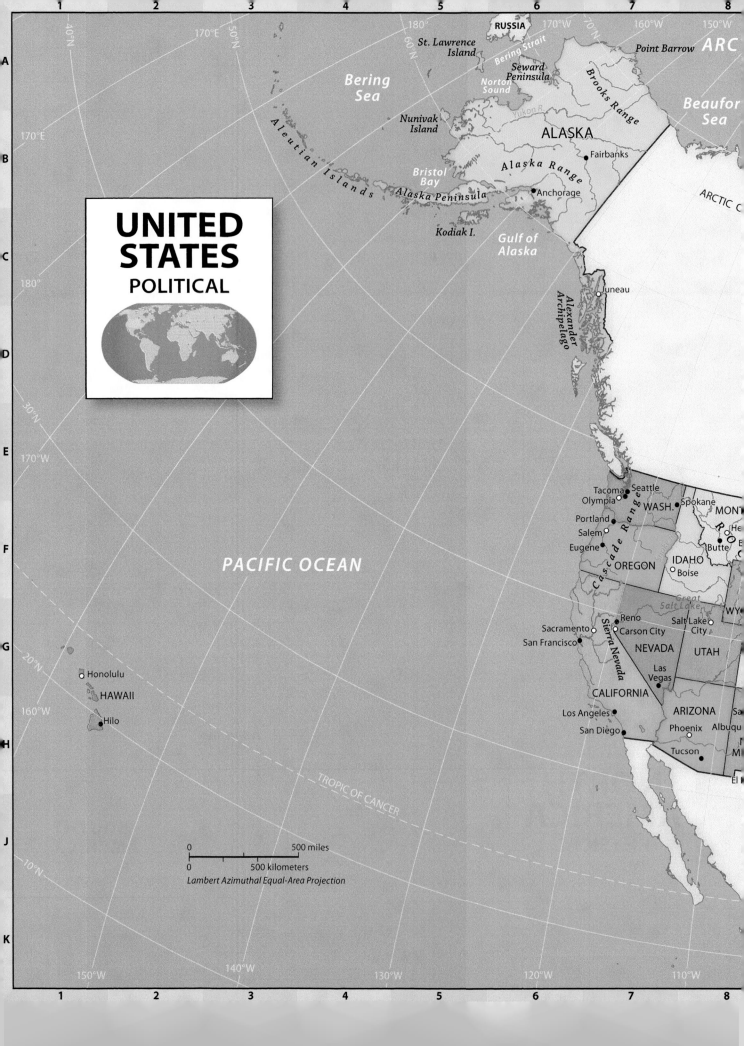

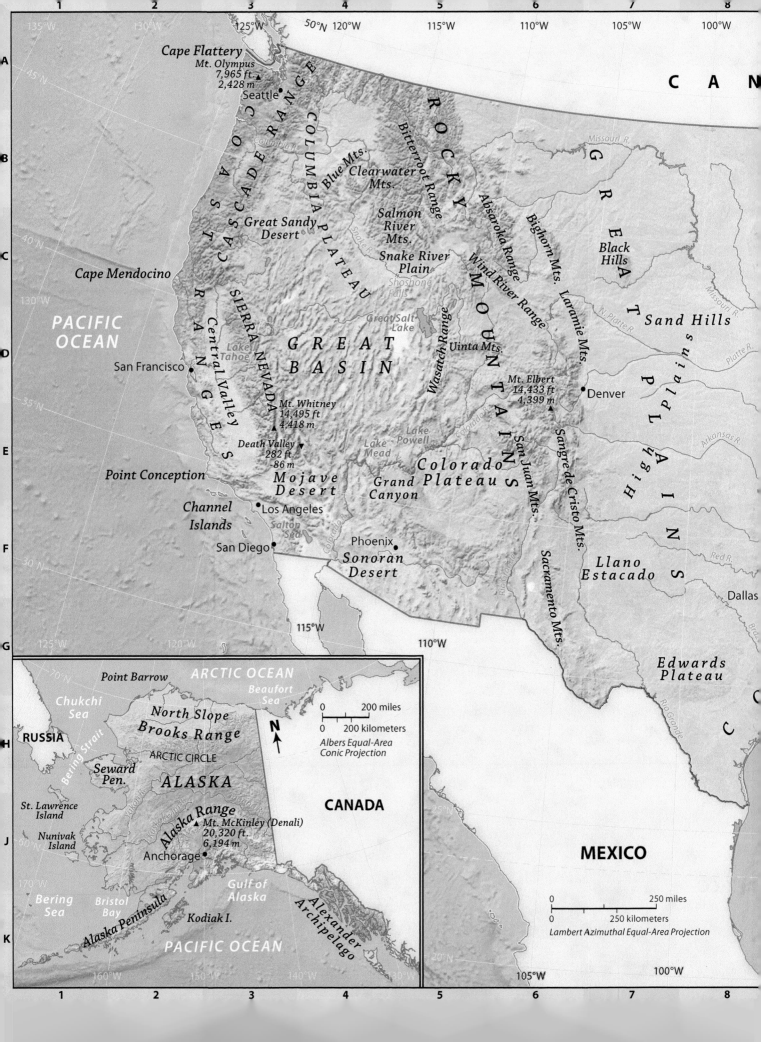

UNITED STATES
PHYSICAL

CANADA

Lake of the Woods
Isle Royale
Lake Superior
Upper Peninsula
Lake Michigan
Lake Huron
Lower Peninsula
Minneapolis
Milwaukee
Chicago
Detroit
Lake Erie
Cleveland

Lake Champlain
Adirondack Mts.
Green Mts.
White Mts.
Gulf of Maine
Lake Ontario
Niagara Falls
Boston
Cape Cod

Appalachian Plateau
Allegheny Mts.
Pittsburgh
New York City
Long Island
Philadelphia
Baltimore
Delaware Bay
Washington, D.C.
Chesapeake Bay

C E N T R A L
L O W L A N D
Indianapolis
Wabash R.
St. Louis
Ohio R.

ATLANTIC OCEAN

Flint Hills
Ozark Plateau
Boston Mts.
Memphis
Ouachita Mts.
Tennessee R.
Cumberland R.

A P P A L A C H I A N   M O U N T A I N S
Cumberland Plateau
Blue Ridge
Mt. Mitchell
6,684 ft
2,037 m

Cape Hatteras

P i e d m o n t

Atlanta
Black Belt

Red R.
Mississippi R.
A S T A L
P L A I N S
Houston
New Orleans
Mississippi River Delta

Jacksonville

Savannah R.

Cape Canaveral

Gulf of Mexico

Lake Okeechobee

The Everglades
Miami

Florida Keys
Straits of Florida

TROPIC OF CANCER

CUBA

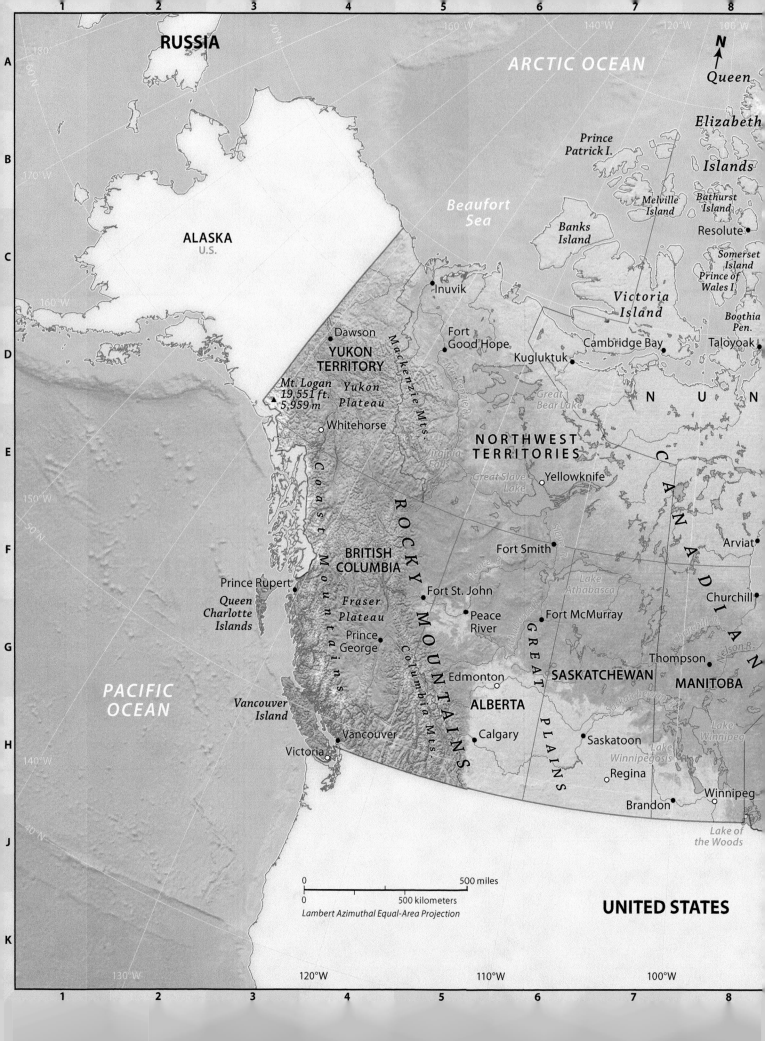

CANADA
PHYSICAL / POLITICAL

ICELAND

Ellesmere Island

Devon Island

GREENLAND
(KALAALLIT NUNAAT)
Den.

Baffin Bay

Arctic Bay

B a f f i n   I s l a n d

Igloolik

Davis Strait

Melville Peninsula

Foxe Basin

N A V U T

Repulse Bay

Iqaluit

Southampton Island

Chesterfield Inlet

Hudson Strait

Ungava Bay

Labrador Sea

Hudson Bay

Kuujjuaq

Belcher Islands

NEWFOUNDLAND

Nain

Cartwright

Fort Severn

Kuujjuarapik

Schefferville

Happy Valley-Goose Bay

Smallwood Reservoir

Churchill Falls

AND LABRADOR

Island of Newfoundland

St. John's

Avalon Peninsula

James Bay

Q U E B E C

Labrador City

Manicouagan Reservoir

Anticosti I.

Sept-Îles

St.-Pierre & Miquelon
Fr.

Gulf of St. Lawrence

Gaspé Pen.

PRINCE EDWARD ISLAND

Sydney

Cape Breton I.

ATLANTIC OCEAN

Lake Nipigon

O N T A R I O

S H I E L D

Chicoutimi

NEW BRUNSWICK

Charlottetown

Fredericton

NOVA SCOTIA

Thunder Bay

Timmins

Rouyn-Noranda

Quebec

Saint John

Halifax

Lake Superior

Sudbury

North Bay

Montreal

St. Lawrence

Bay of Fundy

Ottawa

Lake Michigan

Lake Huron

Toronto

L. Ontario

London

Niagara Falls

Lake Erie

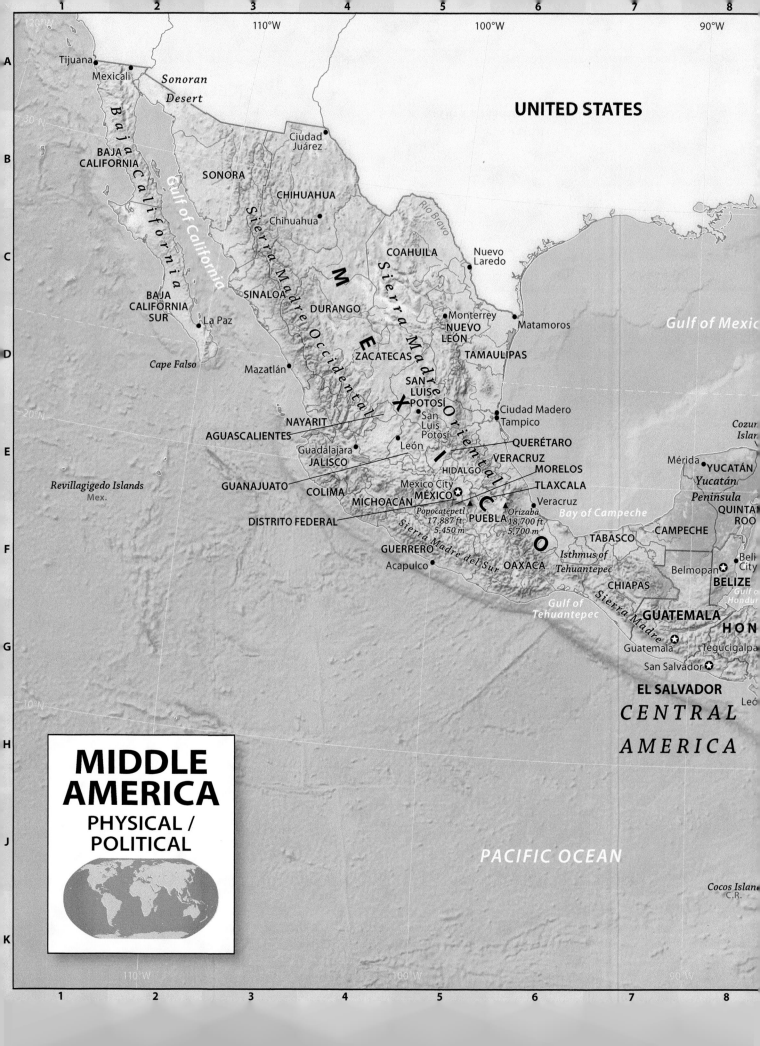

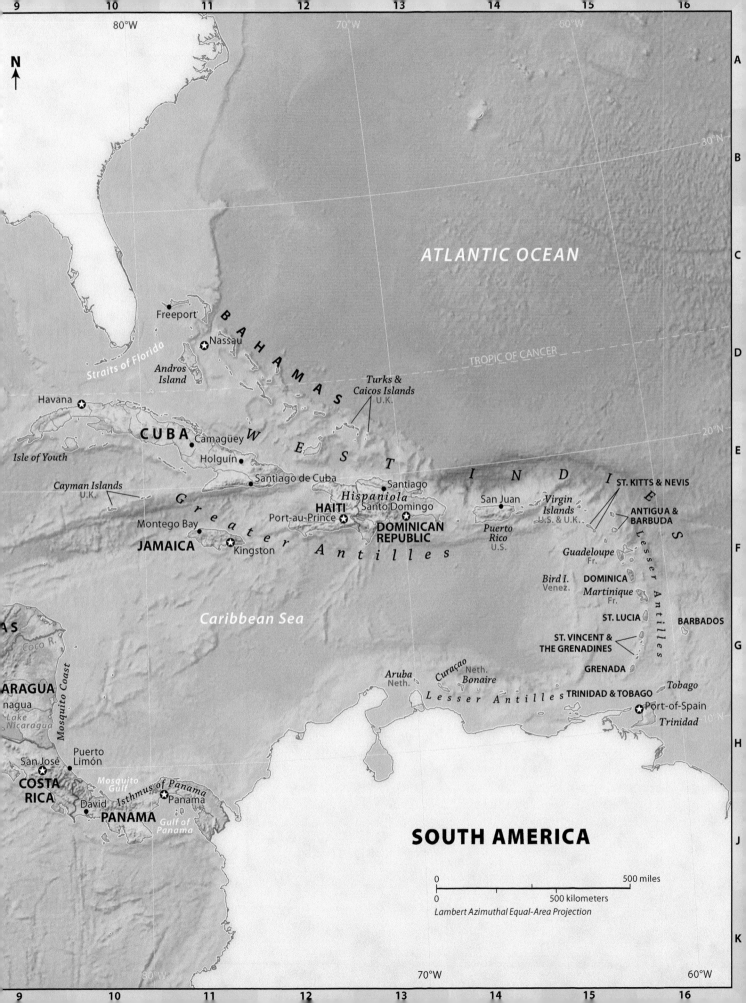

SOUTH AMERICA
POLITICAL

Caribbean Sea

VENEZUELA
Santa Marta
Barranquilla
Cartagena
Maracaibo
Caracas
Valencia
Ciudad Guayana
GUYANA
SURINAME
Bucaramanga
San Cristóbal
Georgetown
Paramaribo
Cayenne
FRENCH GUIANA
Fr.
Medellín
Boundary claimed
by Suriname

Malpelo I.
Col.
Bogotá
Cali
Boa Vista

COLOMBIA
Marajó Island

Esmeraldas
Rio Negro
EQUATOR
Quito
A   M   A   Z   O   N
Amazon R.
ECUADOR
Belém
São Luís
Guayaquil
Iquitos
Manaus
Santarém
Fortaleza
B   A   S   I   N
Amazon R.
Teresina
Campina Grande
Natal
Purus R.
Tapajós R.
Recife
Madeira R.
Xingu R.
PERU
Río Branco
Pôrto Velho
Araguaia R.
Tocantins R.
São Francisco R.
Callao
Machu Picchu
BRAZIL
Lima
Cuzco
Salvador
Ayacucho
Trinidad
Brasília
Lake Titicaca
La Paz
Goiânia
Arequipa
BOLIVIA
Santa Cruz
Uberlândia
Arica
Oruro
Sucre
Campo Grande
Uberaba
Belo Horizonte
Iquique
Tarija
Paraguay R.
Paraná R.
20°S
TROPIC OF CAPRICORN
Antofagasta
PARAGUAY
Londrina
Campinas
Nova Iguaçu
CHILE
Salta
Asunción
São Paulo
Rio de Janeiro
San Félix I.
San Ambrosio I.
Chile
San Miguel de Tucumán
Santos
Curitiba
ATLANTIC OCEAN
La Serena
Coquimbo
Córdoba
Uruguaiana
Pôrto Alegre
Santa Maria
Juan Fernández Is.
Chile
Valparaíso
Santiago
Mendoza
Rosario
Paraná R.
Uruguay R.
URUGUAY
Buenos Aires
Montevideo
Concepción
La Plata
Río de la Plata
ARGENTINA
Mar del Plata
Colorado R.
Negro R.
Bahía Blanca
Puerto Montt
40°S

PACIFIC OCEAN

Comodoro Rivadavia

Falkland Islands (Islas Malvinas)
Stanley
Administered by United Kingdom
Claimed by Arg.
Río Gallegos
Punta Arenas
Ushuaia
Strait of Magellan
Cape Horn
South Georgia Island
U.K.

N

0   1,000 miles
0   1,000 kilometers
Lambert Azimuthal Equal-Area Projection

SOUTH AMERICA

PHYSICAL

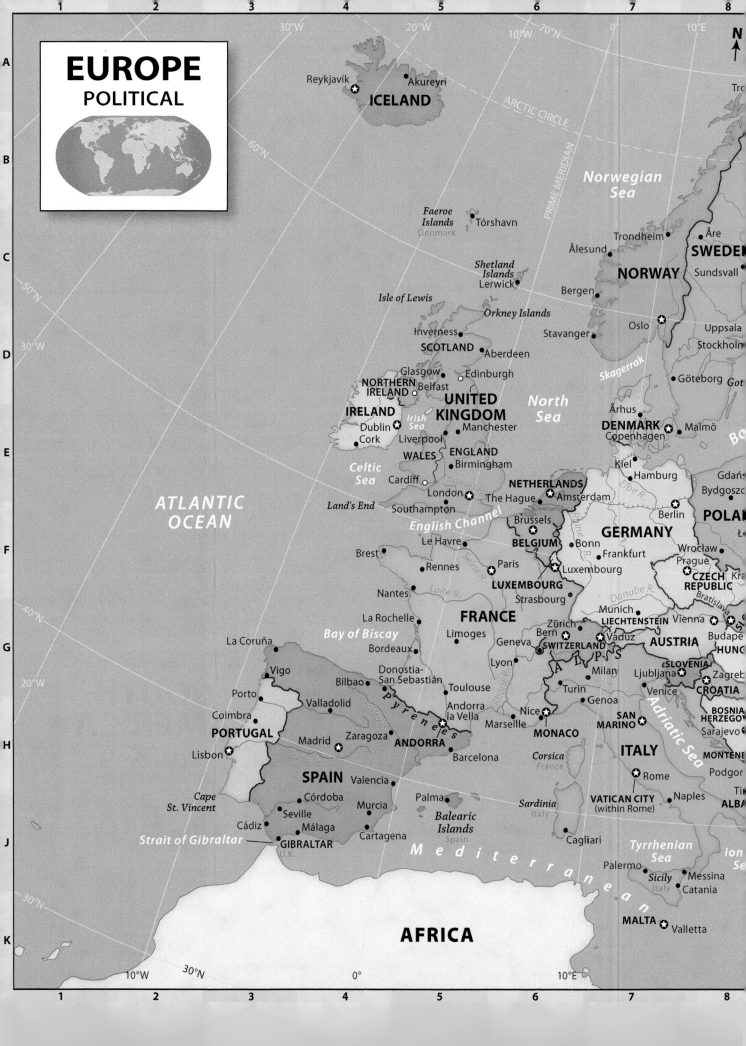

A commonly accepted division between Asia and Europe—here marked by a gray line—is formed by the Ural Mountains, Ural River, Caspian Sea, Caucasus Mountains, and the Black Sea with its outlets, the Bosporus and the Dardanelles.

Europe/Asia boundary

ASIA

Barents Sea

Tobseda

Pechora

URAL MOUNTAINS

Murmansk
Ivalo   Kirovsk
Kola Peninsula
Umba

LAPLAND
Iruna
White Sea

Kem'
Arkhangel'sk
Severodvinsk

Northern Dvina R.

Syktyvkar

Kemi
Luleå   Oulu
Umeå

FINLAND

Perm'

Vaasa   Kuopio
Lake Onega

Pori   Tampere
Lake Ladoga
Turku   Helsinki

Kirov

St. Petersburg

RUSSIA

Ufa

Tallinn
ESTONIA
Novgorod

Yaroslavl'

Kazan'

LATVIA
Riga

Tver'   Moscow

Nizhniy Novgorod

Orenburg

Daugavpils

Samara

Ural R.

LITHUANIA
Vilnius
Vitsyebsk
Smolensk

Ryazan'

Penza

Oral

Kaunas
Kaliningrad

Minsk

Bryansk

Saratov

BELARUS

Kursk

Volga R.

Warsaw

Homyel'

KAZAKHSTAN

Chernihiv

Don R.

Kyiv (Kiev)
Sumy

Kharkiv

Volgograd

L'viv
Vinnytsya

Dnieper R.

Poltava

UKRAINE
Dnipropetrovs'k

Donets'k

Astrakhan

Dniester R.

Rostov

Carpathian Mts.

MOLDOVA
Chișinău

Stavropol'

Caspian Sea

Odessa
Sea of Azov

ROMANIA
Belgrade
Bucharest

Kerch
Crimea
Simferopol'

Grozny

SERBIA
Constanța
Balkan Mts.
Varna

Sevastopol'
Yalta

Caucasus Mountains

GEORGIA

AZERBAIJAN
Baku

KOSOVO
Priština
Sofia

BULGARIA

Bosporus

İstanbul

Black Sea

Skopje
MACEDONIA

T U R K E Y

Thessaloníki

Dardanelles
Sea of Marmara

GREECE
Aegean Sea

Athens
Peloponnese

Rhodes

Nicosia

ASIA

Iraklíon

Crete
Greece

CYPRUS

400 miles

400 kilometers

Lambert Azimuthal Equal-Area Projection

EUROPE
PHYSICAL

N

ICELAND
Reykjavík

Faeroe Islands

Shetland Islands

Norwegian Sea

NORWAY
Oslo

SWEDEN
Stockholm

Gotland

Outer Hebrides

Orkney Islands

British Isles

Highlands

Edinburgh

Belfast

IRELAND
Dublin

Irish Sea

UNITED KINGDOM

North Sea

Skagerrak

Jutland

Kattegat

Zealand

DENMARK
Copenhagen

Baltic

Great Britain

Celtic Sea

Cardiff

Thames R.

London

NETHERLANDS
Amsterdam

Elbe R.

Berlin

N O R T H

POLAND

Land's End

English Channel

Brussels

BELGIUM

GERMANY

Rhine R.

Oder R.

Brittany

Seine R.

Paris

Luxembourg

LUXEMBOURG

Prague

CZECH REPUBLIC

Bratislava

SLOVAKIA

FRANCE

Loire R.

Danube R.

LIECHTENSTEIN

Vienna

Bern

Vaduz

AUSTRIA

Budapest

HUNGARY

ATLANTIC OCEAN

Bay of Biscay

SWITZERLAND

Mont Blanc 15,771 ft. 4,807 m

A L P S

SLOVENIA

Ljubljana

Zagreb

CROATIA

Cantabrian Mountains

Massif Central

Po R.

BOSNIA & HERZEGOVINA

Sarajevo

Douro R.

Ebro R.

Pyrenees

Andorra la Vella

MONACO

Riviera

SAN MARINO

Adriatic Sea

I B E R I A N

Madrid

ANDORRA

Lisbon

Tagus R.

PORTUGAL

SPAIN

P E N I N S U L A

Corsica

ITALY
Rome

MONTENEGRO

Podgorica

Tiranë

Cape St. Vincent

VATICAN CITY
(within Rome)

ALBANIA

Sardinia

Baetic Mountains

Balearic Islands

Strait of Gibraltar

GIBRALTAR

M e d i t e r r a n e a n

Tyrrhenian Sea

Ionian Sea

Sicily

Etna 10,902 ft. 3,323 m

MALTA
Valletta

AFRICA

30°W 20°W 10°W 0° 10°E

60°N

50°N

40°N

ARCTIC CIRCLE

PRIME MERIDIAN

30°W

20°W

40°N

30°N

10°W 30°N 0° 10°E

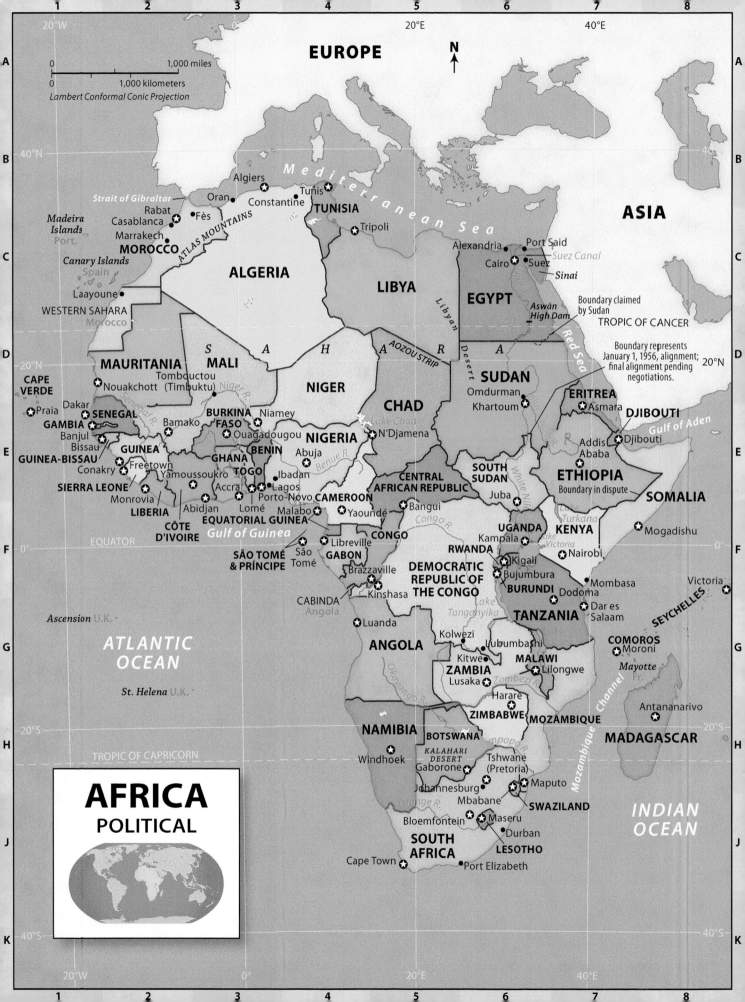

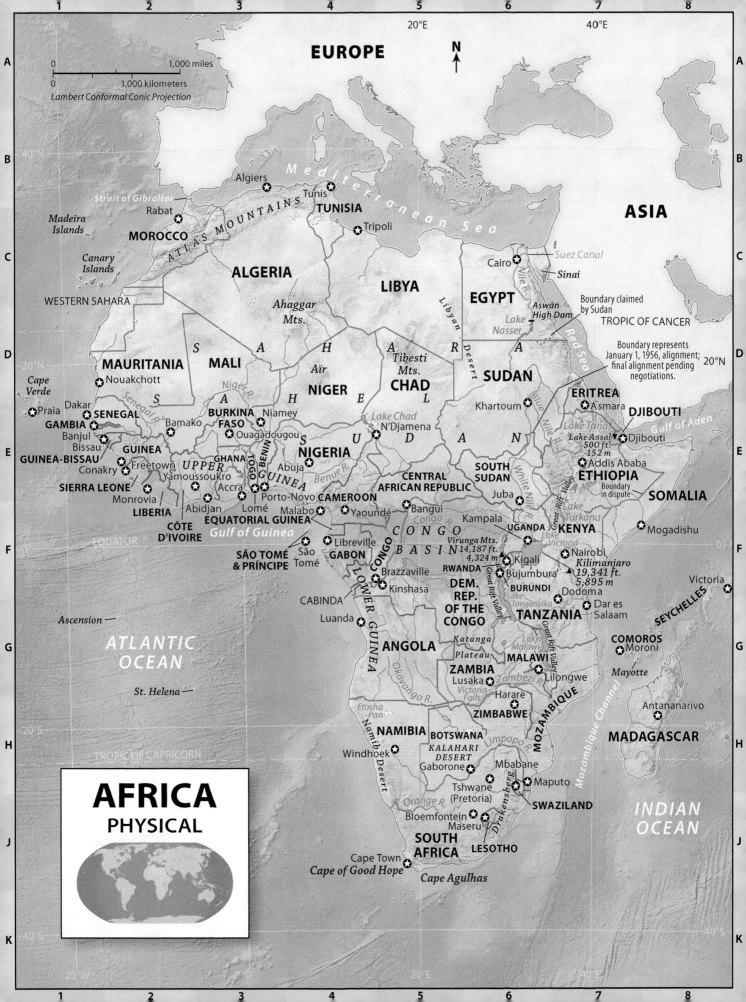

AFRICA
PHYSICAL

EUROPE

N

ASIA

Madeira
Islands

Mediterranean Sea

Algiers
Tunis
TUNISIA
Strait of Gibraltar
Rabat
Tripoli

Cairo
Suez Canal
Sinai

MOROCCO

ATLAS MOUNTAINS

ALGERIA

LIBYA

EGYPT

Canary
Islands

WESTERN SAHARA

*Ahaggar
Mts.*

Nile R.

Aswân
High Dam
Lake
Nasser

Boundary claimed
by Sudan
TROPIC OF CANCER

Boundary represents
January 1, 1956, alignment;
final alignment pending
negotiations.

Cape
Verde

MAURITANIA

Nouakchott

MALI

S   A   H
Air

A
*Tibesti
Mts.*

R
*Libyan
Desert*

A

20°N

Praia
Dakar
SENEGAL
GAMBIA
Banjul
Bissau
GUINEA-BISSAU

Bamako
Niger R.
Senegal R.

S
A
H

NIGER

Niamey

**BURKINA
FASO**
Ouagadougou

E
L

D
Lake Chad
N'Djamena

CHAD

SUDAN

Khartoum

Blue Nile
Lake Tana

N

ERITREA
Asmara
DJIBOUTI
Djibouti
Gulf of Aden

Conakry
GUINEA
Freetown
SIERRA LEONE
Monrovia
LIBERIA

UPPER
GHANA
Yamoussoukro
Accra
Abidjan
**CÔTE
D'IVOIRE**

Abuja
NIGERIA
Benue R.

BENIN
TOGO
GUINEA

S
U
D
A
N

**SOUTH
SUDAN**

Juba

White Nile R.

Addis Ababa
ETHIOPIA
Boundary
in dispute
Lake
Turkana

SOMALIA

Mogadishu

Lomé
Porto-Novo
CAMEROON
Malabo
Yaoundé
Bangui
**CENTRAL
AFRICAN REPUBLIC**

Kampala
UGANDA
Lake
Victoria

Nairobi
KENYA

EQUATOR

EQUATORIAL GUINEA
Gulf of Guinea

*CONGO
BASIN*

Virunga Mts.
14,187 ft.
4,324 m
Kigali
RWANDA
Bujumbura
BURUNDI

Kilimanjaro
19,341 ft.
5,895 m

GABON
Libreville
**SÃO TOMÉ
& PRÍNCIPE**
São
Tomé

CONGO

Great Rift Valley

Dodoma
TANZANIA
Dar es
Salaam

SEYCHELLES
Victoria

Brazzaville
Kinshasa

Lake
Tanganyika

*LOWER
GUINEA*

**DEM.
REP.
OF THE
CONGO**

Ascension

**ATLANTIC
OCEAN**

CABINDA

Luanda

*Katanga
Plateau*

Lake
Malawi

COMOROS
Moroni

Mayotte

St. Helena

ANGOLA
Okavango R.
*Victoria
Falls*
Zambezi R.

ZAMBIA
Lusaka
MALAWI
Lilongwe

Great Rift Valley

Antananarivo

*Etosha
Pan*

Harare

MOZAMBIQUE

MADAGASCAR

20°S

*Namib
Desert*

NAMIBIA
Windhoek
ZIMBABWE

Limpopo R.

Mozambique Channel

TROPIC OF CAPRICORN

BOTSWANA
*KALAHARI
DESERT*
Gaborone
Mbabane
Tshwane
(Pretoria)
SWAZILAND
Maputo

**INDIAN
OCEAN**

Orange R.
Bloemfontein
Maseru

Drakensberg

**SOUTH
AFRICA**
LESOTHO

Cape Town
Cape of Good Hope
Cape Agulhas

40°S

0   1,000 miles
0   1,000 kilometers
Lambert Conformal Conic Projection

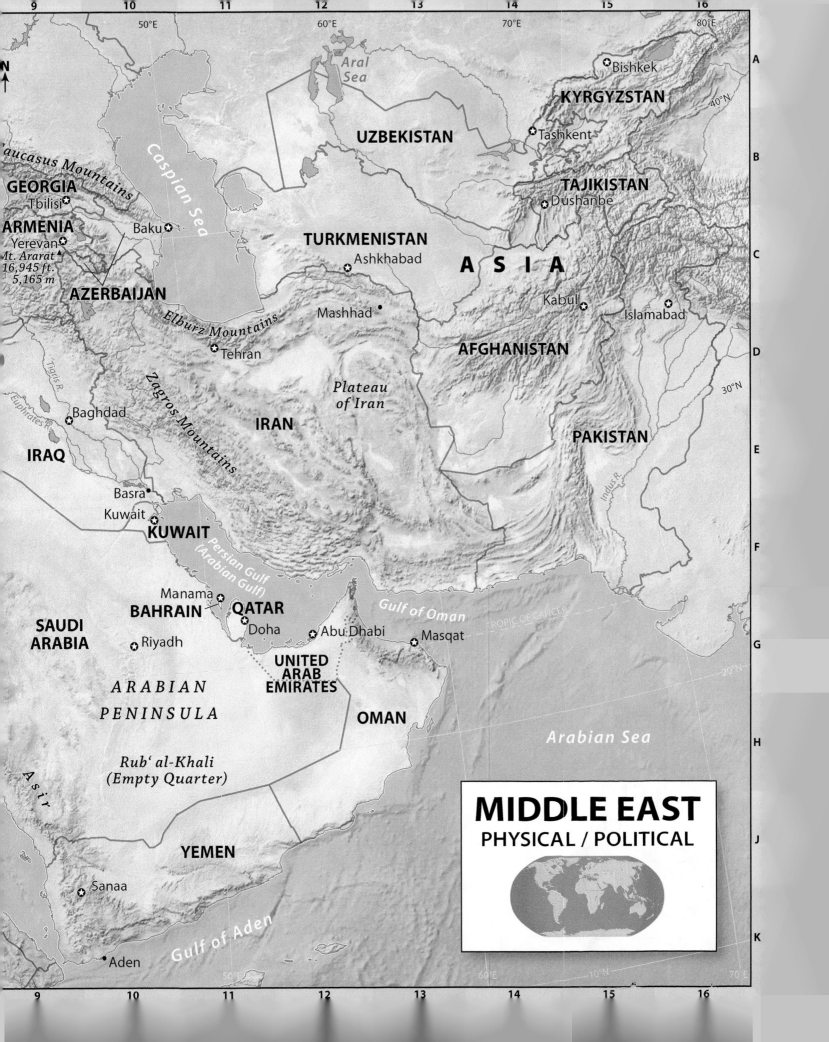

MIDDLE EAST
PHYSICAL / POLITICAL

GEORGIA
Tbilisi

ARMENIA
Yerevan
Mt. Ararat
16,945 ft.
5,165 m
AZERBAIJAN

'aucasus Mountains

Caspian Sea

Baku

Aral Sea

UZBEKISTAN

Bishkek

KYRGYZSTAN

Tashkent

TAJIKISTAN
Dushanbe

TURKMENISTAN

Ashkhabad

A S I A

Kabul

Islamabad

AFGHANISTAN

Elburz Mountains

Mashhad

Tehran

Zagros Mountains

Plateau of Iran

IRAN

PAKISTAN

Tigris R.

Euphrates R.

Baghdad

IRAQ

Indus R.

Basra
Kuwait
KUWAIT

Persian Gulf
(Arabian Gulf)

Gulf of Oman

Manama
BAHRAIN
QATAR
Doha
UNITED ARAB EMIRATES
Abu Dhabi
Masqat

TROPIC OF CANCER

SAUDI ARABIA
Riyadh

OMAN

ARABIAN PENINSULA

Arabian Sea

*Rub' al-Khali
(Empty Quarter)*

Asir

YEMEN

Sanaa

Gulf of Aden

Aden

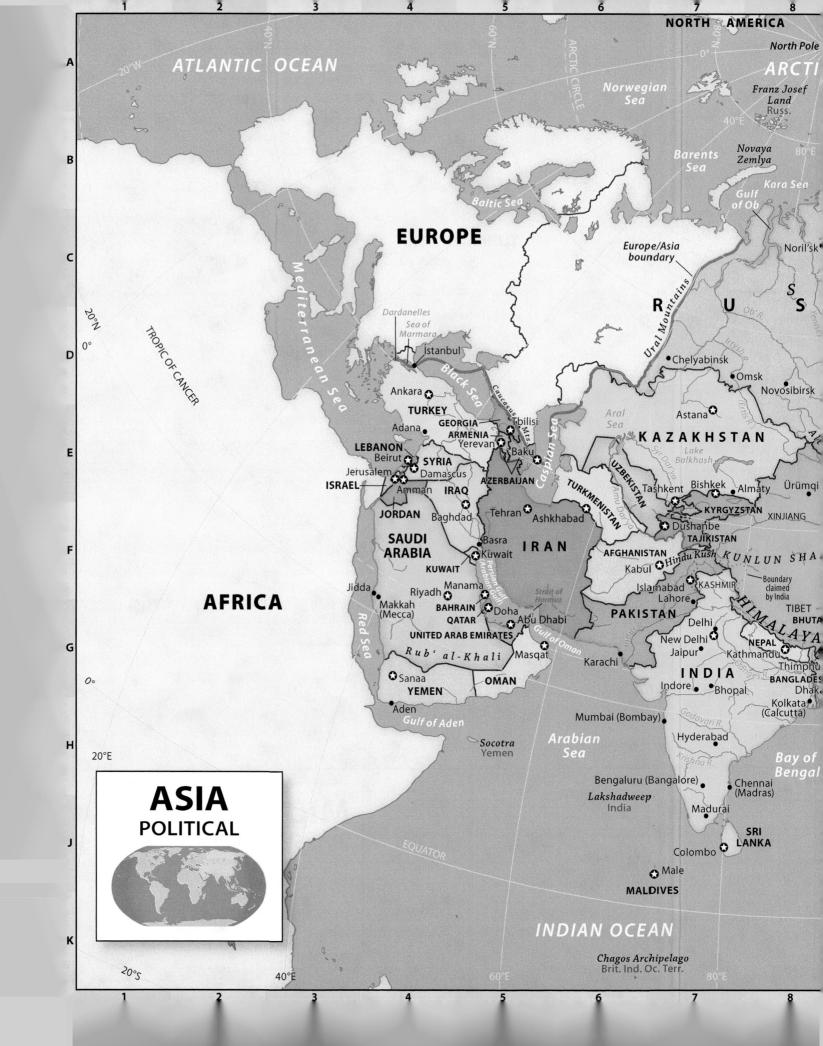

ASIA
POLITICAL

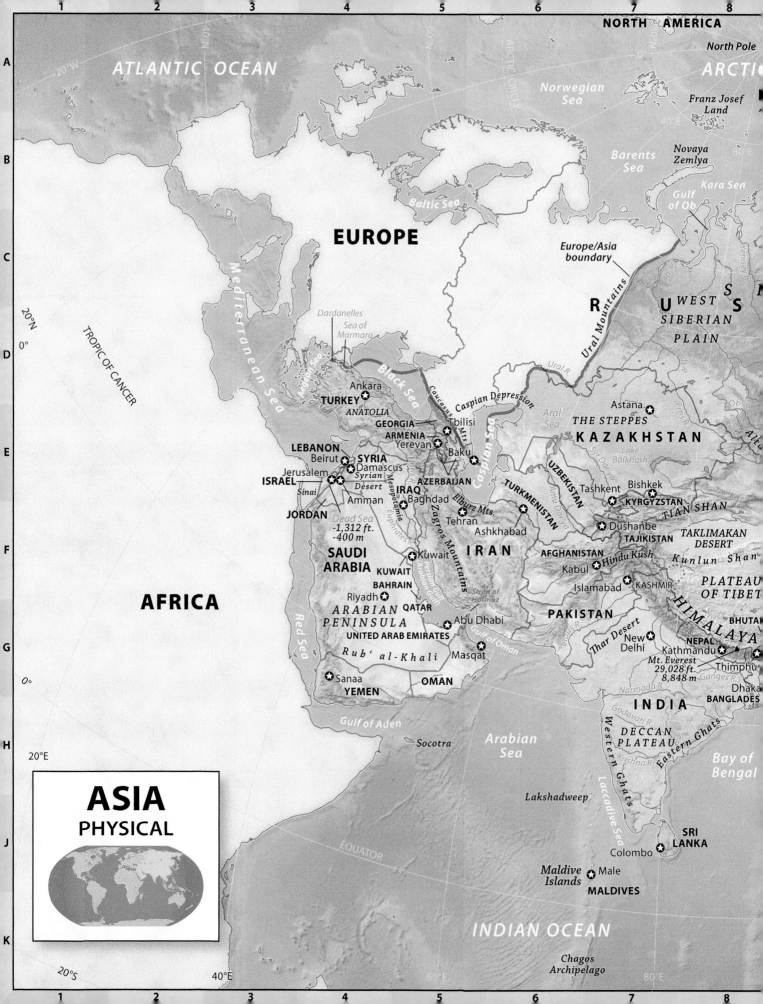

ATLANTIC OCEAN

NORTH AMERICA
North Pole
ARCTIC

Norwegian Sea

Franz Josef Land

Barents Sea

Novaya Zemlya

Kara Sea

Gulf of Ob

Baltic Sea

EUROPE

Europe/Asia boundary

R U S S

WEST SIBERIAN PLAIN

Ural Mountains

Ural R.

Mediterranean Sea

Dardanelles
Sea of Marmara

Aegean Sea

Black Sea

Caucasus

Caspian Depression

Astana

THE STEPPES

KAZAKHSTAN

Lake Balkhash

Altu

Ankara

TURKEY

ANATOLIA

GEORGIA

Tbilisi

Caspian Sea

Aral Sea

ARMENIA

Yerevan

Baku

LEBANON

Beirut

SYRIA

Damascus

Syrian Desert

AZERBAIJAN

UZBEKISTAN

Tashkent

Bishkek

Syr Darya

KYRGYZSTAN

TIAN SHAN

Jerusalem

ISRAEL

Amman

IRAQ

Baghdad

Mesopotamia

Euphrates R.

Elburz Mts.

TURKMENISTAN

Amu Darya

Dushanbe

TAJIKISTAN

TAKLIMAKAN DESERT

Kunlun Shan

JORDAN

Dead Sea
-1,312 ft.
-400 m

Sinai

Zagros Mountains

Tehran

Ashkhabad

IRAN

AFGHANISTAN

Kabul

Hindu Kush

PLATEAU OF TIBET

SAUDI ARABIA

Kuwait

KUWAIT

Persian Gulf
Arabian Gulf

Islamabad

KASHMIR

HIMALAYA

BHUTAN

BAHRAIN

Riyadh

QATAR

ARABIAN PENINSULA

Abu Dhabi

UNITED ARAB EMIRATES

Strait of Hormuz

Gulf of Oman

PAKISTAN

Indus R.

Thar Desert

New Delhi

NEPAL

Kathmandu

Thimphu

Ganges R.

Dhaka

BANGLADES

Mt. Everest
29,028 ft.
8,848 m

Rub' al-Khali

Masqat

OMAN

Sanaa

YEMEN

Red Sea

Gulf of Aden

Socotra

Arabian Sea

Narmada R.

INDIA

Godavari R.

DECCAN PLATEAU

Western Ghats

Krishna R.

Eastern Ghats

Bay of Bengal

AFRICA

TROPIC OF CANCER

20°N

0°

20°E

0°

EQUATOR

Lakshadweep

Laccadive Sea

SRI LANKA

Colombo

Maldive Islands

Male

MALDIVES

INDIAN OCEAN

Chagos Archipelago

20°S

40°E

ASIA
PHYSICAL

9   10   11   12   13   14   15   16

160°W   140°W   120°W

NORTH PACIFIC OCEAN

TROPIC OF CANCER

NORTH AMERICA   A

20°N   B

HAWAII
U.S.

Johnston Atoll
U.S.   C

Kingman
Reef
U.S.   *Palmyra Atoll* U.S.

P
O
L

Line Islands

0 ————————— 1,000 miles
0 ————————— 1,000 kilometers
Mercator Projection   D

*Kiritimati
(Christmas I.)*

EQUATOR   0°

Jarvis I.
U.S.

KIRIBATI

Phoenix Is.

KELAU
N.Z.

AMOA

**AMERICAN
SAMOA**
U.S.

Apia
Samoa Is.   Pago Pago

N
E

Marquesas Is.   E

Tuamotu Archipelago

COOK ISLANDS
N.Z.

Tahiti
Society Is.   Papeete   F

20°S

Niue
N.Z.

FRENCH POLYNESIA
Fr.

S
Austral Is.

TROPIC OF CAPRICORN

—*Henderson Island*
U.K.

—*Pitcairn
Island*
U.K.

—*Easter I.*
Chile   G

A

H

SOUTH PACIFIC OCEAN

INTERNATIONAL DATE LINE

OCEANIA
PHYSICAL /
POLITICAL

J

K

160°W   140°W   120°W

9   10   11   12   13   14   15   16

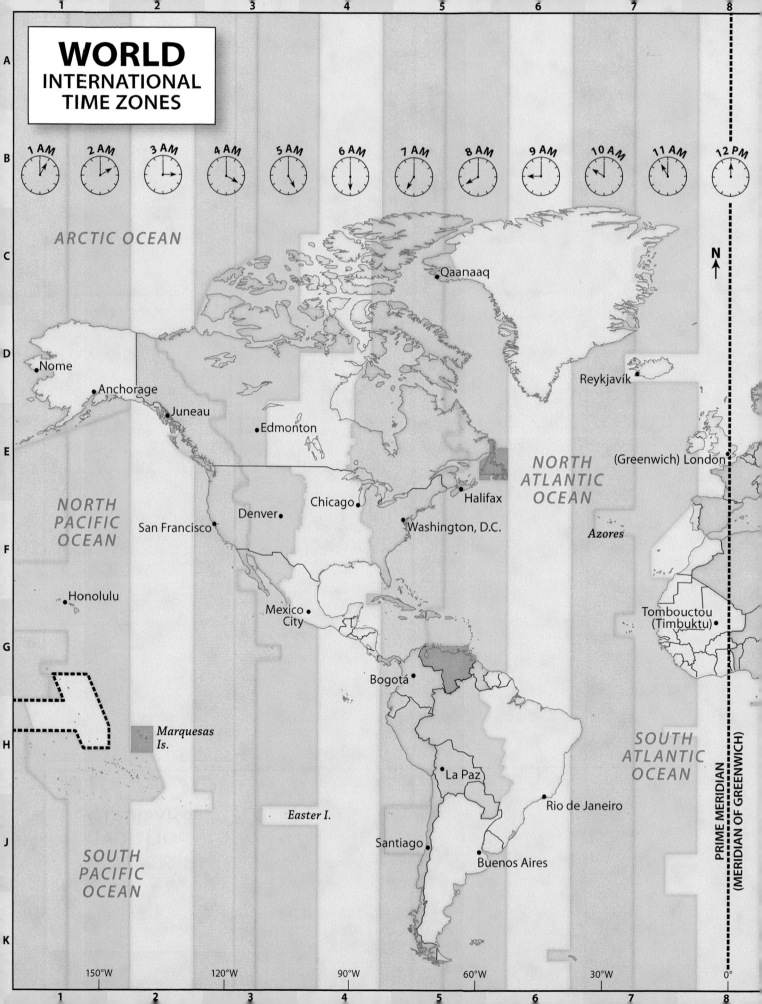

WORLD
INTERNATIONAL TIME ZONES

1 **2** **3** **4** **5** **6** **7** **8**

1 AM **2 AM** **3 AM** **4 AM** **5 AM** **6 AM** **7 AM** **8 AM** **9 AM** **10 AM** **11 AM** **12 PM**

ARCTIC OCEAN

N

Qaanaaq

Nome

Anchorage

Juneau

Reykjavík

Edmonton

(Greenwich) London

NORTH ATLANTIC OCEAN

NORTH PACIFIC OCEAN

Chicago

Denver

Halifax

San Francisco

Washington, D.C.

Azores

Honolulu

Mexico City

Tombouctou (Timbuktu)

Bogotá

Marquesas Is.

SOUTH ATLANTIC OCEAN

La Paz

Rio de Janeiro

Easter I.

Santiago

SOUTH PACIFIC OCEAN

Buenos Aires

PRIME MERIDIAN (MERIDIAN OF GREENWICH)

150°W **120°W** **90°W** **60°W** **30°W** **0°**

1 **2** **3** **4** **5** **6** **7** **8**

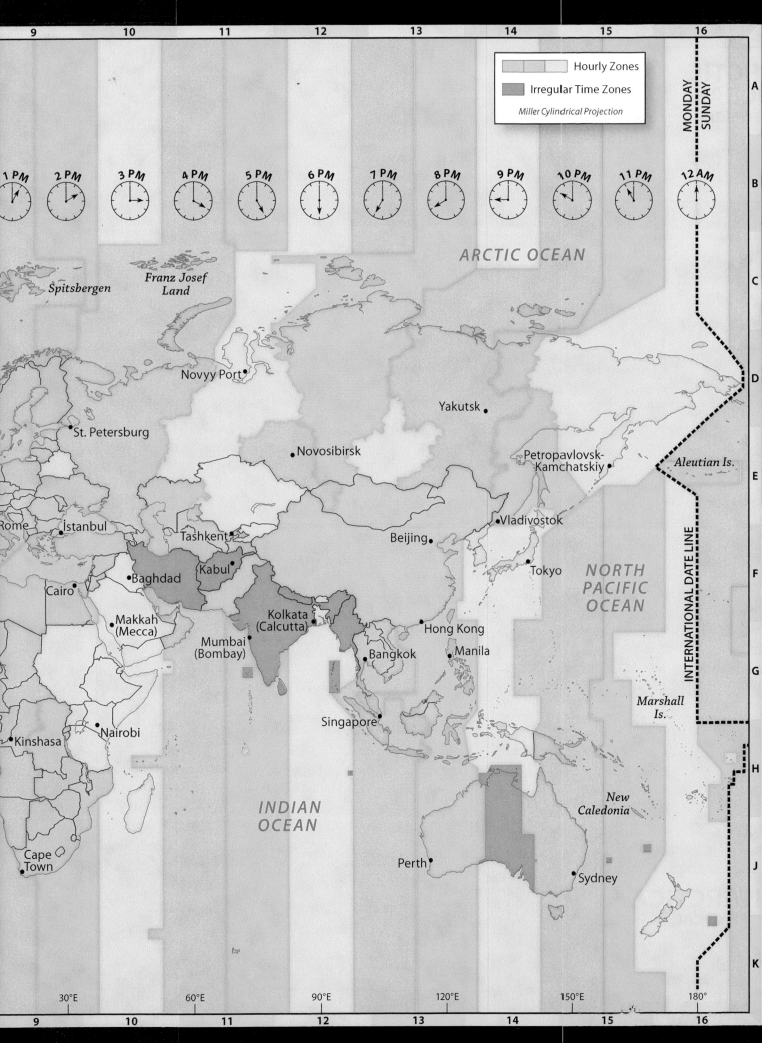

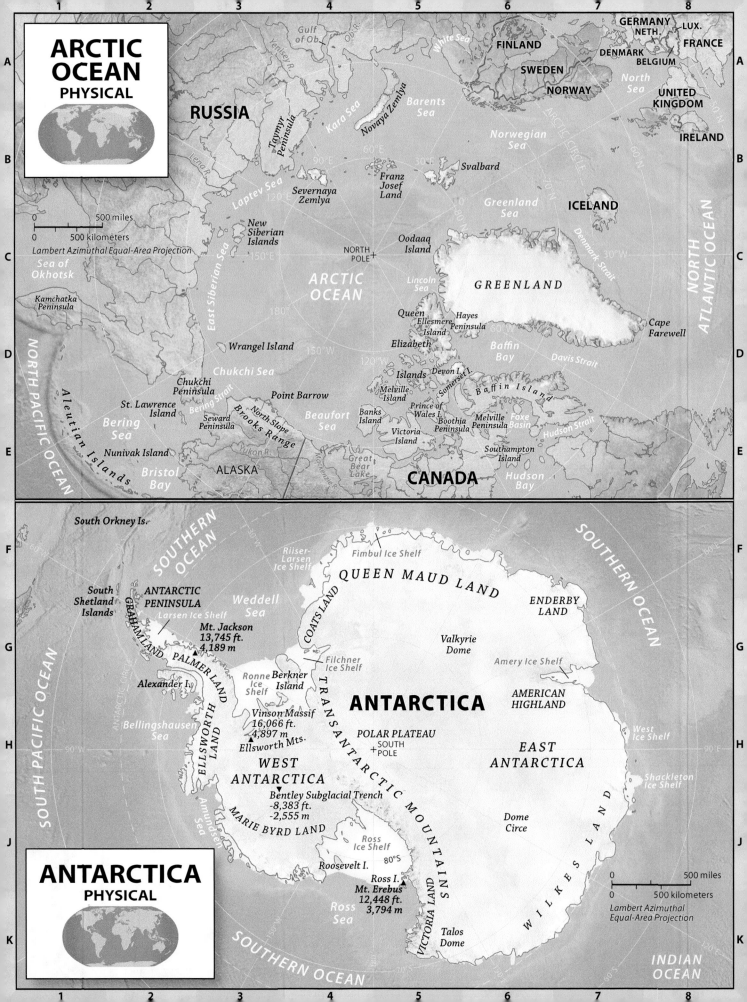

ARCTIC OCEAN PHYSICAL

1 2 3 4 5 6 7 8

A

GERMANY
NETH.
DENMARK
BELGIUM
LUX.
FRANCE
FINLAND
SWEDEN
NORWAY
North
Sea
UNITED
KINGDOM
IRELAND

B

RUSSIA
Gulf of Ob
Yenisey R.
White Sea
Taymyr Peninsula
Kara Sea
Novaya Zemlya
Barents Sea
Norwegian Sea
Svalbard
Franz Josef Land

Laptev Sea
Severnaya Zemlya
Lena R.
Greenland Sea
ICELAND
NORTH ATLANTIC OCEAN

C

500 miles
500 kilometers
Lambert Azimuthal Equal-Area Projection

New Siberian Islands
NORTH POLE +
ARCTIC OCEAN
Oodaaq Island
GREENLAND
Denmark Strait

Sea of Okhotsk
East Siberian Sea
Lincoln Sea
Queen
Ellesmere Island
Hayes Peninsula
Cape Farewell

D

Kamchatka Peninsula
Wrangel Island
Elizabeth
Islands
Devon I.
Somerset I.
Baffin Bay
Davis Strait

Chukchi Sea
Chukchi Peninsula
Point Barrow
Beaufort Sea
Melville Island
Banks Island
Prince of Wales I.
Boothia Peninsula
Baffin Island
Melville Peninsula
Foxe Basin

E

Aleutian Islands
St. Lawrence Island
Bering Strait
Seward Peninsula
North Slope
Brooks Range
Victoria Island
Southampton Island
Hudson Strait

NORTH PACIFIC OCEAN
Bering Sea
Nunivak Island
Bristol Bay
Yukon R.
ALASKA
Mackenzie R.
Great Bear Lake
CANADA
Hudson Bay

ANTARCTICA PHYSICAL

F

South Orkney Is.
SOUTHERN OCEAN
Riiser-Larsen Ice Shelf
Fimbul Ice Shelf
QUEEN MAUD LAND
ENDERBY LAND
SOUTHERN OCEAN

G

South Shetland Islands
ANTARCTIC PENINSULA
GRAHAM LAND
Larsen Ice Shelf
Weddell Sea
COATS LAND
Mt. Jackson 13,745 ft. 4,189 m
PALMER LAND
Alexander I.
Ronne Ice Shelf
Berkner Island
Filchner Ice Shelf
Valkyrie Dome
Amery Ice Shelf

H

SOUTH PACIFIC OCEAN
Bellingshausen Sea
ELLSWORTH LAND
Vinson Massif 16,066 ft. 4,897 m
Ellsworth Mts.
TRANSANTARCTIC MOUNTAINS
ANTARCTICA
POLAR PLATEAU
+ SOUTH POLE
AMERICAN HIGHLAND
EAST ANTARCTICA
West Ice Shelf
Shackleton Ice Shelf

WEST ANTARCTICA
Bentley Subglacial Trench -8,383 ft. -2,555 m
MARIE BYRD LAND
Amundsen Sea

J

Ross Ice Shelf
Roosevelt I.
80°S
Dome Circe
WILKES LAND
INDIAN OCEAN

K

Ross Sea
Ross I.
Mt. Erebus 12,448 ft. 3,794 m
VICTORIA LAND
Talos Dome
SOUTHERN OCEAN

1 2 3 4 5 6 7 8

500 miles
500 kilometers
Lambert Azimuthal Equal-Area Projection

A WORLD OF EXTREMES

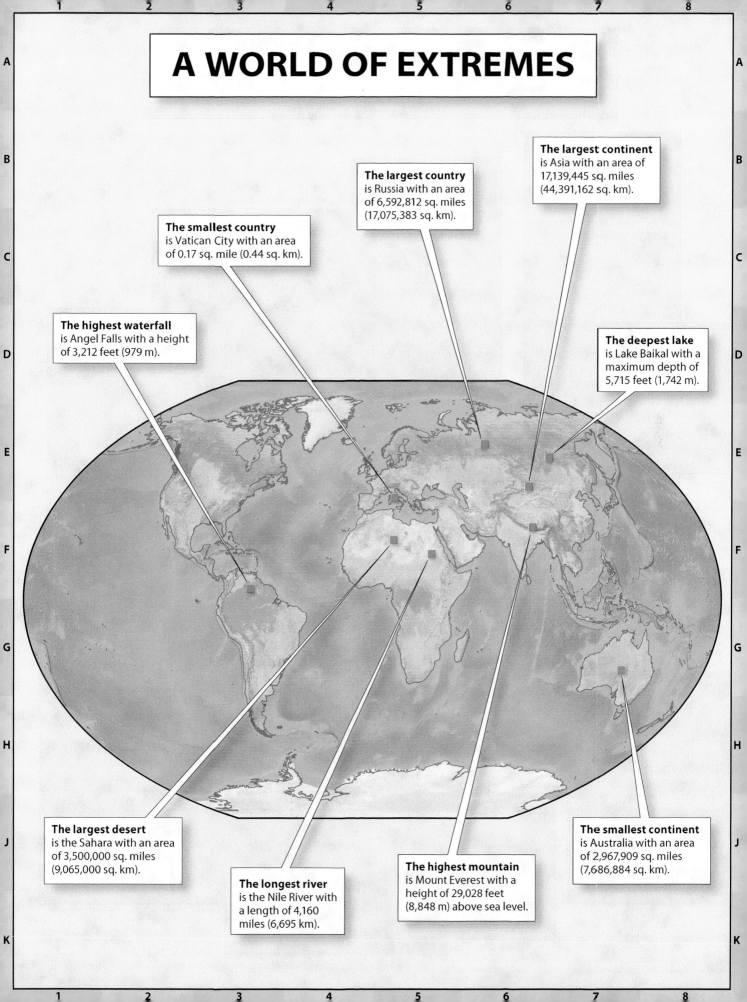

The largest continent
is Asia with an area of
17,139,445 sq. miles
(44,391,162 sq. km).

The largest country
is Russia with an area
of 6,592,812 sq. miles
(17,075,383 sq. km).

The smallest country
is Vatican City with an area
of 0.17 sq. mile (0.44 sq. km).

The deepest lake
is Lake Baikal with a
maximum depth of
5,715 feet (1,742 m).

The highest waterfall
is Angel Falls with a height
of 3,212 feet (979 m).

The largest desert
is the Sahara with an area
of 3,500,000 sq. miles
(9,065,000 sq. km).

The longest river
is the Nile River with
a length of 4,160
miles (6,695 km).

The highest mountain
is Mount Everest with a
height of 29,028 feet
(8,848 m) above sea level.

The smallest continent
is Australia with an area
of 2,967,909 sq. miles
(7,686,884 sq. km).

GEOGRAPHIC DICTIONARY

Ocean · Archipelago · Gulf · Volcano · Reservoir · Isthmus · Plateau · Highlands · Canyon · Cliff · Cape · Reef · Island · Channel · Peninsula · Bay · Harbor

archipelago a group of islands

basin area of land drained by a given river and its branches; area of land surrounded by lands of higher elevations

bay part of a large body of water that extends into a shoreline, generally smaller than a gulf

canyon deep and narrow valley with steep walls

cape point of land that extends into a river, lake, or ocean

channel wide strait or waterway between two landmasses that lie close to each other; deep part of a river or other waterway

cliff steep, high wall of rock, earth, or ice

continent one of the seven large landmasses on the Earth

delta flat, low-lying land built up from soil carried downstream by a river and deposited at its mouth

divide stretch of high land that separates river systems

downstream direction in which a river or stream flows from its source to its mouth

escarpment steep cliff or slope between a higher and lower land surface

glacier large, thick body of slowly moving ice

gulf part of a large body of water that extends into a shoreline, generally larger and more deeply indented than a bay

harbor a sheltered place along a shoreline where ships can anchor safely

highland elevated land area such as a hill, mountain, or plateau

hill elevated land with sloping sides and rounded summit; generally smaller than a mountain

island land area, smaller than a continent, completely surrounded by water

isthmus narrow stretch of land connecting two larger land areas

lake a sizable inland body of water

lowland land, usually level, at a low elevation

mesa broad, flat-topped landform with steep sides; smaller than a plateau

mountain land with steep sides that rises sharply (1,000 feet or more) from surrounding land; generally larger and more rugged than a hill

Desert
Oasis
Mountain Peak
Sound
Basin
Mountain Range
Source of River
Glacier
Tributary
Valley
Hills
Strait
Upstream
Lake
Downstream
River
Mouth of River
Lowland
Escarpment
Delta
Plain
Seacoast

mountain peak pointed top of a mountain

mountain range a series of connected mountains

mouth (of a river) place where a stream or river flows into a larger body of water

oasis small area in a desert where water and vegetation are found

ocean one of the four major bodies of salt water that surround the continents

ocean current stream of either cold or warm water that moves in a definite direction through an ocean

peninsula body of land jutting into a lake or ocean, surrounded on three sides by water

physical feature characteristic of a place occurring naturally, such as a landform, body of water, climate pattern, or resource

plain area of level land, usually at low elevation and often covered with grasses

plateau area of flat or rolling land at a high elevation, about 300 to 3,000 feet (90 to 900 m) high

reef a chain of rocks, coral or sand at or near the surface of the water

river large natural stream of water that runs through the land

sea large body of water completely or partly surrounded by land

seacoast land lying next to a sea or an ocean

sound broad inland body of water, often between a coastline and one or more islands off the coast

source (of a river) place where a river or stream begins, often in highlands

strait narrow stretch of water joining two larger bodies of water

tributary small river or stream that flows into a large river or stream; a branch of the river

upstream direction opposite the flow of a river; toward the source of a river or stream

valley area of low land usually between hills or mountains

volcano mountain or hill created as liquid rock and ash erupt from inside the Earth

SCAVENGER HUNT

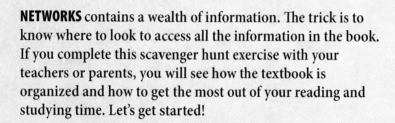

NETWORKS contains a wealth of information. The trick is to know where to look to access all the information in the book. If you complete this scavenger hunt exercise with your teachers or parents, you will see how the textbook is organized and how to get the most out of your reading and studying time. Let's get started!

1 How many lessons are in Chapter 2?
Chapter 2 has three lessons.

2 What does Unit 1 cover?
Unit 1 covers the world.

3 Where can you find the Essential Questions for each lesson?
The Essential Questions are located at the beginning of each lesson, after the lesson title.

4 In what three places can you find information on a Foldable?
Foldables are found on the chapter opener, before each lesson review, and on the chapter activities page.

5 How can you identify content vocabulary and academic vocabulary in the narrative?
Content vocabulary terms are bold and highlighted yellow. Academic terms are bold.

6 Where do you find graphic organizers in your textbook?
Graphic organizers are at the beginning of each lesson in the Reading Helpdesk.

7 You want to quickly find a map in the book about the world. Where do you look?
The Reference Atlas section is easy to find in the front of your book and contains world and regional maps.

8 Where would you find the latitude and longitude for Dublin, Ireland?
You can find latitude and longitude as well as important geographic features and country capitals in the Gazetteer.

9 If you needed to know the Spanish term for *earthquake*, where would you look?
The English-Spanish glossary contains the Spanish terms and definitions for the content and academic vocabulary.

10 Where can you find a list of all the charts in a unit?
The Diagrams, Charts, and Graphs section in the front of your book lists the title and page number of every diagram, chart, and graph in each unit.

Our World: The Western Hemisphere Planner

UNDERSTANDING BY DESIGN®

Enduring Understandings

- People, places, and ideas change over time.
- Over time, people adapt to their environment.
- Countries have relationships with each other.

Essential Questions

- How does geography influence the way people live?
- How do people adapt to their environment?
- What makes a culture unique?
- Why do people make economic choices?

Students will know:

- the five themes of geography (location, place, region, human-environment interaction, movement) and the six essential elements.
- of the parts, styles, and purposes of a world map and use it to identify places.
- the geography, climate, resources, political boundaries, and population of the continents.
- the aspects of life that occur on Earth happen because of Earth's position to the sun, its axis, its rotation, and its revolution.
- Earth has a variety of climates that help to sustain its wide variety of species.
- what a culture is, what makes up cultural regions, and how and why cultures change.
- different forms of government and the definition of globalization.

Students will be able to:

- **use a world map** to identify physical features, political boundaries, population density, economic resources, and climate.
- **identify and apply** a geographer's tools including globes, maps, and geospatial technologies.
- **describe** Earth's six major climate zones and explain what factors determine the climate of an area.
- **describe** the physical characteristics of places including landforms and bodies of water.
- **describe** the physical processes that shape the patterns of Earth's surface including weathering and erosion.
- **explain** human characteristics and how culture and experience influence people's perceptions of places and regions.

Predictable Misunderstandings

- Geography is just the names of states and their capitals.
- Lines of latitude and longitude actually appear on Earth.
- Geography is static and unchanging, serving merely as a backdrop to people's activities.
- Earth is a solid planet.
- The planets in the solar system are all like Earth.
- Humans have very little effect on the environment.
- The ocean floor is flat.
- Families around the world are organized like those found in the student's local community.

- All countries have governments like that found in the United States.
- The customs students enjoy originated in the United States.

Assessment Evidence

Performance Tasks:

- Unit GeoLab Activity
- Environmental Case Study

Other Evidence:

- Physical Location GeoQuiz
- Political Location GeoQuiz
- City Location GeoQuiz
- Physical Geography Activity
- Cultural Geography Activity
- Geography and History Activity
- Geography and Economics Activity
- Geography Skills Activity
- Critical Thinking Skills Activity
- Participation in Interactive Whiteboard Activities
- Contribution to small-group activities
- Interpretation of slide show images and special purpose maps
- Participation in class discussions about the world
- Analysis of graphic organizers, graphs, and charts
- Lesson Reviews
- Chapter Assessments

Key for Using the Teacher Edition

SKILL-BASED ACTIVITIES

Types of skill activites found in the Teacher Edition.

* **V Visual Skills** require students to analyze maps, graphs, charts, and photos.

W Writing Skills provide writing opportunities to help students comprehend the text.

R Reading Skills help students practice reading skills and master vocabulary.

C Critical Thinking Skills help students apply and extend what they have learned.

T Technology Skills require students to use digital tools effectively.

*Letters are followed by a number when there is more than one of the same type of skill on the page.

DIFFERENTIATED INSTRUCTION

All activities are written for the on-level student unless otherwise marked with the leveled labels below.

BL Beyond Level

AL Approaching Level

ELL English Language Learners

All students benefit from activities that utilize different learning styles. Many activities are marked as below when a particular learning style is highlighted.

Intrapersonal	Naturalist
Logical/Mathematical	Kinesthetic
Visual/Spatial	Auditory/Musical
Verbal/Linguistic	Interpersonal

SUGGESTED PACING GUIDE

TOTAL TIME   36 Days

PLANNER

☑ Print Teaching Options

V Visual Skills

☐ **P. 2** Students use photo, text, and prior knowledge of the oceans to identify and catergorize sea plants and animals.

☐ **P. 3** Students interpret an image, then attribute purpose and importance of solar panels to energy needs.

☐ **P. 6** Students contrast a political and physical map of the world, and then answer questions on North America.

☐ **P. 9** Students compare a physical map to a population density map of the world to answer questions.

☐ **P. 10** Students analyze maps to recognize the relationship between natural resources and physical landforms. **ELL**

☐ **P. 12** Students use a climate map to relate climate, physical landforms, and population density. **BL**

W Writing Skills

☐ **P. 14** Students use a photo to write a narrative.

☐ **P. 14** Students summarize what they have learned about the five types of maps studied.

R Reading Skills

☐ **P. 2** Students define what it means to study geography.

☐ **P. 3** Students categorize natural resources as renewable or nonrenewable.

☐ **P. 8** Students use a population map and physical examples to identify population density. **BL**

C Critical Thinking Skills

☐ **P. 2** Students create a list and speculate on how landforms influence how people relate to the environment. **BL**

☐ **P. 4** Students compare and contrast North America and South America on a physical map of the world. **BL**

☐ **P. 5** Students transfer knowledge to write questions and answers about a physical map of the world.

☐ **P. 7** Students make inferences about countries on a political map of the world.

☐ **P. 10** Students use an economic map to draw conclusions about how natural resources affect countries.

☐ **P. 13** Students hypothesize to make connections between Earth's shape and climate. **AL**

T Technology Skills

☐ **P. 14** Student groups create maps and presentations using the unit maps and online research.

☑ Online Teaching Options

V Visual Skills

☐ **MAP** **The World: Physical Map**—Students use a physical map to identify and mark physical features. **AL** Kinesthetic

☐ **MAP** **The World: Population Density Map**—Students use a population map to discuss the impact of high population density. **BL** Visual/Spatial

☐ **MAP** **Regional Map**—Students use the regional map to connect the images from the textbook to their location on the map.

☐ **MAP** **The World: Political Map**—Students use the political map to review the political boundaries of the world.

W Writing Skills

☐ **MAP** **The World: Economic Map**—Students use the resources map to write a paragraph to explain why coastal cities are built. Verbal/Linguistic

☐ **MAP** **The World: Climates Map**—Students use a climate map to write about climate and vegetation regions. **BL** Visual/Spatial

C Critical Thinking Skills

☐ **VIDEO** **A World Tour**—Students watch a video montage and then create charts. Visual

☐ **SLIDE SHOW** **How-To: Read a Map**—Students use the slide show to identify locations on maps. **BL** Visual/Spatial

☐ **CHART** **Precipitation and Temperature Chart**—Students use the interactive chart to study the factors that impact where people live. Verbal/Linguistic

T Technology Skills

☐ **GAME** **The Physical World Game**—Students use a physical map game to drag and drop names of continents and major bodies of water. **AL** Kinesthetic

☐ **GAME** **The Political World Game**—Students use a political map game to drag and drop names of cities and countries. Kinesthetic

☑ Printable Digital Worksheets

W Writing Skills

☐ **WORKSHEET** **Environmental Case Study: Maintenance of Fresh Water Sources**—Students will use the worksheet to review and discuss the significance of Earth as a water planet.

☐ **WORKSHEET** **GeoLab: Desalinization of Water**—Students use the worksheet to understand the process of desalinization.

☐ **WORKSHEET** **Physical Geography Activity**—Students will analyze an elevation profile of the ocean.

☐ **WORKSHEET** **Cultural Geography Activity**—Students will read about the term *culture* and answer questions about the excerpt.

☐ **QUIZ** **Physical Location GeoQuiz**—Use the Physical Location GeoQuiz as a pre- or post-assessment of students' knowledge of the world's landforms and bodies of water.

☐ **QUIZ** **Political Location GeoQuiz**—Use the Political Location GeoQuiz as a pre- or post-assessment of students' knowledge of the world's countries.

☐ **QUIZ** **City Location GeoQuiz**—Use the City Location GeoQuiz as a pre- or post-assessment of students' knowledge of the world's major cities.

OUR WORLD: THE WESTERN HEMISPHERE

McGraw-Hill
netw⊙rks

UNIT 1

| **Chapter 1** | **Chapter 2** | **Chapter 3** |
| What Is Geography? | Earth's Physical Geography | Earth's People |

BILL HATCHER/National Geographic Stock

Global Connections

Discussing The Global Connections issue of this unit is *Social Media in a Changing World*. Begin highlighting this feature by discussing how social media has helped people stay in touch with family and friends, take online classes, and communicate in an emergency. Tell students they will be asked to analyze social media data, to consider Internet safety while online, and to analyze the impact of social media on political situations. Interpersonal

ENGAGE

Bellringer Share with students that the image is of a mountain climber. Ask students to analyze the details in the photo. **Ask:**

- What protective gear does the mountain climber wear? What is the purpose of the gear? *(insulated clothes, hood, gloves, goggles, oxygen mask; to protect against the extreme cold and thin atmosphere at high altitudes)*
- What type of dangers do you think mountain climbers face? *(extreme wind and temperatures, powerful snow storms, lack of shelter, loss of equipment, reduced oxygen, must carry all provisions, confusion, cracks in the ice)* Visual/Spatial

Making Connections Read the following information to students.

The United States has several mountain ranges. Of these, fifty of the highest mountain peaks are located in four states: 28 are located in Colorado, 14 in Alaska, 7 in California, and 1 in Washington.

- The Alaskan Mountain Range has some of the highest mountain elevations in the United States.
- Mount McKinley is the highest peak in the United States and in North America with an elevation of 20,320 ft. When measured from the base of the mountain to the highest peak, it is the tallest mountain on land.
- The first successful climb of Mount McKinley took place in 1913 by the four man team of Hudson Stuck, Harry Karstens, Walter Harper, and Robert Tatum.
- Those who scale these tall mountains face many dangers, including extremely cold temperatures, severe weather conditions, an atmosphere low in oxygen, and the ever-present danger of avalanches.
- Mount McKinley is known for its extremely cold temperatures which average −75.5°F, and with wind chills that can lower the temperature to −118.1°F.
- Mount McKinley is regularly climbed today, even though over 100 people have died trying to climb it.

Tell students they will be learning more about mountains and other aspects of the world's regions and resources.

TEACH & ASSESS

R

R Reading Skills

Naming Have a volunteer read the introductory paragraph aloud. **Ask:**

- What do you learn about when you study geography? (*Earth's land, water, plants, and animals*)
- Why do some people call Earth "the water planet"? (*Water covers almost 70 percent of Earth's surface.*) **AL**
  Verbal/Linguistic

V Visual Skills

V

Identifying Have students discuss what they observe in the image of the SCUBA diver and refer to the paragraph, "Bodies of Water." **Ask:**

- What are the five oceans? (*Pacific, Atlantic, Indian, Southern, Arctic*)
- What can be said about the water that makes up the five oceans? (*It is a continuous body of water that encircles Earth.*)

Have students share what they think undersea explorers might find as they investigate the ocean. Have students categorize items as either sea animals or underwater plants. Create a two-column chart on the board as students generate answers. **Visual/Spatial**

C Critical Thinking Skills

Speculating Have students read the paragraph, "Landforms," and describe what they see in the image corresponding to it. As a class, create a list of all the landforms students can think of. Discuss familiar landforms students have in their community. **Ask:**

- How might landforms influence where people live? (*Students might say that people live near water and food sources.*)
- How do landforms influence how people relate to their environment? (*Students might note that the environment determines the types of shelters people have and the types of food they eat.*) **BL** **Verbal/Linguistic**

EXPLORE the WORLD

Geography is the study of Earth and all of its variety. When you study geography, you learn about the planet's land, water, plants, and animals. Some people call Earth "the water planet." Do you know why? Water—in the form of streams, rivers, lakes, seas, and oceans—covers nearly 70 percent of Earth's surface.

① BODIES OF WATER Underseas explorers can still experience the thrill of investigating uncharted territory—one of Earth's last frontiers. Almost all of Earth's water consists of a continuous body of water that circles the planet. This body of water makes up five oceans: the Pacific, the Atlantic, the Indian, the Southern, and the Arctic.

C

② LANDFORMS Landforms are features of the land, such as mountains, valleys, and canyons. Landforms influence where people live and how they relate to their environment.

2 *Unit 1*

networks *Online Teaching Options*

VIDEO

A World Tour

Creating Charts Display the video montage of images from the unit as an introduction to this lesson. Divide the class into four groups. Assign a region to each group (forest, river valley, open prairie, ocean coast area). Have each group discuss the sights and sounds of the video, and how the region they have been assigned might influence how people living there relate to their environment. Create a group chart of the information generated by the students. Keep the chart to refine with the class during the unit's study. **Visual/Spatial, Auditory/Musical**

Comstock Images/Jupiterimages

③ NATURAL RESOURCES Natural resources are products of Earth that people use to meet their needs. Solar energy is power produced by the heat of the sun. Sun and wind are renewable resources. These resources cannot be used up.

R

V

C

FAST
FACT

Earth's longest mountain range is underwater.

Unit 1 3

R Reading Skills

Categorizing Write *Natural Resources* on the board, and have a volunteer read the paragraph, "Natural Resources." **Ask:** What are natural resources? (*products from Earth that people use to meet their needs*)

Write *renewable* and *nonrenewable* under *Natural Resources*. Ask students to define these resources. To clear up any misconceptions, explain that renewable resources are ones that can be replenished after being used, such as trees used for building houses. Nonrenewable resources are resources that once used are gone forever or for an extremely long period of time. **Ask:**

- What are some examples of renewable resources? (*plants, water, sun*)
- What are some examples of nonrenewable resources? (*oil, coal, natural gas*) **Naturalist**

V Visual Skills

Interpreting Direct students' attention to the image of the solar panels. **Ask:**

- What is the purpose of solar panels? (*to capture solar energy or the energy from the Sun*)
- Where have you seen solar panels? (*Possible answers: on house rooftops; along the highway on lights; on small lights in people's yards*)
- How does solar energy help people meet their energy needs? (*Students answers should reflect an understanding that the solar energy is converted into electrical energy to assist with the energy needs of individuals and communities.*) **Logical/ Mathematical**

C Critical Thinking Skills

Making Connections Read aloud the Fast Fact information. Remind students that landforms can be found both above and below the ocean. Explain that islands, such as the islands of Hawaii, are actually the tops of underwater mountains that rise above the surface of the ocean and provide living space for plants and animals above the water. **Ask:** What benefits do landforms below the ocean's surface serve? (*Possible answer: habitat for fish and other marine animals and plants*)
AL

Environmental Case Study

Evaluating The case study for this unit is about the maintenance of fresh water sources. This topic will help students understand the significance of Earth as a water planet. Divide students into groups and distribute the case study worksheets. Allow students in-class time for planning. Have groups share their findings with the class. **Verbal/Linguistic, Naturalist**

V Visual Skills

Reading a Map Point out to students that this is a physical map, and have students work in pairs to analyze the features of a physical map. Then discuss the map as a group, noting the difference between landforms and bodies of water, types of labeling, and use of color. Identify lines of longitude and latitude for students. Note that lines of latitude run east and west and are parallel to the Equator and each other. Lines of longitude run through the North and South Poles. Point out the map key. **Ask:**

- What does the map key show? *(the elevation of the world's landforms)*
- What do the changes in color signify about those landforms? *(They indicate elevation changes.)*
- What do you notice about the elevation of the world's landforms? *(Students might answer that there are regions of high mountains and lower elevations in all parts of the world.)*

Have students identify regions on the map, then **ask:**

- What are the names of the continents? *(North America, South America, Asia, Africa, Australia, Europe, Antarctica)*
- What are the names of the world's large bodies of water? *(North and South Atlantic Ocean, North and South Pacific Ocean, Indian Ocean, Southern Ocean, Arctic Ocean)*
  AL ELL Visual/Spatial

C Critical Thinking Skills

Compare and Contrast Have students compare and contrast North America and South America. **Ask:**

- What physical features are similar in both North America and South America? *(mountain ranges in western regions, lower elevations in central parts)*
- How do the sizes of North America and South America compare? *(Students might note that North America seems wider and larger than South America.)*
- What is the same about North and South America? *(Both have mountains, rivers, low lying regions, and coastal areas.)*
- What is different about North and South America? *(The Equator runs through South America making it more tropical; the mountains in South America are narrower, but taller.)* **BL**

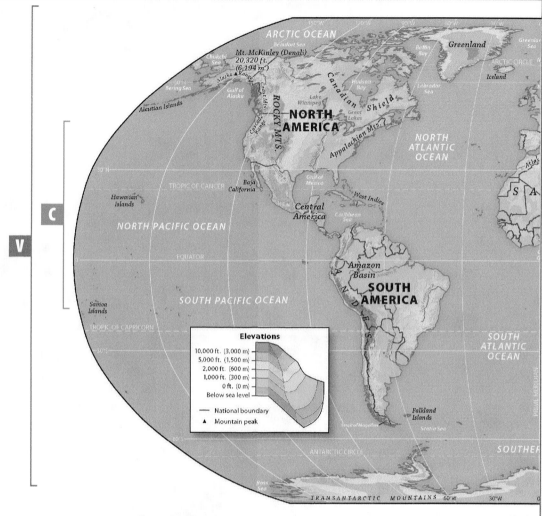

OUR WORLD

4 *Unit 1*

netw⦿rks *Online Teaching Options*

MAP

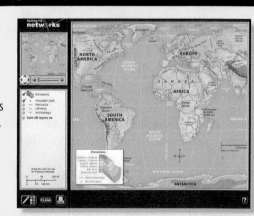

The World: Physical Map

Identifying Display the interactive Physical Map of the World on the whiteboard. As a class, discuss the various physical features. Then have volunteers use whiteboard tools to put an X on the mountain ranges, a circle around the seas, and a star on the continents. **AL** Kinesthetic

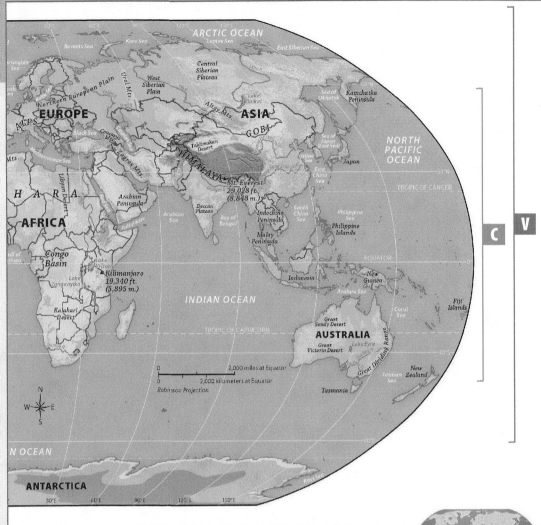

EUROPE ASIA
AFRICA
AUSTRALIA
ANTARCTICA

PHYSICAL

MAP SKILLS

1 **THE GEOGRAPHER'S WORLD** What part of North America has the highest elevation?

2 **THE GEOGRAPHER'S WORLD** Which sea is located east of Central America?

3 **PLACES AND REGIONS** How would you describe much of Europe's landscape?

Unit 1 **5**

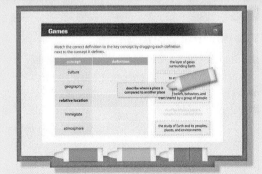

GAME

The Physical World Game

Identifying Display the Physical Map of the World on the interactive whiteboard. Have volunteers identify continents and major bodies of water on the map. Once a student has dragged and dropped the correct location name, have the student ask a question or tell a fact about the location. **AL** Kinesthetic

V Visual Skills

Reading a Map Continue to have students analyze the features found on the map. Explain that the world is divided into the Northern Hemisphere and Southern Hemisphere along the Equator, and into the Eastern Hemisphere and Western Hemisphere along the Prime Meridian and the International Date Line. Have a volunteer identify and point out the Equator and the Prime Meridian. **Ask:**

- In which continent are the highest elevations found in the Eastern Hemisphere? *(Asia)*
- On which continents are elevations below 1,000 feet found? *(all continents)*
- What do you notice about the distribution of land above and below the Equator? *(There is more land above the Equator.)*
- Why is Australia defined as a continent? *(It is a large, disconnected land mass.)*
- Which regions of the world do you think have the hottest climates? *(near the Equator)*
- Which regions of the world do you think are the coldest? *(high mountain ranges, Arctic, Antarctic)* **AL** Visual/Spatial

C Critical Thinking Skills

Transferring Knowledge Write the following questions on the board. Have students write out the questions and answers with a partner. Then as a class, discuss the answers. **Ask:**

- What physical features of Europe and Africa are different? *(Africa is larger and has more areas of higher elevations.)*
- Which continent contains the largest land mass with the highest elevations? *(Asia)*
- Which direction would you travel to get from Japan to the United States in the least amount of time? *(East)*
- How might a ship travel from the Mediterranean Sea to the Indian Ocean? *(Students might answer around Africa or through the Suez Canal.)*

If students answer around Africa, explain that the Suez Canal was made connecting the Mediterranean Sea to the Red Sea to give ships a much easier route. Logical/Mathematical

ANSWERS, p. 5

MAP SKILLS
1. The highest elevation in North America is in the west where the Rocky Mountains are located.
2. Caribbean Sea
3. Much of Europe is lower elevation, called the Northern European Plain. There is little variation in the elevation. Most is green—0 ft.–1,000 ft. (0 m–300 m).

Unit 1 **5**

V1 Visual Skills

Contrasting Explain to students that this is a political map. It shows the divisions between countries and identifies the countries by name. **Ask:** What is the difference between a political map and a physical map? (*A political map shows human-made features such as national boundaries, national capitals, and cities. A physical map focuses on natural landforms and water features such as rivers, mountains, and deserts.*) AL

V2 Visual Skills

Indentifying Allow students to work in pairs as they refer to the previous physical map and this political map of North America. Allow time for students to locate the United States, Mexico, and Canada. **Ask:**

- What bodies of water surround these three countries? (*North Atlantic Ocean, North Pacific Ocean, Gulf of Mexico, Arctic Ocean*)
- Which country has the largest landmass? (*Canada*)
- How can northern Canada be described? (*Northern Canada is made up of a series of islands.*)
- What physical feature separates part of Canada from the United States? (*a series of large lakes*)

Then have the partners analyze and discuss South America. **Ask:**

- Which two countries in South America are landlocked? (*Bolivia and Paraguay*)
- What is the capital city of Guyana? (*Georgetown*)
- What do you notice about the area where North America and South America meet? (*There are several small countries, some of which are island countries.*)

Explain that navigation between the North Atlantic Ocean and the North Pacific Ocean was once very difficult, however, today a large canal exists in Panama that allows ships to travel between the two oceans.

C Critical Thinking Skills

Drawing Conclusions **Ask:** How can landforms both facilitate trade between countries and impede it? (*Landforms such as mountain ranges make it very difficult to travel from one region to another, while landforms with rivers or other water routes facilitate trade.*) ELL Logical/Mathematical

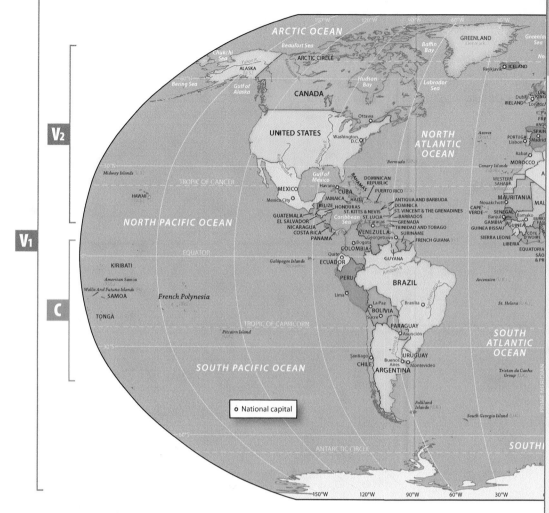

OUR WORLD

Indiana Academic Standards
6.3.1

6 Unit 1

netw⊙rks *Online Teaching Options*

GAME

The Political World Game

Naming Display the Political Map of the World on the interactive whiteboard. Have volunteers drag and drop the names of cities and countries to the proper places as they play the game. Kinesthetic

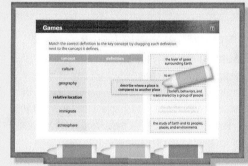

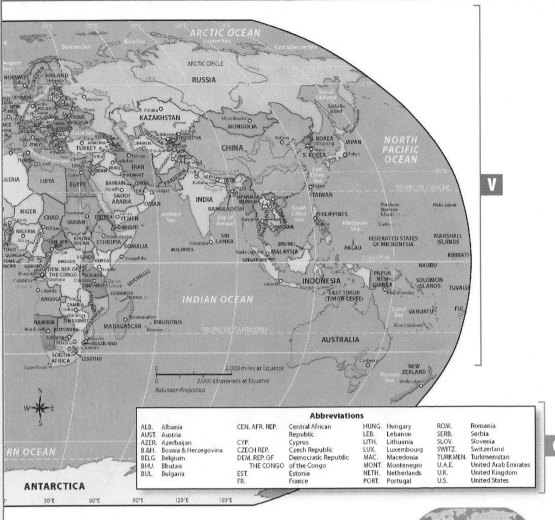

ALB. Albania
AUST. Austria
AZER. Azerbaijan
B.&H. Bosnia & Herzegovina
BELG. Belgium
BHU. Bhutan
BUL. Bulgaria

Abbreviations

CEN. AFR. REP. Central African Republic
CYP. Cyprus
CZECH REP. Czech Republic
DEM. REP. OF THE CONGO Democratic Republic of the Congo
EST. Estonia
FR. France

HUNG. Hungary
LEB. Lebanon
LITH. Lithuania
LUX. Luxembourg
MAC. Macedonia
MONT. Montenegro
NETH. Netherlands
PORT. Portugal

ROM. Romania
SERB. Serbia
SLOV. Slovenia
SWITZ. Switzerland
TURKMEN. Turkmenistan
U.A.E. United Arab Emirates
U.K. United Kingdom
U.S. United States

POLITICAL

MAP SKILLS

1. **PLACES AND REGIONS** Which country in South America has the largest land area?

2. **THE GEOGRAPHER'S WORLD** Which country is located west of Sweden?

3. **PLACES AND REGIONS** What is the capital of Canada?

V Visual Skills

Reading a Map Have students compare the number of political boundaries in the Eastern Hemisphere with that of the Western Hemisphere. Explain that, though physical regions remain the same, political boundaries change through armed conflict and civil uprisings. The names of countries may be different from maps representing different time periods as new governments take over a region, at times dissolving one country and forming others. Direct students' attention to the countries of the Western Hemisphere. **Ask:**

- How does the use of color help you read this map? (Color makes it easy to compare the size and shape of the different countries.)
- How does the key help you read this map? (The key provides the names of different countries.)
- What can be said about the different countries? (have different governments, languages, traditions)
- What might the people who live in the same physical region but in different countries share? (similar ways to use the land)
- What would you expect to happen between countries that share a physical region? (trade, possibly conflict for territorial gain) **BL** Visual/Spatial

C Critical Thinking Skills

Reasoning Focus students' attention on the Abbreviation Key at the bottom of the map. Discuss and pronounce a few of the countries. **Ask:**

- How might size affect the political power of a country? (Possible answer: A larger country may have more political power in the world because it may have more resources that can be traded with others and more people who will purchase goods made in other countries.)
- Which country in Asia might hold a great deal of power in the region? (China or Russia) Logical/Mathematical

Physical Geography Activity

Evaluating Use the Physical Geography Activity worksheet to analyze the elevation profile of the ocean. Have students compare their analyses. Intrapersonal

ANSWERS, p. 7
MAP SKILLS
1. Brazil
2. Norway
3. Ottawa

R Reading Skills

Recognizing Relationships Explain that population density is the number of people living in a certain amount of space. Take two containers that are exactly the same. Fill one with many marbles and fill the other with just a few marbles. Explain that the container with more marbles has a higher density of marbles. Be sure students understand that population density requires a comparison of the number of people living in the same amount of space. If you took the container with the most marbles and spread them out in a larger area, the density would not be the same. **Ask:**

• What is shown on this map? *(The population density of different countries and regions of the world.)*

• How is it possible that a country with a higher population could have a lighter color (lower population density)? *(The country may have more people, but they are living in a larger area, so they are more spread out.)*

Have students point to different parts of the map that show areas of higher population density. Then have them point to areas with a lower population density. BL

V Visual Skills

Interpreting Have students study the population map focusing on the Western Hemisphere. **Ask:**

• Where is the greatest population density in North America? *(East Coast of the United States and central Mexico)*

• Why do you think the population density diminishes in the far northern region of North America and the far southern region of South America? *(Cold environments make it difficult for human habitation.)*

• Why do you think large cities are found on or near coastal areas? *(access to trade and ability of the land to support higher population densities because there is a supply of water)*

• What physical feature do you think has the greatest influence on the growth of a region's population density? *(Students might speculate that a region's abundance of natural resources may be the most influential physical feature.)* Visual/Spatial

C Critical Thinking Skills

Drawing Conclusions Have students discuss the landforms in the local area and which landforms most people tend to live near. **Ask:** Which landforms limit population? *(Landforms such as mountain ranges and deserts.)* Logical/Mathematical

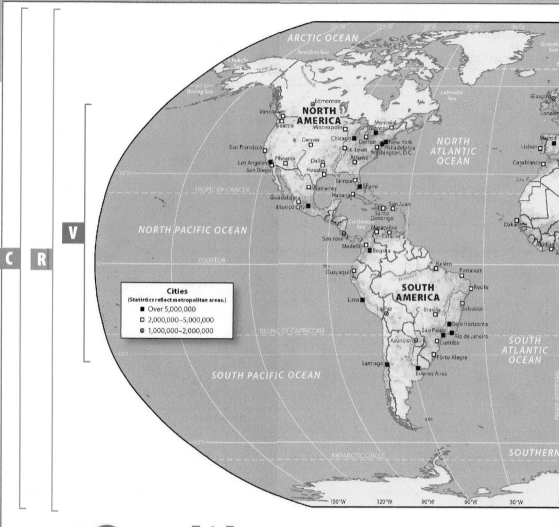

OUR WORLD

network *Online Teaching Options*

MAP

The World: Population Density Map

Speculating Use the interactive Population Density Map of the World to highlight regions of greatest population density. Have students make a list of countries with the highest population densities. Have students discuss how high population density impacts a region's natural resources and speculate on possible problems that could be caused by high population density. BL Visual/Spatial

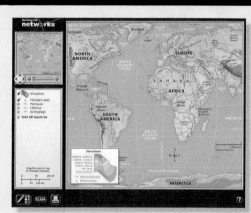

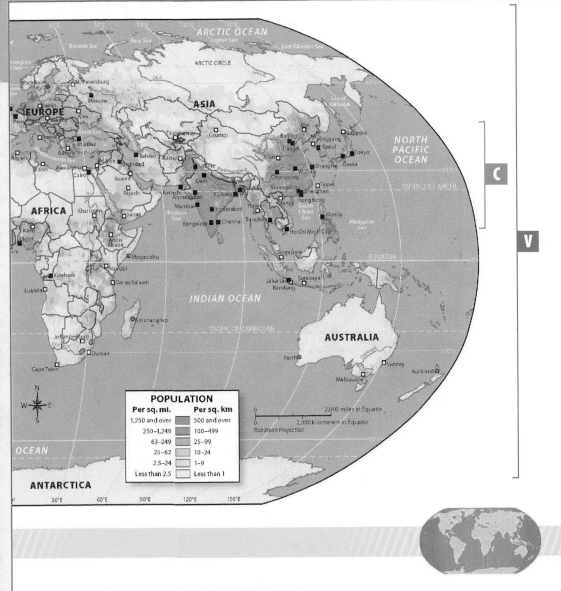

POPULATION DENSITY

POPULATION

Per sq. mi.		Per sq. km
1,250 and over		500 and over
250–1,249		100–499
63–249		25–99
25–62		10–24
2.5–24		1–9
Less than 2.5		Less than 1

2,000 miles at Equator
2,000 kilometers at Equator
Robinson Projection

MAP SKILLS

1 **PLACES AND REGIONS** Which parts of Europe are the least densely populated?

2 **PLACES AND REGIONS** Which part of the United States has the highest population density?

3 **HUMAN GEOGRAPHY** In general, what population pattern do you see in South America?

V Visual Skills

Reading a Map Have students compare the physical map on previous pages with the population density map. Discuss the physical features that create barriers to population expansion, including mountain ranges, deserts, and oceans. **Ask:**

- Where are the highest population densities found in Asia? *(India and Southeast Asia)*
- What can be said about the population density of Europe? *(fairly evenly spread throughout Europe)*
- What do you notice about the population density of Africa? *(High population densities occur both along coastal regions and in parts of the interior of the continent.)*
- What physical feature of the continent allows for greater population density in the interior of Africa? *(rivers that allow for navigation and trade)* Visual/Spatial

C Critical Thinking Skills

Determining Cause and Effect Have students consider the pressures on governments to meet the needs of a country's population when the population density exceeds the country's ability to support the people using its own natural resources. Explain to students that natural resources include such things as fresh water, rich soil to grow food, or trees to build houses. Stress that there are many resources that are necessary to sustain life. There are also natural resources that are not vital to sustaining life, such as gold, diamonds, or other minerals. **Ask:**

- What problems might countries with high population densities experience if they do not have enough natural resources in their country? *(lack of proper housing, poverty, or starvation)*
- Which country in Asia might be experiencing such difficulties? *(Students might speculate that India or China could be experiencing difficulties meeting the needs of the people because the population densities in those countries are very high.)* Logical/Mathematical

SLIDE SHOW

How-To: Read a Map

Synthesizing View the How-To slide show about reading maps. To help students synthesize the information on maps, play "10 questions." Have each student write down a location. Ask for a student volunteer. Have the class take turns asking 10 "yes" or "no" questions to determine the volunteer's location. Have the student who guesses the location be the next volunteer. Visual/Spatial

Slide Show

ANSWERS, p. 9

MAP SKILLS

1. Northern Europe, around Norway, Sweden, and Finland, is the least densely populated.
2. the east coast
3. The most densely populated areas are along the coast. The central area of the continent near the Amazon River is the least densely populated.

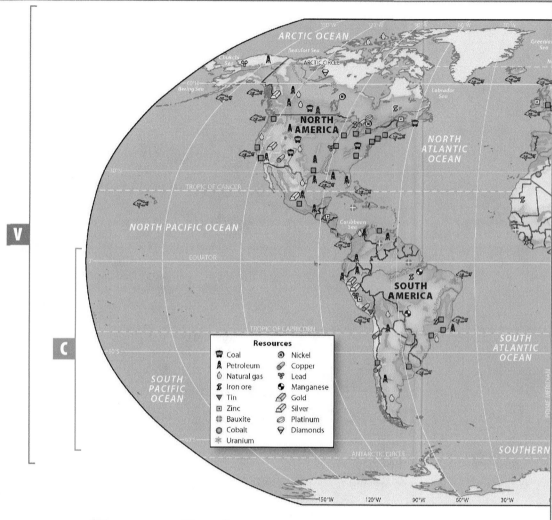

V Visual Skills

Recognizing Relationships Help students recognize the relationship between natural resources and the physical characteristics of a region. Have students analyze both the physical map from previous pages and this economic map. Draw students' attention to the mountain regions along the western regions of North America and South America. **Ask:** What resources are found along these two mountain regions? *(coal, uranium, copper, gold, silver, petroleum)*

Then have students work in teams to analyze the economic resources map. Have them read the map keys and discuss the location of natural resources and land use. **Ask:**

- What types of resources does the map key highlight? *(natural resources of metals, minerals, and fossil fuels)*
- Why do you think these resources are considered "natural"? *(Students' answers may vary but students should reason that natural resources are naturally part of Earth.)*
- What types of resources are found in the central regions of North America? *(petroleum, lead, coal)*
- What types of resources are near the Amazon River? *(bauxite, manganese, iron ore)*
- Which resource is shown by a red symbol on the map key? *(uranium)*
- What types of things does the map key of land use focus on? *(farming, fishing, livestock raising and herding, forestry, and manufacturing and trade)*
- Notice the location of manufacturing and trade areas in North America. Why are these areas located where they are? *(Possible answer: manufacturing and trade areas are located around large cities.)*
- What type of land use covers most of the northern region of South America? *(forests, this area is almost all tropical rain forest area)* **ELL** Visual/Spatial

C Critical Thinking Skills

Drawing Conclusions Have students consider the importance of natural resources to the economic viability of a country. **Ask:**

- Many countries lack some of the natural resources that they need. How can they get these resources? *(trade their resources to get the needed resources from other countries)*
- How might a country's natural resources affect its economy? *(Students may suggest that countries that have a wealth of natural resources are able to bring money into the country by selling those natural resources to other countries that lack them.)* Logical/Mathematical

Resources

🛒	Coal	⊗	Nickel
🛢	Petroleum	⬯	Copper
⬥	Natural gas	⚙	Lead
⅀	Iron ore	◈	Manganese
▼	Tin	▱	Gold
⊡	Zinc	⬭	Silver
⊞	Bauxite	⬮	Platinum
○	Cobalt	▽	Diamonds
✳	Uranium		

OUR WORLD

net**w**🌐rks *Online Teaching Options*

MAP

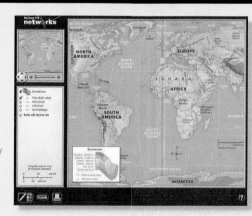

The World: Economic Map

Explaining Display the interactive Economic Map of the World on the whiteboard. As a class, review the regions and the location of resources. Have students write a paragraph explaining why coastal cities were built in certain places. *(Answers will vary but should demonstrate an understanding of the historical importance of coastal areas to trade.)* Verbal/Linguistic, Logical/Mathematical

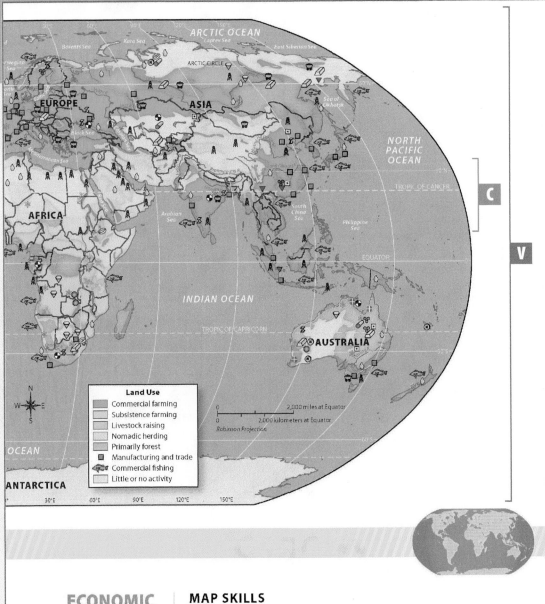

Land Use

- Commercial farming
- Subsistence farming
- Livestock raising
- Nomadic herding
- Primarily forest
- ▣ Manufacturing and trade
- Commercial fishing
- Little or no activity

0   2,000 miles at Equator
0   2,000 kilometers at Equator

Robinson Projection

ECONOMIC RESOURCES

MAP SKILLS

1 **HUMAN GEOGRAPHY** Describe the general use of land in the United States.

2 **HUMAN GEOGRAPHY** What economic activity is found along most coastal regions?

3 **PLACES AND REGIONS** Which resources are located along the Amazon River?

Unit 1 **11**

V Visual Skills

Reading a Map Direct students' attention to the land use map key. Help them understand the relationship between land use and availability of natural resources. **Ask:**

- What is the purpose of the land use map key? *(shows how the land is used by different countries)*
- What type of land use does dark green shading show? *(commercial farming)*
- What type of land use does yellow shading show? *(nomadic herding)*
- Which type of land use occurs in the central region of Australia? *(livestock raising)*
- What type of land use is shown for a large part of the northern region of Africa? *(little or no activity)*
- What would explain this type of land use in northern Africa? *(a desert region)*
- What type of land use occurs in Southeast Asia? *(primarily forest)*
- What explains the difference in land use in North Africa from that in Southeast Asia? *(Students should recognize that the two regions have very different climates and thus different land uses.)* Visual/Spatial

C Critical Thinking Skills

Hypothesizing Point to the northern region of Africa. Explain that all around this area is the Sahara Desert. **Ask:**

- What explains the band of commercial farming in the desert of North Africa? *(The Nile River flows through the desert, so this provides water to the area, which is needed for farming.)*
- What natural resource is also found in this area? Why is this a good place for oil fields? *(Oil, petroleum; students should answer that oil is found there and may speculate that not very many people live in the desert so oil fields will not affect living conditions in the area.)* **AL** Logical/Mathematical

---

WORKSHEET

Cultural Geography Activity

Evaluating Use the Cultural Geography Activity worksheet as a pre- or post-assessment of students' knowledge of culture. Intrapersonal

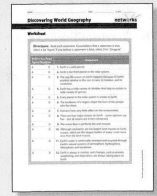

ANSWERS, p. 11

MAP SKILLS

1. commercial farming and livestock raising
2. commercial fishing
3. bauxite, manganese, and iron ore

V1 Visual Skills

Visualizing Ask: What type of map is this? *(a map showing the world's climates)* Explain that maps highlighting the world's climates have a direct relationship to both physical and population density maps. Ask students to visualize a desert environment where little plant or animal life exists because of the lack of rainfall and high daytime temperatures. **Ask:**

- What relationship is there between the physical features of a desert and low population density? *(Few people live in the desert because the land cannot support the population.)*
- What might governments do to increase the ability of a desert region to support a larger population density? *(supply water to the area)* **BL**

V2 Visual Skills

Reading a Map Direct students' attention to the map key. **Ask:**

- What do the colors on the key indicate? *(different climates found throughout the world)*
- Which colors indicate a tropical climate? *(light and dark pink)*
- Which color indicates a Mediterranean climate? *(orange)*
- Which color indicates a tundra? *(dark purple)*
- Where is the tropical climate region located in South America? *(across the northern half of the continent)*
- Where is the desert climate region located in Africa? *(across the top third of the continent)*
- What do you notice about climates as you read the map moving north and moving south of the Equator? *(They get colder and drier.)*
- Which climate region is located mostly in the north central region of the United States? *(humid continental)*
- What can you say about the country of Greenland from reading this map? *(It is a region of extreme cold.)* Visual/Spatial

C Critical Thinking Skills

Formulating Questions Ask: What questions could be answered from reading this climate map? *(Students may suggest such questions as, "Where is it really cold in the world?" or "How do the climates change as you get further away from the Equator?")* Logical/Mathematical

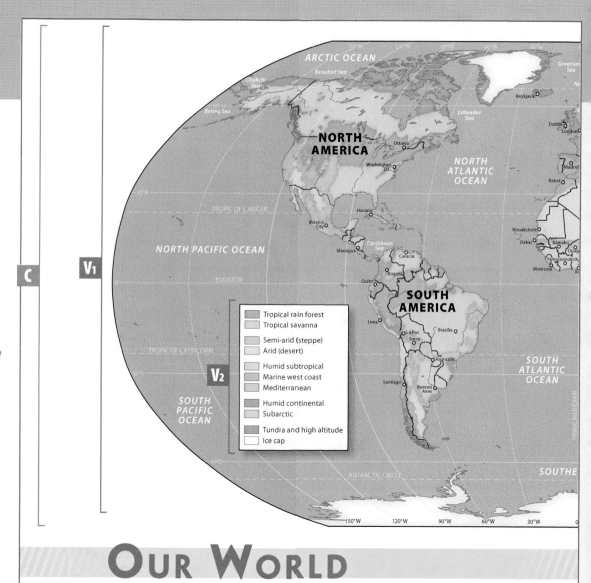

OUR WORLD

Indiana Academic Standards
6.3.1, 6.3.7

12 *Unit 1*

netw⊙rks   *Online Teaching Options*

MAP

The World: Climate Map

Comparing In pairs, have students compare the climate and vegetation regions as they study the interactive Climate Map of the World. Have partners write down four comparisons that they have noted. Then as a class, have students share and discuss their comparisons. **BL**
Visual/Spatial

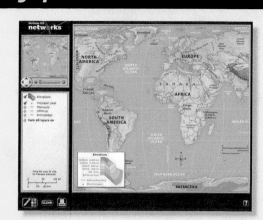

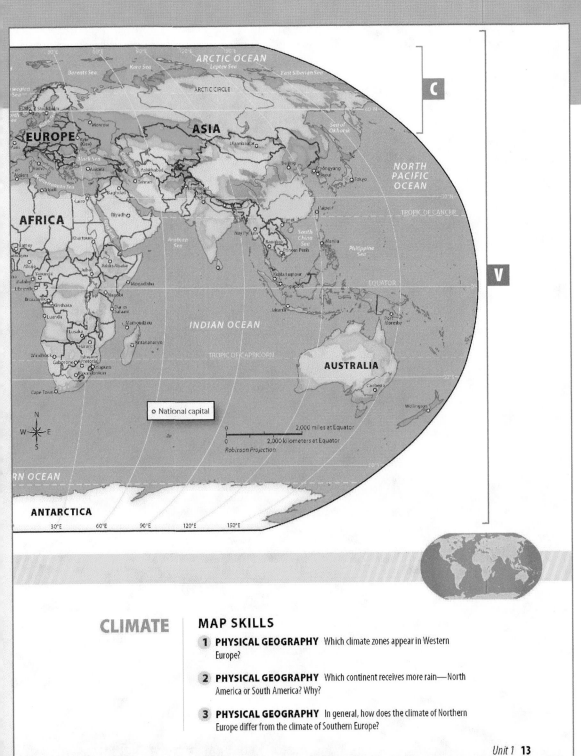

CLIMATE

MAP SKILLS

1. **PHYSICAL GEOGRAPHY** Which climate zones appear in Western Europe?

2. **PHYSICAL GEOGRAPHY** Which continent receives more rain—North America or South America? Why?

3. **PHYSICAL GEOGRAPHY** In general, how does the climate of Northern Europe differ from the climate of Southern Europe?

V Visual Skills

Reading a Map Help students recognize that climates are regionalized. **Ask:**

- What regional aspects to climate do you see? *(Climate areas are located over large areas.)*
- What can you state about climate regions and latitude? *(Students should note that, in general, similar climate zones occur at specific lines of latitude.)*
- What type of climate covers most of Europe? *(marine west coast)*
- What type of climate covers most of the continent of Australia? *(arid and semi-arid)*
- What is the difference between the climate that covers most of Russia and the climate of India? *(While Russia experiences, for the most part, a subarctic climate, most of India experiences a tropical savanna climate.)*
- With the exception of the Middle East region, what can be said about the climates of countries surrounding the Indian Ocean? *(mostly tropical climates)*
- What is the same about the climates of Australia and South Africa? *(They both experience arid climates.)* Visual/Spatial

C Critical Thinking Skills

Recognizing Relationships Have students consider the impact of the shape of Earth on its climate zones. **Ask:**

- Why would areas to the far north and far south of the Equator experience colder climates? *(Areas to the far north and far south do not receive as much direct sunlight.)*
- Look back at the economic map of resources and this map. India has a tropical savanna climate. How do you think its climate affects its land use practices? *(Students might answer that because India has a humid, hot climate, it is able to use its land for agricultural purposes.)* **AL** Logical/Mathematical

CHART

Precipitation and Temperature Chart

Drawing Conclusions Have students use the Climate Map and interactive chart to study the world climates and levels of precipitation and temperature. Guide a class discussion to help students draw conclusions about how levels of precipitation and temperature impact where people live. Verbal/Linguistic, Logical/Mathematical

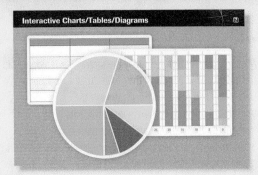

Interactive Charts/Tables/Diagrams

ANSWERS, p. 13

MAP SKILLS

1. marine west coast, Mediterranean, and tundra and high altitude
2. South America receives more rain. Most of South America is covered by tropical rain forest and tropical savanna, while North America has large areas covered by subarctic, semi-arid, and arid climates.
3. Northern Europe has a colder climate—subarctic and tundra, while southern Europe has a warmer, moist climate—marine west coast and Mediterranean.

T Technology Skills

Using Visual Aids Divide students up into six groups. Assign each group one continent (do not assign Antarctica), providing a map of the assigned continent. Tell students they will research cities and countries on their continents and label them on the map. Start by having students transfer the cities shown on the political map to their maps. Have students use the political map, as well as other maps and atlases, to locate additional cities for their continent. Next, have them use other maps to identify and label the physical features and natural resources found on the continents. Make sure that students create a key that will represent the population, natural resources, and physical features for their maps.

Allow class time for groups to research other aspects that are unique to their continent. Groups should prepare index cards that list 5 to 7 facts about their continent that they have learned from their research.

After students have had time to finish, have groups present information about their continent maps. Presentations should include showing and discussing cities and countries on the maps, as well as explaining the researched facts about why their continent is unique.

W Writing Skills

Narrative Have students use the photo to help them visualize what it would be like to see Earth from space. Ask students to imagine that they are astronauts traveling in space. Then have them write a short story about being an astronaut and looking down at this image of Earth.

CLOSE & REFLECT

Summarizing Information Have students reflect on the types of maps they have studied and what they have learned about the maps. Then have students write three sentences that summarize what they learned.

Stocktrek/Getty Images

14 Unit 1

netw⊛rks *Online Teaching Options*

MAP

Regional Map

Making Connections Display the interactive regional map to students. Select some of the images that are connected to the map and place them in context of the map and the textbook. Guide a discussion helping students to identify the content of the images and then to make a connection between the image and the map location. **Visual/Spatial**

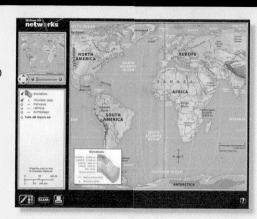

What Is Geography? Planner

UNDERSTANDING BY DESIGN®

Enduring Understandings

- *People, places, and ideas change over time.*

Essential Questions

- *How does geography influence the way people live?*

Predictable Misunderstandings

- *Geography is just the names of states and their capitals.*
- *Lines of latitude and longitude actually appear on Earth.*
- *Geography is static and unchanging, serving merely as a backdrop to people's activities.*

Assessment Evidence

Performance Tasks:

- *Project-Based Learning Digital Hands-On Chapter Project*
- *Project-Based Learning Hands-On Chapter Project*

Other Evidence:

- *Geography Skills Activity*
- *Technology Skills Activity*
- *Participation in Project-Based Learning Activities*
- *Participation in Interactive Whiteboard Activities*
- *Contribution to small-group activities*
- *Interpretation of slide show images and special purpose maps*
- *Participation in completing the Six Essential Elements Digital Chart*
- *Participation in class discussions about the Geographer's World*
- *Lesson Reviews*
- *Chapter Assessments*

Students will:

6.1.17 Discuss the benefits and challenges related to the development of a highly technological society.

6.1.18 Create and compare timelines that identify major people, events and developments in the history of individual civilizations and/or countries that comprise Europe and the Americas.

6.1.19 Define and use the terms decade, century, and millennium, and compare alternative ways that historical periods and eras are designated by identifying the organizing principles upon which each is based.

6.1.20 Analyze cause-and-effect relationships, keeping in mind multiple causations, including the importance of individuals, ideas, human interests, beliefs and chance in history.

6.3.2 Use latitude and longitude to locate the capital cities of Europe and the Americas and describe the uses of locational technology, such as Global Positioning Systems (GPS) to distinguish absolute and relative location and to describe Earth's surfaces.

6.3.3 Describe and compare major physical characteristics of regions in Europe and the Americas.

6.3.11 Define the terms anthropology and archeology and explain how these fields contribute to our understanding of societies in the present and the past.

SUGGESTED PACING GUIDE

Introducing the Chapter..............2 Days	What Do You Think? ....2 Days
Lesson 1 ....2 Days	Chapter Wrap-Up and Assessment......2 Days
Lesson 2 ....2 Days	

TOTAL TIME   10 Days

Key for Using the Teacher Edition

SKILL-BASED ACTIVITIES

Types of skill activities found in the Teacher Edition.

* **V** **Visual Skills** require students to analyze maps, graphs, charts, and photos.

W **Writing Skills** provide writing opportunities to help students comprehend the text.

R **Reading Skills** help students practice reading skills and master vocabulary.

C **Critical Thinking Skills** help students apply and extend what they have learned.

T **Technology Skills** require students to use digital tools effectively.

*Letters are followed by a number when there is more than one of the same type of skill on the page.

DIFFERENTIATED INSTRUCTION

All activities are written for the on-level student unless otherwise marked with the leveled labels below.

BL Beyond Level
AL Approaching Level
ELL English Language Learners

All students benefit from activities that utilize different learning styles. Many activities are marked as below when a particular learning style is highlighted.

Intrapersonal	Naturalist
Logical/Mathematical	Kinesthetic
Visual/Spatial	Auditory/Musical
Verbal/Linguistic	Interpersonal

CHAPTER OPENER PLANNER

Students will know:
- *the parts, styles, and purposes of a world map.*

Students will be able to:
- ***identify** the seven continents using a world map.*
- ***use** a time line to discuss events in history that significantly changed people's view of the world.*

UNDERSTANDING
BY DESIGN®

☑ *Print Teaching Options*

V Visual Skills

P. 16 Students learn about the American cartographer John Paul Goode and use a Goode map of the world to identify the seven continents and other world features.

P. 17 Students use a time line to answer questions about the sequence of events in the development of knowledge of the world and world maps.

☑ *Online Teaching Options*

MAP **Reading a Map**—Students identify aspects and locations of the region on a map.

TIME LINE **Reading a Time Line and Map**—Students use the time line and map to learn about where historical events occurred in the world. **AL** Visual/Spatial

MAP **Interactive World Atlas**—Students use the interactive world atlas to identify the region and describe its terrain.

☑ *Printable Digital Worksheets*

WORKSHEET **Geography Skills: Understanding the Lines on a Map**—Students use the geography skills worksheet to practice and apply the skills of using latitude and longitude lines on a map.

WORKSHEET **Technology Skills: Geospatial Technologies**—Students use the worksheet to investigate the latest forms of geospatial technologies.

Project-Based Learning ✋

Hands-On

Create Maps

Students will create a mental map that shows the route they travel from their homes to their school. Students will then illustrate this map on paper. Maps should include elements such as a compass rose and key. Then in groups, students will analyze the maps to identify the five themes of geography that appear on the map. Students will present their maps to the class, along with identifying where the five themes of geography appear on them.

Digital Hands-On

Create Online Interactive Maps

Students will create digital travel brochures after analyzing locations around the world using an online interactive mapping site. Students should include information about the location and physical features of the location. Travel brochures can be shared with other students so they can make suggestions about including additional geographic information.

edtechteacher
21ˢᵗ Century Learning

Print Resources

ANCILLARY RESOURCES
These ancillaries are available for every chapter and lesson.

- **Reading Essentials and Study Guide Workbook** **AL** **ELL**
- **Chapter Tests and Lesson Quizzes Blackline Masters**

PRINTABLE DIGITAL WORKSHEETS
These printable digital worksheets are available for every chapter and lesson.

- **Hands-On Chapter Projects**
- **What Do You Know? Activities**
- **Chapter Summaries (English and Spanish)**
- **Vocabulary Builder Activities**
- **Quizzes and Tests**
- **Reading Essentials and Study Guide (English and Spanish)** **AL** **ELL**
- **Guided Reading Activities**

More Media Resources

SUGGESTED VIDEOS
NOTE: Be sure to preview any clips to ensure they are age-appropriate.

- **Inside Planet Earth** (120 min.)
- **Six Degrees Could Change the World** (50 min.)
- **Raging Planet** (8 episodes-387 min.)

SUGGESTED READING 📚
- ***National Geographic Student Atlas of the World,*** by The National Geographic Society **BL**
- ***The Coast Mappers,*** by Taylor Morrison
- ***Follow That Map! A First Book of Mapping Skills,*** by Scot Ritchie **AL**

THINKING LIKE A GEOGRAPHER

Students will know:

- the five themes of geography (location, place, region, human-environment interaction, movement).
- meanings of and how to calculate relative and absolute locations.
- meanings of important terms: latitude, longitude, Equator, Prime Meridian, landscape, environment, landform, climate, resource.
- the six essential elements.

Students will be able to:

- *explain* why geographers study more than a place's location and dimensions.
- *identify* examples of human systems.
- *describe* the physical and human characteristics of a community.

UNDERSTANDING
BY DESIGN®

☑ *Print Teaching Options*

V Visual Skills

☐ **P. 19** Students describe physical features of a landscape.

☐ **P. 22** Students identify human and physical features and compose an advertisement for their community. ELL

☐ **P. 22** Students use lines of latitude and longitude to identify absolute location.

☐ **P. 25** Students discuss how visuals such as graphs, charts, diagrams, and photographs convey information. ELL

W Writing Skills

☐ **P. 24** Students write informative paragraphs about the benefits and disadvantages of forms of technology used for communication. AL ELL

R Reading Skills

☐ **P. 18** Students develop a geography vocabulary list of words, meanings, and drawings in their notebooks. ELL

☐ **P. 20** Students make connections between their experiences and the way geography is organized. AL

☐ **P. 21** Students identify relative locations.

☐ **P. 22** Students paraphrase to explain why geographers study regions. AL ELL

☐ **P. 23** Students apply knowledge of key features of the environment to the local area. AL ELL

C Critical Thinking Skills

☐ **P. 18** Students draw conclusions about how physical features on Earth have changed over time. BL

☐ **P. 19** Students use knowledge of human and physical features to make inferences.

☐ **P. 20** Students make connections between their experiences and human and physical features of the world.

☐ **P. 23** Students identify problems that human activities have caused in the environment. AL

☐ **P. 24** Students use chart skills to compare and contrast.

T Technology Skills

☐ **P. 20** Students research how a place has changed over time and how the changes have impacted the place.

☑ *Online Teaching Options*

V Visual Skills

IMAGE **360° View: Times Square**—Students use a 360° image of Times Square, New York, to understand the idea of location.

SLIDE SHOW **The Ninth Ward in New Orleans**—Students interpret the slide show images of New Orleans taken before and after Hurricane Katrina struck the city to describe how a place changes over time. Visual/Spatial

VIDEO **Corals and Oceans**—Students watch a video about the physical geography of the world. They identify the main ideas about the geography of the world portrayed in the video and discuss them with a partner. AL Verbal/Linguistic, Interpersonal

R Reading Skills

GAME **Drag-and-Drop: Vocabulary Game**—Students use the game to build their knowledge of content and academic vocabulary words used in Lesson 1. Verbal, Kinesthetic

CHART **Chart of Six Essential Elements**—Students use a digital chart to apply and reinforce their knowledge of the six essential elements of geography that they learned in the lesson. Verbal/Linguistic, Interpersonal

C Critical Thinking Skills

ANIMATION **Disney World in Orlando, Florida**—Students use the animation to identify the physical and human features and describe the relative location of a place. Visual/Spatial

SLIDE SHOW **How People Are Affected by Geography**—Students use the slide show to discuss how human structures can adversely affect the environment. BL Visual, Interpersonal

T Technology Skills

ANIMATION **Animated Globe**—Students use the animated globe to explain geographic terms. AL Verbal/Linguistic

ANIMATION **Regions of Earth**—Students use the animation to further discuss geographic terms and the concept of a region.

ONLINE SELF-CHECK QUIZ **Lesson 1**—Students receive instant feedback on their mastery of lesson content.

☑ *Printable Digital Worksheets*

W Writing Skills

WORKSHEET **Geography Skills: Understanding the Lines on a Map**—Students use the geography skills worksheet to practice and apply the skills of using latitude and longitude lines on a map.

TOOLS USED BY GEOGRAPHERS

Students will know:
- why geographers study regions.
- the parts, styles, and purposes of different kinds of maps.

Students will be able to:
- *identify* differences in general-purpose maps and thematic maps.
- *analyze* how geospatial technologies could help a business.
- *draw a map* of a place, including the relevant map features.

UNDERSTANDING BY DESIGN®

☑ Print Teaching Options

V Visual Skills

☐ **P. 26** Students create a mental map and sketch it, and then describe the relative location of things on the map.

☐ **P. 28** Students identify the parts of a map and types of information they convey. **ELL**

☐ **P. 29** Students use math and map skills to compute distances on a map.

☐ **P. 30** Students analyze a historical map and connect it to the history of the time it was made.

W Writing Skills

☐ **P. 31** Students work in groups to identify the pros and cons of GPS apps that allow parents to track their children. Then they write persuasive paragraphs.

R Reading Skills

☐ **P. 26** Students paraphrase to explain why a globe is the most accurate way to show places on Earth. **AL** **ELL**

☐ **P. 29** Students define the multiple meanings of the word *scale*.

☐ **P. 29** Students explain different purposes of maps.

☐ **P. 30** Students apply the map skills they are learning to explain elevation.

☐ **P. 31** Students explain the uses of a geographic information system.

☐ **P. 32** Students use context clues to find meaning of unknown words. **ELL**

C Critical Thinking Skills

☐ **P. 27** Students compare and contrast maps and globes, recording their work in a Venn diagram.

☐ **P. 29** Students analyze map projections.

☐ **P. 30** Students make connections and apply map skills to give examples of thematic maps.

☐ **P. 32** Students make inferences about the information gathered by a geographic information system.

T Technology Skills

☐ **P. 33** Students use technology to access NASA weather satellite images and evaluate the importance of the information.

☑ Online Teaching Options

V Visual Skills

☐ **ANIMATION** **Elements of a Globe**—Students use the animated globe to explain geographic terms related to maps. **AL** Visual/Spatial

☐ **SLIDE SHOW** **Special Purpose Maps**—Students use the slide show of various special purpose maps to discuss the kinds of information the maps convey. Visual/Spatial

☐ **SLIDE SHOW** **Mapmaking Over Time**—Students use the slide show to discover how mapmaking has changed over time. Visual/Spatial

W Writing Skills

☐ **VIDEO** **Mapping the World: Google Maps**—Students watch a video and formulate questions about the tools of geography. Verbal/Linguistic, Interpersonal

R Reading Skills

☐ **GRAPHIC ORGANIZER** **Organizing Forms of Technology**—Students use the interactive graphic organizer to review and organize what they have learned about the forms of geospatial technology. Verbal/Linguistic

C Critical Thinking Skills

☐ **GAME** **Map Legends**—Students use a matching game to build their understanding of how the physical features in an area correspond to symbols of those features on a map. Visual/Spatial, Naturalist

T Technology Skills

☐ **ONLINE SELF-CHECK QUIZ** **Lesson 2**—Students receive instant feedback on their mastery of lesson content.

☑ Printable Digital Worksheets

W Writing Skills

☐ **WORKSHEET** **Technology Skills: Geospatial Technologies**—Students use the worksheet to investigate the latest forms of geospatial technologies. Interpersonal

INTERVENTION AND REMEDIATION STRATEGIES

LESSON 1 Thinking Like a Geographer

Reading and Comprehension

Help students understand content vocabulary terms that may be confusing. For example, students may have trouble distinguishing between relative location and absolute location.

Tell students to use flashcards to write six different locations, some relative and some absolute. Have students take turns quizzing each other about which locations are relative and which are absolute.

Then have students make flashcards for other content vocabulary from the lesson to quiz their partners. For example, for the term *latitude,* students might say "I run east to west, but I measure distance north to south."

Text Evidence

Organize students into five groups, and assign one of the five themes of geography to each group. Have students review the lesson and create a pictorial summary of their assigned theme. Students may use images that they found online, magazine photographs, or create their own pictures to convey the theme's meaning. For example, students might create a map to show a certain region. To express human-environment interaction, students might draw people driving along roads, and so on.

LESSON 2 Tools Used by Geographers

Reading and Comprehension

Help students visualize concepts from this lesson by mapping an imaginary trip around the world. Students should work with a partner to plan their journey. Tell students to write a paragraph describing their trip. Have pairs use at least three content vocabulary terms in their paragraphs to demonstrate knowledge of the vocabulary words' meaning as used in the text. For example, students may describe how they used a GPS to help them plan a route from one place to another, or how reading a map's elevation helped them determine how to cross a certain mountain range.

Text Evidence

Organize students into small groups. Tell students they will act as contestants on a television game show called "Tools of the Trade." Students should designate one member of their group to act as host, or two who will then take turns, and ask the contestants a series of questions about geographer's tools.

Tell hosts they may ask multiple-choice or fill-in-the-blank questions. Tell contestants they may refer to the text to find evidence to support their answers. You may wish to use a timer and set a time limit for students to answer each question. For every correct answer, a group gets five points. The team with the most points wins the game.

Online Resources

Leveled Reader

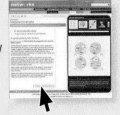

Use this online lower-level text that corresponds directly to the text in the online Student Edition.

Guided Reading Activities

This resource uses graphic organizers and guiding questions to help students with comprehension.

What Do You Know?

Use these worksheets to pre-assess students' background knowledge before they study the chapter.

Reading Essentials and Study Guide Workbook

This resource offers writing and reading activities for the approaching-level student.

Self-Check Quizzes

This online assessment tool provides instant feedback for students to check their progress.

TEACHER NOTES

WHAT IS GEOGRAPHY?

ESSENTIAL QUESTION · *How does geography influence the way people live?*

Prisma/SuperStock

A geographer drills for an ice sample.

networks
There's More Online about Geography.

CHAPTER 1

Lesson 1
Thinking Like a Geographer

Lesson 2
Tools Used by Geographers

The Story Matters...

Since ancient times, people have drawn maps to represent Earth. As people explored, they came into contact with different places and people, which expanded their understanding of the world. Today, our understanding of the world continues to grow as geographers use the latest technology to study Earth's environments. More importantly, by understanding the connections between humans and the environment, geographers can find solutions to significant problems.

FOLDABLES
Study Organizer

Go to the Foldables® library in the back of your book to make a Foldable® that will help you take notes while reading this chapter.

15

ENGAGE

Think-Pair-Share Have students brainstorm reasons why people make maps. Students might cite that people want to share with others how to reach a specific destination or where locations are relative to each other. Then have students read "The Story Matters..." about geographers' use of maps.

Discuss with the class what it means to understand the connections between humans and the environment. **Ask:** What significant problems might a geographer find solutions for? *(Possible answers: Where should a store be located in a city? How does drought affect a region's food production?)*

Tell students in this chapter they will learn about how geographers think and how they use maps and globes.

Making Connections Share the following information with students.

Maps are used for communication. Here are some map facts:

- The oldest known maps were made in Babylon on clay tablets around 2300 B.C.
- By 350 B.C., geographers accepted the idea of Earth being a sphere.
- In 1492, Martin Behaim, a German cartographer, made the first globe. It still exists today.
- Until the use of aerial photography after World War I, much of the world was not shown accurately on maps.

To get students thinking about how maps are used and the types of information they show, have them use their Reference Atlas map of the United States in the front of their Student Editions to determine which city is farther west—Reno, Nevada, or Los Angeles, California. *(Reno, Nevada)*

FOLDABLES
Study Organizer

Go to the Foldables® library for a cumulative chapter-based Foldable® activity that your students can use to help take notes and prepare for assessment.

Letter from the Author

Dear Geography Teacher,

The geographer's world is a mosaic of people, places, and environments, all viewed from a spatial perspective. Geographers have an interest in where people settle and why, along with learning about their various cultures. People move constantly and often settle in places for a variety of reasons. Each place has unique characteristics, both physical (climate, vegetation) and cultural (religion, ethnic origins, occupations, and so on). Geographers try to make sense out of our dynamic, changing world.

Richard H. Boehm

TEACH & ASSESS

Step Into the Place

V Visual Skills

Reading a Map Explain to students that this map presents the entire world on one map and accurately shows the sizes and shapes of the landmasses. Have students compare the sizes and shapes of the continents on this world map to those on the world maps in the Unit 1 Opener.

Next have students identify the seven continents on this map and locate the Equator. Discuss which continents are located primarily north of the Equator and which are located primarily south of the Equator.

Have students speculate why this world map would have been made like this. Discuss how students might make a sphere from the map if they could cut it out. Read the Content Background Knowledge below to students to explain how this type of world map developed and why it is useful.

Then have students use the map to answer the Step Into the Place questions. *Visual/Spatial*

Content Background Knowledge

John Paul Goode (1862–1932) was an American geographer, cartographer, and teacher whose career goal was to make geography an enjoyable and easy-to-understand subject for his students. In 1916, he developed a world map that showed landmasses in proper proportions by "interrupting" the oceans on the map.

Some people describe Goode's map as looking like flattened orange peels. Goode also created an atlas for students, creating many maps and putting them together in one book. The atlas was first published in 1923. It is still used today and is updated every few years using the latest mapping technology.

ANSWERS, p. 16

STEP INTO THE PLACE
1. North and South America, Europe, Asia, Africa, Australia, Antarctica
2. Pacific, Atlantic, Indian, Southern, and Arctic Oceans
3. rivers
4. **CRITICAL THINKING** Possible answer: The map shows the continents, oceans, and Equator.

Chapter 1
WHAT IS GEOGRAPHY?

Geography is the study of Earth and all of its variety. When you study geography, you learn about the physical features and the living things—humans, plants, and animals—that inhabit Earth.

Step Into the Place

MAP FOCUS Use the map to answer the following questions.

1 THE GEOGRAPHER'S WORLD What are the names of the large landmasses on the maps?

2 THE GEOGRAPHER'S WORLD What are the names of the large bodies of water on the map?

3 PLACES AND REGIONS What do you think the blue lines are that appear within the landmasses?

4 CRITICAL THINKING
Identifying How is this world map similar to other maps you have seen?

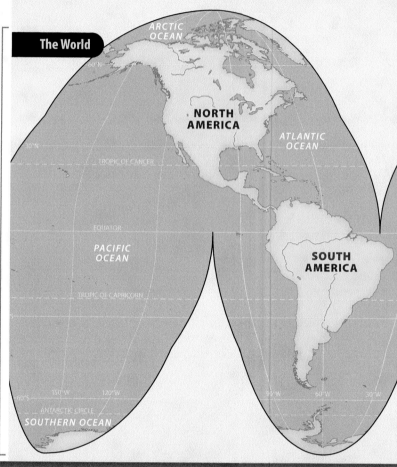

The World

ARCTIC OCEAN

NORTH AMERICA

ATLANTIC OCEAN

TROPIC OF CANCER

EQUATOR

PACIFIC OCEAN

SOUTH AMERICA

TROPIC OF CAPRICORN

150°W   120°W   90°W   60°W   30°W

ANTARCTIC CIRCLE
SOUTHERN OCEAN

Step Into the Time

DRAWING EVIDENCE Choose an event from the time line and write a paragraph describing how it might have changed the way people understood or viewed the world in which they lived.

16 *Chapter 1*

150 A.D.
Ptolemy creates atlas of known world

Universal Images Group/Getty Images

Project-Based Learning ✋

Hands-On

Creating a Mental Map
Students will create a detailed mental map of home to school, including essential parts of a map. In groups, students will analyze the maps to understand the five themes of geography based on their communities. Students will present their maps and their analysis to the class using any visuals decided upon in their groups.

Digital Hands-On

Creating a Travel Brochure
Students will create digital travel brochures after analyzing given locations around the world using an online interactive mapping site. Students will use coordinates, location, place, and other geographic features as well as information from geographic Web sites and the textbook. Travel brochures will be collaboratively shared for students to comment and add other geographic information.

edtechteacher
21st Century Learning

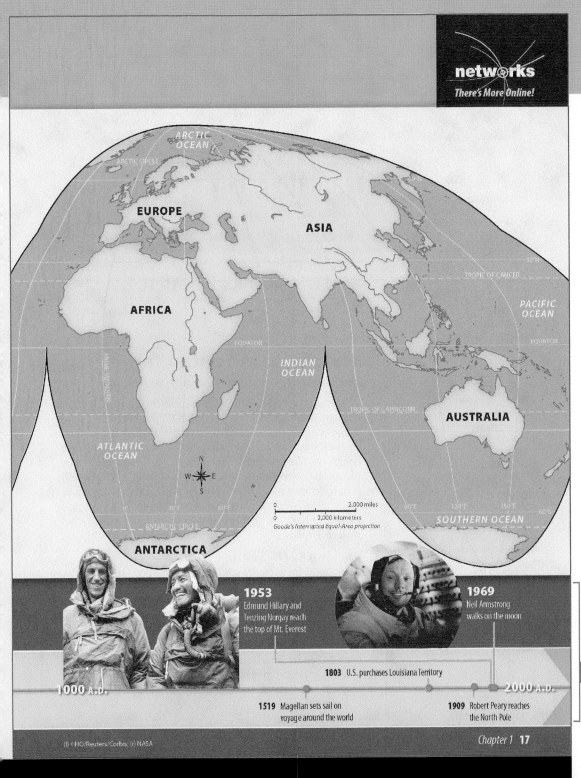

EUROPE

ASIA

AFRICA

INDIAN OCEAN

PACIFIC OCEAN

AUSTRALIA

ATLANTIC OCEAN

ANTARCTICA

SOUTHERN OCEAN

ARCTIC OCEAN

0   2,000 miles
0   2,000 kilometers
Goode's Interrupted Equal-Area projection

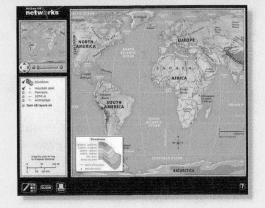

1953
Edmund Hillary and Tenzing Norgay reach the top of Mt. Everest

1969
Neil Armstrong walks on the moon

1000 A.D.

1803 U.S. purchases Louisiana Territory

2000 A.D.

1519 Magellan sets sail on voyage around the world

1909 Robert Peary reaches the North Pole

(l) ©HO/Reuters/Corbis; (r) NASA

Chapter 1   **17**

Step Into the Time

V Visual Skills

Reading a Time Line Remind students that time lines help to sequence events visually in time. Discuss the elements of a time line, such as the title, start and end dates, event markers on the line, and labels for each date. Ask students to share their ideas on other ways time lines can be used. *(to sequence directions and processes)*

Have students review the time line and as a class discuss its major points of interest. **Ask:**

- What period of time is shown on the time line? *(from A.D. 150 to 2000)*
- Ptolemy lived in Alexandria, Egypt. Which continents were most likely not in his atlas of the known world? *(North and South America, Australia, Antarctica)*
- Magellan's fleet was the first to sail around the world. When did it set sail? *(1519)*
- Did Edmund Hillary reach the top of Mt. Everest before or after Neil Armstrong walked on the moon? *(before)*
- Why do you think it took longer for people to reach the top of Mt. Everest than it took to reach the North Pole? *(Students' answers will vary, but they should recognize the extreme cold of both places and the lack of oxygen at the top of the world's tallest mountain as a likely reason why it took longer to reach.)*

Ask students to identify historical events that they know of and tell where they could be added to the time line. *(Students' answers will vary but should include accurate event placement.)*
Visual/Spatial, Verbal/Linguistic

V

CLOSE & REFLECT

Summarizing Have students write one or two sentences to summarize what they learned in the Chapter Opener. Collect and read the summaries to review the information with students. Tell students that they will learn more about geographers and maps as they study this chapter. **AL**

Reading a Time Line and Map

Analyzing Visuals Display the time line and map on the whiteboard. Have volunteers read each event as it is revealed on the time line. Ask students to identify where in the world the event took place and find its location on the map. **AL** Visual/Spatial

See page 15B for other online activities.

ENGAGE

Bellringer Before students begin the lesson, ask them to define the term *geography*. Then read the Essential Question aloud and have students discuss geographical and environmental features in their area that may or may not affect the way people live or where they choose to live. **Ask:** What geographical features would be important to you in choosing a new place to live? Have students explain why these features would be necessary or appealing. *(Student answers will vary but should include mention of specific physical features, such as oceans, mountains, and rivers, or human features, such as cities, states, and human-made attractions.)*

TEACH & ASSESS

R Reading Skills

Determining Word Meanings Explain to students that important academic and content vocabulary words will appear in boldface type throughout a lesson. The meanings of these terms will be given in the text. Have students begin a vocabulary list in their notebooks by writing the word *geography* at the top of a blank piece of paper. As a class, discuss what is included in the study of geography. Have students write their own definition to explain the word. Encourage them to include drawings if desired. Remind students to add words to their lists as they encounter new vocabulary. **ELL** Verbal/ Linguistic

C Critical Thinking Skills

Drawing Conclusions Physical features are landforms and bodies of water that occur naturally on Earth. Have students give examples of physical features that they know. **Ask:** What might scientists conclude after measuring the height, width, and depth of a glacier and determining its distance from other landforms? *(Student answers may vary but should demonstrate an understanding of natural processes, such as erosion that cause changes in landforms.)* **BL** Naturalist

---

ANSWER, p. 18

Taking Notes location, place, region, human-environment interaction, movement

---

---

networks

There's More Online!

- ☑ **CHART/GRAPH** Six Essential Elements of Geography
- ☑ **IMAGES** Places Change Over Time
- ☑ **ANIMATION** Regions of Earth
- ☑ **VIDEO**

Reading HELPDESK

Academic Vocabulary
- dynamic
- component

Content Vocabulary
- geography
- spatial
- landscape
- relative location
- absolute location
- latitude
- Equator
- longitude
- Prime Meridian
- region
- environment
- landform
- climate
- resource

TAKING NOTES: *Key Ideas and Details*

Identifying As you read, list the five themes of geography on a graphic organizer like the one below.

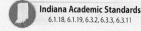

Themes

Indiana Academic Standards
6.1.18, 6.1.19, 6.3.2, 6.3.3, 6.3.11

18

Lesson 1
Thinking Like a Geographer

ESSENTIAL QUESTION • *How does geography influence the way people live?*

IT MATTERS BECAUSE
Thinking like a geographer helps you understand how the world works and to appreciate the world's remarkable beauty and complexity.

The World in Spatial Terms

GUIDING QUESTION *What does it mean to think like a geographer?*

We get our understanding of the world from a combination of many different sources. Biology is the study of how living things survive and relate to one another. History is the study of events that occur over time and how those events are connected. **Geography** is the study of Earth and its people, places, and environments. Geographers look at people and the world in which they live mainly in terms of space and place. They study such topics as where people live on the surface of Earth, why they live there, and how they interact with each other and the physical environment.

Viewing Earth Spatially
Geography, then, emphasizes the spatial aspects of the world. **Spatial** refers to Earth's features in terms of their locations, their shapes, and their relationships to one another.

Physical features such as mountains and lakes can be located on a map. These features can be measured in terms of height, width, and depth. Distances and directions to other features can be determined and measured. The human world also has spatial dimensions. Geographers study the size and shape of cities, states, and countries. They consider how close

(l to r) José Fuste Raga/age fotostock; Aerial Archives/Alamy; Ethan Miller/Getty Images

---

networks *Online Teaching Options*

VIDEO

Coral and Oceans

Finding the Main Idea Use the video to introduce the lesson about geography and life both above and below the oceans. After viewing, have students think about the main ideas that were presented, and then turn to a partner to share these main ideas. Then have volunteers share what they discussed with the class. Discuss with students how coral reef systems and the extreme depths of the ocean are both examples of unique geography in our world. **AL** Verbal/Linguistic, Interpersonal

See page 15C for other online activities.

BBC Motion Gallery Education

or far apart these human features are to one another. Geographers also think about the relationships between human features and physical features.

But thinking spatially is more than just the study of the location or size of things. It means looking at the characteristics of Earth's features. Geographers ask what mountains in different locations are made of. They examine what kinds of fish live in different lakes. The layout of cities and how easy or difficult it is for people to move around in them is also important to geographers.

Characteristics of Place

Locations on Earth are made up of different combinations of physical and human characteristics. Physical features such as climate, landforms, and vegetation combine with human features such as population, economic activity, and land use. These combinations create what geographers call places.

Places are locations on Earth that have distinctive characteristics that make them meaningful and special to people. The places where we live, work, and go to school are important to us. Our home is an important place. Even small places such as our bedroom or a classroom often have a unique and special meaning. In the same way, larger locations, such as our hometown, our country, or even Earth, are places that have meaning to people.

One way that geographers learn about places is by studying landscapes. **Landscapes** are portions of Earth's surface that can be viewed at one time and from one location. They can be as small as the view from the front porch of your home, or they can be as large as the view from a tall building that includes the city and surrounding countryside.

The geography theme of *place* describes all of the characteristics that give an area its own special quality.

▶ **CRITICAL THINKING**
Describing What are the characteristics that make a place like Times Square in New York City special?

Jose Fuste Raga/age fotostock

C Critical Thinking Skills

Making Inferences Explain to students that the relationships between human features and physical features are part of the spatial aspects of the world that are studied by geographers. Students need to think about the issues and relationships such as these that are presented in the text and use what they already know about the world to make inferences about what they are reading. **Ask:**

- How would farming on the side of a mountain be different from farming on flat land? *(Student answers may vary but should discuss the differences in terrain and the affect those differences would have on the types of crops planted and the equipment used.)*
- How would fishing in a lake or river be different from fishing in the ocean? *(Student answers may vary but should discuss the differences in size and currents of the bodies of water that would require different types of boats and fishing techniques to catch the different kinds of fish that live in the different bodies of water.)*

Have students discuss the relationships of the people and the land and water in your area. **Visual/Spatial**

V Visual Skills

Visualizing The landscape surrounding the school is a small portion of Earth that can be viewed. Have students work with a partner to use their five senses to describe the landscape they can view from the classroom window or out the front door of the building. Have partners share their descriptions. **AL** Visual/Spatial, Verbal/Linguistic

Discuss how landscape paintings also show a small portion of Earth that the artist viewed. Have students who are ready for more of a challenge work with a partner to research art books in the library that show landscapes. Have partners write a description of one of the landscapes and share their description and the painting with the class. **BL** Visual/Spatial, Verbal/Linguistic

---

Drag-and-Drop: Vocabulary Game

Reviewing Display the drag-and-drop game on the whiteboard. Have volunteers read each of the vocabulary words. Play the game as a class activity. Then have students choose three to five vocabulary words and use them in a paragraph. **Verbal/Linguistic, Kinesthetic**

See page 15C for other online activities.

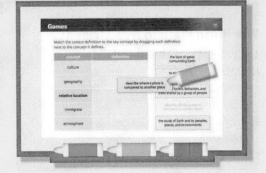

ANSWER, p. 19

CRITICAL THINKING Possible answers: distinctive characteristics include size, large population, many tourists, busyness, noise, bright lights, theatre marquees, souvenir shops

C Critical Thinking Skills

Making Connections Have students make connections between their experiences and their understanding of the world. **Ask:** What physical or human features have you experienced that help you understand the world? *(Student answers may vary but encourage them to tell of experiences that are different from those mentioned in the text, such as experiencing a tornado or flood, body surfing in the ocean, or going to a national park.)* Verbal/Linguistic, Intrapersonal

T Technology Skills

Researching on the Internet and Using Visual Aids Have students think about why places change over time. These changes may be the result of natural processes, natural disasters, or human-made changes. Have students complete the following activity for homework.

Have students choose a place that has changed over time, such as your community, a big city, a forest, a glacier, or a reservoir. Direct them to find pictures on the Internet of what the place looked like in the past and then later after it changed. Then have them write a paragraph to go with the pictures describing the changes, explaining the cause, and identifying the impact the changes had on the place. Visual/Spatial, Logical/Mathematical

R Reading Skills

Making Connections Large topics are often difficult to understand. However, organizing the material into smaller sections makes comprehension easier. Explain that textbooks and other reading material use headings, sections of text, and other elements to help organize material and make it easier to understand. **Ask:** When has understanding parts of a subject helped you understand the whole concept? *(Student answers may vary, but should include relevant details about a large topic and its parts.)* AL Intrapersonal

---

Whether we visit a landscape or look at photographs of one, the landscape can tell us much about the people who live there. Geographers look at landscapes and try to explain their unique combinations of physical and human features. As you study geography, notice the great variety in the world's landscapes.

The Perspective of Experience

C Geography is not something you learn about only in school or just from books. Geography is something you experience every day.

We all live in the world. We feel the change of the seasons. We hear the sounds of birds chirping and of car horns honking. We walk on sidewalks and in forests. We ride in cars along streets and highways. We shop in malls and grocery stores. We fly in airplanes to distant places. We surf the Internet or watch TV and learn about people and events in our neighborhood, our country, and the world.

This is all geography. By learning about geography in school, we can better appreciate and understand this world in which we live.

Academic Vocabulary

dynamic always changing

A Changing World

Earth is **dynamic**, or always changing. Rivers shift course. Volcanoes erupt suddenly, forming mountains or collapsing the peaks of mountains. The pounding surf removes sand from beaches.

The things that people make change, too. Farmers shift from growing one crop to another. Cities grow larger or sometimes shrink. The borders of nations change.

T Geographers, then, study how places change over time. They try to understand what impact those changes have. What factors made a city grow? What effect did a growing city have on the people who live there? What effect did the city's growth have on nearby communities and on the land and water near it? Answering questions like these is part of the field of geography.

☑ READING PROGRESS CHECK

Describing How is geography related to history?

Geography's Five Themes

GUIDING QUESTION *How can you make sense of a subject as large as Earth and its people?*

R To organize information about the world, geographers use five themes. These themes help them view and understand Earth.

Location

Location is where something is found on Earth. There are two types of location. **Relative location** describes where a place is compared to another place. This approach often uses the cardinal directions—north, south, east, and west. A school might be on the east side of town. Relative location can also tell us about the characteristics of a

---

networks *Online Teaching Options*

SLIDE SHOW

The Ninth Ward in New Orleans

Analyzing Images Show the slide show of the Ninth Ward in New Orleans to demonstrate how a geographical location changes over time. Guide students to interpret and analyze the visuals that show the area before Hurricane Katrina made landfall, immediately after Katrina hit, and today with its overgrowth of plants. Visual/Spatial

See page 15C for other online activities.

Slide Show

(l) ©Ocean/Corbis, ©Kryssia Campos/Getty Images, (tr) ©Erica Simone Leeds, (br) ©JG Photography/Alamy

---

ANSWER, p. 20

☑ **READING PROGRESS CHECK** Like history, geography also looks at changes over time.

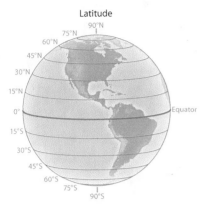

Latitude

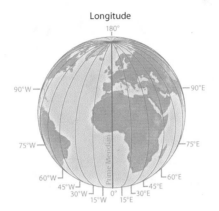

Longitude

place. For example, knowing that New Orleans is near the mouth of the Mississippi River helps us understand why the city became an important trading port.

Absolute location is the exact location of something. An address like 123 Main Street is an absolute location. Geographers identify the absolute location of places using a system of imaginary lines called latitude and longitude. Those lines form a grid for locating a place precisely.

Lines of **latitude** run east to west, but they measure distance on Earth in a north-to-south direction. One of these lines, the **Equator**, circles the middle of Earth. This line is equally distant from the North Pole and the South Pole. Other lines of latitude between the Equator and the North and South Poles are assigned a number from 1° to 90°. The higher the number, the farther the line is from the Equator. The Equator is 0° latitude. The North Pole is at 90° north latitude (90° N), and the South Pole is at 90° south latitude (90° S).

Lines of **longitude** run from north to south, but they measure distance on Earth in an east-to-west direction. They go from the North Pole to the South Pole. These lines are also called *meridians*. The **Prime Meridian** is the starting point for measuring longitude. It runs through Greenwich, England, and has the value of 0° longitude. There are 180 lines of longitude to the east of the Prime Meridian and 180 lines to the west. They meet at the meridian 180°, which is the International Date Line.

Geographers use latitude and longitude to locate anything on Earth. In stating absolute location, geographers always list latitude first. For example, the absolute location of Washington, D.C., is 38°N, 77°W.

Lines of latitude circle Earth parallel to the Equator and measure the distance north or south of the Equator in degrees. Lines of longitude circle Earth from the North Pole to the South Pole. These lines measure distances east or west of the Prime Meridian.

▶ **CRITICAL THINKING**
The Geographer's World At what degree latitude is the Equator located?

Indiana CONNECTION

R | **Locating Capital Cities**

You can use latitude and longitude to locate various places discussed in this text. Using an atlas map, find the approximate absolute location of the following capital cities:
Algiers, Algeria 37°N, 23°E
Bangkok, Thailand 34°N, 58°W
Dakar, Senegal 45°N, 75°W
Makkah, Saudi Arabia 19°N, 99°W
New Delhi, India 55°N, 37°E
Tokyo, Japan 48°N, 2°E
Wellington, New Zealand 59°N, 18°E

R | **Reading Skills**

Identifying and Calculating Explain to students that geographers use relative location and absolute location to tell where something, such as a place or a region, is found on Earth. After students read the section about location, ask them the following questions:

- What terms are used to describe the relative location of a place? *(the cardinal directions—north, south, east, and west—and its relationship to another place)*

- How do geographers identify the absolute location of a place? *(They use a system of imaginary lines called latitude and longitude.)*

- Which way do lines of latitude run? *(east to west)*

- Which location is nearer to the Equator: a city at 25°N latitude or a city at 55°S latitude? *(A city at 25°N latitude is nearer the Equator.)*

- Which way do lines of longitude run? *(north to south)*

- Which location is nearer to the Prime Meridian: a city at 60°W longitude or a city at 90°E longitude? *(A city at 60°W longitude is nearer the Prime Meridian.)*

- What is the relative location of Washington, D.C., in relationship to the location of the Equator and the Prime Meridian? *(It is located north of the Equator and west of the Prime Meridian.)*

- What is the relative location of Sydney, Australia in relationship to the location of the Equator and the Prime Meridian? *(It is located south of the Equator and east of the Prime Meridian.)* **Verbal/Linguistic, Visual/Spatial**

Content Background Knowledge

The International Date Line is an imaginary line that spans north to south across the Pacific Ocean. It is on the opposite side of Earth from the Prime Meridian. It is used to separate two consecutive calendar days. If you travel east across the line, you lose one calendar day, or 24 hours. If you travel west across the line, you gain a calendar day, or 24 hours.

ANIMATION

Animated Globe

Defining with Visuals Display the animated globe on the whiteboard. Use the globe to explain visually the geographic terms related to location: *relative location, absolute location, latitude, longitude, Equator,* and *Prime Meridian.* **AL** **Verbal/Linguistic**

See page 15C for other online activities.

ANSWER, p. 21

CRITICAL THINKING The Equator is at zero degrees latitude.

V1 Visual Skills

Integrating Visual Information Physical and/or human features help define a place. Have students work in a small group to identify physical and/or human features of their community. Challenge them to compose an advertising jingle that promotes these features of their community. ELL
Visual/Spatial, Auditory/Musical

V2

R Reading Skills

Paraphrasing Have students reread the last paragraph in section titled, "Region." Ask them to paraphrase, or use their own words, to explain why geographers study regions. Explain that students need to practice paraphrasing content for all the times they will be researching information that they will need to paraphrase for projects and reports throughout the school year. *(Geographers study regions to find out what physical and human characteristics they have. They can use these characteristics to find out how regions are the same or different.)*
ELL AL Verbal/Linguistic

V2 Visual Skills

Integrating Visual Information Have students identify the lines of latitude and longitude on the photo of Disney World and use them to answer the following question. **Ask:** What is the absolute location of Cinderella's Castle? *(It lies between latitude 28°25'8" N and 28°25'12" N and at longitude 81°34'52" W.)* Visual/Spatial

Content Background Knowledge

To pinpoint the area between latitude and longitude lines more precisely, locations are given in degrees/minutes/seconds. To read the latitude 38°53'55" N, say "38 degrees, 53 minutes, 55 seconds North."

Have students who have used GPS devices to mark the absolute location of a place so that they can find it again later, describe to the rest of the class how this is done.

Disney World, located in Orlando, Florida, attracts millions of visitors every year.
▶ CRITICAL THINKING
Human Geography What effect do you think Disney World has on the surrounding communities?

V1

Place

Another theme of geography is place. The features that help define a place can be physical or human.

Why is Denver called the "Mile High City"? Its location one mile above sea level gives it a special character. Why does New Orleans have the nickname "the Crescent City"? It is built on a crescent-shaped bend along the Mississippi River. That location has had a major impact on the city's growth and how its people live.

Region

Each place is unique, but two or more places can share characteristics. Places that are close to one another and share some characteristics belong to the same **region**. For example, Los Angeles and San Diego are located in southern California. They have some features in common, such as nearness to the ocean. Both cities also have mostly warm temperatures throughout the year.

In the case of those two cities, the region is defined using physical characteristics. Regions also can be defined by human characteristics. For instance, the countries of South America are part of the same region. One reason is that most of the people living in these countries follow the same religion, Roman Catholicism.

R Geographers study region so they can identify the broad patterns of larger areas. They can compare and contrast the features in one region with those in another. They also examine the special features that make each place in a region distinct from the others.

Aerial Archives/Alamy; (inset) Ilene MacDonald/Alamy

netw⊛rks *Online Teaching Options*

ANIMATION

Disney World in Orlando, Florida

Identifying Physical Features Display the animated photo of Disney World in Orlando, Florida. Guide students in identifying the physical and human features that define the place. At the bird's-eye level, have students describe the place in terms of its relative location. Visual/Spatial

See page 15C for other online activities.

Interactive Photos

NASA/NOAA/SPL/Science Photo Library/Getty Images

ANSWER, p. 22

CRITICAL THINKING Possible answers: provides employment; causes more traffic; increases business for hotels, motels, and restaurants; increases tax revenue

Human-Environment Interaction

People and the environment interact. That is, they affect each other. The physical characteristics of a place affect how people live. Flat, rich, well-watered soil is good for farming. Mountains full of coal can be mined. The environment also can present all kinds of hazards, such as floods, droughts, earthquakes, and volcanic eruptions.

People affect the environment, too. They blast tunnels through mountains to build roadways and drain swamps to make farmland. Although these actions can improve life for some people, they can harm the environment. Exhaust from cars on the roadways can pollute the air, and turning swamps into farms destroys natural ecosystems and reduces biological diversity.

The **environment** is the natural surroundings of a place. It includes several key features. One is **landforms**, or the shape and nature of the land. Hills, mountains, and valleys are types of landforms. The environment also includes the presence or absence of a body of water. Cities located on coastlines, like New York City, have different characteristics than inland cities, like Dallas.

Weather and climate play a role in how people interact with their environment. The average weather in a place over a long period of time is called its **climate**. Alaska's climate is marked by long, cold, wet winters and short, mild summers. Hawaii's climate is warm year-round. Alaskans interact with their environment differently in December than Hawaiians do.

Another **component**, or part, of the environment is **resources**. These are materials that can be used to produce crops or other products. Forests are a resource because the trees can be used to build homes and furniture. Oil is a resource because it can be used to make energy.

Movement

Geographers also look at how people, products, ideas, and information move from one place to another. People have many reasons for moving. Some move because they find a better job.

Academic Vocabulary

component a part

In 2005 Hurricane Katrina devastated the Gulf Coast and the city of New Orleans (left). Years later, many houses remain abandoned (right).
▶ **CRITICAL THINKING**
Identifying What hazards does the environment present?

Chapter 1 **23**

(l) ©Ocean/Corbis, ©Kryssia Campos/Getty Images, (tr) ©Erica Simone Leeds, (br) ©JG Photography/Alamy

(l to r) Ethan Miller/Getty Images; ©Julie Dermansky/Corbis

T Technology Skills

Researching on the Internet Have students think about and make a list of what environmental hazards affect the state they live in. Then have small groups each take one of the hazards, such as floods, and research the history of it in their state over the past 50 years. Encourage them to include dates and statistics along with any images available, and to report their findings to the class. **Visual/Spatial, Logical/Mathematical**

C Critical Thinking Skills

Identifying Problems Explain to students that people affect the environment. Have students share what human actions they think could harm the environment. *(Students' answers will vary but might include oil spills, spraying chemicals on lawns, polluting air and water, cutting and/or burning forests.)*

Then have small groups take two sides of an environmental issue on how human actions change the environment for better or for worse, such as draining a marsh or a swamp for farmland or for building houses.

Have one group research the benefits of the environmental issue, such as marshes and swamps help prevent flooding and they support a large biodiversity of life. Have the other group defend the environmental change by explaining the benefits of the change for humans such as providing jobs and usable land.

Have the two sides present their information, and then encourage the two groups to come to some sort of compromise on the issue, explaining that compromise is often needed in these situations. **BL Naturalist, Verbal/Linguistic**

R Reading Skills

Applying After reading about the key features that make up the environment, have volunteers identify each feature as you list it on the whiteboard. *(landforms, climate, resources)* Then have small groups of three to four students brainstorm a list of environmental features for the local area, that is the landforms, the climate, and the natural resources. Bring the class together to share their lists. Encourage students to write the lists and definitions of the features in their notebooks for future reference. **ELL AL**

How People Are Affected by Geography

Understanding Show the slide show about how people are affected by geography. Discuss why people may choose to build structures within the natural environment. Continue by discussing how human structures can adversely affect the environment and how technology can be both helpful and dangerous during times of climate changes. Have students reflect about their community and how the local geography and human-made structures affect people. **BL Visual/Spatial, Interpersonal**

See page 15C for other online activities.

Slide Show

ANSWER, p. 23

CRITICAL THINKING Possible answers: floods, droughts, earthquakes, volcanic eruptions, blizzards, avalanches, mudslides

C Critical Thinking Skills

Reading Charts Using the chart of the six essential elements, read aloud each element of the study of geography and its definition. After discussing each element with students, ask them the following questions:

- **Comparing** Which theme of geography is the essential element Environment and Society similar to? *(Human-environment interaction)*
- **Giving Examples** What is an example of a region of the United States? What makes that area a region? *(Possible answers: Rocky Mountain states have similar physical geography; the corn/soybean/hog belt of the Midwest is a region based on similar farming practices.)*
- **Evaluating** How might a map help you understand the world in spatial terms? *(Possible answer: A map can show where landforms are located and help you compute distances between places.)* **Verbal/Linguistic**

W Writing Skills

Informative/Explanatory Explain to students that the movement of people, products, ideas, and information is an important theme in geography. Have volunteers share reasons why people move within a town, to a different town or region, or even to another country.

Then discuss the movement of products. Have students check product tags on personal items, such as backpacks, shirts, and shoes to determine where items were made. Have students write a list of 10 items that they use frequently and where each was made. **ELL** **AL**

As an alternative exercise, survey the class to determine how many students have cell phones and computers. Have students discuss their ease at using these forms of technology for communication of ideas. Have students write a paragraph to answer these questions: **What communication system do you use most frequently? What are its benefits and disadvantages?** *(Students' answers will vary but may include mention of social networking sites. Their paragraphs should include relevant reasons for using the communication system.)* **BL** Interpersonal

---

ANSWERS, p. 24

☑ **READING PROGRESS CHECK** Possible answer: The location of something determines what landforms and bodies of water are nearby. These physical features help define a place. Every place has two locations—*absolute location* in degrees of latitude and longitude, and *relative location* stated in relation to other places.

CRITICAL THINKING The study of volcanoes, ocean currents, and climate is part of Physical Systems.

CHART SKILLS >

THE SIX ESSENTIAL ELEMENTS

Element	Definition
The World in Spatial Terms	Geography studies the location and spatial relationships among people, places, and environments. Maps reveal the complex spatial interactions.
Places and Regions	The identities of individuals and peoples are rooted in places and regions. Distinctive combinations of human and physical characteristics define places and regions.
Physical Systems	Physical processes, like wind and ocean currents, plate tectonics, and the water cycle, shape Earth's surface and change ecosystems.
Human Systems	Human systems are things like language, religion, and ways of life. They also include how groups of people govern themselves and how they make and trade products and ideas.
Environment and Society	Geography studies how the environment of a place helps shape people's lives. Geography also looks at how people affect the environment in positive and negative ways.
The Uses of Geography	Understanding geography and knowing how to use its tools and technologies helps people make good decisions about the world and prepares people for rewarding careers.

Being aware of the six essential elements will help you sort out what you are learning about geography.

▶ **CRITICAL THINKING**
Identifying The study of volcanoes, ocean currents, and climate is part of which essential element?

Sometimes, people are forced to move because of war, famine, or religious or racial prejudice. Movement by large numbers of people can have important effects. People may face shortages of housing and other services. If new arrivals to an area cannot find jobs, poverty levels can rise.

In our interconnected world, a vast number of products move from place to place. Apples from Washington State move to supermarkets in Texas. Clothes produced in Thailand end up in American shopping malls. Oil from Saudi Arabia powers cars and trucks across the United States. All of this movement relies on transportation systems that use ships, railroads, airplanes, and trucks.

Ideas can move at an even faster pace than people and products can. Communications systems, such as telephone, television, radio, and the Internet, carry ideas and information all around Earth. Remote villagers on the island of Borneo watch American television shows and learn about life in the United States. Political protestors in Greece and Spain use social networking sites to coordinate their activities. The geography of movement affects everyone.

The Six Essential Elements

The five themes are one way of thinking about geography. Geographers also divide the study of geography into six essential elements. Elements are the topics that make up a subject. Calling them *essential* means they are necessary to understanding geography.

☑ **READING PROGRESS CHECK**
Determining Central Ideas How is the theme of location related to the theme of place?

---

netw⊕rks *Online Teaching Options*

CHART

Chart of Six Essential Elements

Evaluating To reinforce understanding, display the interactive chart of the Six Essential Elements on the whiteboard and discuss its contents. You may wish to display the chart with empty cells and have the class work together to add the information. **Verbal/Linguistic, Interpersonal**

See page 15C for other online activities.

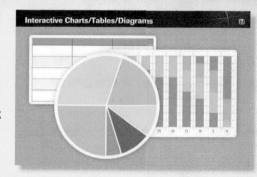

Interactive Charts/Tables/Diagrams

Geographer's Skills

GUIDING QUESTION *How will studying geography help you develop skills for everyday life?*

Have you ever used the GPS feature on a phone or in a car when you were lost? What about using a Web browser to find a route from your home to another place? If you have used these tools, your search took you to a Web site that provides maps. If you followed one of those maps to your destination, you were using a geography skill.

Interpreting Visuals

Maps are one tool geographers use to picture the world. They use other visual images, as well. These other visuals include graphs, charts, diagrams, and photographs.

Graphs are visual displays of numerical information. They can help you compare information. Charts display information in columns and rows. Diagrams are drawings that use pictures to represent an idea. A diagram might show the steps in a process or the parts that make up something.

Critical Thinking

Geographers ask analytical questions. For example, they might want to know why earthquakes are more likely in some places than in others. That question looks at causes. They might ask, How does climate affect the ways people live? Such questions examine effects.

Geographers might ask how the characteristics of a place have changed over time. That is a question of analysis. Or they could ask why people in different nations use their resources differently. That question calls on them to compare and contrast.

Learning how to ask—and answer—questions like these will help sharpen your mind. In addition to understanding geography better, you will also be able to use these skills in other subjects.

☑ **READING PROGRESS CHECK**

Determining Central Ideas How do geographers use visuals?

—Indiana—
CONNECTION

Tools of Discovery

Scientists in other fields assist geographers in understanding societies in the present and the past. For example, archaeologists hunt for evidence in the ground where settlements might once have been. They dig up and study artifacts—weapons, tools, and other things made by humans. They also look for fossils—traces of plants or animals that have been preserved in rock. Anthropologists focus on human society. They study how humans developed and how they related to one another.

FOLDABLES Study Organizer — Geographer's View / Geographer's Tools

Include this lesson's information in your Foldable®.

LESSON 1 REVIEW

Reviewing Vocabulary

1. How do *resources* affect the types of homes people typically build in a region?

Answering the Guiding Questions

2. *Identifying* What is a place within a place that you have been in today?

3. *Determining Central Ideas* What information would you use to give your exact location on Earth?

4. *Determining Word Meanings* What is the difference between environment and landforms?

5. *Identifying* Name an innovation that has greatly affected people's movement.

6. *Informative/Explanatory Writing* Describe how you have experienced geography today.

V Visual Skills

Interpreting Display samples of various kinds of visuals: graphs *(line, bar, circle)*, charts, diagrams, and photographs, or have students find and display examples of each of these from their textbooks. Discuss how visuals show information more clearly, easily, and concisely than can be said in the words of a text. **ELL** Visual/Spatial

C Critical Thinking Skills

Formulating Questions Have students formulate questions about what they want to learn about in geography this year. Make a class list of six questions that the majority of students have in common, and have a small group of volunteers make a poster of these questions for the class to refer to throughout the year. **ELL** **AL** Verbal/Linguistic

Content Background Knowledge

A career in geography involves work that focuses on location. Many jobs are related to map making, such as photogrammetrists who use photography from aerial photographs to measure distances between objects. Another example are surveyors who measure land and map boundaries.

Knowledge of geography may also lead to careers in urban planning, real estate development, tourism, forestry, or climatology. Social science geographers may work for the federal government and study foreign policy.

CLOSE & REFLECT

Making Connections To close this lesson, have students think about what geography is and what geographers do. Ask students to write a paragraph about how geography is visible in their own lives; for example, how it affects the way they get to and from school.

LESSON 1 REVIEW ANSWERS

Reviewing Vocabulary

1. People tend to use the resources of their region because they are readily available and cheaper. Areas with many forests and woodlands, for example, might have more wood-frame houses.

Answering the Guiding Questions

2. **Identifying** Sample answer: I woke up in my bedroom, which is inside my house. I am sitting in my classroom, which is inside my school.

3. **Determining Central Ideas** The line of latitude gives my east-west location. The line of longitude gives my north-south location. A map or globe shows these lines.

4. **Determining Word Meanings** Landforms describe only the appearance of the land. Environment includes landforms plus bodies of water, resources, and climate.

5. **Identifying** Students should cite any of the main innovations in transportation, such as the automobile, train, or airplane.

6. **Informative/Explanatory Writing** Student answers may include reference to the weather, sounds, changing their location, or watching TV.

ANSWER, p. 25

☑ **READING PROGRESS CHECK** Possible answers: Visuals help geographers understand the physical and human processes and systems that operate in the world. Visuals help geographers present information to others. Visuals show interconnections among peoples, places, and regions.

ENGAGE

Bellringer Before students begin this lesson, **ask:** When have you used a map? How did it help you? Display several kinds of maps, such as a road map; a map for an amusement park, museum, or subway; a political map of the world; an economic or resource map; a climate map; and a topographic map. Have students work in small groups to study one of the maps. Then ask each group to explain to the class what information is provided on their map and how someone might use it.

TEACH & ASSESS

V Visual Skills

Creating Visuals Have students close their eyes and picture a room from their home in their mind. Then have them roughly sketch their mental map on paper. Working with a partner, have students use their maps to orally describe the relative locations of objects in their rooms. Tell partners to ask each other questions about where things are located. Visual/Spatial, Verbal/Linguistic

R Reading Skills

Paraphrasing Display a globe. **Ask:** Why are globes the most accurate way to show places on Earth? Tell students to use their own words to answer the question. *(Sample answer: Like Earth, a globe is shaped like a sphere or ball; the shapes of land and bodies of water are correct on globes; distances and directions between places are more correct than those on flat maps.)* ELL AL Verbal/Linguistic

Remind students to add academic and content vocabulary words to their vocabulary lists. Tell students to write their own definitions and to include drawings if desired. This activity can be done as students encounter the words during class or completed as homework. ELL AL

ANSWER, p. 26

Taking Notes Key: explains symbols, colors, and lines; **scale bar:** tells how a measured space on a map corresponds to actual distances on Earth; **compass rose:** shows direction

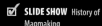

networks

There's More Online!

- ☑ **SLIDE SHOW** History of Mapmaking
- ☑ **ANIMATION** Elements of a Globe
- ☑ **VIDEO**

Reading HELPDESK

Academic Vocabulary

- **sphere**
- **convert**
- **distort**

Content Vocabulary

- **hemisphere**
- **key**
- **scale bar**
- **compass rose**
- **map projection**
- **scale**
- **elevation**
- **relief**
- **thematic map**
- **technology**
- **remote sensing**

TAKING NOTES: *Key Ideas and Details*

Describing As you read the lesson, identify three parts of a map on a graphic organizer. Then, explain what each part shows.

Indiana Academic Standards
6.1.17, 6.1.20, 6.3.2

Lesson 2
Tools Used by Geographers

ESSENTIAL QUESTION · *How does geography influence the way people live?*

IT MATTERS BECAUSE
The tools of geography help you understand the world.

Globes and Maps

GUIDING QUESTION *What is the difference between globes and maps?*

If you close your eyes and imagine your neighborhood, you are using a mental map. You are forming a picture of the buildings and other places and where each is in relation to the others.

Making and using maps is a big part of geography. Of course, geographers make maps that have many parts. Their maps are more detailed than your mental map. Still, their maps are essentially the same as your mental map. Both are a way to picture the world and show where things are located.

Globes

The most accurate way to show places on Earth is with a globe. Globes are the most accurate because globes, like Earth, are **spheres**; that is, they are shaped like a ball. As a result, globes represent the correct shapes of land and bodies of water. They show distances and directions between places more correctly than flat images of Earth can.

The Equator and the Prime Meridian each divide Earth in half. Each half of Earth is called a **hemisphere**. The Equator divides Earth into sections called the Northern and Southern Hemispheres. The Prime Meridian, together with the International Date Line, splits Earth into the Eastern and Western Hemispheres.

(l to r) Lana Sundman/Alamy; Antenna Audio - Inc./Getty Images; Kathy Collins/Getty Images; spacephotos.com/age fotostock; Chris Wallace/Alamy

26

---

networks *Online Teaching Options*

VIDEO

Mapping the World: Google Maps

Writing Questions Use the video to introduce the innovative technology being used for mapping. Ask students if they understand the steps used to map the world with technology. Discuss with students if they have ever used Google Earth, Google Maps, or any other mapping technology. Have students write three questions they have with regard to the video, not placing their names on the questions. Collect the questions and answer a few aloud in class. Then redistribute them and have other students answer the questions. Encourage students to experiment with this technology in their spare time. Verbal/Linguistic, Interpersonal

See page 15D for other online activities.

BBC Motion Gallery Education

Maps

Maps are not round like globes. Instead, maps are flat representations of the round Earth. They might be sketched on a piece of paper, printed in a book, or displayed on a computer screen. Wherever they appear, maps are always flat.

Maps **convert**, or change, a round space into a flat space. As a result, maps **distort** physical reality, or show it incorrectly. This is why maps are not as accurate as globes are, especially maps that show large areas or the whole world.

Despite this distortion problem, maps have several advantages over globes. Globes have to show the whole planet. Maps, though, can show only a part of it, such as one country, one city, or one mountain range. As a result, they can provide more detail than globes can. Think how large a globe would have to be to show the streets of a city. You could certainly never carry such a globe around with you. Maps make more sense if you want to study a small area. They can focus on just that area, and they are easy to store and carry.

Maps tend to show more kinds of information than globes. Globes generally show major physical and political features, such as landmasses, bodies of water, the countries of the world, and the largest cities. They cannot show much else without becoming too difficult to read or too large. However, some maps show these same features. But maps also can be specialized. One map might illustrate a large mountain range. Another might display the results of an election. Yet another could show the locations of all the schools in a city.

☑ **READING PROGRESS CHECK**

Analyzing What is a disadvantage of using maps?

Academic Vocabulary

sphere a round shape like a ball

convert to change from one thing to another

distort to present in a manner that is misleading

A set of imaginary lines divides Earth into hemispheres.
▶ **CRITICAL THINKING**
The Geographer's World
What line divides Earth into Eastern and Western Hemispheres?

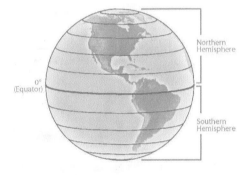

Chapter 1 **27**

C Critical Thinking Skills

Comparing and Contrasting After reading the section titled, "Maps," **ask:** How are maps and globes alike and different? Have students record their ideas in a Venn diagram and then discuss as a class. *(Like a globe, some maps show the whole world and both can show major physical and political features. However, unlike globes, maps distort physical reality and are not as accurate as globes. Maps can show just parts of the world, whereas globes must always show the whole world. Maps can show more details than globes can and can be easily stored and carried. Maps show more kinds of information than globes and can be specialized.)* **Verbal/Linguistic, Visual/Spatial**

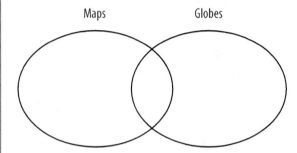

Maps   Globes

Content Background Knowledge

Prime Meridian In the 1600s the determination of longitude was critical to the navigation of ships on the ocean. In 1675 the British established the Royal Observatory at Greenwich to study and create fixed degrees of longitude. Thus the Prime Meridian was set there at Greenwich.

The British and Americans used the resulting system of longitude throughout the 1700s and 1800s. During this time, more and more countries adopted the system of longitude that had been created by the British. When an international conference was held in 1884, enough countries were using this system that it became the established sytem for the world.

Elements of a Globe

Understanding Visuals Display the animated globe on the whiteboard. Use the globe to visually explain the geographic terms related to maps: *hemispheres, key, scale,* and *compass rose*. Then use the animation to show different map projections. **AL Visual/Spatial**

See page 15D for other online activities.

ANSWERS, p. 27

☑ **READING PROGRESS CHECK** Maps distort physical reality, or show it incorrectly.
CRITICAL THINKING The Prime Meridian

Tools Used by Geographers

V1 Visual Skills

Identifying After reading the section titled, "Elements of a Map," display a physical map of the world or the United States, and have students identify the map's elements or features, such as map title, key, scale bar, compass rose, insets, and latitude and longitude lines. Discuss the importance of each map feature, and have students give an example of how they might use each feature to find their way on the map.
ELL Visual/Spatial

V2 Visual Skills

Reading a Map Remind students that maps use tools to visually convey information. Direct students' attention to the maps at the bottom of the page and ask them to identify the parts of each map that are visible. **Ask:**

- What map feature helps you know what information is on a map? *(map title)*
- Identify two streets, areas, or structures on one of the maps and explain their relative location using the compass rose. *(Student answers may vary but should include the use of cardinal directions.)*
- What kinds of information are provided in the key for these maps? *(Student answers should include specific details relative to each map.)*
- How would you use the map of the Canyon Area? *(Student answers may vary but should include finding hiking trails, scenic overlooks, or their way back to the parking lot.)*
- Why does the map of the Canyon Area include the You Are Here label? *(Student answers may vary but should include the understanding that people could be unfamiliar with the area shown on the map and not know where they are in relationship to the trails.)*
- How would you use the map of the National Mall? *(Student answers should include finding the various museums they would want to visit in Washington, D.C.)* Visual/Spatial, Verbal/Linguistic

---

A Closer Look at Maps

GUIDING QUESTION *How do maps work?*

Maps are located in many different places. You can see them in a subway station. Subway maps indicate the routes each train takes. In a textbook, a map might show new areas that were added to the United States at different times. On a company's Web site, a map can locate all its stores in a city. The map of a state park would tell visitors what activities they can enjoy in each area of the park. Each of these maps is different from the others, but they have some traits in common.

Elements of a Map

Maps have several important elements, or features. These features are the tools the map uses to convey information.

The map title tells what area the map will cover. It also identifies what kind of information the map presents about that area. The **key** unlocks the meaning of the map by explaining the symbols, colors, and lines. The **scale bar** is an important part of the map. It tells how a measured space on the map corresponds to actual distances on Earth. For example, by using the scale bar, you can determine how many miles in the real world each inch on the map represents. The **compass rose** shows direction. This map feature points out north, south, east, and west. Some maps include insets that show more detail for smaller areas, such as cities on a state map. Many maps show latitude and longitude lines to help you locate places.

Map Projections

To convert the round Earth to a flat map, geographers use **map projections**. A map projection distorts some aspects of Earth in order to represent other aspects as accurately as possible on a flat

Many different kinds of maps are available because maps are useful for showing a wide range of information.
▶ **CRITICAL THINKING**
Describing What is the difference between a large-scale and a small-scale map?

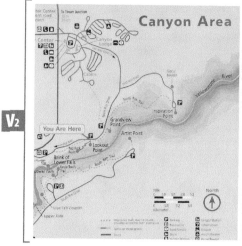

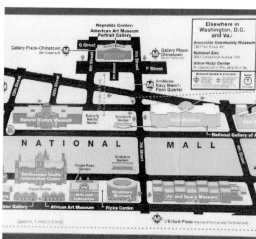

28 Chapter 1

---

networks · Online Teaching Options

GAME

Mapping the Earth

Identifying Display the game on the whiteboard. Have students match the descriptions of the physical features in an area with their corresponding map symbols. As students correctly identify each symbol, drag it to the correct description. Visual/Spatial, Naturalist

See page 15D for other online activities.

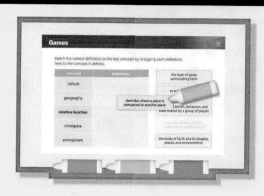

ANSWER, p. 28

CRITICAL THINKING A large-scale map shows details of a small area; a small-scale map shows a large area in less detail, as on a road map.

map. Some projections show the correct size of areas in relation to one another. Other map projections emphasize making the shapes of areas as correct as possible.

Some projections break apart the world's oceans. By doing so, these maps show land areas more accurately. They clearly do not show the oceans accurately, though.

Mapmakers, known as cartographers, choose which projection to use based on the purpose of the map. Each projection distorts some parts of the globe more or less than other parts. Finally, mapmakers think about what part of Earth they are drawing and how large an area they want to cover.

Map Scale

Scale is another important feature of maps. As you learned, the scale bar connects distances on the map to actual distances on Earth. The scale bar is based on the scale at which the map is drawn. **Scale** is the relationship between distances on the map and on Earth.

Maps are either *large scale* or *small scale*. A large-scale map focuses on a smaller area. An inch on the map might correspond to 10 miles (16 km) on the ground. A small-scale map shows a relatively larger area. An inch on a small-scale map might be the same as 1,000 miles (1,609 km).

Each type of scale has benefits and drawbacks. Which scale to use depends on the map's purpose. Do you want to map your school and the streets and buildings near it? Then you need a large-scale map to show this small area in great detail. Do you want to show the entire United States? In that case, you need a small-scale map that shows the larger area but with less detail.

Two Types of Maps

The two types of maps are general purpose and thematic. The type depends on what kind of information is drawn on the map. General-purpose maps show a wide range of information about an area. They generally show either the human-made features of an area or its natural features, but not both.

Political maps are one common type of general-purpose map that shows human-made features. They show the boundaries of countries or divisions within them, like the states of the United States. They also show the locations and names of cities.

Physical maps display natural features such as mountains and valleys, rivers, and lakes. They picture the location, size, and shape of these features. Many physical maps show **elevation**, or how much above or below sea level a feature is. Maps often use colors to present this information. A key on the map explains what height above or below sea level each color represents.

Physical maps usually show **relief**, or the difference between the elevation of one feature and the elevation of another feature near it.

Chapter 1 **29**

Thinking Like a Geographer

Relief

Relief is the height of a landform compared to other nearby landforms. If a mountain 10,000 feet (3,048 m) high rises above a flat area at sea level, the relief of the mountain equals its elevation: 10,000 feet. If the 10,000-foot-high mountain is in a highland region that is 4,000 feet (1,219 m) above sea level, its relief is *less than* its elevation—only 6,000 feet (1,829 m). The difference in height between it and the land around it is much less than its absolute height. *What would be the relief of a mountain 7,500 feet (2,286 m) high compared to its highest foothill, at 3,000 feet (914 m) high?*

SLIDE SHOW

Special Purpose Maps

Analyzing Images Show the slide show of various types of special purpose maps, such as museum, trail, building emergency exit, celestial, and treasure maps. Discuss the purpose and the kinds of information that are drawn on each map. Have students identify any map that is a projection and have them talk about which parts are distorted. **Visual/Spatial**

See page 15D for other online activities.

Slide Show

C Critical Thinking Skills

Analyzing Information Ask: How does knowing that map projections are always distorted help you choose maps to use? *(Possible answer: You would choose a map based on your purpose for study and use one that projects the area you are interested in as accurately, with the least amount of distortion, as possible.)* **Verbal/Linguistic**

R1 Reading Skills

Defining Ask students to define the word *scale* in geographic terms. Then discuss with them that the word *scale* has multiple meanings. Have students use a dictionary to define and draw the different meanings of the word *scale*. **Verbal/Linguistic**

V Visual Skills

Reading a Map Display a political map of the world or the United States. Have students find the scale bar and identify the relationship between distances on the map and on Earth. Choose two cities on the map and have several volunteers use rulers or yardsticks and their multiplication skills to compute the distance between the locations in both miles and kilometers. Possible city combinations include the following:

- New York City, NY and Chicago, IL
- Seattle, WA and San Francisco, CA
- Minneapolis, MN and Tampa, FL
- Denver, CO and Mexico City, Mexico
- Paris, France and Berlin, Germany
- Cairo, Egypt and Baghdad, Iraq **Visual/Spatial, Logical/ Mathematical**

R2 Reading Skills

Explaining Ask: Why wouldn't a map show both country boundaries and land elevations? *(General-purpose maps show either human-made features of an area or its natural features, but not both. Boundaries are human-made features and are shown on political maps. Elevation is a natural feature and is shown on physical maps. Both political maps and physical maps are general-purpose maps.)* **Verbal/Linguistic, Logical/ Mathematical**

ANSWER, p. 29

Thinking Like a Geographer The relief would be 4,500 feet (1,372 m).

V Visual Skills

Analyzing Maps Compare and contrast the two maps of the Western Hemisphere shown at the top of the page. Invite students to infer when each of the maps were made, and have them explain their reasoning. **Ask:** Why do you think only parts of North America are shown on the historical map? *(Possible answer: Explorers had not reached the western part of North America when the map was made and cartographers could not draw what they did not know was there.)* **Verbal/Linguistic, Visual/Spatial**

R Reading Skills

Applying Discuss the difference between elevation and relief and how they are shown on physical maps. Encourage students to consider why it is important to show relief on a map. **Ask:**

- What kind of map shows differences in elevation? *(a physical map)* Why would it have been important to show elevation on a historical map for people traveling west in wagon trains? *(to know what mountain ranges they had to cross and to plan for that kind of travel)*
- What width of colors on a physical map would be used for an area with mountains? *(narrow)* For an area with flat plains? *(wide)*

Have students explain why the width of colors varies. *(It shows the relief.)* **Verbal/Linguistic, Visual/Spatial**

C Critical Thinking Skills

Giving Examples Discuss thematic maps that most students will know such as road maps, maps of a local mall or amusement park, or a map of the school. **Ask:** What kinds of thematic maps are you familiar with or have used? *(Student answers will vary but should demonstrate an understanding of what a thematic map is.)* **Interpersonal**

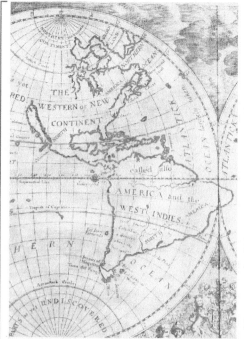

V

Cartography is the science of making maps. As knowledge of Earth grew, maps became increasingly accurate.

▶ **CRITICAL THINKING**
The Geographer's World
Describe two ways in which the historical map differs from the present-day map.

R

Elevation is an absolute number, but relief is relative. It depends on other landforms that are nearby. The width of the colors on a physical map usually shows the relief. Colors that are narrow show steep places, and colors that are wide show gently sloping land.

C

Thematic maps show more specialized information. A thematic map might indicate the kinds of plants that grow in different areas. That kind of map is a vegetation map. Another could show where farming, ranching, or mining takes place. That kind of map is called a land-use map. Road maps show people how to travel from one place to another by car. Just about any physical or human feature can be displayed on a thematic map.

☑ **READING PROGRESS CHECK**

Describing What are the two main types of maps?

Mapping Technology

GUIDING QUESTION *How do geographers use geospatial technologies?*

Electronic maps, such as those on cell phones and mapping devices in cars, are an example of geospatial technologies. **Technology** is any way that scientific discoveries are applied to practical use.

30 Chapter 1

---

netw⊕rks *Online Teaching Options*

WORKSHEET

Geospatial Technologies

Examining Have students investigate the latest forms of geospatial technologies. Have them note their findings on the worksheet. Have students who have used these technologies share their experiences with a partner or with the class. **Interpersonal**

See page 15D for other online activities.

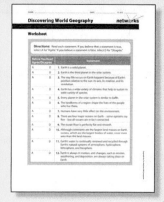

ANSWERS, p. 30

CRITICAL THINKING The historical map is based primarily on speculation or guesswork and on unsophisticated tools. The contemporary map shows greater knowledge and understanding of geography, greater accuracy (as in the shape of continents), and more detail.

☑ **READING PROGRESS CHECK** General-purpose maps show physical or political characteristics of an area. Thematic maps show more specialized information, such as resources or road networks.

Geospatial technologies help us think spatially and provide practical information about the locations of physical and human features.

Global Positioning System

GPS devices work with a network called the Global Positioning System (GPS). This network was built by the U.S. government. Parts of it can be used only by the U.S. armed forces. Parts of it, though, can be used by ordinary people all over the world. The GPS has three elements.

The first element of this network is a set of more than 30 satellites that orbit Earth constantly. The U.S. government launched the satellites into space and maintains them. The satellites send out radio signals. Almost any spot on Earth can be reached by signals from at least four satellites at all times.

The second part of the network is the control system. Workers around the world track the satellites to make sure they are working properly and are on course. The workers reset the clocks on the satellites when needed.

The third part of the GPS system consists of GPS devices on Earth. These devices receive the signals sent by the satellites. By combining the signals from different satellites, a device calculates its location on Earth in terms of latitude and longitude. The more satellite signals the device receives at any time, the more accurately it can determine its location. Because satellites have accurate clocks, the GPS device also displays the correct time.

W GPS is used in many ways. It is used to track the exact location and course of airplanes. That information helps ensure the safety of air travel. Farmers use it to help them work their fields. Businesses use it to guide truck drivers. Cell phone companies use GPS to provide services. GPS in cars helps guide us to our destinations.

Geographic Information Systems

R Another important geospatial technology is known as a geographic information system (GIS). These systems consist of computer hardware and software that gather, store, and analyze geographic information. The information is then shown on a computer screen. Sometimes it is displayed as maps. Sometimes the information is shown in other ways. Companies and governments around the world use this tool.

A GIS is a powerful tool because it links data about all kinds of physical and human features with the locations of those features. Because computers can store and process so much data, the GIS can be accurate and detailed.

People select what features they want to study using the GIS. Then they can combine different features on the same map and analyze the patterns.

Think **Again**

Geographers know the exact height of Mount Everest.

Not true. Mount Everest, on the border of Nepal and China, is the world's tallest mountain. It is said to be 29,028 feet (8,848 m) tall. Scientists disagree on this measurement, however, and the government of Nepal does not accept it. In 2011 Nepal launched a two-year effort to find the exact height using three GPS devices.

W Writing Skills

Argument Explain to students that today parents can download a phone app that uses GPS in real time to keep track of their children through the location of their children's phones. Parents say that they use the app to protect their children. However, children complain that parents are spying on them and that it is an invasion of their privacy.

Have students work together in small groups to brainstorm the pros and cons to these locater apps. Then have students write a persuasive paragraph to answer this prompt: **Should parents use GPS locater apps to keep track of their children?** *(Students' paragraphs need to include a claim either for or against parents using GPS locater apps and at least three ideas or forms of evidence to support the claim.)* Interpersonal, Logical/Mathematical

R Reading Skills

Explaining To make sure students can explain and apply what they are reading about, **ask:** Why is a geographic information system (GIS) an important tool? *(The system links data about all kinds of physical and human features with the locations of those features on Earth. People who use the system can combine different features on the same map and analyze the patterns.)* Verbal/Linguistic

Content Background Knowledge

Geocaching is an activity in which people go on treasure hunts without the use of a treasure map, looking for objects that other people have concealed. The people who conceal the "treasure," which is generally a weather-proof box containing a log book and small objects, use a GPS device to post the GPS coordinates on a Web site. Those who seek the "treasure" use their own GPS device and the posted GPS coordinates to find the hidden object. People can hide whatever they choose to hide.

SLIDE SHOW

Mapmaking Over Time

Analyzing Visuals Show the slide show of how mapmaking has changed over time. Have students identify the various tools used to make maps (for example, pen and ink with scribe, printmaking, film/aerial photography) and discuss how mapmaking has become more accurate. Visual/Spatial

See page 15D for other online activities.

(l) ©Ocean/Corbis, ©Kryssia Campos/Getty Images, (tr) Erica Simone Leeds, (br) ©JG Photography/Alamy

Tools Used by Geographers

C Critical Thinking Skills

Making Inferences After reading about geographic information systems, **ask:** What kinds of questions could be answered with the following information gathered through GIS?

• Geologists use GIS to make a map of areas in a state most likely to suffer damage from earthquakes. *(Possible answers: How should building codes change to insure the least amount of damage during a quake? Is this a good area to build a specific kind of structure, such as an amusement park?)*

• Meteorologists use GIS to study the paths of hurricanes. *(Possible answers: Where might a hurricane occur? How might a hurricane travel? Do people need to evacuate the area?)*

• Police use GIS to map the specific kinds of crimes in each area of a large city. *(Possible answers: Which areas of the city need more police coverage? Which city areas show an increased gang presence? Have crimes increased around schools?)*

Verbal/Linguistic

R Reading Skills

Using Context Clues Have students use context clues to find the meaning of *remote sensing*. (*"getting information from far away"*) **Ask:** How does the definition of remote sensing help you understand how satellites are used? *(Satellites circle the globe in space, which is "far away," collect information about what is happening on Earth, and send the information back to Earth.)* **ELL**

T Technology Skills

Researching the Internet Have students work in small groups to search the Internet for satellite images of their state, community, and neighborhoods. Explain that the cameras on some satellites are so powerful that they can zero in on small areas such as a neighborhood. Have students discuss ways these satellite images could be used. **Visual/Spatial**

GPS satellites are used to measure, as well as determine, location on Earth. Some cell phones receive this satellite information, allowing people to locate places in a city.

▶ CRITICAL THINKING
Analyzing Why is it important for geographers to know exactly where places are located on Earth?

For instance, a farmer might want to compare the amount of moisture in the soil to the health of the plants. At the same time, he or she could add soil types around the farm to the comparison. The farmer could then use the results of the analysis to answer all kinds of questions. What plants should I plant in different locations? How much irrigation water should I use? How can I drive the tractor most efficiently?

Satellites and Sensors

Since the 1970s, satellites have gathered data about Earth's surface. They do so using remote sensing. **Remote sensing** simply means getting information from far away. Most early satellite sensors were used to gather information about the weather. Weather satellites helped save lives during disasters by providing warnings about approaching storms. Before satellites, tropical storms were often missed because they could not be tracked over open water.

Satellites gather information in different ways. They may use powerful cameras to take pictures of the land. They can also pick up other kinds of information, such as the amount of moisture in the

networks *Online Teaching Options*

GRAPHIC ORGANIZER

Organizing: Forms of Technology

Reviewing Display the interactive graphic organizer on the whiteboard and guide students to organize the forms of technology discussed in this chapter: GPS, GIS, Satellites, Sensors. **Verbal/Linguistic**

See page 15D for other online activities.

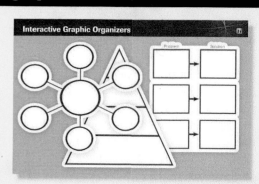

ANSWER, p. 32

CRITICAL THINKING Geographers need to know exactly where places are located on Earth so they can provide information to anyone who needs it. Exact locations are important when predicting storm paths and dispatching emergency equipment, and a matter of convenience and safety for travelers.

soil, the amount of heat the soil holds, or the types of vegetation that are present. In the early 2000s, scientists used GIS technology to help conserve the plants and animals that lived in the Amazon rain forest. Using the technology, scientists can compare data gathered from the ground to data taken from satellite pictures. Land use planners use this information to help local people make good decisions about how to use the land. These activities help prevent the rain forest from being destroyed.

Some satellites gather information regularly on every spot in the world. That way, scientists can compare the information from one year to another. They look for changes in the shape of the land or in its makeup, spot problems, and take steps to fix them.

T

Limits of Technology

Geospatial technologies allow access to a wealth of information about the features and objects in the world and where those features and objects are located. This information can be helpful for identifying and navigating. By itself, however, the information does not answer questions about why features are located where they are. These questions lie at the heart of understanding our world. The answers are crucial for making decisions about this world in which we live. But it is important to go beyond the information provided by geospatial technologies. We must build understanding of people, places, and environments and the connections among them.

R

✓ **READING PROGRESS CHECK**

Determining Central Ideas How could remote sensing be used as part of a GIS?

FOLDABLES Study Organizer — Geographer's View / Geographer's Tools

Include this lesson's information in your Foldable®.

T Technology Skills

Analyzing Data Explain to students that NASA is an excellent source for their research work on the Internet this year. Have students work in small groups to access NASA weather satellite images. Tell them to choose two images and discuss the data and information the images provide and evaluate the importance of the information. Have groups share the images and their analyses with the rest of the class. Visual/Spatial, Verbal/Linguistic

R Reading Skills

Identifying Have students identify the kinds of information that geospatial technologies can and cannot provide. *(They can tell us about physical features and where they are located, but cannot tell us why they are located where they are.)* **Ask:** Why is it important for people to go beyond the information provided by geospatial technologies in their study of geography? *(Students' answers will vary but should include that people need to understand how people interact with places and how they affect the environment, which geospatial technologies cannot tell us.)* AL

Content Background Knowledge

Movement of the Continents The theory of plate tectonics, which students will study in future chapters, was proven with the use of geospatial technologies. These technologies are so precise that they show the continents drifting apart in very small amounts, such as one or two centimeters, over a span of one or more years.

CLOSE & REFLECT

Making Connections To close this lesson, have students think about the different kinds of maps they have used and how the maps helped them find the information they required.

For homework, have students look for maps in their homes that they or their caregivers use. Ask students to discuss what types of maps they found the next day in class.

LESSON 2 REVIEW

Reviewing Vocabulary
1. Which *hemispheres* describe your location?

Answering the Guiding Questions
2. *Identifying* To plan a cross-country trip, would a large-scale or a small-scale map be more helpful? Explain.

3. *Analyzing* If half of the 30 satellites that orbit Earth were unusable, how might GPS be affected?

4. *Integrating Visual Information* Create a map of your school building and grounds. Include the key features of a map.

5. *Identifying* What are the main differences between a map and a globe?

6. *Informative/Explanatory Writing* Can geospatial technology be used to explain all aspects of geography? Explain.

Chapter 1 **33**

LESSON 2 REVIEW ANSWERS

Reviewing Vocabulary

1. Northern Hemisphere; Western Hemisphere

Answering the Guiding Questions

2. **Identifying** A small-scale map shows a larger area in less detail, so it would be more useful.

3. **Analyzing** Some places might not get signals from at least four satellites, which might affect the accuracy of the system.

4. **Integrating Visual Information** Maps should show the layout of the school and include a scale bar, a key, and a compass rose.

5. **Identifying** A globe has less distortion because it is shaped like Earth. It shows much less detail. Maps can show specialized information, such as interstate highways and locations of airports.

6. **Informative/Explanatory Writing** No; it can provide information, but it cannot make connections about information pertaining to people, places, and environments.

ANSWER, p. 33

✓ **READING PROGRESS CHECK** Possible answer: Data from remote sensing could be added to a GIS for an area, providing some of the information needed to study the area.

ENGAGE

Bellringer Before students read the What Do You Think? feature, explain that the feature first presents background information about a topic and then gives two opposing arguments about the topic, much like a debate. The purpose of each argument is to persuade the reader to agree with that position on the controversial subject. **Ask:** When and for what purposes have you used online maps and directions? *(Student answers will vary but should include knowledge of the kinds of information these services and tools provide.)*

TEACH & ASSESS

R Reading Skills

Determining Word Meanings After students read the introductory paragraph, make sure they understand the question that the paragraph ends with. Explain that the word *intrude* has a strong negative connotation and can mean that a person enters into a place or event without being invited or having permission. **Ask:** In which scenario is a classmate intruding: by asking to go with you and a friend to the game or by interrupting a private conversation between you and a friend? *(by interrupting a private conversation between you and a friend)* **ELL** Verbal/Linguistic

C Critical Thinking Skills

Making Connections Discuss with students the argument this writer puts forth. Have students make connections to this side of the issue by relating the example given to their experiences using the Internet. **Ask:** What might happen when images or videos from the Internet are saved to a user's hard drive and disseminated later? Why might such a release of images cause further problems after an objectionable image is removed? *(Possible answer: Since images and videos from the Internet can be saved to any number of personal computers, it would be impossible to be sure that all objectionable images were removed from the Internet after they were released and later removed.)* Interpersonal, Verbal/Linguistic

---

What Do You **Think?**

Are Street-Mapping Technologies an Invasion of People's Privacy?

R Suppose you are curious about a place you have never visited. Instead of going in person, you might be able to get a 360-degree view from your computer. Services like Google Street View and Bing Streetside display panoramic images of public roadways and buildings. The photos are taken by cameras attached to roving vehicles. They capture whatever is happening at the time, which means they sometimes capture random bystanders, too. Some people argue that street-level mapping programs violate the right to privacy. They point out that individuals' pictures can appear on the mapping Web sites without their knowledge or consent. Do tools like Street View intrude too much on people's privacy?

Yes!

PRIMARY SOURCE

C " Privacy encompasses the right to control information disseminated [spread] about oneself. . . . Personal behavior disclosures that occur as a result of Internet street-level mapping technologies almost certainly violate this personal right to choose which face to display to the world . . . A person may not mind that their friends and family know of their participation in certain socially stigmatizing [disapproved of] activities; an entirely new issue arises, however, should the entire public suddenly discover that the person is [doing something questionable.] . . . Internet street-level mapping scenes depart from being simply a record of what a member of the public could have seen on the street [because] on the Internet, images can be—and often are—saved onto users' hard drives for later dissemination. Thus, compromising [reputation-damaging] images, even if removed by Google after the fact, can be released to the public in an ever-widening wake [path]. "

—Andrew Lavoie, Georgia attorney

Users can view high-resolution imagery from Google Earth or Street View on their screens.

34 *Chapter 1*

---

net**works** *Online Teaching Options*

WORKSHEET

Analyzing Primary Sources

Analyzing Have student pairs use this worksheet to analyze two primary sources and the credibility of each writer. Have them share why they think each writer should or should not know about the subject matter. Verbal/Linguistic

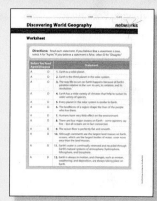

TEXT: By Melissa Lavoie, June 5, 2007, in Freelanonit.com; PHOTO: (t)Sil...

A camera mounted on a car provides the technology for Google Street View.

No!

PRIMARY SOURCE

" At Google we take privacy very seriously. Street View only features imagery taken on public property and is not in real time. This imagery is no different from what any person can readily capture or see walking down the street. Imagery of this kind is available in a wide variety of formats for cities all around the world. While the Street View feature enables people to easily find, discover, and plan activities relevant to a location, we respect the fact that people may not want imagery they feel is objectionable featured on the service. We provide easily accessible tools for flagging inappropriate or sensitive imagery . . . [U]sers can report objectionable images. Objectionable imagery includes nudity, certain types of locations (for example, domestic violence shelters) and clearly identifiable individuals . . . We routinely review takedown requests and act quickly to remove objectionable imagery. "

—Stephen Chau, product manager for Google Maps

What Do You Think? DBQ

1 *Identifying* What types of images does Google consider inappropriate?

2 *Analyzing* What points does Andrew Lavoie make to argue that Street View invades people's privacy?

Critical Thinking

3 *Identifying Point of View* Describe a situation when Street View could be useful and one when it could embarrass or endanger someone. Do you think the benefits of street-mapping tools outweigh the privacy concerns?

Chapter 1 **35**

Supporting Point of View

Citing Text Evidence Have student pairs use this worksheet to identify the text evidence writers use to support their views. Then have students evaluate this text evidence and share why they agree or disagree. **Verbal/Linguistic**

C Critical Thinking Skills

Evaluating Discuss with students the argument this writer puts forth. Have students evaluate this side of the issue by relating the example given to their life experiences. **Ask:** Why might it be difficult to send a takedown request in a timely manner for a personal image that you wish to have removed? *(Answers will vary but should demonstrate an understanding that monitoring images of everywhere you have appeared during a 24-hour period would be impossible to do.)* **Interpersonal, Verbal/Linguistic**

W Writing Skills

Argument Have students choose one of the primary sources and write their own rebuttal to the writer's arguments. Remind students to be polite, to address the writer's arguments specifically, and to make their own case, not to just repeat what was already written. *(Students' paragraphs should include a claim and details or reasons to prove some or all of the writer's arguments wrong or false. Writing should be polite and grammatically correct.)* **Interpersonal**

CLOSE & REFLECT

Summarizing Have students summarize each of the writer's arguments. Take a class vote on which writer was the most convincing. Then discuss the results of the vote and have students analyze why that writer put forth the better argument.

ANSWERS, p. 35

DBQ What Do You Think?

1. those that show nudity, sensitive locations (like domestic violence shelters), or recognizable people
2. He says it takes away people's control over their public image, makes their behavior visible to anyone on the Internet, and turns fleeting moments into permanent images that can be shared widely even after they are removed from Street View.
3. Student answers will vary. Street View might be useful to potential home buyers, vacationers, or anyone exploring an unfamiliar neighborhood, to people with disabilities seeking handicapped-accessible buildings, to users of public transportation searching for bus or subway stops, etc. Embarrassment could arise for people caught jaywalking, littering, picking their noses, leaving a soup kitchen, embracing someone other than a spouse, etc. Some students may feel that anything that happens in public is fair game for the cameras and that Google is taking adequate steps to protect privacy. Other students may be swayed by Lavoie's arguments about Street View's intrusiveness.

CHAPTER REVIEW ACTIVITY

Have students create a two-column chart like the one below. In the first column, have them list and define each of the five themes of geography. In the second column, have them give a physical example of each of the five themes of geography and tell whether a map or a globe would be better to use to show where the example is located. *(In the first column students should list the five themes—location, place, region, human-environment interaction, and movement—and provide definitions similar to those given below. In the second column, students answers will vary but they should give an appropriate example for each of the five themes. Most examples will be better illustrated on a map than on a globe.)*

Five Themes of Geography	
Definition	**Example**
1. **location** – "where something is found on Earth"	
2. **place** – "the physical or human features that make a place unique"	
3. **region** – "places that are close to one another and share some characteristics"	
4. **human-environment interaction** – "how people and the natural surroundings of a place interact"	
5. **movement** – "how people, products, ideas, and information move from one place to another"	

REVIEW THE ENDURING UNDERSTANDINGS

Review this chapter's Enduring Understandings with students:

- *People, places, and ideas change over time.*

Now pose the following questions in a class discussion to apply the Enduring Understandings to this chapter:

- What physical features of our area would have encouraged people to settle in this place? *(Answers will vary but should demonstrate an understanding of the area and how its geography affected settlement.)*

Directions: Write your answers on a separate piece of paper.

❶ Use your **FOLDABLES** to explore the Essential Question.
INFORMATIVE/EXPLANATORY WRITING Research the lifestyles of early Native American people and how their activities were related to the geography of their land. Create a poster explaining what their homes looked like, what foods they ate, and what activities they engaged in. Include images on your poster.

❷ **21st Century Skills**
ANALYZING Select one major geographic change or event that has occurred in the last century, such as the eruption of Mount Saint Helens or Hurricane Katrina. Write an essay that presents facts about the changes that occurred and their effects on the human population.

❸ **Thinking Like a Geographer**
IDENTIFYING Create a graphic organizer using the five themes of geography. Fill in information about your city for each of the five themes.

❹ **GEOGRAPHY ACTIVITY**

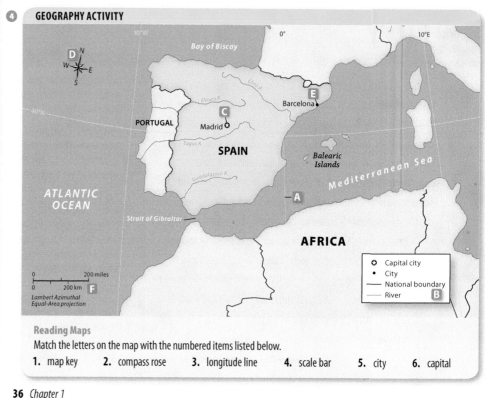

Reading Maps
Match the letters on the map with the numbered items listed below.
1. map key 2. compass rose 3. longitude line 4. scale bar 5. city 6. capital

- Have these physical features changed? If so, how, and what keeps people in this place today? *(Answers will vary but should acknowledge known changes in the area and changes in the community, such as loss or gain of industry or farming or new building developments.)*

- If you were to move, where would you choose to go? What physical or human features would draw you to a new place? *(Answers will vary but students should have a clear understanding of physical and human features and should give a clear description of those features and explain why they would be attractive.)*

ACTIVITIES ANSWERS

Exploring the Essential Question

❶ **INFORMATIVE/EXPLANATORY WRITING** Posters should clearly address the topics of homes, foods, and activities of early Native American peoples and how their activities were related to the geography of their land.

21st Century Skills

❷ **ANALYZING** Students should choose relevant and accurate effects on the lives of the people affected by the changes of one major geographic event in the last century and should write a clear essay of the causes and effects.

REVIEW THE GUIDING QUESTIONS

Directions: Choose the best answer for each question.

1 Children think spatially when they use
   A. snap-together blocks.
   B. crayons.
   C. dress-up clothes.
   D. books.

2 When the appearance of a tree changes from season to season, it is showing that nature is
   F. static.
   G. spatial.
   H. dynamic.
   I. steady.

3 What is an address such as 414 West Third Street giving?
   A. longitude
   B. latitude
   C. absolute location
   D. relative location

4 On a map, which element tells direction?
   F. compass rose
   G. scale bar
   H. relief
   I. the dotted lines

5 A relief map shows differences in
   A. direction.
   B. elevation.
   C. theme.
   D. scale.

6 The Global Positioning System was originally created by
   F. a small committee of mapmaking companies.
   G. the Russians.
   H. a for-profit private business.
   I. the U.S. government.

Chapter 1 **37**

Thinking Like a Geographer

3 **IDENTIFYING** Students should describe their location, place, region, human-environment interactions, and movement that define their area in a graphic organizer that contains each of the five headings.

Geography Activity

4 **READING MAPS**

1. B
2. D
3. A
4. F
5. E
6. C

ASSESSMENT ANSWERS

Review the Guiding Questions

1 **A** Children think spatially when they use snap-together blocks. Make sure students understand that children's use of crayons, dress-up clothes, and books are not activities that involve construction of three-dimensional shapes as the use of snap-together blocks is. Have students who answer incorrectly review, "The World in Spatial Terms," in Lesson 1.

2 **H** A tree changing from season to season is showing that nature is dynamic. Explain that answers F and I, static and steady, would be unchanging and the opposite of the correct answer. Students who answer G spatial should understand that a tree takes up space in every season.

3 **C** An address such as 414 West Third Street is giving absolute location because it is the exact location. Review with students that absolute location can also be given using lines of latitude and longitude. Have students who answer incorrectly review, "Geography's Five Themes," in Lesson 1.

4 **F** The compass rose on a map tells direction. The scale bar is used to calculate distance. The relief on a map is used to understand the difference in elevation of areas on a map. Students should know that dotted lines can be used to show different things on a map and they would use the map key to see what they stand for on a specific map. Have students who answer incorrectly review, "Parts of a Map," in Lesson 2.

5 **B** A relief map shows differences in elevation, such as on a physical map. Explain that all maps show direction and include scale. Maps other than general-purpose maps have a theme. Have students who answer incorrectly review, "Types of Maps," in Lesson 2.

6 **I** The Global Positioning System was originally created by the United States government to be used by the United States armed forces, but now parts of it can be used by ordinary people throughout the world. It involves more than 30 satellites, which a small committee of mapmaking companies or one for-profit private business could not maintain. Have students who answer incorrectly review, "Global Positioning Systems," in Lesson 2.

DBQ Analyzing Documents

7 **B** A geographic realm involves the interaction of cultural and physical properties. Have students who answer incorrectly reread the passage focusing on the second sentence. Point out the word *combination* and have students identify the two things that are combined in a geographic realm, so that they can see why B is the correct answer.

8 **I** One example of a geographic realm is South America. For students who answer incorrectly, explain that growing oranges in Florida is an activity done in a geographic location, a river is a physical feature of a geographic region, and going to school for 12 years is a cultural characteristic of a region.

Short Response

9 Construction companies and related industries most likely would see an increase in business as people repair and rebuild areas damaged by the disaster. Other areas might send workers and supplies to the area impacted by the disaster, which would put more people to work, at least temporarily. However, some businesses that had their buildings and supplies destroyed by the disaster may choose not to rebuild and may leave the area.

10 Students should select a natural event and provide a thoughtful explanation of what steps relief workers should take. Students should note that saving lives and providing medical care is more important than securing property. People who are not injured still need immediate help for food, water, and shelter.

Extended Response

11 Students should select a product and describe its production, beginning with the raw materials. They should point out that when they buy products that are made closer to home, much less energy is needed to ship the product, thus saving costs and resources.

DBQ ANALYZING DOCUMENTS

7 **CITING TEXT EVIDENCE** In the excerpt below, two geographers discuss the content of their geography book.

"*In this book we. . . investigate the world's great geographic realms [areas]. We will find that each of these realms possesses a special combination of cultural . . . and environmental properties [characteristics].*"

—from H.J. de Blij and Peter O. Muller, *Geography*

A geographic realm

A. includes only physical land characteristics.

B. involves the interaction of cultural and physical properties.

C. divides land/water into two categories.

D. makes geographic changes unlikely.

8 **DETERMINING WORD MEANINGS** What is one example of a geographic realm?

F. growing oranges in Florida

G. a river

H. going to school for 12 years

I. South America

SHORT RESPONSE

"*Hurricanes, wildfires, floods, earthquakes, and other natural events affect the Nation's economy, . . . property, and lives. . . . The USGS gathers and disseminates [gives out] real-time hazard data to relief workers, conducts long-term monitoring and forecasting to help minimize the impacts of future events, and evaluates conditions in the aftermath of disasters.*"

—from United States Geological Service, *The National Map—Hazards and Disasters*

9 **ANALYZING** After a natural disaster, some businesses may flourish, while others are destroyed. Explain.

10 **DESCRIBING** Select one type of natural event, and imagine that your community has just suffered from such an occurrence. What steps need to be taken right away, and who should be in charge?

EXTENDED RESPONSE

Write your answer on a separate piece of paper.

11 **INFORMATIVE/EXPLANATORY WRITING** Select a product such as an apple or toothpaste. Trace the path of this product from its start as raw materials through production and shipping until it appears on a store shelf. Explore the concept of buying locally, and explain what advantages it offers.

Need Extra Help?

If You've Missed Question	❶	❷	❸	❹	❺	❻	❼	❽	❾	❿	⓫
Review Lesson	1	1	1	2	2	2	1	1	1	1	1

GEOGRAPHY: REALMS, REGIONS, AND CONCEPTS, Twelfth Edition, by H. J. de Blij and Peter O. Muller. Published by John Wiley & Sons, Inc.; From "THE NATIONAL MAP—HAZARDS AND DISASTERS." National Geospatial Program Office, Fact Sheet 2009-3010. U.S. Geological Survey, Department of the Interior/USGS. The USGS home page is http://www.usgs.gov.

networks *Online Teaching Options*

Evaluation and Assessment

Assessing Use eAssessment to create your own tests from hundreds of available questions. eAssessment helps you design assessments that meet the needs of different types of learners.

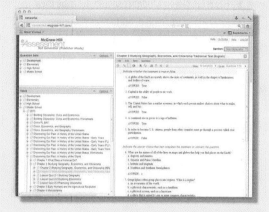

Earth's Physical Geography Planner

UNDERSTANDING BY DESIGN®

Enduring Understandings
- *People, places, and ideas change over time.*

Essential Questions
- *How does geography influence the way people live?*

Predictable Misunderstandings
- *Earth is a solid planet.*
- *The planets in the solar system are all like Earth.*
- *Humans have very little effect on the environment.*
- *The ocean floor is flat.*

Assessment Evidence
Performance Tasks:
- *Project-Based Learning Digital Hands-On Chapter Project*
- *Project-Based Learning Hands-On Chapter Project*

Other Evidence:
- *Geography Skills Activity*
- *Unit GeoLab Activity*
- *Geography and History Activity*
- *Participation in Project-Based Learning Activities*
- *Participation in Interactive Whiteboard Activities*
- *Contribution to small-group activities*
- *Interpretation of slide show images and special purpose maps*
- *Participation in class discussions about physical geography topics*
- *Lesson Reviews*
- *Chapter Assessments*

Indiana Academic Standards

Students will:

6.3.3 Describe and compare major physical characteristics of regions in Europe and the Americas.

6.3.5 Give examples and describe the formation of important river deltas, mountains and bodies of water in Europe and the Americas.

6.3.6 Explain how ocean currents and winds influence climate differences on Europe and the Americas.

6.3.7 Locate and describe the climate regions of Europe and the Americas and explain how and why they differ.

6.3.8 Identify major biomes of Europe and the Americas and explain how these are influenced by climate.

6.3.12 Compare the distribution and evaluate the importance of natural resources such as natural gas, oil, forests, uranium, minerals, coal, seafood and water in Europe and the Americas.

6.3.13 Explain the impact of humans on the physical environment in Europe and the Americas.

6.4.7 Identify economic connections between the local community and the countries of Europe or the Americas and identify job skills needed to be successful in the workplace.

SUGGESTED PACING GUIDE

Introducing the Chapter . . . . .2 Days	Lesson 3 . . . . .2 Days
Lesson 1 . . . . .2 Days	Chapter Wrap-Up and Assessment . . . . . .2 Days
Lesson 2 . . . . .2 Days	

TOTAL TIME   10 Days

Key for Using the Teacher Edition

SKILL-BASED ACTIVITIES

Types of skill activities found in the Teacher Edition.

V Visual Skills require students to analyze maps, graphs, charts, and photos.

W Writing Skills provide writing opportunities to help students comprehend the text.

R Reading Skills help students practice reading skills and master vocabulary.

C Critical Thinking Skills help students apply and extend what they have learned.

T Technology Skills require students to use digital tools effectively.

*Letters are followed by a number when there is more than one of the same type of skill on the page.

DIFFERENTIATED INSTRUCTION

All activities are written for the on-level student unless otherwise marked with the leveled labels below.

BL Beyond Level
AL Approaching Level
ELL English Language Learners

All students benefit from activities that utilize different learning styles. Many activities are marked as below when a particular learning style is highlighted.

Intrapersonal	Naturalist
Logical/Mathematical	Kinesthetic
Visual/Spatial	Auditory/Musical
Verbal/Linguistic	Interpersonal

CHAPTER OPENER PLANNER

Students will know:
- *Earth is a planet in the solar system.*
- *Earth undergoes constant change and movement.*

Students will be able to:
- ***identify*** *places with volcanoes and earthquakes and how these relate to plate tectonics using a map.*
- ***analyze*** *a time line to discuss volcanic eruptions and earthquakes that have occurred throughout history.*

UNDERSTANDING
BY DESIGN®

☑ *Print Teaching Options*

V **Visual Skills**

☐ **P. 40** Students learn about Earth's tectonic plates and use a map to identify plate boundaries and the occurrence of earthquakes and volcanoes along plate boundaries. **AL**

☐ **P. 41** Students use a time line along with the map to answer questions about significant natural disasters in the history of the world. **AL**

☑ *Online Teaching Options*

☐ **MAP** **Reading a Map**—Students identify aspects and locations of the region on a map.

☐ **TIME LINE** **Reading a Time Line and Map**—Students use a time line and a map to learn about where historical events occurred in the world. **Visual/Spatial**

☐ **MAP** **Interactive World Atlas**—Students use the interactive world atlas to identify the region and describe its terrain.

☑ *Printable Digital Worksheets*

☐ **WORKSHEET** **Geography Skills: Reading a Thematic Map**—Students use the worksheet to practice and apply the skills of reading a thematic map on wind currents.

☐ **WORKSHEET** **GeoLab: Desalinization of Water**—Students use the worksheet to analyze how much easily accessible water is on the planet.

☐ **WORKSHEET** **Geography and History: Global Warming Debate**—Students can use the worksheet to review main ideas and key concepts of the global warming debate.

Project-Based Learning

Hands-On

Create Maps
Students will work in groups to create large wall maps of the Earth and symbols that represent Earth's physical forces: volcanoes, hurricanes, cyclones, earthquakes, tsunamis, droughts, and tornadoes. Have students ask fact-based questions about these forces and where they have taken place in the past or recently. Once a student answers the question correctly, he or she can post the cut-out symbol where this event occurred on the map.

Digital Hands-On

Create Online Interactive Maps
Students will work in pairs and use an online map-making program to create a map that shows different physical features of the Earth and the absolute locations of the physical features with an embedded photo or video about them. Students may also write short descriptions about the physical features and embed them in the map. Once completed, students will present their maps to the class and then post them on a class web site or wiki.

Print Resources

ANCILLARY RESOURCES
These ancillaries are available for every chapter and lesson

- **Reading Essentials and Study Guide Workbook** **AL** **ELL**
- **Chapter Tests and Lesson Quizzes Blackline Masters**

PRINTABLE DIGITAL WORKSHEETS
These printable digital worksheets are available for every chapter and lesson.

- **Hands-On Chapter Projects**
- **What Do You Know? Activities**
- **Chapter Summaries (English and Spanish)**
- **Vocabulary Builder Activities**
- **Quizzes and Tests**
- **Reading Essentials and Study Guide (English and Spanish)** **AL** **ELL**
- **Guided Reading Activities**

More Media Resources

SUGGESTED VIDEOS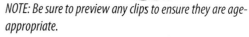
NOTE: Be sure to preview any clips to ensure they are age-appropriate.

- **Twister** (113 min.)
- **Faces of Earth** (180 min.)
- **Violent Earth** (52 min.)

SUGGESTED READING

- ***One Well: The Story of Water on Earth,*** by Rochelle Strauss **AL**
- ***Forces of Nature,*** by Catherine O'Neill Grace
- ***A Child's Introduction to the World: Geography, Cultures, and People—From the Grand Canyon to the Great Wall of China,*** by Heather Alexander
- ***Paths to Peace: People Who Changed the World,*** by Jane Brekin Zalben **BL**

EARTH AND THE SUN

Students will know:
- *Earth is a planet in the solar system.*
- *The aspects of life that occur on Earth happen because of Earth's position to the sun, its axis, its rotation, and its revolution.*
- *Earth is made up of layers.*
- *Earth has a variety of climates that help to sustain its wide variety of species.*

Students will be able to:
- *identify the parts of the solar system.*
- *describe how Earth's orbit causes the seasons.*
- *explain what factors determine the climate of an area.*
- *describe Earth's six major climate zones.*

UNDERSTANDING BY DESIGN®

✓ *Print Teaching Options*

V Visual Skills

- [ ] **P. 42** Students draw a map of the solar system. AL ELL
- [ ] **P. 43** Students diagram Earth's layers and composition.
- [ ] **P. 44** Students draw symbols for four physical systems. AL ELL
- [ ] **P. 45** Students simulate the tilted Earth as it orbits.
- [ ] **P. 46** Students use a world map to explain climate zones.
- [ ] **P. 47** Students analyze a wind patterns map. AL

W Writing Skills

- [ ] **P. 44** Students write a paragraph describing how a drop of water moves through Earth's four physical systems.
- [ ] **P. 48** Students distinguish weather from climate.

R Reading Skills

- [ ] **P. 44** Students use context clues to find meaning. ELL
- [ ] **P. 45** Students use word parts to find meaning. AL ELL
- [ ] **P. 48** Students summarize text on ocean currents.
- [ ] **P. 51** Students summarize information about how human activities affect weather and climate.

C Critical Thinking Skills

- [ ] **P. 42** Students recognize the relationship of the sun to Earth and its importance as the source of all energy. BL
- [ ] **P. 43** Students draw conclusions about Earth's layers.
- [ ] **P. 44** Students synthesize Earth's four physical systems and explain how they are interdependent.
- [ ] **P. 49** Students apply their understanding of the rain shadow effect to the Essential Question. AL
- [ ] **P. 50** Students distinguish climate zones and biomes. BL

T Technology Skills

- [ ] **P. 46** Students make predictions about the climate and use the Internet to check their predictions.
- [ ] **P. 47** Students use calculators to apply information about elevation and climate to a specific situation.

✓ *Online Teaching Options*

V Visual Skills

- **ANIMATION Earth's Daily Rotation**—Students dramatize the daily rotation of Earth after watching the animation. AL ELL Kinesthetic
- **DIAGRAM The Solar System**—Students analyze Earth's position in the solar system.
- **ANIMATION Earth's Layers**—Students label their drawings of Earth's layers after watching the animation. Verbal/Linguistic
- **MAP World Climates**—Students describe the climate of the local region. Verbal/Linguistic
- **MAP Wind and Currents**—Students use map to study effects of ocean currents on climate.

R Reading Skills

- **CHART Temperature and Precipitation Affect Biomes**—Students use the chart to discuss how climate and elevation affect the environment. Interpersonal
- **CHART Climate Zones**—Students identify their climate zone and the zones of other places.
- **GAME Drag-and-Drop: Earth's Physical Systems**—Students can use the game to review.
- **GAME Drag-and-Drop: Climate Terms**—Students can use the game to review the lesson.

C Critical Thinking Skills

- **VIDEO How Mountains Form**—Students watch a video about planet Earth and analyze the images and main ideas. Interpersonal
- **ANIMATION Seasons on Earth**—After watching the animation, students name the season for different countries in different hemispheres at different times of the year. Visual/Spatial
- **SLIDE SHOW Effects of Climate Change**—Students use the slide show to determine causes and effects of climate change and consider possible solutions. Verbal/Linguistic

T Technology Skills

- **DIAGRAM Rain Shadow**—After viewing the diagram, students apply the information to various areas of the United States. Logical/Mathematical
- **MAP Types of Climate**—Students use an animated map to review the various climate types.
- **ONLINE SELF-CHECK QUIZ Lesson 1**—Students receive instant feedback on their mastery of lesson content.

✓ *Printable Digital Worksheets*

W Writing Skills

- **WORKSHEET Geography and History: The Global Warming Debate**—Students can use the worksheet to review main ideas and key concepts of the global warming debate.

FORCES OF CHANGE

Students will know:
- *Earth is made up of layers.*
- *Earth undergoes constant change and movement.*

Students will be able to:
- **describe** *the evidence that tells scientists that Earth's core is solid.*
- **analyze** *how the Ring of Fire got its name.*
- **identify** *evidence that plants cause weathering and erosion.*
- **cite text evidence** *of how human actions change Earth.*

UNDERSTANDING
BY DESIGN®

☑ *Print Teaching Options*

V Visual Skills

☐ **P. 52** Students use a world map to speculate on how the continents may have once fit together.

☐ **P. 53** Students create a chart to summarize information on plate movements.

☐ **P. 53** Students explain the effects of a force below Earth's surface using photographs.

☐ **P. 54** Students analyze a map showing the Ring of Fire and make connections to its effects on states in the United States. BL

W Writing Skills

☐ **P. 55** Students note the eroded landforms in this country's national parks and write an argument for creating additional national parks. BL

☐ **P. 57** Students write a description of how the state's landscape has been altered by people and how much of it remains in a natural state.

R Reading Skills

☐ **P. 54** Students create vocabulary cards for content vocabulary words. AL

☐ **P. 56** Students determine central ideas about the effect of water and ice on landforms. BL

☐ **P. 57** Students list ways humans have changed the environment on Earth.

C Critical Thinking Skills

☐ **P. 55** Students compare and contrast the related processes of weathering and erosion.

T Technology Skills

☐ **P. 52** Students use the Internet to conduct research on the classification of continents.

☑ *Online Teaching Options*

V Visual Skills

☐ **VIDEO** **Water Eroding Mountains**—Students watch a video about the forces that shape Earth's surface and analyze the images and main ideas. Interpersonal

☐ **VIDEOS** **Earth's Forces: Old Faithful and Icelandic Volcano**—Students watch the videos about how landforms shape the life of people in the region, and analyze how landforms in the local region affect people. Verbal/Linguistic

☐ **MAP** **Risk of Earthquakes in the United States**—Students analyze the map to discuss the risk of earthquakes to the United States.

C Critical Thinking Skills

☐ **SLIDE SHOW** **Architecture for Earthquakes**—Students use the slide show to interpret how people have adapted to living with natural disasters. Verbal/Linguistic

☐ **VIDEO** **Erosion in Bryce Canyon**—Students watch a video about erosion and integrate what they learned in the video to landforms that have been eroded in their state or region. Visual

☐ **SLIDE SHOW** **Human Impact on Earth**—Students use the slide show to interpret how people have affected Earth's surface by building canals, dams, levees, roads, and cities. Naturalist

T Technology Skills

☐ **ONLINE SELF-CHECK QUIZ** **Lesson 2**—Students receive instant feedback on their mastery of lesson content.

LANDFORMS AND BODIES OF WATER

Students will know:
- the land of Earth has a wide variety of features.
- the ocean floor of Earth has a wide variety of features.

Students will be able to:
- **give examples** of landforms in their state.
- **describe** how the ocean floor is similar to the surface of dry land.
- **identify** bodies of water as either freshwater or salt water.
- **explain** the water cycle in their own words.

UNDERSTANDING
BY DESIGN®

✓ Print Teaching Options

V Visual Skills

☐ **P. 58** Students draw a landscape with landforms. ELL

☐ **P. 59** Students use a physical map to identify landforms and bodies of water.

☐ **P. 60** Students use a diagram of freshwater and saltwater facts to answer questions and draw conclusions.

☐ **P. 62** Students create word webs to summarize information on bodies of water. AL ELL

☐ **P. 63** Students make a flow chart of the water cycle. ELL

☐ **P. 64** Students analyze a diagram of the water cycle. AL

W Writing Skills

☐ **P. 60** Students conduct research and write an informative report on life in the deepest, darkest places in the ocean.

☐ **P. 62** Students write a narrative about people's use of water and what is happening in one of two photos.

R Reading Skills

☐ **P. 58** Students use a map to identify elevation. AL

☐ **P. 64** Students use context clues to determine meanings of academic vocabulary. BL

C Critical Thinking Skills

☐ **P. 60** Students make connections to prior experiences to discuss coastlines and continental shelves.

☐ **P. 61** Students identify problems with the amount of liquid freshwater that is safe for people to drink. AL

☐ **P. 61** Students make connections to a boy pumping water from a well and identify where the water comes from.

☐ **P. 63** Students connect the changes of state of water to the preparation of a meal.

☐ **P. 64** Students synthesize what they have learned about the water cycle to make a flow chart. AL ELL

T Technology Skills

☐ **P. 59** Students conduct Internet research to determine if Central America belongs to North or South America. BL

☐ **P. 65** Students choose a problem with Earth's water to research and present to the class.

✓ Online Teaching Options

V Visual Skills

☐ **VIDEO** **Changing World—Wild Weather**—Students use the video to create a graphic organizer to analyze the content of the video. Visual/Spatial

☐ **MAP** **Physical Geography of Earth**—Using the map, students identify and describe landforms and waterways of Earth. BL Visual/Spatial

☐ **IMAGE** **Ocean Floor**—Students use the interactive image to describe and discuss the geography of the ocean floor and compare it to the geography of land.

☐ **GRAPHIC ORGANIZER** **Water: Recreation vs. Livelihood**—Using the graphic organizer, students identify the ways water is used for recreation and for making a living. Naturalist

☐ **MAP** **Population of Earth**—Students use this map to discuss the distribution, density, and location of population on Earth. Visual/Spatial

W Writing Skills

☐ **IMAGE** **Garbage**—Using the interactive image to introduce the topic, students write a paragraph that discusses their weekly collection of garbage in their household and how much could be reused or recycled.

R Reading Skills

☐ **LECTURE SLIDE** **Desalinization Process**—Using the lecture slide, review the content of this process with students for understanding.

C Critical Thinking Skills

☐ **INFOGRAPHIC** **Fresh and Salt Water in the World**—Students use the infographic to identify the amounts of fresh and salt water readily available. BL Visual/Spatial

T Technology Skills

☐ **ANIMATION** **How the Water Cycle Works**—Using the animation, students analyze how water sources are replenished and how water moves around the planet. Visual, Naturalist

☐ **ONLINE SELF-CHECK QUIZ** **Lesson 3**—Students receive instant feedback on their mastery of lesson content.

✓ Printable Digital Worksheets

W Writing Skills

☐ **WORKSHEET** **GeoLab: Desalinization of Water**—Students use the worksheet to analyze how much easily accessible water is on the planet. Logical/Mathematical

☐ **WORKSHEET** **Geography Skills: Reading a Thematic Map**—Students use the worksheet to practice and apply the skills of reading a thematic map on wind currents.

INTERVENTION AND REMEDIATION STRATEGIES

LESSON 1 Earth and the Sun

Reading and Comprehension

Organize students into small groups. Assign four different content vocabulary words to each group. Have students in each group work together to write a paragraph, using the four terms they have been assigned.

After groups have completed their paragraphs, ask a volunteer from each group to read the paragraph. Provide guidance as needed, ensuring that students have used each term correctly.

Text Evidence

Have students review the lesson and use the headings and subheadings to create an outline of the lesson. Have students write key words and phrases in their notebooks to remind them about important content under each heading and subheading. Then have students quiz a partner, using the words and phrases from their notebook.

LESSON 2 Forces of Change

Reading and Comprehension

To ensure comprehension of the internal and external forces explained in this lesson, have students take turns acting as the teacher. Assign a key concept, place, or vocabulary word from the lesson for students to explain to the rest of the class.

Have students make a brief presentation to "teach" the topic or term to the rest of the class. Tell students they may use the board to draw diagrams or charts to better explain their assigned concept.

Text Evidence

Organize students into small groups. Tell students they will research a real-life event from one of the following categories: slow change, sudden change, natural force, or human action. Either assign or have students choose the event, ensuring that each group has a different event. Have groups present a summary of their findings to the class, citing textual evidence that supports their research.

LESSON 3 Landforms and Bodies of Water

Reading and Comprehension

Organize students into small groups. Have groups outline key facts and processes related to one of the following topics: surface features on land, the ocean floor, types of water, and the water cycle.

To ensure comprehension of the topics, conduct a question/answer session in which students from each group answer questions about their topic.

Text Evidence

Have students create clues for a "Jeopardy" style game. Have a group of "contestants" provide the correct "question" for each clue. For example, one group might write the clue "a long, narrow cut in the ground that is more than 35,000 feet steep in some places," while the other group writes the question/answer ("What is the Mariana Trench?"). Have groups take turns playing the game.

Online Resources

Level Reader

Use this online lower-level text that corresponds directly to the text in the online Student Edition.

Guided Reading Activities

This resource uses graphic organizers and guiding questions to help students with comprehension.

What Do You Know?

Use these worksheets to pre-assess students' background knowledge before they study the chapter.

Reading Essentials and Study Guide Workbook

This resource offers writing and reading activities for the approaching-level student.

Self-Check Quizzes

This online assessment tool provides instant feedback for students to check their progress.

EARTH'S PHYSICAL GEOGRAPHY

ESSENTIAL QUESTION · *How does geography influence the way people live?*

Carsten Peter/National Geographic/Getty Images

A geologist prepares to enter the crater of Ambrim Island volcano.

Lesson 1
Earth and the Sun

Lesson 2
Forces of Change

Lesson 3
Landforms and Bodies of Water

The Story Matters...

Earth is part of a larger physical system called the solar system. Earth's position in the solar system makes life on our planet possible. The planet Earth has air, land, and water, which make it suitable for plant, animal, and human life. Major natural forces inside and outside of our planet shape its surface. Some of these forces can move suddenly and violently, such as earthquakes and volcanos, causing disasters that can dramatically affect life on Earth.

FOLDABLES
Study Organizer

Go to the Foldables® library in the back of your book to make a Foldable® that will help you take notes while reading this chapter.

39

ENGAGE

Bellringer Setting a time limit of 30 seconds, ask students to think about and jot down major natural forces on Earth that affect their lives. Students might name such forces as gravity, solar radiation, earthquakes, and volcanic eruptions. Call on volunteers to share their lists. Then have students read "The Story Matters..." and identify the natural forces that are implied in the last sentence (*volcanic eruptions and earthquakes*). Tell students that they will be learning more about the natural forces that shape Earth's geography and influence how people live on the planet.

Making Connections Read the following information to students to help them appreciate the uniqueness of Earth's environment within the solar system.

Earth is the only planet in the solar system known to sustain life. It is the third planet from the sun, after Mercury and Venus. The fourth planet is Mars. These four planets are called terrestrial (or land) planets because they have rocky, rather than gaseous, surfaces. The atmospheres of the four planets differ greatly, however.

- Mercury, the planet closest to the sun, has very little atmosphere and extreme temperatures. The side of Mercury that faces the sun gets scorched, while the side away from the sun freezes.
- Venus has a thick, toxic atmosphere, consisting mostly of carbon dioxide plus some poisonous gases. Temperatures on Venus are hot enough to melt lead.
- Earth's atmosphere consists mostly of nitrogen and oxygen. Unique among the planets, Earth contains an abundance of liquid water—and comparatively moderate temperatures.
- Mars has a very thin atmosphere of carbon dioxide. The planet has polar ice caps, but its thin atmosphere and cold temperatures keep the water from becoming liquid. Mars may have had liquid water in the past, as evidenced by signs of ancient floods on its surface.

FOLDABLES
Study Organizer

Go to the Foldables® library for a chapter-based Foldable® activity that your students can use to help take notes and prepare for assessment.

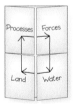

Letter from the Author

Dear Geography Teacher,

The first step in understanding Earth's physical geography is to have a firm understanding of the effects of the Earth-sun relationship. Be sure your students recognize how revolution and rotation affect our climate, wind and ocean currents, length of days, and seasons. In addition, knowledge about physical geography includes an understanding of *insolation*, or how much of the sun's heat and energy reach various parts of the world in the Tropics, mid-latitudes, and polar regions.

Richard H. Boehm

TEACH & ASSESS

Step Into the Place

V Visual Skills

Reading a Map Explain to students that the top layer, or crust, of Earth consists of huge, moving slabs of rock called *tectonic plates*. Over millions of years, the movement of these plates has helped shape the surface of Earth.

These tectonic plates sit on the next layer of Earth, the mantle, which is a layer of hot rock that can be moved, shaped, and melted. This melted rock in the mantle layer can flow to the surface of Earth through cracks in the tectonic plate boundaries. When it flows out through a volcano, this melted rock is called lava. The movement of the mantle and the tectonic plates also can cause earthquakes.

As the map shows, these earthquakes and volcanic eruptions often occur near the boundaries between tectonic plates. These processes will be described more fully in Lesson 2; however, invite students who have had any experiences with earthquakes or volcanic eruptions, such as visiting Hawaii's continually erupting volcanoes, to share their experiences with the class.

Have students examine the map and identify the seven continents. **Ask:**

- What is the symbol on the map for earthquakes? *(yellow circle)*
- Which two states in the United States have had the most earthquakes? *(Alaska and California)*
- What is the symbol on the map for volcanoes? *(red triangle)*
- Where are most of Earth's tectonic plate boundaries located? *(most boundaries are in the oceans and near the edges of continents)*

Then have students answer the Step into the Place questions.

AL Visual/Spatial

ANSWERS, p. 40

STEP INTO THE PLACE
1. near plate boundaries around the Pacific Ocean
2. one
3. The plate underneath the Pacific Ocean borders other plates. Movement of the plates causes numerous volcanoes, thus the name the Ring of Fire.

PHYSICAL GEOGRAPHY

Tectonic Plate Boundaries

ARCTIC OCEAN

ASIA

PACIFIC OCEAN

INDIAN OCEAN

AUSTRALIA

Continents sit on large bases called plates. As these plates move on top of Earth's fluid mantle, the continents move. Sometimes, the plates collide with each other or slide under each other, creating earthquakes or volcanoes.

Step Into the Place

MAP FOCUS Use the map to answer the following questions.

1 PHYSICAL GEOGRAPHY Where are most of the world's volcanoes located?

2 THE GEOGRAPHER'S WORLD How many plates are underneath Australia?

3 CRITICAL THINKING V
Integrating Visual Information Why do you think the edge of the Pacific Ocean is often called the Ring of Fire?

Step Into the Time

DRAWING EVIDENCE Choose one event from the time line and explain how the natural forces that shape the physical geography of a particular place can have a worldwide impact.

79 Mount Vesuvius erupts, burying people and animals under ash

1575 Earthquake brings flooding to central Chile

©Sean Sexton Collection/Corbis

Project-Based Learning ✋

Hands-On

Making a Map of Forces
Students will work in groups to create large wall maps of Earth. Then students will use construction paper to create symbols that represent Earth's physical forces: volcanoes, hurricanes, cyclones, earthquakes, tsunamis, droughts, and tornadoes. Have students ask fact-based questions about these forces and where they have taken place in the past or recently. Once a student answers the question correctly, he or she can post the cut-out symbol where this event occurred on the map.

Digital Hands-On

Making a Physical Features Map
Pairs will use an online map-making program to create a map of different physical features of Earth that includes the absolute locations of the features and an embedded photo, video, or description of them. Pairs will present their maps to the class and then post them on a class Web site or wiki.

edtechteacher
21st Century Learning

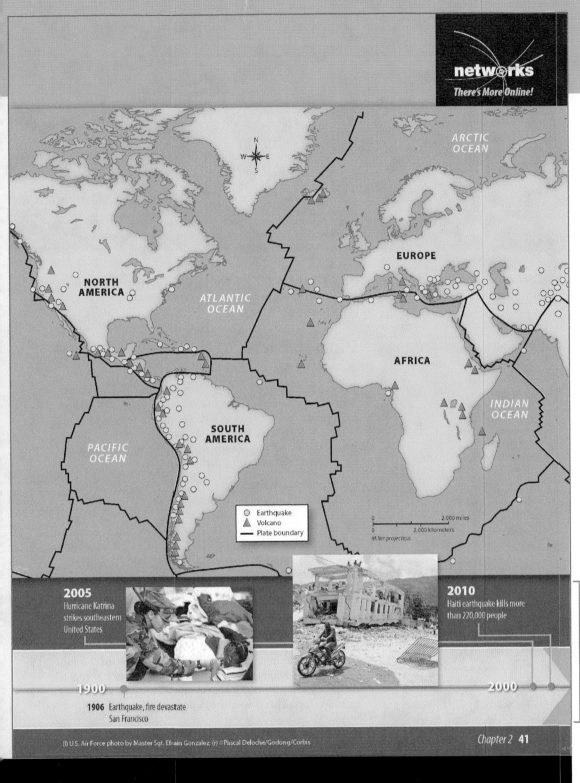

Earthquake ○
Volcano △
Plate boundary —

0   2,000 miles
0   2,000 kilometers
Miller projection

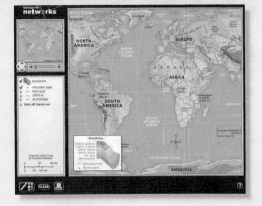

2005
Hurricane Katrina
strikes southeastern
United States

2010
Haiti earthquake kills more
than 220,000 people

1900   2000

1906 Earthquake, fire devastate
San Francisco

(l) U.S. Air Force photo by Master Sgt. Efrain Gonzalez; (r) ©Pascal Deloche/Godong/Corbis

Chapter 2 **41**

Step Into the Time

V Visual Skills

Integrating Visual Information Help students relate the time line to the map by discussing the following questions. **Ask:**

- How might the eruption of Mount Vesuvius in Italy be related to plate tectonics? (*Italy is located near a plate boundary where volcanic eruptions occur.*)
- Why is it not surprising that major earthquakes have occurred in Chile? (*Chile is near particularly active plate boundaries where many earthquakes and volcanic eruptions occur.*)
- Why might the location of San Francisco along the western coast of the United States make it vulnerable to earthquakes? (*A plate boundary runs along the western coast of the United States.*)
- What do you notice about the location of Haiti? (*It, too, is located near a plate boundary.*) **AL** Visual/Spatial

Content Background Knowledge

- Earth's crust has seven major plates which are subdivided into smaller plates.
- These plates are in continual motion, moving from 10 to 130 millimeters in a year.
- At their boundaries, the crustal plates either collide or pull apart.
- Plate tectonics explains why most earthquakes, volcanoes, and mountain ranges are located in narrow zones. These zones coincide with plate boundaries.

V

CLOSE & REFLECT

Predicting Consequences Have students find your community's location on the map and predict the likelihood of earthquakes and/or volcanic eruptions in your area. Discuss the kinds of natural forces that most affect your area and how students can stay safe during natural disasters.

TIME LINE

Reading a Time Line and Map

Analyzing Visuals Display the time line and map on the whiteboard. Have volunteers read each event as it is revealed on the time line. Ask students to identify where in the world the event took place and find its location on the map. Visual/Spatial

See page 39B for other online activities.

ENGAGE

Bellringer Introduce the lesson by having students skim the lesson headings in their book to preview the lesson content, which focuses on how Earth functions in the solar system, its structure, and its seasons and climates. Help students relate this content to the Essential Question: *How does geography influence the way people live?* Note that seasonal and climatic differences around the world greatly affect people's outdoor time and activities.

Have students suggest outdoor jobs that are impacted by the seasons in your area. Make a list of these on the board. Then make another list of recreational outdoor activites that are impacted by the seasons.

TEACH & ASSESS

V Visual Skills

Drawing In pairs have students find diagrams of the solar system to identify Earth's position within the system. Then have them each draw the solar system, labeling the the planets and their distance from the sun. Note that Earth is the third planet from the sun. **AL** **ELL** Visual/Spatial

C Critical Thinking Skills

Recognizing Relationships Emphasize the importance of the sun as the source of *all* the energy that plants and animals need to survive. **Ask:**

- How does the sun provide energy for plants? *(Plants absorb sunlight and convert it into food, from which they get energy.)*
- How does the sun provide energy for animals, including human beings? *(Animals depend on plants and other animals for food, from which they get energy. Since plants get their energy from the sun, animals that eat plants or other animals get their energy indirectly from the sun.)* **BL** Naturalist

---

ANSWERS, p. 42

Taking Notes Answers could include: **Hydrosphere**—all bodies of water; **Lithosphere**—Earth's crust, including land beneath oceans; **Atmosphere**—layer of gases above Earth's surface; **Biosphere**—all living organisms on or near Earth's surface.

---

networks

There's More Online!

- ☑ **CHART/GRAPH** Climate Zones
- ☑ **ANIMATION** Earth's Rotation
- ☑ **IMAGES** Rain Shadow
- ☑ **SLIDE SHOW** Effects of Climate Change
- ☑ **VIDEO**

Reading **HELP**DESK

Academic Vocabulary

- **accurate**

Content Vocabulary

- **orbit**
- **axis**
- **revolution**
- **atmosphere**
- **solstice**
- **equinox**
- **climate**
- **precipitation**
- **rain shadow**

TAKING NOTES: *Key Ideas and Details*

Summarize As you read, complete a graphic organizer about Earth's physical system.

Element	Description
Hydrosphere	
Lithosphere	
Atmosphere	
Biosphere	

Indiana Academic Standards
6.3.3, 6.3.6, 6.3.7, 6.3.8

42

Lesson 1

Earth and the Sun

ESSENTIAL QUESTION · *How does geography influence the way people live?*

IT MATTERS BECAUSE
The processes that change Earth can have sudden and lasting impacts on humans.

Planet Earth

GUIDING QUESTION *What is the structure of Earth?*

The sun is the center of the solar system. Earth is a member of the solar system—planets and the other bodies that revolve around our sun. The sun is just one of hundreds of millions of stars in our galaxy. Because the sun is so large, its gravity causes the planets to constantly **orbit**, or move around, it. Each planet follows its own path around the sun.

Earth and the Sun

Life on Earth could not exist without heat and light from the sun. Earth's orbit holds it close enough to the sun—about 93 million miles (150 million km)—to receive a constant supply of light and heat energy. The sun, in fact, is the source of all energy on Earth. Every plant and animal on the planet needs the sun's energy to survive. Without the sun, Earth would be a cold, dark, lifeless rock floating in space.

As Earth orbits the sun, it rotates, or spins, on its axis. The **axis** is an imaginary line that runs through Earth's center from the North Pole to the South Pole. Earth completes one rotation every 24 hours. As Earth rotates, different areas are in sunlight and in darkness. The part facing toward the sun experiences daylight, while the part facing away has night. Earth makes one **revolution**, or complete trip around the sun, in 365¼ days. This is what we define as one year. Every four

---

networks *Online Teaching Options*

VIDEO

How Mountains Form

Analyzing Images Use this video to introduce the idea that the Earth is made up of layers and plates and that those plates are constantly moving, changing the physical geography of the Earth. After watching the video, have pairs of students analyze the main ideas and write three questions they have about the content. Collect the questions and discuss them as a class. Interpersonal

See page 39C for other online activities.

BBC Motion Gallery Education

years, the extra fourths of a day are combined and added to the calendar as February 29th. A year that contains one of these extra days is called a leap year.

Inside Earth

Thousands of miles beneath your feet, Earth's heat has turned metal into liquid. You do not feel these forces, but what lies inside affects what lies on top. Mountains, deserts, and other landscapes were formed over time by forces acting below Earth's surface—and those forces are still changing the landscape.

If you cut an onion in half, you will see that it is made up of many layers. Earth is also made up of layers. An onion's layers are all made of onion, but Earth's layers are made up of many different materials.

V

Layers of Earth

The inside of Earth is made up of three layers: the core, the mantle, and the crust. The center of Earth—the core—is divided into a solid inner core and an outer core of melted, liquid metal. Surrounding the outer core is a thick layer of hot, dense rock called the mantle. Scientists calculate that the mantle is about 1,800 miles (2,897 km) thick. The mantle also has two parts. When volcanoes erupt, the glowing-hot lava that flows from the mouth of the volcano is magma from Earth's outer mantle. The inner mantle is solid, like the inner core. Magma is melted rock. The outer layer is the crust, a rocky shell forming the surface of Earth. The crust is thin, ranging from about 2 miles (3.2 km) thick under oceans to about 75 miles (121 km) thick under mountains.

C

DIAGRAM SKILLS ›

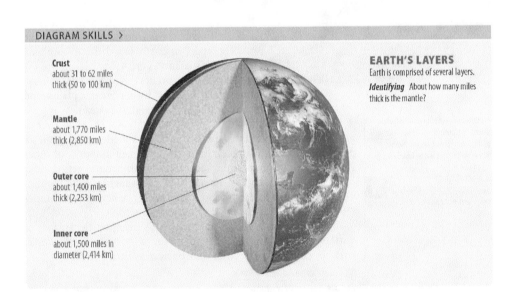

Crust
about 31 to 62 miles thick (50 to 100 km)

Mantle
about 1,770 miles thick (2,850 km)

Outer core
about 1,400 miles thick (2,253 km)

Inner core
about 1,500 miles in diameter (2,414 km)

EARTH'S LAYERS
Earth is comprised of several layers.

Identifying About how many miles thick is the mantle?

V Visual Skills

Diagramming Suggest that, as they read, students draw a diagram of Earth's layers, showing an inner core, an outer core, a thick mantle, and a thin crust. Have students label the layers and note their composition. (***Inner core***—*solid metal;* ***Outer core***—*liquid metal;* ***Mantle***—*hot, denser rock;* ***Crust***—*rock*) Encourage students to draw their diagrams large enough to add future notes on each of Earth's four layers as they continue to read. Visual/Spatial

C Critical Thinking Skills

Drawing Conclusions Note that Earth's outer core consists of melted rock and that the mantle also contains magma, or melted rock. **Ask:**

- What can you deduce about the temperature below Earth's crust? (*It is very hot—hot enough to melt rock.*)
- What happens to magma after it erupts on Earth's surface? (*It cools and solidifies.*)
- How does the new rock that cools on Earth's surface affect Earth's crust? (*It can build new islands in the ocean such as the Hawaiian Islands or build the height of the volcano it erupted from.*)
- What can you deduce about the temperature on Earth's surface as compared to the temperature deep within Earth? (*It is much cooler on Earth's surface than it is deep within Earth.*) Logical/Mathematical

Content Background Knowledge

Since Earth's interior cannot be observed directly, much of the information about its structure comes from analyzing earthquake waves, from laboratory experiments on rocks and minerals, from studies of Earth's movement within the solar system, and from studies of gravity, magnetic fields, and heat flow. Scientists are continually adding to and refining their knowledge of Earth's structure as new technologies make new data available.

ANIMATION

Earth's Daily Rotation

Making Connections After students view the animation, ask a pair of volunteers to dramatize the daily rotation of Earth, using two balls or other round objects to represent the sun and Earth. Mark a large dot on "Earth," and have students identify when it is day and when it is night at that spot. **AL ELL** Kinesthetic

See page 39C for other online activities.

ANSWER, p. 43

Identifying about 1,800 miles (2,897 km)

R Reading Skills

Using Context Clues Have students read the sentence in which the vocabulary word *accurate* appears, as well as the sentences before and after it. **Ask:**

- Based on the way the word is used, what does *accurate* mean? *(correct, true)*
- Can you use the word in another sentence? *(Sample answer: My watch does not keep accurate time.)* **ELL** Verbal/Linguistic

V Visual Skills

Drawing Have students draw symbols to represent the four physical systems. For example, students might draw a drop of water for hydrosphere, a wavy line for atmosphere, a rock for lithosphere, and a leaf for biosphere. Have volunteers share their symbols and explain why each symbol is appropriate for the physical system it represents. **AL ELL** Visual/Spatial

C Critical Thinking Skills

Synthesizing Explain that the four physical systems are useful concepts for studying and thinking about Earth, but that these four systems are interdependent, not separate. Give students a few minutes to jot down all the interconnections they can think of. Students might note, for example, that the atmosphere contains water vapor, soil contains water, people breathe in air from the atmosphere, and so on. While this activity is appropriate for all levels of students, you might expect advanced students to generate more examples. Logical/Mathematical

W Writing Skills

Informative/Explanatory Have students write a paragraph in which they trace a drop of water as it moves through the hydrosphere, atmosphere, lithosphere, and biosphere. Have students who are struggling work together to draw a diagram that shows the movement of the drop of water through the four physical systems, and then write their paragraphs based on their drawing. Have pairs of students exchange their paragraphs and check the movement described against the diagram they have drawn. Encourage partners to make positive comments about each other's writing and to make constructive criticism if revision is needed. Verbal/Linguistic

---

Academic Vocabulary

accurate free from error R

The deepest hole ever drilled into Earth was about 8 miles (13 km) deep. That is still within Earth's crust. The farthest any human has traveled down into Earth's crust is about 2.5 miles (4 km). Still, scientists have developed an **accurate** picture of the layers in Earth's structure. One way that scientists do this is to study vibrations that take place deep within Earth. The vibrations are caused by earthquakes and explosions underground. From their observations, scientists have learned what materials are inside Earth and estimated the thickness and temperature of Earth's layers.

Earth's Physical Systems

Powerful processes operate below Earth's surface. Processes are also at work in the physical systems on the surface of Earth. Earth's physical systems consist of four major subsystems: V the hydrosphere, the lithosphere, the atmosphere, and the biosphere. C

About 71 percent of the earth's surface is water. The hydrosphere is the subsystem that consists of Earth's water. Water is found in the oceans, seas, lakes, ponds, rivers, ice, and groundwater. Only 3 percent of the Earth's water is freshwater.

About 29 percent of Earth's surface is land. Land makes up the part of Earth called the lithosphere. This is Earth's crust. Landforms are the shapes that occur on Earth's surface. They include mountains, hills, plateaus, plains, and ocean basins, the land beneath the ocean.

Earth is sometimes called the "water planet" because about 71 percent of it is covered with water. Almost 97 percent of this water, however, is salt water.
▶ CRITICAL THINKING
Analyzing What causes the cycle from day to night on Earth? W

The air we breathe is part of the **atmosphere**, the thin layer of gases that envelop Earth. The atmosphere is made up of about 78 percent nitrogen, 21 percent oxygen, and small amounts of other gases. The atmosphere is thickest at Earth's surface and gets thinner higher up. Ninety-eight percent of the atmosphere is found within 16 miles (26 km) of Earth's surface. Outer space begins at 100 miles (161 km) above Earth, where the atmosphere ends.

The biosphere is made up of all that is living on the surface of Earth, close to the surface, and in the atmosphere. All people, animals, and plants live in the biosphere.

✓ READING PROGRESS CHECK

Identifying Which of Earth's four major subsystems consists of water?

NASA/NOAA/GSFC/Suomi NPP/VIIRS/Norman Kuring

---

netw⚙rks *Online Teaching Options*

ANIMATION

Earth's Layers

Writing Captions After students view the animation, have them add new information they learned to their own drawings of Earth's layers. They might include this information in the form of a caption for each labeled layer of Earth. Verbal/Linguistic

See page 39C for other online activities.

Sun and Seasons

GUIDING QUESTION *How does Earth's orbit around the sun cause the seasons?*

Fruits such as strawberries, grapes, and bananas cannot grow in cold, icy weather. Yet grocery stores across America sell these ripe, colorful fruits all year, even in the middle of winter. Where in the world is it warm enough to grow fruit in January? To find the answer, we start with the tilt of Earth.

Earth is tilted 23.5 degrees on its axis. If you look at a globe that is attached to a stand, you will see what the tilt looks like. Because of the tilt, not all places on Earth receive the same amount of direct sunlight at the same time.

As Earth orbits the sun, it stays in its tilted position. This means that half of the planet is always tilted toward the sun, while the other half is tilted away. As a result, Earth's Northern and Southern Hemispheres experience seasons at different times.

On about June 21, the North Pole is tilted toward the sun. The Northern Hemisphere is receiving the direct rays of the sun. The sun appears directly overhead at the line of latitude called the Tropic of Cancer. This day is the summer **solstice**, or beginning of summer, in the Northern Hemisphere. It is the day of the year that has the most hours of sunlight during Earth's 24-hour rotation.

Six months later—about December 22—the North Pole is tilted away from the sun. The sun's direct rays strike the line of latitude known as the Tropic of Capricorn. This is the winter solstice—when winter occurs in the Northern Hemisphere and summer begins in the Southern Hemisphere. The days are short in the Northern Hemisphere but long in the Southern Hemisphere.

Midway between the two solstices, about September 23 and March 21, the rays of the sun are directly overhead at the Equator.

R

DIAGRAM SKILLS >

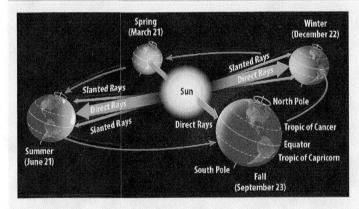

SEASONS
The tilt of Earth as it revolves around the sun causes the seasons to change.

▶ **CRITICAL THINKING**
Integrating Visual Information
When does the Northern Hemisphere receive direct rays from the sun?

V

Seasons on Earth

Applying Information Have students view the animation showing why the seasons differ in the Northern and Southern hemispheres. Then quiz students by naming a few countries in both hemispheres and on different continents, asking what season it is in each location. **Visual/Spatial**

See page 39C for other online activities.

R Reading Skills

Determining Word Meanings Explain to the students that the *solstices* and the *equinoxes* mark the beginnings of the seasons. The longest day of the year is the summer solstice, when summer begins. The shortest day of the year is the winter solstice, when winter begins. During a solstice, the sun is at its greatest distance from the celestial equator.

The equinoxes mark the beginning of spring and fall, when day and night are of equal length. During an equinox, the sun is directly above the celestial equator. You might point out the dates of the solstices and equinoxes on a calendar.

Finally, point out that the Latin root *sol-* in the word *solstice* means "sun," while the root *equi-* comes from a Latin word meaning "equal." **AL** **ELL** **Verbal/Linguistic**

V Visual Skills

Simulating Have students demonstrate the tilted position of Earth as it orbits the sun using a globe and a large ball to represent the sun. Have one student hold the sun, and another student hold the globe tilted at about a 25° angle. Then tell the student holding the sun to stay still while the student holding the globe revolves around the sun making sure that the tilt of the globe remains the same throughout the orbit. Encourage students to use the diagram at the bottom of the page as a guide to the simulation. **Ask:**

- **During summer, how is the Northern Hemisphere tilted?** *(toward the sun)*
- **What season is it in the Southern Hemisphere then? Why?** *(winter, because the Southern Hemisphere is tilted away from the sun)*
- **During winter, how is the Northern Hemisphere tilted?** *(away from the sun)*
- **What season is it in the Southern Hemisphere then? Why?** *(summer, because the Southern Hemisphere is tilted toward the sun)* **Kinesthetic**

ANSWER, p. 45

CRITICAL THINKING about June 21

Earth and the Sun

R Reading Skills

Defining The difference between the content vocabulary words *weather* and *climate* is discussed later in this section of the student textbook, but you might explain to students here that the word *climate* refers to the average weather in a particular area over a long period of time. For example, the weather in both Minneapolis, MN and Houston, TX might be cool and rainy on a particular day, but the two cities have very different climates. Houston is generally warm or hot all year round, while Minneapolis has long, cold winters and warm summers. **AL** **ELL** Verbal/Linguistic

V Visual Skills

Integrating Visual Information Use a world map or globe to show students the location of the Tropics. Emphasize that the Tropics receive direct sunlight year-round and so are always hot. Explain how *latitude*—distance north or south of the equator—affects climate. In general, as you move farther north or south of the tropics, the climate becomes progressively cooler.

To check students' understanding of how latitude affects climate, point to various locations on a world map or globe and ask students to predict features of the area's climate based on its latitude. Have students record their predictions and use them for the following activity. Visual/Spatial

T Technology Skills

Researching on the Internet Direct students to use the Internet to check their predictions about the climate of different areas based on latitude. Call on volunteers to share what their predictions were and what they discovered from their research. Have students speculate on why some of their predictions might have been inaccurate. Some students may be aware that elevation, proximity to the ocean, and other factors also influence climate. Logical/Mathematical

---

These are **equinoxes**, when day and night in both hemispheres are of equal length—12 hours of daylight and 12 hours of nighttime everywhere on Earth.

☑ **READING PROGRESS CHECK**

Identifying When it is winter in the Southern Hemisphere, what season is it in the Northern Hemisphere?

R Climate

GUIDING QUESTION *How do elevation, wind and ocean currents, weather, and landforms influence climate?*

V Low latitudes near the Equator receive the direct rays of the sun year-round. This area, known as the Tropics, lies mainly between the Tropic of Cancer and the Tropic of Capricorn. The Tropics circle the globe like a belt. If you lived in the Tropics, you would experience hot, sunny weather most of the year because of the direct sunlight.

T Outside the Tropics, the sun is never directly overhead. Even when these high-latitude areas are tilted toward the sun, the sun's rays hit Earth indirectly at a slant. This means that no sunlight at all shines on the high-latitude regions around the North and South Poles for as much as six months each year. Thus, climate in these regions is always cool or cold.

A farmer harvests pineapples in Costa Rica.
▶ **CRITICAL THINKING**
Analyzing How is climate affected by elevation?

46 Chapter 2

---

networks   *Online Teaching Options*

MAP

World Climates

Reading a Map Display the climate layer of the Chapter Opener map to introduce students briefly to the variety of climates around the world. Have students write a few sentences describing the climate of the region in which you live or a place they have visited. Verbal/Linguistic

See page 39C for other online activities.

ANSWERS, p. 46

☑ **READING PROGRESS CHECK** summer
CRITICAL THINKING Earth's atmosphere thins as altitude increases. Thinner air retains less heat. As elevation increases, temperatures decrease.

WIND PATTERNS

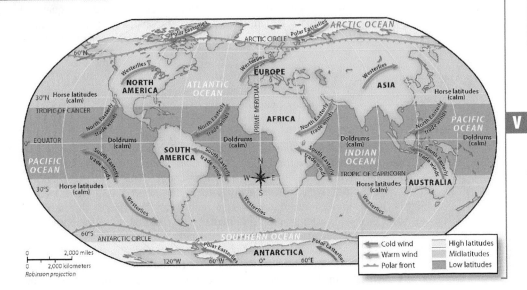

Cold wind
Warm wind
Polar front

High latitudes
Midlatitudes
Low latitudes

0 2,000 miles
0 2,000 kilometers
Robinson projection

Elevation and Climate

At all latitudes, elevation influences climate. This is because Earth's atmosphere thins as altitude increases. Thinner air retains less heat. As elevation increases, temperatures decrease by about 3.5°F (1.9°C) for every 1,000 feet (305 m). For example, if the temperature averages 70°F (21.1°C) at sea level, the average temperature at 5,000 feet (1,524 m) is only 53°F (11.7°C). A high elevation will be colder than lower elevations at the same latitude.

Wind and Ocean Currents

In addition to latitude and elevation, the movement of air and water helps create Earth's climates. Moving air and water help circulate the sun's heat around the globe.

Movements of air are called winds. Winds are the result of changes in air pressure caused by uneven heating of Earth's surface. Winds follow prevailing, or typical, patterns. Warmer, low-pressure air rises higher into the atmosphere. Winds are created as air is drawn across the surface of Earth toward the low-pressure areas. The Equator is constantly warmed by the sun, so warm air masses tend to form near the Equator. This warm, low-pressure air rises, and then cooler, high-pressure air rushes in under the warm air, causing wind. This helps balance Earth's temperature.

> **MAP SKILLS**
>
> **1** PHYSICAL GEOGRAPHY In what general direction does the wind blow over North America?
>
> **2** PHYSICAL GEOGRAPHY What two areas in the Pacific have calm winds?

Chapter 2 **47**

DIAGRAM

Temperature and Precipitation Affect Biomes

Analyzing Use the diagram of biomes in relation to climate and temperature to discuss how climate affects the environment of various areas based on elevation. Invite students who have lived or visited other regions of the world to discuss how that region fits into the diagram. Interpersonal

See page 39C for other online activities.

Interactive Charts/Tables/Diagrams

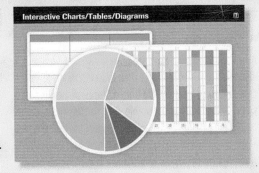

V Visual Skills

Reading Maps Have students examine the wind patterns map and study the key, noting that warm and cold winds are indicated by different colors. Explain that winds are named for the direction *from* which they blow, so the westerlies, for instance, blow from west to east. The map shows the *prevailing*, or most dominant, winds. **Ask:**

- Where do warm winds originate? *(in the low latitudes and midlatitudes)*
- Where do cold winds originate? *(near the poles)*
- How do the prevailing winds over North America, Europe, and Asia differ from those over South America, Africa, and Australia? *(The prevailing winds over North America, Europe, and Asia are westerlies, while those over South America, Africa, and Australia are easterlies.)* **AL** Visual/ Spatial

T Technology Skills

Using Digital Tools Have students use calculators to apply the information about elevation and climate to the following:

A climber is at 5,500 feet, where the temperature is 55°F. She climbs to 9,500 feet. The temperature decreases 3.5° for every 1,000 feet of ascent. What is the temperature at this altitude? *(She ascends 4,000 feet. With the temperature decreasing 3.5°F for every 1,000 feet, the temperature would be 3.5°F x 4, or 14°F, less. 55°F – 14°F = 41°F. The answer is 41°F.)* Logical/ Mathematical

C Critical Thinking Skills

Transferring Knowledge Draw students' attention to the poles on the map and note that cold air currents flow generally away from the poles, while the warm westerlies flow generally toward the poles. Emphasize that the effect of these wind patterns is to circulate the sun's heat. Then help students connect the information about warm air rising to their own experience. **Ask:** In a two-story home, which floor tends to be warmer? Why? *(the upper floor; because warm air rises)*

Students might logically raise the question: **If warm air rises, why is it cooler at higher elevations?** Challenge students to find the answer to this puzzle on the Internet. *(At higher elevations, the air is thin. So warm, rising air expands in these low-pressure conditions. As air expands, it cools. In addition, at high altitudes, more heat escapes into space.)* Logical/ Mathematical

> **ANSWERS, p. 47**
>
> **MAP SKILLS**
> 1. from southwest to northeast
> 2. areas on the Equator, where doldrums are, and areas on the latitudes at 30°N or 30°S.

R Reading Skills

Summarizing Use the following questions to help students summarize the information in the text about ocean currents. **Ask:**

• What pattern occurs in ocean currents? *(Warm water moves away from the Equator to higher latitudes, and cold water moves from the poles toward the Equator.)*

• What is the effect of this pattern? *(It helps to balance the temperature of the planet.)*

• How is this pattern like that of wind currents? *(Both help to circulate heat and balance the planet's temperature.)* **Verbal/Linguistic**

W Writing Skills

Making Connections Emphasize that temperature and precipitation are two major components of both weather and climate. Have students demonstrate their understanding of the difference between weather and climate by writing a paragraph describing the weather in your area today and another describing the climate of your area. Call on volunteers to read their paragraphs aloud. **Verbal/Linguistic**

V Visual Skills

Reading a Diagram Assess students' understanding of the Rain Shadow diagram by discussing the Critical Thinking questions as well as the following ones. **Ask:**

• Which side of the mountain receives a lot of rainfall? *(the side facing the ocean)*

• Which side of the mountain receives little rainfall? *(the side facing away from the ocean)*

• How does the vegetation on the two sides of the mountain reflect the amount of rainfall received? *(The plentiful rainfall on the ocean side generally results in forests, while the lack of rainfall on the other side can produce a desert.)* **Visual/Spatial**

ANSWERS, p. 48

DIAGRAM SKILLS

CRITICAL THINKING

1. Precipitation is water deposited on Earth as rain, snow, sleet, or mist.

2. The air becomes cool and dry.

R Just as winds move in patterns, cold and warm streams of water, known as currents, circulate through the oceans. Warm water moves away from the Equator, transferring heat energy from the equatorial region to higher latitudes. Cold water from the polar regions moves toward the Equator, also helping to balance the temperature of the planet.

Weather and Climate

W Weather is the state of the atmosphere at a given time, such as during a week, a day, or an afternoon. Weather refers to conditions such as hot or cold, wet or dry, calm or stormy, or cloudy or clear. Weather is what you can observe any time by going outside or looking out a window. **Climate** is the average weather conditions in a region or an area over a longer period. One useful measure for comparing climates is the average daily temperature. This is the average of the highest and lowest temperatures that occur in a 24-hour period. In addition to the average temperature, climate includes typical wind conditions and rainfall or snowfall that occur in an area year after year.

Rainfall and snowfall are types of precipitation. **Precipitation** is water deposited on the ground in the form of rain, snow, hail, sleet, or mist. Measuring the amount of precipitation in an area for one day provides data about the area's weather. Measuring the amount of precipitation for one full year provides data about the area's climate.

Landforms

It might seem strange to think that landforms such as mountains can affect weather and climate, but landforms and landmasses change the strength, speed, and direction of wind and ocean

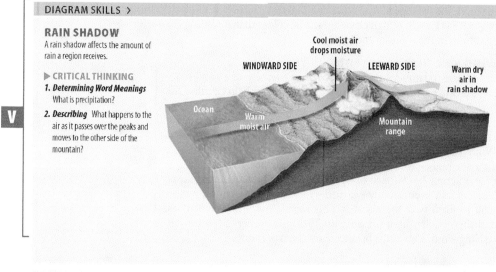

DIAGRAM SKILLS >

RAIN SHADOW
A rain shadow affects the amount of rain a region receives.

▶ **CRITICAL THINKING**

1. *Determining Word Meanings* What is precipitation?

2. *Describing* What happens to the air as it passes over the peaks and moves to the other side of the mountain?

Cool moist air drops moisture

WINDWARD SIDE   LEEWARD SIDE   Warm dry air in rain shadow

Ocean   Warm moist air   Mountain range

48 Chapter 2

DIAGRAM

Rain Shadow

Analyzing Visuals Have students view the diagram of a rain shadow to reinforce their understanding of this concept. Using a map of the United States, point out areas where rain shadows are notable, such as the dry areas east of the Cascade Mountains in Washington and Oregon and east of the Coast Ranges in California. Challenge students to explain how rain shadow is a fitting name for this effect. *(Just as an object casts a shadow by blocking sunlight, a mountain casts a rain shadow by blocking rain.)* **Logical/Mathematical**

See page 39C for other online activities.

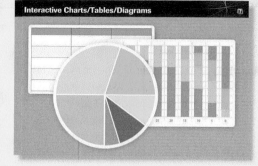

Interactive Charts/Tables/Diagrams

currents. Wind and ocean currents carry heat and precipitation, which shape weather and climate. The sun warms the land and the surface of the world's oceans at different rates, causing differences in air pressure. As winds blow inland from the oceans, they carry moist air with them. As the land rises in elevation, the atmosphere cools. When masses of moist air approach mountains, the air rises and cools, causing rain to fall on the side of the mountain facing the ocean. The other side of the mountain receives little rain because of the rain shadow effect. A **rain shadow** is a region of reduced rainfall on one side of a high mountain; the rain shadow occurs on the side of the mountain facing away from the ocean.

The climate in a zone affects how people live and work.

Identifying What three things are used to define a climate zone?

☑ READING PROGRESS CHECK

Determining Word Meanings Do the terms *weather* and *climate* mean the same thing? Explain.

Climate Regions

GUIDING QUESTION *What are the characteristics of Earth's climate zones?*

Why do Florida and California attract so many visitors? These places have cold or stormy weather at times, but their climates are generally warm, sunny, and mild, so people can enjoy the outdoors all year.

The Zones

In the year 1900, German scientist Wladimir Köppen invented a system that divides Earth into five basic climate zones. Climate zones are regions of Earth classified by temperature, precipitation, and distance from the Equator. Köppen used names and capital letters to label the climate zones as follows: Tropical (A); Desert (B); Humid Temperate (C); Cold Temperate (D); and Polar (E). Years later, a sixth climate zone was added: High Mountain (F).

Chapter 2 **49**

(l) UIG via Getty Images/Universal Images Group/Getty Images; (r) Ira Block/National Geographic/Getty Images

CHART

Climate Zones

Identifying After students view the chart on climate zones, have them identify the climate zone in which they live. Then name some other familiar places and ask students to identify the climate zones. **Visual/Spatial**

See page 39C for other online activities.

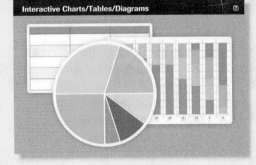

Interactive Charts/Tables/Diagrams

C Critical Thinking Skills

Reasoning Suggest that students apply the Essential Question: *How does geography influence the way people live?* to extend their understanding of the rain shadow effect. **Ask:**

- On which side of a mountain would a person most need a raincoat? *(the side facing the ocean)*
- On which side of a mountain might logging be an important industry? *(the side facing the ocean)*
- On which side of a mountain might farmers need to rely on irrigation? *(the side facing away from the ocean)*
- On which side of a mountain would landslides more likely be a problem? *(the side facing the ocean)*
- On which side of a mountain would snow skiing more likely be better? *(the side facing the ocean)* **AL** Logical/Mathematical

V Visual Skills

Transferring Knowledge After students read the information about climate zones, call on volunteers to apply the information to the photographs at the top of the page. **Ask:**

- How is the climate affecting the woman in the photo on the left? *(It is hot and the heat is making her wear a hat and making her thirsty.)*
- In which of three climate zones could the people with coats be? How do you know? *(Cold Temperate, Polar, or High Mountain; because of the snow and ice and mountains in the background)* Visual/Spatial

T Technology Skills

Researching on the Internet Have students use the Internet to research the climate of a place they would like to visit in the Western Hemisphere. Have them find the climate zone of the place and the average temperature and precipitation at the time of year they would most likely go. Logical/Mathematical

ANSWERS, p. 49

Identifying temperature, precipitation, and distance from the Equator

☑ READING PROGRESS CHECK Both *weather* and *climate* refer to an area's temperature, precipitation, and wind conditions. However, weather is the state of the atmosphere in a region or area at a specific time, whereas climate is the average weather conditions experienced in a region or area over a longer period, such as years.

Earth and the Sun

V Visual Skills

Creating Charts Pair students and have them create a three-column chart like the one below of the six climate zones (tropical, desert, humid temperate, cold temperate, polar, and high mountain) with these three headings: *Climate Zone, Characteristics, Examples*. Students can use the text to list the six climate zones in the first column and their characteristics in the second column. Under Examples in the third column, they should identify three places within each climate zone.

Call on volunteers to share the names of places that have each type of climate and identify a factor that influences the climate in the place, such as latitude or elevation. **AL**
ELL Visual/Spatial, Interpersonal

Climate Zone	Characteristics	Examples
Tropical		
Desert		
Humid Temperate		
Cold Temperate		
Polar		
High Mountain		

C Critical Thinking Skills

Giving Examples To help students understand the relationship between climate zones and biomes, emphasize that the plants and animals within a certain climate zone form a biome.

Write the biomes listed in the text on the board: rain forest, desert, grassland, tundra. Discuss major features of the climate of each biome, and call on volunteers to name some plants or animals that live in each. If students are unable to give examples, direct them to check on the Internet. **BL**
Naturalist

V Each climate zone also can be divided into smaller subzones, but the areas within each zone have many similarities. Tropical areas are hot and rainy, and they often are covered with dense forests. Desert areas are always dry, but they can be cold or hot, depending on their latitude. Humid temperate areas experience all types of weather with changing seasons. Cold temperate climates have a short summer season but are generally cold and windy. Polar climates are very cold, with ice and snow covering the ground most of the year. High mountain climates are found only at the tops of high mountain ranges such as the Rockies, the Alps, and the Himalaya. High mountain climates have variable conditions because the atmosphere cools with increasing elevation. Some of the highest mountaintops are cold and windy and stay white with snow all year.

C Different types of plants grow best in different climates, so each climate zone has its own unique types of vegetation and animal life. These unique combinations form ecosystems of plants and animals that are adapted to environments within the climate zone. A biome is a type of large ecosystem with similar life-forms and climates. Earth's biomes include rain forest, desert, grassland, and tundra. All life is adapted to survive in its native climate zone and biome.

Animals that live in that environment have unique adaptations that help them survive.

50 Chapter 2

Ryan Hagerty/USFWS

networks Online Teaching Options

Effects of Climate Change

Determining Cause and Effect Use the slide show to reinforce students' understanding of global warming and its effects. Encourage students to create a graphic organizer on global warming, identifying its causes, effects, and possible solutions. Verbal/Linguistic

See page 39C for other online activities.

Slide Show

(l) ©Ocean/Corbis, ©Kryssia Campos/Getty Images, (tr) ©Erica Simone Leeds, (br) ©JG Photography/Alamy

Changes to Climate

A thermal image shows heat escaping from the roofs of buildings.

▶ CRITICAL THINKING

Analyzing How do structures in cities affect local weather?

Many scientists say climates are changing around the world. If this is true, the world could experience new weather patterns. These changes might mean more extreme weather in some places and milder weather in others. Human activities can affect weather and climate. For example, people have cut down millions of square miles of rain forests in Central and South America. As a result, fewer trees are available to release moisture into the air. The result is a drier climate in the region.

Metal, asphalt, and concrete surfaces in cities absorb a huge amount of heat from the sun. Because of this, an enormous mass of warmer air builds up in and around the city, which affects local weather.

In recent years, scientists have become aware of a problem called global warming. Global warming is an increase in the average temperature of Earth's atmosphere. Industries created by humans dump polluting chemicals into the atmosphere. Many scientists say that a buildup of this pollution is contributing to the increasing temperature of Earth's atmosphere.

R

If the temperature of the atmosphere continues to rise, all of Earth's climates could be affected. Changes in climate could alter many natural ecosystems. Another consequence is that the survival of some plant and animal species will be threatened. It is also likely to be expensive and difficult for humans to adapt to these changes.

✓ READING PROGRESS CHECK

Identifying Which climate zone experiences all types of weather with changing seasons?

FOLDABLES Study Organizer

Include this lesson's information in your Foldable®.

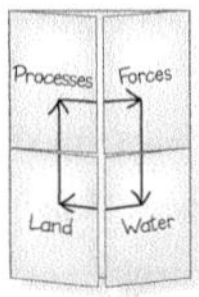

Cultura Science/Joseph Giacomin/Oxford Scientific/Getty Images

LESSON 1 REVIEW

Reviewing Vocabulary

1. Describe the difference between weather and *climate*.

Answering the Guiding Questions

2. ***Describing*** Explain the role of Earth's axis as it relates to rotation.
3. ***Describing*** Describe what happens before, during, and after the equinoxes.
4. ***Analyzing*** If you were climbing a 10,000-foot (3,048 m) mountain, what would you wear and why?
5. ***Identifying*** What has happened in Central and South America that many scientists believe is impacting the world?
6. ***Narrative Writing*** Imagine you are climbing a very tall mountain such as Mont Blanc in the Alps during the summer. Describe how the vegetation would change as you climb higher.

R Reading Skills

Summarizing Discuss with students the changes to climate that scientists say are occurring. Point out that the text gives three examples of how human activities have affected weather and climate. Use the following questions to help students summarize this information. **Ask:**

- What is the effect of cutting down rain forests in Central and South America? *(Fewer trees release moisture into the air, causing the region's climate to become drier.)*
- What effect do metal, asphalt, and concrete surfaces in cities have on weather? *(These surfaces absorb heat, making the air in and around cities warmer.)*
- How do chemical pollutants in the air affect the global climate? *(They contribute to an increase in the average temperature of Earth's atmosphere.)*
- What is the overall effect of these human activities on climate? *(They cause the climate to become hotter and drier.)*
- What do you think people should do considering the effect of these human activities on climate? *(Students' answers will vary, but should include suggestions such as planting more trees, reducing chemical pollutants, and reducing asphalt surfaces.)* BL Verbal/Linguistic

CLOSE & REFLECT

To close the lesson, remind students of Earth's uniqueness in the solar system. Have students summarize the physical features of Earth that make life possible on this planet, and compare these features to the other three rocky planets in the solar system.

Have students write a list of steps each of them could take throughout this school year to help preserve the planet. Encourage students to do research as necessary to create their lists. Then have small groups share their lists and exchange their ideas. Have the groups present the best ideas in a class discussion and make a class list that can be posted for future reference.

LESSON 1 REVIEW ANSWERS

Reviewing Vocabulary

1. *Weather* is the conditions at a particular time. *Climate* is the average of the weather conditions for an area over time.

Answering the Guiding Questions

2. **Describing** The axis is an imaginary line that goes through the middle of Earth at a slight tilt. Earth rotates on this axis once every 24 hours.
3. **Describing** Before the equinox, the sun shines longer on one side of the Equator than the other each day. On the equinox, the sun shines on the Northern and Southern Hemispheres for the same amount of time. After the equinox, it shines on the opposite side of the Equator from before the equinox.
4. **Analyzing** Possible answer: I would wear layers because the temperature would go down about 3.5 degrees for every 1,000 feet I climbed. It would be about 35 degrees colder at the top.
5. **Identifying** Much of the rain forest has been cut for farming, so the air is hotter and drier now.
6. **Narrative Writing** At the bottom, the vegetation would be lush, green, and varied because temperatures are warm. As I climb higher, I will see less variety of plant life and fewer trees because fewer species are adapted to the cold. At the top, I would see very little green because it stays cold and snowy all year.

ANSWERS, p. 51

CRITICAL THINKING Buildings and pavement absorb the sun's heat, causing warmer air to build up in and around cities.

✓ READING PROGRESS CHECK Humid Temperate climate has four seasons, and the temperature and precipitation change quite a bit with the seasons, from over 90 degrees on some summer days to close to zero in the winter, with rainy springs and dry, windy autumns.

ENGAGE

Bellringer Read the "It Matters Because" statement and have students preview the lesson by reading headings and boldface vocabulary words and looking at the photographs. Discuss the topics covered in the lesson: the forces that shape Earth's surface, such as plate movements, erosion, and weathering. Have students predict what caused each of the events shown in the photographs.

TEACH & ASSESS

V Visual Skills

Visualizing Emphasize to students that Earth's surface has changed dramatically over time, but that much of the change has occurred very slowly over many millions of years. Share with students the information in the Content Background Knowledge box below. Then have students look at a world map and speculate on how the continents might have once fit together. Visual/Spatial

T Technology Skills

Researching on the Internet Have students identify the seven continents on a world map. Call on a volunteer to read aloud the definition of a continent. **Ask:** Based on this definition, do you have any questions or doubts about the classification of seven continents? *(Students might logically question why Europe and Asia are considered separate continents. Some people even question whether North and South America should be considered separate continents.)*

Suggest that interested students conduct Internet research on the classification of continents and report back to the class. Logical/Mathematical

Content Background Knowledge

According to the theory of continental drift, today's continents are separate fragments of one supercontinent called *Pangaea*, which began to break apart about 225 million years ago. The word *Pangaea* means "all lands" in Greek. The theory of plate tectonics explains how the continents broke apart and moved into their present locations.

ANSWER, p. 52

Taking Notes weathering, various types of erosion, buildup and movement, human activity

---

---

networks

There's More Online!

- ☑ **ANIMATION** Magnitude of Earthquakes
- ☑ **IMAGES** Human Impact on Earth
- ☑ **MAP** Risk of Earthquakes in the United States
- ☑ **VIDEO**

Reading **HELP**DESK

Academic Vocabulary

- **intense**

Content Vocabulary

- **continent**
- **tectonic plate**
- **fault**
- **earthquake**
- **Ring of Fire**
- **tsunami**
- **weathering**
- **erosion**
- **glacier**

TAKING NOTES: *Key Ideas and Details*

Identify As you read, use a graphic organizer like this one to describe the external forces that have shaped Earth.

External Forces
_____
_____
_____

Indiana Academic Standards
6.3.13

52

Lesson 2
Forces of Change

ESSENTIAL QUESTION · *How does geography influence the way people live?*

IT MATTERS BECAUSE
Internal and external forces change Earth, the setting for human life.

Shaping Earth

GUIDING QUESTION *How did the surface of Earth form?*

Earth's surface has been moving continually since the formation of the planet. Landmasses have shifted and moved over time. Landforms have been created and destroyed. The way Earth looks from space has changed many times because of the movement of continents.

Earth's Surface

A **continent** is a large, continuous mass of land. Continents are part of Earth's crust. Earth has seven continents: Asia, Africa, North America, South America, Europe, Antarctica, and Australia. The region around the North Pole is not a continent because it is made of a huge mass of dense ice, not land. Greenland might seem as big as a continent, but it is classified as the world's largest island. Each of the seven continents has features that make it unique. Some of the most interesting features on the continents are landforms.

Even though you usually cannot feel it, the land beneath you is moving. This is because Earth's crust is not a solid sheet of rock. Earth's surface is like many massive puzzle pieces pushed close together and floating on a sea of boiling rock. The movement of these pieces is one of the major forces that create Earth's land features. Old mountains are worn down, while new mountains grow taller. Even the continents move.

(l to r) ©Jeff Vanuga/Corbis; MARCELLO PATERNOSTRO/AFP/Getty Images; MARTIN BERNETTI/AFP/Getty Images; Stockbyte/Getty Images; Science & Society Picture Library/SSPL/Getty Images

---

networks *Online Teaching Options*

VIDEO

Water Eroding Mountains

Describing Use the video to introduce the lesson topic: the forces that shape Earth's surface, such as plate movements, erosion, and weathering. Have students share what they learned from this video about the internal and external forces of Earth, and tell if anything surprised them. Interpersonal

See page 39D for other online activities.

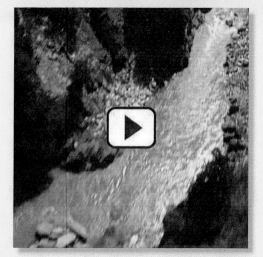
BBC Motion Gallery Education

Plate Movements

Earth's rigid crust is made up of 16 enormous pieces called **tectonic plates**. These plates vary in size and shape. They also vary in the amount they move over the more flexible layer of the mantle below them. Heat from deep within the planet causes plates to move. This movement happens so slowly that humans do not feel it. But some of Earth's plates move as much as a few inches each year. This might not seem like much, but over millions of years, it causes the plates to move thousands of miles.

Movement of surface plates changes Earth's surface features very, very slowly. It takes millions of years for plates to move enough to create landforms. Some land features form when plates are crushed together. At times, forces within Earth push the edge of one plate up over the edge of a plate beside it. This dramatic movement can create mountains, volcanoes, and deep trenches in the ocean floor.

At other times, plates are crushed together in a way that causes the edges of both plates to crumble and break. This event can form jagged mountain ranges. If plates on the ocean floor move apart, the space between them widens into a giant crack in Earth's crust. Magma rises through the crack and forms new crust as it hardens and cools. If enough cooled magma builds up that it reaches the surface of the ocean, an island will begin to form.

V1

Powerful forces within Earth cause the Old Faithful geyser in Yellowstone National Park (left) to erupt. Those forces also cause lava to flow from Mount Etna, a volcano in Italy (right).

▶ **CRITICAL THINKING**
Describing What can happen if plates on the ocean floor move apart?

VIDEO

Earth's Forces: Old Faithful and Icelandic Volcano

Analyzing Use these videos to begin a discussion about how different landforms shape the life of people in a region. Have students identify the major landforms in your region and analyze how they affect the lives of the people in the region.
Verbal/Linguistic

See page 39D for other online activities.

V1 Visual Skills

Creating Charts Help students summarize the information about plate movements by creating a two-column chart with these headings: *Type of Plate Movement* and *Landforms Created*. Suggest that students complete their charts as they read the text. Students' charts should look similar to the one below.

Type of Plate Movement	Landforms Created
Edge of one plate pushes up over another	Mountains, volcanoes, ocean trenches
Plates crush together, causing edges of both plates to crumble and break	Jagged mountain ranges
Plates on ocean floor move apart	New crust, islands

Visual/Spatial

V2 Visual Skills

Analyzing Images Explain that the two photographs at the bottom of the page show the effects of a force below Earth's surface. **Ask:**

- What force is reflected in these two photographs? *(heat within Earth)*
- What does this heat produce? *(geyser, volcano)* Verbal/Linguistic, Visual/Spatial

V2

Content Background Knowledge

Yellowstone National Park sits on a caldera, an ancient crater formed by the blast of a supervolcano, that covers a 25- by 37-mile area in Wyoming. Yellowstone's supervolcano has had major eruptions three times in the past 2.1 million years. Each of these major eruptions was a thousand times more powerful than the eruption of Mount St. Helens in 1980. The extraordinary heat under the ground of Yellowstone causes its sensational geysers, hot springs, mud pots, and other thermal features.

ANSWER, p. 53

CRITICAL THINKING A giant crack in the Earth's crust appears. Magma rises through the crack and forms new crust as it hardens and cools.

Forces of Change

R Reading Skills

Defining and Illustrating Clarify the definition of *fault* for students: a break in Earth's crust that results when two plates grind against each other. Have students create vocabulary cards for the content vocabulary words on this page: *fault, earthquake, Ring of Fire,* and *tsunami.* On one side of each card, students should define the word, and on the other side, create an illustration of the word. Have students write a caption for their illustration that uses the word correctly in a sentence. **AL**
ELL Verbal/Linguistic, Visual/Spatial

V Visual Skills

Analyzing a Map Refer students to the Tectonic Plate Boundaries map in the Chapter Opener and explain that the Ring of Fire borders the continents of Asia, North America, and South America. Have students locate the Ring of Fire, and call on volunteers to identify some countries located near it, such as Japan, Chile, and the United States. Have students analyze the map and find examples of volcanoes and earthquakes that are not on plate boundaries. Encourage interested students to make predictions why a few earthquakes and volcanoes occur far from plate boundaries and to research some of these events and report back to the class. Visual/Spatial

Making Connections Have students identify the states of the United States that are located along the Ring of Fire. *(Alaska, Washington, Oregon, California)* Discuss how these states have been affected by their location near the boundary of the Pacific Plate. For example, California experiences frequent earthquakes, and Washington has active volcanoes. Ask if any students have any personal experience with earthquakes or volcanic eruptions, and have them share their experiences with the class.

Challenge students to research Mount St. Helens, an active volcano in Washington, and make a presentation to the class on its latest eruptions and activity. **BL** Naturalist

---

ANSWERS, p. 54

CRITICAL THINKING Plate movement along fault lines and the force of erupting volcanoes cause earthquakes.
✔ READING PROGRESS CHECK The Earth's plates move so slowly that the movement is too small and slow for people to feel.

A road collapses as a result of a powerful earthquake in Chile.
▶ CRITICAL THINKING
Describing What natural forces cause earthquakes?

Academic Vocabulary

intense great or strong

Sudden Changes

Changes to Earth's surface also can happen quickly. Events such as earthquakes and volcanoes can destroy entire areas within minutes. Earthquakes and volcanoes are caused by plate movement. When two plates grind against each other, faults form. A **fault** results when the rocks on one side or both sides of a crack in Earth's crust have been moved by forces within Earth. **Earthquakes** are caused by plate movement along fault lines. Earthquakes also can be caused by the force of erupting volcanoes.

Various plates lie at the bottom of the Pacific Ocean. These include the huge Pacific Plate along with several smaller plates. Over time, the edges of these plates were forced under the edges of the plates surrounding the Pacific Ocean. This plate movement created a long, narrow band of volcanoes called the **Ring of Fire**. The Ring of Fire stretches for more than 24,000 miles (38,624 km) around the Pacific Ocean.

The **intense** vibrations caused by earthquakes and erupting volcanoes can transfer energy to Earth's surface. When this energy travels through ocean waters, it can cause enormous waves to form on the water's surface. A **tsunami** is a giant ocean wave caused by volcanic eruptions or movement of the earth under the ocean floor. Tsunamis have caused terrible flooding and damage to coastal areas. The forces of these mighty waves can level entire coastlines.

✔ READING PROGRESS CHECK

Determining Central Ideas Earth's surface plates are moving. Why don't we feel the ground moving under us?

External Forces

GUIDING QUESTION *How can wind, water, and human actions change Earth's surface?*

What happens when a stormy ocean tide hits the shore and sweeps over a sand dune? The water wears down the sand dune. Similar changes take place on a larger scale across Earth's lithosphere. These changes happen much slower—over hundreds, thousands, or even millions of years.

---

netw⊙rks   *Online Teaching Options*

Architecture for Earthquakes

Analyzing Visuals Use the slide show to spark a discussion of how human beings have adapted to living with natural disasters, not only earthquakes but also floods, tornadoes, and hurricanes. For example, besides designing buildings to withstand natural disasters, people have developed emergency warning systems and emergency response procedures. They have also built levees and used sandbagging to hold back floodwaters. Have students write a paragraph about one of these examples that they may have experienced in their lives. Verbal/Linguistic

See page 39D for other online activities.

Slide Show

Weathering

Some landforms are created when materials such as rocks and soil build up on Earth's surface. Other landforms take shape as rocks and soil break down and wear away over time. **Weathering** is a process by which Earth's surface is worn away by forces such as wind, rain, chemicals, and the movement of ice and flowing water. Even plants can cause weathering. Plant roots and small seeds can grow into tiny cracks in rock, gradually splitting the rock apart as the roots expand.

You might have seen the effects of weathering on an old building or statue. The edges become chipped and worn, and features such as raised lettering are smoothed down. Landforms such as mountains are affected by weathering, too. The Appalachian Mountains in the eastern United States have become rounded and crumbled after millions of years of weathering by natural forces.

Erosion

Erosion is a process that works with weathering to change surface features of Earth. **Erosion** is a process by which weathered bits of rock are moved elsewhere by water, wind, or ice. Rain and moving water can erode even the hardest stone over time. When material is broken down by weathering, it can easily be carried away by the action of erosion. For example, the Grand Canyon was formed by weathering and erosion caused by flowing water and blowing winds. Water flowed over the region for millions of years, weakening the surface of the rock. The moving water carried away tiny bits of rock. Over time, weathering and erosion carved a deep canyon into the rock. Erosion by wind and chemicals caused the Grand Canyon to widen until it became the amazing landform we see today.

Weathering and erosion cause different materials to break down at different speeds. Soft, porous rocks, such as sandstone and limestone, wear away faster than dense rocks like granite. The spectacular rock formations in Utah's Bryce Canyon were formed as different types of minerals within the rocks were worn away by erosion, some more quickly than others. The result is landforms with jagged, rough surfaces and unusual shapes.

C

Erosion created this rock formation, named Thor's Hammer, in Bryce Canyon National Park, Utah.
▶ CRITICAL THINKING
Explaining Why do materials affected by erosion break down at different speeds?

Stockbyte/Getty Images

W

Chapter 2 **55**

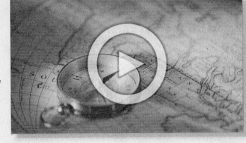

Comstock Images/Jupiterimages

VIDEO

Erosion in Bryce Canyon

Integrating Visual Information Use the video of Bryce Canyon to discuss erosion as a force that reshapes Earth. Have students integrate what they learned in their lives by naming some landforms in your state or region that have been shaped by erosion. **Visual/Spatial**

See page 39D for other online activities.

C Critical Thinking Skills

Comparing and Contrasting Stress that weathering and erosion are related processes and that they occur together. Use the following questions to help students identify the similarities and differences between the two processes. **Ask:**

- What causes weathering? *(wind, rain, chemicals, and the movement of ice and water)*
- What causes erosion? *(wind, moving water and ice)*
- What is the difference between weathering and erosion? *(Weathering is the wearing away of material, while erosion is the movement of that material.)*
- How are weathering and erosion alike? *(They have some of the same causes, such as wind and moving water and ice, and both of them change landforms. They work together.)*

Students may wonder how ice can move. Point out that glaciers are large masses of ice that move very slowly down slopes, pulled by gravity. They are responsible for much eroded landscape. **Verbal/Linguistic**

Making Connections Point out to students that examples of erosion are all around them in the outdoors. For instance, the banks of every stream show the effects of erosion, which often exposes the roots of trees. Challenge students to think of ways to present a simple demonstration of erosion. For example, a student might suggest building a mound of dirt or sand and pouring or running water from a hose down one side. If possible, allow students to set up an erosion demonstration.

W Writing Skills

Argument Note that all of the eroded landforms mentioned as examples in the student text are sites of national parks—the Appalachian Mountains (Great Smoky Mountains National Park), Grand Canyon (Grand Canyon National Park), and Bryce Canyon (Bryce Canyon National Park). Have interested students write a few paragraphs focusing on the importance of national parks in preserving scenic wonders and arguing for the creation of additional national parks in the United States. **BL**
Verbal/Linguistic

ANSWER, p. 55

CRITICAL THINKING Soft, porous rocks, such as sandstone, break down faster than dense rocks like granite.

Forces of Change

R Reading Skills

Determining Central Ideas Point out that the first paragraph on this page focuses on landforms built up by the action of water—either ocean waves and currents or river water. To help students identify the key points, provide them with the following sentence starters and have them complete the sentences:

- Ocean waves and currents deposit sand to build up *(beaches and islands.)*
- Rivers deposit soil where they empty into oceans to build up *(coastal plains and wetland ecosystems).*

Explain the term *wetland ecosystem*. An ecosystem includes all the plants and animals that live in a particular environment. A wetland is an area with wet soil, such as a marsh or swamp.
BL Verbal/Linguistic

Content Background Knowledge

Share with students the following information about glaciers:

- Glaciers are often referred to as rivers of ice that flow downhill. They are found in mountains on all the continents except Australia.
- Glacial ice is very heavy, and as it slowly moves downhill, it grinds away rock and soil, creating valleys and lakes. Ancient glaciers created the Great Lakes.
- The northern United States has many glaciers. They are especially numerous in Alaska, where there are tens of thousands of glaciers.
- Glacier National Park in northern Montana was named the country's tenth national park in 1910. The park borders Waterton Lakes National Park in Canada. The two became the world's first International Peace Park in 1932.
- The rapid melting of glaciers today is one of the many pieces of evidence supporting the theory of global warming. Since 1850, the glaciers in the Alps of Europe have decreased in volume by about one-half.

Huge, tunnel-boring machines were used to dig the Channel Tunnel, or Chunnel. The Chunnel is an undersea rail tunnel connecting the United Kingdom and France.
▶ **CRITICAL THINKING**
Determining Central Ideas Why **R** have humans changed the environment faster and more broadly in the past 50 years than at any other time in history?

Buildup and Movement

The buildup of materials creates landforms such as beaches, islands, and plains. Ocean waves pound coastal rocks into smaller and smaller pieces until they are tiny grains of sand. Over time, waves and ocean currents deposit sand along coastlines, forming sandy beaches. Sand and other materials carried by ocean currents build up on mounds of volcanic rock in the ocean, forming islands. Rivers deposit soil where they empty into larger bodies of water, creating coastal plains and wetland ecosystems.

Entire valleys and plains can be formed by the incredible force and weight of large masses of ice and snow. These masses are often classified by size as glaciers, polar ice caps, or ice sheets. A **glacier**, the smallest of the ice masses, moves slowly over time, sometimes spreading outward on a land surface. Although glaciers are usually thought of as existing during the Ice Age, glaciers can still be found on Earth today.

Ice caps are high-altitude ice masses. Ice sheets, extending more than 20,000 square miles (51,800 sq. km), are the largest ice masses. Ice sheets cover most of Greenland and Antarctica.

56 Chapter 2

netw⬤rks   *Online Teaching Options*

SLIDE SHOW

Human Impact on Earth

Discussing Use the slide show as an introduction into a discussion of the many ways that people affect Earth's surface, such as by building canals, dams, levees, roads, and cities. Have students use the Internet to find more examples of how humans impact geography. **Naturalist**

See page 39D for other online activities.

Slide Show

ANSWER, p. 56

CRITICAL THINKING Demand for food and natural resources is greater than ever and continues to grow.

Human Actions

Natural forces are awesome in their power to change the surface of Earth. Human actions, however, have also changed Earth in many ways. Activities such as coal mining have leveled entire mountains. Humans use explosives such as dynamite to blast tunnels through mountain ranges when building highways and railroads. Canals dug by humans change the natural course of waterways. Humans have cut down so many millions of acres of forests that deadly landslides and terrible erosion occur on the deforested lands.

Pollution caused by humans can change Earth, as well. When people burn gasoline and other fossil fuels, toxic chemicals are released into the air. These chemicals settle onto the surfaces of mountains, buildings, oceans, rivers, grasslands, and forests. The chemicals poison waterways, kill plants and animals, and cause erosion. The buildings in many cities show signs of being worn down by chemical erosion.

Studies show that humans have changed the Earth's environment faster and more broadly in the last 50 years than at any time in history. A major cause of all the change is the demand for food and natural resources is greater than ever before, and it continues to grow.

Changes to Earth's surface caused by natural weathering and erosion happen slowly. These forces create different kinds of landforms that make our planet unique. Erosion and other changes caused by humans, however, can damage Earth's surface quickly. Their effects threaten our safety and survival. We need to protect our environment to ensure that our quality of life improves for future generations.

☑ READING PROGRESS CHECK

Identifying Categorize each of the following events as a change caused by nature or a change caused by humans: coal mining, glaciers melting, air pollution, volcano eruption, acid rain, water erosion, and plate movement.

FOLDABLES
Study Organizer

Include this lesson's information in your Foldable®.

LESSON 2 REVIEW

Reviewing Vocabulary

1. Why can *tsunamis* cause such massive destruction?

Answering the Guiding Questions

2. *Describing* Select one country in Europe. Write about two special or unique landforms of that country. Include photos.

3. *Describing* Describe the importance of tectonic plates.

4. *Determining Central Ideas* How can land features be created by natural forces?

5. *Identifying* How can chemicals contribute to weathering?

6. *Distinguishing Fact from Opinion* Is the following statement a fact or an opinion? Explain.
Although coal mining can damage the environment, it is worth it because the coal is needed to produce electricity.

7. *Describing* Explain the process by which sharp mountain peaks become rounded.

8. *Informative/Explanatory Writing* What human actions have changed the landscape in your area?

LESSON 2 REVIEW ANSWERS

Reviewing Vocabulary

1. A tsunami is a gigantic wave of ocean water. When it hits a populated coastal area, it destroys everything in its path, often with little advance warning.

Answering the Guiding Questions

2. Describing Student responses will vary based on country but should be clear and include photos.

3. Describing When tectonic plates move together, they can form or change landforms. When they move apart, magma can come to the surface and harden.

4. Determining Central Ideas A land feature can form when surface plates are pushed together. Volcanoes can erupt and form new features. Erosion and weathering can also result in new formations

such as the Grand Canyon.

5. Identifying Chemicals from pollution can end up in air and rain, leading to acid rain. Acid rain can kill fish and vegetation, and it can eat away at hard surfaces.

6. Distinguishing Fact from Opinion This is an opinion because some people believe we should be getting our power with solar or wind energy.

7. Describing The process that wears away sharp peaks is weathering. It occurs when wind, water, chemicals, or movement of ice or water wears away a landform.

8. Informative/Explanatory Writing Answers will vary but may include new roadways being cut into a mountain or the building of a dam to prevent flooding.

R Reading Skills

Listing As they read, have students make a list of the ways human beings have changed the environment on Earth. Then have students form small groups, and challenge the groups to add as many items to the list as they can. You might make the activity a contest to see which group develops the longest list within two minutes.

After the small groups have completed and shared their lists, have them classify each of the changes in their list as a positive or a negative change for Earth's environment. Make sure groups include examples of both positive and negative changes made by humans. **Verbal/Linguistic, Interpersonal**

W Writing Skills

Informative/Explanatory Have students view a road map of your state and use it, along with their personal knowledge, to identify areas where streams and landscapes have been changed by people, for example by building dams and creating reservoirs or by building canals.

Direct students to write a paragraph in which they describe how the state's landscape has been altered by people and estimate about how much of it remains in a relatively natural state. If students are struggling, allow pairs to share their ideas or personal knowledge to help those who are struggling. Have pairs then exchange their paragraphs and give constructive criticism to their partner. **Verbal/Linguistic**

CLOSE & REFLECT

Have students reflect on the ways that the land is built up and weathered away naturally on Earth. Have students give examples in the local area of the ways the land has been changed, and identify if those changes occurred naturally or if some of the changes were made by people.

ANSWER, p. 57

☑ READING PROGRESS CHECK **by nature:** volcano eruption, water erosion, plate movement; **by humans:** glaciers melting, coal mining, air pollution, acid rain

ENGAGE

Bellringer Note that many people take the landscape in which they live for granted, but each kind of landscape has its own appeal. Encourage students to identify what is special about the landscape of their home region. Challenge students to write descriptions, draw a local landscape, or bring in photographs they have taken of the local landscape. Then share their thoughts with classmates.

TEACH & ASSESS

R Reading Skills

Applying Have students use a physical map to identify the elevation range within their home state. **Ask:**

- Is there a great difference in elevation from one area of the state to another? *(Students' answers should reflect the geography in their state.)*
- Would you characterize the state as generally flat, hilly, mountainous, or varied? *(Students' answers should reflect the geography in their state.)*
- How does the flat, hilly, mountainous, or varied landscape affect the use of the land by farmers, miners, loggers, or other workers? *(Students' answers should reflect the use of the land for industry in their state.)*
- What relationship, if any, do you see between landscape and population centers? *(Students' answers should reflect the situation in their state.)* **AL** Verbal/ Linguistic

V Visual Skills

Diagramming Have students draw a diagram showing a landscape with a plateau, plain, and valley, and label each landform. Explain that students should make their diagrams large enough to add helpful notes to their diagrams as they read. Then encourage students also to diagram and label other landforms that they read about in this lesson. **ELL** Visual/ Spatial

---

ANSWER, p. 58

Taking Notes Sample answer: **Plateau:** an area of flat land that rises above the surrounding land; **Plain:** flat or gently rolling land; **Ocean:** a large body of salt water; **Gulf:** a large area of ocean water partially surrounded by land

---

networks

There's More Online!

☑ **IMAGE** The Ocean Floor
☑ **ANIMATION** How the Water Cycle Works
☑ **VIDEO**

Reading **HELP**DESK

Academic Vocabulary

- **transform**

Content Vocabulary

- **plateau**
- **plain**
- **isthmus**
- **continental shelf**
- **trench**
- **desalinization**
- **groundwater**
- **delta**
- **water cycle**
- **evaporation**
- **condensation**
- **acid rain**

TAKING NOTES: *Key Ideas and Details*

Describe Using a chart like this one, describe two kinds of landforms and two bodies of water.

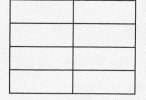

Indiana Academic Standards
6.3.5, 6.3.12, 6.3.13, 6.4.7

Lesson 3

Landforms and Bodies of Water

ESSENTIAL QUESTION · *How does geography influence the way people live?*

IT MATTERS BECAUSE
Earth's landforms and bodies of water influence our ways of life.

Types of Landforms

GUIDING QUESTION *What kinds of landforms cover Earth's surface?*

What is the land like in mountainous areas? Are unique landforms located along a seacoast? Have you ever wondered how different kinds of landforms developed? The surface of Earth is covered with landforms and bodies of water. Our planet is filled with variety on land and under water.

Surface Features on Land

Earth has many different landforms. When scientists study landforms, they find it useful to group them by characteristics. One characteristic that is often used is elevation.

Elevation describes how far above sea level a landform or a location is. Low-lying areas, such as ocean coasts and deep valleys, may be just a few feet above sea level. Mountains and highland areas can be thousands of feet above sea level. Even flat areas of land can have high elevations, especially when they are located far inland from ocean shores.

Plateaus and plains are flat, but a **plateau** rises above the surrounding land. A steep cliff often forms at least one side of a plateau. **Plains** can be flat or have a gentle roll and can be found along coastlines or far inland. Some plains are home to grazing animals, such as horses and antelope. Farmers and ranchers use plains areas to raise crops and livestock for food. A valley is a lowland area between two higher sides. Some

(l to r) Kei Uesugi/Getty Images; Anders Ryman/Alamy; Ingram Publishing/SuperStock; Edwin Remsberg/Taxi/Getty Images

---

networks *Online Teaching Options*

VIDEO

Changing World—Wild Weather

Analyzing Videos Have students view the video about extreme forms of weather and use a graphic organizer to analyze the forms of weather shown in the video. Then have students share what they learned about landforms and their relationship to weather from the video. **Visual/Spatial**

See page 39E for other online activities.

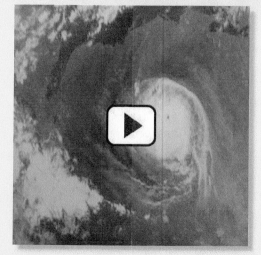

BBC Motion Gallery Education

valleys are small, level places surrounded by hills or mountains. Other valleys are huge expanses of land with highlands or mountain ranges on either side. Because they are often supplied with water runoff and topsoil from the higher lands around them, many valleys have rich soil and are used for farming and grazing livestock.

Another way to classify some landforms is to describe them in relation to bodies of water. Some types of landforms are surrounded by water. Continents are the largest of all landmasses. Most continents are bordered by land and water. Only Australia and Antarctica are completely surrounded by water. Islands are landmasses that are surrounded by water, but they are much smaller than continents.

A peninsula is a long, narrow area that extends into a river, a lake, or an ocean. Peninsulas at one end are connected to a larger landmass. An **isthmus** is a narrow strip of land connecting two larger land areas. One well-known isthmus is the Central American country of Panama. Panama connects two massive continents: North America and South America. Because it is the narrowest place in the Americas, the Isthmus of Panama is the location of the Panama Canal, a human-made canal connecting the Atlantic and Pacific oceans.

Under the Oceans

The ocean floor is also covered by different landforms. The ocean floor, like the ground we walk on, is part of Earth's crust. In many ways, the ocean floor and land are similar. If you could see an ocean without its water, you would see a huge expanse of plains, valleys, mountains, hills, and plateaus. Some of the landforms were shaped by the same forces that created the features we see on land.

If you were to explore the oceans, you would see landforms under the water that are similar to those on land.

Identifying What landforms on the map are classified by elevations?

Kei Uesugi/Getty Images

Chapter 2 **59**

T Technology Skills

Researching on the Internet Students might wonder to what continent Central America belongs. Suggest that interested students conduct Internet research to find out and report back to the class. *(North America)* **BL** Logical/Mathematical

V Visual Skills

Reading a Physical Map Have students use the physical map image of Central America to review the definitions of all the landforms and bodies of water they have read about. Have them point out the underwater ridges that can be seen in the map and relate these to landforms on land.

Suggest that they also use the image of Central America to speculate on the definitions of any unfamiliar terms. Then direct them to the glossary to confirm or refine their definitions. Have them make vocabulary cards or add to the vocabulary lists in their notebooks as needed to keep track of all the new terms they are learning. Visual/Spatial, Verbal/Linguistic

Content Background Knowledge

Mapping the Ocean Floor The ocean covers roughly two-thirds of Earth's surface. Before the 1800s, little was known about the ocean floor. Most people thought of it as being like a bowl, with a smooth surface. Yet even in the 1500s, a few sailors had discovered that different spots in the open ocean varied in depth, based on soundings with hand lines.

In the 1800s, deep-sea line soundings indicated that the central Atlantic Ocean had underwater mountains. In the early 1900s, echo-soundings further revealed the ruggedness of the ocean floor. Exploration of the ocean floor by many countries in the 1950s led to the discovery of an immense mountain chain that winds almost around the globe and rivals any mountain range on land.

MAP

Physical Geography of Earth

Reading a Map Have students view the physical geography layer of the Chapter Opener map and identify an example of a continent, an island, a peninsula, and an isthmus. Call on volunteers to describe the characteristics of each landform. **BL** Visual/Spatial

See page 39E for other online activities.

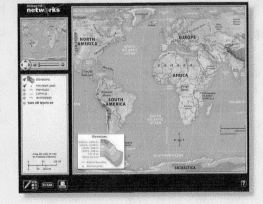

ANSWER, p. 59
Identifying Highland, plateau, lowland, plain

V Visual Skills

Analyzing an Infographic Have students use the infographic about salt water and freshwater at the top of the page to answer the following questions. **Ask:**

- What percentage of the water is salt water? *(about 97 percent)*
- What percentage is freshwater? *(about 3 percent)*
- What percentage of the world's population lacks access to clean drinking water? *(1 in 10, or 10 percent)*
- Even though Earth is largely covered by water, what can you conclude about the amount of water readily available for humans to drink? *(Only a tiny percentage of all the water on Earth is readily available for drinking.)* Logical/Mathematical

C Critical Thinking Skills

Making Connections Ask students if they have had any experience with continental shelves. They should realize that the land along a shoreline is a continental shelf, and so if they have ever waded into the ocean, they have been walking on a continental shelf.

Discuss the variety of coastlines along the eastern United States, from the rocky coastlines of Maine in the north to the sandy shores of Florida in the south. Elicit descriptions of the animal life found along continental shelves, such as crabs, sea stars, and mussels. Naturalist

W Writing Skills

Informative/Explanatory Tell students that even at the deepest, darkest places in the ocean, scientists have found amazing specimens of sea life. Suggest that interested students research the life found in the ocean depths and write a short report. Allow students to present their reports orally and encourage them to include pictures/photographs in their presentations. Verbal/Linguistic

---

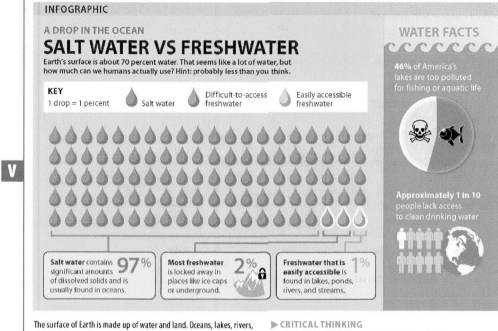

V

INFOGRAPHIC

A DROP IN THE OCEAN
SALT WATER VS FRESHWATER

Earth's surface is about 70 percent water. That seems like a lot of water, but how much can we humans actually use? Hint: probably less than you think.

KEY
1 drop = 1 percent — Salt water — Difficult-to-access freshwater — Easily accessible freshwater

Salt water contains **97%** significant amounts of dissolved solids and is usually found in oceans.

Most freshwater **2%** is locked away in places like ice caps or underground.

Freshwater that is easily accessible is **1%** found in lakes, ponds, rivers, and streams.

WATER FACTS

46% of America's lakes are too polluted for fishing or aquatic life

Approximately 1 in 10 people lack access to clean drinking water

The surface of Earth is made up of water and land. Oceans, lakes, rivers, and other bodies of water make up a large part of Earth.

▶ CRITICAL THINKING
Citing Text Evidence How much of Earth's surface is water?

C One type of ocean landform is the continental shelf. A **continental shelf** is an underwater plain that borders a continent. Continental shelves usually end at cliffs or downward slopes to the ocean floor.

W When divers explore oceans, they sometimes find enormous underwater cliffs that drop off into total darkness. These cliffs extend downward for hundreds or even thousands of feet. The water below is so deep that it is beyond the reach of the sun's light. The deepest location on Earth is the Mariana Trench in the Pacific Ocean. A **trench** is a long, narrow, steep-sided cut in the ground or on the ocean floor. At its deepest point, the Mariana Trench is more than 35,000 feet (10,668 m) below the surface of the ocean.

Other landforms on the ocean floor include volcanoes and mountains. When underwater volcanoes erupt, islands can form because layers of lava build up until they reach the ocean's surface. Mountains on the ocean floor can be as tall as Mount Everest. Undersea mountains can also form ranges. The Mid-Atlantic Ridge, the longest underwater mountain range, is longer than any mountain range on land.

☑ READING PROGRESS CHECK
Determining Word Meanings How is an ocean trench like a canyon?

---

netw☉rks   *Online Teaching Options*

INFOGRAPHIC

Fresh and Salt Water in the World

Analyzing Visuals Have students view this infographic, focusing on major bodies of water. Call on volunteers to identify the oceans and major lakes and rivers and determine if they are freshwater or salt water. Then have students compare the size of these bodies of water. BL Visual/Spatial

See page 39E for other online activities.

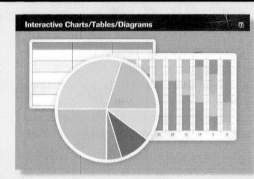

Interactive Charts/Tables/Diagrams

ANSWERS, p. 60

CRITICAL THINKING Water covers about 70% of Earth's surface.

☑ READING PROGRESS CHECK An ocean trench and a canyon both are long, narrow steep-sided cuts in the ground or ocean floor.

The Water Planet

GUIDING QUESTION *What types of water are found on Earth's surface?*

You can find water in many different forms. Water exists in three states of matter—solid, liquid, and gas—can be found all over the world. Glaciers, polar ice caps, and ice sheets are large masses of water in solid form. Rivers, lakes, and oceans contain liquid water. The atmosphere contains water vapor, which is water in the form of a gas.

Two Kinds of Water

Water at Earth's surface can be freshwater or salt water. Salt water is water that contains a large percentage of salt and other dissolved minerals. About 97 percent of the planet's water is salt water. Salt water makes up the world's oceans and also a few lakes and seas, such as the Great Salt Lake and the Dead Sea.

Salt water supports a huge variety of plant and animal life, such as whales, fish, and other sea creatures. Because of its high concentration of minerals, humans and most animals can not drink salt water. However, there is a way to remove minerals from salt water to produce water that is safe to drink. **Desalinization** is a process that separates most of the dissolved chemical elements. People who live in dry regions of the world use desalinization to process seawater into drinking water. But this process is expensive.

Freshwater makes up the remaining 3 percent of water on Earth. Most freshwater stays frozen in the ice caps of the Arctic and Antarctic. Only about 1 percent of all water on Earth is the liquid freshwater that humans and other living organisms use. Liquid freshwater is found in lakes, rivers, ponds, swamps, and marshes, and in the rocks and soil underground.

Water contained inside Earth's crust is called **groundwater**. Groundwater is an important source of drinking water, and it is used to irrigate crops. Groundwater often gathers in aquifers. These are underground layers of rock through which water flows. When humans dig wells down into rocks and soil, groundwater flows from the surrounding area and fills the well. Groundwater also flows naturally into rivers, lakes, and oceans.

Bodies of Water

You are probably familiar with some of the different kinds of bodies of water. Some bodies of water contain salt water, and others hold freshwater. The world's largest bodies of water are its five vast saltwater oceans.

A resident in a village in South America pumps water from a well.
▶ **CRITICAL THINKING**
Describing Why is groundwater important to people?

Anders Ryman/Alamy

Chapter 2 **61**

C1 Critical Thinking Skills

Identifying Problems Emphasize that of all the water on Earth, only 1 percent is liquid freshwater, which is what people and other living organisms require. **Ask:**

• Is all the liquid freshwater on Earth drinkable? *(No)*
• Why not? *(Some of it is polluted with chemicals and waste materials.)*

Explain that people in many regions on Earth struggle to find enough drinkable freshwater. **Ask:** What are some of the effects of a limited supply of drinking water on a people? *(Sample answers: It affects the health of the people in the region. Also, when people need to spend a great deal of energy getting water, they have less time for other activities, such as going to school or work.)* **AL** Verbal/Linguistic

C2 Critical Thinking Skills

Making Connections Draw students' attention to the boy getting water from a well. **Ask:**

• What do you think the boy will do with the water? *(Sample answer: Bring it home to use for drinking and cooking.)*
• Where does the water you use at home and at school come from? *(If students do not know the source of your community's water supply, have them find out by conducting Internet research or by contacting the local government.)* Visual/Spatial

Content Background Knowledge

Desalinization The major users of desalinated water are in the Middle East and North Africa, which are arid regions. In 2002 there were about 12,500 desalinization plants in 120 countries. The technology for desalinization is not new, and it mimics the water cycle in nature. Water is heated, causing it to evaporate, leaving the salt behind. The water vapor is then cooled so that it condenses and again becomes liquid separate from the salt.

WORKSHEET

Desalinization of Water

Interpreting Have students use the Geolab worksheet about desalinization to analyze how much easily accessible drinking water is actually on the planet. Logical/Mathematical

See page 39E for other online activities.

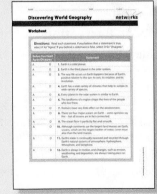

ANSWER, p. 61

CRITICAL THINKING Groundwater is important because it is used for drinking and for irrigating crops.

V Visual Skills

Creating Word Webs Suggest that students create word webs to take notes and then summarize the information about bodies of water. Provide students with the sample word web for *ocean* below, and then have them make their own word webs for *bay, gulf,* and *river.*

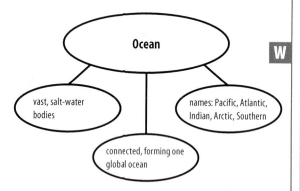

AL **ELL** Visual/Spatial

W Writing Skills

Narrative Suggest that students choose one of the two photographs and write a brief fictional narrative about the people and action depicted. Encourage students to use their imaginations to develop a plot, while focusing on the people's use of water.

Have them create a simple sequence of events for their plot using a flow chart or an outline of sentences that list the events in order. Then have them use their flow chart or outline to write their narrative. Remind them also to include descriptive words that appeal to the senses of their readers.

You might pair or group students for the benefit of those who struggle with writing. Encourage groups to brainstorm several ideas so not all narratives from the group are the same. Have pairs exchange their narratives and provide positive comments and constructive criticism for any revisions that are needed. Verbal/Linguistic, Interpersonal

Humans use bodies of water for recreational activities and to earn a living.
▶ **CRITICAL THINKING**
Describing How do people rely on bodies of water to meet their need for fuel?

From largest to smallest, the oceans are the Pacific, Atlantic, Indian, Southern, and Arctic. The Pacific Ocean covers more area than all of Earth's land combined. The Southern Ocean surrounds the continent of Antarctica. Although it is convenient to name the different oceans, it is important to remember that these bodies of water are actually connected and form one global ocean. Things that happen in one part of the ocean can affect the ocean all around the world.

When oceans meet landmasses, unique land features and bodies of water form. A coastal area where ocean waters are partially surrounded by land is called a bay. Bays are protected from ocean waves by the surrounding land, making them useful for fishing and boating. Larger areas of ocean waters partially surrounded by landmasses are called gulfs. The Gulf of Mexico is an example of ocean waters surrounded by continents and islands. Gulfs have many of the features of oceans but are smaller and are affected by the landmasses around them.

Bodies of water such as lakes, rivers, streams, and ponds usually hold freshwater. Freshwater contains some dissolved minerals, but only a small percentage. The fish, plants, and other life-forms that live in freshwater cannot live in salty ocean water.

Freshwater rivers are found all over the world. Rivers begin at a source where water feeds into them. Some rivers begin where two other rivers meet; their waters flow together to form a larger river. Other rivers are fed by sources such as lakes, natural springs, and melting snow flowing down from higher ground.

A river's end point is called the mouth of the river. Rivers end where they empty into other bodies of water. A river can empty into a lake, another river, or an ocean. A **delta** is an area where sand, silt, clay, or gravel is deposited at the mouth of a river. Some deltas flow onto land, enriching the soil with the nutrients they deposit. River deltas can be huge areas with their own ecosystems.

Bodies of water of all kinds affect the lives of people who live near them. Water provides food, work, transportation, and recreation to people in many parts of the world. People get food and earn a

netw⊙rks *Online Teaching Options*

GRAPHIC ORGANIZER

Water: Recreation vs. Livelihood

Listing Encourage students to think about all the ways that water is used for recreation and for making a living. Set a time limit for completing the graphic organizer—maybe 5 minutes—and have students share their ideas to form a class list. *(Sample answers: Recreation—swimming, canoeing, kayaking, water skiing, fishing, diving, sailing, boating, scuba diving; Livelihood—fishing, mining, oil drilling, shipping, research, tourism, transportation)*
Naturalist

See page 39E for other online activities.

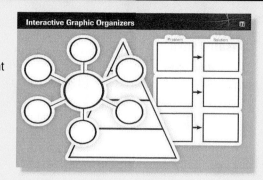

Interactive Graphic Organizers

ANSWER, p. 62

CRITICAL THINKING The ocean floor is drilled for oil and mined for minerals.

living by fishing in rivers, lakes, and oceans. The ocean floor is mined for minerals and drilled for oil. All types of waters have been used for transportation for thousands of years. People also use water for sports and recreation, such as swimming, sailing, fishing, and scuba diving. Water is vital to human culture and survival.

✔ READING PROGRESS CHECK

Describing In what ways do you depend on water?

The Water Supply

GUIDING QUESTION *What is the water cycle?*

Water is a basic need of all living things. Humans and other mammals, birds, reptiles, insects, fish, green plants, fungi, and bacteria must have water to survive. Water is essential for all life on Earth. To provide for the trillions of living organisms that use water every day, the planet needs a constant supply of fresh, clean water. Fortunately, water is recycled and renewed continually through Earth's natural systems of atmosphere, hydrosphere, lithosphere, and biosphere.

A Cycle of Balance

When it rains, puddles of water form on the ground. Have you noticed that after a day or two, puddles dry up and vanish? Where does the water go? It might seem as if water disappears and then new water is created, but this is not true. Water is not made or destroyed; it only changes form. When a puddle dries, the liquid water has turned into gas vapor that we cannot see. In time, the vapor will become liquid again, and perhaps it will fill another puddle someday.

   Scientists believe the total amount of water on Earth has not changed since our planet formed billions of years ago. How can this be true? It is possible because the same water is being recycled. At all times, water is moving over, under, and above Earth's surface and changing form as it is recycled. Earth's water recycling system is called the **water cycle**. The water cycle keeps Earth's water supply in balance.

Water Changes Form

The sun's energy warms the surface of Earth, including the surface of oceans and lakes. Heat energy from the sun causes liquid water on Earth's surface to change into water vapor in a process called **evaporation**. Evaporation is happening all around us, at all times. Water in oceans, lakes, rivers, and swimming pools is constantly evaporating into the air. Even small amounts of water—in the soil, in the leaves of plants, and in the breath we exhale—evaporate to become part of the atmosphere.

C Critical Thinking Skills

Making Connections Note the multitude of experiences that everyone has with water in its various states and with water changing states. Suggest that students think about the ways in which water changes state during the process of preparing a meal. For example, when water is boiled to cook rice, much of the water changes into water vapor. When ice is put into a glass of tea, it begins to melt. Ask students for other examples of water changing state. **Verbal/Linguistic**

V Visual Skills

Creating a Flow Chart Suggest that, as they read, students make a flow chart of the water cycle. If some students have difficulty identifying and paraphrasing the stages in the water cycle, provide them with the following labels:

- Liquid water in ocean, lake, or river
- Liquid water changes to water vapor in air
- Water vapor rises and forms clouds
- Water vapor condenses and forms liquid or solid water
- Liquid or solid water falls as rain, hail, or snow
- Liquid water enters ocean, lake, river, or ground

ELL Visual/Spatial

Content Background Knowledge

Special Properties of Water Tell students that water has many properties that make it an especially valuable substance. Share with students the following information:

- Unique among natural substances, water occurs in all three states (liquid, solid, and gas) at the normal temperatures on Earth.
- With most substances, the solid form is more dense than the liquid form. But solid water, or ice, is less dense than liquid water, which explains why ice floats.
- More substances dissolve in water than in any other liquid. So, unless it has been purified, water normally contains various chemicals and minerals.

MAP

Population of Earth

Identifying Display the population layer of the Chapter Opener map to the students. Have students discuss where populations are largest and how that relates to access to water. **Visual/Spatial**

See page 39E for other online activities.

ANSWER, p. 63

✔ READING PROGRESS CHECK Accept all responses that demonstrate students' understanding of the lesson content regarding the uses and importance of water to human survival and culture. Sample response: Drinking water is important to my health; water provides food to my family in the form of fish, crabs, lobster, and oysters; water provides recreation for my family when we go canoeing and swimming in a local lake or river.

Landforms and Bodies of Water

Reading Skills

Using Context Clues Have students read the sentence in which the academic vocabulary word *transforms* appears. Tell students to use the two or three words that come before and after this vocabulary word to infer its meaning. Have students explain how they determined that *transforms* means "changes."

BL Verbal/Linguistic

C **Critical Thinking Skills**

Synthesizing Ask students if they can think of three separate words that summarize the water cycle *(evaporation, condensation, precipitation)*. Have students draw a simple flow chart of the water cycle containing those three words, such as the following:

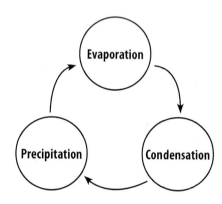

AL **ELL** Visual/Spatial

V **Visual Skills**

Analyzing a Diagram Draw students' attention to the diagram of the water cycle. Call on a volunteer to describe the process shown. **Ask:**

• Is it possible that the water you drank this morning was previously in Canada? *(yes)*

• Is it possible that the same water will be in Europe in the future? *(yes)*

Challenge students to use the diagram to make up a story about the movement of their drinking water through specific places. Call on a volunteer to share such a story. **AL** Visual/Spatial, Verbal/Linguistic

---

Academic Vocabulary

transform to change

Air that contains water vapor is less dense than dry air. This means that moist air tends to rise. As water evaporates, tiny droplets of water vapor rise into the atmosphere. Water vapor gathers into clouds of varying shapes and sizes. Sometimes clouds continue to build until they are saturated with water vapor and can hold no more. A process called **condensation** occurs, in which water vapor **transforms** into a denser liquid or solid state.

Condensation causes water to fall back to Earth's surface as rain, hail, or snow. Hail and snow either build up and stay solid or melt into liquid water. Snow stays solid when it falls in cold climates or on frozen mountaintops. When snow melts, it flows into rivers and lakes or melts directly into the ground.

Liquid rainwater returns water to rivers, lakes, and oceans. Rainwater also soaks into the ground, supplying moisture to plants and refilling underground water supplies to wells and natural springs. Much of the rainwater that soaks into the ground filters through soil and rocks and trickles back into rivers, lakes, and oceans. In this way, water taken from Earth's surface during evaporation returns in the form of precipitation. This cycle repeats all over the world, recycling the water every living organism needs to survive.

DIAGRAM SKILLS >

Water is constantly moving—from the oceans to the air to the ground and finally back to the oceans. The water cycle is the name given to this regular movement of water.

▶ **CRITICAL THINKING**

Analyzing In which part of the water cycle is water vapor changed into a denser liquid or a solid state? Why is this change important?

---

networks *Online Teaching Options*

ANIMATION

How the Water Cycle Works

Have students use the animation of the water cycle to analyze how water sources are replenished and how water moves around the planet. Visual/Spatial, Naturalist

See page 39E for other online activities.

ANSWER, p. 64

CRITICAL THINKING condensation; condensation causes water vapor to fall back on Earth's surface as rain, hail, or snow.

Landforms and Bodies of Water

Human actions have damaged the world's water supply. Waste from factories and runoff from toxic chemicals used on lawns and farm fields has polluted rivers, lakes, oceans, and groundwater. Chemicals such as pesticides and fertilizers seep into wells that hold drinking water, poisoning the water and causing deadly diseases.

The fossil fuels we burn release poisonous gases into the atmosphere. These gases combine with water vapor in the air to create toxic acids. These acids then fall to Earth as a deadly mixture called **acid rain**. Acid rain damages the environment in several ways. It pollutes the water humans and animals drink. The acids damage trees and other plants. As acid rain flows over the land and into waterways, it kills plant and animal life in bodies of water. This upsets the balance of the ecosystem.

☑ **READING PROGRESS CHECK**

Determining Central Ideas Explain how water that evaporates from a puddle can end up in a lake hundreds of miles away.

Some human activities pollute our rivers and oceans.
▶ **CRITICAL THINKING**
Explaining What causes acid rain?

FOLDABLES
Study Organizer

Include this lesson's information in your Foldable®.

LESSON 3 REVIEW

Reviewing Vocabulary
1. What is the role of *evaporation* in the *water cycle*?

Answering the Guiding Questions
2. *Analyzing* Why might life-forms change significantly in the area surrounding a continental shelf?

3. *Identifying* How are aquifers useful to humans?

4. *Determining Central Ideas* Explain why the water that you drink and bathe in today is the same water that the dinosaurs used millions of years ago.

5. *Analyzing* Why is a country that has little or no plains at a disadvantage?

6. *Narrative Writing* Imagine that you are a diver exploring the ocean floor. Describe various features you might see.

Chapter 2 **65**

LESSON 3 REVIEW ANSWERS

Reviewing Vocabulary

1. Evaporation moves water from the surface of Earth into the atmosphere so it can fall again as precipitation.

Answering the Guiding Questions

2. **Analyzing** A continental shelf ends in a sudden drop-off underwater, so the types of life-forms that live beyond the shelf would have to be adapted to much colder, darker waters.

3. **Identifying** Groundwater collects in aquifers, so when people dig wells, they are able to utilize the freshwater.

4. **Determining Central Ideas** The amount of water on Earth never changes. It changes form and is recycled.

5. **Analyzing** Plains are where farmers grow crops and graze livestock for food.

6. **Narrative Writing** Student essays will vary, but they should note that underwater features are similar to land features, but covered with water. They would see trenches, plateaus, mountains, volcanoes, hills, valleys, and plains.

(l) Comstock Images/Alamy; (r) Carey Morishige/NOAA Marine Debris Program

---

Researching on the Internet/Making Presentations Direct students to conduct Internet research either on the Great Pacific Garbage Patch, a huge mass of litter in the Pacific Ocean, or on the effects of acid rain in a specific location. Have students cite the sources for their research and evaluate the reliability of the content of their sources by making a list of their sources and giving each source a reliability score. This list should be turned in after the presentation.

Discuss the difference between paraphrasing content and giving the source credit and plagiarizing, i.e. copying the content of a source and not giving the source credit. Have students practice paraphrasing if needed. Explain that citing sources applies to photographs and images as well as text. Students should list the source of each image they include in their presentation.

Students might work alone or in small groups to prepare presentations on their subject for the class. If students work in small groups, have the groups assign roles so that every member of the group is involved in the presentation. Visual/Spatial

CLOSE & REFLECT

To close the lesson, remind students that they have learned about some of the amazing natural forces and processes that shape our planet. Encourage students to name these natural forces as a quick review. Then have other students name some ways that people have shaped our planet as well.

Place students in pairs. Have each student tell his or her partner one action he or she could take to lessen the negative impact that humans have on Earth. Then come back together and have each member of the pair talk about what their partner's idea is and how easy or difficult it would be to incorporate into the daily life of a student.

ANSWERS, p. 65

CRITICAL THINKING Poisonous gases from fossil fuels combine with water vapor in the air to form acid rain.
☑ READING PROGRESS CHECK The water in the puddle changes form into water vapor (evaporation) and becomes part of the atmosphere as clouds. Via condensation, water changes form and falls to Earth as rain, hail, or snow.

CHAPTER REVIEW ACTIVITY

Note that this chapter covered a great deal of information about Earth's structure, forces, and natural processes. Have students create and complete a two-column chart , listing key facts in column two about topics listed in column one. Then use the chart to lead a review of the chapter's main ideas. *(Students' charts should include the following:* **Earth's rotation on its axis**—*causes day and night;* **Earth's revolution around the sun**—*takes 365 ¼ days, or one year;* **Cause of seasons**—*Earth orbits sun in tilted position, and Northern and Southern hemispheres receive direct rays of sun at different times;* **Earth's layers**—*inner core of solid metal, outer core of liquid metal, mantle of liquid and solid rock, crust of solid rock;* **Earth's physical systems**—*atmosphere, lithosphere, hydrosphere, biosphere;* **Factors that influence climate**—*latitude, elevation, temperature, precipitation, wind and ocean currents, landforms;* **Forces that shape Earth's surface**—*plate movements, earthquakes, volcanic eruptions, weathering, erosion, ocean waves and currents, glaciers, human actions;* **Landforms**—*plateau, plain, valley, continent, isthmus, continental shelf, trench, volcano, mountain, delta;* **Water cycle**—*water evaporates, condenses, and precipitates in a recurring cycle.)*

Chapter 2 Main Ideas	Key Details
Earth's rotation on its axis	
Earth's revolution around sun	
Cause of seasons	
Earth's layers	
Earth's physical systems	
Factors that influence climate	
Forces that shape Earth's surface	
Landforms	
Water cycle	

REVIEW THE ENDURING UNDERSTANDINGS

Review this chapter's Enduring Understandings with students:

• *People, places, and ideas change over time.*
• *Resources are limited, so people must make choices.*

Now pose the following questions in a class discussion to apply these understandings to this chapter:

Chapter 2 ACTIVITIES

Directions: Write your answers on a separate piece of paper.

① Use your **FOLDABLES** to explore the Essential Question.
INFORMATIVE/EXPLANATORY WRITING Starting with the solar system and ending with your bedroom, describe your place in the universe in progressively more specific terms.

② **21st Century Skills**
INTEGRATING VISUAL INFORMATION Work with a partner to research the Isthmus of Panama. Create a PowerPoint presentation that shows its location and special characteristics. Include information about the history of the Panama Canal and its value to the people of the area.

③ **Thinking Like a Geographer**
ANALYZING Use various resources to research the history and evolution of the Appalachian and the Rocky Mountains, including their formation and their current conditions. Make a two-column poster chart describing their similarities and differences in detail.

④ **GEOGRAPHY ACTIVITY**

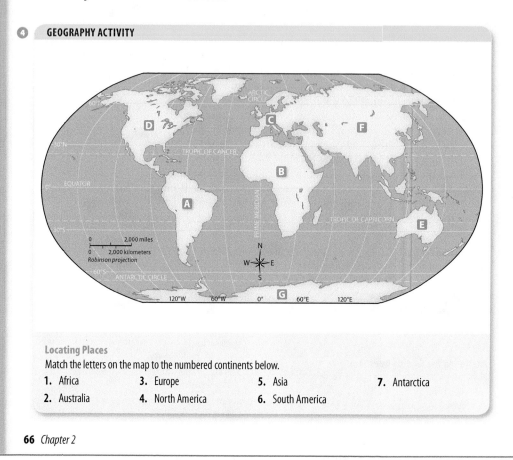

Locating Places
Match the letters on the map to the numbered continents below.

1. Africa   3. Europe   5. Asia   7. Antarctica
2. Australia   4. North America   6. South America

• How has Earth's surface changed over time? *(Answers may include the following facts: the continents have moved, mountains have been built up and eroded, glaciers have carved valleys, and wind and water erosion has created a wide variety of landforms.)*

• How have people changed Earth's surface? *(Answers may include the following facts: people have leveled land to build cities and roads; have polluted oceans, streams, and lakes; have cut down trees and removed other vegetation to create farms and ranches; have littered and polluted the land, oceans, rivers, and lakes with a variety of waste materials.)*

• Fresh drinking water is not readily available to all who need it. What are people doing to meet their needs for water? *(In some parts of the world, people are desalinating saltwater and digging ever-deeper wells to meet their needs for water. However these are expensive processes.)*

ACTIVITIES ANSWERS

Exploring the Essential Questions

① **INFORMATIVE/EXPLANATORY WRITING** Lists should include the Milky Way Galaxy, Earth, the Northern Hemisphere, North America, the United States, your state, your county or its equivalent, your city or town, the student's street name, a house or apartment number, and a bedroom within the home.

REVIEW THE GUIDING QUESTIONS

Directions: Choose the best answer for each question.

1 We walk on Earth's
A. atmosphere.
B. biosphere.
C. hydrosphere.
D. lithosphere.

2 When Earth makes a complete trip around the sun, it makes a
F. revolution.
G. rotation.
H. spin.
I. month.

3 The Ring of Fire was created by
A. an ancient tsunami.
B. movement of Earth's plates.
C. glaciers moving over the surface of Earth.
D. erosion.

4 Damage to buildings from air pollution is an example of
F. human forces.
G. natural forces.
H. global warming.
I. erosion.

5 The Gulf of Mexico is filled with
A. salt water.
B. freshwater.
C. a mixture of freshwater and saltwater fish species.
D. currently inactive volcanoes.

6 How many saltwater oceans does the world have?
F. two
G. three
H. five
I. six

Chapter 2 **67**

21st Century Skills

2 **INTEGRATING VISUAL INFORMATION** Student presentations should clearly show the characteristics of the area and the canal, and explain why the Panama Canal was built.

Thinking Like a Geographer

3 **ANALYZING** Posters should highlight the formation of the mountain ranges and the fact that the Appalachians are eroding, while the Rockies have sharper peaks and have not eroded as much.

Geography Activity

4 **LOCATING PLACES**

1. B

2. E

3. C

4. D

5. F

6. A

7. G

ASSESSMENT ANSWERS
Review the Guiding Questions

1 **D** We walk on Earth's lithosphere, or land. If students answer incorrectly, explain that the atmosphere is the layer of gases around Earth, the biosphere is made up of all the living plants and animals on Earth, and the hydrosphere is Earth's water. Have these students review, "Earth's Physical Systems," in Lesson 1.

2 **F** When Earth makes a complete trip around the sun, it makes a revolution, which takes a year not a month. If students answer incorrectly, explain that Earth's rotation is its spin on its axis, which happens daily causing day and night. Have students who answer incorrectly, review, "Planet Earth," in Lesson 1.

3 **B** The Ring of Fire was created by a collision of Earth's plates. If students answer incorrectly, explain that a tsunami is a giant ocean wave that washes things away, that glaciers carve out valleys and lakes, and that erosion does not create volcanoes. Have students who answer incorrectly, review, "Plate Movements," in Lesson 2.

4 **F** Damage to buildings from air pollution is an example of human forces, not natural forces such as erosion. Air pollution is caused when people burn gasoline and other fossil fuels in factories and modes of transportation such as cars and trucks. Have students who answer incorrectly, review, "Human Actions," in Lesson 2.

5 **A** The Gulf of Mexico is filled with salt water. Explain that the Gulf of Mexico is an example of ocean waters surrounded by continents and islands. Have students who answer incorrectly, review, "The Water Planet," in Lesson 3.

6 **H** The world has five salt-water oceans, the Pacific, Atlantic, Indian, Southern, and Arctic Oceans. Have students who answer incorrectly, review, "The Water Planet," in Lesson 3.

DBQ Analyzing Documents

7 **C** The author infers that the planets that are in the same category are located together as a group. If students answer incorrectly, have them reread the passage and Identify the two categories of planets and where each of them are located within the solar system in relation to the sun.

8 **G** The author would use the hard surface of Earth to classify the type of planet we live on. If students answer incorrectly, have them reread the passage and note that there is no mention of oceans, human beings, or moons for any of the planets and that the author classifies the planets as rocky or gas giants.

Short Response

9 *Rattle* probably refers to sound, and *jar* probably is a kind of surprising movement. The word *great* tells that the whole event was big, not subtle.

10 Twain probably just experienced an earthquake because the ground was moving and it seems to have caused damage. The noises that he describes are likely caused by the grinding of the two tectonic plates in Earth's crust rubbing together causing the earthquake or by the movement and/or collapse of buildings as a result of the earthquake.

Extended Response

11 Student answers will vary but they should choose a specific place and should support their choice with facts based on research about that area's climate, climate zone, landforms, and proximity to areas that suffer from potential natural disasters such as floods or earthquakes. Their writing should be informative and grammatically correct.

Chapter 2 **ASSESSMENT** *(continued)*

DBQ ANALYZING DOCUMENTS

7 **ANALYZING** In this paragraph, a science writer describes the two types of planets in our solar system.

"*The planets can be divided quite easily into two categories—the inner planets, which are small and rocky, and the gas giants that circle through the outer reaches of the solar system. Within each class, the planets bear a striking resemblance to each other, but the two classes themselves are very different.*"

—from James S. Trefil, *Space, Time, Infinity*

The author infers that

A. the planets are all similar.

B. the order of the planets changes.

C. the planets that are in the same category are located together as a group.

D. planets can switch categories as their structure changes.

8 **IDENTIFYING** Which feature of Earth would the author use to classify the type of planet we live on?

F. the presence of oceans

G. a hard surface

H. the existence of human beings

I. our moon

SHORT RESPONSE

"*There was a great rattle and jar. . . . [Then] there came a really terrific shock; the ground seemed to roll under me in waves, interrupted by a violent joggling up and down, and there was a heavy grinding noise as of brick houses rubbing together.*"

—from Mark Twain, *Roughing It*

9 **DETERMINING WORD MEANINGS** What do you think Twain meant by "great rattle and jar"?

10 **DETERMINING CENTRAL IDEAS** What do you think Twain just experienced? Explain how you know.

EXTENDED RESPONSE

11 **INFORMATIVE/EXPLANATORY WRITING** Considering the characteristics of various places in North America, South America, and Europe, where would you most like to live? Support your answer with detailed information about that area's climate, climate zone, landforms, and proximity to areas that suffer from potential natural disasters such as floods or earthquakes.

Need Extra Help?

If You've Missed Question	❶	❷	❸	❹	❺	❻	❼	❽	❾	❿	⓫
Review Lesson	1	1	2	2	3	3	1	1	2	2	1

---

networks *Online Teaching Options*

Remediation and Assessment

Evaluating The *Assess* tab in the online Teacher Lesson Center includes resources to help students improve their test-taking skills. It also contains many project-based rubrics to help you assess students' work.

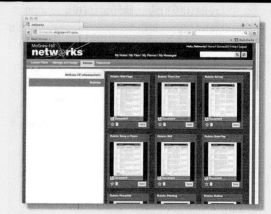

UNDERSTANDING BY DESIGN®

Enduring Understandings

- *Over time, people adapt to their environment.*
- *People, places, and ideas change over time.*
- *Countries have relationships with each other.*

Essential Questions

- *How do people adapt to their environment?*
- *What makes a culture unique?*
- *Why do people make economic choices?*

Predictable Misunderstandings

- *Families around the world are organized like those found in the student's local community.*
- *All countries have governments like that found in the United States.*
- *The customs students enjoy originated in the United States.*

Assessment Evidence

Performance Tasks:

- *Project-Based Learning Digital Hands-On Chapter Project*
- *Project-Based Learning Hands-On Chapter Project*

Other Evidence:

- *Writing Skills Activity*
- *Critical Thinking Skills Activity*
- *Geography and Economics Activity*
- *Participation in Project-Based Learning Activities*
- *Participation in Interactive Whiteboard Activities*
- *Contribution to small-group activities*
- *Interpretation of slide show images and special purpose maps*
- *Participation in class discussions about human geography topics*
- *Lesson Reviews*
- *Chapter Assessments*

SUGGESTED PACING GUIDE

Introducing the Chapter	2 Days	Lesson 3	2 Days
Lesson 1	2 Days	Global Connections	3 Days
Lesson 2	2 Days	Chapter Wrap-Up and Assessment	2 Days

TOTAL TIME 13 Days

Key for Using the Teacher Edition

SKILL-BASED ACTIVITIES

Types of skill activities found in the Teacher Edition.

* **V Visual Skills** require students to analyze maps, graphs, charts, and photos.

W Writing Skills provide writing opportunities to help students comprehend the text.

R Reading Skills help students practice reading skills and master vocabulary.

C Critical Thinking Skills help students apply and extend what they have learned.

T Technology Skills require students to use digital tools effectively.

*Letters are followed by a number when there is more than one of the same type of skill on the page.

DIFFERENTIATED INSTRUCTION

All activities are written for the on-level student unless otherwise marked with the leveled labels below.

BL Beyond Level
AL Approaching Level
ELL English Language Learners

All students benefit from activities that utilize different learning styles. Many activities are marked as below when a particular learning style is highlighted.

Intrapersonal	Naturalist
Logical/Mathematical	Kinesthetic
Visual/Spatial	Auditory/Musical
Verbal/Linguistic	Interpersonal

Indiana Academic Standards

Students will:

6.1.15 Describe the impact of industrialization and urbanization on the lives of individuals and on trade and cultural exchange between Europe and the Americas and the rest of the world.

6.1.16 Identify individuals, beliefs and events that represent various political ideologies during the nineteenth and twentieth century's and explain their significance.

6.1.17 Discuss the benefits and challenges related to the development of a highly technological society.

6.1.18 Create and compare timelines that identify major people, events and developments in the history of individual civilizations and/or countries that comprise Europe and the Americas.

6.1.19 Define and use the terms decade, century, and millennium, and compare alternative ways that historical periods and eras are designated by identifying the organizing principles upon which each is based.

6.1.20 Analyze cause-and-effect relationships, keeping in mind multiple causations, including the importance of individuals, ideas, human interests, beliefs and chance in history.

6.2.1 Compare and contrast major forms of governments in Europe and the Americas throughout history.

6.2.2 Explain how elements of Greek direct democracy and Roman representative democracy are present in modern systems of government.

6.2.4 Define the term nation-state and describe the rise of nation-states headed by monarchs in Europe from 1500 to 1700.

6.2.5 Discuss the impact of major forms of government in Europe and the Americas on civil and human rights.

6.2.7 Define and compare citizenship and the citizen's role throughout history in Europe and the Americas.

6.3.1 Demonstrate a broad understanding of the countries and capitals of Europe and the Americas.

6.3.3 Describe and compare major physical characteristics of regions in Europe and the Americas.

6.3.4 Describe and compare major cultural characteristics of regions in Europe and the Western Hemisphere.

6.3.9 Identify current patterns of population distribution and growth in Europe and the Americas using a variety of geographic representations such as maps, charts, graphs, and satellite images and aerial photography. Evaluate different push and pull factors that trigger migrations.

6.3.10, 6.3.12, 6.3.13, 6.3.14, 6.4.1, 6.4.2, 6.4.3, 6.4.4, 6.4.5, 6.4.7, 6.4.9

CHAPTER OPENER PLANNER

Students will know:
- *that population growth varies around the world.*
- *what a culture is.*

Students will be able to:
- ***identify*** *places on Earth that use the most electricity using a map.*
- ***analyze*** *a time line to discuss development of cultures and immigration movements.*

UNDERSTANDING
BY DESIGN

☑ *Print Teaching Options*

V Visual Skills

☐ **P. 70** Students study a world thematic map to learn about people's use of electricity throughout the world.

☐ **P. 71** Students use a time line along with the map to answer questions about cultures and immigration.

☑ *Online Teaching Options*

☐ **MAP Reading a Map**—Students identify aspects and locations of the region on a map.

☐ **TIME LINE Reading a Time Line and Map**—Students use a time line and a map to learn about where historical events occurred in the world. *Visual/Spatial*

☐ **MAP Interactive World Atlas**—Students use the interactive world atlas to identify the region and describe its terrain.

☑ *Printable Digital Worksheets*

☐ **WORKSHEET Critical Thinking Skills: Investigating Different Forms of Government**—Students use the worksheet to investigate how countries have changed their form of government.

☐ **WORKSHEET Geography and Economics: Pros and Cons of Free Market Trade**—Using the worksheet, students review the arguments for and against trading in a free market.

☐ **WORKSHEET Writing Skills: Investigating Population Movement**—Students use the worksheet to investigate current global population movement. *Verbal/Linguistic*

Project-Based Learning

Hands-On

Create Time Capsules

Students will work in groups to create time capsules that include cultural, economic, and political objects from their present-day communities. Students in each group must justify their choices for including each object. Completed time capsules should accurately reflect what life is like in the students' community today.

Digital Hands-On

Create Digital Scrapbooks

Students will create digital scrapbooks of their family history. Students should research and include information about their ancestral backgrounds using online census information, ancestry web sites, and personal interviews from family members. The digital scrapbooks might also include family photos that students have uploaded. When scrapbooks are complete, have each student share his or hers with the class.

edtechteacher
21ˢᵗ Century Learning

Print Resources

ANCILLARY RESOURCES

These ancillaries are available for every chapter and lesson.

- **Reading Essentials and Study Guide Workbook** AL ELL
- **Chapter Tests and Lesson Quizzes Blackline Masters**

PRINTABLE DIGITAL WORKSHEETS

These printable digital worksheets are available for every chapter and lesson.

- **Hands-On Chapter Projects**
- **What Do You Know? Activities**
- **Chapter Summaries (English and Spanish)**
- **Vocabulary Builder Activities**
- **Quizzes and Tests**
- **Reading Essentials and Study Guide (English and Spanish)** AL ELL
- **Guided Reading Activities**

More Media Resources

SUGGESTED VIDEOS

NOTE: Be sure to preview any clips to ensure they are age-appropriate.

- **History of the World in Two Hours** (120 min.)
- **Human Planet** (3 discs-480 min.)
- **Earth Keepers** (83 min.)

SUGGESTED READING

- *A Life Like Mine: How Children Live Around the World,* by UNICEF
- *What the World Eats,* by Faith D'Aluisio
- *A School Like Mine: A Unique Celebration of Schools Around the World,* by UNICEF AL
- *Green Cities,* by Ronald D. Lankford, Jr.

A Changing Population

Students will know:
- about birthrates and death rates.
- that population growth varies around the world.
- reasons why people move.

Students will be able to:
- **describe** three factors that have contributed to Earth's constantly rising population.
- **determine** why more people live in some parts of the world than in others.
- **list** causes and effects of human migration.

UNDERSTANDING
BY DESIGN®

☑ *Print Teaching Options*

V Visual Skills
- ☐ **P. 73** Students summarize a population pyramid.
- ☐ **P. 74** Students analyze slash-and-burn agriculture.
- ☐ **P. 76** Students compare urban and rural places.
- ☐ **P. 79** Students interpret a photo of refugees. **BL** **ELL**
- ☐ **P. 80** Students create a collage of images of a city. **ELL**

W Writing Skills
- ☐ **P. 79** Students write a paragraph describing how moving could affect a family's culture. **ELL**

R Reading Skills
- ☐ **P. 72** Students identify the main idea. **AL** **ELL**
- ☐ **P. 77** Students paraphrase information. **AL** **ELL**
- ☐ **P. 78** Students identify causes of immigration. **AL** **ELL**
- ☐ **P. 79** Students cite text evidence of the positive effects of the movement of people.
- ☐ **P. 81** Students map largest cities and megalopolises. **ELL**

C Critical Thinking Skills
- ☐ **P. 72** Students analyze information about birthrate and death rate and their impact on population growth. **BL**
- ☐ **P. 73** Students make connections between access to health care and education and population growth.
- ☐ **P. 76** Students infer why some people immigrate.
- ☐ **P. 78** Students determine causes and effects of population distribution and immigration rates. **BL**
- ☐ **P. 80** Students hypothesize about why plant life does better in rural settings than urban settings.

T Technology Skills
- ☐ **P. 74** Students research an alternative energy source and make an oral presentation with visual aids.
- ☐ **P. 75** Students research, draw, and label a diagram of how solar panels work.
- ☐ **P. 80** Students research and plot the top five largest cities on a world map. **AL** **ELL**

☑ *Online Teaching Options*

V Visual Skills
- **VIDEO** **Social Media Impact**—Students watch a video about the impact of social media on the spread of information and human geography. **AL** Visual/Spatial
- **SLIDE SHOW** **Places Around the World**—Students interpret the images and discuss the variety of places in the world. **AL** Visual/Spatial

R Reading Skills
- **SLIDE SHOW** **Population Challenges**—Students list the challenges that the world faces as the population climbs. **BL** Verbal/Linguistic
- **GRAPHIC ORGANIZER** **Why Do People Move?**—Students use the graphic organizer to discuss the meanings of *emigrate* and *immigrate* and analyze why people move. **ELL** Verbal/Linguistic
- **LECTURE SLIDE** **Immigration Definitions**—Students review the lecture slide for understanding of concepts and definitions.
- **LECTURE SLIDE** **Urbanization**—Students review concepts and definitions.

C Critical Thinking Skills
- **CHART** **Understanding Population**—Students analyze a population pyramid and draw conclusions about the data. **BL** Verbal/Linguistic
- **CHART** **Population Pyramids**—Students use the population pyramids of various countries to further explain distribution of population by age and gender.
- **MAP** **Landforms, Waterways, and Population**—Using the physical layer of the world map, students discuss how landforms and waterways affect human settlement. **AL**
- **VIDEO** **Migration**—After watching the video, students discuss the purpose of refugee camps and why people are forced to leave their country. **ELL** Visual/Spatial
- **MAP** **Population Density**—Using the physical and population layers, students relate population density to physical features. **AL** Verbal/Linguistic
- **IMAGE** **Refugee Camps**—Students use the photo to review facts about refugee camps.

T Technology Skills
- **ONLINE SELF-CHECK QUIZ** **Lesson 1**—Students receive instant feedback on their mastery of lesson content.

☑ *Printable Digital Worksheets*

W Writing Skills
- **WORKSHEET** **Writing Skills: Investigating Population Movement**—Students use the worksheet to investigate current global population movement. Verbal/Linguistic

GLOBAL CULTURES

Students will know:
- *what a culture is.*
- *what makes up cultural regions.*
- *how and why cultures change.*
- *different forms of government.*

Students will be able to:
- **analyze** *how clothing, behaviors, language, foods, and music give clues about culture.*
- **explain** *how government affects people's way of life.*
- **give examples** *of how cultures change over time.*
- **write an essay** *explaining their cultural traditions.*

UNDERSTANDING
BY DESIGN®

☑ *Print Teaching Options*

V Visual Skills

☐ **P. 82** Students draw a map of a country that is important to their culture. **AL** **ELL**

☐ **P. 83** Students examine photographs for clues about culture. **ELL**

☐ **P. 88** Students use an image of a port and discuss how global trade affects people's lives.

W Writing Skills

☐ **P. 86** Students write a narrative describing how people living in the colonies felt about Britain and the emergence of a new culture at the time of the signing of the Declaration of Independence.

R Reading Skills

☐ **P. 82** Students examine meanings of *culture*. **AL** **ELL**

☐ **P. 84** Students read a chart of major world religions.

☐ **P. 86** Students note cultural regions in the state. **ELL**

☐ **P. 87** Students use word parts to find meaning. **AL** **ELL**

C Critical Thinking Skills

☐ **P. 83** Students chart roles of ethnic groups. **AL** **ELL**

☐ **P. 85** Students give examples of sports played in international competitions and how they influence culture.

☐ **P. 87** Students make connections between types of government and human rights.

☐ **P. 88** Students suggest solutions for the challenges some cultural groups face when they immigrate.

T Technology Skills

☐ **P. 86** Students use the Internet to research two countries and the top products they produce.

☐ **P. 86** Students use presentation software to add images and music to the narrative they write.

☐ **P. 89** Students research and analyze news features online and evaluate how they affect culture. **AL**

☑ *Online Teaching Options*

V Visual Skills

☐ **MAP** **World Cultural Regions**—Students consider how cultural regions cover different parts of the world. **BL** Visual/Spatial

☐ **VIDEO** **World's Best Ancient Sites: North America**—Students watch a video about traditional cultures and consider how the cultures might be affected by changes such as a new government coming to power or climate change. **BL** Visual/Spatial

☐ **SLIDE SHOW** **Cultural Changes**—Students use the slide show to explain why cultures change and how emigration and immigration affect culture. **ELL**

R Reading Skills

☐ **GRAPHIC ORGANIZER** **Elements of Culture**—Students complete a graphic organizer about the elements of culture and choose one element and write a paragraph about its importance to culture. **AL** Verbal/Linguistic

☐ **LECTURE SLIDE** **Globalization**—Students use the lecture slide to review concepts from the lesson.

☐ **LECTURE SLIDE** **Different Languages**—Using this lecture slide, students review the various languages and pronunciations from around the world.

☐ **LECTURE SLIDE** **Comparing Governments**—Students use the lecture slide to review concepts in the lesson.

C Critical Thinking Skills

☐ **CHART** **Major World Religions**—Students use the chart to consider the similarities and differences of the world's religions and their influence on the culture of a region. **ELL** Visual/Spatial

☐ **CHART** **Types of Government**—Students use the chart to compare and contrast different forms of government, and then choose two of them and make a Venn diagram of their similarities and differences. **AL** Visual/Spatial

T Technology Skills

☐ **ONLINE SELF-CHECK QUIZ** **Lesson 2**—Students receive instant feedback on their mastery of lesson content.

☑ *Printable Digital Worksheets*

W Writing Skills

☐ **WORKSHEET** **Critical Thinking Skills: Investigating Different Forms of Government**—Students use the worksheet to investigate how countries have changed their form of government.

ECONOMIC SYSTEMS

Students will know:
- *different forms of government.*
- *the definition of globalization.*

Students will be able to:
- *describe* resources they use to get what they want and need.
- *identify* the kinds of economic systems used in the world today.
- *determine* how the world's economies interact and affect one another.
- *explain* the benefits of one economic system and write a persuasive paragraph about why the system is better than others.

UNDERSTANDING
BY DESIGN™

☐ *Print Teaching Options*

V Visual Skills

☐ **P. 94** Students sketch resources of wants and needs. ELL

☐ **P. 95** Students evaluate basic problems of economics.

☐ **P. 97** Students relate the factors of production with different economic systems.

☐ **P. 98** Students evaluate the factors of production.

☐ **P. 99** Students analyze a graph about GDP. BL

☐ **P. 100** Pairs of students collaborate and use an image to recognize the advantages and disadvantages of trade. BL

W Writing Skills

☐ **P. 98** Teams debate whether developing countries should be integrated into the world market and write an essay.

R Reading Skills

☐ **P. 94** Students discuss wants and needs of countries. AL

☐ **P. 95** Students use context clues to find meanings. ELL

☐ **P. 96** Students apply opportunity costs to their lives. ELL

☐ **P. 99** Students use word parts to define words. ELL

C Critical Thinking Skills

☐ **P. 95** Students compare and contrast renewable and nonrenewable resources. AL

☐ **P. 97** Students draw a diagram of the three different sectors of economic activities. AL ELL

☐ **P. 98** Students describe the factors of production.

☐ **P. 99** Students make and check predictions about causes and effects of different economies interacting. BL

☐ **P. 101** Students synthesize economic information. AL

T Technology Skills

☐ **P. 96** Students conduct Internet research to find out which type of economic system is most successful. BL

☐ **P. 100** Students evaluate the web site of the World Trade Organization.

☑ *Online Teaching Options*

V Visual Skills

☐ **VIDEO** **Emerging Markets in India Bring Westerners and Trade**—After watching the video, students share surprising information about developing markets in the economy. AL

☐ **IMAGE** **Types of Economic Activities and Sectors**—Students use the interactive image to review the difference between the economic sectors. BL Verbal/Linguistic

☐ **DIAGRAM** **Factors of Production**—Using the diagram, students review the factors of production and review the concepts behind this economic term. ELL Visual/Spatial

R Reading Skills

☐ **GRAPHIC ORGANIZER** **Pros and Cons of Trade**—Students use an interactive graphic organizer about why countries trade and the advantages and disadvantages of trade.

☐ **CHART** **Economic Questions**—Students review the three basic economic questions. Verbal

☐ **GAME** **Bartering and Trade**—Teams provide definitions of terms related to trade. AL

☐ **GAME** **Drag-and-Drop: Needs vs. Wants**—Students review terms from the lesson.

☐ **LECTURE SLIDE** **Renewable Resources**—Students use the lecture slide to enrich understanding of lesson content.

☐ **LECTURE SLIDE** **Economic Terms**—Students use the slide to review concepts and definitions.

☐ **GAME** **Drag-and-Drop: Imports and Exports**— Students play the drag-and-drop game to review concepts of trade and how goods pass from one region to another. Kinesthetic

C Critical Thinking Skills

☐ **GAME** **Drag-and-Drop: Economic Systems**—Teams of students sort a list of details about economic systems, needs, and wants. AL Interpersonal, Kinesthetic

☐ **GRAPH** **GDP Around the World**—Using the graph, students compare and contrast the GDP per capita of the six countries shown. AL Verbal/Linguistic

☐ **CHART** **Opportunity Cost**—Using the chart, students can review, define, and illustrate with examples the concept of this economic term.

T Technology Skills

☐ **ONLINE SELF-CHECK QUIZ** **Lesson 3**—Students receive instant feedback on their mastery of lesson content

☐ *Printable Digital Worksheets*

W Writing Skills

☐ **WORKSHEET** **Geography and Economics: Pros and Cons of Free Market Trade**—Using the worksheet, students review the arguments for and against trading in a free market.

INTERVENTION AND REMEDIATION STRATEGIES

LESSON 1 A Changing Population

Reading and Comprehension

Have students identify cause-and-effect relationships as they read by looking for signal words. Remind students that words and phrases such as *because, since, as a result, due to, therefore, thus, consequently, so, resulted in, cause,* or *effect* all indicate cause or effect.

Have student pairs practice using these words to explain a concept or central idea in this lesson.

Text Evidence

Have students work in small groups to research population changes in different parts of the world. Tell students to present an analysis of their findings, including charts or graphs to show the impact of the change.

After groups have presented their reports, discuss some of the causes and effects of population change.

LESSON 2 Global Cultures

Reading and Comprehension

Have students skim the lesson to look for unfamiliar or confusing words. Tell students to write down what they think the word might mean based on context clues in the text. Then have students look up each word in the dictionary to find its definition. Have students count how many correct definitions they wrote based on context clues.

Text Evidence

Have students work in pairs to research facts about different cultures. Assign each set of partners a different country. Explain that their analysis should answer the following questions about the people within that country: What language do people speak? How do they dress? What do they eat? What religions do people practice? What is the country's form of government? Have students present their findings to the class.

LESSON 3 Economic Systems

Reading and Comprehension

Have students play a guessing game in which one person gives clues about a content vocabulary term, and the other student tries to guess it. Have pairs compete against other pairs to see who knows or can define the most terms correctly in a certain amount of time. Be sure to explain that the students giving the clues should not use the actual vocabulary term in their clue.

Text Evidence

Students may have trouble grasping the different economic systems discussed in this lesson. Organize students into groups and assign each group one type of economic system: traditional economy, market economy, command economy, and mixed economy. Have students in each group work together to summarize how their assigned economic system works. Encourage students to use content vocabulary terms in their summaries.

Online Resources

Level Reader

Use this online lower-level text that corresponds directly to the text in the online Student Edition.

Guided Reading Activities

This resource uses graphic organizers and guiding questions to help students with comprehension.

What Do You Know?

Use these worksheets to pre-assess students' background knowledge before they study the chapter.

Reading Essentials and Study Guide Workbook

This resource offers writing and reading activities for the approaching-level student.

Self-Check Quizzes

This online assessment tool provides instant feedback for students to check their progress.

EARTH'S PEOPLE

There's More Online about Earth's People.

CHAPTER 3

ESSENTIAL QUESTIONS · *How do people adapt to their environment?*
· *What makes a culture unique?* · *Why do people make economic choices?*

©Hugh Sitton/Corbis

**Young girl from
South America**

Lesson 1
A Changing Population

Lesson 2
Global Cultures

Lesson 3
Economic Systems

The Story Matters...

In our study of geography, we study culture, which is the way of life of people who share similar beliefs and customs. A particular culture can be understood by looking at the languages the people speak, what beliefs they hold, and what smaller groups form as parts of their society.

FOLDABLES
Study Organizer

Go to the Foldables® library in the back of your book to make a Foldable® that will help you take notes while reading this chapter.

69

ENGAGE

Think-Pair-Share Read the Essential Questions and have students brainstorm reasons why we study the different cultures of the people of the world. Have pairs of students discuss and share their ideas. Students might say that each culture is different and that learning about other cultures helps us to better understand them. Then have students read "The Story Matters..." about how we can learn about cultures by studying peoples' languages, beliefs, and customs.

Discuss why it is helpful to understand the connections between humans and culture. **Ask:** What attributes make a culture unique from all the other cultures of the world? *(Possible answers: language, clothes, food, traditions, religion, beliefs, etc.)*

Tell students that they will learn about how cultures are similar and different and how people adapt to their environment.

Making Connections Read the following information to students in order for them to make connections to the content of the chapter.

Languages and customs are important to a culture. Cultures are diverse. Here are some facts about cultures and the languages that are spoken throughout the world:

- There is no set number of cultures in the world.
- English is the official language in over 50 countries of the world including the United States.
- Chinese and Chinese dialects are spoken by more human beings than any language.
- Arabic is the official language in 26 countries on two continents, Africa and Asia.
- Both India and Japan have one official language for each country, and that language is not an official language anywhere else in the world.

FOLDABLES
Study Organizer

Go to the Fol...
for a c...
bas...
y...

69

Letter from the Author

Dear Geography Teacher,

In 2012, the United Nations (UN) hosted the Conference on Sustainable Development. The conference addressed critical issues: jobs, energy, cities, food, water, oceans, and disasters. The UN defined sustainability as development that meets the present needs without compromising future generations' needs. Stabilizing population growth was seen as paramount to achieving progress all of the issues. Discuss how different cultures might feel about the conference "issues" and "sustainability."

Richard G. Boehm

ANSWERS, P.70
STEP INTO THE PLAC
1. cities where large amounts o
2. Urban areas use more electricity
No, the lights are not distributed e
Some area
the regions or countries are n
CRITICAL THINKING
s the brightly lit areas.

TEACH & ASSESS

Step Into the Place

V Visual Skills

Reading a Map Explain to students that this map presents the entire world on one map and shows electricity usage by the peoples of the world. Have students identify the regions on each continent where the most and least amount of electricity is used, and have students identify the cities of the world that make the brightest points of light on the map. Discuss how this thematic map would most likely have looked 100 years ago, 50 years ago, and 10 years ago.

Then have students use the map to answer the Step Into the Place questions. Visual/Spatial

Content Background Knowledge

People emigrate and immigrate for a variety of reasons. Jobs, families, education, climate, political factors, and natural disasters are some of the factors that push and pull people to and from places. The heaviest immigration worldwide took place from the early 1800s through the Great Depression in the 1930s. During this time period, about 60 million people moved to a new land. Most of the immigrants came from Europe and more than half of these people settled in the United States. Many came to the United States because of the lure of better farm land or the hope of finding a better job.

In 2010 the United States was the top country in the world to receive immigrants. The Russian Federation, Germany, Saudi Arabia, and Canada followed. However, the United States received more than three times as many immigrants as the next country, the Russian Federation. Today many professional people still emigrate for better job opportunities.

W

TE

f electricity are being used
than rural areas use.
venly.
s have fewer lights
t as developed nor

EARTH'S PEOPLE

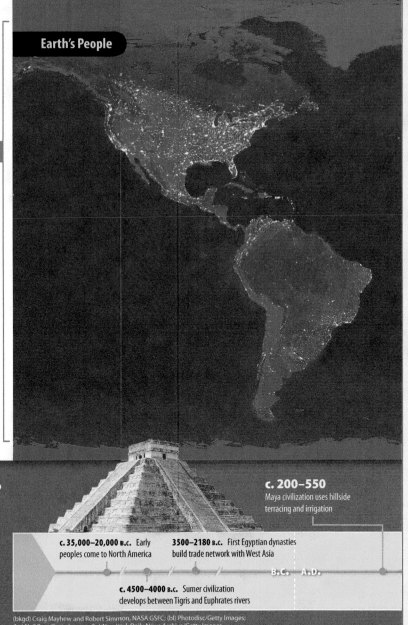

Earth's People

This image shows the world at night. Although the world's population is increasing, people still live on only a small part of Earth's surface. Some people live in highly urbanized areas, such as cities. Others, however, live in areas where they may not have access to electiricty or even running water. **V**

Step Into the Place

MAP FOCUS Use the image to answer the following questions.

1 HUMAN GEOGRAPHY
What do you think the brightly lit areas on the map represent?

2 HUMAN GEOGRAPHY
Why might some areas be brighter than others?

3 ENVIRONMENT AND SOCIETY Are the lights evenly distributed across the land?

4 CRITICAL THINKING
ANALYZING Why do some areas have fewer lights?

Step Into the Time

IDENTIFYING POINT OF VIEW Research one event from the time line. Write a journal entry describing the daily life of the time.

c. 35,000–20,000 B.C. Early peoples come to North America

3500–2180 B.C. First Egyptian dynasties build trade network with West Asia

c. 4500–4000 B.C. Sumer civilization develops between Tigris and Euphrates rivers

B.C. | A.D.

c. 200–550
Maya civilization uses hillside terracing and irrigation

70 *Chapter 3*

(bkgd) Craig Mayhew and Robert Simmon, NASA GSFC; (bl) Photodisc/Getty Images; (bc) Neil Beer/Getty Images; (br) New York Daily News Archive/Getty Images

Project-Based Learning

Hands-On

Making a Time Capsule
Students will work in groups to create time capsules that include cultural, economic, and political objects from their present-day communities. Students in each group must justify their choices for including each object. Completed time capsules should accurately reflect what life is like in the students' community today.

Digital Hands-On

Making a Digital Scrapbook
Students will create digital scrapbooks of their family history. Students should research and include information about their ancestral backgrounds using online census information, ancestry Web sites, and personal interviews from family members. The digital scrapbooks might also include family photos that students have uploaded. When scrapbooks are complete, have each student share his or hers with the class.

edtechteacher
21st Century Learning

1492
Christopher Columbus
lands in Americas

1892–1924
Millions of immigrants
arrive at Ellis Island

1000

1200s West African kingdom
of Benin trade center

1845–1849 Ireland's Great
Famine leads to mass emigration

2000

2011 South Sudan secedes,
forming new nation

Chapter 3 **71**

Step Into the Time

V Visual Skills

Reading a Time Line Remind students that time lines help to show visually the order in which events took place. Discuss the elements of a time line, including the start and end dates, event markers on the line, and labels at each marker. Ask students to share their ideas on how parallel time lines can be used. *(They can be used to compare events that took place in two different countries, regions, or hemispheres.)*

Have students review the time line and as a class, discuss its major points of interest. **Ask:**

- Which event on the time line shows the greatest length of time? *(Early people come to North America)*
- Did Ireland's Great Famine occur before or after millions of immigrants arrived at Ellis Island? *(before)*
- What abbreviation is used on the time line when the exact year is unknown, and what does it stand for? *(c.; circa)*
- Why are events listed from left to right on some time lines? *(Students might say that time lines are easy to read as events flow from left to right, much like the way people read.)*

Ask students to list some historical events that could be added to the time line. *(Student answers will vary but should include accurate event placement.)* Visual/Spatial

W Writing Skills

Narrative Before writing their journal entries, have students brainstorm ideas about how events on the time line changed how people understood or viewed the world in which they lived. Have them share their paragraphs with the class. Verbal/Linguistic

V

CLOSE & REFLECT

Applying Have students write a paragraph to explain how what they learned in the Chapter Opener helps them to better understand different cultures in their daily lives. Invite students to share their paragraphs with the class. Tell them that they will learn more about world cultures as they study this chapter.

TIME LINE

Reading a Time Line and Map

Analyzing Visuals Display the time line and map on the interactive whiteboard. Have students choose an event from the time line and identify where in the world the event took place by finding it on the map. Ask students to research the event further and to share what they learned about the event with the class. Visual/Spatial

See page 69B for other online activities.

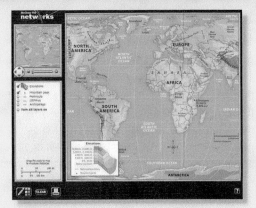

ENGAGE

Bellringer Before students begin the lesson, ask them what they know about population. Then read the Essential Question aloud and have students discuss how the environment of their area affects the way people live or influences how many people choose to live there. **Ask:** In what ways do you need to adapt to the environment in your area? Have them explain why these adaptations would be necessary. *(Student answers will vary but should include mention of how specific environmental factors such as climate or living in a rural or urban area affects the way they live.)*

TEACH & ASSESS

R Reading Skills

Determining Central Ideas Explain to students that finding the main idea of a paragraph will help them to better understand the content and give each paragraph meaning and purpose. Point out that the main idea is often stated in the first few sentences of a paragraph. As a class, locate the main idea of the paragraph. *(Many factors cause populations to increase.)* Encourage them to work with a partner to find the main idea of the next paragraph. Explain that finding the main idea of each paragraph and writing main ideas in their notebooks is an excellent way to keep notes on their reading. **AL ELL**
Verbal/Linguistic

C Critical Thinking Skills

Analyzing Information Population growth is determined by death rate and birthrate. **Ask:** What kind of graph could be used to show data on the death rate and birthrate in a decade and what would it look like? *(A line graph could be used. The line showing the death rate would be decreasing while the line showing the birthrate would be increasing.)* **BL**
Visual/Spatial

ANSWER, p. 72

Taking Notes Responses will vary but should demonstrate an understanding of the main causes and effects of population growth and migration. Sample notes: **Causes of population growth:** relationships between birth and death rates, people living longer and healthier lives; **Effects:** growing human populations, crowding, damage to the environment, emigration and migration, urbanization; **Causes of migration:** war, poverty, lack of opportunities, environmental disasters, human rights issues, family issues; **Effects:** humans emigrate from their homelands and move to new places; **Cause:** humans migrate to different parts of the world; **Effects:** cultures are blended and enriched; cities grow, endangering natural areas; resources are used quickly; environments are polluted.

---

networks

There's More Online!

☑ **IMAGES** Refugee Camps
☑ **MAP** Landforms, Waterways, and Population
☑ **SLIDE SHOW** Places around the World
☑ **VIDEO**

Reading **HELPDESK**

Academic Vocabulary

- mature

Content Vocabulary

- death rate
- birthrate
- doubling time
- population distribution
- population density
- urban
- rural
- emigrate
- immigrate
- refugee
- urbanization
- megalopolis

TAKING NOTES: *Key Ideas and Details*

Determining Cause and Effect As you read, use a graphic organizer like this one to take notes about the causes of population growth and migration.

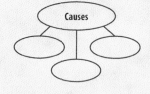

Causes

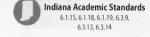

Indiana Academic Standards
6.1.15, 6.1.18, 6.1.19, 6.3.9, 6.3.13, 6.3.14

72

Lesson 1
A Changing Population

ESSENTIAL QUESTION • *How do people adapt to their environment?*

IT MATTERS BECAUSE
Billions of people share Earth. They have many different ways of life.

Population Growth

GUIDING QUESTION *What factors contribute to Earth's constantly rising population?*

The world's population is growing fast. In 1800 about 860 million people lived in the world. During the next 100 years, the population doubled to nearly 1.7 billion. By 2012, the total passed 7 billion.

Causes of Population Growth

How has Earth's population become so large? What has caused our population to grow so quickly? Many factors cause populations to increase. One major cause of population growth is a falling death rate. The death rate is the number of deaths compared to the total number of individuals in a population at a given time. On average, about 154,080 people die every day worldwide. The **death rate** has decreased for many reasons. Better health care, more food, and cleaner water have helped more people—young and old—live longer, healthier lives.

Another major cause of population growth is the global birthrate. The **birthrate** is the number of babies born compared to the total number of individuals in a population at a given time. On average, about 215,120 babies are born each day worldwide. In time, the babies born today will **mature** and have children and grandchildren of their own.

(l to r) Heritage Imagestate/Glow Images; Derek Trask/Photolibrary/Getty Images; Bogdan Bratosin/Flickr/Getty Images; Carlos Spottorno/Getty Images News/Getty Images; Robert Glusic/Photodisc/Getty Images

---

networks *Online Teaching Options*

VIDEO

Social Media Impact

Determining Cause and Effect Use the video about the impact of social media to discuss how technology is making the world a smaller place. Have students point out parts of the video they find interesting. Discuss with students various social media tools that they use that can bring people closer together. Ask students if these changes are positive or negative for human interaction. Highlight current events, protests, and Internet activism impacted by social media. **AL** Visual/Spatial

See page 69C for other online activities.

BBC Motion Gallery Education

This is how more and more people join the human population with each passing day.

However, during the past 60 years, the world's human birthrate has been decreasing slowly, although the global birthrate is still higher than the global death rate. This means that at any given time, such as a day or a year, more births than deaths occur. This results in population growth.

Growth Rates

In some countries, a high number of births has combined with a low death rate to greatly increase population growth. As a result, **doubling time**, or the number of years it takes a population to double in size based on its current growth rate, is relatively short. In some parts of Asia and Africa, for example, the doubling time is relatively short—25 years or less. In contrast, the average doubling time of countries with slow growth rates, such as Canada, can be more than 75 years.

Despite the fact that the global population is growing, the rate of growth is gradually slowing. The United Nations Department of Economic and Social Affairs predicts that the world's population will peak at 9 billion by the year 2050. After that, the population will begin to decrease. This means that for the next few decades, Earth's population will continue to grow. In time, however, this growth trend might stop.

Academic Vocabulary

mature to become fully grown and developed as an adult; also refers to older adults

GRAPH SKILLS >

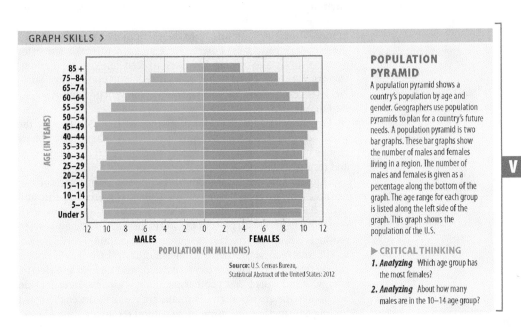

POPULATION PYRAMID

A population pyramid shows a country's population by age and gender. Geographers use population pyramids to plan for a country's future needs. A population pyramid is two bar graphs. These bar graphs show the number of males and females living in a region. The number of males and females is given as a percentage along the bottom of the graph. The age range for each group is listed along the left side of the graph. This graph shows the population of the U.S.

▶ **CRITICAL THINKING**

1. Analyzing Which age group has the most females?

2. Analyzing About how many males are in the 10–14 age group?

Source: U.S. Census Bureau, Statistical Abstract of the United States: 2012

Chapter 3 **73**

Understanding Population Pyramids

Analyzing Charts Display the population pyramid chart on the interactive whiteboard. Have volunteers click on the pyramid to reveal different population trends. Then ask students to analyze the chart, comparing gender and age, and draw conclusions about the data. **BL** Verbal/Linguistic

See page 69C for other online activities.

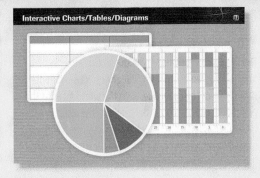

Interactive Charts/Tables/Diagrams

C Critical Thinking Skills

Making Connections Discuss with students the strong relationship between a short doubling time of population growth in certain countries and those countries that do not have adequate access to health care and education. **Ask:** Why do countries in parts of Asia and Africa have short doubling times compared to those in Europe and North America? *(Student answers may vary but should explain how women who live in some countries in Asia and Africa do not have the education or the access to health care as women in Europe and North America do; these women in Asia and Africa do have more children, which contributes to a high population growth and short doubling time.)* Verbal/Linguistic

V Visual Skills

Reading a Graph Explain to students that a graph can show a lot of data in a visual way. When reading a graph, it is important to read all of the labels to become familiar with the data. It is also important to understand what is being measured and the amounts of measurement. To read a population pyramid, look at the data on both sides of the graph. Explain that sometimes lower or abbreviated numbers are used so that the amounts fit or are shown more clearly on a graph. **Ask:**

- What amount is the population being measured in? *(millions)*
- What does the label 60–64 stand for? *(the age group of people who are 60 to 64 years old)*
- According to the graph, what is the population of males under the age of 5? *(10 million)*
- According to the graph, are there more males or females over the age of 85? *(females)*

Have students work individually to write a summary of the data that the graph illustrates. Encourage students to consider the data that shows the highest and lowest values, as well as values that are the same for both females and males or are the same in specific age groups. Remind students that they need to include labels when writing their summaries. Visual/Spatial

ANSWERS, p. 73

CRITICAL THINKING

1. 65–74

2. about 10 million

A Changing Population

V Visual Skills

Creating Visuals Have students look at the picture of the men burning trees. Discuss how these men are farmers who clear land by cutting and burning forests. Explain that slash-and-burn agriculture allows farmers to create farm land quickly, but does not look at longterm effects to the environment. These effects include soil erosion (which can cause deadly mudslides during rainy seasons), reducing spaces for wildlife, polluting the air, eliminating valuable rainforests, and depleting soil nutrients.

Divide students into groups. Have the groups then work on a public service campaign to discourage slash-and-burn farming. A public service campaign tries to educate or persuade citizens to change their behaviors or beliefs. Have the groups create posters or act out skits for their public service campaigns against slash-and-burn practices. **Visual/Spatial, Interpersonal**

T Technology Skills

Making Presentations Have a volunteer read aloud the first two paragraphs under, "Effects on the Environment." **Ask:** What has happened over time to Earth's atmosphere? *(Thousands of factories have polluted the Earth's atmosphere with chemical waste.)*

As a class, discuss other factors that have harmed the environment and how and why these effects have come about. After the discussion, pair up students. Have each pair choose a topic on one of the alternative energy resources from the third paragraph of, "Effects on the Environment," or other alternative energy resources that students may know about.

Provide an opportunity for students to research their topic using the Internet and to prepare an oral presentation. Suggest that they use visual aids, such as photos and graphs to make their presentations more interesting. Then have students share their presentations with the class. **Verbal/Linguistic, Visual/Spatial, Interpersonal**

Farmers in many parts of the world clear land by cutting and burning forests.
▶ CRITICAL THINKING
Analyzing Why do some groups practice slash-and-burn agriculture?

Population Challenges

When human populations grow, the places people inhabit can become crowded. In many parts of the world, cities, towns, and villages have grown and expanded beyond a comfortable capacity. Some cities are now so filled with people that they are becoming dangerously overcrowded.

When the population of an already crowded area continues to grow, serious problems can arise. For example, diseases spread quickly in crowded environments. Sometimes there is not enough work for everyone, and many households live in ongoing poverty. Where many people share tight living spaces, crime can be a serious problem and pollution can increase.

Effects on the Environment

On a global scale, rapid population growth can harm the environment. Each year, more people are sharing the same amount of space. People demand fuel for their cars and power for their homes. Miners drill and dig into the earth in a constant search for more energy resources. Forests are cut down to make farms for growing crops and raising livestock to feed hungry populations. Factory workers build cars, computers, and appliances. Some factories dump chemicals into waterways and vent poisonous smoke into the air.

Over time, and with many thousands of factories all over the world, chemical wastes have polluted Earth's atmosphere. Many groups and individuals are working to clean up the environment and restore once-polluted areas.

Humans have many methods of finding and using the resources we need for survival. Some of these methods are wasteful and destructive. However, humans are also creative in solving modern problems. People in all parts of the world have invented new ways to produce power and harvest resources. For example, some people install solar panels on the roofs of buildings. These panels collect energy from the sun, which can be used to produce heat and electric energy. Wind, solar, and geothermal energy are resources that do not pollute the environment. Humans are rising to the challenge of finding new methods of using these natural resources.

Heritage-Imagestate/Glow Images

---

net**w**rks *Online Teaching Options*

Population Challenges

Drawing Conclusions Show the lecture slide presentation on population challenges. Have students make a list of the challenges that the world faces as the population climbs. Then ask them to write a statement that explains what they think is the greatest challenge caused by population growth. **BL Verbal/Linguistic**

See page 69C for other online activities.

Slide Show

(l) ©Ocean/Corbis, ©Kryssia Campos/Getty Images, (tr) ©Erica Simone Leeds, (br) ©JG Photography/Alamy

---

ANSWER, p. 74

CRITICAL THINKING to clear land to grow crops and raise livestock

Population Growth Rates

Human populations grow at different rates in different areas of the world for many reasons. Often, the number of children each family will have is influenced by the family's culture and religion. In some cultures, families are encouraged to have as many children as they can. Although birthrates have fallen greatly in many parts of Asia, Africa, and South America in recent decades, the rates are still higher than in industrialized nations such as the United States.

In locations with the largest and fastest-growing populations, the need for resources, jobs, health care, and education is great. When millions of people living in a small area need food, water, and housing, there is sometimes not enough for everyone. People in many parts of the world go hungry or die of starvation. Water supplies in crowded cities are often polluted with wastes that can cause diseases. Some areas do not have enough land resources and materials for people to build safe, sturdy homes.

Children in areas affected by extreme poverty often do not receive an education. In areas with job shortages, people are forced to live on low incomes. People living in poverty often live in crowded neighborhoods called *slums*. Slums surround many of the world's cities. These places are often dirty and unsafe. Governments and organizations such as the United Nations are working to make these areas safer, healthier places to live. Because populations grow at different rates some areas experience more severe problems.

R

Solar panels collect energy from the sun.
► **CRITICAL THINKING**
Identifying Why do some people prefer solar energy?

T

☑ **READING PROGRESS CHECK**

Analyzing How can rapid population growth harm the environment?

©George Hammerstein/Corbis

R Reading Skills

Using Context Clues You can look at words around or near a word that is unfamiliar to you to learn its meaning. Have students read the last two paragraphs of this page. **Ask:**

- What words help you to understand the meaning of *sturdy*? *(not enough resources, build, and safe)*
- What words help you to understand the meaning of *slums*? *(poverty, crowded neighborhoods)*
- What other words are unfamiliar to you? *(Possible answer: starvation)*
- What context clues help you to understand their meaning? *(hungry and die)* Verbal/Linguistic, Intrapersonal

T Technology Skills

Diagramming Have students work in small groups to find out how solar panels work using classroom or library print or digital resources. Ask them to draw and label a diagram on a poster or using computer software. **Ask:** Besides not polluting the environment, why is solar energy an ideal alternative resource? *(Student answers may vary but should include that solar energy is an inexhaustible resource that will not run out.)* Visual/Spatial, Interpersonal

V

V Visual Skills

Analyzing Images Have student pairs review the image in the textbook. Encourage them to discuss the image and make notes about the size of the structures and how closely they are placed next to each other. **Ask:**

- Why do you think the buildings are placed so closely together? *(Students' answers should suggest that the buildings are placed closely together so they could fit more buildings in one area.)*
- How does the buildings being placed closely together relate to the population of the area? *(Students' answers should suggest that the area is highly populated and therefore, more housing is needed.)*

Be sure students make the connection between the population density of the region and the creation of places like slums. Visual/Spatial

SLIDE SHOW

Places Around the World

Interpreting Show the slide show on the different types of places in the world. Point out how places can include buildings, streets, or malls, and can be inside or outside places. Discuss how varied places are around the world and within a specific geographic location. Ask students to describe a type of place that is familiar to them. **AL** Visual/Spatial

See page 69C for other online activities.

Slide Show

ANSWERS, p. 75

CRITICAL THINKING It does not pollute the environment.

☑ READING PROGRESS CHECK When a population grows rapidly it can put a strain on available resources. There might not be enough housing, food, clean water, fuel, or jobs. Also the amount of waste the population produces can harm the environment.

A Changing Population

V Visual Skills V

Analyzing Visuals Have students study the images on these two pages and then draw a Venn diagram. Ask them to label one oval "urban," the other "rural," and the middle "both." Explain that they should fill in their diagrams with examples of how urban and rural places are similar and different by comparing the two images. **Ask:** What kind of place do you live in, urban or rural? How do you know? *(Student answers will vary but should include an explanation such as an urban area has more people, streets, and buildings, while a rural area has less population and often has more open and undeveloped land.)* Visual/Spatial, Intrapersonal

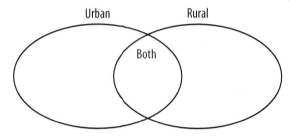

Urban   Rural

Both

C Critical Thinking Skills

Making Inferences Explain that some people migrate to different places to live, while others remain in the same place for a long time. **Ask:** Why do you think that some people move frequently while others never move or stay in the same area? *(Student answers will vary but could include that people often stay in the same area to be close to family, while others move frequently because of economic factors.)* Verbal/Linguistic

Content Background Knowledge

Coastal areas are often the most populated areas around the world. Climate, resources, and economic opportunities are two important factors that affect human settlement and population density and distribution. In 2010, more than half of the world's population lived in urban areas, which marked a milestone in population distribution. Before then, more people lived in rural areas worldwide.

Much of the land surrounding this village is used for farming.
▶ CRITICAL THINKING
Describing What are rural areas?

Where People Live

GUIDING QUESTION *Why do more people live in some parts of the world than in others?*

Throughout history, people have moved from one place to another. People continue to move today, and the population continues to grow.

Population Distribution

Population growth rates vary among Earth's regions. The **population distribution**, or the geographic pattern of where people live on Earth, is uneven as well. One reason people live in a certain place is work. During the industrial age, for example, people moved to places that had important resources such as coal or iron ore to make and operate machinery. People gather in other places because these places hold religious significance or because they are government or transportation centers.

Population Density

One way to look at population is by measuring **population density**—the average number of people living within a square mile or a square kilometer. To say that an area is *densely populated* means the area has a large number of people living within it.

Keep in mind that a country's population density is the average for the entire country. But population is not distributed evenly throughout the country. As a result, some areas are more densely populated than their country's average indicates. In Egypt, for example, the population is concentrated along the Nile River; in China, along its eastern seaboard; and in Mexico, on the Central Plateau.

Derek Trask/Photolibrary/Getty Images

---

net**works** *Online Teaching Options*

MAP

Population Density

Determining Cause and Effect Display the interactive Chapter Opener map on the whiteboard. Use the physical and population layers of the map to show areas of high population density around the world and where populations tend to develop. AL Verbal/Linguistic

See page 69C for other online activities.

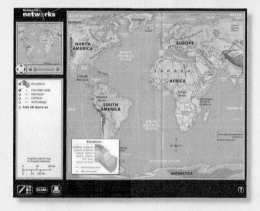

ANSWER, p. 76

CRITICAL THINKING areas with low population density, or which are sparsely populated

Where People Are Located

Urban areas are densely populated. **Rural** areas, in contrast, are sparsely populated. People inhabit only a small part of Earth. Remember that land covers about 30 percent of Earth's surface, and half of this land is not useful to humans. This means that only about 15 percent of Earth's surface is inhabitable. Large cities have dense populations, while deserts, oceans, and mountaintops are uninhabited.

The main reason people settle in some areas and not in others is the need for resources. People live where their basic needs can be met. People need shelter, food, water, and a way to earn a living. Some people live in cities, which have many places to live and work. Other people make their homes on open grasslands where they build their own shelters, grow their own food, and raise livestock.

☑ READING PROGRESS CHECK

Identifying What is the main reason people settle in some areas instead of others?

Changing Populations

GUIDING QUESTION *What are the causes and effects of human migration?*

When people move, either as individuals or in large groups, areas change. When many people leave an area, that area's population decreases.

Guanajuato is a town in central Mexico that began as a major mining center in the mid-1500s.
▶ **CRITICAL THINKING**
Describing What is the main difference between rural areas and urban areas?

Chapter 3 77

Bogdan Bratosin/Flickr/Getty Images

C Critical Thinking Skills

Comparing and Contrasting Have students work in small groups to create a two-column chart that identifies rural and urban places throughout the world.

Rural Places	Urban Places

Students should list real location examples for both rural and urban places on different continents, using their background knowledge and travel experiences as much as possible. Invite students to share their charts with the class. If time allows, compile each group's information into a class graphic organizer.
ELL Verbal/Linguistic

R Reading Skills

Paraphrasing Have students reread the last paragraph in the section, "Where People Are Located." Ask them to paraphrase, or use their own words, to explain why people settle in some areas of the world and not in others. *(Possible answer: People move to areas where they can find resources to meet their basic needs.)*

Then discuss other reasons why people settle in some areas of the world and not in others. *(They also move to more favorable climates to escape cold weather for example or to regions that offer better opportunities for education and jobs.)*

Making Connections Ask students if they have ever been to one of the most populous cities in the United States (New York, NY; Los Angeles, CA; Chicago, IL; or Houston, TX). Have them describe what it was like to be in such a large city. Have them describe what they saw, heard, tasted, and so on. Then do the same for anyone who has been to a rural area. **ELL** **AL**
Interpersonal

MAP

Landforms, Waterways, and Population

Determining Cause and Effect Display the interactive Chapter Opener map on the whiteboard. Use the physical layer of the map to discuss how landforms and waterways affect human settlement and how they may have caused population growth in some areas and not in others. **AL**
Verbal/Linguistic

See page 69C for other online activities.

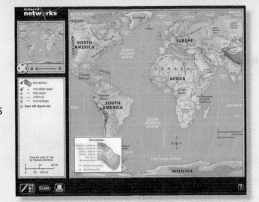

ANSWERS, p. 77

CRITICAL THINKING Urban areas are densely populated, and rural areas are sparsely populated.

☑ READING PROGRESS CHECK Access to basic resources needed to survive is the main reason people choose where to live.

A Changing Population

Applying After students have read the section about the key causes of the migration of people throughout the world, invite volunteers to identify each cause as you list it on the whiteboard. *(push factors such as war or violence force people to leave their homeland and pull factors such as family, education, and economic opportunities encourage people to move to regions with better opportunities)*

Then have small groups brainstorm a list of causes of migration for their area. Remind them to include the natural resources of the area, the climate, opportunities for education, and job opportunites for adults. Bring the class together to share their lists. **ELL AL** Interpersonal

Determining Cause and Effect Explain to students that push and pull factors affect population growth, distribution, and density. They also affect immigration rates. **Ask:** How do push and pull factors affect immigration and population? *(Student answers will vary but should demonstrate an understanding of how immigration will most likely increase where people are pulled, and population will also increase in those locations. Where there are push factors, immigration will decrease as well as the population.)* **BL** Verbal/Linguistic

Content Background Knowledge

According to the UN High Commissioner for Refugees, the number of refugees worldwide decreased from 15.9 million in 2000 to 15.4 million in 2010. Yet the total number of international migrants rose from 150 million in 2000 to 214 million in 2010. Nearly half of those migrants are female. The countries with the fewest number of migrants include South Africa, Slovakia, Turkey, Japan, Nigeria, Romania, India, and Indonesia. Invite students to discuss why they think these countries would have the fewest number of migrants.

People in rural areas often obtain food in outdoor markets such as this one in northern Michigan.

When large numbers of people move into an area, the population of that area increases. Moving from one place to another is called *migration*.

Causes of Migration

R What causes people to leave their homelands and migrate to different parts of the world? To **emigrate** means to leave one's home "to live in another place." Emigration can happen within the same nation, such as when people move from a village to a city inside the same country. Often, emigration happens when people move from one nation to another. For example, millions of people have emigrated from countries in Europe, Asia, and Africa to start new lives in the United States. The term *immigrate* is closely related to *emigrate*, but it does not mean the same thing. To **immigrate** means "to enter and live in a new country."

The reasons for leaving one area and going to another are called push-pull factors. *Push* factors drive people from an area. For example, when a war breaks out in a country or a region, people emigrate from that place to escape danger. People who flee a country because of violence, war, or persecution are called **refugees**. Sometimes people emigrate from an area after a natural disaster such as a flood, an earthquake, or a tsunami has destroyed their homes and land. If the economy of a place becomes so weak that little or no work is available, people emigrate to seek new opportunities. **C**

Think **Again**

Early immigrants came to the United States for both push and pull factors.

True. Some came to avoid war or escape persecution. In addition to these "push" factors, others were "pulled" to gain freedom, education, and economic opportunity.

Dennis MacDonald/age fotostock

netw⊙rks   *Online Teaching Options*

VIDEO

Migration

Interpreting Use the video to discuss what factors would cause people to leave their homes or countries to live in refugee camps, which often have problems and offer very limited opportunites. Be sure to clarify for students the difference between forced migration and other forms of movement. Discuss some of the push-pull factors that affect all people who move from place to place. **ELL** Visual/Spatial

See page 69C for other online activities.

Comstock Images/Jupiterimages

Pull factors attract people to an area. Some people move to new places to be with friends or family members. Many young people move to cities or countries to attend universities or other schools. Some relocate in search of better jobs. Families sometimes move to places where their children will be able to attend good schools.

Effects of Migration

The movement of people to and from different parts of the world can affect the land, resources, culture, and economy of an area. Some of these effects are positive, but others can be harmful.

One positive effect of migration is cultural blending. As people from diverse cultures migrate to the same place and live close together, their cultures become mixed and blended. This blending creates new, unique cultures and ways of life. Artwork and music created in diverse urban areas is often an interesting mixture of styles and rhythms from around the world. Food, clothing styles, and languages spoken in urban areas change when people migrate into that area and bring new influences.

Some families and cultural groups work to preserve their original culture. These people want to keep their cultural traditions alive so they can be passed down to future generations. For example, the traditional Chinese New Year is an important celebration for many Chinese American families. Chinese Americans can be part of a blended American culture but still enjoy traditional Chinese foods, music, and arts, and celebrate Chinese holidays. It is possible to adapt to a local culture yet maintain strong ties to a home culture.

Some people migrate by choice. Others, such as the Libyan refugees shown here, are forced to flee to another country to live.
▶ **CRITICAL THINKING**
Identifying What are examples of "pull" causes of migration?

Chapter 3 **79**

GRAPHIC ORGANIZER

Why Do People Move?

Determining Word Meanings Discuss with students the difference between *emigrate* and *immigrate*. Guide students to interpret their different meanings by pointing out the difference in the prefixes *e* and *im*. Use an interactive graphic organizer to list reasons why people choose to move from or to a place.
ELL Verbal/Linguistic

See page 69C for other online activities.

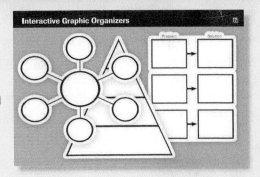

Interactive Graphic Organizers

R Reading Skills

Citing Text Evidence Discuss with students how migration can have beneficial effects for the immigrants as well as the country to which people are moving. **Ask:** What does the text explain is a positive effect of the movement of people? *(cultural blending)* Verbal/Linguistic

W Writing Skills

Informative/Explanatory Explain to students that the migration of people, whether internal, national, or international, affects culture. Have students brainstorm ways in which migration affects culture. Ask them to consider language, customs, and traditions.

Invite students to share if they have moved with their families and how many times. Record the data, including how many students have not moved, on the whiteboard.

Have students write a paragraph to answer these questions. **Ask:**

• **How has moving or not moving affected your family traditions?**
• **How has meeting new people who have moved to your area affected your family traditions and celebrations?** *(Student answers will vary but should demonstrate understanding of the blending of cultures and adoption of cultural aspects through migration.)* **ELL** Interpersonal

V Visual Skills

Interpreting Explain that refugees are often moved from one refugee camp to another as new refugees arrive at a camp that is already full of people escaping violence, war, or persecution. **Ask:** Do you think the refugees in this photograph are coming or going? What details help you to make this interpretation? *(Student answers will vary but should include logical thinking such as people are sitting on their suitcases and appear to be waiting; therefore, they have probably arrived in the camp rather than leaving the camp.)* **ELL** **BL** Logical/ Mathematical, Visual/Spatial

---

ANSWER, p. 79

CRITICAL THINKING Examples of "pull" causes are when people move to be closer to friends or family or move for jobs and schools.

A Changing Population

V Visual Skills

Creating Visuals Discuss with students that urbanization refers to the growth of cities. Cities often include a large population, businesses, and different forms of transportation, all of which contribute to a stress on natural resources and an increase of pollution.

Also discuss that many cities are located near waterways or bodies of water partly because of the need for water to drink, wash, and cook, and partly because water used to be an important means of transportation. Have students create a visual of an urban area, using pictures from magazines, the Internet, or freehand drawings. **ELL** Visual/Spatial

T Technology Skills

Researching on the Internet Have students work with a partner and use the Internet to research the top five urban areas in the world. Then have them plot the five cities on a world map and consider their location to water and other natural resources. **Ask:** What generalizations can you make about the locations of the largest urban areas in the world? *(Sample answer: They are located near bodies of water but are not all on the same continent.)* **ELL** **AL** Logical/Mathematical, Visual/Spatial

C Critical Thinking Skills

Hypothesizing Explain to students that pollution caused from urbanization can have a very harmful effect on the environment. Trees and plants generally do not thrive naturally in urban areas. However, urban areas need the benefits of trees to produce oxygen and to clean pollutants from the air. Many large cities include large parks or forest preserves to address this need for the benefits we gain from trees.

Take students outside to make observations of the vegetation in your area. **Ask:** How might pollution in urban areas also affect the growth of trees and plants in rural areas? *(Sample answer: Pollution in urban areas makes the air and water dirty, and plants need clean air and water to grow. Air pollution from urban areas can blow into rural areas.)* Kinesthetic, Naturalist

---

Nearly half the world's people live in urban areas. Many live in very large cities such as New York City.
▶ **CRITICAL THINKING**
Determining Word Meanings What is a megalopolis?

Causes and Effects of Urbanization

Another effect of migration is the growth of urban areas. **Urbanization** happens when cities grow larger and spread into surrounding areas. Migration is a primary reason that urbanization occurs.

People move to cities for many reasons. The most common reason is to find jobs. Transportation and trade centers draw people primarily by creating new opportunities for business. As the businesses grow and people move into an area, the need for services also grows. Workers fill positions in medical services, education, entertainment, housing, and food sectors.

As more people migrate to cities, urban areas become increasingly crowded. When populations within urban areas increase, cities grow and expand. Farmland is bought by developers to build homes, apartment buildings, factories, offices, schools, and stores to provide for the growing number of people. The loss of farmland means that food must be grown farther from cities, resulting in additional shipping and related pollution.

Urbanization is happening in cities all over the world. In some places, cities have grown so vast that they have reached the outer edges of other cities. The result is massive clusters of urban areas that continue for miles. A huge city or cluster of cities with an extremely large population is called a **megalopolis**. These huge cities are growing larger every day, and they face the challenges that come with population growth and urbanization.

Robert Glusic/Photodisc/Getty Images

80 *Chapter 3*

---

networks   *Online Teaching Options*

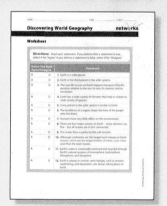

Writing Skills: Investigating Population Movement

Examining Have students investigate current global population movement. Have them note their findings on the Writing Skills worksheet. Then have students write an essay or create a class presentation based on their investigations. Verbal/Linguistic

See page 69C for other online activities.

ANSWER, p. 80

CRITICAL THINKING A megalopolis is a huge city or a cluster of cities that have a large population.

Delhi, one of India's largest cities, is a megalopolis. Its sprawling land area takes in a section called the Old City, dating from the mid-1600s. It also encompasses New Delhi, the modern capital city built by British colonial rulers in the early 1900s.

The largest megalopolis in the Americas is Mexico City. Because of its size and influence, Mexico City is a primate city, an urban area that dominates its country's economy and political affairs. Primate cities include Cairo, Egypt, in Africa, Amman, Jordan, in Asia, and Paris, France, in Europe.

Examples of Urbanization

Urbanization takes place around the world but for different reasons and at different rates. Paraguay, for example, has long been one of the least urbanized regions in the Americas. In 1965, about two of every three Paraguayans lived in rural areas. Most worked in agriculture. Over time, Paraguayans began leaving their rural villages in order to find better job opportunities. Even those who continued to work in agriculture moved closer to urban areas. About 70 percent of all citizens live within 120 miles (193 km) of the capital, Asunción.

Europe is highly urbanized. Beginning in the late 1700s, the Industrial Revolution transformed Europe from a rural, agricultural society to an urban, industrial society. The growth of industries and cities began first in Western Europe. Later, after World War II, the process spread to Eastern Europe.

☑ **READING PROGRESS CHECK**

Describing Explain why Mexico City is a primate city and a megalopolis.

Include this lesson's information in your Foldable®.

LESSON 1 REVIEW

Reviewing Vocabulary
1. Why does *population distribution* vary?

Answering the Guiding Questions
2. *Analyzing* If Canada's population is doubling about every 75 years, is the death rate or the birthrate higher? Explain.

3. *Identifying* Which parts of North America are less densely populated than most other parts? Explain.

4. *Determining Central Ideas* Explain factors that might have led to the formation of the megalopolis of New York City.

5. *Informative/Explanatory Writing* Imagine that you are planning to leave the area where you currently live. Write a paragraph explaining the factors you would consider in selecting a new location. Select a city that is at least 100 miles from where you live now and analyze whether that city meets the criteria you selected. Write another paragraph that includes this analysis.

Chapter 3 **81**

R **Reading Skills**

Labeling Have students use the world maps they created earlier in the lesson with the five largest urban areas. Ask them now to research five to ten megalopolises around the world and then label them on their maps. Encourage them to use different colors to distinguish the areas on the map and to create a key for their map explaining the use of the colors they chose.
ELL Visual/Spatial

Content Background Knowledge

The term *megalopolis* was coined in 1961 by a French geographer Jean Gottmann after spending two decades in an area of the United States that stretches from New Hampshire to Washington, D.C. In his study, he argued that as population growth increased in the cities in this region, people moved to smaller nearby areas that grew into large suburbs and "merged" with other metropolitan regions in the area.

Have students study this area using a map of the eastern United States. Tell students to use the map scale to figure out the distances between the major cities in this area. Then have students compare these distances with the distances between large cities in the Midwest, South, and western United States.

CLOSE & REFLECT

Making Connections To close this lesson, have students think about how population movement and growth affects cultures. Then have a class discussion about population movement and growth in your area, and how it has affected the cultures in your area.

Finally encourage students to make predictions about how population movement and growth will affect the area in which they live in the next ten years.

LESSON 1 REVIEW ANSWERS

Reviewing Vocabulary

1. Among the many reasons people might choose to live in an area is an abundance of resources or jobs. Reasons to avoid an area might be extreme poverty, difficult living conditions such as extreme or frequent droughts, or lack of transportation or education. Populations tend to cluster in more favorable areas.

Answering the Guiding Questions

2. **Analyzing** The birthrate is higher because the population is growing, just not as quickly as in some other places.

3. **Identifying** The desert regions of the United States are not densely populated because the living conditions are not as favorable as in other areas, and there are no manufacturing jobs due to a general lack of resources there. Parts of Canada are also less densely populated due to harsher living conditions.

4. **Determining Central Ideas** The New York City area has easy access to ports, airports, and other transportation methods so products can be shipped in and out of the region. It is also close to the nation's capital, and the weather is moderate.

5. **Informative/Explanatory Writing** Students should first consider factors such as climate, jobs, culture, and lifestyle of the area. Then they should include a thoughtful analysis of the city they selected.

ANSWER, p. 81

☑ **READING PROGRESS CHECK** Mexico City is a megalopolis because of its large size and population. It is a primate city because it dominates the country's economy and politics.

ENGAGE

Bellringer Before students begin this lesson, **ask:** What kinds of food do you and your family eat that are traditional to your family? Display several pictures of different ethnic foods or invite students to bring in a food or recipe that is unique or special to their family to share with the class. Invite students to read the recipes for unique ingredients or sample the food to get a taste of cuisines that might be unfamiliar to them. Ask students to share when they prepare these foods and how the foods represent their culture.

TEACH & ASSESS

R Reading Skills

Specifying Explain that a person's culture can relate to his or her traditions, customs, heritage, beliefs, or even language. A person may follow aspects of more than one culture, especially if he or she has moved from one country to another. **Ask:** Why is the term *culture* used to refer to the set of beliefs, behaviors, and traits shared by a group of people when it is not specific to any one culture? *(Sample answer: Culture is used as a more general term that encompasses a person or group's specific traditions and beliefs from others. It is a way to group those similarities. To be more specific, one would refer to a person's cultural group.)* **ELL** Verbal/Linguistic

Reinforcing Vocabulary Remind students to add academic and content vocabulary words to their vocabulary lists in their notebooks. Tell students to write their own definitions and to include drawings if desired. **ELL AL** Verbal/Linguistic

V Visual Skills

Creating Visuals Using a globe as a model, have students work individually to sketch a map of a country that is important to their culture, such as a home country or a country from which relatives emigrated in the past. Working with a partner, have students use their maps as a starting point for a discussion on elements of their culture. Have partners ask each other questions about special food, clothing, music, or art that is unique to their culture. **ELL AL** Interpersonal

---

ANSWER, p. 82

Taking Notes Sample responses: There are many different forms of government. Governments differ in how their leaders are chosen, who makes the rules, and how much freedom people have and control governments have over their lives. Three of the world's most common forms of government are democracy, monarchy, and dictatorship. Some governments limit or restrict human rights.

Reading HELPDESK

Academic Vocabulary
- behalf

Content Vocabulary
- culture
- ethnic group
- dialect
- cultural region
- democracy
- representative democracy
- monarchy
- dictatorship
- human rights
- globalization

TAKING NOTES: *Key Ideas and Details*

Organize On a graphic organizer like this one, take notes about the different forms of government.

Form of Government

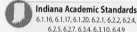

Indiana Academic Standards
6.1.16, 6.1.17, 6.1.20, 6.2.1, 6.2.2, 6.2.4, 6.2.5, 6.2.7, 6.3.4, 6.3.10, 6.4.9

Lesson 2
Global Cultures

ESSENTIAL QUESTION • *What makes a culture unique?*

IT MATTERS BECAUSE
Culture shapes the way people live and how they view the world.

What Is Culture?

GUIDING QUESTION *How is culture part of your life?*

Think about the clothes you wear, the music you listen to, and the foods you eat. These things are all part of your culture. Do you like pizza, rice and beans, pasta, or *samosas*? Have you ever thought about the people and cultures that invented the foods you enjoy eating? Foods are created, grown, or developed by people of different cultures.

Culture is the set of beliefs, behaviors, and traits shared by a group of people. The term *culture* can also refer to the people of a certain culture. For example, saying "the Hindu culture" can mean the Hindu cultural traditions, the people who follow these traditions, or both.

You might be part of more than one culture. If your family has strong ties to a culture, such as that of a religion or a nation, you might follow this cultural tradition at home. You also might be part of a more mainstream American culture while at school and with friends.

If your family emigrated from Somalia to the United States, for example, you might speak the Somali language, wear traditional Somali clothing, and eat Somali foods. Your family might celebrate holidays observed in Somalia as well as American holidays, such as Thanksgiving and Independence Day. When you are with your friends, you might speak English, listen to American music, and watch American sports.

---

networks *Online Teaching Options*

VIDEO

World's Best Ancient Sites: North America

Drawing Conclusions Use the video about traditional cultures in North America to introduce different cultural elements. Ask students to make a list of the ways the different groups described in the video adapt to their environment and the new ways they are continuing to adapt. Then have students describe how these cultural elements might be affected by elements such as changing governments or climate change. **BL** Visual/Spatial

See page 69D for other online activities.

Different Groups

We can look at members of a culture in terms of age, gender, or ethnic group. An **ethnic group** is a group of people with a common racial, national, tribal, religious, or cultural background. Members of the same Native American nation are an example of people of the same ethnic group. Other examples include the Maori of New Zealand and the Han Chinese. Large countries such as China, can be home to hundreds of different ethnic groups. Some ethnic groups in a country are minority groups—people whose race or ethnic origin is different from that of the majority group. The largest ethnic minority groups in the United States are Hispanic Americans and African Americans.

Members of a culture might have special roles or positions as part of their cultural traditions. In some cultures, women are expected to care for and educate children. Most cultures expect men to earn money to support their families or to provide in other ways, such as by hunting and farming. Many cultures respect the elderly and value their wisdom. The leaders of older, traditional cultures are often elderly men or women who have leadership experience. Most cultures have clearly defined roles for their members. From an early age, young people learn what their culture expects of them. It is possible, too, to be part of more than one culture.

Language

Language serves as a powerful form of communication. Through language, people communicate information and experience and pass on cultural beliefs and traditions. Thousands of different languages are spoken in the world. Some languages have become world languages, or languages that are commonly spoken in many parts of the world. Some languages are spoken differently in different regions or by different ethnic groups. A **dialect** is a regional variety of a language with unique features, such as vocabulary, grammar, or pronunciation. People who speak the same language can sometimes understand other dialects, but at times, the pronunciation, or accent, of a dialect can be nearly impossible for others to understand.

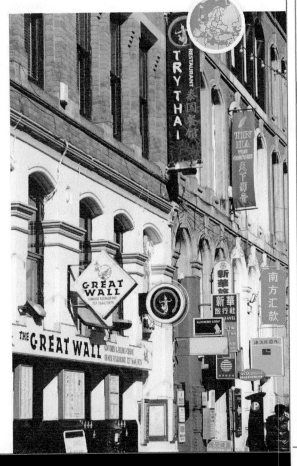

©cunningeye/Alamy

Cities often have communities within them that share a distinct and common culture, language, and customs.

▶ **CRITICAL THINKING**
Describing What is a dialect?

C Critical Thinking Skills

Categorizing Read the section, "Different Groups," aloud to the class. **Ask:** How are roles that are defined in ethnic groups similar and different? *(In some cultures, women care for the children and help to educate them. Most cultures expect men to earn money. Many cultures respect the elderly.)* Record students' ideas on a chart with the headings "Men," "Women," and "Elderly." **ELL AL** Verbal/Linguistic

Men	Women	Elderly

V Visual Skills

Analyzing Images Remind students that images can reveal a lot about the elements of a culture. **Ask:**

- What does this photograph reveal about the culture of this urban area? *(It says that the culture of this area is probably diverse. That is because there are both signs in English and in East Asian languages.)*
- What inferences can you make about the population that lives in this area? What makes you think that? *(One inference is that the area most likely has a large East Asian population, because signs are in East Asian languages.)*
- Why do you think some store owners prefer to have a sign in English and others have chosen a sign in an East Asian language? *(Student answers may include that the owners who have signs written in English want to reach out to English speaking customers as well as East Asian customers.)* **ELL** Visual/Spatial

T Technology Skills

Researching Have students work in groups and spend some time on the Internet finding other places in the world where cultural centers have developed, such as Chinatown in San Francisco or Little Italy in New York City. Students could also choose to research the cultural influences that shape a city such as the Cuban influence in Miami, Florida, or the French influence in New Orleans, Louisiana.

Have the groups create poster presentations with visuals to discuss their chosen city. Then have those groups present their information to the rest of the class. Display the posters in class as you continue to teach this chapter. Visual/Spatial

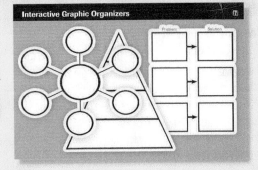

Interactive Graphic Organizers

ANSWER, p. 83

CRITICAL THINKING A dialect is a change in vocabulary, grammar, or pronunciation that is unique to people within a region.

Global Cultures

R Reading Skills

Analyzing Charts Review the chart of major world religions with students. Then ask them the following questions:

- What do Christianity, Judaism, and Islam share in common? *(They are all based on the belief in one God.)*
- How are all of the religions similar? *(They all share the belief in either one God, one leader such as Buddha, or one eternal spirit such as Brahman.)*
- How do you think the artwork and music from some cultures are influenced by religion? *(Student answers may include that the artwork and music depict religious themes, beliefs, leaders, or followers.)* **Verbal/Linguistic**

T Technology Skills

Research Have pairs or small groups of students choose one of the world religions to learn more about by researching it on the Internet. Or you may want to assign a religion to groups to ensure that all religions are covered when class presentations are made.

Make sure students use reliable sources for their research and have them include a list of their sources with their notes. Then have the pairs or groups prepare and give a presentation to the class about the religion they researched. Explain that students should keep the information in their presentation positive and factual, explaining the beliefs of the religion, its history, and the areas in the world where it is predominately followed. **Verbal/Linguistic**

Content Background Knowledge

In some countries, a high percentage of people attend weekly religious services, but it varies widely and regionally. In a study conducted by the Pew Research Center in 2010, ninety-three percent of Jordan's population attended weekly services. The next highest attendance was 65 percent in Indonesia. In the United States the report showed that 35 percent of Americans attend weekly services. Only 4 percent of people living in Japan and Sweden attend religious services.

CHART SKILLS >
MAJOR WORLD RELIGIONS

Religion	Major Leader	Beliefs
Buddhism	Siddhārtha Gautama, the Buddha	Suffering comes from attachment to earthly things, which are not lasting. People become free by following the Eightfold Path, rules of right thought and conduct. People who follow the Path achieve nirvana—a state of endless peace and joy.
Christianity	Jesus Christ	The one God is Father, Son, and Holy Spirit. God the Son became human as Jesus Christ. Jesus died and rose again to bring God's forgiving love to sinful humanity. Those who trust in Jesus and follow his teachings of love for God and neighbor receive eternal life with God.
Hinduism	No one founder	One eternal spirit, Brahman, is represented as many deities. Every living thing has a soul that passes through many successive lives. Each soul's condition in a specific life is based on how the previous life was lived. When a soul reaches purity, it finally joins permanently with Brahman.
Islam	Muhammad	The one God sent a series of prophets, including the final prophet Muhammad, to teach humanity. Islam's laws are based on the Quran, the holy book, and the Sunnah, examples from Muhammad's life. Believers practice the five pillars—belief, prayer, charity, fasting, and pilgrimage—to go to an eternal paradise.
Judaism	Abraham	The one God made an agreement through Abraham and later Moses with the people of Israel. God would bless them, and they would follow God's laws, applying God's will in all parts of their lives. The main laws and practices of Judaism are stated in the Torah, the first five books of the Hebrew Bible.
Sikhism	Guru Nanak	The one God made truth known through 10 successive gurus, or teachers. God's will is that people should live honestly, work hard, and treat others fairly. The Sikh community, or Khalsa, bases its decisions on the principles of a sacred text, the Guru Granth Sahib.

Religion

Religion has a major influence on how people of a culture see the world. Religious beliefs are powerful. Some individuals see their religion as merely a tradition to follow during special occasions or holidays. Others view religion as the foundation and most important part of their life. Religious practices vary widely. Many cultures base their way of life on the spiritual teachings and laws of holy books. Religion is a central part of many of the world's cultures. Throughout history, religious stories and symbols have influenced painting, architecture, and music.

Customs

Customs are also an important outward display of culture. In many traditional cultures, a woman is not permitted to touch a man other than her husband, even for a handshake. In modern European cultures, polite greetings include kissing on the cheeks. People of many cultures bow to others as a sign of greeting, respect, and

---

networks *Online Teaching Options*

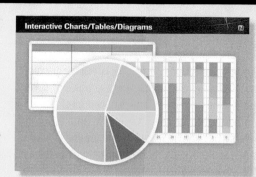
Interactive Charts/Tables/Diagrams

CHART

Major World Religions

Comparing and Contrasting Display the chart on the whiteboard and discuss the different religions listed on the chart. Have students point out the similarities between them *(most of them are monotheistic)*. Discuss with students how religion can become a major influence on how people see and interact with the world. **ELL Visual/Spatial**

See page 69D for other online activities.

goodwill. The world's many cultures have countless fascinating customs. Some are used only formally, and others are viewed as good manners and respectful, professional behavior.

History

History shapes how we view the world. We often celebrate holidays to honor the heroes and heroines who brought about successes. Stories about heroes reveal the personal characteristics that people think are important. Groups also remember the dark periods of history when they met with disaster or defeat. These experiences, too, influence how groups of people see themselves.

The Arts and Sports

Dance, music, visual arts, and literature are important elements of culture. Nearly all cultures have unique art forms that celebrate their history and enrich people's lives. Some art forms, such as singing and dancing, are serious parts of religious ceremonies or other cultural events. Aboriginal peoples of the Pacific Islands have songs, dances, and chants that are vital parts of their cultural traditions. Art can be forms of personal expression or worship, entertainment, or even ways of retelling and preserving a culture's history.

In sports, as in many other aspects of culture, activities are adopted, modified, and shared. Many sports that we play today originated with different culture groups in the past. Athletes in ancient Japan, China, Greece, and Rome played a game similar to soccer. Scholars believe that the Maya of Mexico and Central America developed "ballgame," the first organized team sport. Playing on a 40- to 50-foot long (12m to 15m) recessed court, the athletes' goal was to kick a rubber ball through a goal.

Features of Government

Government is another element of culture. Governments share certain features. They maintain order within an area and provide protection from outside dangers. Governments also provide services to citizens, such as education. Different cultures have different ways of distributing power and making rules.

Jose Luis Pelaez Inc/Blend Images/Getty Images

Soccer is one of the most popular international sports.

▶ CRITICAL THINKING
Identifying Which culture first played the game of soccer?

Chapter 3 **85**

G1 Critical Thinking Skills

Making Connections Invite a volunteer to read the paragraph under, "History." **Ask:**

• In the United States, what holidays are celebrated that honor heroes or heroines? *(Possible answers may include:* **Memorial Day,** *where military men and women who died in service to the United States are honored;* **Veterans Day,** *where former and current military men and women are honored;* **Presidents' Day,** *where past United States presidents are honored;* **Martin Luther King, Jr. Day,** *to honor his efforts to bring about equal rights to all people in the United States.)*

• What types of celebrations usually take place on these holidays? *(parades, memorials, speeches, ceremonies, performances, concerts, or festivals)* Verbal/Linguistic

W Writing Skills

Narrative Have students research more about Aboriginal songs, dances, or chants and write a paragraph about what they learn. Encourage students to use descriptive words that give the reader a vivid picture of their writing.

You may want to allow students who struggle with their writing to enhance their descriptions with drawings, or to perform a song or dance for the class. Auditory/Musical, Visual/Spatial

G2 Critical Thinking Skills

Giving Examples Explain to students that sports can bring together cultures, especially when they are played in international competitions. Some sports have been introduced or influenced by other cultures and other countries. **Ask:**

• What other sports besides soccer are played in countries around the world? *(Possible answers: basketball, golf, ice hockey, baseball, tennis, cycling, skiing)*

• Are there sports that are more popular in other countries than in the United States? *(Possible answers include cricket, rugby, jai alai)* ELL Verbal/Linguistic, Intrapersonal

---

MAP

World Cultural Regions

Analyzing Maps Display the world cultural regions map on the whiteboard. Review with students the various cultural regions. Discuss how some cultural regions cover one country, multiple countries, one continent, or more than one continent. Then ask students to make connections between the locations of similar cultural regions. BL Visual/Spatial

See page 69D for other online activities.

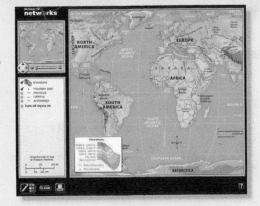

ANSWER, p. 85

CRITICAL THINKING Many different groups from various times and areas played a game similar to soccer. The game cannot be traced back to any one group, however.

Global Cultures

T Technology Skills

Using and Citing Information Have students work in pairs and guide them to recent economic data by country on the Internet, which can often be accessed by going to a country's government web site. Ask them to choose two countries to research and locate the top products or goods that those countries produce. Instruct students to write down the sources they use. As a class, create a world product map or chart in which the data that the students gathered is shown, and have students cite their sources. **Logical/Mathematical, Interpersonal**

R Reading Skills

Discussing Discuss with students the different ethnic groups in your area and how they have influenced traditions, businesses, sports, and other activities in your community. Then relate your area to the state in which you live. **Ask:** What cultural regions are in our state or local region? *(Student answers will vary but should demonstrate understanding of a cultural region.)* **ELL** **Verbal/Linguistic**

W Writing Skills

Narrative Tell students that the signing of the Declaration of Independence is an important event in our nation's history. The signers took a big risk as they declared their independence from Great Britain. They became Americans and formed a new nation, the United States. Ask students to write a short narrative based on this time period in which they describe how people living in the colonies felt about the emergence of a new culture.

Suggest that students use presentation software in which they can add images and music to their narratives, and then show the final product to the class. Have students who are watching the presentations evaluate them based on event sequence, descriptive details, narrative technique, and transition words. **Auditory/Musical, Visual/Spatial**

ANSWERS, p. 86

☑ **READING PROGRESS CHECK** Accept all reasonable responses that demonstrate an understanding of the basic elements of culture.

CRITICAL THINKING Citizens elect government officials to make and carry out laws and policies on their behalf.

Economy

T Economies control the use of natural resources and define how goods are produced and distributed to meet human needs. Some cultures have their own type of economy, but most follow the economy of the country or area where they live. This allows people of different cultures living in an area to trade and conduct other types of business with one another. For example, many people in Benin, West Africa, sell goods in open-air markets. Some people bring items to the markets to trade for the goods they need, but others pay for goods using paper money and coins.

Cultural Regions

R A **cultural region** is a geographic area in which people have certain traits in common. People in a cultural region often live close to one another to share resources, for social reasons, and to keep their cultures and communities strong. Cultural regions can be large or relatively small. For example, one of the world's largest cultural areas stretches across northern Africa and Southwest Asia. This cultural region is home to millions of people of the Islamic, or Muslim, culture. A much smaller cultural region is Spanish Harlem in New York City. This cultural region is home to a large and growing Hispanic culture.

☑ **READING PROGRESS CHECK**

Identifying Point of View What cultural traditions do you practice? Make a list of the beliefs, behaviors, languages, foods, art, music, clothing, and other elements of culture that are part of your daily life.

On July 4, 1776, the Second Continental Congress approved the Declaration of Independence, establishing the United States as an independent country.
► CRITICAL THINKING
Describing What is a representative democracy?

Government

GUIDING QUESTION *How does government affect way of life?*

All nations need some type of formal leadership. What differs among countries is how leaders are chosen, who makes the rules, how much freedom people have, and how much control governments have over people's lives. Many different kinds of government systems operate in the world today. Three of the most common are democracy, monarchy, and dictatorship.

Democracy

In a democracy, the people hold the power. Citizens of a nation make the decisions themselves. A **democracy** is a system of government that is run by the people. In

©PoodlesRock/Corbis

86 *Chapter 3*

---

net**w**⊕rks *Online Teaching Options*

Critical Thinking Skills: Investigating Different Forms of Government

Examining Have students investigate different forms of government such as democracy, monarchy, and dictatorship. Then have them note their findings on the Critical Thinking Skills worksheet. Encourage students to research on the Internet the founding principles behind the idea of a democratic society and government. **BL** **Verbal/Linguistic**

See page 69D for other online activities.

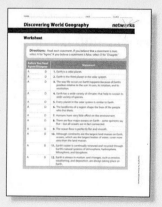

democratic systems of government, people are free to propose laws and policies. Citizens then vote to decide which laws and policies will be set in place. When people run the government, citizens' rights and freedoms are protected.

In some democracies, the people elect leaders to make and carry out laws. A **representative democracy** is a form of democracy in which citizens elect government officials to represent the people; the government representatives make and carry out laws and policies on **behalf** of the people. The United States in an example of a representative democracy.

Monarchy

A **monarchy** is ruled by a king or a queen. In a monarchy, power and leadership are passed down from older to younger generations through heredity. The ruler of a monarchy, called a *monarch*, is usually a king, a queen, a prince, or a princess. In the past, monarchs had absolute power, or total power. Today, most monarchs only represent, or stand for, a country's traditions and values, while elected officials run the government. The United Kingdom is an example of a monarchy.

Dictatorship

A **dictatorship** is a form of government in which one person has absolute power to rule and control the government, the people, and the economy. People who live under a dictatorship often have few rights. With absolute power, a dictator can make laws with no concern for how just, fair, or practical the laws are. North Korea is an example of a dictatorship.

Some dictators abuse their power for personal gain. One negative consequence of abuse of power is lack of personal freedoms and human rights for the general public. **Human rights** are the rights that belong to all individuals. Those rights are the same for every human in every culture. Some basic human rights are the right to life, liberty, security, privacy, freedom from slavery, fair treatment before the law, and marry and have children.

☑ READING PROGRESS CHECK

Describing In your own words, define human rights and list three important human rights.

The queen is the symbolic head of the United Kingdom, but elected leaders hold the power to rule.
▶ CRITICAL THINKING
Describing What is a monarchy?

Academic Vocabulary

behalf in the interest of; in support of; in defense of

Ian Gavan/Getty Images Entertainment/Getty Images

Chapter 3 **87**

R Reading Skills

Determining Word Meanings Explain that by examining Greek and Latin word meanings, students can break down some words to better understand their meaning. In the Greek language, *demos* means "the people" and *kratia* means "power or rule." **Ask:** How does understanding these Greek word meanings help you to determine what democracy means? *(Sample answer: democracy means "power or rule by the people")* **ELL** **AL** Verbal/Linguistic

C Critical Thinking Skills

Making Connections After reading about different kinds of government, **ask:**

- What kind of government affects people more negatively than the others? *(dictatorship)*
- What connection can you make between this form of government and countries in which human rights may not be promoted and protected? *(They are closely connected but not always connected. Very often those who live under a dictator have few rights and have few ways to gain more rights and freedom.)*

Have students model the different types of governments they have learned about in this section. Divide the class into four groups, with each group representing one of the three forms of government and the fourth group acting as the citizens. Take turns having each group model the behavior and decision-making that is characteristic of that form of government toward its citizens. Interpersonal, Kinesthetic

Content Background Knowledge

Ancient Greece was the birthplace of democracy, but the democratic form of government that the ancient Greeks practiced was different than the kind we use today. The ancient Greeks practiced direct democracy, in which citizens voted directly, not through representatives. In the United States and other countries with democratic forms of government, indirect democracy is practiced, which means that citizens vote to elect representatives who represent them.

CHART

Types of Government

Analyze Charts Display the interactive chart on types of government on the whiteboard. Discuss the similarities and differences among different forms of government, including democracy, monarchy, and dictatorship. Have students work with a partner to complete a Venn diagram on two forms of government. **AL** Visual/Spatial

See page 69D for other online activities.

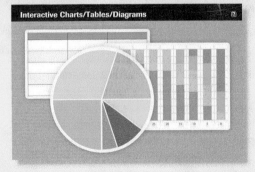

Interactive Charts/Tables/Diagrams

ANSWERS, p. 87

CRITICAL THINKING A government ruled by a royal family. Most monarchs are now only figureheads.
☑ READING PROGRESS CHECK Student answers may vary, but could include the following: Human rights are basic rights every human being should have, such as the right to live, be safe, and be free from slavery.

V Visual Skills

Analyzing Visuals Have students look at the image of the port in Malaysia and discuss the concept of globalization and its effect on culture in pairs. Next discuss how the port in the photo can influence both what is brought into and what leaves the country. **Ask:** In what ways does free trade impact your daily life? *(Students' answers will vary but should demonstrate understanding of how goods are shipped from all around the world and that they use many of these goods on a daily basis.)* Intrapersonal, Visual/Spatial

C Critical Thinking Skills

Suggesting a Solution Explain that when people relocate and bring their cultural traditions with them, they may have to adapt to a new physical environment. Have students consider how people can face these challenges, which may also affect their ability to practice elements of their culture. **Ask:** What is a specific challenge and how would you solve it? *(Students' answers will vary but should demonstrate understanding of how government affects ways of life.)*

Have students work in pairs to answer the question. Then have students share their ideas with the class. Naturalist

Content Background Knowledge

The United Nations (UN), formed in 1945 shortly after World War II ended, originally had fifty-one member countries. The organization formed for many purposes, including maintaining peace and security throughout the world; supporting the self-determination of people; solving global, social, cultural, humanitarian, and economic crises, and protecting human rights. Today, with nearly 200 member countries, the UN protects human rights through nearly 80 treaties and declarations and has aided about 30 countries in their quest to hold democratic elections.

Cargo containers are stockpiled and ready to be loaded onto ships in the port of Johor, Malaysia. International trade is the exchange of goods and services between countries. When people trade, they not only exchange goods, they also exchange customs and ideas.

Shifts in Culture

GUIDING QUESTION *How do cultures change over time?*

Over time, cultures change for a variety of reasons. When people relocate, they bring their cultural traditions with them. The traditions often influence or blend with the cultures of the places where they settle. Over time, as people of many cultures move to a location, the culture of that location takes on elements of all the cultures within it. Cities, such as London and New York, are examples of areas that have richly diverse cultures.

Cultural Change

Change also can occur as a result of trade, travel, war, and exchange of ideas. Trade brings people to new areas to sell and barter goods. Whenever people travel, they bring their language, customs, and ideas with them. They also bring elements of foreign cultures back with them when they return home. Throughout history, traders and explorers have brought home new foods, clothing, jewelry, and other goods. Some of these, such as gold, chocolate, gunpowder, and silk, became popular all over the world. Trade in these items changed the course of history.

88 *Chapter 3*

netw⊕rks   *Online Teaching Options*

SLIDE SHOW

Cultural Changes

Determining Cause and Effect Show the slide show on why cultures change. Explain how some cultures can change over time while some remain the same. Discuss with students how migration, emigration, and immigration affect cultures. In small groups, have students write a list of these effects on cultures and share their findings with the class. ELL

See page 69D for other online activities.

Slide Show

T
Culture can also change as a result of technology. The telegraph, telephones, and e-mail have made communication increasingly faster and easier. Television and the Internet have given people in all parts of the world easy access to information and new ideas. Elements of culture such as language, clothing styles, customs, and behaviors spread quickly as people discover them by watching television and using the Internet.

Global Culture

Today's world is becoming more culturally blended every day. As cultures combine, new cultural elements and traditions are born. The spread of culture and ideas has caused our world to become globalized. **Globalization** is the process by which nations, cultures, and economies become integrated, or mixed. Globalization has had the positive effect of making people more understanding and accepting of other cultures. It also has helped spread ideas and innovations. Technology has made communication faster and easier. Travel also has become faster and easier, allowing more people to visit more places in less time. This is resulting in cultural blending on a wider scale than ever before.

The process of cultural blending through globalization is not always smooth and easy. Sometimes it produces tension and conflict as people from different cultures come into contact with one another. Some people do not want their cultures to change, or they want to control the amount of change. Sometimes the changes come too fast, and cultures can be damaged or destroyed.

Just as no one element defines a culture, no one culture can define the world. All cultures have value and add to the human experience. As the world becomes more globalized, people must continue to respect other ways of life. We have much to learn, and much to gain, from the many cultures that make our world a fascinating place.

Paul J. Richards/AFP/Getty Images

✔ **READING PROGRESS CHECK**

Determining Word Meanings What is globalization?

Widespread use of technology, such as cell phones, allows us to share information with a larger audience.
▶ **CRITICAL THINKING**
Analyzing How does technology help spread new ideas?

FOLDABLES
Study Organizer

Include this lesson's information in your Foldable®.

T **Technology Skills**

Analyzing Have students think about how their lives would be different in regards to technology if they had grown up 40 years ago. If need be discuss the technologies today that were not available or just beginning at that time including personal computers, remote controls on TVs, recorders for TVs, digital cameras, cell phones, the Internet, and so on. **AL**
Verbal/Linguistic

Analyzing News Media Have students work in small groups to access national or international news features online. Ask them to find a news feature that might affect cultural change and evaluate the importance of the information, ideas, or images that are broadcast. Ask groups to consider if there is any form of bias in the news feature.

Then have groups present their findings and evaluations of the news features to the class. Invite discussion of the news features between groups to see if others would have evaluated the features differently. **BL** Visual/Spatial

CLOSE & REFLECT

Making Connections To close this lesson, discuss how today's world is becoming more culturally blended and the positive results that have come about because of globalization.

Then have students think about how cultures change and how they affect the way people live. Have them offer ways their life has changed by the introduction of new cultures in your area, such as ethnic restaurants and new foods available in grocery stores, and new classmates in school.

Ask them to predict a change to various cultures in the United States within their life times. Invite students to write down their predictions and share them with the class for further discussion.

You may want to keep their predictions to review at the end of the school year to see if students have changed their points of view throughout the school year and would want to make changes to their predictions.

LESSON 2 REVIEW

Reviewing Vocabulary
1. What is the difference between a *democracy* and a *representative democracy*?

Answering the Guiding Questions
2. *Determining Central Ideas* Give several examples of parts of a culture that might change over a period of time.

3. *Analyzing* What can be a disadvantage of a representative form of government?

4. *Describing* Describe how the Internet has changed the culture of the countries in which a large percentage of the population utilizes it.

5. *Informative/Explanatory Writing* Write a short essay explaining ways in which globalization has affected your family. Consider foods you eat, things you like to do, and people you have met.

Chapter 3 **89**

LESSON 2 REVIEW ANSWERS

Reviewing Vocabulary

1. A democracy is run directly by the people. In a representative democracy, the people elect representatives to handle laws and policies on their behalf.

Answering the Guiding Questions

2. Determining Central Ideas Food preferences can change, as can attitudes about clothing, music, and art.

3. Analyzing The representatives might decide to vote the way they want to vote instead of the way the people would like them to vote. They can gain power that way, at least until the next election.

4. Describing People have much easier access now to new ideas and products from other places than ever before. This results in more blending of cultures and more familiarity with other ideas.

5. Informative/Explanatory Writing Student essays should address new foods that their family has added to their menu, festivals that they enjoy attending, and alternative views that they accept and understand.

ANSWERS, p. 89

CRITICAL THINKING Technology allows people in all parts of the world easy access to information and the quick spread of ideas.
✔ READING PROGRESS CHECK Globalization is the process by which nations, cultures, and economies become integrated, or mixed.

ENGAGE

Bellringer Before students read the Global Connections feature on social media, explain that this feature in their text provides information and facts on a global issue, such as communication. Have students discuss ways they communicate with friends and family members. Then, **ask:** How many members of your family use social media, such as Facebook and/or Twitter? How much time do you spend each day on social media sites? *(Answers will vary but should include knowledge of how their family uses social media, and about how much time they spend individually on it each day.)*

TEACH & ASSESS

C1 Critical Thinking Skills

Making Inferences Have students infer why social media may at times be the only way to communicate in an emergency. Encourage students to share stories they know about in which social media helped people in an emergency. **Ask:** What more recent emergencies have occurred in the world that social media may have helped? *(Answers will vary but should relate knowledge of current events.)*

Then discuss ways in which social media actually helps us to communicate events faster. **Ask:** What are some advantages to using social media? *(Answers will vary but could include speed and ease of communicating to many people all at one time.)*
BL Interpersonal

R Reading Skills

Explaining Have students explain dangers and abuses of social media and why it is so important to practice safety tips such as the ones described in the textbook on social media sites. **Ask:** How can you protect yourself while using the Internet? *(Answers will vary but should include an understanding of the abuses made on the Internet and how to avoid falling victim to such abuses.)* Verbal/Linguistic, Intrapersonal

---

GLOBAL CONNECTIONS

Social Media in a Changing World

News media, such as newspapers and radio, give us information. Social media, such as Facebook and Twitter, provide information, but they help us communicate, too.

Family and Friends The Internet helps us stay in touch with family and friends. It provides a good way for members of the military and their families and friends to share what is happening in their lives. Online connections also help service members in other ways. Where soldiers have access to the Internet, many have continued taking college courses, even in Iraq and Afghanistan. **C1**

In College Nearly one-third of higher-education students take at least one course online. For several years, online enrollment has grown faster than total higher-education enrollment.

> " It makes it easy to share information. "

In an Emergency At times, social media provides the only way to communicate during an emergency like the tsunami that struck Japan in 2011. Through the use of sites such as Facebook and Twitter, people were able to contact family and friends. Social networks also posted information about shelters, medical help, and relief efforts.

Political Effects The use of social media increases during times of political trouble or change, such as the "Arab Spring" protests. For example, the number of tweets from Egypt rose from 2,300 to 230,000 in the week leading to the resignation of Egyptian president Hosni Mubarak. The tweets spread the message of protest. **C2**

Safety Tips The Internet is a fun way to interact with friends. It makes it easy to share information. But some information should *not* be shared. Remember these safety tips: **R**

- Keep your personal information to yourself. Don't post your full name, Social Security number, address, phone number, or bank account numbers.

- Don't accept as a friend anyone you do not know.

- Post only information that you are comfortable with others seeing—and knowing—about you.

90 *Chapter 3*

(l) Ariel Skelley/the Agency Collection/Getty Images; (t) Daniel Berehulak/Getty Images News/Getty Images

netw⊕rks *Online Teaching Options*

MAP

Global Use of Social Media

Analyzing Maps Have students study the map of global social media usage to identify areas of the world where use is higher and lower. Encourage students to speculate why it varies. Then have small groups pick one country to research and report back on that country's social media use. **BL** Verbal/Linguistic

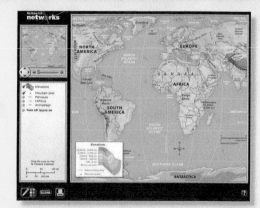

THERE'S MORE ONLINE

HEAR about China's internet restrictions • *SEE* how people influence media • *WATCH* a video on piracy

VIDEO

Social Media Unrest

Integrating Visual Information Show students the video discussing how and why Egypt's government shut down the Internet to its people in early 2011. Further discuss the effects this action had on the people and whether it worked to the government's advantage or not. **AL** Visual/Spatial

C₂ Critical Thinking Skills

Recognizing Relationships Review with students the information about tweets made during the "Arab Spring" protest movement and have them speculate on the content of the messages and how the content related to the rise in number of messages. **Ask:** What do you think the tweets said in the week mentioned in the text? Why would the number of tweets have increased 100 times more than normal? *(Answers will vary but should indicate a call to action and protest by opposition political leaders in Egypt and the need to get as many people involved as possible.)* Verbal/Linguistic

V

V Visual Skills

Interpreting Discuss with students the kinds of information they can gather from photographs. **Ask:** How does the photo in the textbook help you understand the "Arab Spring" protests, and the effect that the numerous tweets had on the protests? *(Students should recognize that the numerous tweets brought out many people to express their opinions through flags and cheers regarding the political leaders of Egypt at the time.)* Visual/Spatial

Content Background Knowledge

Share the following information with students about the "Arab Spring."

- "Arab Spring" is also known as the "Arab Awakening" or the "Arab Revolution."
- The "Arab Spring" began on December 18, 2010.
- The protesters were pro-democracy.
- The "Arab Spring" began in Tunisia, and then it moved to Egypt, Libya, Yemen, and Syria.
- Some causes of the "Arab Spring" were the poor economy and government of these countries.

R1 **Reading Skills**

Stating Have students read the statistics listed on the page. Explain that often a lot of information is communicated in a statistic. **Ask:**

- How much time does the average user spend on social networking sites? *(23 minutes of every hour)*
- What type of online activity is used the most, according to the survey listed in the paragraphs? *(email)*
- In which country is social media most popular, according to the survey listed in the paragraphs? *(Indonesia)*
- What effect do social media sites have on people? *(They are taking up more of people's time.)* **AL**

R2 **Reading Skills**

Determining Word Meanings Have students read aloud the paragraph about the program Instagram with a partner. Then have pairs look up and define the word *filter* as it applies to photography. **Ask:** What does it mean to 'apply a filter on a photograph?' *(adding effects to alter a photograph; examples include enhancing the color or texture, blurring, sharpening, or washing out the photo)*

Point out the "$1 Billion" heading. Discuss ways in which students think the Internet, social media, and other online sites have made many companies and people wealthy over the past several years. **ELL** **Verbal/Linguistic**

C **Critical Thinking Skills**

Analyzing Information Have a small group of student volunteers conduct a class study on social media use. Volunteers will ask their classmates which social media networks they use or participate in. After the survey, have the group report their findings to the rest of the class. As a class, discuss any surprising findings from the survey and whether or not the findings were similiar to the findings found on this page. **Interpersonal**

These numbers and statistics can help you see how social media is changing the world.

840 Million

By 2012, Facebook had more than 840 million users. That's more than the population of every country in the world except China and India.

$1 Billion

In April 2012, Facebook, Inc. purchased the photo-sharing app called Instagram for $1 billion. Instagram allows users to apply a filter on a photograph and share it on any of a number of social networks. The company has 13 employees and has been in business since October 2010.

Fastest to **10 MILLION**

Which social network was the quickest to reach 10 million users? That's Google+, taking only 16 days to reach that number. By contrast, Twitter reached 10 million users in 780 days. It took Facebook 852 days.

23 minutes

Social networks are taking up more and more of our time online. Users spend on average about 23 minutes of every hour of computer time on social networking sites.

62% Of online users worldwide, 62 percent use the Internet for social networking. Social media is most popular in Indonesia, where 83 percent take part. Although the use of social networking is growing, e-mail remains number one. About 85 percent of those surveyed say it remains their top online activity.

55 and older | Nielsen reported that users 55 and older are the fastest-growing group on social networks. However, people between ages 18 and 34 are the most active age group.

Singer from band Train sends a picture from the concert stage

190 Million
That's the number of tweets sent on an average day.

April 23, 2005

On that day, the very first video was uploaded to YouTube. It was called "Me at the Zoo." A little more than a year later, more than 65,000 videos were being uploaded every day.

---

netw⊕rks   *Online Teaching Options*

ANIMATION

How Information Goes Viral

Using and Citing Information Show students the animation that compares the length of time it took information to spread in the past using different forms of media to the length of time it takes now. Have partners propose events in time and research the time it took for such information to spread, such as the time it took to communicate the passing of President Abraham Lincoln compared to how long it would take now to report the death of an entertainer, sports figure, or world leader. **BL**

SOCIAL MEDIA

CLICK HERE TO START.

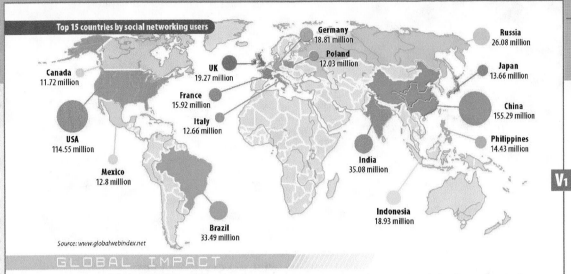

Top 15 countries by social networking users

Canada 11.72 million
USA 114.55 million
Mexico 12.8 million
UK 19.27 million
France 15.92 million
Italy 12.66 million
Germany 18.81 million
Poland 12.03 million
Russia 26.08 million
Japan 13.66 million
China 155.29 million
Philippines 14.43 million
India 35.08 million
Indonesia 18.93 million
Brazil 33.49 million

Source: www.globalwebindex.net

GLOBAL IMPACT

THE GEOGRAPHY OF SOCIAL MEDIA When social media and the Internet were developed, many people said that physical location would no longer matter. People are able to communicate as easily with someone half a world away as with the person next door. However, most communication on social media is with people who are close by. They could go to see the person they are addressing, but they prefer to send a message. Messages on Facebook can be sent to many people at the same time.

Facebook Users

The graph shows the number of Facebook users worldwide from 2004 to 2011.

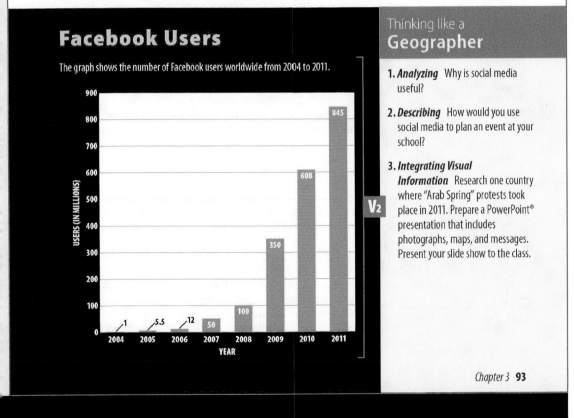

USERS (IN MILLIONS)

- 2004: 1
- 2005: 5.5
- 2006: 12
- 2007: 50
- 2008: 100
- 2009: 350
- 2010: 608
- 2011: 845

YEAR

Thinking like a Geographer

1. **Analyzing** Why is social media useful?

2. **Describing** How would you use social media to plan an event at your school?

3. **Integrating Visual Information** Research one country where "Arab Spring" protests took place in 2011. Prepare a PowerPoint® presentation that includes photographs, maps, and messages. Present your slide show to the class.

Chapter 3 **93**

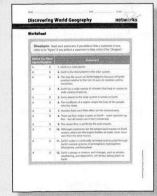

V1 Visual Skills

Reading a Map Have students look at the map and name the top 15 countries that use social networking. **Ask:**

- Which country has more users: China or the United States? *(China)*
- Out of the top 15 countries, which country has the least amount of users? *(Canada)*
- Which continents do not have any countries in the top 15? Why do you think that is? *(Africa, Australia, and Antarctica; student answers will vary but should include the higher number of developing nations in Africa that have less access to computers and the lower populations of Australia and Antarctica.)* **ELL** Visual/Spatial

V2 Visual Skills

Graph Skills Have students look at the graph of Facebook users and answer the following questions. **Ask:**

- How many users were there in 2004? *(One million)*
- How long did it take to jump from one million users to 845 million users? *(seven years)*
- How many more users were there in 2010 than in 2009? *(258 million)*
- Why do you think the amount of users jumped so much from 2010 to 2011? *(Student answers will vary but should include reasons such as lower prices of computers so more people can afford them, more cell phones with Internet access, and increased popularity of sites.)* **AL** Logical/Mathematical

CLOSE & REFLECT

Have students think about all of the social media they know. Then ask them to write survey questions about the different types, uses, or effects of social media. Using the questions, have students survey their classmates, and then write a paragraph or two summarizing the details and results of their surveys.

ANSWERS, p. 93

Thinking Like a Geographer

1. Social media allows individuals to communicate with each other directly, no matter where they are.

2. Social media can be used to issue invitations and track responses and to assign duties for planning the event and the activities that will take place there. It can also be used to tell people near and far what the event is like, using text, photographs, and videos.

3. Presentations should include information about calls for action and reports to the outside world.

ENGAGE

Bellringer Before students begin this lesson, have volunteers explain a time when they have wanted something but could not get it because there were none left of the item in their house or in the local stores. Discuss popular items in limited supply or display photos of a number of items that students would be interested in having, but there are limited supplies of the items. Ask students what solutions they can think of to satisfy their wants as well as others' wants when supplies are limited. List their ideas and discuss possible outcomes of each.

TEACH & ASSESS

V Visual Skills

Drawing Have students make sketches of resources that help to provide us with wants and needs. Suggest that they use their text as a guide but also to include additional resources. Remind students to label their sketches as resources that supply *wants* or *needs*. Invite students to share their drawings in small groups or with the class. **ELL** Visual/Spatial

R Reading Skills

Applying Discuss with students how countries have wants and needs, too. **Ask:** What questions do you think countries must consider when determining what their wants and needs are and how they will fulfill them? Tell students to use their own words to answer the question. *(Possible answer: countries must examine their resources and decide what they will need to acquire through trade.)* Logical/Mathematical

Reinforcing Vocabulary Remind students to add academic and content vocabulary words to the vocabulary lists in their notebooks. Tell students to write their own definitions and to include drawings if desired. **ELL** **AL**

ANSWER, p. 94

Taking Notes Sample notes: **1. Traditional economy:** resources are distributed mainly through families; farming, herding, and hunter-gatherer; developing, mainly agricultural societies often have traditional economies. **2. Market economy (capitalism):** most means of production are privately owned; production is guided and income is distributed through sales and demand for products and resources. **3. Command economy:** means of production are publicly owned and production and distribution are controlled by a central governing authority (communism). **4. Mixed economy:** Parts of the economy may be privately owned and parts may be owned by the government or other authority.

---

networks

There's More Online!

☑ **CHART/GRAPH** Economic Terms

☑ **IMAGE** Renewable Resources

☑ **GAME** Bartering and Trade

☑ **VIDEO**

Reading **HELP**DESK

Academic Vocabulary

- currency

Content Vocabulary

- renewable resource
- nonrenewable resource
- opportunity cost
- economic system
- traditional economy
- market economy
- command economy
- mixed economy
- gross domestic product
- standard of living
- productivity
- export
- import
- free trade
- sustainability

TAKING NOTES: *Key Ideas and Details*

Organize As you read, summarize the key ideas about each economic system.

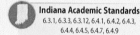

1.   3.

Economic Systems

2.   4.

Indiana Academic Standards
6.3.1, 6.3.3, 6.3.12, 6.4.1, 6.4.2, 6.4.3, 6.4.4, 6.4.5, 6.4.7, 6.4.9

Lesson 3
Economic Systems

ESSENTIAL QUESTION · *Why do people make economic choices?*

IT MATTERS BECAUSE
People strive to meet their basic needs and their desires for a better life.

Economic Principles

GUIDING QUESTION *How do people get the things they want and need?*

All human beings have wants and needs. How do you get the things you want and the things you need? To obtain these items, people use resources. Resources are the supplies that are used to meet our wants and needs. Some types of resources, such as water, soil, plants, and animals, come from the earth. These are called natural resources.

Other resources are supplied by humans. Human resources include the labor, skills, and talents people contribute. Countries also have wants and needs. Like individuals, nations must use resources to meet their needs.

Wants and Resources

What would happen if 14 students each wanted a glass of lemonade from a pitcher that contained only 12 glasses of lemonade? What if even more students wanted a glass of lemonade? No matter how many people want lemonade, the pitcher still contains just 12 glasses. There is not enough for everyone. This is an example of a limited supply and unlimited demand. This situation is not uncommon. It happens to individuals and also to countries. You probably can think of many personal examples, as well as current and historical examples, of limited supply and unlimited demand.

(l to r) Linda Whitwam/Dorling Kindersley/Getty Images; S. Solum/PhotoLink/Getty Images; Walter Hodges/Photodisc/Getty Images; Jens Kuhfs/Photographer's Choice/Getty Images

---

networks   *Online Teaching Options*

VIDEO

Emerging Markets in India Bring Westerners and Trade

Analyzing Use the video about the emerging markets in India with students. Ask students to share what they learned from the video about developing markets and the opportunities for jobs in different parts of the world. Discuss if any of the information was surprising to them. **AL** Visual/Spatial

See page 69E for other online activities.

BBC Motion Gallery Education

One type of resource everyone needs is energy. Energy is the power to do work. Energy resources are the supplies that provide the power to do work. Many types of energy resources exist in our world. Energy resources can be renewable or nonrenewable. **Renewable resources** are resources that can be totally replaced or are always available naturally. They can be regenerated and replenished. Examples of renewable resources include water, trees, and energy from the wind and the sun.

In contrast are nonrenewable resources. **Nonrenewable resources** can not be totally replaced. Once nonrenewable resources are consumed, they are gone. Examples of nonrenewable resources include the fossil fuels oil, coal, and natural gas. These fuels received their name because they formed millions of years ago. Humans' increasing need for energy is taking its toll as supplies of nonrenewable resources shrink.

Making Choices

If the peoples of all nations have unlimited wants but face limited resources, what must happen? We must make choices. Do we continue to use nonrenewable resources? If so, at what rate should we be using them? Should we switch to renewable resources?

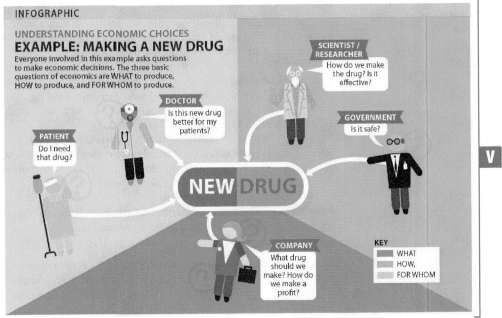

INFOGRAPHIC

UNDERSTANDING ECONOMIC CHOICES

EXAMPLE: MAKING A NEW DRUG
Everyone involved in this example asks questions to make economic decisions. The three basic questions of economics are WHAT to produce, HOW to produce, and FOR WHOM to produce.

SCIENTIST / RESEARCHER — How do we make the drug? Is it effective?

DOCTOR — Is this new drug better for my patients?

GOVERNMENT — Is it safe?

PATIENT — Do I need that drug?

NEW DRUG

COMPANY — What drug should we make? How do we make a profit?

KEY
- WHAT
- HOW,
- FOR WHOM

Every economic system must address three basic questions.

▶ CRITICAL THINKING
Determining Central Ideas How are the three basic economic questions related to the problem of limited supply?

Chapter 3 **95**

R Reading Skills

Using Context Clues Point out to students that by looking at familiar words around or near an unfamiliar word, they can often determine the meaning of the unknown word without having to look the word up in the glossary or dictionary.
Ask: What words help you to infer the meanings of *regenerated* and *replenished* in the first paragraph? *(Sample answer: The definition of renewable resources in the previous sentence tells me that they are resources that can be totally replaced. Resources that can be totally replaced can be used over and over so regenerated and replenished might mean "formed or created again" and "to supply or fill fully.")*
ELL Verbal/Linguistic

C Critical Thinking Skills

Comparing and Contrasting After students have finished reading the section, "Wants and Resources," **ask:** How are renewable and nonrenewable resources alike and different? Record students' responses in a Venn diagram. *(Sample answers: Alike: They are both kinds of resources. Different: Renewable resources can be totally replaced or are always available naturally. Nonrenewable resources cannot be replaced.)*
AL Visual/Spatial

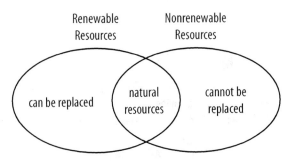

Renewable Resources — can be replaced

natural resources

Nonrenewable Resources — cannot be replaced

V Visual Skills

Interpreting Review the infographic with students. **Ask:** What are the three basic questions of economics according to this graphic? *(what to produce, how to produce, and for whom to produce)* What must people do to solve these questions? *(They must make choices.)* Visual/Spatial

---

CHART

Economic Questions

Analyzing Charts Display the interactive chart on the whiteboard. Review the three basic economic questions and then invite students to fill in the chart, from top to bottom, with the correct answers: unlimited wants, limited resources, scarcity, and choices. Verbal/Linguistic

See page 69E for other online activities

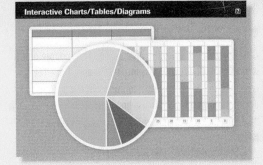

Interactive Charts/Tables/Diagrams

ANSWER, p. 95

CRITICAL THINKING The basic economic questions are questions all societies must ask when dealing with scarcity and efficiently allocating their resources.

Economic Systems

R Reading Skills

Applying Review with students the meaning of opportunity cost and how it works in their everyday lives. For example, ask students to suppose they earned $10 doing chores and wanted to spend some of the money. They have enough money to download a game or music album, but not enough to buy the music or game and go to the movies with friends. They decide to go to the movies with their friends in hopes that they will earn more money later. **Ask:**

- What is the opportunity cost? *(downloading a game or music album)*
- What other choice could you have made? *(Sample answer: I could have downloaded the game or music album and skipped the movie.)* **ELL** Logical/Mathematical

V Visual Skills

Comparing and Contrasting Have students choose two of the different economic systems discussed in the text. Have them draw a Venn diagram to compare and contrast the two systems based on the information in the text and their prior knowledge. **Ask:** How are the two economic systems you chose alike? How are they different? *(Students should be able to verbalize their answers as well as list them in their diagrams.)* Visual/Spatial

T Technology Skills

Evaluating Ask students to work with a partner to research the following question online: **Which type of economic system has had the most successful results?** Remind them to use reliable sources and list their sources along with their findings in their notes. **Ask:** Were you surprised by your findings? Why or why not? *(Sample answer: Yes, I was surprised because I thought a market economy was the most successful. Students should also include facts and reasons why the economic system is successful.)* **BL** Verbal/Linguistic

---

ANSWER, p. 96

☑ READING PROGRESS CHECK Possible answer: Renewable and nonrenewable resources are alike in that they both meet wants and needs. They are different in that renewable resources can be replenished, but once nonrenewable resources are used up, they are gone.

Think **Again** ❓

No countries today rely on a command economic system.

Not true. Some countries still have planned economies, including Cuba, Saudi Arabia, Iran, and North Korea. These nations have an economic system in which supply and prices are regulated by the government, not by the market.

We must weigh the **opportunity cost**, or the value of what we must give up to acquire something else, of using renewable resources versus nonrenewable resources. We must take into account these and many more considerations as we make choices now and in the future. **R**

☑ READING PROGRESS CHECK

Describing How are renewable and nonrenewable resources alike, and how are they different?

National Economies

GUIDING QUESTION *What kinds of economic systems are used in our world today?*

Economic resources are another important resource. Economic resources include the goods and services a society provides and how they are produced, distributed, and used. How a society decides on the ownership and distribution of its economic resources is its **economic system**. Do you ever stop to think about the goods and services you use in a single day? How do these goods and services become available to you?

Different Economic Systems

We can break down the discussion on economic systems into three basic economic questions: *What should be produced? How should it be produced? How should what is produced be distributed?* Different nations have different answers to these questions.

One type of economic system is the traditional economy. In a **traditional economy**, resources are distributed mainly through families. Traditional economies include farming, herding, and hunter-gatherer societies. Developing societies, which are mainly agricultural, often have traditional economies.

Another type of economic system is a **market economy**, also referred to as capitalism. In market economies, the means of production are privately owned. Production is guided and income is distributed through sales and demand for products and resources. **V**

In a **command economy**, the means of production are publicly owned, and production and distribution are controlled by a central governing authority. Communism is a command economy.

What Is a Mixed Economy?

A **mixed economy** is just that—mixed. Parts of the economy may be privately owned, and parts may be owned by the government or another authority. The United States has a mixed market economy. Another economic system is socialism. In socialist societies, property and the distribution of goods and income are controlled by the community. How do individuals get the goods or services they need under each of these economic systems? **T**

---

netw⚙rks   *Online Teaching Options*

GAME

Drag-and-Drop: Economic Systems

Categorizing Display the interactive sorting game on the whiteboard. Divide the class into two teams. Have teams complete the activity matching the economic system to its description. As a class, discuss how each economic system has its benefits and weaknesses. **AL** Interpersonal, Kinesthetic

See page 69E for other online activities.

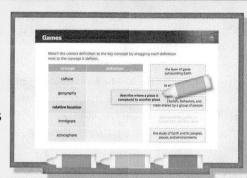

Buyers and sellers come together in an outdoor market in a village in the Central Highlands of Mexico.

▶ **CRITICAL THINKING**

Describing Is the seller involved in a primary, secondary, or tertiary economic activity?

Parts of the Economy

We can break down the economy into parts. In economics, *land* is a factor of production that includes natural resources. Another factor of production is *labor*, which refers to all paid workers within a system. The other factor is *capital*, the human-made resources used to produce other goods. An *industry* is a branch of a business. For example, the *agriculture industry* grows crops and raises livestock. *Service industries* provide services rather than goods. Banking, retail, food service, transportation, and communications are examples of service industries.

Types of Economic Activities

Another way to view the parts of the economy is by the type of economic activity. Economists use the terms *primary sector*, *secondary sector*, and *tertiary sector* to group these activities. The primary sector includes activities that produce raw materials and basic goods. These activities include mining, fishing, agriculture, and logging.

The secondary sector makes finished goods. This sector includes home and building construction, food processing, and aerospace manufacturing. The tertiary sector of the economy is the service industry. Service sectors include sales, restaurants, banking, information technology, and health care.

Indiana CONNECTION

Saving and Investing

In all societies, saving and investing helps increase productivity and economic growth. There are various ways that one can save or invest. One way is to open a savings account at a bank or credit union. These institutions accept people's money, pay them a fairly low rate of interest, and loan the money on deposit to other customers. You can withdraw your money at any time, and the interest you earn is added automatically to your principal, or the amount you initially deposited.

Another way to save is with certificate of deposit (CDs). CDs are a kind of time deposit, in which you agree to deposit a sum of money with a financial institution for a certain amount of time. In return, you are guaranteed a set rate of interest that will be added to your principal when the CD comes due. The rate of interest on a CD is almost always higher than that on a savings account. This is because you have less flexibility to withdraw your money. If you want to withdraw it before the stated date, you must pay a substantial penalty.

Almost all investors also invest in stocks. When you buy shares of stock, you are buying partial ownership in a company. You can sell the shares at any time, hopefully for more than you paid, and the difference is your profit. Stocks generally earn a higher return because they carry greater risk. There is no guarantee that you will make money on your stock investment. In fact, if the company goes out of business, you will lose your entire investment.

Chapter 3 **97**

See page 69E for other online activities.

IMAGE

Types of Economic Activities and Sectors

Identifying Use the interactive image to review the information about the different economic sectors. Have students provide descriptions of each sector and then address which sector is being shown in the image. Ask students which sector is thriving in our current economy.
BL Verbal/Linguistic

V Visual Skills

Integrating Visual Information Have students examine the photograph of the woman selling food to a consumer at a market. Discuss the factors of production that were needed. Then ask students to use this information and integrate it with what they already know about different economic systems.
Ask: How might globalization affect markets such as this one as well as more traditional economic systems? *(Students' answers may vary but should demonstrate an understanding that globalization may help the seller to distribute her product beyond the market and to other countries. It may cause more traditional economies to incorporate aspects of market economies.)* Verbal/Linguistic, Logical/Mathematical

C Critical Thinking Skills

Labeling After you read the section, "Types of Economic Activities," have students draw a diagram to show the three different sectors of economic activities and label each section of the diagram accurately. **Ask:** Why do you think the sectors were divided in this way? What logic was used to determine the structure? *(Sample answer: Raw materials are at the most basic level, which is primary, because they are pure and have not been modified. Building and manufacturing are in the secondary sector because they require raw materials but use machines and other equipment to produce something out of the raw materials. Services are in the tertiary sector because they may require both raw materials and manufactured materials to provide a service.)* **ELL** **AL** Visual/Spatial

Content Background Knowledge

Transportation and communication are not factors of production, but they help to link the factors together. They provide the means for the factors of production to reach the producers, as well as the consumers. Technology, on the other hand, is part of capital, one of the factors of production that includes the tools and equipment needed for production.

ANSWER, p. 97

CRITICAL THINKING Sales is a service. Services are part of the tertiary sector of the economy.

V Visual Skills

Analyzing Charts Review the diagram at the top of the page with students. Explain that this is a graphic organizer and that it displays relationships between items, similar to cause and effect charts. **Ask:** Why do you think the factors of production must begin with the land factor of production? What might happen next? *(Possible answer: Natural resources or raw materials must be first in the sequence because without them products could not be produced. Machines and then labor need to be supplied with the raw materials or natural resources in order to produce a product for consumers. After a product is produced, it needs to be brought to market in order to reach consumers. Entrepreneurs are the factor of production that supply this need.)* Visual/Spatial

C Critical Thinking Skills

Describing After reviewing the factors of production graphic with the class, have students work in small groups to write lyrics for a song with a familiar tune of their choosing that will help them describe the factors of production. Invite groups to perform their songs for the class. Interpersonal, Auditory/Musical

W Writing Skills

Argument Explain that today different groups argue about whether developing countries should be integrated into the global market and about what impact globalization will have on them. Divide the class into two teams to debate this issue. Provide an opportunity for students to gather research on their topic to answer this prompt: **Should developing countries be brought into the global market?** Allow each side to present their argument and then ask students to write a multi-paragraph essay in which they write their argument, support their claim with evidence, acknowledge the opposing argument, and organize their writing logically and clearly. *(Students' essays should include coverage of all of these points and be accurate. They should demonstrate understanding of a developing country and globalization.)* Interpersonal, Verbal/Linguistic

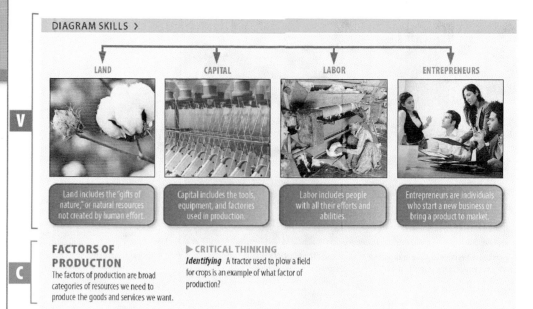

DIAGRAM SKILLS >

| LAND | CAPITAL | LABOR | ENTREPRENEURS |

Land includes the "gifts of nature," or natural resources not created by human effort.

Capital includes the tools, equipment, and factories used in production.

Labor includes people with all their efforts and abilities.

Entrepreneurs are individuals who start a new business or bring a product to market.

FACTORS OF PRODUCTION
The factors of production are broad categories of resources we need to produce the goods and services we want.

▶ **CRITICAL THINKING**
Identifying A tractor used to plow a field for crops is an example of what factor of production?

Economic Performance
Economic performance measures how well an economy meets the needs of society. Economic performance can be determined by several factors that measure economic success. The **gross domestic product (GDP)** is the total dollar value of all final goods and services produced in a country during a single year. The **standard of living** is the level at which a person, a group, or a nation lives as measured by the extent to which it meets its needs. These needs include food, shelter, clothing, education, and health care. Per capita income is the total national income divided by the number of people in the nation.

When referring to economics, **productivity** is a measurement of what is produced and what is required to produce it. Sustainable growth is the growth rate a business can maintain without having to borrow money. The employment rate is the percentage of the labor force that is employed. These factors help determine a nation's economic strength and performance.

Types of National Economies
National economies also can be classified by types. Developed countries are industrialized countries. Developing countries are less industrialized, agricultural countries that are working to become more advanced economically. Developing countries often have weak economies, and most of their population lives in poverty. Newly industrialized countries (NICs) are in the process of becoming developed and economically secure. Their economies are growing

(l to r) S. Solum/PhotoLink/Getty Images; yang yu/Alamy; Ajit Solanki/AP Images; Rubberball/Getty Images

98 *Chapter 3*

netw⊙rks   *Online Teaching Options*

DIAGRAM

Factors of Production

Interpreting Show the diagram about factors of production on the whiteboard and review each factor with students to check for understanding. Then ask students to work in pairs or groups to provide examples of land, capital, labor, and entrepreneurs to bring another product from natural resources to the consumer.
ELL Visual/Spatial

See page 69E for other online activities.

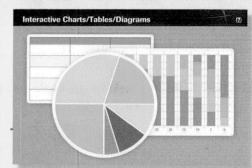

Interactive Charts/Tables/Diagrams

ANSWER, p. 98

CRITICAL THINKING capital

and struggling to become fully developed, but they still face many economic and social challenges.

☑ **READING PROGRESS CHECK**

Describing How is standard of living a sign of economic performance or success?

World Economy

GUIDING QUESTION *How do the world's economies interact and affect one another?*

C

You have read about different economic systems and different types of economies. All the world's nations can be classified into the different economic categories. All nations must find ways to interact with one another. Look at the labels in your clothes or on other products you buy. How many different country names can you find? How and why do we get goods from far across the world?

Trade

Trade is the business of buying, selling, or bartering. When you buy something at the store, you are trading money for a product. On a much bigger scale, nations trade with each other. Countries have different resources. Resources can include raw materials, such as iron ore. Even labor may be cheaper in another country where workers earn lower wages. As a result, goods can be produced in some countries more easily or efficiently than in other countries.

Trade can benefit countries. One country can **export**, or send to another country, a product that it is able to produce. Another country **imports**, or buys that product from another country.

R

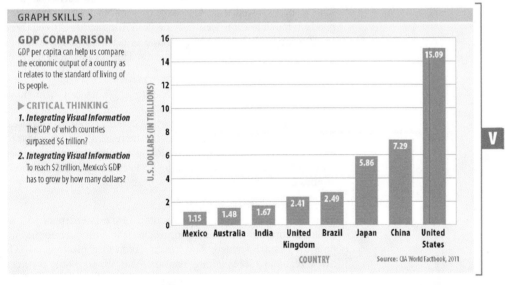

GRAPH SKILLS >

GDP COMPARISON
GDP per capita can help us compare the economic output of a country as it relates to the standard of living of its people.

▶ **CRITICAL THINKING**
1. *Integrating Visual Information*
   The GDP of which countries surpassed $6 trillion?
2. *Integrating Visual Information*
   To reach $2 trillion, Mexico's GDP has to grow by how many dollars?

Graph: GDP Comparison — U.S. DOLLARS (IN TRILLIONS) vs COUNTRY
- Mexico: 1.15
- Australia: 1.48
- India: 1.67
- United Kingdom: 2.41
- Brazil: 2.49
- Japan: 5.86
- China: 7.29
- United States: 15.09

Source: CIA World Factbook, 2011

V

C Critical Thinking Skills

Determining Cause and Effect Have students stop reading and work with a partner to predict what the causes and effects are of different countries' economies interacting. Have pairs write their predictions down. Point out to students that there are often multiple effects or even multiple causes to consider in such complex situations.

After students make their predictions, have them read the rest of the section, "World Economy," and check their predictions for accuracy. Suggest that they make any necessary changes to their predictions. Explain that making predictions helps readers make connections to what they are reading, and that by checking their predictions as they read, they are more actively engaged in the reading which will help them remember the text and do better on exams. **BL** Verbal/Linguistic

R Reading Skills

Defining Discuss the definitions of *export* and *import* and explain that the prefix *ex* means "out of" or "from" and the prefix *im* can mean "in" or "not." Place students into small groups and have them think of other words with the prefixes *ex* and *im*. Come back together, and as a class make a list of all of the words that students came up with. Then ask them to look up and write down the definitions in their vocabulary lists in their notebooks or to make sketches to illustrate the meanings of the words. **ELL**

V Visual Skills

Analyze Graphs Review the GDP Comparison graph with students. **Ask:** What generalizations can you make from the data on this chart about GDP and geographic location? *(Possible answer: There is a wide range of GDP in the Eastern Hemisphere, with China leading the way with the highest GDP of the Eastern countries listed on the graph.)* **BL** Logical/Mathematical

GRAPHS

GDP Around the World

Comparing and Contrasting Show the graph presentation of GDP around the world to students, and discuss the GDP per capita in the six countries shown. Have students compare and contrast the data in small groups, and then explain the economic effects of a high GDP or low GDP orally. **AL** Verbal/Linguistic

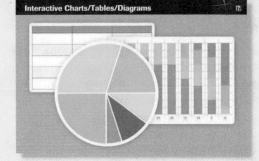

Interactive Charts/Tables/Diagrams

See page 69E for other online activities.

ANSWERS, p. 99

☑ **READING PROGRESS CHECK** Standard of living reveals how well and to what extent the needs and wants of the people of a society are being met.
CRITICAL THINKING
1. China and the United States
2. 0.85 trillion

V Visual Skills

Collaborating Pair students and ask them to discuss how these images reinforce the advantages and disadvantages of trade. **Ask:**

- How do countries with large shipping ports have advantages in global trade over countries without them? *(Possible answer: They may have more trading partners and are able to import and export more goods than countries with fewer or smaller ports.)*

- What effects does shipping have on the environment? What risks are involved? *(Possible answer: Some ships have accidents and petroleum or other harmful substances can leak into the ocean, killing sea life and causing pollution.)*

- How do quotas and tariffs affect global trade? *(Possible answer: They can limit global trade but also protect countries that are importing the goods. With high tariffs, consumers from the importing country may decide to buy a locally produced product over a foreign product.)* **BL** Verbal/Linguistic

T Technology Skills

Evaluating a Web Site Discuss the role of the World Trade Organization (WTO) with students. Have students work in pairs or small groups to evaluate the WTO's web site at http://www.wto.org/. Ask them to each write an evaluation based on this prompt: **Does the WTO clearly state its mission and goals related to regulating trade?** *(Sample answer: Yes, it has a section about its mission and goals and lists information about trade negotiations, implementation and monitoring, dispute settlement, and making trade more effective for developing countries.)*

Discuss students' evaluations and ask them how they would improve upon the web site. Interpersonal, Verbal/Linguistic

Content Background Knowledge

Globalization has changed the way that the World Trade Organization, the World Bank, and the International Monetary Fund work—they now work in cooperation with each other through agreements and within a framework. This greater effort to work together is an attempt to bring about greater policymaking for the global economy.

International trade involves preparing cargo for shipping (left) and transporting goods (right).
▶ **CRITICAL THINKING**
Describing Why do countries trade?

The country that imported the product can in turn export its products to another country. In global trade, extra fees are often added to the cost of importing products by a country's government. The extra money is a type of tax called a tariff. Governments often create tariffs to persuade their people to buy products made in their own country.

Sometimes a quota, a limit on the amount of one particular good that can be imported, is set. Quotas prevent countries from exporting goods at much lower prices than the domestic market can sell them for. A group of countries may decide to set little or no tariffs or quotas when trading among themselves. This is called **free trade**.

Advantages and Disadvantages of Trade

Trade has advantages and disadvantages. Trade can help build economic growth and increase a nation's income. On the other hand, jobs might be lost because of importing certain goods and services. With its benefits and its barriers, increasing trade leads to globalization. Economic globalization takes place when businesses move past national markets and begin to trade with other nations around the world.

Economic Organizations

In recent years, nations have become more interdependent, or reliant on one another. As they draw closer together, economic and political ties are formed. The World Trade Organization (WTO) helps regulate trade among nations. The World Bank provides

(l) Walter Hodges/Photodisc/Getty Images; (r) Jens Kuhfs/Photographer's Choice/Getty Images

net**w**rks *Online Teaching Options*

GAME

Bartering and Trade

Informative/Explanatory Display the game about trade on the whiteboard. Have volunteers read each definition and drag and drop the correct term in order to complete it. Play the game as a class activity or in small groups. Then have each student write a paragraph using these terms to explain trade and its impact on countries and people around the world. **AL** Interpersonal, Kinesthetic

See page 69E for other online activities.

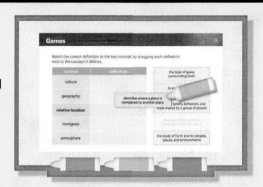

ANSWER, p. 100

CRITICAL THINKING Countries trade to get the resources or goods that they need or cannot produce on their own.

financing, advice, and research to developing nations to help them grow their economies. The International Monetary Fund (IMF) is a group that monitors economic development. The IMF also lends money to nations in need and provides training and technical help. One well-known policy and organization that promotes global trade is the North American Free Trade Agreement (NAFTA). NAFTA encourages free trade among the United States, Canada, and Mexico.

T The European Union (EU) is a group of European countries that operate under one economic unit and one **currency**, or type of money—the euro. The Mercado Camon del Sur (formerly called MERCOSUR) is a group of South American countries that promote free trade, economic development, and globalization. The Mercado Camon del Sur helps countries make better use of their resources while preserving the environment.

The Association of Southeast Asian Nations (ASEAN) is a group of countries in Southeast Asia that promote economic, cultural, and political development. The Dominican Republic-Central America Free Trade Agreement (CAFTA-DR) is an agreement among the United States, five developing Central American countries, and the Dominican Republic. The agreement promotes free trade.

Whether a nation produces its own goods or trades, one basic principle exists: sustainability. The principle of **sustainability** is central to the discussion of resources. When a country focuses on sustainability, it works to create conditions where all the natural resources for meeting the needs of society are available. **C**

What can countries do to ensure sustainability now and into the future? What can you do to plan for your future and the future of your community? Just as every nation is part of a global system, you are part of your community. The choices you make affect you and those around you. What can you do now to plan for a bright economic future?

✓ **READING PROGRESS CHECK**

Analyzing What are some possible disadvantages of trade?

Academic Vocabulary

currency paper money and coins in circulation

FOLDABLES
Study Organizer

Include this lesson's information in your Foldable®.

LESSON 3 REVIEW

Reviewing Vocabulary
1. List examples of *nonrenewable resources*.

Answering the Guiding Questions
2. *Determining Word Meanings* Explain the opportunity cost of buying a new pair of jeans.

3. *Determining Central Ideas* Explain why the United States has a market economy.

4. *Determining Central Ideas* Why is it advantageous to the United States to have a free trade agreement with Mexico and Canada?

5. *Informative/Explanatory Writing* Write a short essay explaining decisions that you can make that help ensure the sustainability of our resources. Consider things you do daily as well as things you do or buy less frequently.

Chapter 3 **101**

LESSON 3 REVIEW ANSWERS

Reviewing Vocabulary

1. Fossil fuels (petroleum/oil, coal, natural gas) are nonrenewable resources. Students may also mention minerals, such as iron ore, silver, and gold, and gem stones, such as diamonds and emeralds.

Answering the Guiding Questions

2. **Determining Word Meanings** If I spend my money on the jeans, I must give up saving it or spending it on something else such as new digital music. That is the opportunity cost.

3. **Determining Central Ideas** The government does not tell our companies what to produce. Companies decide what to make based on demand by consumers and ability to make a profit.

4. **Determining Central Ideas** Allowing free trade makes products cheaper for Americans because we do not have to pay tariffs.

5. **Informative/Explanatory Writing** Essays will vary but might include purchasing items with less packaging, riding bikes instead of using a car, taking shorter showers to conserve water, turning off lights when not in use, and not purchasing every new style if their old clothes still fit.

T **Technology Skills**

Researching Have students choose five different countries from around the world and use the Internet to research what currency is used in each country, and how the currency compares to the dollar used in the United States. **Ask:** Does the currency seem like it would be easier or more difficult to use than the dollar? *(Answers will vary but should show an understanding of the currencies that students researched and how they relate to the United States dollar.)*

Encourage students who have used other currencies in other countries to describe the coins and the bills and how easy or difficult they were to use. **Interpersonal, Verbal/ Linguistic**

C **Critical Thinking Skills**

Synthesizing Have students work in small groups to synthesize the information they have read about the different economic organizations. **Ask:** What are the goals of these economic organizations? How has globalization affected the goals and work of these economic organizations? *(Possible answer: They work to support and finance the economies of developing nations and promote regional and global trade agreements. Globalization has prompted many of these organizations to collaborate and cooperate for the greater good.)* **AL** **Interpersonal**

CLOSE & REFLECT

Making Connections To close this lesson, have students think about the global connections among the following: people's needs and wants, resources, economic systems, and the interaction of economic systems. Have them tell of an item they want, the resources required to produce the item, the country where the item is most likely made, and if the item is an import to the United States, the interaction of economic systems needed to bring the item here.

ANSWER, p. 101

✓ **READING PROGRESS CHECK** There is the potential for the country importing goods in trade to lose jobs associated with the product that is imported.

CHAPTER REVIEW ACTIVITY

Have students create a graphic organizer like the one below with boxes on the left for causes and boxes on the right for effects. Ask them to write "population growth," "movement of people," and "change in government or economy" in the cause boxes. Then lead a discussion that allows students to identify the effects of these causes. (*possible effects of population growth: urbanization, poverty, migration, population density; effects of movement of people: cultural changes, population distribution, urbanization; effects of change in government or economy: migration, globalization, cultural changes, poverty*)

Population growth	→	
Movement of people	→	
Change in government or economy	→	

REVIEW THE ENDURING UNDERSTANDINGS

Review the Enduring Understandings with students:

- *Over time, people adapt to their environment.*
- *People, places, and ideas change over time.*
- *Countries have relationships with each other.*

Now pose the following questions in a class discussion to apply these to this chapter.

- How have people adapted to their environment? *(They find resources in their environment to meet their needs, move to places where their needs can be met, or acquire what they need through trade.)*

- How have migration, population growth, and changes to a country's government or economy affected cultures? *(Some cultures have changed as a result of migration, population growth, and political and economic changes. Many cultures try to preserve elements of their cultures even when affected by these factors.)*

- How has globalization brought countries together and strengthened economic and cultural ties? *(Globalization has enabled countries to have more economic advantages, which has helped to support their populations. It has benefitted some developing countries and strengthened their economies.)*

Chapter 3 ACTIVITIES

Directions: Write your answers on a separate piece of paper.

❶ Exploring the Essential Questions
INFORMATIVE/EXPLANATORY WRITING Research the culture of a South American country. Create a poster with pictures or photos showing some of the unique features, holidays, and celebrations that you learn about.

❷ 21st Century Skills
INTEGRATING VISUAL INFORMATION Select one country in Europe to examine more closely. Create a slide show presentation that includes the following information: population, population density, population patterns, primary language, type of government, customs and other cultural information, resources, and type of economy.

❸ Thinking Like a Geographer
IDENTIFYING Look up the population density and total population figures for North America, South America, and Europe. Make a chart that shows both figures for each continent. Write a narrative explanation of your findings also.

❹ GEOGRAPHY ACTIVITY

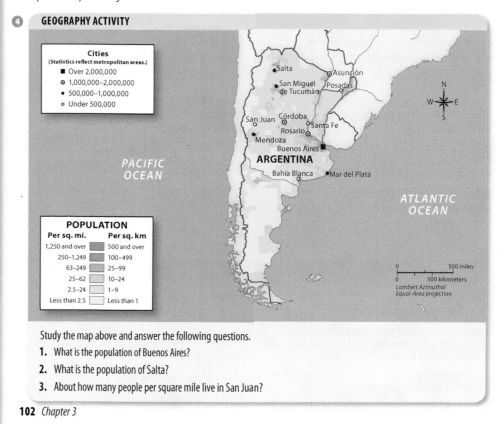

Study the map above and answer the following questions.

1. What is the population of Buenos Aires?
2. What is the population of Salta?
3. About how many people per square mile live in San Juan?

ACTIVITIES ANSWERS

Exploring the Essential Question

❶ INFORMATIVE/EXPLANATORY WRITING Posters about the culture of a South American country will vary but should highlight unique features, holidays, and celebrations such as Cinco de Mayo.

21st Century Skills

❷ INTEGRATING VISUAL INFORMATION
Presentations on a country in Europe will vary but should address the following eight categories: population, population density, population patterns, primary language, type of government, customs and other cultural information, resources, and type of economy.

REVIEW THE GUIDING QUESTIONS

Directions: Choose the best answer for each question.

1 The doubling time refers to the amount of time it takes for
   A. the birthrate to double.
   B. the population to double.
   C. the death rate to double.
   D. a child to reach adulthood.

2 A megalopolis is
   F. a huge urban area.
   G. an area that will not grow any larger.
   H. found in a rural setting.
   I. found most often in inland areas.

3 The American culture encourages
   A. intolerance of diverse religious beliefs.
   B. adherence to common goals.
   C. the same education for everyone.
   D. a blending of lifestyles and backgrounds.

4 Because of globalization,
   F. new languages are forming.
   G. people now travel less.
   H. birthrates are increasing rapidly.
   I. international trade is increasing

5 Choosing between buying a new car or a used car is an example of considering
   A. a quota.
   B. an economic system.
   C. opportunity cost.
   D. an energy resource.

Chapter 3 **103**

Thinking Like a Geographer

3 **IDENTIFYING** Students should create a clear chart with all six figures clearly displayed. They should see that the population density of Europe is much higher than it is for North or South America. Also, Europe's total population is the largest, followed by that of North America, and then South America.

Geography Activity

4 **READING MAPS**

   1. over 2,000,000

   2. 500,000–1,000,000

   3. 2.5–24

ASSESSMENT ANSWERS

Review the Guiding Questions

1 **B** Doubling time refers to the amount of time it takes for the population to double. If students answer A or C, explain that doubling time involves both high birthrate and low death rate. If students answer D, explain that this is the definition of the term *mature*. Have students who answer incorrectly, review the section on population in Lesson 1.

2 **F** A megalopolis is a huge urban area, such as Mexico City, that can either be found on the coast or inland. Make sure students who answer H understand the difference between urban and rural. Have students who answer incorrectly, review the section, "Causes and Effects of Urbanization," in Lesson 1.

3 **D** The American culture encourages a blending of lifestyles and backgrounds. Make sure students who answer A understand that American culture encourages tolerance, not intolerance, of diverse religious beliefs. Have students who answer incorrectly, review the section, "What is Culture," in Lesson 2.

4 **I** Because of globalization, international trade is increasing. If students answer G, explain that with globalization people are traveling more, not less. Although people of different countries are interacting more with globalization, new languages are not forming. Have students who answer incorrectly, review the section, "World Economy," in Lesson 3.

5 **C** Choosing between buying a new car or a used car is an example of considering opportunity cost. People have to make choices about many things including what to do with their money, such as using more of their money to buy a new car or saving some money by buying a used car. Have students who answer incorrectly, review the section, "Making Choices," in Lesson 3.

DBQ Analyzing Documents

6 A The word *surpass* means "to move ahead of" in this story. Have students who answer incorrectly reread the passage and use the context clues "to become the world's most populous country" to help them understand the meaning of *surpass*. Make sure that they understand you do not become the most populous country by falling behind or being the same as.

7 H The increase in population will help India's companies have enough workers. Make sure that students who answer incorrectly understand that a booming population also causes problems, such as not having enough resources, food, or schools for everyone.

Short Response

8 Student answers may vary but should show an understanding that the author would like to see more community schools that can be reached on foot or by bicycle. This will benefit the environment and reduce the air pollution from automobile and bus use transporting children to schools that are not close by. The author would also like to minimize the amount of paved surface around community schools to protect water quality by reducing polluted runoff.

9 Student answers may vary but may conclude that there might be less diversity of students because everyone at a school would come from the same general neighborhood. The development of charter schools would not fit into this plan either.

Extended Response

10 Letters should focus on statistics from research on various countries in Europe and North and South America about which countries have large numbers of immigrants including refugees, where they are primarily from, and the reasons that these people might be moving from one country to another. Students should apply these statistics to this country, state their position on immigration to this country, and back up their position with firm reasons. Students should end with a well-thought-out view of how the United States should handle its immigration policy.

DBQ ANALYZING DOCUMENTS

6 DETERMINING WORD MEANINGS A news story reports on India's population growth.

"*India . . . will surpass China to become the world's most populous country in less than two decades. The population growth will mean a nation full of working-age youth, which economists say could allow the already booming economy to maintain momentum.*"

What does *surpass* mean in this story?

A. to move ahead of   C. to increase in speed

B. to fall behind   D. to be the same as

7 ANALYZING How will the increase in population help India?

F. It will allow the people to use more resources.

G. The farmers will produce more food.

H. India's companies will have enough workers.

I. Schools will be educating more students.

SHORT RESPONSE

"*A school that is . . . easy for students, teachers, [and] parents . . . to reach on foot or by bicycle helps reduce the air pollution from automobile use, protecting children's health. Building schools . . . in the neighborhoods they serve minimizes the amount of paved surface . . ., which can help protect water quality by reducing polluted runoff.*"

—from Environmental Protection Agency, "Smart Growth and Schools"

8 DETERMINING CENTRAL IDEAS Explain in your own words what the author would like to see change.

9 ANALYZING What are some disadvantages to building community schools?

EXTENDED RESPONSE

10 ARGUMENT WRITING From the early years of the founding of this country, debate has raged over how many immigrants to allow in and from where. More recently, discussion has focused on what to do about people who have entered the United States illegally. The debate continues today. Research various countries in Europe and North and South America to collect statistics about which countries have large numbers of immigrants including refugees and where they are primarily from. Also consider the reasons that these people might be moving from one country to another. Write a letter to your congressional representative explaining these facts and how other countries are dealing with their immigration situation. Then state your position on immigration to this country. Back up your position with firm reasons.

Need Extra Help?

If You've Missed Question	1	2	3	4	5	6	7	8	9	10
Review Lesson	1	1	2	3	3	1	1	2	2	1

"India Challenged to Provide Jobs, Education to Young Population," by Anjana Pasricha, October 31, 2011, *Voice of America*, http://voanews.com; "Smart Growth and Schools," The United States Environmental Protection Agency official Web site. http://www.epa.gov/dced/schools.htm

---

networks *Online Teaching Options*

Practicing 21st Century Skills

Practicing Your students can practice important 21st Century skills such as geography, reading, writing, and critical thinking by using resources found in the Skills Builder tab of the online Student Learning Center. Resources include templates, handbooks, and slide shows. These same resources are also available in the Resource Library of the Teacher Lesson Center.

UNDERSTANDING BY DESIGN®

Enduring Understandings

- People, places, and ideas change over time.
- Over time, people adapt to their environment.

Essential Questions

- How does geography influence the way people live?
- Why is history important?
- Why do people make economic choices?
- How does technology change the way people live?
- How do people adapt to their environment?
- What makes a culture unique?
- Why does conflict develop?
- Why do people trade?

Students will Know:

- the United States is made up of various regions that have different industries and agriculture.
- that climate, landforms, and waterways help to shape the United States.
- all of the regions play a role in the history and economy of the United States.
- the geography, climate, and political organization of Canada.
- about the First Nations and the influence of France and England on the people of Canada.
- Canada and the United States have close geographic, economic, and political ties.

- Mexico City is the site of the ancient Aztec capital of Tenochtitlán.
- Mexico's economy is the 11th most productive in the world.
- Mexico has benefited from the North American Free Trade Agreement (NAFTA).
- Central America and the Caribbean went through long periods of colonialism, before achieving independence.

Students will be able to:

- **analyze** a map to identify cities, states, provinces, and islands in North and Central America.
- **use a time line** to discuss significant events in the history of the United States, Canada, Mexico, Central America, and the Caribbean Islands.
- **analyze** the physical landscapes and climates of North America.
- **discuss** modern and historical economies and identify industry and agriculture in North and Central America.
- **discuss** the political and economic relationships between countries in North America.
- **analyze** the path to independence for countries in North and Central America.

Predictable Misunderstandings

- All of the United States has the same geography.
- The only major river in the United States is the Mississippi River.
- The area west of the Mississippi River is desert and sparsely populated.
- It is always cold in Canada.
- The people of Canada originated in England.
- Mexico is a hot, dry country without natural resources.
- Mexico does not have a productive economy.
- The countries of Central America are all the same.

Assessment Evidence

Performance Tasks:

- Unit GeoLab Activity
- Environmental Case Study

Other Evidence:

- Physical Location GeoQuiz
- Political Location GeoQuiz
- City Location GeoQuiz
- Physical Geography Activity
- Cultural Geography Activity
- Geography and History Activity
- Geography and Economics Activity
- Geography Skills Activity
- Critical Thinking Skills Activity
- Participation in Interactive Whiteboard Activities
- Lesson Reviews
- Chapter Assessments

Key for Using the Teacher Edition

SKILL-BASED ACTIVITIES

Types of skill activites found in the Teacher Edition.

* **V Visual Skills** require students to analyze maps, graphs, charts, and photos.

W Writing Skills provide writing opportunities to help students comprehend the text.

R Reading Skills help students practice reading skills and master vocabulary.

C Critical Thinking Skills help students apply and extend what they have learned.

T Technology Skills require students to use digital tools effectively.

*Letters are followed by a number when there is more than one of the same type of skill on the page.

DIFFERENTIATED INSTRUCTION

All activities are written for the on-level student unless otherwise marked with the leveled labels below.

BL Beyond Level

AL Approaching Level

ELL English Language Learners

All students benefit from activities that utilize different learning styles. Many activities are marked as below when a particular learning style is highlighted.

Intrapersonal	Naturalist
Logical/Mathematical	Kinesthetic
Visual/Spatial	Auditory/Musical
Verbal/Linguistic	Interpersonal

SUGGESTED PACING GUIDE

TOTAL TIME   25 Days

PLANNER

☑ Print Teaching Options

V Visual Skills

☐ **P. 107** Students discuss the shape of North America and locate the Baja Peninsula, Atlantic coastline, and Great Plains in the satellite image. **AL**

☐ **P. 108** Students work in pairs to analyze the features of the map. **ELL**

☐ **P. 109** Students analyze the political boundaries on the map and identify information on a political map that is missing from a physical map. **AL**

☐ **P. 110** Students compare political maps and population maps. **ELL**

☐ **P. 111** Students analyze a resource map of North America. **AL**

☐ **P. 112** Students use a map to identify climates in different regions. **AL**

W Writing Skills

☐ **P. 112** Students write a travel log of the landscapes, climate, and resources seen during a trip to a chosen region of North America to reflect on what they've learned.

R Reading Skills

☐ **P. 106** Students identify the three largest countries in North America and discuss what is meant by the term "cultural kaleidoscope." **AL**

☐ **P. 106** Students describe the physical features of the Baja Peninsula and the contrasts they see in photograph 1. **ELL**

C Critical Thinking Skills

☐ **P. 106** Students contrast the landscapes of Nova Scotia and the Baja Peninsula and analyze how a coastal region impacts the lifestyle of people in the area.

☐ **P. 107** Students contrast natural resources found in the Baja Peninsula, Nova Scotia, and the Great Plains. **BL**

☐ **P. 108** Students analyze the role that rivers played in the settlement of North America and the role geography plays in trade and commerce. **AL**

☐ **P. 109** Students contrast Canada and the Caribbean. **BL**

☐ **P. 111** Students discuss how natural resources add to a country's wealth. **BL**

☐ **P. 112** Students examine how a region's climate impacts its economy. **BL**

☑ Online Teaching Options

V Visual Skills

VIDEO **Video Tour of North America**—Students watch a video highlighting North America and share what they found most interesting in a wall map activity. Visual/Spatial

MAP **North America: Physical Map**—Students plot a pre-settlement travel route through North America. Then they present their travel routes to the class. **AL** Kinesthetic

MAP **North America: Political Map**—Students can use the political layer on the Chapter Opener map to review the political boundaries of the region.

MAP **North America: Population Map**—Students can use the population layer on the Chapter Opener map to review the population distribution and density.

W Writing Skills

MAP **North America: Resources Map**—Students use the map of the resources in North America then research a mineral and its impact on exports and the economy of a country. **AL** Verbal/Linguistic

C Critical Thinking Skills

MAP **Regional Map**—Students make connections between the images in the unit and their location on the interactive map.

MAP **North America: Climates Map**—Students work in small groups to create a poster about a climate in North America. **ELL** Kinesthetic, Visual/Spatial

T Technology Skills

GAME **Political Boundaries: North America Game**—Students play a drag and drop to identify and place countries, cities, provinces, and islands of North America. **BL** Visual/Spatial

☑ Printable Digital Worksheets

W Writing Skills

WORKSHEET **Environmental Case Study**—Students will work in groups to study the conservation and sustainability efforts developed by the United States and Canada. Logical

QUIZ **Political Location GeoQuiz**—Use the Political Location GeoQuiz as a pre- or post-assessment of students' knowledge of North America's countries.

QUIZ **Physical Location GeoQuiz**—Use the Physical Location GeoQuiz as a pre- or post-assessment of students' knowledge of North America's landforms and bodies of water.

QUIZ **City Location GeoQuiz**—Use the City Location GeoQuiz as a pre- or post-assessment of students' knowledge of North America's major cities.

WORKSHEET **Physical Geography Activity**—Students will analyze an elevation profile of North America.

WORKSHEET **Cultural Geography Activity**—Students will read about the culture of the North America and answer questions related to the excerpt.

NORTH AMERICA

Philip and Karen Smith/Photographer's Choice RF/Getty Images

UNIT **2**

Chapter 4	Chapter 5	Chapter 6	Chapter 7
The United States East of the Mississippi River	The United States West of the Mississippi River	Canada	Mexico, Central America, and the Caribbean Islands

ENGAGE

Bellringer Share with students the image of the couple canoeing. Ask students to analyze the details in the photo. **Ask:** What are some of the striking features of the landscape? What sounds might the individuals be hearing? What might they be seeing in the distance? *(Student answers may vary, but should reflect answers that relate to the image.)*

Making Connections Explain to students that North America is a diverse continent with a wide variety of landscapes, cultures, geology, and environments. Its diversity offers places of quiet and great awe, from the mountain region in the photo to busy urban settings.

- **Major regions:** United States, Canada, Mexico, Central America, the Caribbean, and Greenland
- **Third largest continent:** includes 23 countries plus territories and possessions
- Located in the Northern and Western Hemispheres, bordered on the north by the Arctic Ocean, on the east by the Atlantic Ocean, and on the west by the Pacific Ocean, and on the Southeast by the Caribbean Sea
- **Lowest point:** Death Valley in California (86 meters/282 feet below sea level)
- **Highest point:** Mt. McKinley in Alaska (6,194 meters/20,320 feet above sea level)
- Mountain ranges include the Rocky Mountains, Appalachian Mountains, Alaska Range, Sierra Madres, and Brooks Range
- **Major languages:** English, Spanish, and French
- **Rank in population:** United States, Mexico, Canada

Ask: What might the canoeists see during their day's adventure on the water? *(Possible answers: wild animals, a variety of plants, fish, birds, contrasting landscapes)*

Tell students they will be learning more about North America, including its landforms, climates, resources, and populations. In particular they will be learning about its three major regions: the United States, Canada, and the southern region including Mexico, Central America, and the Caribbean Islands.

Global Connections

Discussing The Global Connections issue of this unit gives students an opportunity to consider the importance of imports and exports as they learn about the history and impact of NAFTA, the North American Free Trade Agreement. Students will investigate what is meant by free trade and think about the types of products traded between the United States, Canada, and Mexico. The pros and cons of free trade will be debated. **Verbal/Linguistic**

TEACH & ASSESS

R1 Reading Skills

Explaining Have a student volunteer read the paragraph "Landforms" aloud. **Ask:**

- What are the three largest countries of North America? *(Canada, the United States, Mexico)*
- What is meant by "cultural kaleidoscope"? *(mixture of many groups)*
- What word could be used to describe North America? *(Student answers will vary, but could include words such as diverse, interesting, large, varied)* **AL**

R2 Reading Skills

Identifying Have students describe what they see in the image associated with the paragraph about landforms. **Ask:**

- What are the physical features of the Baja Peninsula? *(one of world's longest peninsulas, chain of mountains, four deserts)*
- What contrasts do you notice in the photo? *(Students might note the photo includes both water and a stark landscape with desert cacti.)* **ELL**

C Critical Thinking Skills

Contrasting Have students read the paragraph "Bodies of Water" and contrast the features in Nova Scotia with those of the Baja Peninsula, as discussed in the paragraph "Landforms." **Ask:**

- What is different about the landscapes of Nova Scotia and the Baja Peninsula? *(coastline versus mountain, desert region)*
- How might living in a coastal region impact the lifestyle of the people in the area? *(Student answers may vary, but should include relative details such as people make their living off fishing and use fish as a main food source.)*

Have students work in teams to create a two-column chart contrasting the features seen in the two photos. Have students share the information in their charts. **Verbal/Linguistic**

EXPLORE the CONTINENT

NORTH AMERICA is made up of three large countries—Canada, the United States, Mexico—plus the Caribbean Islands and the countries of Central America. North America is a cultural kaleidoscope—a mixture of the many groups who have settled in the region.

R1

1 LANDFORMS At 800 miles long (1,287 km), the Baja Peninsula of Mexico is one of the world's longest peninsulas. Running nearly its entire length is a chain of mountain ranges. Four deserts are also physical features of Baja.

R2

C

2 BODIES OF WATER Boats line the harbor of a fishing village in Nova Scotia, along Canada's Atlantic coast. In addition to the waters of the Atlantic, the coastal waters of the Pacific Ocean and the Gulf of Mexico are important fisheries.

(bkgd) Konrad and Patty Thomas/Photographer's Choice/Getty Images; (l to r) Rony T B Moore Images/Flickr/Getty Images; Blaine Harrington III/Corbis; Reto Stockli; NOAA National Geophysical Data Center (NGDC)

106 *Unit 2*

networks *Online Teaching Options*

VIDEO

Video Tour of North America

Analyzing Images Display the video montage highlighting North America. Prior to starting the video, tell students that while viewing the video montage they should write down three things they especially like about North America. Afterwards have students share what they found most interesting about North America. Hand three sticky notes to each student have them write their three points of interest on the notes, one per sticky note. Have students place their sticky notes on a wall map of North America. Refer to these over the course of the unit. **Visual/Spatial**

Design Pics/Cory Hochachka/Getty Images

③ NATURAL RESOURCES Wheat is grown on the Great Plains of the United States, a region often called the Wheat Belt. The type of wheat grown depends on the climate. Farmers in the northern plains, with their short growing season, plant wheat in the spring and harvest it in the fall. Farther south, farmers plant winter wheat, which is harvested in early summer.

FAST **FACT**

Canada is the world's second largest country in area.

(tr) NOAA National Geophysical Data Center (NGDC)

Unit 2 **107**

TEACH & ASSESS

C₁ Critical Thinking Skills

Analyzing Write *Natural Resources* on the board and have a student volunteer read the paragraph "Natural Resources." **Ask:**

- What is an important natural resource of the Great Plains? *(wheat)*
- What do you notice about the Great Plains that would allow for the growing of wheat? *(large, treeless area, rolling hills)*

Write *Baja Peninsula, Nova Scotia, Great Plains* on the board as headings. Have students provide information about each region including any natural resources they can identify. Add their information under the correct heading. **Ask:**

- How are these three regions different? *(Students should note differences in landscapes, natural resources, and lifestyles)*
- Which region do you find most interesting? Why? *(Student answers will vary but should support their opinion by identifying an appealing regional feature.)* **BL**

V Visual Skills

Integrating Visual Information Direct student attention to the satellite image at the top of the page. Have students discuss the shape of North America and the locations of the Baja Peninsula, Atlantic coastline, and Great Plains. Point out the Arctic region. **Ask:**

- What can be said about the diversity of the climate of North America? *(from the hot, dry desert to the cold, icy Arctic)*
- What information about North America can you learn from the satellite image? *(Student answers should note differences in the mountain, plains, coastal, and Arctic regions seen in the satellite image.)* **AL**

C₂ Critical Thinking Skills

Locating Have students read the Fast Fact and locate the framed area of the United States shown on the map. Point out that Canada is north of the United States and is the largest country in North America. Explain that Mexico is the third largest country in North America. **Ask:** Where is Mexico on the map? *(south of the United States)* **AL** Visual/Spatial

WORKSHEET

Environmental Case Study

Evaluating The case study for this unit is about the conservation and sustainability efforts between the United States and Canada. Divide the students into groups and distribute the case study, allowing some in-class time for planning. Have groups share their findings with the class. Logical/Mathematical

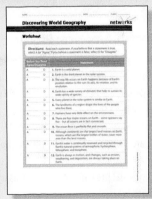

V

V Visual Skills

Reading a Map Have students work in pairs to analyze the features of the physical map. Discuss the map as a group, noting the elevations of different landforms. Point out the Great Lakes and Hudson Bay. Have students identify other large lakes and important rivers. Have students identify lines of longitude and latitude. Note that the Arctic Circle crosses northern Canada, while the Tropic of Cancer crosses Mexico. **Ask:**

- What does the map key show? *(the elevation of the world's landforms)*
- In which country is an area of elevation higher than 3,000 meters above sea level found? *(Greenland)*
- What do you notice about areas of high elevation in North America? *(Students should recognize that high elevations are mostly found along the western region of the continent.)*
- What is shown in the lower left of the map? *(Hawaiian Islands, which are part of the United States but located west of 140°W longitude.)*

Then have students identify regions on the physical map. **Ask:**

- What parts of North America are located north of the Tropic of Cancer? *(Canada, United States, northern part of Mexico, Bermuda Islands)*
- In which region is most of Greenland located? *(above the Arctic Circle)* **ELL** Visual/Spatial

C Critical Thinking Skills

Recognizing Relationships Have students focus on the rivers found in the United States by reviewing the physical map. Remind them that North America was settled by Native Americans thousands of years ago. **Ask:**

- What role do you think rivers played in the settlement of North America? *(navigation, food and fresh water source)*
- How do the physical features of the continent encourage trade and commerce? *(Student answers may vary, but should reflect the understanding that water routes provide access to the interior of the continent and ease of transportation.)* **AL**

NORTH AMERICA

PHYSICAL

MAP SKILLS

1. **PHYSICAL GEOGRAPHY** What physical features probably acted as barriers to settlement in the United States and Canada?

2. **THE GEOGRAPHER'S WORLD** Which body of water is located east of Panama?

3. **PHYSICAL GEOGRAPHY** What mountain range lies in the eastern United States?

108 Unit 2

netw rks *Online Teaching Options*

MAP

North America: Physical Map

Displaying Use the Physical interactive map of North America to help students study and identify features. Then have small groups of students plot a pre-settlement travel route from the East Coast to the West Coast of the regions that make up Canada or the United States. Have each group share their travel route by tracing it on the map. Students should explain the physical features that assist travel and those that present barriers, such as mountain ranges and waterways. **AL** Kinesthetic

---

ANSWER, p. 108

MAP SKILLS

1. the Appalachians, the Rocky Mountains, and the coastal mountains
2. the Caribbean Sea
3. the Appalachians

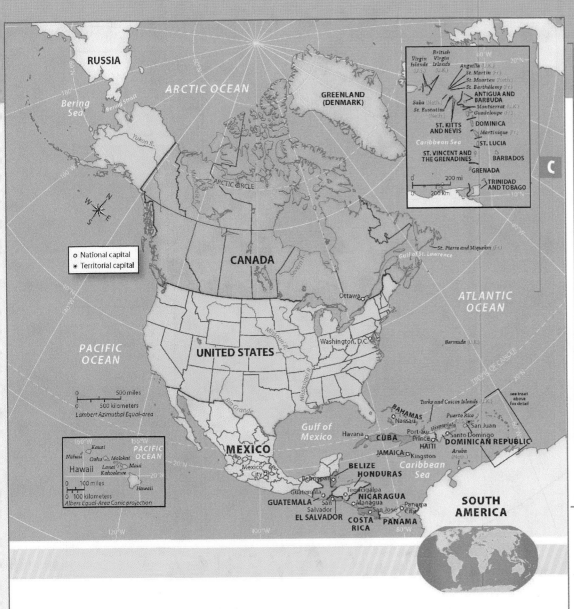

o National capital
● Territorial capital

RUSSIA

ARCTIC OCEAN

Bering Sea

GREENLAND (DENMARK)

ARCTIC CIRCLE

CANADA

Ottawa

ATLANTIC OCEAN

PACIFIC OCEAN

UNITED STATES

Washington, D.C.

Bermuda (U.K.)

500 miles
500 kilometers
Lambert Azimuthal Equal-Area

Hawaii

Kauai
Niihau Oahu Molokai
Lanai Maui
Kahoolawe
Hawaii

PACIFIC OCEAN

100 miles
100 kilometers
Albers Equal-Area Conic projection

MEXICO

Mexico City

Gulf of Mexico

Havana CUBA

JAMAICA Kingston

BELIZE
HONDURAS

Caribbean Sea

BAHAMAS
Nassau

Turks and Caicos Islands (U.K.)

Puerto Rico
San Juan
Port-au- Hispaniola
Prince Santo Domingo
HAITI DOMINICAN REPUBLIC
Aruba (Neth.)

see inset above for detail

Guatemala
GUATEMALA San Salvador
EL SALVADOR COSTA RICA
Belmopan
Tegucigalpa
NICARAGUA
Managua
San Jose Panama City
PANAMA

SOUTH AMERICA

British Virgin Islands
Virgin Islands (U.K.)
Anguilla (U.K.)
St. Martin (Fr.)
St. Maarten (Neth.)
St. Barthélemy (Fr.)
ANTIGUA AND BARBUDA
Saba (Neth.)
St. Eustatius (Neth.)
Montserrat (U.K.)
Guadeloupe (Fr.)
DOMINICA
ST. KITTS AND NEVIS
Martinique (Fr.)
Caribbean Sea ST. LUCIA
ST. VINCENT AND THE GRENADINES BARBADOS
GRENADA
TRINIDAD AND TOBAGO

200 mi
200 km

St. Pierre and Miquelon (Fr.)

Gulf of St. Lawrence

POLITICAL

MAP SKILLS

1 PLACES AND REGIONS What is the capital of Canada?

2 THE GEOGRAPHER'S WORLD What physical feature forms the natural boundary between the United States and Mexico?

3 PLACES AND REGIONS What is the capital of Cuba?

GAME

Political Boundaries: North America Game

Identifying As a class, play the drag-and-drop game to identify country and city names on the map. Then have volunteers use the whiteboard tools to draw a line from one location to another and calculate the distance. Provide students with the locations. **BL** Visual/Spatial, Logical/Mathematical

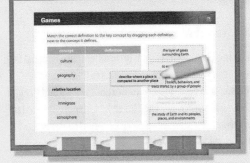

V

V Visual Skills

Analyzing Maps Have students analyze the political boundaries on the map. Encourage them to study the additional information in the map keys. Then have students identify information on a political map that is missing from a physical map. **Ask:**

- What do the additional lines on the region labeled as "United States" indicate? *(state borders)*
- What is shown in the upper right hand frame next to Greenland? *(Lesser Antilles islands found in the Caribbean Sea)*
- What is the capital of Mexico? *(Mexico City)*
- What do you notice about Central America? *(made up of several countries)*
- Have student look back at the Physical map of North America. What information does a political map provide that is not indicated on a physical map? *(governmental units)*
- Aside from governmental units, what other factors are considered when thinking about the political boundaries found in a region? *(Possible answers: language, traditions, cultures, trade, conflict)* **AL** Visual/Spatial

C Critical Thinking Skills

Comparing and Contrasting Have students compare and contrast Canada and the Caribbean Islands on the political map. **Ask:** What do you notice when comparing the political boundaries of Canada and those of the islands found in the Caribbean? *(one government versus several governments)*

Mention to students that the countries of the Caribbean are alike in many ways but also have unique cultures. **Ask:** Do you think that the islands in the Caribbean share the same government, language, and culture? *(Student answers may vary, but should reflect that since each island is a separate country, they do not share the same government, though some of the islands may share the same languages and culture.)*

Mention to students that Canada is just one country, but is divided up into provinces, which are similar to states in the United States. **Ask:** Does the fact that all of Canada has the same government mean that everyone in Canada speaks the same language or follows the same traditions? *(Possible answers: the country of Canada is very large so all the people may not share the same culture and language.)* **BL**

ANSWER, p. 109

MAP SKILLS
1. Ottawa
2. the Rio Grande
3. Havana

V1 Visual Skills

Contrasting Remind students that it is important to analyze and interpret map features. Have students contrast the features of the political and population maps. **Ask:** What are some of the differences between a political map and a population map? *(A political map shows human-made features like national boundaries, national capitals, and the location of cities. A population map shows areas where people live, especially if a lot of people live in a particular area.)* ELL

V2 Visual Skills

Reading a Map Direct students' attention to the population map of North America and to the map key. Point out and discuss the symbols used to identify the size of the cities and the colors used to determine population per square mile and square kilometer. **Ask:**

• What cities exceed a population of 5 million people? *(New York, Philadelphia, Toronto, Chicago, Dallas-Fort Worth, Los Angeles, Mexico City, Miami)*

• Which areas have the highest concentration of people? *(southern Mexico and Central America, the Caribbean, and cities in the eastern half of the United States)*

• Thinking back to the physical map of North America, why do you think the population is not as dense in the west and northwest regions of North America? *(Possible answer: mountains create barriers to settlement)*

• Where is the population least concentrated? *(northern Canada)*

• Why do you think the population is so sparse in this area? *(Because this area is so close to the Arctic Circle and the temperatures are very cold.)*

• In general, what relationship do you notice between population density and coastal regions? *(High population areas are found along the coasts.)*

• What does the population map indicate about the distribution of population in Hawaii? *(the population is most concentrated on just one island, Honolulu)* AL Logical/ Mathematical, Visual/Spatial

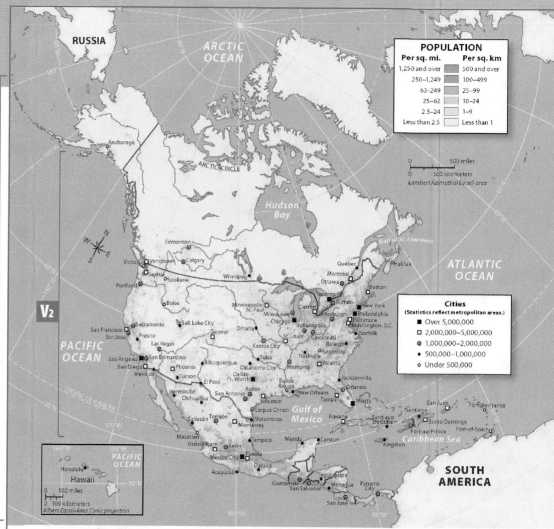

NORTH AMERICA

POPULATION DENSITY

MAP SKILLS

1 **PLACES AND REGIONS** Where is the greatest population density located in the United States?

2 **PLACES AND REGIONS** Contrast the population density of northern Mexico with southern Mexico.

3 **ENVIRONMENT AND SOCIETY** What generalizations can you make about the populations of the Caribbean islands?

110 *Unit 2*

networks   *Online Teaching Options*

MAP

Regional Map

Making Connections Display the interactive regional map to students. Select some of the images that are connected to the map and place them in context of the map and the unit. Guide a discussion helping students to identify the content of the images and then to make a connection between the image and the map location. Visual/Spatial

ANSWER, p. 110

MAP SKILLS
1. along the eastern coast
2. Northern Mexico's population density is not as high as southern Mexico's
3. They appear to be densely populated.

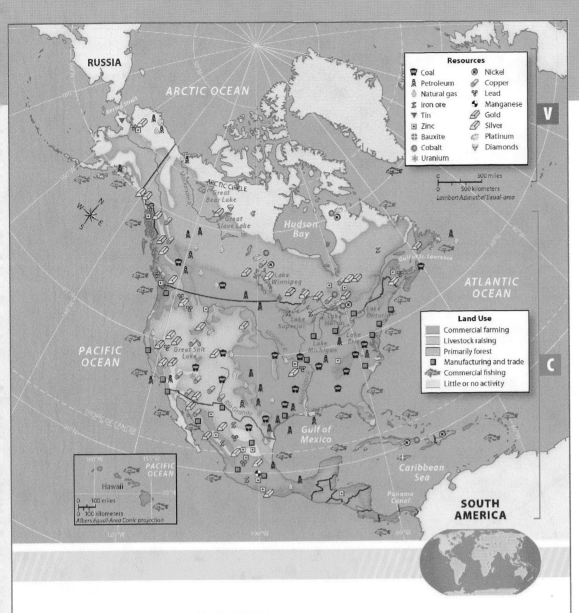

Resources

- ⛏ Coal
- 🅰 Petroleum
- ⬙ Natural gas
- ▨ Iron ore
- ▼ Tin
- ▣ Zinc
- ⬡ Bauxite
- ⬤ Cobalt
- ☀ Uranium
- ⊛ Nickel
- ✿ Copper
- ℣ Lead
- ⚯ Manganese
- ⬭ Gold
- ◎ Silver
- ⬭ Platinum
- ⬦ Diamonds

Land Use

- Commercial farming
- Livestock raising
- Primarily forest
- ■ Manufacturing and trade
- 🐟 Commercial fishing
- Little or no activity

ECONOMIC RESOURCES

MAP SKILLS

1 HUMAN GEOGRAPHY Describe how most land is used throughout the United States.

2 HUMAN GEOGRAPHY What is the main economic activity near Panama?

3 HUMAN GEOGRAPHY Contrast how land is used in northern Canada with Central America.

Unit 2 **111**

North America: Resources Map

Recognizing Relationships Display the interactive Resource map and allow students time to review and discuss the region as each layer is revealed. Then have student teams research a mineral found in North America. Research should include the mineral's value, amount exported from one of the countries being studied, and its impact on the country's economy. **AL** Verbal/Linguistic

V Visual Skills

Reading a Map Help students recognize the relationship between natural resources and the physical characteristics of a region. Have students read the Resources map key. **Ask:**

- What are some of the resources shown on this map? Which symbols are used to indicate those resources? *(Students should identify the resources and indicate which symbols are associated with each resource.)*
- What land uses are shown on this map? *(commercial farming, livestock raising, forest, manufacturing and trade, commercial fishing)*
- Where do you find that information? *(land use map key)*

Continue the class discussion of the map by focusing on specific locations and the natural resources that are located there. **Ask:**

- What type of land use is predominant in the Rocky Mountain region? *(livestock raising)*
- What significant difference do you see in how land is used in the United States with land use in Canada? *(Commercial farming in the United States, forested areas in Canada)*
- What types of resources are mined in Mexico? *(gold, iron ore, coal, lead, copper, and silver)*
- Where is natural gas found? *(Alaska, central United States, Canada)*
- Where does commercial fishing take place? *(along the coastlines of North America)*
- Which resource is shown by a red star-shaped symbol? *(uranium)*
- Which countries have significant manufacturing and trade? *(United States, Mexico)*
- Where is coal mined? *(several areas in the United States, Canada, Mexico)* **AL** Visual/Spatial

C Critical Thinking Skills

Determining Cause and Effect Have students consider the importance of natural resources to the economic viability of a country. **Ask:** How do natural resources add to a country's wealth? *(Possible answers: trade value; ability to sustain resource needs without having to purchase resources from other countries; ability to provide resources for the country)* **BL** Logical

ANSWER, p. 111

MAP SKILLS

1. Land is mostly used for commercial farming and livestock raising.
2. commercial fishing
3. Land is not used for farming, animal raising, or manufacturing in northern Canada. In Central America, however, land is used mostly for commercial subsistence farming.

V Visual Skills

Reading a Map Help students recognize that climates are regionalized. Direct students' attention to the map key. Review each of the different climate groups. **Ask:**

• Where are tropical rain forests found in North America? *(mostly south of the Tropic of Cancer)*

• What type of climate covers most of Greenland? *(ice cap)*

• What type of climate is found north of the Arctic Circle? *(tundra)*

• What type of climate affects much of the American Southwest and northern Mexico? *(semi-arid)*

• Where is a Mediterranean climate found in North America? *(along the west coast of the United States)*

• What is the impact of arid climates on a region? *(Possible answer: that regions impacted by arid climates experience little, if any, rain so water is in short supply and farming is difficult which means the area is not attractive for settlement.)* **AL** Visual/Spatial

C Critical Thinking Skills

Recognizing Relationships Have students consider the importance of climate on a region's economic viability. **Ask:**

• How does a region's climate impact the economy of the region? *(Areas that have warm temperatures and rain are able to grow crops and be more economically independent than an area that must import much of its food.)*

• What can be said about the climate of Canada? *(Much of it is an area of extreme cold.)* **BL** Logical

CLOSE & REFLECT

Narrative Have students reflect on what they have learned so far about North America. Have them write a vacation travel log of the landscapes, climate, and resources seen during a ficticious trip to a chosen region of North America. Encourage students to draw pictures or include images from the Internet in their travel logs. Have students share their travel logs with classmates. Engage interested students in creating a display of the travel logs. **ELL** Verbal/Linguistic

---

ANSWER, p. 112

MAP SKILLS
1. subarctic
2. They share the same types of climate (tropical savanna and tropical rain forest) and lie along approximately the same lines of latitude
3. humid subtropical

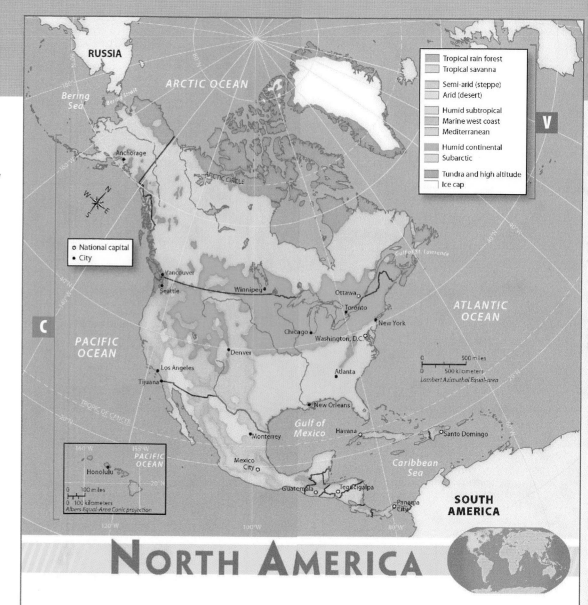

NORTH AMERICA

CLIMATE

MAP SKILLS

1 **PHYSICAL GEOGRAPHY** What type of climate is most common throughout Canada?

2 **PLACES AND REGIONS** The Caribbean islands and central Mexico appear to have two things in common. What are these commonalities?

3 **PHYSICAL GEOGRAPHY** What is the overall climate of the southeastern United States?

112 *Unit 2*

---

netw⊕rks *Online Teaching Options*

MAP

North America: Climates Map

Organizing Use the interactive Climate map to discuss the variety of climates in North America. Divide the class into small groups, one per climate zone. Have each group of students create a poster about the climate emphasizing the precipitation and temperatures in the climate zone. Posters may also include clothing, animals, thermometer showing highest/lowest temperature, rain gauge, and other items of interest. Display the posters in the classroom.
ELL Kinesthetic, Visual/Spatial

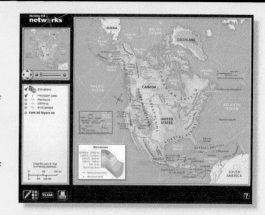

CHAPTER 4

The United States East of the Mississippi River Planner

UNDERSTANDING BY DESIGN®

Enduring Understandings

- *People, places, and ideas change over time.*

Essential Questions

- *How does geography influence the way people live?*
- *Why is history important?*
- *What makes a culture unique?*

Predictable Misunderstandings

- *The United States has the same geography throughout the country.*
- *The only major river in the United States is the Mississippi River.*
- *East of the Mississippi River, the economy is much more stable than in the area West of the Mississippi River.*

Assessment Evidence

Performance Tasks:

- *Project-Based Learning Digital Hands-On Chapter Project*
- *Project-Based Learning Hands-On Chapter Project*

Other Evidence:

- *Geography Skills Worksheet*
- *Technology Skills Worksheet*
- *What Do You Know? Activity*
- *Participation in Project-Based Learning Activities*
- *Participation in Interactive Whiteboard Map Activities*
- *Interpretation of slide show images and special purpose maps*
- *Participation in class discussions about the Geographer's World*
- *Lesson Reviews*
- *Chapter Assessments*

SUGGESTED PACING GUIDE

Introducing the Chapter	2 Days	Lesson 3	2 Days
Lesson 1	2 Days	What Do You Think?	2 Days
Lesson 2	2 Days	Chapter Wrap-Up and Assessment	2 Days

TOTAL TIME   12 Days

Key for Using the Teacher Edition

SKILL-BASED ACTIVITIES

Types of skill activities found in the Teacher Edition.

* **V Visual Skills** require students to analyze maps, graphs, charts, and photos.

W Writing Skills provide writing opportunities to help students comprehend the text.

R Reading Skills help students practice reading skills and master vocabulary.

C Critical Thinking Skills help students apply and extend what they have learned.

T Technology Skills require students to use digital tools effectively.

*Letters are followed by a number when there is more than one of the same type of skill on the page.

DIFFERENTIATED INSTRUCTION

All activities are written for the on-level student unless otherwise marked with the leveled labels below.

BL Beyond Level
AL Approaching Level
ELL English Language Learners

All students benefit from activities that utilize different learning styles. Many activities are marked as below when a particular learning style is highlighted.

Intrapersonal	Naturalist
Logical/Mathematical	Kinesthetic
Visual/Spatial	Auditory/Musical
Verbal/Linguistic	Interpersonal

Indiana Academic Standards

Students will:

6.1.10 Examine and explain the outcomes of European colonization on the Americas and the rest of the world.

6.1.11 Compare and contrast Spanish, Portuguese, French, and British colonies in the Americas.

6.1.15 Describe the impact of industrialization and urbanization on the lives of individuals and on trade and cultural exchange between Europe and the Americas and the rest of the world.

6.1.18 Create and compare timelines that identify major people, events and developments in the history of individual civilizations and/or countries that comprise Europe and the Americas.

6.1.19 Define and use the terms decade, century, and millennium, and compare alternative ways that historical periods and eras are designated by identifying the organizing principles upon which each is based.

6.1.20 Analyze cause-and-effect relationships, keeping in mind multiple causations, including the importance of individuals, ideas, human interests, beliefs and chance in history.

6.1.21 Differentiate between fact and interpretation in historical accounts and explain the meaning of historical passages by identifying who was involved, what happened, where it happened, and relating them to outcomes that followed and gaps in the historical record.

6.2.1 Compare and contrast major forms of governments in Europe and the Americas throughout history.

6.2.5 Discuss the impact of major forms of government in Europe and the Americas on civil and human rights.

6.2.6 Identify and describe the functions of international political organizations in the world today.

6.3.1 Demonstrate a broad understanding of the countries and capitals of Europe and the Americas.

6.3.4 Describe and compare major cultural characteristics of regions in Europe and the Western Hemisphere.

6.3.5 Give examples and describe the formation of important river deltas, mountains and bodies of water in Europe and the Americas.

6.3.7 Locate and describe the climate regions of Europe and the Americas and explain how and why they differ.

6.3.9, 6.3.10

CHAPTER OPENER PLANNER

Students will know:

- the United States east of the Mississippi River is made up of various regions.
- the regions of this area have different industries and agriculture.
- climate, landforms, and waterways help to shape the region.
- there are many major cities in this region of the United States.
- the history of this region in the United States is complex and involves diverse groups of people.

Students will be able to:

- **identify** the cities and states east of the Mississippi River using a map.
- **use a time line** to discuss significant events in the history of the United States east of the Mississippi River.

UNDERSTANDING BY DESIGN®

☑ *Print Teaching Options*

W Writing Skills

☐ **P. 115** Students write a paragraph describing a social, environmental, or economic effect.

V Visual Skills

☐ **P. 114** Students use a political map to identify the eastern region of the United States.

☐ **P. 115** Students use a time line to answer questions about major events between 1620 and 2014.

☑ *Online Teaching Options*

☐ **MAP** **Reading a Map**—Students identify aspects and locations of the region on a map.

☐ **TIME LINE** **Reading a Time Line and Map**—Students learn about where historical events occurred in the eastern United States.

☐ **MAP** **Interactive World Atlas**—Students use the interactive world atlas to identify the region and describe its terrain.

☑ *Printable Digital Worksheets*

☐ **WORKSHEET** **Geography Skills: Mapping the Trail of Tears**—Students use the worksheet to map the forced migration of Native Americans.

☐ **WORKSHEET** **Writing Skills: Immigrating to America**—Students use the worksheet to construct a short essay about immigrating to America

☐ **WORKSHEET** **Primary Source Reading Skills: National Parks**—Students use the information on the worksheet as a guide to research the law that gave presidents power over the national park system.

☐ **WORKSHEET** **Technology Skills: Evaluating a Website**—Students use the worksheet as a guide to evaluate a Web site.

Project-Based Learning

Hands-On

Making a Travel Brochure

Students will create travel brochures highlighting one of the regions east of the Mississippi River. After learning about the physical features, history, and culture of the different subregions, students should identify information to highlight in their brochures. Brochures might include photographs, maps, and fun facts that try to entice travelers to visit places east of the Mississippi. Have students then present their brochures to the class.

Digital Hands-On

Making an Interactive Poster

Students will create an online, interactive poster highlighting one of the subregions east of the Mississippi River. After learning about subregions' physical features, histories, and cultures, students will identify fun facts and other information to highlight in their posters. Students can use state tourist Web sites for photos and videos to add to their posters. Have students then present their posters to the class.

Print Resources

ANCILLARY RESOURCES

These ancillaries are available for every chapter and lesson.

- **Reading Essentials and Study Guide Workbook** AL ELL
- **Chapter Tests and Lesson Quizzes Blackline Masters**

PRINTABLE DIGITAL WORKSHEETS

These printable digital worksheets are available for every *chapter* and *lesson!*

- **Hands-On Chapter Projects**
- **What Do You Know? Activities**
- **Chapter Summaries (English and Spanish)**
- **Vocabulary Builder Activities**
- **Quizzes and Tests (English and Spanish)**
- **Reading Essentials and Study Guide (English and Spanish)** AL ELL
- **Guided Reading Activities**

More Media Resources

SUGGESTED VIDEOS

NOTE: Be sure to preview videos to ensure they are age-appropriate.

- **American Experience: We Shall Remain** (76 min.)
- **Nature Parks: Acadia New England** (45 min.)
- **Sacred Sites and Mound Builders** (82 min.)

SUGGESTED READING

- ***The Breaker Boys,*** by Pat Hughes AL
- ***We've Got a Job: The 1963 Birmingham Children's March,*** by Cynthia Levinson
- ***Chasing the Nightbird,*** by Krista Russell BL

edtechteacher
21st Century Learning

PHYSICAL FEATURES

Students will know:
- the United States east of the Mississippi is made up of various regions.
- the regions of this area have different industries and agriculture.
- climate, landforms, and waterways help to shape the region.

Students will be able to:
- **describe** the different regions that make up the United State east of the Mississippi.
- **identify** industries and agriculture in each region.
- **describe** the physical landscape of the United States east of the Mississippi.

UNDERSTANDING
BY DESIGN®

☑ Print Teaching Options

V Visual Skills

☐ **P. 117** Students locate bodies of water on the subregions map of the United States. **AL**

☐ **P. 119** Students identify the route of a ship transporting goods from Chicago to London might take.

☐ **P. 121** Students locate where the Allegheny and Monongahela rivers combine in western Pennsylvania.

W Writing Skills

☐ **P. 120** Students write paragraphs explaining the benefits and disadvantages of a natural and a man-made boundary.

R Reading Skills

☐ **P. 116** Students describe how subregions are similar to and different from regions. **ELL** **AL**

☐ **P. 117** Students identify subregions based on their characteristics.

☐ **P. 118** Students make connections to remember the names of the Great Lakes by using a mnemonic device.

☐ **P. 123** Students summarize information about mineral and energy resources in the eastern United States.

C Critical Thinking Skills

☐ **P. 117** Students trace the route farmers on the east coast of Mexico and farmers in southern Illinois use for trade.

☐ **P. 119** Students infer how the Mississippi River affects the lifestyle of Americans.

☐ **P. 120** Students compare and contrast the benefits and disadvantages of the Mississippi River.

☐ **P. 122** Students infer what the younger Rocky Mountains look like compared to the worn-down Appalachian Mountains.

T Technology Skills

☐ **P. 118** Students create a visual presentation to show the harmful effects of the 2010 oil spill in the Gulf of Mexico. **ELL** **AL**

☐ **P. 122** Student groups give presentations comparing and contrasting two subregion climates in Eastern United States.

☑ Online Teaching Options

V Visual Skills

MAP **Region Map of East Coast of U.S.**—Students consider why particular states are grouped into a subregion and speculate how each subregion got its name. Visual/Spatial, Logical/Mathematical

IMAGE **The Gulf Coast Region**—Students evaluate the interactive image of the Gulf Coast and discuss the importance of the coast on the local economy. Visual/Spatial, Verbal/Linguistic

VIDEO **The Mississippi River**—Students use the video to trace the path of the Mississippi River and discuss the river's importance to the economy, transportation, and lifestyles of the people living along its banks. **AL** Visual Spatial, Verbal/Linguistic

MAP **The Fall Line**—Students discuss the features of a fall line along the Atlantic coast, then use the map to answer questions. Visual/Spatial, Verbal/Linguistic

IMAGE **360 View: Appalachia**—Students use the 360 view of the Appalachian Mountains to further discuss the landscape.

SLIDE SHOW **Agriculture East of the Mississippi River**—For more on this ahead—use the slide show about agriculture to discuss the important crops grown in this region.

W Writing Skills

VIDEO **Extreme Heat in Urban Areas**—Students watch a video about the extreme temperatures in Eastern United States, then write three questions they have about this region. **AL** Visual/Spatial, Verbal/Linguistic

R Reading Skills

MAP **Political: The Eastern United States**—Students use the political layer of the Chapter Opener map to further explain the ideas of a subregion, connecting to the definitions in the text.

MAP **Resources: Eastern United States**—Students use the resources layer on the Chapter Opener map to extend the connection to the descriptions in the text.

C Critical Thinking Skills

ANIMATION **How the Great Lakes Formed**—Students use the animation to discuss the creation of the landscape and waterways in the area, then explain in their own words how glaciers formed the Great Lakes. **BL** Visual/Spatial, Verbal/Linguistic

MAP **Physical Geography and Climate: The Eastern United States**—Students compare and contrast the physical features and climate conditions in different subregions. Visual/Spatial, Verbal/Linguistic

T Technology Skills

DIAGRAM **Comparing Glaciers to Modern Landmarks**—Students use the diagram to make comparisons of glacier size to modern landmarks.

ONLINE SELF-CHECK QUIZ **Lesson 1**—Students receive instant feedback on their mastery of lesson content

Students will know:

- the regions of this area have different industries and agriculture.
- the history of this region in the United States is complex and involves diverse peoples.

Students will be able to:

- **describe** early America and its indigenous peoples.
- **summarize** European colonization of the area.
- **explain** how the movement of people shaped the culture of the Eastern United States.
- **describe** early industry and agriculture.
- **understand** the Great Migration.

UNDERSTANDING
BY DESIGN®

☑ *Print Teaching Options*

W Writing Skills

☐ **P. 128** Students write a narrative journal entry from the perspective of a colonist headed inland to claim land and start a new life.

R Reading Skills

☐ **P. 125** Students explain how environment shaped the way of life of Native Americans.

☐ **P. 127** Students explain why colonists built towns where they did, what made their lives easier, why they came despite the possibility of illness and death, what caused them to declare independence, and how long it took to become independent.

☐ **P. 128** Students explain why people began to move inland from the Atlantic coast.

☐ **P. 129** Students paraphrase what they have learned about people settling on the east side of the Mississippi River. **ELL** **AL**

☐ **P. 130** Students explain why industry is an important part of the economy of the Eastern United States.

C Critical Thinking Skills

☐ **P. 124** Students use an analogy to help understand the diversity of the United States.

☐ **P. 125** Students make connections to the emotions of Native Americans when their belongings and homes were taken from them.

☐ **P. 126** Students make inferences about how the colonist's desire for wealth hurt the relationship between the colonists and native peoples.

☐ **P. 130** Students make connections to what it would be like to move to a new country with only one small suitcase.

☐ **P. 131** Students reason whether the government was justified in making the Cherokees move.

T Technology Skills

☐ **P. 129** Students work in small groups to evaluate a web site that has information about improved farming methods or equipment. **ELL**

☑ *Online Teaching Options*

V Visual Skills

VIDEO **Life on an Island**—Students watch a video to analyze the aspects of life on an island. Then share unique aspects of the video that surprised them. **AL** Visual/Spatial

MAP **Colonial Expansion**—Students use colonial expansion layer of the Chapter Opener map to discuss settlements and their impact on Native Americans. **AL** Visual/Spatial

SLIDE SHOW **Early Settlements**—Students compare and contrast various cities in different time periods. Then they discuss the changes to the cities. **BL** Visual/Spatial, Verbal/Linguistic

W Writing Skills

GRAPHIC ORGANIZER **Cause and Effect: Colonists and Native Americans**—Students use the graphic organizer to analyze cause and effect relationships.

R Reading Skills

CHART **Words with Native American Origins**—Students use a chart about words and place names to discuss the influence of Native Americans on American culture.

LECTURE SLIDE **Defining: Indigenous and Colonists**—Student use the lecture slide defining indigenous and colonists to help understanding of definitions in the text.

C Critical Thinking Skills

MAP AND CHART **Cultures and Communities on the Mississippi River**—Students discuss the complexity of communities of Native Americans and link the communities to a chart showing the contributions of Native Americans to United States culture. Visual/Spatial, Logical/Mathematical

TIME LINE **Early History of the Eastern United States**—Students use the interactive time line to identify events. Then students make connections between the events and their text by identifying the causes and effects of the events in the time line. Visual/Spatial, Verbal/Linguistic

MAP **Down the Mississippi River**—Students use the Chapter Opener map to reveal cities along the Mississippi to discuss why human development often occurs along major waterways.

T Technology Skills

VIDEOS **Down the Mississippi River**—Students use the videos of various means of travel down the Mississippi to make connections to the text and the map activity. Visual/Spatial, Verbal/Linguistic

ONLINE SELF-CHECK QUIZ **Lesson 2**—Students receive instant feedback on their mastery of lesson content

☑ *Printable Digital Worksheets*

W Writing Skills

WORKSHEET **Geography Skills: Mapping the Trail of Tears**—Students use the worksheet to map the forced migration of Native Americans.

WORKSHEET **Writing Skills: Immigrating to America**—Students research an immigrant group then use their research to write a short essay. Verbal/Linguistic, Logical/Mathematical

LIFE IN THE REGION

Students will know:

- *there are many major cities in this region of the United States.*
- *the regions of this area have different industries and agriculture.*
- *the history of this region in the United States is complex and involves diverse peoples.*

Students will be able to:

- *describe major metropolitan areas in the Eastern United States.*
- *explain how the United States government's actions have affected the land and people of the United States.*
- *identify the three branches of government and their roles.*
- *understand how diversity shapes the culture of the United States.*
- *describe the economy of the United States.*

UNDERSTANDING
BY DESIGN®

☑ *Print Teaching Options*

V Visual Skills

☐ **P. 133** Students identify the five boroughs on a map of New York City and find where the 9/11 Memorial is located.

☐ **P. 134** Students locate the cities of Atlanta and New Orleans on a political map.

W Writing Skills

☐ **P. 134** Students research things to do in a major city. Then they create a brochure about the city. BL

R Reading Skills

☐ **P. 135** Students summarize central ideas in a paragraph. AL

C Critical Thinking Skills

☐ **P. 133** Students infer the skills a person working in tourism should have.

☐ **P. 134** Students explain why Chicago is an important metropolitan area.

☐ **P. 136** Students theorize what a disadvantage of a government in which power is shared equally among three branches might be.

☐ **P. 137** Students draw conclusions about whether the government should have policies that let people or companies pollute or destroy the environment.

☐ **P. 137** Students make connections to segregation.

☐ **P. 138** Students problem solve about how to bring jobs back to America from overseas.

☐ **P. 139** Students infer what jobs in the service industry have been replaced by computers and what jobs in that industry will never be replaced by computers.

T Technology Skills

☐ **P. 132** Have students research the populations of New York, Boston, Philadelphia, and Miami, then create a population chart.

☐ **P. 138** Students create a graph or chart to display United States census information about the American population. ELL AL

☑ *Online Teaching Options*

V Visual Skills

IMAGE 360 View : Times Square, New York City—Students will use the 360 image to make connections to the major cities in this region.

VIDEO Festivals—Students use the interactive image to discuss the different ways people spend their time.

W Writing Skills

VIDEO Cleaning Up Tampa's Rivers: The Green Armada—Students watch a video and write a paragraph about an aspect they found interesting. **Visual/Spatial, Verbal/Linguistic**

LECTURE SLIDE Understanding the U.S. Government's Role in Infrastructure—Students write a brief paragraph about how they have personally benefitted from a government-funded project in their community. **Verbal/Linguistic**

R Reading Skills

GAME Drag-and-Drop: Major Cities—Students take turns dragging and dropping the names of major cities into their locations on the interactive map. Then they discuss unique aspects about each of the cities. **Kinesthetic, Verbal/Linguistic**

LECTURE SLIDE U.S. Government Infrastructure—Students use the lecture slide about the role of United States government in creating infrastructure to make connections to the building of highways.

GRAPHIC ORGANIZER Economy of the Eastern United States—Students use the graphic organizer to review information for understanding.

C Critical Thinking Skills

GRAPHIC ORGANIZER Where People Live—Students use the interactive graphic organizer to show information about different features of rural, suburban, and metropolitan areas. Then they compare and contrast human geography in these areas. **Visual/Spatial, Verbal/Linguistic**

MAP Population: The Eastern United States—Students locate major eastern cities and infer why these places became major metropolitan areas. **Visual/Spatial, Verbal/Linguistic**

CHART The Growth of the Economy—Students use the information on the chart to discuss the growth of America and changes in farming, industry, and services. **Visual/Spatial, Verbal/Linguistic**

T Technology Skills

ONLINE SELF-CHECK QUIZ Lesson 3—Students receive instant feedback on their mastery of lesson content.

☑ *Printable Digital Worksheets*

W Writing Skills

WORKSHEET Primary Sources: National Parks—Students use the information on the worksheet as a guide to research the law that gave presidents power over the national park system. ELL **Verbal/Linguistic, Naturalist**

INTERVENTION AND REMEDIATION STRATEGIES

LESSON 1 Physical Features

Reading and Comprehension

Have students work in pairs to use this lesson's content vocabulary words in sentences. Tell students to write a sentence that uses the first vocabulary word in the lesson as their partner writes a sentence using the second word, and so on. As a lesson review, have students collaborate to write a paragraph using all the terms. Sentences should show an understanding of the technical meaning of each word as it is used in the text.

Text Evidence

Have small groups of students analyze a body of water discussed in this lesson. Students may use information in the text about their assigned body of water or conduct online research to learn about its current condition. Tell students to address these questions in their analyses: Where is it? How big is it? Are there any environmental threats facing this body of water? If so, what are they, and how has the problem been addressed?

LESSON 2 History of the Region

Reading and Comprehension

To help students organize and comprehend the concepts discussed in this lesson, have them create a pictorial outline of the lesson using the content vocabulary terms as headings. As they create their outlines, have them note key ideas and details as subheadings in their outlines. Encourage students to illustrate their timelines to develop a coherent understanding of each concept.

Text Evidence

Have students create a flow chart depicting interactions between different individuals and cultural groups discussed in the lesson. Flow charts should reflect an understanding of the influence that specific events had on different groups or individuals, and the influence that specific groups of people had on various events. Provide students with this example: Hearing stories about new lands in the Americas led to European exploration, which in turn led to colonization.

LESSON 3 Life in the Region

Reading and Comprehension

Have students scan the lesson and use context clues to define the meaning of each content vocabulary word. Ask volunteers to choose one of the words and use it in a sentence that shows an understanding of the word's meaning. Clarify terms students may find confusing, such as Rust Belt. Explain that here the word *belt* is used to describe a specific area with a common characteristic. For example, the term *Snow Belt* refers to a region that receives heavy snowfall.

Text Evidence

Have students select a city or region discussed in this lesson. Tell students they will write an infomercial about the city, describing its cultural attributes and a list of reasons tourists might want to visit. Students may wish to conduct additional research about their location for a brief presentation to the class. After students present their infomercials, guide a question and answer session in which classmates ask questions, acting as prospective tourists. In answering, presenters should use evidence from the text or their research.

Online Resources

Level Reader

Use this online lower-level text that corresponds directly to the text in the online Student Edition.

Guided Reading Activities

This resource uses graphic organizers and guiding questions to help students with comprehension.

What Do You Know?

Use these worksheets to pre-assess students' background knowledge before they study the chapter.

Reading Essentials and Study Guide Workbook

This resource offers writing and reading activities for the approaching-level student.

Self-Check Quizzes

This online assessment tool provides instant feedback for students to check their progress.

THE UNITED STATES EAST OF THE MISSISSIPPI RIVER

CHAPTER 4

ESSENTIAL QUESTIONS · *How does geography influence the way people live?* · *Why is history important?* · *What makes a culture unique?*

Christopher Morris/VII/Corbis

Worker at Michigan auto assembly plant

Lesson 1
Physical Features

Lesson 2
History of the Region

Lesson 3
Life in the Region

The Story Matters...

The eastern United States is a region of diverse physical features and many natural resources. Bordered by the Atlantic Ocean and the Mississippi River, this region is home to mighty rivers, the largest group of freshwater lakes in the world, and old-growth forests. The physical features and wealth of resources found in the eastern United States have played a key role in the region's history. They also influence where and how people live in this region today.

FOLDABLES
Study Organizer

Go to the Foldables® library in the back of your book to make a Foldable® that will help you take notes while reading this chapter.

113

ENGAGE

Think-Pair-Share Have students discuss places they have visited or know about in the eastern United States. Students might name big cities or small towns, national parks, or popular attractions, such as Disney World or the Hall of Fame for baseball or football. Then have students read "The Story Matters..." about the eastern United States.

Discuss with the class what it means for a region to have diverse physical features and many natural resources. How might living next to a swamp not be as attractive as living on a large lake? How might the abundance of coal in an area be both beneficial and harmful?

Tell students that in this chapter they will learn about the region of the United States that lies east of the Mississippi River.

Making Connections Read the following information to students.

The eastern United States is home to over a hundred million people. The region includes urban and rural areas, great bodies of water, mountains, farmland, forests, and swamps. Hurricanes, tornadoes, and floods sometimes ravage the land. Here are some facts about the Mississippi River, the region's western boundary:

- A raindrop falling into the river's headwaters at Lake Itasca, MN, would take about 90 days to reach the Gulf of Mexico.
- In 1922, waterskiing was invented on an area of the river between Wisconsin and Minnesota.
- A bridge over the river in New Orleans is 24 miles long, the world's longest over-water highway bridge.
- The river's depth ranges from less than three feet to over 200 feet deep.
- More than 240 species of fish inhabit the river.

FOLDABLES
Study Organizer

Go to the Foldables® library for a cumulative chapter-based Foldable® activity that your students can use to help take notes and prepare for the assessment.

Letter from the Author

Dear Geography Teacher,

The French geographer, Jean Gottman, was the first person to use the word "megalopolis" to describe the eastern seaboard of the United States. Gottman was referring to the almost continuous urban development stretching from Washington, D.C., to Boston, Massachusetts. Characterized by tall skyscrapers and snakelike transportation routes, the megalopolis plays a large role in the American economy. The region is important for finance, entertainment, fashion, and information technology industries.

Richard H. Boehm

TEACH & ASSESS

Step Into the Place

V Visual Skills

Reading a Map Have students identify the map title *(Cities and States of the Region)* and the features shown on it. *(states, capitals, cities, boundaries, bodies of water, latitude and longitude lines, compass rose)* **Ask:**

- What kind of map is this? *(political)*
- Which Great Lake is not partly in Canada? *(Lake Michigan)*
- In which direction would you travel to get from Jackson, Mississippi, to Charleston, West Virginia? *(northeast)* From New York City to Chicago? *(west)*
- How many states make up the eastern region of the United States? *(27)* Visual/Spatial, Verbal Linguistic

Content Background Knowledge

Fun facts about some of the states in the eastern United States:

- Maine is the only state whose name has one syllable.
- The Tennis Hall of Fame is in Rhode Island.
- The first peanuts grown in the United States were grown in Virginia.
- The sweetest onions in the world, Vidalia onions, can only be grown around Vidalia and Glennville, Georgia.
- Petal, Mississippi is home to the International Checkers Hall of Fame.
- In 1856, the first enamel bathtub was made in Louisville, Kentucky.
- Michigan is known as the Wolverine State, but there are no longer any wolverines there.
- The Toilet Paper Capital of the World is in Green Bay, Wisconsin.
- The official state gem of Arkansas is the diamond. Crater of Diamonds State Park is the only diamond-producing site in the world open to the public.

ANSWERS, p. 114

STEP INTO THE PLACE
1. Atlantic Ocean
2. Florida
3. Wisconsin, Illinois, Kentucky, Tennessee, Mississippi
4. **CRITICAL THINKING** Rivers act as natural borders. When state borders were first identified, there was little technology for crossing natural features, such as rivers, so they were used as boundaries.

V The United States east of the Mississippi River is one of the two regions that make up the United States. As you study the map, identify the geographic features of the region.

Step Into the Place

MAP FOCUS Use the map to answer the following questions.

1 **THE GEOGRAPHER'S WORLD** Which body of water lies to the east of the United States?

2 **THE GEOGRAPHER'S WORLD** Which state has the longest coastline?

3 **PLACES AND REGIONS** Name the states that use the Mississippi River as all or part of their western border.

4 **CRITICAL THINKING** **ANALYZING** Why do you think rivers such as the Mississippi and the Ohio were used as state borders?

THE CAPITOL The U.S. Capitol in Washington, D.C., is the meeting place of Congress, the nation's legislature.

THE GREAT SMOKY MOUNTAINS Part of the Appalachian Mountain Range, the Smoky Mountains are named for the blue-gray mist that seems to hang above the peaks and valleys.

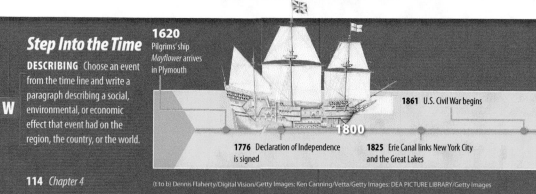

Step Into the Time

DESCRIBING Choose an event from the time line and write a paragraph describing a social, environmental, or economic effect that event had on the region, the country, or the world.

W

1620 Pilgrims' ship *Mayflower* arrives in Plymouth

1776 Declaration of Independence is signed

1800

1825 Erie Canal links New York City and the Great Lakes

1861 U.S. Civil War begins

114 *Chapter 4*

(t to b) Dennis Flaherty/Digital Vision/Getty Images; Ken Canning/Vetta/Getty Images; DEA PICTURE LIBRARY/Getty Images

Project-Based Learning ✋

Hands-On

Making a Travel Brochure
Students will create travel brochures highlighting one of the regions east of the Mississippi River. After learning about the physical features, history, and culture of the different subregions, students should identify information to highlight in their brochures. Brochures might include photographs, maps, and fun facts that try to entice travelers to visit places east of the Mississippi. Have students then present their brochures to the class.

Digital Hands-On

Making an Interactive Poster
Students will create an online, interactive poster highlighting one of the subregions east of the Mississippi River. After learning about subregions' physical features, histories, and cultures, students will identify fun facts and other information to highlight in their posters. Students can use state tourist Web sites for photos and videos to add to their posters. Have students then present their posters to the class.

edtechteacher
21st Century Learning

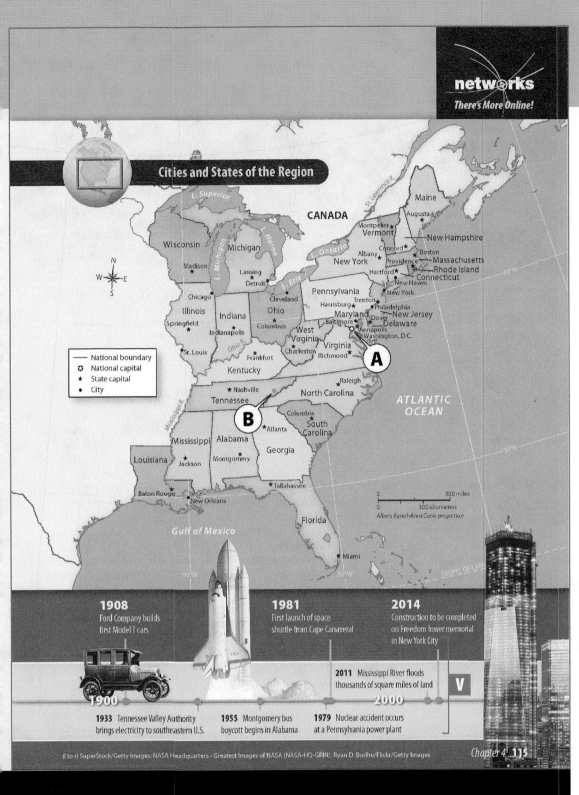

Cities and States of the Region

- —— National boundary
- ✪ National capital
- ★ State capital
- • City

0   300 miles
0 300 kilometers
Albers Equal-Area Conic projection

1908 Ford Company builds first Model T cars

1981 First launch of space shuttle from Cape Canaveral

2014 Construction to be completed on Freedom Tower memorial in New York City

2011 Mississippi River floods thousands of square miles of land

1900

2000

1933 Tennessee Valley Authority brings electricity to southeastern U.S.

1955 Montgomery bus boycott begins in Alabama

1979 Nuclear accident occurs at a Pennsylvania power plant

(l to r) SuperStock/Getty Images; NASA Headquarters - Greatest Images of NASA (NASA-HQ-GRIN); Ryan D. Budhu/Flickr/Getty Images

Chapter 4   115

Step Into the Time

V Visual Skills

Reading a Time Line Have students review the time line and as a class, discuss its major points of interest. **Ask:**

- What period of time is shown on the time line? *(from 1620 to 2014)*
- What "first" did the Ford Company accomplish and when did it happen? *(built first Model T cars in 1908)*
- Did the Civil War happen before or after the Declaration of Independence was signed? *(after)*
- How do the pictures next to certain events help you? *(Possible answer: The pictures help to locate events quickly.)*

Ask students to list some historical events that could be added to the time line. *(Student answers will vary but should include accurate event placement.)* Visual/Spatial, Verbal/Linguistic

W Writing Skills

Informative/Explanatory Read aloud the activity described at the beginning of the time line. Before writing their paragraphs, have students brainstorm ideas about the social, political, or economic effects the different events on the time line had on the region, country, or world. Have students share their completed paragraphs with the class.

CLOSE & REFLECT

Hypothesizing Have students identify the state in the eastern region that is not wholly east of the Mississippi River. *(Louisiana)* Have students hypothesize about why this state is included in the region. *(Possible answers: Louisiana shares more characteristics with the eastern region in the United States than with the western region; the Mississippi River is an important geographical influence in the state and defines it as being part of the east.)* Verbal/Linguistic

---

TIME LINE

Reading a Time Line and Map

Integrating Visual Information Display the time line and map on the whiteboard. Have volunteers read each event as it is revealed on the time line. Ask students to identify where in the eastern United States the event took place and find its location on the map. If students are unsure of where an event took place, have them conduct research to find out. Visual/Spatial

See page 113B for other online activities.

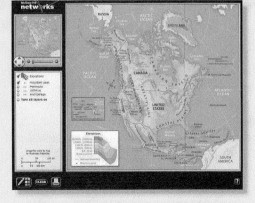

ENGAGE

Bellringer Before students begin the lesson, have them review the definition of *region*. *(places that are close to one another and share some characteristics)* Then read the Essential Question aloud and have students discuss how the physical geography in an area might influence what they do in their free time. **Ask:** How might leisure activities done during the month of January in Florida be different from those done during the same time in Vermont? *(Student answers will vary but should include mention of specific physical features such as the ocean, mountains in Vermont, and the climate of the two different regions.)*

TEACH & ASSESS

R **Reading Skills**

Explaining Discuss with students the difference in terminology between *regions* and *subregions* and how the discussion of subregions might impact their study of the eastern United States. **Ask:** How are subregions similar to and different from regions? *(Both have features that make them unique; however a subregion is smaller than a region.)*

Remind students to add academic and content vocabulary words to their vocabulary lists in their notebooks. Tell students to write their own definitions and to include drawings if desired.

ELL **AL** **Verbal/Linguistic**

V **Visual Skills**

Analyzing Maps Display a physical map of the United States. Have a volunteer locate the Mississippi River and point out the area east of the river and the area west of it. Discuss how the Mississippi River divides the country in two parts, and how it was integral to travel in the 1700s and 1800s. **Ask:** Which region is physically larger—the eastern United States or the western United States? *(western United States)* **Visual/Spatial**

ANSWER, p. 116

Taking Notes Students may note that the major bodies of water in the eastern United States include the Atlantic Ocean, the Great Lakes, the Mississippi River, and the Ohio River; the physical landscape of the eastern United States varies greatly and includes a large coastal plain, several mountain ranges, forests, plains, beaches, and marshes; the land is rich in natural resources and is used for a variety of purposes, including farming, mining, and industry.

---

netw⊙rks

There's More Online!

☑ **MAP** Atlantic Coast Fall Line

☑ **SLIDE SHOW** Agriculture East of the Mississippi River

☑ **ANIMATION** How the Great Lakes Formed

☑ **VIDEO**

Reading **HELP**DESK

Academic Vocabulary

- **parallel**

Content Vocabulary

- **subregion**
- **lock**
- **tributary**
- **levee**
- **coastal plain**
- **fall line**
- **hurricane**

TAKING NOTES: *Key Ideas and Details*

Organize As you read about the region's physical landscape, take notes on a graphic organizer like this one.

U.S. East of the Mississippi

Landscape   Bodies of Water

Indiana Academic Standards
6.1.18, 6.1.19, 6.3.5, 6.3.7

116

Lesson 1
Physical Features

ESSENTIAL QUESTION · *How does geography influence the way people live?*

IT MATTERS BECAUSE
The United States can be divided into regions based on physical characteristics. Learning about each region will help you better understand our nation's geographic diversity.

The Regions

GUIDING QUESTION *How do the physical features of the eastern United States make the region unique?*

The United States is a vast and varied land. If you were to view our entire nation from outer space, you would notice dramatic differences between its various parts. To better study the United States as well as other countries, geographers divide these parts into large geographic areas called regions. Each region's characteristics make it distinctly different from the others.

R Geographers can further divide regions into smaller parts called **subregions**. Like a region, a subregion has special features that make it unique. The most basic way to divide the **V** United States is into two regions: the United States east of the Mississippi and the United States west of the Mississippi. The Mississippi River is the dividing line between the two regions. In this lesson, you will learn about the United States east of the Mississippi and its four subregions: New England, the Mid-Atlantic, the Midwest, and the Southeast.

New England
New England is the subregion located in the northeastern corner of the United States, between Canada and the Atlantic Ocean. Many of the first English colonists who came to

(l to r) Karl Weatherly/The Image Bank/Getty Images; Scenics of America/PhotoLink/Getty Images; J. R. Factor/Photo Researchers; Kennan Harvey/Getty Images

---

netw⊙rks *Online Teaching Options*

VIDEO

Extreme Heat in Urban Areas

Formulating Questions Use this video about extreme heat in urban areas of the eastern United States to introduce the lesson. Ask students to write three questions they have about this effect from watching the video. Collect the questions and see if you can answer them as a class after reading the lesson. Discuss with students that because of the major cities in the eastern United States and the number of people living in those cities, this is example of human-environment interaction, which is of major importance to the cities in the eastern United States. **AL** **Visual/Spatial, Verbal/Linguistic**

See page 113C for other online activities.

BBC Motion Gallery Education

America during the 1600s settled in this area. The settlers named the area New England in honor of their distant homeland. New England includes the states of Maine, New Hampshire, Vermont, Massachusetts, Rhode Island, and Connecticut.

The Mid-Atlantic

Located along the Atlantic coast, just south of New England, is the Mid-Atlantic subregion. The Mid-Atlantic includes the states of Delaware, Maryland, New Jersey, New York, and Pennsylvania. These states were part of America's original thirteen colonies. Our nation's capital, Washington, D.C., is also located in the Mid-Atlantic.

The Midwest

The states of Illinois, Indiana, Michigan, Ohio, and Wisconsin are part of the subregion called the Midwest. All five of these states share borders with one or more of the Great Lakes. The Midwest is nicknamed "the nation's breadbasket" because a large percentage of America's food crops are grown in its rich soil.

The Southeast

R The Southeast is the largest subregion in the eastern United States. The Southeast is made up of 11 states: Alabama, Florida, Georgia, Kentucky, Louisiana, Mississippi, North Carolina, South Carolina, Tennessee, Virginia, and West Virginia. Some Southeastern states have long coastal borders where they meet the Atlantic Ocean or the Gulf of Mexico.

☑ **READING PROGRESS CHECK**

Determining Central Ideas Why do you think geographers divide the United States at the Mississippi River instead of dividing it through the middle into equal halves?

Bodies of Water

V

GUIDING QUESTION *Which of North America's major bodies of water are located east of the Mississippi?*

C Oceans, lakes, and rivers have helped make this region prosperous. Oceans link the region to other countries for trade. An abundant supply of freshwater provides power for homes and industries.

MAP SKILLS

1 **PLACES AND REGIONS**
Which subregion includes the state of Alabama?

2 **THE GEOGRAPHER'S WORLD** Which subregion extends the farthest north?

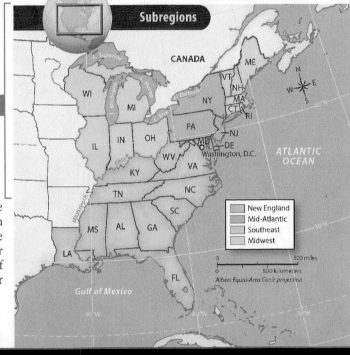

Subregions

R Reading Skills

Applying After reading about the four subregions east of the Mississippi River and looking at the map, **ask:**

- Which subregion produces much of the food grown in the United States? *(the Midwest)*
- Which subregion would you be in if you were visiting the White House? *(the Mid-Atlantic)*
- Which subregion has access to two major bodies of water? *(the Southeast)*
- Which subregion has an international border? *(New England)*
- Which subregion touches 4 out of 5 of the Great Lakes? *(the Midwest)* **Verbal/Linguistic, Visual/Spatial**

V Visual Skills

Reading a Map Have students locate the following bodies of water on the Subregions map of the eastern United States: Atlantic Ocean, Great Lakes, Mississippi River, Gulf of Mexico. Invite students to talk about how these bodies of water connect to one another and which subregions each body of water is near. **AL** **Visual/Spatial**

C Critical Thinking Skills

Problem-Solving Have students use the map to consider how waterways affect trade and the shipping of products from one region, subregion, or country to the next. **Ask:** Farmers in southern Illinois want to trade wheat for tropical fruit grown by farmers on the east coast of Mexico. How might the farmers in these two countries use waterways to complete their trade successfully? Have students trace the route on the map. *(Possible answer: The wheat can be put on a boat traveling south on the Mississippi River, and then transferred to a larger ship in New Orleans traveling southwest to Mexico. The tropical fruit can then make the reverse trip.)* **Visual/Spatial, Logical/Mathematical**

MAP

Region Map of East Coast of U.S.

Analyzing Use the Region Map of East Coast of U.S. to lead a discussion on subregions. Discuss why geographers find it helpful to divide regions into smaller parts. Then have students hypothesize why specific states are grouped into a particular subregion and speculate how each subregion got its name. **Visual/Spatial, Logical/Mathematical**

See page 113C for other online activities.

ANSWERS, p. 117

MAP SKILLS

1. Southeast

2. New England

☑ **READING PROGRESS CHECK** Student answers will vary but may include: The Mississippi River forms a natural dividing line; there are no natural divisions through the exact middle of the United States; the Mississippi River is a historical waterway recognized by most Americans.

C Critical Thinking Skills

Comparing and Contrasting Have students compare and contrast the Atlantic Ocean and the East Coast with the Gulf of Mexico and the Gulf Coast. **Ask:** How does the Atlantic Ocean and the East Coast compare to the Gulf of Mexico and the Gulf Coast? *(Possible answers include: the East Coast borders more states than the Gulf Coast does; the East Coast can be jagged, rocky, smooth, or sandy, while the Gulf Coast varies from sandy beaches to marshes, bays, and lagoons; waters in the Gulf of Mexico are warmer and generally calmer than those of the Atlantic; both contain saltwater; the Atlantic Ocean is larger than the Gulf of Mexico.)* Verbal/Linguistic

T Technology Skills

Creating Visuals Explain to students that in April 2010, there was an explosion on the Deepwater Horizon drilling rig that killed 11 workers and released millions of barrels of crude oil into the waters of the Gulf of Mexico. This accidental marine oil spill caused extensive environmental damage to marine and wildlife habitats and greatly harmed the fishing and tourism industries in Louisiana, Mississippi, Alabama, and Florida. Have students use the Internet to research photos showing the harmful effects of the oil spill on the environment and on the people in the area. Students may choose to use a software presentation program to show the visuals along with captions to the class or make hard copies of the visuals and display them along with captions on a poster. ELL AL Visual/Spatial

R Reading Skills

Making Connections To help students remember the names of the five Great Lakes, share this mnemonic device: HOMES (Huron, Ontario, Michigan, Erie, Superior). Intrapersonal

Content Background Knowledge

Both the Atlantic Ocean and the Gulf of Mexico contain water that is salty. Most of the salt in the water comes from rocks on land. Water in rivers picks up small amounts of salts and minerals as it flows over the rocks to the oceans and seas. As water in the oceans evaporates or freezes, the salt does not evaporate or freeze but remains dissolved in the ocean. Over time, the water gets saltier and saltier. The Great Lakes contain water that is fresh with no salt because they were made from melted glacial ice that does not contain salt.

The Atlantic Ocean and the Gulf Coast

The eastern United States is nearly surrounded by water. The largest body of water east of the Mississippi is the Atlantic Ocean. This enormous salt-water ocean borders the states along the East Coast. The East Coast is a shoreline that stretches for more than 2,000 miles (3,219 km), from Maine in the north to Florida in the south. It is jagged and rocky in New England but smooth and sandy in the Mid-Atlantic and Southeast. The Atlantic Ocean affects the region's land, weather, economy, and people in many ways.

The East Coast borders the Atlantic Ocean. The Gulf Coast borders a smaller body of water called the Gulf of Mexico. The Gulf of Mexico covers an area of about 600,000 square miles (1,550,000 sq. km) and is nearly surrounded by land. Several currents flow through the Gulf of Mexico like giant underwater rivers. One of the currents feeds into the Gulf Stream, a powerful current that flows through the Atlantic Ocean.

The Gulf Coast extends from Florida to Texas and Mexico. The land along the Gulf Coast varies from sandy beaches to marshes, bays, and lagoons. Waters in the Gulf of Mexico are warmer and generally calmer than those of the Atlantic.

The Great Lakes

The term *Great Lakes* refers to a cluster of five huge lakes located in the American Midwest and central Canada. These lakes were formed thousands of years ago when massive glaciers carved out the ground and melted over time. The Great Lakes form the largest group of freshwater lakes in the world. Together, the Great Lakes hold more liquid freshwater than any other location on Earth.

Moving from west to east, the Great Lakes are Lake Superior, Lake Michigan, Lake Huron, Lake Erie, and Lake Ontario. The five lakes are connected. Water flows west to east from one lake to the next, eventually making its way to the long St. Lawrence River.

Destin Beach is located on the Florida Panhandle along the Gulf of Mexico.
▶ CRITICAL THINKING
Describing How far does the Gulf Coast extend?

118 Chapter 4

Karl Weatherly/The Image Bank/Getty Images

---

netw⚡rks *Online Teaching Options*

IMAGE

The Gulf Coast Region

Evaluating Display the interactive image of the Gulf Coast region and discuss the importance of the coast on the local economies in the region. Ask students how the Gulf of Mexico may influence the way people live. Visual/Spatial, Verbal/Linguistic

See page 113C for other online activities.

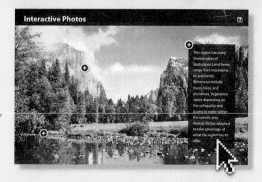
Interactive Photos
Purestock/Getty Images

ANSWER, p. 118

CRITICAL THINKING from Florida to Texas and Mexico

The St. Lawrence Seaway

The St. Lawrence River carries the water eastward for 750 miles (1,207 km), until it empties into the Atlantic Ocean. Because the Great Lakes border the United States and Canada, these nations work together to set up environmental programs for the region. Important goals include addressing population threats and protecting the health and safety of people living in the Great Lakes region.

During the 1950s, the United States and Canada worked together to build canals and gated passageways called **locks** between the Great Lakes and into the St. Lawrence River. The locks and canals made it possible for ships to travel the entire length of the Great Lakes and the St. Lawrence River. The final passageway, extending 2,340 miles (3,766 km) from Lake Superior to the Atlantic Ocean, is called the St. Lawrence Seaway. The St. Lawrence Seaway connects the Midwest to seaports all over the world. This has made it faster and easier for businesses in the Midwest to ship their products to buyers worldwide.

V

The Mississippi River

The "Mighty Mississippi" is one of the longest rivers in North America. Many people consider it the most important river in the United States. From its source in Minnesota, the Mississippi River winds its way southward for 2,350 miles (3,782 km). **Tributaries** such as the Missouri and Ohio rivers feed into the Mississippi, adding to its strength and volume. The Mississippi River ends at the point where it empties into the Gulf of Mexico.

C

Since early settlers arrived in America, the Mississippi River has affected the settlement patterns, the economy, and the lifestyles of countless Americans. People have used the river for transportation for hundreds of years.

The Welland Canal (left) begins on Lake Ontario. The St. Lawrence Seaway connects Chicago's harbors to the Atlantic Ocean. (right)
▶ **CRITICAL THINKING**
Describing How do canals aid ship travel?

(l to r) Henry Georgi/age fotostock; ©Alan Schein Photography/Corbis

Chapter 4 **119**

ANIMATION

How the Great Lakes Formed

Paraphrasing Use the animation about how the Great Lakes were formed to discuss the creation of the landscape and waterways in the area. Ask students to use their own words to explain how glaciers formed the Great Lakes.
BL Visual/Spatial, Verbal/Linguistic

See page 113C for other online activities.

V Visual Skills

Interpreting Visual Information Display a map of North America that shows the political boundaries between countries. Have a volunteer locate the St. Lawrence River and trace its path from Lake Ontario to the Atlantic Ocean. Point out the boundary lines in the Great Lakes that divide the United States and Canada. **Ask:** What route might a ship transporting goods from Chicago to London travel to get to the open waters of the Atlantic Ocean? *(Students should trace a route from Chicago on Lake Michigan's shore north to Lake Huron and onward through Lakes Erie and Ontario, then up the St. Lawrence River and out to the Atlantic Ocean.)* Visual/Spatial

C Critical Thinking Skills

Making Inferences Have students use their prior knowledge along with what they have read about major rivers to help them make an inference to answer the question. **Ask:** How might the Mississippi River affect the lifestyles of Americans? *(Student answers will vary but should include knowledge of careers or recreation associated with large rivers.)* Verbal/Linguistic

Content Background Knowledge

The United States and Canada began work on the St. Lawrence Seaway in 1954. It is known as one of the most difficult engineering accomplishments in history. The completed seaway is a 189-mile deepwater navigation channel in the St. Lawrence River between Montreal and Ogdensburg, New York.

It cost the United States and Canada around 470 million dollars. Workers had to move more than 200 million cubic yards of earth.

President Eisenhower and Her Majesty Queen Elizabeth formally opened the Seaway on June 26, 1959, at the lock in St. Lambert, Canada. Then the President and the Queen took a 5-hour cruise on the royal yacht *Britannia* down the seaway to mark the symbolic opening of the waterway.

ANSWER, p. 119

CRITICAL THINKING Canals make it possible for ships to travel larger bodies of water in shorter timeframes.

Physical Features

C Critical Thinking Skills

Comparing and Contrasting Divide students into two groups. Have one group brainstorm and list benefits that the Mississippi River provides and the other brainstorm and list the river's disadvantages. After groups share their lists, as a class discuss if the river's benefits out-weigh its disadvantages. Logical/Mathematical

W Writing Skills

Informative/Explanatory A boundary is used to divide one area from another. A river is a natural boundary that can separate states, countries, cities, and private property such as farms or ranches.

Have students research both natural and man-made boundaries used by pioneers to mark their homestead. Then have them write two paragraphs explaining the benefits and disadvantages of one natural and one man-made boundary. *(Student paragraphs should identify the types of boundaries and explain at least one benefit and disadvantage of each. For example, pioneers used streams as natural boundaries between properties. A stream is easily visible; however, streams can dry up or change course and cause arguments about where the boundary lies. Pioneers used man-made fences as boundaries. Fences are easily visible and for the most part prevent people and animals from entering; however, fences can be moved or fall into disrepair.)* Verbal/Linguistic

Content Background Knowledge

When the Mississippi River was originally used to establish state borders, the middle of the riverbed was identified as the boundary line. However, during periods of big floods, the river can change course and reroute itself through new channels. This happened in 1876 when the Mississippi River changed course and cut the settlement of Reverie, TN, off from the rest of the state. Even though the settlement became attached to Arkansas, the boundary line in the old river channel was still recognized as the official one.

The Mississippi River is the largest river system in North America.
▶ CRITICAL THINKING
Analyzing How do its many tributaries change the Mississippi River?

C Ships and steamboats filled with passengers and cargo can follow the wide river and its tributaries for thousands of miles. This vast stretch makes the Mississippi one of the world's busiest commercial waterways.

In the past, the Mississippi would often flood its banks, dumping millions of tons of water and sediment onto the land. The sediment enriched the soil in farm fields, but the floods also destroyed homes and washed away entire fields of crops. The government built **levees**—embankments to control the flooding and reduce the damage to homes and crops. Unfortunately, levees also block the sediment that used to replenish farm fields.

The powerful Mississippi River has influenced the nation's history more than any other river. The river's importance, and the respect humans have for it, is shown in its name: *Mississippi* is a Choctaw word meaning "Great Water" or "Father of Waters."

Rivers as Boundaries

Rivers make natural boundaries. The Mississippi River forms much of the western border of the states of Wisconsin, Illinois, Kentucky, Tennessee, and Mississippi.

Rivers are boundaries for counties and cities, too. For example, **W** the Tennessee River in northwest Alabama forms the border between Lauderdale County and Colbert County.

Rivers are examples of physical systems that form political boundaries. Mountains and lakes are other physical features that may be used as political boundaries. Structures that humans make, such as streets and roads, can also set boundaries.

netw⊙rks   *Online Teaching Options*

The Mississippi River

Discussing Show the video of the Mississippi River and trace its path from its source in Minnesota to its mouth at the Gulf of Mexico. Have students discuss its importance to the economy, transportation, and the lifestyles of people living along its banks. **AL** Visual Spatial, Verbal/Linguistic

See page 113C for other online activities.

ANSWER, p. 120

CRITICAL THINKING The tributaries add to the river's strength and volume.

The Ohio River

The Ohio River carries more water to the Mississippi River than any of the other tributaries. The Ohio River begins where the Allegheny and Monongahela rivers combine in western Pennsylvania. From Pennsylvania, the Ohio River flows westward for 981 miles (1,579 km), forming a wide, watery border that separates the states of Ohio, Indiana, and Illinois that lie along the north side of the river from West Virginia and Kentucky on its south side. Like the Mississippi, the Ohio River has long been an important shipping and transportation route. The Ohio River connects much of the Midwest to the Mississippi River. Both of these river systems have affected our nation's land, its people, and its history.

☑ **READING PROGRESS CHECK**

Determining Central Ideas How could a logging company in Kentucky send logs to a buyer on the Gulf of Mexico using an all-water route?

Physical Landscape

GUIDING QUESTION *What characteristics make the physical landscape east of the Mississippi unique?*

The Atlantic Coastal Plain

The East Coast of the United States sits at the edge of a huge continental platform. Most of this platform is underwater, forming a shelf around the Atlantic coastline. But over time, a large area of the platform rose above sea level. Ocean waves washed over the platform for millions of years, leaving behind layers of sandy sediment. As the sediment built up, a flat lowland called the **coastal plain** formed. The coastal plain stretches from the northeastern U.S. to Mexico. In places, the coastal plain was crushed under the weight of glaciers, pushing the land below sea level. These areas often become flooded by fierce storms and heavy rains.

The Appalachian Mountains

The Appalachian Mountain system is the oldest, longest chain of mountains in the United States east of the Mississippi River. It begins in Alabama and continues 1,500 miles (2,414 km) northeast to the Canadian border. Dense forests cover much of the Appalachian Mountains, which are known for their rugged beauty.

The mountains of the Appalachian system stand side by side in **parallel** ranges. Two of the most well-known Appalachian Mountain ranges are the Blue Ridge Mountains in Virginia and the Great Smoky Mountains in Tennessee.

Even though central New York is more than 200 miles (322 km) from the Atlantic Ocean, scientists have found fossils of marine organisms there.

▶ **CRITICAL THINKING**

Analyzing What is an explanation for finding the marine fossils so far from the ocean?

Academic Vocabulary

parallel extending side by side in the same direction, always the same distance apart

Chapter 4 **121**

J.R. Factor/Photo Researchers

V Visual Skills

Reading a Map Display a political map of the eastern United States and have volunteers locate where the Allegheny and Monongahela rivers combine in western Pennsylvania to form the headwaters of the Ohio River. Have another volunteer trace the river's westward flow into the Mississippi. Point out the Wabash River, an eastern boundary of Illinois that is a tributary of the Ohio. Then have students identify the states that border the river to the north and south. Visual/Spatial

C Critical Thinking Skills

Making Inferences Remind students that they learned in Unit 1 about how physical changes such as weathering and erosion change the physical features of the environment. **Ask:** What might happen when fierce storms cause winds to blow and waves to crash on beaches along the Atlantic Coastal plain? *(Students' answers will vary but should include an understanding of the effects of wind and water erosion on beaches.)* Verbal/Linguistic

Content Background Knowledge

The Appalachian Trail stretches about 2,180 miles through 14 states from Springer Mountain, Georgia, to Katahdin, Maine.

- It is one of the longest continuously marked footpaths in the world.
- About 2 to 3 million people walk part of the trail each year, while over 1,800 "thru-hikers" a year walk the trail in a continuous journey that takes an average of 6 months to complete.
- Most thru-hikers start in Georgia in the spring and finish in the fall in Maine.
- Only about 25% of people who try to be a thru-hiker actually make it all the way through.
- It is easiest to hike through Maryland and West Virginia and hardest to hike through New Hampshire and Maine.

MAP

Physical Geography and Climate: The Eastern United States

Comparing and Contrasting Display the physical and climate layers of the Chapter Opener map for the eastern United States. Have students compare and contrast the physical features and climate conditions in different subregions. Ask students to identify the area they would be most comfortable living in and explain why. Visual/ Spatial, Verbal/Linguistic

See page 113C for other online activities.

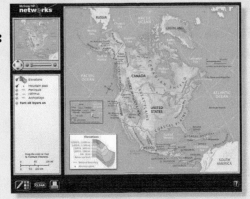

ANSWERS, p. 121

CRITICAL THINKING Ocean waves washed up sediment and organisms, creating a flat lowland inland.

☑ READING PROGRESS CHECK The Ohio River borders Kentucky, and the Ohio River eventually connects to the Mississippi River, so the logging company could ship its products by river from Kentucky to the Gulf of Mexico.

Physical Features

C Critical Thinking Skills

Drawing Conclusions Explain to students that they can apply what they are learning about the physical features in one region to the physical features of another region to make comparisons and draw conclusions. Encourage students to think deeply and critically about what they read, without having to be told everything in a text. **Ask:** Knowing that the Appalachian Mountains in the eastern United States have worn down over time and are rounded in appearance, how might you characterize the younger Rocky Mountains in the western United States? *(Possible answer: The Rockies would have sharper peaks and not look as worn or show as much erosion.)* Logical/Mathematical

R Reading Skills

Explaining After reading the section on climate in the eastern United States, ask students whether they would rather live in the Midwest or the Southeast and to explain why they feel that way. *(Answers should include reasons why they chose the subregion that they did, such as: I would prefer to live in the Midwest because I like to see the seasons changing, or I would prefer to live in the Southeast because I would like to live closer to the ocean.)* Verbal/Linguistic

T Technology Skills

Integrating Visual Information Have students work in small groups to gather seasonal photographs of two of the four subregions in the eastern United States.

Explain that photographs are like text and that students should not use other people's photographs without giving them credit. Have students list the source of each of the photographs they gather for their presentation.

Then using a software presentation program or hard copies of the photographs displayed on poster board, have each group give a five minute presentation to the class comparing and contrasting the climate of the two subregions. ELL Visual/Spatial

The Pisgah National Forest in western North Carolina is a land of heavy forests and many waterfalls.
▶ CRITICAL THINKING
Explaining What is a fall line?

These mountain ranges were formed from sedimentary rock by powerful upheavals within Earth's crust. The mountains have worn down over time because of natural erosion. Compared to younger mountain ranges such as the Rockies in the western United States, the Appalachian Mountains show their age in their worn, rounded appearance.

The Appalachian Mountains are home to many natural wonders. Old-growth forests are filled with diverse plant and animal life. Some of the most spectacular features of the Appalachians are the thousands of waterfalls that decorate the landscape. The many waterfalls are evidence that a fall line runs through the region. A **fall line** is an area where waterfalls flow from higher to lower ground. In this region, a fall line stretches for hundreds of miles between New Jersey and South Carolina. This fall line is a long, low cliff that runs parallel to the Atlantic coast. Throughout New England, the Mid-Atlantic, and the Southeast, waterfalls spill over this fall line. The fall line forms a boundary between higher, upland areas and the Atlantic coastal plain. Many cities originally located along the fall line because waterfalls provide water power, a renewable resource.

R Climate in the Eastern United States

The climate of the eastern United States is as varied as the landscape. The changing seasons in most places east of the Mississippi are quite noticeable. New England and the Midwest see the most dramatic seasonal changes. These regions have cold winters and hot, humid summers. Autumn is cool and colorful as the leaves change color. Springtime brings rainy and snowy weather and strong storms.

Coastal areas tend to have mild climates. States along the East Coast still experience seasons, but temperatures are less extreme than they are inland. States located farther south experience milder changes in seasons.

Much of the Southeast has a humid subtropical climate. Summers are rainy and hot, and winters are cooler and drier. In general, climates of the eastern United States are more humid and rainy than climates of the West. In late summer and early autumn, **hurricanes**—ocean storms that span hundreds of miles with winds of at least 74 miles per hour (119 km per hour)—can pound the coastline. One of the most damaging hurricanes in history, Hurricane Katrina, struck the Gulf Coast in August 2005. More than 1,800 people died, and hundreds of thousands lost their homes.

netw◉rks   *Online Teaching Options*

MAP

The Fall Line

Making Inferences Display the map of the fall line along the Atlantic coast. Discuss the features of a fall line. **Ask:** Why would people decide to live along the fall line? *(Students' answers will vary but should demonstrate an understanding of waterfalls being a source for electricity.)* Visual/Spatial, Verbal/Linguistic

See page 113C for other online activities.

ANSWER, p. 122

CRITICAL THINKING   an area where waterfalls flow from higher to lower ground

Minerals and Energy Resources

A wealth of resources is hidden below the surface of the region, and two of the most valuable materials are minerals and energy resources. Minerals are natural substances such as iron ore, gold, and zinc. These minerals can be processed into metals. Metals and other forms of minerals are used in manufacturing and construction.

Energy resources, such as coal, oil, and natural gas, are called fossil fuels. Burning coal can produce electricity. Oil is processed into fuel for cars and other vehicles. Natural gas is used to heat our homes and to generate electricity. The demand for mineral and energy resources is huge. Mining them is a major industry in the U.S. east of the Mississippi River. Minerals and energy resources are mined from inside mountains and from deep under the ground. Some mining methods harm the environment by damaging the land and polluting the water, soil, and air.

R

Farming and Industry

One of the most valuable resources east of the Mississippi River is farmland. The rich soil is excellent for growing crops such as grains, fruits, and vegetables. Sandy soils in the Southeast are good for growing cotton. Excellent growing conditions have helped the region become a major producer of meat, dairy foods, wood, cotton, sugar, corn, wheat, soybeans, and other food crops.

Industries such as logging, mining, and fishing are a way of life throughout the region. Products such as automobiles, electronics, and clothing are made in factories in these cities. Information technology (IT) and tourism are also important. Plentiful resources and hard-working people make the eastern United States one of the most productive regions in the world.

C

FOLDABLES
Study Organizer

Include this lesson's information in your Foldable®.

☑ **READING PROGRESS CHECK**

Explaining Why is farmland considered a natural resource?

LESSON 1 REVIEW

Reviewing Vocabulary

1. How does a *tributary* affect the amount of water flowing through a river?

Answering the Guiding Questions

2. *Determining Central Ideas* Why do you think geographers divide the eastern U.S. into four subregions?

3. *Identifying* Which of the four subregions of the Eastern United States does not border the Atlantic Ocean?

4. *Analyzing* In what ways are the East Coast and the Eastern Gulf Coast alike? In what ways are they different?

5. *Describing* How do locks in the Great Lakes and the St. Lawrence Seaway affect transportation in the Midwest?

6. *Analyzing* Think about how mining minerals and energy resources can damage the environment. Brainstorm a creative solution to this problem. Describe your solution.

7. *Identifying* Crops of citrus fruits, such as oranges and lemons, will die in freezing temperatures. Which subregion of the Eastern U.S. has the best climate for growing citrus fruits?

8. *Argument Writing* Write a persuasive letter encouraging a friend or family member to visit one of the four subregions of the eastern U.S. Include details about the region's physical features, resources, and climate in your letter.

Chapter 4 **123**

LESSON 1 REVIEW ANSWERS

Reviewing Vocabulary

1. Tributaries feed water into rivers, adding to the amount of water flowing through a river.

Answering the Guiding Questions

2. **Determining Central Ideas** Geographers divide large regions into smaller subregions to organize and categorize locations in the region.

3. **Identifying** The Midwest

4. **Analyzing** Alike: Both border lands in the eastern United States and large bodies of water; both have long coastlines; Different: The East Coast borders the Atlantic Ocean, while the Gulf Coast borders a gulf; waters along the Gulf Coast are warmer and calmer than those found on the East Coast.

5. **Describing** Locks in the Great Lakes allow ships to travel between all five lakes and the St. Lawrence Seaway. The St. Lawrence Seaway enables ships to travel to the Atlantic Ocean and on to seaports all over the world.

6. **Analyzing** Solutions might mention reducing destructive mining practices, reducing the amount of resources mined, or using alternative energy sources.

7. **Identifying** The Southeast, because it is the warmest subregion with less risk of freezing temperatures.

8. **Argument Writing** Letters will vary, but should include details about one of the four subregions of the eastern United States.

R **Reading Skills**

Summarizing Have students work with a partner to summarize the information about mineral and energy resources in the eastern United States. Remind students that summaries are short and tell just the main ideas.

Have partners share their summaries with others. *(Possible answer: The Eastern United States has a wealth of minerals and energy resources. The minerals are processed into metals and used in manufacturing and construction. The energy resources are used to produce electricity, fuel for vehicles, and heat. Mining is a major industry in the eastern United States, but some mining methods harm the environment.)* Logical/Mathematical

C **Critical Thinking Skills**

Making Connections Discuss with students how it is easier to remember material that they read when they make personal connections between the material and how it applies to their lives. **Ask:** How are products produced in the eastern United States important to you? *(Students' answers will vary but should include relevant details about how they personally use products produced in the eastern United States.)* Intrapersonal, Verbal/Linguistic

CLOSE & REFLECT

Comparing and Contrasting To close this lesson, have students think about the special features of the subregions of the eastern United States that make these subregions interesting and unique.

Ask them to think about how these features will help them better understand and appreciate our nation's geographic diversity and be able to explain how these features have affected our nation's history. Invite volunteers to share their ideas with the rest of the class.

ANSWER, p. 123

☑ **READING PROGRESS CHECK** Farmland occurs naturally and can be used to produce resources, such as food, animal feed, meat, dairy, other food crops, and cloth.

ENGAGE

Bellringer Before students begin the lesson, ask them to remember something that happened in their past that influenced how they think or act today. Explain that each person's past is his or her own personal history. Then make a connection to past events in students' lives to the Essential Question: *Why is history important?* **Ask:**

- What have you learned from past events in your life? *(Students' answers will vary but should include mention of either general or specific learning experiences.)*
- Do you find you learned more from making mistakes in the past or from the successes in your life? Why do you think so? *(Students' answers will vary but should include mention of either mistakes or successes that have been learning experiences.)* **Intrapersonal**

TEACH & ASSESS

C Critical Thinking Skills

Making Comparisons Explain that the purpose of the analogy between our nation and a quilt is to use something familiar (a quilt) to understand an unfamiliar idea. Maybe students have heard the metaphor comparing our nation to a melting pot. Both a quilt and a melting pot combine many parts to make a whole.

Ask: How does using an analogy help you understand the concept that our nation is diverse and complex? If needed, review the meanings of the words *diverse* ("having a lot of variety") and *complex* ("having many different and connected parts; complicated"). *(Students' answers should include a reference to our nation being made up of people from different nationalities and backgrounds.)* Then have students come up with other analogies about our nation. *(One analogy could include comparing our nation to a salad, where all of the ingredients are good by themselves, but together, they are great.)* **Verbal/Linguistic**

ANSWER, p. 124

Taking Notes Students may note that colonists took lands away from Native Americans and changed their ways of life; settlers moved westward and farmed the land east of the Mississippi River; the United States government forced Native Americans to relocate to distant areas, damaging their cultural traditions; many African-American people migrated in the Great Migration after the Civil War. Starting in the 1800s, people began migrating to urban areas to work in factories. People from all over the world immigrated to America to start new lives; the blending of people and cultures over hundreds of years has made the United States a culturally diverse nation.

netw⊙rks

There's More Online!

☑ **IMAGE** Early Settlements

☑ **MAP** Cultures and Communities on the Mississippi River

☑ **VIDEO**

Reading HELPDESK

Academic Vocabulary
- isolate

Content Vocabulary
- indigenous
- colonists
- agriculture
- industry

TAKING NOTES: *Key Ideas and Details*

Organize Use the graphic organizer below to take notes about the effects of migration on the people and the land of the region.

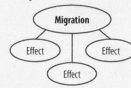

Migration

Effect   Effect

Effect

Indiana Academic Standards
6.1.10, 6.1.11, 6.1.15, 6.3.9

Lesson 2

History of the Region

ESSENTIAL QUESTION • *Why is history important?*

IT MATTERS BECAUSE
Learning about our nation's past helps us understand and appreciate its diversity and complexity.

Early America

GUIDING QUESTION *Who were the first peoples to live in the eastern United States?*

Looking back into history to learn about America's past is like examining a colorful quilt. A quilt is made up of bits and pieces of fabrics of many different colors and patterns. Each piece is made up of thousands of threads woven together. These threads were joined together into fabric pieces, and the pieces were joined together to make a quilt.

Like the quilt, our nation is a whole made up of many smaller parts. These parts are peoples and their cultures, interacting with places and environments. Over time, cultures, beliefs, and ways of living have become woven together like the threads of a quilt. The result is a unique and extraordinary nation.

Earlier, you read about the physical geography of the United States east of the Mississippi River and its many different kinds of landforms and bodies of water. This region has a variety of climates and resources. In this lesson, you will learn about the variety of peoples, cultures, and ways of life in the eastern United States, as well as how people have changed the land. You will discover how natural resources have influenced human settlement and how the land, the people, and the cultures of the eastern United States are connected.

(l to r) ©Burstein Collection/Corbis; ©Jose Fusta Raga/Corbis; ©Corbis; Ingram Publishing

---

netw⊙rks   *Online Teaching Options*

VIDEO

Life on an Island

Analyzing Visuals Use this video about life on an island in Maine to analyze the visual aspects of life on this island. Ask students to describe some of the visuals and what they learned from the video about aspects of life in early America that still have a place in modern society. Have students share unique aspects of the video that may have surprised them.

AL Visual/Spatial

See page 113D for other online activities.

BBC Motion Gallery Education

Native Americans

Native American peoples were the first humans to settle in North America. Historians believe these peoples came to North America by crossing a land bridge from Asia around 14,000 to 19,000 years ago. Over time, these groups migrated in all directions. Hundreds of different groups settled in locations throughout North and South America. Each group developed a unique culture with its own language, religion, and lifestyle. Some of the groups that settled on lands east of the Mississippi River were the Cherokee, the Iroquois, the Miami, and the Shawnee. These groups are considered **indigenous** to North America. *Indigenous* means "living or occurring naturally in a particular place."

Native American peoples satisfied their needs by using the plants, animals, stones, water, and soil around them. Their way of life was shaped by their environment. For example, peoples who lived in northern woodland areas made their homes out of bark and wood. They burned wood to heat their homes during cold winters. They hunted woodland animals for food and used the animals' skins to make clothing.

Native peoples of the Americas built shelters suitable for the climates where they lived. People who lived in hot climates used grasses, vines, and reeds to build open-air homes. Other groups used stones, caves, and earth to build solid structures and mound cities. Their homes reflected their environments.

Some native groups were **isolated** from other groups, while others had contact with neighboring peoples. Sometimes groups interacted peacefully, such as when trading. Other times, wars over land and resources would develop.

For most of their history, Native Americans had little or no contact with people from other parts of the world. Native peoples lived off the land for thousands of years, resulting in only a minor impact on the natural environment. Then, suddenly, the land that they had relied on for everything was taken from them. When the first Europeans arrived in the Americas in the 1400s, native peoples' ways of life were changed forever.

European Colonization

Across the Atlantic Ocean, Europeans grew interested in the Americas. They heard tales about these wild, bountiful lands. Explorers who had been to the Americas told of endless forests, rivers overflowing with fish, and mountains filled with gold and silver. Kings and queens from England, France, Italy, and Spain wanted to claim land in North America. They wanted to control America's gold and natural resources.

©Burstein Collection/Corbis

Academic Vocabulary

isolated being alone or separated from others

Sequoyah spent many years developing 86 symbols to represent all the syllables of the Cherokee language.
▶ **CRITICAL THINKING**
Drawing Conclusions Why is having a written language essential for a culture?

Chapter 4 **125**

R Reading Skills

Explaining Discuss with students how people throughout history have used the natural resources around them and adapted to the environment in which they lived. **Ask:** How was the way of life of Native Americans shaped by their environments? *(Students' answers will vary but should include relevant details from the text specifically citing evidence that tells how food, clothing, and shelters of native people reflected where they lived.)*

Remind students to continue adding academic and content vocabulary to the vocabulary lists in their notebooks along with their own definitions and drawings. **Verbal/Linguistic**

C Critical Thinking Skills

Making Connections Explain to students the importance of making personal connections to the text to help them understand and remember what they read. **Ask:** How would you feel if something you relied on was suddenly taken away from you? *(Students' answers will vary but should demonstrate an understanding of personal feelings they may have when something important is taken away and never returned.)* **Intrapersonal**

Content Background Knowledge

During the Pleistocene Ice Age ten to twenty-five thousand years ago, large parts of North America, Europe, and Asia were covered by glaciers up to two miles thick. Because much of Earth's water was in the glaciers, sea levels dropped. Land that was once under water became dry land. A land bridge connecting the continents of Asia and North America in the present-day Bering Strait became exposed. The area, known as Beringia, formed a flat, grassy, treeless plain that stretched 1,000 miles from north to south. Many species of animals, including the wooly mammoth, mastodon, brown bear, moose, and horse moved between the continents along with plant life and people, some of whom brought diseases and parasites.

Cultures and Communities on the Mississippi River

Integrating Visual Information Display the map showing the complexity of the communities of the Native Americans in the eastern United States. Discuss how evolved these native peoples of the Americas were by linking the map to the chart showing contributions of Native Americans to United States culture. **Visual/Spatial, Logical/Mathematical**

See page 113D for other online activities.

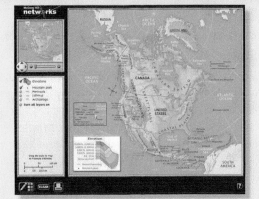

ANSWER, p. 125

CRITICAL THINKING Possible answers: for communication, for recordkeeping as a historical document

History of the Region

C Critical Thinking Skills

Making Inferences Explain to students that making inferences requires readers to piece togther information in a text and make decisions regarding that information. **Ask:** How might the desire to control America's riches and claim land for their home countries have hurt the relationship between the colonists and the Native Americans? *(Students' answers will vary but should include an understanding of colonists upsetting the balance of nature the Native Americans had with the environment and the colonists taking land that the Native Americans valued.)* **Verbal/Linguistic**

R Reading Skills

Explaining After students read this page, check for understanding. **Ask:** Why were colonists sent to the Americas and where did they settle? *(to live in a new place and claim land for their home country; they settled along the Atlantic Ocean in North America)*

Content Background Knowledge

The Spanish military post of **St. Augustine** was founded by Spanish explorer Admiral Pedro Menendez de Aviles in 1565. Having arrived off the coast of Florida on the feast day of St. Augustine, Menendez named the settlement after the saint. His mission was to protect the colony of Florida, originally claimed for Spain by Juan Ponce de Leon in 1513, from British invaders.

From the fort that was built at St. Augustine, Menendez and his men eliminated a nearby French settlement and controlled the Timucuan Indians. Menendez and his men were also aided by an approaching hurricane that destroyed the ships of an invading force.

An entire town of Spanish settlers developed around the fort of St. Augustine. The Spanish settlers introduced cattle ranching, citrus growing, and raising pigs to the area. If you travel to St. Augustine, Florida, you can tour the Spanish fort that still exists today.

In the 1500s, Spanish priests, soldiers, and settlers built military and religious outposts in the Americas. Included was St. Augustine in Florida. Originally founded as a settlement in 1565, settlers soon realized the need for protection after a series of pirate attacks. Settlers were also concerned by the arrival of English settlers. Construction on a stone fort began around 1672. This was the first permanent European settlement in what would become the United States. In the early 1600s, the English began to send **colonists** to the Americas. Colonists are people who are sent to live in a new place and claim land for their home country.

The first English colonists settled along the Atlantic coast of North America. They started early settlements in Jamestown, Virginia, in 1607 and Plymouth, Massachusetts, in 1620. Other settlements soon followed, built on lands that had been home to native peoples. The colonists turned native peoples' hunting grounds into farmland. They used many resources that were important to the Native Americans' survival.

Over the years, more and more Europeans journeyed across the Atlantic Ocean to America. Their colonies grew quickly. By 1650, about 52,000 colonists lived in America. Over the next 50 years, the

Visitors tour the Castillo de San Marcos National monument in St. Augustine, Florida. The fort is over 300 years old and took 23 years to complete.

▶ **CRITICAL THINKING**
Identifying Why do you think settlers chose a site along the water for the fort?

©Jose Fuste Raga/Corbis

126 Chapter 4

---

netw⚙rks   *Online Teaching Options*

TIME LINE

Early History of the Eastern United States

Making Connections Display the interactive time line and have students identify the events shown as they are revealed. Have students make connections between events and their text by identifying causes and effects of the events in the time line. **Visual/Spatial, Verbal/Linguistic**

See page 113D for other online activities.

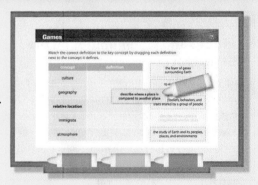

ANSWER, p. 126

CRITICAL THINKING Locations along the coast made it easier to receive supplies from Europe and provides a clear view of approaching enemy ships and pirates.

number of colonists grew to about 250,000. By 1760, an estimated 1.7 million colonists lived in America. People built towns along the Atlantic coast. Large cities such as Boston and New York City started out as tiny settlements. By the 1750s, thirteen English colonies had been established in North America.

Life was hard for the first colonists. The food supplies they brought from England soon ran out. Many people got sick or died from starvation. In time, however, the colonists learned how to plant crops and hunt for food in this new land. They also adapted the natural resources they found there to make things they needed, such as candles, soap, pots, clothing, tools, and medicine.

The colonies built by English settlers were controlled by English rulers thousands of miles away. In 1707 England and Scotland united to form Great Britain. The colonists did not like the laws and taxes forced upon them by the British government. They made plans to break away and become free from British rule. In 1776, American colonists declared their independence from British rule, which led to the Revolutionary War. The war ended in 1781 when the British surrendered. The thirteen colonies became an independent nation called the United States of America, and the colonists called themselves *Americans*.

☑ READING PROGRESS CHECK

Identifying Point of View Why did European nations want to control land in North America?

R

©Corbis

European goods important to the survival of the colonists were received in Boston Harbor.
▶ CRITICAL THINKING
Determining Central Ideas Why were early colonists dependent on supplies from England?

Chapter 4 **127**

MAP

Colonial Expansion

Discussing Display the colonial expansion layer on the Chapter Opener map to discuss the arrival of Europeans to the eastern United States. Have students discuss the established settlements and the impact the settlements had on Native Americans. **AL** Visual/Spatial

See page 113D for other online activities.

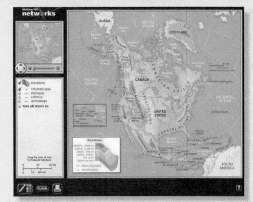

R Reading Skills

Explaining After reading about the first colonists in America, ask the following questions:

- Why do you think the colonists built towns along the Atlantic coast? *(Possible answer: The colonists came from Europe, got off the boats along the coast, and built towns where they landed.)*
- What are some things that helped to make life in the colonies easier? *(Possible answers: learning how to plant or hunt for food and learning how to use natural resources to make things they needed.)*
- Why do you think the possibility of sickness or death from starvation did not stop colonists from coming to America? *(Students' answers will vary but should demonstrate an understanding of the strong desire colonists had for a better life in America.)*
- What caused the colonists to declare their independence from British rule? *(laws and taxes forced upon the colonists by the British government)*
- How long did it take for the American colonies to become an independent nation? *(5 years)* Verbal/Linguistic, Logical/Mathematical

Content Background Knowledge

The Declaration of Independence was a document that gave colonists freedom from British rule. Signing the Declaration of Independence was an act of treason against Britain, and each man who signed his name knew he could be hanged for doing so. Therefore, the large signature of John Hancock on the Declaration of Independence was a statement of bravery by Hancock, who was declaring that he wanted everyone who saw the Declaration to know that he had signed it.

The original document was written on parchment, which is actually animal skin.

Even though we celebrate Independence Day on July 4th every year, the Declaration of Independence was not signed until August 2, 1776.

History of the Region

R Reading Skills

Explaining Make sure students can explain in their own words what they are reading. **Ask:** Why did people start moving inland, away from the Atlantic coast? *(Possible answers: to get away from crowded coastal areas, to build new lives, to claim land to farm, to look for gold and silver)* Verbal/Linguistic

W Writing Skills

Narrative Read the following to students: Imagine that you and your family headed inland during the early 1800s to claim land and start a new life. When you began your journey, you had great expectations for a better life, but along the way you encountered many hardships.

Have students write a journal entry about the day their family stopped traveling and set down roots in the land west of the Appalachians. Encourage students to use descriptive adjectives and vivid verbs to describe their feelings and emotions about what they had gone through in their travels and their reaction to their new "home." *(Students' journal entries will vary but should show an understanding of the physical geography of the area west of the Appalachian Mountains and the misfortunes often encountered by the early settlers heading west.)* Verbal/ Linguistic, Intrapersonal

Content Background Knowledge

Daniel Boone's father, Squire Boone, came from England. Daniel Boone was a wandering hunter and trapper. He was one of the earliest explorers of Kentucky and was the person who wanted to make it the 14th colony.

He spent two years making a trail, which was called the Wilderness Road, to help settlers who wanted to move into the territory of Kentucky.

He was not only an explorer. He also spent three terms serving in the Virginia legislature.

Settling the Land

GUIDING QUESTION *How has the movement of people shaped the culture of the eastern United States?*

The new nation officially stretched from the Atlantic Ocean to the Mississippi River. However, the land west of the Appalachian Mountains was a mystery to most Americans. The few explorers and settlers who traveled west brought back stories of a wild and dangerous land. Many people were afraid to venture into the West. Others were willing to take their chances to seek new opportunities.

As more European settlers arrived, towns along the Atlantic coast became crowded. People began moving inland, away from the crowded coastal areas, to build new lives. They wanted to claim land for themselves. Many settlers packed everything they owned into wagons and headed west. Some looked for gold or silver. Some hunted animals and sold or traded the animals' skins. Most of these settlers stopped traveling, however, when they found land that looked suitable for farming.

These settlers quickly built homes and planted crops on the land. They hoped to grow enough food to feed their families. Many families of settlers were isolated from other people. They had no neighbors, and they were hundreds of miles from the closest town. These people had to make or grow everything they needed. Like the Native Americans, the early settlers lived off the land.

Daniel Boone helps lead settlers through the Cumberland Gap. This well-traveled path for settlers moving west later became known as the Wilderness Road.
▶ **CRITICAL THINKING**
Analyzing Primary Sources Why would the journey west have been difficult for early settlers?

©Bettmann/Corbis

---

net**w**©rks   *Online Teaching Options*

SLIDE SHOW

Early Settlements

Comparing and Contrasting Display the slide show of various East Coast cities in different time periods. Have volunteers read the information contained in the slide show. Discuss with students how the cities have changed through the years. **BL** Visual/Spatial, Verbal/ Linguistic

See page 113D for other online activities.

Slide Show

© Ocean/Corbis; Kryssia Campos/Flickr RF/Getty Images; Erica Simone Leeds; © JG Photography/Alamy

---

ANSWER, p. 128

CRITICAL THINKING The land was mountainous and unsettled. Settlers had to take everything they might need with them. There were no stores or even paved roads. Traveling was slow and laborious.

New Territory

Between 1700 and 1800, thousands of settlers built homes along the Mississippi River. The Mississippi formed a natural boundary because it was wide, deep, and difficult to cross. When they arrived at the banks of the Mississippi, travelers either settled on the eastern side of the river or turned back. Those who did try to drive their horse-drawn wagons through the powerful river risked being swept away by its swift waters.

The young U.S. government wanted to claim as much of America's land as possible. The Land Ordinance of 1785 gave the United States legal claim to lands known as the Ohio Country. These lands were located north of the Ohio River and east of the Mississippi River. The Land Ordinance of 1785 allowed American settlers to buy sections of this land for one dollar per acre. The government divided up some land among settlers and also set aside land to be used for schools. Native Americans living on this land were forced to leave. The United States was slowly settling all territory east of the Mississippi River.

New Technology Changes Farming

Americans have been farming the land east of the Mississippi River for centuries. Much of our country's fruits, vegetables, grains, and cotton are raised on farms in this region. Growing crops and raising livestock to sell is called commercial **agriculture**. Good soil and frequent rains make the region one of the best places in the world for agriculture.

Until recently, planting and harvesting crops was hard work, performed mainly by hand and with the help of animals, such as horses and oxen. In the late 1700s, people designed and built new kinds of machines to do farmwork. Some machines planted large amounts of seeds quickly or harvested crops faster and more thoroughly than was possible by hand. For example, a Massachusetts man named Eli Whitney invented a machine called the cotton gin. The cotton gin made processing cotton faster and easier. This increased profits for cotton farmers.

Over the years, machines began to replace human workers on farms. With the help of machines, farmers planted and harvested more crops. This made farms more productive. As more and more farmwork was done with machines, however, fewer people were

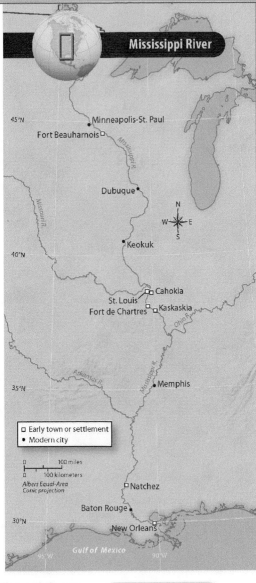

Mississippi River

- 45°N — Minneapolis-St. Paul
- Fort Beauharnois
- Dubuque
- 40°N — Keokuk
- Cahokia
- St. Louis — Kaskaskia
- Fort de Chartres
- 35°N — Memphis
- Natchez
- Baton Rouge
- 30°N — New Orleans
- Gulf of Mexico

☐ Early town or settlement
● Modern city

100 miles
100 kilometers
Albers Equal-Area Conic projection

MAP SKILLS

Throughout history, many cities and towns were built and grew along the Mississippi River.
▶ **CRITICAL THINKING**
Describing How does a river contribute to the growth of a city or town?

Chapter 4 **129**

R Reading Skills

Paraphrasing After reading about people settling on the east side of the Mississippi River, have students work with a partner to paraphrase what they learned. Remind students that they must use their own words when they paraphrase. Have partners share their paraphrases with others. (*Possible answer: People going west settled on the east side of the Mississippi River because the river was too difficult to cross or they turned around and went back east. The river's fast and powerful waters could sweep a horse-drawn wagon down river.*) **ELL** **AL** Verbal/Linguistic

T Technology Skills

Evaluating a Web Site Have small groups work together to evaluate a Web site that gives information about people who invented machines to improve farming methods, such as Eli Whitney, or about specific farm equipment, such as the tractor or the baler. Have students ask the following questions and use the worksheet for their evaluations: What is the site's purpose? What information is given? Is the information current? Who wrote or sponsored the site? Can I trust that the information is true? Is the site easy to navigate? Remind students that just because something is found on the Internet, it is not necessarily true. Have groups share their evaluations with the class. **ELL** Visual/Spatial, Logical/Mathematical

Content Background Knowledge

The Land Ordinance of 1785 not only provided for selling sections of land one-mile square or 640 acres at $1 per acre, but the federal government also surveyed the land to prevent boundary squabbles between landowners. Section sixteen in each township of 36 sections was to be used for public education. The government wanted to make education mandatory. Up until this time, only the New England states wanted all capable children to go to school. The Mid-Atlantic states focused on educating children for religious or political careers, and the Southern states educated children through apprenticeships. The Ordinance also set aside section twenty-nine for religious purposes. The government took the provision of separation of church and state in the Constitution very seriously.

MAP

Down the Mississippi River

Making Inferences Display the layer of the Chapter Opener map that reveals cities along the Mississippi River. As you move down the river, revealing the cities that developed around the water, have students discuss why they think human development often occurs along major waterways. Visual/Spatial, Verbal/Linguistic

See page 113D for other online activities.

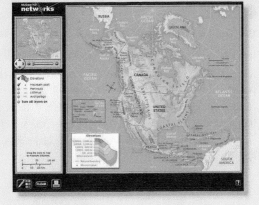

ANSWER, p. 129

CRITICAL THINKING Possible answer: A city or town's proximity to a river means more trade, visitors, ease of travel.

Explaining Discuss how the industry of the eastern United States encouraged more immigrants to come to America looking for jobs and opportunities. **Ask:** Why is industry an important part of the economy of the eastern United States? *(Students' answers will vary but should include an understanding of the consumer products that are produced in the region.)* **Verbal/Linguistic**

Making Connections Explain to students that many immigrants arrived in America with very little. They might have carried all their belongings in one small suitcase or worn all their clothing in layers as they made the journey to the United States because there was very little room on the ships to store possessions. The immigrants' reasons for coming to America were much more important to them than arriving with material possessions. Others were so poor that they had sold everything they had to pay for passage on the ship. **Ask:** If you had to move to another country and were only allowed to take one small suitcase filled with your belongings, including clothes, what would you pack and why? *(Students' answers will vary but should reflect the space constraints of small luggage.)* **Intrapersonal, Logical/Mathmatical**

Interpreting Visual Information Have students examine the picture of the immigrants arriving in America. After reading aloud the caption that goes with the picture, **ask:** How do you think these immigrants felt coming to a new place? What makes you say that? How would you feel if you had to move to a new country? *(Students' answers will vary but should reflect the emotions of the people in the picture and whether they think they would feel the same way or differently about immigrating to a new country.)* **Visual/Spatial**

Immigrants arrive in New York Harbor in the late 1800s.
▶ CRITICAL THINKING
Identifying State three reasons immigrants came to live in the United States.

needed to work on farms. This left thousands of people without work, and many moved to the cities. Today, most farmwork is done with the help of machines, such as tractors and combines.

Industrial Growth
New technology led to jobs in factories for millions of people. Manufacturing, making products to sell, is called **industry**.

Industry is an important part of the economy of the United States east of the Mississippi. This region has been one of the world's leading industrial regions for more than two centuries. Thousands of factories have been built all over the region during this time. Today, factories produce an endless variety of products including clothing, computer parts, shoes, baby formula, and medicines. Some factories process foods and bottled drinks. Cars are also built at automobile assembly plants. Products made east of the Mississippi River are shipped and sold all over the world.

Influence of Immigration
The history of the United States east of the Mississippi River is the history of many cultures. The cultures have become woven together over time, blending and changing into something new. Since the colonial days, people have been moving to the eastern United States from other countries. People immigrate to America because they want to be free. They also want jobs, education, and other opportunities. As a result, an amazing variety of languages, religions, cultures, and customs can be found east of the Mississippi. The cultural traditions brought by people from all over the world have made America a unique and diverse nation.

Forced Migration
In the 1830s, gold was discovered in the Southeast. Word quickly spread, and settlers poured into the southern states. Most did not find gold, but many stayed to start cotton farms in Alabama, Georgia, Mississippi, and the Carolinas. Some of these lands were home to the Cherokee, a large group of Native Americans. U.S. citizens wanted these lands—and their valuable resources.

Ingram Publishing

networks   *Online Teaching Options*

Writing Skills: Immigrating to America

Informative/Explanatory Have students research an immigrant group who migrated to America in the 1700s or 1800s. Use the worksheet to record what you learn about when the immigrants came to America, their reasons for coming, where in America most of them first settled, and customs and traditions the immigrants brought with them that have become part of American life. Then use your information to write a short essay about immigrants coming to America. **Verbal/Linguistic, Logical/Mathematical**

See page 113D for other online activities.

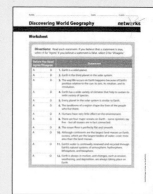

ANSWER, p. 130

CRITICAL THINKING freedom, jobs, education, land, search for gold (Student answers should include three of these.)

The government forced the Cherokee to leave their lands. In 1838 thousands of Cherokee men, women, and children were rounded up by U.S. soldiers. These people were forced to make the long and difficult journey to Indian Territory in Oklahoma, far west of the Mississippi River and 1,000 miles (1,609) from their homeland. The land they were given to live on was dry and difficult to farm, which was very different from the land they were forced to leave. Thousands of Cherokee died during and after the journey. This terrible event became known as the Trail of Tears.

The Trail of Tears was just one of many forced migrations in America's history. Native American groups all over the continent were forced to leave the lands that had shaped their ways of life for thousands of years. This movement destroyed some of their cultural traditions. As America gained territory, Native Americans lost their lands and their ways of life.

The Great Migration

The years after the Civil War were a time of change in the Southeast. Slavery became illegal in all states. Angry that slavery was outlawed, many states passed laws that took away the rights the freed Americans had recently gained. During the late 1800s, thousands of African Americans moved to states in the Mid-Atlantic, New England, and the Midwest. The relocation of people from the South to the North was called the Great Migration.

The Great Migration was part of the larger rural-to-urban migration occurring in the United States. This migration increased during the 1900s, when millions more people left rural areas and moved to cities to work in factories. This rural-to-urban movement of people is one of the largest migrations in America's history.

FOLDABLES
Study Organizer

Include this lesson's information in your Foldable®.

☑ **READING PROGRESS CHECK**

Analyzing How did the invention of farm machinery lead to unemployment in the eastern United States?

LESSON 2 REVIEW

Reviewing Vocabulary

1. What makes the United States east of the Mississippi River a good region for *agriculture*?

Answering the Guiding Questions

2. *Determining Central Ideas* How did the early Native American peoples utilize resources from their environment?

3. *Identifying Point of View* What are reasons why English rulers sent colonists to America in the 1600s?

4. *Analyzing* What factors helped the U.S. economy change and grow?

5. *Identifying Point of View* How did laws ending slavery affect different populations of people in the Southeast after the Civil War?

6. *Narrative Writing* Imagine you are a young Native American living in the 1800s. Your family is being forced to leave its home as colonists take over the land. Write a narrative telling how you feel about what is happening to you and your people. Include details from the lesson in your narrative.

Chapter 4 **131**

C Critical Thinking Skills

Reasoning The Cherokee Nation was forced to leave their lands in the eastern United States and move to lands west of the Mississippi River in what is now Oklahoma because the U.S. government wanted the lands that the Cherokee people lived on along with the valuable resources on the lands. **Ask:** Was the United States government justified in making the Cherokee people move? Explain your reasoning. What might be a good reason for a government to force people to make a permanent move? *(Student's answers will vary but should demonstrate an understanding of the forced migration of the Cherokees.)* **Verbal/Linguistic, Logical/ Mathematical**

T Technology Skills

Have students research how slavery became illegal in all of the states and territories of the United States after the Civil War. Remind students to use reliable resources in their research and to include a list of their sources in their notes.

Then have students present their findings in a five-minute oral presentation or in a written essay. *(Presentations and essays should include information about President Abraham Lincoln's Emancipation Proclamation and the Union's success over the Southern states that forced the southern states to follow the Emancipation Proclamation.)* **Verbal/Linguistic**

CLOSE & REFLECT

Making Connections To close this lesson, have students think about something that they have learned in this lesson that helps them understand the diversity and history of the subregions in the eastern United States. Ask students to think about how this knowledge might change their views of American history that they had learned prior to reading this chapter.

LESSON 2 REVIEW ANSWERS

Reviewing Vocabulary

1. The eastern United States has good soil and frequent rains, which is good for agricultural crops.

Answering the Guiding Questions

2. **Determining Central Ideas** Responses should mention: Native people got everything they needed from the natural resources where they lived; their environments shaped they way they lived, such as the foods they ate and the types of houses they lived in.

3. **Identifying Point of View** to control the land and its natural resources

4. **Analyzing** New technology and machinery improved agricultural productivity. New technology also led to improvements in manufacturing and other

industries. Industrialization needs workers. Many people left farms to find work in the cities. Many immigrants came to the United States and worked in industry.

5. **Identifying Point of View** After slavery was abolished, freed African Americans were targeted by unfair laws and threats of harm. Many African Americans left the Southeast and migrated north. As thousands of African Americans left southern states, the population of the Southeast decreased.

6. **Narrative Writing** Responses should be written from the perspective of a Native American person. Narratives should describe the narrator's personal feelings about forced relocation and the actions of the colonists.

ANSWER, p. 131

☑ READING PROGRESS CHECK New machinery was faster and more efficient than humans and produced larger crops and larger profits for farmers. With machines doing so much of the work, many farmworkers were no longer needed and lost their jobs.

ENGAGE

Bellringer Before students begin the lesson, ask them to think about a big city that they know. It may be a city they have visited or read about or even one they have lived in previously or presently live in. **Ask:** What is special or unique about this big city? *(Students' answers will vary but should include details such as city attractions, area, climate, ethnic neighborhoods and restaurants, and physical features of its location.)* Then have students make a connection between their answers and the Essential Question: *What makes a culture unique?*

TEACH & ASSESS

R Reading Skills

Determine Word Meanings Have students locate the word *megalopolis* in the text. Explain that knowing the meanings of word parts can help readers figure out the meanings of unfamiliar words. Guide students to identify the prefix *mega,* meaning "large," and the Greek root *poli,* meaning "city." Have them use the meaning of the word parts to figure out the meaning of the word: "a very large, heavily populated urban area." Ask them to name other words that they know that contain the same prefix or root. *(Possible answers: megabuck, megabyte, megaphone; metropolitan, metropolis, cosmopolitan, police, political)* Verbal/Linguistic

T Technology Skills

Researching on the Internet/Making a Chart Have students conduct research to find out what the actual populations are for New York, Boston, Philadelphia, and Miami today. Direct students to the latest census of these cities by the United States government. Then have students put the population information of these large cities in a chart in ascending order. Visual/Spatial

---

ANSWER, p. 132

Taking Notes Students' sentences may vary, but answers include: **Metropolitan areas:** Metropolitan areas are centers of culture, education, business, and recreation; Tourism is an important industry.
U.S. Government: The Constitution establishes three branches (legislative, executive, judicial) of the U.S. government. The Constitution separates the powers of government so that no one person or part of government has all the power; Government actions have had good and bad effects on people and the environment.
Economy: Manufacturing industries have been in decline. Service industries are providing more and more jobs.

---

netw⦿rks

There's More Online!

☑ **IMAGE** Festivals
☑ **ANIMATION** Role of Government
☑ **VIDEO**

Reading **HELP**DESK

Academic Vocabulary

- **revenue**

Content Vocabulary

- **metropolitan area**
- **tourism**
- **civil rights**
- **Rust Belt**
- **service industry**

TAKING NOTES: *Key Ideas and Details*

Organize As you read about life in the eastern United States, write a one-sentence summary for each of the listed topics.

Topic	Summary Sentence
Metropolitan areas	
U.S. government	
Economy	

Indiana Academic Standards
6.1.20, 6.1.21, 6.2.1, 6.2.5, 6.2.6, 6.3.1, 6.3.4, 6.3.10

Lesson 3
Life in the Region

ESSENTIAL QUESTION • *What makes a culture unique?*

IT MATTERS BECAUSE

Learning about the human geography of the United States—its people, government, economy, and culture—can help you better understand and appreciate the nation as a whole.

Major Metropolitan Areas

GUIDING QUESTION *What is it like to live in a large metropolitan area in the eastern United States?*

People in the United States live in many different environments. Farmers and ranchers live in rural areas with open land for farming and livestock. Suburbs are popular places for people who want larger homes and their own pieces of property. People who enjoy urban environments often live in large cities called **metropolitan areas**. Metropolitan areas are centers of culture, education, business, and recreation. Large cities such as New York, Boston, Philadelphia, and Miami are home to millions. The populations of metropolitan areas in the eastern United States are large and diverse. The Boston-Washington corridor is a metropolitan area, home to about 50 million people. It is often referred to as a megalopolis.

(l to r) Randy Wells/Stone/Getty Images; Enzo Figueres/Flickr/Getty Images; Richard Freeda/Aurora/Getty Images; ©Nik Wheeler/Corbis; (b) Enzo Figueres/Flickr/Getty Images

132

---

netw⦿rks *Online Teaching Options*

VIDEO

Cleaning Up Tampa's Rivers: The Green Armada

Narrative Use this video about this group cleaning up rivers in Tampa to introduce the lesson about challenges and issues in the eastern United States. Have students write a paragraph about one aspect of the video that was interesting to them. Make sure that students give a reason as to why that aspect was interesting. Visual/Spatial, Verbal/Linguistic

See page 113E for other online activities.

BBC Motion Gallery Education

Some metropolitan areas serve as hubs for international cooperation. The member countries of the United Nations (UN), located in New York City, work together to find and share solutions to problems related to education, science, and culture. For example, the UN's World Heritage program promotes and protects natural and cultural sites around the world. World Heritage sites in the eastern United States include the Everglades National Park in Florida and the Statue of Liberty in New York Harbor.

Tourism is one industry that provides jobs to people in and around metropolitan areas. The **tourism** business provides services to people who are traveling for enjoyment. Businesses such as restaurants, hotels, resorts, travel agencies, and tour companies are part of the tourism industry. The money tourists spend brings **revenue** to the state and local economies.

Academic Vocabulary

revenue income generated by a business

Some metropolitan areas on the East Coast began as port cities along the shores of the Atlantic Ocean. Port cities are large, busy towns where ships dock and depart. Trade between the United States and the rest of the world began in port cities such as Baltimore; Boston; Charleston, South Carolina; New Haven, Connecticut; and New York.

New York and Chicago

New York and Chicago are two of the largest metropolitan areas east of the Mississippi River. New York City, located on the Atlantic coast at the mouth of the Hudson River, is the most populous city in the United States. This famously diverse city is home to more than 9 million people, making it one of the most heavily populated cities in the world. New York began as a Dutch colonial port city called New Amsterdam. Although it is better known today as a hub of culture and commerce, New York is still home to one of the busiest ports in North America.

New York City is a dense cluster of urban areas, called boroughs, connected by streets, bridges, trains, and water passages. The five boroughs that make up the city are Manhattan, Brooklyn, Queens, the Bronx, and Staten Island. Though it is the smallest of the five boroughs, covering an area of only 22.6 square miles (58.5 sq. km), the island of Manhattan is the cultural, political, and economic center of New York City.

New York City is the most populous city in the United States.
▶ **CRITICAL THINKING**
Determining Central Ideas What are some of the advantages of living in a large city? What are some disadvantages?

See page 113E for other online activities.

GRAPHIC ORGANIZER

Where People Live

Organizing Use the interactive graphic organizer to show information about rural, suburban, and metropolitan areas, listing types of housing, kinds of work available, and environmental features for each area. Have students compare and contrast the human geography of the areas. Visual/Spatial, Verbal/Linguistic

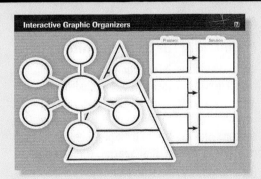

Interactive Graphic Organizers

C Critical Thinking Skills

Making Inferences Discuss with students their prior experiences with people who helped their families while they were traveling. Encourage them to share positive experiences with helpful people at hotels, restaurants, museums, and so forth, as well as negative experiences with these people. **Ask:** What kind of skills do you think someone who works in the tourism industry should have? Explain. *(Students' answers will vary but should include an understanding of the importance of being able to work with and communicate with people.)* Verbal/Linguistic, Logical/Mathematical

V Visual Skills

Reading a Map Display a map of New York City and guide students to identify its five boroughs. Point out where the 9/11 Memorial is located in lower Manhattan. Explain that the 9/11 Memorial is a national tribute of remembrance and honor to the men, women, and children killed in the terror attacks of September 11, 2001 and February 26, 1993. It is a tribute to the past and a place of hope for the future. Visual/Spatial

Content Background Knowledge

On February 26, 1993, the World Trade Center was attacked for the first time. Terrorists detonated 1,500 pounds of explosives in a van parked in an underground parking lot of the towers. Six people were killed and more than a thousand injured. The explosion created a five-story crater beneath the towers.

On September 11, 2001, terrorists hijacked four commercial United States jets. They deliberately crashed two of the planes into the Twin Towers of the World Trade Center and one plane into the Pentagon in Arlington County, Virginia. A fourth hijacked airplane crashed into an empty field in western Pennsylvania after the passengers and crew attempted to overtake the terrorists. In all, almost 3,000 people were killed.

ANSWER, p. 133

CRITICAL THINKING **Advantages:** jobs, education, cultural opportunities; **Disadvantages:** pollution, crowdedness, traffic congestion.

C Critical Thinking Skills

Evaluating Discuss with students why cities are important in the middle of a large country, as well as on the edges or coasts of a country like the United States. Make sure students understand that these central cities are often transportation centers with large airports and train stations. **Ask:** Why is Chicago an important metropolitan area? *(Students' answers will vary but should include relevant details about its location, waterways, transportation systems, and manufacturing industries.)* Verbal/Linguistic

V Visual Skills

Reading a Map Display a political map of the United States, or have students use the Reference Atlas map of the United States in the front of their student editions. Have students locate the cities of Atlanta and New Orleans and discuss the subregion in which they are located. **Ask:** Why is this area referred to as the Southeast? *(Students' answers should make reference to direction using the compass rose and note that the area is the southeast section of the 48 contiguous United States.)* Visual/Spatial, Logical/Mathematical

W Writing Skills

Informative/Explanatory Have students research both educational and fun things to do in one of the cities of Chicago, Atlanta, or New Orleans and make travel brochures explaining why people should visit there and the kinds of attractions that would make them want to visit the city.

Have students include hand-drawn pictures and/or photographs in their brochures. Remind students to include the sources for photographs as well as the text that they use in their brochure. Invite interested students to share their brochures with the class, or post them on a classroom bulletin board for others to read. *(Students can include human-made things such as art museums, historical and science museums, planetariums, zoos, sports stadiums, and amusement parks as well as physical features such as Lake Michigan in Chicago.)* BL Verbal/Linguistic, Visual/Spatial

---

Thinking Like a Geographer

Population Centers

Geographers study why certain cities became places where many people live. Many population centers in the United States lie in coastal areas where healthy economies support large populations. Some cities are important world trade centers because of their coastal or near-coastal locations. Some population centers are located inland, yet many are situated near rivers and lakes. Other inland cities such as Atlanta grew from agricultural and trading centers.

Manhattan is home to people of every racial, ethnic, and religious background in the world. It is also known worldwide as a center of finance, advertising, and entertainment. An endless variety of visual and performing arts—such as music, dance, drama, painting, sculpture, fashion, and architecture—bring the city to life.

More than 30 million tourists visit New York City each year. The city has an extensive public transportation system that includes subways and buses to help eliminate dependency on cars.

Chicago began as a small settlement between Lake Michigan and the Mississippi River in the early 1800s. The settlement developed into a thriving city after it was connected to the rest of the country by railroads and canals. By the mid-1800s, Chicago had become the center of all railroad travel in the United States. Chicago's importance as a transportation center increased when the St. Lawrence Seaway opened in the mid-1900s. Today, an elevated train system in the center of Chicago helps move its many tourists and residents.

Chicago remains one of the nation's most important centers of shipping, transportation, and industry. The city is one of America's leading producers of steel, machinery, and manufactured products. Several large printing and publishing companies are located in Chicago, as well as major financial institutions such as the Chicago Stock Exchange. **C**

Atlanta and New Orleans

Atlanta and New Orleans are two of the most vibrant cities in the Southeast. Serving as Georgia's capital city, Atlanta is a historic city and a modern metropolis. Its location at the southern edge of the Appalachian Mountain range made it a popular passageway for settlers and other travelers. As railroads brought people and cargoes through the area, Atlanta grew into a thriving economic, cultural, and political center of the South. **V**

During the Civil War, Atlanta served as a supply depot for the Confederate army. Most of the city's buildings were burned to the ground during a devastating invasion by the Union army in 1864. When Atlanta was rebuilt after the war, it became a symbol of strength and rebirth in the South.

Today, Atlanta is a strong center of transportation, industry, trade, education, and culture. It has been called the commercial center of the modern South. A wide array of industries, including publishing, telecommunications, banking, insurance, military supply, and manufacturing, have headquarters in Atlanta. The city's major factories produce electrical equipment, chemicals, packaged foods, paper products, and aircraft.

New Orleans began as a shipping town along the Mississippi River. During times of peace, New Orleans was an important center of transportation and trade. In times of war, such as during the Revolutionary War, the War of 1812, and the Civil War, New Orleans **W**

134 Chapter 4

---

networks   Online Teaching Options

MAP

Population: The Eastern United States

Integrating Visual Information Display the population layer of the Chapter Opener map. Have students locate the major cities of New York, Chicago, Atlanta, and New Orleans. Then have them use information about the cities' locations and population to infer why these places became major metropolitan areas. Visual/Spatial, Verbal/Linguistic

See page 113E for other online activities.

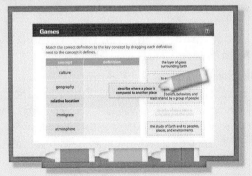

Randy Wells/Stone/Getty Images

Millions visit the city of New Orleans every year to take part in the festivities of Mardi Gras.
▶ **CRITICAL THINKING**
Identifying Besides Mardi Gras, what attractions draw tourists to New Orleans?

became a major stop along supply lines that served the military and civilians. Located only 110 miles (177 km) from the Gulf of Mexico, New Orleans eventually was connected to the Gulf by river channels, making it easier for ships to enter and leave the city.

R In 2005, Hurricane Katrina struck the Gulf of Mexico's coast. The storm raged from Louisiana to Florida. In New Orleans, levees failed when the storm surged, flooding low-lying areas and trapping many people. Thousands of people were left homeless and many people died. Hurricane Katrina was one of the worst natural disasters in U.S. history. Some neighborhoods and areas of New Orleans have been rebuilt. Other areas have not recovered.

New Orleans remains an important commercial trade center in the eastern United States. Manufacturing and transportation still contribute to the city's economy. New Orleans is renowned for its rich cultural traditions including its spicy Cajun and Creole foods, original musical styles, and colorful celebrations such as Mardi Gras. New Orleans was one of the first centers of jazz music. The city and its people, art, music, language, and architecture are a bold and unique mixture of French, Spanish, Caribbean, and African cultures. Tourism has long been vital to the economy of New Orleans.

New York, Chicago, Atlanta, and New Orleans each have a unique character. These remarkable cities are just a few of the places that make the eastern United States such a fascinating region.

☑ **READING PROGRESS CHECK**

Citing Text Evidence How are New York and New Orleans alike? How are they different?

Chapter 4 **135**

T **Technology Skills**

Making Presentations Have students work in small groups to give multimedia presentations on one aspect of the unique culture of New Orleans, such as Creole cuisine, jazz, jazz funerals, or the language of New Orleans. After brainstorming and narrowing one of these topics to manageable size, have students use the Internet for research. Make sure students use reliable sources and include a list of their sources.

Then have each group divide the information so that each member of the group has the chance to learn how to use a presentation software program and other visual aids to present their findings to the class. **Visual/Spatial, Verbal/Linguistic**

R **Reading Skills**

Summarizing Explain to students that combining main ideas and details into a succinct summary is an important reading skill that will benefit them throughout middle and high school. A summary should include the central idea of a paragraph or section of text along with the most important supporting details. **Ask:** How would you summarize the paragraph on "Hurricane Katrina"? *(Sample answer: The hurricane was a horrible natural disaster. It devastated many areas and caused thousands of people to have no place to live.)* **AL** **Verbal/Linguistic**

C **Critical Thinking Skills**

Drawing Conclusions Explain to students that one of the reasons why Hurricane Katrina caused so much damage to New Orleans was because of the levees breaking and ensuing flood of waters. **Ask:** How might the damage to New Orleans have been prevented? *(Answers may vary but should include examples such as having the government hire workers to build, reinforce, and maintain critical infrastructure such as the levees in New Orleans to prevent such disasters.)*

GAME

Drag-and-Drop Game: Major Cities

Discussing Display the Drag-and-Drop game on the Interactive Whiteboard. Have students take turns dragging and dropping the names of major cities into their proper locations on the map. Have students discuss the unique aspects of each city. **Kinesthetic, Verbal/Linguistic**

See page 113E for other online activities.

ANSWERS, p. 135

CRITICAL THINKING The city is known for its cultural traditions, special foods, original music styles, and its unique mixture of French, Spanish, Caribbean, and African culture.
☑ **READING PROGRESS CHECK** **Alike:** both cities are important centers of transportation and trade; both have diverse cultural backgrounds; both are known for their unique cultures; both attract many tourists; **Different:** New York is larger and is located on the East Coast, while New Orleans is located in the Southeast near the Mississippi River and the Gulf of Mexico; New York is famous for its skyscrapers; New Orleans is famous for its spicy food, original music, and celebrations such as Mardi Gras.

Life in the Region

C Critical Thinking Skills

Theorizing Explain to students that one of the major benefits to living in a free country such as the United States is that ordinary citizens such as themselves can be critical of the government without fear of reprisal. Encourage students to consider whether the three branches of the United States government form a good structure for government or if they could come up with a better system. **Ask:** What might be a disadvantage of having a government in which power is shared equally among three branches? *(Possible answers: When branches disagree decisions may not be made; one branch can undo what another branch has done.)* Verbal/Linguistic

W Writing Skills

Informative/Explanatory After reading about the three branches of government, have students make a chart detailing these branches of government. The heads should be: *Legislative Branch, Executive Branch,* and *Judicial Branch.* The rows should be: *Who Is the Leader?* and *What Do They Do?.* Then have students use their charts to write an informative paragraph about one of the three branches of government. Have partners exchange paragraphs and make constructive criticisms on how each other's writing could be more clear or more detailed. Verbal/Linguistic, Visual/Spatial

Content Background Knowledge

The first ten amendments to the Constitution, added in 1791, are known as the Bill of Rights. They give individuals specific rights that cannot be taken away by the government. Included in these ten amendments are the rights of freedom of religion, speech, and the press; the right to bear arms; protection against unreasonable search and seizures; and the rights to a speedy and public trial, having a jury trial, and not being forced to testify against yourself.

Discuss why the Bill of Rights is important to every citizen, and why or why not similar rights should be given to all people of the world.

Thinking Like a Geographer

The Nation's Capital

The planned city of Washington, D.C., is the capital of the United States. Washington, D.C., is located along the banks of the Potomac River between the states of Virginia and Maryland. These two states gave land to the government to form the federal District of Columbia. Thus, the District was free of any single state's influence. Why was the capital located in the eastern United States near the Atlantic Coast?

The U.S. Government

GUIDING QUESTION *How have the government's actions affected the land and people of the United States?*

The United States declared its independence from Great Britain on July 4, 1776. On that day, Americans became citizens of a free and independent nation. Like all nations, the new country needed a system of government. It was important to Americans that their government protect the rights and freedoms of the people. The U.S. government was designed as a representative democracy, a system in which the people elect representatives to operate the government.

In 1787 representatives from each of the 13 states gathered to write a plan of government called a constitution. The U.S. Constitution is still the law of our country. The United States is a federal republic. The national government shares power with the states. Government leaders must promise to obey the Constitution. Amendments, or changes to the Constitution, have been made to meet the nation's changing needs. The first 10 amendments—the Bill of Rights—guarantee the basic rights of citizens.

The Three Branches of Government

C One of the main functions of the U.S. Constitution is to make sure government power is shared. The men who wrote the Constitution did not want a single person or group to have all the power to make laws and decisions for the country. They divided the government into three separate but equal branches. Each branch has important functions, and each branch must work with the other two branches to govern the country. The three parts of the U.S. government are the executive, legislative, and judicial branches. The U.S. government's system of shared power was created to ensure that all parts of the government work together in a balance of power.

The legislative branch, called Congress, makes laws for the nation. Congress has two parts: the House of Representatives and the Senate. Members of Congress are elected by the people and come from all 50 states. To pass a law, the House of Representatives and the Senate must agree on what the law states.

The executive branch is the office of the president of the United States. The president's main duties are to carry out laws, to lead the military, to appoint judges to the Supreme Court, to plan the national budget, to meet with foreign leaders, and to appoint advisors to help make decisions for the nation.

W The judicial branch is made up of state and federal courts. The role of the government's judicial branch is to decide if laws are fair and if they follow the Constitution. The Supreme Court, with nine judges called justices, is the most powerful court in America.

136 *Chapter 4*

---

networks   *Online Teaching Options*

LECTURE SLIDE

Understanding the U.S. Government's Role in Infrastructure

Informative/Explanatory After students review the lecture slide on government actions affecting the nation's infrastructure, lead a discussion about similar projects in your community that are likely funded by the government. Identify how these projects benefit area residents and others not living in the community. Once students have had a chance to contribute their ideas, have them write a brief paragraph about how they personally have benefitted from one of the projects identified. Verbal/Linguistic

See page 113E for other online activities.

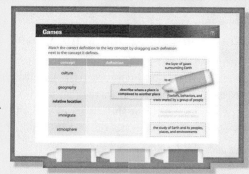

ANSWER, p. 136

THINKING LIKE A GEOGRAPHER

When the nation was formed, the United States consisted of states in the eastern part of the country only.

Government Actions Affect the Land

The three branches of the U.S. government make laws and decisions that affect our nation's land. Some laws and decisions protect the environment. For example, the president has the authority to set aside land for use as national parks. This protects plant and animal habitats and creates recreational areas. Local governments enforce laws that reduce water pollution and littering.

Another environmental program is Superfund. The purpose of the program is to clean up abandoned hazardous waste sites. Superfund was implemented after the discovery of toxic waste sites such as Love Canal and Times Beach in the 1970s. The federal government works in conjunction with the state government and the communities to implement cleanup plans.

Government Actions Affect People

Some actions of the United States government that affected Native American peoples had severe consequences. Other government actions—such as building roads and bridges, providing aid to people in need, and establishing national parks—help people and enrich our lives.

One example of how government actions have affected Americans positively is the civil rights movement. **Civil rights** are basic rights that belong to all citizens, such as the right to be treated equally under the law. To answer the demand for civil rights for African Americans, the federal government made laws ending segregation. These laws were meant to help people. Some local governments, however, did not agree with these laws and refused to enforce them.

Another example of positive action is how the government helps people during emergencies. Government agencies such as the Federal Emergency Management Agency (FEMA) provide food, water, medical care, and transportation to people affected by tornadoes, hurricanes, earthquakes, floods, terrorist attacks, and other disasters. FEMA has saved many lives, but some people claim the agency does too little to help and is slow to respond.

When thinking about how government actions affect people and the land, it is important to remember that no government is perfect. The U.S. government is made up of many different people doing many different jobs.

✓ **READING PROGRESS CHECK**

Determining Central Ideas Why is the U.S. government divided into three branches?

National parks, such as Maine's Acadia National Park, are pieces of land that are protected by the federal government.
▶ **CRITICAL THINKING**
Describing What are the purposes of national parks?

Richard Freeda/Aurora/Getty Images

C₁ Critical Thinking Skills

Drawing Conclusions Explain to students that one of the questions that political parties debate is the amount of laws and regulations the United States government should be able to impose on individuals, companies, and states. **Ask:** Do you think the United States government should have policies that let people or some companies pollute or destroy the environment? Explain. *(Students' answers will vary but should include an understanding of how government and private interests affect legislation.)* Verbal/Linguistic

C₂ Critical Thinking Skills

Making Connections Tell students that *segregation* means "the forced separation or isolation of a race, class, or ethnic group." This forced separation may restrict people to certain areas, prevent people from socializing with others of a different race, class, or ethnic group, establish separate schools, or discriminate by other means. **Ask:**

- How would you feel if you were not allowed to be friends with someone? *(Students' answers will vary but should demonstrate an understanding of segregation.)*
- What do you think about local governments not enforcing national laws? Do you feel local governments have that right? Explain. *(Students' answers will vary but should include relevant reasons to support their ideas.)* Intrapersonal, Logical/Mathematical

T Technology Skills

Research Place students in small groups. Have each group research a different Civil Rights Activist on the Internet. Make sure students explain how their person helped the Civil Rights movement of the 1950s and 1960s in the United States and whether the person used a non-violent approach or not. Have each group present their findings to the class. Verbal/Linguistic

---

WORKSHEET

Primary Sources: National Parks

Researching on the Internet President Theodore Roosevelt enacted a law to protect landmarks, structures, and objects of historic or scientific interest by designating them as national monuments. Using the worksheet as a guide, have students find two sources to answer each of the following questions: 1) What is the name of the law that gave presidents the power to designate sites as national monuments? *(Antiquities Act of 1906);* 2) What was the first national park and when was it established? *(Yellowstone National Park, 1872)*

ELL Verbal/Linguistic, Naturalist

See page 113E for other online activities.

ANSWERS, p. 137

CRITICAL THINKING to protect plants and animals, and create places for recreation

✓ READING PROGRESS CHECK The Constitution outlines a three-part government to prevent any one person or group from having all of the authority to make laws and decisions; the three branches of government work together in a balance of power.

Creating Visuals Have students use a word-processing or spreadsheet program to create a chart or graph (circle, line, or bar) to display the United States census information about the classification of the American population.

Have students present their graphs to the class. If students have used different types of graphs, have them discuss how each graph displays the information differently and which type of graph works best for displaying this type of information. **ELL**
AL Visual/Spatial

C Critical Thinking Skills

Problem-Solving Explain to students that many people in the United States have lost their jobs because U.S. companies have outsourced their production of goods to foreign countries. The companies claim that it is cheaper to produce their products overseas and that this savings is then passed on to the U.S. consumer, who benefits from the opportunity to buy cheaper goods.

Explain that there is a movement in our country to buy products "Made in America." **Ask:** How do you feel about buying a product made overseas? How do you think jobs could be brought back to American soil? How would this help the economy? *(Students' answers will vary but should reflect an understanding of the economic principle of supply and demand.)* Verbal/Linguistic, Logical/Mathematical

V Visual Skills

Reading a Graph Have students study the bar graph at the bottom of the page and write three questions about how the percentages of the population have changed in the last 30 to 40 years in the United States. Tell students to write the answers to their questions on a separate piece of paper and exchange their questions with a partner. Next have students use the bar graph to answer their partner's questions, and then to check each other's answers. Have partners discuss any discrepancies they have in the answers to their questions. Logical/Mathematical

---

ANSWERS, p. 138

GRAPH SKILLS
CRITICAL THINKING
1. Hispanics and Asian Americans
2. Caucasians

Everyday Life

GUIDING QUESTION *How has diversity shaped the culture of the United States?*

Religion and Ethnicity
In the United States, the religion with the largest number of followers is Christianity. The influence of the Christian faith in the United States has continued since colonial times. However, many Americans practice the Jewish, Muslim, Buddhist, or Hindu faith. Research shows that 16 percent of Americans do not participate in organized religion. Nearly half of all American adults say they have changed their faiths or beliefs at least once in their lives.

T In gathering population statistics, the Census Bureau classifies the people of the United States into several different categories. The most recent data collected from the 2010 Census show that the four most populous ethnic groups are Caucasian, Latino, African American, and Asian American. In the last two censuses, people of Hispanic or Latin-American origin comprised the second largest ethnic group after Caucasians. In the Census of 1990, African Americans made up the second most-populous group.

Economy
C America has one of the largest and strongest economies in the world. Advancements in technology help keep industries such as farming and manufacturing productive. The U.S. economy has slowed in the past decade, however. Many Americans remain unemployed. It could take years for the economy and employment rate to rebound.

Agriculture has long been an important industry. Today, the businesses of farming and raising animals for food are changing. Farms owned and operated by families are being replaced by corporate farms. They are managed by people who do not own or live on the land. Some Americans believe the growth of corporate farms is bad for the economy and the nation's people. They believe corporate farms agree to sell crops to large grocery-store chains at

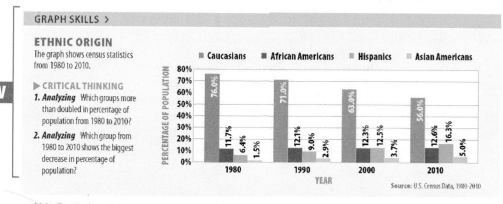

V

GRAPH SKILLS >

ETHNIC ORIGIN
The graph shows census statistics from 1980 to 2010.

► CRITICAL THINKING
1. *Analyzing* Which groups more than doubled in percentage of population from 1980 to 2010?
2. *Analyzing* Which group from 1980 to 2010 shows the biggest decrease in percentage of population?

■ Caucasians   ■ African Americans   ■ Hispanics   ■ Asian Americans

Caucasians: 1980 76.0%, 1990 71.0%, 2000 63.0%, 2010 56.0%
African Americans: 1980 11.7%, 1990 12.1%, 2000 12.3%, 2010 12.6%
Hispanics: 1980 6.4%, 1990 9.0%, 2000 12.5%, 2010 16.3%
Asian Americans: 1980 1.5%, 1990 2.9%, 2000 3.7%, 2010 5.0%

PERCENTAGE OF POPULATION / YEAR

Source: U.S. Census Data, 1980-2010

138 *Chapter 4*

---

netw⊕rks   *Online Teaching Options*

CHART

The Growth of the Economy
Interpreting Display the chart about the growth of the United States economy. Have students use the information on the chart to discuss the growth of America and the changes in farming, industry, and services from 1800 to the present. Have them write two or three sentences telling which change they think had the most impact on the economy of the United States. Visual/Spatial, Verbal/Linguistic

See page 113E for other online activities.

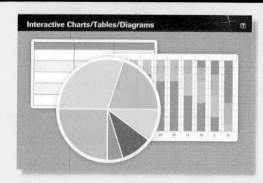

Interactive Charts/Tables/Diagrams

such low prices that family farms can not compete. A growing number of Americans now support organic farming. Organic farms use only natural pesticides and fertilizers. Some people believe that organically-grown foods are safer and healthier than foods that have been treated with chemicals.

In the late 1800s and early 1900s, the U.S. shifted away from an agricultural-based economy to a more industrial economy. Factories producing automobiles, appliances, machinery, electronics, and other items have employed millions of Americans. During the 1980s, however, the manufacturing industry began to weaken. Businesses closed, and factories were abandoned. Workers lost their jobs. So many factories closed across the Midwest, the Mid-Atlantic, and New England that these areas earned the nickname "the **Rust Belt**."

In recent years, more Americans have found jobs in service industries. **Service industries** are businesses that provide services rather than products. Child care centers, restaurants, grocery stores, hair salons, electricians, moving companies, and auto repair shops are some examples of service industries. Other industries such as finance, insurance, and education still provide many jobs and revenue today. Many businesses, including banks and insurance companies, are located in cities east of the Mississippi River.

Different types of industries are important to the economy of the eastern U. S. Today, another shift is taking place as the nation moves from a service-based economy to an economy that is connected to the computer-information age.

☑ **READING PROGRESS CHECK**

Citing Text Evidence What is the main difference between service industries and manufacturing industries?

Every March, Cuban Americans in Miami celebrate Calle Ocho, the single largest Latino celebration in the United States.

▶ **CRITICAL THINKING**
Analyzing Why are ethnic celebrations important for the community as well as for the people?

C

FOLDABLES
Study Organizer

Include this lesson's information in your Foldable®.

C Critical Thinking Skills

Making Inferences Explain that students often need to apply their background knowledge and experince to information in the text to make inferences about material that is not stated specifically in the text. **Ask:**

- Why might many jobs in the service industries never be replaced by computers? Give a job example. *(Students' answers will vary but should demonstrate an understanding of the importance of human-to-human contact in areas such as teachers, financial advisors, doctors, police officers, and so on.)*

- What jobs in the service industries have already been replaced by computers? *(Possible answers: automated tellers in banks have replaced some tellers, online ordering of products have replaced salespeople, self-check outs at grocery stores have replaced clerks)* **Verbal/Linguistic, Logical/ Mathematical**

Making Connections Discuss with students whether any of their family members work in the service industries. Encourage students to talk with adult family members about the types of jobs they have or had before retiring, and how the adult family members felt about their work and its impact on others. **Ask:** What connections can you make between the experiences of your family members and the text? *(Students' answers will vary but should demonstrate an understanding of the kinds of jobs their family has had and the kinds of occupations discussed in the text.)*

CLOSE & REFLECT

Making Connections To close this lesson, have students think about what makes their own culture unique. Ask them to think about how their culture is the same as and different from other parts of the nation. Have them suggest ways their culture contributes to the United States economy through food, festivals, common occupations, and so forth.

LESSON 3 REVIEW

Reviewing Vocabulary
1. What are the names of the major *metropolitan* areas located in your state?

Answering the Guiding Questions
2. ***Integrating Visual Information*** What are some of the largest metropolitan areas located in the eastern United States?
3. ***Determining Central Ideas*** How have the government's actions affected the land and people of the United States?

4. ***Determining Central Ideas*** How have cultures from other parts of the world shaped the culture and character of the United States?
5. ***Citing Text Evidence*** What types of businesses and industries are important to the economy of the eastern United States today?
6. ***Informative/Explanatory Writing*** Write a paragraph explaining how tourism might affect the economy of a major metropolitan area.

Chapter 4 **139**

LESSON 3 REVIEW ANSWERS

Reviewing Vocabulary

1. Students' answers should be the names of large cities within the state.

Answering the Guiding Questions

2. **Integrating Visual Information** Answers should include New York City, Boston, Atlanta, and New Orleans, but may mention other major cities located east of the Mississippi River.

3. **Determining Central Ideas** Answers will vary but should summarize the section on government actions. Government actions have both helped and harmed America's people and land. Helpful government actions include aid after disaster, building roads and bridges, establishing national parks, and enacting fair laws. Harmful actions include policies that allow the destruction of the environment and decisions to involve Americans in foreign wars.

4. **Determining Central Ideas** The cultures brought to America by immigrants have combined to become a new, original culture that is uniquely American.

5. **Citing Text Evidence** manufacturing, farming, service industries, and businesses such as education, finance, and insurance companies

6. **Informative/Explanatory Writing** Responses should demonstrate an understanding of the contributions of the tourist industry and mention job creation and increased revenue for businesses such as restaurants, hotels, tour companies, airlines, travel agencies, and amusement parks.

ANSWERS, p. 139

CRITICAL THINKING
Responses include: to showcase unique cultures and customs, share experiences, increase learning and understanding
☑ **READING PROGRESS CHECK** Service industries provide services to people, while manufacturing industries make products to sell.

ENGAGE

Bellringer Before students read the What Do You Think? feature, explain that this debate will center around fracking, or hydraulic fracturing, which is a process used to obtain natural gas and oil. **Ask:** How dependent is your family on natural gas and oil? How do high gas prices affect your family? (*Student answers will vary but should include knowledge of how their family uses natural gas and oil, such as for heating their homes or fueling their cars.*)

TEACH & ASSESS

R Reading Skills

Paraphrasing Have students identify the question that will be debated. Then ask them to explain in their own words what *fracking* is. You may wish to have volunteers illustrate the process through drawings or act out the process through pantomime. **Ask:** Would you describe fracking as a gentle process or a violent one? (*a violent process*)
ELL Kinesthetic

C Critical Thinking Skills

Recognizing Bias Explain to students that different propaganda devices are used to persuade readers to agree with a writer's position. Loaded words and phrases, such as *proven, well-regulated,* and *strong environmental track record,* appeal to the readers' emotions. Referencing important government agencies, such as the EPA and GWPC, lend credibility to the argument. Quotes from authority figures, such as the EPA administrator, support the writer's position. Stating supporting facts that can be checked makes the argument appear to be trustworthy.

Explain that recognizing the tools of persuasion will help readers make an informed judgment about the information presented. **Ask:** In your opinion, what information makes the strongest argument to go along with the American Petroleum Institute's position? What information makes a strong argument to go along with the Food and Water Watch's position? (*Students' answers will vary but should include an understanding of the tools of persuasion*) Verbal/ Linguistic, Logical/Mathematical

What Do You Think?

Is Fracking a Safe Method for Acquiring Energy Resources?

R Fracking is a process for obtaining natural gas and oil through high-pressure blasting of underground rock. Fracking involves pumping a specially blended liquid—a mix of water, sand, and chemicals—into wells drilled deep below Earth's surface. The fluids pour in with such force that the rock formations fracture, or crack, releasing precious oil and natural gas. Oil and gas are key resources for heating our homes, creating electricity, and fueling our cars. But critics of fracking worry that the process is harming the environment and people's health. Is fracking a safe way to meet our energy needs?

No !
PRIMARY SOURCE

C " The form of natural gas drilling called fracking has caused livestock and crops to die from tainted water, people in small towns to black out and develop headaches from foul air, and flames to explode from kitchen taps. . . . [I]n recent years, we have learned that extracting gas through fracking poses unacceptable risks to the public. Fracking uses large quantities of water and a cocktail of toxic chemicals that have been shown to poison water resources. To date, thousands of cases of water contamination have been reported near drilling sites around the country. In many cases, residents can no longer drink from their taps, and in one instance, a home near a fracking site exploded after a gas well leaked methane into its tap water. . . . [S]tudies . . . found that 25 percent of fracking chemicals can cause cancer and 40 to 50 percent can affect the nervous, immune and cardiovascular [heart and blood vessel] systems. "

—Sam Schabacker, senior organizer for Food & Water Watch

Environmental activists protest fracking in New York.

netw○rks   *Online Teaching Options*

How to Analyze a Primary Source

Analyzing Primary Sources Have students use the worksheet to analyze the information from each primary source. Remind students to recognize the bias shown in the arguments and to be aware of the persuasive tools the writers use in their arguments, especially loaded words that appeal to the emotions. Verbal/Linguistic

TEXT: From ENERGY TOMORROW: http://www.energyfromshale.org/what-is-fracking © Copyright 2012 API.
All Rights Reserved. Reproduced courtesy of the American Petroleum Institute.
PHOTO: Bloomberg/Getty Images

Water is unloaded from trucks at a treatment plant. The plant will separate water, oil, and sediment that is mixed during the fracking process.

Yes!

PRIMARY SOURCE

" "Typically, steel pipe known as surface casing is cemented into place at the uppermost portion of a well for the explicit (specific) purpose of protecting the groundwater. ... As the well is drilled deeper, additional casing (large pipe) is installed ... which further protects groundwater. ...

Casing and cementing are critical parts of the well construction that not only protect any water zones, but are also important to successful oil or natural gas production. ... Industry well design practices protect sources of drinking water from ... oil and natural gas well with multiple layers of impervious (hard to pass through) rock.

"While 99.5 percent of the fluids used consist of water and sand, some chemicals are added to improve the flow." "

—American Petroleum Institute

What Do You Think? DBQ

C
1. **Identifying Point of View** According to Sam Schabacker, how does fracking put people's health at risk?

2. **Identifying Point of View** How does each side support its position?

Critical Thinking

W
3. **Analyzing** Some people believe that fracking should be halted until experts have studied the risks more thoroughly. Do you think a temporary ban on fracking is reasonable? What would be the advantages and disadvantages?

Chapter 4 **141**

C Critical Thinking Skills

Recognizing Bias Have volunteers identify examples of loaded words in this writer's argument and explain how the words affect the reader. **Ask:** How does the writer's use of loaded words make you feel about the use of fracking to obtain natural gas and oil? Identify some of the loaded words and phrases. *(Students' answers will vary but should demonstrate an understanding of propaganda techniques used in persuasive writing.)* Interpersonal, Verbal/Linguistic

W Writing Skills

Informative/Explanatory Have students identify an emotional appeal and a fact used in the Yes argument, and explain the difference between the two to a partner. Then have each students write a paragraph explaining the difference and what to watch for to distinguish emotional appeals from facts in persuasive arguments and appeals. *(Students' paragraphs should cite a specific use of loaded words and a hard fact that can be proven. Students' answers should demonstrate the understanding of the use of propaganda techniques to influence readers.)* Interpersonal, Verbal/Linguistic

CLOSE & REFLECT

Divide the class in half. Assign one group as the people who want to use fracking to reach valuable natural resources and the other group as the people who do not want it used in their region of the country because of its possible impact on the environment.

Then have the groups do a mock debate, using the information in this section. If students need more more information to support their side of the argument, have them conduct research on fracking using reliable resources on the Internet.

ANSWER, p. 141

DBQ What Do You **Think?**

1. It can pollute the drinking water and the air with chemicals that may cause headaches, blackouts, cancer, and damage to peoples' nervous, immune, and cardiovascular systems.

2. The American Petroleum Institute says that EPA and GWPC studies have found no cause-and-effect relationship between fracking and water contamination. Sam Schabacker cites studies about the dangers of fracking chemicals to the human body.

3. Students' answers will vary. Possible answers: A ban would allow time to assess the risks and recommend appropriate government regulations, and it might prevent environmental harm and save lives. But stopping fracking would also reduce energy production and mean a loss of jobs and income for those in the oil and gas industry.

CHAPTER REVIEW ACTIVITY

Have students create a five-column chart like the one below. Tell students to list the four subregions of the eastern United States as column heads. For the four row titles, have them list bodies of water; physical landscape; climate; and metropolitan areas. Tell students to complete the chart for each subregion with examples for each category. *(Possible answers: **New England**—Atlantic Ocean; coastal plain, fall line, northern range of Appalachians; cold winters, hot and humid summers, cool autumns, rainy springs; Boston; **Mid-Atlantic**—Atlantic Ocean; coastal plain, Appalachian Mountains, fall line; mild climate with less extreme temperatures; New York, Philadelphia, Washington, DC; **Midwest**—Great Lakes, Mississippi River, Ohio River; plains with rich soil; cold winters, hot and humid summers, cool autumns, rainy springs; Chicago; **Southeast**—Atlantic Ocean, Gulf of Mexico, Mississippi River; coastal plain, Appalachians, Great Smoky Mountains; humid subtropical climate with rainy and hot summers and cooler and drier winters; New Orleans)*

REVIEW THE ENDURING UNDERSTANDINGS

Review this chapter's Enduring Understanding with students:

• *People, places, and ideas change over time.*

Now pose the following questions in a class discussion to apply this to this chapter.

• How did bodies of water affect the development of the eastern United States? *(Sample answers: The Atlantic Ocean was used as a means of transportation for immigrants coming to America and as a source of food and jobs. The Mississippi River affected settlement patterns, the economy, and people's lifestyles.)*

• How did the arrival of more European settlers after the Revolutionary War affect the growth of the United States? *(Sample answer: As towns along the Atlantic Coast became crowded, people began moving inland and building new homes and towns. The government claimed new land, and the country got bigger.)*

• How could tourism change an area? *(Sample answer: Tourism would provide jobs for the local people and more businesses, such as restaurants and hotels, which would be built in the area.)*

Directions: Write your answers on a separate piece of paper.

1 Exploring the Essential Question
INFORMATIVE/EXPLANATORY WRITING Choose one of the subregions located in the United States east of the Mississippi. Write an essay explaining how the physical geography of the subregion influenced its settlement and economic development.

2 21st Century Skills
INTEGRATING VISUAL INFORMATION Use a map to trace the Ohio River from its birthplace at the mouths of the Allegheny and Monongahela Rivers in Pennsylvania and the Mississippi River from its birthplace in Minnesota to the point where they meet. Then follow the path of the Mississippi to the Gulf of Mexico. List the states that border these two rivers and five cities along the rivers' banks.

3 Thinking Like a Geographer
INTEGRATING VISUAL INFORMATION Create a graph showing how quickly the population of the colonies grew between 1650 and 1700 and from 1700 to 1750.

4 GEOGRAPHY ACTIVITY

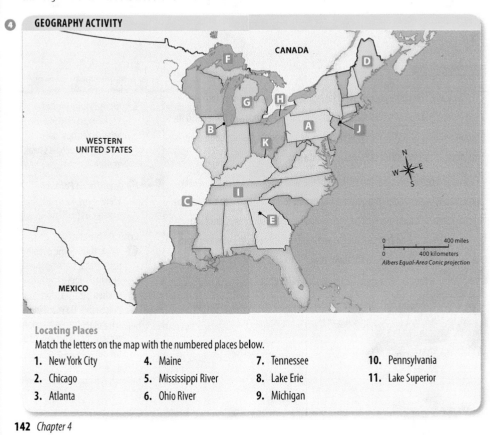

Locating Places
Match the letters on the map with the numbered places below.

1. New York City
2. Chicago
3. Atlanta
4. Maine
5. Mississippi River
6. Ohio River
7. Tennessee
8. Lake Erie
9. Michigan
10. Pennsylvania
11. Lake Superior

ACTIVITIES ANSWERS

Exploring the Essential Question

1 **INFORMATIVE/EXPLANATORY** Students' writings will vary but should demonstrate what they have learned from their text and any other sources used about the subregion they chose to write about.

21st Century Skills

2 **INTEGRATING VISUAL INFORMATION** States include: Pennsylvania, Ohio, West Virginia, Kentucky, Indiana, Illinois, Minnesota, Wisconsin, Iowa, Missouri, Tennessee, Arkansas, Mississippi, and Louisiana. Students' answers for names of cities might include any of the following: Pittsburgh, Cincinnati, Parkersburg, Louisville, Evanston, Dubuque, Davenport, St. Louis, Memphis, Baton Rouge, New Orleans.

REVIEW THE GUIDING QUESTIONS

Directions: Choose the best answer for each question.

1 In which subregion of the United States is the nation's capital located?

A. Southeast

B. Midwest

C. Mid-Atlantic

D. New England

2 What is the name of the river system that connects the Great Lakes to the Atlantic Ocean?

F. the Hudson River

G. the St. Lawrence Seaway

H. the Ohio and Mississippi rivers

I. the Monongahela and Allegheny rivers

3 Why did Europe's kings and queens claim lands in North America?

A. They wanted to spread Catholicism to the Western Hemisphere.

B. They wanted control over America's gold and natural resources.

C. They wanted to reduce the population in overcrowded cities.

D. They wanted to protect the native population from exploitation.

4 Why were the Cherokee people forced to leave their land in the Southeast and walk 1,000 miles (1,609 km) to Oklahoma?

F. A hurricane destroyed their homes.

G. Their land was needed for forts to protect America from the Spanish.

H. White settlers wanted their land and the resources on it.

I. Locusts destroyed their crops.

5 New York City is made up of five unique urban areas called

A. counties.

B. boroughs.

C. townships.

D. districts.

6 Whose job is it to carry out the laws passed by Congress, appoint federal judges, lead the military, meet with foreign leaders, and plan the budget?

F. the Senate

G. the Speaker of the House of Representatives

H. the president of the United States

I. the secretary of state

Chapter 4 **143**

Thinking Like a Geographer

3 **INTEGRATING VISUAL INFORMATION** In 1650—the population was 52,000; 1700—it had increased to 250,000; 1750—it had grown to 1,700,000.

Geography Activity

4 **LOCATING PLACES**

1. J   7. I

2. B   8. H

3. E   9. G

4. D   10. A

5. C   11. F

6. K

ASSESSMENT ANSWERS

Review the Guiding Questions

1 **C** For this question, students will need to visualize a map of the eastern United States. Knowing that Washington, DC, is located between Maryland and Virginia and that those states are in the Mid-Atlantic subregion will help them to choose the correct answer. Providing a map of the United States may be helpful to students.

2 **G** For this question, choices F, H, and I can be eliminated because none of those rivers connect with the Great Lakes. Providing a map of the United States showing bodies of water may be helpful to students.

3 **B** To answer this question, students will need to know about early European colonization in the Americas. Refer students to Lesson 2 for help. A helpful clue in this question is the word *lands*. The clue will help students to associate gold and natural resources with being found in the land.

4 **H** Knowing that homes can be rebuilt after hurricanes and that destroyed crops can be replanted will help students eliminate choices F and I. Understanding that the Trail of Tears occurred after the Spanish had left the area will eliminate choice G.

5 **B** Knowing that counties, townships, and districts can include both urban and rural areas will help students eliminate choices A, C, and D. Refer students to Lesson 3 for help.

6 **H** To answer this question, students need to recall the duties of the three branches of government. A helpful clue in this question is *carry out the laws passed by Congress.* Knowing that the Senate and the House of Representatives make up Congress will help eliminate choices F and G. The Secretary of State is an appointed advisor to the President who helps the President carry out foreign policies. This knowledge will eliminate choice I. Refer students to Lesson 3 for help.

Assessment Answers

DBQ Analyzing Documents

7 **B** Since this job is expected to grow much faster than the average, more software developers will be needed in the future than is the case with most other jobs. Point out that the last sentence of the passage says the healthcare industry is greatly increasing their use of computers which is contradictory to answer C. Students should also be able to eliminate answer D as there is no mention of the government in the passage.

8 **I** A decline in sales of smart phones is likely to lower demand for mobile technology software. Since that technology is one of the reasons for rapid job growth among software developers, the need for these jobs is likely to either grow less rapidly or decrease.

Short Response

9 The purpose of this section of the Constitution is to explain the goals that people had when they wrote the Constitution, and to include all people of the United States, not just a select few.

10 Possible answer: By using the phrase "Blessings of Liberty," the writers of the Constitution have in mind the benefits that all Americans enjoy because they are free to live where and as they wish with relatively little interference from the government.

Extended Response

11 Students' writings will vary but should make a choice of a state in the eastern United States and reasons why they would like to live there. Students should support their choice with information from the chapter and adequate supporting details of the physical features, culture, human attractions, natural resources, and other benefits of the state they have chosen.

DBQ ANALYZING DOCUMENTS

7 **DETERMINING CENTRAL IDEAS** The government reports on the future need for workers who create software:

"*Employment of software developers is projected to grow . . . much faster than the average for all occupations. . . . The main reason . . . is a large increase in the demand for computer software. Mobile technology requires new applications. Also, the healthcare industry is greatly increasing its use of computer systems.*"

—from the *Occupational Outlook Handbook*

Which generalization can you make from the information in this quote?

A. Computer use is expected to go down in the future.

B. More software developers will be needed than most other jobs.

C. Software developers are not likely to work for health care companies.

D. The government will be the biggest employer of software developers.

8 **ANALYZING** What will happen to the number of software developer jobs if smartphone sales go down in the future?

F. increase at the expected rate   H. stay the same instead of increase

G. increase more rapidly than expected   I. decrease or increase at a slower rate

SHORT RESPONSE

"*We the People of the United States, in Order to form a more perfect Union, establish Justice, insure domestic Tranquility [calm], provide for the common defence, promote the general Welfare, and secure the Blessings of Liberty . . ., do . . . establish this Constitution.*"

—from the United States Constitution

9 **IDENTIFYING** What is the purpose of this section of the United States Constitution?

10 **DETERMINING WORD MEANINGS** What do you think the writers of the Constitution meant by "the Blessings of Liberty"?

EXTENDED RESPONSE

11 **INFORMATIVE/EXPLANATORY WRITING** If you could choose to live in any state east of the Mississippi River, which one would it be and why? Have you ever lived in or visited that state? Do you have friends or family who live there? Write a report explaining your choice. Be sure to give details about the state's features that appeal to you. Consider things like climate, job opportunities, education, and recreational opportunities when making your choice.

Need Extra Help?

If You've Missed Question	❶	❷	❸	❹	❺	❻	❼	❽	❾	❿	⓫
Review Lesson	1	1	2	2	3	3	3	3	3	3	1

---

networks   *Online Teaching Options*

Evaluation and Assessment

Assessing Use eAssessment to create your own tests from hundreds of available questions. eAssessment helps you design assessments that meet the needs of different types of learners.

CHAPTER 5

The United States West of the Mississippi River Planner

UNDERSTANDING BY DESIGN®

Enduring Understandings

- *People, places, and ideas change over time.*

Essential Questions

- *How does geography influence the way people live?*
- *Why do people make economic choices?*
- *How does technology change the way people live?*

Predictable Misunderstandings

- *The area west of the Mississippi River is desert and sparsely populated.*
- *Only California produces goods and services.*
- *The culture and history west of the Mississippi River is only shaped by Americans arriving there during westward expansion.*

Assessment Evidence

Performance Tasks:

- *Project-Based Learning Digital Hands-On Chapter Project*
- *Project-Based Learning Hands-On Chapter Project*

Other Evidence:

- *What Do You Know? Worksheet*
- *Critical Thinking Skills Worksheet*
- *Participation in Project-Based Learning Activities*
- *Participation in Interactive Whiteboard Map Activities*
- *Contribution to small-group activities*
- *Interpretation of slide show images and special purpose maps*
- *Participation in class discussions about physical geography topics*
- *Lesson Reviews*
- *Chapter Assessments*

Indiana Academic Standards

Students will:

6.1.10 Examine and explain the outcomes of European colonization on the Americas and the rest of the world.

6.1.11 Compare and contrast Spanish, Portuguese, French, and British colonies in the Americas.

6.1.17 Discuss the benefits and challenges related to the development of a highly technological society.

6.1.18 Create and compare timelines that identify major people, events and developments in the history of individual civilizations and/or countries that comprise Europe and the Americas.

6.1.19 Define and use the terms decade, century, and millennium, and compare alternative ways that historical periods and eras are designated by identifying the organizing principles upon which each is based.

6.3.5 Give examples and describe the formation of important river deltas, mountains and bodies of water in Europe and the Americas.

6.3.7 Locate and describe the climate regions of Europe and the Americas and explain how and why they differ.

6.3.14 Explain and give examples of how nature has impacted the physical environment and human populations in specific areas of Europe and the Americas.

SUGGESTED PACING GUIDE

Introducing the Chapter.............. 2 Days	Lesson 3 .... 2 Days
Lesson 1 .... 2 Days	Chapter Wrap-Up and Assessment..... 2 Days
Lesson 2 .... 2 Days	

TOTAL TIME   10 Days

Key for Using the Teacher Edition

SKILL-BASED ACTIVITIES

Types of skill activities found in the Teacher Edition.

* **V** **Visual Skills** require students to analyze maps, graphs, charts, and photos.

W **Writing Skills** provide writing opportunities to help students comprehend the text.

R **Reading Skills** help students practice reading skills and master vocabulary.

C **Critical Thinking Skills** help students apply and extend what they have learned.

T **Technology Skills** require students to use digital tools effectively.

*Letters are followed by a number when there is more than one of the same type of skill on the page.

DIFFERENTIATED INSTRUCTION

All activities are written for the on-level student unless otherwise marked with the leveled labels below.

BL Beyond Level
AL Approaching Level
ELL English Language Learners

All students benefit from activities that utilize different learning styles. Many activities are marked as below when a particular learning style is highlighted.

Intrapersonal	Naturalist
Logical/Mathematical	Kinesthetic
Visual/Spatial	Auditory/Musical
Verbal/Linguistic	Interpersonal

CHAPTER OPENER PLANNER

Students will know:
- *the area west of the Mississippi River is a large area with a variety of climates, landforms, and waterways.*

Students will be able to:
- *identify states, cities, and towns in the western United States, using a map.*
- *use a time line to discuss significant events in the history of the western United States.*

UNDERSTANDING
BY DESIGN®

☑ *Print Teaching Options*

V Visual Skills

☐ **P. 146** Students identify the states that make up the western region of the United States and some of their features on a map.

☐ **P. 147** Students use a time line to answer questions about major events in the history of the western region of the United States.

W Writing Skills

☐ **P. 147** Students choose an event on the time line and write a paragraph describing how social, political, ecological, and/or economic factors led to the event.

☑ *Online Teaching Options*

☐ **MAP** **Reading a Map**—Students identify aspects and locations of the region on a map.

☐ **TIME LINE** **Reading a Time Line and Map**—Students identify where in the western United States events on the timeline took place and locate the places on a map. *Visual/Spatial*

☐ **MAP** **Interactive World Atlas**—Students use the interactive world atlas to identify the region and describe its terrain.

☑ *Printable Digital Worksheets*

W Writing Skills

☐ **WORKSHEET** **Geography and Economics: NAFTA**—Students use the worksheet about the history of NAFTA and its influence on trade to learn more about this trade agreement.

☐ **WORKSHEET** **Critical Thinking Skills: The Rise of Silicon Valley**—Students use the worksheet to evaluate the rise of Silicon Valley.

Project-Based Learning ✋

Hands-On

Writing a Narrative
Students will work in small groups to write a fictional account of their travels throughout the region of the United States west of the Mississippi River. The fictional story should include information about the physical geography, along with historical facts about the subregion in which they are traveling. Students may also compare and contrast details about the different lifestyles they witness along the journey.

Digital Hands-On

Creating Flashcards
Students will work in groups or independently to create online flashcards based on the content from the chapter. Online flashcards can include fact-based questions or activities where students are quizzed about vocabulary words. The flashcards can be published online for the class to see. When completed, the flashcards can be used in class as a review game for the chapter.

Print Resources

ANCILLARY RESOURCES
These ancillaries are available for every chapter and lesson.

- **Reading Essentials and Study Guide Workbook** AL ELL
- **Chapter Tests and Lesson Quizzes Blackline Masters**

PRINTABLE DIGITAL WORKSHEETS
These printable digital worksheets are available for every chapter and lesson!

- **Hands-On Chapter Projects**
- **What Do You Know? Activities**
- **Chapter Summaries (English and Spanish)**
- **Vocabulary Builder Activities**
- **Quizzes and Tests (English and Spanish)**
- **Reading Essentials and Study Guide (English and Spanish)** AL ELL
- **Guided Reading Activities**

More Media Resources

SUGGESTED VIDEOS MOVIES
NOTE: Be sure to preview videos to ensure they are age-appropriate.

- **Oregon Ghost Towns** (54 min.)
- **Just Say Go: Colorado Western Slopes** (23 min.)
- **Yellowstone: Battle for Life** (three 60 min. episodes)

SUGGESTED READING
- *Away to the Goldfields!* By Pat Derby BL
- *York's Adventures With Lewis and Clark: An African American's Part in the Great Expedition,* by Rhonda Blumberg
- *My Name is Not Easy,* by Dahl Edwardson BL

PHYSICAL FEATURES

Students will know:
- the area West of the Mississippi River is a large area with a variety of climates, landforms, and waterways.
- all areas in the region play a role in the U.S. economy.

Students will be able to:
- *identify* and describe landforms and waterways in the western United States.
- *describe* the different climates found in the western United States.
- *identify* resources found in the western United States.

UNDERSTANDING
BY DESIGN®

☑ *Print Teaching Options*

V Visual Skills

☐ **P. 148** Students sketch a map of the Great Plains. **BL**

☐ **P. 149** Students create a human map of the dominant mountain ranges in the Western United States. **ELL**

☐ **P. 151** Students create a chart to compare and contrast the lakes of the western region. **AL**

☐ **P. 152** Student groups create a diagram that show parts of a dam, power generated, and how dams work. **AL**

☐ **P. 154** Students compare and contrast climates by creating a Venn diagram. **BL**

☐ **P. 155** Students use a blackline map of the western region to create a resource map for the region. **BL**

W Writing Skills

☐ **P. 152** Students write an argument over controlling the flow of the Colorado River and present their argument to the class. **BL**

R Reading Skills

☐ **P. 149** Students determine the main idea of the text. **AL**

☐ **P. 150** Students think of a song or saying to remember the Hawaiian islands. **AL**

☐ **P. 151** Students locate the major ports in the Western United States.

C Critical Thinking Skills

☐ **P. 148** Students compare and contrast the eastern and western regions of the United States. **ELL** **AL**

☐ **P. 151** Students infer a cause for fewer lakes in the western region as compared to the eastern region.

☐ **P. 153** Students make charts to classify climates in the Western United States. **AL**

☐ **P. 155** Students make connections between products made in the Western United States and the importance of these products to the region where they live.

T Technology Skills

☐ **P. 150** Students evaluate how scientists measure mountains and discuss the methods. **BL**

☐ **P. 154** Students make a collage of images and words that depict the climates of Alaska and Hawaii. **ELL**

☑ *Online Teaching Options*

V Visual Skills

☐ **MAP** **Physical Geography: Western United States**—Students review the different landscapes and waterways in the region and determine which region is best for settlement. Visual/Spatial

☐ **SLIDE SHOW** **Hoover Dam**—Students veiw the slide show and discuss the need for water resource management. Visual/Spatial, Verbal/Linguistic

☐ **VIDEO** **Crater Lake**—Students use the video of this landform and body of water to discuss the unique physical geography of the region.

☐ **ANIMATION** **Chinooks**—Students use the animation on Chinooks to discuss what they are, what they cause, and how they form.

☐ **MAP** **Resources: Western United States**—Students can use the resources layer on the Chapter Opener map to make connections to the content of the lesson.

W Writing Skills

☐ **VIDEO** **Death Valley, USA**—Students watch a video about the physical features of the Death Valley and create an advertisement to attract tourists. **AL** Visual/Spatial, Verbal/Linguistic

☐ **SLIDE SHOW** **Bodies of Water: Western United States**—Students view a slide show and write a paragraph about the similarities and differences between bodies of water. **BL** Visual/Spatial, Verbal/Linguistic

☐ **MAP** **Climate: Western United States**—Students review the different climates in the Western United States and write two descriptive paragraphs to explain how people adapt to different climates. Visual/Spatial

R Reading Skills

☐ **GRAPHIC ORGANIZER** **Landforms: Western United States**—Students provide definitions for landforms found in the Western United States and explain how the landforms might affect the way people live. Visual/Spatial, Verbal/Linguistic

☐ **GAME** **Drag and Drop: Resources of the Western United States**—Students work in teams to play a game sorting the region's resources. **AL** Kinesthetic

☐ **LECTURE SLIDE** **Defining: Geography Terms**—Students use the lecture slide with definitions of timberline, cordillera, and contiguous to review the content of the lesson for understanding.

☐ **LECTURE SLIDE** **Defining: Bodies of Water**—Students use the lecture slide containing the types of bodies of water and definitions to review the content of the lesson.

☐ **GAME** **Climate Vocabulary: Climate Zones**—Students use the drag and drop game on general climate terms to review the lesson.

☐ **GRAPHIC ORGANIZER** **Resources in the Western United States**—Students use the interactive graphic organizer about the resources discussed in the narrative to assess understanding.

T Technology Skills

☐ **VIDEOS** **Landscapes of the Western United States**—Students use the videos of various landforms in the region to make connections to the visuals in the lesson.

☐ **ONLINE SELF-CHECK QUIZ** **Lesson 1**—Students receive instant feedback on their mastery of lesson content.

HISTORY OF THE REGION

Students will know:

- the culture and the history of the area west of the Mississippi River are shaped by all the individuals who have lived there.
- all areas in the region play a role in the U.S. economy.

Students will be able to:

- **describe** Native American ways of life.
- **explain** what the western United States was like during colonial times.
- **describe** westward expansion.
- **understand** the history of industry and agriculture in the West.

UNDERSTANDING
BY DESIGN

☑ *Print Teaching Options*

V Visual Skills

☐ **P. 157** Students make inferences based on questions about mission-style and Pueblo-style buildings. **ELL**

☐ **P. 159** Students answer questions about the Westward Expansion map. **BL**

☐ **P. 162** Students interpret an image of the cattle industry to determine how economic activities in the western region adapted to the environment.

W Writing Skills

☐ **P. 160** Students write a narrative from the perspective of a young person traveling west with his or her family in the late 1800s to seek a new life.

☐ **P. 161** Students write a summary about how the United States acquired land in the late 1800s.

R Reading Skills

☐ **P. 157** Students create a T-chart on how lives of Native Americans changed as a result of Spanish settlement.

C Critical Thinking Skills

☐ **P. 156** Students use a chart to classify the information about Native American life. **ELL**

☐ **P. 158** Students infer why President Jefferson sent Lewis and Clark to explore and map the land west of the Mississippi.

☐ **P. 162** Students suggest solutions for how a region can modify its economic activities once a resource has run out. **AL**

☐ **P. 163** Students describe what makes up the tertiary sector and why they think it developed.

☐ **P. 163** Students describe what makes up the tertiary sector and why they think it developed in the late twentieth century and early twenty-first centuries.

T Technology Skills

☐ **P. 159** Students groups create parallel time lines for events happening in the western United States and eastern United States and other parts of the world.

☑ *Online Teaching Options*

V Visual Skills

☐ **MAP** **Westward Expansion**—Students use the westward expansion layer of the Chapter Opener map to discuss established settlements and their impact on Native Americans. Then discuss how and why settlers moved West. **AL** Visual/Spatial

☐ **MAP** **Resources: Western United States**—Students discuss the locations where towns sprung up near where gold was discovered by using the resources map. Then they choose a Gold Rush town to research further and present their findings to the class. **BL** Visual/Spatial

☐ **MAP** **Trail of Tears**—Students use the map to discuss the forced movement of the Native Americans to reservations. Then have students discuss how these groups might have had to adjust to their new environment. Visual/Spatial, Verbal/Linguistic

☐ **IMAGE** **The Transcontinental Railroad**—Students can use the interactive image with historical information about the construction of the railroad to analyze how westward expansion was boosted by industrialization.

☐ **IMAGES** **Ranching in the West**—Students can use the interactive image of the cattle drives that includes comparing historical cattle drive to a modern cattle drive to discuss ranching in the west.

☐ **IMAGES** **Chicago: Before and After Industrialization**—Students use the interactive images to make comparisons of the city of Chicago pre-industrial revolution and post-industrial revolution.

W Writing Skills

☐ **VIDEO** **The Southwest is in Need of Water**—Students watch a video about the water crisis and drought in the Southwest and write about a topic or event they thought was of primary importance. **AL** Visual/Spatial

☐ **MAP** **Agricultural and Industrial Expansion**—Students work in small groups to identify a major agricultural or industrial center that developed as a result of the cattle drives and create a 5-minute report about it. Visual/Spatial, Logical/Mathematical

C Critical Thinking Skills

☐ **IMAGES** **Missions and Pueblos**—Students use an interactive image to compare and contrast a pueblo and a mission and to describe their different purposes. Visual/Spatial, Verbal/Linguistic

☐ **TIME LINE** **Notable Events: Western United States**—Students make connections between events on the interactive time line and the text by identifying causes and effects of events. Visual/Spatial, Verbal/Linguistic

☐ **GRAPHIC ORGANIZER** **Relationship between Spanish and Native Americans**—Students use the graphic organizer to analyze the relationship between Native Americans and the Spanish.

T Technology Skills

☐ **ONLINE SELF-CHECK QUIZ** **Lesson 2**—Students receive instant feedback on their mastery of lesson content.

LIFE IN THE UNITED STATES WEST OF THE MISSISSIPPI

Students will know:
- the culture and the history of the area west of the Mississippi River are shaped by all the individuals who have lived there.
- all areas in the region play a role in the U.S. economy.

Students will be able to:
- *identify* major cities and rural areas.
- *analyze* challenges facing the region.
- *describe* the economy of the region.

UNDERSTANDING
BY DESIGN®

☑ *Print Teaching Options*

V Visual Skills

☐ **P. 165** Students locate port cities on the Gulf of Mexico and Pacific Coast and discuss their importance.

☐ **P. 167** Students trace the borders between U.S. and Canada and U.S. and Mexico on a map and discuss how physical landscapes along the borders may make illegal immigration easy or difficult.

W Writing Skills

☐ **P. 168** Students choose one of the environmental challenges facing the western United States, research it, and write one or two paragraphs explaining what experts suggest as possible solutions.

R Reading Skills

☐ **P. 166** Students summarize text information about life in rural areas.

☐ **P. 167** Students determine the meanings of the words *exports* and *imports* by using roots and prefixes. ELL AL

C Critical Thinking Skills

☐ **P. 164** Students compare and contrast cities in the western region to the eastern urban areas. AL

☐ **P. 165** Students infer advantages and disadvantages to having 90 different languages spoken in one city. BL

☐ **P. 166** Students infer why there is much racial diversity in Hawaii, California, New Mexico, and Texas where non-Hispanic whites are the minority.

☐ **P. 169** Students determine what causes volcanoes to erupt, wildfires to occur, and mudslides to happen.

☐ **P. 170** Students draw conclusions about how crops grown in the Great Plains are used in other areas. BL

☐ **P. 171** Students discuss how advances in the computer industry and new technology affect them personally.

T Technology Skills

☐ **P. 167** Student groups research either the Medicare program or the Social Security system.

☐ **P. 168** Student groups create a slideshow of Dust Bowl photos with captions and background music. ELL AL

☐ **P. 169** Student groups research and present what to do during an earthquake in different situations.

☑ *Online Teaching Options*

V Visual Skills

▪ **SLIDE SHOW** **History of Drought and Irrigation**—Students learn about the history of the water problem in the west and discuss efforts to fight drought. Visual/Spatial, Verbal/Linguistic

▪ **MAP** **Population: Western United States**—Students can use the population map to understand the population distribution and density of the Western United States.

W Writing Skills

▪ **VIDEO** **The Iowa State Fair**—Students watch a video about the Iowa State Fair and write three questions about an aspect they found interesting. AL Visual/Spatial, Verbal/Linguistic

▪ **LECTURE SLIDE** **NAFTA**—Students can use the lecture slide with facts about NAFTA to reinforce the content of the worksheet in this lesson.

▪ **GRAPHIC ORGANIZER** **Industries in the Western United States**—Students use the graphic organizer to define industries in the United States and list examples of each. BL Visual/Spatial

R Reading Skills

▪ **LECTURE SLIDES** **Population Changes**—Students use the lecture slide presentation to discuss the different ethnicities in the West. Visual/Spatial, Verbal/Linguistic

▪ **GAME** **Drag and Drop: Renewable vs. Nonrenewable Resources**—Students take turns playing this game to explain the differences between the two resources. AL Visual/Spatial

▪ **GAME** **Fill-in-the-Blank**—Students take turns playing this game to reinforce content of this lesson.

▪ **LECTURE SLIDE** **Economic Terms: Private and Public Sector**—Students can use the lecture slide to understand and explain the difference between public and private sectors of economy.

C Critical Thinking Skills

▪ **MAP** **Population: Major Cities in the Western United States**—Students use the population map to discuss the population density of major cities in the region. Visual/Spatial

▪ **GRAPH** **Industries in the Western United States**—Students identify and read information presented on interactive circle graphs about industry and discuss current aspects of industry, services, and agricultural industries.

▪ **GRAPH** **Hispanic Population Growth**—Students can use the graph containing census data about Hispanic population from 1980–2010 to discuss the increase in Hispanic population.

T Technology Skills

▪ **ONLINE SELF-CHECK QUIZ** **Lesson 3**—Students receive instant feedback on their mastery of lesson content.

☑ *Printable Digital Worksheets*

W Writing Skills

▪ **WORKSHEET** **Geography and Economics: NAFTA**—Students use the worksheet to understand the history of NAFTA and its influence on trade.

▪ **WORKSHEET** **Critical Thinking Skills: The Rise of Silicon Valley**—Students use the worksheet to evaluate the rise of Silicon Valley.

INTERVENTION AND REMEDIATION STRATEGIES

LESSON 1 Physical Features

Reading and Comprehension

Have students review physical features that are east of the Mississippi River (Chapter 4 Lesson 1). Then have them analyze physical features noted in this lesson that are similar to and different from features in regions east of the Mississippi River. Remind students to look for compare-contrast signal words, such as *same* or *differ from,* and comparative words such as *larger, wider,* and so on. Have students create a list of these similarities and differences in a Venn diagram.

Text Evidence

Organize students into four groups and assign them one of the following topics: physical landscape, bodies of water, climate, and resources. Have students select aspects of their topic covered in the text or conduct online research to learn more about it. Ask groups to come up with at least two questions about their topic to answer in a short report. Then have groups present their analyses to the class.

LESSON 2 History of the Region

Reading and Comprehension

Have students skim the lesson to look for unfamiliar or confusing words or phrases. Tell students to look up the words using a print or online dictionary to define the words. Have student pairs play the dictionary game in which one student reads either a real or made up definition, and partners guess which is the real definition. The student who guesses the most correct definitions wins the game.

Text Evidence

Have student groups create posters featuring people who lived and settled in the western states. You may wish to assign specific groups of people—such as Native Americans, the Pueblo, Spanish settlers, and so on—to student groups. Posters should depict facts about the group based on evidence in the text, or from additional research, and should answer the following questions: What specific part of the country did this group live in, or migrate to? What was their way of life? How did they dress? What did they eat? Have groups present their findings to the class.

LESSON 3 Life in the United States West of the Mississippi

Reading and Comprehension

To ensure comprehension of the issues and challenges discussed in this lesson, have students write sentences using the content vocabulary terms. Tell students their sentences should show an understanding of the meaning of each word. Ask volunteers to read their sentences and explain how the term relates to lesson content.

Text Evidence

Assign student groups one of the challenges discussed in this lesson based on headings in the text: population changes, relations with neighbors, the water problem, human actions and the environment, nature and the environment. Have students in each group work together to summarize the problems related to their topic and determine how or if the problems are being solved. Encourage students to use content vocabulary terms in their summaries.

THE UNITED STATES WEST OF THE MISSISSIPPI RIVER

ESSENTIAL QUESTIONS · *How does geography influence the way people live?* · *How do people make economic choices?* · *How does technology change the way people live?*

Modern-day cowhands still ride in the cattle country of the West.

Just One Film/The Image Bank/Getty Images

netw rks
There's More Online about The United States West of the Mississippi River.

CHAPTER 5

Lesson 1
Physical Features

Lesson 2
History of the Region

Lesson 3
Life in the United States West of the Mississippi

The Story Matters...

Within the region are several mountain ranges, including the Rocky Mountains, the longest mountain range in North America. Its many mountains, plateaus, basins, and valleys mean that this region contains a range of elevations. The region is rich in land, mineral, and energy resources, all of which contributed to westward expansion to the Pacific Ocean in the 1800s, and continues to influence the way of life of its residents.

FOLDABLES
Study Organizer

Go to the Foldables® library in the back of your book to make a Foldable™ that will help you take notes while reading this chapter.

145

ENGAGE

Think-Pair-Share Have students discuss places they have visited or know about in the western United States. Students might name cities or towns, national parks, ghost towns, or popular attractions, such as Hollywood or Disneyland. Then have students read "The Story Matters..." about the western United States.

Discuss with the class what it means for a region to have dominant mountain ranges, diverse physical features, and rich natural resources. How might living in a desert be different or more desirable than living near the ocean? How might abundant sunshine year-round be beneficial to humans and the economy? Tell students that in this chapter they will learn about the region of the United States that lies west of the Mississippi River.

Making Connections Read the following information to students.

Today, the western states are experiencing the most growth of all other areas of the country. The region includes urban and rural areas, great bodies of water, mountains, deserts, farmland, and forests. Natural disasters that affect the region include tornadoes east of the Rocky Mountains, earthquakes and tsunamis along the Pacific Coast, and wild fires and floods throughout.

Share with students these facts about the Pacific Ocean, which is on the region's western boundary:

- It is the largest ocean in the world and covers about one-third of Earth's surface.
- *Pacific* means "peaceful" from a similar Latin word. The ocean was named by Portuguese explorer Ferdinand Magellan in 1521.
- The total size of the ocean is larger than all of Earth's continents combined.
- It contains about 25,000 different islands.
- The Mariana Trench is the deepest trench in any of Earth's oceans. It reaches its deepest point at about 36,000 feet.

Letter from the Author

Dear Geography Teacher,

Diversity is a common feature found throughout the United States west of the Mississippi River. Western United States cities are populated by Italians, Germans, Greeks, Czechs, Irish, Poles, Bosnians, and others. Louisiana is defined by its unique language and culture and even has its own flag. In California, Asian cultures are prevalent. The largest minority group in the United States are Latinos. Latinos are playing an increasingly important role in economics and politics.

Richard H. Boehm

FOLDABLES
Study Organizer

Go to the Foldables® library for a cumulative chapter-based Foldable® activity that your students can use to help take notes and prepare for the assessment.

TEACH & ASSESS

Step Into the Place

V1 Visual Skills

Reading a Map Have students identify the states that make up the western United States. *(Washington, Montana, North Dakota, Minnesota, Iowa, South Dakota, Nebraska, Wyoming, Idaho, Oregon, California, Nevada, Utah, Colorado, Kansas, Missouri, Arkansas, Oklahoma, New Mexico, Texas, Arizona, Hawaii, Alaska)* Then have students identify the features shown on the map. *(states, capitals, cities, national boundaries, bodies of water, compass rose, map key or legend)* **Ask:**

- What kind of map is this? *(political)*
- What body of water borders the western region on the southeast? *(Gulf of Mexico)*
- In which direction would you travel to get from San Francisco, California, to Phoenix, Arizona? *(southeast)* From Jefferson City, Missouri, to Seattle, Washington? *(northwest)*
- How many states of the western region lie outside the continental United States? *(2)* Visual/Spatial, Verbal Linguistic

Content Background Knowledge

Fun facts about some of the states in the western region:

- Santa Fe, New Mexico is the highest capital city in the nation.
- Seventeen of the nation's twenty highest mountain peaks are located in Alaska.
- The amount of copper in the dome of the Capitol building in Phoenix, Arizona is enough to mint nearly 5 million pennies.
- Sabula is Iowa's only town that is located on an island.
- Dodge City, Kansas is the windiest city in the United States.
- The Mall of America in Bloomington, Minnesota is large enough to fit 78 football fields.
- Kansas City, Missouri has more boulevards than Paris, France and boasts the second-most number of fountains in the world after Rome, Italy.
- The state of Washington is the only state in the Union that is named for a United States president.
- The National Cowboy Hall of Fame is located in Oklahoma City, Oklahoma.

ANSWERS, p. 146

STEP INTO THE PLACE
1. Iowa
2. Utah, Colorado, New Mexico, Arizona
3. Rio Grande
4. CRITICAL THINKING Alaska and Hawaii

146

The United States west of the Mississippi River is one of the two regions that make up the United States. As you study the map, identify the states and cities of the region.

Step Into the Place

V1 MAP FOCUS Use the map to answer the following questions.

1 THE GEOGRAPHER'S WORLD What is the name of the state just north of Missouri?

2 THE GEOGRAPHER'S WORLD Which four states meet at one point?

3 PLACES AND REGIONS What natural feature separates Texas from Mexico?

4 CRITICAL THINKING Identifying The contiguous United States consists of the states between Canada and Mexico. Which two states are not contiguous?

A MONUMENT VALLEY Buttes are a common landform in Arizona's Monument Valley Navajo Tribal Park.

B GOLDEN GATE BRIDGE Named after the Golden Gate Strait, the bridge stands where water from the Pacific Ocean enters San Francisco Bay.

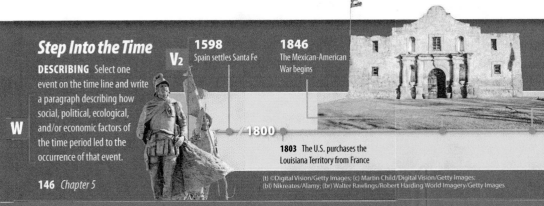

Step Into the Time

V2 DESCRIBING Select one event on the time line and write a paragraph describing how social, political, ecological, and/or economic factors of the time period led to the occurrence of that event.

W

1598 Spain settles Santa Fe

1846 The Mexican-American War begins

1800

1803 The U.S. purchases the Louisiana Territory from France

146 Chapter 5

(t) ©Digital Vision/Getty Images; (c) Martin Child/Digital Vision/Getty Images; (bl) Nikreates/Alamy; (br) Walter Rawlings/Robert Harding World Imagery/Getty Images

Project-Based Learning

Hands-On

Writing a Narrative
Students will work in small groups to write a fictional account of their travels throughout the region of the United States west of the Mississippi River. The fictional story should include information about the physical geography, along with historical facts about the subregion in which they are traveling. Students may also compare and contrast details about the different lifestyles they witness along the journey.

Digital Hands-On

Creating Flashcards
Students will work in groups or independently to create online flashcards based on the content from the chapter. Online flashcards can include fact-based questions or activities where students are quizzed about vocabulary words. The flashcards can be published online for the class to see. When completed, the flashcards can be used in a class review game for the chapter.

edtechteacher
21st Century Learning

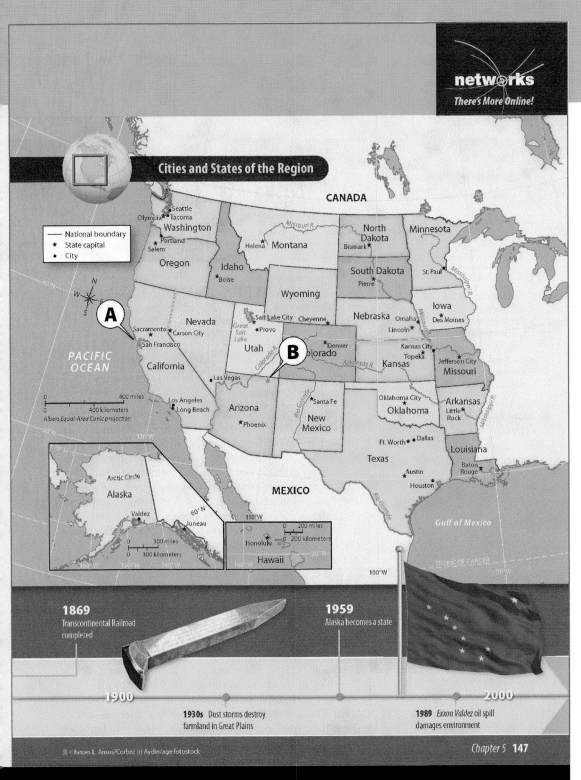

Cities and States of the Region

CANADA

- National boundary
- ★ State capital
- • City

Seattle
Olympia ★ Tacoma
Washington
Portland
Salem
Oregon

Helena ★ Montana
★ Boise
Idaho

Missouri R.

North Dakota
Bismark ★

Minnesota

St. Paul

Wyoming

South Dakota
★ Pierre

Iowa
Des Moines ★

A

Nevada
Sacramento ★ ★ Carson City
San Francisco

PACIFIC OCEAN

Salt Lake City Cheyenne ★
Great Salt Lake
• Provo
Utah

Nebraska Omaha •
Lincoln ★

B
Denver ★
Colorado
Colorado R.

Kansas City
Topeka ★
Kansas

Jefferson City ★
Missouri

California

Las Vegas

Arkansas R.

0   400 miles
0   400 kilometers
Albers Equal-Area Conic projection

Los Angeles
Long Beach

Arizona
★ Phoenix

Rio Grande

Santa Fe ★
New Mexico

Oklahoma City ★
Oklahoma

Arkansas
Little ★
Rock

Ft. Worth • • Dallas

Louisiana

Texas

Austin ★

Baton
Rouge ★

Houston •

MEXICO

Arctic Circle

Alaska

Valdez
Juneau

60° N

0   300 miles
0   300 kilometers

110°W

Gulf of Mexico

0   200 miles
0   200 kilometers
Honolulu ★
Hawaii

100°W

TROPIC OF CANCER

1869
Transcontinental Railroad completed

1959
Alaska becomes a state

1900

2000

1930s Dust storms destroy farmland in Great Plains

1989 *Exxon Valdez* oil spill damages environment

(l) ©James L. Amos/Corbis; (r) Aydin/age fotostock

Chapter 5 **147**

Step Into the Time

V₂ Visual Skills

Reading a Time Line Have students review the time line and as a class, discuss its major points of interest. **Ask:**

- What time span is shown on the time line? *(from 1598 to 2000)*
- What happened first, the Mexican-American War or the purchase of the Louisiana Territory? *(the purchase of the Louisiana Territory)*
- Which event best connected the region? *(the building of the Transcontinental Railroad)*
- Why do you think dust storms destroying farmland in the Great Plains would be important? *(Possible answer: It would hurt the economy of the region, cause an increase in food prices nationwide, and might force people to migrate to other places both inside and outside the region.)*

Ask students to list additional historical events that could be added to the time line. *(Student answers will vary but should include accurate event placement.)* Visual/Spatial

W Writing Skills

Informative/Explanatory Read aloud the activity described at the beginning of the time line. Before writing their paragraphs, have students brainstorm ideas about the social, political, or economic effects that the different events on the time line had on the region, the country, or the world. Have students share their completed paragraphs with the class. Verbal/Linguistic

CLOSE & REFLECT

Identifying Discuss with students how the Mississippi River forms a natural boundary between the eastern and western regions of the United States. Then ask them to identify other waterways or bodies of water that form boundaries in the western region. *(Possible answers: The Colorado River forms part of the boundary between the states of California, Nevada, and Arizona. The Pacific Ocean forms the western boundary of the mainland United States and West region. The Rio Grande forms a boundary between the state of Texas and the country of Mexico. The Gulf of Mexico forms the southeastern boundary of the West region.)* Visual/Spatial, Verbal/Linguistic

---

TIME LINE

Reading a Time Line and Map

Integrating Visual Information Display the time line and map on the whiteboard. Have volunteers read each event as it is revealed on the time line. Ask students to identify where in the western United States the event took place and find its location on the map. If students are unsure of where an event took place, have them work with a partner to find out. Visual/Spatial

See page 145B for other online activities.

ENGAGE

Bellringer Before students begin the lesson, have them review what a region is compared to a place. *(A region includes places that are close to one another and share some characteristics, while a place is self-contained.)* Then read the Essential Question aloud and have students discuss how the physical geography of an area might influence people's activities. **Ask:** How might activities done in the winter in Arizona differ from activities done in the winter in Montana? *(Student answers will vary but should include mention of climate, location, and physical features having an affect on the activities that people do in these states.)*

TEACH & ASSESS

C Critical Thinking Skills

Comparing and Contrasting Show students a political map of the United States and point to the dividing line, the Mississippi River, between the eastern and western regions. **Ask:** How are the eastern and western regions alike and different? *(**Alike:** The Mississippi River forms a boundary for each region; **Different:** The western region has more states and is larger.)* Visual/Spatial

Remind students to add academic and content vocabulary words to their vocabulary lists in their notebooks. Tell students to write their own definitions and to include drawings if desired. ELL AL Verbal/Linguistic

V Visual Skills

Visualizing Have partners or small groups work together to sketch a map of the Great Plains based on the description in the text and any additional research or prior knowledge they have of the subregion. Ask them to include a map key that indicates elevation as well as symbols for economic activities and products and plants and animals.

Remind students that all maps should include a map title and compass rose and to add these to their map. Invite students to share their maps with the class and ask other students questions so that they can practice their map skills. BL Visual/Spatial, Naturalist

---

ANSWER, p. 148

Taking Notes Sample answer: rolling hills; tilted downward to east; once covered by grasses; fertile soil good for farming; generally dry climate; southern part called "Tornado Alley"

---

netw⊙rks

There's More Online!

☑ **SLIDE SHOW** Bodies of Water: West of the Mississippi

☑ **Animation** Chinooks

☑ **VIDEO**

Reading **HELP**DESK

Academic Vocabulary

- **significant**
- **create**

Content Vocabulary

- **cordillera**
- **timberline**
- **contiguous**
- **Continental Divide**
- **irrigation**
- **chinook**
- **ethanol**
- **national park**

TAKING NOTES: *Key Ideas and Details*

Organize As you read, take notes on different characteristics of the Great Plains.

Great Plains

Indiana Academic Standards
6.1.18, 6.1.19, 6.3.5, 6.3.7

148

Lesson 1
Physical Features

ESSENTIAL QUESTION · *How does geography influence the way people live?*

IT MATTERS BECAUSE
The region includes many resources, but its rapidly growing population is causing overuse of some of them.

Physical Landscape

GUIDING QUESTION *How do the physical features of the western United States make the region unique?*

The Mississippi River divides the United States into two parts. These two regions are not equal in size. The area west of the Mississippi River is larger than the area to the east.

The states to the west differ from each other in some ways. At the same time, they have more in common with each other than with the states east of the Mississippi River. The western states are typically larger than the eastern states. Their human populations are generally more spread out across these vast distances. Their landforms are steeper and rockier than in the eastern states, and their climates overall are much drier. Many of the western states are rich in natural resources.

The Great Plains

Just west of the Mississippi River lie the Great Plains. In many places, the Plains appear flat. In other places, the Plains are gently rolling land. In spite of their flat appearance, however, the Plains are tilted downward toward the east. In eastern Nebraska, for example, the elevation of the land is less than 1,500 feet (457 m) above sea level. But on western edge of Nebraska, the land rises to about 6,000 feet (1,829 m).

The Great Plains were once covered by wild grasses. Vast herds of bison and pronghorn—an American antelope—grazed there. Today, the Great Plains are covered by farms and ranches.

---

netw⊙rks *Online Teaching Options*

VIDEO

Death Valley, USA

Formulating Questions Use this video about Death Valley, a physical feature of the western United States, to introduce the lesson. Ask students to share what they learned from watching the video and to create an advertisement pointing out interesting features in Death Valley to attract tourists. AL Visual/Spatial, Verbal/Linguistic

See page 145C for other online activities.

BBC Motion Gallery Education

Mountains and Hills

Toward the north, the Great Plains are interrupted by the Black Hills. These hills were once mountains, but over time they eroded. Evergreen trees appear to darken the hills, giving them their name.

West of the Great Plains tower the Rocky Mountains. The Rockies are not a single mountain chain, but a cordillera. A **cordillera** is a region of parallel mountain chains. The Rockies include dozens of different mountain systems. They extend from the Canadian border to the Mexican border. Peaks soar up to 14,000 feet (4,267 m), and valleys plunge thousands of feet below. Many of the mountains are snow capped. Trees cover the slopes, but not above the **timberline**. At that elevation, the climate is too cold for trees to grow.

Several different mountain ranges tower over the Pacific coast. Many of these mountains formed because plate tectonics exert pressure on Earth's lithosphere. This causes the lithosphere to crack and the broken land to rise into steep, rugged mountains. Among them are the Olympic Mountains of Washington. Heavy rainfall and cold temperatures form glaciers on these mountains.

About 150 miles (241 km) east of the Pacific coast are two higher ranges. The Cascades run from north to south through western Oregon and Washington State. The Cascades are volcanic, and some of the volcanoes are still active. The Sierra Nevada range runs along the California-Nevada border. The name *Sierra Nevada* comes from the Spanish for "snowy mountains." These mountains include Mount Whitney, which at about 14,500 feet (4,419 m) is the highest point in the 48 contiguous states. **Contiguous** means "connected to." The contiguous states are those that stretch from the Atlantic to the Pacific oceans. Alaska and Hawaii are not among them.

Think Again?

The bison and buffalo are the same animal.

Not true. The bison and buffalo are animals that belong to the *Bovidae* biological family, but they differ in their physical appearance and habitat. The buffalo is native to Asia and Africa. The bison is native to North and South America. *Bison* is the correct scientific name for the American animal, but the term *buffalo* is widely used.

Today, bison live mainly in parks and reserves.

Identifying In what area do most bison live?

Chapter 5 **149**

MAP

Physical Geography: Western United States

Evaluating Use the physical geography layer of the Chapter Opener map to review the different landscapes and waterways in the western United States. Ask students to determine which landscape is best for settlement and to explain their choice. Visual/Spatial

See page 145C for other online activities.

R Reading Skills

Determining Main Ideas Explain to students that finding the main ideas in a text will give them the critical information that they need to know about what they are reading. Tell them that a good writer will use only details that support the main ideas and that main ideas are often restated at the end. **Ask:**

- What is the main idea of the section "Mountains and Hills?" *(West of the Great Plains, the western region is made up of mountains and hills.)*
- What supporting details does the text provide about the main idea? *(The text provides details on the Great Plains, mountain ranges, and mountain peaks.)*
- Is the main idea restated in the last paragraph of the section? If not, write a possible restatement of the main idea of the section. *(No; sample answer: Beyond the Great Plains, the western region of the United States is made up of hills and several mountain ranges.)* **AL** Verbal/Linguistic

V Visual Skills

Creating Maps Ask volunteers to stand up and form a human map of the three dominant mountain ranges in the western United States. Using the classroom as their base map of the western region, have some students stand in the correct location of the Rocky Mountains, others as the Cascades, and the last volunteers as the Sierra Nevada.

Then turn to the rest of the class and **ask:** Are the students standing in the correct locations? Have the other students use intermediate directions to tell student volunteers who are not standing in the correct position to move to the correct position of the mountain ranges. **ELL** Visual/Spatial, Kinesthetic

Content Background Knowledge

The American bison blanketed the Great Plains and other areas of North America until settlers migrated westward in search of land and opportunity. As many as 50 million bison were slaughtered in the nineteenth century, leaving many Native Americans without a resource that they had relied on for centuries. Today, some 200,000 bison are protected on ranches and preserves.

ANSWER, p. 149

Identifying plains or the Great Plains

Physical Features

T1 Technology Skills

Using Visual Aids Have students work with a partner and choose one of the three landform groups described in the section "Basins and Plateaus"—Colorado Plateau, Basin and Range, or Columbia Basin. Ask students to find out more about one of these landform groups and to find images of it online to use in a display. Suggest to students that they also include a map to show the location of the landform group. Students may use poster board to mount their visuals and information. **Visual/Spatial, Interpersonal**

T2 Technology Skills

Using Digital Tools There has been some debate among scientists on what the tallest mountain in the world is—Mount McKinley or Mount Everest. If measured from sea level, Mount Everest is the highest mountain. However, if measured from base to summit, Mount McKinley is taller than that of Mount Everest, by more than 1,000 feet. Explain that by the time mountain climbers reach the base of Mount Everest, they are already about 12,000 ft above sea level. Have students use technology skills to find out how scientists measure mountains, and then ask the following questions:

- What tools could you use to measure a mountain? *(topographic map)*
- Which method do you think is more accurate, measuring from sea level, its base, or from the land on which the mountain sits? Explain your answer. *(Possible answer: from its base because a mountain's base could be above or below sea level)*
- Why do you think Mount McKinley is called "Denali"? *(Possible answer: It probably refers to something that is very high or the highest.)* Have interested students research the names of this mountain and report back to the class.
BL Logical/Mathematical

R Reading Skills

Naming Using a physical map of the United States, review with students the main islands of Hawaii *(Niihau, Kauai, Oahu, Maui, Molokai, Lanai, Kahoolawe, and Hawaii)*. Then ask them to think of a saying that will help them to remember the names of the eight main islands. *(Sayings will vary but should include the names of the eight main islands.)* **Intrapersonal, Auditory/Musical**

ANSWERS, p. 150

Identifying Colorado Plateau, Basin and Range region, Columbia Basin

✓ **READING PROGRESS CHECK** Sample answer: The states west of the Mississippi are similar in being larger than the eastern states, having a more spread-out population, having similar landforms, and having many natural resources.

Hikers stroll toward the peaks called the Maroon Bells. The peaks are part of the Elk Mountains near the ski town of Aspen, Colorado.

T1

Identifying What three sections of landforms are located between the Rocky Mountains and the mountain ranges along the Pacific Coast?

150 *Chapter 5*

Between the coastal mountains and the line of the Sierras and the Cascades are long, low valleys. This lowland area is called Central Valley in California. In Oregon, it is called the Willamette Valley.

Basins and Plateaus

Between the Rockies and the Sierra Nevada and Cascade Range is a mix of landforms. They can be grouped into three sections.

To the south and east is the Colorado Plateau. A plateau is a large area of generally flat land. This highland area is marked by smaller, flat-topped features called mesas that are sometimes separated by canyons. In addition, many canyons cut deep into the Colorado Plateau. Among these canyons is the Grand Canyon. Winding along the canyon floor, more than a mile (1.6 km) below the rim, is the Colorado River. Rising up to the plateau are rocks of many colors and shapes. The spectacular sight attracts more than 4 million visitors every year.

West of the Colorado Plateau and extending to the north is the Basin and Range region. This name refers to a pattern on the land in which clusters of steep, high mountains are separated by low-lying basins.

To the north is the Columbia Basin. This large area was formed mainly by vast amounts of lava that flowed from volcanoes and then cooled and hardened. Much of the area is flat, but rivers cut deep valleys and canyons.

Landforms of Alaska

Alaska—the largest U.S. state in land area—lies to the west of Canada. Mountains run along its southern and northern edges. The Alaska Range, also in the south, is the home of the highest point in the United States, Mount McKinley. Also called Denali, the mountain soars 20,320 feet (6,194 m) high. Lowland plains cover the area between the Alaska Range and the northern mountains.

Landforms of Hawaii

Nearly 2,400 miles (3,862 km) southwest of California is Hawaii. An archipelago, Hawaii includes more than 130 islands. The eight largest ones are in the eastern part of this chain of islands. Volcanoes formed these islands. Two volcanoes—Mauna Loa and Kilauea—are still active. Wind and the sea have eroded some mountains to make steep cliffs. Along the shore, some islands have sandy beaches that draw many tourists.

✓ **READING PROGRESS CHECK**

Citing Text Evidence What are two ways in which the states west of the Mississippi River are similar to each other?

---

networks   *Online Teaching Options*

GRAPHIC ORGANIZER

Landforms: Western United States

Interpreting Display the interactive graphic organizer on landforms of the western United States. Ask students to provide the definitions and then click to reveal them. Have them explain how these landforms might affect the way people live and the activities they do. **Visual/Spatial, Verbal/Linguistic**

See page 145C for other online activities.

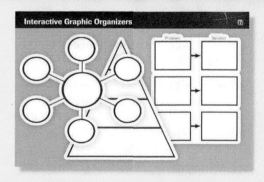

Interactive Graphic Organizers

Bodies of Water

GUIDING QUESTION *How do the bodies of water in the region affect people's lives?*

The United States west of the Mississippi River is much drier than the eastern part of the country. As a result, it has fewer rivers and lakes. Those that do exist play **significant** roles in the area's economy.

Ocean and Gulf

The chief body of water for this region is the Pacific Ocean. This vast ocean meets the western shores of the continental United States and of Alaska. Hawaii sits in its midst. Inlets from the ocean **create** many excellent harbors along the Pacific coast. As a result, the coast has many major ports. They include San Diego, Long Beach, and Los Angeles, California; Portland, Oregon; and Seattle and Tacoma, Washington. Valdez, Alaska, and Honolulu are also important Pacific ports.

Louisiana and Texas border the Gulf of Mexico. They both have several major ports, including those of New Orleans and Houston. The coastlines of the Pacific Ocean and the Gulf of Mexico are very different. Plate tectonics are active along the Pacific coast. This not only causes earthquakes but also makes for a steep coastline with rocky cliffs. The Gulf coast is much more stable and very flat. It has many swamps and shallow water.

Lakes of the Region

Because the western United States has a fairly dry climate, lakes are not as common in this region as east of the Mississippi. But thousands of years ago, the climate was wetter. A huge, freshwater lake covered many of the basins that are located in what are now Utah, Idaho, and Nevada. Today, only a few isolated lakes remain.

Academic Vocabulary

significant important

Academic Vocabulary

create to cause to form

Tall cliffs surround volcanic Crater Lake in Oregon. A volcanic hill rises out of the middle of the lake.
▶ **CRITICAL THINKING**
Analyzing Are lakes more plentiful in the western United States than in the eastern region? Explain.

©Doug Sherman/Geofile

SLIDE SHOW

Bodies of Water: Western United States

Comparing and Contrasting After students have viewed the slide show, ask them to write a paragraph about the similarities and differences among Crater Lake, the Great Salt Lake, the Columbia River, and Lake Mead.
BL Visual/Spatial, Verbal/Linguistic

See page 145C for other online activities.

Slide Show

R Reading Skills

Locating Display a map of North America and have students locate the major ports of the western United States as they are listed in the text. Encourage students to discuss why the ports are located where they are and to look at the map for the safe bays and harbors that are needed for ships. **AL** Visual/Spatial

C Critical Thinking Skills

Determining Cause and Effect Tell students that geographers study the physical features of a region and ask themselves why regions have the features they have. Encourage students also to ask such questions and conduct research as needed to find the answers. **Ask:** Why do you think there are fewer lakes in the western United States as compared to the eastern United States? *(Possible answer: The western United States has a drier climate and much of the region's water is lost through evaporation.)* Verbal/Linguistic

V Visual Skills

Creating a Chart Have students work in small groups to use information from the text and the image of Crater Lake to compare and contrast the lakes of the western region in a chart. Provide an opportunity for students to gather additional research material. Then ask them to create a chart in which they plot the data. Invite groups of students to present their data to the class. **AL** Visual/Spatial, Interpersonal

Content Background Knowledge

The Great Salt Lake is the largest inland body of salt water in the Western Hemisphere. It is located in northern Utah. It also ranks as the one of the saltiest bodies of water around the globe. The lake was first drawn on eighteenth-century maps, when it was at its largest—nearly 2,400 square miles. In 1963, it had shrunk to 950 square miles. Towns and cities are now located far from the lake.

When the transcontinental railroad was completed in 1869, two railroad companies met at the Great Salt Lake. One company had started in Nebraska and gone west. The other had started in California and gone east. They joined the two sides of the railroad with the last spike near the Great Salt Lake's shore.

ANSWER, p. 151

CRITICAL THINKING No, the West has a drier climate, thus fewer lakes than the eastern United States.

C Critical Thinking Skills

Hypothesizing Tell students that geographers not only ask why a region has the physical features it has, but they also hypothesize about how conditions have changed throughout its history and how conditions could change in the future. **Ask:** If the climate in the western United States were wetter, how might this affect the Great Salt Lake? *(Possible answer: It could be larger and contain a lower percentage of salt.)* Naturalist

W Writing Skills

Argument Controlling the flow of the Colorado River via dams, such as the Hoover Dam, in order to provide drinking water, water for irrigation, and to generate hydroelectric power is an ongoing debate. Ask students to take a side, pro or con, to the building of these dams. They should support their opinion with facts and details, acknowledge the opposing opinion, and use a convincing and reasoned argument to challenge the opposing opinion.

Suggest that they conduct additional research as needed. Invite students to present their arguments to the opposing side and the class. *(Students' arguments should demonstrate understanding of the topic and take a side. They should support their argument with facts and details, acknowledge the opposing side, and be convincing.)* **BL** Verbal/Linguistic, Naturalist

V Visual Skills

Diagramming Divide students into small groups. Have each group research and create a diagram to show how dams work, the parts of a dam, and the amount of power generated by dams in the western United States. Point out that students should assign group members different tasks, such as researching, drawing the diagram, labeling the diagram, writing the facts, and plotting the data on power production on a chart or graph. **AL** Visual/Spatial, Logical/Mathematical, Interpersonal

Hoover Dam is located on the Colorado River along the border between Arizona and Nevada.
▶ CRITICAL THINKING
Describing How do dams benefit the people of the region?

152 Chapter 5

One of them is Utah's Great Salt Lake. It is the largest salt lake in the Americas. The lake changes in size gradually because a varying amount of water evaporates from it. The lake is salty because it does not have an outlet. Tributary rivers bring salt to the lake. Evaporation takes the water away but leaves the salt behind.

Two other important lakes in the region are Lake Tahoe and Lake Mead. Lake Tahoe sits high in the Sierra Nevada. Lake Mead is a human-made lake formed when Hoover Dam was built on the Colorado River. Both lakes are used for boating and other water recreation.

Rivers

Rivers are important in the western United States. The Colorado is one of the major rivers of the region. It begins along the western slope of the Rocky Mountains and twists its way south and west to the Gulf of California. At many places along its course, the Colorado has been dammed. So much of the river's water is used for farming and in cities that no water at all reaches the Gulf of California. To the north, the Columbia River flows from the Rocky Mountains to the Pacific Ocean. It has been dammed in several places to provide hydroelectric power. The Snake and Willamette rivers feed into this river.

All these rivers flow west. But some of the rivers in the region flow east toward the Gulf of Mexico. The **Continental Divide**, an imaginary line through the Rocky Mountains, separates these two sets of rivers. The eastward-flowing rivers include the Missouri, the Platte, the Kansas, the Arkansas, and the Rio Grande. The first four of these rivers feed into the Mississippi.

The dams on all the rivers bring much benefit to the people in the region. They control floods, generate hydroelectric power, and provide water for urban and rural areas. The dams also greatly affect the hydrosphere and biosphere. Without dams, the rivers flow fast and cold during springtime when snows are melting. Then in summer, they flow slowly and are warmer.

✓ READING PROGRESS CHECK

Integrating Visual Information What landform is crossed by the rivers that flow from the Rocky Mountains to the Mississippi River?

networks   *Online Teaching Options*

Slide Show

Climates of the Region

GUIDING QUESTION *What factors influence the climates of the region?*

The United States west of the Mississippi River has many different climates. Tropical rain forests cover parts of Washington and Oregon because of the many storms that come from the North Pacific Ocean. Dry, hot deserts cover large parts of the Southwest.

Coastal and Highland Climates

High mountains play a role in forming climates in the region. The western mountains cause what is called a rain shadow. West-facing slopes of the Pacific Coast Ranges, the Cascades, and the Sierra Nevada receive plentiful rain and snow from Pacific Ocean storms. Heavy rains give northern California, Oregon, and Washington a marine west coast climate. Vast forests grow there.

The valleys to the east of the coastal ranges lie in the rain shadow, so they are dry. Although California's Central Valley lies in the rain shadow, it is a major farming region. It is hot and dry, but it is located near the western slopes of the Sierra Nevada, which receive abundant rain. Mountain rainwater is used for irrigation in the valley. **Irrigation** is the process by which water is supplied to dry land.

Climates in the Interior

The high mountains of the Cascades and the Sierra Nevada produce a rain shadow effect that keeps the interior of the region dry. This dry climate is what causes so much evaporation from Great Salt Lake. Some areas are covered by large deserts.

Advances in technology have produced new methods of watering farmland.

Determining Word Meaning What is irrigation?

Chapter 5 **153**

See page 145C for other online activities.

MAP

Climate: Western United States

Describing Use the climate layer of the Chapter Opener map to review the different climates in the western United States. Ask students to write two descriptive paragraphs in which they explain how people adapt to two different climates in the region. Visual/Spatial

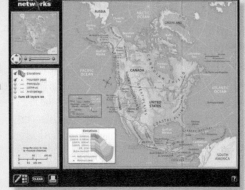

C Critical Thinking Skills

Classifying Before students read this section, have them make a chart to classify the information about the climates in the western United States. Suggest that the students make their charts large enough to draw small sketches in the chart as a quick guide to the diverse climates of the region.

Explain to students that they should add information to their charts as they read more about the different climates of the region. *(Students' charts should show that parts of Washington and Oregon have a wet, cool climate; large parts of the Southwest have a desert climate; northern California, Oregon, and Washington have a marine climate; California's Central Valley has a hot, dry climate; and the region's interior has a dry climate.)* **AL** Visual/Spatial

R Reading Skills

Describing Have students work with a partner taking turns describing the diverse climates of the western United States. Remind them that they may use their climate charts as a guide and encourage them to modify their charts as they learn more about each subregion of the region. **Ask:** How could you best describe the climates of the western United States? *(Students' answers will vary but should include an understanding of the diverse climates of the region.)* Verbal/Linguistic, Interpersonal

Content Background Knowledge

The western United States has a vast area that is hot and dry. This makes irrigation necessary in order to grow crops. However, irrigation is not a new practice in this area. It was used by Native Americans in the southwest long before white settlement of the region. For example, the Hohokam people used irrigation canals hundreds of years ago. At Pueblo Grande Museum and Archeological Park in Phoenix, you can visit the remains of 1,500-year-old Hohokam canals that may have been used to irrigate more than 10,000 acres of land to grow corn and other crops for the tribe.

ANSWER, p. 153

Determining Word Meaning the process by which water is supplied to dry land

Physical Features

V Visual Skills

Analyzing Images Have students study the two photos. Then **ask:**

- How do these photographs illustrate the diverse climates of the region? *(Possible answer: The image of the person mountain biking shows that the climate is mild and dry, which is ideal for this activity. The person snowboarding in the snow-covered mountains shows the other extreme in climate in the region, cold with precipitation.)*

- How have these people learned to adapt to their climate in order to enjoy recreational activities? *(Possible answer: They have found recreational activities that are suited for their climates. Someone would not want to mountain bike in the snow-covered mountains or be able to snowboard without snow.)*

- Which climate would you prefer to live in? Why? *(Answers will vary depending on whether students like a warm climate or a cold climate. Make sure students give a reason why they chose the climate they did.)*

Ask students to complete a Venn diagram comparing and contrasting the climates shown in the images as well as the ways in which the people have adapted their recreational activities. *(Possible answer: Same: western region, mountainous; Different: humid, subtropical; cold, snowy)* **BL** Visual/Spatial

T Technology Skills

Contrasting Have students work in small groups to make a collage of images and words that depict the contrasting climates of Alaska and Hawaii. Provide an opportunity for students to use presentation software or hard copies of photographs. Remind students to include the sources of the images they use to give the proper credit to their owners. Suggest that they also create or print out a map and graphs to illustrate and contrast the data of the two climates, such as temperature and precipitation. Have groups deliver a five minute presentation to the class contrasting the climates of the two subregions. **ELL** Visual/Spatial, Logical/Mathematical

The mountain regions in Colorado can have large variations in climate. Snow-covered mountains have cold nighttime temperatures in winter. Bright sunshine can make summer days comfortably warm.

Identifying What area of the region has a humid subtropical climate?

The western Great Plains have a semiarid climate. A semiarid area receives more rain than a desert but not enough for trees to grow. Instead, semiarid areas have bushes and grasslands. Temperatures in the Great Plains get hot in the summer and cold in the winter. This is what is known as a humid continental climate. Sometimes in the winter, a dry wind called the **chinook** blows over the region. It originates in the mountains where it is cold. But the air heats up as it blows down the eastern slopes of the mountain.

The eastern half of the Plains has two climate types. The northern part has a humid continental climate. It is influenced by cold air masses moving down from the Arctic. The climate of the southern part is humid subtropical. It is shaped by warm, moist air from the Gulf of Mexico. It has higher temperatures than the northern Plains. When cold, dry air from the north collides with warm, moist air from the south, thunderstorms and even tornadoes can result.

Climates of Alaska and Hawaii

Climates in Alaska are generally moderate but cool to cold. More moderate temperatures occur toward the south and colder ones to the north. Winters are cold in the far north. Snow can be heavy in the south and southeast. Valdez can receive as much as 200 inches (508 cm) of snow per year.

Hawaii has a tropical rain forest climate with high temperatures and high levels of rainfall. Rain tends to be heaviest in the winter. More rain falls on the northeastern side of mountains because the moist wind comes from that direction. Steady ocean breezes keep the air comfortable even when temperatures are high.

☑ READING PROGRESS CHECK

Citing Text Evidence Why does so much water evaporate from Great Salt Lake?

netw⊛rks *Online Teaching Options*

GAME

Drag-and-Drop: Resources of the Western United States

Categorizing Display the drag-and-drop game on the whiteboard. Divide the class into two teams. Have volunteers read each resource. Then ask each team to sort the resources by location within the region or type. The team with the most correct answers within a given time frame wins.
AL Kinesthetic

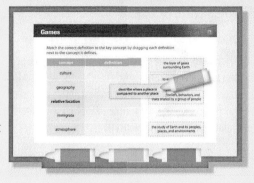

See page 145C for other online activities.

ANSWERS, p. 154

Identifying southeastern part of the Great Plains
☑ **READING PROGRESS CHECK** Possible answer: The rain-shadow effect keeps the area dry and hot. The heat causes high levels of evaporation.

Resources of the Region

GUIDING QUESTION *What resources does the region have?*

The United States west of the Mississippi River has a great variety of natural resources. In addition to land that supports raising livestock, rich reserves of petroleum, minerals, and a variety of energy sources are found here.

Energy Resources

The United States west of the Mississippi River has large reserves of energy resources. Petroleum is found in the Gulf of Mexico, near Louisiana and Texas; in the southern Great Plains; in California; and in Alaska. Natural gas is found in the same areas. Coal is abundant in Wyoming.

A growing source of energy coming from the region is ethanol. **Ethanol** is a liquid fuel made from plants. In the United States, ethanol is made from corn and blended with gasoline. The United States is one of the world's leading producers of ethanol.

Hydroelectric power is an important source of energy in this region. Dams along the Columbia and Colorado rivers supply this power. Wind power is a growing source of energy here. South Dakota gets nearly a quarter of its electricity from wind power—more than any other state. Solar power is also becoming more important.

Minerals and Other Resources

The Rocky Mountains are important sources of gold, silver, copper, zinc, and lead. Timber is an important resource, too. Fertile soil makes the Plains, California's Central Valley, and parts of Oregon and Washington major farming regions.

Another important resource in the region is its natural beauty. Large areas of great natural beauty have been set aside in **national parks**. These parks attract millions of visitors every year.

☑ **READING PROGRESS CHECK**

Analyzing Does this region of the United States rely too much on one energy resource? Explain?

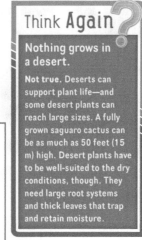

Think Again

Nothing grows in a desert.

Not true. Deserts can support plant life—and some desert plants can reach large sizes. A fully grown saguaro cactus can be as much as 50 feet (15 m) high. Desert plants have to be well-suited to the dry conditions, though. They need large root systems and thick leaves that trap and retain moisture.

FOLDABLES
Study Organizer

Include this lesson's information in your Foldable®.

LESSON 1 REVIEW

Reviewing Vocabulary

1. Why is *irrigation* needed in California's Central Valley?

Answering the Guiding Questions

2. *Determining Central Ideas* How would the landforms and climate of the region affect where people live?

3. *Identifying* What are two characteristics that Washington and Hawaii share?

4. *Describing* What can result in the Great Plains when cold, dry air collides with warm, moist air?

5. *Analyzing* Are you more likely to find hydroelectric power in Washington and Oregon or on the Great Plains? Why?

6. *Informative/Explanatory Writing* In a paragraph, describe the scenery you would see on a drive from the Mississippi River to the Pacific coast.

Chapter 5 **155**

LESSON 1 REVIEW ANSWERS

Reviewing Vocabulary

1. Irrigation is needed to grow crops in California's Central Valley because the area is largely dry due to the rain-shadow effect caused by the coastal mountains.

Answering the Guiding Questions

2. **Determining Central Ideas** Possible answer: People are not able to live in great numbers in parts of the region because of the forbidding landforms, such as high mountains, and difficult climates, such as desert or extreme cold.

3. **Identifying** Any two: Washington and Hawaii are both influenced by their Pacific Ocean location, both have active volcanoes, and both have areas with climates that feature heavy rain.

4. **Describing** thunderstorms and even tornadoes

5. **Analyzing** You are more likely to find hydroelectric power in Washington and Oregon because dams to produce this kind of power have been built on the Columbia River.

6. **Informative/Explanatory Writing** Students' paragraphs should describe the rolling hills of the Great Plains; the gradually rising land on the western edge of the Plains; the dramatic, high peaks of the Rocky Mountains; the rough landscape of either the Colorado Plateau, the Basin and Range region, or the Columbia Basin; the high peaks of the Sierra Nevada or Cascades; the lowlands to their west; and the coastal ranges near the ocean.

V **Visual Skills**

Creating Maps Provide students with a blackline political or physical map of the western United States, and have them work with a partner to create a resource map of the region. Explain that they may use their text as a guide, but they should also check out other electronic or print resources to gather more information on the resources of the region. Remind them to include a map key and map title. *(Possible answer: Students' maps should at least show petroleum and natural gas near Louisiana and Texas, in the southern Great Plains, and in California and Alaska; coal in Wyoming; gold, silver, copper, lead, and zinc in the Rocky Mountains; hydroelectric power along the Columbia and Colorado Rivers.)* **BL** Visual/Spatial

C **Critical Thinking Skills**

Making Connections Discuss with students the goods they use that are grown, developed, or produced in the western United States, such as fruits and vegetables and the beef they eat, the movies they watch, and the cell phones and computers they use every day.

Ask: How are the products produced in the western United States important to your region? *(Students' answers will vary but should include relevant details about how they use products produced in the western United States or live in the western region and how the production of these goods helps their local economy.)* Interpersonal, Verbal/Linguistic

CLOSE & REFLECT

Comparing and Contrasting To close this lesson, have students think about the unique features of the western United States that make these states special and diverse. Ask them to think about how these features help them better understand our nation's geographic diversity and to name at least one of the geographic features they would love to see.

ANSWER, p. 155

☑ **READING PROGRESS CHECK** Possible answer: No; the states west of the Mississippi River have diverse sources of energy, including oil, natural gas, coal, hydroelectric power, and solar and wind power.

ENGAGE

🔔 **Bellringer** Before students begin the lesson, ask them to think about an economic choice or decision that affected their lives. Explain that economic choices and decisions can change how we live or what we do. Then make a connection to the Essential Question: *How do people make economic choices?* **Ask:** What economic choice or decision affected your life or how you live? *(Students' answers will vary but should include mention of a specific economic choice or decision that impacted their life.)* Intrapersonal

TEACH & ASSESS

C Critical Thinking Skills

Classifying Explain that just as the region has diverse climates, the cultures and ways of life of the many different tribes of Native Americans in the western United States were also diverse. Have students work with a partner to classify the information in the section "Native American Ways of Life" in a chart. **Ask:** How does the chart you created illustrate the diversity of cultures and ways of life in the western region? *(Students' charts should classify the three groups mentioned in the text, including their homes, resources, food, economic activities, and clothing. Students should explain how the chart shows diversity in many aspects of life.)* ELL
Verbal/Linguistic, Visual/Spatial

Content Background Knowledge

Many Native Americans of the Great Plains lived in teepees, which were practical homes for their nomadic way of life.

- It was sometimes difficult to find 15-foot wooden poles to make the teepees, so people would often trade one horse for five poles.
- Some teepees could hold 30–40 people.
- A hide flap made of animal skin was used as a doorway.
- Women were in charge of the teepee, including building it, repairing it, placing it, and taking it down when the family would move.
- Men were in charge of getting the skins and poles for the teepees and painting the outside.

ANSWER, p. 156

Taking Notes Sample answer: **Louisiana Purchase:** most of the Great Plains up to the Rocky Mountains; **Agreement with Britain:** Oregon and Washington; Annexation of Texas: Texas; **War with Mexico:** All or part of western states from New Mexico to California and north to Wyoming; **Purchase from Russia:** Alaska; **Annexation:** Hawaii

---

---

networks

There's More Online!

☑ **IMAGE** Chicago: Before and After Industrialization

☑ **TIME LINE** Notable Events: West of the Mississippi

☑ **VIDEO**

Reading **HELP**DESK

Academic Vocabulary
- establish
- data

Content Vocabulary
- nomadic
- pueblo
- mission
- frontier
- Manifest Destiny
- annex
- extinct
- reservation

TAKING NOTES: *Key Ideas and Details*

Organize As you read about westward expansion, use a graphic organizer like the one below to identify two land acquisitions and how the land was acquired.

Land Acquired	How Acquired

Indiana Academic Standards
6.1.10, 6.1.11

Lesson 2
History of the Region

ESSENTIAL QUESTION · *How do people make economic choices?*

IT MATTERS BECAUSE
Westward expansion is an important story in U.S. history.

Early Settlements

GUIDING QUESTION *How did life in the region change for Native Americans?*

The first people to live in the western states of what is now the United States were Native Americans. Native Americans belonged to dozens of different groups. Each group had its own language and culture and followed a lifestyle well-suited to the area where they lived.

Native American Ways of Life

The tribes of the Great Plains adopted different ways to live on these grasslands. Some farmed and hunted. They settled along rivers, where they tended fields that grew corn, squash, and other foods.

Other Native Americans of the Plains hunted the herds of bison. Along with obtaining meat, the people used other parts of the animals for clothing and homes. These peoples were **nomadic**, always on the move. Few trees grew there, so the nomadic peoples of the Plains built homes called teepees, using animal hides stretched over long poles. Teepees could be folded up and moved fairly easily, allowing Plains peoples to take their homes with them as they traveled.

The Pueblo people of the Southwest lived in villages that the Spanish called **pueblos** ("towns" or "villages" in Spanish). These villages' multistoried homes were made of dried mud. The Pueblo practiced dry farming, conserving scarce water to grow corn, beans, and squash.

(l to r) ©George H.H. Huey/Corbis; ©Bettmann/Corbis; ©Corbis; ©Corbis

---

networks *Online Teaching Options*

VIDEO

The Southwest is in Need of Water

Interpreting Use this video about the changes in water levels in recent history across various locations of the western United States to introduce the lesson. Ask students to share what they learned from the video about the water crisis in the western United States. Ask them to choose and write about one event or topic that they thought was of primary importance to our nation's history. AL Visual/Spatial

See page 145D for other online activities.

BBC Motion Gallery Education

In the Northwest, Native Americans fished for salmon and hunted sea mammals. On land, they hunted small game. Taking advantage of the thick forests that grew in the region's climate, they built large homes of wood.

When Europeans came to North America, the lives of Native Americans changed dramatically. For example, Europeans introduced new animals such as horses and sheep. Horses made hunting bison easier for the Plains peoples. The Navajo of the Southwest began herding sheep. But Europeans also brought diseases that killed large numbers of Native Americans.

Colonial Times

The Spanish were the first Europeans to come to this region. In 1598 they **established** the first European settlement in the region near what is now El Paso, Texas. By the early 1600s, they had founded Santa Fe, New Mexico. Soon they spread out along the upper reaches of the Rio Grande.

In the 1700s, the Spanish settled parts of California and Texas. Central to some settlements were **missions**. These church-based communities led by Catholic priests were meant to house native peoples. The priests hoped the Native Americans would adopt Christianity and the Spanish way of life. They relied on the work of the native peoples to grow food.

The land and climate across much of the region were similar to what they had left in Spain. The Spanish settlers introduced numerous types of crops that grew in Spain but did not exist in the Western Hemisphere. These included oranges, grapes, apples, peaches, pears, and olives. The Spanish also adopted crops that grew in the Western Hemisphere but not in Spain. These crops included corn, tomatoes, and avocados.

Academic Vocabulary

establish to start

This ancient pueblo (left) is near Taos, New Mexico. Located near Tucson, Arizona, San Xavier del Bac (right) was founded as a Catholic mission by Father Eusebio Kino.
▶ CRITICAL THINKING
Describing In what ways was life for Native Americans in pueblos similar to life in the mission? In what ways was it different?

IMAGES

Missions and Pueblos

Comparing and Contrasting Display the interactive images of the pueblos and the mission on the whiteboard. Use the information in the photos so that students can discuss how the appearance of the structures is similar. Then ask students to point out how these buildings were used for different purposes. Visual/Spatial, Verbal/Linguistic

See page 145D for other online activities.

Interactive Photos

This region has many diverse types of landforms. Land forms range from mountains to grasslands. Waterways include rivers, lakes, and shorelines. Vegetation varies depending on the soil quality and access to water within the specific area. Animal life has adapted to take advantage of what the region has to offer.

C Critical Thinking Skills

Classifying Have students add to their charts of Native American life that they created for the activity on page 156 by adding and classifying the information on the Native Americans of the Northwest and the Navajo of the Southwest. Then ask students to discuss with a partner how the ways of life differed among the groups of this region. **AL** Verbal/Linguistic, Interpersonal

R Reading Skills

Describing Work with the class to create a T-chart to show how the lives of Native Americans in the western United States changed as a result of Spanish settlement. Use the headings "Before" and "After" at the top of the chart, and ask students to brainstorm examples. **Ask:** How did the Spanish integrate their culture into the lives of Native Americans? *(Possible answer: They convinced Native Americans to adopt Christianity and live on missions. They introduced crops that grew in Spain but were new to the region.)*

Remind students to continue adding academic and content vocabulary to the vocabulary lists in their notebooks along with their own definitions and drawings. Verbal/Linguistic

V Visual Skills

Integrating Visual Information Ask students to look at the images of the mission-style and Pueblo-style buildings. Then have them use these images, information in the text, prior knowledge, and their own ideas to make inferences based on these questions:

• Why are the styles of the buildings similar? *(Possible answer: They both appear to use similar materials and use a main square structure, although the mission is more ornate probably because it is a religious building.)*

• Was one culture influenced by the other? Explain. *(Possible answer: The Spanish may have been influenced by the pueblo-style building because the pueblo was already built when the Spanish arrived. The Spanish missionaries may have incorporated the pueblo style so that the mission would look familiar to the Pueblo people and would be more comfortable for them to attend.)*

• How did resources in the environment affect their building styles? *(Possible answer: Because the region was hot and dry, dried mud, or adobe, would have been a plentiful resource to build with, especially in the absence of wood from a treeless area.)* **ELL** Visual/Spatial

ANSWER, p. 157

CRITICAL THINKING **Similar:** Both served as homes and shelters for Native Americans; **Different:** Native Americans lived freely in the pueblos; but worked for the priests in the missions and adopted Christianity and the Spanish way of life.

History of the Region

C Critical Thinking Skills

Making Inferences Explain to students that the job of surveying land was an important occupation in colonial America and the early republic, and that even George Washington was a surveyor before he embarked on a military career and later became president of the United States.

Tell students that the task that President Thomas Jefferson gave to the Lewis and Clark expedition was a bit different and more involved than just surveying the land. **Ask:** Why do you think President Jefferson sent Lewis and Clark to explore and map the land west of the Mississippi? *(Students' answers will vary but should demonstrate an understanding that he wanted them to not only learn about the land but also the people who inhabited it. He was likely interested in the available resources in the area and wanted them to make peace with the people they encountered.)*

T Technology Skills

Researching Have students research more information about the challenges faced by the Lewis and Clark expedition, including the benefits they gained by having Sacajawea as a member of the group. Remind students to use reliable sources and to include a list of their sources. Invite volunteers to share what they learned with the class in an oral presentation or a written report. **Verbal/Linguistic, Interpersonal**

Content Background Knowledge

The French founded New Orleans in 1717 as a trading port, but the first settlers did not arrive until a few years later. Hurricanes that hit in 1721 and 1722 delayed the construction of the city. The city was later named the capital of the Louisiana Territory. To the disappointment of the French, the port city was anything but productive, so they gave it to the Spanish in 1763.

Under Spanish rule, the port began to thrive, as trade with Britain increased. In 1800, the Spanish gave New Orleans back to France, who sold it to the United States for a bargain price in 1803 when they needed the money for their war with Britain.

ANSWER, p. 158

☑ READING PROGRESS CHECK Sample answer: Before the Europeans came, Native American groups followed different ways of life, each one suited to the environment in which they lived.

Thinking Like a Geographer

Into the Unknown

What lay in the vast Louisiana Territory? How far was it to the Pacific Ocean? While exploring the Louisiana Territory, William Clark recorded his observations in a journal. The explorers carefully mapped the entire trip, which covered about 8,000 miles (12,875 km). The pages of Clark's journal also include drawings of the animals the expedition encountered.

Academic Vocabulary

data information

In the 1680s, France claimed the land drained by the Mississippi River, which included much of the land east of the Rocky Mountains. It called this vast area Louisiana. Over the years, the French placed a few settlements along the Mississippi River. The most important was New Orleans. It was founded in the early 1700s as a port for shipping goods from the river's valley.

☑ READING PROGRESS CHECK

Determining Central Ideas What was the Native American lifestyle like before Europeans came to the region?

Westward Expansion

GUIDING QUESTION *Why and how did Americans move into this region?*

When the American Revolution ended in 1783, the territory of the United States was entirely east of the Mississippi River. Much of this land was still unsettled by white Americans. But after the Revolution, they quickly began moving to the frontier in large numbers. A **frontier** is a region just beyond or at the edge of a settled area. Soon, Americans turned their eyes west of the river, eager for more land.

Exploring the West

In 1803 President Thomas Jefferson purchased the vast Louisiana Territory from France. The Louisiana Purchase gave the United States most of the land between the Mississippi River and the Rocky Mountains.

Soon after, Meriwether Lewis and William Clark led nearly 50 men to explore parts of the area. The Lewis and Clark expedition lasted more than two years, as they traveled from St. Louis to what is now the coast of Oregon and back. They traveled along the Missouri River as far as they could, and then they proceeded overland by horseback. They mapped the land and rivers they saw. They recorded **data** about the plants and animals living there. They also made peaceful contact with Native American peoples. By reaching the Pacific Ocean, they helped set an American claim to Oregon and Washington.

Over the next decades, other explorers helped open new areas. Meanwhile, hardy adventurers called mountain men began to trap beavers in the Rocky Mountains. Their travels added more knowledge about the geography of the American West. They also discovered ways through the mountains that settlers would use later.

Settling the West

By the 1830s, some Americans had come to believe in the idea of **Manifest Destiny**. According to this concept, the United States had a right to extend its boundaries to the Pacific Ocean. This belief helped promote the nation's westward movement.

158 *Chapter 5*

---

netw⊙rks *Online Teaching Options*

TIME LINE

Notable Events: Western United States

Making Connections Display the interactive time line and have students identify the newspaper headlines shown as they are revealed and the location on the map where the event happened. Have students make connections between events by identifying causes and effects of the events in the time line. **Visual/Spatial, Verbal/Linguistic**

See page 145D for other online activities.

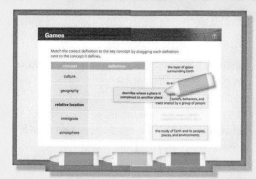

Settlers began moving to the rich farmlands in what is now Oregon. Traveling in wagons, they took a long route called the Oregon Trail. It carried them across the Great Plains and through passes in the Rocky Mountains. Over the years, thousands of people moved to Oregon. What is now Oregon and Washington, however, were claimed by both the United States and Great Britain. In 1846 the two countries reached an agreement. Under the deal, the United States gained control of those two future states. Britain kept control of lands to the north, which became part of Canada.

Meanwhile, some American settlers had moved to what is now Texas, which belonged to Mexico at the time. In the next decade, they declared independence. They set up an independent country, though many Texans wanted to join the United States. In 1845 the United States **annexed**, or took control of, Texas.

Some Americans hoped to gain California and other lands that were part of Mexico. This desire led to a war with Mexico, which the United States won. In the Treaty of Guadalupe Hidalgo (1848), Mexico gave the United States a vast area that later formed all of California, Utah, and Nevada and parts of Colorado, Arizona, Wyoming, and New Mexico. This territory added a sizable Spanish-speaking population to the United States.

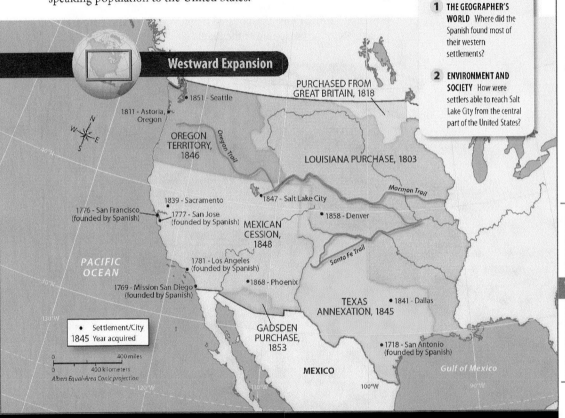

Westward Expansion

PURCHASED FROM GREAT BRITAIN, 1818
• 1851 - Seattle
1811 - Astoria, Oregon
OREGON TERRITORY, 1846
LOUISIANA PURCHASE, 1803
1839 - Sacramento
• 1847 - Salt Lake City
Mormon Trail
1776 - San Francisco (founded by Spanish)
1777 - San Jose (founded by Spanish)
• 1858 - Denver
MEXICAN CESSION, 1848
PACIFIC OCEAN
1781 - Los Angeles (founded by Spanish)
Santa Fe Trail
1769 - Mission San Diego (founded by Spanish)
• 1868 - Phoenix
TEXAS ANNEXATION, 1845
• 1841 - Dallas
GADSDEN PURCHASE, 1853
• 1718 - San Antonio (founded by Spanish)
MEXICO
Gulf of Mexico
• Settlement/City
1845 Year acquired
0   400 miles
0   400 kilometers
Albers Equal-Area Conic projection

MAP SKILLS

1 **THE GEOGRAPHER'S WORLD** Where did the Spanish found most of their western settlements?

2 **ENVIRONMENT AND SOCIETY** How were settlers able to reach Salt Lake City from the central part of the United States?

When gold was discovered in California, thousands of people streamed there in hopes of making their fortunes. This mass migration is called the California Gold Rush. San Francisco and other cities grew rapidly as a result.

Western Lands in the Late 1800s

Later in the 1800s came more discoveries of mineral wealth in other areas in the region. Each new discovery brought more people to the region in hopes of becoming wealthy. A huge reserve of silver lured them to Nevada in the 1870s. Also during that decade, gold attracted people to South Dakota's Black Hills and to Colorado.

At the same time, the nation was building railroads to join the eastern and western areas. The first line from the Mississippi River to the Pacific Ocean was completed in 1869. Others followed. Trains carried settlers to the western states. Some started farms or ranches. Others settled in towns that sprang up along rail lines or near mines.

As a result of these changes, the population of the West grew rapidly. In 1900 more than twice as many people lived in the West as in 1880, just 20 years earlier.

The Great Plains changed dramatically during this time. The vast grasslands were turned into farms and ranches. Settlers hunted the huge herds of bison and other animals. Some of the animals became **extinct**, or disappeared from Earth. These were huge changes to the biosphere of the Plains.

Passengers board stagecoaches in Virginia City, Nevada. The discovery of silver drew settlers to the town and made the area wealthy almost overnight.

Identifying What other western areas drew settlers as a result of the discovery of minerals?

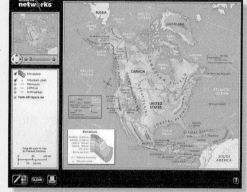

W Writing Skills

Narrative Explain that students will write a narrative from the perspective of a young person traveling west with his or her family during the late 1800s to claim land, gold, other opportunities, or seek a new life. They should write three short journal entries to describe their feelings and experiences before, during, and after traveling on the Oregon Trail.

Remind students to use descriptive adjectives and verbs to describe their feelings and emotions before, during, and after the journey, as well as to use sequence words. Invite students to sketch a picture or map of what they saw on their journey or when they arrived at their destination. *(Students' journal entries will vary but should show an understanding of the physical geography of the area and the challenges encountered by the early settlers heading west. Each entry should describe appropriate feelings before, during, and after the journey.)* Verbal/ Linguistic, Intrapersonal

V Visual Skills

Analyzing Images Point out to students that the discovery of minerals such as gold, silver, and copper in states like California, Nevada, and Arizona led to the birth of towns and cities in the western United States. From this image and from making inferences, **ask:** What buildings and services were important to the towns that sprung up quickly as settlers and prospectors migrated westward in search of riches and opportunities? *(Possible answers: banks or exchanges, hotels, transportation, mining supplies, restaurants, general stores, horses or mules)* **AL** Visual/Spatial

Content Background Knowledge

- James Marshall found gold at Sutter's Mill, which started the California Gold Rush.
- People who left their homes to search for gold in the West were called "forty-niners" because many left in 1849.
- Many people made their living or fortunes not by finding gold, but serving the travelers who came to the area looking for gold. For example, travelers paid anywhere from $1.00 to $100.00 for a glass of water.

networks *Online Teaching Options*

MAP

Resources: Western United States

Analyzing Display the resources layer of the Chapter Opener map. Discuss the various resources of the region and the locations of towns that sprung up near where gold was discovered. Discuss the concepts of a boom town and a ghost town. Ask students to choose a Gold Rush town to research further and present their findings to the class.
BL Visual/Spatial

See page 145D for other online activities.

ANSWER, p. 160

Identifying California, South Dakota, and Colorado

The spread of white settlements came at the expense of Native Americans. Native Americans suffered from the changes to the environment and the growth of the population. Farms, ranches, railroads, and mines took away land that Native Americans had farmed or hunted on. Some Native American groups resisted the changes, but they were outnumbered. Finally, Native Americans were forced to live on **reservations**. These are lands that were set aside for them. Reservations were often located in areas with poor soil that made farming difficult.

Gaining New Lands

During the late 1800s, the United States made its last land acquisitions. The first new territorial gain was Alaska. In 1867, the United States purchased Alaska from Russia for just over $7 million. The future state was so large that the cost was only about two cents per acre. The purchase of Alaska was not entirely popular. Some newspaper editors criticized Secretary of State William Seward for agreeing to the sale. They called the area "Seward's Icebox" or "Seward's Folly." In 1898, however, gold and copper were found in Alaska. These discoveries awakened new interest in the land.

Americans also took an interest in Hawaii in the late 1800s. Businesspeople began to grow sugar there. By the late 1880s, American sugar planters feared Hawaii's royal family would take away the power and land they had acquired. Instead, they seized the government and requested that the United States annex Hawaii. In 1900 the government agreed to do so.

W

Shows as He Goes, a Native American chief (left), fought U.S. pioneers and soldiers on the Great Plains. Native American boys in uniform (right) attended a white-run school opened in Pennsylvania during the late 1800s.
▶ **CRITICAL THINKING**
Determining Central Ideas How did Native Americans in the West live before the arrival of white settlers? How did they live after whites settled the area?

(l to r) ©Corbis ©Bettmann/Corbis

✓ **READING PROGRESS CHECK**
Analyzing How were the acquisitions of Texas and Hawaii similar?

W Writing Skills

Summarizing After reading the section "Gaining New Lands," have students write a summary about how the United States acquired land in the late 1800s. Remind students that a summary should contain the main ideas of a text and any supporting details that are necessary to understand the main ideas. Then ask them to work with a partner to read aloud their summaries.

Challenge students to compare and contrast their summaries and to make any modifications if necessary. Tell them to keep their summaries as they are great tools when preparing for a test. *(Possible summary: During the late 1800s, the United States gained land through the purchase of Alaska and the annexation of Hawaii.)* **Verbal/Linguistic, Auditory/Musical**

Content Background Knowledge

1758 The first Native American reservation was set up by the colony of New Jersey. Native Americans agreed that they no longer had rights to New Jersey. However, they were still allowed to hunt and fish throughout the colony.

1830 The Indian Removal Act is signed by President Andrew Jackson, forcing the removal of a large number of tribes from the eastern United States to west of the Mississippi.

1851 The Fort Laramie Treaty is signed between the United States Government and the Sioux Nation, promising a large area of land in the west for a reservation. However, in 1877, that promise is not upheld, and the United States Government takes control, and Native Americans are left without a home or land.

1887 Dawes Act encourages the assimilation of Native Americans into American society and the discouragement of Native American unity. Congressman Henry Dawes sponsored this act because he wanted to give Native Americans land so they could be independent farmers and citizens.

MAP

Trail of Tears

Discussing Use the map of the Trail of Tears to discuss the movement of Native Americans to reservations. Highlight how some groups were forced to move from the eastern United States to the western United States due to new western settlements. Discuss with students how these groups might have had to adapt to this new environment. **Visual/Spatial, Verbal/Linguistic**

See page 145D for other online activities.

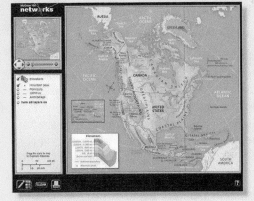

ANSWERS, p. 161

CRITICAL THINKING Before the arrival of whites, Native Americans lived independent lives, hunting, farming, and following traditional ways. After the coming of white settlers, Native Americans lost their land and their independence. They were forced to live on reservations and to adopt white American ways.

✓ **READING PROGRESS CHECK** Both Texas and Hawaii were independent territories that were annexed by the United States government. In Texas, American settlers first rebelled to win independence from Mexico. In Hawaii, American businessmen first seized power from the islands' king and formed an independent government.

G Critical Thinking Skills

Suggesting a Solution Provide some background to students about industries that have declined in the western United States such as mining and fishing because of the depletion of resources, as well as the environmental factors that have impacted the region. **Ask:** How does a region modify its economic activities once resources run out? How does it maintain a growing economy while also protecting the environment and preserving its resources? *(Students' answers will vary but should include solutions that describe looking into new industries or taking measures to preserve resources and to protect the environment.)* **AL** Logical/Mathematical, Naturalist

V Visual Skills

Interpreting Discuss with students why ranching and cattle drives became important industries in the West in the 1800s, yet they were not economic activities performed in the eastern United States. **Ask:** What does this panorama of the ranching and the cattle industry reveal about how people in the western region adapted their economic activities to their environment? *(Possible answer: Much of the climate in the Southwest is dry and hot, unlike the climate in the eastern United States. It was a good match with ranching and the cattle industry because cattle herders did not have to worry about harsh weather when moving cattle long distances. Vast open areas were ideal for cattle drives and large ranches.)* Visual/Spatial

C2 Critical Thinking Skills

Inferencing Explain to students that it was due to the Homestead Act that many immigrants to the United States had the opportunity to own land. **Ask:** Do you think people who claimed land became successful farmers and kept the land? Why or why not? *(Answers will vary but should include reasons why people would or would not be successful.)* Verbal/Linguistic, Interpersonal

---

ANSWER, p. 162

CRITICAL THINKING They enabled ranchers to send their cattle east, where meatpacking companies turned the animals into meat that could be sold in growing eastern cities.

Agriculture and Industry

GUIDING QUESTION *How did people in the states west of the Mississippi live?*

As people moved into the states west of the Mississippi, they developed various ways of earning a living. For many decades, their choices depended on the resources of the area where they settled. Most made their living in primary economic activities that extract resources directly from the earth. These include farming, ranching, mining, lumbering, and fishing.

Farming and Ranching

In the 1800s, many Americans were farmers. Many dreamed of starting farms in the West. In 1862 Congress made that easier by passing the Homestead Act. This law made public land in the western states free to anyone who claimed the land, built a farm, and stayed on it for five years. Hundreds of thousands of people settled on the Great Plains to start farms.

Life on these farms was not easy. The lack of trees made it difficult to find wood to build homes. People covered homes with sod—chunks of soil held together by the roots of grasses.

Another important activity in the western states was raising cattle. Cowboys in places such as Texas herded the cattle and drove them north to towns in Colorado and Kansas that had railroad

Cowboys on horseback round up cattle near Colorado's Cimarron River.
▶ CRITICAL THINKING
Describing How did railroads help the cattle industry grow?

©Corbis

162 *Chapter 5*

networks *Online Teaching Options*

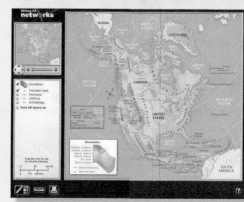

MAP

Agricultural and Industrial Expansion

Analyze Maps Display the animated map for students on the whiteboard. Discuss the routes of the cattle drives in the West and how those affected agricultural and industrial expansion in the region. Have students work in small groups to identify a major agricultural or industrial center in the region today that developed as a result of the cattle drives. Suggest that they include production data in the form of a chart or graph. Allow groups to present 5-minute reports to the class. Visual/Spatial, Logical/Mathematical

See page 145D for other online activities.

stations. There, the animals were shipped east to cities like Chicago. Meatpacking companies butchered the animals into meat that could be sold in growing eastern cities. Cities like Denver; Kansas City, Missouri; and Omaha, Nebraska, became major centers for processing crops and meat.

Industry

The first industries in the western states were also primary economic activities. The industries concentrated on using the resources of the region. Companies set up silver and copper mines. Others cut trees in the Northwest to provide lumber for building homes and ships. Fish canneries were important along the Pacific coast and the Gulf coast.

In the 1900s, new primary industries developed. The growing popularity of cars created rising demand for oil. The oil industry boomed in Texas, Oklahoma, and California. Oil in northern Alaska became usable in the 1970s with completion of a major construction project: the Trans-Alaska Pipeline System (TAPS). That project built a pipeline from the northern oil fields to the port of Valdez in the south so that oil could be shipped to the continental states.

Although primary economic activities remained dominant as the region developed, more secondary economic activities began to emerge. These are industries that turn raw materials into manufactured goods. Many cities across the region became major manufacturing centers. Los Angeles specialized in machine tools and automobiles. San Francisco became a major shipbuilding center.

Recreation and Entertainment

Other new industries focused on recreation and entertainment. Southern California became home to the movie industry. Las Vegas turned into a major resort city known for its casino-hotels, shops, and restaurants. Areas in the Rockies with great natural beauty—or excellent slopes for skiing—became favored vacation spots.

☑ **READING PROGRESS CHECK**

Determining Central Ideas What resources attracted Americans to the western region in the 1800s?

Include this lesson's information in your Foldable®.

LESSON 2 REVIEW

Reviewing Vocabulary
1. How did *pueblos* and *missions* differ?

Answering the Guiding Questions
2. ***Describing*** What was one change in the way of life for Native Americans after the Spanish and French came to this region?

3. ***Determining Central Ideas*** Why was the Lewis and Clark expedition important?

4. ***Identifying*** Why did the movement of white settlements into the West cause problems for Native Americans?

5. ***Analyzing*** In what way was the recreation industry in the region similar to farming, ranching, and mining in earlier times?

6. ***Informative/Explanatory Writing*** In a paragraph, explain how the industries that developed in the region late in the 1900s were different from those of earlier times.

Chapter 5 **163**

LESSON 2 REVIEW ANSWERS

Reviewing Vocabulary

1. Pueblos were Native American villages of homes made of dried mud. Missions were communities built by the Spanish to convince Native Americans to adopt Christianity and the Spanish way of life.

Answering the Guiding Questions

2. **Describing** Possible answer: adoption of horses by the Plains people, adoption of sheep herding by the Navajo, the move of some Native Americans in California and Texas to missions

3. **Determining Central Ideas** The expedition resulted in more accurate maps and information and helped the United States gain a claim to territory that later became the states of Washington and Oregon.

4. **Identifying** Possible answer: The whites took the land away from the Native Americans who then could no longer live on it as they had in the past.

5. **Analyzing** Like farming, ranching, and mining, the recreation industry depended on the physical environment. In this case, it was the natural beauty rather than resources such as soil or minerals.

6. **Informative/Explanatory Writing** Students' paragraphs should point out that industries like farming and ranching are based on resources and have been engaged in for centuries. The entertainment, aviation, aerospace, and computer industries, however, are based on technology and require highly developed technical skills.

C Critical Thinking Skills

Applying Explain to students that secondary economic activities such as manufacturing became important to the region's economy in the mid-twentieth century. Economic activities in the tertiary sector began to develop a little later and greatly expanded in the late twentieth and early twenty-first centuries. **Ask:** What makes up the tertiary sector, and why do you think it developed and expanded in the late twentieth and early twenty-first centuries? *(services and the service industry; Possible answer: With a decline of raw materials, manufacturing declined. Tourism became an important industry, especially with the growth in popularity of Hollywood and Las Vegas.)* Logical/Mathematical

CLOSE & REFLECT

Making Connections To close this lesson, have students think about what they found most fascinating about the expansion into the western United States that they did not know before. Ask them to consider how it relates to the way people in the West live today.

Have a group discussion of whether students would have wanted to live east or west of the Mississippi back in the 1800s and which region they find most appealing.

Content Background Knowledge

U.S. Highway 66, known as "Route 66," was the nation's first all-weather highway linking Chicago to Los Angeles. It is not America's oldest or longest road; however, what sets this segment of national highway apart is that it was the shortest, year-round route between the Midwest and the Pacific Coast. Route 66 reduced the distance between Chicago and Los Angeles by more than 200 miles compared to other routes during its period of popularity from 1926 to 1970. Route 66 symbolized the importance of the automobile as a technological achievement, and it symbolized the unprecedented freedom and mobility for every American citizen who could afford to own and operate a car to travel across the country.

ANSWER, p. 163

☑ **READING PROGRESS CHECK** In the 1800s, Americans were attracted to the west by rich farmland, minerals such as gold and silver, timber, fishing grounds, grasslands that could support herds of cattle, and land in general.

CHAPTER 5, Lesson 3
Life in the United States
West of the Mississippi

ENGAGE

Bellringer Before students begin the lesson, ask them to think about something they use everyday that their parents or grandparents did not have. **Ask:** How does this item make your life different from the life your parents or grandparents lived at your same age? *(Students' answers will vary but should include details of the availability of recent technology.)*

Then ask students to make a connection between their answers and the Essential Question: *How does technology change the way people live?*

TEACH & ASSESS

C1 Critical Thinking Skills

Comparing and Contrasting Have students name cities in the western United States that they have visited or have lived in and write the list of western city names on the whiteboard. Then have students name two characteristics of each city on the list, and have volunteers write the characteristics next to the city name. Have students compare and contrast the western cities to the eastern urban areas that they studied in Chapter 4 including New York, Chicago, Atlanta, and New Orleans. Verbal/Linguistic, Logical/Mathematical

C2 Critical Thinking Skills

Making Connections Discuss with students some of the tallest skyscrapers in the United States (One World Trade Center and the Empire State Building in New York City, Willis Tower and the John Hancock Building in Chicago, etc.) Ask students if they have ever been in a skyscraper. Have volunteers talk about what their experiences were like. Then have students speculate how skyscrapers in California might be built differently than skyscrapers in the East. AL

ANSWER, p. 164

Taking Notes Sample answers: **Urban and Rural Life**—major ports include Los Angeles, Long Beach, San Francisco, Tacoma, Seattle, several on Gulf Coast; important interior cities include Denver, Austin, Boise, Las Vegas, Phoenix, Provo, Riverside, and Dallas-Ft. Worth; rural life mixes traditional ways of life with modern technology; **Challenges**—elderly population; relations with neighbors (including issue of illegal immigration); need for water, especially with growing populations; environmental challenges such as protecting environment from oil spills, effects of natural disasters; **Economy**—agricultural products vary from area to area; major industries include aerospace, computers; service industries include software, information, telecommunications, entertainment, tourism

164

net*w*rks

There's More Online!

☑ **MAP** Major Cities

☑ **VIDEO**

Reading **HELP**DESK

Academic Vocabulary
- **annual**
- **decline**

Content Vocabulary
- **Mormon**
- **Dust Bowl**
- **topsoil**
- **agribusiness**
- **aerospace**

TAKING NOTES: *Key Ideas and Details*

Organize As you study the lesson, take notes on the topics shown below.

Urban and Rural Life
Challenges
The Economy

Indiana Academic Standards
6.1.17, 6.3.14

Lesson 3

Life in the United States West of the Mississippi

ESSENTIAL QUESTION · *How does technology change the way people live?*

IT MATTERS BECAUSE
The states west of the Mississippi are a source of technological change.

The Region's Cities and Rural Areas

GUIDING QUESTION *Where do the people of the region live?*

Modern cities are in many ways similar. Glass, steel, and concrete skyscrapers rise into the sky. Networks of highways carry heavy traffic. Cities in this region have distinct characters, though. The French flavor of New Orleans differs from the Spanish style of Santa Fe, New Mexico. Denver, near towering mountains, is unlike Omaha, Nebraska, on the relatively flat Plains. What could be more different than tropical Honolulu and cold Anchorage?

One characteristic common to almost all cities in the western United States is dependence on the automobile for transportation. Most western cities have limited or no subway or light-rail systems. In addition, most large cities are spread out, and the distances between cities are often great.

Major Port Cities
The region has many major ports. Los Angeles and Long Beach in California are essentially one port. They handle more than one-half the value of all imports into the United States that come through Pacific ports. San Diego and San Francisco in California, and Seattle and Tacoma in Washington State, are also vital to U.S. trade with Asia.

164

---

net*w*rks *Online Teaching Options*

VIDEO

The Iowa State Fair

Formulating Questions Use this video about the Iowa State Fair, one of the biggest fairs in the western United States, to introduce the lesson. Have students write three questions about one aspect of the video that was interesting to them and they would like to know more about. Discuss with students how fairs and festivals can be used to bring people together and to celebrate certain cultures. AL Visual/Spatial, Verbal/Linguistic

See page 145E for other online activities.

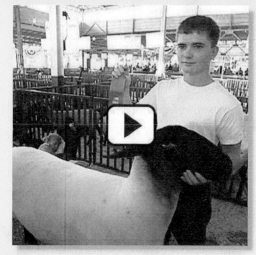

V1 Although only a small part of the region is located along the Gulf of Mexico, Gulf ports are important. Three of the nation's top 10 ports in terms of the **annual**, or yearly, value of goods they handle are the Texas port cities of Houston, Beaumont, and Corpus Christi.

C Many of these cities are diverse. Los Angeles—the nation's second-largest city—is home to people who collectively speak about 90 languages other than English at home. Los Angeles County has more Latinos and Native Americans than any other county in the United States. The city of Los Angeles has more people from South Korea and Nicaragua than any other city outside those nations.

Academic Vocabulary

annual yearly; each year

Interior Cities

Denver has an unusual location for a major city. It is not a seaport or on the navigable part of a river. Denver owes its vibrance to the mountains nearby. It originally grew as a mining town. In the late 1900s, the city attracted people who wanted to enjoy the mountains. Its economy is based on software, finance, and communications.

Some of the nation's most rapidly growing cities are in the interior of the United States west of the Mississippi. They include Austin, Texas; Boise, Idaho; Las Vegas; Phoenix; Provo, Utah; and Riverside, California. In Texas, the location of San Antonio, Dallas, and Fort Worth near Mexico makes them important to trade with that country.

V2 Many urban schools today reflect the growing ethnic diversity of America's cities.

Somos/Veer/Jupiterimages

Chapter 5 **165**

Population: Major Cities in the Western United States

Making Inferences Use the population layer of the Chapter Opener map to discuss the population density and distribution of major cities in the region. Click on each city for more information. Ask students to make inferences about why these areas became population hubs. Visual/Spatial

See page 145E for other online activities.

V1 Visual Skills

Interpreting Display a world political map or have students use the Chapter Opener map for the western United States. Have volunteers locate the port cities of Los Angeles, Long Beach, San Diego, San Francisco, Seattle, Tacoma, Houston, Beaumont, and Corpus Christi. **Ask:**

• Before the Panama Canal opened, where do you think most foreign goods entering a Pacific Coast port came from? *(Asia)*

• Where do you think most foreign goods entering a Gulf Coast port came from? *(Europe)*

• How would ports on two coasts benefit the region? *(Students' answers will vary but should demonstrate an understanding of being able to trade with the whole world.)* Visual/Spatial, Logical/Mathematical

C Critical Thinking Skills

Making Inferences Ask: What would be some advantages and disadvantages to having about 90 different languages spoken in one city? *(Students' answers will vary but should demonstrate an understanding of the difficulties that occur when people do not speak or understand the same language and of the benefits that different cultures give to an area.)* BL Verbal/Linguistic, Logical/Mathematical

V2 Visual Skills

Reading a Map Display a political map of the United States or have students use the Chapter Opener map to locate the following interior cities: Denver, CO; Austin, TX; Boise, ID; Las Vegas, NV; Phoenix, AZ; Provo, UT; Riverside, CA; San Antonio, TX; Dallas and Fort Worth, TX. Visual/Spatial

Content Background Knowledge

In 1882, the French began work on a canal through the Isthmus of Panama to connect the Atlantic and Pacific Oceans. But after working for over seven years on the project and losing over 25,000 people, mostly from malaria and yellow fever, the French offered to sell their equipment and infrastructure to the United States for $40 million. In 1904, the United States accepted the French offer, paid Panama an additional $10 million for rights to the Canal Zone, and began construction on what would become a 52-mile-long waterway. The Canal was completed in 1914. On December 31, 1999, the United States handed control of the Canal to Panama. A project to enlarge the Canal to accommodate larger ships began in 2000.

CHAPTER 5, Lesson 3
Life in the United States
West of the Mississippi

R Reading Skills

Summarizing Have students summarize the information in the first section, "Life in Rural Areas." Remind them that summaries are generally short—two or three sentences—and focus on the main ideas, and that they include supporting details only when necessary to explain a main idea. Remind students to keep their summaries as a study tool when reviewing the chapter. *(Possible summary: Millions of people live in rural areas west of the Mississippi. They depend on the rich resources of the land and sea to provide work and food. Modern technology often makes their jobs easier.)* Verbal/Linguistic

C Critical Thinking Skills

Making Inferences Remind students to use their background knowledge along with what they read to make inferences.
Ask: Why do you think there is much racial diversity in Hawaii, California, New Mexico, and Texas with non-Hispanic whites being in the minority? *(Students' answers will vary but should include reference to the original settlers of the areas as being of Asian or Pacific Islander descent in Hawaii and of Spanish and Mexican descent in the other states.)* Logical/Mathematical

Content Background Knowledge

There are different ways that someone can become a citizen of the United States. One way is to be born in the United States. Children can be born outside of the country and still be a citizen if they have a parent or parents who are already citizens of the United States when they were born. Finally, a person can apply for naturalization.

People can qualify for naturalization if they have lived as a permanent resident in the United States for at least five years. Another way to qualify is to have lived in the United States for three years and be married to a United States citizen. Most people who apply for naturalization have to pass tests on English and United States' history and government.

ANSWERS, p. 166

☑ **READING PROGRESS CHECK** Sample answer: (any two) Las Vegas and Phoenix are interior cities with more quickly rising populations than Los Angeles and Seattle; they are not port cities, which the other two cities are.
CRITICAL THINKING Native Americans, Asians, Latinos, white Europeans; the western United States is closer and more accessible to Asia.

Life in Rural Areas

R Small towns and villages remain home to millions of people in the states west of the Mississippi. Many rural Americans rely on the rich resources of the land and sea. They might be farmers of the Plains or fishers in rural Alaska. They may drill for oil in Texas or run a ranch in Montana. Although these occupations have existed for centuries, modern technology often makes these jobs easier. For example, farmers and ranchers use GPS devices to map regions, manage the land, and track cattle.

☑ READING PROGRESS CHECK

Citing Text Evidence In what ways are Las Vegas and Phoenix different from Los Angeles and Seattle?

A man from East Asia takes the oath to become a U.S. citizen. He was part of a group of 7,000 candidates who became U.S. citizens in a ceremony held in Los Angeles, California.
▶ CRITICAL THINKING
Identifyng What are some of the ethnic groups that make up the diverse population of the western United States? Why do you think many people from East Asia have settled in this region?

Kevork Djansezian/Getty Images News/Getty Images

Challenges Facing the Region

GUIDING QUESTION *What issues will face the region in the coming years?*

Americans celebrate their ethnic and religious diversity. Diversity has long been a strength of the nation. While diversity enriches American life, other population changes pose challenges to the region's future.

Population Changes

In recent decades, much of the growth in U.S. population has taken place in the states west of the Mississippi River. This region attracts new residents because of the mild climate and growing businesses. But more people means a strain on natural resources such as water, which is already scarce in much of the region.

C Ethnic and racial diversity are common in the states in this region. In Hawaii, Asian Americans and other distinct ethnic or racial groups form the majority of the population. In California, New Mexico, and Texas, Latinos constitute a large part of the population. In these four states, non-Hispanic whites are in the minority.

---

netw🌐rks   *Online Teaching Options*

LECTURE SLIDE

Population Changes

Discussing Dipslay the lecture slide presentation that shows the population changes of the western United States. Use the information to discuss the ethnic diversity of the region and the movement from the east to the west to discuss with students the continued growth in the western United States. Encourage students to discuss reasons why people may be moving West. *(Students' answers may suggest: job availability, land, different types of recreation, etc.)* Ask students if they would ever consider moving when they are adults. Visual/Spatial, Verbal/Linguistic

See page 145E for other online activities.

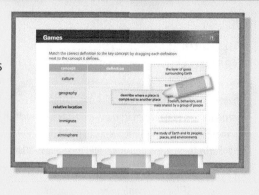

The United States west of the Mississippi is also marked by great religious diversity. A few Christian groups are particularly important in this region. Lutherans are numerous in the northern Great Plains states. Catholics are prominent in the states from New Mexico to California. Utah and some neighboring states have many Mormons. **Mormons** are members of the Church of Jesus Christ of Latter Day Saints. Large numbers of Mormons settled in Utah in the mid-1800s.

Another population trend raises important economic challenges. The share of the population over age 65 has been growing. Many older people require extensive health care. That increases the costs for Medicare, a government-run program that pays the health care costs of the elderly. Most older people collect monthly retirement checks from the Social Security system. Meeting the costs of Social Security and Medicare will be a challenge in the coming years.

Relations With Neighbors
Relations between the United States and neighboring Canada and Mexico are strong. In the early 1990s, the three nations signed a trade agreement called the North American Free Trade Agreement (NAFTA). In that treaty, they pledged to remove all barriers to trade among themselves. This created the world's largest free trade area.

Today, Canada and Mexico are the largest markets for exports from the United States. They are also the second- and third-largest sources of U.S. imports, behind China. States west of the Mississippi form a vital part of this trade. Their food products and manufactured goods form a share of the exports to these nations. In addition, much of the trade that takes place flows into and out of the United States through ports in this region.

Open borders help trade. They also make it possible for people to enter the country illegally. In the late 1900s, the problem of illegal immigrants drew a great deal of attention. The U.S. government has taken steps to reduce the flow of illegal immigrants. These efforts have had some success. Illegal immigration dropped from about 550,000 people in 2005 to around 300,000 in 2008. Changes in Mexico also help explain this reduction. A better economy, smaller families, and better education have meant better chances of landing good jobs in Mexico.

The Water Problem
Most of the United States west of the Mississippi usually receives little rain. Years of low rainfall can easily lead to drought. Between 1930 and 1940, a severe drought dried the southern Great Plains so thoroughly that crops died. Strong winds carried dry soil away, covering other areas with dust. The area came to be called the **Dust Bowl**. Many farmers lost their homes and left the area looking for work.

Chapter 5 **167**

Thinking Like a Geographer

Making the Desert Bloom
Why did Mormon pioneers settle in Utah? Utah in the mid-1800s was a harsh desert land. The Mormons, however, needed a safe, isolated place where they could practice their religion free of persecution. In 1847 the first Mormon settlers reached Utah after traveling 1,000 difficult miles (1,609 km) from the Midwest. The land was dry and wild. Nevertheless, the Mormons stayed in Utah. They built irrigation canals to support farms and towns. Life at first was difficult, but the Mormons made their Utah communities prosper because of their hard work and determination to succeed. By 1860, many other Mormons had arrived, and numerous Mormon settlements dotted the Utah region.

T Technology Skills

Researching on the Internet Have students work in small groups to research information about either the Medicare program or the Social Security system. Have each student present at least two facts to the class about their topic. **Ask:** Why do you think the population over age 65 has been growing in recent decades? *(Students' answers will vary but should demonstrate an understanding about advances in medical technology and diagnosis and preventive medicine.)* Verbal/Linguistic, Logical/Mathematical

R Reading Skills

Determining Word Meanings Explain that students can use the meanings of Latin roots and the meanings of prefixes to figure out the meanings of words. Have students locate the words *exports* and *imports* in the text and identify the Latin root, *port*, meaning "to carry." Knowing that *ex-* is a prefix meaning "out," **ask:** What does the word *export* mean? *("to carry out")*

Explain that knowing that the words *exports* and *imports* are antonyms, or opposites, **ask** What does the word *import* mean? *("to carry in")* ELL AL

V Visual Skills

Integrating Visual Information Display a physical map of the United States or have students use the United States Reference Atlas map found in the front of their textbooks. Have volunteers trace the border between the United States and Canada and between the United States and Mexico. Remind students that the middle of a riverbed is used as a border in a body of water. **Ask:** How might the physical landscape along our country's borders make illegal immigration easy or difficult? *(Students' answers will vary but should include details such as desert, forest, and mountainous landscape that could hinder or help the flow of illegal immigrants. Also, the length of the border makes it difficult to patrol all areas at all times.)* Verbal/Linguistic, Logical/Mathematical

GAME

Fill-in-the-Blank
Identifying To reinforce the content of this lesson, have students complete the Fill-in-the-Blank game on the interactive whiteboard. Challenge students to create their own fill-in-the-blank game on a piece of paper and give it to a partner to complete. AL Visual/Spatial, Verbal/Linguistic

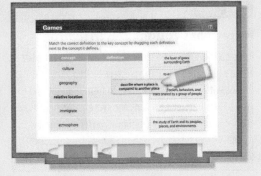

CHAPTER 5, Lesson 3
**Life in the United States
West of the Mississippi**

T Technology Skills

Creating Visuals Have students work in small groups to find Dust Bowl photos from the 1930s. Using a software presentation program, have students present a slide show of their photos along with captions and background music. Remind them to list the sources of the photos at the end of their presentations. **ELL** **AL** **Visual/Spatial, Auditory/ Musical**

W Writing Skills

Informative/Explanatory Have students choose one of the environmental challenges facing the western United States: water shortages, damage from oil spills, or erosion from deforestation. After researching possible solutions to one of the problems, have students write one or two paragraphs explaining what experts suggest as possible answers to these challenges. Then invite volunteers to share their findings with the class. **Verbal/Linguistic**

R Reading Skills

Inference After students read the section "Human Actions and the Environment," **ask,** Why do you think the oil spill severely hurt the local economy? *(Answers will vary but one possible response could be that many of the fish in the sea were killed because of the oil spill, and therefore, many people who catch and sell fish would not be able to make any money.)* **Naturalist**

Content Background Knowledge

On April 14, 1935, Black Sunday, a dust cloud with winds of 60 mph hit the southern Plains. It was so dark that chickens went to roost, thinking it was night. The wind blew trucks down streets and seeds out of the ground.

There had been dust storms in previous years, but this one was the worst. People wore dust masks and hung wet sheets over windows, trying to keep the dust out of their homes—it did not work. In some places, the dust drifted so high that it covered entire homesteads.

ANSWER, p. 168

CRITICAL THINKING The cartoon is about resources or, more generally, economic issues. Answers will vary regarding the cartoonist's opinion. Possible answer: The senator does not know the definition of "unlimited resources."

" Bad news . . we've run out of unlimited resources. "

An editorial cartoon makes a point about a political issue or event.
▶ **CRITICAL THINKING**
Analyzing What issue do you think this cartoon is about? What do you think the cartoonist's opinion on this issue is?

The Dust Bowl resulted in new practices in land use and farming. These practices were intended to reduce the chance of another dust bowl. Nevertheless, unusually low rainfall for several years could cause similar difficulties in the future.

The lack of water is more of a challenge because of population growth. As more and more people settle in the area, more water is needed. When farmers expand their operations, they also need more water. This strains the limited amount of water present in the region, which could limit economic growth.

Limited water resources have prompted scientists to develop ways to remove salt from seawater to make it usable for drinking and farming. This process, called desalination, is expensive but might provide a long-term solution to the problem in the future.

Human Actions and the Environment

Oil—another precious resource—is also a potential cause of environmental damage. In 1989 the oil tanker *Exxon Valdez* ran aground in Alaska's Prince William Sound. Its shattered hull released more than 250,000 barrels of oil into the sea. The oil killed plants and animals and severely hurt the local economy. Even worse was the Deepwater Horizon disaster of 2010. An explosion destroyed an oil drilling platform deep in the Gulf of Mexico. By the time the underwater leak was stopped, 5 million barrels of oil had gushed into the sea. It devastated the coastal economy.

Erosion and the Environment

Erosion is another environmental problem in the region. Harvesting trees for lumber has left some mountain slopes bare. With no tree roots to hold the soil in place, soil runs off with the rain. This runoff affects the surface of the mountain. Pieces of the mountain become smaller pieces and go down the side. Erosion of rich **topsoil**, the fertile soil that crops depend on to grow, is a problem in some farming areas.

The region west of the Mississippi River also experiences a variety of natural disasters. Washington, Alaska, and Hawaii have active volcanoes that can cause damage if they erupt. Wildfires and

---

netw⊕rks   *Online Teaching Options*

History of Drought and Irrigation

Problem Solving Show the slide show about the history of the water problem in the western United States. Discuss with students the efforts to fight drought and the interactions between humans and the environment that are necessary to fight this natural disaster. Encourage students to do research on the Internet about the most current drought issues. **Visual/Spatial, Verbal/ Linguistic**

See page 145E for other online activities.

Slide Show

In 1994 the deadly Northridge earthquake struck near Los Angeles. It resulted in 57 deaths and was one of the costliest natural disasters in U.S. history.
Citing Text Evidence Why is California so prone to earthquakes?

C mud slides can also strike the region. The wildfires occur when wooded areas become too dry. Mud slides can result from heavy rains or severe shaking from an earthquake. During a mud slide, the soil moves like a liquid, flowing downhill in a sea of mud that dislodges trees and buries houses in its path.

T Some parts of the region are prone to earthquakes. A major fault system called the San Andreas Fault, cuts through western California. Movement along this fault has caused several major earthquakes over the years. Scientists think more are likely to occur. As a result, severe damage is possible—as well as the loss of many lives—in major cities such as Los Angeles and San Francisco.

☑ READING PROGRESS CHECK

Determining Central Ideas Why is the high likelihood of a major earthquake along the San Andreas Fault so worrisome?

The Economy

GUIDING QUESTION *How do the people of the region make their living?*

Land and resources have attracted many Americans to the western states. Some people of the region still rely on these advantages to earn their living. Most people, however, work in modern settings that are far removed from the land.

Modern Agriculture

Agriculture remains an important part of life west of the Mississippi River. The Great Plains are the center of the nation's wheat industry with eight of the nation's top wheat-producing states. Spring wheat—planted in spring and harvested in autumn—is grown on the

HAL GARB/AFP/Getty Images

Chapter 5 **169**

C Critical Thinking Skills

Determining Cause and Effect **Ask:** What causes volcanoes to erupt, wildfires to occur, and mud slides to happen? *(pressure from gasses on hot magma inside the earth; wooded areas that are too dry; too much rain that makes hillsides too heavy, or severe shaking from an earthquake)* Verbal/Linguistic

T Technology Skills

Researching on the Internet Divide the class into four groups. Have each group research what to do during an earthquake in one of the following situations: you are indoors, you are outdoors, you are in a moving vehicle, you are trapped under debris. Have groups present their findings to the class. Verbal/Linguistic, Logical/Mathematical

Content Background Knowledge

The San Francisco earthquake of April 18, 1906 was one of the biggest earthquakes of all time. It ruptured the northernmost 296 miles of the San Andreas Fault and lasted between 45 and 60 seconds. The strong shaking toppled buildings, ruptured gas lines, and was felt from southern Oregon to south of Los Angeles and east to central Nevada. It is estimated that the ground moved at a speed of 4 to 5 feet/second or approximately 3 mph.

The quake triggered a fire in San Francisco that destroyed over 28,000 buildings and burned an area of the city covering 4.7 square miles. More than 3,000 people died in the quake and fire, most of those in deaths occurring in the San Francisco area. Many survivors lost their homes and had to live in tents in city parks.

Scientists estimate that another quake like the one that occurred in 1906 will not happen again until around 2106. However, earthquakes on other fault lines pose real threats to the region.

Drag-and-Drop: Renewable vs. Nonrenewable Resources

Identifying Display the game about renewable vs. non-renewable resources on the Interactive Whiteboard. Have students take turns dragging and dropping the resources to their proper locations on the map. After the activity is completed, have students explain using their own words the difference between the two resources. Continue to use this game to review the content of this section of the lesson. **AL** Visual/Spatial

See page 145E for other online activities.

ANSWERS, p. 169

Citing Text Evidence The San Andreas Fault system cuts through western California. Movement along this fault and many others has caused major earthquakes in California over the years.

☑ READING PROGRESS CHECK The high likelihood of a major earthquake along the San Andreas Fault is so worrisome because major cities like Los Angeles and San Francisco are near the fault; if a quake hits one of these cities, there could be widespread destruction and possibly deaths.

Life in the United States West of the Mississippi

C₁ Critical Thinking Skills

Drawing Conclusions Remind students that it is important to think critically about what they are reading and to draw conclusions based on the text and their previous knowledge and experiences. **Ask:**

• How might crops grown and harvested in the Great Plains be used by people in other areas of the country? *(Students' answers will vary but should demonstrate an understanding of how these crops provide ingredients for producing other products, such as bread.)*

• Why is both spring wheat and summer wheat grown? *(Possible answer: to provide a year-round source of wheat)* **BL** Verbal/Linguistic, Logical/Mathematical

C₂ Critical Thinking Skills   **V**

Making Connections Have students name the different resources that are a part of the economy of this region. **Ask:** How might each of these resources of the western United States be used by people throughout the country? *(Possible answers: oil—heating oil, gasoline, diesel fuel, asphalt, plastics; natural gas—heat homes and businesses, fuel vehicles; copper—wires for machinery, vehicles, and telecommunication systems and in plumbing fixtures; uranium—nuclear power, shield against radiation, to color glass; timber—paper products, building supplies)* Verbal/ Linguistic, Logical/Mathematical

V Visual Skills

Comparing and Contrasting Have students look at the photograph of the airplane on this page and compare and contrast it with some of the first airplanes developed.

Have interested students research how planes have evolved since the early 1900s and make a report of their research to the class. Encourage students to include photographs to show the progress of development in air travel, and to credit their sources for both text and photos. Then have them give an oral presentation to the class. Verbal/Linguistic, Visual/Spatial

---

Academic Vocabulary

decline to reduce in number

Workers install an engine cover on a passenger plane at an aerospace factory in Washington state. **Identifying** What other states became important centers of the aerospace industry?

northern Plains. Winter wheat—planted in the fall and harvested in the spring—grows in the southern Plains. Wheat plants would wither in this southern region if they faced the hot summer temperatures. Other important crops in the Plains include cotton, corn, hay, and sorghum, another grain. Cattle and sheep ranching are major activities from Montana to New Mexico.

Other areas in the region are known for other crops. Washington and Oregon produce dairy products and fruit. Idaho is famous for potatoes. California, with its warm, year-round Mediterranean climate, provides fruits and vegetables throughout the year.

Today, the number of small family farms in the region is **declining**. They are being replaced by large **agribusinesses**, firms that rely on machines, advanced technology, and mass-production methods to farm large areas.

The Mining Industry

Mining the region's vast resources remains a vital part of its economy. Oil and gas fields in the southern Plains, Wyoming, and southern California provide energy. Mines in Montana furnish copper, and those in the Colorado Plateau provide uranium. The Northwest is still a major producer of timber.

The Aerospace Industry

In the early 1900s, the airplane industry was born. Decades later, the states of Washington, California, and Texas became important to the aerospace industry. The **aerospace** industry makes vehicles that

Stephen Brashear/Getty Images News/Getty Images

---

networks   *Online Teaching Options*

GRAPHS

Industries in the Western United States

Analyzing Graphs Display the interactive circle graphs about various types of industry in the western United States. Have volunteers identify and read the information presented on the graphs. Discuss with students the current aspects of industry, service, and agricultural industries. **BL** Visual/Spatial

See page 145E for other online activities.

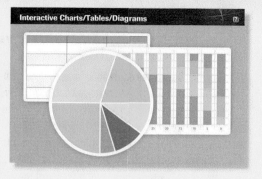

Interactive Charts/Tables/Diagrams

ANSWER, p. 170

Identifying California and Texas

travel in the air and in outer space. This industry brought many engineers and other highly skilled workers to the United States west of the Mississippi.

The aerospace industry remains important in southern California and around Seattle. Employment in this industry has declined in recent years, however. Taking its place has been the computer industry. The first area to experience rapid growth from this field was California's Silicon Valley. Today, centers of computer research and manufacturing are also found in Texas, Washington, and New Mexico.

Service Industries in the Region

Advanced technologies, such as robotics and computerized automation, have transformed manufacturing in the region. As with farming, the region's factories produce greater quantities of goods with fewer workers than in the past.

The growth of computer technology has spawned other industries. Software and information science companies are based in the same areas that are home to computer manufacturing. Utah and Colorado have also become important in these fields. Los Angeles, San Francisco, Denver, Dallas, and Seattle have become major financial centers. Telecommunications—telephone and related services—is an important industry in Denver and Dallas.

Over time, new industries have focused on tertiary economic activities such as retail sales, entertainment, and tourism. Visitors flock to the area to see the soaring mountains, stunning rock formations, and dense forests. They enjoy unusual features like Alaska's glaciers and Hawaii's tropical beaches. The western region includes some of the most-visited national parks in the country.

☑ **READING PROGRESS CHECK**

Citing Text Evidence Why did tourism and the tourist industry develop in the United States west of the Mississippi?

Include this lesson's information in your Foldable®.

LESSON 3 REVIEW

Reviewing Vocabulary
1. Why would the loss of *topsoil* threaten *agribusiness*?

Answering the Guiding Questions
2. *Determining Central Ideas* Why is it unusual that Denver developed into a major city?

3. *Identifying* What are the advantages and disadvantages of open borders?

4. *Analyzing* What steps could be taken to prevent the damage caused by mud slides? Explain your answer.

5. *Describing* Would you describe the economy of these states as diversified? Explain.

6. *Informative/Explanatory Writing* Write a short essay explaining why water conservation is important in the region.

Chapter 5 **171**

C1 Critical Thinking Skills

Making Connections Explain to students that articles can be found every day online or in newspapers about advances in technology and new products being introduced to the public. Have students discuss how advances in the computer industry and new technology affect them personally. *(Students' answers should include relevant and specific details about how they use technology and the types of products they buy.)* Verbal/ Linguistic, Intrapersonal

C2 Critical Thinking Skills

Hypothesizing Discuss with students how most people today have cell phones, computers, and/or tablets or have access to these forms of modern technology through libraries or schools. Lead a discussion with students about what life would be like without these forms of modern technology. Ask students to consider whether they think life would be easier or more difficult. *(Students' answers should give reasons why life would be different and explain that communicating and researching information are now much easier but that escaping from the stresses of life may be more difficult with these forms of technology.)* Verbal/Linguistic, Interpersonal

W Writing Skills

Narrative Have students choose one form of technology that they feel they could not live without and describe its benefits in a paragraph. Verbal/Linguistic

CLOSE & REFLECT

To close this lesson, have students think about the economy of the western region of the United States. Have a group discussion about how technology can either help or hurt the local economy there.

LESSON 3 REVIEW ANSWERS

Reviewing Vocabulary

1. The loss of topsoil would threaten agribusiness because less topsoil would make the land less fertile, and thus hamper the mass-production of crops on which agribusiness depends.

Answering the Guiding Questions

2. **Determining Central Ideas** Denver is not a port city or located on the navigable part of a river, both of which would have helped its growth by promoting trade.

3. **Identifying** Advantages: the ease of trade and of the movement of visitors from one nation to another. Disadvantage: is that it makes it easy for illegal immigrants to enter the country.

4. **Analyzing** Banning construction where mudslides are likely to occur would prevent those disasters from causing damage.

5. **Describing** The economy of the states west of the Mississippi River is diversified because it has farming and ranching and the businesses tied to agriculture; manufactures important goods like aerospace equipment and computers; and is home to important service industries, such as software, finance, entertainment, and tourism.

6. **Informative/Explanatory Writing** The region is dry and the rising population and increasing need for water for agriculture puts a strain on the limited amount of water available, thus making it important to conserve water by using it wisely.

ANSWER, p. 171

☑ READING PROGRESS CHECK The western United States has a wide variety of geographical features that attract visitors. The region also includes many picturesque national parks.

CHAPTER REVIEW ACTIVITY

Have students create a four-column chart like the one below with the following column heads: *Physical Landscape, Bodies of Water, Climate, Resources.* Tell students to complete the chart for the western United States with examples for each category. *(Possible answers:* **Physical Landscape**—*plains, mountains, hills, basins, plateaus, mesas, canyons, islands, volcanoes;* **Bodies of Water**—*Pacific Ocean, Gulf of Mexico, Great Salt Lake, Crater Lake, Lake Tahoe, Lake Mead, and other lakes, Colorado River, Columbia River, Snake River, Willamette River, and other rivers;* **Climate**—*varies by region—wet (rain/snow), hot and dry, semi-arid, humid continental climate, or humid subtropical, cold and heavy snow in Alaska, tropical rain forest climate in Hawaii;* **Resources**—*vast amount of land, petroleum, natural gas, hydroelectric power, wind power, solar power, gold, silver, copper, zinc, lead, timber, fertile soil, natural beauty)*

Western United States			
Physical Landscape	Bodies of Water	Climate	Resources

REVIEW THE ENDURING UNDERSTANDING

Review this chapter's Enduring Understanding with students:

People, places, and ideas change over time.

Now pose the following questions in a class discussion to apply this idea to this chapter.

- **How might people change their use of petroleum and natural gas to avoid using up those resources?** *(Sample answers: use less oil and gas by switching to alternative fuels, such as electricity to power vehicles; use wind and solar power for heating and cooling homes and buildings)*

- **How did Native Americans adapt their way of life to the physical landscape and climate of the western United States?** *(Sample answer: They settled along rivers so that they would have a source of water; they built houses that could be moved as they traveled; some used mud to build homes to keep the interiors cool and provide insulation from the desert heat.)*

- **How did port cities change the kind of products consumers bought?** *(Sample answer: Port cities opened up international trade and allowed foreign goods to enter the marketplace.)*

Chapter 5 ACTIVITIES

Directions: Write your answers on a separate piece of paper.

1 Use your **FOLDABLES** to explore the Essential Question.
INFORMATIVE/EXPLANATORY WRITING Write an essay explaining why the physical geography of the area west of the Mississippi River made settlement of the region difficult.

2 21st Century Skills
ANALYZING Working in small groups, research and prepare a presentation explaining how an alternative resource can be used to reduce America's dependence on foreign oil.

3 Thinking Like a Geographer
CITING TEXT EVIDENCE Create a time line like the one shown and place these six events in the correct order on it.
- Lewis and Clark expedition
- The American Revolution
- Louisiana Purchase
- Spanish establish settlements in the West
- Alaska is purchased from Russia
- The Pueblo flourish in the Southwest

4 GEOGRAPHY ACTIVITY

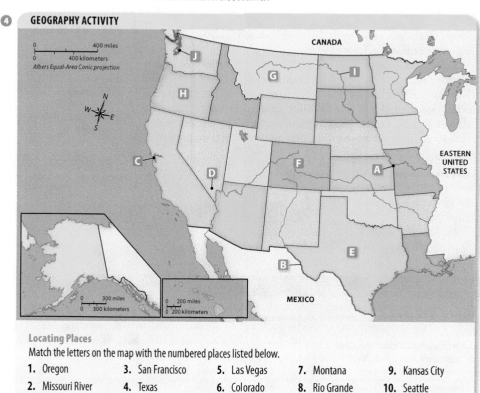

Locating Places
Match the letters on the map with the numbered places listed below.
1. Oregon
2. Missouri River
3. San Francisco
4. Texas
5. Las Vegas
6. Colorado
7. Montana
8. Rio Grande
9. Kansas City
10. Seattle

ACTIVITIES ANSWERS

Exploring the Essential Question

1 **INFORMATIVE/ EXPLANATORY WRITING** Students' writing should refer to the rugged physical features of the region including steep, rocky mountain trails, vast deserts, rushing rivers in some areas and a lack of water in other areas. They might also mention the lack of roads and rail lines and the harsh weather conditions as obstacles to settlement. Essays should be well thought out and display good grammar and spelling.

REVIEW THE GUIDING QUESTIONS

Directions: Choose the best answer for each question.

1 The Rocky Mountains are
   A. the shortest mountain range in the United States.
   B. a cordillera that extends from Canada to Mexico.
   C. an archipelago.
   D. worn down from erosion.

2 Which of the following is a contiguous state?
   F. Puerto Rico
   G. Alaska
   H. Colorado
   I. Hawaii

3 How did western settlement affect Native Americans?
   A. They were able to sell their lands for a great deal of money.
   B. Those who did not die of disease were forced onto reservations.
   C. They moved east to work in coal mines and factories.
   D Many became cowboys or joined the army.

4 During the Civil War, Congress passed the Homestead Act, which
   F. guaranteed low-interest loans to home buyers.
   G. established the border with Canada.
   H. set aside land to be used for schools.
   I. gave away western lands to people who were willing to move there and build farms.

5 Population in the states west of the Mississippi River is
   A. growing slowly.
   B. declining.
   C. growing rapidly.
   D. showing little change.

6 Which resource is the most critical factor to further development in the western states?
   F. oil
   G. natural gas
   H. solar power
   I. freshwater

Chapter 5 **173**

21st Century Skills

2 **ANALYZING** Presentations should reflect thorough research. They should be factual, interesting, well-organized, and make use of charts, graphs, or other visual materials to tell their story.

Thinking Like a Geographer

3 **CITING TEXT EVIDENCE** Order of events on the timeline: The Pueblo people flourish in the Southwest; Spanish establish settlements in the West; The American Revolution; Louisiana Purchase; Lewis and Clark expedition; Alaska is purchased from Russia

Geography Activity

4 **LOCATING PLACES**

1. H	6. F
2. I	7. G
3. C	8. B
4. E	9. A
5. D	10. J

ASSESSMENT ANSWERS

Review the Guiding Questions

1 **B** For this question, students will need to think about what they know about the Rockies and other mountains. Knowing that the Rockies extend from Canada, through the United States, to Mexico eliminates choice A. Remembering that the Appalachians in the east are worn down from erosion eliminates choice D. Knowing that an archipelago is a group of islands, like Hawaii, eliminates choice C. Refer students to Lesson 1 for help in understanding what a cordillera is.

2 **H** Remind students that *contiguous* means "connected to." Puerto Rico is not a state, so students should be able to eliminate this choice immediately. Alaska and Hawaii, while both states, are not connected to the other states, so these answers can be rejected. Colorado, which is bordered by other states, is the correct answer choice.

3 **B** To answer this question, students will need to remember that the spread of white settlements came at the expense of Native Americans. Most white settlers did not pay for the Native Americans' lands; they just took them. In the end, Native Americans were forced to live on reservations. The word *reservations* is a helpful clue in answer choice B. Refer students to Lesson 2 for help.

4 **I** A helpful clue in this question is the word *Homestead*. Associating the word with the idea of *building a farm* helps students to eliminate choices F, G, and H. If needed, refer students to Lesson 2 to review the provisions of the Homestead Act.

5 **C** To answer this question, students need to remember that some of the nation's most rapidly growing cities are in the interior of the United States, west of the Mississippi River. Also visualizing people traveling to the vast, open spaces of the West helps students understand that the population is getting bigger, which eliminates choices A, B, and D.

6 **I** A helpful clue in this question is the word *critical*, meaning "having the potential to become disastrous." Thinking about things that people could potentially live without eliminates choices F, G, and H; however, people need water to survive.

Assessment Answers

DBQ Analyzing Documents

7 **C** Students should understand that growth rate measures the difference from one year to another of the number of people in a region, not the number of states or amount of land that do not change. Since the statistics are about population, they refer to the number of people.

8 **G** By reading the passage carefully students should realize that the population of the Northeast increased by only 6 percent, while that of the West increased by 20 percent. By using simple math, students should know that 20 percent is more than three times greater than 6 percent.

Short Response

9 Possible answer: The western states have a dry climate that creates challenges for having enough water for a growing population and for agriculture and other uses. If climate changes and rainfall lessens, farming will become even more difficult in the region and people who farm will most likely have to change their ways of life.

10 Students' answers will vary but might include such steps as conservation to use less water and preventing wasteful uses of water. Their responses should also include an explanation of why they think the steps they suggest would be effective in solving the problem.

Extended Response

11 Press releases should be well written and show evidence of sufficient research using reliable resources. Students' writing should highlight well-known attractions in the state and include lesser-known places of special interest to the student. Writing should also be grammatically correct, use sentence variety, and be interesting to read.

DBQ ANALYZING DOCUMENTS

7 **DETERMINING WORD MEANING** Read the following quotation about the American population.

"With an overall 20 percent growth rate, the [population of the] West grew more rapidly than any other region. The South was the second fastest growing region, increasing 17 percent. The Midwest and the Northeast grew almost 8 percent and 6 percent, respectively."

—from *National Atlas of the United States*

What does the term *growth rate* in the passage refer to?

A. the number of states in one year compared to another
B. the amount of land in one year compared to another
C. the number of people in one year compared to another
D. the economic output in one year compared to another

8 **CITING TEXT EVIDENCE** How did population growth in the West compare to that in the Northeast?

F. much lower
G. more than three times higher
H. about the same
I. nearly twice as high

SHORT RESPONSE

"In the Western United States, the availability of water has become a serious concern. . . . The climate . . . in the West . . . is best known for its low precipitation, aridity [dryness], and drought. . . .The potential for departures from average climatic conditions threatens to disrupt society and local to regional economies."

—from Mark T. Anderson and Lloyd H. Woosley, Jr.,
Water Availability in the Western United States

9 **IDENTIFYING** Why might a change in climate threaten to disrupt societies and economies?

10 **ANALYZING** What do you think the people of the western states should do in light of this problem? Why would it work?

EXTENDED RESPONSE

11 **INFORMATIVE/EXPLANATORY WRITING** Imagine that you are the governor of any one of the states west of the Mississippi River and you want to bring more tourism dollars into your state. Use what you have learned from the chapter and do additional Internet research on that state. Write a press release to newspaper travel editors that promotes all the reasons people should vacation in your state.

Need Extra Help?

If You've Missed Question	❶	❷	❸	❹	❺	❻	❼	❽	❾	❿	⓫
Review Lesson	1	1	2	2	3	3	3	3	3	3	1

174 *Chapter 5*

From "Water Availability for the Western United States—Key Scientific Challenges" by Mark T. Anderson and Lloyd H. Woosley, Jr., U.S. Geological Survey Circular 1261. Department of the Interior/USGS. The USGS home page is http://www.usgs.gov.

---

networks   *Online Teaching Options*

Remediation and Assessment

Evaluating The *Assess* tab in the online Teacher Lesson Center includes resources to help students improve their test-taking skills. It also contains many project-based rubrics to help you assess students' work.

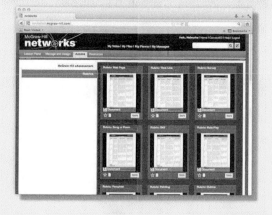

CHAPTER 6
Canada Planner

UNDERSTANDING BY DESIGN®

Enduring Understandings

- *Over time, people adapt to their environment.*
- *People, places, and ideas change over time.*

Essential Questions

- *How do people adapt to their environment?*
- *What makes a culture unique?*

Predictable Misunderstandings

- *It is always cold in Canada.*
- *The people of Canada originated from England.*
- *The is just one main language spoken in Canada.*

Assessment Evidence

Performance Tasks:

- *Project-Based Learning Digital Hands-On Chapter Project*
- *Project-Based Learning Hands-On Chapter Project*

Other Evidence:

- *What Do You Know? Activity*
- *Geography Skills Worksheet*
- *Participation in Interactive Whiteboard Activities*
- *Contribution to small-group activities*
- *Interpretation of slide show images and special purpose maps*
- *Participation in completing the Six Essential Elements Digital Chart*
- *Participation in class discussions about the Geographer's World*
- *Lesson Reviews*
- *Chapter Assessments*

SUGGESTED PACING GUIDE

Introducing the Chapter.............. 2 Days	Lesson 3 .... 2 Days
Lesson 1 .... 2 Days	Chapter Wrap-Up and Assessment..... 2 Days
Lesson 2 .... 2 Days	

TOTAL TIME   10 Days

Key for Using the Teacher Edition

SKILL-BASED ACTIVITIES

Types of skill activities found in the Teacher Edition.

* **V** **Visual Skills** require students to analyze maps, graphs, charts, and photos.

W **Writing Skills** provide writing opportunities to help students comprehend the text.

R **Reading Skills** help students practice reading skills and master vocabulary.

C **Critical Thinking Skills** help students apply and extend what they have learned.

T **Technology Skills** require students to use digital tools effectively.

*Letters are followed by a number when there is more than one of the same type of skill on the page.

DIFFERENTIATED INSTRUCTION

All activities are written for the on-level student unless otherwise marked with the leveled labels below.

BL Beyond Level
AL Approaching Level
ELL English Language Learners

All students benefit from activities that utilize different learning styles. Many activities are marked as below when a particular learning style is highlighted.

Intrapersonal	Naturalist
Logical/Mathematical	Kinesthetic
Visual/Spatial	Auditory/Musical
Verbal/Linguistic	Interpersonal

Indiana Academic Standards

Students will:

6.1.11 Compare and contrast Spanish, Portuguese, French, and British colonies in the Americas.

6.1.18 Create and compare timelines that identify major people, events and developments in the history of individual civilizations and/or countries that comprise Europe and the Americas.

6.1.19 Define and use the terms decade, century, and millennium, and compare alternative ways that historical periods and eras are designated by identifying the organizing principles upon which each is based.

6.2.6 Identify and describe the functions of international political organizations in the world today.

6.3.1 Demonstrate a broad understanding of the countries and capitals of Europe and the Americas.

6.3.5 Give examples and describe the formation of important river deltas, mountains and bodies of water in Europe and the Americas.

6.3.8 Identify major biomes of Europe and the Americas and explain how these are influenced by climate.

6.3.12 Compare the distribution and evaluate the importance of natural resources such as natural gas, oil, forests, uranium, minerals, coal, seafood and water in Europe and the Americas.

6.3.14 Explain and give examples of how nature has impacted the physical environment and human populations in specific areas of Europe and the Americas.

6.4.7 Identify economic connections between the local community and the countries of Europe or the Americas and identify job skills needed to be successful in the workplace.

CHAPTER OPENER PLANNER

Students will know:

- *the geography and climate of Canada.*
- *how Canada is organized politically.*
- *the importance of Canada's major bodies of water.*
- *about the First Nations and the influence of France and England on the people of Canada.*

Students will be able to:

- *identify provinces, cities, and towns in Canada, using a map.*
- *use a time line to discuss significant events in the history of Canada.*

UNDERSTANDING
BY DESIGN®

☑ *Print Teaching Options*

V Visual Skills

☐ **P. 176** Students read a map to answer questions about the unique features of Canada's geographic location. **AL**

☐ **P. 177** Students review the time line about the history of Canada, discuss the major events, and answer questions about the time line.

C Critical Thinking Skills

☐ **P. 177** Students infer the meanings of events on the time line and do an Internet search to identify the meanings of those that they cannot infer.

☑ *Online Teaching Options*

☐ **MAP** **Reading a Map**—Students identify aspects and locations of the region on a map.

☐ **TIME LINE** **Reading a Time Line and Map**—Students identify where in Canada events on the timeline took place and locate the places on a map. **AL** Visual/Spatial

☐ **MAP** **Interactive World Atlas**—Students use the interactive world atlas to identify the region and describe its terrain.

☑ *Printable Digital Worksheets*

☐ **WORKSHEET** **Geography Skills: Understanding the St. Lawrence Seaway**—Students can use the worksheet to understand how the St. Lawrence Seaway works.

☐ **WORKSHEET** **Cultural Geography Activity: The VIA and Travel in Canada**—Students can use the worksheet to review how the VIA was constructed and its current role in tourism in Canada, along with the movement of goods and people for employment.

Project-Based Learning ✋

Hands-On

Making a Giant Puzzle
In small groups, students will create a giant puzzle of Canada's regions. Assign each group a region of Canada, and have them research information about it. On poster board, students will draw and cut out an outline of the region, creating a puzzle piece. Puzzle pieces may include physical features and illustrate the region's resources using photos, drawings, or text. Have groups present and display their puzzles.

Digital Hands-On

Creating Digital Essay
Students will work in pairs to analyze the historical, physical, economic, and cultural characteristics of Canada. Pairs will create a digital essay that describes what life is like in Canada including relevant vocabulary words, content, and time lines in their essays. As they analyze, have them take notes in an online note-taking system and write a script, which can be stored online. Students may also include links to online movies or audio podcast programs.

edtechteacher
21ˢᵗ Century Learning

Print Resources

ANCILLARY RESOURCES
These ancillaries are available for every chapter and lesson.

- **Reading Essentials and Study Guide Workbook** **AL** **ELL**
- **Chapter Tests and Lesson Quizzes Blackline Masters**

PRINTABLE DIGITAL WORKSHEETS
These printable digital worksheets are available for every chapter and lesson!

- **Hands-On Chapter Projects**
- **What Do You Know? Activities**
- **Chapter Summaries (English and Spanish)**
- **Vocabulary Builder Activities**
- **Quizzes and Tests (English and Spanish)**
- **Reading Essentials and Study Guide (English and Spanish)** **AL** **ELL**
- **Guided Reading Activities**

More Media Resources

SUGGESTED VIDEOS
NOTE: Be sure to preview videos to ensure they are age-appropriate.

- **Nanook of the North** (79 min)
- **St. Lawrence: Stairway to the Sea** (96 min)
- **For Future Generations** (54 min)

SUGGESTED READING 📚
- ***Mabel Riley: A Reliable Record of Humdrum, Peril, and Romance,*** by Marthe Jocelyn
- ***Crazy About Canada!: Amazing Things Kids Want to Know*** by Vivian Bowers **AL**
- ***Canada: The Culture (Lands, People, & Cultures)*** by Bobbie Kalman **AL**
- ***Blizzard of Glass: The Halifax Explosion of 1917,*** by Sally Walker **BL**

The Physical Geography of Canada

Students will know:
- the geography and climate of Canada.
- how Canada is organized politically.
- the importance of Canada's major bodies of water.

Students will be able to:
- **identify, locate, and describe** the provinces of Canada in terms of geography and climate.
- **analyze** the importance of Canada's major bodies of water.

UNDERSTANDING
BY DESIGN

☑ *Print Teaching Options*

V Visual Skills

☐ **P. 179** Students draw an outline map of Canada, labeling the regions, provinces, territories, and physical features.

☐ **P. 179** Students create word squares for the words *coniferous* and *deciduous*. **ELL**

☐ **P. 180** Students analyze photographs to compare and contrast the physical features of two national parks.

☐ **P. 181** Students draw a simple diagram of the landscape of the Far North.

☐ **P. 182** Students create a chart to summarize information about bodies of water in Canada, their effects on climate, and their economic importance.

☐ **P. 182** Students interpret the diagram and map about the impact of the St. Lawrence Seaway.

W Writing Skills

☐ **P. 183** Students research the environmental effects of the St. Lawrence Seaway and write a short report on it. **BL**

R Reading Skills

☐ **P. 178** Students express the difference between a province and a territory. **ELL**

☐ **P. 179** Students summarize the features of Quebec and Ontario. **AL**

☐ **P. 180** Students summarize information on the dominant landform and the climate in the Prairie Provinces. **AL**

C Critical Thinking Skills

☐ **P. 178** Students infer the relationship between the U.S. and Canada based on their shared undefended border. **AL**

☐ **P. 181** Students identify and analyze snowmobiling and other outdoor recreational activities.

T Technology Skills

☐ **P. 180** Students conduct research to locate photographs of the Prairie Provinces and British Columbia and prepare and present a slide show. **BL**

☑ *Online Teaching Options*

V Visual Skills

☐ **VIDEOS** **Landscapes of Canada**—Students watch videos on the landscapes of Canada and identify the various kinds of landforms and biomes. Then they create charts describing the climate of each region. **Visual/Spatial, Naturalist**

☐ **MAP** **Regions of Canada**—Students can use the regional layer of the Chapter Opener map to review the regions and provinces of Canada.

☐ **VIDEO** **Niagara Falls**—Students can use the video of the Niagara Falls to discuss this body of water on the border of Canada and the United States.

W Writing Skills

☐ **VIDEO** **Around the World—British Columbia**—Students watch a video about British Columbia's physical geography. Then they write three questions about Canada and British Columbia. **Visual/Spatial**

R Reading Skills

☐ **GRAPHIC ORGANIZER** **Canada's Land**—Students use the graphic organizer to organize information in this lesson.

C Critical Thinking Skills

☐ **GAME** **Drag-and-Drop: Comparing Landforms**—Students play a game where they sort and categorize the landforms of Canada and compare these to landforms in the United States. **Kinesthetic, Logical/Mathematical**

☐ **MAP** **Physical Geography: Canada**—Students use the physical geography map to compare and contrast the landscapes of the Prairie Provinces and British Columbia and choose one region to draw a picture of showing contrasts in elevation. **AL** **Visual/Spatial**

T Technology Skills

☐ **ANIMATION** **The St. Lawrence Seaway**—Students watch an animation of a ship going through the lock system of the St. Lawrence Seaway and make connections to elevators in tall buildings. **Logical/Mathematical**

☐ **ONLINE SELF-CHECK QUIZ** **Lesson 1**—Students receive instant feedback on their mastery of lesson content.

☑ *Printable Digital Worksheets*

W Writing Skills

☐ **WORKSHEET** **Geography Skills: Understanding the St. Lawrence Seaway**—Students can use the worksheet to understand how the St. Lawrence Seaway works.

THE HISTORY OF CANADA

Students will know:

- about the First Nations and the influence of France and England on the people of Canada.
- Canada gained its independence from England in the 1900s.

Students will be able to:

- **describe** the ways of life of the First Nations of Canada.
- **explain** how exploration and settlement changed Canada.
- **describe** westward expansion in Canada and growth into the 1900s.

UNDERSTANDING
BY DESIGN®

☑ *Print Teaching Options*

V Visual Skills

☐ **P. 185** Students create a three-column chart to take notes on the ways the people of the eastern woodlands, Pacific Coast, and Far North lived. ELL AL

☐ **P. 185** Students analyze a photograph of a mother and infant to determine when it was taken.

☐ **P. 187** Students analyze Canadian postage stamps.

R Reading Skills

☐ **P. 184** Students determine the meaning of the word *aboriginal* and make connections between the Ice Age and migration of people from Asia to North America. ELL

☐ **P. 185** Students determine the central ideas during the period of French settlement. AL

☐ **P. 186** Students identify the main idea of each paragraph in the section on how the British controlled Canada. AL

☐ **P. 187** Students make connections between Canadian history and United States history.

☐ **P. 188** Students summarize how Canada became industrialized in the 1900s. AL

☐ **P. 189** Students calculate how many years after the United States Canada gained its independence. AL

C Critical Thinking Skills

☐ **P. 188** Students make connections between United States holidays and the photograph showing Canada Day.

T Technology Skills

☐ **P. 187** Students conduct Internet research on either the role of the métis in the creation of Manitoba or on the expulsion of Native peoples from their lands during Canada's westward expansion. BL

☐ **P. 188** Students research how Canadians celebrate Canada Day.

☑ *Online Teaching Options*

V Visual Skills

VIDEO **The Separation Vote**—Students watch a video about the separation vote that occurred in Quebec and share with partners what they learned. AL Visual/Spatial

SLIDE SHOW **The First Nations of Canada**—Students discuss the aboriginals' ways of life in Canada and how they made adaptations to their environment. Visual/Spatial, Logical/Mathematical

W Writing Skills

GRAPHIC ORGANIZER **People in Canada**—Students continue discussing treatment of different cultural and ethnic groups and compare the issues of civil rights to those of the U.S. government in the 1900s as they fill in information. BL Verbal/Linguistic

R Reading Skills

LECTURE SLIDES **Government Policies and Native Groups**—Students discuss the ways the Canadian government has treated different cultural and ethnic groups in Canada and compare this to policies of the U.S. government toward Native Americans. Interpersonal

C Critical Thinking Skills

GAME **Drag-and-Drop: Comparing U. S. and Canadian History**—Students play a game where they drag and drop events into one of two categories—unique to Canada or similar to the United States. Kinesthetic

T Technology Skills

ONLINE SELF-CHECK QUIZ **Lesson 2**—Students receive instant feedback on their mastery of lesson content.

LIFE IN CANADA

Students will know:

- that most of Canada's people live in cities or suburbs.
- how Canada is organized politically.
- Canada and the United States have close geographic, economic, and national defense ties.
- Canada is an active world leader and supports peacekeeping efforts.

Students will be able to:

- **identify** where Canadians live.
- **describe** Canada's economic and political relationships with other countries.
- **analyze** Canada's peacekeeping role in the world.
- **understand** challenges Canada faces.

UNDERSTANDING BY DESIGN®

☑ *Print Teaching Options*

V Visual Skills

☐ **P. 192** Students create a graphic organizer to summarize the main ideas about Canada's ties to the United States. **AL ELL**

☐ **P. 195** Students create a graphic organizer to summarize the effects of climate change and acid rain.

W Writing Skills

☐ **P. 195** Students research the environmental concerns about producing oil from the Athabasca Tar Sands and write a brief report on the issue. **BL**

R Reading Skills

☐ **P. 191** Students learn about the root, prefix, and meaning of the word *bilingual* and share other words with the prefix *bi-*. **AL**

☐ **P. 191** Students group Canadian cities into categories. **AL**

☐ **P. 193** Students recall the type of government that both Britain and Canada have.

C Critical Thinking Skills

☐ **P. 192** Students draw conclusions about why a foreign country might want to eliminate trade barriers with another country.

☐ **P. 194** Students discuss reasons for the separatist movement in Canada and the potential problems it could cause.

T Technology Skills

☐ **P. 194** Students research the creation of the new territory of Nunavut and give a brief oral report on their findings. **BL**

☑ *Online Teaching Options*

V Visual Skills

☐ **MAP** **Population: Canada**—Students use the population map to discuss population density in Canada and they identify where the majority of Canadians live. **Visual/Spatial**

☐ **MAP** **VIA Train Route across Canada**—Students take a "trip" across Canada using the train route map describing the terrain, provinces, and towns they pass. **BL Logical/ Mathematical, Kinesthetic**

☐ **IMAGE** **360 View: Toronto**—Students can use the 360 image of the space needle in Toronto to discuss the major cities of Canada.

☐ **IMAGES** **Bilingual Signs in Canada**—Students can use the interactive images of common signs presented in two languages to discuss bilingualism in Canada.

W Writing Skills

☐ **VIDEO** **Northern Canada Climate Change**—Students watch a video about the climate change in Canada and write a paragraph about an aspect they found interesting. **AL Verbal/ Linguistic**

☐ **MAP** **Resources: Canada**—Students use the interactive map to discuss the resources and economy of Canada and Canada's role in NAFTA. Then students write a descriptive paragraph about the relationship between the United States and Canada based on resources. **Verbal/ Linguistic, Naturalist**

R Reading Skills

☐ **LECTURE SLIDE** **NAFTA**—Students can use the lecture slide about NAFTA facts to discuss Canada's role in NAFTA.

☐ **GAME** **Canada's Environment**—Students can use the drag-and-drop game to discuss Canada and the environment.

C Critical Thinking Skills

☐ **GRAPHIC ORGANIZER** **Canada Compared to the U.S. and the UK**—Students complete the graphic organizer by identifying similarities among the cultures of the three countries. **Verbal/ Linguistic**

☐ **IMAGE** **Separatist Movement in Canada**—Students can use the interactive image to discuss the separatist movement in Quebec.

T Technology Skills

☐ **ONLINE SELF-CHECK QUIZ** **Lesson 3**—Students receive instant feedback on their mastery of lesson content.

☑ *Printable Digital Worksheets*

W Writing Skills

☐ **WORKSHEET** **Cultural Geography: The VIA and Travel in Canada**—Students can use the worksheet to review how the VIA was constructed and its current role in tourism in Canada, along with the movement of goods and people for employment.

INTERVENTION AND REMEDIATION STRATEGIES

LESSON 1   The Physical Geography of Canada

Reading and Comprehension

Students may find some of the academic and content vocabulary words in this lesson confusing, such as the term *comprise* (sometimes confused with *compose*). Students may also be confused by the difference between a *province* and a *territory*, or the definitions of *coniferous* and *deciduous*. Have students work with a partner to make flashcards of each term and quiz each other. Circulate to provide corrective guidance to clarify meaning and pronunciation of terms as needed.

Text Evidence

Have students work in five groups to research the five provinces of Canada discussed in this lesson. Tell students to present an analysis of their findings, comparing information in the text with information found in their research. Tell students to include an objective summary of the information. Remind students to use reliable sources and to distinguish claims supported by evidence from those that are not.

LESSON 2   The History of Canada

Reading and Comprehension

Have students work in pairs to define and distinguish between the academic vocabulary terms *occupy* and *migrate*. Have students use each word in sentences that show any nuances or connotations of the words. For example, the phrase "soldiers *occupied* the town" has a different connotation than "she *occupied* the apartment for six months." Ask students to turn to a partner and discuss reasons people might *occupy* a place or *migrate* somewhere.

Text Evidence

Have students work in small groups to present a skit about different segments of Canada's history. You may wish to use the lesson's headings to assign students their skit titles: *First Nations, Exploration and Settlement,* and *Canada Grows and Unites.* Have students collaborate to use evidence from the text on which to base their script and present their skits to the class.

LESSON 3   Life in Canada

Reading and Comprehension

Have students work in pairs or small groups to outline important aspects of daily life in Canada. Tell partners to take turns summarizing portions of the text, dividing the text into segments using the lesson's headings and subheadings. To ensure comprehension of the concepts in this lesson, have students write two or three sentences describing life in Canada today.

Text Evidence

Organize students into small groups. Have each group create a list of challenges Canadians face, and what is being done to remedy these challenges. Tell students they may conduct additional research about these problems, but to use reliable sources, not tourism sites, for example. After groups have presented their lists, moderate a class debate in which students either defend or denounce the following statement: Canada should remain one unified nation. Have students defend their arguments based on facts gleaned from the text or their research.

Online Resources

Level Reader

Use this online lower-level text that corresponds directly to the text in the online Student Edition.

Guided Reading Activities

This resource uses graphic organizers and guiding questions to help students with comprehension.

What Do You Know?

Use these worksheets to pre-assess students' background knowledge before they study the chapter.

Reading Essentials and Study Guide Workbook

This resource offers writing and reading activities for the approaching-level student.

Self-Check Quizzes

This online assessment tool provides instant feedback for students to check their progress.

CANADA

ESSENTIAL QUESTIONS · *How do people adapt to their environment?*
· *What makes a culture unique?*

Blackfoot girl takes part in First Nations Pow Wow held in Alberta, Canada.

Michelle Gilders Canada West/Alamy

netw⊕rks
There's More Online about Canada.

CHAPTER 6

Lesson 1
The Physical Geography of Canada

Lesson 2
The History of Canada

Lesson 3
Life in Canada

The Story Matters...

Nearly 4 million square miles (10.4 million sq. km) in total area, Canada is the second-largest country in the world. The landscape of this immense country is known for its beauty and bountiful natural resources. Even though Canada is immense in size, it is sparsely populated. Canada's population of First Nations and Inuit people, French, English, and immigrants from around the world reflects its history and diversity.

FOLDABLES
Study Organizer

Go to the Foldables® library in the back of your book to make a Foldable® that will help you take notes while reading this chapter.

175

ENGAGE

Bellringer Ask students to think about ways in which Canada and the United States are similar and ways in which they are different. Draw a Venn diagram on the board, and write the labels *Canada* and *United States* above the two circles. Call on volunteers to come to the board and write similarities in the overlapping section. *(Examples include "large size," "democratic government," and "many immigrants.")* Then call on other volunteers to come to the board and write features that are unique to each country in the appropriate side section. *(Examples for Canada include "two official languages" and "far north location." Examples for the United States include "one official language" and "wide range of climates.")*

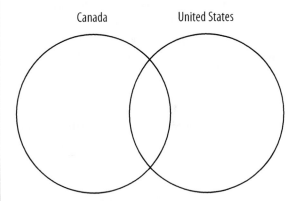

Canada   United States

Making Connections

Have students view the photograph and read "The Story Matters...." Then have them add any new information they have learned from the text to the Venn diagram. **Ask:** What conclusions can you draw about the two countries of Canada and the United States from the diagram? *(Students might conclude that the two countries have more similarities than differences, or vice versa.)*

Tell students that they will learn much more about the features that make Canada unique in this chapter.

Letter from the Author

Dear Geography Teacher,

The United States and Canada are similar. It is useful for students to understand, however, that diversity has existed in both countries from their early settlements. In the Quebec province of Canada, French language is very dominant. Tell them that they might have more fun in Quebec if they are able to speak French. Then ask students to predict why this is so. Tell them that they will learn about Canada's history in this chapter, which will help them understand what you meant by the statement.

Richard H. Boehm

FOLDABLES
Study Organizer

Go to the Foldables® library for a cumulative chapter-based Foldable® activity that your students can use to help take notes and prepare for assessment.

TEACH & ASSESS

Step Into the Place

V Visual Skills

Reading a Map After students read the introductory paragraph and look at the map on the next page, explain that Russia is the only country that is physically larger in size than Canada. Then use the following questions for students to practice their map reading skills and to reinforce the unique features of Canada's geographic location. **Ask:**

- In what latitude range is most of Canada? *(between about 40°N and 70°N)*
- Based on this latitude range, what conclusion can you draw about the climate of much of Canada? *(Much of the country has a generally cold climate.)*
- What major circle of latitude runs through Canada? *(the Arctic Circle)*
- What major bodies of water border the country? *(Pacific Ocean, Arctic Ocean, Hudson Bay, and Atlantic Ocean)*
- Where do you think most of Canada's people live? Why? *(in the southern part of the country, because the climate is not as cold there)* **AL** Visual/Spatial

Content Background Knowledge

- More than 40 percent of Canada's landmass lies within the Arctic region.
- Along with the polar bears shown in the photograph on this page, more than 100,000 Canadians make their homes in this icy region north of the Arctic Circle, many of them indigenous people.
- The Canadian government and international environmental groups have focused attention on the dangers that global climate change pose to the animals of this region.
- With the rise in global temperatures, Arctic sea ice has been melting and polar bear litters are decreasing in size.

ANSWERS, p. 176

STEP INTO THE PLACE
1. Ontario
2. Hudson Bay
3. Ottawa
4. CRITICAL THINKING northwest

Chapter 6

CANADA

V *In land area, Canada is the second-largest country in the world. It occupies most of the northern part of North America and is bordered by three major oceans. As you study the map, look for the geographic features that make Canada unique.*

Step Into the Place

MAP FOCUS Use the map to answer the following questions.

1. **THE GEOGRAPHER'S WORLD** Which Canadian province borders the Great Lakes?
2. **THE GEOGRAPHER'S WORLD** What body of water divides Canada nearly in half?
3. **PLACES AND REGIONS** What is the national capital of Canada?
4. **CRITICAL THINKING** Analyzing What direction would you travel when flying from Winnipeg to Yellowknife?

A CANADIAN ARCTIC Canada's polar bears live in icy Arctic terrain surrounded by open water.

B VICTORIA, BRITISH COLUMBIA British Columbia's Legislative Assembly assembles in the Parliament Buildings to pass laws for the province.

Step Into the Time

DESCRIBING Select one event from the time line and write a paragraph describing how that event changed Canada.

1000 Vikings arrive in Canada

1534 Cartier explores Gulf of St. Lawrence **1608** Quebec founded **1670** Hudson's Bay Company formed **1700**

176 *Chapter 6*

(t to b) PhotoAlto/PunchStock; ©David Pillinger/Corbis; North Wind/North Wind Picture Archives

Project-Based Learning ✋

Hands-On

Making a Giant Puzzle

In small groups, students will create a giant puzzle of Canada's regions. Assign each group a region of Canada, and have them research information about it. On poster board, students will draw and cut out an outline of the region, creating a puzzle piece. On the puzzle piece, students can draw or list the physical features found in that region, and illustrate the importance of the region's resources to Canada and the world using photos, drawings, or text. After groups have presented their puzzle pieces, affix them to a classroom wall to create a complete map of Canada.

Digital Hands-On

Creating a Digital Essay

Pairs will work to analyze the historical, physical, economic, and cultural characteristics of Canada and create a digital essay that describes life in Canada. Students should include vocabulary words, content, and time lines in their essays and could include links to online movies or audio podcasts. Have them take notes in an online note-taking system and write a script that can be stored online.

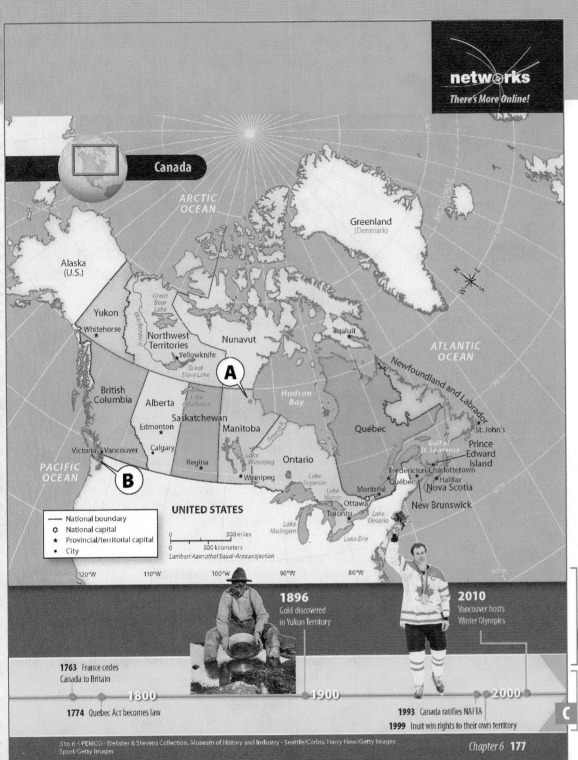

Canada

ARCTIC OCEAN

Greenland (Denmark)

Alaska (U.S.)

Yukon
Whitehorse ★

Northwest Territories
Yellowknife ★

Nunavut

Iqaluit

ATLANTIC OCEAN

Newfoundland and Labrador

British Columbia

Alberta

Saskatchewan

Manitoba

Edmonton ★

Great Bear Lake

Great Slave Lake

Lake Athabasca

Hudson Bay

Québec

A

Calgary ●

Regina ★

Lake Winnipeg

Ontario

St. John's ★

Prince Edward Island

Victoria ★ Vancouver ●

Winnipeg ★

Fredericton Charlottetown

PACIFIC OCEAN

B

Lake Superior

Lake Huron

Montréal ● Québec

Halifax ★

Nova Scotia

UNITED STATES

Ottawa ⊙

New Brunswick

Toronto ★

Lake Ontario

Lake Michigan

Lake Erie

— National boundary
⊙ National capital
★ Provincial/territorial capital
● City

0   500 miles
0   500 kilometers
Lambert Azimuthal Equal-Area projection

120°W   110°W   100°W   90°W   80°W

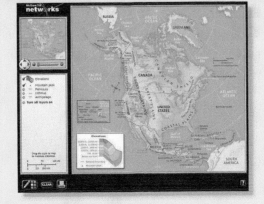

1896
Gold discovered in Yukon Territory

2010
Vancouver hosts Winter Olympics

1763 France cedes Canada to Britain

1800

1900

2000

1774 Quebec Act becomes law

1993 Canada ratifies NAFTA
1999 Inuit win rights to their own territory

(l to r) ©PEMCO - Webster & Stevens Collection, Museum of History and Industry - Seattle/Corbis; Harry How/Getty Images Sport/Getty Images

Step Into the Time

V Visual Skills

Reading a Time Line Have students review the time line, and as a class, discuss the major events depicted. **Ask:**

- What period of time is shown on the time line? *(from A.D. 1000 to 2010)*
- Who were the first Europeans to arrive in Canada? What do you know about this group? *(the Vikings; students may or may not know that the Vikings were seafaring Scandinavian pirates.)*
- What European countries claimed Canada? *(France and then Britain)*

Tell students that Canada did not gain its political independence from Britain until 1931, which was much later than the United States. **Visual/Spatial**

C Critical Thinking Skills

Making Inferences Students may not know the significance of some of the historical events included on the time line. Encourage them to infer the meaning of any events they can. Then have small groups each take an event on the time line and do a quick Internet search to identify the significance of each event and have them report back to the class about what they learned. Encourage them to explain how the event not only affected Canada, but how it may have affected other parts of the world. **Verbal/Linguistic**

V

CLOSE & REFLECT

Formulating Questions Have each student in the class generate a list of questions they have about Canada based on the chapter introduction. Place students in pairs and have them compare their questions to see how many they have in common. Suggest that students look for answers to these questions as they read the chapter.

C

TIME LINE

Reading a Time Line and Map

Display the time line and map on the whiteboard. Have volunteers read each event as it is revealed on the time line. Ask students to identify where in Canada the event took place and find its location on the map. **AL**
Visual/Spatial

See page 175B for other online activities.

ENGAGE

Bellringer Note that this first lesson focuses on Canada's physical geography. Have students look again at the Venn diagram they created for the chapter's opening activity and highlight the items that deal with physical geography. Use these items to begin a discussion of students' prior knowledge of Canada's landscape. **Ask:** What else do you know about the landscape of Canada? *(Students may know that Canada has many mountains, large coniferous forests, and large areas of tundra.)* Tell students that they will learn more about Canada's landscape in this lesson.

TEACH & ASSESS

C Critical Thinking Skills

Making Inferences Draw students' attention to the fact that the United States and Canada share the longest undefended border in the world. **Ask:**

- What does this fact suggest about the relationship between the two countries? *(It suggests that the two countries trust each other and that each country has no concern about being invaded by the other.)* Then discuss the fact that Canada has much land but few people, most of whom live in the southern part of the country.
- Why might northern Canada be sparsely populated? *(because of its cold climate)* **AL** Verbal/Linguistic

R Reading Skills

Expressing Make sure students understand and can express the difference between a *province* and *territory*. **Ask:** How does a *province* differ from a *territory*? *(A* province *is like a state and has its own government. A* territory *is not like a state and does not have its own government.)* How are a *province* and a *territory* similar? *(Both come under the rule of the national government.)* **ELL** Verbal/Linguistic

---

ANSWER, p. 178

Taking Notes Sample answers: **Atlantic Provinces:** Newfoundland and Labrador, Prince Edward Island, Nova Scotia, New Brunswick; Separated by Gulf of St. Lawrence; Mainly lowlands; Humid continental climate; **Ontario and Quebec:** Ontario, Quebec; Most populous region; From St. Lawrence and Great Lakes in south to Hudson Bay in north; Fertile land in south; **Prairie Provinces:** Manitoba, Saskatchewan, Alberta; Mostly flat land except for Canadian Shield in east and Rocky Mountains in west; little rainfall; Cold in winter, hot in summer; **British Columbia:** British Columbia; Mountainous; On Pacific Coast; Marine west coast climate; **Northern Territories:** Nunavut, Northwest Territory, Yukon Territory; Flat in center, highlands in east, and mountains in west; Very cold

---

Reading **HELP**DESK

Academic Vocabulary

- comprise
- access

Content Vocabulary

- province
- territory
- shield
- coniferous
- deciduous
- archipelago
- tundra
- fishery

TAKING NOTES: *Key Ideas and Details*

Summarizing As you read about Canada's regions, take notes about them using the graphic organizer below.

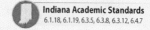

Region	Provinces or Territories	Key Facts
Atlantic Provinces		

Indiana Academic Standards
6.1.18, 6.1.19, 6.3.5, 6.3.8, 6.3.12, 6.4.7

178

Lesson 1
The Physical Geography of Canada

ESSENTIAL QUESTION · *How do people adapt to their environment?*

IT MATTERS BECAUSE
Canada shares many physical features with the United States.

Canada's Physical Landscape

GUIDING QUESTION *How is Canada's physical geography similar to and different from that of the United States?*

For millions of U.S. residents, another nation, Canada, is a short drive away. Canada is a vast and sprawling land of some 3.86 million square miles (10 million sq. km). That size makes it six times larger than the state of Alaska. Canada is larger than every nation in the world except Russia.

Canada and the United States share the longest undefended border in the world. Several of the crossings along this 5,523-mile (8,888-km) border are busy. About 400,000 people and $1.4 billion worth of goods cross it every day.

Overview of Canada

Although huge, Canada is home to relatively few people. Its population ranks thirty-sixth in the world. The great majority of those people live in the southern part of the country. Almost 90 percent of them live within 150 miles (241 km) of the Canada-U.S. border.

Canada is divided into smaller units. The main divisions are Canada's 10 provinces. **Provinces** are administrative units similar to states. Each province has its own government. Canada also has three territories. The **territories** are lands administered by the national government. Canada's provinces and territories can be grouped into five regions.

(l to r) Design Pics/Bilderbuch; Design Pics/Richard Wear; Design Pics/Carson Ganci/Getty Images; Anita Erdmann/Flickr/Getty Images

---

VIDEO

Around the World—British Columbia

Formulating Questions Use this video about the physical geography of British Columbia to introduce the lesson. Ask students to write three questions they have about British Columbia and Canada after watching the video. Collect the questions and discuss them as a class after the lesson. Visual/Spatial

See page 175C for other online activities.

BBC Motion Gallery Education

The Atlantic Provinces

V1

Nova Scotia, New Brunswick, Prince Edward Island, and Newfoundland and Labrador are called the Atlantic Provinces. These four relatively small provinces border the Atlantic Ocean. Except for Newfoundland and Labrador, they are distinguished mainly by lowlands and plateaus. Highlands cover western Newfoundland and Labrador.

Much of the Atlantic Provinces has a humid continental climate. Winters are cold, and summers are warm. Toward the north, winters can last as long as six months. To the south, winters last only four months. More rain falls here than in Canada's interior.

Quebec and Ontario

R

The provinces of Quebec and Ontario reach from the St. Lawrence River and Great Lakes to northern Canada. They are the heart of Canada and home to more than 6 out of every 10 Canadians.

The land along the St. Lawrence River and the Great Lakes tends to be lowland plains with fertile soil. A massive plateau called the Canadian Shield covers the northern area of these two provinces. A **shield** is a large area of relatively flat land **comprised** of ancient, hard rock. This plateau extends south, east, and west of Hudson Bay. The Shield holds many valuable minerals, such as iron ore, uranium, gold, and copper.

Like the Atlantic Provinces, the southern parts of Ontario and Quebec have a humid continental climate. Temperatures are colder to the north than to the south, and winters are longer. In the northern part of these two provinces, a subarctic climate prevails. These areas have long, cold winters and mild summers. Much of the northern part of these provinces is covered by forests that include coniferous and deciduous trees. **Coniferous** evergreen trees produce cones that hold seeds, and they have needles instead of leaves. **Deciduous** trees shed their leaves in the autumn.

V2

Rainfall and relatively mild temperatures give the southern edge of these two provinces a longer growing season than areas in northern Canada. That, combined with fertile soil, makes it a productive farming area.

Academic Vocabulary

comprise to make up

MAP SKILLS

1 PLACES AND REGIONS What subregion lies directly north of the Great Lakes?

2 THE GEOGRAPHER'S WORLD What subregions border the Pacific Ocean?

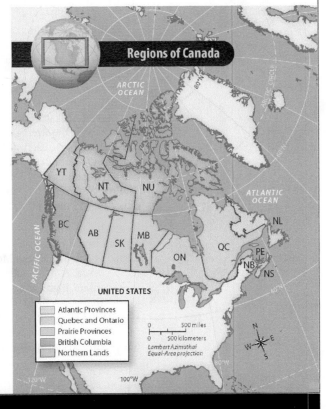

Regions of Canada

ARCTIC OCEAN

ARCTIC CIRCLE

YT

NT

NU

ATLANTIC OCEAN

BC

AB

SK

MB

NL

ON

QC

PE

NB

NS

PACIFIC OCEAN

UNITED STATES

- Atlantic Provinces
- Quebec and Ontario
- Prairie Provinces
- British Columbia
- Northern Lands

0   500 miles
0   500 kilometers
Lambert Azimuthal Equal-Area projection

N E S W

100°W

120°W

V1 Visual Skills

Creating Maps Before students begin to read about the regions of Canada, have them draw a large outline map of the country. As they read the lesson, have them label the regions, provinces, and territories of Canada and make notes on the physical features of each region of the country directly on the map. Encourage them to keep these maps as a study tool to review at the end of the chapter. **Visual/Spatial**

R Reading Skills

Summarizing After students read the section on Quebec and Ontario, have them find the two provinces on the map. Emphasize the description used in the first paragraph of this section that Quebec and Ontario are the "heart of Canada." Have students summarize what this phrase actually means. **Ask:** What features of Quebec and Ontario make these provinces the "heart of Canada"? *(These provinces are home to a majority of Canadians, have many valuable minerals, have large forests, and have fertile soil.)* **AL Verbal/Linguistic**

V2 Visual Skills

Creating Visuals The words *coniferous* and *deciduous* are key terms in geography, earth science, and biology, and thus are words that students should become familiar with. A good aid in learning content vocabulary words is to create word squares. Have students create a word square for each of these terms, in which they identify the word, write its definition, write a sentence using the word, draw a picture, and give a few examples. **ELL Visual/Spatial, Verbal/Linguistic**

Definition		Examples
	Word	
Sentence		Drawing

GAME

Drag-and-Drop: Comparing Landforms

Categorizing Display the drag-and-drop landforms game on the whiteboard. Have students sort the landforms of Canada into two groups: those shared with the United States and those unique to Canada. Encourage students to create a different graphic organizer to review the information from the game. **Kinesthetic, Logical/Mathematical**

See page 175C for other online activities.

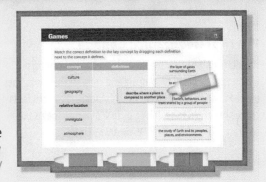

Games

Match the correct definition to the key concept by dragging each definition next to the concept it defines.

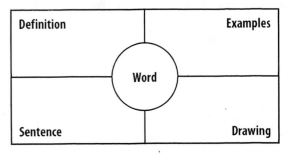

ANSWER, p. 179

MAP SKILLS
1. Ontario
2. Yukon Territory, British Columbia

The Physical Geography of Canada

R Reading Skills

Summarizing Help students summarize the information on the Prairie Provinces by focusing on the dominant landform of the region and the climate. **Ask:** What is the main landform of the Prairie Provinces? *(plains)* How would you describe the climate of the Prairie Provinces? *(cold winters, warm summers, little precipitation)* Then have students use this information to write a summary of the section. **AL** Verbal/Linguistic

T Technology Skills

Researching on the Internet and Using Visual Aids Have students conduct Internet research to locate photographs of the Prairie Provinces and of British Columbia. Suggest that students prepare and present their own slide show contrasting the landscape of the Prairie Provinces with that of British Columbia. Remind students to include the sources of the photos they use. **BL** Visual/Spatial

V Visual Skills

Analyzing Visuals Have students look at both photographs on the page and compare and contrast the physical features shown. Have them decide which of these two national parks they would like to visit. Ask volunteers to share their choice and the reason(s) why they would prefer one over the other. Visual/Spatial, Naturalist

Content Background Knowledge

The five national parks in the Canadian Rockies are Banff, Jasper, Kootenay, Waterton Lakes, and Yoho. Like the United States, Canada has an extensive national park system that preserves many of the country's spectacular wilderness areas. Banff, Canada's first national park, was established in 1885. By 1888, a 250-room hotel was built in the park. Many people began to use Banff as a stopover on the transcontinental railroad. In 1911, a road was built to allow people to access the park in their cars.

Cape Breton Highlands National Park (left) is located in Nova Scotia. Alberta's Jasper National Park (right) is one of Canada's oldest and largest national parks.

▶ CRITICAL THINKING

Describing What is the climate of Alberta and the other Prairie Provinces?

The Prairie Provinces

The Prairie Provinces comprise Manitoba, Saskatchewan, and Alberta. They are covered chiefly by plains extending north from the United States. As in the United States, the plains are tilted from west to east. Their elevation is higher in Alberta than in Manitoba.

Highland areas rim the plains to the northeast and the west. The northeastern highlands, in Manitoba, are part of the Canadian Shield. The western highlands, in Alberta, are the eastern edge of the Canadian Rockies.

The flat land of the Prairie Provinces receives cold blasts of Arctic air from the north. The average daily temperature in January for Regina, Saskatchewan, is –1°F (–18°C). Summers are much warmer, with the average temperature in July being 67°F (19°C). The prairies have reached the highest temperature ever recorded in Canada. On one hot day in 1937, two communities in Saskatchewan had temperatures of 113°F (45°C).

Precipitation in the Prairie Provinces is light. The area receives only about 15 inches (38 cm) of rain or snow each year.

British Columbia

The landscape of British Columbia is like that of the northwestern United States. The Rocky Mountains tower over the eastern edge of the province. A deep valley and plateaus separate the mountains from another high range farther west, the Coast Mountains. The Canadian Rockies include 30 mountain peaks that reach more than 10,000 feet (3,048 m). They are also home to five of Canada's national parks. The Coast Mountains rise even higher—several of them soar more than 15,000 feet (4,572 m).

(t to r) Design Pics/Bilderbuch; Design Pics/Richard Wear

netw**o**rks *Online Teaching Options*

MAP

Physical Geography: Canada

Reading a Map Use the physical geography layer on the Chapter Opener map to compare and contrast the landscapes of the Prairie Provinces and British Columbia. Have students choose one region and draw a picture of it that shows the contrast in elevation. **AL** Visual/Spatial

See page 175C for other online activities.

ANSWER, p. 180

CRITICAL THINKING humid continental climate; cold winters and warm summers

Inlets of the Pacific Ocean cut into the mountains along British Columbia's coast. Steep cliffs rise directly from the water to heights of more than 7,000 feet (2,134 m).

British Columbia has a marine west coast climate. Temperatures are mild because warm air blows west from the ocean. Rainfall is heavy in some areas—as much as 100 inches (254 cm) per year.

Northern Lands

Canada's three territories—Nunavut, Northwest Territories, and Yukon Territory—lie to the north. The Arctic Ocean laps their northern shores. Within that ocean lies an archipelago. An **archipelago** is a group of islands. Some of the roughly 1,000 islands are tiny. Baffin Island, though, is nearly 200,000 square miles (518,000 sq. km)—larger than the state of California.

The vast center of these territories is covered by lowland plains. To the east, the rim of the Canadian Shield rises. The Shield continues onto the islands north of Hudson Bay.

The western part of the far north has high mountains. Among them is Mount Logan, Canada's highest peak, at 19,524 feet (5,951 m).

Much of the land of the territories, called the far north, is covered by a subarctic climate zone marked by cold winters and mild summers. The areas farthest north, however, have a tundra climate. The name of this climate zone comes from the landscape. A **tundra** is a flat, treeless plain with permanently frozen ground.

☑ **READING PROGRESS CHECK**

Determining Central Ideas Why do most of Canada's people live in southern Canada?

Cold and ice do not stop Yellowknife residents in the Northwest Territories from enjoying outdoor activities (left). Canada's wettest area, in terms of rain and snow, is the Pacific coast.

▶ **CRITICAL THINKING**

Describing What is the climate of the far north?

Think Again

Northern Canada receives a huge amount of snow.

Not true. The cold Arctic air that controls the climate of northern Canada holds little moisture. The dry air brings little snowfall to northern Canada. The Rocky Mountains and the Gulf of St. Lawrence region receive more snow than the far north.

Chapter 6 **181**

C **Critical Thinking Skills**

Analyzing Visuals Have students identify the recreational activity shown in the photograph on the left. *(snowmobiling)*
Ask:

• What other recreational activities might be common in areas with long, cold, snowy winters? *(snowshoeing, skiing, tobogganing, sledding, ice skating)* Direct students' attention to the cloudy, gray, rainy weather in the photograph on the right.

• In which climate do you think it would be easier to be active outdoors, a snowy one or a rainy one? *(Students' opinions may vary. Students may note that proper clothing is essential for outdoor activities in both climates.)* **Visual/Spatial, Naturalist**

V **Visual Skills**

Diagramming Suggest that students draw a simple diagram of the landscape of the far north as they read the description in the text. Remind students that the Canadian Shield is a large, flat, rocky plateau. Call on volunteers to share their diagrams with the class. **Visual/Spatial**

Content Background Knowledge

Tundras are the coldest biomes on Earth, and because they receive so little precipitation, they are similar to deserts. In fact, tundras receive less precipitation than most of the world's largest deserts. Also, tundras do not have any trees. The tundra biome covers about half of Canada. During the dark, cold winters on the tundra, the mean temperature can be below freezing for 6 to 10 months a year. As a result, the layer of ground just below the surface is permanently frozen; it is called permafrost. In the short summer, the sun shines almost 24 hours a day, and the temperature can get up to 50 degrees Fahrenheit.

VIDEOS

Landscapes of Canada

Integrating Visual Information Show the videos on the landscapes of Canada and have students identify the various kinds of landforms and biomes. Have students use visual clues to infer and create charts that describe the types of climate in each region. **Visual/Spatial, Naturalist**

See page 175C for other online activities.

ANSWERS, p. 181

CRITICAL THINKING subarctic
☑ **READING PROGRESS CHECK** Most of Canada's people live in southern Canada where the climate is warmer and the land is more fertile, and where there are more natural resources that are easier to obtain.

(l to r) Design Pics/Carson Ganci/Getty Images; Anita Erdmann/Flickr/Getty Images

Comstock Images/Jupiterimages

The Physical Geography of Canada

V1 Visual Skills

Creating a Chart Point out that this section focuses on the climatic and economic impact of Canada's major bodies of water. As they read, have students create and complete a chart like the one below to summarize the information in the text. Note that students will not find climate information for every body of water, so you may want them to do research to complete the chart. *(Pacific Ocean: brings rain and mild temperatures to western Canada, transportation of imports and exports and fishing; Arctic Ocean: chills northern and central Canada, some ship traffic; Atlantic Ocean: moderates temperatures of eastern Canada, Grand Banks fishery; Gulf of St. Lawrence: provides access to Canada's interior; Hudson Bay: provides fish and sea mammals for native peoples; Great Lakes and St. Lawrence Seaway: provide access to deep within Canada's interior; Fraser River: farming, fishing, and mining) Visual/Spatial*

Body of water	Effects on climate	Economic importance
Pacific Ocean		
Arctic Ocean		
Atlantic Ocean		
Gulf of St. Lawrence		
Hudson Bay		
Great Lakes and St. Lawrence Seaway		
Fraser River		

V2 Visual Skills

Analyzing an Image and a Map Have students use the Chapter Opener map that shows the distribution of Canada's resources and the physical geography of Canada to discuss the waterways used for shipping. Then, have students analyze the image of the logs being shipped down the waterway. **Ask:**

- How does the St. Lawrence Seaway contribute to the movement of goods? *(It allows ships to travel from the Atlantic Ocean, through the St. Lawrence River, and through all of the Great Lakes.)*
- Do you think it would be difficult to move goods if the St. Lawrence Seaway didn't exist? *(Students' answers may vary but should suggest that the St. Lawrence Seaway provides access to the interior of Canada and that if it didn't exist, it would make it harder to move goods.)* Visual/Spatial, Logical/Mathematical

Bodies of Water

V1

GUIDING QUESTION *What bodies of water are important to Canada?*

Some bodies of water shape Canada's climate. Others have economic importance.

Oceans, Bays, and Gulfs

Three oceans border Canada—the Atlantic, the Pacific, and the Arctic. The Pacific Ocean brings rain and mild temperatures to western Canada. Cold air blows over the Arctic Ocean to chill northern and central Canada. The Atlantic Ocean moderates the temperatures of eastern Canada.

The Atlantic and Pacific oceans are also important economically. Ships cross the oceans to bring goods to and from Canada. They are important for another reason, too. East of the Atlantic Provinces is an area called the Grand Banks. This part of the Atlantic Ocean is one of the world's great fisheries. A **fishery** is an area where fish come to feed in huge numbers. The Grand Banks is visited by fishing fleets from all over the world. However, overfishing has severely hurt the populations of some kinds of fish in recent years.

Tugboats tow logs along the Fraser River to sawmills. Forest industries have always been an important part of the country's economy.

182 *Chapter 6*

---

netw⊕rks *Online Teaching Options*

ANIMATION

The St. Lawrence Seaway

Integrating Visual Information Display the animation of a ship going through the lock system at the St. Lawrence Seaway to demonstrate how locks work. To help students make connections ask what feature in a tall building works somewhat like a lock. *(an elevator)* **Ask:** In what ways do you think a waterway of this type could shape transportation and trade? *(Students' answers may vary but should discuss that canals can speed up water travel.)* Logical/Mathematical

See page 175C for other online activities.

The Pacific coast is another important fishery. Many transitions are occurring in the Arctic Ocean because of climate change. Less ice is forming, which allows more ship traffic through the region. It is also altering how native peoples live.

The Gulf of St. Lawrence is another important body of water. It is an extension of the Atlantic Ocean and serves as the mouth of the St. Lawrence River. It provides **access**, or a way in, to the interior of Canada.

An inland sea called Hudson Bay covers much of east central Canada. Native peoples live around its shores. They catch fish and hunt sea mammals for food.

Lakes and Waterways

The Gulf of St. Lawrence connects to the St. Lawrence River, which flows into the Great Lakes. For centuries, rapids and steep drops in elevation blocked ships from moving along the river west of Montreal. In the 1950s, though, the United States and Canada worked together to build the St. Lawrence Seaway. They made canals and a system of locks that can raise and lower ships from water at two different levels. As a result, oceangoing ships can reach as deep into the interior as western Lake Superior.

Canada shares four of the five Great Lakes with the United States. The one it does not share is Lake Michigan. Three other major lakes are found in lowland areas west of the Canadian Shield. They are Great Slave Lake and Great Bear Lake in the Northwest Territories, and Lake Winnipeg in Manitoba.

The Mackenzie River and its tributaries dominate much of the lowlands of the far north. Beginning at Great Slave Lake, the Mackenzie flows north and west to empty into the Arctic Ocean. It is a wide river—from 1 mile to 4 miles (1.6 km to 6.4 km) across—and flows for more than 1,000 miles (1,609 km). The Fraser River flows through the mountains of British Columbia. The river basin is important for many activities such as farming, fishing, and mining.

☑ READING PROGRESS CHECK

Analyzing Why is the St. Lawrence River economically more important to Canada than the Mackenzie River?

FOLDABLES
Study Organizer

Include this lesson's information in your Foldable®.

LESSON 1 REVIEW

Reviewing Vocabulary

1. What is the difference between a *province* and a *territory* in Canada?

Answering the Guiding Questions

2. *Identifying* What landforms in Canada are similar to those in the United States?

3. *Analyzing* Why do most of Canada's people live in southern Ontario and Quebec?

4. *Identifying Point of View* Which body of water do you think is most important to Canada? Why?

5. *Analyzing* Which of Canada's regions do you think has benefited most from the fisheries of the Grand Banks? Why?

6. *Informative/Explanatory Writing* Write a paragraph describing the physical geography of one of Canada's regions and the impact of its landforms and climate on the people in that region.

Chapter 6 **183**

W **Writing Skills**

Informative/Explanatory Have students conduct research to find out the environmental effects of the St. Lawrence Seaway on the surrounding area or how the locks on the seaway work and enable ship travel. Make sure students use reliable sources and include a list of their sources.

Have students write a short explanation of how the seaway impacts the environment or how the building of the locks makes the passage of ships on the seaway possible. Encourage interested students to give a brief oral report on either subject to the class. **BL** Naturalist, Verbal/Linguistic

CLOSE & REFLECT

Have students think about living in both the United States and Canada. Ask them to list positives and negatives about living in both places. Then have a class discussion comparing life in the two countries.

Content Background Knowledge

Share the following information with students to help them appreciate how important the St. Lawrence Seaway is to the economies of Canada and the United States:

The St. Lawrence Seaway has great economic importance to both Canada and the United States. Since the completion of the seaway in 1959, the Great Lakes-St. Lawrence River system has become one of the most heavily traveled trade routes in the world, despite the fact that the shipping season generally lasts only about 8½ months because of severe winter weather. Grain from Canada's prairies and the American Midwest is the main commodity shipped through the seaway. Other commodities include iron ore, coal, and steel. Ships from many nations besides Canada and the United States use the seaway.

LESSON 1 REVIEW ANSWERS

Reviewing Vocabulary

1. In Canada, a *province* is a smaller administrative unit with its own government; *territories* are larger areas of land governed by the central government.

Answering the Guiding Questions

2. **Identifying** Central Canada has plains that are an extension of the Great Plains in the United States. Both nations also share the Rocky Mountains, a series of plateaus, and high coastal mountains.

3. **Analyzing** Most people live in southern Ontario and Quebec because these areas have a mild climate, fertile soil, and a long growing season, which are good for growing crops; and they have access to world trade through the St. Lawrence Seaway.

4. **Identifying Point of View** Students may mention either the Atlantic or Pacific Oceans, which affect the climate of parts of Canada, have important fisheries, and are avenues of trade. They may mention the St. Lawrence Seaway because it provides access for oceangoing ships to carry goods into and out of Canada's interior regions.

5. **Analyzing** The Atlantic Provinces have benefited the most from the fisheries of the Grand Banks because the region is located closest to those fishing grounds.

6. **Informative/Explanatory Writing** Student should detail the landforms, bodies of water, and climate of the chosen region and discuss how these characteristics impact the life of the people in that region.

ANSWER, p. 183

☑ READING PROGRESS CHECK The St. Lawrence River is economically more important to Canada because it is vital to the country's international trade. It connects the most populous part of Canada to nations around the world by linking the Great Lakes with the Atlantic Ocean. In contrast, the Mackenzie River flows through a remote region with few people.

The History of Canada

ENGAGE

 Bellringer Tell students that this lesson provides a summary of Canada's history, which has many similarities to the history of the United States. Have students preview the lesson by skimming the headings and guiding questions and by looking at the photographs. **Ask:** Based on your preview of the lesson, what similarities do you notice between Canada's history and the United States' history? *(Students may note that Native Americans originally lived in both places, Europeans explored and claimed the lands, the British governed the lands for a time, both became independent countries, immigrants flocked to both countries, and both became industrialized and economically strong.)* Tell students that they will also learn about the unique features of Canada's history in this lesson.

TEACH & ASSESS

R Reading Skills

Determining Word Meanings Write the word *aborigine* on the board, and explain that it is a Latin word meaning "original inhabitants." Tell students that *aboriginal* means the same thing. Some students may be familiar with the word used as the name for the original inhabitants of Australia. Explain that the words *aboriginal, native,* and *indigenous* all refer to the same thing—the original inhabitants of an area. Emphasize that the ties of aboriginals to the land go back thousands of years in Canada. **Ask:** What are Native Americans called in Canada? *(First Nations)* **ELL** Verbal/Linguistic

Making Connections Remind students that Earth's surface, and even the location of continents, has changed dramatically over millions of years. Elicit from students what they know about the Ice Age and the migration of people from Asia to North America. If students are not familiar with this history, display a map that focuses on the area where northern Asia and North America come close to meeting. Share this information with students:

- Sheets of ice have covered large parts of the continents at various times in Earth's history. The most recent episode is commonly called the Ice Age, and it began about 1.6 million years ago and ended about 11,000 years ago.
- During the Ice Age, Alaska and Siberia were connected by a land mass that was up to 1,000 miles wide. Scientists believe people crossed into North America using this land bridge.
- Even though this land bridge no longer exists, the distance between Alaska and Siberia is only about 55 miles.

ANSWER, p. 184

Taking Notes 1530s: Cartier claims St. Lawrence River and lands around it for France; **1763:** British gain almost all of New France; **1867:** Dominion of Canada is formed; **1931:** Canada gains more independence from Britain

---

networks

There's More Online!

☑ **IMAGE** the First Nations of Canada

☑ **VIDEO**

Reading **HELP**DESK

Academic Vocabulary

- **occupy**
- **eventually**
- **migrate**

Content Vocabulary

- **aboriginal**
- **Métis**
- **transcontinental**
- **granary**

TAKING NOTES: *Key Ideas and Details*

Sequencing Events As you read about Canada's history, use the graphic organizer below to record important dates and events.

1530s	Cartier claims St. Lawrence River and lands around it for France
1763	
1867	
1931	

Indiana Academic Standards
6.1.11

184

Lesson 2

The History of Canada

ESSENTIAL QUESTION • *What makes a culture unique?*

IT MATTERS BECAUSE
Canada has one of the world's largest economies.

The First Nations of Canada

GUIDING QUESTION *How did native peoples of Canada live before Europeans came to the area?*

R In the United States, the **aboriginal**, or native, peoples who lived in North America before Europeans are called Native Americans. Canadians call them the First Nations.

Coming to Canada
The first people to arrive in Canada came from Asia. They came during a long period of intense cold called the Ice Age. The first groups to arrive moved south because Canada was covered with ice. Over thousands of years, though, Earth's climate warmed. The ice sheets over most of Canada melted. As Canada warmed, people **occupied** the land there. Their way of life depended on the resources where they lived.

Different Ways of Life
The peoples of the eastern woodlands lived by farming, hunting, and fishing. They built villages where they lived for most of the year. They traded with one another. Two important eastern groups were the Huron and the Iroquois. The two nations were rivals and often fought.

The peoples of the Pacific coast lived in a region of plenty. Rivers and the waters of the Pacific Ocean provided fish and sea mammals. They hunted game animals in the forests. They used wood from the region's trees to make houses. They also made oceangoing canoes, which they used to hunt and fish.

(l to r) ©Bettmann/Corbis; World History Archive/Alamy; Courtesy of Canada Post - 2012; ©Zou Zheng/Xinhua Press/Corbis

---

networks *Online Teaching Options*

VIDEO

The Separation Vote

Analyzing Visuals Use this video about the separation vote that occurred in Quebec to introduce the lesson. Discuss with students the reasons why Quebec wanted to be independent. Ask partners to share what they learned about Quebec from the video. Did anything surprise them? If so, have them share what was unexpected. **AL** Visual/Spatial

See page 175D for other online activities.

V1

Life was more difficult in the far north. There, peoples like the Inuit had to find food in a land where few plants grow. Shelters had to be built without using trees. They had to protect themselves from fierce cold. They hunted caribou, a large animal related to deer, on land and seals and whales on the water. Caribou skins were used to make clothes and shoes to keep them warm in winter.

✓ READING PROGRESS CHECK

Determining Cause and Effect How did the presence and absence of ice affect the early settlement of Canada?

Exploration and Settlement

GUIDING QUESTION *How did migration and settlement change Canada?*

The first Europeans to reach what is now Canada were Vikings. They began their travels around A.D. 1000 and settled in southern Newfoundland. They soon abandoned their settlements and left, however. More than 500 years later, other Europeans came to the Americas.

Europeans in Canada

R

The next Europeans to explore Canada were the French. An explorer named Jacques Cartier sailed up the St. Lawrence River in the 1530s. He claimed the St. Lawrence and the lands around it for France. The whole area of French control **eventually** was called New France.

In the 1600s, the French made the first serious effort to settle the region. Explorer Samuel de Champlain founded the first French settlement, Quebec, in 1608.

Over time, more French settlers **migrated** to Canada. Some became fur traders. These traders exchanged European goods with the Huron, a First Nations people. The French received beaver furs that could be shipped back to Europe. Some settlers were priests. They came to Canada to minister to the French settlers, who were Roman Catholic. They also hoped to convert native peoples to Christianity. Some settlers farmed. Their crops fed the other settlers.

Academic Vocabulary

occupy to settle in a place
eventually at some later time
migrate to move to an area to settle

Inuit and other native North Americans lived in Canada long before European settlers arrived.

▶ CRITICAL THINKING

Describing How did the lives of the First Nations people of the far north differ from the lives of the Pacific coast people?

©Bettmann/Corbis

Chapter 6 **185**

SLIDE SHOW

The First Nations of Canada

Analyzing Visuals Use the slide show to expand students' awareness of the diverse ways of life among the aboriginal peoples of Canada. Lead a discussion on how each group's way of life reflected adaptations to the environment. Visual/Spatial, Logical/Mathematical

See page 175D for other online activities.

Slide Show

V1 **Visual Skills**

Creating Charts Suggest that students create a three-column chart to take notes on the ways the people of the eastern woodlands, Pacific Coast, and Far North lived. (*Eastern Woodlands: farmed, hunted, and fished; built permanent villages; traded; Huron and Iroquois fought each other; Pacific Coast: fished, hunted sea mammals and game animals, made wooden houses and oceangoing canoes from forest wood; Far North: hunted caribou, seals, and whales, made clothes and shoes from caribou skins*) ELL AL Visual/Spatial

V2

Eastern Woodlands	Pacific Coast	Far North

R **Reading Skills**

Determining Central Ideas Note that the first European settlers who stayed in Canada were the French. Use the following questions to help students identify the main ideas about the period of French settlement. **Ask:**

• Who were important French explorers of Canada? *(Jacques Cartier and Samuel de Champlain.)*

• What area of Canada did they claim and settle? *(the lands around the St. Lawrence River)*

• Who were the groups of French settlers, and what did they do in Canada? *(Some were fur traders who traded European goods for beaver furs; some were priests who ministered to French settlers and hoped to convert the Native Americans; some were farmers who fed the other settlers.)* AL Verbal/Linguistic

V2 **Visual Skills**

Analyzing Images Direct students' attention to the photograph of the mother and infant. **Ask:** Do you think this photograph of people of the Far North is from long ago or fairly recent? How can you tell? *(It is fairly recent. You can tell because the woman is wearing modern clothes and the building in the background is made of wood.)* Visual/Spatial

ANSWERS, p. 185

✓ READING PROGRESS CHECK When much of the Northern Hemisphere was covered by ice, people did not settle in Canada. Only when the climate warmed and the ice melted did they begin to live in Canada.

CRITICAL THINKING Life was more difficult in the Far North because of relatively fewer resources, sparser vegetation and trees, and a colder climate. In contrast, the people of the Pacific Coast enjoyed a much milder climate and an abundance of resources. Crops were easily grown in the Pacific Coast region, the forests teemed with wildlife for hunting, and wood was readily available for building comfortable homes.

R Reading Skills

Determining Central Ideas Note that this page focuses on the time period from the late 1600s through the 1800s, during most of which the British controlled Canada. Use the following questions to help students identify the main ideas of each paragraph. **Ask:**

• What two countries competed for control of Canada? *(Britain and France)*

• Who formed the Hudson Bay Company, and what was its purpose? *(Some British merchants formed the company and set up trading posts around Hudson Bay to gain some of the fur trade.)*

• How did Britain gain control of Canada? *(Britain defeated the French in war in 1763, and France was forced to give up most of its land in North America to Britain.)*

• What was the Quebec Act? *(a British act that allowed French settlers in Canada to keep their language, religion, and system of laws)*

• How did the American Revolution affect Canada? *(Many Americans who remained loyal to Britain moved to what are now the Atlantic Provinces and Ontario.)*

• How did the Dominion of Canada form? *(Fearing a United States takeover, the colonies of Quebec, Ontario, Nova Scotia, and New Brunswick united as provinces and formed the Dominion of Canada.)*

• What was the Dominion of Canada's relationship with Great Britain? *(The Dominion of Canada was partly self-governing within the British Empire.)* **AL** Verbal/Linguistic

Content Background Knowledge

Share the following information with students to provide some context for understanding the photograph at the bottom of the page:

The war between France and Great Britain for dominance in North America has several names. It is called the Seven Years' War in Europe, the French and Indian War in the United States, and the War of the Conquest in Canada. It officially started in 1756 (though the war had been waged in North America since 1754), and ended in 1763. France and Britain fought each other in many parts of the world and expended immense resources in the conflict.

ANSWER, p. 186

CRITICAL THINKING After the British victory, France was forced to give up most of its land in Canada.

British Canada

France was a powerful nation in the 1600s and 1700s. It had a rival for power, however. Britain competed with France in the Americas. In the late 1600s, some British merchants formed a company called the Hudson's Bay Company. They set up trading posts around the bay in the hope of gaining some of the profitable fur trade.

The two nations fought wars in the 1700s. As a result of a British victory in 1763, France was forced to give up much of its land in North America. However, the Quebec Act, passed by the British in 1774, gave French settlers in Canada the right to keep their language, religion, and system of laws.

The next big change in Canada came in the 1770s and 1780s. When the American Revolution broke out, thousands of Americans remained loyal to Britain. During and after the war, many of them moved to Canada. Some settled in what are now the Atlantic Provinces and others in modern Ontario.

During the early 1800s, English and French communities disagreed over colonial government policies. Fears of a U.S. takeover, however, forced them to work together. In 1867 the British colonies of Quebec, Ontario, Nova Scotia, and New Brunswick united as provinces of the Dominion of Canada. This new nation was partly self-governing within the British Empire. Other territories would join Canada over the next 100 years.

Known as outstanding commanders, the British General Wolfe (below) and the French General Montcalm lost their lives in the Battle of Quebec. The war ended in 1763.
▶ CRITICAL THINKING
Analyzing What was the result of the war?

World History Archive/Alamy

186 *Chapter 6*

networks *Online Teaching Options*

LECTURE SLIDES

Government Policies and Native Groups

Comparing and Contrasting Use the lecture slide series to discuss the ways the Canadian government has treated different cultural and ethnic groups in Canada, particularly the First Nations. Compare the policies of the Canadian government toward the First Nations to the policies of the United States government toward Native Americans.
Interpersonal

See page 175D for other online activities.

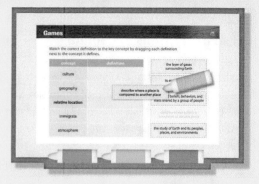

Canada Expands Westward

Canada's leaders began looking westward. They hoped to expand the nation all the way to the Pacific. In 1869 Canada gained the vast territory held by the Hudson's Bay Company. Many Métis lived on some of this land. **Métis** are the children of French and native peoples. They wanted more say in governing themselves. The province of Manitoba was created to give them that chance.

By this time, settlers had already arrived in British Columbia on the Pacific coast. There, they traded furs and searched for gold. The people of British Columbia agreed to join Canada in 1871. In the 1880s, Canadians built a **transcontinental**, or continent-crossing, railroad that united the eastern and western parts of their nation.

New Provinces

Canada's leaders made agreements with some native peoples of the west. According to the government, the native peoples agreed to give up their lands in exchange for aid. Native people believed they gave settlers only the right to use the land for farming. Canada's westward expansion came at a price. New settlers pushed native peoples off their lands. In 1905 Saskatchewan and Alberta entered Canada as provinces.

Meanwhile, gold had been discovered in the Yukon Territory. This discovery led to a gold rush. Helping create order in the west was a police force that formed in 1873. Called the North West Mounted Police, the group is known today as the Royal Canadian Mounted Police.

☑ **READING PROGRESS CHECK**

Determining Central Ideas How did European rivalries affect the development of Canada?

Courtesy of Canada Post - 2012

Canada honored two African Canadian heroes in 2012. John Ware (left) was important in starting the ranching industry in western Canada. Viola Desmond (right) worked to repeal unjust laws.

▶ **CRITICAL THINKING**
Describing Who were the Métis? What right did they obtain?

T **R**

Thinking Like a
Geographer

Why was a mounted police force needed in western Canada?

The vast size and sparse population of the region explain it. Police needed to be able to ride horses to travel quickly from one place to another. Because settlements were far-flung, they had to travel often. The Mounties filled an important need in a time before car travel.

Chapter 6 **187**

V

R **Reading Skills**

Making Connections Encourage students to make connections between Canadian history and United States history. For example, they might note the following similarities:

- Both the United States and Canada had a period of westward expansion, extending their boundary all the way to the Pacific Ocean.
- Both countries built transcontinental railroads to unite far-flung regions of the countries.
- In both countries, Native Americans were pushed off their lands.
- Both countries experienced a gold rush—the United States in California and Canada in the Yukon Territory.

Note some major differences in their histories as well. For example, Canada did not fight a war to gain independence from Britain, and Canada did not have plantations on which large numbers of enslaved people worked, though some slavery did exist in Canada.

V **Visual Skills**

Analyzing Images To provide background on the stamps, tell students that John Ware was born into slavery in South Carolina, moved to Texas after the Civil War, and settled in Canada in the late 1800s. Viola Desmond was arrested in 1945 for sitting in the "white" section of a theater and worked for the repeal of segregation laws in Nova Scotia. **Ask:** How does each stamp convey the story of the person featured? *(The stamp of John Ware includes a lariat and silhouette of a man on a horse to convey that Ware was a rancher, and the stamp of Desmond shows a movie ticket and theater seats to convey that Desmond fought against segregation in a theater. You may have to define the word* lariat *for students.)* **Visual/Spatial**

T **Technology Skills**

Researching on the Internet Have students conduct Internet research to find out more about one of these two subjects: the role of the métis in the creation of the province of Manitoba or the expulsion of Native Americans from their lands during Canada's westward expansion. Ask students to give brief oral reports on their findings. **BL** **Verbal/Linguistic**

ANSWERS, p. 187

CRITICAL THINKING The Métis were children of French and native people. Manitoba was created to give them more say in governing themselves.

☑ READING PROGRESS CHECK France and Britain were rivals for power in Europe and in the Americas. Though France settled Canada first, the British wanted to gain control of New France. The two nations fought several wars that resulted in France being forced to give up much of its land in North America. After that, Canada was closely tied to Britain.

GRAPHIC ORGANIZER

People in Canada

Comparing Use the interactive graphic organizer on the whiteboard to organize and further discuss the treatment of different cultural and ethnic groups in Canada by the Canadian government. Compare the issues of civil rights for African Americans and Asians in Canada to those of the U.S. government in the 1900s. **BL** **Verbal/Linguistic**

See page 175D for other online activities.

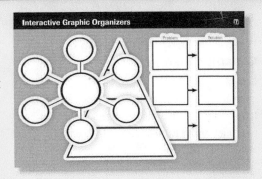

Interactive Graphic Organizers

The History of Canada

GUIDING QUESTION *How did Canada change in the 1900s?*

During the 1900s, Canada grew into a prosperous, independent country. Its population grew and became more diverse. Canada also reached the territorial size it is today. In 1949 Newfoundland and Labrador became the last territory to join Canada as a province.

Economic Growth and Immigration

Early in the 1900s, however, Canada had many economic problems. The country's economy was based on agriculture and mining. When prices for those resources fell, Canada suffered. In the late 1900s, Canada became an industrial nation. Canadians built factories and took advantage of their mineral resources. They developed hydroelectric projects and transportation systems. Agriculture also grew as farmers in the west increased production. Granaries stored wheat to feed the growing population. A **granary** is a building used to store harvested grain.

To help increase the nation's industrial power, Canada needed more workers. Canada's leaders made it easier for people to enter the country. Canada's population began to grow, particularly after World War II, which helped Canada meet its need for more workers. Canada's population jumped from 12 million people in 1945 to nearly 35 million in 2012.

R **Reading Skills**

Summarizing In the early 1900s, Canada had many economic problems. Help students summarize how Canada became industrialized in the late 1900s. **Ask:** How did Canada become an industrial nation in the late 1900s? *(Canadians built factories, hydroelectric projects, and transportation systems. They developed their mineral resources and increased their agricultural production. They added to their workforce by making it easier for people to immigrate to the country.)* **AL** Verbal/Linguistic

C **Critical Thinking Skills**

Making Connections Use the following questions to help students connect to the photograph at the bottom of the page. **Ask:**

- What United States holiday is somewhat like Canada Day? *(Fourth of July or Independence Day)*
- How is the event that Independence Day in the United States commemorates different from the event that Canada Day commemorates? *(On July 4, 1776, the United States became an independent country separate from the British Empire. On July 1, 1867, the Dominion of Canada formed as a partly self-governing nation within the British Empire.)* Visual/Spatial

T **Technology Skills**

Researching Have students research online using reliable resources what Canadians do to celebrate Canada Day. Have students pair up and exchange what information each other found and share their sources.

Next have partners compare the celebrations of the Canadians with the celebrations we hold on the Fourth of July, such as parades, picnics, and fireworks. Have volunteers give presentations to the class that include photographs or other visuals of the celebrations held on Canada Day. Interpersonal, Visual/Spatial

The Royal Canadian Mounted Police take part in Canada Day celebrations in Ottawa. The annual celebration commemorates when Canada became a self-governing dominion within the British Empire.
▶ CRITICAL THINKING
Identifying What major change in Canada occurred in 1931?

©Zou Zheng/Xinhua Press/Corbis

netw⊙rks *Online Teaching Options*

GAME

Drag-and-Drop: Comparing U.S. and Canadian History

Comparing and Contrasting Display the drag-and-drop game on the interactive whiteboard. Have students take turns dragging and dropping events into one of two categories: unique to Canada or similar to United States. Kinesthetic

See page 175D for other online activities.

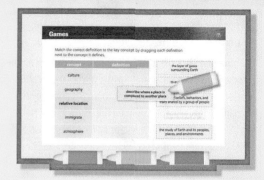

ANSWER, p. 188

CRITICAL THINKING Canada gained almost complete independence from Great Britain.

In recent decades, Canada has welcomed immigrants from all over the world. Today it is a multicultural society. People descended from settlers who came from the British Isles or France account for only about half the population. Another 15 percent trace their background to some other European country. About 6 percent of the people have an African or an Asian background. About 2 percent of Canada's people are from the First Nations. More than a quarter of Canadians have mixed backgrounds.

Independence

A major change came to Canada in 1931. That year, Britain granted almost complete independence to Canada. Canadians were now able to make their own laws without interference from Britain. The British government, however, maintained the right to approve changes to Canada's constitution. This link to Britain finally ended in 1982.

During the later 1900s, Canada became less connected to Britain. Instead, Canada developed closer ties to the United States. It also became active in international bodies, such as the United Nations.

R

The Growth of Industry

Canada's industries boomed after World War II. Part of the boom was the result of increased demand for Canada's mineral resources. Part was the result of industrial growth. Part, too, came from population growth and movement. More people meant more demand for more goods. Also, people were moving from rural areas to cities and suburbs. That created a need for construction of homes, stores, offices, and roads.

Construction of the St. Lawrence Seaway helped the economy grow, too. Canada could more easily—and cheaply—ship its products around the world. It also could bring in needed goods at lower costs. At the same time, agriculture expanded. Farmers in the Prairie Provinces boosted production. Granaries were built. By 2013, Canada's economy was strong in all sectors: agriculture, industry, services, and information technology (IT).

FOLDABLES
Study Organizer

Include this lesson's information in your Foldable®.

☑ **READING PROGRESS CHECK**

Identifying What are two ways that Canada changed in the 1900s?

LESSON 2 REVIEW

Reviewing Vocabulary
1. Why do the Prairie Provinces have *granaries*?

Answering the Guiding Questions
2. *Describing* Why did people of the First Nations have different ways of life in different parts of Canada?

3. *Analyzing* Why was the province of Manitoba created?

4. *Analyzing* Why do you think people settled what is now British Columbia before settling the Prairie Provinces?

5. *Determining Central Ideas* Why has Canada developed closer ties to the United States?

6. *Informative/Explanatory* Write a summary that highlights the key points of Canada's development as a nation.

Chapter 6 **189**

LESSON 2 REVIEW ANSWERS

Reviewing Vocabulary

1. There are granaries in the Prairie Provinces because those areas have highly productive farms.

Answering the Guiding Questions

2. **Describing** People of the First Nations had different ways of life in different parts of Canada depending on the resources in the area where they lived. Because resources differed, their ways of life differed.

3. **Analyzing** The Métis wanted more political freedom.

4. **Analyzing** People probably settled British Columbia before the Prairie Provinces because it was easier to reach that area by boat than to travel over land to the Prairie Provinces.

5. **Determining Central Ideas** Possible answer: Canada has developed closer ties to the United States because the two nations are close neighbors and share a common history and language. The United States is Canada's biggest trading partner.

6. **Narrative Writing** Students' summaries should mention the French settlement of part of modern Canada, the French and British rivalry in North America that resulted in British control, the various changes in British governance over Canada, Canada's expansion to the west, and its population and economic growth.

R **Reading Skills**

Calculating Point out that Canada gained its independence from Britain much later than the United States did. Have students calculate how many years later. *(1931 − 1776 = 155; 155 years)* Explain that some people who were loyal to Britain at the time the United States declared independence actually moved to Canada rather than stay in what they saw was a rebellious country. Then have students discuss why they think the Canadian people did not rebel, but were content to remain as a colony of Britain until the 1930s. **AL** Logical/Mathematical

CLOSE & REFLECT

To close the lesson, have students discuss any new or surprising information they learned about Canadian history. Encourage students to provide specific information, such as facts about how the population has changed throughout its history, why different languages are spoken there, how the government has changed, and other details of its history. Then ask students to reflect on how Canada's history is different from that of the United States. Interpersonal

Content Background Knowledge

Canada actively encourages immigration, especially of skilled and educated workers, and has developed a highly diverse population.

Encourage students to look at the location of Toronto on a map and discuss why its location would make it an important business center. Have them share any information that they know about Toronto.

- Toronto is one of the country's most diverse cities.
- Much of Toronto's population is made up of immigrants.
- The city's people speak more than 140 languages and dialects.

ANSWER, p. 189

☑ **READING PROGRESS CHECK** Students might give any two of the following answers: In the 1900s, Canada grew in population. It became more industrial. Its economy grew. It gained independence from Great Britain. It developed closer ties to the United States. It became active in international organizations.

ENGAGE

Bellringer Ask students to finish this sentence: *I would like to live in Canada because...* Call on students to read their sentences aloud, and then discuss what Canadians lives are like based on students' responses. Tell students to see if their ideas of Canadian life are confirmed by this lesson. Then have students preview the lesson by scanning the headings, guiding questions, and photographs.

TEACH & ASSESS

R1 Reading Skills

Determining Word Meanings Write the academic vocabulary words *via* and *vary* on the board. Tell students that *via* means "through," "by way of," or "by means of." Provide these two example sentences: *I biked from Walton to Brody via Grant's Trail. I sent the letter via overnight mail.* Then tell students that *vary* means "to differ" or "to change." Provide this example sentence: *Temperatures vary throughout the year.* Then ask students to generate example sentences of their own. **ELL** Verbal/Linguistic

R2 Reading Skills

Determining Central Ideas Use the following questions to help students identify and understand the main ideas in the text. **Ask:**

- What city is the capital of Canada? *(Ottawa, Ontario)*
- How is Canada's government like the United States' government? *(It has a national government and provincial governments, which are like state governments.)*
- How is its government different from the United States' government? *(It has a parliamentary system. Voters elect the members of parliament and then the party with the most members chooses the prime minister, who carries out the laws. In the United States, the voters elect the president, who carries out the laws.)*
- How is Toronto's location ideal for shipping Canadian products around the world? *(It has access to the Atlantic Ocean via the St. Lawrence Seaway, it has rail lines and highways connecting to the rest of Canada, and about half of the country's manufactured goods are made in Ontario.)*

ANSWERS, p. 190

Taking Notes Sample answers: **Cities:** Toronto—largest city; Toronto, Montreal, and Vancouver—major ports; Ottawa—national capital; Montreal and Quebec—French influence; **Relations with the World:** close economic and defense ties to United States, close relations with Britain, major role in giving aid to poorer countries and peacekeeping; **Challenges:** unity—challenge of Quebec separatists not settled; Environmental—climate change and acid rain

---

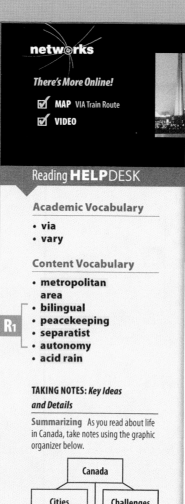

netw**o**rks

There's More Online!

☑ **MAP** VIA Train Route
☑ **VIDEO**

Reading **HELP**DESK

Academic Vocabulary

- via
- vary

Content Vocabulary

R1

- metropolitan area
- bilingual
- peacekeeping
- separatist
- autonomy
- acid rain

TAKING NOTES: *Key Ideas and Details*

Summarizing As you read about life in Canada, take notes using the graphic organizer below.

Canada
Cities
Challenges
Relations With the World

Indiana Academic Standards
6.2.6, 6.3.1, 6.3.14

190

Lesson 3
Life in Canada

ESSENTIAL QUESTION • *What makes a culture unique?*

IT MATTERS BECAUSE
Canada plays a major role in world affairs.

City and Country Life

GUIDING QUESTION *Where and how do Canadians live?*

Where do you think most Canadians live? Do you think of a fishing village or a farm? Do you picture a remote settlement in the far north? Actually, four out of every five Canadians live in cities or suburbs. Canada is a modern urban society.

Ottawa and Toronto

Ottawa is located in the province of Ontario. It is Canada's capital city and home to the national government. Canada's government is similar to those of the United States and the United Kingdom. Like the United States, Canada has national and regional governments. In Canada, those regions are the provinces. Like the United Kingdom, Canada has a parliamentary system. Voters elect members of the legislature, or Parliament. The party with the most members chooses the prime minister, who carries out the laws.

Another Ontario city, Toronto, is Canada's largest metropolitan area. A **metropolitan area** is a city and its surrounding suburbs. Metropolitan Toronto has more than 5 million people. Toronto has access to the Atlantic Ocean **via** the St. Lawrence Seaway. As a result, it is a major port. Rail lines and highways make it possible to ship imported goods from the seaway across Canada. About half of Canada's manufactured goods are made in Ontario. Toronto is an ideal location for shipping Canadian products around the world.

R2

(l to r) Brand X Pictures/PunchStock; Garry Black/All Canada Photos/Getty Images; Ken Paul/All Canada Photos/Getty Images; ©Earl & Nazima Kowall/Corbis

---

netw**o**rks   *Online Teaching Options*

VIDEO

Northern Canada Climate Change

Simulating Use this video about climate change in Northern Canada to introduce the lesson about life in Canada. Have students write a paragraph about the aspect of Canadian life that they found most appealing. Discuss with students that climate change in Canada does not only affect Canadians. **AL** Verbal/Linguistic

See page 175E for other online activities.

BBC Motion Gallery Education

Each summer, Toronto is home to the Canadian National Exhibition, a combination fair and business meeting. The city also has major sports teams and a wide array of cultural opportunities. Its restaurants offer food from many different ethnic groups.

Montreal and Quebec

Montreal and Quebec are the major cities of Quebec Province. Canada's French heritage remains strong throughout this province. Canada is a **bilingual** nation, meaning it has two official languages—English and French. Most people in Quebec speak French.

Montreal is Canada's second-largest city. It is the economic hub, or center of activity, of Quebec Province. Like Toronto, it is a major port because of the St. Lawrence Seaway. Montreal is an important center of manufacturing, banking, and insurance. It offers a special combination of historic European charm and modern life.

Quebec, the capital of Quebec Province, attracts tourists who are eager to see buildings that reflect its 400-year history. Costumed performers reenact life in the early days of New France to make that history come alive.

Western Cities

Canada's third-largest metropolitan area is Vancouver, in British Columbia. It is Canada's busiest port. Vancouver's port ships food products from the nearby Prairie Provinces. Because of its Pacific Ocean location, it is a vital center of trade with Asia. Many people have moved to the city from Asian nations in recent years.

Canada's other major western cities are Calgary and Edmonton in Alberta. Both benefit from Alberta's large oil and natural gas reserves, which have fueled an economic boom in the province. The cities have grown rapidly in recent years. Both are centers for processing the grain and meat produced in the province.

Life in Rural Areas

Life in rural Canada **varies** from place to place. People of the First Nations who live in the far north live in a harsh landscape. Many follow traditional ways, although modern aspects of life can be found as well. For example, they may travel on snowmobiles instead of dogsleds. Fishing villages in the Atlantic Provinces have suffered in recent years. Overfishing has reduced fish stocks—and thus income from fishing.

Brand X Pictures/PunchStock

✓ **READING PROGRESS CHECK**

Analyzing Why are Toronto and Vancouver more important to trade than Calgary and Edmonton?

Academic Vocabulary

via through

vary to differ

Canada's National Tower in Toronto is a symbol of the country, and it is the tallest, free-standing structure in the Western Hemisphere.

▶ **CRITICAL THINKING**
Identifying What are Canada's two most populous cities?

R1 Reading Skills

Determining Word Meanings Explain that the word *bilingual* consists of the prefix *bi-*, which means "two," and the root word *lingual,* which comes from a Latin word meaning "tongue" or "language." When the prefix and root word are put together, it means "able to speak two languages."

Share some other words that have the prefix *bi-* and have students state the meaning of each: (bicycle: a vehicle that has two wheels, biweekly: happens every two weeks). **AL** Verbal/Linguistic

R2 Reading Skills

Categorizing To help students assimilate the information about Canada's major cities, suggest that they group the cities into categories. Provide students with the categories listed below and have them place Ottawa, Toronto, Montreal, Quebec, Vancouver, Calgary, and Edmonton into one or more of the following categories:

• Capital *(Ottawa)*
• Major ports *(Toronto, Montreal, Vancouver)*
• Cities with French heritage *(Montreal, Quebec)*
• Grain- and meat-processing centers *(Calgary, Edmonton)*
  AL Verbal/Linguistic

Content Background Knowledge

With its lofty antenna, Canada's National Tower shown in the picture on this page took 4 years to build, and it opened in 1976. It functions as a broadcast and telecommunications tower, but has other uses as well.

Rising 1,815 feet, the tower is not only a telecommunications center but also an important tourist attraction. It features a revolving restaurant at the circular top beneath the antenna, observation decks, and an entertainment complex. About 2 million people come to visit Canada's National Tower every year.

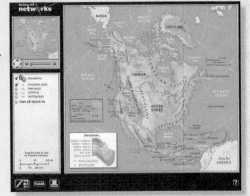

ANSWERS, p. 191

CRITICAL THINKING Toronto and Montreal
✓ **READING PROGRESS CHECK** Toronto and Vancouver are more important to trade than Calgary and Edmonton because they are port cities with access by water to nations around the world. Calgary and Edmonton are deep in Canada's interior and have no water access to other locations.

C Critical Thinking Skills

Drawing Conclusions Explain to students that trade barriers are regulations that tend to restrict trade, such as the addition of taxes, called tariffs, on imports. Placing a tax on an import increases its price, which may make it more costly than an item produced within a country. **Ask:**

• Why do you think a foreign country might want to eliminate trade barriers with another country? *(It would want to eliminate trade barriers so that its products would be competitive in price with those produced within a country and then would be easier to sell there.)*

• Why do you think a country might want to impose trade barriers on the products from another country? *(It would want to impose trade barriers to protect its manufacturers so that their products will be cheaper in price than those produced outside the country and then will be easier to sell.)* Logical/Mathematical

V Visual Skills

Creating a Graphic Organizer To help students summarize the main ideas about Canada's ties to the United States, have them complete a graphic organizer like the one below filling in the main ideas for its economic, defense, and cultural ties to the United States. *(Economic—¾ of all exports to United States, ¾ of all imports from United States; Defense—joint air defenses against possible plane or missile attack, work together to fight terrorism; Cultural—Canadians watch American movies and TV shows, Canadian singers and actors work in United States, Canadians worry about United States cultural dominance)* AL ELL Visual/Spatial

Canada's Ties to U.S.

Economic — Defense — Cultural

ANSWER, p. 192

CRITICAL THINKING to emphasize the culture of Canada and to make sure that U.S. culture does not overwhelm Canada's

Outdoor winter sports are a popular pastime in both Canada and the northern United States.
▶ CRITICAL THINKING
Analyzing Why is Canada's government making a strong effort to promote the nation's culture?

Economic and Political Relationships

GUIDING QUESTION *What is Canada's relationship with other nations?*

Canada has one of the world's largest economies. It also plays a leading role in many world issues.

Canada and the United States

Canada has close economic, defense, and cultural ties to the United States. In the early 1990s, Canada joined the United States and Mexico in signing the North American Free Trade Agreement (NAFTA). This agreement eliminated trade barriers in North America. In 2010 three-quarters of all of Canada's exports went to the United States. The same year, three-quarters of its imports came from the United States.

Canada and the United States also cooperate in defense. They work together to defend the air space against possible attack from planes or missiles. They also work together to combat terrorism.

Canada and the United States share many cultural features. Canadians watch American movies and television shows. Many Canadian singers and actors enjoy success in the United States. Canadians worry, though, about cultural dominance from the United States. Canada's government promotes the production of Canadian movies and television shows.

Garry Black/All Canada Photos/Getty Images

192 *Chapter 6*

networks   *Online Teaching Options*

MAP

Resources: Canada

Writing a Narrative Use the resources layer of the Chapter Opener map to discuss the resources and the economy of Canada. Be sure to discuss Canada's role in NAFTA. Have students write a descriptive paragraph about the relationship between the United States and Canada that is solely based on resources. Verbal/Linguistic, Naturalist

See page 175E for other online activities.

Canada and Britain

Canada's government is modeled on Britain's. So are its laws, except in Quebec Province. Canadian culture draws on British culture. Many Canadians trace their ancestry to Britain. For these reasons, Canada maintains close ties with that nation. The British king or queen is officially Canada's king or queen, as well. A Canadian official called the governor-general acts in his or her place, though.

R

Canada and the World

Canada is active in many world organizations. It is a member of the United Nations and the North Atlantic Treaty Organization (NATO). NATO links Canada, the United States, and many nations of Europe in defense matters. Canada has worked in recent years to connect more closely with Asian nations.

Canada plays a major role in efforts to aid poorer nations. It has often taken part in peacekeeping efforts. **Peacekeeping** is sending trained members of the military to crisis spots to maintain peace and order.

☑ **READING PROGRESS CHECK**

Analyzing Why is Canada more similar to the United States and the United Kingdom than to other nations?

An efficient and comfortable train system is an important part of Canada's economic development.

▶ CRITICAL THINKING

Identifying Point of View The nation's transcontinental train makes only eight planned stops en route from Toronto to Vancouver. How does this help travelers?

Ken Paul/All Canada Photos/Getty Images

R Reading Skills

Discussing Use the following questions to help students recall and summarize the type of government that both Canada and Britain have. Then have them compare this form of government with the type of government in the United States. **Ask:**

- What is the name of the type of government that both Canada and Britain have? *(parliamentary)*
- What is distinctive about a parliamentary type of government? *(Voters elect the members of the parliament, or the legislature. The party with the most members chooses the prime minister, who runs the country.)*
- How is that different from the system of government in the United States? *(The United States has a democratic system of government. The citizens/voters choose the president, who runs the country.)* **Verbal/Linguistic**

Content Background Knowledge

- **Commonwealth of Nations** Along with many other lands that were formerly part of the British Empire, Canada belongs to the Commonwealth of Nations. This organization is a free association of independent countries that choose to maintain close ties with Britain and one another. The symbolic head of the Commonwealth is the British monarch. A symbolic head of state does not exercise real power; instead, he or she has primarily ceremonial duties.
- **NATO** is an alliance of independent countries that agree to take joint political and military action to defend its members against threats and attacks. For example, in response to the terrorist attacks of 9/11, a coalition of NATO forces invaded Afghanistan. The alliance also seeks to achieve peace and stability through the promotion of democracy and cooperation with other countries. NATO members consist of Canada, the United States, and 26 European nations.

MAP

VIA Train Route Across Canada

Analyzing Information Suggest that students take a "trip" across Canada using the VIA train route map. With the scale counter, students can identify the travel time and distance between the cities where the VIA train stops. As students manipulate the slider bar to manually move the train along, have them describe the terrain, provinces, and towns they pass. **BL** Logical/Mathematical, Kinesthetic

See page 175E for other online activities.

ANSWERS, p. 193

CRITICAL THINKING The transcontinental trek is very long. The fewer stops mean completing the route in less time.

☑ **READING PROGRESS CHECK** Canada is similar to the United States because it shares economic, defense, and cultural ties; it is similar to the United Kingdom because its government, legal system, and culture draw on British traditions.

C Critical Thinking Skills

Identifying Central Issues and Problems Lead a discussion of the reasons for the separatist movement in Canada and the potential problems it could cause. **Ask:**

- Why do some Quebec residents support a separatist movement? *(They believe they have been treated as second-class citizens, and they resent English speakers' control of Quebec's economy.)*

- What does it mean to be treated as second-class citizens? *(It means to lack equal rights or opportunities.)*

- If Quebec were to become a separate country, what difficulties might the new country face? *(Sample answers: Its English-speaking citizens might want to move, it would have to provide for its own defense and its own social welfare programs, it would have to establish a national government, and its economy might be disrupted.)*

- How might Canada be harmed if Quebec separates from the country? *(Sample answers: It would lose Quebec's contributions to the national economy and culture, people might be demoralized, and the country would be physically divided.)* Logical/Mathematical

T Technology Skills

Researching on the Internet Have interested students conduct Internet research using reliable resources on the creation of the new territory of Nunavut in Canada. Encourage students to give brief oral reports to the rest of the class on the territory's government, economy, and culture.
BL Verbal/Linguistic

Content Background Knowledge

The Constitution for the United States is in a single text that has been amended many times in its history. In Canada, they have a number of constitutional enactments. In both places, the country's Constitution contains the laws that everyone is required to follow.

Canada's Challenges

GUIDING QUESTION *What challenges do Canadians face?*

Canada's biggest challenge might be staying together as a nation. Some people in Quebec want to create their own nation.

Unity and Diversity

Canada's constitution guarantees the rights of French-speaking people in Quebec and elsewhere. Still, tension is evident. English speakers have dominated the nation. They controlled the economy of Quebec for many years. As a result, some French speakers felt they were treated as second-class citizens.

In the late 1900s, some Quebec leaders launched a separatist movement. **Separatists** are those who want to break away from control by a dominant group. Voters in Quebec have twice defeated attempts to make it independent. Still, the issue remains unsettled.

The government did succeed in giving more power to people of the First Nations. In 1999 the government created the new territory called Nunavut. Most of its people are from the First Nations. The government gave them greater **autonomy**, or self-government, than they had in the past.

A Montreal rally calls for a "No" vote on independence for Quebec.
▶ **CRITICAL THINKING**
Identifying Point of View Why do some Canadians support independence for Quebec?

©Earl & Nazima Kowall/Corbis

---

netw⊕rks *Online Teaching Options*

GRAPHIC ORGANIZER

Comparing Canada, the United States, and the United Kingdom

Comparing Display the graphic organizer on the interactive whiteboard. Have students complete the graphic organizer by identifying similarities among the cultures of Canada, the United States, and the United Kingdom. Verbal/Linguistic

See page 175E for other online activities.

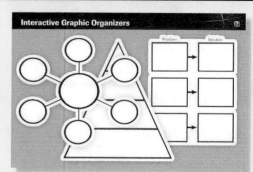

Interactive Graphic Organizers

ANSWER, p. 194

CRITICAL THINKING French-speaking Canadians argue that English speakers dominate Canada and the economy.

Environmental Challenges

Some scientists worry about the effects of climate change. Milder weather threatens plants and animals that are adapted to the cold of the far north. Experts also believe fisheries will suffer further. In addition, they fear water shortages and more extreme weather. Extreme weather includes long periods of drought and sudden damaging storms.

Canada's government is taking some steps to reduce its use of fossil fuels such as oil, coal, and natural gas. Burning these fuels is thought to contribute to climate change. The government is also encouraging research into clean energy.

Nevertheless, Canada depends greatly on fossil fuels to power its industries, transportation systems, and homes. Primary economic activities such as fossil fuel production are a large part of Canada's economy. Fossil fuel extraction has become an environmental concern in Athabasca Tar Sands in northwestern Alberta. This area has sand located near Earth's surface that contains a form of crude oil that is as thick as tar. The tar can be refined into oil, but the process is difficult and requires a great deal of energy and water.

Acid Rain

Another environmental problem for Canada is acid rain. **Acid rain** is produced when chemicals from air pollution combine with precipitation. When the rain falls to Earth, the chemicals may kill fish, land animals, and trees. Even when they do not kill living things, the chemicals weaken them. That makes them more vulnerable to damage from pests, disease, or severe weather.

Damage from acid rain has been particularly bad in eastern Canada. The government has made efforts to reduce acid rain. But many of the chemicals that cause acid rain in Canada enter the air in the United States. Canada cannot solve its problem without U.S. help. Canada's government wants to reach an agreement that includes tough steps to prevent acid rain.

FOLDABLES
Study Organizer

Include this lesson's information in your Foldable®.

☑ **READING PROGRESS CHECK**

Determining Central Ideas Why can Canada not meet its environmental challenges by itself?

V Visual Skills

Creating a Graphic Organizer Encourage students to summarize the effects of climate change and of acid rain by creating a cause–and–effect diagram for each environmental issue, similar to the one below. (***Cause:*** *Climate change;* ***Effects:*** *Threatens plants and animals adapted to the cold of the Far North, Fisheries will suffer further, Water shortages, More extreme weather;* ***Cause:*** *Acid rain;* ***Effects:*** *Kills fish, land animals, and trees, Weakens organisms that it does not kill and makes them more vulnerable to damage from pests, disease, or severe weather)* Visual/Spatial

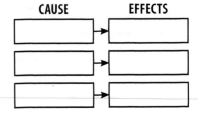

W Writing Skills

Informative/Explanatory Suggest that students research on the Internet the environmental concerns about producing oil from the Athabasca Tar Sands and write a brief informational report on the issue. Remind students that this is an informational report so they should not be taking sides on the issue, but should report their research in an unbiased manner. If time permits, have one or more students present their reports to the class. **BL** Verbal/Linguistic

CLOSE & REFLECT

To close the lesson, note that Canada is a beautiful, interesting, and varied country. Ask students what part of Canada they would most like to visit now that they have learned more about the country. Encourage students to give reasons to support their selection.

LESSON 3 REVIEW

Reviewing Vocabulary
1. What does it mean to say that Canada is a *bilingual* nation?

Answering the Guiding Questions
2. *Determining Central Ideas* How do the cultures of Quebec and Montreal reflect Canada's history?

3. *Describing* How does life in Calgary and Edmonton relate to Alberta's resources?

4. *Describing* In what ways has Canada tried to build a better world?

5. *Identifying Point of View* Why is separatism in Quebec an ongoing problem for Canada?

6. *Argument Writing* Take the role of Canada's prime minister. Write a letter to the president of the United States urging stronger American action to reduce air pollution that causes acid rain.

Chapter 6 **195**

LESSON 3 REVIEW ANSWERS

Reviewing Vocabulary

1. Canada is bilingual because it has two official languages that people speak: English and French.

Answering the Guiding Questions

2. **Determining Central Ideas** Quebec and Montreal were both settlements of New France. They have a French flavor to their culture that reflects their history.

3. **Describing** Calgary and Edmonton have both grown in recent years because of the boom in Alberta's oil and gas industries. Both cities have plants that process food produced on the farms and ranches of Alberta's prairies.

4. **Describing** Canada tries to build a better world by giving aid to poor nations and by joining in peacekeeping efforts.

5. **Identifying Point of View** Possible answer: Separatism is a problem for Canada because many people want Quebec to separate from Canada and be its own country. If Quebec were to become independent, Canada would lose one of its most populous provinces and key economic resources, including the city of Montreal. This would also divide the Atlantic Provinces from the rest of Canada.

6. **Argument Writing** Students' letters should indicate the severity of the acid rain problem, point to the major contribution to the problem by pollution from the United States, and give persuasive reasons for greater U.S. efforts to reduce pollution.

ANSWER, p. 195

☑ **READING PROGRESS CHECK** Canada cannot solve its environmental challenges by itself because climate change is a worldwide phenomenon and requires global cooperation.

CHAPTER REVIEW ACTIVITY

To summarize the chapter, have students complete an outline like the one below. Tell students to list five main ideas under each of the three headings. Note that students may list different main ideas, since the chapter has more than five main ideas for each topic. Discuss the main ideas that students generate. *(Students' answers may vary but should reflect main ideas covered in each of the three lessons of the chapter.)*

A. Physical Geography of Canada

1. _____
2. _____
3. _____
4. _____
5. _____

B. History of Canada

1. _____
2. _____
3. _____
4. _____
5. _____

C. Life in Canada

1. _____
2. _____
3. _____
4. _____
5. _____

REVIEW THE ENDURING UNDERSTANDINGS

Review this chapter's Enduring Understandings with students:

- *Over time, people adapt to their environment.*

- *People, places, and ideas change over time.*

Pose the following questions in a class discussion to apply these ideas to this chapter.

- How did the first people to settle in to what is now Canada adapt to their environment? *(Sample answer: In each region where they lived, they hunted and fished for the animals that were available and they built shelters from the natural materials that were available.)*

- How have peoples' ways of life in Canada changed over time? *(Sample answer: People in Canada used to depend on their immediate environment for food and clothing. Now people obtain food, clothing, and other goods from all over the world, and live in homes made from materials that may come from far away.)*

Directions: Write your answers on a separate piece of paper.

❶ Use your **FOLDABLES** to explore the Essential Questions.

ANALYZING Look at the population map of Canada at the beginning of the unit. In a short essay, explain why Canada's major cities and population centers developed where they did.

❷ 21st Century Skills

ANALYZING In a small group, research to find a historical painting about an important event in Canada's history. Find a secondary source about the same event. Compare the two sources and develop an answer to the question: Did one of the sources help you better understand the event? Why?

❸ Thinking Like a Geographer

INTEGRATING VISUAL INFORMATION Reseach the benefits and disadvantages of separatism for Quebec and list them in a chart like the one shown.

Benefits	Disadvantages

❹ GEOGRAPHY ACTIVITY

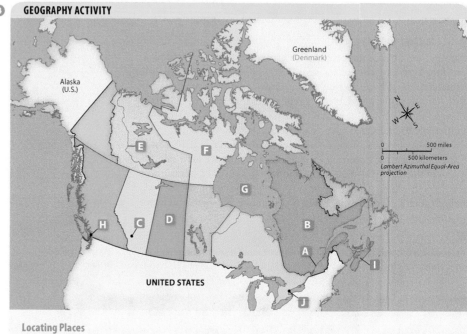

Locating Places

Match the letters on the map with the provinces, territories, or locations listed below.

1. Vancouver
2. Quebec
3. Calgary
4. Toronto
5. Mackenzie River
6. Nunavut
7. Hudson Bay
8. St. Lawrence River
9. Nova Scotia
10. Saskatchewan

ACTIVITIES ANSWERS

Exploring the Essential Question

❶ ANALYZING Students should recognize that 90 percent of Canada's population lives within 150 miles of the border with the United States because the weather in much of the country is too cold and harsh to support large numbers of people.

21st Century Skills

❷ ANALYZING Student groups should provide a thoughtful analysis of the two sources and be able to explain why one source is better than the other for understanding the event.

REVIEW THE GUIDING QUESTIONS

Directions: Choose the best answer for each question.

❶ Manitoba, Saskatchewan, and Alberta are called the
   A. archipelago.
   B. Northwest Territories.
   C. Prairie Provinces.
   D. Atlantic Provinces.

❷ Canada's highest mountain is
   F. Mount McKinley.
   G. Mount Logan.
   H. Hudson Mountain.
   I. Pikes Peak.

❸ The man who founded Quebec and led the French effort to settle Canada was
   A. Henry Hudson.
   B. Father Junipero Serra.
   C. Samuel de Champlain.
   D. the Métis.

❹ Which of Canada's provinces is predominately French in language and culture?
   F. Nova Scotia
   G. Prince Edward Island
   H. Quebec
   I. Yukon Territory

❺ Canada's largest metropolitan area, which includes the city and its surrounding suburbs, is
   A. Ottawa.
   B. Vancouver.
   C. Montreal.
   D. Toronto.

❻ The territory created in 1999 to give the First Nations greater self-government is
   F. Nunavut.
   G. Saskatchewan.
   H. Northwest Territory.
   I. Yukon Territory.

Chapter 6 **197**

Thinking Like a Geographer

❸ INTEGRATING VISUAL INFORMATION Possible benefits: greater local power; strengthening of French culture; appease French Canadian nationalists; less political tension between English-speaking and French-speaking factions; Possible disadvantages: loss of the English-speaking population who might move out of the province; separation of the Atlantic provinces from the rest of Canada; need to renegotiate trade agreements, including NAFTA; other nations may be slow to recognize independence; loss of the support of a strong established central government; foreign and domestic investment might stop

Geography Activity

❹ LOCATING PLACES

1. H	6. F
2. B	7. G
3. C	8. A
4. J	9. I
5. E	10. D

ASSESSMENT ANSWERS

Review the Guiding Questions

❶ C If students answer incorrectly, have them study the chapter maps and review Lesson 1. Lesson 1 in the student text names Manitoba, Saskatchewan, and Alberta as the Prairie Provinces.

❷ G If students answer incorrectly, again have them review Lesson 1. Students should be able to eliminate Pikes Peak and Mount McKinley as answers because they are both mountains in the United States, not in Canada. Hudson Mountain is not mentioned in the student text. Lesson 1 identifies Mount Logan as Canada's highest peak.

❸ C If students answer incorrectly, have them review Lesson 2. Students can eliminate answer C because the métis are a group of people of mixed French and aboriginal background, not an individual man. Henry Hudson and Father Junipero Serra are not mentioned in the student text. Lesson 2 identifies explorer Samuel de Champlain as the founder of the settlement of Quebec.

❹ H If students answer incorrectly, have them review Lesson 3. Lesson 3 identifies Quebec as the province where French heritage remains strong and where most people speak French.

❺ D If students answer incorrectly, have them review Lesson 3. Lesson 3 identifies Toronto as Canada's largest metropolitan area.

❻ F If students answer incorrectly, have them review Lesson 3. Lesson 3 explains how the Canadian government created the territory of Nunavut in 1999 to give First Nations people greater autonomy. Students should recognize the names of the other three choices as previously existing provinces or territories of Canada.

DBQ Analyzing Documents

7 **D** Immigrants accounted for two-thirds of Canada's population growth, so they were the major factor in that growth. Canada's population would have grown without immigration but to a lesser degree; therefore, students could eliminate choice A. The quotation does not mention the United States, so students should be able to eliminate choice C also.

8 **H** The sentence describes where in Canada the immigrants have settled. There is no mention of their occupations, where they have immigrated from, or their economic status.

Short Response

9 Possible answer: Champlain benefited from France not being the first to place colonies in the Americas by being able to see what happened in the Spanish colonies and learn from any mistakes and problems they had.

10 Possible answer: Peaceful relations with Native Americans would give French colonists benefits such as the absence of war and its cost in human life and money; the chance of becoming allies with Native Americans, who could help if conflicts arose with other European powers; the possibility of trade with Native Americans; and the possibility of receiving aid from the Native Americans if the colony struggled.

Extended Response

11 Students' essays are likely to show that they would choose an area of Canada that is similar to the area where they live in the United States. Details should draw parallels between the countries' regions and the lifestyles of the regions' inhabitants. Essays should be grammatically correct, contain a variety of sentence types, and make clear comparisons.

DBQ DOCUMENT-BASED QUESTIONS

7 **DETERMINING CENTRAL IDEAS** Read the following statement about Canada's people.

"Immigration . . . was responsible for two-thirds of [Canada's] population growth in the period 2001 to 2006. . . . The effect of immigration is mostly felt in Canada's largest urban [centers] and their surrounding municipalities."

—from *The Atlas of Canada*

Which generalization can be made from this quotation?
A. Without immigration, Canada's population would have declined.
B. The immigration rate is higher in Canada today than ever before.
C. The immigration rate to Canada is higher than to the United States.
D. Immigrants were the major reason for Canada's population growth.

8 **DETERMINING CENTRAL IDEAS** What does the second sentence in the quotation tell you about Canada's immigrants?
F. their occupations
G. their origin in urban or rural areas
H. their settlement patterns
I. their economic status

SHORT RESPONSE

"[Samuel de Champlain] thought that the conquering spirit in which the Spanish usually approached the new Indian groups was itself mistaken. . . . A new colony should seek friends and allies amidst the indigenous peoples."

—from Arthur Quinn, *A New World*

9 **ANALYZING** How did Champlain benefit from France not being the first European nation to place colonies in the Americas?

10 **IDENTIFYING** In what ways could French colonists benefit from peaceful relations with Native Americans?

EXTENDED RESPONSE

11 **INFORMATIVE/EXPLANATORY WRITING** Choose the Canadian province or territory where you think you would be most comfortable living. Write an essay describing the province or territory, and explain why you chose it over the others. Your essay should show your understanding of the similarities and parallels between life in Canada and the United States.

Need Extra Help?

If You've Missed Question	❶	❷	❸	❹	❺	❻	❼	❽	❾	❿	⓫
Review Lesson	1	1	2	3	3	3	2	2	2	2	1

---

networks   *Online Teaching Options*

Practing 21st Century Skills

Practicing Your students can practice important 21st Century skills such as geography, reading, writing, and critical thinking by using resources found in the Skills Builder tab of the online Student Learning Center. Resources include templates, handbooks, and slide shows. These same resources are also available in the Resource Library of the Teacher Lesson Center.

CHAPTER 7

Mexico, Central America, and the Caribbean Islands Planner

UNDERSTANDING BY DESIGN®

Enduring Understandings

- Over time, people adapt to their environment.

Essential Questions

- How does geography influence the way people live?
- Why does conflict develop?
- Why do people trade?

Predictable Misunderstandings

- Mexico is a hot, dry country without natural resources.
- Mexico does not have a productive economy.
- The countries of Central America are all the same.

Assessment Evidence

Performance Tasks:

- Project-Based Learning Digital Hands-On Chapter Project
- Project-Based Learning Hands-On Chapter Project

Other Evidence:

- Geography Skills Activity
- Critical Thinking Skills Activity
- Geography and History Activity
- Informational Map Activity
- Global Connections
- Participation in Project-Based Learning Activities
- Participation in Interactive Whiteboard Map Activities
- Contribution to small-group activities
- Interpretation of slide show images and special purpose maps
- Lesson Reviews
- Chapter Assessments

SUGGESTED PACING GUIDE

Introducing the Chapter	2 Days	Lesson 3	2 Days
Lesson 1	2 Days	Global Connections	3 Days
Lesson 2	2 Days	Chapter Wrap-Up and Assessment	2 Days

TOTAL TIME   13 Days

Key for Using the Teacher Edition

SKILL-BASED ACTIVITIES

Types of skill activities found in the Teacher Edition.

* **V Visual Skills** require students to analyze maps, graphs, charts, and photos.

W Writing Skills provide writing opportunities to help students comprehend the text.

R Reading Skills help students practice reading skills and master vocabulary.

C Critical Thinking Skills help students apply and extend what they have learned.

T Technology Skills require students to use digital tools effectively.

*Letters are followed by a number when there is more than one of the same type of skill on the page.

DIFFERENTIATED INSTRUCTION

All activities are written for the on-level student unless otherwise marked with the leveled labels below.

BL Beyond Level
AL Approaching Level
ELL English Language Learners

All students benefit from activities that utilize different learning styles. Many activities are marked as below when a particular learning style is highlighted.

Intrapersonal	Naturalist
Logical/Mathematical	Kinesthetic
Visual/Spatial	Auditory/Musical
Verbal/Linguistic	Interpersonal

Indiana Academic Standards

Students will:

6.1.1 Summarize the rise, decline, and cultural achievements of ancient civilizations in Europe and Mesoamerica.

6.1.6 Identify trade routes and discuss their impact on the rise of cultural centers and trade cities in Europe and Mesoamerica

6.1.10 Examine and explain the outcomes of European colonization on the Americas and the rest of the world.

6.1.11 Compare and contrast Spanish, Portuguese, French, and British colonies in the Americas.

6.1.18 Create and compare timelines that identify major people, events and developments in the history of individual civilizations and/or countries that comprise Europe and the Americas.

6.1.19 Define and use the terms decade, century, and millennium, and compare alternative ways that historical periods and eras are designated by identifying the organizing principles upon which each is based.

6.1.20 Analyze cause-and-effect relationships, keeping in mind multiple causations, including the importance of individuals, ideas, human interests, beliefs and chance in history.

6.1.22 Form research questions and use a variety of information resources to obtain, evaluate and present data on people, cultures and developments in Europe and the Americas.

6.2.5 Discuss the impact of major forms of government in Europe and the Americas on civil and human rights.

6.3.3 Describe and compare major physical characteristics of regions in Europe and the Americas.

6.3.4 Describe and compare major cultural characteristics of regions in Europe and the Western Hemisphere.

6.3.5 Give examples and describe the formation of important river deltas, mountains and bodies of water in Europe and the Americas.

6.3.7 Locate and describe the climate regions of Europe and the Americas and explain how and why they differ.

6.3.10 Explain the ways cultural diffusion, invention, and innovation change culture.

6.3.11 Define the terms anthropology and archeology and explain how these fields contribute to our understanding of societies in the present and the past.

6.3.12, 6.4.1, 6.4.2, 6.4.7

CHAPTER OPENER PLANNER

Students will know:

• Mexico City is on the site of the ancient Aztec capital of Tenochtitlán.

• Central America and the Caribbean went through a long period of colonialism, but finally achieved independence.

Students will be able to:

• *identify* countries and cities in Central America and the Caribbean Islands using a map.

• *use a time line* to discuss significant events in the history of Mexico, Central America, and the Caribbean Islands.

UNDERSTANDING
BY DESIGN®

☑ *Print Teaching Options*

V Visual Skills

☐ **P. 200** Students study a map of the region and identify different countries and discuss the oceans and islands in the region.

☐ **P. 201** Students discuss the major points of interest on the timeline.

W Writing Skills

☐ **P. 201** Students choose one of the entries on the timeline and write a paragraph about how the event may have affected people's lives.

T Technology Skills

☐ **P. 200** Students research about ancient ruins and make presentations to show what they learned to the class. BL

☑ *Online Teaching Options*

☐ **MAP** **Reading a Map**—Students identify aspects and locations of the region on a map.

☐ **TIME LINE** **Reading a Time Line and Map**—Students identify where in the region events on the timeline took place and locate the places on a map. Visual/Spatial

☐ **TIME LINE** **Interactive World Atlas**—Students use the interactive world atlas to identify the region and describe its terrain.

☑ *Printable Digital Worksheets*

☐ **WORKSHEET** **Geography and History: The Building of the Panama Canal**—Students can use the worksheet that goes into more detail about the construction of the canal.

☐ **WORKSHEET** **Geography Skills: Using an Informational Map**—Students can use the worksheet to understand how to read an informational map.

☐ **WORKSHEET** **Critical Thinking Skills: Making Generalizations**—Students can use the worksheet to make generalizations about the Ring of Fire.

Project-Based Learning ✋

Hands-On

Making a News Map
Have students read and clip news articles about recent events that have occurred in Mexico, Central America and the Caribbean Islands. On a large classroom map of this region, have students use string to connect the clipped articles to the map. Refer to this news map to stimulate discussion about this region's physical features, history, culture, and current events as students study the chapter.

Digital Hands-On

Creating Virtual Tours
Have students work in teams to create a virtual tour highlighting locations in Mexico, Central America and the Caribbean Islands. Students should select interactive, multimedia Web sites for each destination and prepare a text or audio guide to enrich the tour. When students have completed the assignment, have them share their tours with the rest of the class.

ⓔdtechteacher
21ˢᵗ Century Learning

Print Resources

ANCILLARY RESOURCES
These ancillaries are available for every chapter and lesson.

• **Reading Essentials and Study Guide Workbook** AL ELL
• **Chapter Tests and Lesson Quizzes Blackline Masters**

PRINTABLE DIGITAL WORKSHEETS
These printable digital worksheets are available for every chapter and lesson!

• **Hands-On Chapter Projects**
• **What Do You Know? Activities**
• **Chapter Summaries (English and Spanish)**
• **Vocabulary Builder Activities**
• **Quizzes and Tests (English and Spanish)**
• **Reading Essentials and Study Guide (English and Spanish)** AL ELL
• **Guided Reading Activities**

More Media Resources

SUGGESTED VIDEOS
NOTE: Be sure to preview videos to ensure they are age-appropriate.

• **Introducing the People and Land of Mexico** (32 min)
• **Three Cubans** (59 min)
• **Dawn of the Maya** (60 min)

SUGGESTED READING 📚
• *Mexico & Central America: A Fiesta of Cultures, Crafts, and Activities for Ages 8-12,* by Mary Turck, AL
• *Hurricane Dancers,* by Margarita Engle
• *El Beisbol: Travels Through the Pan American Pastime,* by John Krich BL

PHYSICAL GEOGRAPHY

Students will know:
- *Mexico City is the site of the ancient Aztec capital of Tenochtitlán.*
- *about landforms and waterways of Mexico, Central America, and the Caribbean Islands.*

Students will be able to:
- *discuss* the physical geography of Mexico and Central America.
- *describe* climates in Mexico and Central America.
- *analyze* a graph of climate zones.
- *identify* important resources in Mexico and Central America.

UNDERSTANDING
BY DESIGN®

☑ *Print Teaching Options*

V Visual Skills

☐ **P. 203** Students sketch a mental map as they read the description of the physical geography of Mexico. **BL**

☐ **P. 204** Students look at the photo of the volcano and analyze why it might be in the "Ring of Fire." **ELL**

☐ **P. 206** Student groups discuss and compose a song that describes the features of a climate zone. **ELL**

☐ **P. 208** Students draw a mental map of the Lesser Antilles and Greater Antilles as they read about them. **ELL**

W Writing Skills

☐ **P. 208** Students read a primary source and write a narrative essay describing what Columbus saw when he arrived in the Americas. **BL**

R Reading Skills

☐ **P. 202** Students determine the meaning of *isthmus*. **ELL**

☐ **P. 205** Students discover the meanings of *terra caliente, terra templada,* and *terra fría.* **ELL**

☐ **P. 207** Students identify the central idea of the paragraph under the head "Major Islands." **ELL**

☐ **P. 208** Students take notes on the climate of the Caribbean Islands. **AL**

C Critical Thinking Skills

☐ **P. 202** Students give examples of how geographic location affects a region's culture and economy. **BL**

☐ **P. 203** Student partners list reasons why the Aztecs chose Mexico City as the center of their empire. **AL**

☐ **P. 207** Students draw a Venn diagram to compare and contrast the mineral resources in Mexico and Central America. **AL**

T Technology Skills

☐ **P. 204** Students research the effects of earthquakes on the economies of Mexico and Central America and how the region has prepared for natural disasters. **BL**

☐ **P. 209** Students research the tourist industry in the Caribbean and analyze it. **BL**

☑ *Online Teaching Options*

V Visual Skills

MAP **Climates: Mexico, Central America, and the Caribbean Islands**—Students use the climate map to determine how the location of landforms and waterways affect the climate. **ELL** Verbal/Linguistic

VIDEOS **Caribbean Island Views**—Students watch a video to review the Caribbean's water, climate, and resources and then discuss the similarities and differences. Kinesthetic

MAP **Physical Geography: Mexico, Central America, and the Caribbean Islands**—Students use the physical geography map to discuss the landforms and bodies of water in the region. Interpersonal

MAP **Political: Mexico, Central America, and the Caribbean Islands**—Students can use the political map to review the countries of the region and make connections to the lesson.

MAP **Resources: Mexico, Central America, and the Caribbean Islands**—Students can use the resources map to review the resources of this region.

W Writing Skills

VIDEO **Chiapas Coffee**—Students watch a video about coffee farmers in Chiapas and discuss the physical geography that goes into growing coffee. Then they summarize the main ideas they learned. Visual/Spatial, Verbal/Linguistic

IMAGE **360° View: Mexico City**—Students use the interactive image of Mexico City to write three questions they would like to find answers to about the city. Visual/Spatial, Verbal/Linguistic

GRAPHIC ORGANIZER **Climates of Mexico, Central America, and the Caribbean**—Students can use the graphic organizer to review the climate zones of the region.

GRAPHIC ORGANIZER **The Caribbean Islands**—Students can use the graphic organizer about the organization of the Caribbean Islands to understand how these islands are grouped.

R Reading Skills

GRAPHIC ORGANIZER **Landforms and Waterways of Mexico, Central America, and the Caribbean Islands**—Students organize the landforms and waterways by region and discuss the "Ring of Fire" and its effect on the region. **ELL** Visual/Spatial

C Critical Thinking Skills

ANIMATION **Waterways as Political Boundaries**—Students view the animation showing how the rivers and oceans form the boundary lines between places. Visual/Spatial

T Technology Skills

ONLINE SELF-CHECK QUIZ **Lesson 1**—Students receive instant feedback on their mastery of lesson content

☑ *Printable Digital Worksheets*

W Writing Skills

WORKSHEET **Critical Thinking Skills: Making Generalizations**—Students can use the worksheet to make generalizations about the Ring of Fire.

HISTORY OF THE REGIONS

Students will know:

- *Spanish forces led by Hernán Cortés defeated the Aztec and took over their empire.*
- *Many Native Americans died from diseases brought from Europe.*
- *Central America and the Caribbean went through a long period of colonialism, but finally achieved independence.*

Students will be able to:

- **describe** *early civilizations in Mexico and Central America and the Caribbean Islands.*
- **analyze** *conflicts and the path to independence for Mexico and countries in Central America and the Caribbean Islands.*

UNDERSTANDING
BY DESIGN®

☑ *Print Teaching Options*

V Visual Skills

☐ **P. 210** Students work with a partner to create a timeline and plot events they read about in the text. ELL AL

☐ **P. 213** Students analyze how the image of the barge supports the text. ELL

☐ **P. 214** Students describe the items on the map that surprised them as being brought to the Americas. ELL

W Writing Skills

☐ **P. 212** Students write an informative essay comparing and contrasting European rule of Mexico and Central America and their moves for independence. BL

R Reading Skills

☐ **P. 210** Students use context clues to determine the meaning of *specialize*. ELL AL

☐ **P. 212** Students work together in pairs to write summaries of text sections. ELL

☐ **P. 214** Students describe why different nations would want to colonize in the same area and what physical features made it easy for countries to colonize the Caribbean Islands. AL

C Critical Thinking Skills

☐ **P. 211** Students compare and contrast the Maya and the Aztec.

☐ **P. 213** Students interpret how the colonial system took advantage of the resources of Central America for European gain and whether the end of colonialism brought economic change. AL

☐ **P. 214** Students discuss how diseases spread and how Europeans could have prevented the spread of diseases they brought to the Americas.

☐ **P. 215** Students infer why the Caribbean Islands became independent faster than elsewhere in the region and the effect later independence movements had on the Caribbean.

T Technology Skills

☐ **P. 211** Students create and deliver a brief presentation about the causes and effects of the Spanish conquest of Mexico.

☑ *Online Teaching Options*

V Visual Skills

VIDEO Aztec Lake—Students watch a video about the region's history and make connections between the location of lakes and the civilizations of the Aztec. AL Interpersonal

MAP The Panama Canal: Before and After—Students analyze before and after maps of the Panama Canal and discuss how trade, travel, and access affected the economy of Panama, the region, and the Western Hemisphere. Visual/Spatial

MAP The Columbian Exchange—Students identify items and diseases that were exchanged between Europe and the Americas. Visual/Spatial, Logical/Mathematical

IMAGE Tenochtitlán—Students can use the interactive image about Tenochtitlán to discuss this ancient city's importance.

R Reading Skills

LECTURE SLIDE Goods in the Columbian Exchange—Students can use the lecture slide to reinforce the information on the map and from the lesson.

C Critical Thinking Skills

IMAGES Lake Farming: Then and Now—Students describe the differences they see in photographs of the *chinampas* and photographs of modern farming practices in a T-chart. ELL Visual/Spatial

MAP The Colonization of Central America—Students compare and contrast the locations of colonies and write sentences about the resources in areas colonized by Europeans. Visual/Spatial

MAP Colonial Expansion in Mexico, Central America, and the Caribbean Islands—Students can use the map to review nations that colonized the region, the major settlers of the area, and when the nations gained their independence.

T Technology Skills

VIDEO Panama Canal Construction—Students can use the video of the ship passing through the Panama Canal to analyze the lock system and the technology it uses.

ONLINE SELF-CHECK QUIZ Lesson 2—Students receive instant feedback on their mastery of lesson content.

☑ *Printable Digital Worksheets*

W Writing Skills

WORKSHEET Geography and History: The Building of the Panama Canal—Students can use the worksheet that goes into more detail about the construction of the canal.

WORKSHEET Geography Skills: Using an Informational Map—Students can use the worksheet to understand how to read an informational map.

LIFE IN THE REGION

Students will know:
- Mexico's economy is the 11th most productive in the world.
- Mexico has benefited from the North American Free Trade Agreement (NAFTA).

Students will be able to:
- **analyze** the economy, culture, and challenges of modern Mexico, Central America, and the Caribbean Islands.

UNDERSTANDING
BY DESIGN®

☑ *Print Teaching Options*

V Visual Skills

☐ **P. 216** Students work with a partner to create a map that shows the member nations of NAFTA. ELL AL

☐ **P. 217** Students work in groups to create a mural that shows an event in Mexico's history or is part of Mexico's culture. ELL

☐ **P. 218** Students visualize what Mexico's economy will be like in a decade or fifty years. AL

☐ **P. 220** Students analyze the photo of Haiti's barren landscape and discuss whether that is what they envision when they think of islands.

W Writing Skills

☐ **P. 219** Students write an essay about how the United States and other nations should intervene to help Central America solve its economic and political challenges. BL

R Reading Skills

☐ **P. 216** Students make a list of the important economic activities in Mexico and draw pictures or write descriptions of the products Mexico produces. ELL AL

C Critical Thinking Skills

☐ **P. 217** Students synthesize how tourism affects the tertiary sector of Mexico's economy. BL

☐ **P. 218** Students draw and complete a Venn diagram to compare and contrast the economies of Mexico and Central America. ELL

☐ **P. 219** Students explain how forming economic relationships with the United States helped strengthen Central America's economy.

☐ **P. 219** Students explain how forming economic relationships with the United States helped strengthen Central America's economy.

☐ **P. 220** Students discuss why economic and political problems in the Caribbean Islands, Central America, and Mexico are similar. AL

☐ **P. 221** Students work in pairs to classify the information in the Island Cultures section. ELL

T Technology Skills

☐ **P. 221** Students research and find examples of the music of the Caribbean Islands.

☑ *Online Teaching Options*

V Visual Skills

☐ **VIDEO** **Ecotourism in Costa Rica**—Students watch a video about ecotourism in Costa Rica and write four descriptive sentences to tell how ecotourism has contributed to the economy. Visual/Spatial, Verbal/Linguistic

☐ **SLIDE SHOW** **Central American Culture**—Students watch a slide show about the culture of Central America and discuss different aspects of life in the region and then make an arts and crafts item that represents Central American culture. ELL Auditory/Musical, Visual/Spatial

W Writing Skills

☐ **VIDEO** **The Border between the United States and Mexico**—Students watch a video about the border between Mexico and the United States and the influence of the border on thier relationship. They discuss how the economies of both countries influence the development of cities along the border. Then students write three questions about the video. AL Verbal/Linguistic

☐ **MAP** **Hispaniola**—Students analyze the map of Hispaniola and write a travelogue entry from the perspective of a visitor, describing the uniqueness of the land. Visual/Spatial, Logical/Mathematical

R Reading Skills

☐ **GRAPHIC ORGANIZER** **Cultural Aspects of Mexico, Central America, and the Caribbean Islands**—Students use the interactive graphic organizer about Central America to summarize culture, economy, and challenges.

☐ **WORKSHEET** **Mexico, Central America, and the Caribbean Islands**—Students use a worksheet to reinforce their comprehension of content and academic vocabulary words. Verbal/Linguistic, Interpersonal

T Technology Skills

☐ **ONLINE SELF-CHECK QUIZ** **Lesson 3**—Students receive instant feedback on their mastery of lesson content.

INTERVENTION AND REMEDIATION STRATEGIES

LESSON 1 Physical Geography

Reading and Comprehension

Students may find some of the content vocabulary words in this lesson difficult to pronounce. Write the word terrestrial on the board and ask volunteers to offer a definition. *(relating to the Earth)* Have students work in mixed-ability pairs to pronounce the vocabulary words and identify their meanings. Encourage Spanish speakers to assist classmates in correct pronunciation. Have student pairs practice using these words to explain a concept in this lesson.

Text Evidence

Have students work in small groups to research natural resources in Mexico and Central America. Tell students to present an analysis of their findings to answer this question: What issues do these regions face that relate to its natural resources? Tell students to use evidence in the text and from their research to support their answer. After groups have presented their reports, discuss some of the problems faced by countries in Central America with regard to natural resources (Mexico's oil production has declined, Nicaragua is too poor to mine its resources, and so on).

LESSON 2 History of the Region

Reading and Comprehension

Have students work with a partner to identify this lesson's content vocabulary words that have more than one meaning, such as *staple* and *revolution*. Have pairs review the list of words to identify root words or words with similar meanings, such as *conquest, colony,* and *revolt*. Then have them write sentences using the meanings of the vocabulary words as they are used in the text. Tell students their sentences should show a clear understanding of the meaning of each word.

Text Evidence

Assign pairs or small groups a topic from the lesson to research and analyze, drawing comparisons to information presented in the text. Tell students to note information found in their research that supports or conflicts with evidence in the text. As students research their topic, have them note key ideas and details about their topic to answer the essential question: Why does conflict develop? Have students present their findings to the class.

LESSON 3 Life in the Region

Reading and Comprehension

Have students skim the lesson to identify words that are unfamiliar or confusing. Have students use print or online dictionaries to define the words. Then have students work with a partner to play a guessing game in which one person gives clues about a word, and the other student tries to guess it. To ensure comprehension of concepts in this lesson, guide a class discussion about complex concepts and terms, such as NAFTA or the unique qualities of island economies.

Text Evidence

Organize students into small groups and tell students they will act as members of an economic and development committee. Their job is to bring economic growth to one of the regions discussed in the lesson. (You may wish to assign specific regions to avoid duplication.) Have groups use evidence from the text and additional research to identify the type of economy in their region and what might help increase economic growth (business, tourism, etc.). Have groups present their reports to the class, using visuals to clarify concepts and ideas.

Online Resources

Level Reader

Use this online lower-level text that corresponds directly to the text in the online Student Edition.

Guided Reading Activities

This resource uses graphic organizers and guiding questions to help students with comprehension.

What Do You Know?

Use these worksheets to pre-assess students' background knowledge before they study the chapter.

Reading Essentials and Study Guide Workbook

This resource offers writing and reading activities for the approaching-level student.

Self-Check Quizzes

This online assessment tool provides instant feedback for students to check their progress.

MEXICO, CENTRAL AMERICA, AND THE CARIBBEAN ISLANDS

ESSENTIAL QUESTIONS · *How does geography influence the way people live?* · *Why does conflict develop?* · *Why do people trade?*

Girl from the highlands of Guatemala

Sergio Pitamitz/Robert Harding World Imagery/Corbis

networks
There's More Online about Mexico, Central America, and the Caribbean Islands.

CHAPTER 7

Lesson 1
Physical Geography

Lesson 2
History of the Region

Lesson 3
Life in the Region

The Story Matters...

Early advanced civilizations developed in this region of the Americas. Their people developed economies based on farming and trade. They built planned cities and developed highly organized societies and governments. The arrival of the Spanish and other Europeans had a dramatic impact on the region and its indigenous peoples. The influence of European colonial rule and the struggles for independence can still be seen in the economies, politics, and cultures of the region today.

FOLDABLES
Study Organizer

Go to the Foldables® library in the back of your book to make a Foldable® that will help you take notes while reading this chapter.

199

Letter from the Author

Dear Geography Teacher,

As students study Mexico, you might want to address the illegal drug trafficking and the violence that has resulted from it with students. Discuss ways that the Mexican government has tried to stop the drug trade and evaluate whether these methods are effective. Tell students that despite these problems, Mexico is poised to assume a strong leadership role in Latin America. The economy is booming, partly fueled by a dynamic tourist industry that lures European and American visitors every year.

Richard G. Boehm

ENGAGE

Bellringer Show students a map or a globe and point to the region of Mexico, Central America, and the Caribbean Islands. Invite students who have visited the region or who are from the region to share their experiences. Have students brainstorm words that describe the region. Then have students read "The Story Matters..." about the region's culture and history.

Discuss with the class what it means to study the geography and history of a region in order to better understand the way people live. **Ask: How does understanding a region's geography and history reveal aspects about its culture?** *(Possible answer: A region's geography and history can help to explain the ways of life of the people who live there.)* Tell students that in this chapter they will learn about the region of Mexico, Central America, and the Caribbean Islands.

Making Connections Read the following information to students.

Mexico, Central America, and the Caribbean are located in the Western Hemisphere. Here are some facts about the region:

- Mexico City, Mexico, has one of the largest populations of any city in the world.
- Mexico is a country with much biodiversity, or diversity of plant and animal life.
- The island of Hispaniola is located in the present-day country of the Dominican Republic in the Caribbean. Christopher Columbus landed on Hispaniola in 1492, where he interacted with the local people, yet many call this event the "discovery" of America.
- Spanish is the most widely spoken language in the region, but some indigenous languages are still heard today. One such language is Mayan, which has been spoken in the region since ancient times.

To get students thinking about how geography and history influence the way people live, have them choose one of the cities in the region and use the Internet to search for key events in their city's history. Ask them to write a paragraph about how the geography and history of the area affected the way people lived in the city long ago or today. *(Answers will vary but should demonstrate an understanding of how geography and history affect how people live.)*

FOLDABLES
Study Organizer

Go to the Foldables® library for a cumulative chapter-based Foldable® activity that your students can use to help take notes and prepare for assessment.

TEACH & ASSESS

Step Into the Place

V Visual Skills

Reading a Map Explain to students that this map shows the region of Mexico, Central America, and the Caribbean Islands. Have students identify each of the different countries in the region. Discuss with students how oceans surround the region and how they most likely influence the way of life of the people living in these countries. Point out Puerto Rico on the map and discuss the prominence of islands in the region. **Visual/Spatial**

T Technology Skills

Research Have students look at the two pictures on this page and read aloud the captions. Have students compare and contrast the buildings in the two images. Explain that the Maya lived in the area that is now Mexico, Guatemala, and Belize and that they built huge pyramids that people still visit today. Have students who are interested in learning more about the Mayan people do some research about their ancient ruins and present what they learned to the class. **BL Verbal/Linguistic, Interpersonal**

Content Background Knowledge

- Puerto Rico is a self-governing commonwealth and is associated with the United States.
- It was acquired by the United States in 1898 after its victory in the Spanish-American War.
- Puerto Ricans are United States citizens, but they cannot vote in presidential elections and do not have to pay federal income tax.
- Puerto Rico's population density is very high and is primarily urban.
- About 3.8 million people live in Puerto Rico, but another 2 million people from Puerto Rico live in the United States.

200

Chapter 7 MEXICO, CENTRAL AMERICA, AND THE CARIBBEAN ISLANDS

V Mexico, Central America, and the Caribbean islands sit between North America and South America. The region is surrounded by oceans and seas and is located close to the Equator. As you study the map, look for the geographic features that make this area unique.

Step Into the Place

MAP FOCUS Use the map to answer the following questions.

1. **THE GEOGRAPHER'S WORLD** What is the largest country in this region?

2. **ENVIRONMENT AND SOCIETY** Why was the Panama Canal built where it is?

3. **THE GEOGRAPHER'S WORLD** Which of the Caribbean islands is part of the United States?

4. **CRITICAL THINKING** Analyzing Given their location, what might be a key economic industry of the Caribbean islands?

A HISTORIC CITY Willemstad, capital of the Caribbean island of Curacao, was founded in 1634 by Dutch settlers.

B MAYAN RUINS Early Americans known as the Maya built cities in the rain forests of southern Mexico.

Step Into the Time

DESCRIBING Select one location on the time line and describe the impact of European colonization on the lives and environment of the people who lived there.

1325 Aztec found Tenochtitlán

1300

1492 Christopher Columbus arrives in Americas

1500

200 Chapter 7

Project-Based Learning

Hands-On

Making a News Map
Have students read and clip news articles about recent events that have occurred in Mexico, Central America, and the Caribbean Islands. On a large classroom map of this region, have students use string to connect the clipped articles to the map. Refer to this news map to stimulate discussion about this region's physical features, history, culture, and current events as students study the chapter.

Digital Hands-On

Creating a Virtual Tour
Have students work in teams to create a virtual tour highlighting locations in Mexico, Central America, and the Caribbean Islands. Students should select interactive, multimedia Web sites for each destination and prepare a text or audio guide to enrich the tour. When students have completed the assignment, have them share their tours with the rest of the class.

edtechteacher
21st Century Learning

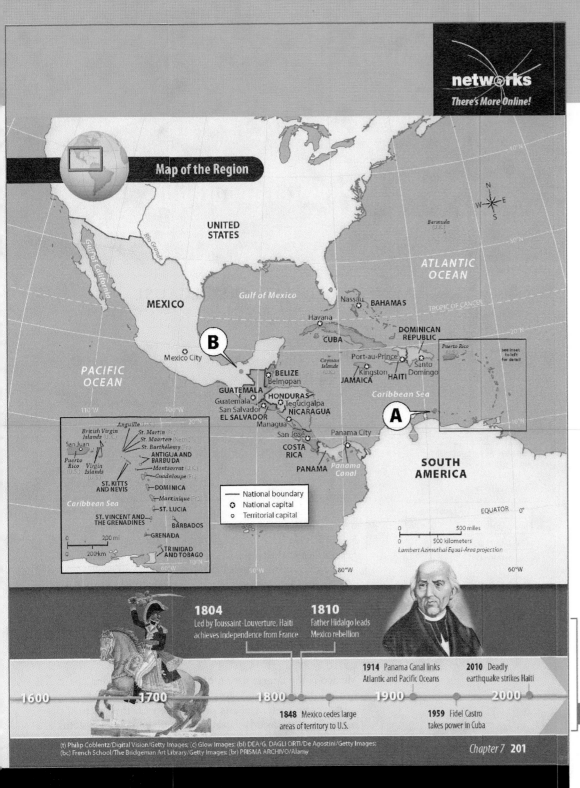

Map of the Region

Step Into the Time

V Visual Skills

Reading a Time Line Remind students that time lines help show the correct order of events. Discuss how events over hundreds of years can appear on the same time line. Ask students how much time is shown between the first event on this time line to the last event. *(685 years)*

Have students review the time line and, as a class, discuss its major points of interest. **Ask:**

- Which century is most represented on this time line? *(the 1800s)*
- When did the Panama Canal connect the Atlantic and Pacific Oceans? *(1914)*
- Why do you think Mexico gave large areas of territory to the United States in 1848? *(Possible answer: They were at war and the United States won.)*
- Was the Panama Canal built in the nineteenth or twentieth century? *(twentieth)*

Ask students to identify additional historical events for this region and ask where they would place them on the time line. *(Students' answers will vary but should include accurate event placement.)* Visual/Spatial

W Writing Skills

Informative/Explanatory Have students brainstorm ideas about how events on the time line might have affected the lives of the people in the region. Then have students choose one of the entries and write a paragraph about how the event may have actually affected people's lives. Have the students share their paragraphs with the class. Verbal/Linguistic

V

1804 Led by Toussaint-Louverture, Haiti achieves independence from France

1810 Father Hidalgo leads Mexico rebellion

1914 Panama Canal links Atlantic and Pacific Oceans

2010 Deadly earthquake strikes Haiti

1848 Mexico cedes large areas of territory to U.S.

1959 Fidel Castro takes power in Cuba

1600 1700 1800 1900 2000

(t) Philip Coblentz/Digital Vision/Getty Images; (c) Glow Images; (bl) DEA/G. DAGLI ORTI/De Agostini/Getty Images; (bc) French School/The Bridgeman Art Library/Getty Images; (br) PRISMA ARCHIVO/Alamy

Chapter 7 **201**

CLOSE & REFLECT

Summarizing Have students write two or three sentences to summarize what they learned from the Chapter Opener. Collect and read a few of the summaries to the class. Tell students that they will learn more about how events in this region affected the way people lived as they read the chapter.

TIME LINE

Reading a Time Line and Map

Display the time line and map on the whiteboard. Have volunteers read each event as it is revealed on the time line. Ask students to identify where in the region the event took place and find its location on the map. Visual/Spatial

See page 199B for other online activities.

ENGAGE

Bellringer Before students begin the lesson, ask for five volunteers to model what an isthmus looks like. Have two students stand next to each other to form the continent of North America. Then have two more students stand next to each other about 4 feet away (and to the south) of the other students. Then have the fifth student lie down on the floor and touch his or her hands to North America and his or her feet to South America. Then read the Essential Question aloud and have students discuss geogaphical features in their area that may or may not influence the way people live. **Ask:** How might living on an isthmus affect the way people live? *(Student answers will vary but should include that living on an isthmus would give people easy access to travel on bodies of water but at the same time could be isolating.)* Have students explain why living on an isthmus might be appealing or challenging.

TEACH & ASSESS

R Reading Skills

Determining Word Meanings Have students add the word *isthmus* to their vocabulary lists in their notebooks. As a class, discuss how an isthmus is different from a continent. Have students write their own definitions to explain the word and draw sketches to show where an isthmus is located between North and South America. Remind students to add words to their lists as they encounter new vocabulary in their reading of the chapter. **ELL** Verbal/Linguistic

C Critical Thinking Skills

Making Connections Explain to students that geographic location influences the cultural and economic ties that a region maintains. Have students give examples of how geographic location affects their region's culture and economy. **Ask:** How do cultural influences and economic relationships with other regions affect the way people live? *(Student answers may vary but should demonstrate an understanding of adapting aspects of culture and the strengthening and growth of an economy through economic ties with other regions.)* **BL** Verbal/Linguistic

---

ANSWER, p. 202

Taking Notes Sample answers: **Mexico:** Mountains along west and east coast; Central Plateau between them; Low coastal plains; Mountains in south; Baja and Yucatán Peninsulas. **Central America:** Highlands in center; Low plains on both coasts. **Caribbean Islands:** Formed by partly submerged mountain chain created by volcanoes.

---

netw⚫rks

There's More Online!

☑ **GRAPHIC ORGANIZER**
Landforms and Waterways

☑ **IMAGE** 360° View: Mexico City

☑ **ANIMATION** Waterways as
Political Boundaries

☑ **VIDEO**

Reading **HELP**DESK

Academic Vocabulary

- similar
- benefit

Content Vocabulary

- isthmus
- *tierra caliente*
- *tierra templada*
- *tierra fría*
- bauxite
- extinct
- dormant

TAKING NOTES: *Key Ideas and Details*

Organize As you read about the region, take notes on the physical geography using a graphic organizer like the one below.

Area	Landforms
Mexico	
Central America	
Caribbean islands	

Indiana Academic Standards
6.1.18, 6.1.19, 6.3.5, 6.3.7, 6.3.12, 6.4.7

Lesson 1
Physical Geography

ESSENTIAL QUESTION · *How does geography influence the way people live?*

IT MATTERS BECAUSE
Mexico and Central America are southern neighbors to the United States.

Physical Geography of Mexico and Central America

GUIDING QUESTION *What landforms and waterways do Mexico and Central America have?*

Mexico and the seven nations of Central America act like a bridge between two worlds. Geographically, they form an isthmus that connects North and South America. An **isthmus** is a narrow piece of land that connects two larger landmasses. Culturally, they join with South America and some Caribbean islands to make up Latin America. Latin America is a region of the Americas where the Spanish and Portuguese languages, based on the Latin language of ancient Rome, are spoken. Economically, the nations have close ties to the United States. They also trade with their Latin American neighbors.

Shaped like a funnel, the region is wider in the north than in the south. To the north, Mexico has a 1,951-mile (3,140-km) border with the United States. At the southern end, the Central American country of Panama is only about 40 miles (64 km) wide.

Land Features
Mexico is the largest nation of the region, occupying about two-thirds of the land. Imagine a backwards *y* along the western and eastern coasts of Mexico, with the tail to the south. That backwards *y* neatly traces the mountain systems

(l to r) Wendy Connett/Robert Harding World Imagery/Getty Images; ©Francisco Guasco/epa/Corbis; ©iStockphoto.com/yuhirao; Pixtal/age fotostock

---

netw⚫rks *Online Teaching Options*

VIDEO

Chiapas Coffee

Summarizing Use this video about this family of coffee farmers in Chiapas to introduce the lesson. Discuss with students the various apsects of physical geography that go into growing coffee, such as weather, climate, soil, and human-environment interaction. Ask students to summarize the main ideas after watching the video. Collect the summaries and review them as a class after the lesson. Visual/Spatial, Verbal/Linguistic

See page 199C for other online activities.

BBC Motion Gallery Education

on Mexico's two coasts and south central region. The coastal ranges are called the Sierra Madre Occidental (Spanish for "western") and the Sierra Madre Oriental (Spanish for "eastern"). They join in the southern highlands. Coastal plains flank the western and eastern mountains. The eastern plain is wider.

Between the two arms of the y is a vast highland region called the Central Plateau. It is the heartland of Mexico. This plateau is home to Mexico City, which is the capital, and a large share of the nation's people.

Mexico has two peninsulas. The Yucatán Peninsula bulges northeast into the Gulf of Mexico. Baja California (*baja* means "lower" in Spanish) extends to the south in western Mexico.

Central America has landforms **similar** to those of south central Mexico. Mountains run down the center of these countries. Narrow coastal lowlands flank them on the east and west.

Mexico and Central America lie along the Ring of Fire that rims the Pacific Ocean. Earthquakes and volcanoes are common in the Ring of Fire. The Sierra Madre Occidental are made of volcanic rocks, but they have no active volcanoes. The mountains in the southern part of the central plateau and in Central America, however, do have numerous active volcanoes. These volcanoes bring a **benefit**. Volcanic materials weather into fertile, productive soils.

V

Academic Vocabulary

similar much like

benefit advantage

Mountains appear on the hazy horizon of Mexico City. Mexico's capital lies about 7,800 feet (2,377 m) above sea level.

Wendy Connett/Robert Harding World Imagery/Getty Images

IMAGE

Interactive Photos

This region has many diverse types of landscapes. Land forms range from mountains to grasslands. Waterways include rivers, lakes, and shorelines. Vegetation varies depending on the soil quality and access to water within the specific area. Animal life has adapted to take advantage of what the region has to offer.

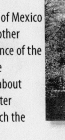

360° View: Mexico City

Formulating Questions Display the 360° image of Mexico City and point out details that show industry and other economic activities. Discuss the economic importance of the city to the region. Then ask students to write three questions that they would like to find answers to about Mexico City. If students do not find the answers after reading the chapter, allow time for them to research the answers. Visual/Spatial, Verbal/Linguistic

See page 199C for other online activities.

V Visual Skills

Diagramming Explain to students that Mexico is a region of diverse landforms. Have students read the section on Mexico's land features and sketch a mental map as they read the description of the physical geography of the country. Invite students to share and compare their sketches in small groups. **Ask:** How is the land diverse in Mexico? (*Student answers may vary but should explain how Mexico has mountains and volcanoes, coastal ranges and plains, highlands and plateaus, and two peninsulas.*) **BL** Visual/Spatial

C Critical Thinking Skills

Drawing Conclusions Discuss with students how Mexico City is flanked by mountains. Have students study the photograph of Mexico City at the bottom of the page. Then, with a partner, have them make a list of the reasons why the Aztecs might have chosen this location as the center of their empire and why it grew to become Mexico's largest city and capital. Have partners share their lists with the class. **AL** Naturalist, Interpersonal

C

Content Background Knowledge

Fun Things to Do in Mexico City

- Visit the National Museum of Anthropology that contains a hall dedicated to each cultural group from the region today and throughout its history.
- Go see the Pyramids of Teotihuacan that echo the shape of the mountains surrounding the city.
- Explore the Metropolitan Cathedral, which is the oldest and largest cathedral in the Americas.
- Take a sightseeing or a hot-air balloon tour to see the diversity of the area's physical features and human-made features.
- Go shopping in the cuturally diverse marketplace and barter with the merchants.

Physical Geography

Visual Skills

Analyzing Photos Have students look at the photo on this page and read the caption about Popocateptl Volcano. Discuss why the volcano is known as the "smoking mountain." **Ask:** Why do you think this volcano might be in "the Ring of Fire"? *(Possible answer: This volcano is probably in the Ring of Fire because Mexico lies on this ring of active volcanoes that lie near tectonic plate boundaries that circle the Pacific Ocean.)*
ELL Verbal/Linguistic

Technology Skills

Researching on the Internet and Using and Citing Information Have students work with a partner to research the effects of earthquakes on the economies of Mexico and Central America and what the region has done to prepare for such natural disasters.

Remind students to use reliable sources and record the list of sources they used to gather facts. Review the need for students to paraphrase rather than copy the information word-for-word. Ask students to each write an informative piece on their findings or to diagram the information in an appropriate chart or graph. Then invite volunteers to present their findings to the class. **BL** Visual/Spatial, Logical/Mathematical

Reading Skills

Summarizing Explain to students that combining main ideas and details into a succinct summary is an important skill because it helps them better understand what they are reading. Summaries are also excellent ways to take notes and to review material in preparation for a test. A summary should include the central idea of a paragraph or section along with the main details that support the central idea. **Ask:** How would you summarize the section "Bodies of Water"? *(Sample answer: Mexico and Central America are surrounded by oceans but have few major rivers. The Panama Canal is a very important waterway.)* **AL** Verbal/Linguistic

Popocatépetl volcano stands in the background as a farmer plows the land. Popocatépetl, also known as "smoking mountain," has experienced eruptions since ancient times.
▶ **CRITICAL THINKING**
Explaining Why are earthquakes common in some parts of Mexico and Central America?

Earthquakes are common in the area, too. A magnitude 8.0 earthquake that hit Mexico City in 1985 killed thousands of people. One that struck El Salvador in 2001 produced another kind of disaster. A hill weakened by the earth's movement collapsed onto the town of Las Colinas. It crushed homes and killed hundreds of people.

Bodies of Water

Mexico and Central America are bordered by the Pacific Ocean to the west. The Gulf of California, an inlet of that ocean, separates Baja California from the rest of Mexico. To the east, the region is surrounded by the waters of two arms of the Atlantic Ocean. They are the Gulf of Mexico and the Caribbean Sea.

The region has few major rivers. In the northern half of Mexico, the climate is dry. This means that few rivers flow across the rocky landscape. Southern Mexico and Central America receive more rain, but the landscape is steep and mountainous, and the rivers are short. An important river is the Río Bravo. In the United States, this river is called the Rio Grande. The largest lake in the region is Lake Nicaragua, in Nicaragua.

©Francisco Guasco/epa/Corbis

netw**o**rks *Online Teaching Options*

GRAPHIC ORGANIZER

Landforms and Waterways of Mexico, Central America, and the Caribbean Islands

Categorizing Display the graphic organizer and guide students to organize the landforms and waterways by region. Discuss with students the "Ring of Fire" and its effect on the region. **ELL** Visual/Spatial

See page 199C for other online activities.

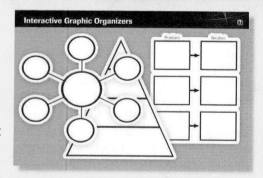

Interactive Graphic Organizers

ANSWER, p. 204

CRITICAL THINKING Earthquakes are common because these countries lie along plate boundaries and the movement and collision of the plates cause earthquakes.

An important waterway in the region is not a river, but a feature built by people. It is the Panama Canal, built in the early 1900s. The Panama Canal makes it possible for ships to pass between the Atlantic and Pacific oceans without journeying around South America. It saves thousands of miles of travel, which in turn saves time and money. It is one of the world's most important waterways.

Climates

Most of Mexico and Central America lie in the Tropics. Because of their location near the Equator, it might seem that the climate would be hot. Although the coastal lowlands are hot, areas with higher elevation are not. The highlands are much cooler.

Nearly the entire region can be divided into three vertical climate zones. Soil, crops, animals, and climate change from zone to zone. The *tierra caliente*, or "hot land," is the warmest zone. It reaches from sea level to about 2,500 feet (762 m) above sea level. Major crops grown here are bananas, sugarcane, and rice.

Next highest is the *tierra templada*, or "temperate land." This climate zone has cooler temperatures. Here farmers grow such crops as coffee, corn, and wheat. Most of the region's people live in this climate zone.

Higher in elevation is the *tierra fría*, or "cold land." This region has chilly nights. It can be used only for dairy farming and to grow hearty crops such as potatoes, barley, and wheat.

Think **Again**

Because the Panama Canal connects the Atlantic and Pacific oceans, it must go east to west.

Not really! Central America twists to the east where Panama is located. As a result, the Panama Canal is cut from the north to the south.

R

The Rio Bravo, or Rio Grande, carves its way through rugged countryside. It forms part of the border between Mexico and the United States.
▶ **CRITICAL THINKING**
Describing Why are there so few rivers in the northern part of Mexico?

©iStockphoto.com/yuhirao

Chapter 7 205

ANIMATION

Waterways as Political Boundaries

Analyzing Visuals Display the animation on the whiteboard to visually explain how bodies of water such as rivers and oceans form boundary lines between places. Ask students to point out three examples on the map of how waterways or bodies of water form boundaries and discuss the reasons that waterways are often used as political boundaries. **Visual/Spatial**

See page 199C for other online activities.

R Reading Skills

Determining Word Meanings Explain to students that geographers often use words from the language of the region to describe geographical features or conditions in an area. Since the predominant language in this region is Spanish, geographers have used the terms *tierra caliente, tierra templada,* and *tierra fría* to describe the climate zones of the region. Based on each climate zone description, students can try to understand the words' meanings. After students read the section on climates, **ask:**

- What word part do all three climate zones share, and what do you think it means? *(tierra, land)*
- Which climate zone refers to a zone that is milder? How do you know? *(tierra templada; because templada sounds like the word "temperate" and a synonym for temperate is "mild")*
- What word do you think describes land that is cold? Why? *(fría, because it sounds like the word "freezing," and if you are freezing, you are cold)* **ELL** Verbal/Linguistic

Content Background Knowledge

The Panama Canal is considered one of the "Wonders of the Modern World." For hundreds of years, people throughout the world wanted to build a canal across Central America to reach the Pacific Ocean without having to travel completely around South America. Though the French began building the canal, they were unable to complete it as so many workers were plagued by the malaria-carrying mosquitoes of the jungle region.

The equipment and rights to the canal were eventually bought by the United States, who completed the canal for about 400 million dollars and operated it from 1914 until 1979. The United States signed a treaty with Panama which allowed joint control of the canal from 1979 until 1999. On December 31, 1999, Panama assumed all of the control, including setting toll rates for use of the canal. From start to finish, it takes about 9 hours for a ship to navigate through the canal.

ANSWER, p. 205

CRITICAL THINKING The dry climate means there is little rainfall for rivers to form.

Physical Geography

V Visual Skills

Integrating Visual Information Climate zones have been designated for regions around the world. Place students into small groups and assign a climate zone to each group. Have each group talk about its climate zone. Then challenge the group to compose a song that describes the features of its climate zone and present the song to the class. **ELL** Auditory/Musical

T Technology Skills

Problem Solving The region's tropical location makes it vulnerable to natural disasters such as hurricanes. Ask students to work with a partner to research on the Internet what steps and measures the Mexican government has taken to prepare the Mexican people when a hurricane hits. Then ask students to answer the following questions:

- What action has Mexico's government taken to help protect its people and resources in the event of a hurricane? *(Answers will vary but should demonstrate understanding of steps that the Mexican government has taken to protect its people, infrastructure, and resources from damage caused by hurricanes.)*
- What success has Mexico had in implementing these safety measures? *(Answers will vary but should give specific examples of the effects of Mexico's preparation.)*
- How do you think nations should prepare for natural disasters, such as hurricanes, and how can they best protect their resources based on your research? *(Answers will vary but should offer viable solutions to providing protection and being prepared during a hurricane.)* Verbal/ Linguistic, Interpersonal

Content Background Knowledge

Mexico is among the top 10 oil-producing nations in the world and is among the top 20 natural gas producing nations. The oil sector alone contributes 14 percent of Mexico's earnings from exports. Mexico's economy places high importance on oil and natural gas exports because the revenue gained from it accounts for about 1/3 of the Mexican government's total revenue.

V CLIMATE ZONES

Although the region is located in the Tropics, many inland areas of Mexico and Central America have relatively cool climates.

▶ **CRITICAL THINKING**

1. **Identifying** What products are grown in *tierra caliente*?

2. **Analyzing** Why are many inland areas of Mexico and Central America relatively cool?

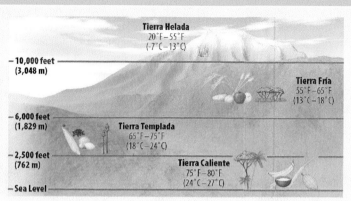

Tierra Helada
20°F – 55°F
(-7°C – 13°C)

−10,000 feet
(3,048 m)

Tierra Fría
55°F – 65°F
(13°C – 18°C)

−6,000 feet
(1,829 m)

Tierra Templada
65°F – 75°F
(18°C – 24°C)

−2,500 feet
(762 m)

Tierra Caliente
75°F – 80°F
(24°C – 27°C)

−Sea Level

Geographers also designate other vertical climate zones. Few human activities take place on the *tierra helada,* or "frozen land". This vertical climate zone is more common in other regions of the Americas.

Tropical Wet/Dry Climate

Much of Mexico and Central America have a tropical wet/dry climate. The climate is characterized by two distinct seasons. The wet season, during the summer months, is when most of the precipitation falls. The dry season occurs during the winter months. The dry season is longer in the areas farther from the Equator and closer to the polar regions.

The region's tropical location exposes it to another natural hazard. Ferocious hurricanes can strike in the summer and early autumn months. These storms do great damage. For example, a 1998 hurricane killed more than 9,000 people in Honduras and destroyed 150,000 homes.

Natural Resources

Oil and natural gas are Mexico's most important resources. They are found along the coast of the Gulf of Mexico and in the gulf waters. Mexico is an important oil-producing country. It has enough oil and gas to meet its own needs and still export a large amount. The exports help fuel the nation's economy. However, Mexico's oil production has declined since 2004. Many oil fields are old and are starting to run out of oil.

When Spanish explorers first came to Mexico, they were attracted to the area's gold and silver. Mexico still produces silver, which is mined in the central and north central parts of the country. Gold also is still mined in Mexico. Other minerals include copper, iron ore, and **bauxite**. Bauxite is used to make aluminum.

---

netw⦿rks *Online Teaching Options*

MAP

Climates: Mexico, Central America, and the Caribbean Islands

Determining Cause and Effect Display the climate layer on the Chapter Opener map to show the location of landforms and waterways and how they affect the climates of the region. Ask students to explain to a partner how physical features affect climate. **ELL** Verbal/Linguistic

See page 199C for other online activities.

ANSWER, p. 206

CRITICAL THINKING

1. tropical agricultural products, such as bananas and sugar
2. because of higher elevation

The seven smaller nations of Central America have few mineral resources. Nicaragua is an exception, with gold, silver, iron ore, lead, zinc, and copper. The nation is so poor, however, that it has not been able to take advantage of these deposits. Guatemala also has some oil, and its mountains produce nickel.

✓ READING PROGRESS CHECK

Analyzing Why are different climate zones found in this region, even though most of the region is in the Tropics?

Physical Geography of the Caribbean Islands

GUIDING QUESTION *How are the Caribbean islands alike and different from one another?*

Hundreds of islands dot the Caribbean Sea. The islands are home to more than 30 countries or territories belonging to other countries. Some are large, with millions of people living on them. Others are tiny and home to only thousands.

Major Islands

The Caribbean islands can be segmented into three different groups. The first group is the Greater Antilles. The four islands, the largest Caribbean islands, include Cuba, Jamaica, Hispaniola, and Puerto Rico. Cuba and Jamaica are independent countries. Hispaniola is home to two countries: Haiti in the west and the Dominican Republic

This scenic bay in the Caribbean island of Antigua provides an ideal harbor for yachts and other sailing ships. Antigua is part of the Lesser Antilles.
▶ **CRITICAL THINKING**
Describing What islands make up the Greater Antilles?

Pixtal/age fotostock

VIDEOS

Caribbean Island Views

Determining Central Ideas Use these videos about the various Caribbean islands to review the region's land, water, climate, and resources. Have students discuss the similarities and differences between the videos.
Kinesthetic

See page 199C for other online activities.

G1 Critical Thinking Skills

Comparing and Contrasting Have students draw a Venn diagram to compare and contrast the mineral resources in Mexico and Central America. (**Alike:** *gold, copper, iron ore:* **Different:** *Mexico: bauxite; Central America: silver, lead, zinc*)
AL Visual/Spatial

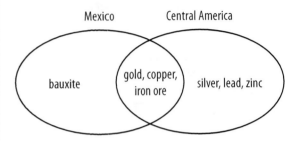

Mexico   Central America

bauxite   gold, copper, iron ore   silver, lead, zinc

R Reading Skills

Determining Central Ideas Explain to students that breaking down a large amount of text can help locate the main idea. Review with students the first paragraph under the Guiding Question to discuss what the central idea is for the paragraph. *(The central idea is that there are islands of different sizes in the Caribbean.)* Point out that the main idea is not always in the first sentence of the paragraph. **Ask:** What is the central idea of the section "Major Islands"? *(The Caribbean islands are made up of three different groups of islands.)* **ELL** Verbal/Linguistic

C2 Critical Thinking Skills

Classifying After students read the last paragraph, have them begin a chart of the three different groups of islands to complete as they read the next page. Encourage them to take notes in their charts and to classify the different islands of the Caribbean by size. **AL** Visual/Spatial

Making Connections Discuss with students if any of them have ever lived on or visited an island in the Caribbean. Have these students share what experiences they had on the islands. Encourage them to talk about what the area looked like, what foods they had to eat, what the temperature and weather was like, what unusual things they saw or did, or any other experiences they or a family member had during the visit.

ANSWERS, p. 207

CRITICAL THINKING Cuba, Jamaica, Hispaniola, and Puerto Rico.
✓ READING PROGRESS CHECK Different areas of the region have different climate zones because they are at different elevations. The higher the elevation, the cooler the climate is.

Physical Geography

V Visual Skills

Making Connections Review with students the islands that make up the Lesser Antilles and the Greater Antilles. Then have students read the paragraphs on both sets of islands and draw a mental map of both island groups as they read each detail. **Ask:** Why do you think these island groups are called the Lesser Antilles and Greater Antilles? Use details and evidence from the text and the maps you drew in your response. *(Students' answers may vary but should include that the Lesser Antilles are made up of smaller islands formed by individual volcanoes, while the Greater Antilles are the largest islands in the Caribbean Sea and are the tops of a nearly submerged chain of mountains.)* **ELL** Visual/Spatial

W Writing Skills

Narrative Explain to students that the "discovery" of the Bahamas by Christopher Columbus opened up the exploration and settlement of the Americas. Have them read a primary source such as an excerpt from his journal and then write a narrative essay in which they describe what Columbus saw when he arrived in the region from his point of view. Remind them to be as descriptive as possible about the physical geography, plants and animals, and people he encountered. *(Students' essays should have a strong and engaging opening, use the first-person point of view, include dialogue, transition and descriptive words, and a reflective conclusion.)* **BL** Naturalist

R Reading Skills

Explaining Have students read the last section on the page about the climate of the Caribbean Islands. Suggest that they jot down notes to help them remember key ideas and details. Then have them choose a partner and take turns explaining orally what they read. If possible, have them include details that they already read about the climate of Mexico and Central America in their explanations. **AL** Interpersonal, Verbal/Linguistic

---

Thinking Like a Geographer

Why are the Caribbean islands hit so often by earthquakes and volcanoes?

The islands of the Caribbean are not along the edge of the Pacific Ocean. So why do they experience these disasters? The Ring of Fire is not the only place where tectonic plates meet. Many Caribbean islands are located at the boundaries of different plates where volcanoes form and earthquakes occur. Hence, the islands are vulnerable to these disasters. A 2010 earthquake near Haiti's capital of Port-au-Prince might have killed as many as 200,000 people and forced 1 million others out of their homes.

---

in the east. Puerto Rico is a commonwealth of the United States. Although it is a possession of the United States, it has its own government. The people of Puerto Rico are American citizens. They can travel freely between their island and the United States.

The second group of islands is the Lesser Antilles. Dozens of smaller islands make up this group. They form an arc moving east and south from Puerto Rico to northern South America. Most of the islands are now independent countries. At one time, they were colonies of France, Britain, Spain, or the Netherlands. Each has a culture reflecting its colonial period.

The third island group is the independent nation of the Bahamas. The islands lie north of the Greater Antilles and east of Florida. The Bahamas include more than 3,000 islands, although people live on only about 30 of them.

The Greater Antilles are a mountain chain, much of which is under water. On a map, you can see that this chain extends eastward from Mexico's Yucatán Peninsula. These islands include some mountains, such as the Sierra Maestra in the eastern part of Cuba and the Blue Mountains of Jamaica. The highest point in the Caribbean is Duarte Peak, in the Dominican Republic. The Lesser Antilles are formed by volcanic mountains. Many of the volcanoes are **extinct**, or no longer able to erupt. Some islands have **dormant** volcanoes, or ones that can still erupt but show no signs of activity.

The Caribbean Sea

The Caribbean Sea is a western arm of the Atlantic Ocean. In the past, sailing ships traveling west from Europe followed trade winds blowing east to west to reach the sea. Christopher Columbus used the winds to reach the Bahamas in 1492. There, he first sighted land in the Americas. Columbus explored the Caribbean, too. These voyages sparked European settlement of the Americas.

The warm waters of the Caribbean help feed the Gulf Stream. This current carries warm water up the eastern coast of the United States.

The Climate of the Caribbean Islands

The Caribbean islands have a tropical wet/dry climate. Temperatures are high year-round, though ocean breezes make life comfortable. Humidity is generally high, but rainfall is seasonal and varies significantly. Islands like Bonaire receive only about 10 inches (25 cm) of rain per year. Dominica, on the other hand, receives about 350 inches (899 cm) of rain each year. That is an average of almost an inch of rain every day.

Like Central America and Mexico, the Caribbean islands are prone to hurricanes. These storms are more likely to occur in the northern areas, toward the Gulf of Mexico, than to the south. On average, seven hurricanes strike the Caribbean islands each year.

208 Chapter 7

---

netw⊙rks   *Online Teaching Options*

MAP

Physical Geography: Mexico, Central America, and the Caribbean Islands

Determining Cause and Effect Display the physical geography layer on the Chapter Opener map to discuss with students the various landforms, oceans, and waterways. Be sure to highlight the Caribbean Sea and how it contributes to the warm weather of the Caribbean Islands and encourages tourism there. Also discuss with students how the tectonic plates create the unique landforms and islands in the region. **Interpersonal**

See page 199C for other online activities.

ANSWER, p. 208

THINKING LIKE A GEOGRAPHER The islands are located near tectonic plates.

Natural Resources

The waters of the Caribbean are rich in fish. Some are fished for food and others for sport. The islands have few timber resources today. People have cut down most of the trees already to use for fuel or to make farmland.

Mineral resources are generally lacking too, although some Caribbean islands have important resources. Trinidad and Tobago has reserves of oil and natural gas. The Dominican Republic exports nickel, gold, and silver. Cuba is a major producer of nickel. Jamaica has large amounts of bauxite.

Perhaps the most important resources of the Caribbean are its climate and people. Warm temperatures and gracious hosts attract millions of tourists to the region each year. Some enjoy the white sandy beaches and clear blue water. Some scuba dive to see the colorful fish darting through coral reefs.

✓ **READING PROGRESS CHECK**

Citing Text Evidence How did the islands of the Caribbean form?

Tourists on a boat near the French-ruled island of Guadeloupe learn to dive in Caribbean waters.

Identifying What natural resource of the Caribbean Sea benefits the region's island nations?

FOLDABLES
Study Organizer

Include this lesson's information in your Foldable®.

LESSON 1 REVIEW

Reviewing Vocabulary

1. What is the *tierra templada*? Why do most people in Mexico and Central America live in this vertical climate zone?

Answering the Guiding Questions

2. ***Describing*** How are the physical geography of Mexico and Central America similar?

3. ***Analyzing*** What impact does the Panama Canal have on the cost of shipping goods? Why?

4. ***Determining Central Ideas*** How do the locations of Mexico and Central America increase the possibility of natural hazards striking the region?

5. ***Determining Word Meanings*** Why are some islands in the Caribbean called the *Greater* Antilles and others called the *Lesser* Antilles?

6. ***Narrative Writing*** Imagine you are taking a cruise that stops at a Caribbean island, a port in Central America, and a port in Mexico. Write three diary entries describing what you would see in each place.

Chapter 7 **209**

LESSON 1 REVIEW ANSWERS

Reviewing Vocabulary

1. The *tierra templada* is the climate zone between the *tierra caliente* lowlands and the *tierra fría* highlands. Most people live in the *tierra templada* because it has more moderate temperatures than the hot lowlands and colder highlands.

Answering the Guiding Questions

2. **Describing** The physical geography of Mexico and Central America are similar because these areas have a highland interior flanked by coastal lowlands. They also have the same climate zones based on elevation.

3. **Analyzing** Possible answer: The Panama Canal made it cheaper to ship goods between the Atlantic Ocean and Pacific Ocean because cutting the travel distance saves time and fuel, which saves money.

4. **Determining Central Ideas** Mexico and Central America are located on the edge of the Ring of Fire, where volcanoes and earthquakes are common. Because they are located in the tropics, they are also prone to hurricanes.

5. **Determining Word Meanings** The four islands that make up the Greater Antilles are the largest islands in the Caribbean. The islands of the Lesser Antilles are smaller.

6. **Narrative Writing** Students' diary entries should note the physical differences between the island and the mainland areas, the similarities between the coastal plains of Central America and Mexico, and the warm climate of the Caribbean and lowland areas.

V Visual Skills

Analyzing Images Point to the image on the page, and review with students what natural resources are and how they are used. **Ask:** How does this image illustrate the economic importance of people using the natural resources in the Caribbean? *(It shows people using water, a natural resource, that is readily available all around them, to create income from the tourist industry thus growing the local economy.)* **ELL** Visual/Spatial

T Technology Skills

Analyzing Data Have students work with a partner to find statistics on the Internet for tourism and the tourist industry in the Caribbean. After they have gathered the data, have them analyze it. **Ask:**

• How important is the tourist industry to the Caribbean's economy? How much does it contribute to the economy? *(Sample response: Tourism is important to the Caribbean's economy, but it is more important in some countries than in others. For example, in Antigua and Barbuda, it contributes more than 80 percent of the GDP, while in Trinidad and Tobago it contributes about 10 percent of the GDP.)*

• After reading about the climate and physical features of the region, how likely would you be to visit the islands and contribute to the economy? Why? *(Students' answers will vary but should include an explanation of why or why not they would want to visit the area based on the facts given in the text.)* **BL** Logical/Mathematical

CLOSE & REFLECT

Making Connections To close this lesson, have students think about how the geography and the climate of Mexico, Central America, and the Caribbean Islands affect the region's economy. Ask students to make a list of the important economic activities in the region.

ANSWERS, p. 209

Identifying fishing

✓ **READING PROGRESS CHECK** The Greater Antilles are a section of a partially submerged mountain chain that extends from the Yucatán Peninsula. The Lesser Antilles were formed by volcanoes.

ENGAGE

Bellringer Before students read the lesson, explain that civilizations rise and fall, and that archaeologists try to piece together a people's early history by examining evidence such as artifacts. **Ask:** What artifacts would you leave behind so that an archaeologist in the future could determine how you lived? Make a list of students' responses on the board. Then **ask:** How would an archaeologist figure out how a civilization collapsed? Have students write down their ideas and discuss them as a class.

TEACH & ASSESS

V Visual Skills

Creating Time Lines Have students work with a partner to read the page and create a time line, plotting events that they read about in the text. Point out that for long periods of time between events, they can create a break in the time line and then continue the time line in even increments. Model an example on the board. Ask students how creating the time line helped them understand key events in Mexico's early history. Suggest that students add events to their time lines as they read the lesson. **ELL AL** Visual/Spatial, Interpersonal

R Reading Skills

Using Context Clues Explain that words around a word that is unfamiliar can help a reader determine its meaning. **Ask:**

- What words provide a clue in determining the meaning of the word *specialize*? ("jobs other than getting food")

- What do you think the meaning of the word is based on knowing these context clue words? (Possible answer: a specific skill or job) **ELL AL** Verbal/Linguistic

Reinforcing Vocabulary Remind students to add academic and content vocabulary words to their vocabulary lists. Tell students to write their own definitions and include drawings if desired. This activity can be done as students encounter the words during class or completed as homework. **ELL AL**

ANSWER, p. 210

Taking Notes Native American Civilizations: Maya—lived in Mexico, Guatemala, Belize; had city-states; skilled at building, astronomy; Aztec—lived in central Mexico; conquered other peoples; priests performed rituals to win favor of the gods; skilled builders and farmers. **Colonial Period:** Conquest of Aztec by Spanish; death of Native Americans by disease; Spanish people had wealth, Native Americans poor. **1800s:** Mexico gains independence; political turmoil for many decades. **1900s:** Revolution early in 1900s; many reforms instituted; land given to poor people

---

There's More Online!

☑ **SLIDE SHOW** Tenochtitlán
☑ **VIDEO**

Reading **HELP**DESK

Academic Vocabulary
- **feature**
- **transform**

Content Vocabulary
- **staple**
- **surplus**
- **conquistador**
- **colonialism**
- **revolution**
- **plantation**
- **cash crop**
- **caudillo**
- **Columbian Exchange**

TAKING NOTES: Key Ideas and Details

Summarize As you read about the history of Mexico, take notes using the graphic organizer below.

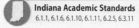

Mexico

Indiana Academic Standards
6.1.1, 6.1.6, 6.1.10, 6.1.11, 6.2.5, 6.3.11

Lesson 2
History of the Regions

ESSENTIAL QUESTION · Why does conflict develop?

IT MATTERS BECAUSE
The region was home to highly developed Native American civilizations.

Mexico's History

GUIDING QUESTION How did economic and governmental relationships between Spanish and Native Americans in Mexico change over time?

V Mexico was first inhabited by Native American groups. Later, Spanish soldiers conquered the groups and ruled them. Since the early 1800s, Mexico has been independent. Its history is long and rich, and its accomplishments are many.

Early Civilizations
Native peoples first grew corn in Mexico about 7,000 years ago. They also grew other foods that have become **staples**, or foods that are eaten regularly, such as corn, squash, chilies, and avocados. Farming allowed people to produce food **R** **surpluses**, or more than they needed to survive. Surpluses helped people specialize in jobs other than getting food.

About 3,000 years ago, the Maya formed the major civilization in the region. They lived mainly in the lowland plains of Mexico's Yucatán Peninsula and in what is now Guatemala and Belize. One **feature** of their culture was great cities. The Maya erected pyramids with stepped sides and temples on top. They invented a complex system of writing. By studying astronomy, they were able to make accurate calendars. The height of Maya civilization was from about A.D. 300 to A.D. 900. Then their power suddenly collapsed. Archaeologists do not know exactly why.

---

netw⊕rks *Online Teaching Options*

VIDEO

Aztec Lake

Summarizing Use this video about the history of the Aztec to introduce the lesson. Be sure students make connections between the lakes and the development of the civilization of the Aztec. Discuss why this civilization developed near water. Ask students to summarize what they already know about the history of Mexico, Central America, or the Caribbean Islands or early civilizations like the Maya or Aztec. Have students share their summaries with a partner to activate prior knowledge.

AL Interpersonal

See page 199D for other online activities.

The Aztec ruled the region next. They settled in central Mexico in about 1300. Their impressive capital city was Tenochtitlán. Mexico City occupies the site where it once stood. Tenochtitlán was built on an island in the middle of a lake. Causeways connected it to the mainland.

The Aztec had a complex social and religious system. They conquered many of their neighbors and made slaves of captured soldiers. Priests performed rituals to win the favor of their gods. The Aztec were also skilled farmers. They built up land in the lake to form small islands called *chinampas*, which they used to grow crops.

The Spanish Arrive

In the early 1500s, a rival power appeared. Around 1520, Hernán Cortés led a small force of Spanish **conquistadors**, or conquerors, to Mexico. Within two years, these explorers and soldiers had defeated the Aztec and taken control of their empire.

How could the Spanish conquer the Aztec with only a few hundred men? Spanish guns and armor were better weapons than Aztec spears. Another major factor was European diseases. The diseases did not exist in the Americas until Europeans unknowingly brought them. Native Americans had no resistance to them, so the diseases killed many thousands. Cortés also took advantage of the anger of other native peoples who resented Aztec rule. Several groups joined him as allies.

Winning the Aztec Empire brought Spain riches in gold and silver mines. The conquest completely **transformed** life in Mexico. Roman Catholic priests converted native peoples to Catholicism. Conquistadors forced native peoples to work on farms or in mines. Spanish rule in Mexico was an example of colonialism.

DE/A.G. DAGLI ORTI/DEA PICTURE LIBRARY/Getty Images

Academic Vocabulary

feature a characteristic
transform to change

C

T

The Aztec city of Tenochtitlán was linked by canals, bridges, and raised streets built across the water.
▶ **CRITICAL THINKING**
Describing How were the Aztec able to build a city and farms in an area covered by a lake?

IMAGES

Lake Farming: Then and Now

Contrasting Display the images of the *chinampas* and modern farming practices side-by-side to show how lake farming changed over time. Ask students to describe the differences by listing them on a T-chart. **ELL** Visual/ Spatial

See page 199D for other online activities.

Interactive Photos

C Critical Thinking Skills

Comparing and Contrasting After reading the section "Early Civilizations", **ask:** How were the Maya and the Aztec alike and different? Have students record their ideas in a Venn diagram and then discuss as a class. (***Alike:*** *They both had thriving civilizations in Mexico, farmed, and had a religious system;* ***Maya:*** *They built pyramids, invented a complex writing system, created a calendar, and studied astronomy;* ***Aztec:*** *built a capital city, built causeways and* chinampas, *and conquered and captured other people.*) Verbal/Linguistic, Visual/Spatial

T Technology Skills

Making Presentations Divide the class into small groups. Ask them to read the section "The Spanish Arrive" and take detailed notes. Have students create and deliver a brief presentation about the causes and effects of the Spanish conquest of Mexico. Explain to students that they may use presentation software to create their presentations and that they should use the Internet or an electronic database in which to gather additional information on the causes and effects. While groups are presenting, have the students in the audience prepare an evaluation for each group. Point out to them that the evaluation should not be critical but include useful feedback. Verbal/ Linguistic, Visual/Spatial

Content Background Knowledge

Facts about Hernán Cortés:

- He studied law as a young man.
- He helped conquer Cuba in 1511 and became the mayor of Santiago de Cuba.
- The governor of Cuba let him lead the expedition into Mexico.
- He befriended a native group, the Tlaxcalans, who helped him against the Aztecs.
- After conquering the Aztec, he built Mexico City on their ruins.

ANSWER, p. 211

CRITICAL THINKING The Aztecs built up land in the lake to form small islands called *chinampas*.

R Reading Skills

Summarizing Explain to students that when you summarize, you state the main points. Summarizing what you read helps you understand a large chunk of text better. While reading the sections on colonialism, independence, conflict, revolution, and stability, ask students to write one sentence that summarizes each section.

Then pair together students and have them work together to write a summary of all of the sections. Suggest that they add transitions between each summary sentence to connect each idea. *(Sample summary: Mexico was a colony of Spain for nearly 300 years. Mexico rebelled against Spanish rule in 1810 and finally gained independence in 1821. However, many Mexicans remained poor, and political conflict led to a revolution in the early 1900s.)*
ELL Verbal/Linguistic

W Writing Skills

Informative/Explanatory Review with students how civilizations thrived in Mexico and Central America before the arrival of the Spanish in the 1500s, and how matters changed after their arrival.

After reading the section "A History of Central America," ask students to do more research and write an informative essay comparing and contrasting European rule of Mexico to that of Central America, as well as the movements for independence in these regions. Remind students that their essays will be evaluated using the following criteria:

- introducing the topic clearly
- developing the topic with relevant facts, details, and other information
- making clear comparisons of similarities
- supporting differences with examples
- using transitions, precise language, and formal style
- including a concluding statement or paragraph that supports the information presented **BL** Verbal/Linguistic

---

Under **colonialism**, one nation takes control of an area and dominates its government, economy, and society. The colonial power uses the colony's resources to make itself wealthier. In colonial Mexico, settlers from Spain had the most wealth.

Independence and Conflict

After almost 300 years of Spanish rule, a priest named Miguel Hidalgo led a rebellion in Mexico in 1810. The goal of the rebellion was to win independence from Spain. Some people hoped it would also create a more nearly equal society. The Spanish captured and executed Hidalgo, but by 1821 Mexico had gained its independence. Spanish rulers, though, were replaced by wealthy Mexican landowners. Native peoples remained poor.

Through much of the 1800s, Mexico was troubled by political conflict. Rival groups fought one another for power. Most of Mexico's people remained poor.

Revolution and Stability

By the early 1900s, dissatisfaction was widespread. A revolution erupted in Mexico. A **revolution** is a period of violent social and political change. One change was the land reform plan, which divided large estates into parcels of land that were then given to poor people to farm. National public schools were established, and a new constitution was written detailing the responsibilities of the government toward the people. Only one political party, however, held power until the 1990s.

☑ READING PROGRESS CHECK

Determining Central Ideas How were the Spanish able to conquer the Aztec?

A History of Central America

GUIDING QUESTION *How did the nations of Central America develop?*

The nations of Central America developed in similar ways to Mexico. But there were differences, as well.

W Early Civilizations and Conquest

The Maya had flourished in Guatemala and Belize, as well as in southern Mexico. Even after their great cities were abandoned, the Maya continued to live in the region. After conquering Mexico, the Spanish moved south. By the 1560s, Spain had seized control of most of Central America. During the early 1800s, Britain claimed the area that is now Belize.

Independence

Central America gained its independence soon after Mexico. In 1823 the territories of Central America united to form one government. By 1840, they had separated into five independent

---

netwⓞrks   *Online Teaching Options*

MAP

The Colonization of Central America

Compare and Contrast Display the colonization layer of the Chapter Opener map to discuss European colonization in Central America. Have students compare and contrast the locations of the colonies. Ask them to write 3–4 sentences about the resources in the region that the European nations may have wanted. Encourage students to compare the colonization of this region to the colonization of the United States by Europeans. **Visual/Spatial**

See page 199D for other online activities.

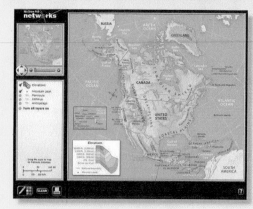

ANSWER, p. 212

☑ READING PROGRESS CHECK The Spanish had better weapons than the Aztec, and they had armor; European diseases killed many Aztec; Cortés gained fighters by turning enemies of the Aztec into allies.

countries: Guatemala, Honduras, El Salvador, Nicaragua, and Costa Rica. The area that is now Belize was still a British colony. Panama was part of Colombia.

Central American countries were subjected to economic colonialism. This means that foreign interests dominate a people economically. These foreign interests were large companies from other countries. They set up **plantations**, or large farms, where poorly paid workers produced cash crops. **Cash crops** are crops sold for profit. The most important were bananas, coffee, and sugarcane.

Heading the governments for much of this time were military strongmen called **caudillos**. The caudillos helped ensure the foreigners' success. In turn, the foreigners made sure that the caudillos remained in power.

Conflict in Modern Times

Around 1900, Panama gained its independence from Colombia. It was helped by the United States, which wanted to build a canal there. The United States controlled the canal until 2000. Then, by agreement, Panama took control of the canal.

The late 1900s was a time of conflict. New wealth came to the upper classes, but most people remained poor. Various groups demanded reforms. Several countries were ravaged by civil wars. Only Costa Rica and Belize remained peaceful. One of Costa Rica's presidents, Óscar Arias Sánchez, helped bring peace to the region.

✓ READING PROGRESS CHECK

Analyzing How did Central America and Mexico's history differ?

Russell Kord/Alamy

Built by the United States in the early 1900s, the Panama Canal is now owned and operated by the Republic of Panama.

Identifying Which country held Panama shortly before the United States built the Panama Canal?

Chapter 7 **213**

MAP

The Panama Canal: Before and After

Analyzing Maps Show the map that displays the routes of sea trade and travel before and after the construction of the Panama Canal. Discuss with students how trade, travel, and access to new regions changed after the construction of the Panama Canal. Visual/Spatial

See page 199D for other online activities.

History of the Regions

V Visual Skills

Reading a Map Have students study the map of the Columbian Exchange. **Ask:** What items on the map surprised you as being brought to the Americas, rather than being native to the Americas? Why? *(Answers will vary but should be supported with a reason.)* **ELL** Visual/Spatial

C Critical Thinking Skills

Problem Solving Ask students what they know about how to avoid spreading the germs that cause a cold or flu. Explain that when the Europeans brought diseases to the Americas, they often brought them unknowingly because the germs were carried in the systems of the travelers who were immune to them. Both the Europeans and Native Americans had little understanding of how disease spreads; therefore, many Native Americans who were not resistant to the diseases died. **Ask:**

• What measures could the Europeans have taken to prevent the spread of the diseases they brought? *(Possible answer: They could have kept ill people away from the native people.)*
• How do diseases spread? *(Possible answer: from contact through droplets in the air from an infected person to a healthy person or by touching something a sick person touched)* Provide an opportunity for students to use resource materials or the Internet to better understand how diseases spread. Naturalist, Logical/Mathematical

R Reading Skills

Applying Have students read the section "Colonialism" independently. **Ask:** Why would different nations want to colonize in the same area? *(Possible answer: resources, easily accessible)* What physical features made it easy for different nations to colonize the Caribbean Islands? *(Possible answer: The Caribbean Islands are a group of islands, which makes them individual entities geographically. With the ocean as borders, each island was easier to colonize by a different nation.)* **AL** Verbal/Linguistic

---

ANSWER, p. 214

MAP SKILLS
1. The Exchange brought about the transfer or flow of products, diseases, ideas, and people throughout the Atlantic world.
2. Enslaved Africans in large numbers were brought from their homelands to work on plantations in the Americas.

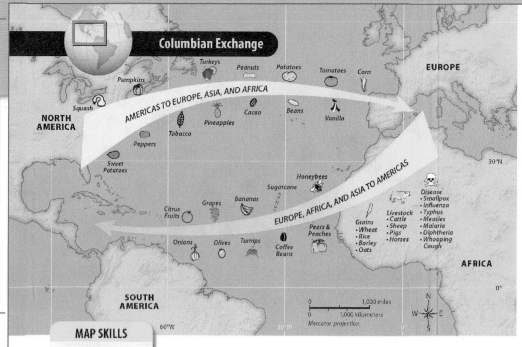

Columbian Exchange

AMERICAS TO EUROPE, ASIA, AND AFRICA

EUROPE, AFRICA, AND ASIA TO AMERICAS

NORTH AMERICA — Turkeys, Peanuts, Potatoes, Tomatoes, Corn, Pumpkins, Squash, Cacao, Beans, Vanilla, Pineapples, Tobacco, Peppers, Sweet Potatoes

EUROPE — 30°N

Honeybees, Sugarcane, Citrus Fruits, Grapes, Bananas, Livestock • Cattle • Sheep • Pigs • Horses, Grains • Wheat • Rice • Barley • Oats, Pears & Peaches, Onions, Olives, Turnips, Coffee Beans

Disease • Smallpox • Influenza • Typhus • Measles • Malaria • Diphtheria • Whooping Cough

AFRICA

SOUTH AMERICA

0°

60°W 30°W 0°

0 1,000 miles
0 1,000 kilometers
Mercator projection

MAP SKILLS

1 **THE USE OF GEOGRAPHY** What happened as a result of the Columbian Exchange?

2 **HUMAN GEOGRAPHY** How did the Columbian Exchange affect African peoples?

History of the Caribbean Islands

GUIDING QUESTION *How did the Caribbean islands develop?*

The history of the Caribbean islands is similar to that of Mexico and Central America. The islands have greater diversity, though, because several European countries ruled them as colonies.

Indigenous Peoples and European Settlers

Europeans changed the way the native peoples of the Caribbean lived. Like the Native Americans of the mainland, they suffered from diseases carried by the Europeans. This is why their numbers declined sharply soon after the arrival of the Europeans. Overwork and starvation also reduced their numbers. The Spanish set up colonies in what are now Cuba, the Dominican Republic, and Puerto Rico. Later, the French settled in what is now Haiti and on other smaller islands. The British and Dutch had some colonies, too.

Colonialism

During the 1600s, the Caribbean colonies became the center of the growing sugar industry. European landowners hoped to make money by selling the sugar in Europe. Because so many Native American workers had died, Europeans brought in hundreds of thousands of enslaved Africans to work the plantations.

The transport of enslaved Africans was part of the **Columbian Exchange**. This term refers to the transfer of plants, animals, and

214 *Chapter 7*

---

netw⊙rks   *Online Teaching Options*

See page 199D for other online activities.

MAP

The Columbian Exchange

Analyzing Maps Display the map of the Columbian Exchange and ask students to identify the items and diseases that were exchanged between Europe and the Americas. Then ask students to write a paragraph to explain how the Columbian Exchange influenced colonization in the region. Visual/Spatial, Logical/Mathematical

people between Europe, Asia, and Africa on one side and the Americas on the other. Foods such as wheat, rice, grapes, and apples were introduced to the Americas as were cattle, sheep, pigs, and horses. At the same time, products from the Americas were introduced into Europe, Africa, and Asia. They included corn, chocolate, and the potato. The Columbian Exchange also resulted in the introduction of new diseases into different parts of the world.

Independence

The first area in the Caribbean to gain independence was Haiti, then called Saint Domingue. Led by Toussaint-Louverture, Haiti gained its independence from France in 1804. The Dominican Republic won its independence in 1844. Cuba and Puerto Rico remained Spanish until 1898. When Spain lost the Spanish-American War, it gave independence to Cuba. Puerto Rico passed into American hands. Other islands of the Caribbean did not win the right to self-government until the middle 1900s.

C

Turmoil in the Twentieth Century

Independence did not mean freedom or prosperity. Rule by caudillos and widespread poverty have remained a problem in Haiti and the Dominican Republic.

Cuba, too, was often subject to dictatorial rule following its independence. Then in 1959, revolutionaries led by Fidel Castro took over. Castro soon cut all ties with the United States. He said his government would follow the ideas of communism. Communism involves government control of all areas of the economy and society. His rule did not bring economic success to Cuba.

W

The other islands of the Caribbean have had their own difficulties. Some countries in the region are trying to improve conditions and bring economic benefits to all their citizens. Small and with few resources, they have been unable to develop strong economies. Many of the islands depend on aid from the governments that used to run them as colonies.

FOLDABLES
Study Organizer

✔ **READING PROGRESS CHECK**

Analyzing What caused the population of the Caribbean islands to grow in colonial times?

Include this lesson's information in your Foldable®.

LESSON 2 REVIEW

Reviewing Vocabulary
1. What is the difference between a *conquistador* and a *caudillo*?

Answering the Guiding Questions
2. *Describing* How did the Maya and the Aztec differ?
3. *Analyzing* How were relations between people with European and Native American heritage similar in Mexico during colonial times and the 1800s?

4. *Determining Central Ideas* How did economic colonialism affect the nations of Central America?
5. *Analyzing* How was the development of Cuba and of Haiti similar and different?
6. *Informative/Explanatory Writing* Write a summary of the history of Mexico, Central America, or the Caribbean islands after independence.

Chapter 7 **215**

LESSON 2 REVIEW ANSWERS

Reviewing Vocabulary

1. A *conquistador* is a Spanish explorer and soldier who conquered Native American peoples. A *caudillo* is a military strongman who ruled a country.

Answering the Guiding Questions

2. **Describing** The Maya lived in city-states in what is now southern Mexico, Guatemala, and Belize; the Aztec lived around modern Mexico City. The Maya had achievements in writing, building, astronomy, and calendar making. The Aztec conquered a large empire and were skilled builders and farmers.

3. **Analyzing** Mexicans of European heritage had the most wealth and power; those with Native American heritage were poor and had little power.

4. **Determining Central Ideas** Possible answer: Economic colonialism hurt the poor people of Central America who had to work hard on large plantations owned by foreigners and were paid little. Also the profits from the plantations went to foreigners and helped support rule by caudillos.

5. **Analyzing** Haiti gained independence much earlier than Cuba; both experienced the problems of rule by dictators; both have remained poor; Cuba has been under communist rule since 1959.

6. **Narrative Writing** Students' summaries should highlight the key points of the history of the chosen area after it became independent. It should include problems caused by dictators, the division of society into rich and poor, and any efforts to reform.

C Critical Thinking Skills

Making Inferences Remind students that they need to put together information from throughout the chapter to make inferences that are not directly stated in the text. **Ask:**

- Why do you think the Caribbean Islands became independent faster than areas elsewhere in the region? *(Possible answer: It was most likely because the Caribbean was colonized by many different nations and the islands were self-contained.)*

- What effect do you think later independence movements had on the political climate in the Caribbean? *(Possible answer: Since the other independence movements happened later than in the Caribbean, it may have led to more political turmoil in the Caribbean whose people compared their government to the others.)* **Verbal/ Linguistic, Logical/Mathematical**

W Writing Skills

Finding Information Have small groups of students research Fidel Castro to find out more information about the political leader and about communism. Then have groups write a short biography about Castro, which includes his communist views and ideas on leadership. Provide time for the groups to research and write. Encourage them to include photographs or drawings to show as they share their research with the class. Be sure the students provide at least two reliable sources and include the sources for any photos. **Verbal/Linguistic**

CLOSE & REFLECT

Making Connections To close this lesson, have students think about how the climate, physical features, and natural resources influenced the way people have lived in this region throughout its history. Then have a class discussion about their thoughts on the region.

ANSWER, p. 215

✔ **READING PROGRESS CHECK** The population of the Caribbean Islands grew in colonial times because European landowners wanted to make money by growing and selling sugar. To do this, they imported large numbers of enslaved Africans.

Life in the Region

ENGAGE

Bellringer Before students begin the lesson, **ask:** Have you ever traded something with a friend? If so, what did you trade? Make a list of students' examples on the board. Then **ask:** Why did you want the item that you traded for, and what did you give to your friend in exchange? Ask students to write a paragraph explaining what they traded and why, and then discuss some of the paragraphs as a class.

TEACH & ASSESS

V Visual Skills

Create Maps Have students work with a partner to create a map that shows the member nations of NAFTA (Canada, the United States, and Mexico). Ask them to include information on the map about the percentage of exports and imports between Mexico and the other NAFTA members. Explain that they can use arrows to show in which direction exports and imports move. **ELL AL** Visual/Spatial

R Reading Skills

Listing Ask students to make a list of the important economic activities in Mexico and to draw pictures or write specific examples of the products Mexico produces in agriculture or manufacturing. **Ask:** What products do you think are most important to Mexico's economy? Why? *(Possible answer: crops and textiles; they bring in a lot of money.)*

Have students underline or circle the products that they think are most important. At the end of the lesson, have them go back and check their lists and make any necessary changes based on what they read. They may also do research online to find out which products are most important to the nation's economy. **ELL AL** Logical/Mathematical

Reinforcing Vocabulary Remind students to add academic and content vocabulary words to their vocabulary lists. Tell students to write their own definitions. This activity can be done as students encounter the words during class or completed as homework. **ELL AL** Verbal/Linguistic

---

ANSWER, p. 216

Taking Notes Economy: importance of trade with United States and Canada; growth in manufacturing; agriculture varied and differs by region; service industries important, especially tourism. **Culture:** blend of Spanish and Native American influences; seen in art, dance; influence of Spain and United States seen in sports

---

netw⊙rks

There's More Online!

☑ **MAP** Hispaniola
☑ **VIDEO**

Reading **HELP**DESK

Academic Vocabulary

- **circumstance**
- **initiate**

Content Vocabulary

- **maquiladora**
- **mural**
- **dependence**
- **free-trade zone**
- **remittance**
- **reggae**

TAKING NOTES: *Key Ideas and Details*

Summarize As you read about Mexico, use the graphic organizer below to take notes about its economy and culture.

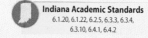

Indiana Academic Standards
6.1.20, 6.1.22, 6.2.5, 6.3.3, 6.3.4, 6.3.10, 6.4.1, 6.4.2

216

Lesson 3
Life in the Region

ESSENTIAL QUESTION · *Why do people trade?*

IT MATTERS BECAUSE
Mexico and other countries in the region have close ties to the United States.

Modern Mexico

GUIDING QUESTION *What is life like in Mexico today?*

When you think of Mexico, you might think of Mexican food like tacos. You might think of mariachi musicians playing lively music and wearing large sombreros. But Mexico has a rich and complex culture and is a rising economic power.

The Economy

Mexico has close economic ties to the United States and Canada. These ties are a result of joining with them in the North American Free Trade Agreement (NAFTA). About 80 percent of Mexico's exports go to NAFTA partners. More than 60 percent of Mexico's imports come from members of NAFTA. Most of this trade is with the United States.

In recent decades, Mexico has developed its manufacturing industry. Factories account for about a third of Mexico's output. Some of them are **maquiladoras**. These are factories where parts made elsewhere are assembled into products. Many of the factories are located in northern Mexico. The goods are then exported. Food processing is another major industry in Mexico. The textile and clothing industries are important, too. Mexico also has heavy manufacturing, producing iron, steel, and automobiles.

Farming remains important. Cotton and wheat are grown in the dry north using irrigation. Along the southeastern coast, farms produce coffee, sugarcane, and fruit. On the

(l to r) ©Patrick Frilet/Hemis/Corbis; Christopher Pillitz/Photonica World/Getty Images; Steve Bly/Photographer's Choice/Getty Images; James P. Blair/National Geographic/Getty Images

---

netw⊙rks *Online Teaching Options*

VIDEO

The Border between the United States and Mexico

Comparing and Contrasting Use this video about the border between the United States and Mexico to introduce the influence of the border on the relationship between these countries. Discuss with students how the economies of both countries influence the development of cities and businesses along the border. Have students write three questions about the content of the video. Review the questions and then use them throughout the lesson to connect the text to the video. **AL** Verbal/Linguistic

See page 199E for other online activities.

BBC Motion Gallery Education

central plateau, farmers grow corn, wheat, and fruits and vegetables. In the poor south, many farmers engage in subsistence farming—growing just enough food to feed themselves and their families.

C Service industries are important in Mexico. Banking helps finance economic growth. A major service industry is tourism. Visitors from around the world come to visit ancient Maya sites or to see the architecture of Spanish colonial cities. Tourists also come to relax in resorts along the warm and scenic tropical coasts.

Culture

V Mexicans are proud of their blend of Spanish and native cultures. They have long celebrated the folk arts that reflect native traditions. In the early 1900s, several Mexican painters drew on these traditions to paint impressive murals celebrating Mexico's history and people. **Murals** are large paintings made on walls. The Ballet Folklorico performs Mexican dances.

Sports reflect Mexico's ties to Spain and the United States. Soccer is popular there, as it is in Spain. So is baseball.

Challenges

With nearly 9 million people, Mexico City is one of the largest cities in the world. Including the city's suburbs, it has more than 21 million people—nearly 20 percent of Mexico's population. Overcrowding is a major problem.

Pollution is another problem, particularly air pollution. Because Mexico City is at a high elevation, the air has less oxygen than at sea level. This makes breathing difficult for some people in normal **circumstances**, but conditions in Mexico City are not normal. A great deal of exhaust from cars and factories is released into the air. The polluted air is held in place by the mountains around the city.

©Patrick Frilet/Hemis/Corbis

Think Again?

All Mexican food is spicy.

Not true! Mexican food varies from region to region. Most dishes are based on traditional native foods —corn, beans, and squash—along with rice, introduced from Spain. Not all Mexican food is spicy, although chilies are used in many dishes.

Academic Vocabulary

circumstance a condition

Farmers sell produce at a village market in Mexico.
▶ **CRITICAL THINKING**
Describing What is farming like in southern Mexico?

C Critical Thinking Skills

Synthesizing Discuss with students the importance of putting together different ideas presented in a text and making their own decisions of how these ideas affect and impact one another. These kinds of critical thinking skills will help students read and understand more challenging texts as they continue through middle school and go into high school.

Ask: How does tourism affect the tertiary sector of Mexico's economy? What draws tourists to Mexico? *(Tourism is a major service industry in Mexico, which contributes greatly to the tertiary sector. Visitors come to see the ancient Mayan ruins and Spanish architecture from colonial days. They also come for the warm weather and beautiful beaches in the coastal areas of the country.)* **BL** Verbal/Linguistic

V Visual Skills

Creating Visuals Divide the class into small groups. After they read the section on Mexico's culture, have them share their ideas and create a mural that shows an event that happened in Mexico's history or is part of Mexican culture.

Students may incorporate graphics printed out from the computer in their murals, and/or they may use markers to draw pictures and write words that depict the event. Allow 5 minutes for each group to present their murals to the class and explain the event that the murals depict and how it is an important part of Mexico. **ELL** Visual/Spatial, Interpersonal

Making Connections Have students who have either lived in Mexico, visited Mexico, or learned about Mexican culture through their family members or immigrant neighbors share their experiences of Mexico with the class. Have them describe what physical and cultural features they have seen, the kinds of traditional or popular Mexican music they have heard, and the kinds of Mexican food they have tasted. Then invite students to name other sights, sounds, and tastes of Mexico that they would like to experience.

Mexico, Central America, and the Caribbean Islands

Defining Have students use the worksheet to reinforce their comprehension of this chapter's content and academic vocabulary words. Instruct students to work in pairs to complete the worksheet and then to check their answers as you review the exercise as a class. **Verbal/Linguistic, Interpersonal**

Discovering World Geography networks

Worksheet

ANSWER, p. 217

CRITICAL THINKING In the poor south, many farmers practice subsistence farming—growing only enough food to survive.

Life in the Region

Visualizing Ask students to think about what Mexico's economy might be like in a decade or even 50 years from now. Have them consider effects of pollution, poverty, and the growth of manufacturing. **Ask:** Do you think that Mexico's economy will continue to grow? Will it rely more or less on manufacturing? *(Sample answers: Yes, but it will probably be slow; yes, but with limited resources, Mexico will probably rely more and more on manufacturing.)* **AL** Logical/Mathematical

C **Critical Thinking Skills**

Comparing and Contrasting Have students draw and complete a Venn diagram that compares and contrasts the economies of Mexico and Central America. Then put students in pairs and have them share and discuss their Venn diagrams. *(Students' Venn diagrams should show that tourism, cash crops, and manufacturing are important in both economies. However, Central America has the Panama Canal, which provides economic benefits, and Mexico does not. Mexico has more natural resources than Central America does.)* **ELL** Verbal/Linguistic, Visual/Spatial

Content Background Knowledge

Tropical rain forests can be found only in a few geographical areas: parts of South America and Central America; Africa, specifically the Zaire and Congo basins in West Africa and eastern Madagascar; and Indo-Malaysia, which includes the western coast of India, Sumatra, and New Guinea; and Queensland, Australia.

The rarity of tropical rain forests in the world makes each one highly prized by scientists who want to explore the vast diversity of plant and animal life in them and by environmentalists who worry that some of these rare plants and animals could become extinct before people even know of them.

Nicaraguan workers make clothing in a factory.
▶ **CRITICAL THINKING**
Identifying What types of products have Central American manufacturers recently begun to make?

V

Sometimes a layer of cold air high in the atmosphere keeps the pollution from rising. The result can be a serious threat to health.

Another challenge facing Mexico is the power of criminals who sell illegal drugs. Drug lords use violence to fight police and to intimidate people. Mexico has mounted a major effort to battle this problem with some success.

Poverty is yet another major challenge facing Mexico. Anywhere from one-fifth to nearly half of Mexico's people are poor. Continued economic growth would help, and seems to be working. Some economists are predicting that Mexico will overtake Brazil in the 2010s as the leading economy in Latin America.

☑ **READING PROGRESS CHECK**

Analyzing How have close ties with the United States helped Mexico's economy?

Modern Central America

GUIDING QUESTION *What is life like in Central America?*

The nations of Central America have fewer resources than Mexico. The region must also deal with political problems.

Central America's Economies
The countries of Central America long showed **dependence**, or too much reliance, on cash crops. In recent years, some have begun to escape this trap. A good sign is the growth of manufacturing. This consists mostly of food processing and production of clothing and textiles. Tourism has grown as well. Tourists come to Belize and Guatemala to see ancient Maya sites. They travel to Costa Rica to see the varied plants and animals in its rain forests.

Panama benefits economically from the Panama Canal. Working for additional benefit, Panama **initiated** a major building program to expand the canal so it can accept larger cargo ships.

C

Academic Vocabulary

initiate to begin

Christopher Pillitz/Photonica World/Getty Images

netw⊙rks *Online Teaching Options*

VIDEO

Ecotourism in Costa Rica

Describing After showing the video on ecotourism in Costa Rica to students, have them write four descriptive sentences that tell how ecotourism has contributed to the nation's and region's economy. Visual/Spatial, Verbal/Linguistic

See page 199E for other online activities.

Design Pics/Corey Hochachka/Getty Images

ANSWERS, p. 218

CRITICAL THINKING food processing and production of clothing and textiles
☑ **READING PROGRESS CHECK** Close ties with the United States have helped Mexico's economy because the United States imports things from Mexico, which brings money into Mexico.

High rates of population growth create an economic challenge. The countries need to grow their economies fast to provide enough jobs. One hope for promoting growth is trade agreements between the countries of the region and other countries.

In the 2000s, the United States and the Dominican Republic signed a series of agreements with five Central American countries (Costa Rica, El Salvador, Guatemala, Honduras, and Nicaragua). The agreement, called the Central America Free Trade Agreement (CAFTA-DR), was the first agreement among the United States and smaller developing economies. CAFTA-DR creates a **free-trade zone** that lowers trade barriers between the countries. Often, however, such trade agreements help the United States more than the other countries.

Challenges Facing the Region

Another challenge to the area is natural disasters. Earthquakes and hurricanes can have a devastating effect on the region's fragile economies. Nicaragua was making some economic progress in the 1990s when Hurricane Mitch hit. The destruction set the nation's economy back significantly.

The need to solve long-standing political problems also holds the region back. The civil wars of the 1980s and 1990s are over, but some of the issues that caused them remain unsolved. If these issues again become more severe, conflict may resume.

Culture

The culture of Central America is strongly influenced by European and native traditions. Spanish is the chief language in all countries except Belize, where English is the official language. English is spoken in many cities in the region as well. In rural Guatemala, native languages are common.

The population is mainly of mixed European and native heritage. Some people of African and Asian descent live there as well. Most people of the region are Roman Catholics. In recent years, however, Protestant faiths have gained followers.

☑ **READING PROGRESS CHECK**

Identifying What are the causes of poverty in Central America?

A tourist descends from a tree in a rain forest in Costa Rica.
▶ **CRITICAL THINKING**
Identifying Point of View Why do visitors travel to Costa Rica's rain forests?

C Critical Thinking Skills

Explaining After students read the paragraph on economic agreements in the region, **ask:** How have forming economic relationships with the United States helped to strengthen Central America's economy? *(Sample answer: The CAFTA-DR has lowered trade barriers between the United States and Central American countries, which has strengthened the region's economy.)*

Ask students to stand behind their desks if they think the United States should provide more economic assistance or aid in Central America's attempts to further develop its economy. If they do not agree, they should remain seated. Then, as a class, discuss arguments for and against this issue and make a class list of possible solutions. **Verbal/Linguistic, Kinesthetic**

W Writing Skills

Argument Review with students some of the economic and political problems that Central American nations have faced and continue to face. Ask them to respond to this writing prompt: *Should the United States and other nations intervene to help Central America solve its economic and political challenges?*

Provide time for students to do additional research to support their opinion on this issue. Remind them to use reliable resources and to follow these guidelines when planning and writing their persuasive essays:

- Introduce your argument or claim clearly.
- Support your argument or claim with clear reasons and relevant evidence.
- Anticipate the argument of the opposing view and cite reasons why their view is faulty.
- Use credible sources and cite information correctly.
- Include a concluding statement in which you restate your argument or claim. **BL** **Verbal/Linguistic**

SLIDE SHOW

Central American Culture

Creating Visuals Display the slide show for students on the culture of Central America and discuss with them the different aspects of life in the region. Provide different arts and crafts materials to students so they can make an item that represents Central American culture. Students may also compose music that would be representative of Central American culture. Display students' work in a class exhibit. **ELL** **Auditory/Musical, Visual/Spatial**

See page 199E for other online activities.

Slide Show

ANSWERS, p. 219

CRITICAL THINKING Visitors travel to Costa Rica's rain forests to see varied plants and animals.

☑ **READING PROGRESS CHECK** Poverty is a problem in Central America because the nations have few resources and because political turmoil has gotten in the way of economic development. Economic colonialism has also slowed improvements in the income that people can earn.

V Visual Skills

Analyzing Have students analyze the image of the physical terrain shown in the picture on the page. **Ask:**

• When you think of islands, do you envision a landscape such as this one? Why or why not? *(Possible answer: No, I think of a land that is sandy, surrounded by water, and dotted with palm trees.)*

• How do people's perceptions of islands affect their thinking about this region? *(Possible answer: People may think that the Caribbean Islands are unproductive and without resources, but in reality they do have natural resources and the land is diverse.)* Verbal/Linguistic, Naturalist

C Critical Thinking Skills

Making Comparisons After students read the section "Island Economies", discuss with them the common economic and political problems that the Caribbean islands share with Mexico and Central America. **Ask:**

• Why are economic and political problems similar among nations in this region? *(Possible answer: Their geographic location, culture, and history are similar and therefore they have some of the same economic and political challenges.)*

• Why have the smaller islands had more success? *(Possible answer: There is less political corruption on the smaller islands.)* AL Verbal/Linguistic

Content Background Knowledge

• The earthquake that hit Haiti on January 12th, 2010, was the most powerful earthquake the country had experienced in over 200 years.

• More than 220,000 people were killed.

• About 300,000 people were injured.

• More than one million people were left without homes, jobs, food, and water.

Haiti's brown, barren landscape contrasts sharply with the richly forested terrain of the neighboring Dominican Republic.
▶ **CRITICAL THINKING**
Analyzing Why has economic development been held back in Haiti?

The Caribbean Islands

GUIDING QUESTION *What is life like on the Caribbean islands?*

The Caribbean islands are mostly small countries with small populations and few resources. Although they have a rich and vibrant culture, they face many challenges.

Island Economies

The biggest challenge for the islands is to develop economically. Many people on the islands are poor. Even in Puerto Rico, a large share of the population lives in poverty. One reason for the poverty is high unemployment.

Cuba's economy is in poor condition after decades of communism. The government has been unable to promote economic development. It relied on aid first from the Soviet Union and more recently from Venezuela. Conditions are worse now than in the 1980s. Cubans also have little political freedom. Those who criticize the government are often arrested.

In Haiti, a history of poor political leadership has held back economic development. Haiti ranks among the world's poorest nations. Poverty is not the country's only problem. Widespread disease is another threat. In addition, as many as one in eight Haitians have left the country. Many of those who emigrated were among Haiti's most educated people. This loss hurts efforts to improve the economy. Finally, the country has not yet recovered from a deadly 2010 earthquake. Despite these problems, Haiti's people are determined to succeed.

Trinidad and Tobago has one of the more successful economies in the region. Sales of its oil and natural gas have funded economic development. Its location near Venezuela and Brazil has helped

James P. Blair/National Geographic/Getty Images

netw⊙rks *Online Teaching Options*

MAP

Hispaniola

Analyzing Maps Display the map of Hispaniola and then show the images of the different countries on the island. Ask students to note the similarities and differences of the island and the two countries. Then ask students to write a travelogue entry from the perspective of a visitor to one of the countries on the island, describing the uniqueness of the land. Visual/Spatial, Logical/Mathematical

See page 199E for other online activities.

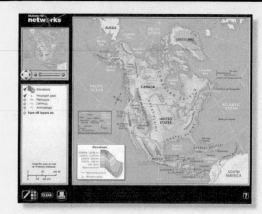

ANSWER, p. 220

CRITICAL THINKING Poverty, disease, and poor political leadership have held back Haiti's economic development make its ports busy. The smaller Caribbean islands have had more political success than the larger ones. Governments are democratic and stable, but the economies are plagued by few resources and poverty.

Another important economic factor in the region is remittances. A **remittance** is money sent back to the homeland by people who migrated someplace else to find work. Many Dominicans came to the United States for work and send money home to support their families.

Tourism is a major part of the economy of several islands. Resorts in the Bahamas, Jamaica, and other islands invite tourists to come and relax in pleasant surroundings. The resorts often separate tourists from the lifestyle of the islanders, but they provide jobs for island citizens.

Island Cultures

The cultures of the Caribbean islands show a mix of mainly European and African influences. Large numbers of Asians also came to some of the islands in the 1800s and 1900s. Those from China went mainly to Cuba. South Asians settled in Jamaica, Guadalupe, and Trinidad and Tobago.

The languages spoken on the islands reflect their colonial heritage. English is the language of former British colonies such as the Bahamas and Jamaica. Spanish is spoken in Cuba, the Dominican Republic, and Puerto Rico. English is also taught in Puerto Rico's schools. French and Creole, a blend of French and African languages, are spoken in Haiti.

The Caribbean islands have strongly influenced world music. Much of the music blends African and European influences. Cuba is famous for its salsa, and Jamaica for reggae. Both forms of music rely on complex drum rhythms. **Reggae** has become popular around the world not only for its musical qualities but also for lyrics that protest poverty and lack of equal rights.

☑ READING PROGRESS CHECK

Citing Text Evidence How do economic conditions in Jamaica relate to the development of reggae?

C

T

FOLDABLES®
Study Organizer

Include this lesson's information in your Foldable®.

LESSON 3 REVIEW

Reviewing Vocabulary
1. What is a *free-trade zone*, and why do the nations of the region want to be in one?

Answering the Guiding Questions
2. *Determining Central Ideas* Do you think Mexico has a strong economy? Why or why not?

3. *Identifying* What challenges does Mexico face?

4. *Describing* How have the economies of the Central American countries changed in recent years?

5. *Analyzing* How do the languages of the Caribbean islands reflect their colonial history?

6. *Argument Writing* Take the role of a government official in one of these countries. Write a brief report to the nation's president explaining whether you think promoting tourism is good or bad for the nation's economy. Give reasons.

Chapter 7 **221**

LESSON 3 REVIEW ANSWERS

Reviewing Vocabulary

1. A *free-trade zone* is an area in which two or more countries have no barriers to trade with each other. Countries want to be in this zone to increase trade.

Answering the Guiding Questions

2. **Determining Central Ideas** Mexico's economy is strong in manufacturing, agriculture, and service industries. Mexico benefits financially from trade with the United States and Canada through NAFTA. Mexico's economy is weakened due to its rapidly growing population of people living in poverty.

3. **Identifying** Mexico faces the challenges of high population growth and poverty, pollution, and illegal drugs and related violence.

4. **Describing** Central American countries have developed a greater manufacturing capacity, and tourism has become more important. These changes have improved their economies by bringing in money and reducing the emphasis on growing cash crops.

5. **Analyzing** The islands speak different languages based on who colonized them. English is the language of former British colonies like the Bahamas and Jamaica. Spanish is spoken in Cuba, the Dominican Republic, and Puerto Rico. French and Creole, a blend of French and African languages, are spoken in Haiti.

6. **Argument Writing** Students should clearly state whether they think tourism is good or bad for economic development and give supporting reasons.

C Critical Thinking Skills

Classify Have students work with a partner to classify the information in the section "Island Cultures." Explain that they should classify information such as the island nation, the country that colonized the nation, and cultural aspects of the island nation such as languages spoken and other cultural characteristics. When students have completed classifying the information, **ask:** How would you describe the culture of the Caribbean Islands? *(Possible answer: They have combined European, African, and Asian aspects of culture to produce a unique culture of their own.)* **ELL** Verbal/Linguistic, Visual/Spatial

T Technology Skills

Researching on the Internet Ask students to find examples of the music of the Caribbean Islands on the Internet and to play examples of each of them for the rest of the class. Be sure that they include both salsa and reggae and examples of the complex drum rhythms that both forms of music contain. **Ask:** Which of these types of music do you prefer? Why do you think reggae has become popular around the world? *(Students' answers will vary but should include that the lyrics of reggae speak to many people world wide as they protest poverty and the lack of equal rights for all people. They may also note that since Cuba is a Communist country, their music may not be shared as much with others.)*

Have students take a quick class vote of which example of music they prefer and then have volunteers explain why they feel this way. **Auditory/Musical**

CLOSE & REFLECT

Making Connections To close this lesson, have students think about how resources and political corruption have affected the economies of this region. Then have a class discussion about what they think could be done to improve daily life for the people of the region.

ANSWER, p. 221

☑ READING PROGRESS CHECK The lyrics of reggae songs protest poverty and the lack of equal rights, which reflect the poverty and difficult conditions in Jamaica.

ENGAGE

🔔 **Bellringer** Before students read the feature on the effects of NAFTA, have students suggest ways that they participate in global trade through their purchases of various goods. Then **ask:**

- How many of you purchase clothing made outside of the United States? Where are these clothing items made? *(Answers will vary but should include an awareness that many clothing items sold in the United States today are made in other countries, including India, Mexico, and China.)*
- What do you think is meant by the phrase "the global market"? *(Answers should show an awareness that countries engage in trade worldwide.)*

Direct students to the quote on this page. Have a volunteer read it aloud and state an opinion as to what it means. Then explain that the term NAFTA in the title means North American Free Trade Agreement. Have students read the introduction sentence and identify the countries NAFTA includes *(United States, Canada, and Mexico).*

TEACH & ASSESS

C Critical Thinking Skills

Recognizing Relationships Have students list the types of items that are traded between countries. Create a class list of items traded globally. Help students recognize how the global market assists the economies of nations. **Ask:** In what way does the global market help the economies of nations, especially the economies of developing nations? *(Answers will vary but should recognize that trade puts people to work and grows an economy.)* **AL** Logical/Mathematical

R Reading Skills

Defining Define for students the terms *tariffs* and *quotas* as needed and provide examples. Have students define free trade. **Ask:**

- What is meant by free trade? *(a lack of trade barriers, such as tariffs and quotas)*
- What are the disadvantages of free trade? *(costs jobs, hurts small business)* What advantages are there? *(allows for lower cost trades and greater market choice)* Verbal/Linguistic

---

GLOBAL CONNECTIONS

NAFTA and Its Effects

The North American Free Trade Agreement (NAFTA) was created to grow trade among the United States, Canada, and Mexico to help these countries become more competitive in global markets.

C1 **Why Do Nations Trade?** No country produces all the goods and services it needs. Because most countries have more than they need of some things but not enough of others, trade is important.

Trade Barriers Sometimes countries try to protect their industries from competition by setting up trade barriers such as **R** tariffs and quotas. A tariff is a tax on imports. Tariffs raise the prices of imported goods so a country's own industries can produce and sell those goods at competitive prices. A quota restricts the amount of certain goods that can be imported from other countries.

Free Trade The United States, Mexico, and Canada agreed to free trade, or getting rid of trade barriers, in 1994. The United States also has free trade agreements with 17 other nations, including Australia, Israel, and Peru.

> "No country produces all the goods and services it needs."

Disadvantages Critics of NAFTA say that the agreement has cost U.S. jobs. Workers in Mexico are paid less. As a result, many U.S. industries moved all or part of their production to Mexico. Critics also argue that NAFTA hurt Mexican farmers. Mexico imported more corn and other grains when tariffs on those items were removed. Small farmers in Mexico could not compete with technologically advanced U.S. farms.

Advantages Supporters of NAFTA say that it creates the largest free trade area in the world. With tariffs removed, the NAFTA countries can trade with one another at lower cost. It allows the 463 million people in the three countries greater choice in the marketplace. The three countries produced an estimated $18 trillion worth of goods and services in 2011.

A worker assembles parts at a U.S. automobile plant. Critics argued that NAFTA resulted in U.S. job losses, especially in the manufacturing industry. ▶

(tr) Joe Raedle/Getty Images News/Getty Images; (bl) David McNew/Getty Images News/Getty Images; (r) Bloomberg/Getty Images

222 *Chapter 7*

---

netw❂rks *Online Teaching Options*

VIDEOS

Borders with the United States

Integrating Visual Information Have students view the two short videos that show the border with Mexico and the border with Canada. Encourage students to compare and contrast what the borders look like and their differences and similarities. Then have small groups identify and research an international border issue with either Mexico or Canada and explain how the issue contrasts with the purpose of NAFTA. **BL** Visual/Spatial

Design Pics/Corey Hochachka/Getty Images

THERE'S MORE ONLINE

SEE the political boundaries of the U.S., Canada, and Mexico • WATCH changes in migration patterns

Chapter 7 **223**

CHAPTER 7
Global Connections

C Critical Thinking Skills

Identifying Central Issues Direct student attention to the photograph of the person holding the "Need Work" sign on page 222. **Ask:**

- How does an increase in trade grow jobs? *(Students should recognize that as countries increase their trade, businesses add jobs to meet the market demand.)*
- How could an increase in trade hurt jobs? *(Students should recognize that some jobs in one country could be lost to similar manufacturers in another country.)* Visual/Spatial

Making Connections Direct students' attention to the border crossing photo on page 222. Discuss the image with students. Point out the sign and explain to students that the sign is written in Spanish, so it can probably be inferred that this photo was taken in Mexico or another Spanish speaking coutry. **Ask:**

- How does trade help industries beyond those which are manufacturing the product? *(trade also feeds the transportation and communication industries)*
- Which businesses in our community manufacture products or sell products that are part of the global market? *(Answers will vary but students should identify businesses that produce products that are traded worldwide including farm products.)* Verbal/Linguistic

V

V Visual Skills

Interpreting Have students look at the photo on page 223. **Ask:**

- What is being manufactured in the photo? *(a type of engine)*
- How does the global market help a variety of manufacturers from start to finish? *(Students should recognize that there are several industries and workers involved in the manufacturer of a complex product such as machinery, from the raw material, to the parts, to the finished product.)* Visual/Spatial

---

GRAPHIC ORGANIZER

Pros and Cons of NAFTA

Interpreting Share the interactive graphic organizer with students. Record the class discussion on the pros and cons of NAFTA. Have small groups create a poster supporting or opposing NAFTA. Have a group of students create a display with the posters. ELL Verbal/Linguistic

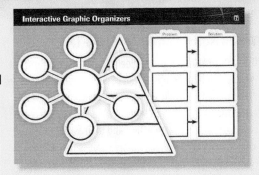

Interactive Graphic Organizers

R Reading Skills

Listing Have students identify each of the statistics noted on the page. Create a list on the board as they are identified. **Ask:** What do you think these statistics indicate? *(Students should be able to recognize that global trade significantly impacts the global economy through job creation.)* Logical/Mathematical

C Critical Thinking Skills

Analyzing Information Review the list of statistics with students and explain that after statistics are measured, people need to analyze them and apply them to local situations so that others can understand their importance. **Ask:** How does job growth as a result of global trade help grow the economies of local communities like ours? *(Students should be able to recognize that employed workers spend money locally, creating more jobs and growing the local economy.)* Intrapersonal

V Visual Skills

Integrating Visual Information Discuss with students how the large numbers and images affect the impact of this page on the reader. Then focus their attention on the image of the cars at the bottom of the page. **Ask:**

- Now that the car has been manufactured, what other types of jobs are created? *(sales, car services, parts sales)*

- How does car manufacturing help the economy? *(It helps create more jobs for people, which in turn helps the economy because if people are making money, then they are spending money.)*

- How does free trade help manufacturers meet the demands of the global economy? *(Students should recognize that manufacturers respond to the purchasing preferences of other countries and produce products to meet that demand.)* Logical/Mathematical

---

R *These numbers and statistics can help you learn about the effects of NAFTA.*

Growth Triples

In 1993, the year before NAFTA went into effect, U.S. trade with Mexico and Canada totaled $276.1 billion. In 2010 U.S. exports and imports of goods with its NAFTA partners amounted to $918 billion.

U.S. Surplus in Services

A trade deficit occurs when a nation imports (buys) more goods and services than it exports (sells). In 2010 the U.S. experienced a trade deficit of $94.6 billion in *goods* with its NAFTA partners. A trade surplus occurs when a nation exports (sells) more than it buys. In 2009 the United States had a $28.3 billion trade surplus with its NAFTA partners in the value of *services*. The main services exported are financial services and insurance.

$1 million a minute

Almost 400,000 people—truckers, businesspeople, commuters, and tourists—cross the U.S.-Canada border daily. U.S.-Canada two-way trade amounts to $1.4 billion a day. That's almost a million dollars every minute.

One-fifth

Canada is the world's largest supplier of energy to the United States. Canada provides 20 percent of U.S. oil imports and 18 percent of U.S. natural gas imports.

21,444

V the number of U.S. Border Patrol agents in 2011. This is double the number of agents in 2003.

700,000 Jobs

Critics of NAFTA say the agreement has cost the jobs of U.S. workers. According to the Economic Policy Institute, the transfer of production to Canada, Mexico, and other countries has resulted in the loss of about 700,000 jobs in the United States since NAFTA began.

FIFTEEN THOUSAND

This is the number of workers at the new Volkswagen plant in Puebla, Mexico, making it one of the country's largest employers.

224 Chapter 7

---

netw⊛rks *Online Teaching Options*

ANIMATION

Trade Before and After NAFTA

Using Digital Tools Have students form small groups. Use the animation for groups to choose a few goods as examples of items created, produced, manufactured, and shipped across the border. First present the time as 1993, one year before NAFTA became effective, and then as 1995, one year after NAFTA became effective. Have groups tell how the two times impact their goods and present their work to the class. BL Visual/Spatial

TOP 10 COUNTRIES IN EXPORTS
Countries with exports in excess of $300 billion

CHINA
U.S.
GERMANY
JAPAN
NETHERLANDS
FRANCE
ITALY
U.K.
SOUTH KOREA
RUSSIA

KEY:
■ $1 trillion or more ■ $500 billion–$999 billion ■ $300 billion–$499 billion

U.S. TRADE WITH OTHER NATIONS
Trade in billions of dollars
(imports and exports combined, 2011)

CANADA
$597*
CHINA $503
MEXICO $461*
JAPAN $195
SOUTH KOREA $100
NETHERLANDS $66
GERMANY $148
U.K. $107
BRAZIL $74
SAUDI ARABIA $61

♣ *NAFTA countries

GLOBAL IMPACT

EXPORTS AND IMPORTS Based on 2011 statistics, the exports of three countries—China, the United States, and Germany—exceeded $1 trillion in value. China's major exports to the U.S. include electrical machinery and toys, guns, and sports equipment. Top U.S. exports to China include oil seeds, fruits, vehicles, and aircraft.

The U.S. did more trade, if exports and imports are combined, with Canada in 2011 than with any other nation.

NAFTA Signing 1992

Mexican President Carlos Salinas, U.S. President George H.W. Bush, and Canadian Prime Minister Brian Mulroney look on as the chief trade representatives sign the NAFTA agreement in 1992. NAFTA was ratified by the three countries in 1993.

©Bettmann/Corbis

Thinking Like a Geographer

1. **Human Geography** What is the purpose of NAFTA?

2. **The Uses of Geography** Find a product in a store or at home that has a label in another language in addition to English. Is that language used in one of the NAFTA countries? Why would a product be labeled in more than one language?

3. **Human Geography** Hold a debate in your class on this statement: NAFTA has been good for U.S. workers and consumers.

Chapter 7 **225**

V Visual Skills

Infographic Have students look at the left side of the infographic at the top of the page and name the top 10 countries that export goods. **Ask:**

- Which countries export more than one trillion dollars worth of goods? *(China, United States, and Germany)*
- Out of the top 10, which two countries make the least amount of money exporting goods? *(United Kingdom, Russia)*

Have students look at the right side of the infographic at the top of the page and name the countries with which the United States both imports and exports. **Ask:**

- Which country does the United States trade with the most? The least? *(Canada, Saudi Arabia)*
- Why are there asterisks by some of the amounts of trade dollars ? *(These countries are part of NAFTA, the North American Free Treaty Agreement.)*
- Why do you think the United States trades the most with Canada? *(Answers will vary but should reflect that Canada is the neighbor of the United States and they are both a part of NAFTA.)* **ELL** Visual/Spatial

CLOSE & REFLECT

Have the students turn back the clock to act out a 1994 press conference on NAFTA. Have three students represent the United States, Canada, and Mexico. These students will be presenting NAFTA to the "press" in the form of a press conference. Have the remaining students be journalists assigned to the press conference. The "press" should pose questions to the three countries on the pros and cons of NAFTA.

After the "press conference," divide the class into small groups to create an oral or written "press release" summarizing the press conference.

MAP

Map of North America

Reading a Map Have students view the map of the United States, Canada, and Mexico. Use callout text for examples of exports for all three countries. Then have students work in pairs to list ten items they have purchased as part of the global market. Have them highlight any items imported from Canada or Mexico. Have students share their lists. **AL** Logical/Mathematical

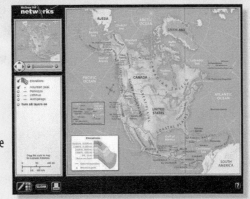

ANSWERS, p. 225

Thinking Like a Geographer
1. The North American Free Trade Agreement, or NAFTA, was established to promote free movement of goods and capital among the United States, Canada, and Mexico.
2. Many products are labeled in French and/or Spanish as well as English. Spanish is widely used in the United States and it is the national language of Mexico. French is one of Canada's official languages. Products labeled in French and/or Spanish as well as English are readily exported to Canada and Mexico.
3. Both debate teams should back up their statements with evidence. They may consider job security, working conditions, cost of living, and environmental impacts.

CHAPTER REVIEW ACTIVITY

Have students create three-column charts like the one below with column heads: Mexico, Central America, and the Caribbean Islands. Tell students to complete a different chart for each of the following categories: physical geography, climate, natural resources, history, economy, and culture. *(Possible answers: **Mexico**—coastal plains, plateaus, peninsulas, mountains, highlands, volcanoes, Pacific Ocean, Gulf of Mexico, Caribbean Sea, tropical/wet, dry, oil, natural gas, gold, silver, copper, iron ore, bauxite, colonized by Spanish, gained independence, revolution, slow-growing economy, economic agreement (NAFTA), agriculture, manufacturing, blend of Spanish and native cultures; **Central America**—coastal plains, plateaus, peninsulas, mountains, highlands, volcanoes, Pacific Ocean, Gulf of Mexico, Caribbean Sea, tropical/wet, dry, gold, silver, copper, iron ore, colonized by Spanish, gained independence, instability, too much reliance on cash crops, tourism, some manufacturing, economic agreements (CAFTA-DR), blend of European and native cultures; **Caribbean Islands**—islands, Caribbean Sea, mountains, tropical wet/dry, fish, oil, natural gas, nickel, colonized by Europeans, plantation economy, gained independence, communism in Cuba, slow economic development, tourism, some natural resources development; blend of Africa, European, and native cultures)*

	Climate	
Mexico	**Central America**	**Caribbean Islands**

REVIEW THE ENDURING UNDERSTANDINGS

Review this chapter's Enduring Understandings with students:

• *Over time, people adapt to their environment.*

• *People, places, and ideas change over time.*

Now pose the following questions in a class discussion to apply this to this chapter.

• How have people in this region adapted to their environment? *(Sample answers: They have used the natural resources in the region, such as fish and minerals, and have populated the coastal areas.)*

Directions: Write your answers on a separate piece of paper.

❶ Use your **FOLDABLES** to explore the Essential Question.
INFORMATIVE/EXPLANATORY WRITING Write a couple of paragraphs explaining how geographical features led the Aztec and then much later the founders of Mexico City to build their cities on the same site.

❷ **21st Century Skills**
INTEGRATING VISUAL INFORMATION Choose a country or one of the islands mentioned in this chapter. Find out more about it by researching it on the Internet. Use the information to create a travel poster or slide show highlighting the country's or island's best features and include any places you would like to see.

❸ **Thinking Like a Geographer**
INTEGRATING VISUAL INFORMATION Draw a graphic organizer like the one shown here and use it to record information about the islands of the Caribbean.

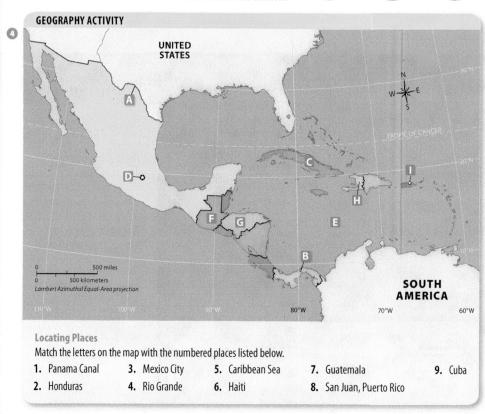

GEOGRAPHY ACTIVITY

Locating Places
Match the letters on the map with the numbered places listed below.

1. Panama Canal
2. Honduras
3. Mexico City
4. Rio Grande
5. Caribbean Sea
6. Haiti
7. Guatemala
8. San Juan, Puerto Rico
9. Cuba

• Why has there been much political unrest in this region? What are some possible solutions? *(Sample answer: Many of these nations were colonized by European countries and had to develop a new government and economy once they gained independence. Through democratic elections, the countries dealing with political corruption might have a better chance of strengthening and developing their economies.)*

• How have the nations of Mexico, Central America, and the Caribbean tried to strengthen and develop their economies? *(Sample answer: They have tried to diversify their economies so that they are not as reliant on cash crops, by utilizing their limited resources wisely, and increasing manufacturing and tourism.)*

ACTIVITIES ANSWERS

Exploring the Essential Question

❶ **INFORMATIVE/EXPLANATORY WRITING** A possible answer: Because Mexico lies within the tropics, most of the country is hot all year long. The Aztec built their capital city, Tenochtitlán, on the site of a lake on the Central Plateau because such highlands are much cooler. Later in time, Mexico City was built on that same, now-dry lake bed for the same reason.

21st Century Skills

❷ **SUMMARIZING** Although all students' work will reflect personal choices, it should be well-researched and organized.

REVIEW THE GUIDING QUESTIONS

Directions: Choose the best answer for each question.

1 What are Mexico's two most important natural resources?
- A. gold and silver
- B. oil and natural gas
- C. iron ore and copper
- D. bauxite and zinc

2 Which is one of the most important waterways in the world?
- F. Lake Nicaragua
- G. Río Bravo
- H. Panama Canal
- I. Caribbean Sea

3 A civilization that flourished in Southern Mexico, Belize, and Guatemala about 3,000 years ago and built pyramids like the Egyptians was the
- A. Anasazi.
- B. Olmec.
- C. Aztec.
- D. Maya.

4 Europeans established plantations and brought enslaved people to Cuba, Puerto Rico, and Hispaniola in order to grow
- F. tobacco.
- G. bananas.
- H. sugar.
- I. coffee.

5 Which country is Mexico's biggest trading partner?
- A. Canada
- B. China
- C. Venezuela
- D. the United States

6 What is the most serious economic challenge facing Central American countries?
- F. high rate of population growth
- G. fluctuating oil prices
- H. food shortages
- I. debt

Chapter 7 **227**

Thinking Like a Geographer

3 **INTEGRATING VISUAL INFORMATION** Greater Antilles: big islands including Cuba, Jamaica, Puerto Rico, Hispaniola (Haiti and Dominican Republic); Lesser Antilles: dozens of small islands stretching from Puerto Rico to South America; Bahamas: 3,000 islands east of Florida

Geography Activity

4 **LOCATING PLACES**

1. B
2. G
3. D
4. A
5. E
6. H
7. F
8. I
9. C

ASSESSMENT ANSWERS

Review the Guiding Questions

1 **B** For this question, students will need to think about the two resources that the text refers to for all parts of this region. Knowing that gold and silver were what drew the conquistadors to Mexico but that they are not as plentiful as they used to be eliminates choice A. Iron ore and copper as well as bauxite and zinc are important to some nations in the region but not all, therefore eliminating both answer choices C and D.

2 **H** A helpful clue in this question is the word *waterway*, because a body of water is an ocean, lake, or sea, which eliminates answer choices F and I. Knowing that the Panama Canal is a waterway that shortens the journey around South America and helps the economy of Panama makes answer choice H the best one. Refer students to Lesson 1 for help.

3 **D** To answer this question, students will need to remember that the Maya civilization was spread out over several modern-day nations in the region. The Olmec and Aztec only lived in Mexico (refer students to Lesson 2), which eliminates answer choices B and C. The Anasazi are not mentioned in the chapter at all, which leaves answer choice D.

4 **H** Two helpful clues in this question are *plantations* and *enslaved people*. The chapter discusses the plantation economy and the cultivation of sugar in Lesson 2. The other three crops are not mentioned in the text.

5 **D** To answer this question, students will need to think about the biggest trade agreement in which Mexico is a member nation, NAFTA. The members of NAFTA are Mexico, Canada, and the United States, which eliminates answer choices B and C. Refer students to Lesson 3, where NAFTA and Mexico's most important trader partner, the United States, is discussed.

6 **F** All of the answer choices are challenges, however the question asks for the most serious economic challenge. Fluctuating oil prices, food shortages, and debt are all challenges to the economy, but the region can rely on the help of other countries in order to overcome them. Population growth is different because other nations cannot help Central America overcome that challenge.

DBQ Analyzing Documents

7 **C** Farming maize is an important economic activity today and was one in ancient times. Students should be able to eliminate choices A and B as activities that were not done in ancient times.

8 **I** The men leave the villages to find work in the cities, so there must be a lack of jobs in the villages. Students should be able to eliminate choices A and B as there is no mention of their wives or the government in the passage.

Short Response

9 Possible answer: Widespread growing of sugar led to the destruction of the environment because the passage says entire jungles were cut down to make room for the sugar plantations and the homes of the workers and other immigrants. Major changes to the population came about when people from Africa, Asia, and Europe arrived.

10 Possible answer: By this phrase, the author means that it took many people to work on the islands to harvest the sugar, and the lives of these people were not sweet. The first workers were slaves brought from Africa who were forced to work. When slavery was abolished, they were replaced by a "cheap work force" from Asia meaning that these people were not paid well.

Extended Response

11 Student reports should reflect adequate research of the cotton and rice plantations of the American South and the sugar plantations of the Caribbean islands to make valid comparisons and distinctions between the two. Reports should also make logical consideration of the question, be grammatically correct, and use a variety of sentence styles.

DBQ ANALYZING DOCUMENTS

7 **IDENTIFYING** Read this passage about the Maya.

"About six million Maya live in Central America. Like their ancestors, many of them survive by growing maize (Indian corn) or other crops on their land, or by producing woven textiles for sale. In some villages, the men have to leave their families to find work in the cities, or on coffee and cotton plantations."

—from *How People Live*, DK Publishing

Which Maya activity today is similar to one from ancient times?

A. working in tourism
B. working in factories
C. growing maize
D. working in cities

8 **DETERMINING CENTRAL IDEAS** Which best explains why some men have to leave their villages?

F. They leave to seek wives elsewhere.
G. They're forced to do so by the government.
H. The villages are overcrowded.
I. They face a lack of jobs within the villages.

SHORT RESPONSE

"At the beginning of the 17th century the sweet crystal [sugar] transformed the Caribbean Islands into the Sugar Islands, though the islands did not turn sweet themselves. . . . Entire jungles were leveled; a slave or, later, cheap work force was massively imported from Africa and Asia; [and] a huge wave of European settlers arrived to stay."

—from Alfonso Silva Lee, *Natural Cuba/Cuba Natural*

9 **DESCRIBING** In what ways were the Caribbean islands transformed by the spread of sugar farming?

10 **DETERMINING WORD MEANINGS** What does the author of the passage mean by the phrase "the islands did not turn sweet themselves"?

EXTENDED RESPONSE

11 **INFORMATIVE/EXPLANATORY WRITING** Research and then write a brief report comparing and contrasting the cotton and rice plantations of the American South with the sugar plantations of the Caribbean islands.

Need Extra Help?

If You've Missed Question	**1**	**2**	**3**	**4**	**5**	**6**	**7**	**8**	**9**	**10**	**11**
Review Lesson	1	1	2	2	3	3	3	3	2	2	3

networks *Online Teaching Options*

Evaluation and Assessment

Assessing Use eAssessment to create your own tests from hundreds of available questions. eAssessment helps you design assessments that meet the needs of different types of learners.

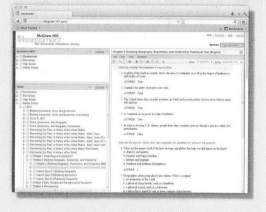

South America Planner

UNDERSTANDING BY DESIGN®

Enduring Understandings

- People, places, and ideas change over time.
- Over time, people adapt to their environment.

Essential Questions

- How does geography influence the way people live?
- How do governments change?
- What makes a culture unique?
- Why does conflict develop?
- Why do civilizations rise and fall?

Students will know:

- there is more influence on the area and the population than just the Amazon River.
- Brazil is home to forests, minerals, and farmland.
- colonized by Portugal in the 1500s, many of the indigenous peoples were enslaved or killed.
- Brazilian population contains a variety of racial and ethnic groups and has a rich culture and heritage.
- the landforms and waterways make up the unique landscapes of the Tropical North.
- there are many various resources in the Tropical North.
- the Andean countries have a unique geography that shapes their landscape and their culture.
- the Andean and Midlatitude countries both have unique geography that affects their industry, travel, trade, and agriculture.

Students will be able to:

- **use a map** to identify Brazil, countries of the Tropical North, and Andean and Midlatitude countries.
- **use a time line** to discuss significant events in the history of the countries.
- **discuss** how development has impacted the environments and the economies.
- **describe** the physical geography and various climates, including climate extremes.
- **identify** natural resources and major crops.
- **describe** indigenous populations.
- **analyze** how countries gained independence.
- **discuss** the governments of modern Brazil.
- **examine** the different ethnic and language groups.
- **discuss** European colonization.
- **discuss** the instability of governments in the Tropical North that have resulted in revolutions.
- **describe** religions, daily life, and the arts.
- **describe** the effect of latitude on climate.
- **explain** the rise and fall of the Inca Empire.
- **discuss** major population patterns in South America.

Predictable Misunderstandings

- All of Brazil is rain forest.
- Brazilians are Spanish with no other influence.
- The climate has no effect on the landscape.

- The geography of the Tropical North is the same as other places in Central America.
- The Andean countries have the exact same geography as the Tropical North.
- The culture of these countries is the same as the other nations in South America.

Assessment Evidence

Performance Tasks:

- Environmental Case Study

Other Evidence:

- Physical Location GeoQuiz,
- Political Location GeoQuiz
- City Location GeoQuiz
- Physical Geography Activity
- Cultural Geography Activity
- Geography and History Activity
- Geography and Economics Activity
- Reading Skills Activity
- Geography Skills Activity
- Critical Thinking Skills Activity
- Technology Skills Activity
- Participation in Interactive Whiteboard Activities
- Analysis of graphic organizers, graphs, and charts
- Lesson Reviews
- Chapter Assessments

Key for Using the Teacher Edition

SKILL-BASED ACTIVITIES

Types of skill activites found in the Teacher Edition.

* **V** Visual Skills require students to analyze maps, graphs, charts, and photos.

W Writing Skills provide writing opportunities to help students comprehend the text.

R Reading Skills help students practice reading skills and master vocabulary.

C Critical Thinking Skills help students apply and extend what they have learned.

T Technology Skills require students to use digital tools effectively.

*Letters are followed by a number when there is more than one of the same type of skill on the page.

DIFFERENTIATED INSTRUCTION

All activities are written for the on-level student unless otherwise marked with the leveled labels below.

BL Beyond Level

AL Approaching Level

ELL English Language Learners

All students benefit from activities that utilize different learning styles. Many activities are marked as below when a particular learning style is highlighted.

Intrapersonal	Naturalist
Logical/Mathematical	Kinesthetic
Visual/Spatial	Auditory/Musical
Verbal/Linguistic	Interpersonal

SUGGESTED PACING GUIDE

Introducing the Unit	3 Days
Chapter 8	10 Days
Chapter 9	10 Days
Chapter 10	10 Days
Global Connections	3 Days
What Do You Think?	2 Days

TOTAL TIME   38 Days

PLANNER

☑ *Print Teaching Options*

V Visual Skills

☐ **P. 231** Students discuss the shape of South America and other features they can see in the satellite image. **AL**

☐ **P. 232** Students analyze the features of and identify regions on the map of South America. **AL**

☐ **P. 233** Students analyze the political boundaries on a physical map and identify information on a political map that is not shown on a physical map. **ELL**

☐ **P. 234** Students discuss the symbols in the map key of the population map of South America and answer questions about the map. **AL** Logical/Mathematical

☐ **P. 235** Students learn about the relationship between natural resources, land uses, and the physical characteristics of a region using the Resources map. **ELL**

☐ **P. 236** Students use the map to explore climates of South America. Visual/Spatial

W Writing Skills

☐ **P. 236** Students work in small groups to design a brochure for tourists visiting a country in South America. **AL** Verbal/Linguistic

R Reading Skills

☐ **P. 230** Students describe what they see in the photograph and discuss bio-reserves. **AL**

C Critical Thinking Skills

☐ **P. 229** Students compare and contrast what they know from their study of North America with basic information about South America. Verbal/Linguistic

☐ **P. 230** Students consider the global significance of rivers such as the Amazon River. **BL**

☐ **P. 231** Students discuss the glacier and landforms found in the Los Glaciares National Park and the climate of the area. **BL**

☐ **P. 232** Students analyze elevations on the physical map of South America. **BL**

☐ **P. 234** Students discuss how physical features impact population density. **ELL** Visual/Spatial

☐ **P. 236** Students discuss the pressure to convert forested areas to agriculture or to develop mining in regions that hold mineral wealth. **AL**

☑ *Online Teaching Options*

V Visual Skills

VIDEO **Video Tour of South America**—Students watch a video montage highlighting South America and share what they found most interesting in a wall map activity. **ELL**

MAP **South America: Physical Map**—Students identify areas of elevation and name the major rivers of South America using the physical map. **AL** Visual/Spatial

MAP **South America: Political Map**—Students can use the political map to review the political boundaries of the region. Visual/Spatial

MAP **South America: Population Map**—Students use the population map to review the population distribution and density. Visual/Spatial

W Writing Skills

MAP **South America: Resources Map**—Students use the resources map to review and discuss the resources as each layer is revealed, and then they conduct research about the natural resources of that country. Visual/Spatial, Naturalist

C Critical Thinking Skills

MAP **Regional Map**—Students make connections between the images in the unit and their location on the interactive map. Visual/Spatial

MAP **South America: Climates Map**—Students use the climate map to discuss the precipitation and temperatures, then small groups of students create scenarios describing the impact of a particular climate on the people who live in the region. **AL** Interpersonal

T Technology Skills

GAME **Political Boundaries: South America Game**—Students drag and drop the country and city names into the map. **AL** Kinesthetic

☑ *Printable Digital Worksheets*

W Writing Skills

WORKSHEET **Physical Location GeoQuiz** Use the Physical Location GeoQuiz as a pre- or post-assessment of students' knowledge of the region's landforms and bodies of water.

WORKSHEET **Political Location GeoQuiz** Use the Political Location GeoQuiz as a pre- or post-assessment of students' knowledge of the region's countries.

WORKSHEET **City Location GeoQuiz** Use the City Location GeoQuiz as a pre- or post-assessment of students' knowledge of the region's major cities.

WORKSHEET **Physical Geography Activity**—Students will analyze an elevation profile of the region.

WORKSHEET **Cultural Geography Activity**—Students will read about the culture of the region and answer questions related to the excerpt.

WORKSHEET **Environmental Case Study**—Students will conduct an environmental case study on alternative energy sources and how these sources can impact the environment. **BL**

SOUTH AMERICA

McGraw-Hill networks™

UNIT 3

MIKE THEISS/National Geographic Stock

Global Connections

Discussing The Global Connections issue for this unit gives students an opportunity to learn about rain forest resources, its people, and its global economic and environmental importance. Students will investigate the challenges faced by rain forest regions, including pressures on the regions for farming and exploitation of its natural resources. Students also will investigate the pressures placed on native populations of the rain forest. **AL** Verbal/Linguistic

Rain Forest
Resources

ENGAGE

Bellringer Share with students the image of the South American man standing in front of the ancient ruins. Encourage a general discussion to analyze the details in the photo. **Ask:** What do you notice about the landscape? What do you think is behind the individual and how is it built into the mountainside? How do you think this individual feels about his heritage? How can you tell? **ELL** Visual/Spatial

Making Connections Share the following information about South America with students.

- It is the fourth largest continent and includes 12 independent countries.
- The Amazon river system empties into the Atlantic Ocean and the Caribbean Sea.
- South America includes tropical, desert, and high alpine climate zones.
- The South American economy relies on natural gas and oil reserves. Iron ore deposits and copper are also important economic resources.
- Small farms are limited by unfavorable climate conditions and terrain in much of South America.
- The large scale plantations of South America include coffee, bananas, sugarcane, tobacco, and grains.
- Fishing is an important industry in coastal regions.
- The two major languages of South America are Portuguese and Spanish.

C

C Critical Thinking Skills

Comparing and Contrasting Have students compare and contrast what they know from their study of North America with this basic information about South America. **Ask:** What does the image and our discussions tell you about this diverse continent? *(Students may speculate that there are many different types of cultures, landscapes, climates, and a rich history.)*

Tell students they will be learning more about South America and its resources. In particular they will be learning about three major regions: Brazil, the Tropical North, and the Andean and Midlatitude countries. Verbal/Linguistic

TEACH & ASSESS

R1

R1 Reading Skills

Naming Have a student volunteer read the opening paragraph aloud. **Ask:**

- What two rivers flow through Brazil and the Tropical North? *(Orinoco and the Amazon)*
- What is the most distinctive landform in South America? *(the Andes)*
- Why do you think the Andes mountain are considered "distinctive"? *(Students should mention that the Andes are the world's longest mountain range, and might speculate that they are quite high and rugged looking.)* **AL**

R2 Reading Skills

Identifying Have a volunteer read aloud the section "Natural Resources." Discuss the section and the photo associated with it in a class discussion. **Ask:**

- What natural resources are highlighted here? *(potatoes and the soil of the Peruvian Andes)*
- What do you think a bio-reserve is? *(Students might speculate that it is a region reserved for farming or conservation.)*
- Why is it important for local communities to manage the bio-reserve? *(best utilization of resources, so local people benefit)* **AL**

C Critical Thinking Skills

Analyzing Visuals With a partner, have students read the paragraph, "Bodies of Water," and analyze the photo while they discuss possible goods that might be transported throughout the region and globally. Give the pairs time to formulate a list of goods that may be imported or exported to and from the region. **Ask:**

- In what way are South America's waterways like a circulation system? *(movement to and from an area as goods are picked up and dropped off)*
- Why do rivers, such as the Amazon River, have global significance to people living in the interior of the continent? *(provide the ability to export goods to other regions and import needed resources to the interior)*

With the same partner, have pairs create a two-column chart contrasting the life styles of South Americans working on bio-reserves (#1) with those working in South American port cities (#2). Have students share the information in their charts. **BL**
Verbal/Linguistic

EXPLORE the CONTINENT

SOUTH AMERICA At nearly 7 million square miles (18 million sq. km) in area, South America is the fourth-largest continent in the world. Two great rivers—the Orinoco and the Amazon—flow through Brazil and the Tropical North. The most distinctive landform in the region is the Andes mountain ranges. The Andes, 4,500 miles (7,242 km) long, is the world's longest continental mountain range.

R2

① NATURAL RESOURCES Farmers grow a variety of potatoes in plots located in the Peruvian Andes. El Parque de la Papa, also known as "Potato Park," is a bio-reserve that is managed by the local communities surrounding it.

② BODIES OF WATER Oil tankers travel near the port of Maracaibo, Venezuela. Like a circulatory system, the region's many waterways serve as arteries that transport people and goods throughout the region and to the world.

C

netw⊙rks   *Online Teaching Options*

VIDEO

Video Tour of South America

Analyzing Images Display the video montage highlighting South America. Prior to starting the video, tell students that while viewing the video montage they should write down three things they especially like about South America. Afterwards have students share what they found most interesting about the continent. Hand three post-it notes to each student. Then have them write their three points of interest on the post-its, one per post-it. Have students "park" their post-its on a wall map of South America. Refer to these over the course of the unit.
ELL **Visual/Spatial**

Tongro Image Stock/age fotostock

3 LANDFORMS Los Glaciares National Park in Argentina is an area of rugged mountains and many glacial lakes. Its name refers to the glaciers that are part of the Patagonian ice field. The ice field is the largest ice mantle outside Antarctica. Los Glaciares is located along Argentina's border with Chile.

G₁

FAST FACT

Earth's driest place is in South America.

C₂

WORKSHEET

Environmental Case Study

Evaluating The case study for this unit is about developing alternative energy sources and how the use of these sources will impact the environment. Divide the students into groups and distribute the case study, allowing in-class time for the planning, preparing, and presentation process. Have groups share their findings with the class. **BL** Logical/Mathematical

TEACH & ASSESS

G₁ Critical Thinking Skills

Contrasting Write *Glaciers* on the board and have a student volunteer read the "Landforms" paragraph. **Ask:**

- What is a *glacier*? *(Students should recognize that a glacier is a huge sheet of ice that slowly moves across a land mass.)*
- What do you notice about the landforms found in the Los Glaciares National Park? *(rugged landscape, jagged rock cliffs, snow, ice)*

Have students provide information about glaciers. Add their information to the board. **Ask:** What do you think the climate is like in this region? *(Students might speculate that the region is cold year-round and not supportive of large plants or settlement.)* **BL**

V Visual Skills

Integrating Visual Information Direct student attention to the satellite image at the top of the page. Have students discuss the shape of South America. Point out that the region extends across the Equator and stretches toward the Antarctic Circle. Discuss what that means in terms of contrasting climates. **Ask:**

- What can be said about the diversity of climate of South America? *(from tropical rain forest, to hot, dry desert, to cold, icy Antarctic)*
- What information about South America can you learn from the satellite image? *(Student answers should note differences in the mountain, plains, and coastal regions seen in the satellite image.)* **AL**

C₂ Critical Thinking Skills

Analyzing Visuals Have students read the Fast Fact and identify the framed area of South America as an outline of the United States so that students can compare the size of the continent to what they know. Point out that although rain forests are found in South America, the driest place on Earth is also in South America. **Ask:** What does the diversity of climates suggest to you about the lifestyles of the people of South America? *(Students might suggest that the lifestyles also are diverse as people adapt to the climates and make use of available resources for survival.)* **BL**

V Visual Skills

Reading a Map Have students work in pairs to analyze the features of the physical map. Discuss the map as a group, noting the difference between landforms throughout the continent. Point out the areas of higher elevations along the western region and explain that the Andes run the entire length of the continent. Have students identify the size of the Amazon Basin and estimate what percentage of the continent it covers. Have students identify lines of longitude and latitude. Note that the Equator and Tropic of Capricorn both cross South America. **Ask:**

• What does the map key show? *(the elevation of South America's landforms)*

• Where are elevations of at least 10,000 ft. (3,000 m) found in South America? *(along western ridge)*

• What is the name of this mountain ridge? *(Andes)*

• What do you notice about the flow of the major river systems in South America? *(drain to the Atlantic Ocean or Caribbean Sea)*

Have students identify regions on the map. **Ask:**

• Where is the Atacama Desert found? *(along the west coastline above and below the Tropic of Capricorn)*

• Where are the Falkland Islands found? *(near the southern tip of the continent)* **AL** Visual/Spatial

C Critical Thinking Skills

Analyzing Visuals Have students focus on the elevations shown on the physical map. **Ask:**

• What do you notice about the elevation of most of South America? *(Students should note that low elevations extend across most of South America.)*

• How do the elevations of eastern South America compare to the elevations of western South America? *(Students should note that eastern South America has low elevations compared to the high elevations of western South America.)*

• Where would you expect to find the lowest elevations? *(along river valleys, coastlines)* **BL** Visual/Spatial

SOUTH AMERICA

PHYSICAL

MAP SKILLS

1 **THE GEOGRAPHER'S WORLD** What is the easternmost river in Brazil?

2 **PLACES AND REGIONS** Describe the elevation differences between western South America and eastern South America.

3 **PLACES AND REGIONS** Explain why elevation of land in the Amazon Basin makes travel easier.

232 Unit 3

networks   Online Teaching Options

MAP

South America: Physical Map

Identifying Display the physical map of South America on the whiteboard. Have students identify areas of elevation and name the major rivers of South America. Have students determine the distance a ship would need to travel to navigate from the Caribbean Sea to the Galapagos Islands. Have students speculate on the climates the ships would encounter. Point out the importance of the Panama Canal to navigation and commerce. **AL** Kinesthetic

ANSWERS, p. 232

MAP SKILLS
1. São Francisco River
2. 10,000 ft. (3,000 m) to below sea level
3. River waters run from elevated land to lower land (Amazon Basin).

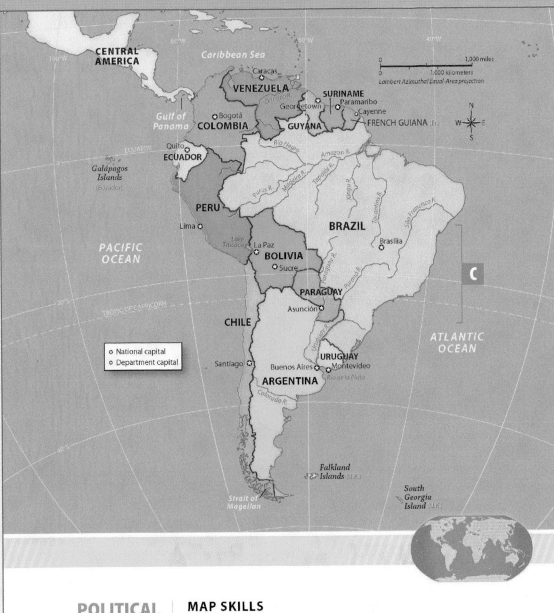

CENTRAL AMERICA
Caribbean Sea
Caracas
VENEZUELA
Georgetown
SURINAME
Paramaribo
Cayenne
FRENCH GUIANA (Fr.)
Gulf of Panama
Bogotá
COLOMBIA
GUYANA
Quito
ECUADOR
Galápagos Islands (Ecuador)
Rio Negro
Amazon R.
Purus R.
Madeira R.
Tapajós R.
Xingu R.
Tocantins R.
São Francisco R.
PERU
Lima
Lake Titicaca
La Paz
BOLIVIA
Sucre
BRAZIL
Brasília
PACIFIC OCEAN
Juruá R.
Paraguay R.
Paraná R.
PARAGUAY
Asunción
CHILE
ATLANTIC OCEAN
National capital
Department capital
Uruguay R.
URUGUAY
Santiago
Buenos Aires
Montevideo
Río de la Plata
ARGENTINA
Colorado R.
TROPIC OF CAPRICORN
EQUATOR
Falkland Islands (U.K.)
South Georgia Island (U.K.)
Strait of Magellan

0 1,000 miles
0 1,000 kilometers
Lambert Azimuthal Equal-Area projection
N W E S

POLITICAL

MAP SKILLS

1 **PLACES AND REGIONS** What is the capital of Uruguay?

2 **PHYSICAL GEOGRAPHY** Which two countries in South America do not have coastlines?

3 **THE GEOGRAPHER'S WORLD** Which country in South America shares its border with the most countries?

Unit 3 **233**

V Visual Skills

Reading a Map Have student analyze the political boundaries on the map. Have students identify information on a political map that is missing from a physical map. **Ask:**

- What is the largest country in South America, and how does it compare in size to the other countries? *(Brazil; it is much larger)*
- Which countries have coastlines on the Pacific Ocean? *(Colombia, Ecuador, Peru, Chile)*
- Which countries are landlocked, or do not have a coastline on an ocean or a sea? *(Bolivia and Paraguay)*
- Which country has a coastline on both the Caribbean Sea and the Pacific Ocean? *(Colombia)*
- What is the capital of Chile? *(Santiago)*
- Which countries border Venezuela? *(Colombia, Brazil, Guyana)* **ELL** Visual/Spatial

V

C Critical Thinking Skills

Drawing Conclusions Have students consider the advantages of a coastline for a country versus a country that is landlocked. **Ask:**

- What are the economic advantages of having a coastline for a country? *(ports that facilitate the import and export of goods)*
- What economic difficulties might Bolivia and Paraguay experience? *(Students might speculate that the two countries could have difficulty shipping goods into and out of the country and participating in the global market due to their landlocked positions.)*
- Which country appears to hold the greatest economic advantage due to its location on the continent? *(Students' answers will vary but should show an understanding of the advantages of size, political position, available resources such as rivers or river systems and mineral wealth, and available coastline.)* **BL**

GAME

Political Boundaries: South America Game

Identifying Display the interactive political map of South America on the whiteboard. As a class, play the drag and drop game to identify the countries and city names on the map. Then have volunteers use the whiteboard tools to draw a line from one location to another and calculate the distances. **AL** Kinesthetic, Logical/Mathematical

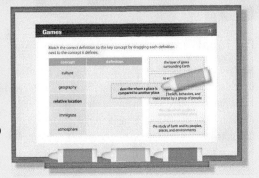

Games

Match the correct definition to the key concept by dragging each definition next to the concept it defines.

concept	definition
culture	
geography	describe where a place is compared to another place
relative location	
immigrate	
atmosphere	the study of Earth and its peoples, places, and environments

---

ANSWERS, p. 233

MAP SKILLS
1. Montevideo
2. Bolivia and Paraguay
3. Brazil

C Critical Thinking Skills

Comparing Have students compare the population map with the two previous maps showing the political and physical features of South America. Using the maps, discuss how physical features impact population density and how political boundaries can impact population location. **Ask:**

• How does the information shown on a population map add to the information we gain from a political map? *(A population map shows population density, and gives us an indication of the development of each country)*

• How do you read a population map? *(by looking for symbols and colors)* **ELL** Visual/Spatial, Verbal/ Linguistic

V Visual Skills

Reading a Map Direct students' attention to the population map of South America. Point out and discuss the symbols used in the map key. Then note how the map key uses color to show regions of population density. **Ask:**

• Which cities exceed a population of 5 million people? *(Bogata, Lima, Santiago, Buenos Aires, São Paulo, Rio de Janeiro, Belo Horizonte)*

• Where are most areas of high population density located? *(along coastal regions)*

• What do you notice about population patterns in the continent's interior? *(Students might mention that settlement seems to be along river systems.)*

• Where is the population least concentrated? *(within the deep interior of the continent, pockets in the northeast region)*

• What city found in the Amazon Basin has a population of at least one million people? *(Manaus)*

• Why might a city deep within the interior of the continent have a large population density? *(central point for goods and service, availability of housing, education, employment, resources, tourism)* **AL** Logical/ Mathematical

---

ANSWERS, p. 234

MAP SKILLS
1. along the coasts
2. more than 5 million
3. Rio de Janeiro, São Paulo

SOUTH AMERICA

POPULATION DENSITY

Cities
(Statistics reflect metropolitan areas.)
■ Over 5,000,000
□ 2,000,000–5,000,000
⊙ 1,000,000–2,000,000
• 500,000–1,000,000
○ Under 500,000

POPULATION

Per sq. mi.	Per sq. km
1,250 and over	500 and over
250–1,249	100–499
63–249	25–99
25–62	10–24
2.5–24	1–9
Less than 2.5	Less than 1

MAP SKILLS

1 **HUMAN GEOGRAPHY** Where do most people in South America live?

2 **HUMAN GEOGRAPHY** About how many people live in Lima?

3 **PLACES AND REGIONS** What are the largest cities on South America's eastern coast?

---

networks *Online Teaching Options*

MAP

Regional Map

Making Connections Display the interactive regional map to students. Select some of the images that are connected to the map and place them in the context of the map and the unit. Guide a discussion helping students to identify the content of the images and then to make a connection between the image and the map location. Visual/Spatial

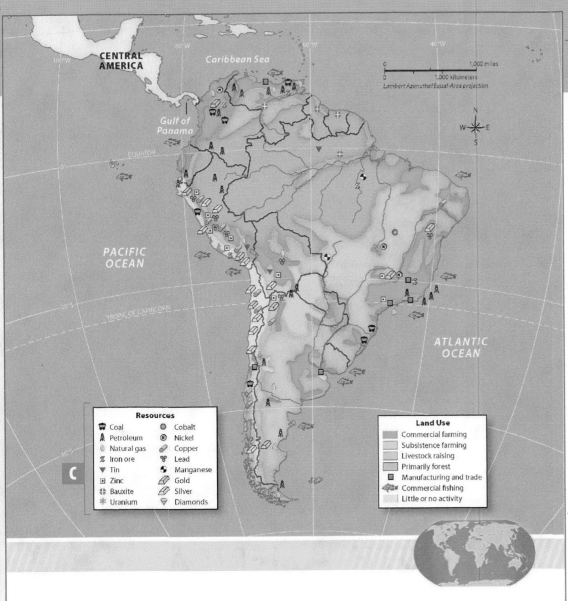

Resources

🦪 Coal	○ Cobalt
⚒ Petroleum	⊗ Nickel
◌ Natural gas	◎ Copper
✻ Iron ore	✿ Lead
▼ Tin	⚓ Manganese
⊡ Zinc	◿ Gold
✤ Bauxite	◿ Silver
✳ Uranium	▽ Diamonds

Land Use

- Commercial farming
- Subsistence farming
- Livestock raising
- Primarily forest
- ▪ Manufacturing and trade
- Commercial fishing
- Little or no activity

ECONOMIC RESOURCES

MAP SKILLS

1 **HUMAN GEOGRAPHY** Is there more commercial farming or livestock raising in South America?

2 **PHYSICAL GEOGRAPHY** Where is the greatest concentration of minerals and ores?

3 **ENVIRONMENT AND SOCIETY** Is South America a manufacturing center?

Unit 3 **235**

South America: Resources Map

Recognizing Relationships Display the interactive Resources map to review and discuss the resources as each layer is revealed. Ask students to choose one of the countries and using the Internet further research the natural resources found in the country. Then have students create a graph that includes the resources and the market value of the resources. **Visual/Spatial, Naturalist**

V

V Visual Skills

Reading a Map Help students recognize the relationship between natural resources, land uses, and the physical characteristics of a region. Direct students' attention to the resources map key. **Ask:**

- What are some of the resources shown on this map? Which symbols are used to indicate those resources? *(Students should identify the resources and indicate which symbols are associated with each resource.)*
- What land uses are shown on this map? *(commercial farming, subsistence farming, livestock raising, forest, manufacturing and trade, commercial fishing)*
- Where did you find that information? *(land use map key)*

Continue to discuss the resources map with students. **Ask:**

- What are the two primary land uses in South America? *(forest, livestock raising)*
- Where is subsistence farming found? *(in areas along the western coast and in Bolivia, Paraguay, and Argentina)*
- What type of resources are concentrated along the western coast? *(gold and silver)*
- What resource is found at the southern tip of the continent? *(oil, gold, silver)*
- What is an important land use for coastal regions? *(commercial fishing)*
- Which land use is shown by a red square? *(manufacturing and trade)*
- Where does this activity mostly occur? *(in Brazil)*
- Where is copper mostly found? *(along the western coast)*
- What land use pressure is placed on forested areas? *(livestock grazing, commercial farming)*
- Where is there little or no land use in South America? *(in the Andes)* **ELL**

C Critical Thinking Skills

Determining Cause and Effect Help students understand that a continent's natural resources help to support economic growth and stability among individual countries. **Ask:** How do natural resources add to a country's economic strength? *(ability to export, develop businesses, provide jobs)* **BL** Logical/Mathematical

---

ANSWER, p. 235
MAP SKILLS
1. more livestock raising
2. along the west coast
3. no

V Visual Skills

Reading a Map Help students recognize that climates are regionalized. Direct students' attention to the map key. **Ask:**

- What type of climate covers the Amazon Basin? *(tropical)* **V**

- What do you notice about the climates from north to south? *(change from tropical to subtropical to desert)*

- What do you notice about the extremes of climate along the western coast? *(includes both desert and tundra)*

- What landform explains the presence of a tundra climate along South America's western region? *(high mountains of the Andes)*

- Why is a tundra climate found along South America's southern tip? *(high latitudes, near Antarctic Circle)*

- What relationship does climate have with agricultural land use in South America? *(Students should recognize that climate includes regional rainfall and temperatures, which influence whether a region can support sustainable agricultural practices.)* **Visual/Spatial**

C Critical Thinking Skills

Reasoning Have students consider the pressure to convert forested areas to agriculture or to develop mining. **Ask:** Where might pressure be placed to convert land to agriculture? Why? *(along the edges of the Amazon Basin because of climate and availability of land; increase wealth of a region)*

Discuss the effects of farming and other deforestation processes. Have students consider what types of concerns develop when too much land is used for either purpose. **Ask:** How might opening up a region to agriculture or to mining impact the region? *(environmental changes, job creation)* **AL**

CLOSE & REFLECT

Narrative Divide the class into groups of five and assign each group a country in South America. Have each group design a brochure inviting tourists to their country. Students should first visit the country's website. Tasks of writing, gathering images, and developing the brochure can be divided among student interests. *(Student brochures should highlight a country's landscape, climate, people, and resources.)* **AL** Verbal/Linguistic

ANSWERS, p. 236

MAP SKILLS
1. tropical savanna
2. at continent's southernmost region and northward on and near the west coast
3. Mediterranean

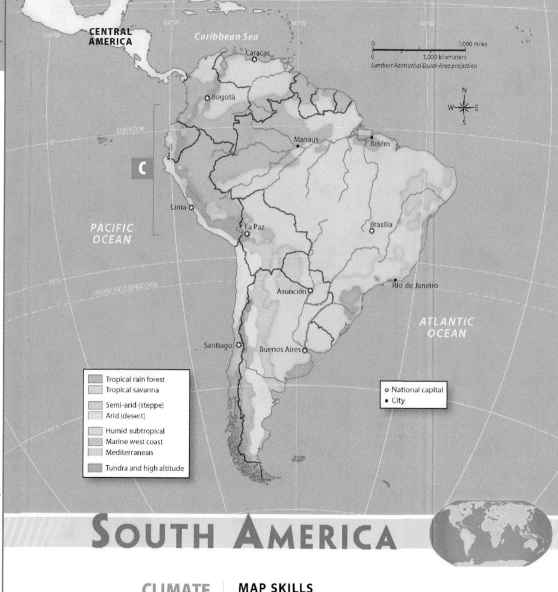

Map Key:
- Tropical rain forest
- Tropical savanna
- Semi-arid (steppe)
- Arid (desert)
- Humid subtropical
- Marine west coast
- Mediterranean
- Tundra and high altitude

- ○ National capital
- ● City

SOUTH AMERICA

CLIMATE

MAP SKILLS

1 **PHYSICAL GEOGRAPHY** What is the most prevalent climate in South America?

2 **PHYSICAL GEOGRAPHY** Where is South America's desert climate?

3 **PLACES AND REGIONS** In which type of climate is Santiago, Chile, located?

netw⊛rks   *Online Teaching Options*

MAP

South America: Climate Map

Describing Have students use the interactive climate map to discuss the precipitation and temperatures of South America as a post assessment. Then have small groups of students create three "You Are There" scenarios describing the impact of a particular climate on the people who live in the region without mentioning the climate name. Each group should then present its scenarios to the class. Have the other groups identify the climate that is being described in a game-like format. **AL** Interpersonal

CHAPTER 8
Brazil Planner

UNDERSTANDING BY DESIGN®

Enduring Understandings
- *Over time, people adapt to their environment.*

Essential Questions
- *How does geography influence the way people live?*
- *How do governments change?*
- *What makes a culture unique?*

Predictable Misunderstandings
- *All of Brazil is rainforest.*
- *The independence of Brazil came quickly to the nation.*
- *Brazilians are Spanish with no other influence.*

Assessment Evidence

Performance Tasks:
- *Project-Based Learning Digital Hands-On Chapter Project*
- *Project-Based Learning Hands-On Chapter Project*

Other Evidence:
- *Geography and Economics Activity*
- *Primary Sources Reading Skills Activity*
- *Geography Skills Activity*
- *Critical Thinking Skills Activity*
- *Participation in Project-Based Learning Activities*
- *Participation in Interactive Whiteboard Activities*
- *Interpretation of slide show images and special purpose maps*
- *Participation in class discussions*
- *Lesson Reviews*
- *Chapter Assessments*

SUGGESTED PACING GUIDE

Introducing the Chapter	2 Days	Lesson 3	2 Days
Lesson 1	2 Days	Global Connections	3 Days
Lesson 2	2 Days	Chapter Wrap-Up and Assessment	2 Days

TOTAL TIME   13 Days

Key for Using the Teacher Edition

SKILL-BASED ACTIVITIES

Types of skill activities found in the Teacher Edition.

* **V Visual Skills** require students to analyze maps, graphs, charts, and photos.

W Writing Skills provide writing opportunities to help students comprehend the text.

R Reading Skills help students practice reading skills and master vocabulary.

C Critical Thinking Skills help students apply and extend what they have learned.

T Technology Skills require students to use digital tools effectively.

*Letters are followed by a number when there is more than one of the same type of skill on the page.

DIFFERENTIATED INSTRUCTION

All activities are written for the on-level student unless otherwise marked with the leveled labels below.

BL Beyond Level
AL Approaching Level
ELL English Language Learners

All students benefit from activities that utilize different learning styles. Many activities are marked as below when a particular learning style is highlighted.

Intrapersonal	Naturalist
Logical/Mathematical	Kinesthetic
Visual/Spatial	Auditory/Musical
Verbal/Linguistic	Interpersonal

Students will:

6.1.6 Identify trade routes and discuss their impact on the rise of cultural centers and trade cities in Europe and Mesoamerica

6.1.10 Examine and explain the outcomes of European colonization on the Americas and the rest of the world.

6.1.18 Create and compare timelines that identify major people, events and developments in the history of individual civilizations and/or countries that comprise Europe and the Americas.

6.1.19 Define and use the terms decade, century, and millennium, and compare alternative ways that historical periods and eras are designated by identifying the organizing principles upon which each is based.

6.2.7 Define and compare citizenship and the citizen's role throughout history in Europe and the Americas.

6.3.5 Give examples and describe the formation of important river deltas, mountains and bodies of water in Europe and the Americas.

6.3.7 Locate and describe the climate regions of Europe and the Americas and explain how and why they differ.

6.3.8 Identify major biomes of Europe and the Americas and explain how these are influenced by climate.

6.3.12 Compare the distribution and evaluate the importance of natural resources such as natural gas, oil, forests, uranium, minerals, coal, seafood and water in Europe and the Americas.

6.4.7 Identify economic connections between the local community and the countries of Europe or the Americas and identify job skills needed to be successful in the workplace.

CHAPTER OPENER PLANNER

Students will know:

- *There is a variety of climate in Brazil.*
- *There is more influence on the area and the population than just the Amazon River.*
- *Brazil is home to forests, minerals, and farmland.*
- *Brazilian population contains a variety of racial and ethnic groups.*
- *Brazil has a rich culture and heritage.*

Students will be able to:

- ***analyze*** *a map to identify Brazil on a map of South America*
- ***use a time line*** *to discuss significant events in the history of Brazil*
- ***discuss*** *how development has impacted the environment and the economy of Brazil*

UNDERSTANDING BY DESIGN®

☑ *Print Teaching Options*

V **Visual Skills**

☐ **P. 238** Students use a map of South America to answer the Step Into the Place questions and identify countries that share Brazil's border. **AL**

☐ **P. 239** Students discuss the major points of interest on the time line.

W **Writing Skills**

☐ **P. 239** Students write a persuasive paragraph about the environmental or economic impact of the 2016 Olympics on Rio de Janeiro.

☑ *Online Teaching Options*

☐ **MAP** **Reading a Map**—Students identify aspects and locations of the region on a map. **AL**

☐ **TIME LINE** **Reading a Time Line**—Students identify where in the region events on the time line took place and locate the places on a map. **AL**

☐ **MAP** **Interactive World Atlas**—Students use the interactive world atlas to identify the region and describe its terrain.

☑ *Printable Digital Worksheets*

☐ **WORKSHEET** **Geography Skills: Reading a Bar Graph**—Students can use the worksheet to learn how to read bar graphs for statistics.

☐ **WORKSHEET** **Primary Sources Reading Skills: Jesuits and Their Opinions on Slavery**—Students use this worksheet to learn more about the connections between Jesuits and slavery.

☐ **WORKSHEET** **Critical Thinking Skills: Production of Ethanol**—Students can use the worksheet to analyze and interpret information about ethanol production.

☐ **WORKSHEET** **Geography and Economics: The Trans-Amazonica Highway**—Students can use the worksheet to learn more about this roadway's impact on the region.

Project-Based Learning

Hands-On

Graphic Novel about Brazil

Students may work independently or in pairs to create graphic novels about Brazil. Topics may include information about the history of Brazil, the differences between urban or rural life, or the numerous physical features found throughout the country. After researching their chosen topic, students should create a story about it. Once the story is approved, they can begin to create storyboards for their graphic novels. Have students share their completed graphic novels with the class.

Digital Hands-On

Online Digital Story about Brazil

Have students work in pairs to create an online digital story about Brazil. Students might write a story that highlights a historical event that occurred in Brazil or describes what life is like for someone who lives in a rural or urban region. Students should go online to find photographs, videos, or art about Brazil and link these in the stories. Have student pairs present their online digital stories to the class.

Print Resources

ANCILLARY RESOURCES

These ancillaries are available for every chapter and lesson.

- **Reading Essentials and Study Guide Workbook** **AL** **ELL**
- **Chapter Tests and Lesson Quizzes Blackline Masters**

PRINTABLE DIGITAL WORKSHEETS

These printable digital worksheets are available for every chapter and lesson.

- **Hands-On Chapter Projects**
- **What Do You Know? Activities**
- **Chapter Summaries (English and Spanish)**
- **Vocabulary Builder Activities**
- **Quizzes and Tests**
- **Reading Essentials and Study Guide (English and Spanish)** **AL** **ELL**
- **Guided Reading Activities**

More Media Resources

SUGGESTED VIDEOS MOVIES

NOTE: Be sure to preview videos to ensure they are age-appropriate.

- **Discovery Atlas: Brazil Revealed** (97 min.)
- **7 Days BRAZIL** (52 min.)
- **Nature's Deadliest: Season 1, Ep. 3 "Brazil"** (44 min.)

SUGGESTED READING

- ***Tropical Rain Forest,*** by Donald Silver **AL**
- ***Kids Around the World: We Live in Brazil,*** by Francois-Xavier Freeland
- ***Brazil: the Land, the People, the Culture,*** by Malika Hollander **AL**

edtechteacher
21ˢᵗ Century Learning

PHYSICAL GEOGRAPHY OF BRAZIL

Students will know:
- *There is a variety of climate in Brazil.*
- *There is more influence on the area and the population than just the Amazon River.*
- *Brazil is home to forests, minerals, and farmland.*

Students will be able to:
- *discuss the physical geography of Brazil, including landforms and waterways*
- *describe the various climates in Brazil*
- *identify Brazil's natural resources and major crops*

UNDERSTANDING BY DESIGN®

☑ Print Teaching Options

V Visual Skills

☐ **P. 240** Pairs create a short skit based on text information.

☐ **P. 241** Students locate the Amazon River on a map.

☐ **P. 241** Students create a drawing of the Amazon Basin.

☐ **P. 242** Students create a two-column chart to visualize facts about the Brazilian Highlands.

☐ **P. 245** Students match areas of Brazil with their climate zones. AL

☐ **P. 246** Students chart forest and timber resources.

W Writing Skills

☐ **P. 244** Small groups write a Brazilian weather report.

☐ **P. 246** Students write a report on the positive and negative effects of drilling for potential oil reserves.

R Reading Skills

☐ **P. 240** Pairs identify the meaning of *tributaries*. ELL

☐ **P. 241** Students practice using content vocabulary. ELL

☐ **P. 243** Students discuss the word *tropics*. ELL

☐ **P. 244** Students fill in a chart with statistics. BL

C Critical Thinking Skills

☐ **P. 241** Students work to solve problems experienced by Native Americans in the Amazon Basin. BL

☐ **P. 243** Students use a map to infer how Brazil's geography affects how people live. BL

☐ **P. 245** Students discuss the issues that arise when developing natural resources for economic gain.

T Technology Skills

☐ **P. 242** Small groups research what sort of environmental problems rapid growth has caused in Brazil. BL

☐ **P. 246** Small groups research Brazil's deforestation rates. BL

☐ **P. 247** Small groups make a visual of Brazil's major crops.

☑ Online Teaching Options

V Visual Skills

VIDEO **Pampas**—Students can use the short video of the pampas to create a visual connection to the definition.

VIDEO **Monsoons**—Students can use the short video of a monsoon to create a visual connection to the definition.

VIDEO **The Brazilian Rain Forest**—Students use the video as a guide to discuss the flora and fauna of the Brazilian Rain Forest.

ANIMATION **Elements of a Globe**—Students use the animation about Earth's hemispheres to discuss how to make connections to concepts.

MAP **Climates: Brazil**—Students use a climate map to discuss the climate features of Brazil. ELL

W Writing Skills

VIDEO **Wild Worlds—The Amazon**—Students create flashcards about what they find interesting while watching a video about the physical geography of Brazil.

IMAGE **The Amazon River**—Students write an informative paragraph explaining how the Amazon River influences people's lives.

R Reading Skills

GRAPHIC ORGANIZER **Organizing Information: Landforms**—Students use the graphic organizer to take notes about a particular region and share their findings with the class.

C Critical Thinking Skills

SLIDE SHOW **Landforms of Brazil**—Students discuss the importance of the escarpment and grassland and how it influences the way people live. AL

GAME **Drag-and-Drop: Brazil's Resources**—Students will use the drag-and-drop game with the chapter resources map to discuss the various resources of the region, their locations, and their uses.

DIAGRAM **How Coffee Works**—Students use the flow chart to elaborate on the role of the production of coffee in Brazil.

IMAGE **Transportation of Goods on Rivers**—Students use the photos of people transporting goods using river systems to compare the Amazon River system to various other rivers.

T Technology Skills

ONLINE SELF-CHECK QUIZ **Lesson 1**—Students receive instant feedback on their mastery of lesson content.

☑ Printable Digital Worksheets

W Writing Skills

WORKSHEET **Geography Skills: Reading a Bar Graph**—Students can use the worksheet to learn how to read bar graphs for statistics.

HISTORY OF BRAZIL

Students will know:
- *Brazil is home to forests, minerals, and farmland.*
- *Colonized by Portugal in the 1500s, many of the indigenous peoples were enslaved or killed.*
- *Brazilian population contains a variety of racial and ethnic groups.*

Students will be able to:
- **describe** *indigenous populations*
- **discuss** *colonial rule in Brazil including resources that were valuable to colonists*
- **explain** *how Brazil became independent*
- **discuss** *the government of modern Brazil*

UNDERSTANDING
BY DESIGN®

☑ *Print Teaching Options*

V Visual Skills

☐ **P. 248** Students make a time line of Brazil's history.

☐ **P. 252** Students create a class time line.

☐ **P. 254** Students explore why Brazil used the United States Constitution as a model for its own government. **BL**

W Writing Skills

☐ **P. 249** Students write a short skit depicting a scene that might have taken place during Brazil's colonization.

☐ **P. 253** Students do a think-pair-share activity to create a list of words for the word *independence*. **AL**

☐ **P. 255** Students write about Getúlio Vargas's rule.

R Reading Skills

☐ **P. 248** Students explore the word *indigenous*. **AL**

☐ **P. 251** Students identify cause and effect signal words.

☐ **P. 252** Students paraphrase the information. **AL**

☐ **P. 253** Pairs write quiz questions about independence.

C Critical Thinking Skills

☐ **P. 248** Students explore cause and effect.

☐ **P. 250** Students create a diagram of events in trade.

☐ **P. 251** Students draw conclusions about the spread of Christianity. **ELL**

☐ **P. 253** Students discuss the difference between a republic and a constitutional monarchy.

☐ **P. 254** Students consider differing viewpoints people had about slavery and emancipation in Brazil in the 1850s.

☐ **P. 255** Students consider how industrial growth has affected the people of Brazil.

T Technology Skills

☐ **P. 249** Students research slash-and-burn agriculture and present a report based on their findings. **BL**

☐ **P. 255** Students conduct online research and make a presentation about Dilma Vana Rousseff.

☑ *Online Teaching Options*

V Visual Skills

SLIDE SHOW **Brazil's Natural Products**—Students view and discuss the slide show of the various products that are made from Brazil's natural resources.

MAP **The Colonization of Brazil**—Students explore features showing how Brazil's colonization compares to nations that border it.

W Writing Skills

VIDEO **Brazil Fights Deforestation**—Students watch a video about Brazil's history of deforestation and write three questions they have. **ELL**

R Reading Skills

LECTURE SLIDE **Suffragists in Brazil**—Students use the lecture slide presentation to help students sequence key events in Brazil's changes in government. **ELL**

LECTURE SLIDE **Comparing Governments**—Students use the lecture slide to compare governments.

C Critical Thinking Skills

CHART **Emancipation in Brazil**—Students use information in the text about emancipation and the chart information to compare the history of the slave trade in Brazil and other parts of the world.

IMAGE **Contributions of Indigenous People**—Students create a flow chart to show how indigenous peoples affected trade.

T Technology Skills

GAME **Drag-and-Drop: Economics of Brazil**—Students drag and drop words and phrases to show cause-and-effect relationships between resources and the history of colonization in Brazil.

ONLINE SELF-CHECK QUIZ **Lesson 2**—Students receive instant feedback on their mastery of lesson content.

☑ *Printable Digital Worksheets*

W Writing Skills

WORKSHEET **Primary Sources Reading Skills: Jesuits and Their Opinions on Slavery**—Students use this worksheet to learn more about the connections between Jesuits and slavery. **BL**

LIFE IN BRAZIL

Students will know:
- *Brazilian population contains a variety of racial and ethnic groups.*
- *Brazil has a rich culture and heritage.*

Students will be able to:
- **describe** *the diverse population of Brazil and where they live*
- **examine** *the different ethnic and language groups in Brazil*
- **explain** *environmental concerns in developing rain forest*

UNDERSTANDING
BY DESIGN®

☑ *Print Teaching Options*

V Visual Skills

☐ **P. 259** Small groups create a poster of the emergence of Brazil's different ethnic and language groups.

☐ **P. 261** Students review and interpret the information about Brazil's economy to create a bar graph.

W Writing Skills

☐ **P. 258** Students write a story, poem, or play about a family that lives in the *favelas*.

☐ **P. 263** Students develop and write arguments either in favor of or against colonization of Brazil's interior.

R Reading Skills

☐ **P. 256** Students define *diverse*.

☐ **P. 259** Students paraphrase the text. **AL**

C Critical Thinking Skills

☐ **P. 256** Students explore issues that might result from having a large population.

☐ **P. 257** Students discuss what life was like for former enslaved people.

☐ **P. 258** Students brainstorm different ways to solve the issues facing people living in the *favelas*. **BL**

☐ **P. 260** Students create a Venn diagram comparing and contrasting rural and urban life in Brazil.

☐ **P. 262** Students discuss the issues of poverty and transportation in interior regions of Brazil.

T Technology Skills

☐ **P. 257** Students conduct research on one of four areas and create a presentation with visuals that describes the culture, education, and way of life for people in that area.

☐ **P. 260** Students create a presentation about their assigned topic incorporating music and visuals.

☐ **P. 261** Students conduct research about MERCOSUR and make a short presentation based on specific questions. **BL**

☐ **P. 262** Students research programs that have been set up to improve Brazil's poverty, overcrowding, and poor educational facilities. **BL**

☐ **P. 263** Small groups gather information and give a short report about ethanol and other alternative fuel sources.

☑ *Online Teaching Options*

V Visual Skills

☐ **MAP** **Population: Brazil**—Students use the population layer on the Chapter Opener map to identify where the majority of Brazil's population lives.

☐ **IMAGE** **360° View: Rio de Janeiro, Brazil**—Students use a 360° image to discuss the region, the city, the location of the city, and its growth.

☐ **IMAGE** **360° View: São Paulo, Brazil**—Students use a 360° image to discuss the region, the city, the location of the city, and its growth.

☐ **SLIDE SHOW** **Brazilian Culture**—Students discuss some of the cultural influences in Brazil.

☐ **IMAGE** **What is a *Favela*?**—Students use the interactive image to have a visual representation of vocabulary.

W Writing Skills

☐ **VIDEO** **Brazil's Economic Boom**—Students watch a video about the economic boom in Brazil and create a brochure to highlight tourist attractions.

R Reading Skills

☐ **GRAPHIC ORGANIZER** **Resources and Economics in Brazil**—Students use a graphic organizer to review the various aspects of Brazil's resources and economy.

C Critical Thinking Skills

☐ **CHART** **Brazil's Population**—Students use the population pyramid to show population distribution and density.

☐ **CHART** **Languages of Brazil**—Students discuss the influence of colonists on the culture and language of Brazil. **AL**

☐ **CHART** **Education in Brazil**—Students discuss the growing importance of education in Brazil with a chart showing attendance changes in the last decade. **ELL**

T Technology Skills

☐ **GAME** **Drag-and-Drop: Brazil's Goods**—Students use a drag-and-drop game to review the various aspects of Brazil's resources and their environmental impact.

☐ **ONLINE SELF-CHECK QUIZ** **Lesson 3**—Students receive instant feedback on their mastery of lesson content.

☑ *Printable Digital Worksheets*

W Writing Skills

☐ **WORKSHEET** **Geography and Economics: The Trans-Amazonica Highway**—Students can use this worksheet to learn more about this roadway's impact on the region.

☐ **WORKSHEET** **Critical Thinking Skills: Production of Ethanol**—Students can use this worksheet to analyze and interpret information about ethanol production.

INTERVENTION AND REMEDIATION STRATEGIES

LESSON 1 Physical Geography of Brazil

Reading and Comprehension

Have students work with a partner to create flash cards for each of the content vocabulary words by writing the word on one side and the definition on the other. Students may also draw sketches to serve as clues to each word's meaning. Have pairs use their flashcards to take turns quizzing each other. Then have them practice using the words in sentences to explain concepts in the lesson.

Text Evidence

Organize students into four groups, and assign groups the following topics: waterways, landforms, climate, and natural resources. Have groups create a visual display to describe their topic in the form of an outline, poster, or a digital slide presentation. Tell students to present an analysis of their topic using evidence from the text to support the concepts presented in their displays.

LESSON 2 History of Brazil

Reading and Comprehension

To help students make connections between concepts in this lesson, have students look for signal words as they read. Tell students that comparisons are often signaled by words such as *also, as well as, too, like,* and *similarly*. Words such as *yet, but, however,* and *though* indicate concepts being contrasted. Have students skim the lesson to look for signal words and note which concepts and ideas are being compared or contrasted. For example, students might note similarities and differences of Brazil's presidents and their rule.

Text Evidence

Organize students into three groups and assign groups the following topics: Group A/Early History, Group B/Colonial Rule, and Group C/Independence. Have students collaborate to write a summary of their topic. Tell students their summaries should answer the guiding questions: Group A/How did Brazil's early peoples live?, Group B/How did the Portuguese colony in Brazil develop?, and Group C/How did Brazil gain independence and become a democracy? Have a member of each group read the group's summary to the class.

LESSON 3 Life in Brazil

Reading and Comprehension

Have students skim the lesson to find unfamiliar or challenging words. Tell students to use print or online dictionaries to define each word. Then have pairs play a guessing game in which one student reads the definition for partners to guess. To help students make connections to lesson concepts, ask volunteers to explain how one or two of the words on their list is used in a sentence.

Text Evidence

Students may have trouble grasping the economic dichotomy that exists in modern Brazil. Organize students into small groups and have each group research a different Brazilian city. Tell students their research should provide information about the city's population, education, economic diversity, and challenges. Have students in each group collaborate to answer questions such as: What is the city's population? What percentage of the population has a college degree? What are some of the ways people earn a living? After groups present their findings, discuss various issues facing Brazilian cities.

Online Resources

Level Reader

Use this online lower-level text that corresponds directly to the text in the online Student Edition.

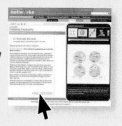

Guided Reading Activities

This resource uses graphic organizers and guiding questions to help students with comprehension.

What Do You Know?

Use these worksheets to pre-assess students' background knowledge before they study the chapter.

Reading Essentials and Study Guide Workbook

This resource offers writing and reading activities for the approaching-level student.

Self-Check Quizzes

This online assessment tool provides instant feedback for students to check their progress.

BRAZIL

ESSENTIAL QUESTIONS · *How does geography influence the way people live?*
· *How do governments change?* · *What makes a culture unique?*

Soccer ("football") player Robinho has many fans in Brazil and around the world.

networks
There's More Online about Brazil.

CHAPTER 8

Lesson 1
Physical Geography of Brazil

Lesson 2
History of Brazil

Lesson 3
Life in Brazil

The Story Matters...

Brazil is located in the eastern half of South America. Brazil's vast land area makes it the giant of South America. Water is also important in defining the country. The great Amazon River flows through Brazil for more than 2,000 miles (3,219 km) and carries as much as one-fourth of the world's freshwater. This river drains the Amazon Basin, which stretches across the northern half of Brazil and contains the world's largest remaining tropical rain forest.

FOLDABLES
Study Organizer

Go to the Foldables® library in the back of your book to make a Foldable® that will help you take notes while reading this chapter.

237

ENGAGE

Think-Pair-Share Point to Brazil on a map of South America. Have students locate the Amazon River and brainstorm ways that the river most likely is important to the region. Pairs should consider and share the importance of the river to people for transportation and irrigation, or its importance to the animals and the plants that live in or near it. Then have students read "The Story Matters. . ." introducing the region's geography.

Discuss with the class how the Amazon River affects the way people live. **Ask:** How might the Amazon River both help and hurt people in the region? *(Students may suggest that the Amazon River helps people by serving as a waterway for transportation. They may also conclude that such a large body of water could pose a threat to the region because of flooding.)*

Tell students in this chapter they will learn about the physical features, the history, and the cultures of South America's largest country, Brazil.

Making Connections Ask students to list on the board items that consumers buy that come to mind when they think of the country of Brazil. *(Answers will vary but could include Brazil nuts or Brazilian coffee or rain forest woods such as mahogany.)* Have them consider how Brazilian products are made as you read the following information aloud.

- Brazil is home to a wide variety of plants and animals that live in the Amazon rain forest, the world's largest tropical rain forest.
- Some of Brazil's natural resources include gold, iron, nickel, and other rare elements.
- Some human activity, such as deforestation and illegal mining, threaten the survival of the plants and animals in the Amazon rain forest.
- The climate of Brazil is very diverse. During the dry season, droughts occur in northeastern Brazil. At other times of the year, heavy rainfall can cause flooding in the southern region of the country.

Letter from the Author

Dear Geography Teacher,

A concern among Brazil's government leaders is that most development has occurred along the southeast coast. To solve this problem, the government encouraged people to settle deeper within the Amazon Basin. The capital, Brasilia, was established there, and the Transamazonica Highway was built; however, this has led to deforestation of the rain forest. Divide the class into two groups to debate the issue. Have groups research arguments for and against deforestation for economic development.

FOLDABLES
Study Organizer

Go to the Foldables® library for a cumulative chapter-based Foldable® activity that your students can use to help take notes and prepare for assessment.

TEACH & ASSESS

Step Into the Place

V Visual Skills

Reading a Map Explain to students that this map shows the continent of South America with the country of Brazil in green. Have students use the map to answer the "Step Into the Place" questions. Then have students identify the countries that share Brazil's border. *(French Guiana, Suriname, Guyana, Venezuela, Colombia, Peru, Bolivia, Paraguay, Argentina, Uruguay)* **Ask:**

- Which countries do not share Brazil's border? *(Ecuador, Chile)*
- Where is the Amazon River located? *(in the northern part of Brazil)* Which direction does it run? *(east from Peru to the Atlantic Ocean)*
- Approximately how many miles is it to travel from Brasília to São Paulo? *(about 600)* **AL** Visual/Spatial, Logical/Mathematical

Content Background Knowledge

Here are some interesting facts about the country of Brazil and its people:

- Brazil is one of the world's largest countries, covering close to half of South America, with a population of about 194 million people.
- Brazil's largest city is São Paulo with more than ten million people; it is the largest city in the Southern Hemisphere.
- Portuguese is the official language of Brazil, but most people in other South American countries speak Spanish.
- While about 75 percent of Brazil's population is Roman Catholic, some Brazilians practice local religions that combine African beliefs with Catholicism.
- A popular religious holiday in Brazil is Carnival, a Roman Catholic celebration highlighted by street parades, music, masks, costumes, and dancing.

ANSWERS, p. 238

STEP INTO THE PLACE

1. the Amazon
2. ten
3. Much of Brazil will have a hot climate. Regions near the Equator and the Tropics tend to experience a hot climate.
4. **CRITICAL THINKING** approximately 580 miles (933 km)

Brazil is the largest country in South America with almost 3.3 million square miles (8.5 million sq. km) of land. It accounts for most of the eastern coast of South America. Brazil contains more than 4,665 miles (7,508 km) of coastline along the Atlantic Ocean. The Equator and the Tropic of Capricorn run through the country. As you study the map, look for the geographic features that make this area unique.

Step Into the Place

MAP FOCUS Use the map to answer the following questions.

1. **PHYSICAL GEOGRAPHY** What is the main river in Brazil?
2. **PLACES AND REGIONS** How many countries share a border with Brazil?
3. **THE GEOGRAPHER'S WORLD** Why is it significant that the Equator and the Tropic of Capricorn both run through Brazil?
4. **CRITICAL THINKING**
   ANALYZING Use the scale bar on the map to measure the distance between the cities of Brasília and Rio de Janeiro.

RIO, AERIAL VIEW The huge "Christ the Redeemer" statue overlooks Rio de Janeiro. Set between beautiful mountains and the Atlantic coast, Rio de Janeiro was Brazil's capital from 1763 to 1960.

BRAZIL'S CAPITAL Brasília is a planned city, built in Brazil's central wilderness area. Brasília has been the country's capital since 1960.

Step Into the Time

ANALYZING Select at least two events on the time line and explain how they illustrate the importance of the Amazon Basin to Brazil's development, as well as the environmental concerns caused by that development.

238 Chapter 8

1500 Cabral is first European to reach Brazil's coast

1800

1822 Brazil gains independence from Portugal

(t to b) ©Mike Theiss/Ultimate Chase/Corbis; Luiz Felipe Castro/Flickr/Getty Images; giulio andreini/Marka/age fotostock

Project-Based Learning

Hands-On

Writing a Graphic Novel

Students may work independently or in pairs to create graphic novels about Brazil. Topics may include information about the history of Brazil, the differences between urban and rural life, or the numerous physical features found throughout the country. After researching their chosen topic, students should create a story about it. Once the story is approved, they can begin to create storyboards for their graphic novels. Have students share their completed graphic novels with the class.

Digital Hands-On

Creating an Online Digital Story

Have students work in pairs to create an online digital story about Brazil. Students might write a story that highlights a historical event that occurred in Brazil or describes what life is like for someone who lives in a rural or urban region. Students should go online to find photographs, videos, or art about Brazil and link these in the stories. Have student pairs present their online digital stories to the class.

edtechteacher
21st Century Learning

Brazil

Brazil

National capital ◆
City •

1889
Brazil is proclaimed a republic

1888 Slavery is abolished in Brazil

1960 Capital moves from Rio de Janeiro to Brasília

2009 Rio de Janeiro chosen to host 2016 Olympic Games

2010
Dilma Rousseff elected president

1900

2000

(l to r) Photodisc/Getty Images; Globo/Getty Images

Chapter 8 **239**

Step Into the Time

V Visual Skills

Reading a Time Line Have students review the time line as a class and discuss its major points of interest. **Ask:**

- What key event occurred in 1822? *(Brazil gained independence from Portugal.)*
- When was the capital of Brazil moved and to which city? *(in 1960, from Rio de Janeiro to Brasília)*
- Who was elected president in 2010? *(Dilma Rousseff)*

To help students gain a global perspective, highlight key cultural and political events that occurred in different parts of the world *(**1492:** Christopher Columbus sails to America; **1503:** Leonardo da Vinci paints the Mona Lisa; **1597:** William Shakespeare's play Romeo and Juliet is published; **1607:** English settlers colonize Jamestown, Virginia; **1804:** Lewis and Clark start expedition of Louisiana Purchase; **1914–1918:** World War I; **1939–1945:** World War II; **1963:** U.S. President John F. Kennedy assassinated; **2001:** Terrorist attacks on United States).*

Have students work with a partner to identify additional historical events and tell where they would place them on the time line. *(Students' answers will vary but should include accurate event placement.)* Visual/Spatial, Interpersonal

W Writing Skills

Argument Read aloud the "Step Into the Time" activity and briefly discuss how development may cause environmental problems but can also boost the region's economy. Tell students that they have been assigned to a development committee to plan for the Olympic Games in Rio de Janeiro. Have students write a persuasive paragraph about the environmental or economic impact of the Olympics on the city. Remind students to write a concluding statement, and have them share their paragraphs with the class. Verbal/Linguistic

CLOSE & REFLECT

Listing Draw a three-column chart on the board labeled *Geography, Government,* and *Culture.* Call on students to use information they learned from the Chapter Opener to list facts in each column. Tell students that they will learn more about Brazil's geography, government, and culture as they read this chapter.

TIME LINE AND MAP

Reading a Time Line and Map

Display the time line and map on the whiteboard. Have volunteers read each event as it is revealed on the time line. Ask students to identify where in the region the event took place and find its location on the map.

AL Visual/Spatial

See page 237B for other online activities.

ENGAGE

Bellringer Have students think of a nearby body of water or one they have visited. Guide a class discussion about how people use oceans, rivers, and lakes for work and play. Then read the Essential Question aloud and have students discuss how Brazil's physical geography affects what people do for work and recreation. **Ask:**

• What different geographical features can help people earn a living? (*Answers may vary but should include specific physical features such as fertile land for farming and ranching, forests for logging, and the ocean and rivers for fishing.*)

• What geographical features allow people to enjoy recreational activities? (*Answers may include beaches for swimming and surfing, and rivers and lakes for boating.*)

TEACH & ASSESS

Ⓥ Visual Skills

Collaborating Have students work in pairs to create a short skit or debate based on the information from the text. Have one student represent the Amazon River, and the other represent the Mississippi River. Students should create "dialogue" for their characters based on the content of the text. Have students present their skits and allow time for a brief question/answer session. **Ask:**

• How is the Amazon River different from the Mississippi River? (*The Amazon River moves more than 10 times the water volume.*)

• How might the Amazon River's size affect the shipping industry in Brazil? (*The large river benefits the shipping industry because it allows for ships to carry freight long distances.*) Naturalist, Kinesthetic, Verbal/Linguistic

Ⓡ Reading Skills

Using Context Clues Call on volunteers to identify and determine the meaning of *tributaries* using context clues in the text (*smaller rivers, feed into*). Then have students begin a vocabulary list by writing the boldface terms and definitions in their notebooks. Encourage students to include drawings of vocabulary words to help them remember each word's meaning. ELL Verbal/Linguistic

---

ANSWER, p. 240

Taking Notes Notes should include facts about each topic, such as: The major waterway in Brazil is the Amazon River; Most of Brazil has some type of warm, humid, rainy climate; Brazil's greatest natural resources are its plentiful forests, minerals, and farmlands.

---

net**works**

There's More Online!

☑ **IMAGE** Brazilian Rain Forest

☑ **SLIDE SHOW** Landforms: Brazil

☑ **VIDEO**

Reading **HELP**DESK

Academic Vocabulary
• area
• occur

Content Vocabulary
• tributary
• basin
• rain forest
• canopy
• plateau
• escarpment
• pampas
• Tropics
• temperate zone

TAKING NOTES: *Key Ideas and Details*

Summarize As you read, use a graphic organizer to write a summary sentence about each topic.

Topic	Summary
Waterways	
Climate	
Resources	

Ⓙ **Indiana Academic Standards**
6.1.18, 6.1.19, 6.3.5, 6.3.7, 6.3.8, 6.3.12, 6.4.7

Lesson 1
Physical Geography of Brazil

ESSENTIAL QUESTION · *How does geography influence the way people live?*

IT MATTERS BECAUSE
Brazil is the world's fifth-largest country in size and population.

Waterways and Landforms

GUIDING QUESTION *What are Brazil's physical features?*

Brazil is the largest country in South America. It occupies about half the continent. Rolling lowland plains and flat highland plateaus cover most of the country.

The Amazon

The Amazon River is one of Brazil's amazing natural features as well as a great natural resource. It begins high in the Andes of Peru and flows east across northern Brazil to the Atlantic Ocean. The river is the Western Hemisphere's longest river and the world's second longest, after the Nile River in Africa.

Ⓥ The Amazon is the largest river in terms of the amount of freshwater it carries. It moves more than 10 times the water volume of the Mississippi River. Of all the water that Earth's rivers empty into the oceans, about 25 percent comes from the Amazon. Its massive flow pushes freshwater more than 100 miles (161 km) out into the Atlantic Ocean. The river's depth allows oceangoing ships to travel more than 2,000 miles (3,219 km) upstream to unload or pick up cargo.

The Amazon Basin

Ⓡ One reason the Amazon carries so much water is that it has more than 1,000 **tributaries**. These smaller rivers feed into the Amazon as it flows from the Andes to the Atlantic Ocean. Several tributaries are more than 1,000 miles (1,609 km) long.

(l to r) SambaPhoto/Milton Carelo/Getty Images; E. Hanazaki Photography/Flickr/Getty Images; Rodrigo Baleia/LatinContent/Getty Images; Kevin Schafer/Photographer's Choice/Getty Images; Benjamin Lowy/Getty Images News/Getty Images

---

net**works** — *Online Teaching Options*

▶ **VIDEO**

Wild Worlds—The Amazon

Categorizing Use this video about the Amazon rain forest to introduce the lesson. Have students create flashcards of topics and terms they found interesting or want to learn more about after watching the video. Collect the flashcards and discuss as a class. Distribute the flashcards to students after completing the lesson and have them categorize the topics and terms as follows: *Waterways, Landforms, Climate, Natural Resources.* Visual/Spatial, Verbal/Linguistic

See page 237C for other online activities.

BBC Motion Gallery Education

R The **area** that a river and its tributaries drain is called a **basin**. The Amazon Basin covers more than 2 million square miles (5.2 million sq. km). Nearly half of Brazil's land lies within this vast region. Its wet lowlands cover most of the country's northern and western areas.

Much of the Amazon Basin is covered by the world's largest **rain forest**. A rain forest is a warm woodland that receives a great deal of rain each year. Tall evergreen trees form a **canopy**, or an umbrella-like covering. The Amazon rain forest is called the Selva. It is the world's richest biological resource. The Selva is home to several million kinds of plants, insects, birds, and other animals.

Only about 6 percent of Brazil's population live in the Amazon Basin. Most of the region contains fewer than two people per square mile. Some are Native Americans who live in small villages and have little contact with the outside world.

C

Brazilian Highlands

South and east of the Amazon Basin are the Brazilian Highlands. This is mainly a region of rolling hills and areas of high, flat land called **plateaus**. These highlands are divided into western and eastern parts.

(t) Manfred Gottschalk/Workbook Stock/Getty Images; (b) altrendo travel/Getty Images

Visual Vocabulary

Tributary A tributary is a smaller river or stream that flows into a larger one, or into a lake.

V1

Academic Vocabulary

area a geographic region

South America's Amazon River and North America's Mississippi River cross vast distances and carry enormous amounts of water.

▶ **CRITICAL THINKING**

Comparing How are the Amazon and Mississippi Rivers similar? How are they different?

Chapter 8 **241**

IMAGE

The Amazon River

Interpreting Use the interactive photo of the Amazon River to elaborate on the Amazon River's role in affecting the environment and population of Brazil and the world. Ask students to write an informative paragraph explaining how rivers influence people's lives. Encourage students to use graphics such as charts and tables to help convey the information. **Visual/Spatial, Verbal/Linguistic**

See page 237C for other online activities.

Interactive Photos

This region has many diverse types of landscapes. Land forms range from mountains to grasslands. Waterways include rivers, lakes, and shorelines. Vegetation varies depending on the soil quality and access to water within the specific area. Animal life has adapted to take advantage of what the region has to offer.

R Reading Skills

Applying Ask a volunteer to read the first paragraph. Next have students work in pairs to determine the various uses of the word *area*. Then have each pair write a sentence using the word. Sentences should focus on the Amazon Basin or the Brazilian Highlands. Circulate to provide corrective guidance as needed. **ELL** Verbal/Linguistic, Interpersonal

V1 Visual Skills

Drawing Have students interpret the text about the Amazon Basin to create a drawing of the region. Tell students to use clues from the text to imagine what the Amazon Basin and rain forest looks like. Call on volunteers to give a "guided tour" of their drawings, explaining what each element in their drawing represents. Visual/Spatial, Naturalist

V2

C Critical Thinking Skills

Problem-Solving Have students use their drawings of the region and the information in the text to discuss problems and solutions. **Ask:** What problems might Native Americans living in the Amazon Basin have? How might these problems be resolved? *(Possible answers: The Native Americans living in the Amazon Basin are isolated, so they have limited access to modern health care, education, and technology. Constructing a community health center and library with Internet service could help give inhabitants better health care and more access to the rest of the world.)* **BL** Logical/Mathematical, Verbal/Linguistic

V2 Visual Skills

Analyzing Maps Display a physical map of Brazil. Have a volunteer locate the Amazon River. **Ask:**

- In which country does the Amazon River begin? *(Peru)*
- Where does the river end? *(in northeastern Brazil at the Atlantic Ocean)* Visual/Spatial

---

ANSWER, p. 241

CRITICAL THINKING **Similar:** They both cross vast distances and carry large amounts of water. **Different:** The Amazon River moves more than 10 times the water volume of the Mississippi River.

Physical Geography of Brazil

Creating Charts To help students visualize and comprehend facts about the Brazilian Highlands, have them create a two-column chart labeled *Eastern Highlands* and *Western Highlands*. Have students use information from the text to complete their charts. **Ask:** What physical features define the western part of the highlands? *(grassland covered with shrubs and small trees)* Continue to ask similiar questions, as students fill out their charts. **Visual/Spatial**

T Technology Skills

Researching on the Internet Tell students that Brasília is a planned city that was designated a UNESCO World Heritage Site in 1987 because of its distinctive architecture and design. However, rapid growth has caused some problems. Have students work in small groups to research what sort of environmental problems this growth has caused for people living in and around the city. Have groups present a summary of their findings in a short report that includes visuals and a list of sources students used to collect reliable geographic data.
BL Interpersonal

V₂ Visual Skills

Diagramming Have students use information from the text to create a Venn diagram comparing and contrasting the cities of Brasília and São Paulo. **Ask:** What do these two cities have in common? How do they differ? *(Both are large cities. Brasília is the capital of Brazil, but São Paulo is much larger with a population of more than 17 million people.)* **Visual/Spatial**

Brasília   São Paulo

C Critical Thinking Skills

Comparing Have students review the last two paragraphs on the page. **Ask:** What similarities do the Atlantic lowlands share with the pampas? *(They are both farming areas.)* **Verbal/Linguistic**

ANSWER, p. 242

CRITICAL THINKING Escarpments have hindered development of Brazil's inland areas.

V₁ The western part of the highlands is largely grassland that is partly covered with shrubs and small trees. Farming and ranching are the major economic activities in this part of the highlands. Farther west is the Mato Grosso Plateau, a flat, sparsely populated area of forests and grasslands that extends into Bolivia and Peru.

Low mountain ranges form much of the eastern Brazilian Highlands, although some peaks rise above 7,000 feet (2,134 m). In other places, highland plateaus plunge to the Atlantic coast, forming **escarpments**, or steep slopes. These escarpments, rising from coast to highlands, have hindered development of inland areas.

T Brazil's third-largest city, Brasília, is located in the Brazilian Highlands. It was built in the 1950s as Brazil's new capital to encourage settlement in the country's interior. Some 3.5 million people live in and around the city.

V₂ About 600 miles (966 km) south of Brasília is São Paulo. This huge city is located on a plateau at the highland's eastern edge, just 30 miles (48 km) from the Atlantic coast. With more than 17 million people, São Paulo is the largest city in the Southern Hemisphere. It is also South America's most important industrial city.

Farther south are grassy, treeless plains called **pampas**. The grass and fertile soil make the pampas one of Brazil's most productive ranching and farming areas.

C **Atlantic Lowlands**
Brazil has one of the longest strips of coastal plains in South America, wedged between the Brazilian Highlands and the Atlantic Ocean. This narrow plains region, called the Atlantic lowlands, is just 125 miles (201 km) wide in the north; it becomes even narrower in the southeast. The rural parts of this region are another important area for farming.

An escarpment slopes down to an Atlantic Ocean beach near the city of São Paulo.
▶ **CRITICAL THINKING**
Describing How have escarpments affected Brazil's development?

networks   *Online Teaching Options*

SLIDE SHOW

Landforms of Brazil

Analyzing Visuals Use the slide show to guide a class discussion about the importance of landforms to people who live in the region. Ask students how these landforms influence the way people live. Tell students to use clues from the slide show to give them ideas. For example, the grass and fertile soil in the pampas help ranchers and farmers raise livestock and produce crops in rural areas.
BL Verbal/Linguistic

See page 237C for other online activities.

Slide Show

E. Hanazaki Photography/Flickr/Getty Images

Although the coastal lowlands cover only a small part of Brazil's territory, most of the nation's people live here. More than 12 million live in and around Rio de Janeiro, Brazil's second-largest city. Rio's beautiful beaches and vibrant lifestyle make it Brazil's cultural and tourist center.

T

☑ READING PROGRESS CHECK

Analyzing Why do many Brazilians live in the Brazilian Highlands?

A Tropical Climate

GUIDING QUESTION *What are Brazil's climate and weather like?*

Most of Brazil is located in the **Tropics**. This is the zone along Earth's Equator that lies between the Tropic of Cancer and the Tropic of Capricorn. Brazil's climate varies. In fact, the huge country has several different climates.

Wet Rain Forests

R

The area along the Equator in northern Brazil has a tropical rain forest climate. In this climate, every day is warm and wet. Daytime temperatures average in the 80s Fahrenheit (27°C to 32°C). It feels hotter than this because the wet rain forest makes the air humid.

Ranchers herd cattle on the Mato Grosso Plateau of west-central Brazil.

▶ CRITICAL THINKING

Describing What are the main features of the Mato Grosso Plateau?

Chapter 8 **243**

Organizing Information: Landforms

Organizing Organize students into three groups and assign them to the following regions: basins, highlands, and lowlands. Use the interactive graphic organizer to help students take notes on facts in the text about each area. When students have completed their charts, have groups present their findings to the rest of the class. Allow time for a question-answer session and for the students to complete the section of the chart they were not assigned in groups. **Visual/Spatial, Verbal/Linguistic**

See page 237C for other online activities.

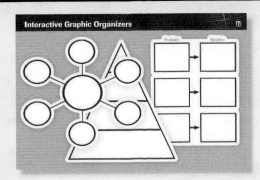
Interactive Graphic Organizers

C Critical Thinking Skills

Making Inferences Display a map of Brazil that shows the physical features of the highlands and lowlands. Then have students look at the photograph on the page as they consider how Brazil's geography affects how people live. **Ask:**

- What might life be like for a Brazilian farmer living on the Mato Grosso Plateau? *(Answers may vary, but students should mention that the life of a farmer would be hard since a farmer works seven days a week and never works just an 8-hour day; they might also have limited transportation and less access to technology.)*
- How would this lifestyle differ from someone who lives in Rio de Janeiro? *(Answers may vary, but students should mention that the life of a resident of Rio de Janeiro would be faster paced with more access to culture, public transportation, and technology.)* **BL** Verbal/Linguistic

T Technology Skills

Researching Have students choose one of Brazil's two largest cities São Paulo or Rio de Janeiro to research on the Internet. Remind students to use reliable sources for both fun facts about the city and for photographs. Have students make a travel poster advertising the city's attractions using the facts and pictures they have found. Logical/Mathematical, Visual/Spatial

R Reading Skills

Determining Word Meanings Have students locate the words *tropics* and *tropical* in the text. To help clarify the definitions, use the *tropics* in a sentence that hints at the meaning. For example, "This winter, I will escape the cold temperatures by flying to the *tropics*." Point out that the sentence in the last paragraph that contains the word *tropical* is followed by an explanation. Read aloud the last paragraph on this page, emphasing the words, *"every day is warm and wet."* **ELL** Verbal/Linguistic

---

ANSWERS, p. 243

CRITICAL THINKING The Mato Grosso Plateau is flat, sparsely populated, and covered by forests and grasslands.

☑ READING PROGRESS CHECK Farmers live in the tropical savanna in the western half of the Highlands, while other farmers have settled in the prairie grasslands to the south. The capital city of Brasília draws people to live there, as does the city of São Paulo, an important industrial city.

Physical Geography of Brazil

R Reading Skills

Calculating Students may have trouble comprehending the statistics mentioned on this page. Draw a chart on the board labeled *Rainfall, Wind,* and *Temperatures.* Ask volunteers to read the first paragraph aloud. As students read, fill in the chart with pertinent information. Continue to complete the chart as students read the rest of the page. **Ask:**

- When does the most rainfall occur along the Amazon River? *(during monsoon season)*
- Where do tropical wet/dry climates often exist? *(along the outer edges of the tropical rain forest climates)*
- What seasons occur in the northern and central Brazilian Highlands? *(summer and winter)* **BL** Visual/ Spatial, Logical/Mathematical

W Writing Skills

Informative/Explanatory Have students work in small groups to write a weather report for a Brazilian newscast. Tell students to use information from the text to formulate what sort of weather each region might experience. Have groups assign different regions of Brazil to each member. Encourage students to use visuals and graphics and to be creative. For example, they might alert viewers about what to wear, if storms are in the forecast, and so on. Have groups present their weather reports. Verbal/Linguistic, Kinesthetic

Content Background Knowledge

Some scientists believe the Amazon to be the world's longest river. Others believe Egypt's Nile River is longer. The true source and length of the Amazon River has been debated for many years. In the 1950s, creeks near mountains in Peru were listed as the river's source. This data changed in 1971, when explorers identified the Carruhasanta Creek near Peru's Mount Mismi as the river's actual source. However, in 1983 a Polish expedition stated the Apacheta Creek was the true source. Finally, using technological advances such as Global Position Systems (GPS), scientists calculated more accurate readings. A 2007 expedition determined that the Apacheta Creek was six miles (10 km) longer than the Carruhasanta Creek, and was the true source of the Amazon River. The researchers included the Amazon's southern estuary, which lengthened the river's earlier measurement by over 200 miles. The same team used GPS technology to measure the length of the Nile River, which they determined was close to 90 miles shorter than the Amazon. Still, the Amazon's varying climate and streambeds make accurate measurement tricky, so the river's exact length continues to be debated.

During periods of drought, the Amazon River carries less water, which exposes sandbars in the river and low-lying areas along the shoreline.
▶ CRITICAL THINKING
Identifying What type of climate is found in areas along the Amazon River?

R

Academic Vocabulary

occur to happen or take place

Areas along the Amazon River have a tropical rain forest climate. They experience winds called monsoons that bring a huge amount of rain—120 inches to 140 inches (305 cm to 356 cm) per year. During the monsoon season, flooding swells the Amazon River in some places to more than 100 miles (161 km) wide. These areas also have a dry season when little rain **occurs**. During the dry season, forest fires are a danger, even in a rain forest.

Tropical Wet/Dry Climate
Tropical wet/dry climates usually exist along the outer edges of tropical rain forest climates. Most of the northern and central Brazilian Highlands has a tropical wet/dry climate. This climate has just two seasons—summer, which is wet, and winter, which is dry. Daily average temperatures change very little. Summers average in the 70°F range (21°C) and winters in the 60°F range (16°C). But even this slight difference is enough to change wind patterns, which affect rainfall. Between 40 inches and 70 inches (102 cm to 178 cm) of rain fall during the summer months. Winters get almost no rain.

Dry and Temperate Climates
The northeastern part of the Brazilian Highlands has a semiarid climate. This region is the hottest and driest part of the country. The daily high temperature during the summer often reaches 100°F (38°C). Frequent and severe droughts have caused many of the region's farms to fail. Even so, the desertlike plant life supports some light ranching.

W

Rodrigo Baleia/LatinContent/Getty Images

244 *Chapter 8*

network s *Online Teaching Options*

MAP

Climates: Brazil

Summarizing Display the climate layer of the Chapter Opener map. Guide students to integrate information presented on the map with facts in the text. Lead a class discussion about the different climate features of Brazil. Have students write a short summary that describes Brazil's tropical wet/dry climate and its dry and temperate climates.
ELL Visual Spatial, Verbal/Linguistic

See page 237C for other online activities.

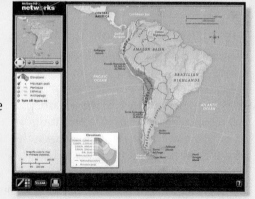

ANSWER, p. 244

CRITICAL THINKING The Amazon areas have a tropical monsoon climate, with rainy and dry seasons.

Southeastern Brazil, including São Paulo and Rio de Janeiro, is located in the **temperate zone**—the region between the Tropic of Capricorn and the Antarctic Circle. It has a temperate climate called humid subtropical. It is the same type of climate that the southeastern United States experiences.

Temperatures vary according to location and elevation in this part of Brazil. Summers are generally warm and humid, and winters are mild. Rainfall occurs year-round. In the southern parts of this climate zone, snow can fall.

☑ READING PROGRESS CHECK

Identifying What factors make farming in the northeastern part of Brazil difficult?

Natural Resources

GUIDING QUESTION *What resources are most plentiful and important in Brazil?*

Brazil has some of the world's most plentiful natural resources. Many of the resources have been developed for years, especially in the south and southeast. Recent transportation improvements have made the resources in Brazil's vast interior available to its growing industries and population. Agriculture, mining, and forestry have been important for centuries. The natural riches of Brazil attracted European settlers to the region. They found abundant trees, rich mineral resources, and fertile farmland.

River floodwaters surge through an area of the Amazon rain forest in northwestern Brazil.
▶ CRITICAL THINKING
Identifying What yearly natural event causes flooding in the Amazon Basin?

V

Think Again ?

Summer and winter occur at about the same time everywhere.

Not true. While American teens enjoy their summer vacation, young people in Brazil are going to school! That's because south of the Equator, the seasons are reversed. The summer months in the United States are winter months in Brazil.

C

Chapter 8 **245**

VIDEO

The Brazilian Rain Forest

Integrating Visual Information Lead a discussion about the flora and fauna that inhabit the Brazilian rain forest. Assign small groups the following topics to research: jungle animals, birds and fish, lizards and snakes, bats and spiders, and trees and plants. Have groups integrate what they have learned from their research with information presented in the video. Tell students to compare and contrast the information found in their research with facts presented in the video. Call on groups to present their topics. Prepare a classroom exhibit titled "Rain Forest Flora and Fauna." **Verbal/Linguistic, Naturalist**

See page 237C for other online activities.

V Visual Skills

Simulating Play a game of "You're Getting Warmer" with students. Designate certain parts of the classroom as northern Brazil, central Brazil, southern Brazil, and so on. As you slowly read aloud the paragraphs about the different climate zones of Brazil, have students move to the designated area. Encourage students moving towards a warm climate by saying, "You're getting warmer." If they should move toward a cooler climate, say, "You're getting colder." **AL** Visual/Spatial, Kinesthetic

C Critical Thinking Skills

Identifying Central Issues Explain to students that Brazil has abundant natural resources, but developing these resources can present problems for the environment. Discuss what some of these issues might be. Guide students to understand that extracting natural resources can have a potentially harmful impact on Brazil's ecosystem. For example, toxic compounds from mining can seep into surrounding rivers creating agricultural concerns, and deforestation can make the land sparse and susceptible to forest fires. **Ask:**

- How might agriculture, mining, and forestry adversely affect Brazil's environment? *(Answers may vary. Sample answer: Mining, logging, and other development can strip the land of nutrients essential for some plants and animals to survive.)*
- What are some of the positive effects of developing Brazil's natural resources? *(Developing natural resources by mining coal or developing forests for lumber can help the economy.)* Verbal/Linguistic

Content Background Knowledge

As students study the photo at the top of the page, read the following to them. When the Amazon River floods during the wet season, the river overflows its banks and covers the forest sometimes up to the treetops. The yearly flooding of the forest helps maintain the Amazonian ecosystem. It helps many of the fish as they swim through the forest feasting on the fruits, nuts, and seeds that fall from the trees. This helps the plants because the hard outer shell of many of the seeds is softened as they pass through the digestive system of the fish. The seeds then can grow into new plants as the waters recede.

ANSWERS, p. 245

CRITICAL THINKING Flooding is caused by monsoons, winds that bring a heavy amount of rain.
☑ READING PROGRESS CHECK The area is very hot and dry and often experiences droughts. These droughts make farming difficult, and have caused many farms to fail.

Kevin Schafer/Photographer's Choice/Getty Images

Tongro Image Stock/agefotostock

Physical Geography of Brazil

V Visual Skills

Creating Charts Have students use the information in the first paragraph to create a graph or diagram that gives a visual representation of Brazil's forests and timber resources. **Ask:** How has logging affected Brazil's forests? *(Areas in the northeast and south no longer have forests due to the excessive logging that was done in the past.)* Logical/Mathematical, Visual/Spatial

T Technology Skills

Analyzing Data Have students work in small groups to research Brazil's deforestation rates in the past twenty years and find out what is being done to preserve the trees of the rain forest. Remind students to use reliable sources and to cite their sources. Have groups present their findings in a report with visual representations of the data collected in their research, such as charts and graphs. Reports should end with a concluding statement supported by textual evidence from online or library supported resources. BL Logical/ Mathematical, Visual/Spatial

W Writing Skills

Argument As students read the third paragraph on the page, have them consider the environmental challenges posed by digging for oil beneath the ocean floor. For homework, have students prepare a report in which they research both the positive and negative effects of drilling for potential oil reserves. Students may wish to use examples of successful offshore oil drilling, and disasters in offshore oil drilling such as the 2010 BP oil spill in the Gulf of Mexico.

Have students write an argumentative essay that is either in favor of or against drilling for oil reserves below the ocean floor. Tell them to support their view with facts from their research. Call on volunteers to present their reports and conduct a discussion about the pros and cons of digging for oil reserves. Verbal/Linguistic

A worker on a Brazilian coffee plantation picks ripe coffee berries. After picking, the coffee berries are separated for quality and packed in sacks to send to market.
▶ **CRITICAL THINKING** V

Identifying Where are Brazil's major coffee-growing areas?

Abundant Forests

Forests cover about 60 percent of Brazil, accounting for about 7 percent of the world's timber resources. Most of the forests in the northeast and south were cleared long ago. Heavy logging continues in the Atlantic lowlands.

Logging in the Amazon Basin is increasing as more roads are built and settlement grows. The rain forest's mahogany and other hardwoods are highly desirable for making furniture. The rain forest is also a source of natural rubber, nuts, and medicinal plants. Logging, mining, and other development have become a major environmental issue. However, the rate of deforestation, or clearing land of forests or trees, has declined in recent years.

Minerals

Brazil has rich mineral resources that are only partly developed. They include iron ore, tin, copper, bauxite, gold, and manganese. At one time, most mining was done in the Brazilian Highlands. Recently, major deposits of minerals have been found in the Amazon basin. The new deposits might make Brazil the world's largest producer of many of the minerals. Brazil also has huge potential reserves of petroleum and natural gas deep under the ocean floor off its coast. Getting to the oil is a challenge, however.

Benjamin Lowy/Getty Images News/Getty Images

netw⊙rks *Online Teaching Options*

DIAGRAM

How Coffee Works

Sequencing Use the diagram to elaborate on the role of various resources in Brazil, specifically the production of coffee. Have students create a flow chart that shows the steps in the coffee-making process, from planting the beans, to consumers' purchase of coffee in supermarkets and coffee shops. Encourage students to use graphics such as charts and tables to help convey the information.
Logical/Mathematical, Visual/Spatial

See page 237C for other online activities.

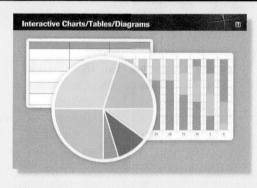

Interactive Charts/Tables/Diagrams

ANSWER, p. 246

CRITICAL THINKING The major coffee-growing areas are the eastern Brazilian Highlands and the Atlantic lowlands.

Productive Farmland

Brazil is the world's largest producer of coffee, sugarcane, and tropical fruits. The country also produces great amounts of soybeans, corn, and cotton.

Brazilian farmers produce most of their country's food supply. Agriculture is also important in trade, accounting for more than one-third of Brazil's exports. It is a leading exporter of coffee, oranges, soybeans, and cassava. Cassava is used to make tapioca.

Major Crops

R Production of coffee throughout the world was estimated to set an all-time high in 2012–2013, up 10 million bags from the previous year. Brazil and Vietnam accounted for most of the increase. The eastern Brazilian Highlands and the Atlantic lowlands are the main coffee-growing areas. Coffee was once Brazil's main export. Today, soybeans provide more income for the country. China is increasing its soybean imports, mostly for animal feed, and much of it comes from Brazil.

Most soybeans are grown in the south, but they are an important crop in the Brazilian Highlands, too. Farming has become easier in the highlands as farmers have begun using tractors and fertilizer to work the savanna soils.

Brazil grows one-third of the world's oranges, making it the world's leading supplier of the citrus fruit. Brazil is also the largest beef exporter in the world. Most of the country's grazing land is in the south and southeast.

In a recent year, Brazil's sugarcane production was more than two and a half times that of India, the second-leading producer. **T** Brazilian sugarcane is used to make ethanol, which is mixed with gasoline and used as fuel for cars and trucks. For many years, the government has required cars to use ethanol. The country's car manufacturers make flexible-fuel vehicles that can use fuel with high levels of ethanol.

☑ **READING PROGRESS CHECK**

Identifying Which two regions are Brazil's most important agricultural areas?

FOLDABLES
Study Organizer

Include this lesson's information in your Foldable®.

Valuable Natural Resources
Urban Population

LESSON 1 REVIEW

Reviewing Vocabulary

1. How does Brazil's location in the Tropics affect its climate?

Answering the Guiding Questions

2. *Determining Central Ideas* Why is the Amazon Basin a unique region?

3. *Analyzing* How do a tropical rain forest climate and a tropical wet/dry climate differ?

4. *Describing* What resources are important Brazilian exports?

5. *Informative/Explanatory Writing* In which of Brazil's physical regions would you most like to live? Write a paragraph to explain why.

Chapter 8 **247**

R Reading Skills

Summarizing Have students work with a partner to summarize the information about Brazil's major crops. Remind students that summaries should include the main ideas of a text stated in as few words as possible. Have partners share their summaries with others, and then keep their summaries to review at the end of the chapter. **Ask:** How are some of Brazil's products important to you? *(Students' answers will vary but should include relevant details about how they personally use products produced in Brazil.)* **Interpersonal, Verbal/Linguistic**

T Technology Skills

Using Visual Aids Have students work in small groups to create an accurate visual representation of the information about Brazil's major crops using presentation software. **Visual/Spatial, Interpersonal**

Making Connections Have students think about the ways they may use some of Brazil's crops, such as sugar and corn. Then explain that many crops are used for purposes other than eating. Read the following information to students:

- Ethyl alcohol is a chemical compound used in important industries, such as an additive to gasoline for cars and trucks.
- Ethyl alcohol is produced by fermenting raw sugar and corn.
- In 2011, the high price of sugar caused Brazilian President Dilma Rousseff to order the reduction of ethanol levels in Brazilian gasoline.

CLOSE & REFLECT

Comparing and Contrasting To close this lesson, have students think about the geographical features of Brazil that make the country unique. Ask them to think about how these features are similar to and different from the geography where they live. Have students share information that they did not know about Brazil before reading this lesson. **AL Verbal/Linguistic**

LESSON 1 REVIEW ANSWERS

Reviewing Vocabulary

1. They make most of Brazil warm, humid, and wet most of the year.

Answering the Guiding Questions

2. **Determining Central Ideas** It covers almost half of Brazil and contains the world's largest rain forest, which is the world's richest biological resource. The rain forest is home to several million kinds of plants, insects, birds, and other animals.

3. **Analyzing** Tropical rain forest climates get heavy rain year-round. Tropical wet/dry climates have rainy summers and dry winters.

4. **Describing** mahogany and other hardwoods; mineral resources such as iron ore, tin, copper, manganese, bauxite, and gold; food resources such as coffee, cassava, soybeans, oranges, and beef

5. **Informative/Explanatory Writing** Students should state an opinion of where in Brazil they would like to live and back up their opinion with facts about the regions of Brazil.

ANSWER, p. 247

☑ **READING PROGRESS CHECK** The eastern Brazilian Highlands and the Atlantic lowlands are Brazil's most important agricultural areas.

History of Brazil

ENGAGE

Bellringer To help students connect to Brazil's history and the formation of its government, guide a class discussion about the United States' system of government. Explain that the United States is a federal republic with a democratic system of government. Remind them that the United States began as a series of colonies governed by the British. **Ask:** When did the United States gain its independence from British rule? (1776) Have students consider how governments in other countries were formed. Tell students that in this lesson they will learn about Brazil's history and path to independence.

TEACH & ASSESS

V Visual Skills

Creating Time Lines Have students use the information on this page to start a pictorial time line of Brazil's history. As students read the lesson, have them add key events to their time lines and use them as a review tool. Visual/Spatial

C Critical Thinking Skills

Determining Cause and Effect Have students read and take notes on the first two paragraphs. **Ask:**

- What was the Treaty of Tordesillas? (The Treaty of Tordesillas divided lands east and west between Spain and Portugal so that neither country could claim all of the land for itself.)
- What year did the Treaty of Tordesillas go into effect? (It was signed in 1494.)
- What caused Brazil to have a unique cultural heritage? (After the Treaty of Tordesillas went into effect, the eastern part of South America, where Brazil is, became Portuguese territory. This is why Brazil is the only South American country that has a Portuguese heritage.) Interpersonal

R Reading Skills

Determining Word Meanings Point to the word indigenous. Ask a volunteer to tell the meaning of the word, using context clues (native). Explain that the term can apply to people as well as plants and animals. **AL** Verbal/Linguistic

---

ANSWER, p. 248

Taking Notes Notes should include main events from Brazil's history, such as: Portugal's government moves to Brazil; Portugal's king returns home; Brazil declares independence and becomes a kingdom; king is overthrown and Brazil becomes a republic; Vargas seizes power from "coffee presidents" and becomes dictator; military overthrows Vargas and takes power; civilian rule returns and Brazil becomes a true democracy.

There's More Online!

☑ **MAP** Colonization of Brazil

☑ **SLIDE SHOW** Brazil's Natural Products

☑ **VIDEO**

Reading **HELPDESK**

Academic Vocabulary
- **comprise**
- **extract**

Content Vocabulary
- **indigenous**
- **slash-and-burn agriculture**
- **emancipate**
- **compulsory**

TAKING NOTES: *Key Idea and Details*

Sequencing As you read about Brazil's history, use the graphic organizer below to note how Brazil became a modern democratic republic.

Portugal's government moves to Brazil.

↓

↓

Indiana Academic Standards
6.1.6, 6.1.10, 6.2.7, 6.4.1

248

14.1%

Lesson 2

History of Brazil

ESSENTIAL QUESTION • *How do governments change?*

IT MATTERS BECAUSE
Brazil is one of the world's leading industrial powers.

Early History

GUIDING QUESTION *How did Brazil's early peoples live?*

In 1493 Christopher Columbus returned to Spain with news of his explorations and of new lands. The Spanish worried that neighboring Portugal, a powerful seafaring rival, would try to claim these lands for itself. So they asked the pope to find a solution. The pope decided that all new lands west of a certain line should belong to Spain. Lands east of the line would belong to Portugal. The two countries agreed to this division in 1494 by signing the Treaty of Tordesillas.

Almost nothing was known of the region's geography, so neither side realized how unequal the division was. Almost all of the Americas lay west of the line, which became Spanish territory. The only exception was the eastern part of South America, which became Portuguese territory. Today, this part of South America is Brazil. That is why Brazil is the only South American country that has a Portuguese heritage.

Indigenous Populations

The first Portuguese ships stopped in Brazil in 1500. Their destination was India, so they did not stay in Brazil for long. They had peaceful encounters with some of the **indigenous**, or native, peoples who lived along the coast. The Portuguese commander, Pedro Cabral, claimed the land for Portugal. After just 10 days, the Portuguese left. They had no idea of the vast region and many peoples included in Cabral's claim.

(l to r) Mike Goldwater/Alamy; Diego Frichs Antonello/Getty Images; Eraldo Peres/AP Images

---

netw✺rks   *Online Teaching Options*

VIDEO

Brazil Fights Deforestation

Formulating Questions Use this video to introduce the lesson. Ask students to write three questions they have about Brazil's history of deforestation after watching the video. Collect the questions and set them aside. Then after completing the lesson, discuss and answer the questions as a class. **ELL** Verbal/Linguistic

See page 237D for other online activities.

BBC Motion Gallery Education

The people the Portuguese met were the Tupi. They lived along the coast and in the rain forests south of the Amazon River, where they grew cassava, corn, sweet potatoes, beans, and peanuts. They hunted fish and other water animals with arrows and harpoons from large log canoes, but they did little hunting on land.

Brazil's native peoples had lived there for more than 10,000 years when the Portuguese arrived. Estimates are that the population was between 2 million and 6 million by 1500. Besides the Tupi, it included the Arawak and Carib people of the northern Amazon and coast, and the Nambicuara in the drier grasslands and highlands. These are not the names of native peoples; they were Brazil's four main language groups. Each group **comprised** many different peoples.

Daily Life

Like the Tupi, Brazil's other lowland and rain forest peoples were mainly farmers. They lived in permanent, self-governing villages and practiced **slash-and-burn agriculture**. This is a method of farming in forests that involves cutting down trees and burning away underbrush to create fields for growing crops. Farther south, most of the Nambicuara of the Brazilian Highlands were nomads, people who move from place to place and have no permanent home. In the dry season, they lived as hunter-gatherers, people who get their food by hunting, fishing, and collecting seeds, roots, and other parts of trees and wild plants. In the wet season, they built temporary villages and practiced slash-and-burn agriculture.

Europeans Arrive

For more than 30 years after Cabral's visit, the Portuguese did not pay much attention to Brazil. Their main focus was on their colonies and trade in Asia. Their trading ships sailed south and east around Africa on their way to Asia. Portuguese sailors established a few trading posts along Brazil's coast and collected brazilwood. The red dye **extracted** from this wood was highly valued in Europe. It was because of this trade that the Portuguese named the region Brazil.

Mike Goldwater/Alamy

Academic Vocabulary

comprise to be made up of

extract to remove or take out

An Ashaninka family fishes from a boat in Brazil's Amazon rain forest.
▶ CRITICAL THINKING
Describing How did indigenous peoples make a living when the first Europeans arrived in Brazil?

Chapter 8 **249**

Elena Kalistratova/Vetta/Getty Images

PHOTO

Contributions of Indigenous People

Creating Charts Use the interactive photo to help students make connections between indigenous people and later cultural and economic development. Have students use information from the text and the photo to create a flow chart that shows how indigenous peoples affected trade. *(Charts should show that as hunter-gatherers, indigenous peoples cultivated plants later used in the Columbian Exchange.)* Visual/Spatial, Logical/Mathematical

See page 237D for other online activities.

Interactive Photos

This region has many diverse types of landscapes. Land forms range from mountains to grasslands. Waterways include rivers, lakes, and shorelines. Vegetation varies depending on the soil quality and access to water within the specific area. Animal life has adapted to take advantage of what the region has to offer.

T Technology Skills

Making Presentations Have students work in small groups to research other parts of the world that have used slash-and-burn agriculture. Students should present a report based on their findings that answers the following questions:

• What parts of the world have used slash-and-burn agriculture?
• What are the effects on the environment?
• How does slash-and-burn agriculture work?

Students' presentations should include diagrams and maps, a concluding statement, and a list of sources used to support their findings. **BL** Interpersonal, Verbal/Linguistic

W Writing Skills

Narrative Have students use the information about daily life and the arrival of Europeans in Brazil to write a short skit depicting a scene that might have taken place during this time. After students write their skits, allow time for small groups to rehearse and present the skits. **Ask:**

• What was an important part of daily life in Brazil? *(trade)*
• What was an important natural resource for Portuguese sailors? *(brazilwood, a valuable material to Europeans)* Kinesthetic, Verbal/Linguistic

Content Background Knowledge

Share the following information with students to provide context for understanding some of the founding cities in Brazil:

• In January 1502, Portuguese explorers came upon the large bay in Rio de Janeiro. Thinking it was a river, they named it River of January, or Rio de Janeiro. Though the city was later renamed in 1565 for the Portuguese king, the name Rio de Janeiro has lasted through the centuries.
• The city of São Paulo got its name from Jesuit missionaries in 1554 who named the city for St. Paul on the anniversary of his conversion.
• Though the idea for building an inland capital city was posed back in 1789, Brazil's current capital of Brasília was not selected until 1956. In 1960, the federal government relocated from the former capital city, Rio de Janeiro.

ANSWER, p. 249

CRITICAL THINKING Indigenous people grew various crops, such as cassava and beans, and hunted fish and water animals with arrows and harpoons from log canoes.

History of Brazil

C1 Critical Thinking Skills

Determining Cause and Effect Have students work with a partner to read the first paragraph. Have partners create a cause and effect diagram that shows the events involving trade and settlement of Brazil that are described in the paragraph. **Ask:**

• What caused Europeans to become more interested in Brazil? *(valuable brazilwood)*

• What did King John III do as a result of French traders coming into the region to collect brazilwood? *(He set up a permanent colony and government in Brazil.)*

• Why did King John III establish a permanent colony and government in Brazil? *(to bring the region under tighter Portuguese control, and to try to keep the French and other Europeans out of the region)* **Visual/Spatial**

C2 Critical Thinking Skills

Making Inferences Discuss with students that this page focuses on the time during which the Portuguese ruled Brazil, which began in 1533 and lasted more than 300 years. Have students think about the United States and compare the time frame described for Brazil to the time when the United States was colonized and then became an independent country. Then note that in the United States Native American groups are considered its indigenous people. **Ask:**

• What problems do you think might have occurred for Brazil's indigenous people? *(Answers will vary but students may say that Indigenous people likely felt threatened by Portuguese explorers. Their way of life probably changed dramatically after the development of Portuguese settlements. They may have caught diseases from the explorers.)*

• What sort of issues might have arisen for Portuguese explorers? *(Answers will vary but students may say that Portuguese explorers were probably unfamiliar with the new land, climate, and people. Their demands for expansion and colonization were probably met with resistance from indigenous people.)* **Verbal/Linguistic**

ANSWERS, p. 250

CRITICAL THINKING The Jesuits built mission villages to convert indigenous people to Christianity and to protect them from slavery imposed by European slave hunters.

✓ **READING PROGRESS CHECK** The brazilwood that Portuguese traders collected was valued in Europe. When the French threatened to compete for this trade, Portugal's king decided to bring Brazil under better control by founding a permanent colony.

The church of São Miguel das Missões was built about 1740 as the center of a Jesuit mission village in southern Brazil.
▶ **CRITICAL THINKING** **C1**
Explaining Why did the Jesuits build mission villages in Brazil and other parts of South America?

Diego Frichs Antonello/Getty Images

The valuable brazilwood trade made other Europeans more interested in Brazil. French traders began collecting the wood and shipping it to France. To bring Brazil under tighter Portuguese control, Portugal's King John III established a permanent colony and government there. The first Portuguese settlers arrived in 1533.

✓ **READING PROGRESS CHECK**
Determining Central Ideas Why did the Portuguese colonize Brazil?

Colonial Rule

GUIDING QUESTION *How did the Portuguese colony in Brazil develop?*

Portugal's rule of Brazil lasted more than 300 years. During that time, Portuguese settlements spread all along the coast. Explorers and others traveled up rivers and deep into Brazil's interior. The expansion brought wealth to Portugal, though much of it came at great cost to Brazil's indigenous peoples.

C2 The Portuguese Conquest
King John III gave wealthy supporters huge tracts of land in Brazil. These tracts extended west from the coast about 150 miles (241 km) inland. In return, the people who received a land grant were responsible for developing it. They founded cities and gave land to colonists to farm.

250 Chapter 8

---

networks   *Online Teaching Options*

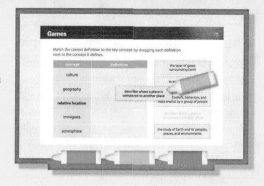

Because the colonists could not do all the work that was required, they soon began enslaving nearby native peoples as laborers. Many of them resisted and were killed. Thousands more died from exposure to European diseases to which they had no natural resistance. Others fled into Brazil's interior. These conditions and other complaints caused King John to end the land-grant system in 1549. He put Brazil under royal control and sent a governor from Portugal to rule the colony.

Spread of Christianity

The new governor brought more colonists with him. They included a number of Jesuit Catholic priests who belonged to a missionary group called the Society of Jesus. The king asked the Jesuits to go to Brazil to help the native peoples and convert them to Christianity. Those who converted were settled in special Jesuit villages and were protected from slavery.

Those Portuguese colonists who held enslaved people complained to the king about the Jesuits' work. In 1574 he ruled that native peoples who did not live in Jesuit villages could be enslaved only if they were captured in war. This ruling sent Jesuits into Brazil's interior to protect and convert peoples there. Slave hunters also moved into the interior to attack and enslave the native peoples. Cattlemen and prospectors followed, slowly spreading development inland.

Sugar and Gold

As Brazil's sugar industry expanded, cattlemen needed new land. The rise of large sugarcane plantations, mainly in the northeast, pushed ranching westward.

Plantation workers carry sugarcane into a Brazilian mill, 1845.
▶ **CRITICAL THINKING**
Identifying Besides sugarcane, what else did large plantations grow?

Hulton Archive/Getty Images

Chapter 8 **251**

R Reading Skills

Identifying Tell students that identifying signal words can help them understand cause-and-effect relationships in a text. Explain that words and phrases such as *because, so, therefore, since,* and *as a result* usually show cause or effect. Have students identify cause-and-effect signal words in the first paragraph. *(Because, caused)*

Then have students answer the following question using a signal word. **Ask:** What happened to indigenous people after European colonists came to Brazil? *(As a result of colonists' arrival in Brazil, many indigenous people were forced to become slaves, were killed, or died from European diseases.)* Encourage students to find other signal words as they read to help them better understand the text. **AL** Verbal/Linguistic

C Critical Thinking Skills

Drawing Conclusions Have students read the information about the spread of Christianity by Jesuit Catholic priests sent from Portugal to Brazil. As a class, discuss the king's role in spreading Christianity and later his role in spreading development inland. *(The king asked the Jesuits to go to Brazil to convert the indigenous people to Christianity. Later the king's ruling pushed slave hunters into Brazil's interior to find indigenous people to enslave, which brought about inland development.)* **Ask:** What were the pros and cons for indigenous people who converted to Christianity? *(Pro: they were protected from slavery. Con: they were forced to adopt religious beliefs that may have differed from their own.)* **ELL** Verbal/Linguistic

T Technology Skills

Researching on the Internet Have students work in small groups to conduct online research about either the sugar industry or the cattle industry in Brazil and how their chosen industry has affected the development of the region. Tell students they can choose how to present the information they find, possibly in a chart, time line, or written report. Remind students to assess the credibility and accuracy of online sources. Interpersonal, Visual/Spatial

WORKSHEET

Primary Sources: Jesuit Missionaries' View of Slavery

Making Connections Have students use this primary source worksheet to learn more about the connections between Jesuit missionaries and slavery. Then encourage students to write essays and have students explain what missionaries did to protect people from slavery or to stop it. After students have written their essays, ask volunteers to read their essays to the class. **BL**

See page 237D for other online activities.

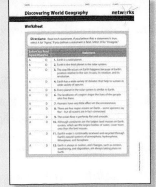

ANSWER, p. 251

CRITICAL THINKING cotton and coffee

History of Brazil

R Reading Skills

Paraphrasing Help students paraphrase the information contained in the text and on the map. Explain that restating information in your own words shows that you understand it and helps you to remember it.

Model how to paraphrase the first sentence. Then have partners take turns paraphrasing the remaining sentences in the paragraph. Encourage students to pair up and use the skill of paraphrasing whenever they have read a section of the text that is confusing or contains a lot of information. **AL** Verbal/Linguistic

V Visual Skills

Creating Visuals Help students interpret the information presented so far in this lesson to create a class time line. Have students skim the text looking for dates and use the dates on the map that tell when the cities shown were settled. Have volunteers come up to the board and draw a visual representation of the information in sequential order. Start the time line with the date 1493 and end it with 1820. Have students copy the time line in their notebooks. As a class, discuss any questions or concerns that arise as students copy the time line. **Ask:**

• What could be the title of this time line? *(Possible answers might include "Sugar and Gold," "Enslaved Workers," "Brazil: 1493 to 1820")*

• What does the red line stand for on the map, and why is this date and event important to include on the time line? *(The red line represents the division line between Spain and Portugal. The date, 1494, and the event, the Treaty of Tordesillas, are important to include on the time line because this division line gave Spain the rights to almost all of the Americas.)*

• What happened in the 1720s that added to the population boom of Brazil? *(the discovery of diamonds in the region)*

Once the class time line is complete, provide guidance to students as they answer the "Map Skills" questions. Visual/Spatial

---

In the 1600s, sugar became Brazil's main export and Portugal's greatest source of wealth. Coffee and cotton plantations also developed. The discovery of gold in the eastern highlands in the 1690s further boosted the development of the interior. Towns sprang up as thousands of colonists rushed to the area. Large numbers of new colonists arrived from Europe, as well. The discovery of diamonds in the region in the 1720s added to the population boom.

Plantation agriculture and mining required large numbers of workers. This increased the need for enslaved workers. When native populations could not fill the need, the Portuguese began importing large numbers of enslaved Africans. By the 1780s, more than 150,000 enslaved Africans worked in the mining districts. This was twice the size of the Portuguese population. By 1820, some 1.1 million enslaved people accounted for nearly one-third of Brazil's total population.

☑ **READING PROGRESS CHECK**

Determining Central Ideas Why did King John III send Jesuits to Brazil?

MAP SKILLS

1 **PLACES AND REGIONS** Where did the Portuguese settle in South America?

2 **HUMAN GEOGRAPHY** Why was the division of South America between Spain and Portugal so unequal?

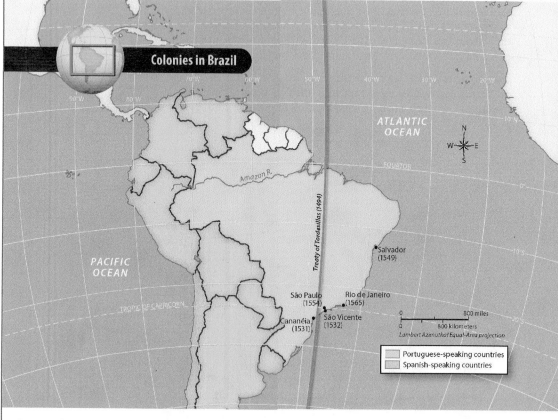

Colonies in Brazil

---

net**w**rks *Online Teaching Options*

MAP

The Colonization of Brazil

Analyzing Visuals Use the colonization map, focusing on Brazil, and discuss with students the information contained on the map. Point out features showing how Brazil's colonization compares to nations that border it. Be sure students understand how and why Brazil was colonized. Have students then discuss the independence of Brazil in relation to its surrounding countries. Visual/Spatial

See page 237D for other online activities.

ANSWERS, p. 252

☑ **READING PROGRESS CHECK** to convert Brazil's indigenous people to Christianity and protect them from enslavement

MAP SKILLS

1. The Portuguese settled coastal areas in the eastern part of South America that bordered the Atlantic Ocean.

2. When the treaty marking the division was signed, Europeans knew little of the region's geography and so were unaware how unequal the division was.

GRAPH SKILLS >

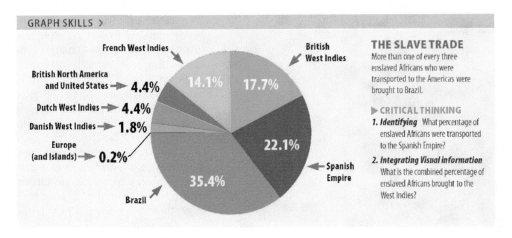

French West Indies
British North America and United States → **4.4%**
Dutch West Indies → **4.4%**
Danish West Indies → **1.8%**
Europe (and Islands) → **0.2%**
Brazil **35.4%**
British West Indies
14.1% **17.7%**
22.1%
Spanish Empire

THE SLAVE TRADE
More than one of every three enslaved Africans who were transported to the Americas were brought to Brazil.

▶ **CRITICAL THINKING**
1. *Identifying* What percentage of enslaved Africans were transported to the Spanish Empire?
2. *Integrating Visual information* What is the combined percentage of enslaved Africans brought to the West Indies?

Independent Brazil

GUIDING QUESTION *How did Brazil gain independence and become a democracy?*

Brazil gained independence from Portugal in an unusual way. It came gradually, fairly easily, and with little bloodshed. It was also the indirect result of the actions of the French emperor Napoleon Bonaparte. **W**

Independence and Monarchy

In 1805, Britain joined by its allies Russia, Austria and Sweden, went to war with France to crush Napoleon. Instead, Napoleon defeated them and conquered much of Europe. In 1807 Napoleon invaded Portugal. As the French army closed in on Portugal's capital city of Lisbon, ruler Dom João, the royal family, and other government leaders fled to Brazil. Rio de Janeiro became the new capital of the Portuguese Empire. Brazil's status within the empire changed from a colony to a kingdom. This action gave Brazil equal status with Portugal within the empire. **R**

After Napoleon was defeated, the Portuguese people wanted their king back. In 1821 Dom João and the rest of the government returned to Portugal. He left his son Pedro to rule Brazil. In 1822 Portugal's legislature restored Brazil's status as a colony and ordered Pedro to return. Pedro refused to give up the Brazilian throne. He declared independence and crowned himself Emperor Pedro I. Most other independent American nations became republics, but independent Brazil became a constitutional monarchy. In this form of government, a king, a queen, or an emperor acts as head of state. **C**

Most Brazilians had supported independence from Portugal, but they soon tired of Pedro's harsh rule. In 1831 he was forced to turn over the throne to his five-year-old son.

Chapter 8 **253**

CHART

Emancipation in Brazil

Analyzing Charts Use the interactive chart to elaborate on the slave trade in Brazil. Have students use information in the text about emancipation and the chart information to compare the history of the slave trade in Brazil and other parts of the world. Visual/Spatial

See page 237D for other online activities.

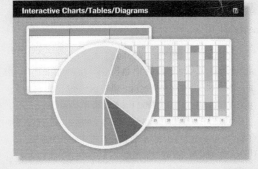

Interactive Charts/Tables/Diagrams

W Writing Skills

Think-Pair-Share In a think-pair-share activity, have students write a list of words that come to mind when they think of the term *independence*. First discuss the term as a class and have students write the definition. Then have students make their lists and have pairs share their lists of words.

Next compare the concept of independence with dependence. **Ask:** What does it mean to depend on someone or something? *(It means to rely on or need someone or something.)* Have students write two or three sentences about the difference between being independent or dependent upon someone or something. As a class, discuss how and why some countries' governments change from being dependent to independent. **AL** Verbal/Linguistic

R Reading Skills

Organizing Have students work with a partner to generate quiz questions using the information in the first paragraph under "Independence and Monarchy." Have students create flashcards with their questions on one side and answers on the other side. Have small groups of students take turns asking and answering their questions to help them better understand the text. Verbal/Linguistic

C Critical Thinking Skills

Comparing and Contrasting Guide a class discussion about the difference between a republic and a constitutional monarchy. Remind students that the United States is a federal republic with a democratic form of government. Then discuss Brazil's change from a colony to a kingdom. **Ask:**

- Why did the people of Brazil like having King Dom João living there when Napoleon took over Portugal? *(Having a king allowed Brazil to have equal status with Portugal)*
- Why did the Portuguese people want King Dom João to return after Napolean was defeated? *(Their country needed its leader in Europe, not in South America.)*
- Why did Brazil remain a monarchy after King Dom João returned to Portugal? *(His son Pedro was ruling Brazil.)* Verbal/Linguistic

ANSWER, p. 253

CRITICAL THINKING
1. 22.1 percent
2. 38 percent

C Critical Thinking Skills

Identifying Points of View After students read the first three paragraphs on this page, have them consider the differing viewpoints people had about slavery and emancipation in Brazil in the 1850s. **Ask:**

• What did plantation owners think about emancipation? *(They were angry because emancipation caused them to lose their enslaved workers.)*

• How did Pedro II feel about slavery? *(He opposed it.)*

• Once Pedro II gradually ended slavery, who do you think should have been the first group of freed slaves? *(Students' answers will vary, but should include a specific group of people and clear reasoning to support their answer.)* Verbal/Linguistic, Intrapersonal

V Visual Skills

Diagramming Help students put Brazil's quest for independence into context by reminding them that the United States declared independence from British rule in 1776.
Ask: Why do you think Brazil used the United States Constitution on which to model its own government? *(Just as the United States sought and gained independence from British rule, Brazil sought independence from Portugal.)*

In pairs, have students use the information in the first two paragraphs of the section "The Brazilian Republic" to create a Venn diagram comparing and contrasting Brazil's constitution with the Constitution of the United States. Partners may wish to conduct research using the Internet to find more information about the two governments and their constitutions to include in their Venn diagrams. Remind students to use reliable online sources. **BL** Visual/Spatial

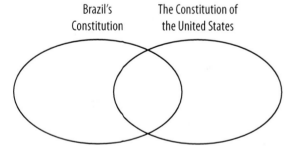

Brazil's Constitution   The Constitution of the United States

---

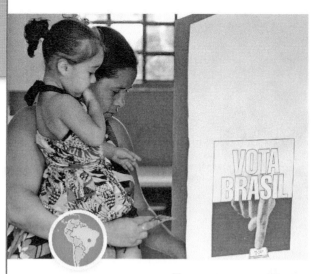

As in the United States, voters in Brazil elect a president every four years.
▶ CRITICAL THINKING **C**
Identifying Which group controlled the election of Brazil's president in the early republic?

A series of advisers ruled in the boy's name until he was old enough to rule on his own. In 1840, at age 14, he became Emperor Pedro II.

Pedro II ruled Brazil for nearly 50 years. His reign was marked by great progress. Brazil's population grew from 4 million to 14 million during his rule. He offered land to attract large numbers of Germans, Italians, and other European immigrants to Brazil. Sugar, coffee, and cotton production rose. Brazil's first railroads were built to get these and other products to the coast for export.

In 1850 Brazil stopped importing enslaved people from Africa. In the 1860s, a new movement began to **emancipate**, or free, the enslaved. Pedro II opposed slavery, but he thought it should be ended gradually. An 1871 law granted freedom to all children born to people in slavery. An 1885 law freed enslaved people who were over age 60. Finally, in 1888, all remaining enslaved people were freed.

The Brazilian Republic

Brazil's powerful plantation owners were angered by the loss of their enslaved workers. In 1889 they supported Brazil's army in overthrowing Pedro II. A new government was established, with a constitution based on the Constitution of the United States. Brazil became a republic, a system in which the head of state is an elected ruler instead of a king, a queen, or an emperor. In this republic, the right to vote was limited to wealthy property owners. In 1910, for example, out of a population of 22 million, only 627,000 people could vote.

Most of the power in the early republic was held by the governors of Brazil's southeastern states. Governors were elected by their state's wealthy voters. State governors controlled the election of Brazil's president, who usually came from the highly populated, coffee-rich states of São Paulo and Minas Gerais (General Mines).

These presidents followed economic policies that benefited southeastern Brazil. Coffee became Brazil's main export. By 1902, Brazil was supplying 65 percent of the world's coffee. São Paulo, Minas Gerais, and Rio de Janeiro also became the country's industrial and commercial centers. Over time, some people became unhappy with government policies that continued to favor the coffee growers and other rich Brazilians. In 1930 Getúlio Vargas overthrew the newly elected "coffee president" and seized power. He ruled for the

---

net works *Online Teaching Options*

Suffragists in Brazil

Sequencing Use the lecture slide presentation to help students sequence key events in Brazil's changes in government. Display the lecture slide presentation as a review tool after completing the lesson to help students understand the chronology of events. Point out the specific changes from monarchy, to dictatorship, to democracy.
ELL Visual/Spatial

See page 237D for other online activities.

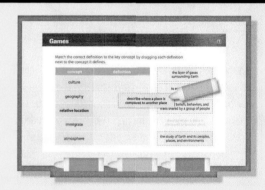

ANSWER, p. 254

CRITICAL THINKING State governors, elected by wealthy voters, controlled the election of Brazil's president during the early republic.

next 15 years. Vargas's reforms made him a hero to most Brazilians. He raised wages, shortened work hours, and let workers form labor unions. Yet for much of his rule, Vargas governed as a dictator. He dissolved the legislature and banned political parties. In 1945 military leaders forced Vargas to resign.

Brazil Under Military Rule

Vargas was elected president again in 1950, but again was forced from office by the military in 1954. For over 30 years, government in Brazil alternated between dictators and elected leaders. Manufacturing thrived throughout this period. Foreign investments brought rapid growth in the steel, auto, and chemical industries.

Industrial growth was accompanied by changes and unrest in Brazilian society. As a result, the military took control of Brazil in 1964, and a series of generals became the heads of government. An elected legislature was allowed, but the army controlled the elections. People who opposed the government were arrested. Many others were frightened into silence. The military gave up power in 1985 and allowed the election of a civilian president.

Modern Brazil

Today Brazil is a democratic republic in which people elect a president and other leaders. In Brazil, voting is **compulsory**. This means that citizens have no choice in deciding whether or not to vote. People from ages 18 to 70 are required by law to vote.

Because Brazil has a high number of well-supported political parties, coalition governments are common. A coalition government is one in which several political parties cooperate to do the work of government. In 2003 a democratically elected president replaced another democratically elected president for the first time in more than 40 years. In 2010 voters elected Dilma Vana Rousseff as the thirty-sixth president of Brazil. She is the first woman president in the country's history.

Include this lesson's information in your Foldable®.

☑ **READING PROGRESS CHECK**

Identifying Central Ideas Why did Brazil's monarchy come to an end?

LESSON 2 REVIEW

Reviewing Vocabulary
1. What kind of agriculture did some *indigenous* farmers practice?

Answering the Guiding Questions
2. *Analyzing* How were the Nambicuara similar to and different from the other main indigenous peoples of early Brazil?

3. *Identifying* Why did African slavery increase in Brazil before it was abolished completely in 1888?

4. *Describing* What were the main steps in Brazil's transition from a colony to a democratic country?

5. *Argument Writing* Take the role of a Brazilian living in 1889. Write a letter to the editor of your local newspaper supporting or opposing the establishment of the republic. Be sure to state the reasons for your opinion.

LESSON 2 REVIEW ANSWERS

Reviewing Vocabulary

1. Brazil's lowland and rain forest people practiced slash-and-burn agriculture.

Answering the Guiding Questions

2. **Analyzing** They were similar to other groups in that they practiced slash-and-burn agriculture. They were different in that they lived in the highlands instead of the rain forests and were nomads and hunter-gatherers who lived in villages for only part of the year.

3. **Identifying** The growth of sugar plantations and mining created a need for more slave labor. When enslaved indigenous people were not enough, more slaves were imported from Africa.

4. **Describing** From 1807 to 1821, Portugal's monarch ruled the empire from Brazil. After he returned to Portugal, Brazil declared its independence. His son and grandson ruled Brazil from 1822 to 1889. In 1889 the monarchy was overthrown and Brazil became a republic governed by elected leaders. In 1930 Getúlio Vargas overthrew the elected president and ruled as dictator until he was overthrown in 1945. Elected presidents governed again until 1964, when the military took control. Civilian rule returned in 1985 and continues today.

5. **Argument Writing** Letters should show the reasons for the emperor's overthrow and the formation of the republic and state a position that is appropriate for the role they have taken.

W Writing Skills

Informative Have students use the information in the text about Getúlio Vargas to write an informative essay about his rule. Students may wish to conduct online research to enhance their essays. Have students exchange papers with a partner and conduct a brief peer review session in which students critique each other's papers. Tell students to note factual errors as well as grammatical or stylistic ones. Encourage them to give positive comments as well as constructive criticism. Allow time for students to correct and revise their essays based on their partner's comments. **Verbal/Linguistic**

C Critical Thinking Skills

Making Generalizations After students read the fourth paragraph, have them consider how industrial growth has affected the people of Brazil. **Ask:** What are some positive and negative effects of industrial growth that have had an impact on Brazilian society? *(Answers may vary but students should conclude both kinds of effects. Positive: economic stability and growth; negative: pollution, overcrowding)* **Logical/Mathematical**

T Technology Skills

Analyzing News Media Have students work in small groups to conduct online research about Dilma Vana Rousseff. Tell students they will make a brief presentation about her policies and how she is perceived by Brazilians. Remind students that as they gather information, they should assess the credibility and accuracy of online sources, especially news media. Tell students to consider the source when choosing whether to quote it for their presentation. **Interpersonal, Verbal/Linguistic**

CLOSE & REFLECT

To close the lesson, guide a class discussion about how Brazil's history is similar to and different from that of the United States. Have students discuss any new or surprising information they learned about Brazil's history.

ANSWER, p. 255

☑ **READING PROGRESS CHECK** Plantation owners were upset over the freeing of the enslaved workers and supported the army in overthrowing the emperor.

ENGAGE

Bellringer Have students look at the images on the top of this page. Guide a class discussion about what students think daily life is like in Brazil based on these images. **Ask:** What similarities do you notice between Brazil and the United States based on these images? *(Students may note that Brazil shares similar recreation and sporting activities; both have modern cities.)* Tell students that they will learn more about Brazil's culture and daily life in this lesson.

TEACH & ASSESS

C₁ Critical Thinking Skills

Predicting Consequences Discuss Brazil's size and population with the class. Then have them recall how a large population can cause problems for a country and make predictions. **Ask:** What sort of issues might result for Brazil from having such a large population? *(overcrowding in cities, poverty, pollution)* Verbal/Linguistic

R Reading Skills

Determining Word Meanings Point to the word *diverse*. Have a volunteer read the definition of the word. **Ask:** What makes Brazil's population diverse? *(Brazil's population is made up of people of different ancestry.)* Encourage students to find opportunities to use the word *diverse* throughout the day. Remind students to add content and academic vocabulary words to the vocabulary lists in their notebooks. Verbal/Linguistic

C₂ Critical Thinking Skills

Analyzing Have students calculate how many Brazilians have mixed racial ancestry. **Ask:** What is 40 percent of Brazil's current population of 200 million people? How many people in Brazil have mixed racial ancestry? *(80 million people)* Logical/Mathematical

---

ANSWER, p. 256

Taking Notes Notes should include at least one fact from each section, such as: **Population:** almost 200 million people; world's fifth largest country in population; **Culture:** More than half of Brazilians have European origins and nearly 40 percent have a mixed racial ancestry; Brazil's African heritage has had major influences on Brazilian culture; **Challenges:** efforts to settle and develop Brazil's sparsely-populated interior threaten the world's largest rain forest.

---

networks

There's More Online!

☑ **IMAGE** Rio de Janeiro
☑ **SLIDE SHOW** Brazilian Culture
☑ **VIDEO**

Reading HELPDESK

Academic Vocabulary
- **diverse**
- **unique**

Content Vocabulary
- **hinterland**
- **metropolitan area**
- **central city**
- **favela**

TAKING NOTES: *Key Ideas and Details*

Organize As you read the lesson, use the graphic organizer below to organize information about Brazil by adding one or more facts to each box.

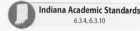

Modern Brazil

Population — Culture

Challenges

Indiana Academic Standards
6.3.4, 6.3.10

256

Lesson 3
Life in Brazil

ESSENTIAL QUESTION • *What makes a culture unique?*

IT MATTERS BECAUSE
Brazil's cultures have influenced many people around the world.

People and Places

GUIDING QUESTION *What cultures are represented by Brazilians?*

With some 200 million people, Brazil is the world's fifth-largest country in population. Only China, India, the United States, and Indonesia are home to more people. About half of all South Americans live in Brazil.

Brazil's Diverse Population

Brazil is a mix of several cultures. Many people have a combination of European, African, and native American ancestry. Many are of Portuguese origin or immigrants from Germany and Italy. To a lesser degree, people came from Russia, Poland, and Ukraine. São Paulo, in particular, has a **diverse** population, including a large Japanese community.

Nearly 40 percent of Brazilians have mixed ancestry. This is largely because marriages between people of different ethnic groups have been more acceptable in Brazil than in many other countries. The largest group of multiethnic Brazilians are persons with European and African ancestors. People of European and Native American ancestry are a smaller group.

The smallest multiethnic group is persons of African and Native American descent. About 4 million Africans had been enslaved and brought to Brazil by the 1800s. Many escaped into the **hinterland**, the often remote inland regions, far from the coasts. The Africans lived there with the indigenous Native Americans or formed their own farming communities.

(l to r) Stuart Dee/Photographer's Choice RF/Getty Images; Felipe Borges/Flickr/Getty Images; Buda Mendes/LatinContent WO/Getty Images; EVARISTO SA/AFP/Getty Images; ©Paulo Fridman/Sygma/Corbis

---

networks *Online Teaching Options*

VIDEO

Brazil's Economic Boom

Analyzing Visuals Use this video about the thriving economy of Brazil to introduce the lesson. Have students write a brochure for a Brazilian tourism bureau highlighting features seen in the video that might appeal to visitors or people moving there for work. After students complete the lesson, have them revise their brochures to include more specific information about where tourists and new immigrants should visit. Verbal/Linguistic

See page 237E for other online activities.

BBC Motion Gallery Education

Today, about 80 percent of Brazilians live within 200 miles (322 km) of the Atlantic coast. After slavery ended, many formerly enslaved people left their homes and settled in other agricultural areas or towns. The northeast, however, still has Brazil's highest African and mixed populations. They also form the major population groups in coastal cities and towns north of Rio de Janeiro.

Most Brazilians of European descent live in southern Brazil. Indigenous Native Americans live in all parts of the country. The Amazon rain forest holds the greatest number, but about half of Brazil's Native Americans now live in cities.

Crowded Cities

For most of Brazil's history, the majority of Brazilians lived in rural areas, mainly on plantations, on farms, or in small towns. In the 1950s, millions of people began migrating to cities to take jobs in Brazil's growing industries. By 1970, more Brazilians lived in urban areas than in rural ones. Today, 89 percent of Brazilians live in and around cities.

São Paulo, Brazil's industrial center, is one of the world's largest cities. Some 17 million people live in its **metropolitan area**, or the city and built-up areas around the central city. The **central city** is the largest or most important city in a metropolitan area. São Paulo and Brazil's other large cities look much like cities in the United States. Skyscrapers line busy downtown streets. Cars and trucks jam highways in the mornings and evenings as people travel to and from their jobs. People work in office buildings, shops, and factories. Many own small businesses.

Favelas

Many middle-class urban dwellers live in apartment buildings. Others live in small houses in the suburbs, which are largely residential communities on the outskirts of cities. Wealthy Brazilians live in luxury apartments and mansions.

Most of Brazil's large cities also have shantytowns called **favelas**. Favelas are makeshift communities located on the edges of the cities.

Stuart Dee/Photographer's Choice RF/Getty Images

Academic Vocabulary

diverse differing from one another; varied

C

Sugarloaf Mountain looms above Rio de Janeiro's Copacabana Beach.
▶ CRITICAL THINKING
Explaining What has led to the growth of Brazil's cities since the 1950s?

C Critical Thinking Skills

Theorizing Guide a class discussion about what life was like for former enslaved people in Brazil. **Ask:** Why do you think many former enslaved people left their homes after slavery ended in Brazil? *(Answers will vary. Sample response: They probably wanted to move to areas where they could work on farms to support their families.)* Verbal/Linguistic

T Technology Skills

Researching on the Internet Organize students into three groups and assign each group one of the following topics: *Rural Life, City Life,* or *Favelas.* Have students conduct research using reliable resources on the Internet to find information about their topic.

Tell students to make a presentation with visuals such as copies of photographs and/or their own drawings and present it to the class. Students' presentations should include an explanatory paragraph that describes the culture, education, and way of life for people living in that area. After students make their presentations, discuss what makes the culture unique in each area. Interpersonal, Verbal/Linguistic

Content Background Knowledge

The Yanomami The indigenous people of Brazil are still under threat today from outside people trying to exploit the natural resources of the area in which these people live. For example, the Yanomami are an indigenous people that inhabit rural parts of the Amazon region in Brazil. About 30 years ago in 1987, gold prospectors invaded Yanomami land after gold was discovered there. This influx of people looking for gold brought diseases, pollution, and violence to the region. As a result, the Yanomami population decreased substantially. Today, a small number of Yanomami people still live in remote villages along the northern border that Brazil shares with Venezuela.

Chapter 8 **257**

MAP

Population: Brazil

Analyzing Visuals Use the population layer of the Chapter Opener map to discuss the population of Brazil. Be sure to discuss with students the idea of population density. **Ask:** Where does most of Brazil's population live? *(more Brazilians live in cities)* Have students point out where the major cities are located. Ask students to explain the similarties of these cities and their locations. Visual/Spatial

See page 237E for other online activities.

ANSWER, p. 257

CRITICAL THINKING Millions of people from rural areas have moved to Brazil's cities to find jobs in growing industries. Migrants with few skills and little education have settled in crowded slums called *favelas.*

W Writing Skills

Narrative Have students use information in the text to write a story, poem, or play about a family that lives in the favelas. Students should elaborate on information in the text to create vivid images using descriptive details to write about the members of the family, where the family lives, what the setting looks like, possible activities that the family does on a daily basis, etc.

Encourage students to write about both the positive and negative aspects of living in the favelas, as students may tend to focus on the negatives. If needed, guide students to understand that even though these families are very poor, there are still positive aspects to living with your family; these may include close family bonds, a family living together rather than separated, or frequent communication.

Allow students time to develop and edit their writing. During the editing process, encourage students to add more descriptive details. Call on volunteers to read their narratives to the class. **Ask:** What do you think it is like for families living in favelas? *(Answers will vary but students should mention crowded living conditions, poor housing, and widespread crime and disease.)* Verbal/Linguistic

C Critical Thinking Skills

Problem Solving Tell students they have been elected to serve as a member of Rio de Janeiro's City Council. Have students brainstorm different ways to solve the various issues faced by people living in the favelas. **Ask:** What is a possible solution to combat overcrowding and crime in the favelas? *(Answers will vary. Sample response: the Rio de Janeiro City Council could initiate and implement fundraisers or grants to support low-cost housing in the suburbs; a government program to train residents in community policing might help reduce crime in the favelas.)*

For homework, have students conduct research to identify specific problems in the favelas, and have them write a list of possible solutions to the problems. BL Verbal/Linguistic

The Estaiada Bridge, opened in 2008, is one of São Paulo's landmarks. It is known for its curved appearance and X-shaped tower. **W**

▶ CRITICAL THINKING
Describing What role does São Paulo play in Brazil's economy?

Felipe Borges/Flickr/Getty Images

Favelas arose as millions of poor, rural Brazilians with few skills and little education migrated to cities to seek better lives. These people could not afford houses or apartments. Instead, they settled on land they did not own and built shacks from scraps of wood, sheet metal, cinder blocks, and bricks. Some favelas lack sewers and running water. In many, disease and crime are widespread.

C São Paulo and Rio de Janeiro have the most and largest favelas. Rio has about 1,000 of them. About one of every three of the city's residents live in a favela. Rio officials have tried to deal with this problem by offering favela dwellers low-cost housing in the suburbs. Many do not want to move because the long commute from the suburbs to jobs in the city can take hours.

☑ READING PROGRESS CHECK

Analyzing Why does Brazil have such a large percentage of people with multiethnic ancestry?

258 Chapter 8

net**w**⚙rks   *Online Teaching Options*

IMAGE

360° View: São Paulo, Brazil

Analyzing Images Use a 360-degree photo of São Paulo to discuss geography of this major city including the region, the place, the location, and its growth. Have students write a paragraph about what life might be like in the city based on the photograph. Encourage students to do research on the Internet to find interesting things to do in São Paulo if they were to ever visit there. Visual/Spatial

See page 237E for other online activities.

Interactive Photos

Elena Kalistratova/Vetta/Getty Images

ANSWERS, p. 258

CRITICAL THINKING São Paulo is Brazil's major industrial center.

☑ READING PROGRESS CHECK Marriages between people of different races have been more acceptable in Brazil than in many other countries, and for a longer time.

People and Cultures

GUIDING QUESTION *What is it like to live in Brazil?*

Brazilians get along well for a country whose population includes such a variety of racial and ethnic groups. This is largely due to Brazilians' reputation for accepting other people's differences. Personal warmth, good nature, and "getting along" are valued in Brazilian culture. These attitudes and behaviors are an important part of what is known as the "Brazilian Way."

R

Tensions exist in Brazilian society, but they involve social and economic issues more than ethnic or cultural ones. Ethnicity still plays a factor, though, because Brazilians of European origins have often had better educational opportunities. They hold many of the better jobs as a result.

Ethnic and Language Groups

Until the late 1800s, nearly all European immigrants to Brazil were from Portugal. After slavery ended, large numbers of Italians arrived to work on the coffee plantations.

During the same period, settlers from Germany started farming colonies in southern Brazil. In the early 1900s, the first Japanese arrived to work in agriculture in the Brazilian Highlands. Many of their descendants moved to cities. The first Middle Easterners, mainly Lebanese and Syrians, arrived at about the same time. They became involved in commerce in cities and towns around the country.

V

The diversity of Brazil's people has given the country a **unique** culture. Portuguese is Brazil's official language. Almost all Brazilians speak it. Brazilian Portuguese is quite different from the language spoken in Portugal. In fact, many Brazilians find it easier to understand films from Spanish-speaking countries in South America than films from Portugal. This is because Brazil's many ethnic groups have introduced new words to the language. Thousands of words and expressions have come from Brazil's indigenous peoples. Dozens of Native American languages are still spoken throughout Brazil.

C

Academic Vocabulary

unique unlike anything else; unusual

Religion and the Arts

About two-thirds of Brazilians are Roman Catholics, but only about 20 percent attend services regularly. Women go to church more often than men, and older Brazilians are more active in the Church than the young.

Chapter 8 **259**

R Reading Skills

Paraphrasing Call on students to take turns reading aloud sentences in the first two paragraphs on the page. Have students work with a partner to paraphrase the text. **Ask:**

- Why do Brazilians get along with each other despite having a mix of racial and ethnic groups? *(Brazilians are accepting of other people's differences and are known for being warm and good-natured.)*
- What role does race play with regards to employment in Brazil? *(Brazilians of European origin often have better educational and job opportunities.)* **AL** Verbal/Linguistic

V Visual Skills

Creating Visuals Have students work in small groups to create a poster showing the emergence of Brazil's different ethnic and language groups. **Ask:** How have all of these different groups contributed to Brazil's culture? *(Having a mixture of different ethnic groups has given Brazil a unique culture comprised of people who speak different languages. Many people from different cultures have introduced new words to the Portuguese language spoken there.)* Visual/Spatial

C Critical Thinking Skills

Drawing Conclusions Have students who have had experience in multi-language classrooms or whose families speak more than one language share experiences with the other students of how easily words from one language can be adopted in another language. **Ask:**

- Why do most Brazilians speak Portuguese? *(because Portuguese is the official language of Brazil)*
- Why is Brazilian Portuguese quite different from the language spoken in Portugal? *(Brazilian Portuguese has developed in a different way than the language spoken in Portugal. The many different ethnic groups in Brazil have introduced new words and expressions to the language that are not used in Portugal.)* Verbal/Linguistic

CHART

Interactive Charts/Tables/Diagrams

Languages of Brazil

Analyzing Charts Use the chart on the different languages in the region to discuss the influence of the colonists on the culture and language of Brazil. Explain what life must be like where many different languages are spoken. Approach a student and say a phrase in a foreign language you know that they likely do not. Repeat the phrase if needed or asked and see if any student can translate the phrase. Then, discuss how language barriers can potentially cause communication problems. **AL** Verbal/Linguistic

See page 237E for other online activities.

Life in Brazil

T Technology Skills

Making Presentations Divide students into six groups and assign each group one of the following topics: the music, food, dance, holidays, literature, and films and plays of Brazil. Have students find information on the Internet about important events and people related to their topic. Have groups assign tasks to each member to create a presentation about their assigned topic. Encourage students to incorporate music and a variety of visuals in their presentations.

Conduct a "Brazilian Cultural Fair" in which students bring in Brazilian food to share with the class. Encourage students to show photos of traditional Brazilian clothing, perform dances, and play or perform Brazilian music. **Kinesthetic, Auditory/Musical**

C Critical Thinking Skills

Comparing and Contrasting Have students use information from the text to create a Venn diagram comparing and contrasting rural and urban life in Brazil. After students have had time to complete their diagrams, **ask:**

- **What do Brazil's rural and urban areas have in common?** *(Many of Brazil's city dwellers and people in rural areas are poor and they eat the same foods.)*
- **What are differences between Brazil's rural and urban life?** *(City life moves at a faster pace and many city residents have access to government services and modern conveniences, such as cars and buses.)* **Verbal/Linguistic**

Content Background Knowledge

The Indigenous Games Similar to the Olympic Games, Brazil's Indigenous Peoples' Games feature athletic competitions among various indigenous groups. The event, which began in 1996, is held in a different Brazilian city every two years. One event is a type of soccer in which players use only their heads. Another event is a type of bowling game in which ears of corn are used as bowling pins.

ANSWER, p. 260

READING PROGRESS CHECK a unique and lively blend of African, European, and Native American influences that emphasize personal warmth, tolerance, and getting along with others

Most of the rest of Brazil's population follows the Protestant faith. Those who practice Islam and Eastern religions such as Buddhism are growing in numbers. Many Brazilians blend Christian teachings with beliefs and practices from African religions.

T

Other African influences on Brazilian culture include foods, popular music, and dance, especially the samba. Brazilians blended samba rhythms with jazz to introduce the world to music called bossa nova. Several Brazilian writers have gained world fame for their books exploring regional and ethnic themes. Brazilian movies and plays also have gained worldwide attention.

Each February, Brazilians celebrate a four-day holiday called Carnival. Millions of working-class and middle-class Brazilians spend much of the year preparing for it by making costumes and building parade floats. Nearly all city neighborhoods are strung with lights. Rio de Janeiro's Carnival is the largest and is world famous. Elaborately costumed Brazilians ride equally elaborate floats in dazzling parades. They are accompanied by thousands of costumed samba dancers moving to the lively music.

Rural Life

Family ties are strong in Brazil. Family members usually live close to one another. They hold frequent reunions or gather at a family farm or ranch on weekends and holidays. Life in rural Brazil has changed little over the years. Most rural families are poor. They work on plantations or ranches or own small farms. They live in one- or two-room houses made of stone or adobe—clay bricks that are dried and hardened in the sun. Their chief foods are beans, cassava, and rice. A stew of black beans, dried beef, and pork is Brazil's national dish.

Urban Life

C

Many city dwellers are poor, too, and they eat a similar diet. For those who can afford it, U.S. fast-food chains are rapidly expanding in larger Brazilian cities. In general, people in the industrial cities of southern Brazil have a better life than people in the more rural northeast.

Life in Brazil's cities moves at a faster pace. Government services and modern conveniences are available there. Many workers have good jobs and enjoy a decent quality of life. Most middle-class families have cars. Poor families rely on buses to get to work and to the beach or countryside on weekends.

Soccer ("football") is Brazil's most popular sport. It is played nearly everywhere on a daily basis. Matches between professional teams draw huge crowds in major cities. Brazil's national team is recognized as one of the best in the world.

READING PROGRESS CHECK

Describing Describe one element of Brazil's culture. Explain why that element of culture is important to Brazilians.

networks Online Teaching Options

SLIDE SHOW

Brazilian Culture

Interpreting Use the slide show about Brazilian culture to discuss some of the influences in Brazil. Have students point out some of the aspects of Brazilian culture that they find interesting or unique. Make connections between the culture of Brazil and its importance to Brazilians and the importance of other cultures (like United States culture or Canadian culture) to the people in those countries. Encourage students to research the cultural aspects of Brazil they wish to learn more about. **Visual/Spatial**

See page 237E for other online activities.

Soccer ("football") players scramble for the ball during a match at a Rio de Janeiro stadium.

▶ **CRITICAL THINKING**
Describing How important is football to Brazilians?

Contemporary Brazil

GUIDING QUESTION *What challenges does Brazil face?*

Brazil has the world's seventh-largest economy. It ranks among the leaders in mining, manufacturing, and agriculture. These activities have produced great wealth for some people and a growing middle class. However, only 10 percent of Brazilians receive about half the country's income, while the bottom 40 percent receive only 10 percent of the total income. At the same time, 1 in 10 Brazilians is forced to live on less than $2 a day. About 1 in 5 workers is employed in agriculture, mainly on large farms and ranches owned by corporations or wealthy Brazilians.

Brazil is a member of several organizations designed to promote free trade. MERCOSUR, established in 1991, is South America's leading trading bloc. In 2008 the leaders of 12 South American nations created the Union of South American Nations (UNASUR).

Education and Earning a Living

Education is an important key to success in Brazil. College graduates earn twice as much as high school graduates do, and high school graduates earn four times as much as those with little or no schooling.

Buda Mendes/LatinContent WO/Getty Images

Chapter 8 **261**

Education in Brazil

Analyzing Charts Use the chart comparing education numbers in Brazil to the United States and then discuss the growing importance of education in Brazil. Have students make connections between the growth of education in Brazil and its impact on the economy. To ensure comprehension of the information on the chart, have students work in groups to review the information. **ELL** Logical/Mathematic, Interpersonal

See page 237E for other online activities.

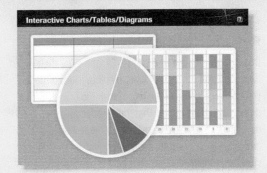

Interactive Charts/Tables/Diagrams

Creating Graphs Have students work in pairs to review and interpret the information about Brazil's economy to create a bar graph. Circulate to provide corrective guidance as needed. Remind students that Brazil's population is about 200 million people. You may wish to break down the information on the board for students who may struggle with comprehending the different figures. Call on volunteers to present their graphs and guide a class discussion about Brazil's economic challenges. Logical/Mathematical, Visual/Spatial

Analyzing Data Have students conduct online research to learn more about MERCOSUR. Have students make a short presentation based on their findings that answers the following questions:

- What does MERCOSUR stand for?
- What are some of the specific things that the organization does?
- Who benefits from MERCOSUR?
- Has the organization faced any criticism? If so, from whom, and what is it about?

Remind students to use reliable sources in their research. Have students present their findings in a short report. Allow time to discuss the findings as a class and to compare and contrast any conflicting information. **BL** Verbal/Linguistic

Making Generalizations Have students read the last paragraph on the page about education and earning a living. Discuss whether this information is surprising or not. Have students consider how education impacts earning a living in the United States. Have them make generalizations regarding the relationship of education and earning a living in any country in the world. **Ask:** Why would students in Brazil drop out of high school when their prospects for earning a living are so poor? *(Students' answers will vary but will likely include that the student has to help the family rather than go to school.)* Verbal/Linguistic

ANSWER, p. 261

CRITICAL THINKING Soccer is Brazil's favorite sport, played nearly everywhere on a daily basis. Professional matches draw huge crowds, and Brazil's national team is one of the best in the world.

Life in Brazil

Technology Skills

Researching on the Internet Have students research programs that have been set up to improve Brazil's problems with poverty, overcrowding, and inadequate educational facilities. Encourage students to identify social and government programs in addition to the ones mentioned in the text. Have students present their findings to the class. Reports should answer the following questions:

- When was the program founded, and by whom?
- What is the primary goal of the program?
- What are the requirements of the program?
- How do poeple find out about the program?
- Who benefits the most from this program (women, children, elderly)?
- Has the program been successful in reaching its goal? Why, or why not? **BL** Verbal/Linguistic

Critical Thinking Skills

Reasoning Read aloud the first paragraph under "Connections and Challenges" in the text. Explain any unknown words or concepts to students. Stress that the Transamazonica Highway is an important interior road. Then guide a class discussion about the issues of poverty and transportation in the interior regions of Brazil. **Ask:** Why are building roads an important part of improving the quality of life for people who live in interior regions of Brazil? *(Building roads would allow poor Brazilians in rural interior regions to have access to services.)* Interpersonal

Writing Skills

Informative/Explanatory Have interested students research the transcontinental railroad built across the western United States in the 1860s and make comparisons between it and the Transamazonica Highway. Students should write a short informative report about the importance of transportation in opening up an area to development. They should also include that both countries offered free land to people who would travel west and develop the land. Verbal/Linguistic

Boys read in front of the class at a public school in Brazil's Amazon area.
▶ CRITICAL THINKING
Describing How well educated are most Brazilians?

School is free up to age 17. Yet 60 percent of Brazilians have only four years of schooling or less. These people have a hard life. They work long hours for low pay. In 2011 the government launched "Brazil Without Poverty," a program aimed at raising the standard of living and improving access to education and health care.

Seeking to create a skilled workforce, Brazil's government is trying to improve education at all levels. It has increased funds to build better primary and secondary schools. At the university level, Brazil has introduced the "Science Without Borders" program, which aims to send thousands of students to universities abroad, including to colleges in the United States.

Connections and Challenges

Improving citizens' quality of life is just one of the challenges facing Brazil. The government is sponsoring a program to colonize the country's sparsely populated interior. Several highways have been built across the country. The most important is the Transamazonica Highway, from the coastal city of Recife to the border with Peru. To relieve poverty and overcrowding, poor rural Brazilians have been offered free land in the Amazon if they will develop it. Thousands have followed new roads into the Amazon Basin to take advantage of this offer.

Brazilians also have worked to develop the energy resources the country needs for continued economic development. Large power

EVARISTO SA/AFP/Getty Images

netw⊕rks   *Online Teaching Options*

Resources and Environmental Impact

Determining Cause and Effect Expand upon the environmental concerns of Brazil by reintroducing the resources and goods of the region with the drag-and-drop game. Discuss the impact that their production or development can have on the environment. Have students match the goods with their environmental impact. As students correctly identify each good, have them drag and drop the information to the correct location. Visual/Spatial, Kinesthetic

See page 237E for other online activities.

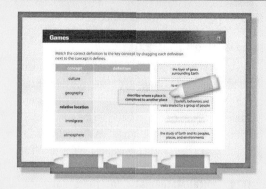

ANSWER, p. 262

CRITICAL THINKING About 60 percent of Brazilians have only four years of schooling or less.

plants along several major rivers use water power to produce most of Brazil's electricity. In the 1970s, the high cost of oil caused the government to develop a program that substitutes ethanol, a fuel made from sugarcane, for gasoline. Recent discoveries of oil and natural gas off Brazil's coast provide the country with the energy it needs.

Environmental Concerns

Programs to develop Brazil's interior have resulted in great concern for the future of the Amazon rain forest. Logging has long been a problem, as trees are cut down to sell as wood. The Transamazonica Highway and other new roads have increased this destruction by making it easier to get into the rain forest and to get the logs out.

The farmers, ranchers, miners, and other settlers the roads have brought into the region have become cause for even greater concern. About 15 percent of the rain forest is already gone, and the rate of its destruction has attracted worldwide attention.

It is easy to think that good soils must lie underneath tropical rain forests. However, this is often not true. The heat and moisture of the area keep the nutrients in the biosphere, that is, in the living organisms, particularly the plants. As a result, the soil is poor. When the forest is cleared for farming, the soil cannot support crops.

☑ **READING PROGRESS CHECK**

Identifying What are reasons for allowing development in the rain forest?

A highway cuts through Brazil's Amazon rain forest.
▶ **CRITICAL THINKING**
Explaining How do new roads benefit and harm Brazil's development, especially in rain forest areas?

FOLDABLES
Study Organizer

Include this lesson's information in your Foldable®.

©Paulo Fridman/Sygma/Corbis

LESSON 3 REVIEW

Reviewing Vocabulary
1. What is Brazil doing to develop some of its *hinterlands*?

Answering the Guiding Questions
2. *Identifying* In what parts of Brazil do most of its population live?
3. *Determining Central Ideas* How has Brazil's African heritage affected its culture today?

4. *Analyzing* How do education issues contribute to economic inequalities in Brazil?
5. *Argument Writing* Choose one challenge Brazil faces today and write a short essay suggesting how to solve it.

Chapter 8 **263**

Chapter 8 **263**

ENGAGE

Bellringer Before students read the Global Connections feature on rain forest resources, explain that all of the Global Connections features in their textbook provide information and facts on global issues. In this case it is focused on the importance of the world's rain forests. Have students share what they know about rain forests. Then **ask:**

- Where are rain forests found? *(in areas where the climate is warm and receives a great deal of rain, including the Amazon Basin in South America, the Congo Basin in Africa, and the Indonesian Archipelago in Southeast Asia)*

- Why do you think rain forests are called the "Lungs of the Planet"? *(Answers should include an understanding that all people and animals need a large contribution of oxygen for survival.)* Direct students to the quote on this page. Have a student read it aloud and explain what is meant by "deforestation." Help students recognize that as the rain forests are deforested, the ability of the world's rain forests to act as the "planet's lungs" diminishes as well.

TEACH & ASSESS

C1 Critical Thinking Skills

Evaluating Have students use the images in the text book to discuss apsects of life for indigenous people who lived in rain forest regions before deforestation began to take place. **Ask:**

How do you think indigenous people lived in the rain forests before contact with the outside world? *(Answers will vary but students should recognize that the rain forests satisfied indigenous peoples' needs for food, shelter, and medicine, allowing them to survive in isolation.)* **AL** Logical/Mathematical

R Reading Skills

Determine Central Ideas Have students recognize the cause of deforestation. **Ask:**

- Why is the deforestation of the world's rain forest occurring? *(cutting for livestock grazing, agriculture, wood and mining of the land's minerals)*

- What is the environmental impact of deforestation? *(reduction in the world's biological diversity)*

- What efforts are being made to preserve the world's rain forests? *(plant trees on deforested land, companies operate in ways to minimize damage to rain forests)* Verbal/Linguistic

---

Rain Forest Resources

Many medicines that we use today come from plants found in rain forests. From these plants, we derive medicines to treat or cure diabetes, heart conditions, glaucoma, and many other illnesses and physical problems.

Largest Rain Forests The world's largest rain forests are located in the Amazon Basin in South America, the Congo Basin in Africa, and the Indonesian Archipelago in Southeast Asia. The Amazon rain forest makes up more than half of Earth's remaining rain forest. **C2**

The Planet's Lungs Rain forests are often called the "lungs of the planet" for their contribution in producing oxygen, which all animals need for survival. Rain forests also provide a home for many people, animals, and plants. Rain forests are an important source of medicine and foods. **C1**

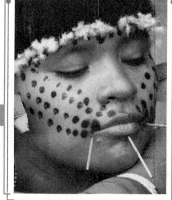

The Yanomami People
An ancient indigenous people, the Yanomami live in the Amazon rain forest regions of Brazil and Venezuela. For many years, the Yanomami lived in isolation. They rely on their environment for their food, shelter, and medicine.

Deforestation Every year, less and less of the rain forest remains. Human activity is the main cause of this deforestation. Humans cut rain forests for grazing land, agriculture, wood, and the land's minerals. Deforestation harms the native peoples who rely on the rain forest. The loss of rain forests also has an extreme impact on the environment because the rich biological diversity of the rain forest is lost as the trees are cut down.

Preserving Rain Forests More and more people realize that keeping the rain forests intact is critical. Groups plant trees on deforested land in the hope that forests will eventually recover. More companies are operating in ways that minimize damage to rain forests. **C3**

More Research Thirty years ago, very little research on the medicines of the rain forest was being done. Today, many drug companies and several branches of the U.S. government, including the National Cancer Institute, are taking part in research projects to find medicines and cures for viruses, infections, cancer, and AIDS.

Ashaninka children are at play in the rain ▶ forest. The Ashaninka comprise one of the largest indigenous groups in South America.

> " Every year, less and less of the rain forest remains. Human activity is the main cause of this deforestation. " **R**

---

networks Online Teaching Options

SLIDE SHOW

Medical Treatments from the Rain Forest

Analyzing Images Display the slide show of plants and the uses of plants for medical needs to help students understand the importance of rain forest plants. In teams have students choose one or two plants from the slide show presentation to research where the plants are found and how they are used for medicinal purposes. Teams should provide drawings or diagrams to explain what they learned. Then have volunteers create a display with the visuals. **AL** **ELL** Visual/Spatial, Interpersonal

Slide Show

THERE'S MORE ONLINE

HEAR why the rain forest is important • SEE the loss of the rain forest • WATCH plants become medicine

C₂ Critical Thinking Skills

Analyzing Visuals Direct attention to the picture of the young woman in the center column. **Ask:**

- Why is it important to respect the traditions and culture of indigenous people? *(Answers will vary, but students should recognize that different does not mean wrong and that indigenous people have great knowledge to share about the rain forest environment.)*
- What might the Yanomami be able to teach the world about the rain forests? *(plants that are of medicinal value)* **Verbal/Linguistic**

V

C₃ Critical Thinking Skills

Speculating Help students become aware of why rain forest environments are limited. **Ask:**

- Most rain forest environments are found near the equator. Why is this? *(little variation in climate yearlong)*
- How might continued deforestation of the world's rain forests impact the indigenous people who live there? *(Answers will vary but students should recognize that further destruction of the environment indigenous people depend on may threaten their ability to survive in the rain forest.)* **Visual/Spatial**

V Visual Skills

Integrating Visual Information Have students analyze the full page image. **Ask:**

- How is the rain forest environment a safe environment for indigenous people? *(Indigenous people understand the plants and animals of the rain forest, know which plants are safe, use the rain forest for shelter and for play.)*
- What indications are there that the Ashaninka children and the Ashaninka community no longer live in isolation? Is no longer living in isolation advantageous for Ashaninka children? *(clothing worn by the children; Answers will vary but students should recognize both positive and negative effects for the children no longer living in isolation.)* **Visual/Spatial**

INFOGRAPHIC

Rain Forest Biome

Simulating Share the infographic with the class. Ask students to explain the rain forest biome. Have students research images and create a visual "snapshot" of the rain forest from the rain forest floor through the canopy to show the variety of animals and plants that inhabit the rain forest. Students who enjoy technology may wish to create an interactive presentation to visually build their "snapshot." Have students share their work. **BL Verbal/ Linguistic**

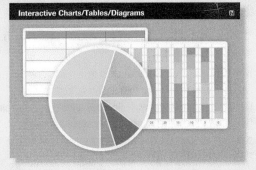

Interactive Charts/Tables/Diagrams

R Reading Skills

Citing Text Evidence Create a chart on the board with three headings: *Value for Animals*, *Value for Medicine*, and *Value for Agriculture*. Have the class identify individual statistics on page 266 and determine in which category the statistic belongs. Review the information in the chart. **Ask:**

What does the evidence say about the value of the world's rain forests? *(Students should recognize and provide specific examples from the text to articulate that rain forests benefit the world in a variety of ways.)* Logical/Mathematical

C1 Critical Thinking Skills

Identifying Problems Add a fourth column to the chart on the board. Label the column *Problems*. Have students quantify the ongoing deforestation. **Ask:**

What has happened to the rain forests in recent times? *(In 1950 rain forests covered 14 percent of Earth's land, today 7 percent; 32 million acres lost yearly; at current rate rain forests will disappear in 40 years.)* Logical/Mathematical

C2 Critical Thinking Skills

Analyzing Ask:

• How does use of the rain forest threaten its survival? *(Continued deforestation for agriculture and mineral extraction reduces the total acreage of the rain forest and leaves it difficult for the region to recover.)*

• How does use of the rain forest threaten the survival of those living there? *(Accept all answers. Students should recognize that without the plants, animals that depend on the rain forest for food and shelter will perish, as well.)*

Content Background Knowledge

Scientists are working with the Brazilian government and an indigenous group in the western Amazon in Brazil to develop medicines from the slime of a poisonous tree frog. The group has been using the slime as a remedy for illness and pain for centuries. The slime contains compounds with anesthetic and tranquilizing properties. Scientists hope to isolate these compounds and then reproduce them using modern technology in genetics.

Today's scientists are realizing that the traditional knowledge of these indigenous groups in the rain forest is an extremely valuable resource, because they know the many plants and animals of the rain forest much better than anyone else. For example, there are more than 100 frog species in the Amazon rain forest, and the indigenous people know which one of these many frogs to use.

R These numbers and statistics can help you learn about the resources of the rain forest.

1.4 Billion Acres

The Amazon rain forest covers 1.4 billion acres (2,187,500 sq km). If the rain forest were a nation, it would be the 13th-largest country in the world.

OVER SEVEN PERCENT

Tropical rain forests make up about 7 percent of the world's total landmass. But found within the rain forest are half of all known varieties of plants.

80%

About 80 percent of the diets of developed nations of the world originated in tropical rain forests. Included are such fruits as oranges and bananas; corn, potatoes, and other vegetables; and nuts and spices.

120

Today, 120 prescription drugs sold worldwide are derived from rain forest plants. About 65 percent of all cancer-fighting medicines also come from rain forest plants. An anticancer drug derived from a special kind of periwinkle plant has greatly increased the survival rate for children with leukemia.

EIGHTY PERCENT

For centuries, people who live in rain forests have used the plants and trees to meet their health needs. The World Health Organization (WHO) estimates that about 80 percent of the indigenous peoples still rely on traditional medicine.

ONE PERCENT

Although ingredients for many medicines come from rain forest plants, less than 1 percent of plants growing in rain forests have been tested by scientists for medicinal purposes.

40 Years

In 1950 rain forests covered about 14 percent of Earth's land. Rain forests cover about 7 percent today. Scientists estimate that, at the present rate, all rain forests could disappear from Earth within 40 years.

50,000 Square Miles

When rain forests are cleared for land, animal and plant life disappears. Almost half of Earth's original tropical forests have been lost. Every year, about 32 million acres—50,000 square miles (129,499 sq. km)—of tropical forest are destroyed. That's roughly the area of Nicaragua or the state of Alabama.

266 Chapter 8

---

net**wo**rks   *Online Teaching Options*

ANIMATION

Costs and Benefits of Human Activity in the Rain Forest

Interpreting Use this animation to help students weigh the costs and benefits of using the rain forest, from medical treatment to loss of species, indigenous cultures, habitat, and future medical cures. As a group, have students create a wall-size costs and benefits chart that includes visual images.

ELL Kinesthetic, Interpersonal

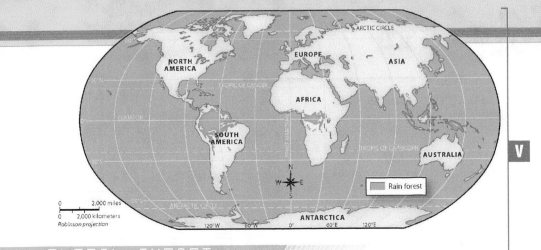

GLOBAL IMPACT

THE WORLD'S RAIN FORESTS Rain forests are located in a belt around Earth near the Equator. Abundant rain, relatively constant temperatures, and strong sunlight year-round are ideal conditions for the plants and animals of the rain forest.

Rain forests cover only a small part of Earth's surface. The Amazon Basin in South America is the world's largest rain forest area.

Rain Forest Research

Laboratories provide a research base for scientists to conduct environmental research. This laboratory in Mumbai attracts rain forest scientists from around the world.

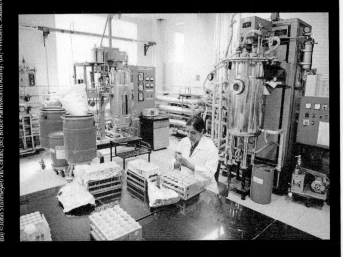

(t) Imagestate Media Partners Limited - Impact Photos/Alamy; (c) A.T. White/The Image Bank/Getty Images; (bl) ©John Stanmeyer/VII/Corbis; (br) ©Bruce Farnsworth/Alamy; (br) ©Frederic Soltan/Corbis

Thinking Like a Geographer

1. *Environment and Society* Why do you think scientists only know about a small fraction of potential medicines from the rain forest?

2. *Environment and Society* How do you think native doctors in the Amazon rain forest discovered medical uses for plants?

3. *Human Geography* List two reasons to explain why some people support saving rain forests. List two reasons to explain why some people support cutting down rain forests. Write a paragraph to state which position you support. Include facts to support your position.

Chapter 8 **267**

GAME

Rain Forest Facts

Collaborating Play this game as a class to allow students to use what they have learned about the rain forest. Afterwards, have the class design an advertising campaign to save the world's rain forests. Group students to make use of technology to create different parts of the advertising campaign. **ELL** Visual/Spatial, Verbal/Linguistic

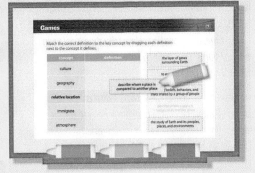

V Visual Skills

Interpreting Visual Information Discuss with students how the map at the top of the page showing the areas of rain forest left in the world relates to the photograph of the scientist working in a laboratory. First have a volunteer apply the map key to interpret and explain the map. Then have other volunteers apply what they have learned in the previous pages to both the map and photograph. **Ask:**

Why is the rain forest an important resource for scientists? *(The scientists want to explore the plants and animals of the rain forest to develop medicines to help humans. The scientists want to work with the indigenous people who understand the plants and animals of the rain forest, and who already use some plants and animals for medicines for the tribe.)* Visual/Spatial

W Writing Skills

Arguing As students prepare to write the paragraph for question #3 in Thinking Like a Geographer, discuss with them the proper format and structure appropriate for writing a paragraph. Explain that students should state their opinions in the paragraph clearly and support them with convincing facts. Verbal/Linguistic

CLOSE & REFLECT

Divide the class into small groups. Have each group search the Internet for private and governmental efforts to save the rain forests. Provide sticky note sheets for each group. Have students write on a sticky note sheet information on the efforts of a private or government group that is working to save a part of the rain forest. Students should attach their notes to a large world map. Have each group lead a discussion to evaluate efforts to save the world's rain forests.

ANSWERS, p. 267

Thinking Like a Geographer
1. Because travel in the rain forest is challenging, scientists have not explored the region completely. Scientists may also distrust native medical practitioners, preferring to use chemistry and other laboratory-based methods of finding new medicines.
2. Much of the knowledge develops through trial and error. A plant may have been ingested by accident but be found to be beneficial. Some trials come about because of a plant's appearance, for example, resemblance to an organ or a disease condition like a rash.
3. Students may cite that people who support saving the rain forest argue that it is home to unique people and habitats. Those who support cutting down the rain forest argue that it is needed for economic development and could be used to develop medicines.

CHAPTER REVIEW ACTIVITY

Have students create a three-column chart like the one below, labeled "Geography", "History", and "Culture". Tell students that they will use their completed charts to create a travel guide for tourists who visit Brazil. Have students think about what they learned in this chapter relating to Brazil's geography, history, and culture that they might want to include in their guide. For example, are there any geographical points of interest that should be highlighted? What historical facts might be of interest to visitors? Are there travel tips about Brazilian society and culture that should be included? Display students' brochures in a classroom exhibit. *(Students' charts and guides may vary but should include information from the chapter, such as facts about **geography:** Amazon River and the Amazon Basin, rain forest, tropical climate; **history:** indigenous people, slash-and-burn agriculture, Portuguese conquest, emancipation and independence; and **culture:** ethnically and racially diverse population, crowded cities, beautiful beaches.)*

Geography	History	Culture

REVIEW THE ENDURING UNDERSTANDINGS

Review this chapter's Enduring Understandings with students:

- ***Over time, people adapt to their environment.***

Now pose the following questions in a class discussion to apply this to this chapter.

- What physical features of Brazil affect the way people live? *(Answers may mention that the Amazon River basin is sparsely populated, while Brazil's major cities such as São Paulo, an important industrial city, are overcrowded. Farmers live in the tropical savannah in the western half of the Highlands, while other farmers have settled in the prairie grasslands to the south. The capital city of Brasília draws people to live there, as does the city of Rio de Janeiro, which has beautiful beaches.)*

- What is an example of a challenge that Brazilians face and how has it impacted the environment? *(Answers will vary but might mention that overcrowding in big cities, such as Rio de Janeiro and São Paulo, has caused poverty, crime, and pollution. Many city dwellers live in favelas, or slums, by building makeshift housing using cardboard and scrap metal.)*

- How would you describe Brazil's culture and people? *(Sample answer: Brazil has a diverse culture because it has a variety of ethnic groups and races. Brazilians are known for being warm and good natured.)*

Chapter 8 ACTIVITIES

Directions: Write your answers on a separate piece of paper.

1 Use your FOLDABLES to explore the Essential Question.
INFORMATIVE/EXPLANATORY Write an essay explaining how the Brazilians' conversion of rain forest land to farmland may affect the environment of the rest of the world.

2 21st Century Skills
IDENTIFYING POINT OF VIEW Given what you have learned about the benefits of rain forests, do you think Brazil has an obligation to maintain what remains of them? Write two or three paragraphs to explain your viewpoint.

3 Thinking Like a Geographer
DESCRIBING On a graphic organizer, note important differences between Brazilians who live in the major cities and those who do not. Add other categories you think are important in describing the differences.

	City dwellers	Country dwellers
Wealth		
Housing		
Work		

4 GEOGRAPHY ACTIVITY

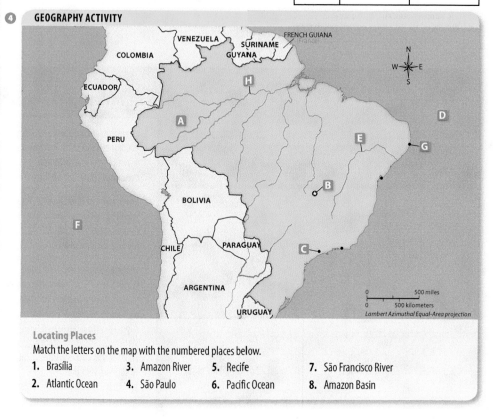

Locating Places
Match the letters on the map with the numbered places below.
1. Brasília
2. Atlantic Ocean
3. Amazon River
4. São Paulo
5. Recife
6. Pacific Ocean
7. São Francisco River
8. Amazon Basin

ACTIVITIES ANSWERS

Exploring the Essential Question

1 **INFORMATIVE/EXPLANATORY** Students' essays will vary in opinion, but should show careful thought and analysis as well as meet your standards for grammar and spelling.

21st Century Skills

2 **IDENTIFYING POINT OF VIEW** Opinions will vary, but paragraphs should address the question, be organized, and meet your high standards for spelling and grammar.

Chapter 8 ASSESSMENT

REVIEW THE GUIDING QUESTIONS
Directions: Choose the best answer for each question.

1 Brazil is the world's largest exporter of
- A. beef.
- B. clocks.
- C. peanut butter.
- D. tropical plants.

2 Most of Brazil's population lives in
- F. the rain forest.
- G. the coastal lowlands.
- H. the Amazon Basin.
- I. northeastern Brazil.

3 The first Portuguese explorer to lay claim to Brazil was
- A. Ferdinand Magellan.
- B. a Jesuit priest.
- C. Getúlio Vargas.
- D. Pedro Cabral.

4 When Napoleon invaded Portugal in 1807 and the Portuguese royal family and government leaders fled to Brazil, which city became the new capital of the Portuguese Empire?
- F. São Paulo
- G. Campinas
- H. Rio de Janeiro
- I. Brasília

5 Brazil's largest metropolitan area, or city and surrounding suburbs, is
- A. Brasília.
- B. Buenos Aires.
- C. São Paulo.
- D. Rio de Janeiro.

6 The official language of Brazil is
- F. Spanish.
- G. Brazilian.
- H. Portuguese.
- I. English.

Chapter 8 **269**

Thinking Like a Geographer

3 DESCRIBING

	City dwellers	Country dwellers
Wealth	Poor, middle class, & rich	Mostly poor
Housing	Poor live in favelas. Middle class live in small homes and apartments. Rich live in luxury apartments & condominiums	Most live in one- or two-room adobe homes
Work	Industry and commerce	Own small farms or work on ranches and plantations

Geography Activity

4 LOCATING PLACES

1. B
2. D
3. H
4. C
5. G
6. F
7. E
8. A

ASSESSMENT ANSWERS
Review the Guiding Questions

1 A Choices B and C can be eliminated because these products do not relate to products that Brazil exports and are not mentioned in the chapter. Choice D may appear to be an option because of the word *tropical;* however, students need to remember that Brazil's farmers raise livestock. Students may remember coffee as the main product in Brazil, but the text mentions Brazil as the largest beef exporter. Refer students to Lesson 1 for help.

2 G Students will need to recall the different regions of Brazil. It may help to look at a map of Brazil to review the different regions. Students should recall that choices F and H are not correct because those regions are sparsely populated. Choice I is also not correct because northeastern Brazil is the hottest and driest climate in the country. Reviewing the text in Lesson 1 may be helpful to students.

3 D To answer this question, students will need to recall that Pedro Cabral was the first explorer to lay claim to Brazil. Reviewing Brazil's early history in Lesson 2 will help students eliminate choices A, B, and C.

4 H Students may be confused by Choice I, because Brasília is Brazil's current capital city. Choice F may also be confusing, as São Paulo is Brazil's largest city. Refer students to the section "Independence and Monarchy" in Lesson 2 for help.

5 C Students should recall that Choice C is correct because São Paulo is one of the world's largest cities. They should be able to eliminate Choice B as being incorrect because Buenos Aires is a large city in Argentina, not Brazil. Choices A and D may cause confusion, as they are also large cities. Refer students to Lesson 3 for help.

6 H To answer this question, students need to recall that nearly all European immigrants to Brazil were from Portugal. While Choice F seems like a viable option, students should remember that Brazil is unique because of its Portuguese heritage. Refer students to Lesson 3 for help.

Assessment Answers

DBQ Analyzing Documents

7 **B** Since the people being discussed are farmers, they must want to clear the land to be able to grow more crops so they can increase their sales and thus their profits.

8 **H** If the law that the farmers support is passed, many farmers will probably clear the additional land permitted under law. As a result, deforestation in the Amazon will increase at a faster rate.

Short Response

9 Possible answer: Brazil's economy has benefited from the nation's large size because its size makes possible the vast natural resources it can use, including the large expanse of land in the interior, which can be developed in many different ways. In turn, Brazil's physical size has made the nation home to a large population, which provides a large workforce.

10 Possible answer: If income is unequally distributed, a nation is likely to have a large number of poor people. With little money, these people cannot consume large amounts of goods. That reduces demand for a nation's products, which hurts the economy.

Extended Response

11 Possible answer: The governments of the two countries share similarities, although Brazil has gone through a longer and more dramatic time to reach its current version of a representative democracy, especially given the dictatorships of its recent past. Its constitution was modeled after that of the United States. As the most industrialized of the South American countries, Brazil's economy is also similar to that of the United States. Brazil's industrial growth has thus far given it the strongest economy of the South American countries. In general, thanks to its industry and its many natural resources, it has a solid trade surplus. Brazil has a vast difference in incomes between the wealthy and the poor, and about one-third of the population lives in poverty. Culturally, Brazilians have a wide mix of ancestries, including indigenous people, Portuguese and other Europeans, and Africans, as well as, more recently, Asians. Art and music are a mix of elements from all these backgrounds. The citizens of Brazil are a warm and accepting people.

DBQ ANALYZING DOCUMENTS

7 **IDENTIFYING POINT OF VIEW** Read the following news report:

"Brazilian farmers meanwhile have been demanding the country's Congress ease environmental laws in the Amazon region. They support a bill that would let them clear half the land on their properties in environmentally sensitive areas. Current law allows farmers to clear just 20 percent of their land in the Amazon zone."

—from Marco Sibaja, "Amazon Deforestation in Brazil Increases"

Why do Brazilian farmers want to be able to clear more land?

A. They oppose any environmental protection laws.

B. They want more land for crops to increase their profits.

C. They plan to sell the cleared land for new housing developments.

D. They hope to drive Native Americans from the land.

8 **ANALYZING** What is likely to happen if the bill the farmers support becomes law?

F. Brazil's economy will suffer from too much emphasis on agriculture.

G. Agriculture in Brazil will decline because the land is unproductive.

H. Deforestation in the Amazon will increase at a faster rate.

I. Environmentalists will stop fighting over deforestation.

SHORT RESPONSE

"Exploiting vast natural resources and a large labor pool, [Brazil] is today South America's leading economic power. . . . Highly unequal income distribution and crime remain pressing problems."

—from *CIA World Factbook*

9 **ANALYZING** How has Brazil's economy benefited from the nation's large size?

10 **IDENTIFYING** Why is unequal income distribution in Brazil a problem?

EXTENDED RESPONSE

11 **INFORMATIVE/EXPLANATORY WRITING** Compare and contrast the cultures of the United States and Brazil, including political, economic, and social factors.

Need Extra Help?

If You've Missed Question	1	2	3	4	5	6	7	8	9	10	11
Review Lesson	1	1	2	2	1	3	3	3	1	3	3

networks *Online Teaching Options*

Remediation and Assessment

Evaluating The *Assess* tab in the online Teacher Lesson Center includes resources to help students improve their test-taking skills. It also contains many project-based rubrics to help you assess students' work.

UNDERSTANDING BY DESIGN®

Enduring Understandings

- *Over time, people adapt to their environment.*

Essential Questions

- *How does geography influence the way people live?*
- *Why does conflict develop?*
- *What makes a culture unique?*

Predictable Misunderstandings

- *The geography of the Tropical North is the same as other places in Central America.*
- *The region of the Tropical North has no resources.*
- *The climate of the region has no effect on the landscape.*
- *People in the Tropical North are all of similar backgrounds.*

Assessment Evidence

Performance Tasks:

- *Project-Based Learning Digital Hands-On Chapter Project*
- *Project-Based Learning Hands-On Chapter Project*

Other Evidence:

- *Technology Skills Activity*
- *Geography and History Activity*
- *Primary Sources Reading Skills Activity*
- *Participation in Project-Based Learning Activities*
- *Participation in Interactive Whiteboard Activities*
- *Participation in class discussions about physical geography topics*
- *Interpretation of slide show images and special purpose maps*
- *Lesson Reviews*
- *Chapter Assessments*

SUGGESTED PACING GUIDE

Introducing the Chapter	2 Days	Lesson 3	2 Days
Lesson 1	2 Days	Chapter Wrap-Up and Assessment	2 Days
Lesson 2	2 Days		

TOTAL TIME   10 Days

Key for Using the Teacher Edition

SKILL-BASED ACTIVITIES

Types of skill activities found in the Teacher Edition.

* **V Visual Skills** require students to analyze maps, graphs, charts, and photos.

W Writing Skills provide writing opportunities to help students comprehend the text.

R Reading Skills help students practice reading skills and master vocabulary.

C Critical Thinking Skills help students apply and extend what they have learned.

T Technology Skills require students to use digital tools effectively.

*Letters are followed by a number when there is more than one of the same type of skill on the page.

DIFFERENTIATED INSTRUCTION

All activities are written for the on-level student unless otherwise marked with the leveled labels below.

BL Beyond Level
AL Approaching Level
ELL English Language Learners

All students benefit from activities that utilize different learning styles. Many activities are marked as below when a particular learning style is highlighted.

Intrapersonal	Naturalist
Logical/Mathematical	Kinesthetic
Visual/Spatial	Auditory/Musical
Verbal/Linguistic	Interpersonal

Students will:

6.1.6 Identify trade routes and discuss their impact on the rise of cultural centers and trade cities in Europe and Mesoamerica.

6.1.18 Create and compare timelines that identify major people, events and developments in the history of individual civilizations and/or countries that comprise Europe and the Americas.

6.1.19 Define and use the terms decade, century, and millennium, and compare alternative ways that historical periods and eras are designated by identifying the organizing principles upon which each is based.

6.3.4 Describe and compare major cultural characteristics of regions in Europe and the Western Hemisphere.

6.3.10 Explain the ways cultural diffusion, invention, and innovation change culture.

6.3.12 Compare the distribution and evaluate the importance of natural resources such as natural gas, oil, forests, uranium, minerals, coal, seafood and water in Europe and the Americas.

6.4.1 Give examples of how trade related to key developments in the history of Europe and the Americas.

6.4.3 Explain why international trade requires a system for exchanging currency between various countries.

6.4.6 Analyze current economic issues in the countries of Europe or the Americas using a variety of information resources.

6.4.7 Identify economic connections between the local community and the countries of Europe or the Americas and identify job skills needed to be successful in the workplace.

6.4.8 Identify ways that societies deal with helpful and harmful externalities (spillovers*) in Europe or the Americas.

CHAPTER OPENER PLANNER

Students will know:
- *the landforms and waterways make up the unique landscapes of this area.*
- *the climate varies in the region.*
- *there are many various resources in the Tropical North.*
- *there are a large variety of people in the Tropical North.*

Students will be able to:
- ***analyze a map** to identify countries of the Tropical North*
- ***use a time line** to discuss significant events in the history of countries in the Tropical North*
- ***discuss** the variety of people and cultures in the Tropical North*

UNDERSTANDING
BY DESIGN®

☑ *Print Teaching Options*

V Visual Skills

- **P. 272** Students compare and contrast living in a small rural village on the river with living in an urban center.

- **P. 272** Students reinforce their map skills by answering questions.

- **P. 273** Students review the timeline and discuss its major points of interest.

W Writing Skills

- **P. 273** Students write a paragraph describing the social, political, or environmental effect that one of the events on the timeline had on the region and the world.

☑ *Online Teaching Options*

- **MAP** **Reading a Map**—Students identify aspects and locations of the region on a map.

- **TIME LINE** **Reading a Time Line**—Students identify where in the region events on the time line took place and locate the places on a map. **ELL**

- **MAP** **Interactive World Atlas**—Students use the interactive world atlas to identify the region and describe its terrain.

☑ *Printable Digital Worksheets*

- **WORKSHEET** **Geography and History: Devil's Island**—Students use the worksheet to learn more about the history of Devil's Island.

- **WORKSHEET** **Primary Sources: Hugo Chávez**—Students can use the worksheet to understand more about the controversial presidency of Hugo Chávez.

- **WORKSHEET** **Technology Skills: Finding an International Pen Pal**—Students can use this worksheet to find reliable Web sites for international pen pals.

Project-Based Learning

Hands-On

Making a Culture Poster
Have student pairs research a specific indigenous group who live in the Tropical North. Students should gather information about the group's music, art, clothing, writing and language, economy, and religious beliefs, as well as facts about their history. Have students display their information on poster boards using photos to highlight the indigenous group's culture. Display students' posters around the classroom.

Digital Hands-On

Creating a Web Page for a Country
Have small groups or pairs create a Web page for a country in the Tropical North. Assign countries or allow students to choose one. Web pages should include facts and photos about their country's physical features, climate, natural resources, commerce, history, and culture. Each category of information can be a separate section. Completed Web pages can be presented to the class, or students can review them online.

edtechteacher
21ˢᵗ Century Learning

Print Resources

ANCILLARY RESOURCES
These ancillaries are available for every chapter and lesson.
- **Reading Essentials and Study Guide Workbook** **AL** **ELL**
- **Chapter Tests and Lesson Quizzes Blackline Masters**

PRINTABLE DIGITAL WORKSHEETS
These printable digital worksheets are available for every chapter and lesson!
- **Hands-On Chapter Projects**
- **What Do You Know? Activities**
- **Chapter Summaries (English and Spanish)**
- **Vocabulary Builder Activities**
- **Quizzes and Tests**
- **Reading Essentials and Study Guide (English and Spanish)** **AL** **ELL**
- **Guided Reading Activities**

More Media Resources

SUGGESTED VIDEOS
NOTE: Be sure to preview videos to ensure they are age-appropriate.
- **Galapagos, Ep. 2, "The Islands That Changed the World"** (49 min.)
- **Wild Venezuela Venezuelan Birds of Diversity** (24 min.)
- **Subtle Voices: Cries from Colombia** (60 min.)

SUGGESTED READING
- ***Island: A Story of the Galapagos,*** by Jason Chin **AL**
- ***Colombia (Enchantment of the World, Second)*** by Marion Morrison
- ***Ecuador in Pictures (Visual Geography)*** by Alison Behnke

PHYSICAL GEOGRAPHY OF THE REGION

Students will know:
- the landforms and waterways make up the unique landscapes of this area.
- the climate varies in the region.
- there are many various resources in the Tropical North.

Students will be able to:
- **discuss** the physical geography of the Tropical North, including landforms and waterways
- **describe** the various climates in the Tropical North
- **identify** natural resources and major crops of the Tropical North

UNDERSTANDING
BY DESIGN®

☑ *Print Teaching Options*

V Visual Skills

☐ **P. 274** Students reference the political map of the United States and the map of the Tropical North and compare sizes of individual countries and their relationships. ELL

☐ **P. 275** Students use the location descriptions in the text along with the compass rose on the physical map to pinpoint where landforms are located. ELL AL

☐ **P. 278** Students interpret an infographic and in small groups research precious gems.

W Writing Skills

☐ **P. 279** Students work in pairs to create a list of foods they like and then write paragraphs describing the foods.

R Reading Skills

☐ **P. 274** Students determine the meaning of the word *elevations* using context clues. ELL AL

☐ **P. 277** Students use context clues to define *trade winds* and how they benefit an area.

☐ **P. 277** Students paraphrase the main idea of a paragraph about natural resources.

C Critical Thinking Skills

☐ **P. 275** Students make inferences based on knowing that rivers flow across much of northern South America.

☐ **P. 276** Students draw conclusions about what makes a river navigable by commercial ships.

☐ **P. 277** Students contrast a tropical monsoon climate with a tropical wet-dry climate. BL

☐ **P. 278** Students reason why a lack of roads and the physical geography of Venezuela might not interfere with Venezuela's oil production.

T Technology Skills

☐ **P. 276** Students research one unusual native animal that lives on the Galapagos Islands. ELL AL

☑ *Online Teaching Options*

V Visual Skills

VIDEO **Angel Falls**—Students use the video of Angel Falls to further connect to the images in the lesson.

SLIDE SHOW **Emeralds**—Students use the slide show about mining to understand the process of extracting minerals from the Earth.

SLIDE SHOW **Landforms and Waterways: Tropical North**—Students discuss various landforms and waterways of the Tropical North using the slide show. AL

MAP **Physical Geography: Tropical North**—Students use the physical geography layer on the Chapter Opener map to discuss the absolute location of the items in the slide show.

LECTURE SLIDE **The Latin *terra* in English and Spanish**—Students can use the lecture slide about *tierra templada* to understand adaptation to the environment of the Tropical North.

W Writing Skills

GRAPHIC ORGANIZER **Comparing the Coastline**—Students use the interactive graphic organizer to review the coastline of the region.

VIDEO **Around the World—Galapagos Islands**—Students watch a video about the Galapagos Islands and write three questions they have about this subregion. AL

R Reading Skills

GRAPHIC ORGANIZER **Definitions: Landforms and Waterways of the Tropical North**—Students explain the characteristics of landforms and waterways.

LECTURE SLIDE **Geo Facts: Ecuador**—Students can use the lecture slide to make a connection between the term *Equator* and the name of the country Ecuador.

C Critical Thinking Skills

MAP **Climates: Tropical North**— Students compare and contrast the different climates of the Tropical North.

MAP **Resources: Tropical North**—Students use a resources map to explore resources found in the Tropical North and make connections to agriculture and emerald mining. AL

T Technology Skills

ONLINE SELF-CHECK QUIZ **Lesson 1**—Students receive instant feedback on their mastery of lesson content.

HISTORY OF THE COUNTRIES

Students will know:
- there are a large variety of people in the Tropical North.
- the climate varies in the region.
- there are many various resources in the Tropical North.

Students will be able to:
- **describe** early peoples of the Tropical North
- **discuss** European colonization of the Tropical North
- **explain** how Spanish colonies gained independence
- **discuss** the instability of governments that has resulted in revolutions

UNDERSTANDING
BY DESIGN®

☑ *Print Teaching Options*

V Visual Skills

☐ **P. 281** Students use the Chapter Opener map to locate the capital cities of countries in the Tropical North.

☐ **P. 284** Students study the map showing dates of independence of countries in the Tropical North and answer map skills questions.

W Writing Skills

☐ **P. 283** Students work in small groups to research and write about the characteristics of a dictatorship.

R Reading Skills

☐ **P. 280** Students determine what motivated the Spanish to explore the Tropical North.

☐ **P. 281** Students explain how the Spanish chose the areas for their capitals.

☐ **P. 284** Students speculate about why independence came slowly for Guyana and Suriname.

☐ **P. 285** Students discuss the benefits of having a stable government.

C Critical Thinking Skills

☐ **P. 281** Students make generalizations about Spanish rule in the Tropical North. ELL

☐ **P. 282** Students make inferences from the fact that the Spanish brought thousands of enslaved Africans to the Tropical North. BL

☐ **P. 282** Students identify problems that might arise when the ruler of a colony is thousands of miles away.

T Technology Skills

☐ **P. 283** Students use the Internet to research facts and find pictures of Devil's Island and use a software presentation program to create a presentation about Devil's Island.

☑ *Online Teaching Options*

V Visual Skills

☐ **VIDEO** **Caracas, Venezuela**—Students watch a video about the recent historical events in Venezuela and share what they learned about life for the people. AL

☐ **SLIDE SHOW** **Caracas Cityscape**—Students discuss the development of the city of Caracas in the context of the early history of the region.

☐ **MAP** **Colonialism and Independence: Tropical North**—Students analyze the map to discuss changes in government in the Tropical North. BL

☐ **IMAGE** **Simon Bolivar**—Students can use the interactive image of Simon Bolivar to discuss this explorer and the impact of Europeans on Native American populations.

W Writing Skills

☐ **GRAPHIC ORGANIZER** **Colonialism in the Tropical North**—Use the interactive graphic organizer to review the nations that transported workers to the Tropical North.

R Reading Skills

☐ **LECTURE SLIDE** **Important Crops: Tropical North**—Students devise a recruiting strategy to attract workers to the plantations of the Tropical North. Logical/Mathematical, Interpersonal

☐ **LECTURE SLIDE** **Disease and Native American Populations** —Students create cause and effect charts using the lecture slide presentation that discusses the spread of disease and its impact on Native American population. BL

C Critical Thinking Skills

☐ **LECTURE SLIDE** **Important Crops: Tropical North**—Students devise a recruiting strategy to attract workers to the plantations of the Tropical North. Logical/Mathematical, Interpersonal

T Technology Skills

☐ **ONLINE SELF-CHECK QUIZ** **Lesson 2**—Students receive instant feedback on their mastery of lesson content.

☑ *Printable Digital Worksheets*

W Writing Skills

☐ **WORKSHEET** **Geography and History: Devil's Island**—Students use the worksheet to learn more about the history of Devil's Island.

LIFE IN THE TROPICAL NORTH

Students will know:
- *there are many various resources in the Tropical North.*
- *there are a large variety of people in the Tropical North.*

Students will be able to:
- **describe** *indigenous populations of the Tropical North*
- **identify** *where people in the Tropical North live*
- **identify** *languages spoken in the Tropical North*
- **describe** *various religions, daily life, and the arts in the Tropical North*
- **examine** *ongoing issues and struggles in countries in the Tropical North*

UNDERSTANDING
BY DESIGN®

☑ *Print Teaching Options*

W Writing Skills

☐ **P. 290** Students work in groups to write a paragraph about whether free movement of people between countries is in the best interests of governments.

R Reading Skills

☐ **P. 286** Students use context clues to determine the meaning of the word *mestizos*.

☐ **P. 289** Students explain why most people in Guyana speak English.

C Critical Thinking Skills

☐ **P. 286** Students infer why they think the Tropical North has such a culturally diverse population.

☐ **P. 287** Students compare the population of French Guiana and Ecuador and French Guiana and Colombia.

☐ **P. 288** Students make generalizations about why people live in certain regions of the Tropical North.

☐ **P. 288** Students identify problems that might arise when people from Ecuador, Colombia, and Venezuela try to communicate in Spanish. BL

☐ **P. 289** Students explore why most of the people of Ecuador, Colombia, and Venezuela practice the Roman Catholic faith.

☐ **P. 291** Students analyze contradictions between the goals of FARC and its means to reach those goals.

T Technology Skills

☐ **P. 287** Students use the Internet to research an urban city or rural town in one of the countries in the Tropical North and design a travel brochure for the city or town.

☐ **P. 289** Students research the music and/or the food of these countries and play the music or present a recipe to the class. BL

☐ **P. 290** Students use the Internet to research regional music or dances of the Tropical North and create and present audio clips or videos of the music and dances.

☑ *Online Teaching Options*

V Visual Skills

☐ **IMAGE** **360° View: Bogotá, Columbia**—Consider using the 360° view of Bogotá, Columbia to discuss the size and population of this city.

☐ **LECTURE SLIDES** **What Is Carnival?**—Students use the lecture slide presentation to discuss the cultural and social impact and the religious elements of carnival. ELL

W Writing Skills

☐ **VIDEO** **Panama Hats**—Students watch a video about this unique element to the economy of the Tropical North. AL

☐ **GRAPHIC ORGANIZER** **Challenges in the Tropical North**—Students use the interactive graphic organizer to discuss the challenges facing Venezuela, Colombia, and Ecuador. BL

R Reading Skills

☐ **LECTURE SLIDE** **Language in the Tropical North**—Students use the lecture slide to review the languages in the region.

☐ **LECTURE SLIDE** **Defining: Tariffs**—Students use the lecture slide defining tariff and discussing UNASUR to review the content of the lesson.

C Critical Thinking Skills

☐ **MAP** **Population: Tropical North**—Students discuss the population density of the Tropical North and why people chose certain areas to settle.

☐ **GRAPHS** **The Populations of the Nations of the Tropical North**—Students use the bar graphs to compare the populations and the ethnic groups of the Tropical North. AL

☐ **GRAPHS** **Religion in the Tropical North**—Students use the circle graphs to discuss religious affiliation by country.

T Technology Skills

☐ **ONLINE SELF-CHECK QUIZ** **Lesson 3**—Students receive instant feedback on their mastery of lesson content.

☑ *Printable Digital Worksheets*

W Writing Skills

☐ **WORKSHEET** **Primary Sources: Hugo Chávez**—Students can use the worksheet of primary sources to understand more about the controversial presidency of Hugo Chávez.

☐ **WORKSHEET** **Technology Skills: Finding an International Pen Pal**—Students can use the worksheet to find reliable Web sites for pen pals.

INTERVENTION AND REMEDIATION STRATEGIES

LESSON 1 Physical Geography of the Region

Reading and Comprehension

Have students scan the lesson and use context clues to define the meaning of each content vocabulary word. Have students write a sentence using each vocabulary word that demonstrates their understanding of each word's meaning. To assess students' comprehension of lesson concepts, have students write a paragraph that uses all three words. Ask volunteers to read their paragraphs to the class. Challenge students to also use the academic vocabulary terms in their paragraphs.

Text Evidence

Assign six student groups one of the following regions discussed in the lesson: Ecuador, Colombia, Venezuela, Guyana, Suriname, and French Guiana. Have groups use information from the text to identify key facts about each region. Students should use a graphic organizer to list important landforms and waterways, natural resources, and climate conditions. Then have groups present a list of reasons for and against living in the region, defending each side with evidence from the text.

LESSON 2 History of the Countries

Reading and Comprehension

To help students organize and comprehend the concepts discussed in this lesson, have them work in pairs to create an outline or flow chart using the lesson's main headings: *Early History and Colonization, Independence,* and *Challenges and Change.* As students gather information, have them note key ideas and details as subheadings. Encourage students to illustrate their outlines and charts to develop a coherent understanding of each concept. Ask volunteers to present their outlines and charts to the class.

Text Evidence

Have students write a summary of interactions between groups of the Tropical North and other people discussed in the lesson. Summaries should demonstrate an understanding of the influence that specific events had on of different groups. Encourage students to use content vocabulary words in their summaries. Provide students with this example: Invasions by Spanish explorers led to colonization of regions occupied by the indigenous people of the Tropical North. This led to enslavement under the *encomienda* system, which led to conflict and eventually independence for Spain's colonies.

LESSON 3 Life in the Tropical North

Reading and Comprehension

Have students use a dictionary to look up the definitions for the words *ratio, migrate* and *tariff.* Then tell students to use a print or online thesaurus to find synonyms for each word. Have students write sentences using each word, showing a clear understanding of each word's meaning as it is used in the lesson. Then have students work with a partner to brainstorm ways to use each word as it pertains to a real life situation. Have students write a sentence using each word in a sentence beyond lesson content. Circulate to provide corrective guidance.

Text Evidence

Read aloud this lesson's essential question: What makes a culture unique? Assign student groups a country discussed in this lesson. Tell students they will create a series of storyboards for a television commercial about their country seeking to boost tourism. Storyboards should use simple sketches and phrases to describe the country's cultural features and a list of reasons tourists might want to visit. Students may wish to conduct additional research about their country to give them ideas for their storyboards. After students present their storyboards, guide a class discussion about what makes each country's culture unique.

Online Resources

Level Reader

Use this online lower-level text that corresponds directly to the text in the online Student Edition.

Guided Reading Activities

This resource uses graphic organizers and guiding questions to help students with comprehension.

What Do You Know?

Use these worksheets to pre-assess students' background knowledge before they study the chapter.

Reading Essentials and Study Guide Workbook

This resource offers writing and reading activities for the approaching-level student.

Self-Check Quizzes

This online assessment tool provides instant feedback for students to check their progress.

THE TROPICAL NORTH

ESSENTIAL QUESTIONS · *How does geography influence the way people live?*
· *Why does conflict develop?* · *What makes a culture unique?*

Farmer Juan Lucas harvests palms in Ecuador's tropical coastal lowlands.

©Pablo Coral V/Corbis

network

There's More Online about
The Tropical North.

CHAPTER 9

Lesson 1
Physical Geography
of the Region

Lesson 2
History of the Countries

Lesson 3
Life in the Tropical North

The Story Matters...

The countries of the Tropical North are home to some of the most ethnically diverse populations in the world. Native Americans, Europeans, Africans, and Chinese are among those who live in this subregion of South America. It is also home to some of the most diverse environments in the world. Landscapes include jungles, towering mountain ranges, broad river plains, plunging waterfalls, and an archipelago renowned for its unique animal life.

V

FOLDABLES
Study Organizer

Go to the
Foldables®
library in the
back of your
book to make
a Foldable® that will help you take
notes while reading this chapter.

271

Letter from the Author

Dear Geography Teacher,

The Soviet Union's communist government collapsed in 1991. Surviving communist countries, like Cuba, lost financial aid from the former Soviet Union. Cuba was forced to ask other countries for economic aid. Tell students that this is an example of contemporary political geography. Political geography is a form of human geography that focuses on governments and the boundaries of political units. As students read through their textbooks, have them identify other examples of political geography.

Richard H. Boehm

ENGAGE

Think-Pair-Share Have students recall what they learned about the physical landscape and climate of Brazil. Students might cite that Brazil has lowland plains and flat highland plateaus along with the second largest river in the world, the Amazon. Its climate is tropical. **Ask:** How might the subregion to the north be the same as or different from Brazil? *(Students' answers should cite specific physical features and climate characteristics when making comparisons.)*

Then have students read "The Story Matters..." about the countries of the Tropical North, a subregion of South America that lies to the north of Brazil and Peru.

Discuss with the class what it means for a region to have an ethnically diverse population. Have students make a comparison between the population of Brazil and the Tropical North. *(Both have diverse populations.)* Then discuss the following questions: **What do you think it would be like to live in a jungle? Why would there be unique animal life in an archipelago?** Tell students that in this chapter, they will learn about the subregion of the Tropical North.

V Visual Skills

Interpreting Have students look at the picture and read the caption about the farmer harvesting palms. **Ask:** What do you think of when you see palm trees? *(Student answers may include: sunshine, warm beaches, relaxation, a laid-back life, trips to Florida)*

Explain that the coconuts from palms are used in many edible products and drinks. In the 1800s, South American native people used the branches of palms to make thatched roofs for their homes, blowpipes for shooting poisoned arrows, bassoon-like musical instruments, and fishing lines.

Have students conduct online or library research in school or as homework to find different uses for palm trees and report their findings to the class. Make a class list of the many ways people use this valuable renewable resource. Visual/Spatial

FOLDABLES
Study Organizer

Go to the Foldables® library for a cumulative chapter-based Foldable® activity that your students can use to help take notes and prepare for assessment.

TEACH & ASSESS

Step Into the Place

V1 Visual Skills

Analyzing Images Have students compare and contrast the image of living in a small rural village on the river with the image of living in an urban center. Draw a Venn diagram on the board, and write the labels *Rural Village* and *Urban Center* above the two circles. Call on volunteers to list similarities in the overlapping section. *(Students may say that families can live in both places.)* Then call on other volunteers to list features that are unique to each area in the appropriate side section. *(Answers may include: **Rural**—Small boats are used for travel, village populations are small, pace of life is laid-back; **Urban**—Tall buildings are used for living and working, vehicles are used for transportation, populations are large, pace of life is fast.)*

Ask: In which setting would you prefer to live? *(Students' answers will vary but should include relevant details and reasons for choosing one lifestyle over another.)* **Visual/Spatial, Verbal Linguistic**

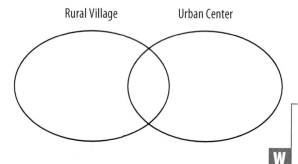

Rural Village   Urban Center

W

V2 Visual Skills

Reading a Map Use the following questions to discuss the map and to reinforce students' map skills. **Ask:**

- In what latitude range is most of this subregion? *(between 0° and 10°N)*
- What is the name for the 0° latitude line? *(Equator)*
- Based on this latitude range, what conclusion can you draw about the climate of the area? *(Much of the area is hot and humid.)*

ANSWERS, p. 272

STEP INTO THE PLACE
1. Colombia
2. west
3. Possible answer: The Galápagos Islands are closest to Ecuador and were probably discovered and claimed by Ecuador.
4. **CRITICAL THINKING** Both are bordered by the Atlantic Ocean to the north and Brazil to the south. Both have capital cities that are on their northern coast. Both share a north-south border with each other.

Ecuador, Colombia, Venezuela, Guyana, Suriname, and French Guiana are the lands that make up South America's Tropical North.

Step Into the Place

MAP FOCUS Use the map to answer the following questions.

1 **THE GEOGRAPHER'S WORLD** Which country in the Tropical North is connected to Central America?

2 **THE GEOGRAPHER'S WORLD** In which direction would you go if you were traveling from French Guiana to Suriname?

3 **PLACES AND REGIONS** Why do you think the Galápagos Islands belong to Ecuador?

4 **CRITICAL THINKING** **DESCRIBING** Use the map to help you describe how Guyana and Suriname are similar geographically.

A

RIVER TRAVEL Indigenous peoples, such as the Makushi, live in small villages on the banks of rivers that wind their way through Guyana's rain forests.

V1

B

URBAN CENTER With about 4 million people, Caracas is the capital and largest city of Venezuela.

Step Into the Time

DESCRIBING Choose one event from the time line and write a paragraph describing the social, political, or environmental effect that event had on the region and the world.

1821 Simón Bolívar frees Venezuela from Spanish rule

1667 The Netherlands acquires Suriname from Britain

1800

1835 English naturalist Charles Darwin arrives on Galápagos Islands

272 Chapter 9

(t to b) Les Gibbon/Alamy; Hisham Ibrahim/Getty Images; ©Hisham Ibrahim/Photov.com/Alamy

---

Project-Based Learning

Hands-On

Making Culture Posters

Have student pairs research a specific indigenous group who live in the Tropical North. Students should gather information about the group's music, art, clothing, writing and language, economy, and religious beliefs, as well as facts about their history. Have students display the information on poster boards using photos to highlight the indigenous group's culture. Display students' posters around the classroom.

Digital Hands-On

Creating a Web Page

Students may work in groups or pairs to create a Web page for a country in South America's Tropical North. Web pages should include facts and photos about the country's physical features, climate, natural resources, commerce, history, and culture. Each category of information can be a separate section on the Web page. Completed Web pages can be presented to the class, or students can review them online independently.

edtechteacher
21st Century Learning

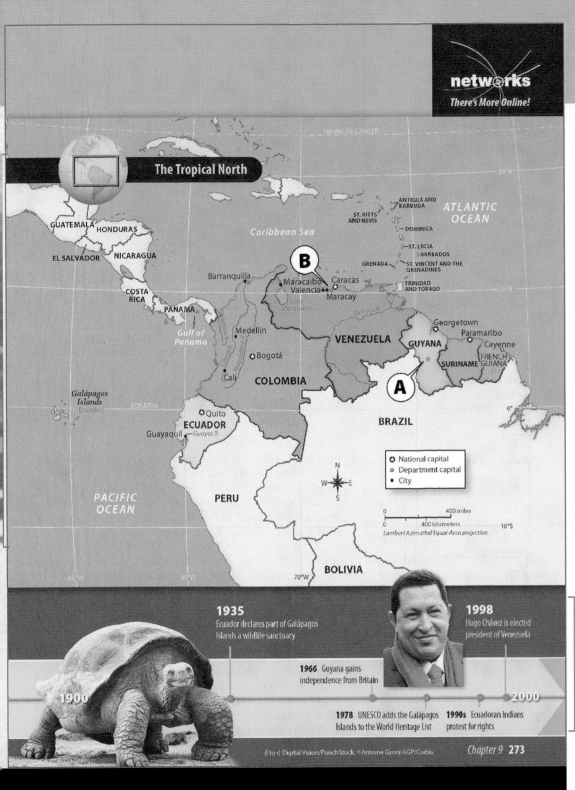

The Tropical North

GUATEMALA
HONDURAS
EL SALVADOR
NICARAGUA
COSTA RICA
PANAMA
Gulf of Panama

ATLANTIC OCEAN
Caribbean Sea
ANTIGUA AND BARBUDA
ST. KITTS AND NEVIS
DOMINICA
ST. LUCIA
BARBADOS
GRENADA
ST. VINCENT AND THE GRENADINES
TRINIDAD AND TOBAGO

Barranquilla
Maracaibo
Valencia
Caracas
Maracay
Lake Maracaibo

Medellín
Bogotá
Cali
COLOMBIA

Galápagos Islands (Ecuador)
EQUATOR
Quito
ECUADOR
Guayaquil — Guayas R.

VENEZUELA
GUYANA
SURINAME
Georgetown
Paramaribo
Cayenne
FRENCH GUIANA

BRAZIL

PERU

PACIFIC OCEAN

BOLIVIA

National capital
Department capital
City

0 400 miles
0 400 kilometers
Lambert Azimuthal Equal-Area projection

10°S

1935
Ecuador declares part of Galápagos Islands a wildlife sanctuary

1966 Guyana gains independence from Britain

1900

1978 UNESCO adds the Galápagos Islands to the World Heritage List

1998
Hugo Chávez is elected president of Venezuela

1990s Ecuadoran Indians protest for rights

2000

(l to r) Digital Vision/PunchStock; ©Antoine Gyori/AGP/Corbis

Chapter 9 **273**

Reading a Time Line and Map

Integrating Visual Information Display the time line and map on the whiteboard. Have volunteers read each event as it is revealed on the time line. Ask students to identify where in the world the event took place and find its location on the map. **ELL** Visual/Spatial

See page 271B for other online activities.

Step Into the Time

V₃ Visual Skills

Reading a Time Line Have students review the time line and then, as a class, discuss its major points of interest. **Ask:**

- What period of time is shown on the time line? *(from 1667 to 2000)*
- How many years after the Galápagos Islands became a wildlife sanctuary were the islands added to the World Heritage List? *(43 years)*
- Did the acquisition of Suriname by the Netherlands happen before or after Darwin arrived on the Galápagos Islands? *(before)*
- What can you assume from the time line showing that the Ecuadorian Indians protested for rights in the 1990s? *(The protest lasted for more than one year, possibly for several years.)*

Ask students to list other historical events that could be added to the time line. *(Student answers will vary but should include accurate event placement.)* Visual/Spatial, Verbal/Linguistic

W Writing Skills

Informative/Explanatory Read aloud the activity described at the beginning of the time line. Before writing their paragraphs, have students brainstorm ideas about the social, political, or economic effects the different events on the time line had on the region, country, or world. Have students share their completed paragraphs with the class.

V₃

CLOSE & REFLECT

Drawing Conclusions Have students use the Key to identify the city that is a Department capital. *(Cayenne, French Guiana)* **Ask:** What can you conclude about a Department capital from the map? *(Possible answer: The Key symbol suggests that a Department capital is not the same as the capital of a country but still has political importance. It can be concluded that French Guiana is not independent but is still part of France. The "Fr." in parentheses confirms this.)* Verbal/Linguistic, Logical/Mathematical

ENGAGE

Bellringer Before students begin the lesson, have them think about the importance of having something others want. **Ask:** What would you be willing to pay or trade for something you can not produce yourself? *(Students' answers will vary but should include details about specific products or services.)* Then read the Essential Question and the "It Matters Because" statement. Have students discuss how trade between countries helps people get what they need or want.

TEACH & ASSESS

V Visual Skills

Integrating Visual Information Have students reference a political map of the United States along with the map of the Tropical North countries in the Chapter Opener. Ask volunteers to read the size comparisons made between individual countries in the Tropical North and United States. Have students locate the countries and states on the maps and make visual comparisons between the two areas. Ask volunteers to describe sizes and relationships in their own words. **ELL**
AL Visual/Spatial

R Reading Skills

Determining Word Meanings Tell students that knowing the meaning of related words can help in understanding the meaning of unfamiliar ones. Point out the word *elevations* and have students find its definition using the context clues. *(height above the level of the sea)* Point out that *elevate,* meaning "to lift up or raise," is a related word and knowing its meaning can help understand the meaning of *elevations.* **Ask:** What other words that you know are related to elevations? *(elevated, elevator)*

Remind students to add academic and content vocabulary words to their lists. Tell students to write their own definitions and to include drawings if desired. This activity can be done as students encounter the words during class as they read or completed as homework. **ELL** **AL** Verbal/Linguistic

---

ANSWER, p. 274

Taking Notes Notes should include facts about each country's resources, such as: Colombia's emeralds, Venezuela's oil, Suriname's bauxite, and so on.

net works
There's More Online!

- ☑ **GRAPHIC ORGANIZER**
- ☑ **MAP** Tropical North
- ☑ **SLIDE SHOW** Emeralds
- ☑ **VIDEO**

Reading **HELP**DESK

Academic Vocabulary

- **exceed**
- **despite**

Content Vocabulary

- **elevation**
- **trade winds**
- **cash crop**

TAKING NOTES: *Key Ideas and Details*

Identify As you read the lesson, use a graphic organizer like this one to record the important resources of each of these countries.

Country	Resources
Ecuador	
Colombia	
Venezuela	
Guyana	
Suriname	

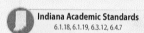
Indiana Academic Standards
6.1.18, 6.1.19, 6.3.12, 6.4.7

274

Lesson 1
Physical Geography of the Region

ESSENTIAL QUESTION · *How does geography influence the way people live?*

IT MATTERS BECAUSE
The land and waters of the Tropical North provide oil, bauxite, and emeralds, along with shrimp and other food products that people and industries in the United States and around the world need or want.

Landforms and Waterways

GUIDING QUESTION *What are the major physical features of the Tropical North?*

South America's Tropical North consists of five countries and a colony. From west to east, they are Ecuador, Colombia, Venezuela, Guyana, Suriname, and French Guiana.

Colombia is the Tropical North's largest country, and Venezuela is the second largest. Each is more than twice the size of California. Ecuador and Guyana, the third and fourth largest, are about the size of Colorado and Kansas, respectively. Suriname is about the size of Washington State; French Guiana, the smallest, is the size of Maine. Together, the countries of the Tropical North total only about one-third the size of nearby Brazil.

Landforms of the Tropical North
Ecuador, Colombia, and Venezuela have the region's most diverse physical geography. The Andes mountain ranges, which extend the length of western South America, run through each country. Some of the peaks have **elevations**, or height above the level of the sea, that **exceed** 18,000 feet (5,486 m)—almost 3.5 miles (5.6 km) high. Many peaks are covered with snow year-round. About 40 peaks are volcanoes.

(l to r) Fabio Filzi/Vetta/Getty Images; Tips Italia Srl a socio unico/Alamy; ©Last Refugee/Robert Harding World Imagery/Corbis

---

net works *Online Teaching Options*

VIDEO

Around the World—Galapagos Islands
Formulating Questions Use this video about the Galapagos Islands in the Tropical North to introduce the lesson. After watching the video, ask students to write three questions they have about the islands or this subregion. Collect students' questions, and then discuss them as a class.
AL Visual/Spatial, Verbal/Linguistic

See page 271C for other online activities.

BBC Motion Gallery Education

Cotopaxi in Ecuador, at 19,347 feet (5,897 m), is the world's highest active volcano. In Colombia, the Sierra Nevada de Santa Marta mountains along the Caribbean coast are the world's highest coastal range.

Colombia is the only country in South America with coastlines on both the Pacific Ocean and the Caribbean Sea. The mountains make travel between the coasts difficult. So does the Darién, a wilderness region of deep ravines, swamps, and dense rain forest along Colombia's border with Panama.

West of the Andes, Colombia and Ecuador have narrow lowlands that border their Pacific coasts. East of the mountains, more lowlands extend into Peru, Brazil, and Venezuela. The southern half of the lowlands is part of the Amazon Basin. The northern half is a grassy plain called the Llanos. This plain also covers most of northern Venezuela.

Southern Venezuela contains a heavily forested region of rolling hills, low mountains, and plateaus called the Guiana Highlands. Along the border with Brazil, groups of forest-covered mesas called *tepuis* rise to heights of 9,000 feet (2,743 m) in places. The Guiana Highlands extend east into Guyana, Suriname, and French Guiana. Rain forest covers most of this region except for a narrow band of low and sometimes swampy plains along the Atlantic coast.

Abundant Waterways

Rivers flow across much of northern South America. The 1,300-mile-long (2,092 km) Orinoco River is the continent's third-longest river. Its more than 400 tributaries form the north's largest river system. The Orinoco crosses Venezuela in a giant arc, dropping from the Guiana Highlands through the Llanos to the Atlantic Ocean. One of its tributaries flows over Angel Falls, the world's highest waterfall. Angel Falls is more than 20 times higher than Niagara Falls. From the top of a *tepui*, the water plunges more than a half-mile to the fall's base.

(t) ©Last Refuge/Robert Harding World Imagery/Corbis; (b) Tips Images/Tips Italia Srl a socio unico/Alamy

© Ocean/Corbis; Kryssia Campos/Flickr RF/Getty Images; Erica Simone Leeds; © JG Photography/Alamy

Academic Vocabulary

exceed to be greater than; to go beyond a limit

Visual Vocabulary

Mesa A mesa is a small, elevated area of land that has a flat top and sides that are usually steep cliffs.

A shepherd tends alpaca below the western slope of the Cotopaxi volcano in Ecuador.
▶ **CRITICAL THINKING**
Analyzing Why is there snow on Cotopaxi even though the volcano lies close to the Equator?

V Visual Skills

Reading a Map Display a physical map of the Tropical North or of South America. Have students locate the landforms named in this section, beginning with the Andes Mountains. Have them use the location descriptions in the text along with the compass rose on the map to pinpoint where the landforms are located. Landforms to identify include:

- Cotopaxi in Ecuador
- the Sierra Nevada de Santa Marta mountains
- the coastline of Colombia
- the Darián wilderness region
- the narrow lowlands of Colombia and Ecuador
- the Llanos plain
- the Guiana Highlands
- mesas along Venezuela's border with Brazil
- the Galapagos Islands **ELL** **AL** Visual/Spatial, Logical/Mathematical

C Critical Thinking Skills

Making Inferences Have students work in pairs to read the content of the page. Then have students create charts detailing the information about the mountain ranges and the waterways mentioned in the content. This content may extend to the following page. Circulate to help students format and create their charts. To help guide student learning, **ask:**

- What might you infer from knowing that rivers flow across much of northern South America? *(Students' answers will vary but should demonstrate an understanding of using rivers for transportation of people and products.)*
- What landforms of the Tropical North make travel difficult? *(Steep mountains, active volcanoes, deep ravines, swamps, and dense rain forest.)*
- How would the rivers of the Tropical North help travel through northern South America? *(Since it would be difficult to build roads through many of these landforms, rivers are probably the main route of transportation of people and products.)*
- The height of Niagara Falls is about 165 feet. According to the text, approximately what is the height of Angel Falls? *(Since Angel Falls is about 20 times higher than Niagara Falls, multiply 20 by 165, which comes to 3,300 ft.)*

Encourage those students who wish to learn more to research Angel Falls and compare it to other waterfalls or the tallest building they know of. Verbal/Linguistic, Logical/Mathematical

See page 271C for other online activities.

SLIDE SHOW

Landforms and Waterways: Tropical North

Discussing As a class, view the slide show images of the landforms and waterways of the Tropical North. Have volunteers read the captions. Point out and discuss as a class the various terrains shown. Discuss with students how these different terrains can influence where people live and trade. **AL** Visual/Spatial, Naturalist

ANSWER, p. 275

CRITICAL THINKING Despite a tropical location, the volcano has a high elevation, rising 19,347 feet (5,897 m).

C Critical Thinking Skills

Drawing Conclusions Display to students the physical geography map from the Chapter Opener. Have a student volunteer point out the rivers mentioned in this section of the text on the map as other student volunteers read the text aloud. Encourage students to either draw or take notes on the information described. **Ask:** What might you conclude about a river that can be navigated by commercial ships? *(Possible answer: The river is wide and deep.)* **Logical/Mathematical**

T Technology Skills

Researching on the Internet The Galápagos Islands are located in an isolated area of the Pacific Ocean where three ocean currents come together. The islands have been called a "melting pot" of marine species. Have students research one unusual, native animal that lives on the islands, such as the giant tortoise; the land iguana or other lizard or gecko; one of many native birds, such as the Galápagos flightless cormorant or Galápagos penguin; or one of many native mammals, such as the Galápagos fur seal or sea lion. Have students use a software presentation program to present visuals and facts about their animals. **ELL** **AL** **Visual/Spatial**

Content Background Knowledge

Share these facts about the Galápagos Islands with students.

- Because the abundant wildlife on the islands is not afraid of humans, visitors can get close to some very rare animals.
- "Lonesome George," the only surviving giant Pinta tortoise, is estimated to be 90 years old. He is considered one of the rarest animals in the world and lives at the Charles Darwin Research Station on Santa Cruz Island.
- The islands were discovered in 1535 by Bishop Fray Tomas de Berianga of Panama. He used the old Spanish word *galapagos*, meaning "saddle," to describe the giant tortoises.
- Estimates put the age of the islands as between three and ten million years old.
- The islands have two seasons: December to May, which is warm and wet, and June to December, which is cool and dry.
- The Galápagos Islands are a UNESCO World Heritage site. (1978)

Academic Vocabulary

despite in spite of

C

The waters of Venezuela's Angel Falls drop from such a height that they are vaporized by the wind and turn into mist before reaching the ground.
▶ CRITICAL THINKING
Identifying Angel Falls is part of what major river system?

The Tropical North region has coastlines on three bodies of ocean water. Ecuador and western Colombia lie along the Pacific Ocean. Northern Colombia and Venezuela lie along the Caribbean Sea. The Atlantic Ocean washes the shores of Guyana, Suriname, and French Guiana.

Colombia's two main rivers, the Magdalena and the Cauca, flow north across Andes plateaus and valleys to the Caribbean Sea. These rivers form important routes into the country's agricultural and industrial interior. Both can be navigated by commercial ships for much of their length.

Other rivers that begin in the Andes flow west to the Pacific. Of these, Ecuador's Guayas River is the most important because it has made Guayaquil the country's largest city and a major port.

Rivers in Guyana, Suriname, and French Guiana flow north and empty into the Atlantic. Most are shallow, slow moving, and responsible for the region's swampy coastline. They are not useful for long-distance transportation into the interior.

Galápagos Islands

The Galápagos Islands lie in the Pacific, about 600 miles (966 km) west of Ecuador. They consist of 13 major islands, six smaller ones, and many tiny islands called islets. These rocky islands, which were formed by underwater volcanoes, are owned by Ecuador. Most have no human population.

The islands' isolation makes them home to many unusual animals, such as lizards that swim and birds with wings although they do not fly. In the 1800s, British scientist Charles Darwin studied the islands' animals to develop his theory of evolution. Today, the islands are tourist attractions. Many are protected as national parks.

T

☑ READING PROGRESS CHECK

Analyzing How do Colombia's rivers help the nation's economy?

Climates

GUIDING QUESTION *How and why do climates vary in the Tropical North?*

South America's Tropical North lies along the Equator. **Despite** its location, the region has a variety of climates. Many of the variations result from differences in elevation and location, and from the influence of ocean currents and winds.

Tropical Climates

The region's coasts, interior lowlands, plains, and highlands all have some type of tropical climate. This means warm temperatures throughout the year.

Fabio Filzi/Vetta/Getty Images

---

networks *Online Teaching Options*

GRAPHIC ORGANIZER

Definitions: Landforms and Waterways of the Tropical North

Explaining Display the interactive graphic organizer to highlight the landforms and waterways of the region. Have students review and define the characteristics of each as they are displayed. Have students make comparisons to other landforms discussed in previous chapters.

BL **Visual/Spatial, Naturalist**

See page 271C for other online activities.

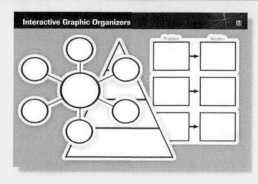
Interactive Graphic Organizers

Much of the coastal and eastern lowlands of Ecuador and Colombia have a tropical monsoon climate, with a short, dry season and a long, wet season of heavy rainfall. In Colombia's coastal Chocó region, which includes the rugged Darién, it rains more than 300 days per year. This produces more than 400 inches (1,016 cm)—about 33 feet (10 m)—of rainfall each year, making it one of the wettest places on Earth.

The Llanos of Colombia and Venezuela have a tropical wet-dry climate, with an annual rainfall of 40 inches to 70 inches (102 cm to 178 cm). Most rain falls between May and October. Average daily temperatures are above 75°F (24°C) throughout the year. The Guiana Highlands have a tropical monsoon climate in some places. In other areas, a tropical rain forest climate (which has no dry season) is normal.

Guyana, Suriname, and French Guiana have the same climate as Venezuela's highlands. Yearly rainfall ranges from 70 inches to 150 inches (178 cm to 381 cm). Their coasts are not as hot as might be expected because of the **trade winds**, steady winds that blow from higher latitudes toward the Equator. The Caribbean coast of Venezuela and Colombia is also cooler. It has a semiarid climate, receiving less than 20 inches (51 cm) of rain per year.

Cooler Highlands

Mountain climates depend on elevation. From 3,000 to 6,500 feet (914 m to 1,981 m) is the *tierra templada*, or "temperate land." This zone has moderate rainfall and temperatures with daily averages between 65°F (18°C) and 75°F (24°C). Next is the *tierra fria*, or "cold land," reaching to about 10,000 feet (3,048 m). A colder zone called the *páramo* begins at about 10,000 feet (3,048 m); daily average temperatures in this zone are below 50°F (10°C). Wind, fog, and light drizzle are common in this zone. Vegetation is mainly grasses and hardy shrubs. Above 15,000 feet (4,572 m), the ground is permanently covered with snow and ice.

✓ READING PROGRESS CHECK

Identifying How do the climates of the Pacific coast, the Atlantic coast, and the Caribbean coast differ?

Natural Resources

GUIDING QUESTION *Which natural resources are most important to the economies of the Tropical North's countries?*

Tropical rain forests cover much of the North, but lack of roads and the region's physical geography have made it difficult for any of its countries to exploit this natural resource. The North's largest countries, Venezuela and Colombia, are its richest and most diverse in other resources, as well.

Think Again?

Angel Falls was named after a pilot.

True. The falls are called Salto Ángel in Spanish. They are named for Jimmie Angel, a Missouri-born pilot who was the first person to fly over the falls in a plane in 1933. In 2009, however, Venezuelan president Hugo Chávez declared that the falls should be known as Kerepakpai Merú, which means "waterfall of the deepest place" in the language of the local Pemón people. He believed that Venezuela's most famous natural wonder should have an indigenous name. At the time of Chávez's death in early 2013, the name of the falls remained in dispute.

C Critical Thinking Skills

Comparing and Contrasting Discuss with students how the climates of the Tropical North of South America compare or contrast with their own climates, including the change in seasons, in weather, in amounts of precipitation, and in temperature. Then have students consider the difference in the two climates of the Tropical North. **Ask:**

- What is one difference between a tropical monsoon climate and a tropical wet-dry climate in the Tropical North? *(Places with a tropical monsoon climate receive more than 400 inches of rain per year. Places that have a tropical-wet climate have an annual rainfall of 40 to 70 inches)*
- What is something that all tropical climates have? *(warm temperatures throughout the year)* BL Verbal/Linguistic

R1 Reading Skills

Using Context Clues Remind students that as they are reading, they can use other words or sentences to help them figure out unknown words or terms without having to use the glossary or dictionary. **Ask:**

- What words helped you figure out what the term *trade winds* meant? *(Steady winds that blow from higher latitudes toward the Equator came right after the words* trade winds.*)*
- What benefit do you think that trade winds bring to an area? *(cooler air)* Verbal/Linguistic

R2 Reading Skills

Paraphrasing Remind students that paraphrasing means to tell something in your own words. To aid understanding, ask students to paraphrase the paragraph and give the main idea. *(Students may state that the Tropical North has many natural resources, but because of tropical rainforests, mountains, and not many roads, it's difficult to get to the region's natural resources or get them out to people who would buy them.)* Verbal/Linguistic

---

MAP

Climates: Tropical North

Comparing and Contrasting Display the climate layer of the Chapter Opener map to review and discuss the various climates found in the region. Click on each climate for more information. Have students compare and contrast the different climates to each other and to other nations from previous chapters. BL Visual/Spatial, Verbal/Linguistic

See page 271C for other online activities.

ANSWER, p. 277

✓ READING PROGRESS CHECK Much of the Pacific coast has a Tropical Monsoon climate, while the Atlantic coast is cooler and dryer, and the Caribbean coast has a semiarid climate.

C Critical Thinking Skills

Reasoning Use the resources map from the Chapter Opener to point out the resources mentioned in the sections called "Fossil Fuels" and "Minerals and Gems." When reviewing the text, have student volunteers point out the geographic locations described in the text. Encourage students to make connections between the physical geography of the location and the resources found there, then **ask:**

- Why might lack of roads and the physical geography of the region not interfere with Venezuela's oil production? *(Students' answers will vary but should demonstrate an understanding of where Venezuela's oil reserves are located—along the coast, at the mouth of the Orinoco River, and offshore in the Caribbean. The location makes transporting the oil possible. Transportation of oil is not hampered by physical geography or lack of infrastructure.)*

- What reasons are there that the countries of Suriname and Guyana do not export oil? *(Possible answer: Those countries do not have enough oil to export. They do not even have enough for their own people.)* Logical/Mathematical, Verbal/Linguistic

V Visual Skills

Interpreting Visual Information Have students point out the two parts of the infographic: the left side that shows the percentage of the world's emeralds that are mined in the four countries shown in the mining buckets and the right side of the infographic that shows the four most valuable gems in the world and the range of prices per carat that they sell for. Have students read the caption about mining emeralds and identify which two of the four countries shown are South American countries *(Colombia and Brazil)*. Have students add the percentages on the two buckets for the South American countries to find the total percentage of the world's emeralds that come from South America *(67%)*.

Then have small groups of students pick one of the other three precious gems on the right side of the infographic to research. Encourage students to find facts about the gem that they can represent in an infographic similar to the one shown. Have groups divide the work appropriately. Some students could do the research, others could plan how to represent the information, while others could draw the infographic on poster board. Logical/Mathematical, Visual Spatial

---

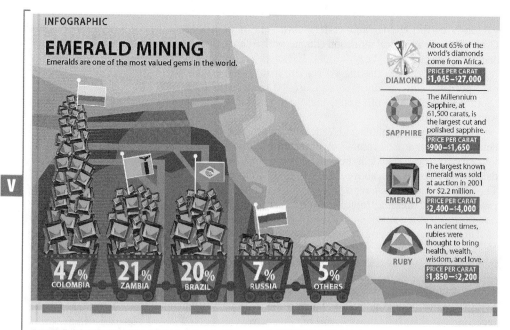

INFOGRAPHIC

EMERALD MINING
Emeralds are one of the most valued gems in the world.

47% COLOMBIA **21%** ZAMBIA **20%** BRAZIL **7%** RUSSIA **5%** OTHERS

DIAMOND — About 65% of the world's diamonds come from Africa. **PRICE PER CARAT** $1,045–$27,000

SAPPHIRE — The Millennium Sapphire, at 61,500 carats, is the largest cut and polished sapphire. **PRICE PER CARAT** $900–$1,650

EMERALD — The largest known emerald was sold at auction in 2001 for $2.2 million. **PRICE PER CARAT** $2,400–$4,000

RUBY — In ancient times, rubies were thought to bring health, wealth, wisdom, and love. **PRICE PER CARAT** $1,850–$2,200

Emeralds were first mined in South America by indigenous peoples centuries ago. Later, the Spanish mined emeralds and shipped them to Europe as part of the valuable treasure from their American empire.

▶ CRITICAL THINKING
Analyzing Why do you think emeralds, gold, and diamonds are considered to be valuable?

Fossil Fuels

Oil is found across much of the Tropical North. Venezuela is South America's top producer of oil and ranks eleventh in the world. Some of the world's largest known reserves are in the Llanos, at the mouth of the Orinoco River, and offshore in the Caribbean. Large amounts also exist around Lake Maracaibo, South America's largest lake, along the country's northwestern coast. Venezuela has some of the world's largest natural gas deposits and is South America's second-largest coal producer. Most of the coal lies along the country's southwestern border with Colombia.

Colombia is South America's largest coal producer, with major deposits in its lowlands. It is also South America's third-largest oil producer (Brazil is second), with deposits in the Amazon lowlands, the Llanos, and the Magdalena River valley.

Ecuador produces less oil than Colombia, but it accounts for 40 percent of Ecuador's exports. It is piped over the Andes from oil fields in the east. Suriname and Guyana also have oil resources, but they do not produce enough to even meet their needs.

Minerals and Gems

Gold is found throughout the Tropical North. The largest deposits are in Colombia's mountains, eastern Ecuador, and Venezuela's

---

net works *Online Teaching Options*

MAP

Resources: Tropical North

Making Connections Display the resource layer of the Chapter Opener map to review and discuss the various resources found in the region. Click on each resource for more information. Have students make connections to agriculture and emerald mining, by discussing why they are important to the economy of the Tropical North.

AL Visual Spatial, Verbal/Linguistic

See page 271C for other online activities.

ANSWER, p. 278

CRITICAL THINKING Answers may vary but should give reasons or evidence to support their ideas.

Guiana Highlands. In Ecuador, thousands of miners live in remote jungle regions and do dangerous work in tunnels that sometimes collapse in heavy rains.

Diamonds are mined from Colombia to Suriname, but Colombia is better known for high-quality emeralds and is the world's leading emerald producer. Guyana is one of the world's largest producers of bauxite, a mineral used to make aluminum. Venezuela and Suriname also have major bauxite deposits. In addition, the four countries have important deposits of copper, iron ore, and other minerals. Except for gold, Ecuador's mineral resources are limited, and French Guiana has no important mining industries.

Agriculture and Fishing

The differing elevations and climates in Ecuador and Colombia allow farmers to grow a variety of crops. Both countries export bananas from their tropical lowlands and coffee from the *tierra templada*. Ecuador's agriculture, however, is not well developed. The amount of farmland is limited, and most rural Ecuadorans grow only enough to feed their families. Corn, potatoes, beans, and cassava are common crops in both countries. Colombia produces rice, wheat, sugarcane, and cattle for sale, as well as cotton for the country's large textile industry.

Coffee is Venezuela's main **cash crop**, a product raised mainly for sale. Venezuela's main food crops are corn and rice. Most farming takes place in the northwest, and most ranching happens on the Llanos. Only about 10 percent of Venezuelans are farmers or ranchers, and much the same is true of Venezuela's neighbors to the east. Guyana, Suriname, and French Guiana have little farming because much of the land is covered by rain forest. Any farming takes place mainly along the coast.

Fishing is not a major economic activity in the Tropical North, which is unusual for countries that border the sea. The region's people do not eat much fish. The major catch of its small fishing industry is shrimp, most of which is exported.

W

✓ **READING PROGRESS CHECK**

Identifying Which fossil fuel, mineral, and gem are most widespread in the Tropical North?

FOLDABLES
Study Organizer

Include this lesson's information in your Foldable®.

LESSON 1 REVIEW

Reviewing Vocabulary

1. What *cash crops* are important to the economy of the Tropical North?

Answering the Guiding Questions

2. *Analyzing* Why are Venezuela's Orinoco and Colombia's Magdalena rivers so important?

3. *Identifying* How are climate and elevation related in the Tropical North?

4. *Analyzing* Why is agriculture more important in Colombia than elsewhere in the Tropical North?

5. *Informative/Explanatory Writing* Which of the Tropical North's countries would you most like to visit? Write a paragraph to explain why.

Chapter 9 **279**

LESSON 1 REVIEW ANSWERS

Reviewing Vocabulary

1. coffee, bananas, sugarcane, rice, wheat, cotton

Answering the Guiding Questions

2. **Analyzing** The Orinoco crosses Venezuela and is the continent's third-longest river. With its tributaries, it forms the region's largest river system. Colombia's Magdalena provides an important route into the interior in a country where the mountainous geography makes travel difficult.

3. **Identifying** Lowland areas are hot and rainy, with Tropical Monsoon or Tropical Rain Forest climates, while mountain climates get cooler as elevations increase.

4. **Analyzing** Colombia has good farmland and produces important cash crops. In Ecuador, Guyana, Suriname, and French Guiana, farmland is limited. Few Venezuelans are farmers.

5. **Informative/Explanatory Writing** Students should state which country they would like to visit and provide information that explains why.

W **Writing Skills**

Narrative Even though the region's people do not eat much fish, other tasty dishes are cooked and served. In Colombia, toasted fire ants, or *hormiga*, are a specialty, and in Ecuador, barbecued guinea pigs, or *cuy*, are popular.

In a think-pair-share activity, have students create a list of foods they enjoy or dislike that have their roots or origins in other countries or cultures. Have students compare their lists to the students around them to see if they have any foods in common. Then have students write a few paragraphs describing the food they enjoy eating the most, the food's origin, and when and why they enjoy eating it. Encourage students to use descriptive details of the smells and tastes of the food. **Verbal/Linguistic**

Content Background Knowledge

Cassava is a tropical plant with edible leaves and starchy roots. It has twice the fiber content and a higher level of potassium than potatoes and is used the same way potatoes are used in the United States.

Cassava roots and leaves can be used in salads and vegetable dishes, grated to make pancakes, dried and ground into tapioca flour, or sliced and made into snack chips. Cassava must be processed—dried, soaked in water, rinsed, and baked—before eating. If the plant is poorly processed, it can produce cyanide and cause cyanide poisoning.

CLOSE & REFLECT

Specifying To close this lesson, have students think about the challenges that the physical geography of the region presents to the people of the Tropical North. Ask them to think about how the people have adapted to the parts of the environment that they cannot change and how they have changed what they could. Then discuss these adaptations as a class.

ANSWER, p. 279

✓ **READING PROGRESS CHECK** Oil is found almost everywhere. Gold and diamonds are present throughout the region.

ENGAGE

Bellringer Before students begin the lesson, have them discuss what sometimes happens when a popular product is in high demand but short supply. Have them talk about how serious disagreements or arguments, or maybe even fights, can break out between consumers wanting the same item. Then make a connection to the Essential Question: *Why does conflict develop?* **Ask:** How would compromise help settle conflicts? *(Students' answers will vary but should include mention of both sides making acceptable concessions.)*

TEACH & ASSESS

R Reading Skills

Synthesizing Information After reading the section "Early Peoples of the Tropical North" aloud to students, have students make a chart of the different Native American groups and their locations in the Tropical North. As students proceed through this section, encourage them to add a column to the chart entitled *Conquered By*, filling in the correct European country that conquered that Native American group. **Ask:**

- Which group of explorers conquered the majority of these Native American groups? *(the Spanish)*
- What motivated the Spanish to explore the Tropical North? *(The Spanish were looking for gold.)*
- What can you conclude about the Spanish colonization of the Tropical North? *(Students' answers will vary but should demonstrate an understanding that the Spanish were invaders and conquerors who took what they wanted rather quickly, in less than 50 years.)* Verbal/Linguistic, Logical/Mathematical

Content Background Knowledge

Share the following facts about the Incas with the class:

- In the late 1400s, more than one million people were part of the Inca Empire.
- The Incan Empire was known as the "land of the four quarters" because it was divided into four sections. The four sections met at Cuzco, Peru, the Incan capital.
- The language of the Incas was called Quechua.
- The Incas did not have a system of writing.

ANSWER, p. 280

Taking Notes Summary sentences should include important events in the region's history.

networks

There's More Online!

☑ **GRAPHIC ORGANIZER**
☑ **IMAGE** Caracas Cityscape
☑ **VIDEO**

Reading **HELP**DESK

Academic Vocabulary

- **conflict**
- **stable**

Content Vocabulary

- **immunity**
- *encomienda*
- **hacienda**

TAKING NOTES: *Key Ideas and Details*

Analyze As you read the lesson, write summary sentences about five important events in the history of the Tropical North on a graphic organizer like the one below.

Important Events
• Native Americans settle in villages along the region's coast.
•
•
•
•

 Indiana Academic Standards
6.1.6

R

280

Lesson 2
History of the Countries

ESSENTIAL QUESTION • *Why does conflict develop?*

IT MATTERS BECAUSE
The countries of the Tropical North export products that are sought after and highly valued by the rest of the world.

Early History and Colonization
GUIDING QUESTION *How did Europeans colonize the Tropical North?*

The Tropical North's indigenous peoples lived there for thousands of years before encountering Spanish explorers. These explorers invaded the region in the early 1500s. Less than 50 years later, the Spanish had conquered and colonized most of the region.

Early Peoples of the Tropical North
The Native Americans of the Tropical North included Carib, Arawak, and other hunter-gatherer peoples. They settled in villages along the Caribbean and Atlantic coasts.

To the west, the Cara and other peoples built fishing villages along the Pacific coast. Over time, groups like the Chibcha and Quitu moved inland to mountain valleys in the Andes. There they created advanced societies that farmed, made cloth from cotton and ornaments of gold, and traded with the Inca, an advanced civilization that developed to the south. In the late 1400s, some of the groups were conquered by the Inca and became part of the Inca Empire.

Arrival of the Europeans
In the early 1500s, Spanish adventurers landed on the Caribbean and Atlantic coasts, seeking gold and enslaving native peoples. When they met resistance and found no gold, they lost interest. The first Spanish settlements did not appear

---

networks *Online Teaching Options*

VIDEO

Caracas, Venezuela

Interpreting Use this video about recent historical events in Venezuela to introduce the lesson. Ask students to share what they learned from the video about life for people in Caracas, Venenzuela. Students should ask if anything surprised or concerned them. **AL** Visual/Spatial, Verbal/Linguistic

See page 271D for other online activities.

gold, they lost interest. The first Spanish settlements did not appear on the Caribbean coast—in Venezuela and Colombia—until 1523 and 1525. The Spanish made no effort to colonize east of Venezuela.

On the Pacific coast, the Spanish conquered the Inca in 1530 and seized their silver and gold. Driven by hunger for more wealth, they invaded Ecuador in 1534. By the mid-1500s, the conquest of the area that is now Ecuador, Colombia, and Venezuela was complete.

Spanish Colonies

To control their new colonies, the Spanish set up governments. Bogotá, which the Spanish founded in 1538, became the capital of Colombia in 1549. The Spanish placed Ecuador's government at the native town of Quito in 1563. Caracas, which the Spanish founded in 1567, eventually became Venezuela's capital. The Spanish located these cities where Native Americans already had settlements. Most were located inland, in the higher elevations where climates are milder than on the tropical coasts. For many years, Venezuela was ruled from Peru. In the 1700s, Spain placed Venezuela, Ecuador, and Colombia under a single government located at Bogotá.

Native American peoples suffered greatly under the Spanish. As in Brazil, thousands died from European diseases to which they had no natural **immunity**, or protection against illness. Others found themselves forced to work for the Spanish under a system called *encomienda*. This system allowed Spanish colonists to demand labor from the Native Americans who lived in a certain area.

The *encomienda* provided workers for Spanish mines and for the

Under Spanish rule, the Native American village of Teusaquillo became known as Bogotá. Life in Spanish Bogotá focused on the main plaza, or square, surrounded by a cathedral and government buildings.

▶ **CRITICAL THINKING**
Describing What role did location play in the selection of Bogotá and other cities as centers of government in northern South America?

DEA/M. SEEMULLER/De Agostini Picture Library/Getty Images

V Visual Skills

Integrating Visual Information In pairs, have students use the Chapter Opener map to locate the capital cities of Bogotá, Colombia; Quito, Ecuador; and Caracas, Venezuela; and the country of Peru. Encourage students to point out the locations of these cities on a map and discuss their locations in comparison to each other. Then have students create a time line indicating the founding of the major cities discussed in this lesson. **Visual/Spatial**

R Reading Skills

Explaining Have volunteers read aloud the "Spanish Colonies" section on the page and discuss the main ideas of the text. Encourage students to write down the main idea using only one sentence. **Ask:**

- How did the Spanish choose the areas for their capitals? *(They chose areas that were already settled by Native Americans and that were inland, in the higher elevations with mild climates.)*
- Why did so many Native Americans die from European diseases? *(The Native Americans did not have any immunity against these illnesses.)*
- What did *encomienda* allow the Spanish colonists to do? *(It allowed the Spanish colonists to make the Native Americans work for them if they lived in a certain area.)* **Verbal/Linguistic**

C Critical Thinking Skills

Making Generalizations Discuss with students how the native people of the Tropical North were treated by the Spanish colonists. Have students speculate why the Spanish might have treated the natives the way that they did. **Ask:**

- How did the Native American people suffer under the Spanish? *(The Native Americans died from European diseases and were forced to work for the Spanish.)*
- What generalization could you make from this information about Spanish rule in the Tropical North? *(Students' answers will vary but should demonstrate an understanding of the harsh rule of the Spanish and that the Native Americans lost their freedom and were treated as slaves.)* **ELL Verbal/Linguistic, Logical/Mathematical**

LECTURE SLIDE

Disease and Native American Populations

Synthesizing Information Display the lecture slide that discusses how diseases spread through Native American populations. Have students create a cause and effect chart that displays the connections between the arrival of the Europeans, the spread of disease, and the deaths of Native American populations, and the need for a different labor force as a result. Circulate to help students with this activity. **BL Visual/Spatial, Verbal/Linguistic**

See page 271D for other online activities.

ANSWER, p. 281

CRITICAL THINKING Spanish and later independent government leaders wanted capitals located inland, in the higher elevations where climates are milder than on the tropical coasts.

C1 Critical Thinking Skills

Making Inferences Using the information about Native Americans from the previous page, work with students to analyze the cause and effect relationship between their deaths, the need for labor, and the arrival of enslaved Africans to the Tropical North. **Ask:** What can you infer from the fact that the Spanish brought thousands of enslaved Africans to the Tropical North? *(Possible answer: The haciendas became so large that a larger labor force was needed. The local labor pool had gotten smaller because many Native Americans had died from European diseases or were already enslaved so outside help was needed.)* **BL** Verbal/Linguistic, Logical/Mathematical

C2 Critical Thinking Skills

Identifying Problems Help students make connections to the fact that the European rulers of the nations of the Tropical North did not often know what was happening in their colonies. Ask student volunteers to describe which country controlled which nation in the Tropical North. Then, **ask:** What problems might arise when the ruler of a colony lives thousands of miles away? *(Students' answers will vary, but should include an understanding of the problems caused by long-distance rule, lack of timely communication between the colony and the ruler, and the impossibility of being in two places at the same time.)* Verbal/Linguistic, Logical/Mathematical

Content Background Knowledge

Simón Bolívar was born in Caracas on July 24, 1783, the son of wealthy parents who died when Simón was a child. Simón inherited a lot of money that allowed him to complete his education in Spain and to travel extensively in Europe. He was influenced by both the American and French Revolutions and vowed to free his country from Spanish rule. In 1807 Bolívar joined the resistance movement against Spain. He and his followers successfully freed Venezuela from Spain in 1813, and Bolívar became known as *El Libertador* (The Liberator). He became president of the independent republic of Gran Colombia and then dictator of Peru. His dream was to create a union of states similar to the United States, but he faced resistance from factions throughout the independent republic of Gran Colombia. In 1830 Bolívar made plans for exile in Europe, but died in December of that year from tuberculosis. The republic of Bolivia was named after Simón Bolívar in 1825.

ANSWERS, p. 282

☑ **READING PROGRESS CHECK** Spain colonized Ecuador, Colombia, and Venezuela. Guyana became a British colony, Suriname a Dutch colony, and French Guiana a French colony.

Most haciendas became plantations that grew coffee, tobacco, sugarcane, or other cash crops. Others, mostly on the Llanos, were cattle ranches. As the hacienda system grew, the Spanish brought in thousands of enslaved Africans to provide more labor. African slavery was most common in Venezuela.

European Colonization

The French, British, and Dutch fought over and colonized Guyana, Suriname, and French Guiana. The British and the Dutch established sugar plantations and brought the first enslaved Africans to the area. Control of these colonies changed hands several times in the 1600s and 1700s. Eventually, what is now Guyana became British Guiana. Suriname was called Dutch Guiana, and French Guiana became a colony of France.

☑ READING PROGRESS CHECK

Identifying Which European nations founded colonies in the Tropical North, and which countries did each nation colonize?

Simón Bolívar, also known as "the Liberator," led the movement that won freedom for several countries in the Americas.

©Bettmann/Corbis

Independence

GUIDING QUESTION *How did Spain's colonies become independent countries?*

By the late 1700s, many Spanish colonists who were born in the Americas wanted independence from their Spanish rulers. Their chance came in 1808, when the French ruler Napoleon invaded and conquered Spain. Spain found it difficult to fight the French in Europe and to rule its colonies. Some of the colonists in the Americas took this opportunity to fight for independence from Spain.

Overthrow of Colonial Rule

Ecuadorans rose up against Spanish rule in 1809. Colombians and Venezuelans soon followed. A long war began, at first mainly between groups who remained loyal to Spain and those who favored independence. After the Spanish expelled the French from Spain in 1814, Spain's king sent troops to South America to try to restore Spanish control. In the south, resistance to the Spanish was led by Argentine general José de San Martín. In the north, Venezuela's Simón Bolívar led the revolt.

Spanish forces were not finally defeated until 1823. In 1819, however, Bolívar united Venezuela, Colombia, Panama, and Ecuador to form an independent republic called Gran Colombia. He became its first president.

---

networks   *Online Teaching Options*

IMAGE

Simón Bolívar

Comparing and Constrasting Display the interactive image of Simón Bolívar to students and review the information. Read the Content Background Knowledge section to them. As a class, discuss his role in the exploration of the Americas and compare and constrast him to any other explorers students may remember from previous chapters. Visual/Spatial, Verbal/Linguistic

See page 271D for other online activities.

Interactive Photos

Elena Kallistratova/Vetta/Getty Images

Independent Countries

Gran Colombia broke apart after Bolívar's death in 1830. Ecuador and Venezuela formed independent countries. Colombia and Panama remained united as one country. In the early 1900s, Panama separated from Colombia and became independent.

Independence and self-government did not bring democracy and peace. Wealthy landholders competed with wealthy city businesspeople for control of the government. **Conflict** over the Catholic Church's role in society added to the unrest. The tensions resulted in civil wars in Colombia and Venezuela. Throughout the history of Ecuador, Colombia, and Venezuela, military or civilian leaders often ruled as dictators.

Labor and Immigration

While Ecuador, Colombia, and Venezuela struggled with self-government, British, Dutch, and French Guiana remained colonies. The British abolished slavery in their colony in 1838. The French and the Dutch followed in 1863.

To replace the once-enslaved workers, British and Dutch plantation owners recruited laborers from India and China. The Dutch also imported workers from their colony in Indonesia. The immigrants had to work on their colony's sugar, rice, coffee, or cacao plantations for a required length of time. At the end of their contract, they were free. Many stayed in the colony and, like the formerly enslaved people they replaced, founded towns along the coast.

In 1852 France began sending convicted criminals to its colony. More than 70,000 convict laborers arrived between 1852 and 1939. The worst convicts were imprisoned off the coast on notorious Devil's Island.

✓ **READING PROGRESS CHECK**

Determining Central Ideas How did British, Dutch, and French colonists find workers after slavery ended in their colony?

Danita Delimont/Gallo/Getty Images

British and Dutch colonial rulers recruited foreign workers from India, China, and other parts of Asia to harvest various tropical crops in their South American colonies. The prison on Devil's Island (above) housed convict laborers.

▶ **CRITICAL THINKING**
Describing How did the arrival of foreign workers in British Guiana and Dutch Guiana change these territories in a way that made them different from other parts of South America?

Academic Vocabulary

conflict a serious disagreement

Chapter 9 **283**

W Writing Skills

Argument In small groups, have students research the characteristics of a dictatorship. Record the characteristics on the board as groups present their findings to the class. Then have students write a persuasive essay for the following argument: **A dictatorship is/is not a preferred form of government.** *(Students' essays should make a claim either for or against the argument of a dictatorship as a form of government and support the claim with at least three reasons.)* Logical/Mathematical

C Critical Thinking Skills

Inferring Discuss with students the section "Labor and Immigration." Make sure to include a discussion on how plantation owners replaced the slaves they had lost in the changes of government. **Ask:** Why do you think people would want to leave their homes to work in a new place for a required length of time? *(Students' answers will vary but should mention that after working hard for a certain length of time, the laborers were then free. The laborers may then decide what to do, many staying in the colony and helping to develop towns along the coast.)* Verbal/Linguistic

T Technology Skills

Using Visual Aids Devil's Island was closed in 1946 after 94 years as a French penal colony. It is now a tourist attraction. Explain that penal colonies were set up in various places around the world to house dangerous prisoners and exiled convicts. Have students work with a partner to use the Internet to research Devil's Island, finding facts and pictures of the penal colony. Partners may choose to use a software presentation program to show the visuals or to make hard copies and display the pictures on a poster. Have partners present their visual displays to the class, which includes an oral presentation of facts about Devil's Island. Encourage other class members to ask questions about the presentations. Visual/Spatial, Verbal/Linguistic

Important Crops: Tropical North

Problem Solving Use the lecture slide to begin a discussion about haciendas and their subsequent growth into plantations. Remind students that after slavery was abolished, plantation owners turned to immigrants to provide necessary labor. Have students pretend to be plantation owners and, working in pairs, devise a recruiting strategy to attract workers to their plantation. When completed, ask each pair to present their strategy to the class. Logical/Mathematical, Interpersonal

See page 271D for other online activities.

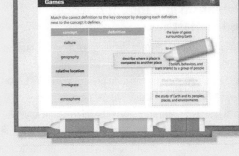

ANSWERS, p. 283

CRITICAL THINKING The arrival of workers brought to British Guiana and Dutch Guiana added a different cultural influence not found in the Spanish and Portuguese-influenced areas of South America.

✓ **READING PROGRESS CHECK** The British and Dutch imported contract workers from India, China, and Indonesia. The French sent convicted criminals to their colony to do forced labor.

History of the Countries

V Visual Skills

Reading a Map Have students study the map showing the countries in the Tropical North of South America and their dates of independence. Have volunteers identify the year of independence and from what country it was achieved. Discuss why Ecuador, Colombia, and Venezuela may have achieved independence about 150 years earlier than Guyana, Suriname, and French Guiana. Then have students answer the Map Skills questions. **Visual/Spatial, Verbal/Linguistic**

R Reading Skills

Explaining Have student volunteers read aloud the "Challenges and Change" section on the next two pages and discuss the main ideas of this section of text.

As you progress through this section, draw a time line of events on the whiteboard. Use this time line until the section is complete. Encourage students to copy down this information for use when they study for the test at the end of the chapter. **Ask:**

• Which countries had political and social problems even after gaining independence? *(Ecuador, Colombia, and Venezuela)*

• When did Venezuela finally achieve a peaceful transfer of power? *(1969)*

• How many years passed from the time Venezuela gained its independence from Spain until its first peaceful transfer of power? Why do you think it took so long? *(158 years. Students answers should include the struggles between opposing groups in the country that included military and civilian dictators.)*

• Why did it take so long for Guyana and Suriname to gain independence? *(Students' answers will vary but should include plausible explanations as to why independence was so slow in coming, such as the citizens of the countries being unsure that independence was a better option than being governed by an overseas power.)* **Logical/Mathematical, Verbal/Linguistic**

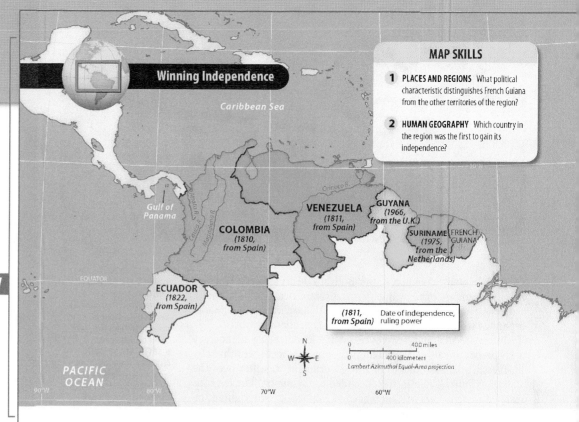

Winning Independence

MAP SKILLS

1 PLACES AND REGIONS What political characteristic distinguishes French Guiana from the other territories of the region?

2 HUMAN GEOGRAPHY Which country in the region was the first to gain its independence?

Caribbean Sea

VENEZUELA (1811, from Spain)

GUYANA (1966, from the U.K.)

COLOMBIA (1810, from Spain)

SURINAME (1975, from the Netherlands)

FRENCH GUIANA

Gulf of Panama

ECUADOR (1822, from Spain)

(1811, from Spain) Date of independence, ruling power

0 400 miles
0 400 kilometers
Lambert Azimuthal Equal-Area projection

PACIFIC OCEAN

EQUATOR

90°W   80°W   70°W   60°W

Challenges and Change

GUIDING QUESTION *What challenges do the countries of the Tropical North face?*

The political and social problems that plagued Ecuador, Colombia, and Venezuela after independence continued through most of the twentieth century. Venezuela, for example, did not achieve a peaceful transfer of power between opposing groups until 1969. Meanwhile, the region's other countries, which gained independence in the twentieth century, experienced similar issues and challenges.

Gaining Independence

Independence came slowly for Guyana and Suriname. The British granted their colony limited self-government in 1891. In 1953 all colonists were given the right to vote and allowed to elect a legislature. Guyana finally gained independence in 1966.

Colonists in Dutch Guiana obtained the right to vote in 1948 and self-government in 1953. The colony became the independent country of Suriname in 1975.

The people of French Guiana became French citizens and gained the right to vote in 1848. In 1946 French Guiana's status changed from

networks Online Teaching Options

MAP

Colonialism and Independence: Tropical North

Visualizing Display the map showing the modern states in the Tropical North with the layer on colonial rule. Have volunteers identify the information presented. Guide students to analyze the changes of the boundaries from colonial rule to modern states. Use the information about when the colonies gained independence to create a time line that includes dates and events to visualize the information. **BL Visual/Spatial, Verbal/Linguistic, Logical/Mathematical**

See page 271D for other online activities.

ANSWER, p. 284

MAP SKILLS

1. French Guiana still has ties to a European power—France, while the other territories are fully independent nations.
2. Colombia, in 1810

a colony to an overseas department, or district, of the country of France. French Guiana remains part of France and has representatives in France's national legislature.

Revolutions and Borders

The Tropical North's lack of strong, **stable** governments has resulted in major unrest in its countries, as well as conflicts between them. In Colombia, assassinations and other violence between feuding political groups took as many as 200,000 lives between 1946 and 1964. In the 1960s and 1970s, small rebel groups began making attacks throughout the country in hopes of overthrowing the government.

Ecuador's government has not maintained control over its remote region, which lies in the Amazon Basin, to the east of the Andes. In the 1940s, Peru seized some of this land. The two countries often clashed, until a settlement was finally reached in 1968. In 2008 tensions between Ecuador and Colombia were strained after Colombian forces attacked a Colombian rebel camp in Ecuador's territory. In 2010 Colombia accused Venezuela of allowing Colombian rebels to live in its territory. War was narrowly avoided.

Guyana's independence renewed an old border dispute with Venezuela that arose when Guyana was a British colony. The dispute was not settled until 2007. Another dispute arose on Guyana's eastern border after Suriname gained independence in 1975. Several clashes took place before that boundary was settled in 2007. Guyana also experienced years of social and political unrest as its African and South Asian populations competed for power.

Like Guyana, Suriname has faced internal unrest since independence. The military removed civilian leaders in 1980 and again in 1990. Meanwhile, rebel groups of Maroons, the descendants of escaped slaves, disrupted the country's bauxite mining in an effort to overthrow the government. The army responded by killing thousands of Maroon civilians. Thousands more fled to safety in French Guiana.

☑ **READING PROGRESS CHECK**

Identifying Which of the region's nations have experienced serious internal unrest since gaining independence?

Academic Vocabulary

stable staying in the same condition; not likely to change or fail

R

T

FOLDABLES
Study Organizer

Include this lesson's information in your Foldable®.

LESSON 2 REVIEW

Reviewing Vocabulary
1. How were the *encomienda* and the *hacienda* related?

Answering the Guiding Questions
2. ***Analyzing*** Why were the Spanish more interested in colonizing Ecuador, Colombia, and Venezuela than Guyana, Suriname, and French Guiana?

3. ***Identifying*** How did conflicts in society lead to independence for Spain's colonies and cause unrest afterward?

4. ***Determining Central Ideas*** Why do the Tropical North's nations have a history of tense relations and internal unrest?

5. ***Argument Writing*** Write a short speech calling for or opposing independence for French Guiana. Support your view.

Chapter 9 **285**

R Reading Skills

Finding the Main Idea After reading the section "Revolution and Borders," have students write down the main ideas of the section. Have student volunteers read their sentences aloud and compare their responses. Encourage students to use the suggestions made by other students to help reinforce the main idea. Then, **ask:** What would be the benefits of having a stable government? *(Students' answers will vary but should demonstrate an understanding of the academic vocabulary word,* stable. *Possible answer: A stable government would provide citizens with consistent laws and fewer conflicts and unrest.)* **Verbal/Linguistic, Logical/Mathematical**

T Technology Skills

Using and Citing Information Assign small groups of students one of the countries discussed in the chapter, and have them research the current political situation in the country. Make sure students use reliable sources and that they include a list of their sources in their notes. Have each group compare and contrast the political situation in the country assigned with the government we have in the United States. Have students consider the human rights of the citizens of their assigned country in the Tropical North compared to the human rights of citizens of the United States.

Ask the groups to pretend that they live in their assigned country. Have them decide whether they would support the current government or not. Then have the groups make political posters or commercials in support or critical of the current government for the country assigned. Have students consider whether or not they would have the freedom of speech in the assigned country to be critical of the government in power, and would be able to display their posters or commercials there without being persecuted or arrested. **Visual/Spatial**

CLOSE & REFLECT

Formulating Questions To close this lesson, have students think about the unrest and conflicts this part of the world has experienced from colonial times to the present. In small groups, have students formulate questions they still have about the countries of the Tropical North. Then have them use the Internet or library to research possible answers.

LESSON 2 REVIEW ANSWERS

Reviewing Vocabulary

1. The *encomienda* system forced Native Americans to provide labor that early Spanish *haciendas* needed to grow cash crops.

Answering the Guiding Questions

2. **Analyzing** Ecuador and Colombia had more gold, more advanced Native Americans and, with Venezuela, more and better farmland than did Guyana, Suriname, and French Guiana.

3. **Identifying** Some Spanish colonists who wanted self-government declared independence, whereas others remained loyal to Spain. After independence was won, conflicts between wealthy business and rural groups over control of the government led to further unrest.

4. **Determining Central Ideas** Their governments have been unstable and not strong enough to control their territories.

5. **Argument Writing** Speeches should demonstrate reasoned judgment and an understanding of issues, such as French Guiana's current status and general political trends in the region.

ANSWER, p. 285

☑ **READING PROGRESS CHECK** Colombia, Guyana, and Suriname

Life in the Tropical North

ENGAGE

Bellringer Before students begin the lesson, ask them to think about something that makes their family unique. It could be a family custom, a tradition or maybe a shared event or even a second language.

Then make a connection to the Essential Question: *What makes a culture unique?* **Ask:** What is special or unique about your family? *(Students' answers will vary, but should include specific details about activities or traditions that are special or remarkable about their families.)*

TEACH & ASSESS

C Critical Thinking Skills

Making Inferences Have students think back to the history of the Tropical North countries that they read in Lesson 2. Have them identify the nationality of the European explorers of the region, the countries that colonized the region, and the slaves and workers that the colonists brought to the region. **Ask:** Why do you think the Tropical North has such a culturally diverse population? *(Students' answers will vary, but should include an understanding of the history of the European colonization of the area, the use of slave labor from Africa, and the recruitment of workers from Asia.)* Verbal/Linguistic, Logical/Mathematical

R Reading Skills

Using Context Clues Have students locate the word *mestizos* in the text and use context clues to determine its meaning. *(people of white and native American blood)* Tell students that in Spanish, the word *mestizo* means "mixed." The first known use of the word to refer to people of mixed ancestry was in 1582. **Ask:** Why do you think the Spanish word *mestizo* gained a new meaning in the late 1500s? *(Possible answer: By that time, the Spanish had conquered Ecuador, Colombia, and Venezuela, the people of mixed ancestry were part of the population.)* Verbal/Linguistic, Logical/Mathematical

---

ANSWER, p. 286

Taking Notes Notes should include at least one fact from each section, such as: Most people are mestizos; most people live in cities; people's location influences their culture; and so on.

networks

There's More Online!

☑ **GRAPHIC ORGANIZER**
☑ **VIDEO**

Reading **HELP**DESK

Academic Vocabulary
- **ratio**
- **migrate**

Content Vocabulary
- **Creole**
- **tariff**

TAKING NOTES: *Key Ideas and Details*

Organize As you read the lesson, use a graphic organizer to list information about life in the Tropical North.

Indiana Academic Standards
6.3.4, 6.3.10, 6.4.1, 6.4.3, 6.4.6, 6.4.8

Lesson 3
Life in the Tropical North

ESSENTIAL QUESTION • *What makes a culture unique?*

IT MATTERS BECAUSE
Many nations of the world, including the United States, have important trade relations with countries of the Tropical North.

People and Places

GUIDING QUESTION *What ethnic groups populate the Tropical North, and where do they live?*

People of European, African, Native American, and mixed descent are the major population groups of the countries that border the Pacific and Caribbean coasts. African, South Asian, and ethnically mixed peoples form the majority in the Atlantic coast countries.

Population Groups

Ecuador has the Tropical North's greatest indigenous population. About one in four Ecuadorans is Native American. If mestizos, or people of white and Native American descent, are added, the **ratio** becomes 9 of every 10 Ecuadorans.

Venezuela and Colombia have the opposite distribution. Some 20 percent of their populations are white, and 1 to 2 percent are Native American. Colombia's native population is the lowest of any Andean country. Mestizos are the largest group, accounting for more than two-thirds of Colombians and Venezuelans. The African populations of Venezuela, Ecuador, and Colombia are small, although some 15 percent of Colombians have mixed African and European ancestry.

The descendants of contract laborers from India are Suriname's largest group, making up nearly 40 percent of the population. An equal number are people of African and

(l to r) John Coletti/AWL Images/Getty Images; Kristin Piljay/Lonely Planet Images/age fotostock; Kymri Wilt/DanitaDelimont.com "Danita Delimont Photography"/Newscom

---

networks *Online Teaching Options*

VIDEO

Panama Hats

Stating Use this video about where and how the misnamed "Panama Hat" is made to discuss this small market, but unique element, of the economy of the Tropical North. Have pairs of students discuss the video and individually write a paragraph about one aspect of the video that was interesting to them. **AL** Visual/Spatial, Verbal/Linguistic

See page 271E for other online activities.

BBC Motion Gallery Education

mixed-African descent. A large Indonesian population is also present. Whites and Native Americans total less than 5 percent of Surinam's population.

Neighboring Guyana is home to more Native Americans; this group makes up almost 10 percent of the country's population. Ethnic Africans make up one-third of the population, and East Indians account for more than 40 percent. The country has no significant white population. About one in six Guyanese is of mixed ancestry.

People of mixed descent make up most of French Guiana's population. Small groups of French, Native Americans, Chinese, East Indians, Laotians, Vietnamese, Lebanese, Haitians, and Africans also live in French Guiana.

Where People Live

Guyana's population remains largely rural. Elsewhere in the Tropical North, most people live in cities. Bogotá, Colombia's capital on a high Andes plateau, is home to almost 5 million people. It is the north's largest city and the fifth largest in South America.

Colombia's Caribbean lowlands are home to about 20 percent of its people, mainly in Cartagena and other port cities along the coast.

John Coletti/AWL Images/Getty Images

Academic Vocabulary

ratio the relationship in amount or size between two or more things

The Iglesia de San Francisco, built by Catholic missionaries in about 1560, is the oldest restored church in Bogotá, Colombia.
▶ CRITICAL THINKING
Describing How important is the city of Bogotá in the Tropical North region today?

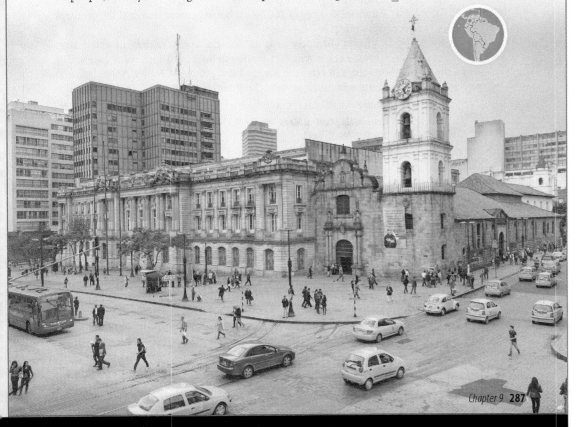

Life in the Tropical North

C Critical Thinking Skills

Comparing Have students make population comparisons between other countries in the Tropical North. **Ask:** What comparison could you make between the population of French Guiana and Ecuador? Between French Guiana and Colombia? *(Possible answers: Both the populations of French Guiana and Ecuador are mostly made up of people of mixed ancestry, although Colombia has more white people than French Guiana.)* Verbal/Linguistic, Logical/Mathematical

T Technology Skills

Making Presentations Have students work in small groups to use the Internet to research an urban city or rural town in one of the countries in the Tropical North. Then have groups use a word processing program to design a travel brochure for the city or town and present it to the class. The brochures should include photos, as well as fun and interesting facts about the city or town. Visual/Spatial

Content Background Knowledge

Santa Cruz de Mompox, founded in 1540, is a remote interior town located on an island in the middle of the Magdalena River in Colombia. It was an important and wealthy city during the colonial era. A royal mint was located there along with storehouses of precious metals and jewels. The river provided transportation from the city to the coast.

In the 1800s, the Magdalena River became unusable to large boats because of an accumulation of silt. Other trade routes were used and Mompox became isolated. In modern times, the region became off-limits to visitors because of warring factions in the area. However, the Magdalena Valley is now safe for tourists and Mompox was designated a World Heritage Site in 1995. Its well-preserved historic town center and the colonial architecture of the buildings are basically the same as they were in colonial times. Many of the churches, schools, and even a hospital are still being used the same way they were used almost 500 years ago. The making of gold jewelry is an important trade in this city of about 30,000 people.

MAP

Population: Tropical North

Integrating Visual Information Display the population layer of the Chapter Opener map. Have volunteers define the ideas of population distribution and density. Have students discuss the population density of this region and make inferences as to why people chose certain areas in which to settle. Visual/Spatial, Verbal/Linguistic, Logical/Mathematical

See page 271E for other online activities.

ANSWER, p. 287

CRITICAL THINKING Bogotá is Colombia's capital. Having almost 9 million people, Bogotá is the north's largest city and the fifth-largest city in South America.

Chapter 9 287

C1 Critical Thinking Skills

Making Generalizations Discuss with students where the current populations of the countries of the Tropical North live and why they most likely live where they do. **Ask:**

- What generalization could you make about why most people in the Tropical North live in or near a big city? *(Possible answer: Big cities offer the best job opportunities, which in turn, generally means more money.)*

- Think back to the physical landforms of these countries which you read about in Lesson 1. Why might the interior of some of these countries have few roads? Why might most of the population live along the coast? *(Possible answer: The interiors of these countries contain mountains, deep ravines, and dense rain forest that would make building roads extremely difficult, leaving the land along the coast the easiest for people to access.)* Logical/ Mathematical, Verbal/Linguistic

C2 Critical Thinking Skills

Identifying Problems Discuss with students that even though Spanish is the common language of the Tropical North, there may be regional differences in how the words are spoken. Ask students to theorize why this may occur. Point out to students that people who speak English can also have differences in how words and phrases are spoken. **Ask:** What problem might arise when people from Ecuador, Colombia, and Venezuela try to communicate in Spanish? *(Students' answers may vary, but should demonstrate an understanding of the different Spanish dialects spoken in each country because of the influence of Native American languages in the regions.)*
BL Logical/Mathematical, Verbal/Linguistic

Content Background Knowledge

Share with the class these interesting facts about Quito, Ecuador.

- Quito, the capital city of Ecuador, lies near the active Pichincha Volcano.
- Quito has had many earthquakes rock the city throughout its history.
- Quito has an elevation of 9,350 ft.

ANSWER, p. 288

✓ **READING PROGRESS CHECK** in cities along the coasts

The country's Pacific coast is sparsely settled. Most of the people there are descendants of enslaved Africans who worked on plantations near the Caribbean Sea. As they were freed or they escaped, they migrated into remote areas in western Colombia. The Llanos, where cattle ranching is the main activity, is another area with few people.

Quito, Ecuador, is another mountain capital city, with nearly 2 million people. Most of Ecuador's Native Americans live in or around Quito, or they farm rural mountain valleys nearby. Most other Ecuadorans live along the coast. Guayaquil, the country's largest city and major port, is located there.

C1 Most Venezuelans live along the coast. As in Colombia and Ecuador, Venezuelans began **migrating** to cities in the mid-1900s for the jobs and opportunities they offered. Today, more than 90 percent of the country's people live in Caracas, the capital city of 3 million, and other cities on or near the coast.

The countries of Guyana, Suriname, and the territory of French Guiana are sparsely populated. The population of the three combined totals only about half the population of Caracas. The interior of French Guiana has few roads and is largely uninhabited. In Suriname, small groups of Native Americans live in the Guiana Highlands. Nearly everyone else lives along the coast. Suriname's capital, Paramaribo, a city of 260,000, is home to more than half the country's population.

Most Guyanese also live on the coast, mainly in small farm towns. Each town's farmlands extend inland for several miles. The country's interior is home to a few groups of Native Americans and scattered mining and ranching settlements.

✓ **READING PROGRESS CHECK**

Determining Central Ideas Where do the greatest number of people in the Tropical North live?

Academic Vocabulary

migrate to move from one place to another

People and Cultures

GUIDING QUESTION *What is the Tropical North's culture like?*

Despite its largely Spanish heritage, no one culture unifies the Tropical North. Instead, its culture can be defined by the wide variety of ethnic groups that populate the region.

Language Groups

Spanish is the official language of Ecuador, Colombia, and Venezuela. There are differences in Ecuadoran Spanish because of the influence of Native American languages in each region of the country. More **C2** than 10 native languages are spoken in Ecuador. More than 25 native languages are spoken in Venezuela and some 180 in Colombia. Colombians, however, have taken great care to preserve the purity of the Spanish language.

288 *Chapter 9*

networks   *Online Teaching Options*

GRAPHS

The Populations of the Nations of the Tropical North

Comparing Visual Information Display the population pyramids showing the population distribution of the nations of the Tropical North across age and gender. Have volunteers identify the information each pyramid represents. In pairs, have students use the information to compare the populations of the various countries of the Tropical North. Then have the partners write a paragraph explaining their findings. AL Visual/Spatial, Verbal/Linguistic

See page 271E for other online activities.

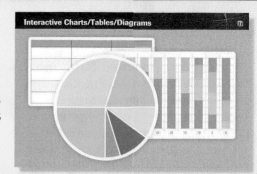
Interactive Charts/Tables/Diagrams

Languages in Guyana, Suriname, and French Guiana reflect their colonial heritage as well as their ethnic populations. **Creole**, a group of languages that enslaved people from various parts of Africa developed to communicate on colonial plantations, is widely spoken. Most people in Guyana speak English. In Suriname, the official language, Dutch, is spoken only as a second language. Native American languages, Hindi, and other South Asian languages are heard in both countries.

Whether they come from the region's rural or urban areas, many people enjoy a celebration called Carnival. This festival is celebrated just before the beginning of Lent, the Christian holy season that comes before Easter.

R

Religion, Daily Life, and the Arts
Ecuador, Colombia, and Venezuela are overwhelmingly Roman Catholic. No more than 10 percent of the people in these countries practice other religions. The religions practiced in Guyana, French Guiana, and Suriname reflect the variety of ethnic groups that live there. Suriname's population is made up of about equal numbers of Roman Catholics, Protestants, Hindus, and Muslims. Guyana's population is largely Protestant and Hindu, with sizable Catholic and Muslim minorities. In all countries, some Native Americans practice indigenous religions.

C

Each country's foods, music, and other cultural elements reflect its ethnic and religious makeup. Venezuela, Colombia, and Ecuador celebrate Carnival, though the festivities are not as colorful or as lively as those in Brazil. Regional religious festivals are celebrated in many Andes communities.

T

Kristin Piljay/Lonely Planet Images/age fotostock

Chapter 9 **289**

Explaining After students read the first paragraph, discuss the difficulties that we would have in the United States if people in each state spoke a different language. Have students consider the proximity of the countries of the Tropical North and compare them in size and proximity to the states in subregions of the United States.

Then have students consider the history of the countries in the Tropical North. **Ask:** Why would most people in Guyana speak English? *(The area was colonized by the English-speaking British and the country did not gain independence from Great Britain until 1966. English is the official language of Great Britain.)* Logical/Mathematical, Verbal/Linguistic

C Critical Thinking Skills

Synthesizing Have students recall what European country conquered and controlled the region of Ecuador, Colombia, and Venezuela, and consider what religion was primarily practiced in that country at that time. **Ask:** Why would most of the people of Ecuador, Colombia, and Venezuela practice the Roman Catholic faith? *(Students may state that Roman Catholic missionaries came to the area with the Spanish and worked to convert the native population to Christianity—specifically the Roman Catholic Church.)* Logical/Mathematical, Verbal/Linguistic

T Technology Skills

Transferring Knowledge Have interested students research the music of these countries that the women in the photo could be dancing to, and have them make recordings that they can play for the class.

As an alternative, some students could find pictures and recipes of different foods that people in these countries eat. Then share the pictures of the dishes along with the ingredients that are used in everyday foods or special foods eaten on holidays celebrated in these countries. **BL** Auditory/Musical

---

LECTURE SLIDES

What Is Carnival?

Discussing Display the lecture slide presentation about the historical and religious aspects of Carnival. Have volunteers read some of the information from the slides aloud. As a class, discuss the cultural and social impact and the religious elements of this event. **ELL** Visual/Spatial, Verbal/Linguistic

See page 271E for other online activities.

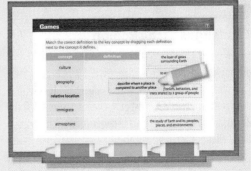

Life in the Tropical North

Making Presentations Place students in small groups. Have them use reliable sources on the Internet to research cultural and regional dances of the Tropical North. Encourage each group to either perform one of the dances they learn about by watching the videos or to show and explain a video of the music and dances to the rest of the class.

Then discuss the characteristics of this cultural heritage. **Ask:** What aspects about the music or dances of the Tropical North countries do you enjoy or not enjoy? Why? *(Students' answers will vary, but should reflect valid opinions supported by appropriate details or constructive criticism of the music or dance moves.)* **Kinesthetic, Auditory/Musical**

W Writing Skills

Argument Explain to students that another goal of UNASUR is the free movement of people between member countries. For example, in the past, if a person from Colombia wanted to travel to Ecuador, he or she had to have a valid Colombian passport along with a visa from Ecuador. A visa is an official government document that gives the holder permission to enter a country and to stay for a specific length of time. Obtaining a visa can take several weeks and requires filling out various government forms.

In small groups, have students brainstorm advantages and disadvantages of allowing people of member countries to move freely between the UNASUR countries. Encourage groups to list these advantages and disadvantages in a two-column chart that all members can use or copy.

Tell students to take a side on the issue and have at least three reasons to support the side they take. Then have individuals use their group's two-column charts to write a paragraph to answer the question: **Is free movement of people between countries in the best interests of governments?** *(Students' paragraphs should make a claim and have at least three details to support the position.)* **Logical/Mathematical, Verbal/Linguistic**

A girl in the Andes of Ecuador plays a pan flute, one of the most popular instruments of Andean music.
▶ **CRITICAL THINKING**
Describing In addition to music, what other cultural traditions are practiced by people in the region?

Culture often differs by geographic area. Native Americans in mountain regions weave baskets and cloth using designs that are hundreds of years old. They play Andean music using drums, flutes, and other traditional instruments. Along the coast of Colombia and Venezuela, a dance called the *cumbia* blends the region's Spanish and African heritages. Other Venezuelan coastal music and dance, such as salsa and merengue, show Caribbean island influences. Maracas and guitars are used to perform the music of the Llano.

☑ **READING PROGRESS CHECK**

Analyzing What language and religion are most common in the region?

Ongoing Issues

GUIDING QUESTION *What challenges do the countries of the Tropical North face?*

Many people who live in the Tropical North are poor, although natural resources in the region are plentiful. For generations, those resources have mostly benefited only a wealthy few. This situation has created tensions within and between countries.

Trade Relations

Many South American leaders believe that one way to strengthen their countries' economies is to expand trade. In 2008 the countries in the Tropical North joined with the rest of South America to form the Union of South American Nations (UNASUR). One of the organization's goals is ending **tariffs**—taxes on imported goods—on trade between member nations. Another goal is adopting a uniform currency, similar to the euro.

A Northern Neighbor

Another challenge is improving the region's relationship with the United States. The relationship has sometimes been rocky in the past, as when the United States helped Panama gain independence

---

net**w**rks *Online Teaching Options*

GRAPHIC ORGANIZER

Challenges of the Region

Suggesting a Solution Use the interactive graphic organizer to identify the challenges that Venezuela, Colombia, and Ecuador face. Discuss the challenges with the class and have volunteers list each challenge. Continue the discussion by asking students to suggest solutions to each of the challenges listed on the graphic organizer. Then have students write a paragraph explaining what they feel is the most serious challenge. **BL Verbal/Linguistic**

See page 271E for other online activities.

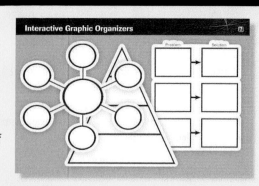

Interactive Graphic Organizers

ANSWERS, p. 290

☑ **READING PROGRESS CHECK** Spanish and Roman Catholic

CRITICAL THINKING basket making, cloth weaving, and dancing that blend indigenous, Spanish, and African cultural influences

from Colombia in the early 1900s. Relations between the United States and Colombia have improved greatly. The United States and the Colombian government are working together to stop the flow of illegal drugs.

Challenges in Venezuela

In 1998 Venezuelans elected Hugo Chávez, a former military leader, as president. Chávez frequently criticized the United States and became friendly with anti-U.S. governments in Cuba and Iran.

After his election, Chávez promised to use Venezuela's oil income to improve conditions for the country's poor. Among other actions that angered U.S. leaders, in 2009 he seized control of U.S. companies that were developing oil resources in Venezuela. His strong rule split Venezuela into opposing groups. Working-class people supported Chávez, but middle-class and wealthy Venezuelans opposed his policies.

Struggles in Colombia and Ecuador

Colombia has undergone a long and bitter struggle between the country's government and a Colombian organization called the Revolutionary Armed Forces of Colombia (FARC). One of FARC's goals is to curtail the role of foreign governments and businesses in Colombia's affairs. Another goal is to provide help and support for the nation's poor farmers. FARC is funded through various means, including the production and sale of illegal drugs.

In Ecuador, indigenous peoples protested for rights and blamed President Rafael Correa for not keeping his promises. Correa had promised to rewrite Ecuador's constitution. Among other things, he pledged to extend the rights of the people. Disappointed when Correa did not act, indigenous peoples organized to win rights for access to land, basic services, and political representation.

FOLDABLES
Study Organizer

Include this lesson's information in your Foldable®.

☑ **READING PROGRESS CHECK**
Determining Central Ideas How did Hugo Chávez increase tensions between Venezuela and the United States?

LESSON 3 REVIEW

Reviewing Vocabulary
1. Why did enslaved Africans create *Creole*?

Answering the Guiding Questions
2. *Identifying* Why is the Tropical North home to so many ethnic groups?

3. *Analyzing* Why are there Hindu and Muslim populations in northern South America?

4. *Analyzing* How and why is UNASUR likely to affect the economies and people of the Tropical North's countries?

5. *Informative/Explanatory Writing* Choose one of the challenges the Tropical North faces, and write a short essay suggesting how to solve it.

C Critical Thinking Skills

Analyzing Have one or two volunteers read aloud the section called "Struggles in Colombia and Ecuador" and discuss it as a class. **Ask:** What contradiction do you see between the goals of FARC and its means to reach those goals? *(Students' answers will vary, but should discuss the contrast of positive goals with the negative means to fund them.)* Logical/Mathematical, Verbal/Linguistic

W Writing Skills

Argument Have students research more about Hugo Chávez. Have students use reliable sources, and encourage them to read about people who endorsed him and those who did not. Tell students after they have considered the arguments of both sides to take a side, pro or con, with those who endorsed him or those who did not.

Then have students write a paragraph explaining whether they agree with the working class people who supported him or the middle class and wealthy people who did not agree with him. Students should clearly state their opinion in their paragraphs and support their opinion with facts from their research. Verbal/Linguistic

CLOSE & REFLECT

Formatting Questions To close this lesson, have each student write a question about the ongoing issues that challenge the countries of the Tropical North and how these issues could affect the people of those countries or affect the people of the United States.

Collect the questions, and have a volunteer read and post them. Tell students to watch for international news stories about the Tropical North countries and report to the class any breaking news they hear of or read about, especially any news that answers or addresses one of their questions.

LESSON 3 REVIEW ANSWERS

Reviewing Vocabulary

1. Many came from different parts of Africa and needed a language that all could use to communicate.

Answering the Guiding Questions

2. **Identifying** The Spanish conquered much of the region from the natives. Then they, as well as the Dutch, French, and English, brought African slaves to the region. Intermingling of the races produced mixed populations. Later, South Asian workers replaced African slaves.

3. **Analyzing** In colonial times, after slavery ended, plantation owners in Guyana and Suriname imported large numbers of contract workers from India

and Indonesia to work on their plantations. Most Hindus and Muslims living in the region today are descendants of those workers.

4. **Analyzing** Removal of tariffs will encourage trade between nations. Increased trade will lead to more jobs making goods for export. More exports, jobs, and income will enlarge the country's economy.

5. **Informative/Explanatory Writing** Answers should demonstrate an accurate understanding of the issue and reasoned judgment in proposing a solution.

ANSWER, p. 291

☑ **READING PROGRESS CHECK** He frequently criticized the United States, took control of American companies in Venezuela, and developed close ties with communist Cuba.

CHAPTER REVIEW ACTIVITY

Have students create a four-column chart like the one below for the Tropical North. Have students list *Settled by, Physical Geography, Climate, Economy-Major Exports* as the four column headings. Tell students to complete the chart for each category with information and examples from the text. (Possible answers: **Settled by**—*Spanish, British, Dutch, French;* **Physical Geography**—*Andes Mountains, Darién lowlands, Llanos plains, Guiana highlands, rainforests, rivers, waterfalls, Galápagos Islands;* **Climate**—*tropical (monsoon, wet-dry, rain forest),* mountain *(tierra templada, tierra fria, páramos);* **Economy**—*bananas, coffee, oil, coal, diamonds, emeralds, bauxite, shrimp)* Visual/Spatial

The Tropical North			
Settled by	Physical Geography	Climate	Economy— Major Exports

REVIEW THE ENDURING UNDERSTANDINGS

Review this chapter's Enduring Understandings with students:

• **Over time, people adapt to their environment.**

Now pose the following questions in a class discussion to apply the Enduring Understanding to this chapter.

• How do rivers help the people in the Tropical North? (*Possible answer: People use the rivers as a means of transportation through the rugged lands of these countries where it would be difficult to build roads. The rivers form important routes from the coast to the interior of the countries.*)

• How did the Native Americans of the Tropical North adapt to their environment before Europeans arrived in the region? (*Possible answer: The Native Americans were hunter-gatherers at first, fishing the rivers and coasts of the ocean. They continued to adapt to their environment by moving inland to the mountain valleys in the Andes and began to farm the land and mine natural resources such as gold.*)

Directions: Write your answers on a separate piece of paper.

❶ Use your **FOLDABLES** to explore the Essential Questions.
INFORMATIVE/EXPLANATORY WRITING Choose one of the region's countries or colonies. Compare the physical and population maps found at the beginning of the unit. Then write at least two paragraphs explaining how the physical geography affects where people live and work.

❷ **21st Century Skills**
ANALYZING Working in small groups, choose one of the countries or the colony found in the region and research the most common occupations practiced by its people. Are any of those jobs unique to that country and its culture? Present your findings to the class in a slideshow or a poster.

❸ **Thinking Like a Geographer**
IDENTIFYING Create a two-column chart. List the name of the Tropical North country or colony in the first column. List the primary languages spoken in the second column.

❹ **GEOGRAPHY ACTIVITY**

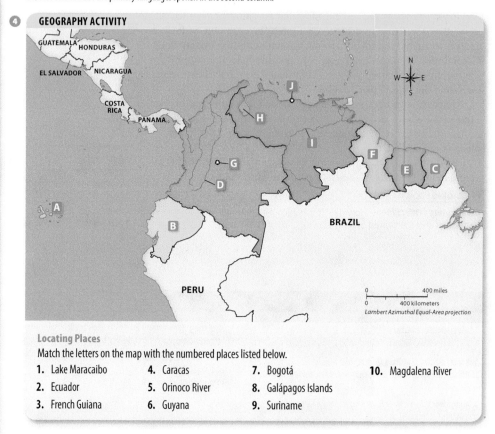

Locating Places
Match the letters on the map with the numbered places listed below.

1. Lake Maracaibo
2. Ecuador
3. French Guiana
4. Caracas
5. Orinoco River
6. Guyana
7. Bogotá
8. Galápagos Islands
9. Suriname
10. Magdalena River

• The Spanish conquered the Tropical North in the 1500s, and the region came under the rule of governments set up by the Spanish. How did the Native Americans adapt to the presence of the Spanish? (*Sample answer: Native Americans suffered greatly under the Spanish. Many of them died from European diseases that the Spanish had brought with them, or they were enslaved by the Spanish and forced to work in Spanish mines and on Spanish haciendas.*)

• How might the creation of UNASUR help the people of the region? (*Students may state that the trade between nations would not be taxed and people will have access to more and varied types of products.*)

ACTIVITIES ANSWERS

Exploring the Essential Question

❶ **INFORMATIVE/EXPLANATORY WRITING** Students' writings will vary, but should demonstrate an understanding of the physical geography of the country or colony chosen and how it affects population areas and growth.

21st Century Skills

❷ **ANALYZING** Students' work should be well-researched, interesting, informative, and meet standards for spelling and grammar.

REVIEW THE GUIDING QUESTIONS

Directions: Choose the best answer for each question.

❶ The Galápagos Islands were the site of
A. Christopher Columbus's second landing in the Americas.
B. an outpost of the Incas.
C. Charles Darwin's study that resulted in the theory of evolution.
D. Ecuador's largest volcanic eruption.

❷ The world's leading producer of emeralds is
F. Venezuela.
G. Colombia.
H. Ecuador.
I. French Guiana.

❸ South America's native populations were forced into laboring for the Spanish under a system called
A. *encomienda.*
B. immunity.
C. hacienda.
D. Quito.

❹ The transition from colonial governments to independence in the Tropical North of South America
F. happened suddenly in 1550.
G. took place slowly over a period of more than 100 years.
H. began in Brazil.
I. was a result of the War of 1812.

❺ The most populous spot in the Tropical North is
A. Ecuador.
B. Bogotá.
C. the Llanos.
D. Cartagena.

❻ Of the languages used in the Tropical North countries, Spanish is used in its purest form in
F. Ecuador.
G. French Guiana.
H. Venezuela.
I. Colombia.

Chapter 9 **293**

ASSESSMENT ANSWERS

Review the Guiding Questions

❶ **C** For this question, knowing that Columbus and the Incas have no connection to the Galápagos Islands will help students eliminate choices A and B. Choice D is the distracter because the islands are part of Ecuador and have active volcanoes, but not necessarily the *largest* volcanic eruption. Refer students to Lesson 1 for help.

❷ **G** To answer this question students need to recall that gold is found throughout the Tropical North and diamonds are mined from Colombia to Suriname, but Colombia is known for high-quality emeralds. Refer students to Lesson 1 for help.

❸ **A** The phrase *forced into laboring* in the question gives a clue to the meaning of the word needed to complete the item. Knowing that *encomienda* is a system that allowed Spanish colonists to demand labor from the Native American will help students eliminate choices B, C, and D. Refer students to Lesson 2 for help.

❹ **G** To answer this question, students need to recall the information on the map in Lesson 2 on about when the countries in the region gained their independence. Some quick mental math will eliminate choices F and I. Knowing that Brazil is not part of the region will eliminate choice H.

❺ **B** Remembering that most people in the region live in cities will help eliminate choices A and C, a country and a vast tropical plain. Students then need to recall that Bogota is the north's largest city with almost 9 million people. Refer students to Lesson 3 for help.

❻ **I** The word *Spanish* in the question gives a clue to the origin of the language and eliminates choice G immediately. Since Spanish is spoken in the three remaining countries, students will need to recall that Colombians have taken great care to preserve the purity of the Spanish spoken in that country. Refer students to Lesson 3.

Thinking Like a Geographer

❸ **IDENTIFYING**

Ecuador	Quito, Spanish and 10 native languages
Colombia	Bogota, Spanish and 180 native languages
Venezuela	Caracas, Spanish and 25 native languages
Guyana	Georgetown, English and Creole
Suriname	Paramaribo, Creole and Dutch
French Guiana	Cayenne, Creole, French, native, Hindi

Geography Activity

❹ **LOCATING PLACES**

1. H
2. B
3. C
4. J
5. I
6. F
7. G
8. A
9. E
10. D

Assessment Answers

DBQ Analyzing Documents

7 C Make sure that students understand that the question is asking about public lands and not the lands in the hands of indigenous people and farmers. Public lands are owned by the nation and are controlled by the government, which has the responsibility to use them on behalf of all of Ecuador's people.

8 F Since the indigenous people and farmers are among Ecuador's poorest citizens, they are likely to want to be better off than they are, so they would be most likely to sell the land to have a better way of life.

Short Response

9 Possible answer: Improving child development and education would help make children better able to become productive workers and good citizens, which would help the economy and government of their nation.

10 Students might suggest such steps as better health care or nutrition to improve children's health so they can learn better and live more healthful lives. Whatever suggestions students make to improve child development should then be supported by explanations or reasons why the suggestions would improve children's lives.

Extended Response

11 Students' reports should show evidence of good research from credible sources, be interesting, well-written and not plagiarized from the sources, and meet your standards for spelling and grammar. The writing should describe school life for children of the Tropical North and contain appropriate transitions to address related issues.

DBQ ANALYZING DOCUMENTS

7 CITING TEXT EVIDENCE Read the following passage:

"*With one of the highest deforestation rates in Latin America, Ecuador is losing 200,000 hectares (494,211 acres) of forest every year . . . Although most of the forests of the country are public lands, an important percentage of what is left is in the hands of indigenous people and farmers, among the country's poorest citizens.*"

—from Steve Goldstein, "A Grand Plan: Ecuador and 'Forest Partners'" (2008)

What group in Ecuador controls the forests on public lands?

A. indigenous people
B. farmers
C. the government
D. businesses

8 ANALYZING Which most likely explains why the indigenous people and the farmers might be willing to sell their land?

F. to enjoy a better way of life
G. so they can buy more productive land
H. so they can move to the city
I. to rid themselves of the burden of the land

SHORT RESPONSE

"*Latin American pop superstar Shakira will be at this weekend's gathering of the Western Hemisphere's leaders advocating for [promoting] her favorite issues: early childhood development and universal education.*"

—from Gregory M. Lamb, "Shakira Advocates for Children at the Summit of the Americas" (2012)

9 IDENTIFYING POINT OF VIEW How would improving child development and education benefit the countries of the region?

10 ANALYZING What step do you think nations in this region should take to improve child development? Why?

EXTENDED RESPONSE

11 INFORMATIVE/EXPLANATORY WRITING What is school like for children who live in the Tropical North of South America? Research and then describe the educational system in this part of the world in a detailed report. Find out how many months of the year school is in session, how long the typical day is, and what kinds of subjects are taught. You might also want to find out how education is funded. Then compare the results with your school experience.

Need Extra Help?

If You've Missed Question	1	2	3	4	5	6	7	8	9	10	11
Review Lesson	1	1	2	2	3	3	1	3	3	3	3

---

networks   *Online Teaching Options*

Practicing 21st Century Skills

Practicing Skills Your students can practice important 21st Century skills such as geography, reading, writing, and critical thinking by using resources found in the Skills Builder tab of the online Student Learning Center. Resources include templates, handbooks, and slide shows. These same resources are also available in the Resource Library of the Teacher Lesson Center.

CHAPTER 10

Andes and Midlatitude Countries
Planner

UNDERSTANDING BY DESIGN®

Enduring Understandings

- *People, places, and ideas change over time.*

Essential Questions

- *How does geography influence the way people live?*
- *Why do civilizations rise and fall?*
- *What makes a culture unique?*

Predictable Misunderstandings

- *The Andean countries have the exact same geography as the Tropical North.*
- *The culture of these countries is the same as the other nations in South America.*
- *The Andes mountain range is a small mountain chain that has no effect on the landscape.*

Assessment Evidence

Performance Tasks:

- *Project-Based Learning Digital Hands-On Chapter Project*
- *Project-Based Learning Hands-On Chapter Project*

Other Evidence:

- *Participation in Project-Based Learning Activities*
- *Participation in Interactive Whiteboard Activities*
- *Contribution to small-group activities*
- *Interpretation of slide show images and special purpose maps*
- *Participation in class discussions about physical geography topics*
- *Lesson Reviews*
- *Chapter Assessments*

Students will:

6.1.6 Identify trade routes and discuss their impact on the rise of cultural centers and trade cities in Europe and Mesoamerica.

6.1.20 Analyze cause-and-effect relationships, keeping in mind multiple causations, including the importance of individuals, ideas, human interests, beliefs and chance in history.

6.1.21 Differentiate between fact and interpretation in historical accounts and explain the meaning of historical passages by identifying who was involved, what happened, where it happened, and relating them to outcomes that followed and gaps in the historical record.

6.2.5 Discuss the impact of major forms of government in Europe and the Americas on civil and human rights.

6.3.3 Describe and compare major physical characteristics of regions in Europe and the Americas.

6.3.4 Describe and compare major cultural characteristics of regions in Europe and the Western Hemisphere.

6.3.10 Explain the ways cultural diffusion, invention, and innovation change culture.

SUGGESTED PACING GUIDE

Introducing the Chapter .... 2 Days	Lesson 3 .... 2 Days
Lesson 1 .... 2 Days	What Do You Think? .... 2 Days
Lesson 2 .... 2 Days	Chapter Wrap-Up and Assessment .... 2 Days

TOTAL TIME   12 Days

Key for Using the Teacher Edition

SKILL-BASED ACTIVITIES

Types of skill activities found in the Teacher Edition.

* **V Visual Skills** require students to analyze maps, graphs, charts, and photos.

W Writing Skills provide writing opportunities to help students comprehend the text.

R Reading Skills help students practice reading skills and master vocabulary.

C Critical Thinking Skills help students apply and extend what they have learned.

T Technology Skills require students to use digital tools effectively.

*Letters are followed by a number when there is more than one of the same type of skill on the page.

DIFFERENTIATED INSTRUCTION

All activities are written for the on-level student unless otherwise marked with the leveled labels below.

BL Beyond Level
AL Approaching Level
ELL English Language Learners

All students benefit from activities that utilize different learning styles. Many activities are marked as below when a particular learning style is highlighted.

Intrapersonal	Naturalist
Logical/Mathematical	Kinesthetic
Visual/Spatial	Auditory/Musical
Verbal/Linguistic	Interpersonal

CHAPTER OPENER PLANNER

Students will know:

- *the Andean countries have a unique geography that shapes their landscape.*
- *this unique geography affects their industry, travel, trade, and agriculture.*

Students will be able to:

- *analyze a world map to identify Andes and Midlatitude countries*
- *use a time line to discuss various events in the history of this region*

UNDERSTANDING
BY DESIGN®

☑ *Print Teaching Options*

V **Visual Skills**

☐ **P. 296** Students identify countries in the region and explore their landscape. Visual/Spatial

☐ **P. 297** Students review the time line and use it to answer questions about the history of the region. **AL**

W **Writing Skills**

☐ **P. 297** Students write a paragraph to discuss how people would have reacted to the discovery of a valuable resource, such as silver, by drawing on what they know about the Gold Rush in the United States. Verbal/Linguistic

☑ *Online Teaching Options*

☐ **MAP** **Reading a Map**—Students identify aspects and locations of the region on a map.

☐ **TIME LINE** **Reading a Time Line** —Students learn about where historical events occurred in the region and identify the locations where events took place on the map. Visual/Spatial

☐ **MAP** **Interactive World Altas**—Students use the interactive world atlas to identify current location of the Andean region and its terrain. Visual/Spatial

☑ *Printable Digital Worksheets*

☐ **WORKSHEET** **Primary Sources: Juan and Eva Perón**—Students can use the worksheet to learn more about the government of Argentina under Perón. Verbal/Linguistic

☐ **WORKSHEET** **Critical Thinking Skills: Salmon Farming**—Students can use this worksheet to analyze the impact of salmon farming on the environment.

Project-Based Learning

Hands-On

Making a Photo Collage

Have students make a photo collage that illustrates the diversity found in the Andean and mid-latitude countries in South America. Student groups will create a collage that includes information about the region's physical features, economy, and culture. After students have created their collages, have them display them on a bulletin board or wall. Students will then conduct a gallery walk to review the collages. As students examine each group's work, have them analyze the photos and describe why certain ones are part of the display.

Digital Hands-On

Making an Online Video

Have pairs create an online video about the history of one of the Andes or mid-latitude countries. Students should find historical online photos, put them in order, and create storyboards with captions or short summaries about each photo. Students might also want to link sounds or music to different photos for enrichment. Have students upload the videos to a class wiki or Web site and have a class video day.

Print Resources

ANCILLARY RESOURCES

These ancillaries are available for every chapter and lesson.

- **Reading Essentials and Study Guide Workbook** **AL** **ELL**
- **Chapter Tests and Lesson Quizzes Blackline Masters**

PRINTABLE DIGITAL WORKSHEETS

These printable digital worksheets are available for every chapter and lesson.

- **Hands-On Chapter Projects**
- **What Do You Know? Activities**
- **Chapter Summaries (English and Spanish)**
- **Vocabulary Builder Activities**
- **Quizzes and Tests**
- **Reading Essentials and Study Guide (English and Spanish)** **AL** **ELL**
- **Guided Reading Activities**

More Media Resources

SUGGESTED VIDEOS

NOTE: Be sure to preview videos to ensure they are age-appropriate.

- **180° South** (documentary, 87 min.)
- **The Great Inca Rebellion** (52 min.)
- **Globe Trekker: Argentina** (48 min.)

SUGGESTED READING

- *Pablo Neruda: Poet of the People,* by Monica Brown **AL**
- **Trapped: How the World Rescued 33 Miners from 2,000 Feet Below the Chilean Desert,** by Marc Aronson **BL**
- **Argentina (South America Today),** by Charles J. Shields
- **The Lost City: The Discovery of Machu Picchu** by Ted Lewin **AL**

PHYSICAL GEOGRAPHY OF THE REGION

Students will know:
- the Andean countries have a unique geography that shapes their landscape.
- this unique geography affects their industry, travel, trade, and agriculture.

Students will be able to:
- **identify** the different landforms and waterways in the Andes countries.
- **describe** the effect of altitude on climate.
- **discuss** the climate extremes found in the region.
- **describe** important natural resources in the region.

UNDERSTANDING
BY DESIGN®

☑ Print Teaching Options

V Visual Skills

☐ **P. 298** Students relate the photograph of the mountains to the essential question of how geography affects where people live by imagining what it would be like to live there. **Naturalist, Interpersonal**

☐ **P. 299** Students create word squares to reinforce vocabulary. **ELL Visual/Spatial**

☐ **P. 300** Students use the photographs of the mountains and village to make inferences about life in the village.

☐ **P. 300** Students mark and label the areas they read about on an outline map of South America. **Visual/Spatial**

☐ **P. 302** Students create a two-column chart to take notes on the climates of the midlatitude countries. **Visual**

☐ **P. 303** Students create a stair-step diagram to illustrate the effects of latitude on climate in Andean countries.

☐ **P. 305** Students complete a chart showing the natural resources in Bolivia, Chile, and Peru. **AL**

R Reading Skills

☐ **P. 301** Students summarize the relationship between altitude and temperature and the relationship between altitude and oxygen content. **Logical/Mathematical**

☐ **P. 304** Students identify the most important ideas about El Niños and Las Niñas. **Verbal/Linguistic**

C Critical Thinking Skills

☐ **P. 299** Students compare and contrast distinctive features of the Andes with features around the world.

☐ **P. 302** Students add latitude ranges to the climate chart they made and relate latitude changes to differences in climate. **Logical/Mathematical**

T Technology Skills

☐ **P. 303** Students research the 2010 Chilean mine cave-in and rescue in Copiago and give a brief report on it. **BL**

☑ Online Teaching Options

V Visual Skills

☐ **MAP Physical Geography: Andean Region**—Students use the physical geography layer of the Chapter Opener map to highlight the various landforms and the scope of the Andes.

☐ **MAPS Winds and Currents**—Students use the maps to discuss the climate factors that shape the landscape of the Andean region. **Visual/Spatial**

☐ **MAP Climates: Andean Region**—Students view the climate layer of the Chapter Opener map and discuss how climate varies with elevation. **AL Visual/Spatial, Verbal/Linguistic**

☐ **IMAGE Uses of Wool**—Students use the interactive image to discuss the importance of alpaca wool to the region. **ELL Interpersonal**

☐ **MAP Resources: Andean Region**—Students can use the resources layer of the Chapter Opener map to discuss the various resources of the region. **Visual/Spatial**

W Writing Skills

☐ **SLIDE SHOW Landforms: Andean Region**—Students use the slide show information to write a paragraph about how mountains have influenced development of the region. **BL Visual/Spatial**

R Reading Skills

☐ **LECTURE SLIDE The Latin *terra* in English and Spanish**—Students use the lecture slide to discuss climate by analyzing the root word *terra* and how it connects to the way elevation is described. **BL Verbal/Linguistic**

☐ **LECTURE SLIDE Impact of Altitude**—Students use the lecture slide to make connections to the content of the lesson.

C Critical Thinking Skills

☐ **VIDEO Around the World—Chile**—Students watch a video about the physical geography and cities of Chile and compare and contrast it with the geography of their own region. **AL**

☐ **INFOGRAPHIC How Elevation Affects Life**—Students can use the infographic to discuss the impact of elevation on plants, animals, and humans. **ELL Visual/Spatial, Verbal/Linguistic**

☐ **MAP Comparing Mountain Ranges**—Students use the map to compare the Andes Mountains to other mountain ranges discussed in previous chapters. **ELL Verbal/Linguistic**

T Technology Skills

☐ **ONLINE SELF-CHECK QUIZ Lesson 1**—Students receive instant feedback on their mastery of lesson content.

HISTORY OF THE REGION

Students will know:
- *the Andean culture is unique due to geography.*

Students will be able to:
- **explain** *the rise and fall of the Inca empire.*
- **describe** *how the countries of the region gained their independence.*
- **discuss** *economic challenges and political instability in the region.*

UNDERSTANDING
BY DESIGN®

☑ *Print Teaching Options*

V Visual Skills

☐ **P. 306** Students use a map to discuss the advantages and disadvantages of the location of the Inca Empire.

☐ **P. 307** Students analyze the image of Machu Picchu.

☐ **P. 308** Students study a map of native civilizations and answer questions to help them grasp the significance of the Inca Empire. **AL** Visual/Spatial

☐ **P. 311** Students create a time line of political changes in Argentina and Chile beginning in 1946. **AL**

W Writing Skills

☐ **P. 309** Pairs of students conduct Internet research and write biographies of Simón Bolívar and José de San Martin to share with the class. **BL** Verbal/Linguistic

R Reading Skills

☐ **P. 307** Students determine the meaning of the word *hierarchy.* **AL** **ELL** Visual/Spatial

☐ **P. 309** Students determine the main ideas about independence movements in South America.

☐ **P. 310** Students answer questions to focus on the central ideas about the history of the Andean region in the late 1800s and 1900s. Logical/Mathematical

☐ **P. 311** Students summarize recent political trends in the region in one sentence. Verbal/Linguistic

C Critical Thinking Skills

☐ **P. 307** Students complete a T-chart to compare and contrast American civilization and Inca civilization.

T Technology Skills

☐ **P. 310** Students research the life of Eva Perón and write a short biographical essay. Verbal/Linguistic

---

☑ *Online Teaching Options*

V Visual Skills

☐ **MAP** **Native American Civilizations**—Students use the map to discuss the expanse of the Incan Empire and their colonization by Europeans. **AL** Kinesthetic, Interpersonal

☐ **MAP** **Independence: Andean Region**—Students use the map to identify the order in which various nations in the region became independent. **BL** Visual/Spatial

W Writing Skills

☐ **VIDEO** **World's Wonders—Machu Picchu**—Students watch a video about the history of Machu Picchu and write a paragraph about an aspect they found interesting. **AL** Visual/Spatial

R Reading Skills

☐ **GRAPHIC ORGANIZER** **Andean Economic Challenges**— Students use the interactive graphic organizer to discuss the economic challenges of the region. Visual/Spatial

☐ **LECTURE SLIDE** **How Spain Conquered the Inca**— Students use the lecture slide to review the various methods through which Spain concuqered the Incan Empire. Visual/Spatial

☐ **LECTURE SLIDE** **Aspects of Incan Society**— Students use the lecture slide to understand more about the Inca. Visual/Spatial

C Critical Thinking Skills

☐ **TIME LINE** **Rise and Fall of the Incan Empire**—Students use the interactive time line about the rise and fall of the Incan empire to discuss the impact of colonization on native people. **AL**

☐ **TIME LINE** **Dates of Independence**—Students use the time line on independence to review the process of independence from European rule in the region. Visual/Spatial

☐ **CHART** **Dictators in the Andean Regions**—Students use the chart to discuss the civil unrest in the Andean region during the 1800s and 1900s. **BL** Kinesthetic, Interpersonal

T Technology Skills

☐ **ONLINE SELF-CHECK QUIZ** **Lesson 2**—Students receive instant feedback on their mastery of lesson content.

☑ *Printable Digital Worksheets*

W Writing Skills

☐ **WORKSHEET** **Primary Sources Reading Skills: Juan and Eva Perón**—Students can use the worksheet to learn more about the government of Argentina under Perón. Verbal/Linguistic

LESSON 3 PLANNER

LIFE IN THE REGION

Students will know:
- this unique geography affects their industry, travel, trade, and agriculture.
- the Andean culture is unique due to geography.

Students will be able to:
- *discuss* the major population patterns in the region.
- *describe* the ethnic and language groups in the region.
- *discuss* daily life.
- *explain* how economic and environment issues are affecting the region.

UNDERSTANDING BY DESIGN®

☑ Print Teaching Options

V Visual Skills

☐ **P. 313** Students identify the two main ideas in the first two paragraphs about large cities and communities that are represented in the photograph of the city.

☐ **P. 314** Students create a two-column chart to identify in which country each ethnic or language group is found.

☐ **P. 315** Students create a Venn diagram to compare city life and country life in the region. Visual/Spatial

☐ **P. 316** Students create a circle graph about the important sectors of the economy based on the percentages given in the text. **BL** Visual/Spatial

W Writing Skills

☐ **P. 315** Students experiment with writing a story in the style of magic realism. **BL** Verbal/Linguistic

R Reading Skills

☐ **P. 312** Students answer questions to help summarize information about the ethnic background of the region's population. Verbal/Linguistic

☐ **P. 313** Students determine the meaning of the phrase *pueblos jóvenes.* **AL** Verbal/Linguistic

C Critical Thinking Skills

☐ **P. 316** Students answer questions to focus on the main ideas about the economies of Peru and Bolivia. **AL**

T Technology Skills

☐ **P. 317** Students work in groups to research the transportation of one of the Andean countries, Mercosur, or environmental problems in the region and present their findings. Verbal/Linguistic

☑ Online Teaching Options

V Visual Skills

MAP **Population: Andean Region**—Students use the population map to discuss the "population rim" along the coast of the Andean region. **ELL** Visual/Spatial

IMAGE **Cultures of the Andean Region**—Students use the interactive image to discuss cultural traditions in the region. **AL** Interpersonal

W Writing Skills

SLIDE SHOW **Traditional and Modern Lifestyles**—Students use the slide show to discuss aspects of traditional and modern life in the region and write a paragraph about an aspect that appeals to them. **BL** Verbal/Linguistic

MAP **Comparing Highway Systems**—Students use the map to compare the Incan roads to the Pan-American Highway and write a paragraph describing transportation challenges. **BL**

R Reading Skills

GRAPHIC ORGANIZER **Andean Economic Activities Today**—Students will work in small groups to organize the main economic activities of the region.

C Critical Thinking Skills

VIDEO **Greener Sources of Power in the Andes**—Students watch a video to learn more about finding lithium in the Andes Mountains. **AL** Visual/Spatial, Intrapersonal

VIDEO **Buenos Aires, Argentina**—Students watch a video about life in this city and compare and contrast ways of life in the video to their own lives. Visual/Spatial

GRAPHS **Population of the Andean Region**—Students use the graphs to analyze the change and distribution of population in the region. Visual/Spatial

GRAPHIC ORGANIZER **Pro vs. Con: The Highway System**—Students use the interactive graphic organizer to analyze the pros and cons of the highway system and its impact on the region. Verbal/Linguistic

T Technology Skills

GAME **Drag-and-Drop: Major Cities of the Andean Region**—Students use the game to learn more about the major cities in the region and their populations. Verbal/Linguistic

ONLINE SELF-CHECK QUIZ **Lesson 3**—Students receive instant feedback on their mastery of the lesson content.

☑ Printable Digital Worksheets

W Writing Skills

WORKSHEET **Critical Thinking Skills: Salmon Farming**—Students can use the worksheet to analyze the impact of salmon farming on the environment.

INTERVENTION AND REMEDIATION STRATEGIES

LESSON 1   Physical Geography of the Region

Reading and Comprehension

Students may have trouble with the meaning and pronunciation of some of the content vocabulary words. Have students play a guessing game in which one person gives clues about a content vocabulary term, and the other student tries to guess it. Have pairs compete against other pairs to see who can guess the most terms correctly in a certain amount of time. Encourage Spanish speaking students to offer guidance with pronunciation of vocabulary words and locations referred to in the text.

Text Evidence

Have students work in small groups to analyze two of the physical features described in the lesson. Students should choose various aspects of their feature covered in the text, or they may wish to conduct additional research using reliable online sources. Tell students to present an analysis of their findings, including answers to the following questions: Where is this physical feature located? How does it impact the people who live in that region? What are some of its unique characteristics?

LESSON 2   History of the Region

Reading and Comprehension

Have students scan the lesson to identify cause-and-effect relationships. Tell students to look for signal words as they read. Remind students that words and phrases such as *because, since, as a result, due to, therefore, consequently, so, resulted in,* and *affected* all indicate cause or effect. Have students work with a partner to practice using these words to explain concepts and cause-and-effect relationships in this lesson.

Text Evidence

Have students work in pairs or small groups to research facts about Native American civilizations referred to in the lesson. Tell students their analyses should answer the following questions: In what region were these civilizations located? What language did they use? What was a significant contribution made by this civilization? Have students present their findings to the class. Encourage students to use visual displays to enhance their presentations.

LESSON 3   Life in the Region

Reading and Comprehension

Have students skim the lesson to find challenging or unfamiliar words and try to determine each word's meaning by using context clues. Then have students look up the words' definitions using an online or print dictionary to clarify the meanings. Have students work in pairs to practice using these words to explain a concept in this lesson.

Text Evidence

Have students work in pairs or small groups to create a visual representation of the issues facing cities discussed in this lesson. For example, students may choose to create a flow chart or diagram that shows the impact of population growth. Have students in each group work together to summarize how these issues impact daily life for people living in cities. Encourage students to use content vocabulary terms in their summaries.

Online Resources

Level Reader

Use this online lower-level text that corresponds directly to the text in the online Student Edition.

Guided Reading Activities

This resource uses graphic organizers and guiding questions to help students with comprehension.

What Do You Know?

Use these worksheets to pre-assess students' background knowledge before they study the chapter.

Reading Essentials and Study Guide Workbook

This resource offers writing and reading activities for the approaching-level student.

Self-Check Quizzes

This online assessment tool provides instant feedback for students to check their progress.

ANDES AND MIDLATITUDE COUNTRIES

ESSENTIAL QUESTIONS · *How does geography influence the way people live?* · *Why do civilizations rise and fall?* · *What makes a culture unique?*

©iStockphoto.com/hadynyah

Woman from the town of Tarabuco in south central Bolivia

---

networks

There's More Online about Andes and Midlatitude Countries.

CHAPTER 10

Lesson 1
Physical Geography of the Region

Lesson 2
History of the Region

Lesson 3
Life in the Region

The Story Matters...

Running the length of the Pacific coast of South America, the Andes define the countries of Peru, Bolivia, and Chile. For the people who have made the Andes their home, the grandeur of the high mountain peaks often contrasts sharply with the challenges of life in such a rugged location. And yet, it was in this very location of mountains, high plateaus, plains, and deserts that the ancient Inca built their powerful and highly developed civilization.

V

FOLDABLES
Study Organizer

Go to the Foldables® library in the back of your book to make a Foldable® that will help you take notes while reading this chapter.

295

ENGAGE

Bellringer To activate students' prior knowledge of the Andean region, have them begin a KWL chart. Divide the class into groups of 3 or 4 students, and direct each group to make a chart like the one below. In the first column, students should list what they already know about the Andean region of South America. In the second column, they should list questions they have about the region.

Allow about 5 minutes for the groups to share the information and questions they have generated with the class. Then have students read "The Story Matters...". Have each group add the responses to the following questions to their KWL charts: **Ask:** What do you know about the Inca people who lived in Peru? What do you want to know?

Tell students that they will complete the last column of the chart, what they learned about the region, after they read the chapter. Remind students that the information they gather should not come only from the text. It can come from pictures, maps, graphs, captions, and time lines in the chapter, as well as any additional research they perform on various topics in the chapter or unanswered questions they have.

What I Know	What I Want to Know	What I Learned

V Visual Skills

Interpreting Have students look at the picture and read the caption about the woman. **Ask:** What are some unique aspects to the way she is dressed? *(She is wearing is a broad brimmed hat and a colorful shawl. that could be handwoven. She is warmly dressed.)* Visual/Spatial, Verbal/Linguistic

FOLDABLES
Study Organizer

Go to the Foldables® library for a chapter-based Foldable® activity that your students can use to help take notes and prepare for assessment.

Letter from the Author

Dear Geography Teacher,

Have students identify the Amazon Basin and the Andes on a map. In this chapter, students will study the countries located near this mountain chain. The Andes stretch from Venezuela in the north to Tierra del Fuego in the south. With many peaks as high as 20,000 ft (6096 m), the Andes have a profound effect on the people that live near them. The high altitudes require people to live and work differently. This chapter gives students the opportunity to learn about vertical climate zones.

TEACH & ASSESS

Step Into the Place

V1 Visual Skills

Analyzing Images Have students look at the two pictures. Have them compare and contrast the different geographic features and plants showing in the images. Call on volunteers to list the similarities, such as the large rocks, blue skies, and sparse vegetation. List the similarities on the board.

Then do the same with the differences. Discuss whether there are more similarities or differences in the two images of the region. *(Students should point out that a similarity is that they are both in the same region. They should also point out that picture A has mountains and grass, while picture B has cacti. There are more differences than similarities.)* Visual/Spatial, Verbal/Linguistic

V2 Visual Skills

Direct students' attention to the political map of the Andes and midlatitude countries of South America and point out that the Andes Mountains run through several of these countries and that they hug the Pacific Coast along much of their range. **Ask:**

- What countries does this chapter cover? *(Peru, Bolivia, Chile, Argentina, Uruguay, and Paraguay)*
- What is the latitude range for these countries? *(from 0° to 50° South)*
- Which of these countries have a significant portion of land dominated by the Andes? *(Peru, Bolivia, and Chile)*
- Why does this map not show the Andes Mountains? **W** *(because it is a political map, not a physical map)* Have students find these mountains on a physical map of South America from the unit opener. Then have students answer the Step Into the Place questions. Visual/Spatial

---

ANSWERS, p. 296

STEP INTO THE PLACE
1. Bolivia; La Paz and Sucre
2. Atlantic Ocean and Pacific Ocean
3. Montevideo
4. CRITICAL THINKING Possible answer: A natural feature, such as a mountain ridge, may have determined the country's border.

STEP INTO THE TIME
the discovery of silver in Potosi, Bolivia, in 1545

The world's longest mountain system runs parallel to the Pacific coast of South America. The Andes stretch about 4,500 miles (7,242 km) and include many high mountain peaks. As you study the map, look for other geographic features that make this area unique.

Step Into the Place

MAP FOCUS Use the map to answer the following questions.

1. **PLACES AND REGIONS** Which country has two capitals? Name them.

2. **THE GEOGRAPHER'S WORLD** Which two bodies of water does the Strait of Magellan connect?

3. **THE GEOGRAPHER'S WORLD** What is Uruguay's capital city?

4. **CRITICAL THINKING** **ANALYZING** Why do you think Chile has such a unique shape?

A

RUGGED TERRAIN Gigantic cacti dot the hilly landscape on Bolivia's Incahuasi Island. The island is in the middle of the world's largest salt flats.

B

HANDICRAFTS The people of the small island of Taquile on Lake Titicaca are known for making some of Peru's highest-quality handwoven clothing.

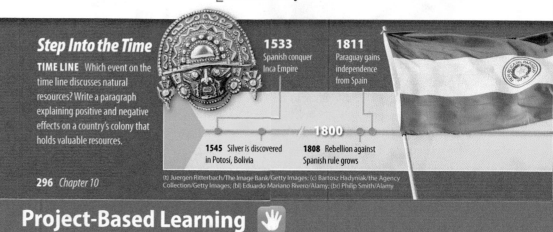

Step Into the Time

TIME LINE Which event on the time line discusses natural resources? Write a paragraph explaining positive and negative effects on a country's colony that holds valuable resources.

1533 Spanish conquer Inca Empire

1811 Paraguay gains independence from Spain

1800

1545 Silver is discovered in Potosí, Bolivia

1808 Rebellion against Spanish rule grows

296 Chapter 10

(t) Juergen Ritterbach/The Image Bank/Getty Images; (c) Bartosz Hadyniak/the Agency Collection/Getty Images; (bl) Eduardo Mariano Rivero/Alamy; (br) Philip Smith/Alamy

Project-Based Learning

Hands-On

Making a Photo Collage
Have students make a photo collage that illustrates the diversity found in the Andean and midlatitude countries in South America. Student groups will create a collage that includes information about the region's physical features, economy, and culture. After students have created their collages, have them display them on a bulletin board or wall. Students will then conduct a gallery walk to review the collages. As students examine each group's work, have them analyze the photos and describe why certain ones are part of the display.

Digital Hands-On

Creating an Online Video
Have pairs create an online video about the history of one of the countries using online photos that reflect the historical development of the country. Have them create storyboards and write captions or short summaries about each photo. Students might link sounds or music to photos. Have students upload the videos to a class Web site. Whenstudents are finished, have a video day where they present their final products.

edtechteacher
21st Century Learning

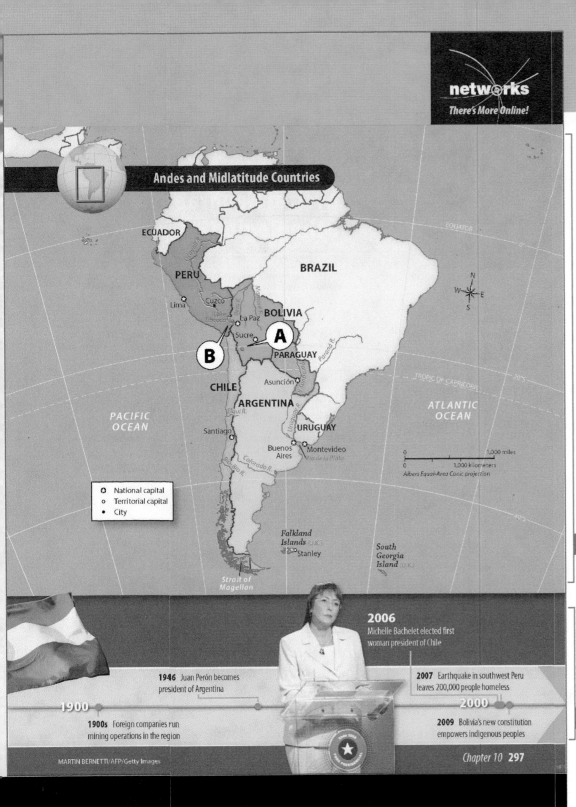

Andes and Midlatitude Countries

ECUADOR
PERU
Lima
Cuzco
La Paz
BOLIVIA
Sucre
A
B
PARAGUAY
CHILE
Asunción
ARGENTINA
Elqui R.
Santiago
URUGUAY
Buenos Aires
Montevideo
Río de la Plata
BRAZIL

PACIFIC OCEAN

ATLANTIC OCEAN

TROPIC OF CAPRICORN

EQUATOR

Falkland Islands (U.K.)
Stanley
South Georgia Island (U.K.)
Strait of Magellan

0   1,000 miles
0   1,000 kilometers
Albers Equal-Area Conic projection

⊙ National capital
○ Territorial capital
● City

2006 Michelle Bachelet elected first woman president of Chile

1946 Juan Perón becomes president of Argentina

2007 Earthquake in southwest Peru leaves 200,000 people homeless

1900

1900s Foreign companies run mining operations in the region

2000

2009 Bolivia's new constitution empowers indigenous peoples

MARTIN BERNETTI/AFP/Getty Images

Chapter 10 **297**

TIME LINE

Reading a Time Line and Map

Display the time line and map on the interactive whiteboard. Have volunteers read each event as it is revealed on the time line. Ask students to identify the country or countries where the event took place and find its location on the map. Visual/Spatial

See page 295B for other online activities.

Step Into the Time

V₃ Visual Skills

Interpreting Have students review the time line and use it to answer the following questions. **Ask:**

- What might you deduce from the fact that silver was discovered in Bolivia in 1545? *(Possible answers: that silver mining became an important economic activity in Bolivia; that explorers and settlers were attracted to the area because of this important mineral)*
- What European country conquered much of the region, and in what year? *(Spain, 1533)*
- About how long did Spain control the region before people began to rebel against Spanish rule? *(almost 300 years)*
- What country broke away from Spain in 1811? *(Paraguay)*
- What country suffered a massive earthquake in 2007? *(Peru)*

Tell students that they will learn more about Juan Perón and Michelle Bachelet, two leaders mentioned in the time line, in Lesson 2. **AL** Visual/Spatial

V₂

W Writing Skills

Informative/Explanatory Using the event on the time line about the discovery of silver in Bolivia, discuss how people would have reacted to the discovery of such a valuable resource. Have students recall what they know about the gold rush in the United States as an example of how people behave when a valuable resource is discovered. Then have students write their paragraphs. Verbal/Linguistic

V₃

CLOSE & REFLECT

Formulating Questions Ask if students have any questions they would like to add to their KWL charts. Suggest that students look for answers to their questions as they study this chapter.

ENGAGE

Bellringer To introduce the lesson, draw a concept web on the board with the word *Andes* in the middle. For 5 minutes, have students describe the thoughts, words, or images that they associate with the Andes mountain ranges. At the end, have a student summarize the impression of the Andes that the class has created by the concept web.

Point out that this lesson focuses on the physical geography of the Andean region, which includes Peru, Bolivia, and Chile, as well as the physical geography of the midlatitude countries, which are Uruguay, Argentina, and Paraguay. Have students preview the lesson by scanning the visuals, guiding questions, and headings.

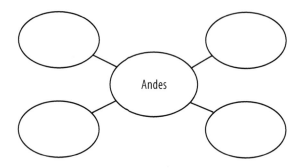

TEACH & ASSESS

V Visual Skills

Analyzing Images Help students relate the photograph at the bottom of the page with the Essential Question: *How does geography influence the way people live?*. Then, have students imagine living in the region shown. **Ask:**

- What challenges do you think you might face living in this mountainous area? *(Sample answers: Transportation would be slow and difficult. Towns and stores might be far away. You might have to travel a long distance to get food and other goods. The weather might be cold and unpredictable.)*
- What would be appealing about living in such an area? *(Sample answers: It would probably be incredibly beautiful. You might hike, ski, and hunt. You might learn to be very independent and self-sufficient.)* Naturalist, Intrapersonal

net✦rks

There's More Online!

☑ **SLIDE SHOW** Landforms: Andean Region

☑ **IMAGES** Uses of Wool

☑ **MAP** Comparing Mountain Ranges

☑ **VIDEO**

Reading **HELP**DESK

Academic Vocabulary

- isolate

Content Vocabulary

- cordillera
- altiplano
- pampas
- estuary
- altitude

TAKING NOTES: *Key Ideas and Details*

Integrate Visual Information
As you read, use a graphic organizer like this one to identify significant physical features of the region.

Physical Features

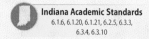

Ⓘ **Indiana Academic Standards**
6.1.6, 6.1.20, 6.1.21, 6.2.5, 6.3.3, 6.3.4, 6.3.10

Lesson 1
Physical Geography of the Region

ESSENTIAL QUESTION • *How does geography influence the way people live?*

IT MATTERS BECAUSE
Much of the terrain of the southern and western part of South America is extremely rugged. The geography of the area presents unique challenges to the people who live there.

Andes Countries

GUIDING QUESTION *What are the physical features of the Andean region?*

Three countries make up the bulk of the Andean region in South America. They are Peru, Bolivia, and Chile. From north to south, these countries span from the Equator to the southern tip of the continent of South America. The physical landscape includes towering mountains, sweeping plains, and significant waterways.

(l to r) Duane Miller/Flickr/Getty Images; Steve Allen Travel Photography/Alamy; ©VICTOR ROJAS/dpa/Corbis; Imágenes del Peru/Flickr/Getty Images; (b) Duane Miller/Flickr/Getty Images

net✦rks *Online Teaching Options*

VIDEO

Around the World—Chile

Comparing and Contrasting Use this video about the cities and landscapes of Chile to introduce the physical geography of the Andes and midlatitudes region and to preview the lesson content. Ask students how the geography of this region compares and contrasts with the geography of their own region. **AL** Visual/Spatial, Naturalist

See page 295C for other online activities.

BBC Motion Gallery Education

The Andes

On a map of South America, one of the first features you might notice is the system of mountain ranges running parallel to the continent's Pacific coast. These are the Andes, the longest continuous group of mountain ranges in the world and the tallest in the Western Hemisphere. The Andes include high plateaus and high plains, with even higher mountain peaks rising above them. The entire series of the Andes range stretches for 4,500 miles (7,242 km).

The peaks that make up the Andes are not arranged in one neat line. Instead, they form a series of parallel mountain ranges. The parallel ranges are called **cordilleras**. The rugged terrain of the cordilleras makes travel difficult. These ranges **isolated** human settlements from one another for centuries.

In Peru and Bolivia, the two main branches of the Andes border a high plain called the **altiplano**. In fact, *altiplano* means "high plain" in Spanish. About the size of Kentucky, the altiplano has an elevation of 11,200 feet to 12,800 feet (3,414 m to 3,901 m) above sea level.

The Andes mountain ranges are the result of collisions between tectonic plates. This kind of geologic activity comes as no surprise. After all, the Andes are part of the Ring of Fire. All around the rim of the Pacific Ocean, plates are colliding, separating, or sliding past each other. Those forces make earthquakes and volcanic eruptions a part of life throughout much of the Andes.

Plains and Deserts

The Andes run parallel to the Pacific coast but lie 100 miles to 150 miles (161 km to 241 km) inland from the coast. The land between the Andes and the coast averages more than 3,500 feet (1,067 m) above sea level. In most places, the land rises steeply from the ocean. The area has tall cliffs and almost no areas of coastal plain. In Peru and northern Chile, the area between the Pacific and the Andes is a coastal desert. On the Atlantic side of South America, broad plateaus and valleys spread across Uruguay and eastern Argentina.

Academic Vocabulary

isolate to separate

Spectacular mountains are part of Torres del Paine National Park in southern Chile.
▶ CRITICAL THINKING
Describing How were the Andes mountain ranges formed?

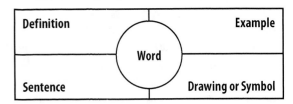

V Visual Skills

Creating Word Squares To reinforce the content vocabulary, have students create a word square for each word, using the model below. To help students remember the meaning of the word *altiplano*, point out the two parts of the word, *alti* and *plano*. Note that *alti*, which means "high," is related to *altitude*, and *plano* is similar to *plain*. ELL Visual/Spatial

Definition		Example
	Word	
Sentence		Drawing or Symbol

C Critical Thinking Skills

Comparing and Contrasting Pose the following questions to reinforce the distinctive features of the Andes mountain ranges as compared to other mountain ranges previously studied. **Ask:**

- How do the Andes compare with other mountain ranges in the world in terms of length? *(They are the longest continuous group of mountain ranges in the world.)*
- How do the Andes compare with other mountain ranges in the Western Hemisphere in terms of height? *(They are the tallest in the Western Hemisphere.)*
- What is distinctive about the form of the Andes? *(They form a series of parallel mountain ranges called cordilleras.)*
- How are the Andes similar to other mountain ranges in the way they were formed? *(Like other mountain ranges, the Andes were formed as a result of collisions between tectonic plates.)*
- How are they similar to other mountain ranges in the obstacles they pose to human settlement? *(Their rugged terrain makes travel difficult and isolates human settlements from one another. They also are the site of earthquakes and volcanic eruptions.)* Logical/Mathematical

---

MAP

Comparing Mountain Ranges

Analyzing a Map Display the interactive map that compares the different features of the Andes to various other mountain regions previously discussed in other chapters. Work with students to make comparisons of the various features of the Andes including the size of mountain range, highest peak of the mountain range, how they formed, and the age of the mountain range.
ELL Verbal/Linguistic

See page 295C for other online activities.

ANSWER, p. 299

CRITICAL THINKING They formed as a result of collisions between tectonic plates.

V1 Visual Skills

Analyzing Images Have students use the photograph at the top of the page to make inferences about life in this Bolivian village. **Ask:**

- What economic activity do you see in the photograph? (cattle raising)
- What can you infer about the elevation of this village? How can you tell? (The elevation is fairly high. The village appears to be at about the same elevation as the snow line on the mountain in the distance.)
- How does your inference compare with the information in the text? (It corresponds with the text. The text says that the Andean region has high plateaus and high plains.)
- Does the village appear prosperous or poor? How can you tell? (The village appears prosperous. The buildings appear to be well-made and well-maintained.) Visual/Spatial

V2 Visual Skills

Creating Maps As students read about the plains, deserts, and plateaus of this region, have them mark these areas on an outline map of South America, using different colors of shading and labels. Then direct students to add the main waterways to their maps. Suggest that students use their maps as study aids when they review the chapter. Visual/Spatial

Content Background Knowledge

Share these facts about the Atacama Desert with students.

- More than one million people live there.
- It is about 600 miles long but only about 100 miles wide.
- It is known as one of the driest places on Earth.
- Farmers use aquifers to grow olives, tomatoes, and cucumbers.
- In the summer, the average temperature in the desert is only 66 degrees Fahrenheit.

The Illimani mountains tower over a small village in the plains of western Bolivia.
▶ CRITICAL THINKING
Describing What are the main economic activities in the area?

This plain is called the **pampas**. Its thick, fertile soils come from sediments that have eroded from the Andes. The pampas, like North America's Great Plains, provide land for growing wheat and corn and for grazing cattle.

Coastal Peru and Chile and most of southern Argentina have deserts. Wind patterns, the cold Peru Current, and high elevations are the causes of the low precipitation. The Atacama Desert in Peru and northern Chile is so arid that in some places no rainfall has ever been recorded. The Patagonia Desert in Argentina lies in the rain shadow of the Andes.

Waterways

The Paraná, the Paraguay, and the Uruguay rivers combine to create the second-largest river system in South America, after the Amazon. This river system drains much of the eastern half of South America. The system is especially important to Paraguay, because Paraguay is a landlocked country. The river system provides transportation routes and makes possible the production of hydroelectric power. Along the Paraguay River is the Pantanal, one of the world's largest wetlands. This area produces a diverse ecosystem of plants and animals.

Steve Allen Travel Photography/Alamy

300 Chapter 10

netw⊙rks   Online Teaching Options

SLIDE SHOW

Landforms: Andean Region

Analyzing Use the slide show to reinforce and discuss the information on landforms presented in the student text. Ask students to consider how mountains have influenced the development of the region, including the development of cities and settlements, and have them write a paragraph on the subject. BL Visual/Spatial

See page 295C for other online activities.

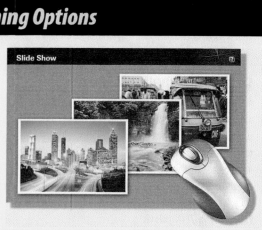

Slide Show

© Ocean/Corbis; Kryssia Campos/Flickr RF/Getty Images; Erica Simone Leeds; © IG Photography/Alamy

ANSWER, p. 300

CRITICAL THINKING growing wheat and corn and raising cattle

The Paraná-Paraguay-Uruguay river system flows into the Río de la Plata (Spanish for "river of silver"). This river then empties into the Atlantic Ocean on the border of Argentina and Uruguay. The Río de la Plata meets the ocean in a broad estuary. An **estuary** is an area where the ocean tide meets a river current.

South America has few large lakes. The largest lake in the Andean region is Lake Titicaca. It lies on the border between Bolivia and Peru. Lake Titicaca is on the altiplano at 12,500 feet (3,810 m) above sea level. It is the world's highest lake that is large enough and deep enough to be used by small ships.

☑ READING PROGRESS CHECK

Analyzing How do you think the geography of the Andean region affects the lives of the people who live there?

Climate Diversity

GUIDING QUESTION *How does climate affect life in the Andean region?*

Climate is part of a region's physical geography. The varying mountains, plains, and other landforms in the Andean region and midlatitude countries of South America mean that the region's climate is extremely diverse.

The Effect of Altitude

The main factor that determines climate in the Andes is **altitude**, or height above sea level. The higher the altitude, the cooler the temperatures are. This is true even in the warm tropics. Conditions in the region can range from hot and humid at lower elevations to freezing in the mountain peaks.

Farming is a challenge in the rugged Andean region. Farmers have successfully terraced the hillsides to grow crops such as potatoes, barley, and wheat.

Visitors to the Andes may find the altitude at the higher elevations hard to handle. Oxygen is thin. This results in heavy breathing and tiring easily. The region's inhabitants are adapted to the thinner air, as are various native species of plants and animals.

Think Again?

The Atacama Desert is unpopulated.

Not true. More than a million people live in this region. They live in mining towns, fishing villages, and coastal cities. Farmers use irrigation to grow olives and tomatoes. The Atacama is also a favorite place for teams of astronomers. They take advantage of the area's crystal-clear night skies to probe the secrets of the universe.

Chapter 10 **301**

C Critical Thinking Skills

Inferring Discuss with students the fact that Lake Titicaca is large and deep enough for small ships. **Ask:** Why would people on small ships want to travel on the lake? *(They may want to travel on the lake to go fishing or to go from Bolivia to Peru.)* Verbal/Linguistic

R Reading Skills

Summarizing Call on a student to summarize the relationship between altitude and temperature as well as the relationship between altitude and oxygen content. *(As altitude increases, temperature and oxygen decrease.)* Discuss how these relationships affect the life of the people living in the Andes region.

You might help students visualize this relationship by drawing a mountain on the board with an arrow pointing down at the top of the mountain and the words *temperature* and *oxygen* by the arrow. Remind students of the relationship they learned about altitude and temperature in Chapter 2: temperatures decrease by about 3.5°F for every 1,000 feet in elevation gain. Verbal/Linguistic, Logical/Mathematical

Content Background Knowledge

- The shores of Lake Titicaca are dotted with towns, and its waters contain many islands. For example, the island of Taquile, where the people are known for their colorful, high-quality, handwoven clothing, is located on Lake Titicaca.
- There are no cars on the island—and no electricity—and the people still follow their traditional way of living.
- The Inca people considered Lake Titicaca a sacred place. According to Incan mythology, the god Viracocha arose from the lake and created the first people as well as the sun and stars.

MAP

Climates: Andean Region

Reading a Map Display for students the climate layer on the Chapter Opener map and discuss how climate varies with elevation. Be sure to highlight all the different climates in the region, including the climates as related to mountain elevations. Discuss with students the climate events of El Niño and La Niña. **AL** Visual/Spatial, Verbal/Linguistic

See page 295C for other online activities.

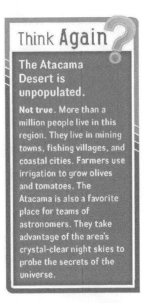

V Visual Skills

Creating Charts Remind students that the midlatitude countries are Paraguay, Uruguay, and Argentina. Point out that these countries enjoy a generally moderate climate. Suggest that students create a two-column chart like the one below to take notes on the climates of these countries. (**Uruguay:** *midwinter temperatures in the low 50s, mid-summer temperatures in the 70s, rainfall even throughout year;* **Argentina:** *varies from subtropical in north to tundra in far south; hot, humid summers in northern Argentina, warm summers and cold winters with heavy snowfall in southern Argentina;* **Paraguay:** *temperate or subtropical climate with strong winds)* Visual/Spatial

Midlatitude Country	Climate
Uruguay	
Argentina	
Paraguay	

C Critical Thinking Skills

Making Comparisons and Generalizations Direct students to use the Chapter Opener map to identify the latitude ranges of the three midlatitude countries. (**Uruguay:** *about 30°S to 35°S;* **Paraguay:** *about 20°S to 28°S;* **Argentina:** *about 22°S to 55°S)* Tell students to add those latitude ranges to the climate charts they made. Use the following questions to help students relate these latitude ranges to differences in climate. **Ask:**

- Which country has the largest range in latitude? (*Argentina*)
- Which country has the greatest variation in climate? (*Argentina*)
- What generalization can you make about the relationship between latitude range and climate? (*In general, the greater the range in latitude, the greater the differences in climate.*)

Then direct students to the infographic at the bottom of the page to identify the altitudes of the three midlatitude countries and how altitude affects human survival. Logical/Mathematical

---

ANSWER, p. 302

CRITICAL THINKING The temperature drops as altitude increases. As elevation increases, humans may experience shortness of breath and more exertion when undertaking physical activity.

Midlatitude Variety

Climates of the midlatitude countries of South America are quite different from the Andean region. These countries enjoy a generally temperate, or moderate, climate. In Uruguay, for example, the average daily temperature in the middle of winter are a mild 50°F to 54°F (10°C to 12°C). In mid-summer, the average daily temperatures reach a comfortable 72°F to 79°F (22°C to 26°C). There is no wet or dry season—rainfall occurs throughout the year. Inland areas, however, are drier than the coast.

Argentina is much larger than Uruguay and includes a greater variety of landforms. As you might expect, Argentina's climate is extremely diverse. It varies from subtropical in the north to tundra in the far south. Northern Argentina has hot, humid summers. Southern Argentina has warm summers and cold winters with heavy snowfall, especially in the mountains.

Paraguay presents yet a different climate. Paraguay is a landlocked country. The climate is generally temperate or subtropical. Strong winds often sweep the pampas in Paraguay because the country lacks mountain ranges to serve as wind barriers.

INFOGRAPHIC

EFFECTS OF ALTITUDE

30,000 ft

Average height of commercial aircraft; cabins are pressurized and oxygenized

29,527 ft
Highest elevation considered possible for human survival without an oxygen supply

20,000 ft
Less than half the oxygen available at sea level; physical activity becomes taxing; breathing is difficult

10,000 ft
Shortness of breath from simple movements, such as walking uphill

1,000 ft above sea level
No effects felt

SEA LEVEL

At all latitudes, altitude, or the height above sea level, influences climate. Earth's atmosphere thins as altitude increases. Thinner air retains less heat.

▶ CRITICAL THINKING
Describing What happens to temperatures as altitude increases? How do higher elevations affect humans?

networks *Online Teaching Options*

INFOGRAPHIC

The Effects of Altitude

Making Connections Display the infographic to students and discuss the impact of altitude on plants, animals, and specifically people. Have students relate the information to their own environment and write a paragraph explaining how altitude influences life in their region. ELL Visual/Spatial, Verbal/Linguistic

See page 295C for other online activities.

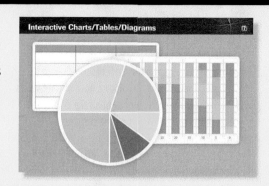

Interactive Charts/Tables/Diagrams

(l to r) ©VICTOR ROJAS/dpa/Corbis; ©CEZARO DE LUCA/epa/Corbis

Climate Extremes

Extremes of climate can be experienced in the Andean countries without changing latitude. Altitude is all that has to change. The climate changes tremendously in the Andes from the lower to the higher elevations. The *tierra caliente*, or "hot land," is the land near sea level. The hot and humid conditions do not change much from month to month. In this zone, farmers grow bananas, sugarcane, cacao, rice, and other tropical crops.

From 3,000 feet to 6,000 feet (914 m to 1,829 m), the air is pleasantly cool. Abundant rainfall helps forests and a great variety of crops grow. This zone is the *tierra templada*, or "temperate land." It is the most densely populated area. Here, farmers grow a variety of crops, such as corn, coffee, cotton, wheat, and citrus fruits.

Higher up, the climate changes. This is the *tierra fría*, or "cold land." It extends from 6,000 feet to 10,000 feet (1,829 m to 3,048 m). The landscape is a combination of forests and grassy areas. Farmers here grow crops that thrive in cooler temperatures, including potatoes, barley, and wheat.

The land at the highest altitude is the *tierra helada*, or "frozen land." Here, above 10,000 feet (3,048 m), conditions can be harsh. The winds blow cold and icy, and temperatures fall well below freezing. Vegetation is sparse, and few people live in this zone.

Mining (left), especially copper mining, is an important part of the Chilean economy. Mining can be dangerous. Miners celebrate their rescue on October 12, 2010 (right), after being trapped underground for 69 days.

Identifying Besides minerals and metals, what natural resources are abundant in the Andean and midlatitude countries?

Chapter 10 **303**

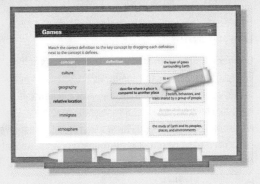

R Reading Skills

Determining Central Ideas Use the following questions to help students identify the most important ideas about Los Niños and Las Niñas. **Ask:**

• How does the weather along the Pacific coast of South America change during an El Niño? *(It becomes much warmer and wetter. Floods occur, especially along the coast of Peru.)*

• When does an El Niño occur? *(It occurs when cold winds from the east are weak.)*

• How often do Los Niños occur? *(They occur about every 3 years.)*

• What kind of weather occurs with La Niña? *(The opposite kind of unusual weather from El Niño occurs, which would be cooler and drier weather.)* **Verbal/Linguistic**

Content Background Knowledge

Tell students that Los Niños and Las Niñas affect weather in the United States as well as in South America. Share with them the following information:

• Sea surface temperatures affect global weather, and Los Niños and Las Niñas are changes in the temperature of the sea surface—with an El Niño bringing warmer temperatures and La Niña bringing cooler temperatures.

• When an El Niño occurs, the southern United States typically has a wetter winter, the Northeast has a stormy winter, and the Northwest has milder weather.

• When a La Niña occurs, the South has a drier and milder winter, the Northeast has short cold periods, and the Northwest is wetter than normal.

Suggest that students check the Internet to see if either event is occurring in the current year and what that means for the weather in the area they live in. Explain that farmers, construction workers, and others who work outside and whose livelihoods are linked to the weather need to keep a close watch on Los Niños and Las Niñas.

ANSWERS, p. 304

Identifying alpacas

☑ **READING PROGRESS CHECK** It is the temperate zone. It has mild temperatures and can support a variety of crops, so many people choose to live here.

Llamas are camelids, relatives of camels. They are bred and raised for food, wool, and as pack animals for pulling carts.

Identifying What other camelids are common in the region?

El Niño and La Niña

Every few years, changes in wind patterns and ocean currents in the Pacific Ocean cause unusual and extreme weather in some places in South America. One of these events is called El Niño. During an El Niño, the climate along the Pacific coast of South America becomes much warmer and wetter than normal. Floods occur in some places, especially along the coast of Peru.

El Niños form when cold winds from the east are weak. Without these cold winds, the central Pacific Ocean grows warmer than usual. More water evaporates, and more clouds form. The thick band of clouds changes wind and rain patterns. Some areas receive heavier-than-normal rains. Other areas, however, have less-than-normal rainfall.

Scientists have found that El Niños occur about every three years. They also found that in some years, the opposite kind of unusual weather takes place. This event is called La Niña. Winds from the east become strong, cooling more of the Pacific. When this happens, heavy clouds form in the western Pacific.

☑ **READING PROGRESS CHECK**

Identifying Why is the *tierra templada* the most populated climate zone by altitude in the Andean region?

Imagenes del Peru/Flickr/Getty Images

networks **Online Teaching Options**

IMAGES

Uses of Wool

Comparing and Contrasting Display the images of the llamas to students. Use the side-by-side comparisons of the uses of wool to discuss the wool of alpacas and how this important resource improves the life of the people of this region. Discuss with students the traditional and modern ways that wool is used. Be sure to make connections with students about the importance of the llama and wool as a resource.

ELL Interpersonal

See page 295C for other online activities.

Interactive Photos

This region has many diverse types of landscapes. Land forms range from mountains to grasslands. Waterways include rivers, lakes, and shorelines. Vegetation varies depending on the soil quality and access to water within the specific area. Animal life has adapted to take advantage of what the region has to offer.

Elena Kalistratova/Vetta/Getty Images

Natural Resources

GUIDING QUESTION *Which natural resources are important to the region?*

The Andean and midlatitude countries are rich in natural resources. Energy sources are especially important. Bolivia holds the second-largest reserves of natural gas in South America, trailing behind only Venezuela. Bolivia also has extensive deposits of petroleum. Paraguay's hydroelectric power plants produce nearly all the country's electricity. The governments want to use these resources to develop and strengthen their economies.

Minerals and Metals

Besides energy resources, the region has a number of mineral resources. Most of the area's mines are in the Andes. Chile leads the world in exports of copper. Tin production is important to the Bolivian economy. Bolivia and Peru have deposits of silver, lead, and zinc, and Peru also has gold.

Wildlife

The region's varied geography and climate support a variety of wildlife, including many species of birds and butterflies. The ability of plants and animals to thrive in the region varies with altitude.

A group of mammals called camelids is especially important in this region. Camelids are relatives of camels, but they do not have the typical humps of camels. Two kinds of camelids are the llama and the alpaca. The llama is the larger of the two. Llamas serve as pack animals and are a source of food, wool, and hides. Native Americans throughout the Andes tend herds of llamas. These animals are used to carry goods or pull carts. They are also raised for food, hides, and wool.

Alpacas are found only in certain parts of Peru and Bolivia. The animal's thick, shaggy coat is an important source of wool. Alpaca wool is strong yet soft and repels water. It is used for all kinds of clothing and as insulation in sleeping bags.

☑ READING PROGRESS CHECK

Analyzing What metal is important to Chile's economy?

FOLDABLES
Study Organizer

Include this lesson's information in your Foldable®.

LESSON 1 REVIEW

Reviewing Vocabulary

1. Why is *altitude* an important feature in the Andean region?

Answering the Guiding Questions

2. *Determining Central Ideas* Why do earthquakes and volcanoes occur in the Andes?

3. *Analyzing* Why is the climate wet on the western slopes of the Andes in southern Argentina but dry on the eastern slopes?

4. *Describing* How does the climate of the Andes countries compare with that of the midlatitude countries?

5. *Identifying* Give a specific example of how a family living in the Andes might use llamas.

6. *Narrative Writing* You are living with a relative for a month somewhere in the Andes. Choose the country and the area where you are staying. Then write a letter to a friend describing where you are and what you did yesterday.

Chapter 10 **305**

V Visual Skills

Creating a Chart After students read about natural resources in this region, have them copy the chart below and place check marks to indicate each country's resources. *(Bolivia: Natural gas, petroleum; tin; silver, lead, zinc; Chile: Copper; Peru: Silver, lead, zinc; gold)* **Ask:** Which country has the most kinds of natural resources? *(Bolivia)* **AL** Visual/Spatial, Naturalist

	Bolivia	Chile	Peru
Natural gas, petroleum			
Copper			
Tin			
Silver, lead, zinc			
Gold			

Content Background Knowledge

Llamas, which are common in the Andes and midlatitude countries, are also fairly common in the United States. Llamas can be seen on farms and ranches in many parts of our country. Some sheep ranchers in the United States use llamas as guard animals to protect their sheep from coyotes and wild dogs. Llamas seem to instinctively react defensively to coyotes and wild dogs. They will sound an alarm and often will run toward a threatening animal and kick it.

CLOSE & REFLECT

To close the lesson, remind students of the KWL chart they made at the beginning of the chapter. Have them make a list of five facts they learned about the physical geography of the Andean region. Have students add these facts to their KWL charts labeling them for Lesson 1. Tell students that they will add more items to the chart at the end of Lessons 2 and 3.

LESSON 1 REVIEW ANSWERS

Reviewing Vocabulary

1. Altitude affects climate, settlement patterns, and transportation.

Answering the Guiding Questions

2. **Determining Central Ideas** The Andes are the result of colliding tectonic plates, which also produce earthquakes and volcanoes.

3. **Analyzing** The western slopes receive rain from the moist air blowing in from the Pacific Ocean. By the time this air reaches the eastern slopes, the moisture is gone. The eastern slopes are in a rain shadow.

4. **Describing** The Andes countries often have extreme climate conditions, depending on altitude. The midlatitude countries generally have more temperate climates.

5. **Identifying** Sample answer: They might use llamas to carry goods and equipment between a farm and a town.

6. **Narrative Writing** Answers will vary. Students' letters should describe the location as well as its landforms and climate.

ANSWER, p. 305

☑ READING PROGRESS CHECK copper

ENGAGE

Bellringer To introduce the lesson, draw a T-chart on the board and write the word *Civilization* above it. Remind students that the word *civilization* refers to the culture of a specific group or groups at a certain time and place and that *culture* refers to the way of life of a group of people, including their language, technology, government, religion, and arts. On one side of the T-chart, write *American* and on the other side write *Inca*.

Ask students to think of five significant features or achievements of American civilization and write their responses. Then tell students that they will begin this lesson on the history of the Andean region by learning about the Inca. Suggest that, as they read, students think about features of Inca civilization to compare with American civilization.

Civilization

American	Inca

TEACH & ASSESS

V Visual Skills

Visualizing On a map of South America, show students the extent of the Inca Empire, from northern Ecuador through Peru and into Chile. **Ask:**

- What challenges do you think the Inca faced in ruling this mountainous area? *(Sample answer: They probably had significant transportation and communication problems in this mountainous region.)*
- What advantages might the location have had? *(Sample answer: It might have afforded protection from invaders.)* Visual/Spatial

---

ANSWER, p. 306

Taking Notes Sample answers: **Inca Empire**—highly structured society with no written language; **Spanish rule**—able to conquer the Inca because they had firearms; **Independence movements**—led by Simón Bolívar and José de San Martín

---

networks

There's More Online!

☑ **MAP** Native American Civilizations

☑ **VIDEO**

Reading HELPDESK

Academic Vocabulary

- **hierarchy**

Content Vocabulary

- **smallpox**
- **guerrilla**
- **multinational**
- **coup**

TAKING NOTES: *Key Ideas and Details*

Describe As you read this lesson, use a graphic organizer like this one to write an important fact about each topic.

Topic	Fact
Inca Empire	
Spanish rule	
Independence movements	

Indiana Academic Standards
6.1.6, 6.2.5

306

Lesson 2
History of the Region

ESSENTIAL QUESTION • *Why do civilizations rise and fall?*

IT MATTERS BECAUSE
In the Andean and midlatitude countries of South America, history and government have developed in very different ways.

Early History and Conquest

GUIDING QUESTION *How has history influenced the region?*

Native Americans and European colonizers made major contributions to the history of this region of South America. The actions and achievements of both groups continue to influence life today. Almost all the countries in the region have been independent for nearly two centuries. Still, their history continues to influence their culture.

Rise and Fall of the Inca Empire

Before the rise of the Inca in the 1100s, the Andean region was the home of small Native American societies such as the Moche, the Mapuche, and the Aymara. These societies were based primarily on agriculture. The Moche settled on the arid coastline of northern Peru. Archaeological finds show that they were talented at engineering and irrigation. They used a complex irrigation system to grow corn (maize), beans, and other crops.

The Inca developed a highly sophisticated civilization. They first settled in the Cuzco Valley in what is now Peru. It was not until their fifth emperor, Capac Yupanqui, that they began to expand outside the valley. In the 1400s, under the rule of Pachacuti Inca Yupanqui, the Inca made extensive conquests. By the early 1500s, the Inca ruled a region stretching from northern Ecuador through Peru and then southward into Chile. Historians estimate that the area was

---

networks *Online Teaching Options*

VIDEO

World's Wonders—Machu Picchu

Informative/Explanatory Writing Use this video about the history of the Inca and Machu Picchu to generate interest in the lesson content. Have students write a paragraph about some aspect of the video that was particularly interesting to them. **AL** Visual/Spatial

See page 295D for other online activities.

home to 12 million people. This population included dozens of separate cultural groups, who spoke many different languages.

The Inca state was called Tawantinsuyu. The name means "the land of the four quarters." The imperial capital was located where the four quarters, or provinces, of the Inca Empire met, at Cuzco. Inca society was highly structured. At the top of the **hierarchy** were the emperor, the high priest, and the commander of the army. The nobility served the emperor as administrators. At the bottom of the social pyramid were farmers and laborers.

Inca technology and engineering were highly advanced. The Inca built extensive irrigation systems, roads, tunnels, and bridges that linked regions of the empire to Cuzco. Today you can still see the remains of Inca cities and fortresses. Some of the most impressive ruins are at Machu Picchu, located about 50 miles (80 km) northwest of Cuzco.

The Inca had no written language. Instead, they created a counting system called quipu for record keeping. A quipu was a series of knotted cords of various colors and lengths.

Messengers carrying quipu could travel as far as 150 miles (241 km) per day on the roads. The Inca became extremely wealthy because of their vast natural resources of gold and silver.

Spain Conquers Peru
Unfortunately for the Inca, however, their advanced culture could not turn back the invasion that led to the empire's downfall. The Spanish conquests in Mexico encouraged them to move into South America. In 1532 a Spanish adventurer named Francisco Pizarro landed in Peru with a small band of soldiers.

(tr) ©Werner Forman/Corbis; (b) HUGHES Hervé©hemis.fr/Getty Images

Academic Vocabulary

hierarchy a classification that is arranged by rank

Visual Vocabulary

quipu The quipu was an Inca counting device.

The ruins of the city of Machu Picchu are high in the Andes.
▶ CRITICAL THINKING
Describing How did the Inca build a large empire?

R Reading Skills

Determining Word Meanings Note that a *hierarchy* is a system of ranking people in a society or organization. The people at the top of a hierarchy have the most power and, typically, the most wealth. To help students visualize the Inca hierarchy, draw a pyramid on the board. At the top, write emperor and then high priest and commander of the army. In the middle, write nobility or administrators. At the bottom, list farmers and laborers. To check students' understanding of the word *hierarchy*, you might have them identify a hierarchy in American society. **ELL** **AL** Visual/Spatial

C Critical Thinking Skills

Comparing and Contrasting Have students complete the T-chart they started as an introduction to the lesson by listing five significant features or achievements of the Inca civilization. *(Sample answers: highly structured society, highly advanced technology and engineering, quipu for recordkeeping, extensive road system, vast natural resources of gold and silver)* **Ask:**

- How is American civilization similar to Inca civilization? *(Sample answers: Both have a highly structured society, highly advanced technology and engineering, an extensive road system, and vast natural resources.)*
- How do the two differ? *(Sample answer: American civilization has a written language; uses computers for recordkeeping; and has cars, airplanes, ships, and trains for transportation.)* Verbal/Linguistic

V Visual Skills

Analyzing Images Draw students' attention to the photograph of Machu Picchu at the bottom of the page. **Ask:**

- What advantages might such a location have for a capital city? *(It would be difficult for invaders to attack.)*
- What disadvantages might it have? *(Transportation of people and goods would be difficult.)* Visual/Spatial

TIME LINE

Rise and Fall of the Incan Empire

Reading a Time Line Display the interactive time line about the rise and fall of the Inca Empire to discuss with students how colonization affected native peoples in South America. Explain that, for the most part, the impact was negative. Discuss with students that most native groups declined in population and lost much of their culture, while some groups were completely wiped out. **AL** Visual/Spatial

See page 295D for other online activities.

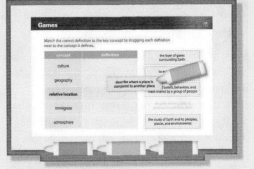

ANSWER, p. 307

CRITICAL THINKING through conquest of other groups

History of the Region

V Visual Skills

Reading a Map After students examine the map of native civilizations, use the following questions to help students appreciate the significance of the Inca Empire. **Ask:**

- How did the Inca Empire compare in size with the lands of the Maya and the Aztec? *(The Inca Empire was much larger by far.)*
- Which empire lasted the longest? How long? *(The Mayan Empire lasted 590 years.)*
- How would you describe the shape, location, and extent of the Inca Empire? *(Sample answer: It formed a narrow band extending along most of the Pacific coast of South America.)*
- What do you think the terrain of the empire is like? *(It is all mountainous land.)* **AL** Visual/Spatial, Verbal/Linguistic

V

Content Background Knowledge

In 1532 Pizzaro advanced into the Inca Empire with an army of fewer than 200 soldiers. At that time, two brothers vied for control of the empire in a civil war. Because of the turmoil, the Inca failed to forcefully and decisively deal with Pizzaro and his soldiers.

The first battle between the Spaniards and the Inca resulted in a slaughter of the Inca people because they panicked when faced with the unfamiliar, noisy, and terrifying artillery and cavalry of the Spaniards. The Spaniards suffered no casualties, while killing thousands of Inca soldiers.

After taking the Inca emperor Atahualpa hostage, Pizzaro made a bargain with the Inca people: his freedom in exchange for a room filled to half its height with gold and filled entirely with silver twice. After Pizzaro obtained the gold and silver, however, he did not hold up his side of the bargain; instead he had Atahualpa executed.

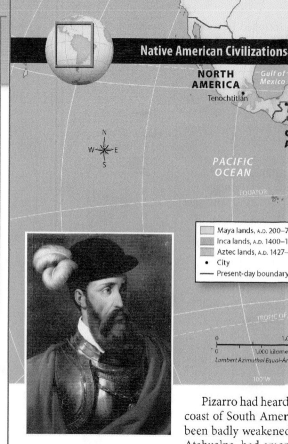

Native American Civilizations

NORTH AMERICA

Gulf of Mexico

Tenochtitlan

Tikal

CENTRAL AMERICA

PACIFIC OCEAN

EQUATOR

SOUTH AMERICA

Cuzco

20°S

TROPIC OF CAPRICORN

	Maya lands, A.D. 200–790
	Inca lands, A.D. 1400–1525
	Aztec lands, A.D. 1427–1520
•	City
—	Present-day boundary

0   1,000 miles
0   1,000 kilometers
Lambert Azimuthal Equal-Area projection

100°W   80°W   60°W

MAP SKILLS

1 PLACES AND REGIONS What was the capital of the Inca Empire?

2 THE GEOGRAPHER'S WORLD Francisco Pizarro (pictured) was a Spanish adventurer. What empire did he conquer?

Spanish conquistador Francisco Pizarro conquered the empire of the Inca.

Pizarro had heard tales of the fabulously rich cities on the Pacific coast of South America. He also learned that the Inca empire had been badly weakened by a civil war from which the new emperor, Atahualpa, had emerged victorious. When the Spanish confronted Atahualpa, the Inca army, unprepared to face Spanish artillery, was nearly destroyed. Within a few years, the Spanish controlled the entire empire. The Spanish also seized control of the region's precious metals. The road system that the Inca developed became an important transportation route for Spanish goods. The Inca are the ancestors of the Native Americans who live in the Andes region today.

The Spanish also branched out from Peru to create colonies in Argentina, Chile, and other parts of South America. The Spanish military victors were called conquistadors, from the Spanish word for "conqueror." The Spanish colonies became sources of wealth for Spain. Some Spanish settlers prospered from gold and silver mining. Spanish rule of the Andean and midlatitude areas in the region continued for nearly 300 years.

After the Inca lost their empire to the Spanish, they and other Native Americans in the region endured great hardships. Their numbers declined drastically as a result of **smallpox**, a highly

DEA/G. DAGLI ORTI/De Agostini/Getty Images

netw**o**rks *Online Teaching Options*

MAP

Native American Civilizations

Analyzing Visuals Display and discuss the map that shows the different Native American civilizations in Central and South America. Explain that Spain's conquest and colonization of the Inca Empire was driven by its desire to gain the silver and gold resources of the empire. Have students interact with the map and discuss its features, including the fact that the Inca Empire reached throughout the entire Andean region. **AL** Kinesthetic, Interpersonal

See page 295D for other online activities.

ANSWERS, p. 308

MAP SKILLS

1. Cuzco

2. the Inca Empire

infectious disease introduced by the Europeans. The introduction of epidemic diseases also affected numerous Native American groups in North America.

✓ READING PROGRESS CHECK

Analyzing How were the Spanish, under conquistador Francisco Pizarro, able to conquer such a mighty empire as the Inca?

Independent Countries

GUIDING QUESTION *How did the countries of the Andean region gain their independence?*

By the early 1800s, most of South America had been under Spanish control for nearly 300 years. History was about to change once again. The reasons for this shift were local as well as international.

Overthrow of Spanish Rule

In the early 1800s, revolution and liberation movements were occurring around the world. The United States threw off British rule, and the French replaced the monarchy with a republic. Struggles for independence also occurred in Mexico and the Caribbean. People in South America were encouraged by these events. It was exactly the right time for two South American revolutionary leaders to lead the fight against Spanish rule. These two leaders were Simón Bolívar and José de San Martín.

The two leaders were able to rally support for independence. San Martín pioneered many elements of **guerrilla** warfare—the use of troops who know the local landscape so well that they are difficult for traditional armies to find. By the mid-1800s, many South American countries had gained independence.

W

Power and Governance

After the Spanish left South America, several different countries formed. Their borders mostly followed the divisions set in place by the Spanish colonizers. But despite gaining independence, political and economic hardships continued on the continent.

In contrast to the United States, there was no strong momentum for unity in South America. In fact, the rulers of many of the newly independent states were wealthy aristocrats, powerful landowners, or military dictators. Their mindset was more European than South American. In addition, communication between countries was difficult because of the mountainous terrain.

The new countries lacked a tradition of self-government. The British colonies in North America had elected representatives in their colonial legislatures. The new states of South America, however, did not have a structure in place for a government to function. The newly independent countries drafted constitutions.

R

Thinking Like a Geographer

A Land of Two Capitals

A map of Bolivia reveals an unusual feature. Bolivia has two capitals: Sucre and La Paz. When Bolivia gained its independence, the question of which city would serve as the nation's capital was never resolved. Today, La Paz is the home of the country's executive and legislative branches, and Sucre serves as the center of the country's judicial system.

Chapter 10 **309**

W Writing Skills

Informative/Explanatory Have students who are interested do some Internet research and write one-page biographies of Simón Bolívar and José de San Martín. Then have them give a short presentation about what they learned to the class.
BL Verbal/Linguistic

R Reading Skills

Determining Central Ideas Use the following questions to help students identify the main ideas about independence movements in South America. **Ask:**

- What helped spark the independence movements in South America in the early 1800s? *(liberation movements occurring in places around the world, including the United States, France, Mexico, and the Caribbean)*
- What two men led the fight against Spanish rule in South America? *(Simón Bolívar and José de San Martín)*
- Why did the newly independent states in South America struggle politically and economically after gaining independence? *(There was no strong momentum for unity. The continent's rugged terrain made communication between regions difficult. The new countries lacked a tradition of self-government and a structure for government. The wide divide between the rich and the poor caused social and economic instability. Several countries battled over boundary disputes and mineral rights.)* Verbal/Linguistic

Content Background Knowledge

Explain that guerrilla warfare involves small bands of fighters who make sudden, sneak attacks on a larger, more conventional army. The fighters then disperse and disappear into the local landscape, making capture or return attacks impossible. This type of warfare often enables a smaller force to defeat a larger, more powerful enemy. Guerrilla warfare has been used successfully against the United States in the Vietnam War, and more recently, in the war in Afghanistan.

MAP

Independence: Andean Region

Reading a Map Display the colonization and independence layer of the Chapter Opener map on the whiteboard. Using the colonization information first, have students identify the order in which the various nations in the Andean region and midlatitude region were colonized. Then, using the independence information, discuss when and how they became independent nations. Encourage students to make a graphic organizer like an outline or a time line to organize the information discussed.
BL Visual/Spatial

See page 295D for other online activities.

ANSWER, p. 309

✓ READING PROGRESS CHECK The Spanish were aided by firearms, the Inca transportation network of roads, and the Inca civil war.

R Reading Skills

Determining Central Ideas Use the following questions to focus students' attention on the central ideas about the history of the Andean region in the late 1800s and the 1900s. **Ask:**

• What interest did industrialized countries have in the Andean region in the late 1800s and the 1900s? *(They wanted the region's natural resources.)*

• Who benefited from the mining and smelting operations in the region that were started by multinational companies? *(wealthy landowners and multinational companies)*

• What happened to the workers and farmers as the economies expanded? *(They remained poor.)*

Point out that industrialization in the United States helped enlarge the middle class, but that did not happen in the Andean region in the late 1800s and the 1900s. Instead, most people remained either rich or poor, which caused much discontent and political instability in the region. **Logical/Mathematical**

T Technology Skills

Researching Have interested students research the life of Eva Perón, as an actress and as the First Lady of Argentina. **Verbal/Linguistic**

Content Background Knowledge

Eva Perón, affectionately called Evita, appealed to the common people of Argentina partly because she was one of them. Her father, a poor village landowner, died while Eva was still a child; her mother then opened a boarding house to support the family.

Eva was a radio and movie actress when she met the much older Juan Perón, a rising politician. She was only 26 when he became President of Argentina and she became First Lady of the country.

Eva became a champion of the poor, setting up offices that gave food, medicine, and money to the needy. To them, she was "la dama de la esperanza"—the lady of hope. Eva Perón died of cancer at the age of 33.

A Broadway musical called *Evita* and a subsequent movie musical (1996) was made of her life. Interested students can most likely find a DVD of the musical in their library or local video store.

ANSWERS, p. 310

✓ **READING PROGRESS CHECK** They were the most important leaders in the struggle of several countries for independence from Spain.

CRITICAL THINKING Perón was overthrown in 1955. The military ruled Argentina after Perón.

Eva Perón was married to Juan Perón, president of Argentina. She won admiration for her efforts to support the woman suffrage movement and to improve the lives of the poor.
▶ **CRITICAL THINKING**
Identifying How was Juan Perón removed from office? Who ruled Argentina after Perón?

The enormously uneven distribution of wealth between rich and poor, however, resulted in social and economic instability. Several countries engaged in bloody conflicts over boundary disputes and mineral rights. These conflicts led to much loss of life and weakened economies.

✓ **READING PROGRESS CHECK**

Describing Why are Simón Bolívar and José de San Martín important in the history of the region?

History of the Region in the Modern Era

GUIDING QUESTION *What challenges did the countries of the region face in the late 1800s and 1900s?*

The Andean and midlatitude countries continued to face challenges during the late 1800s and 1900s. With military backing, dictators seized power, and they ignored democratic constitutions. Economies were still dependent on outside powers.

Economic Challenges

The countries of the region faced economic challenges. Among the challenges were developing and controlling resources, building roads and railroads, and establishing trade links. Before independence, the countries of the region depended economically on Spain and Brazil. After independence, the economies of the region remained tied to countries outside South America.

Rapidly industrializing countries in Europe exploited the region for its raw materials. Wealthy landowners, cattle grazers, and mining operators refused to surrender their ties to European investors. Beginning in the early 1900s, large U.S. and European **multinational** firms—companies that do business in several countries—started mining and smelting operations in the region. As the economies expanded, profits grew for wealthy landowners and multinational companies. But many workers and farmers and their families remained mired in poverty.

Political Instability

Economic woes led to calls for reform. Political leaders promised changes for the better. In 1946 Argentinians elected General Juan Perón as the nation's president. Perón and his wife, Eva, were popular with the people. The new government enacted economic reforms to benefit the working people. However, the Perón government limited

netw⊕rks   *Online Teaching Options*

CHART

Dictators in the Andean Region

Analyzing Use the interactive chart about dictators in the Andean region to discuss the civil unrest and upheaval that took place in the Andean region and midlatitude states during the late 1800s and 1900s. Have students interact with the chart and discuss the information about the various dictators during this time period. Encourage students to research on the Internet to find out more information about these individuals. **BL Kinesthetic, Interpersonal**

See page 295D for other online activities.

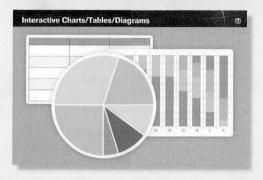

Interactive Charts/Tables/Diagrams

free speech, censored the press, and added to the country's debt. After Perón was overthrown in 1955, the military government ruled Argentina.

The new government moved to put an end to unrest. The rulers imprisoned thousands of people without trial. Some were tortured or killed. Others simply "disappeared." Argentina was also troubled by conflict over the Falkland Islands. Argentina and Great Britain both claimed the Falklands. After a brief war in 1982, Argentina was defeated, and the Falklands remain a British territory.

Significant changes were also taking place in the country of Chile. In the presidential election of 1970, Chileans elected a socialist candidate named Salvador Allende. Allende took action to redistribute wealth and land. The government took over Chile's copper industry and banking system. Allende's economic reforms were popular with workers but angered the upper classes. In 1973 Chilean military officers staged a **coup**, an illegal seizure of power, and killed Allende. A military dictatorship, headed by General Augusto Pinochet, ruled Chile for the next 16 years.

Movements for Change

In recent years, democracies have replaced dictatorships. Yet the countries in the region are still struggling to end corruption in government, shrink the gap between rich and poor, provide jobs, and protect human rights.

Voters also have elected new leaders. In 2005 Bolivians elected Evo Morales, the country's first indigenous president. Morales introduced a new constitution and land reforms, brought industries under government ownership, and moved to limit U.S. corporate involvement in the country's politics. In 2006 Chileans elected the country's first female president, Michelle Bachelet. A year later, Cristina Fernández de Kirchner became Argentina's first elected female president. Both female leaders started efforts to improve human rights and equal opportunity.

☑ READING PROGRESS CHECK

Determining Central Ideas After independence, why did the countries in this region continue to experience economic hardship?

FOLDABLES
Study Organizer

Include this lesson's information in your Foldable®.

LESSON 2 REVIEW

Reviewing Vocabulary
1. What is one advantage of *guerrilla* warfare?

Answering the Guiding Questions
2. *Identifying* What were some of the strengths and achievements of the Inca culture?

3. *Describing* What were two events in North America and Europe that set the stage for the independence movement in the Andes and midlatitude countries?

4. *Determining Central Ideas* What can you infer about democratic government based on what you learned about Juan Perón in Argentina and Salvador Allende in Chile?

5. *Argument Writing* You are either Simón Bolívar or José de San Martín. The year is 1822, when the two men met face to face in Guayaquil (now located in Ecuador). Write a paragraph or two in which you urge your fellow leader to pursue the struggle for independence from Spain.

Chapter 10 **311**

LESSON 2 REVIEW ANSWERS

Reviewing Vocabulary

1. Soldiers in guerrilla warfare know the local terrain so well that their opponents have difficulty finding them.

Answering the Guiding Questions

2. **Identifying** The Inca established the most important empire of their time. They were accomplished engineers. Deposits of precious metals made the Inca enormously wealthy. The Inca developed a highly efficient road system in rugged terrain.

3. **Describing** The United States threw off British rule, and the French declared a republic.

4. **Determining Central Ideas** Students may respond that stable democratic government is hard to achieve since it may be threatened by dictatorships or by military takeovers.

5. **Argument Writing** Student answers will vary, but should be supported by historical facts about the independence of South American colonies.

V Visual Skills

Creating Time Lines Work with the class to create on the board a time line of political changes in Argentina and Chile, beginning in 1946. Have volunteers come to the board and add an event discussed in the text. Make sure events are added in the proper sequence. *(The time line should include these events: **1946:** Juan Perón elected president of Argentina, enacts economic reforms to help working people; **1955:** Military government takes over Argentina; **1970:** Salvador Allende is elected the president of Chile, enacts economic reforms popular with workers; **1973:** Military government takes over Chile.)*

After completing the time line, ask students what pattern they notice in Argentina and Chile. *(After an elected president makes economic reforms that benefit working people, the military steps in and takes over.)* **AL** Visual/Spatial

R Reading Skills

Summarizing Challenge students to summarize the recent political trends in the region in only one sentence. *(Democracies have replaced dictatorships, and people have elected the first indigenous president in Bolivia and the first female presidents in Chile and in Argentina.)* Verbal/Linguistic

CLOSE & REFLECT

To close the lesson, remind students of the KWL chart they made at the beginning of the chapter. Have students review the second column to see if the lesson answered any of the questions they had listed. Then have students make a list of five facts they learned about the history of the Andes region and midlatitude states.

Have students add these five items to the last column of the chart, labeling them for Lesson 2. Discuss how the chart will be a good summary when they complete it at the end of the chapter.

ANSWER, p. 311

☑ READING PROGRESS CHECK Their economies remained tied to Europe. Wealthy landowners, cattle grazers, and mining operators remained linked to European investors. Workers and farmers remained mired in poverty, while profits grew for wealthy landowners and for United States and European multinational companies.

ENGAGE

Bellringer Remind students that the Andean region includes the countries of Peru, Bolivia, and Chile, and that the midlatitude countries are Uruguay, Paraguay, and Argentina. Pose these questions to students: *If you could choose to live in one of these countries, which one would you choose? Why?*

Call on a few students to share their responses. Make sure that they give good reasons to back up their feelings. Then explain to students that they will learn more about life in these countries in this lesson. Have students preview the lesson by skimming the headings, guiding questions, and visuals. Encourage them to make predictions about what they will learn based on their preview. Ask if they expect any of their unanswered questions to be answered in this final lesson.

TEACH & ASSESS

R Reading Skills

Summarizing Note that some of the information about the ethnic background of the region's population applies to all the countries in the region. For example, all the countries have people of Spanish descent and of other European descent. **Ask:**

- What country also has descendants of enslaved Africans? *(Peru)*
- What two countries have large Native American populations? *(Peru and Bolivia)*
- What additional ethnic groups live in Peru? *(people with origins in Japan and Southwest Asia)*
- Which country seems to be the most ethnically diverse? Where do people come from who live there? *(Peru; Europe, Japan, Southwest Asia)*
- Why is an area in the Andean region called the "population rim?" *(The population is densest in the coastal areas, which are along the edge of the area.)* Verbal/Linguistic

---

ANSWER, p. 312

Taking Notes People and Places: densest population along coastlines, cities have many people in shantytowns; **People and Cultures:** many Bolivians rely on natural healers, outstanding literature; **Ongoing Issues:** high population growth, difficult to build strong economies

---

net✷✷rks

There's More Online!

☑ **IMAGES** Cultures of the Andean Region

☑ **MAP** Comparing Highway Systems

☑ **SLIDE SHOW** Traditional and Modern Lifestyles

☑ **VIDEO**

Reading **HELP**DESK

Academic Vocabulary
- impact
- contemporary

Content Vocabulary
- pueblo jóven

TAKING NOTES: *Key Ideas and Details*

Describe As you read this lesson, use a graphic organizer like this one to write an important fact about each topic.

Topic	Fact
People and Places	
People and Cultures	
Ongoing Issues	

R

Indiana Academic Standards
6.1.20, 6.1.21, 6.3.3, 6.3.4, 6.3.10

Lesson 3
Life in the Region

ESSENTIAL QUESTION · *What makes a culture unique?*

IT MATTERS BECAUSE
The population of the Andean and midlatitude countries is ethnically diverse. People, places, and cultures have been shaped by physical geography, urban growth, migration, and immigration.

People and Places

GUIDING QUESTION *What are the major population patterns in the Andean region?*

The population of the Andean region is not evenly distributed. Population patterns in this region reflect the changing **impact** of politics, economics, and the availability of natural resources and jobs.

Population Density and Distribution
The people of the region came from many different places. Three centuries of colonization by Spain have left their mark on the population. Enslaved Africans were brought as laborers, especially in Peru; this was less common in other countries of the region. After independence, immigrants from many European countries traveled to settle in South America. Immigrants also came from Asia.

Today, Bolivia and Peru have large Native American populations. Argentina and Chile have many people of European ancestry, including Spanish, Italian, British, and German backgrounds. Peru has descendants of people from Europe, but also people with origins in Japan and Southwest Asia.

In the Andean and midlatitude countries, as with the whole continent, the population is densest in the coastal areas. This area is sometimes called the "population rim." The rugged,

(l to r) WINFIELD PARKS/National Geographic Stock; ©David Mercado/Reuters/Corbis; ©Paul Thompson/Corbis

---

net✷✷rks   *Online Teaching Options*

VIDEO

Greener Sources of Power in the Andes

Analyzing Use this video about finding lithium in the Andes region and midlatitude countries, and its use as an alternative power source, to generate interest in the lesson content. Ask how the ways the current issues discussed in the video affect the students' current or potential way of life. AL Visual/Spatial, Intrapersonal

See page 295E for other online activities.

BBC Motion Gallery Education

mountainous areas and the tropical rain forest have discouraged settlement in many inland areas. Transportation is difficult, and communication can be slow or nonexistent. Coastal regions offer fertile land, favorable climates, and easy transportation.

Large Cities and Communities

The largest city in the region is Buenos Aires, the capital of Argentina. This is a bustling port and cultural center. It resembles a European city with its parks, buildings, outdoor cafes, and wide streets. About 2.8 million people live in the central city of Buenos Aires, but the metropolitan area includes 11.5 million people. This is more than one-fourth of Argentina's entire population. Although Argentina as a whole is not densely populated, the area in and around Buenos Aires is.

Buenos Aires and many other large cities in the region have shantytowns. These makeshift communities often spring up on the outskirts of a city. Poor people migrate here from remote inland areas to seek a better life. They cannot afford houses or apartments in the city or suburbs, so they settle in the shantytowns. They build shacks from scraps of sheet metal, wood, and other materials. Shantytowns often lack sewers, running water, and other services. They tend to be dangerous places with widespread crime.

In Lima, the capital and largest city in Peru, the shantytowns are called **pueblos jóvenes**. The name means "young towns." One pueblo jóven was home to María Elena Moyano. She worked to improve education, nutrition, and job opportunities in the pueblo jóven. She refused to give in to the demands of the government or to the communist rebels, who assassinated her in 1992. She has become recognized as a national hero for her courage.

✓ **READING PROGRESS CHECK**

Analyzing What limits the population in many inland areas?

WINFIELD PARKS/National Geographic Stock

Academic Vocabulary

impact an effect

Shacks made of metal, wood, and other materials stand in front of high-rise apartments in Buenos Aires.

▶ **CRITICAL THINKING**
Describing What challenges do people living in the shantytowns face?

MAP

Population: Andean Region

Analyzing Maps Display the population density layer of the Chapter Opener map and point out the "population rim" along the coast of the region. Note that the rugged terrain of the Andes discourages the settlement and movement of people. Be sure students make connections between the "population rim" and the development of cities along the coastline. **ELL** Visual/Spatial

See page 295E for other online activities.

V Visual Skills

Integrating Visual Information Point out that the photograph at the bottom of the page is a visual representation of the two main ideas in the first two paragraphs under the heading "Large Cities and Communities." Call on students to identify these two main ideas and explain how they are represented in the photograph. *(The majority of the population in this region lives in large cities. The migration of people from remote areas to the cities has resulted in the building of shantytowns around the large cities.)* Visual/Spatial, Verbal/Linguistic

R Reading Skills

Determining Word Meanings Tell students that unlike English where adjectives that describe nouns generally come before the noun, in Spanish, an adjective comes after the noun. One example of this is the phrase *pueblos jóvenes*. The Spanish word *pueblo* means "town" and the word *jóven* means "young." Together, the words mean "young town." **AL** Verbal/Linguistic

Content Background Knowledge

Severe poverty in Peru and other South American countries contributes to political turmoil and violence in the region. One instance of such violence was when María Elena Moyano, an activist in Peru, was killed at the age of 33.

Even though only 50 people turned up for a peace march that María was leading against an organization of revolutionary guerillas called Shining Path, she continued with the march. The next night while she was attending a fundraising event, she was gunned down by the people she was opposing. The organization used terror tactics against all opponents in its drive to overthrow the Peruvian government.

ANSWERS, p. 313

CRITICAL THINKING Crime is widespread, and shantytowns lack sewers and running water.
✓ READING PROGRESS CHECK The mountains and rain forests in the area make settlement difficult.

Life in the Region

V Visual Skills

Creating Charts Remind students that different countries within a region can have people who speak different languages. As students read about the ethnic and language groups of the region, have them create a two-column chart identifying the country where each group is found. Then have pairs of students compare the information in their charts with each other. (**Guarani:** Paraguay; **Sirionó:** Bolivia; **Quechua:** Peru)

AL Visual/Spatial

Ethnic or Language Group	Country
Guarani	
Sirionó	
Quechua	

Content Background Knowledge

Although more than 25 percent of modern drugs come from plants, scientists have only tested a tiny percentage of the world's plants for their potential medical use. In recent decades, however, scientists have become more interested in learning about and preserving the plant knowledge of traditional healers such as the Kallawayas of Bolivia.

The Western medical profession long ago adopted some of the plants used by the Kallawayas, such as quinine from the dried bark of the cinchona tree and cocaine from the coca plant. Quinine was formerly used to treat malaria, and cocaine was used as a topical anesthetic. Pan American Health Organization has supported the compilation of books that preserve the Kallawayas' knowledge of medicinal plants and traditional medicine.

People and Cultures

GUIDING QUESTION *How do ethnic and religious traditions influence people's lives?*

The Andean and midlatitude regions are home to a wide range of ethnic groups. Although many people trace their ancestry back to Europe, Asia, and Africa, Native American groups still thrive in parts of the region.

Ethnic and Language Groups

V

The Guarani is a Native American group that lives mainly in Paraguay, but people of Guarani descent also can be found in Argentina, Bolivia, and Brazil. The Guarani lived in tropical forests and practiced slash-and-burn agriculture—cutting and burning small areas of forest to clear land for farming. After a few years, the soil's nutrients were used up, and the people moved to a new area.

Today, Guarani customs and folk art are an important part of the culture in Paraguay. Guarani is one of the country's official languages. A related language is Sirionó. The Sirionó live in eastern Bolivia. In Peru, Quechua, a surviving language of the central Andes, is still widely spoken, along with Spanish.

Traditional Medicine

In Bolivia, the custom of Kallawaya medicine is widespread. The word *Kallawaya* might come from the Aymara word for "doctor." Kallawaya healers use traditional herbs and rituals in their cures. Many Bolivians seek the help of Kallawayas when they get sick, either because they prefer these healers or because they cannot afford other doctors. In fact, 40 percent of the Bolivian population relies on the natural healers, who travel from place to place.

Religion and the Arts

During the centuries of Spanish colonization, the Roman Catholic Church was one of the region's most important institutions. The influence of the Catholic Church continues. Millions of people practice mixed religions. Many of the native peoples of the Andes combine their indigenous rituals and beliefs with Roman Catholicism. Others have adopted Protestant religions.

Traditional arts, crafts, music, and dance thrive in the Andean and midlatitude countries. In literature, two Chilean poets, Gabriela Mistral and Pablo Neruda, have won the Nobel Prize for Literature. The works of writers from Argentina,

Kallawaya healers use traditional methods in efforts to cure the sick. The customs and languages of the indigenous peoples are an important part of the culture of the region.
▶ **CRITICAL THINKING**
Identifying What are some of the languages that are spoken in the region?

©David Mercado/Reuters/Corbis

---

netw⊙rks   *Online Teaching Options*

IMAGE

Cultures of the Andean Region

Examining Use the interactive image of the Kallawaya healer to discuss the various cultures in the Andean region. Use the extra information provided to further the discussion with regard to other cultures of the region. Be sure to discuss these traditional ways and their role in modern traditions.

AL Interpersonal

See page 295E for other online activities.

Interactive Photos

Elena Kalistratova/Vetta/Getty Images

ANSWER, p. 314

CRITICAL THINKING Guarani, Sirionó, Quechua

including Jorge Luis Borges and Manuel Puig, are popular with readers around the world. Isabel Allende from Chile, a cousin of the country's former president Salvador Allende, is a **contemporary** writer of great distinction. Many writers have been praised for their use of magic realism. This style combines everyday events with magical or mythical elements. It is especially popular in Latin America.

Academic Vocabulary

contemporary living or happening now

W

Daily Life

In large cities and towns and in wealthier areas, family life revolves around parents and children. In the countryside, extended families are more common. In the region, the *compadre* relationship is still valued. This relationship is a strong bond between a child's parents and other adults who serve as the child's godparents.

V

In a megacity like Buenos Aires, people can wander through large, modern shopping malls. They may dine in outdoor cafes or fancy restaurants. They may work in modern office buildings. Traditional Andean foods of the countryside include *pachamanca* in Peru. This is a mixture of lamb, pork, and chicken baked in an earthen oven. Pachamanca dates back to the time of the Inca Empire.

Soccer, or football, is the most popular sport in the region. Football is Argentina's national game, and its teams have won several World Cup titles. Equestrian sports, or sports featuring riders on horseback, are popular in the region. Argentina's polo teams have long dominated international competition. The Argentina team won the first ever Olympic polo gold medal in 1924.

The Larcomar Shopping Mall in Lima, Peru, is a popular attraction for international tourists.

Football is also the national sport for many of the other countries in the region. The top professional league, the American Football Confederation, is made up of teams from 10 South American nations. League teams are eligible for the World Cup and the America Cup. Other popular sports include basketball, golf, boxing, and rugby. Social life focuses on family visits, patriotic events, religious feast days, and festivals.

✓ **READING PROGRESS CHECK**

Analyzing How is Kallawaya medicine different from the modern medicine that is practiced in most Western countries?

Chapter 10 **315**

W Writing Skills

Narrative Explain to students that magic realism weaves fantastic elements into a realistic story and presents these elements in a straightforward way, as though they were real. For example, a character may come back from the dead, may have telepathic powers, or may levitate.

Discuss examples of stories that students know that use magic realism. Have interested students research stories written by Isabel Allende that use the genre of magic realism. Then have students experiment with writing a story in this style. **BL** Verbal/Linguistic

V Visual Skills

Creating a Graphic Organizer Direct students to create a Venn diagram comparing city life and country life in this region. One circle should be labeled *Rural Life* and the other circle *Urban Life*. Remind students that facts that apply to both should appear in the overlapping area. (***Rural Life:*** *extended families common; pachamanca popular in Peru;* ***Urban Life:*** *family life revolves around parents and children; people go to shopping malls, outdoor cafes, fancy restaurants; people work in modern office buildings;* ***Both:*** *compadre relationship valued; soccer (football) most popular sport; basketball, golf, boxing, and rugby popular; social life focuses on family visits, patriotic events, religious feast days, festivals)* Visual/Spatial, Verbal/Linguistic

Rural Life   Urban Life

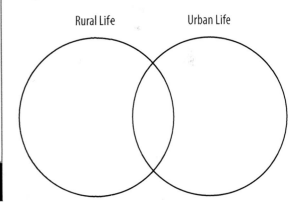

SLIDE SHOW

Traditional and Modern Lifestyles

Integrating Visual Information After students view the slide show, discuss the traditional and modern aspects of life in the Andean and midlatitude regions. **BL** Verbal/Linguistic

See page 295E for other online activities.

Slide Show

ANSWER, p. 315

✓ **READING PROGRESS CHECK** Kallawaya medicine uses traditional herbs and rituals.

C Critical Thinking Skills

Finding the Main Idea Pose the following questions to focus students' attention on the main ideas about the economies of Peru and Bolivia. **Ask:**

- What economic activities are important in Peru? *(agriculture; mining of silver, zinc, copper, and other minerals; production of oil and natural gas; fishing)*
- What important natural resource does Bolivia have? *(natural gas)* **AL** Verbal/Linguistic

V Visual Skills

Creating Charts Explain that the categorization of economic activities into primary, secondary, and tertiary sectors is based on increasing distance from the natural environment, or from raw materials.

To help students visualize the relative importance of these sectors in the region's economy, have them create a circle graph based on the percentages given in the text. *(20% in the secondary, or manufacturing, sector; 65% in the tertiary, or services, sector; leaving 15% in the primary sector, which includes agriculture, mining, and fishing)* **BL** Visual/Spatial

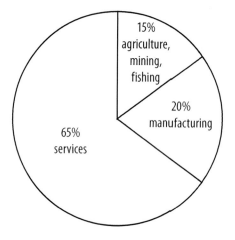

15%
agriculture,
mining,
fishing

20%
manufacturing

65%
services

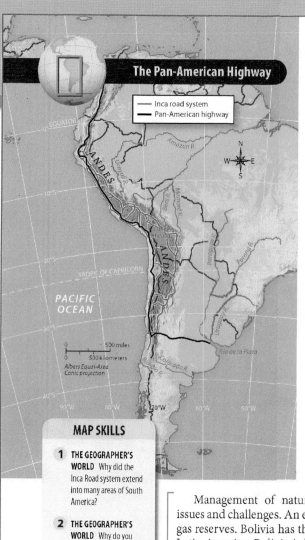

The Pan-American Highway

— Inca road system
— Pan-American highway

0   500 miles
0   500 kilometers
Albers Equal-Area
Conic projection

MAP SKILLS

1 **THE GEOGRAPHER'S WORLD** Why did the Inca Road system extend into many areas of South America?

2 **THE GEOGRAPHER'S WORLD** Why do you think the Pan-American Highway links many capital cities?

316 Chapter 10

Ongoing Issues

GUIDING QUESTION *How are economic and environmental issues affecting the region?*

The population growth rate in the Andean and midlatitude countries is generally not high. However, population is growing enough in some places to add to today's challenges of earning a living.

Earning a Living

It is difficult to build strong economies in the Andean region largely because of the rugged terrain. Many countries rely heavily on agriculture, which is limited and difficult in the mountains. About one-third of Peruvians, for example, are farmers. They grow potatoes, coffee, and corn on terraces built into the mountain slopes. Farms in the valleys along the coast produce sugarcane, asparagus, mangoes, and many other crops.

Mining and fishing are other important economic activities in Peru. Mines in the mountains produce silver, zinc, copper, and other minerals. Peru also produces oil and natural gas. The country's coastal waters are rich fishing grounds. Much of the fish catch is ground into fishmeal for animal feed and fertilizer.

Management of natural resources presents many important issues and challenges. An example is conflict between countries over gas reserves. Bolivia has the second-largest reserve of natural gas in Latin America. Bolivia is landlocked. So, to export the gas, it must move through Peru or Chile.

In 2003 the Bolivian government proposed moving the natural gas through Chile, because it would be cheaper than an alternate plan to go through Peru. The Bolivian people turned out in huge numbers to protest. In Bolivia, suspicion and anger against Chile are widespread. These feelings date back to the Pacific War of the early 1880s, when Chile took over Bolivia's former coastal lands.

As the economies in the region develop, the primary economic activities of agriculture, mining, and fishing remain important. Other activities have become important as well. About 20 percent of the workers in the region are employed in the secondary, or manufacturing, sector. They work in factories making products.

network*s* *Online Teaching Options*

MAP

Comparing Highway Systems

Comparing Display the interactive map of the Incan roads and the Pan-American Highway and have students compare the two road systems, including the length of the roadway, the time it took to build the roadway, and other aspects of these two means of travel. Then direct students to write a paragraph describing the transportation challenges in the region. **BL** Verbal/Linguistic

See page 295E for other online activities.

ANSWERS, p. 316

MAP SKILLS

1. The Inca built an extensive network of roads to connect different parts of their empire.
2. A great deal of transporting goods and people take place in capital cities and from one capital city to another. Having a direct link between the cities saves time and money.

316

About 65 percent find jobs in the tertiary, or services, sector. They work in a wide variety of occupations, ranging from transportation and retail sales to banking and education.

Transportation and Trade

This region has many geographic and regional barriers. The Andes limit construction of roads and railroads. Yet highways do link large cities. The Pan-American Highway, for example, runs from Argentina to Panama, then continues northward after a break in the highway. A trans-Andean highway connects cities in Chile and Argentina. Peru and Brazil are building the Transoceanic Highway. Parts of it opened in 2012. Eventually, this road will link Amazon River ports in Brazil with Peruvian ports on the Pacific Ocean. Unlike other countries, Argentina has an effective railway system.

Trade also connects countries. In 1991 a trade agreement, known as MERCOSUR, was signed by Argentina, Paraguay, Uruguay, and Brazil. In 2011 MERCOSUR merged into a new organization—the Union of South American Nations (UNASUR). The Union set up an economic and political zone modeled after the European Union (EU). Its goals are to foster free trade and closer political unity.

Addressing Challenges

Looking toward the future, the Andean and midlatitude countries must address many challenges. Environmental issues are among the most important. Air and water pollution is a major problem, especially in the shantytowns of urban areas, where the lack of sewage systems and garbage collection increases disease.

Disputed borders have presented challenges for years. For example, Bolivia and Paraguay long disputed rights to a region thought to be rich in oil. In 1998 Peru and Ecuador finally settled a territorial dispute after years of tensions marked by episodes of armed conflict. Border wars use up resources of people, money, time, and brainpower that could be used to address economic development and environmental concerns.

T

R

FOLDABLES
Study Organizer

Include this lesson's information in your Foldable®.

☑ **READING PROGRESS CHECK**

Determining Central Ideas How does the physical landscape hamper transportation? What actions are being taken to improve transportation?

LESSON 3 REVIEW

Reviewing Vocabulary
1. Why might someone live in a *pueblo jóven*?

Answering the Guiding Questions
2. ***Describing*** How are the populations of Peru and Bolivia different from the populations of Argentina and Chile?

3. ***Analyzing*** Why might the Kallaway of Bolivia have an important influence on people's lives?

4. ***Identifying*** What are two important industries in Peru today?

5. ***Informative/Explanatory Writing*** Write a paragraph or two to explain what you think is the most pressing problem facing the people who live in shantytowns.

Chapter 10 **317**

LESSON 3 REVIEW ANSWERS

Reviewing Vocabulary

1. Someone might live in a pueblo jóven, or shantytown, because he or she cannot afford a house or apartment in the city.

Answering the Guiding Questions

2. **Describing** Peru and Bolivia have large populations of Native Americans, while Argentina and Chile do not.

3. **Analyzing** For a large percentage of Bolivians, who are of Native American descent, the Kallaway are their preferred doctors; for others they are the only doctors they can afford.

4. **Identifying** Mining and fishing are two important industries in Peru today.

5. **Informative/Explanatory Writing** Students should select a pervasive problem such as health and offer supporting arguments stating why this is most pressing.

ENGAGE

Bellringer Before students read the What Do You Think? feature, make sure they understand the concepts of globalization and indigenous culture. *Globalization* refers to the linkage of the economies of countries around the world through international trade, communication, and travel, while an *indigenous culture* is the traditional way of life of a group of native people. Remind students of the effects of colonization on indigenous cultures in North and South America: it wiped out some cultures and caused many others to decline. Ask students to imagine how globalization might have similar effects, and tell them that this feature presents two views on the conflict between globalization and indigenous cultures. Then have students read the introductory paragraph and the *No!* viewpoint.

TEACH & ASSESS

C Critical Thinking Skills

Analyzing Primary Sources Pose the following questions to help students analyze the *No!* viewpoint. **Ask:**

- What is the source of the *No!* viewpoint? *(the United Nations Development Programme)*
- Would you expect this source to be knowledgeable on this issue? *(yes)*
- Does this source regard globalization's effect on indigenous cultures as positive or negative? *(positive)*
- What benefit of globalization does the source cite? *(Globalization makes it easier for indigenous people to organize, raise funds, and network with other groups around the world.)*
- According to this source, what protection do indigenous groups have from encroachment by foreign investors and settlers? *(Many states have laws recognizing indigenous people's rights over their resources. Respecting cultural identity is possible as long as decisions are made democratically by states, companies, international institutions, and indigenous people.)*
- Do all these groups—states, companies, international institutions, and indigenous people—usually make decisions democratically? *(No, companies do not typically make decisions democratically.)*
- Do you find this argument convincing? Why or why not? *(Some students may agree with the argument, citing the power of the Internet as an organizing tool to gain worldwide support. Other students may disagree with the argument, noting that indigenous groups tend to have little political power while companies tend to have a lot of power and money and little respect for the needs of individuals.)* Logical/Mathematical, Verbal/Linguistic, Interpersonal

---

What Do You **Think?**

Is Globalization Destroying Indigenous Cultures?

Globalization makes it easier for people, goods, and information to travel across borders. Customers have more choices when they shop. Costs of goods are sometimes lower. However, not everyone welcomes these changes. Resistance is particularly strong among indigenous peoples. They see the expansion of trade and outside influences as a threat to their way of life. Is globalization deadly for indigenous cultures?

No !
PRIMARY SOURCE

C

" Indigenous people have struggled for centuries to maintain their identity and way of life against the tide of foreign economic investment and the new settlers that often come with it. ... But indigenous groups are increasingly assertive. Globalization has made it easier for indigenous people to organize, raise funds and network with other groups around the world, with greater political reach and impact than before. The United Nations declared 1995–2004 the International Decade for the World's Indigenous People, and in 2000 the Permanent Forum on Indigenous Issues was created. ... Many states have laws that explicitly recognize indigenous people's rights over their resources. ... Respecting cultural identity [is] possible as long as decisions are made democratically—by states, by companies, by international institutions and by indigenous people. "

—Report by the United Nations Development Programme (UNDP)

A Quechuan family shops at an open air market in a Peruvian village. The Quechua is the term for several native groups who speak a common language. They live in many countries throughout the region.

318 *Chapter 10*

---

networks *Online Teaching Options*

WORKSHEET

How to Analyze a Visual

Analyzing Visuals Divide the class into small groups and have each group follow the steps in the How to Analyze a Visual worksheet using the two photographs in this feature. Allow the groups to share their analyses with the class. **ELL** Visual/Spatial

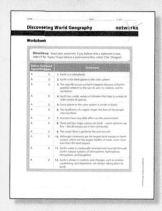

A woman carries water home in a mining town in central Peru. Protesters contend that aggressive mining practices contaminate the environment and destroy the way of life of indigenous people.

Yes!

PRIMARY SOURCE

" Globalization ... is a multi-pronged attack on the very foundation of [indigenous people's] existence and livelihoods. ... Indigenous people throughout the world ... occupy the last pristine [pure and undeveloped] places on earth, where resources are still abundant [plentiful]: forests, minerals, water, and genetic diversity. All are ferociously sought by global corporations, trying to push traditional societies off their lands. ... Traditional sovereignty [control] over hunting and gathering rights has been thrown into question as national governments bind themselves to new global economic treaties. ... Big dams, mines, pipelines, roads, energy developments, military intrusions all threaten native lands. ... National governments making decisions on export development strategies or international trade and investment rules do not consult native communities. ... The reality remains that without rapid action, these native communities may be wiped out, taking with them vast indigenous knowledge, rich culture and traditions, and any hope of preserving the natural world, and a simpler ... way of life for future generations. "

—International Forum on Globalization (IFG), a research and educational organization

C

What Do You Think? DBQ

1 *Citing Text Evidence*
According to the IFG, why are indigenous people at risk?

2 *Describing* According to the United Nations report, how has globalization given indigenous people more power?

Critical Thinking

3 *Identifying* One effect of globalization is that more tourists are visiting remote places such as rain forests in South America and wildlife areas in Africa. How do you think indigenous peoples feel about the growth of tourism in their communities?

Chapter 10 **319**

C Critical Thinking Skills

Analyzing Primary Sources Use the following questions to help students analyze the *Yes!* viewpoint. **Ask:**

- What is the source of the *Yes!* viewpoint? *(International Forum on Globalization)*
- Does this source regard globalization's effect on indigenous cultures as positive or negative? *(negative)*
- According to this source, how is globalization a threat to indigenous cultures? *(Global corporations want natural resources on native lands. Dams, mines, pipelines, roads, energy developments, and military intrusions all threaten native lands.)*
- According to this source, can native communities count on support from national governments? *(No, the source says national governments do not consult native communities when making decisions on international trade and investments.)*
- According to this source, why should native communities be saved? *(to preserve their vast indigenous knowledge and rich culture as well as the natural world and a simpler way of life)*
- Do you find this argument that globalization is a serious threat to native peoples convincing? Why or why not? *(Some students may agree with the argument, noting that historically native peoples have often lost out to more powerful groups. Other students may disagree with the argument, noting that indigenous groups have gained legal rights to their lands.)* Verbal/Linguistic, Interpersonal

CLOSE & REFLECT

To close this lesson, have students write a paragraph presenting their own view on this issue. Tell them to support their opinion with facts, and to give reasons for their view.

Allow time for volunteers to share their paragraphs with the class. Remind students to be considerate of opposing viewpoints.

WORKSHEET

Writing Skills: Supporting Opinion with Facts

Have students use the Writing Skills worksheet for this feature to practice researching and writing convincing arguments supported with clear reasons for both sides of a debatable issue. **BL** Verbal/Linguistic

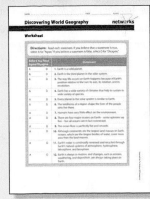

ANSWERS, p. 319

DBQ What Do You Think?

1. Indigenous people live on lands with valuable natural resources that international corporations want to exploit.
2. Globalization has made it easier for indigenous people to organize, raise funds, network, and gain political recognition of their rights.
3. Possible answers: Indigenous people might resent tourists and the environmental damage caused by building hotels, roads, and other infrastructure to support the tourist industry; they might worry about increased commercialization and the loss of traditional values; they might appreciate the jobs created and the chance to educate others about their cultures.

CHAPTER REVIEW ACTIVITY

To summarize the chapter, divide the class into four groups and assign each group one of the concept webs below to complete. Tell the groups to identify five or more main ideas about their subject. Have the groups share their completed concept webs. *(Students' answers may vary but should reflect main ideas covered in each of the three lessons of the chapter.)*

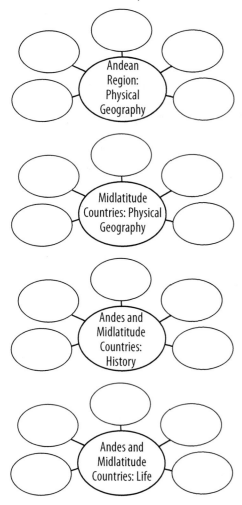

REVIEW THE ENDURING UNDERSTANDINGS

Review this chapter's Enduring Understandings with students:

• **People, places, and ideas change over time.**

Pose the following questions in a class discussion to apply this idea to this chapter:

• How did the rise of the Inca in the 1100s affect the Andean region? *(Sample answer: The small, independent Native American societies were united into a large empire. The empire developed a highly sophisticated, highly structured society that had advanced technology and engineering, including an extensive road system.)*

Directions: Write your answers on a separate piece of paper.

❶ Use your **FOLDABLES** to explore the Essential Questions.
INFORMATIVE/EXPLANATORY WRITING Write a short essay to answer the question: Why are people who live in the Andes more likely to follow a traditional way of life than those who live in cities?

❷ **21st Century Skills**
DESCRIBING Write a radio script for a two-minute segment about what people do for recreation in one of this region's countries. Research the topic, and outline the information you want to include in your script. Share your notes with an adult, and ask: (a) Is my outline clear and well-organized? (b) Does the outline have too much or too little information? Revise your outline as needed, and then use it to write the script. Exchange scripts and compare your script with a classmate's. Discuss strong and weak points in each script.

❸ **Thinking Like a Geographer**
ANALYZING Think about why industrialization requires good transportation and communication systems. Then, describe obstacles that slow the development of these systems.

❹ **GEOGRAPHY ACTIVITY**

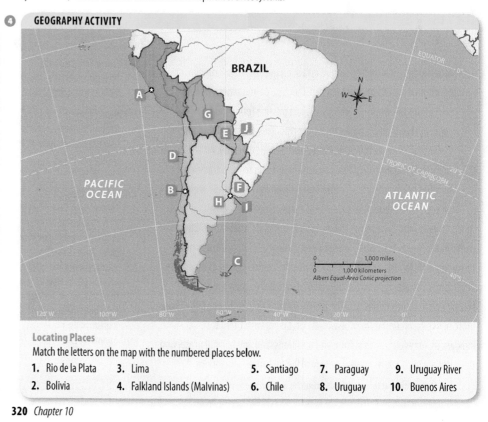

Locating Places
Match the letters on the map with the numbered places below.

1. Rio de la Plata
2. Bolivia
3. Lima
4. Falkland Islands (Malvinas)
5. Santiago
6. Chile
7. Paraguay
8. Uruguay
9. Uruguay River
10. Buenos Aires

320 *Chapter 10*

• How did the arrival of the Spanish in the 1500s change the Andean region? *(Sample answer: The Native American groups declined drastically because of the violence of the Spanish overthrow and from the introduction of European diseases. Also the region was plundered for its mineral wealth, especially gold and silver.)*

• What economic activity was dominant in the early Native American societies in the Andean region? *(agriculture)* In what type of economic activity are most people of this region employed today? *(services)*

ACTIVITIES ANSWERS

Essential Question

❶ **INFORMATIVE/ EXPLANATORY WRITING** Answers could include that Andean communities are somewhat isolated. The residents continue their traditional ways of life because they are physically separated from outside influences.

21st Century Skills

❷ **CREATING A COMMUNICATIONS PRODUCT** Students should revise their outline to clarify information and organize the outline logically. Students will obtain appropriate feedback from a peer to revise the radio script.

REVIEW THE GUIDING QUESTIONS

Directions: Choose the best answer for each question.

1 The ocean tide meets a river current at a(n)

A. cordillera.

B. altiplano.

C. estuary.

D. *tierrra templada.*

2 Chile leads the world in exports of

F. emeralds.

G. copper.

H. lead.

I. gold.

3 The Inca became extremely wealthy because of

A. the system called quipu.

B. rich farmland.

C. huge deposits of gold and silver.

D. a lucrative fur trade.

4 The broad plain that spreads across Uruguay and eastern Argentina is called

F. the pampas.

G. the Atacama.

H. the Rio Blanco.

I. the Río de la Plata.

5 The group of South American animals called camelids includes

A. horses and donkeys.

B. sheep and goats.

C. llamas and alpacas.

D. mules and llamas.

6 The Spanish explorer who took the Inca emperor Atahualpa hostage was

F. Pizarro.

G. Columbus.

H. Magellan.

I. Fernandez.

ASSESSMENT ANSWERS

Review the Guiding Questions

1 **C** An estuary is an area where the ocean tide meets a river current. A cordillera is a series of parallel mountain ranges. An altiplano is a high plain. The *tierra templada* is the second lowest of four climate zones in the Andes.

2 **G** If students do not get this answer correct, refer them to Lesson 1 where it states that Chile leads the world in exports of copper.

3 **C** Students can eliminate answers B and D because the text makes no mention of rich farmland or a fur trade. Answer A refers to quipu, which was a useful counting tool but not a source of wealth. Refer students to Lesson 2 where it states that the Inca became extremely wealthy because of their vast natural resources of gold and silver.

4 **F** If students do not get this answer correct, refer them to Lesson 1 where it identifies this plain as the pampas. The Atacama is a desert in Peru and northern Chile. The Rio Blanco and Rio de la Plata are rivers in the region.

5 **C** Camelids are relatives of camels, and the resemblance among llamas, alpacas, and camels is obvious even though alpacas and llamas do not have humps.

6 **F** If students do not get this answer correct, refer them to Lesson 2 where it identifies Pizarro as the one who captured the Inca emperor Atahualpa. Columbus, Magellan, and Fernandez are not mentioned in this chapter because they did not directly play a role in the history of the region.

Thinking Like a Geographer

3 **ANALYZING** Industrialization requires good transportation systems to bring raw materials to factories and to deliver manufactured products to customers; good communication systems help link producers and consumers and speed the flow of information. The rugged mountains in the Andes make it difficult to build roads and railroads, to transport goods over waterways, and to develop reliable communication systems.

Geography Activity

4 **LOCATING PLACES**

1. I	**6.** D
2. G	**7.** E
3. A	**8.** F
4. C	**9.** J
5. B	**10.** H

DBQ Analyzing Documents

7 **B** The writer is saying that Argentina's government might take over other companies as it has done with the oil companies because it wants to make sure that it will receive a large amount of the money that comes from selling Argentina's oil, rather than having those profits go to private investors such as occurs with the oil companies in the United States.

8 **H** Companies might be afraid that the Argentinian government may have intentions to nationalize other companies, including the companies that these people own. This will make these companies very reluctant to invest in developing their operations in Argentina, for fear they will not benefit from their investment.

Short Response

9 Visitors' impressions that much of Inca Cuzco has survived is incorrect. That is because streets and the Incan system of roads that made it famous have been greatly changed and most Inca buildings have been thoroughly destroyed.

10 Possible answer: The Spanish probably made many of these changes in an effort to turn native people away from their old ways of thinking and living and to adopt Spanish culture and ways of life. Some of the changes may have occurred in modern times because of modernization or new technologies.

Extended Response

11 If students are having trouble responding to this question, refer them back to lesson 1 where they learned that elevation, climate, and proximity to water are the geographic features that influence where people in the Andes and Midlatitude countries live.

DBQ ANALYZING DOCUMENTS

7 **CITING TEXT EVIDENCE** Read the following passage:

"*[Argentina's] President [Cristina] Kirchner . . . announce[d] the nationalization of the Argentine oil company. . . . The move . . . raised concerns that this may be the first of many expropriations [government takeovers] of privately run companies.*"

—from Jonathan Gilbert, "The Next Venezuela?" (2012)

What does the writer say that Argentina's government might do in the future?

A. break the nation's dependence on imported oil

B. take over other companies

C. replace nuclear power with oil as the main source of energy

D. end high unemployment in Argentina

8 **IDENTIFYING** What impact will Argentina's action probably have on foreign companies doing business there?

F. They probably will try to sell their businesses to the government.

G. They will expect to have lower costs when oil prices fall.

H. They are likely to fear that their companies will be taken over, too.

I. They will seek to buy the oil company from the government.

SHORT RESPONSE

"*Visitors to modern Cuzco frequently marvel at the exquisite [very fine] workmanship of its many Inca walls. The . . . impression is that a great deal of Inca Cuzco has survived. . . . [Actually,] new streets have been created, ancient ones lost, and the bulk of the city's former palaces, halls, temples, and shrines [holy places] have been demolished.*"

—from Brian S. Bauer, *Ancient Cuzco: Heartland of the Inca* (2004)

9 **DETERMINING CENTRAL IDEAS** Is the impression visitors have that much of Inca Cuzco has survived correct? Why or why not?

10 **IDENTIFYING** Who do you think was responsible for these changes to ancient Cuzco? Why?

EXTENDED RESPONSE

11 **INFORMATIVE/EXPLANATORY WRITING** Think about what you have read about the physical geography of the Andes and midlatitude countries. What geographic factors influence where people have settled in the region?

Need Extra Help?

If You've Missed Question	**1**	**2**	**3**	**4**	**5**	**6**	**7**	**8**	**9**	**10**	**11**
Review Lesson	1	1	2	1	1	2	3	3	2	2	1

Jonathan Gilbert, BA (Hons), PgDip. This article first appeared in THE CHRISTIAN SCIENCE MONITOR. http://CSMonitor.com; From ANCIENT CUZCO: HEARTLAND OF THE INCA, by Brian S. Bauer, Copyright © 2004. By permission of the University of Texas Press.

---

networks   *Online Teaching Options*

Evaluation and Assessment

Assessing Use eAssessment to create your own tests from hundreds of available questions. eAssessment helps you design assessments that meet the needs of different types of learners.

EUROPE Planner

UNDERSTANDING BY DESIGN®

Enduring Understandings
- *People, places, and ideas change over time.*
- *Countries have relationships with each other.*

Essential Questions
- *How does geography influence the way people live?*
- *How do governments change?*
- *How do people adapt to their environment?*
- *Why do civilizations rise and fall?*
- *How do new ideas change the way people live?*

Students will Know:
- *that each region of Europe has a unique geography and history.*
- *that Europeans speak many languages and have different cultures.*
- *that Europe incorporates many nations.*
- *that Northern and Southern Europe share similar modern struggles as Western Europe.*
- *that Eastern Europe and Western Russia have had similar governments, and share similar climates, cultural aspects, and economic issues.*

Students will be able to:
- **analyze a map** *to identify countries, cities, and geographic features of Europe.*
- **time line** *to discuss countries of Europe.*
- **identify** *landforms and waterways in Europe.*

- **discuss** *the history of Europe through 1800.*
- **describe** *how the Industrial Revolution changed Europe.*
- **discuss** *World War I, World War II, and the Cold War and their affects on Europe.*
- **discuss** *how the collapse of the Soviet Union affected Europe.*
- **describe** *ethnic and language groups in Europe.*
- **discuss** *religion, literature, music, and the arts.*
- **describe** *the Renaissance and how it changed Europe.*
- **discuss** *daily life in different regions of Europe.*
- **discuss** *the early history of Northern and Southern Europe.*
- **explain** *the rise of communism.*
- **discuss** *social and economic changes in Russia after the fall of the Soviet Union.*
- **examine** *economic issues and current challenges that face Europe.*

Predictable Misunderstandings

Students may think:
- *Western Europe is only the British Isles.*
- *All people in Western Europe speak English.*
- *Western Europeans share the same culture.*
- *Northern and Southern Europe have the same geographic landscape as Western Europe.*

- *Northern and Southern Europeans share the same language and cultures as Western Europeans.*
- *Eastern Europe has more similarity to the other European nations*
- *Western Russia has had no influence on the development of Eastern Europe. Eastern Europe and Western Russia have little cultural connection.*

Assessment Evidence

Performance Tasks:
- *Environmental Case Study*

Other Evidence:
- *Physical Location GeoQuiz*
- *Political Location GeoQuiz*
- *City Location GeoQuiz*
- *Physical Geography Activity*
- *Cultural Geography Activity*
- *Geography and History Activity*
- *Geography and Economics Activity*
- *Writing Skills Activity*
- *Geography Skills Activity*
- *Critical Thinking Skills Activity*
- *Technology Skills Activity*
- *Participation in Interactive Whiteboard Activities*
- *Analysis of graphic organizers, graphs, and charts*
- *Lesson Reviews*
- *Chapter Assessments*

Key for Using the Teacher Edition

SKILL-BASED ACTIVITIES

Types of skill activites found in the Teacher Edition.

V **Visual Skills** require students to analyze maps, graphs, charts, and photos.

W **Writing Skills** provide writing opportunities to help students comprehend the text.

R **Reading Skills** help students practice reading skills and master vocabulary.

C **Critical Thinking Skills** help students apply and extend what they have learned.

T **Technology Skills** require students to use digital tools effectively.

DIFFERENTIATED INSTRUCTION

All activities are written for the on-level student unless otherwise marked with the leveled labels below.

BL Beyond Level

AL Approaching Level

ELL English Language Learners

All students benefit from activities that utilize different learning styles. Many activities are marked as below when a particular learning style is highlighted.

Intrapersonal	Naturalist
Logical/Mathematical	Kinesthetic
Visual/Spatial	Auditory/Musical
Verbal/Linguistic	Interpersonal

SUGGESTED PACING GUIDE

TOTAL TIME   38 Days

PLANNER

☑ Print Teaching Options

V Visual Skills

☐ **P. 325** Students infer what climates can be found in Europe based on the large coastal regions seen in the satellite image. **BL** Logical/Mathematical

☐ **P. 326** Students explore a physical map of Europe identifying landforms and waterways. **AL** Visual/Spatial

☐ **P. 327** Students analyze political boundaries and locate European countries on the map. **ELL** Visual/Spatial

☐ **P. 328** Students make generalizations about population density in Europe and use the cities key to identify European cities with populations over 5 million people.

☐ **P. 328** Students use the population map to discuss locations of cities and population densities. **ELL**

☐ **P. 329** Students use the resources map to identify resources found in different parts of Europe and connect land use to economics and population density. **ELL**

W Writing Skills

☐ **P. 329** Students write a short essay about which regions in Europe likely have economic advantages due to their abundance of natural resources. **BL** Logical

R Reading Skills

☐ **P. 324** Students use the context clues and the photo of the individual fishing to make inferences about harbors and coastal industries. **AL**

☐ **P. 325** Students compare size of Europe and the United States and express ideas on the diversity of cultures. **ELL**

C Critical Thinking Skills

☐ **P. 323** Students share their prior knowledge about Europe. Verbal/Linguistic

☐ **P. 325** Students discuss the landscape of Tuscany and speculate about its main industry. Verbal/Linguistic

☐ **P. 327** Students discuss the importance of cooperation among the countries of Europe. **BL** Logical

☐ **P. 330** Students consider the relationship between climate, latitude, and land use. **BL** Logical

T Technology Skills

☐ **P. 330** Students research and develop a "You Are There" presentation on one country in Europe.

☑ Online Teaching Options

V Visual Skills

☐ **MAP** **Europe: Political Map**—Students can use the political layer on the Chapter Opener map to review the political boundaries of the region. Visual/Spatial

☐ **MAP** **Europe: Population Map**—Students can use the population layer on the Chapter Opener map to review the population distribution and density. Visual/Spatial

W Writing Skills

☐ **VIDEO** **Video Tour of Europe**—Students watch a video montage highlighting Europe and write three questions they have about Europe. **ELL** Visual/Spatial

☐ **MAP** **Europe: Resources Map**—Students use the map of the resources in Europe and then research a mineral and its impact on exports and the economy of a country. **AL** Visual/Spatial

☐ **MAP** **Europe: Climates Map**—Students work in groups to research a specific climate and recognize how climate affects the lifestyle and industry of the people in that region. Visual/Spatial, Interpersonal

C Critical Thinking Skills

☐ **MAP** **Europe: Physical Map**—Students identify areas of elevation, calculate distance, and speculate on the difficulty of navigating ships. **AL** Kinesthetic

☐ **MAP** **Regional Map**—Students make connections between the images in the unit and their location on the interactive map. **ELL** Visual/Spatial

T Technology Skills

☐ **GAME** **Political Boundaries: Europe Game**—Students play a drag and drop game to identify and place countries, cities, provinces, and islands of Europe. **AL** Kinesthetic

☑ Printable Digital Worksheets

W Writing Skills

☐ **WORKSHEET** **Environmental Case Study**—Students will use the environmental case study worksheets to evaluate effective land use in Europe. Logical/Mathematical

☐ **QUIZ** **Physical Location GeoQuiz**—Use the Physical Location GeoQuiz as a pre- or post-assessment of students' knowledge of Europe's landforms amd bodies of water.

☐ **QUIZ** **Political Location GeoQuiz**—Use the Political Location GeoQuiz as a pre- or post-assessment of students' knowledge of Europe's countries.

☐ **QUIZ** **City Location GeoQuiz**—Use the City Location GeoQuiz as a pre- or post-assessment of students' knowledge of Europe's major cities.

☐ **WORKSHEET** **Physical Geography Activity**—Students will analyze an elevation profile of the region.

☐ **WORKSHEET** **Cultural Geography Activity: Scandinavian Culture**—Students compare and contrast daily life of Northern Europe to Southern Europe using a collaborative worksheet, and use a Venn diagram to visualize their comparisons.

EUROPE

Chapter 11	**Chapter 12**	**Chapter 13**
Western Europe	Northern and Southern Europe	Eastern Europe and Western Russia

UNIT **4**

Global Connections

The Global Connections feature for this unit gives students an opportunity to think about Europe's aging population and the impact an aging population has on the region's economy. Students will consider how European countries are responding to the problems associated with an aging population, and they will gain an understanding of the problems seniors face when countries have limited resources to address an aging population. **Verbal/Linguistic**

c

ENGAGE

Bellringer Share with students the Unit Opener image of cyclists in Europe. Explain that Europe is a diverse continent with a dynamic history, quaint villages, large cities, and varied landscapes and climates. Guide students in a discussion of the image by asking:

- What do you notice about the landscape?
- What event is taking place?
- What type of landscape are the bicyclists having to manage?
- What type of lifestyle is evident in the photo?

Making Connections Share the following information with students. Encourage students to volunteer what they may already know about Europe. Then, access students' prior knowledge with the following facts about Europe:

- It is the second smallest continent by surface area.
- It includes the mountainous regions of the Alps, Pyrenees, and Carpathians, as well as a lowland called the Great European Plain.
- It is bounded by the Atlantic Ocean to the west, the Arctic Ocean to the north, and six seas to the south: Tyrrhenian, Mediterranean, Adriatic, Aegean, Black, and Caspian.
- Its biomes include tundra, forest, and dry steppe.
- Twenty-seven countries in Europe belong to the European Union.
- Many cultures and languages are represented throughout the region.

C Critical Thinking Skills

Transferring Knowledge Have students share their prior knowledge and experiences of Europe with the class. **Ask:** What are some facts you know about Europe, such as its history, its many cultures, its traditions, languages, or climates? *(Encourage students to share their prior knowledge.)*

Tell students they will be learning more about Europe, its people, and its resources and climate. In particular they will be learning about four major regions: Western Europe, Northern Europe, Southern Europe, and Eastern Europe and Western Russia. **Verbal/Linguistic**

TEACH & ASSESS

C Critical Thinking Skills

Synthesizing Review the importance of different landscape features to the establishment of communities. Have a student volunteer read the introduction aloud. **Ask:**

- How would you describe the landscape of Europe? *(Students might answer that the landscape is varied with coastlines, plains, hills, and mountains.)*
- What advantage does a jagged coastline offer European countries? *(access for fishers, transportation, defense)*
- What advantage does a series of rivers offer Europeans? *(transportation routes, commerce)*
- How might an area's industry change as the landscape changes? *(fishing to farming to forestry)* Naturalist

R Reading Skills

Using Context Clues Have students read the paragraph "Bodies of Water" and describe what they see in the image associated with the paragraph. **Ask:** What is the individual doing? *(pulling in his fish net)*

Point out that the text states "Europe's deep bays and well-protected inlets shelter fine harbors." **Ask:**

- What inference can you make about the harbors from this statement? *(Possible answers: They would be good for ships since they are deep and well-protected, also they are likely abundant in fish and other natural resources.)*
- In what way might coastal industries depend on inland population centers? *(Students might answer that the coastal industries depend on the sale of products to inland population centers.)* **AL** Naturalist

V Visual Skills

Analyzing Images Have students read the paragraph, "Landforms" and study the image associated with the paragraph. **Ask:**

- What makes the Great Hungarian Plain a good place for raising livestock? *(plenty of grass for grazing, availability of water, large open spaces to keep large herds of cattle)*
- Along with raising livestock, what other type of industry is found on a plain? *(growing grains, fruits, and vegetables)*
- Why might the North European Plain have attracted settlers? *(Fertile land and an abundance of rivers provided the resources needed to survive on the plain.)* Verbal/Linguistic

EXPLORE the CONTINENT

EUROPE

Europe is a relatively small continent with a long, jagged coastline. Fertile plains extend across much of northern Europe. Farther south, the plains become rugged hills, and then mountains. Great rivers wind their way through Europe's landscape, linking inland areas with the seas.

R

1 BODIES OF WATER A fisher uses a net to catch salmon on Loughros Bay in northwest Ireland. Europe's deep bays and well-protected inlets shelter fine harbors. For centuries, the rivers of Europe have provided links between coastal ports and inland population centers.

2 LANDFORMS A herder tends to cattle on the Great Hungarian Plain in the eastern part of Hungary. Farmers raise livestock and cultivate grains, fruits, and vegetables here. In the northern part of the region, the North European Plain stretches from France to Russia. The plain's fertile soil and wealth of rivers originally drew farmers to the area.

V

324 *Unit 4*

netw✪rks *Online Teaching Options*

VIDEO

Video Tour of Europe

Formulating Questions Prior to starting the video montage, tell students that while viewing the video, they should write down three questions they have about Europe. Hand three sticky notes to each student and have them write their three questions on the note sheets, one per piece of paper. Have students place their sticky notes on a wall or bulletin board. As the questions are answered throughout the unit, take down the sticky notes. **ELL** Visual/Spatial

Medioimages/Photodisc/Getty Images

3 NATURAL RESOURCES Located in west central Italy, the region of Tuscany is known for its natural resources as well as its beautiful landscape. In the mountains, iron and magnesium are produced, and marble is quarried. Carrara marble is in high demand for building and statues worldwide. Along the northern coast, pine forests are abundant.

FAST **FACT**

Europe is only about 10 percent larger than the United States.

(tr) NOAA National Geophysical Data Center (NGDC)

Unit 4 **325**

WORKSHEET

Environmental Case Study

Interpreting The Environmental Case Study for this unit is about land use. Divide the students into groups and distribute the case study, allowing in-class time for planning and completing the study. Have groups share their findings with the class. Logical/Mathematical

TEACH & ASSESS

V Visual Skills

Transferring Knowledge Direct students' attention to the satellite image at the top of the page. Have students discuss the shape of Europe. Point out the large coastal regions of the continent and remind students of the location of Europe. Have students consider what they know about the contrasting climates found in the United States and how they might compare to the climates in Europe. **Ask:**

- Based on the satellite image, what type of climates do you think are found in Europe? *(temperate, cold and snowy, and semi-arid)*
- What other information about Europe can you learn from the satellite image? *(Students might answer that the amount of water surrounding Europe is very prominent in the image.)* **BL** Logical/Mathematical

C Critical Thinking Skills

Evaluating Have a student volunteer read the paragraph "Natural Resources" and locate Tuscany om the satellite image. **Ask:** From the information in the paragraph, how would you describe Tuscany? *(rich in natural resources and beauty)*

Have students list the natural resources found in Tuscany based on the text. **Ask:** What industries do you think this region could support? Why? *(Possible answer: the region could support farming due to its location and abundance of natural resources.)* Verbal/Linguistic

R Reading Skills

Expressing Have students read the Fast Fact and locate the outline of the United States over the continent of Europe. Remind students that while the United States is a country, Europe is a continent, and that while the United States is made up of a union of states, Europe is made up of a union of countries. **Ask:** Why do you think there is such diversity of cultures in Europe? *(Students might suggest that each country has its own set of languages, religions, and traditions that define the country as unique and separate from the others.)* **ELL**

V Visual Skills

Identifying Discuss the physical map as a group, including the lines of longitude and latitude and the map key. Point out that the Arctic Circle crosses the northern region of Europe. Have students work in pairs to identify the following features of the map: the Northern European Plain, the Alps, Carpathian Mountains, and Pyrenees Mountains. Have students identify regions on the map. **Ask:** **V**

- Where is the Hungarian Plain found? *(between the Carpathian Mountains and mountains that border the Adriatic Sea)*
- Where is the Iberian Peninsula located? *(in the southwest region of the continent)*

Have students identify important landforms on the physical map. **Ask:**

- What types of landforms do you notice about the continent? *(Possible answers: the many peninsulas and islands, several seas that surround the continent)*
- Where are the highest elevations found in Europe? *(Alps, Pyrenees Mountains, Caucasus Mountains)*
- Which mountain range separates Europe from Asia to the west? *(Ural Mountains)*
- Which islands are found below 40° N latitude? *(Balearic Islands, Part of Sardinia, Sicily, Ionian Islands, Crete, Cyprus)*
- What is the highest mountain in Europe? *(Mt. Elbrus)*
- What must ships pass through in order to enter the Mediterranean Sea? *(Strait of Gibraltar)* **AL** Visual/ Spatial

C Critical Thinking Skills

Assessing Have students focus on the elevations shown on the physical map. **Ask:**

- What do you notice about the elevation of most of Europe? *(Students should observe that most of Europe is less than 2000 ft, or 600 m, above sea level.)*
- What role might mountains have played in European history? *(Possible answers: were natural boundaries; made invasion difficult; prevented easy migration from one region to another)* **BL** Visual/Spatial

---

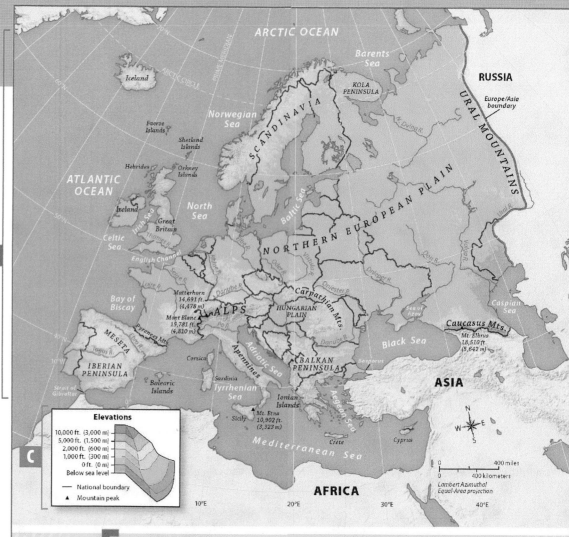

EUROPE

PHYSICAL

MAP SKILLS

1. **PHYSICAL GEOGRAPHY** How would you describe the landforms of central Europe?

2. **PLACES AND REGIONS** How high is the Meseta in the Iberian Peninsula?

3. **PLACES AND REGIONS** What body of water separates Great Britain from Europe's mainland?

326 Unit 4

---

net**w**rks   *Online Teaching Options*

MAP

Europe: Physical Map

Locating Display the physical map of Europe on the interactive whiteboard. Have students determine the distance a ship would need to travel to navigate the Mediterranean Sea from the Strait of Gibraltar to Sicily, and then to Crete, and finally to Cyprus. Have students speculate on the difficulty of navigating from the Mediterranean to the Black Sea. Point out the importance of rivers as water routes through the continent's interior. **AL** Kinesthetic

ANSWERS, p. 326

MAP SKILLS
1. mountainous
2. between 2,000 ft. (600 m) and 5,000 ft. (1500 m)
3. English Channel

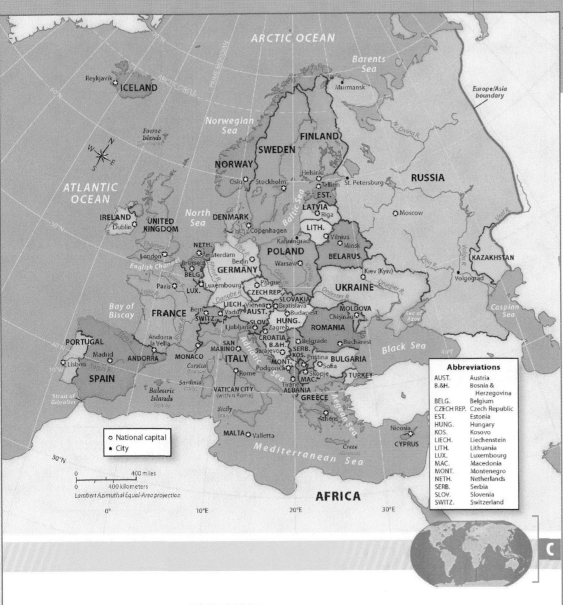

ABBREVIATIONS

AUST.	Austria
B.&H.	Bosnia & Herzegovina
BELG.	Belgium
CZECH REP.	Czech Republic
EST.	Estonia
HUNG.	Hungary
KOS.	Kosovo
LIECH.	Liechtenstein
LITH.	Lithuania
LUX.	Luxembourg
MAC.	Macedonia
MONT.	Montenegro
NETH.	Netherlands
SERB.	Serbia
SLOV.	Slovenia
SWITZ.	Switzerland

POLITICAL

MAP SKILLS

1 THE GEOGRAPHER'S WORLD Where is Monaco located?

2 PLACES AND REGIONS What country lies between Belarus and Romania?

3 PLACES AND REGIONS Which countries border the Baltic Sea?

Unit 4 **327**

V Visual Skills

Reading a Map Have students analyze the political boundaries on the map. Call out the names of several countries and have the students locate them. **Ask:**

- Which countries are found on the Iberian Peninsula? *(Portugal, Spain)*
- Which is the largest country in Europe? *(Russia)*
- Which countries border the Black Sea? *(Turkey, Bulgaria, Romania, Ukraine, Russia)*
- Which countries have land areas that extend into the Arctic Ocean? *(Norway, Russia)*
- What is the capital of France? *(Paris)*
- Which country borders Germany, Poland, Slovakia, and Austria? *(Czech Republic)*
- Where is Moscow found? *(in Russia)* **ELL** Visual/Spatial

V

C Critical Thinking Skills

Reasoning Remind students about the physical size of Europe. Point to the world map as a reference to the landmass as compared to the remainder of the world. Have students use this information to reason about the importance of cooperation among the countries of Europe. **Ask:**

- Which countries would appear to be the most powerful? Why? *(Students might suggest that larger countries might be more powerful than smaller countries, or those with coastlines have a political advantage over countries that are landlocked.)*
- Why do you think there are so many countries in Europe? *(Possible answers: history tells us that the first civilizations were started near this region, so as religions, beliefs, cultures, and languages changed new countries were created; natural boundaries separated civilizations; travel was difficult in early periods, so new groups of people settled in areas close together)*
- Why is economic and political cooperation among the countries of Europe important? *(Students' answers will vary but should address cooperation is important to avoid the potential for armed conflict to maintain political borders as countries try to meet the needs of their people with available land and resources.)* **BL** Logical/Mathematical

GAME

Political Boundaries: Europe Game

Labeling Display the political interactive map of Europe on the whiteboard. Have students study the political boundaries on the map. Then have students play the drag-and-drop game by labeling the names of the cities and countries on the interactive map. After the game, you may want to give students the Political Location GeoQuiz as a pre-assessment tool for this unit. Then use the geoquiz at the end of the unit as a post-assessment.

AL Kinesthetic

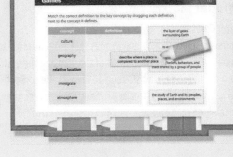

ANSWERS, p. 327

MAP SKILLS
1. on the Mediterranean coast of France
2. Ukraine
3. Sweden, Finland, Estonia, Latvia, Lithuania, Russia, Poland, Germany, and Denmark

V1 Visual Skills

Making Comparisons Direct attention to the two map keys associated with the population map. **Ask:**

- In looking at the map and population key, what general statement can you make about population density in Europe? *(Answers will vary, but students should recognize that population seems to be concentrated in the central region of Europe.)*

- In looking at the cities map key and using it to find where large cities are located, which cities in Europe have a population of over 5 million people? *(Madrid, London, Paris, Moscow, Istanbul)* **ELL** **V1**

V2 Visual Skills

Reading a Map Direct students' attention to the cities shown on the population map. Lead a class discussion reviewing why many major cities are located near a waterway or body of water. Have students find cities that are located near, but not necessarily along a body of water. **Ask:** What major city in Russia is not located along a sea or river? *(Moscow)*

Continue the class discussion by discussing some of the unique features of Europe's population. **Ask:**

- Which island country has a high population? *(Great Britain)*

- Where is population least concentrated? *(in the northern and far eastern regions)*

- In thinking back to the physical map, what does the continent's interior have that would encourage higher population densities? *(Possible answer: areas for farming and livestock raising)*

- What is the population of Iceland? *(less than 2.5 persons per square mile; less than 1 person per square kilometer)*

- Why do you think the population of Iceland is sparse? *(harsh, cold climate)* **Visual/Spatial**

POPULATION

Per sq. mi.		Per sq. km
1,250 and over		500 and over
250–1,249		100–499
63–249		25–99
25–62		10–24
2.5–24		1–9
Less than 2.5		Less than 1

Cities
(Statistics reflect metropolitan areas.)
- ■ Over 5,000,000
- ▢ 2,000,000–5,000,000
- ◉ 1,000,000–2,000,000
- ● 500,000–1,000,000
- ○ Under 500,000

EUROPE

POPULATION DENSITY

MAP SKILLS

1. **PLACES AND REGIONS** How would you describe the population in the area north of St. Petersburg?

2. **THE GEOGRAPHER'S WORLD** What cities are located in Europe's most densely populated area?

3. **PLACES AND REGIONS** What part of Europe has a low population density?

328 Unit 4

---

networks *Online Teaching Options*

MAP

Regional Map

Making Connections Display the interactive regional map to students. Select some of the images that are connected to the map and place them in context of the map and the unit. Guide a discussion helping students to identify the content of the images and then to make a connection between the image and the map location. **ELL** **Visual/Spatial**

ANSWERS, p. 328

MAP SKILLS
1. lightly populated
2. London, Amsterdam, the Hague, Brussels, Lille, Frankfurt, Munich, and Pristina
3. Northern Europe

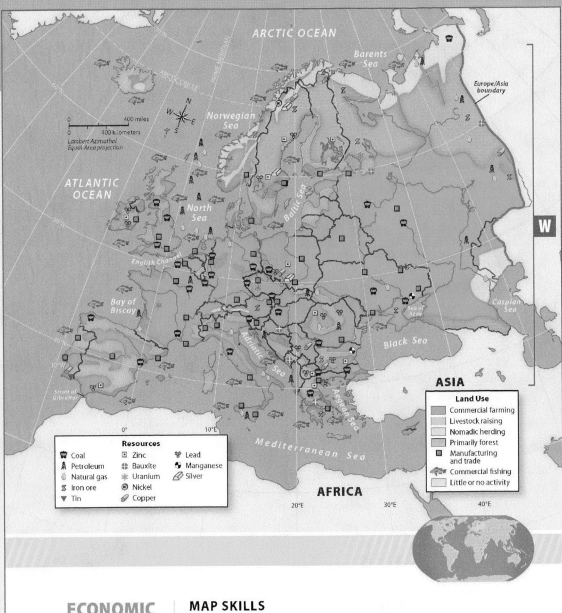

ARCTIC OCEAN

Barents Sea

Europe/Asia boundary

Norwegian Sea

ATLANTIC OCEAN

North Sea

Baltic Sea

English Channel

Bay of Biscay

Adriatic Sea

Caspian Sea

Sea of Azov

Black Sea

ASIA

Mediterranean Sea

Aegean Sea

Strait of Gibraltar

0°   10°E   20°E   30°E   40°E

AFRICA

Land Use
- Commercial farming
- Livestock raising
- Nomadic herding
- Primarily forest
- Manufacturing and trade
- Commercial fishing
- Little or no activity

Resources
- ♛ Coal
- ☒ Zinc
- ♉ Lead
- 🅰 Petroleum
- ⠿ Bauxite
- 🜨 Manganese
- ⬡ Natural gas
- ☀ Uranium
- ⬭ Silver
- ⋝ Iron ore
- ⊛ Nickel
- ▽ Tin
- ⬤ Copper

400 miles
400 kilometers
Lambert Azimuthal
Equal-Area projection

ECONOMIC RESOURCES

MAP SKILLS

1 PLACES AND REGIONS In what part of Europe is bauxite found?

2 ENVIRONMENT AND SOCIETY How is land used in the far northern areas of Europe?

3 PLACES AND REGIONS What mineral resources are located under the North Sea?

V Visual Skills

Analyzing a Map Help students recognize the economic importance of natural resources to a region's industry. Direct students' attention to the resources map key. **Ask:**

- What are some of the resources shown on this map? *(Students should identify the various resources in the map key)*
- Which natural resources seem to be most plentiful throughout the continent? *(coal, oil, lead)*
- What land uses are shown on this map? *(commercial farming, livestock raising, nomadic herding, forest, manufacturing and trade, commercial fishing)*
- In general, what land use is most common across the continent? *(commercial farming)*

Write the questions listed below on the board. With a partner, have students analyze the resources map and write the answers to the following questions on the board. **Ask:**

- What land use does Europe's extensive coastlines offer? *(commercial fishing)*
- Where is manufacturing and trade found in Europe? *(throughout the region except far eastern and northern regions)*
- What type of land use do countries in the far north depend on for economic stability? *(mining, fishing)*
- What type of land use occurs most often in Iceland? *(livestock raising)*
- How does land use change from north to south? *(nomadic herding to forest, to commercial farming)*
- Where is oil and natural gas most concentrated in Europe? *(under the North Sea)*
- What natural resources are found in Spain? *(zinc, copper, tin, coal, lead)*
- What relationship is there between land use and population density? *(Students might suggest that the highest population densities occur where the greatest land use is possible.)* **ELL** Verbal/Linguistic

W Writing Skills

Informative/Explanatory Have students write a short essay in which they use the resource map and the population density map to answer: **Which region in Europe might have an economic advantage due to its abundance of natural resources?** Essays should provide an answer to the question in a topic sentence and the remaining text should support their answers that connect manufacturing and trade, oil production, mining, and commercial farming with the economic advantages of stability and growth. **BL** Logical/Mathematical

---

MAP

Resources Map: Europe

Recognizing Relationships Display the interactive resource map and allow students time to review and discuss the region as each layer is revealed. Ask students to choose one of the countries and further research the natural resources found in the country using the Internet. Then have students create a graph that includes the resources and the current market value of the resources. **AL** Visual/Spatial

ANSWERS, p. 329

MAP SKILLS
1. Southeastern Europe (Balkan Peninsula)
2. nomadic herding
3. petroleum and natural gas

V Visual Skills

Discussing Direct students' attention to the climate map key and review each of the climate types. **Ask:**

- What type of climate covers the far north? *(subarctic)*
- In general, what do you notice about the change of climates from north to south? *(change from subarctic to humid continental to marine west coast, to Mediterranean)*
- What landform is associated with the tundra section found in the southern region of Europe? *(high mountains)*
- Where is a semi-arid (steppe) region found in Europe? *(southeastern region bordering the Caspian Sea)*
- Where are humid subtropical regions located? *(in south central Europe near the Black Sea)* Visual/Spatial

C Critical Thinking Skills

Recognizing Relationships Have students consider the relationship between climate, latitude, and land use. **Ask:**

- What challenges might commercial farmers experience in the humid continental region of Europe? *(cold winters, snow, rugged terrain to the east near mountains)*
- How does climate affect the type of land use in Europe? *(Climate includes precipitation, winds, and temperatures, which all impact land use.)* **BL** Logical

T Technology Skills

Making Presentations Divide the class into groups of three and assign each group a country. Students should develop a 5-minute "You Are There" presentation on their country, possibly including its history, recent past, industry, education, economy, resources, population, cultures, traditions, languages, and/or religions. Encourage students to make their presentations creative and visual. Verbal/Linguistic

CLOSE & REFLECT

To close the lesson, distribute outline maps of Europe to pairs of students. Tell students that Europe can be divided into four subregions: northern Europe, western Europe, southern Europe, and eastern Europe. Have partners work together and use the chapters in this unit to identify the countries in each subregion. Have them color code each region, and then label each country and subregion on their maps.

ANSWERS, p. 330
MAP SKILLS
1. Iberian Peninsula and Caspian Sea area
2. marine west coast
3. eastern Europe and western Russia

EUROPE

CLIMATE

MAP SKILLS

1 **THE GEOGRAPHER'S WORLD** Where are Europe's driest areas located?

2 **PLACES AND REGIONS** What type of climate do people in Paris experience?

3 **PLACES AND REGIONS** What area of Europe has a largely humid continental climate?

330 *Unit 4*

netw⊛rks   *Online Teaching Options*

MAP

Europe: Climates Map

Creating Graphic Organizers In small groups, have students study the interactive climate map. Assign each group a climate. Have students research the elements that define the assigned climate and apply those elements to a region in Europe. Use these types of questions as research prompts: **What makes up a (subarctic) climate? How does a (subarctic) climate affect the lifestyle and industry of the people in that region?** Have groups create a graphic organizer and attach a title or catchy logo for the climate as it applies to Europe. Display the graphic organizers in the classroom. Visual/Spatial, Interpersonal

CHAPTER 11
Western Europe Planner

UNDERSTANDING BY DESIGN®

Enduring Understandings
- *People, places, and ideas change over time.*

Essential Questions
- *How does geography influence the way people live?*
- *Why do civilizations rise and fall?*
- *How do governments change?*

Predictable Misunderstandings
- *Western Europe is only the British Isles.*
- *All people in Western Europe speak English.*
- *Western Europeans share the same culture.*

Assessment Evidence

Performance Tasks:
- *Project-Based Learning Hands-On Digital Chapter Project*
- *Project-Based Learning Hands-On Chapter Project*

Other Evidence:
- *Geography and Economics Activity*
- *Techonlogy Skills Activity*
- *Participation in Interactive Whiteboard Activities*
- *Contribution to small-group activities*
- *Interpretation of slide show images and special purpose maps*
- *Participation in class discussions about physical geography topics*
- *Lesson Reviews*
- *Chapter Assessments*

SUGGESTED PACING GUIDE

Introducing the Chapter	2 Days	Lesson 3	2 Days
Lesson 1	2 Days	What Do You Think?	2 Days
Lesson 2	2 Days	Chapter Wrap-Up and Assessment	2 Days

TOTAL TIME 12 Days

Key for Using the Teacher Edition

SKILL-BASED ACTIVITIES

Types of skill activities found in the Teacher Edition.

* **V** **Visual Skills** require students to analyze maps, graphs, charts, and photos.

W **Writing Skills** provide writing opportunities to help students comprehend the text.

R **Reading Skills** help students practice reading skills and master vocabulary.

C **Critical Thinking Skills** help students apply and extend what they have learned.

T **Technology Skills** require students to use digital tools effectively.

*Letters are followed by a number when there is more than one of the same type of skill on the page.

DIFFERENTIATED INSTRUCTION

All activities are written for the on-level student unless otherwise marked with the leveled labels below.

BL Beyond Level
AL Approaching Level
ELL English Language Learners

All students benefit from activities that utilize different learning styles. Many activities are marked as below when a particular learning style is highlighted.

Intrapersonal	Naturalist
Logical/Mathematical	Kinesthetic
Visual/Spatial	Auditory/Musical
Verbal/Linguistic	Interpersonal

Indiana Academic Standards

Students will:

6.1.1 Summarize the rise, decline, and cultural achievements of ancient civilizations in Europe and Mesoamerica.

6.1.2 Describe and compare the beliefs, the spread and the influence of religions throughout Europe and Mesoamerica.

6.1.3 Explain the continuation and contributions of the Eastern Roman Empire after the fall of the Western Roman Empire.

6.1.4 Identify and explain the development and organization of political, cultural, social and economic systems in Europe and the Americas.

6.1.5 Analyze the diverse points of view and interests of those involved in the Crusades and give examples of the changes brought about by the Crusades.

6.1.7 Describe how the Black Death, along with economic, environmental and social factors led to the decline of medieval society.

6.1.12 Describe the Reformations and their effects on European and American society.

6.1.13 Explain the origin and spread of scientific, political, and social ideals associated with the Age of Enlightenment/Age of Reason.

6.1.14 Describe the origins, developments and innovations of the Industrial Revolution and explain the impact these changes brought about.

6.1.15 Describe the impact of industrialization and urbanization on the lives of individuals and on trade and cultural exchange between Europe and the Americas and the rest of the world.

6.1.18 Create and compare timelines that identify major people, events and developments in the history of individual civilizations and/or countries that comprise Europe and the Americas.

6.1.19 Define and use the terms decade, century, and millennium, and compare alternative ways that historical periods and eras are designated by identifying the organizing principles upon which each is based.

6.1.20 Analyze cause-and-effect relationships, keeping in mind multiple causations, including the importance of individuals, ideas, human interests, beliefs and chance in history.

6.1.21 Differentiate between fact and interpretation in historical accounts and explain the meaning of historical passages by identifying who was involved, what happened, where it happened, and relating them to outcomes that followed and gaps in the historical record.

6.2.3, 6.2.4, 6.3.1, 6.3.4, 6.3.7, 6.3.9, 6.3.10, 6.3.12, 6.4.1, 6.4.6, 6.4.7, 6.4.8

CHAPTER OPENER PLANNER

Students will know:

- *Western Europe has a unique geography.*
- *Western Europeans speak many languages and have different cultures.*
- *Western Europe incorporates many nations.*
- *Western Europe has similar struggles to other countries of the world.*

Students will be able to:

- *analyze* a world map to identify countries of Western Europe
- *use a time line* to discuss various events in the history of Western Europe

UNDERSTANDING
BY DESIGN®

☑ *Print Teaching Options*

V **Visual Skills**

☐ **P. 332** Students identify bodies of water, islands, peninsulas, and mountain ranges on a map of Western Europe and discuss which physical features form boundaries. Visual/Spatial

☐ **P. 333** Students review the time line and use it to answer questions about the history of Western Europe. Verbal/ Linguistic

☑ *Online Teaching Options*

☐ **MAP** **Reading a Map**—Students identify aspects and locations of the region on a map.

☐ **TIME LINE** **Reading a Time Line and Map**—Students learn about where historical events occurred in the region and identify places where events took place. **AL** Visual/Spatial

☐ **MAP** **Interactive World Atlas**—Students use the interactive world atlas to identify the region and describe its terrain.

☑ *Printable Digital Worksheets*

☐ **WORKSHEET** **Technology Skills: The Bronze Age**—Students use this worksheet to learn more about the Bronze Age.

☐ **WORKSHEET** **Geography and Economics: Banking Crisis in the European Union**—Students can use this worksheet to research newspaper and magazine articles about the current financial crisis affecting the banks in Western Europe.

Project-Based Learning

Hands-On

Tour Western Europe

Students may work independently or with partners to take a fictional trip through a country in Western Europe. Students will create a travel journal describing the physical features, climate, food, and culture of the country. The travel journal should include photos or drawings of sites or artifacts found throughout the Western European country.

Digital Hands-On

My European Trip

Have students work in pairs to create an online scrapbook about a fictional trip through a Western European country. The online scrapbook should describe the physical features, climate, and food of the country. Scrapbooks might also contain audio clips of the different types of music heard throughout the country. Have students vote as a class for which online scrapbook is the most interesting.

Print Resources

ANCILLARY RESOURCES

These ancillaries are available for every chapter and lesson.

- **Reading Essentials and Study Guide Workbook** **AL** **ELL**
- **Chapter Tests and Lesson Quizzes Blackline Masters**

PRINTABLE DIGITAL WORKSHEETS

These printable digital worksheets are available for every chapter and lesson.

- **Hands-On Chapter Projects**
- **What Do You Know? Activities**
- **Chapter Summaries (English and Spanish)**
- **Vocabulary Builder Activities**
- **Quizzes and Tests**
- **Reading Essentials and Study Guide (English and Spanish)** **AL** **ELL**
- **Guided Reading Activities**

More Media Resources

SUGGESTED VIDEOS

NOTE: Be sure to preview videos to ensure they are age-appropriate.

- **Cave of Forgotten Dreams** (91 min.)
- **Third Man on the Mountain** (108 min.)
- **Rob Roy** (139 min.)

SUGGESTED READING

- ***Hana in the Time of the Tulips,*** by Deborah Noyes **AL**
- ***Charles Dickens and the Street Children of London,*** by Andrea Warren
- ***If I Lived in Germany,*** by Rosanne Knorr **AL**

PHYSICAL GEOGRAPHY OF WESTERN EUROPE

Students will know:
- The countries of Western Europe have a unique geography that shapes their landscape.
- This unique geography affects their industry, travel, trade, and agriculture.

Students will be able to:
- *identify* the different landforms and waterways in Western Europe
- *discuss* the different climates found in Western Europe
- *describe* important natural resources in Western Europe

UNDERSTANDING BY DESIGN®

☑ *Print Teaching Options*

V Visual Skills

- **P. 336** Students create visuals tying the North Sea to economic advantages. Visual/Spatial
- **P. 337** Students review an image and analyze the content of the photograph. ELL Visual/Spatial, Interpersonal
- **P. 338** Students study the Danube River image and make a T-chart of physical and human-made features.
- **P. 341** Partners make two web diagrams to describe types of trees in Western Europe. ELL Visual/Spatial

W Writing Skills

- **P. 339** Students describe their favorite season in a narrative. BL Verbal/Linguistic
- **P. 340** Students write an informative essay about alternative energy. BL Naturalist

R Reading Skills

- **P. 334** Students find the main idea of a paragraph. ELL
- **P. 335** Students connect how Britain's geography affected its history. BL Verbal/Linguistic
- **P. 337** Students discuss the importance of rivers for boundaries and trade. AL Verbal/Linguistic
- **P. 337** Students read about the Rhine and Danube rivers and compare and contrast them. AL Verbal/Linguistic
- **P. 339** Students reread the section "Mediterranean Climate Area" and paraphrase it. AL Verbal/Linguistic
- **P. 340** Students give examples of economic development in the Northern European Plain. AL Verbal/Linguistic

C Critical Thinking Skills

- **P. 334** Students discuss Western Europe and list three questions about the region. AL Verbal/Linguistic
- **P. 338** Pairs trace Western Europe and connect longitude/latitude with climate. ELL Visual/Spatial

T Technology Skills

- **P. 341** Students research and present images and text on a bird, plant or animal brought to the United States by immigrants. BL Verbal/Linguistic
- **P. 341** Students research a bird, animal, or plant that is native to Western Europe and create a computer presentation. BL Verbal/Linguistic

☑ *Online Teaching Options*

V Visual Skills

- **VIDEO Fault Lines: UK Earthquake**—Students watch a video and make a map of the region to discuss natural disasters. AL Visual/Spatial
- **MAP The British Isles**—Students use the map of the British Isles to discuss the geography, location, and unique aspects of this region. AL Verbal/Linguistic
- **MAP The Westerlies**—Students use the map to extend their knowledge of world climate and the Westerlies.
- **MAP Resources: Western Europe**—Students use the resources map to review resources in the region.

W Writing Skills

- **MAP Interesting Facts: Western Europe**—Students analyze the Geofacts layer of the Chapter Opener Map and write facts that they can use to quiz each other. BL Visual/Spatial
- **VIDEOS Major Rivers in Western Europe**—Small groups create a poem that describes the features and benefits of one of the rivers in the video slide show. Auditory/Musical
- **SLIDE SHOW Agriculture in Western Europe**—Students make a list of important crops in Western Europe and write details about where they are grown. ELL Visual/Spatial
- **IMAGE Dikes and Sea Polders**—Students use this interactive image to discuss this example of human-environment interaction.

R Reading Skills

- **LECTURE SLIDE Defining: Estuaries**—Students use the lecture slide with information on estuaries to discuss the human-environment interaction with this structure.
- **LECTURE SLIDE Comparing Water Diverting Systems**—Students can use the lecture slide comparing dams and dikes to learn more about human-environment interaction.
- **GRAPHIC ORGANIZER Temperate Lowlands and the Mediterranean**—Students will use the graphic organizer to discuss the lowlands and Mediterranean climates.
- **LECTURE SLIDE Defining: Deciduous and Coniferous Forests**—Students use the lecture slide that defines deciduous and coniferous forests to discuss this aspect of the environment.
- **GRAPHIC ORGANIZER Resources of Western Europe**—Students will use the graphic organizer to review the resources mentioned in the lesson.

C Critical Thinking Skills

- **IMAGE How the Chunnel was Built**—Students examine the interactive image of the Chunnel to discuss its architectures and its impact on tourism. AL Visual/Spatial
- **IMAGE How Windmills Work**—Students use the interactive image to learn how windmills convert wind to energy.
- **MAP Climates: Western Europe**—Students complete a chart or Venn diagram to compare and contrast the climate regions of Western Europe. AL

T Technology Skills

- **ONLINE SELF-CHECK QUIZ Lesson 1**—Students receive instant feedback on their mastery of lesson content.

HISTORY OF WESTERN EUROPE

Students will know:
- Western Europeans speak many languages and have different cultures
- Western Europe incorporates many nations
- Western Europe has similar struggles to other countries of the world

Students will be able to:
- *discuss* the history of Western Europe through 1800
- *describe* how the Industrial Revolution changed Western Europe
- *discuss* World War I, World War II, and the Cold War and their affects on Western Europe

UNDERSTANDING
BY DESIGN®

☑ Print Teaching Options

V Visual Skills

☐ **P. 343** Students make a T-chart to show the groups that conquered Western Europe. **ELL** Visual/Spatial

☐ **P. 344** Students write questions based on the Black Plague infographic. **AL** Verbal/Linguistic

☐ **P. 348** Students study maps and discuss how the German Army took control of such a large area. **AL** Visual/Spatial

W Writing Skills

☐ **P. 345** Students write an essay in arguing for or against the Church's ruling on Martin Luther. **AL** Verbal/Linguistic

☐ **P. 349** Students write short essays about industrialization. **BL** Interpersonal

R Reading Skills

☐ **P. 342** Small groups show how the Romans conquered areas and brought their way of life. **ELL** Kinesthetic

☐ **P. 342** Students define vocabulary words and include drawings as allowed. **ELL** **AL**

☐ **P. 346** Students discuss the ideas that led to reform and revolution in France. **AL** Verbal/Linguistic

☐ **P. 346** Students discuss how they think the industrial system would change Western Europe. **ELL** Verbal/Linguistic/Interpersonal

C Critical Thinking Skills

☐ **P. 342** Students discuss why people decided to farm the land instead of hunt animals and gather food. **AL**

☐ **P. 344** Students discuss the causes and effects of the crusades. Verbal/Linguistic

☐ **P. 345** Students make a chart to classify the people and ideas described in "Enlightenment." **ELL** Logical/Mathematical

T Technology Skills

☐ **P. 345** Students research how deadly the Black Death was and collect data. Logical/Mathematical

☐ **P. 347** Students study and make generalizations about population data and rate of industrial growth by country in Western Europe. **BL** Logical/Mathematical

☑ Online Teaching Options

V Visual Skills

☐ **SLIDE SHOW** World War II—Students make a time line to sequence the events of World War II. **AL** Verbal/Linguistic

W Writing Skills

☐ **VIDEO** Ancient Mysteries—Stonehenge—Students watch a video about the history, construction, and mystery of Stonehenge and make a time line of key events. **BL** Verbal/Linguistic

☐ **GRAPHIC ORGANIZER** History of Western Europe—Students use a graphic organizer that is designed like a note-taking chart to organize this information. **AL**

R Reading Skills

☐ **LECTURE SLIDES** Enlightenment Reforms—Students use the lecture slide presentation to review changes during the Enlightenment. **ELL** Intrapersonal

☐ **LECTURE SLIDE** Declaration of the Rights of Man—Students use a lecture slide to learn more about changes in government.

☐ **LECTURE SLIDE** Defining: Nationalism— Students use a lecture slide to review content of the text.

C Critical Thinking Skills

☐ **INFOGRAPHIC** The Black Death—Students use the infographic and discuss the spread of the Plague and its impact on society and feudalism. Visual/Spatial, Naturalist

☐ **TIME LINE** Religious Upheaval and Change—Students use the time line to review religious changes in Western Europe. **AL** Visual/Spatial

☐ **CHART** Cause and Effect: The Industrial Revolution—Students use the cause and effect flow chart to review the Industrial Revolution.

☐ **MAP** Religion: Western Europe—Include the interactive map about the spread of religion in Western Europe to discuss the cultural influences of religion. Visual/Spatial

T Technology Skills

☐ **ANIMATION** How Bronze is Made—Students use the animation to review bronze making and the Bronze Age. **ELL** Visual/Spatial

☐ **ONLINE SELF-CHECK QUIZ** Lesson 2—Students receive instant feedback on their mastery of lesson content.

☑ Printable Digital Worksheets

W Writing Skills

☐ **WORKSHEET** Technology Skills: The Bronze Age—Students use this worksheet to learn more about the Bronze Age.

LIFE IN WESTERN EUROPE

Students will know:
- Western Europeans speak many languages and have different cultures
- Western Europe incorporates many nations
- Western Europe has similar struggles to other countries of the world

Students will be able to:
- **discuss** how the collapse of the Soviet Union affected Western Europe
- **describe** ethnic and language groups in Western Europe
- **discuss** religion, literature, music, and the arts in Western Europe
- **explain** current challenges facing Western Europe

UNDERSTANDING
BY DESIGN®

☑ *Print Teaching Options*

V Visual Skills

☐ **P. 350** Pairs create a map of the European Community nations of Western Europe. **ELL** **BL** Visual/Spatial

☐ **P. 351** Students amend the maps with additional nations. **ELL** **BL** Visual/Spatial

☐ **P. 352** Students discuss immigrant contribution to Western Europe's economy and culture. **AL** Logical/Mathematical

☐ **P. 354** Students make flash cards of the European roots of English words and meanings. **ELL** Verbal/Linguistic

W Writing Skills

☐ **P. 357** Students write whether the countries of Western Europe should restrict immigration. Verbal/Linguistic

R Reading Skills

☐ **P. 350** Students work with vocabulary words. **AL** **ELL** Visual/Spatial

☐ **P. 352** Students make a list of all the religions that are practiced in Western Europe. **ELL** Verbal/Linguistic

☐ **P. 356** Students cite evidence of the recent economic events in Western Europe. **AL** Verbal/Linguistic

C Critical Thinking Skills

☐ **P. 351** Students discuss early Western European history and its languages and ethnicities. Verbal/Linguistic

☐ **P. 354** Students compare the sports they play to the sports played in Western Europe. **ELL** Intrapersonal

☐ **P. 355** Students compare and contrast school in Western Europe with United States schools. Verbal/Linguistic

T Technology Skills

☐ **P. 351** Small groups search for economic data about the European Union and create a chart based on the data.

☐ **P. 353** Students research influential Western European artistic and cultural contributions. **BL** Verbal/Linguistic

☐ **P. 356** Student groups present economic information on a nation in Western Europe. **BL** Verbal/Linguistic

☑ *Online Teaching Options*

V Visual Skills

☐ **MAP** **The European Union**—Students discuss regional trade pacts and statistics and make connections between countries that are part of economic pacts and their GDPs. Visual/Spatial

☐ **IMAGE** **360° View: The Louvre**—Students compare and contrast the types of structures and items they have seen in a museum with those in the image of The Louvre. **ELL** Visual/Spatial

☐ **MAP** **Empires of Western Europe**—Students use the map to point out changes they see in different areas of Europe between 1900 and the present. **AL** Visual/Spatial

☐ **MAP** **Population: Western Europe**—Students use the Chapter Opener map with the population layer to further discuss the population of the region. **BL**

W Writing Skills

☐ **MAP** **Language: Western Europe**—Students look at the regions where similar languages are spoken and compare those results to the chart on page 354 that shows European roots of English words and write about any connections. **BL** Visual/Spatial, Logical/Mathematical

R Reading Skills

☐ **GRAPHIC ORGANIZER** **Comparing Art**—Students use an interactive graphic organizer to compare contemporary to classic art.

C Critical Thinking Skills

☐ **VIDEO** **French School Lunches**—Students watch a video about school life in France and explain the cultural impact of this program. **AL** Verbal/Linguistic

☐ **CHARTS** **Population Distribution: Western Europe**—Students write a paragraph to explain why the areas that are the most densely populated are those areas that have received the most immigrants. **BL** Logical/Mathematical

☐ **GRAPH** **Religions of Western Europe**—Students identify the religion that is the most widely practiced and explain how the region's past might have contributed to this. Visual/Spatial, Logical/Mathematical

☐ **VIDEO** **Railways and Highways**—Students use the video and stats and info on the speed, types, and use of railroads and highways in the region.

T Technology Skills

☐ **ONLINE SELF-CHECK QUIZ** **Lesson 3**—Students receive instant feedback on their mastery of lesson content.

☑ *Printable Digital Worksheets*

W Writing Skills

☐ **WORKSHEET** **Geography and Economics: Banking Crisis in the European Union**—Students can use this worksheet to research articles about the financial crisis in Europe.

INTERVENTION AND REMEDIATION STRATEGIES

LESSON 1 Physical Geography of Western Europe

Reading and Comprehension

Students may have trouble with the meaning and pronunciation of some of the content vocabulary words, such as *deciduous* and *coniferous*. Have student pairs play a guessing game in which one person gives clues about a content vocabulary term, and the other student tries to guess it. Have pairs compete against other pairs to see who can guess the most terms correctly in a certain amount of time. As a "bonus" question, have each team use the academic vocabulary term *adapt* correctly in a sentence.

Text Evidence

Have students work in small groups to analyze the impact of one of the landforms or waterways described in the lesson. Students should describe key aspects of their feature covered in the text, or they may wish to conduct additional research. For example, students may wish to analyze the English Channel as it relates to transportation. Tell students to present an analysis of their findings, including answers to the following questions: Where is this landform or waterway located? How does it impact the people who live in that region? What are some of its unique characteristics?

LESSON 2 History of Western Europe

Reading and Comprehension

Have students skim the lesson to look for unfamiliar or confusing words. Tell students to write down what they think the word might mean based on context clues in the text. Then have students look up each word in the dictionary to find the definition of each word. Have students count how many definitions they guessed correctly. Circulate to ensure correct pronunciation of words with confusing vowel combinations such as the digraphs in *feudalism* and *Parliament*.

Text Evidence

Have student groups create a flow chart showing the change Western Europeans endured through 1800. Flow charts should depict facts about groups of people based on evidence in the text, or from additional research, and should answer the following questions: How were people affected by the practice of agriculture? What events affected people in Western Europe during the Middle Ages? How did illness and conflict affect countries in Western Europe? Have groups present their findings to the class.

LESSON 3 Life in Western Europe

Reading and Comprehension

Have students skim the lesson to find challenging or unfamiliar words and try to determine each word's meaning by using context clues. Then have students look up the words' definitions using an online or print dictionary to clarify the meanings. Have students work in pairs to practice using these words in sentences. Then ask students to explain a concept in this lesson using one of the academic vocabulary terms. Clarify the pronunciation of the separate sounds and syllables of the vowel pair in *cooperate*.

Text Evidence

Assign student pairs or groups one of the Western European countries discussed in this lesson. Tell students to write a summary explaining their assigned country's involvement in (or absence from) the European Union. Students may wish to conduct research using reliable Web sites to learn about each country's history with the European Union. After students have had time to compile and summarize information from their research, have them present their summaries to the class.

Online Resources

Level Reader

Use this online lower-level text that corresponds directly to the text in the online Student Edition.

Guided Reading Activities

This resource uses graphic organizers and guiding questions to help students with comprehension.

What Do You Know?

Use these worksheets to pre-assess students' background knowledge before they read the chapter.

Reading Essentials and Study Guide Workbook

This resource offers writing and reading activities for the approaching-level student.

Self-Check Quizzes

This online assessment tool provides instant feedback for students to check their progress.

WESTERN EUROPE

ESSENTIAL QUESTIONS · *How does geography influence the way people live?* · *Why do civilizations rise and fall?* · *How do governments change?*

©Alex Masi/Corbis

Coal mine worker in South Wales

Lesson 1
Physical Geography of Western Europe

Lesson 2
History of Western Europe

Lesson 3
Life in Western Europe

The Story Matters...

Western Europe has always been a crossroad of cultures. Today, this is reflected in the diversity of cultures represented in the population, particularly in large cities, such as Paris, France. Long before modern times, however, the geography and resources of Western Europe influenced early civilizations and their rise to economic and political power, shaping the history and governments of this region.

FOLDABLES
Study Organizer

Go to the Foldables® library in the back of your book to make a Foldable® that will help you take notes while reading this chapter.

331

ENGAGE

Think-Pair-Share Read the Essential Questions and have students brainstorm how geography influences not only the way people live but also the development of civilizations. Have pairs of students share their ideas. Students might say that civilizations that are surrounded by natural barriers may be isolated from other civilizations. Others may suggest that civilizations are also protected by those same barriers. Then have students read "The Story Matters..." about how Western Europe has served as a crossroads of cultures for centuries.

Discuss why it is helpful to understand how geography and resources influence the development of civilizations. **Ask:** How do geography and resources affect a civilization's economy? *(Possible answers: Basic economic questions about what to produce are often based on available resources. If a civilization has few resources, it may have to trade with others for common tools and food products.)*

Tell students that they will learn about how Western Europe's geography and resources attracted diverse cultures and made the region an economic and political power.

Content Background Knowledge

- Western Europe is comprised of 11 countries.
- The Population Reference Bureau estimates that the United Kingdom will have the largest population by 2050, surpassing that of both Germany and France.
- Historians typically point to the ancient Greeks as the founders of Western European culture.
- Europe was politically divided into Eastern and Western Europe during the Cold War when eastern-bloc nations joined the Warsaw Pact and western nations became members of the North Atlantic Treaty Organization (NATO).
- In a March 1946 speech, British Prime Minister Winston Churchill spoke of an "iron curtain . . . descend[ing] across Europe" when he referred to the Soviet Union taking control of Eastern European countries. Citizens of these Soviet bloc countries did not have the freedoms to speak, travel, work, and worship as Western European countries.

FOLDABLES
Study Organizer

Go to the Foldables® library for a cumulative chapter-based Foldable® activity that your students can use to help take notes and prepare for assessment.

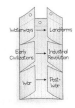

Letter from the Author

Dear Geography Teacher,

One factor that helped Western Europe regain its economic strength after World War II was the formation of an economic union. The European Union developed from the European Coal and Steel Community in 1956, to the Common Market in 1958, and then the European Free Trade Association (EFTA). Finally, in 1993, the European Union (EU) emerged. The EU allows goods, services, and workers to move freely among member countries.

TEACH & ASSESS

Step Into the Place

V Visual Skills

Reading a Map Explain to students that the map presents the region of Western Europe. Have students identify the countries of Western Europe and their capitals, the bodies of water in and around these countries, the islands, and the peninsulas. Ask them to note which rivers and other bodies of water form the boundaries of these countries. Then have students compare this political map to a physical map of Western Europe and look for mountain ranges that also form boundaries between countries. Visual/Spatial

Content Background Knowledge

The Rhine River has been an international and economic artery in Europe for centuries. The ancient Romans used the river as a major route for their military, and it was used for expanded trade during the Middle Ages. In 1815 the delegates at the Congress of Vienna decided that navigation of the river would be free. Since that decision, the river has been used for transportation, industry, and agriculture, for urban drinking water and sanitation, for hydroelectric production, and for recreation. Great cities have risen along its banks, and it has served as a point of political and cultural unity for much of its modern history. Improvements were made to the navigation of the river in the late nineteenth and early twentieth centuries. But the multipurpose, overused river still experienced high levels of environmental degradation until restoration efforts were begun in the 1970s.

Today, the Rhine River also serves as a major tourist attraction. Each year thousands of people enjoy boat tours along the river, where they can view Germany's beautiful scenery, lavish castles, as well as its modern cities and quaint villages.

ANSWERS, p. 332

STEP INTO THE PLACE
1. the United Kingdom and France
2. Ireland
3. Bern
4. CRITICAL THINKING The rivers and waterways could allow people to travel and to ship goods between countries besides being a possible food source.

STEP INTO THE TIME
Students' answers should identify an event and include several possible consequences. Answers should demonstrate the ability to make predictions based on historical information provided in the lesson.

332

V Islands and peninsulas branch out from Western Europe into the various oceans, seas, bays, and channels that border the region. In the past, these landforms and waterways isolated groups of people. As a result, many different cultures developed. As you study the map, look for other geographic features that make this area unique.

Step Into the Place

MAP FOCUS Use the map to answer the following questions.

1 THE GEOGRAPHER'S WORLD
Which two countries does the English Channel separate?

2 PLACES AND REGIONS Which island country in Western Europe lies farthest west?

3 THE GEOGRAPHER'S WORLD
What is the capital city of Switzerland?

4 CRITICAL THINKING
ANALYZING In what ways might the large number of rivers and waterways be important to the people of Western Europe?

A

SWISS ALPS A train begins its climb to the summit. The railway, completed in the early 1900s, makes this scenic trip popular with visitors.

B

BRANDENBURG GATE Completed in the late 1700s, the Brandenburg Gate is one of the well-known landmarks in Berlin, Germany.

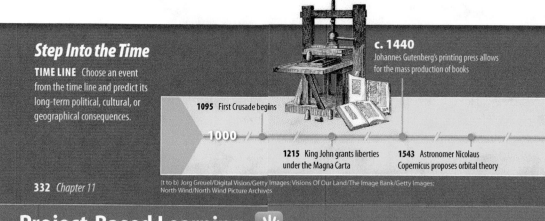

Step Into the Time

TIME LINE Choose an event from the time line and predict its long-term political, cultural, or geographical consequences.

1000

1095 First Crusade begins

1215 King John grants liberties under the Magna Carta

1543 Astronomer Nicolaus Copernicus proposes orbital theory

c. 1440 Johannes Gutenberg's printing press allows for the mass production of books

332 *Chapter 11*

(t to b) Jorg Greuel/Digital Vision/Getty Images; Visions Of Our Land/The Image Bank/Getty Images; North Wind/North Wind Picture Archives

---

Project-Based Learning ✋

Hands-On

Tour Western Europe
Students may work independently or with partners to make a fictional trip through a country in Western Europe. Students will create a travel journal describing the physical features, climate, food, and culture of the country. The travel journal should include photos or drawings of sites or artifacts found throughout the Western European country.

Digital Hands-On

My European Trip
Have students work in pairs to create an online scrapbook about a fictional trip through a Western European country. The online scrapbook should describe the physical features, climate, and food of the country. Scrapbooks might also contain audio clips of the different types of music heard throughout the country. Have students vote as a class which online scrapbook is the most interesting.

edtechteacher
21st Century Learning

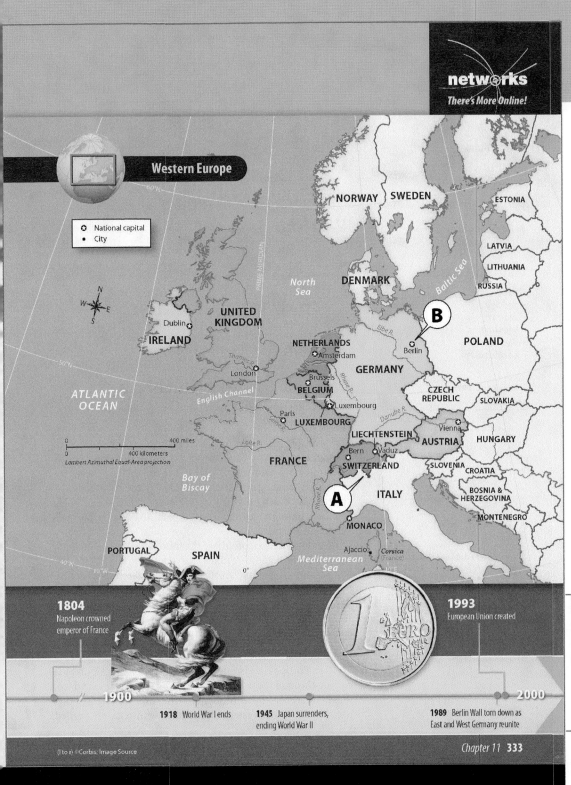

Western Europe

- National capital
- City

1804 Napoleon crowned emperor of France

1993 European Union created

1900

1918 World War I ends

1945 Japan surrenders, ending World War II

1989 Berlin Wall torn down as East and West Germany reunite

2000

(l to r) ©Corbis; Image Source

Chapter 11 **333**

Step Into the Time

V Visual Skills

Reading a Time Line Remind students that time lines can show a number of events that took place over time. Discuss the time span shown on the time line. Ask students to share their ideas on why it is beneficial to look at events that happened over a long span of time on a time line. *(A time line that shows a long span of time can provide a quick glance at a region's history.)*

Have students review the time line and as a class, discuss its major points of interest. **Ask:**

- Which event on the time line describes an important invention? *(Gutenberg's printing press)*
- Did the Berlin Wall come down before or after the European Union was created? *(before)*
- Why would the event listed for 1215 be important to the region's history? *(Possible answer: It is the historical event that happened when King John was forced by his noblemen to sign the Magna Carta marking the very first time liberties were granted to the people.)*
- Why does the time line stop at the year 2000? *(The last event listed happened in 1992; therefore, the time line does not need to extend past the year 2000.)*

Ask students to list some historical events that could be added to the time line. *(Student answers will vary but should include accurate event placement.)* **Verbal/Linguistic**

V

CLOSE & REFLECT

Summarizing Have students write a paragraph to explain how what they learned in the Chapter Opener helps them better understand how physical geography can separate cultures as well as unite them. Tell them that they will learn more about how cultures developed in Western Europe as they study this chapter.

Before writing their paragraphs, have students brainstorm ideas about how religious events can affect a region's history. Have them share their paragraphs with the class.

TIME LINE

Reading a Time Line and Map

Display the time line and map on the interactive whiteboard. Have students choose an event from the time line and identify where in the region the event took place by finding it on the map. Ask students to research the event further and to share what they learned about the event with the class. **AL Visual/Spatial**

See page 331B for other online activities.

ENGAGE

Bellringer Before students begin the lesson, ask them what they know about the landforms and waterways of Western Europe. Then read the Essential Question aloud and have students discuss how the physical features of the area where they live makes it unique. **Ask: What physical features in your area provide advantages to your community?** *(Student answers will vary but should include how the resources, climate, or location of their area is beneficial to the community.)*

Have a volunteer read the "It Matters Because" statement. Point out the words, "several advantages." Ask students to explain why these elements are advantages.

TEACH & ASSESS

C Critical Thinking Skills

Formulating Questions Ask students what they already know about the countries of Western Europe. Make a list of their answers on the board. **Ask: What three questions do you have about the countries of Western Europe?** *(Sample questions: What languages do people speak in the Netherlands? Which country in Western Europe has the largest population? What products are made in Germany?)*

Encourage students to refer back to this list of questions as they read through the chapter content and to write down the answers for their questions. **AL** Verbal/Linguistic, Interpersonal

R Reading Skills

Determining Central Ideas Explain that locating the main idea of a paragraph will help improve their understanding of the content and provide each paragraph of the text with meaning and purpose. Point out that the main idea is often stated in the first few sentences of a paragraph. As a class, locate the main idea of the paragraph. *(Western Europe's landscape consists of plains with mountains that cut through in some places.)* Have students work with a partner to find the main idea of the next paragraph. **ELL** Verbal/Linguistic

---

ANSWER, p. 334

Taking Notes oil and natural gas in the North Sea; electric power from the flow of rivers; dried peat for heating; rich soils

---

networks

There's More Online!

☑ **IMAGE** How Windmills Work

☑ **SLIDE SHOW** Agriculture in Western Europe

☑ **VIDEO**

Reading HELPDESK

Academic Vocabulary

- adapt

Content Vocabulary

- dike
- polder
- estuary
- Westerlies
- deciduous
- coniferous

TAKING NOTES: *Key Ideas and Details*

Identify Use a graphic organizer like this one to list important resources in Western Europe.

Resources

Indiana Academic Standards
6.1.18, 6.1.19, 6.3.1, 6.3.7, 6.3.12, 6.4.7

Lesson 1

Physical Geography of Western Europe

ESSENTIAL QUESTION · *How does geography influence the way people live?*

IT MATTERS BECAUSE

The geography of Western Europe has provided the people who live there with several advantages: closeness to the sea, abundant resources, and temperate climates.

Landforms and Waterways

GUIDING QUESTION *How do the physical features of Western Europe make the region unique?*

You probably have seen images of Europe on television or in photographs. Maybe you have seen a movie showing a Dutch windmill on a windswept plain. You might have watched news clips showing cyclists racing through the rolling French countryside during a yearly sports event called the Tour de France. These images show just a part of Western Europe's varied landscape.

Western Europe comprises the following nations: Ireland, the United Kingdom, France, Luxembourg, Germany, the Netherlands, Belgium, Austria, and Switzerland. Belgium, the Netherlands, and Luxembourg are often referred to as the Benelux Countries. Western Europe also includes the tiny countries of Monaco and Liechtenstein, which have a combined population of fewer than 70,000 people.

Low-Lying Plains

Western Europe's landscape consists of plains with mountains cutting through some places. Shaped by wind, water, and ice, these landforms have influenced the lives of the region's peoples. Much of Western Europe lies within an area called

(l to r) TADAO YAMAMOTO/a.collectionRF/Getty Images; Willfried Gredler/age fotostock; Arterra Picture Library/Alamy; Philippe Huguen/AFP/Getty Images

---

networks · *Online Teaching Options*

VIDEO

Fault Lines: UK Earthquake

Creating Maps Use the video to begin the discussion about the physical geography of Western Europe. Have students make a map of the entire region, highlighting the countries mentioned in the video. Discuss with students whether natural disasters can occur in other parts of Western Europe. Consider referencing the tectonic plates map from an earlier chapter to make connections to the content of the video. **AL** Visual/Spatial

See page 331C for other online activities.

BBC Motion Gallery Education

the Northern European Plain. France, Belgium, the Netherlands, Luxembourg, and most of Germany are located on this plain.

Massive sheets of ice shaped the Northern European Plain during the last ice age, which ended about 11,000 years ago. In some places, the melting glaciers left behind fertile soil, but also thick layers of sand and gravel. Ocean waves, currents, and winds have eroded these deposits into sand dunes along some of the North Sea coastline. The glaciers also left behind areas of poorly drained wetlands along the North Sea and Atlantic coasts in Ireland and the United Kingdom.

Mountains and Highlands

Two mountain ranges—the Pyrenees (PIR•eh•NEES) and the Alps—separate Western Europe from neighboring nations in Southern Europe. Both mountain ranges divide the cooler climates of the north from the warm, dry climate of the Mediterranean region to the south. To the southwest, the Pyrenees form a natural barrier between France and Spain. This mountain range stretches 270 miles (435 km) from east to west. Pico de Aneto—the tallest mountain in the Pyrenees—reaches a height of 11,169 feet (3,404 m). The average height of the Pyrenees, however, is only about 5,300 feet (1,615 m).

To the east of the Pyrenees lie the Alps. Like the Pyrenees, the Alps were created by the folding of rocks as a result of plate tectonics. Then these mountains were further shaped by glaciers. The Alps extend about 750 miles (1,207 km) along the southeastern border of France through Switzerland, Austria, and Germany. The Alps are much larger and higher than the Pyrenees. The tallest mountain in the Alps is Mont Blanc, at 15,771 feet (4,807 m).

The Alps and Pyrenees are geologically younger than other mountainous areas in Western Europe that have been worn down by glaciers. The most extensive is a plateau called the Middle Rhine Highlands in Germany, Belgium, Luxembourg, and France. Its highest elevations are about 3,000 feet (914 m).

Seas, Islands, and Waterways

Western Europe has long, irregular coastlines that touch many bodies of water, including the Atlantic Ocean and the North, Baltic, and Mediterranean seas. This closeness to the sea has long shaped European life.

The North Sea is part of the Atlantic Ocean but shallower. Separating the island of Britain from the rest of Europe, the North Sea is a rough, dangerous body of water to navigate. It is also a rich fishing ground for the Netherlands and the United Kingdom. The North Sea has long been important for trade between the United Kingdom and the rest of Europe. It is also the location of large oil and natural gas reserves.

Windmills are used to pump water into a reservoir for this village in the plains of the Netherlands.
► **CRITICAL THINKING**
Identifying What is the major plain in the region?

Chapter 11 **335**

C Critical Thinking Skills

Determining Cause and Effect Explain to students that landforms and bodies of water can affect the climate of a region. **Ask:** How do the mountain ranges in Western Europe affect its climate? (*Areas to the south are warmer than areas to the north. There is also less rainfall to the south of the mountains.*) Verbal/Linguistic

V Visual Skills

Analyzing Share with students that the Netherlands are famous for their many windmills and that the windmills have been a source of many famous pieces of literature. There are still over 1,000 remaining windmills in the region. Further share that the windmills served an important function. Strong winds blew across the plains of the Netherlands. People used these winds to their advantage by building windmills. The mill sails transmit the force of the wind on to large paddle wheels that scoop up the water. Not only did the windmills supply villages with water, but later they also provided electrical power. Though there are still many working windmills, most cities now use power-driven engines to do these things.

Explain to students that adapting to the environment in which they live is an important skill. **Ask:** How is using a windmill to pump water for a village an example of people adapting to their environment? (*Student answers may vary but should explain how people in the Netherlands recognized the power of the wind and used technology to move water from one place to another to make both the land and the water usable.*) Logical/Mathematical

R Reading Skills

Applying Explain to students that because Britain did not have the protection of the mountains like some countries of mainland Europe, Britain became a great sea power. Because they live on an island, and attacks for much of their history would come from the sea, the British knew they needed a strong navy to defend their shores. Ask students to think about what physical features have shaped their lives where they live. **BL** Verbal/Linguistic

MAP

Interesting Facts: Western Europe

Analyzing Maps Display the GeoFacts layer on the Chapter Opener map. Have students write the facts on note cards and then take turns quizzing each other on facts about Western Europe. Discuss with students some of the facts they find most interesting and have them compare the facts with some of the other countries previously discussed. **BL** Visual/Spatial

See page 331C for other online activities.

ANSWER, p. 335

CRITICAL THINKING Northern European Plain

Physical Geography of Western Europe

V Visual Skills

Creating Visuals Have students work with a partner to create a visual that shows the importance of the North Sea to Western Europe. Explain to students that they should be creative and include a map and a map key with specific examples depicted. Students should use this question to guide their work. **Ask:** What economic benefits has the North Sea provided for the region? *(economic benefits such as trade; resources such as fish, oil, and natural gas; protection and defense.)* Visual/Spatial

T Technology Skills

Making Presentations Have students work with a partner and choose a waterway of Western Europe. Provide an opportunity for students to research their topic using the Internet and prepare an oral or digital presentation. They should research the waterway's importance for trade, transportation, recreation, and energy production, providing historical and present-day information. Suggest that they use visual aids to make their presentations more interesting. Verbal/Linguistic, Visual/Spatial, Interpersonal

Content Background Knowledge

The United Kingdom as it is known today became united over a long period of time. At one point in history, Great Britain controlled nearly one-third of the world. Wales was the first area that became part of the United Kingdom in 1282 through conquest. However, the political union of England and Wales occurred much later, in 1536. In 1603 James I of England ruled both England and Scotland for the first time, but the two countries were formally united in 1707. Despite much struggle and conflict, Ireland was joined with Great Britain in 1801, creating the United Kingdom. However, movements for Irish independence were on-going, and in 1921, the Irish Free State was formed. Today, only six Irish counties in northern Ireland are part of the United Kingdom.

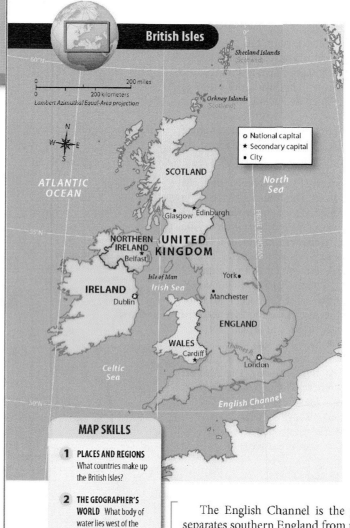

British Isles

MAP SKILLS

1 **PLACES AND REGIONS** What countries make up the British Isles?

2 **THE GEOGRAPHER'S WORLD** What body of water lies west of the United Kingdom?

Academic Vocabulary

adapt to change a trait to survive **T**

336 Chapter 11

The North Sea has helped but also hindered the Dutch, the people of the Netherlands. The Netherlands sits at a low elevation—25 percent of the country is below sea level. To **adapt**, the Dutch have built **dikes**, which are walls or barriers to hold back the water. The Dutch call the land they reclaim from the sea **polders**. This land is used for farming and settlement. Stormy seas, however, have broken dikes and caused flooding in recent times. **V**

Just off the northern coast of France lie the British Isles, or the Atlantic Archipelago—the islands of Britain and Ireland. You might think each main island is its own country, but that is not the case. There are four parts of the United Kingdom: England, Wales, Scotland, and Northern Ireland. Three parts—England, Wales, and Scotland—occupy the island of Britain. The fourth part, Northern Ireland, is the northeastern section of Ireland. The country of Ireland, or Eire, occupies all but the northeastern section of the island of Ireland.

The English Channel is the part of the Atlantic Ocean that separates southern England from northern France. The channel is a busy sea route connecting the North Sea with the Atlantic Ocean. In addition to the ships that travel the route, trains pass beneath this waterway. A tunnel runs through the rock under the water. Called the Chunnel, it houses a high-speed train that connects Britain to mainland Europe.

Western Europe has a wealth of rivers and smaller waterways. The region's rivers have played an important role in how Europe developed over the centuries. Rivers determined the locations of cities, such as London, Paris, and Hamburg. Rivers provide transportation routes for goods and people. They also form some political borders. Rivers linked by canals provide transportation

---

netw☉rks   *Online Teaching Options*

MAP

The British Isles

Summarizing Use the map of the British Isles to discuss this unique island formation with students. Discuss the different waterways that surround the area and the five distinct areas that form the British Isles. Use the informative callouts for further discussion. Encourage students to research the history of a particular area they would like to learn more about. **AL**

See page 331C for other online activities.

ANSWERS, p. 336

MAP SKILLS

1. Ireland, Britain

2. Atlantic Ocean

networks from inland areas to the sea. They also provide water for farming and electric power.

The Thames River in southern England is one of the most well-known rivers in the world. The Thames flows for 205 miles (330 km) from the Cotswold Hills to the city of London. When it reaches London, the Thames becomes an **estuary** and extends for another 65 miles (105 km) before it enters the North Sea. An estuary is where part of the sea connects to the lower end of a river.

The Rhine River is the busiest waterway in Europe. It begins high in the Swiss Alps and empties into the North Sea. Along its course, it plunges over waterfalls, cuts deeply into the Middle Rhine Highlands, and connects industrial areas to the port in Rotterdam. The Rhine meanders lazily across the plains of the Netherlands to the North Sea. The river serves as part of the political boundary between France and Germany. It runs through the most populated region of Europe.

Another important waterway in Germany is the Elbe River, which also empties into the North Sea. Historically, the Elbe formed part of the border between West Germany and East Germany when that country was split into two from 1945 to 1990 (after World War II). Another important river in Germany, the Danube, is different from the other rivers because it flows toward the east. It passes through southern Germany and Austria on its way into Eastern Europe. The Danube is Eastern Europe's most important waterway. The Main (MINE) River, a tributary of the Rhine, is linked to the Danube by the Main-Danube Canal. The canal links the North Sea with the Black Sea at the southeastern end of Europe.

This seaport in Dover, England, is one of the busiest in the world.
▶ **CRITICAL THINKING**
Analyzing What are some of the important waterways in Western Europe?

Think Again?

London has black fogs that can kill people.

Not true. At one time, London had "pea soupers," thick, black and greenish fog. The fogs were caused in part by the burning of soft coal in homes and industry, which produced soot and poisonous sulfur dioxide. This mixed with the mist and fogs of the Thames Valley. In 1952 the Great Smog killed 4,000 London residents. Coal burning has been outlawed in London, but fumes from automobiles still produce smog in the city.

Chapter 11 **337**

Visual Skills

Analyzing Images Have students read the photo caption and discuss the image of a harbor on the English Channel at Dover. **Ask:** Why do you think safe harbors would be critical to the country of Britain? *(since Britain is an island it needs safe harbors on important waterways such as the English Channel for trade)* **ELL** Visual/Spatial, Interpersonal

Reading Skills

Comparing and Contrasting Have students reread the text about the rivers in this region. Tell students that they should note that both the Rhine River and the Danube River are very important waterways in Europe. **Ask:**

- How do both rivers help the region's economy? *(They both serve as important waterways for trade.)*
- What boundaries do they form? *(The Rhine serves as part of the boundary between France and Germany. The Danube does not form a political boundary.)*
- How is the flow of the rivers different? *(The Rhine flows toward the north, while the Danube flows toward the east.)*

Continue with a class discussion about the Elbe and Main Rivers. Have students compare and contrast the boundaries, location, flow, and importance of each river. **AL** Verbal/Linguistic

Content Background Knowledge

The Channel Tunnel, also called "The Chunnel," opened in 1994 and stretches about 31 miles beneath the English Channel. It is the longest undersea structure of its kind. At speeds greater than 100 mile per hour, trains can get passengers from the coast of England to the coast of France in just over a half hour. To build the tunnel, English workers had to dig through massive amounts of chalk rock. Chalk deposits are plentiful along the English Channel and are an important resource in Britain.

IMAGE

How the Chunnel Was Built

Analyzing Images Show the interactive image of the Chunnel and its construction to students. Draw a chart with the headings "Architecture," "Human-Environment Interaction," and "Tourism." Have students examine the image and the informative callouts and give examples for each category on the chart. **AL** Visual/Spatial

See page 331C for other online activities.

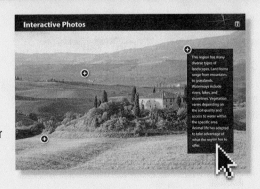

Interactive Photos

V Visual Skills

Analyzing Images Read the photo caption and have a volunteer answer the "Critical Thinking" question. Have students draw a T-chart and study the image on the page. Ask them to list physical features on one side of the chart and human-made features on the other. Explain that they should fill in their charts with examples of how the image shows both natural features, as well as human-made features.

Lead a class discussion that compares and/or contrasts both the physical and human-made features shown in the image with the features of the students' community. **Ask:**

• What kind of physical features are in your region? *(Student answers will vary but should include accurate examples of physical features in their area.)*
• What kind of human-made features are in your region? *(Student answers will vary but should include accurate examples of human-made features in their area.)*
• Do you feel that the human-made features in your community have helped or hurt the area? *(Student answers will vary but should include either support or opposition to the features and supply valid reasons for their answers.)*
Visual/Spatial, Intrapersonal

C Critical Thinking Skills

Making Connections Provide copies of a world map for pairs of students to use as a reference and to draw on. Ask students to work with a partner to trace Western Europe and the grid of latitude and longitude lines over Western Europe. Have them explain the difference between latitude and longitude as a review. Then have them plot the locations of Western Europe; Southern France; Halifax, Nova Scotia; and the Atlantic Ocean. Discuss the connection between the Atlantic Ocean and the mild climate of Western Europe. Ask students to draw lines from the ocean to Western Europe to illustrate the Westerlies. The lines will remind students how the warm winds off the Atlantic affect the climate of the region. ELL Visual/Spatial

Roadways run along the Danube River in Vienna, Austria.
▶ CRITICAL THINKING
Describing How is the Danube different from other rivers in the region?

In France, the longest river is the Loire River, at a length of 634 miles (1,020 km). It passes through the Loire Valley, the most important agricultural region in France. It is the Seine River, however, which runs through the capital city of Paris, that carries far more of the country's inland water traffic.

☑ READING PROGRESS CHECK

Analyzing How did the rivers in Western Europe affect its economic development?

Climate

GUIDING QUESTION *Why is the climate mild in Western Europe?*

Western Europe is located at northern latitudes, but it has a milder climate than other places at the same latitudes. For example, southern France is at roughly the same latitude as Halifax, Nova Scotia, in Canada, but southern France experiences a milder climate. Why? Western Europe is located near the Atlantic Ocean. Warm winds off the ocean are the primary factor that shapes the region's climate.

Temperate Lowlands

Most of Western Europe lies in the path of the **Westerlies**, strong winds that travel from west to east. The Westerlies blow a constant stream of relatively warm air from the sea to the land. Why is the air so warm this far north? The answer is found on the other side of the Atlantic Ocean, in the tropical waters of the Caribbean Sea. Here, an

net**w**♦rks *Online Teaching Options*

VIDEOS

Major Rivers in Western Europe

Describing Show the videos on major rivers of Western Europe to students. Then have students work in small groups to create a poem that describes the features and benefits of one of the rivers featured in the slide show, such as the Danube or the Thames, and read the poem to the class. Auditory/Musical

See page 331C for other online activities.

ANSWERS, p. 338

CRITICAL THINKING because it flows toward the east
☑ READING PROGRESS CHECK Possible answer: The rivers served as trade routes among cities and countries, allowing goods and people to travel easily among the different regions.

ocean current called the Gulf Stream moves warm tropical water north along the eastern coast of North America. The Gulf Stream then flows across the Atlantic Ocean, where its eastern extension, the North Atlantic Current, approaches the European coast. The current's warm water heats the air above it. This warm, moist air moves inland on the Westerlies and brings mild temperatures and rain to most of Western Europe throughout the year. Summers are cool, and winters are mild. This climate is known as a marine west coast climate.

Most places that have a marine west coast climate have mountain ranges running north-south along the coast. The mountains block the warm, moist air from moving farther inland. Western Europe, however, does not have coastal mountain ranges, so the Westerlies blow farther across the European continent.

Mediterranean Climate Area

Other areas of Western Europe, such as southern France, have a drier climate. A high-pressure system called the Azores High travels north over the Atlantic Ocean during the summer months. This pressure system pushes moist air northward. As a result, summers in southern France are hot and dry. In winter, the nearby Mediterranean Sea moderates the climate so that winters are mild or cool. Most of the rainfall occurs in spring and autumn. This is called a Mediterranean climate.

✓ READING PROGRESS CHECK

Describing How do the Westerlies affect the climate of Western Europe?

Walkers take an autumn stroll through a forest in southern Belgium. In this area, autumns start mild but soon become cool. Winters are cold and snowy.

Arterra Picture Library/Alamy

Chapter 11 **339**

R1 Reading Skills

Citing Text Evidence Have students read the first two paragraphs independently. Then as a class, have students answer each of the following questions as they point out and read aloud the passage or sentences directly from that text citing where they found their answers. **Ask:**

- Does it rain most of the time in Western Europe? *(Yes; students should cite: This warm, moist air moves inland on the Westerlies and brings mild temperatures and rain to most of Western Europe throughout the year.)*
- Do mountains help create a marine west coast climate? *(Yes; students should cite: The mountains block the warm, moist air from moving farther inland.)*
- Do mountains play an important role in controlling the weather in Western Europe? *(No; students should cite: Western Europe, however, does not have coastal mountain ranges, so the Westerlies blow farther across the European continent.)* **ELL** Naturalist, Kinesthetic

R2 Reading Skills

Paraphrasing Have students reread the section called "Mediterranean Climate Area." Ask them to paraphrase, or use their own words, to describe the Mediterranean climate area in Western Europe. *(Possible answer: Areas in Western Europe such as southern France enjoy a Mediterranean climate, with drier, warmer conditions.)* **AL** Verbal/Linguistic

W Writing Skills

Narrative Remind students that in the Northern Hemisphere there are seasons and that in most regions, the weather changes with the season. Have students write a short essay describing their favorite season. Tell students to provide details about what that season is like in the area in which they live. **BL** Verbal/Linguistic

---

MAP

Climates: Western Europe

Comparing and Contrasting Display the climate layer of the Chapter Opener map. Have students complete a chart or Venn diagram to compare and contrast the different climate regions of Western Europe. **AL**

See page 331C for other online activities.

ANSWER, p. 339

✓ READING PROGRESS CHECK Westerlies blow warm, moist air from sea to land, bringing mild temperatures and rain.

W Writing Skills

Informative/Explanatory Energy resources are important to the people and economy of Western Europe. Have students make a list of the energy sources that are predominantly used in the region. Then ask them to research an alternate energy source other than peat, which people in the region are using because it is a resource that is available in their environment. Ask students to write an informative essay to describe this alternate energy resource and explain how people in the region are using it. **BL** Naturalist

R Reading Skills

Giving Examples After reading about the Northern European Plain, ask students to give examples of how people in Western Europe have used this physical feature to develop their economy. **Ask:** To what economic sector does the Northern European Plain contribute? What type of economic activity makes up this sector? *(primary sector, agriculture)* **AL** Verbal/Linguistic

Content Background Knowledge

The Northern European Plain is one of the largest and most continuous plains on Earth. Even though the plain is large, it is quite narrow in length in some areas. In Western Europe, the plain is only about 200 miles wide. However, the width of the plain widens as it stretches to the east. In Western Russia, it widens to over 2,000 miles. Though the plain is generally flat, there are parts in the west that are covered with rolling hills.

Scientists believe that the area was glaciated several times during the Pleistocene Epoch (about 2,600,00 to 11,700 years ago), which flattened most of the plain. Hilly terminal moraines mark the edge of the glacier's ice sheets. In between the moraines are long parallel paths where water from the glacier melted and flowed to the sea. These areas are made up of flat wetlands or windblown sandy dunes, except for the large delta plain of The Netherlands. This area that was formed by the deposits of the Rhine River has left behind rich, fertile soil. Overall, the plain creates an enormous lowland that gives Europe a lower average elevation than any other continent.

Natural Resources

GUIDING QUESTION *How do the people of Western Europe use the region's natural resources?*

Western Europe has many important natural resources. Layers of coal lie beneath rich, fertile soils. Beneath the North Sea are large pockets of oil and natural gas. Western Europeans use these natural resources to support their economies and populations.

Energy Sources

Deposits of coal are plentiful throughout Britain, Belgium, the Netherlands, France, and Germany. Coal was used to fuel machines invented during the Industrial Revolution of the 1800s. Today, coal production is declining in Northern Europe. Much less coal is available than in the past, so the region is importing more coal. Coal has also become less important as a source of energy as people rely more on other energy sources to meet their needs. In places where other fuels are scarce, Europeans burn peat. A peat bog is a wetland in which large masses of vegetable matter decay in the poorly drained soil. Peat—the name for the decaying vegetable matter—can be used as fuel for heating. The peat is dug up, cut into blocks, and dried so that it can be burned.

In 1959 oil and natural gas were discovered under the North Sea. Since then, the North Sea has become the region's most important source for these resources. The United Kingdom and the Northern European nation of Norway are the leading producers of oil and natural gas from North Sea oil fields. The Netherlands and Germany also produce oil and natural gas from the North Sea.

Other countries in Western Europe use their rivers to supply energy. Switzerland, for example, uses its fast-flowing rivers to produce electricity. Hydroelectricity supplies more than half of Switzerland's electricity needs.

Rich Soils

The Northern European Plain has some of the richest soils in Europe so people can farm there. Soils of the Northern European Plain contain humus. Humus is decomposed plant and animal material that makes soils rich and fertile, and is good for growing crops and raising livestock.

France is Western Europe's leading agricultural producer. France devotes more surface area to agriculture than any other country in the region. Large wheat fields stretch across northern France. Orchards and vineyards are common in the central and southern parts of the country. On the Northern European Plain, farmers grow a variety of crops and raise cattle and hogs. In the Netherlands, dairy farming is important for the country's economy.

netw⊕rks *Online Teaching Options*

SLIDE SHOW

Agriculture in Western Europe

Listing Use the slide show to discuss the important crops that are grown in the region. While students view the images, ask them to make a list of the crops mentioned or shown and draw pictures of them. Ask them to write details about where the crops are grown, and then discuss students' lists as a class. Outline the locations on a regional map. **ELL** Visual/Spatial

See page 331C for other online activities.

Plants and Wildlife

The moderate climate and abundance of rainfall in most of Western Europe support a wide variety of plant and animal life. The British Isles have dense forests, grasslands, scrublands, and wetlands. The natural vegetation in most of the British Isles is **deciduous** forest, which includes trees such as oak, maple, beech, and chestnut, that lose their leaves in autumn. The climate on the mainland of Europe is more diverse than the climate of the British Isles. As a result, mainland Europe has a wider variety of plant life.

Farther inland, in Germany, Austria, and Switzerland, the drier climate as well as highlands and mountain ranges support other kinds of plants. Coniferous forests have become more common. **Coniferous** trees, such as fir and pine trees, have cones and needle-shaped leaves, and they keep their leaves during the winter. Many peaks in the Alps and Pyrenees lie above the tree line. Here, grasses and shrubs are the most common plants. Much of Western Europe was once covered in forests. Most of these forests were destroyed to make towns, cities, and roads.

Wildlife

Animals have had to adapt to these changes. Deer, wild boars, hare, and mice are common. Wildcats, lynx, and foxes roam the forests. Small populations of brown bears live in the Pyrenees. In the British Isles, the population of large mammals, such as wolves, reindeer, and boars, has decreased. The islands have more than 200 kinds of birds, many of which have adapted to life in towns and cities.

☑ **READING PROGRESS CHECK**

Determining Central Ideas What effect did coal have on the Industrial Revolution?

France is one of the largest producers of wheat in the world; it is the largest European producer.

▶ CRITICAL THINKING

Analyzing What makes the soils of the Northern European Plain good for growing crops?

Phillipe Huguen/AFP/Getty Images

FOLDABLES
Study Organizer

Include this lesson's information in your Foldable®.

V Visual Skills

Diagramming Emphasize that deciduous means "falling off" and refers to trees that shed their leaves each year. Coniferous refers to trees that keep or retain their leaves or needles all year long. Have students work with a partner to make two web diagrams of the two types of trees. Each diagram should have either "Deciduous" or "Coniferous" in the center circle. Students should fill in the outer circles with examples or descriptions of these types of trees found in Western Europe. Suggest that students either draw or provide an image as an example of each type of tree on both diagrams. Invite students to share their diagrams and drawings in small groups. **ELL** Visual/Spatial

T Technology Skills

Making Presentations Ask students to use the Internet or other electronic or print resources to learn more about a bird, animal, or plant that is native to Western Europe and is not native to the United States or that was brought to the United States by European immigrants. Have students put together a brief presentation of images and text describing the chosen bird, animal, or plant.

Provide an opportunity for students to use computer presentation software for their research projects, and allow five minutes for each student to present to the class. Students who are listening to the presentations should take notes on each bird, animal, and plant presented, and then write a paragraph explaining which one was the most interesting to them and why. **BL** Verbal/Linguistic

CLOSE & REFLECT

Making Connections To close this lesson, have students think about how the people of Western Europe have used the natural resources and physical features of their environment to live and meet their needs. Have students provide and explain specific examples that they recall. Write these on the board and use them as a class review of the lesson.

LESSON 1 REVIEW

Reviewing Vocabulary

1. How do the *Westerlies* affect the climate in Western Europe?

Answering the Guiding Questions

2. *Identifying* What landmasses make up the British Isles, and what countries do they form?

3. *Describing* Why is the North Sea important to Western Europe?

4. *Analyzing* How does the marine west coast climate in Western Europe differ from marine west coast climates in other parts of the world?

5. *Describing* Why has the use of coal dwindled in Western Europe? What discovery in the North Sea helped bring about that change?

6. *Informative/Explanatory Writing* Write a paragraph describing how Europe's rivers contribute to the region's industry.

LESSON 1 REVIEW ANSWERS

Reviewing Vocabulary

1. The Westerlies blow warm, moist air from the Atlantic Ocean, providing Western Europe with a mild, wet climate.

Answering the Guiding Questions

2. **Identifying** The British Isles consist of the islands of Britain and Ireland. The United Kingdom occupies all of Britain and the northern part of the island of Ireland. The nation of Ireland occupies the rest of the island of Ireland.

3. **Describing** It is a rich fishing ground. It is an important trade route between the United Kingdom and mainland Europe. It is a source of oil and natural gas.

4. **Analyzing** In most parts of the world, the effects of a marine west coast climate are cut short by coastal mountain ranges. Western Europe does not have coastal mountain ranges. Thus the Westerlies can blow farther across Europe, providing a mild climate.

5. **Describing** Coal is used less because much less of it is available and oil and natural gas have become more important sources of energy. Petroleum was discovered in the North Sea in 1959, giving Western Europe a nearby source for oil and natural gas.

6. **Informative/Explanatory** Responses should mention that the Rhine and the Danube can accommodate large ships and barges. Because of their links to seas, Europe's rivers provide important trade outlets for the continent's cities and industries.

ANSWERS, p. 341

CRITICAL THINKING It contains humus, made up of decomposed plant and animal material, which is essential for fertility of the soil.

☑ READING PROGRESS CHECK Coal was used to fuel the machines invented during the Industrial Revolution.

ENGAGE

Bellringer Before students begin this lesson, ask students to name one cultural tradition or background fact from within their family. Invite students who have family members or ancestors from Western Europe to share information about the region, its culture, or its history. Point out that many cultures make up the region today and much of that is a result of its history. Have students think about the influence that multiple cultures can have on a region.

TEACH & ASSESS

C Critical Thinking Skills

Making Inferences After students read the text about how people in Europe changed from hunter-gatherers to practicing agriculture, **ask:** Why might people decide to farm the land instead of hunt animals and gather fruit and nuts? *(Possible answer: A hunter-gatherer lifestyle is one that is nomadic, while farming the land requires settlement. People decided to settle instead of moving around in search of food.)*
AL Verbal/Linguistic

R1 Reading Skills

Illustrating Explain to students that the Romans conquered a vast area of land in Europe. They brought their culture, language, and technology to the areas that they conquered. Have students work in small groups to illustrate how the Romans conquered areas of Europe and brought their way of life with them. Tell students that they should show how the Romans spread across the region and how their culture changed the existing culture of Europe. **ELL** Kinesthetic

R2 Reading Skills

Reinforcing Vocabulary Remind students to add academic and content vocabulary words to their vocabulary lists in their notebooks. Tell students to write their own definitions and to include drawings if desired. **ELL** **AL**

ANSWER, p. 342

Taking Notes Notes should include the following: **Britain:** The people in Britain were proud that their nation was a leader in scientific research, in trade and commerce, and in political thought. **France:** Napoleon used the French people's sense of loyalty to their country to build a great army.
Germany: The German people wanted the German states to unify into one country.

---

netw⊕rks

There's More Online!

☑ **GRAPHIC ORGANIZER**
☑ **SLIDE SHOW** WWII
☑ **VIDEO**

Reading **HELP**DESK

Academic Vocabulary

• **theory**

Content Vocabulary

• **smelting**
• **feudalism**
• **Middle Ages**
• **pilgrimage**
• **Parliament**
• **industrialized**
• **Holocaust**

TAKING NOTES: *Key Ideas and Details*

Summarize Use a chart like this one to describe the different ways nationalism affected people in Britain, France, and Germany.

Britain	France	Germany

Indiana Academic Standards
6.1.1, 6.1.2, 6.1.3, 6.1.4, 6.1.5, 6.1.7, 6.1.12, 6.1.13, 6.1.14, 6.1.15, 6.2.3, 6.2.4

Lesson 2
History of Western Europe

ESSENTIAL QUESTION • *Why do civilizations rise and fall?*

IT MATTERS BECAUSE
Even though the nations of Western Europe are not geographically large, their culture and technology have had a worldwide impact.

History of the Region Through 1800

GUIDING QUESTION *How did Western Europe change from a land controlled by loose-knit tribes to a region of monarch-ruled nations?*

Western Europeans were not the first Europeans to begin farming, but the rich soil and moderate climate drew many early people to the region. As the forests were cleared for farmland, people began a long struggle to control the land.

Beginnings

Modern humans have lived in Europe for about 40,000 years. The early people were hunters and gatherers, but over time the practice of agriculture was introduced in Western Europe. Populations began to grow, and settlements became towns. People began to make tools from metal, especially bronze. To make bronze, people needed to know how to melt and fuse tin and copper, a process called **smelting**.

Roman Empire

Meanwhile, the Romans were spreading throughout Southern Europe and advancing into Western Europe. By A.D. 14, all of France and most of Germany were under Roman control. Within 100 years, Rome also controlled most of the island of Britain.

(l to r) Celtic/The Bridgeman Art Library/Getty Images; ©Stefano Bianchetti/Corbis; ©Heritage Images/Corbis; Hulton Archive/Getty Images

---

netw⊕rks *Online Teaching Options*

VIDEO

Ancient Mysteries - Stonehenge

Creating Time Lines Use the video to introduce the history, construction, and mystery surrounding the use of Stonehenge. As they watch the video, ask students to make a time line that includes key events in the artifact's history. Students could also draw one of the representations of Stonehenge from the video. **BL** Verbal/Linguistic

See page 331D for other online activities.

BBC Motion Gallery Education

The Romans did not just conquer people and territories. They brought their beliefs, their language (Latin), and their technologies with them. They built concrete roads and bridges throughout the empire. They also built aqueducts, which carried water long distances, from remote areas to cities and towns. Some of these structures are still visible today.

Over the centuries, Rome's empire in Western Europe began to weaken. The Huns, a warrior people from Asia, invaded from the east, driving invading groups of Germanic peoples, such as the Visigoths, westward. Rome could no longer protect its colonies in Western Europe. Some Germanic groups settled there and created kingdoms. The Franks ruled what is now France, and the Angles and Saxons ruled what is today England.

Christianity and Western Europe

Christianity, which became Europe's major religion, began in the eastern Roman Empire. It gradually spread throughout the empire. Once Emperor Constantine converted to Christianity in A.D. 312, Christianity began to spread quickly. By the time Rome's western empire fell in A.D. 476, Christianity was common throughout most of Western Europe. The Christian Church played a key role in education and developed religious communities called monasteries. The Roman Catholic Church became a major force in Western European life.

The Middle Ages

As time went on, invaders threatened the region. No strong governments existed to help Western Europeans fight off invasion. To bring order, a system called **feudalism** arose. Under feudalism, kings gave land to nobles. The nobles in turn gave kings military service. Many nobles became knights, or warriors on horseback. Today, we call this period of time the **Middle Ages**, or the Medieval Age. This term describes a period of transition between ancient and modern times.

Conflicts also arose over religious beliefs. One of the most important rituals in medieval European society was the religious **pilgrimage**, a visit to lands that were important to the history of Christianity. Jerusalem was the most important destination for pilgrims, but in the late 1000s, Muslims controlled the city. Pope Urban II, leader of the Catholic Church, called for a crusade to conquer Jerusalem for Christianity. The kings and noblemen of Western Europe formed great armies to meet the pope's demand. They won Jerusalem in the First Crusade. More crusades followed, but they were not successful. Muslims regained control of Jerusalem, and Muslim power continued to grow.

Celtic/The Bridgeman Art Library/Getty Images

Thinking Like a Geographer

The Channel in History

Because the English Channel is the most direct route from continental Europe to the island of Britain, it has served as the route of many invasions. When Julius Caesar first invaded Britain in 55 B.C., the Roman army crossed the English Channel. In World War II, American, British, and Canadian troops invaded from the opposite direction, from Britain to the beaches of Normandy in France.

This iron and bronze helmet dates from the 300s B.C.

▶ **CRITICAL THINKING**

Identifying What warrior people from Asia invaded Western Europe?

Chapter 11 **343**

V Visual Skills

Making a Chart After reading about different groups that conquered Western Europe, have students make a chart to show the places and names of each group. *(Students' charts should show the following:* **Romans** *(France, Germany, England),* **Huns** *(Germany),* **Visigoths** *(Germany and parts of France),* **Franks** *(France),* **Angles and Saxons** *(England).)* **Ask:** How does the chart illustrate the culture of Western Europe? *(Possible answer: It shows how Western Europe attracted many cultures and even though some of the groups came to the area and left, aspects of their culture remained and contribute to the overall culture of the region.)* **ELL** Visual/Spatial

R Reading Skills

Explaining Remind students that culture includes more than language and customs. Religion and government are also aspects of culture. **Ask:**

• What important element was introduced during the invasions and changed life in Western Europe? *(Christianity)*

• What was *feudalism*? Explain how and why it worked. *(It was a system created to help the kings bring about order; the kings gave land to nobles, and in exchange for the land, the nobles fought for the king's military.)*

• What influence did the Roman Catholic Church have? *(It greatly influenced life in Western Europe by improving education and bringing about Roman order.)*

• Why did the governments of Western Europe fail to prevent the invasions during the Middle Ages? *(They were not strong or unified.)*

• What challenge did Christianity face in the late 1000s? *(Possible response: Muslims controlled Jerusalem, where Christians made their pilgrimages. As a result, Christians fought against the Muslims in the crusades, which was an effort to take back the Holy Land and to control Jerusalem.)* Verbal/Linguistic

ANIMATION

How Bronze is Made

Creating Visuals Display the animation of how bronze is made and have students take turns reading about different aspects of bronze work and smelting in Western Europe. Discuss as a class how the people of the region used metal and the influence of the Romans on metal and technology. Ask students to draw a tool made of metal that was important to the region. They should write 1–2 sentences to explain how it was used. **ELL** Visual/Spatial

See page 331D for other online activities.

ANSWER, p. 343

CRITICAL THINKING the Huns

C Critical Thinking Skills

Determining Cause and Effect Discuss with students that the crusades resulted in a substantial loss for Christianity but also had other effects. After students read about the crusades, **ask:**

- How did the crusades affect the culture of Western Europe? *(People who fought in the crusades had traveled to lands in the east, bringing back new ideas and cultural elements.)*

- How did the economy of Western Europe change? *(Towns grew and trade expanded. Work became more specialized, which also helped trade.)*

- Do you think Christians should have gone on the crusades? Explain your answer. *(Possible answers: Yes, I think that even though they were not successful in taking back Jerusalem, they brought new ideas back to Western Europe. These new ideas helped the region's economy to grow and culture to flourish. No, the Crusades just created more division between the cultures of Europe and the Middle East.)* Verbal/Linguistic

V Visual Skills

Interpreting In pairs, have students read and discuss the infographic on Black Death. Have each partner write three questions based on the information provided in the infographic. Next have partners exchange questions, allowing time for the other student to provide the answers. Then as a class, discuss the questions and answers that the pairs created. AL

Content Background Knowledge

The Hundred Years' War was not a war that was ongoing for one hundred years. It was a series of conflicts that related to English and French claims to the crown to rule France. It lasted from about 1337 to 1453, which is just over one hundred years. The result of these warring years was that England and France were looking at their own internal problems rather than focusing on regional dominance. England and France continued to have differences throughout much of history.

ANSWER, p. 344

CRITICAL THINKING Possible Answer: If there are more workers than are needed, wages will drop as there are more people competing for the same job(s). At the same time, if there are more jobs than people wanting those jobs, wages would probably go up as the supply of workers is less.

As the Crusades ended, monarchs began to lay the foundations of what became Europe's modern nation-states. A nation state is a political organization controlling a specific territory. It also includes a population that shares something in common, such as language, history, or ethnic background. In building new nations, Europe's monarchs strengthened control over territories as the power of local nobles declined. Promoting law and order, monarchs won the support of the rising merchant class, whose wealth provided the taxes needed for government services and whose writing and business skills were used in running new government offices.

Many of the crusaders returned to their European homes with changed ideas. They had seen a richer, more powerful, more modern world in the east. These ideas from the east began to spread across Northern Europe.

The economy in Western Europe was changing. Villages grew into towns. Traders and merchants began to play a bigger role in town life. Work became more specialized. People with important skills—metalsmiths, butchers, carpenters—began to organize into guilds. Guilds were not as powerful as the noblemen or the Church, but they helped the towns grow stronger.

Hundred Years' War

The threat of war between France and England flared throughout the 1200s and early 1300s. When war finally broke out between the two countries in 1337, the fighting lasted for a total of more than 100 years. England won important battles early on, gaining land in France. By the end of the Hundred Years' War, France had won all that land back. Several truces were agreed to during the war, some of them lasting many years. One of the most important developments of the war though was not a truce. It was the rapid spread of a terrible disease called a plague.

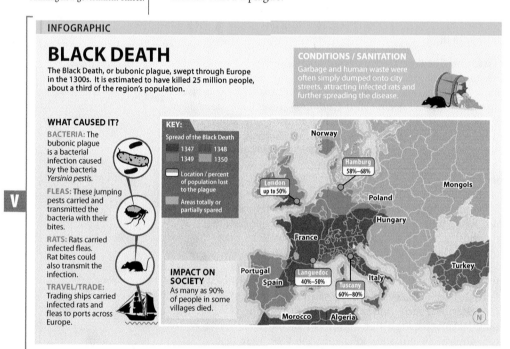

INFOGRAPHIC

BLACK DEATH

The Black Death, or bubonic plague, swept through Europe in the 1300s. It is estimated to have killed 25 million people, about a third of the region's population.

CONDITIONS / SANITATION
Garbage and human waste were often simply dumped onto city streets, attracting infected rats and further spreading the disease.

WHAT CAUSED IT?

BACTERIA: The bubonic plague is a bacterial infection caused by the bacteria *Yersinia pestis*.

FLEAS: These jumping pests carried and transmitted the bacteria with their bites.

RATS: Rats carried infected fleas. Rat bites could also transmit the infection.

TRAVEL/TRADE: Trading ships carried infected rats and fleas to ports across Europe.

KEY:
Spread of the Black Death
1347 — 1348
1349 — 1350
Location / percent of population lost to the plague
Areas totally or partially spared

Norway
Hamburg 58%–68%
London up to 50%
Poland
Mongols
Hungary
France
Turkey
Portugal
Spain
Languedoc 40%–50%
Tuscany 60%–80%
Italy
Morocco
Algeria

IMPACT ON SOCIETY
As many as 90% of people in some villages died.

With the great loss of population, the production of food and goods also decreased. Workers demanded higher wages and farmers increased the price of their goods.

▶ CRITICAL THINKING
Analyzing Explain the effect of supply and demand on wages.

---

networks *Online Teaching Options*

INFOGRAPHIC

The Black Death

Reading an Infographic Display the infographic on the Black Death to discuss the spread of this disease from Asia to Europe. Ask students to explain how the virus spread from person to person and how much of the population of Europe it killed. Be sure to make connections with students that the results of the Black Death caused a shortage of workers and began to restructure society. Visual/Spatial, Naturalist

See page 331D for other online activities.

Interactive Charts/Tables/Diagrams

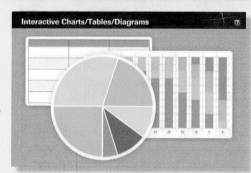

In 1347 the plague, called the Black Death, reached Western Europe, where it raged for four years. Whole towns were wiped out. Four more outbreaks struck Europe by the end of the century. Victims of the Black Death often stayed in monasteries and hospitals run by Roman Catholic officials.

Early Modern Europe

The Roman Catholic Church was wealthy and had power over numerous aspects of society. Many people wanted to reform, or change, some Church teachings and practices. For example, most people did not speak Latin. Yet, the Bible was largely available only in Latin. People began to demand translations of the Bible in their languages so that they could read and interpret it on their own.

People also began questioning the moneymaking practices of Church officials. This included the sale of indulgences, pardons from the Church for a person's sins. A German priest named Martin Luther protested this practice. He declared that only trust in God could save people from their sins. In 1517 Luther wrote the Ninety-Five Theses, a document that attacked the practice of selling indulgences. The Church expelled Luther for his beliefs, but his ideas spread quickly. His followers became known as Lutherans, and his efforts spurred a religious movement called the Protestant Reformation.

As the Catholic Church's power weakened, England's kings also were being forced to share power with a new government institution called **Parliament**. This lawmaking body was made up of two houses. The House of Lords represented the wealthy, powerful nobles. The "lower" house, or House of Commons, represented the common citizens, usually successful guild members and business owners.

The Enlightenment

A wave of discovery and scientific observation swept over Europe in the 1600s and 1700s. During this time, European explorers were traveling and mapping the world, and European astronomers were mapping the solar system.

In 1543 the Polish astronomer Nicolaus Copernicus proposed the **theory** that Earth and the other planets orbit the sun instead of the sun and other planets orbiting Earth, as was then believed. Philosophers began to consider ways of improving society. People began to use reason to observe and describe the world around them. Reason transformed the way people thought about how to answer questions about the natural world. This period is called the Enlightenment.

English philosophers John Locke and Thomas Hobbes used reason to study society itself. Locke believed that the best form of government was a contract, or agreement, between the ruler and the people. People began to question the authority of kings and of the Church.

Think Again?

Johannes Gutenberg invented the printing press.

Not true. The earliest printing was probably done with stamps that were pressed into clay or soft wax to create an image. The Chinese started printing on paper using wooden blocks with text carved into the wood. The Chinese also invented movable type, which used carved blocks of individual characters. Gutenberg did not invent the first printing press. His design for a movable-type printing press, however, is the one that was adopted and used going forward.

Indiana CONNECTION

England's Political Heritage

During the Middle Ages and early modern period, important documents (the Magna Carta, the Petition of Right, and the English Bill of Rights) limited the power of English kings and recognized the rights of landowners—rights that eventually came to apply to all English people. As a result, Parliament, which came to be made up of the people's representatives, emerged as the most powerful government institution. England's system of parliamentary government shaped the political life of the United States and other countries that were for a time under English rule.

Academic Vocabulary

theory an explanation of why or how something happens

Chapter 11 **345**

T Technology Skills

Create Charts Have students use the Internet to research how deadly the Black Death was. Ask them to include data such as the number of deaths by year or deaths by country or region. **Ask:** How do you think the Black Death affected trade in Europe? Explain. *(Possible answer: It decreased trade because there were fewer people to produce goods and fewer people with whom to trade.)* Logical/Mathematical

W Writing Skills

Argument Explain to students that Martin Luther was only one of several reformers who wanted the Roman Catholic Church to change some of its practices. Review the section on Luther with students and discuss how he was expelled from the Church for his beliefs. Have students use this question as a writing prompt for a short essay in which they argue for or against the Church's ruling against Luther: **Was Luther treated fairly by the Roman Catholic Church?**

Remind them to follow these guidelines when writing their essay:

- introduce the argument or claim clearly
- support the argument or claim with clear reasons and relevant evidence
- use credible sources and cite information correctly
- include a concluding statement and restate your argument or claim

(Students' arguments should demonstrate understanding of the topic and take a side. Students should support their argument with facts and details, acknowledge the opposing side, and be convincing.) AL Verbal/Linguistic

C Critical Thinking Skills

Categorizing Explain to students that by putting information into categories, it is easier to see how things are grouped. Make a list of the people and ideas described in the section called "The Enlightenment." Ask students to study the list, make a chart, and classify the information by topic. *(Explorers: mapped the world; astronomers: mapped the solar system, Copernicus's theory that the planets orbit the sun; philosophers: used reason to observe and describe the world and society).* ELL Logical/Mathematical

---

TIME LINE

Religious Upheaval and Change

Determining Cause and Effect Display the time line and discuss the causes and events for religious changes in Europe. Be sure to highlight the role of the Roman Catholic Church and Martin Luther, along with the weakening of the Church and the creation of Parliament. Ask students to identify those events that were effects of the Catholic Church-Martin Luther controversy.
AL Visual/Spatial

See page 331D for other online activities.

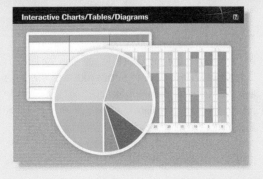

Interactive Charts/Tables/Diagrams

R1 Reading Skills

Applying After students have read the section on reform in France, discuss the ideas that led to reform and revolution in the country. Point out the year in which revolution broke out (1789). **Ask:**

- What event had taken place recently across the Atlantic Ocean that may have influenced the way the French people thought about government and the rights of citizens? *(Student answers will vary but should demonstrate understanding of the American Revolution.)*
- Do you think the revolution in France influenced movements for reform in other countries? Explain. *(Possible answer: Yes, I think that the movement for reform became more global and affected other countries in Europe and elsewhere.)* **AL** Verbal/Linguistic

R2 Reading Skills

Discussing Divide the class into small groups. Have them read the Guiding Question on this page and discuss how they think the industrial system would change Western Europe. Ask them to brainstorm a list of possible outcomes. Then have each group share their list with the class. At the end of this lesson, have each group revisit their lists to remove or add any of the outcomes. **ELL** Verbal/Linguistic, Interpersonal

Content Background Knowledge

After *The Declaration of the Rights of Man and of the Citizen* was written, a young French woman named Olympe de Gouges wrote her response in the *Declaration of the Rights of Woman and of the Female Citizen* in 1791. She asserted that representatives of the National Assembly did not acknowledge any voting rights for women when they wrote their *Declaration* and that women should be treated as equal partners. She also contended that women should receive the same opportunities in education as men.

During the French Revolution in July 1789, a huge mob stormed the Bastille, an old fort used as a prison and a weapons armory.
▶ **CRITICAL THINKING**
Analyzing What was the result of the French Revolution?

©Stefano Bianchetti/Corbis

Reform

In 1789 France was a powerful country, ruled by a king. Most of the people in France were peasants, living in poverty. But a growing, successful middle class resented not having a voice in government. In July of that year, a revolution limited the king's power and ended the privileges of nobles and church leaders. An important document was written: *The Declaration of the Rights of Man and of the Citizen.* It stated that government's power came from the people, not the king. A few years later, the king was removed and executed.

Not everyone in France supported the revolution. Violence raged in France for the next 10 years. Finally, in 1799 a young French general named Napoleon Bonaparte quickly took military and political control of the country. With a powerful army, he brought much of Europe under French control. By 1814, the combined might of France's enemies in conquered lands led to Napoleon's defeat and removal from power.

✓ **READING PROGRESS CHECK**

Identifying What roles did the Reformation and the Enlightenment play in changing the balance of power in Western Europe?

Change and Conflict

GUIDING QUESTION *How did the industrial system change life in Western Europe?*

During the 1800s, some Western European nations **industrialized**, or changed from an agricultural society to one based on industry. As a result, many people moved from the countryside to the city to

346 *Chapter 11*

netw⊕rks   *Online Teaching Options*

LECTURE SLIDES

Enlightenment Reforms

Determining Cause and Effect As you show the lecture slide presentation to students, discuss with them the causes and effects of ideas of the Enlightenment on movements for reform. Ask students to think of a time that ideas influenced them to do something or change the way they did something. Invite volunteers to share their examples.
ELL Intrapersonal

See page 331D for other online activities.

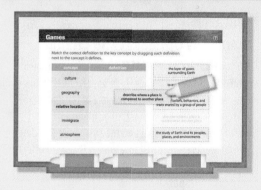

ANSWERS, p. 346

CRITICAL THINKING The revolution limited the king's power and ended the privileges of the nobles and church leaders. A few years later, the king was executed.
✓ **READING PROGRESS CHECK** Possible answers: The Reformation and the Enlightenment both encouraged people to think more for themselves. They began to question those who held power over them.

find work in factories. The urban population grew, and the cities became powerful. At the same time, some Europeans began to feel strong loyalty to their country. A new, national spirit was rising.

The Industrial Revolution

A big change took place in Britain in the period from 1760 to 1830. People began to use steam-powered machines to perform work that had been done by humans or animals. For example, weavers in small villages once wove cloth on looms in their own homes, but new machines were invented to weave more cloth at greater speed for lower cost.

Machines of the Industrial Revolution did not affect only urban populations; they improved farm labor so much that fewer people were needed to work the land. People began to leave farms and villages for industrial cities where they could work in the factories.

As nations industrialized, loyalties shifted. Former enemies Great Britain and France grew closer as Germany gained military strength. As the possibility of war increased, alliances formed between countries.

T1

World War I

Rivalries among European powers for new territory and economic power helped lead to World War I. Political changes also contributed as monarchies and empires were being replaced by modern nation-states.

T2

©Heritage Images/Corbis

A steam hammer in an English factory molds steel and iron into engine and machine parts.
▶ CRITICAL THINKING
Describing How did the Industrial Revolution affect rural populations?

T1 Technology Skills

Analyzing Data Write the following statistics on the board, and ask students to study them. Then provide students with the chart "Rate of Industrial Growth by Country" as seen below.

Population Estimates: Europe
1750: 132 million
1800: 190 million
1850: 260 million

Rate of Industrial Growth by Country			
	United Kingdom	France	Germany
1781–90	3.8	10.9	-
1801–14	7.1	12.3	-
1825–34	18.8	21.5	-
1845–54	27.5	33.7	11.7

Ask: What generalizations can you make about this data regarding industrial growth in Europe and the rise in population? *(Sample answers: Industrial growth expanded greatly, especially after 1845. Industrial growth increased with the growth in population. The United Kingdom had the greatest rate of industrial growth.)* **BL** Logical/Mathematical

T2 Technology Skills

Analyzing News Media Ask a group of volunteers to search reliable Internet sites for news stories from 1914 about the beginning of World War I. Have students read aloud a few of the news stories to the class. Discuss and ask questions about the information in the articles to help provide students with an understanding of the significance of the war. Verbal/Linguistic

GRAPHIC ORGANIZER

Cause and Effect: The Industrial Revolution

Analyzing Charts Display the interactive graphic organizer to discuss the reasons behind the movement from an agricultural society to one based on industry. Make connections with students that industrialization also causes movement of populations and changes in ideas. Work with students to complete the graphic organizer and answer any questions students may have.
AL Visual/Spatial

See page 331D for other online activities.

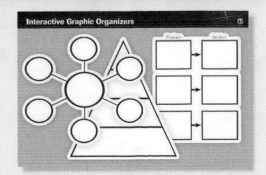

Interactive Graphic Organizers

ANSWER, p. 347

CRITICAL THINKING Because of new technology, fewer farm workers were needed. Rural population migrated to cities to work in the factories.

History of Western Europe

V Visual Skills

Integrating Visual Information Have students study the map of the countries under Axis control. **Ask:** How could Hitler and the German army have taken control of such a large area? How long do you think it took to conquer this area? *(Students' answers may vary.)*

Provide students with a map of the area shown and have them do reliable Internet research to learn when each of the different countries fell to the Axis powers. Students should include the dates on their maps. Then, revisit the questions and see if their answers change or become more detailed. **AL** Visual/Spatial

C Critical Thinking Skills

Comparing and Contrasting After students read the sections on World War I and World War II, ask them to work with a partner to complete a Venn diagram. Their diagrams should show very generally how the wars were similar and different, and list the nations that fought in each of the wars. Point out additional references for students to use or have students do additional research to help them with their charts. *(Students' Venn diagrams should show under **Differences:** World War I was a rivalry among several nations for economic power and colonies. World War II was an alliance of Germany, who wanted to expand its territory and get rid of the Jews and other minorities, and Japan who wanted to increase its influence in the Pacific and expand into Asia. **Similarities:** Germany lost in both wars. Britain won in both wars.)*

Content Background Knowledge

Of the six million Jews who were murdered during the Holocaust, the highest number in Western Europe came from Germany. The Jewish population in Germany was about 566,000, and those who perished during the Holocaust comprised more than one-third of the total population of Germany. The next highest number of deaths was in the Netherlands and those deaths were nearly three-fourths of the nation's total Jewish population.

Axis Control in World War II

NORWAY SWEDEN FINLAND
ESTONIA
IRELAND GREAT DENMARK LATVIA
BRITAIN EAST LITHUANIA
PRUSSIA
NETHERLANDS USSR
ATLANTIC BELGIUM GERMANY POLAND
OCEAN
FRANCE SLOVAKIA
SWITZERLAND HUNGARY
ITALY ROMANIA
PORTUGAL YUGOSLAVIA Black Sea
SPAIN BULGARIA
ALBANIA
GREECE TURKEY
MOROCCO ALGERIA
TUNISIA Mediterranean Sea
Maximum extent of territory
under Axis control
LIBYA EGYPT

500 miles
500 kilometers
Lambert Azimuthal Equal-Area projection

MAP SKILLS

1 PLACES AND REGIONS Which country in central Europe did not fall under Axis control?

2 THE GEOGRAPHER'S WORLD Why would control of Southern Europe and northern Africa be important?

Fought between 1914 and 1918, World War I resulted in millions of deaths and great destruction. Germany lost the war, and the victorious countries—led by Great Britain, France, Italy, and the United States—demanded that Germany pay for damages.

The defeat nearly wrecked the German economy. Germans believed they were being punished too harshly for their role in the war. A political radical named Adolf Hitler used the people's anger to build a political party called the Nazi Party. By 1933, he was the dictator, or absolute ruler, of Germany. The Nazis believed the Germans were a superior race. They carried out the **Holocaust**, the government-sponsored murder of 6 million Jews. Other minorities also suffered at the hands of the Nazis. Hitler and his Nazi Party envisioned a new German empire.

World War II

War came when Hitler's armies began seizing other countries. World War II stretched far beyond Western Europe. Germany allied with Italy and Japan to form the Axis Powers. Great Britain, the United States, and the Soviet Union formed the Allied Powers. The war was fought in Western and Southern Europe, in Africa, and in the Pacific. A combination of American, British, and Canadian troops invaded

348 Chapter 11

netw⊕rks   *Online Teaching Options*

World War II

Determining Cause and Effect Show the slide show on World War II. Explain the main points to the students. Discuss each event and make a time line so that students can see the sequence of events. Ask students to write a summary of the causes and effects of World War II. Then have students read their summaries to a partner.
AL Verbal/Linguistic

Slide Show

See page 331D for other online activities.

(l) ©Ocean/Corbis, ©Kryssia Campos/Getty Images, (tr) ©Erica Simone Leeds, (br) ©JG Photography/Alamy

---

ANSWERS, p. 348

MAP SKILLS

1. Switzerland

2. controlling these regions gains control of the Mediterranean Sea

France in June 1944 and liberated it from the Germans.

After Hitler's death and Germany's surrender in May 1945, the war continued in East Asia and the Pacific for another three months. The fighting ended after the United States used atomic bombs on the cities of Hiroshima and Nagasaki in Japan. Worldwide, between 40 million and 60 million people died in World War II. More civilians died than military forces.

The Cold War

Before World War II, Britain, France, and Germany were among the most powerful nations in the world. However, World War II had weakened them. After the war, the United States and the Soviet Union emerged as the leading world powers. Both superpowers were interested in Europe's fate. The Soviet Union took control of most of Eastern Europe. The United States was a strong ally to nations in Western Europe. Germany was split in half, with Britain, the United States, and France occupying western Germany, and the Soviet Union controlling the eastern half.

For more than 40 years, the United States and the Soviet Union engaged in a cold war, a conflict that never erupted into war, but the threat of war always existed. Both sides stockpiled nuclear weapons. In the 1980s, Soviet influence began to weaken. Protest movements spread in European countries under Soviet control. The Cold War ended when the government of the Soviet Union collapsed in 1991.

☑ READING PROGRESS CHECK

Determining Central Ideas How were the causes of World War I and World War II similar? How were the causes different?

Hulton Archive/Getty Images

Nazi soldiers post a notice urging Germans not to buy from this establishment because it is owned by a Jew. Nazi actions against Jews became violent.

▶ CRITICAL THINKING

Describing What was the Holocaust?

FOLDABLES
Study Organizer

Include this lesson's information in your Foldable®.

LESSON 2 REVIEW

Reviewing Vocabulary
1. Describe how *feudalism* worked.

Answering the Guiding Questions
2. *Identifying* What was the economic result of the plague?

3. *Determining Central Ideas* How did thinking change during the historical period known as the Enlightenment?

4. *Analyzing* How did the Industrial Revolution change life in Western Europe?

5. *Identifying* What factors led to World War I?

6. *Informative/Explanatory Writing* Write a paragraph to discuss this statement: The printing press was one of the greatest inventions in history. Explain why you agree or disagree with the statement.

Chapter 11 **349**

W Writing Skills

Argument Discuss with students how becoming industrialized advanced Western European economies and enabled the region to make an impact globally. However, technology and industrialization also enabled nations to make more powerful weapons. Have students write a short essay about their feelings on the industrialized advances that they have learned about in this lesson. Ask students to consider:

- *Was industrialization worthwhile?*
- *Were the benefits worth the cost?*

(Students' essays will vary but should be supported with specific examples and show a clear evaluation of how industrialization was good or bad for Western Europe's advancement.) BL
Interpersonal

C Critical Thinking Skills

Evaluating As a class, have volunteers take turns reading the section on the Cold War. Discuss the similarities and differences between the Cold War and World War I and World War II. **Ask:**

- What cause of the Cold War was similar to a cause of World War II? *(Possible answer: both wars were over gaining control of other countries or regions.)*
- What was the major difference between the Cold War and both World War I and World War II ? *(The Cold War was a conflict that never erupted into war.)* **Visual/Spatial**

CLOSE & REFLECT

Making Connections To close this lesson, have students think about how different cultures made Western Europe unique, and how Western Europe advanced through technology and industrialization.

LESSON 2 REVIEW ANSWERS

Reviewing Vocabulary

1. Kings gave land to nobles. In return, nobles served in the kings' military.

Answering the Guiding Questions

2. **Identifying** The plague wiped out towns. Victims stayed in monasteries and hospitals run by Roman Catholic officials.

3. **Determining Central Ideas** Possible answer: People emphasized the importance of reason to describe the world around them.

4. **Analyzing** Possible answers: Fewer goods were handmade by people living in small villages. More goods were produced on machines. Most of the machines were housed in factories that were located in cities. More people started moving to the cities so they could work in factories. The Industrial Revolution made Britain the most powerful nation in Western Europe.

5. **Identifying** France and Britain were allies with Russia. Germany allied with Austria-Hungary. When a Serbian nationalist assassinated the Archduke of Austria-Hungary, Austria-Hungary declared war on Serbia. Russia sided with Serbia, which meant that France and Britain were drawn into war against Austria-Hungary. Germany sided with Austria-Hungary.

6. **Informative/Explanatory** Paragraphs should include valid reasons in support of the position taken.

ANSWERS, p. 349

CRITICAL THINKING the murder of 6 million Jews by Hitler's Nazis

☑ READING PROGRESS CHECK Possible answer: The causes for World War I and World War II were similar in that both were sparked by strong feelings of nationalistic pride. Some of this pride was because of each country's colonial expansion; some was because of each country's economic power in World War I. This same pride in Germans caused them to believe they were a superior race when they started World War II. The causes were different because in World War I many countries were filled with nationalistic pride, but in World War II, it was the pride of Germans that led to the war.

ENGAGE

Bellringer Before students begin the lesson, discuss historical landmarks and why people preserve the past in such landmarks. **Ask:** Have you ever visited a historical landmark or tourist attraction? What was special or unique about it?

Make a list of students' responses on the board. Then, **ask:** What made you want to visit the attraction or the city? What did you learn?

Ask students to tell a partner why they visited the place, a unique fact about it, or something they learned that was interesting.

TEACH & ASSESS

R Reading Skills

Reinforcing Vocabulary Remind students to add academic and content vocabulary words to the vocabulary lists in their notebooks. Tell students to write their own definitions, and encourage them to include any sketches or example sentences that will remind them of how to use the word. This activity can be done as students encounter the words during class or can be completed as homework. **ELL AL** Verbal/Linguistic

V Visual Skills

Create Maps Have students work with a partner to create a map that shows the member nations of the European Community (EC) that represent Western Europe. Point out that students should make a map key because on the next page they will add the Western European members of the European Union (EU) to their maps, as not all members of the EU are members of the EC. Discuss as a class the benefits of this united effort by European countries. **ELL BL** Visual/Spatial

---

There's More Online!

☑ **GRAPHIC ORGANIZER**
☑ **IMAGE** Dublin, Ireland
☑ **MAP** Empires: Western Europe
☑ **VIDEO**

Reading HELPDESK

Academic Vocabulary

- **cooperate**
- **regulate**
- **diverse**

Content Vocabulary

- **postindustrial**

TAKING NOTES: *Key Ideas and Details*

Identify Use a graphic organizer like the one here to identify three characteristics of major European cities.

Major European Cities

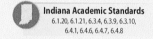

Indiana Academic Standards
6.1.20, 6.1.21, 6.3.4, 6.3.9, 6.3.10, 6.4.1, 6.4.6, 6.4.7, 6.4.8

350

Lesson 3
Life in Western Europe

ESSENTIAL QUESTION · *How do governments change?*

IT MATTERS BECAUSE
Western European nations recognize that in a global economy, they need to work together if their region is to prosper.

People, Places, and Cultures

GUIDING QUESTION *What are contributions of Western Europe to culture, education, and the arts?*

Western Europe's great cities are major population centers. They are also historical landmarks and tourist attractions. National capitals such as London, Dublin, Berlin, and Paris are among the world's most famous cities.

A Changing World

Political events in the 1900s threatened all of Europe. In order to survive and compete in a changing world, the nations of Western Europe needed to learn to work together.

When Western Europe began to rebuild after World War II, countries made efforts to **cooperate**. In April 1951, the Treaty of Paris called for an international agency to supervise the coal and steel industries in France, West Germany, Belgium, the Netherlands, Luxembourg, and Italy.

Those six nations then created the European Economic Community, or EEC, in 1958 to make trade among its member nations easier. The spirit of cooperation among these countries continued when they created the European Commission, or EC, in 1967. Two more Western European nations, the United Kingdom and Ireland, joined the EC in 1971. By the late 1980s, Denmark, Greece, Spain, and Portugal had also joined.

(l to r) Paul M O'Connell/Flickr/Getty Images; Buena Vista Images/The Image Bank/Getty Images

---

networks · *Online Teaching Options*

VIDEO

French School Lunches

Determining Cause and Effect Use this video about school life in France to discuss the reasons behind such elaborate lunches for public school students, including shopping for ingredients in local markets, preparation of meals by professional chefs, and a menu that focuses on French cultural dishes. Ask students to list the interesting facts that they learned while watching this video. **AL** Verbal/Linguistic

See page 331E for other online activities.

BBC Motion Gallery Education

ANSWER, p. 350

Taking Notes Major population centers; Historical landmarks; Tourist attractions

Forming the European Union

Those 12 nations formed the European Union, or EU, in 1993 with one goal being to strengthen trade among the countries of Europe. Member nations have control over their own political and economic decisions, but they also follow EU laws to **regulate** the use of natural resources and the release of pollutants. They also have agreements on law enforcement and security.

When the Soviets lost control of Eastern Europe in the late 1980s, those nations began forming their own governments. With the Soviet threat gone, East Germany and West Germany reunited. A united Germany became a strong voice in the EU.

The European Union now has 27 members. Eight of those nations lie in Western Europe: Austria, Belgium, France, Germany, Ireland, Luxembourg, the Netherlands, and the United Kingdom.

Ethnic and Language Groups

Celts, Saxons, Romans, Vikings, Visigoths, and others fought for dominance in ancient Western Europe. Those traditional ethnic divisions faded as the modern nations of Europe began to take shape. The people of a nation share a common language and a common history. Ethnic groups such as the French, the Germans, and the British rule entire countries. Their languages are the main languages of those nations.

Paul M O'Connell/Flickr/Getty Images

Academic Vocabulary

cooperate to act or work with others

regulate to adjust or control something according to rules or laws

O'Connell Street is Dublin, Ireland's, main thoroughfare. Dublin is among the world's most famous cities.

V1 Visual Skills

Create Maps Have students work with their partners to add to their maps the member nations of the European Community (EC) that represent Western European nations. They should also add the Western European members of the European Union (EU) to their maps and change their map keys to reflect this new information. Discuss as a class how the breakup of the Soviet Union affected membership in the EU. ELL BL Visual/Spatial

T Technology Skills

Creating Charts Divide the class into small groups. After they read the section on the European Union, ask them to search for economic data on the Internet about the European Union. Point out that students should use reliable sources and look for the most recent data available. Remind students that data can probably be found on the EU Web site. Ask students to create a chart based on the economic data that they find. They may show data over a period of time for all countries, or different economic data over a one-year time period for individual countries involved in the European Union. Allow 5 minutes for each group to present their charts to the class, explaining how the chart is set up, the data it shows, and conclusions they can draw about the data. Visual/Spatial, Interpersonal

C Critical Thinking Skills

Synthesizing Explain to students that when they synthesize information, they combine information from different parts of a text with what they already know about the subject into a whole or into one new main idea. **Ask:** How has the early history of Western Europe affected the languages and ethnicities of each country in the region? *(Possible answer: After the invasions by different groups, modern nations formed, each with a unique culture and a language common to most of the people who lived in each of those nations.)* Verbal/Linguistic

V2 Visual Skills

Visualizing Ask students to visualize what their town or city looks like in the business district or along the main thoroughfare. Then have them study the image and ask them to find several things in the picture of Dublin, Ireland, that are familiar and can be found in their own communities. **Ask:** How are towns and cities in Western Europe like those that are near to us? How are they different? *(Students' answers will vary but should demonstrate understanding of common buildings and infrastructure.)* Invite students to share their examples of how the image shows things that are like those in their communities. Visual/Spatial, Intrapersonal

---

CHART

Population Distribution: Western Europe

Analyze Charts Display the interactive chart on the whiteboard and discuss the population distribution and immigration into Western Europe. Have students write a paragraph that makes connections between why the areas that are the most densely populated are those areas that have received the most immigrants. BL

See page 331E for other online activities.

Interactive Charts/Tables/Diagrams

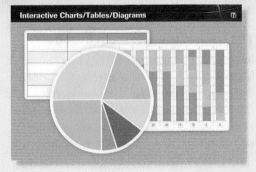

Life in Western Europe

V Visual Skills

Analyzing Ask students to think about how immigrants have contributed to the culture and economy of Western Europe. Have them analyze the photograph of the immigrant, and then **ask:** What kinds of jobs do you think this and other immigrants have? How is their work important to the economy of the region? *(Answers will vary but should indicate that immigrant workers can have blue- or white-collar jobs, and that immigrants are either filling a void in the workforce or may even be competing for jobs with citizens.)* **AL** Logical/ Mathematical

R Reading Skills

Listing Have students make a list of all of the religions that are practiced in Western Europe. Next to each religion on their list, have students write the names of the countries in which the religion is widely practiced. Then ask them to circle the religion that is the most widely practiced in the region. *(Christianity, Islam, Judaism; Christianity: France, United Kingdom, Germany, Ireland, Belgium; Islam and Judaism are not practiced widely in any one country but practiced throughout the region. Students should circle Christianity as the most widely practiced religion.)* **ELL** Verbal/Linguistic

Content Background Knowledge

Even though Corsica is nearer to the Italian Peninsula (only 56 miles west) than it is to France, the main language spoken on the island is French. This is due to the fact that Corsica became a province of France in 1769.

Despite the French influence, Corsican is a language that is also spoken on the island. Like French, it is a romance language. Even though only a small percentage of the island's population speaks Corsican, it remains important to the people of Corsica in preserving the culture and traditions of the island.

Employees prepare a food order at a fast-food restaurant that caters to the city's large Islamic population.

Identifying From what areas did many Muslims come to Western Europe?

Western Europe is home to significant numbers of other ethnic groups who are minorities in the country. Many are immigrants. They often speak the language of their homeland and continue their own culture and way of life.

Most people in the region speak one of the Indo-European languages. Indo-European is a family of related languages. It includes languages spoken in most of Europe, parts of the world that were colonized by Europeans, Persia, India, and some other parts of Asia.

Two major divisions of Indo-European languages spoken in Western Europe are Romance and Germanic. Romance languages are based on Latin, the language of the Roman Empire. The most common Romance language in Western Europe is French. The Germanic languages spoken in Western Europe include German, Dutch, and English, although about half of the English vocabulary comes from the Romance languages. Not all European languages are Indo-European, however. For example, Basque, a language spoken in the Pyrenees region of France and Spain, is unrelated to any other language spoken today. It is common for Western Europeans to speak more than one language—their native language in addition to English, French, or German.

Religion in Western Europe

Romans accepted Christianity, and Christian missionary-monks spread their religion during the Middle Ages. Christianity continues as Europe's major religion. Germany was the birthplace of the Protestant Reformation, and Western Europe was the first place that Protestantism took hold. Today, most Western European Christians are either Catholic or Protestant. The Roman Catholic faith is strongest in France, Ireland, and Belgium. Protestant churches are strongest in the United Kingdom and Germany.

Immigration from Africa and Asia has brought many Muslims to Western Europe, especially to the United Kingdom, France, Germany, Austria, the Netherlands, and Switzerland. Muslims follow the religion of Islam.

World War II and the Holocaust nearly wiped out Europe's Jewish population. Today, Europe's Jewish communities are growing in Western Europe, especially in France, the United Kingdom, and Germany.

netw⊛rks   *Online Teaching Options*

GRAPH

The Religions of Western Europe

Interpreting Show the graph on religions in Western Europe to students. Ask them which religion is the most widely practiced in the region. Then have them orally explain how the region's past might contribute to Christianity being the predominant religion in Western Europe. Visual/Spatial, Logical/Mathematical

See page 331E for other online activities.

Interactive Charts/Tables/Diagrams

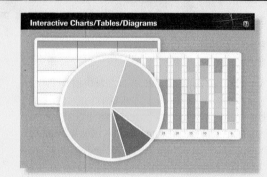

ANSWER, p. 352

Identifying from Africa and Asia

Literature, Music, and the Arts

For centuries, Western Europe has been a world leader in the arts and culture. As European explorers spread European culture to other parts of the globe, the names of their greatest artists became known worldwide. England's William Shakespeare is one of the most famous playwrights in the world, nearly 400 years after his death. The music of German and Austrian composers such as Bach, Mozart, Beethoven, and Schubert is among the most important in all of classical music. The paintings of great artists from France, the Netherlands, and Belgium are among the most treasured in the world.

The arts are an important part of Western European culture. Museums and cultural institutions celebrate each nation's art and history, and national governments support the arts. The German government, for example, funds hundreds of theaters, and concerts and plays attract large audiences. Most important is the influence Western European culture has had on the rest of the world. German architects from the Bauhaus School influenced buildings in cities throughout the 1900s. British popular music and television have had an impact, especially on American culture.

T

MAP SKILLS

1 **THE GEOGRAPHER'S WORLD** The original members of the EU are from what part of Europe?

2 **HUMAN GEOGRAPHY** From a geographical standpoint, would you predict that the EU in the future will grow, stay the same, or decrease in members? Explain.

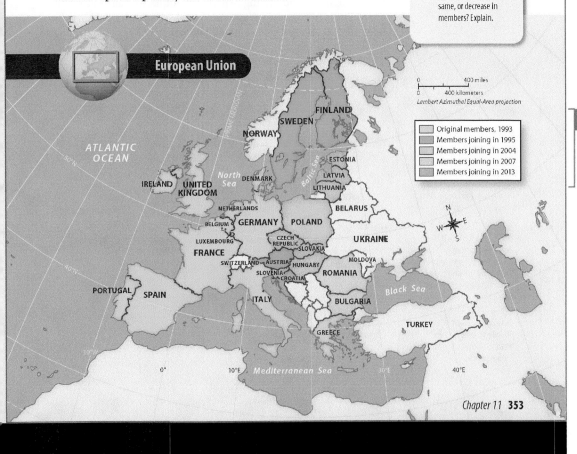

European Union

Original members, 1993
Members joining in 1995
Members joining in 2004
Members joining in 2007
Members joining in 2013

400 miles
400 kilometers
Lambert Azimuthal Equal-Area projection

MAP

The European Union

Making Connections Display the European Union map on the whiteboard. Use the different layers to discuss regional trade pacts and statistics such as gross domestic product (GDP). Have students make connections between those countries in the region that are members of economic pacts and their GDP. Ask them to explain which countries have the strongest economies based on the data in the map. **Visual/Spatial**

See page 331E for other online activities.

T **Technology Skills**

Classifying Read the paragraph on the art, literature, and music of Western Europe. Have students work with a partner to research additional artists, architects, writers, or musicians or styles or movements that came from or were influenced by Western Europe. Or you may want to assign pairs of students a particular artist or topic to research to avoid students duplicating one another.

Ask students to share their findings and write them on the board. Then add the following artists that are described in the text to the list, and have students classify the information in a chart: William Shakespeare, Bach, Mozart, Beethoven, Schubert, and Bauhaus. **Ask:** What headings did you use to classify the information? Were you surprised by how many contributions Western Europe has made in these areas? *(Possible answer: Artists, Architects, Musicians, Writers; Yes, I was surprised. I did not realize that so many famous people in these areas came from Western Europe.)* **BL** **Verbal/Linguistic**

V

V **Visual Skills**

Analyzing Maps Have students make a five-column chart with the years that are given in the map key as the five headings. Next have students use the map to identify the European countries that joined the European Union in one of the five years and list the names of those countries under the correct year. Then have students list the countries that have not joined the EU under their chart.

Ask students to use their charts and the map to write three to five questions about the European Union on one piece of paper and the answers to their questions on another piece of paper. Have partners exchange and answer each other's questions and make constructive comments on how to word questions more clearly, make questions more challenging, or make them simpler. **Ask:** How does writing your own questions help you remember the content better? *(Student answers will vary, but should include that writing questions makes them think more about the content than just answering questions in the text.)* **Verbal/Linguistic**

ANSWERS, p. 353

MAP SKILLS
1. Original members of the EU are from Western Europe.
2. Grow slightly as the majority of nations already belong to the EU, but there are still a few that have not joined.

Life in Western Europe

C Critical Thinking Skills

Comparing Before reading the section on daily life in Western Europe, **ask:** What sports do you watch, play at school, or play as recreation with friends or family? *(Answers will vary but should indicate a recreational sport that is televised or played by middle school students.)*

Then read the section "Daily Life" with students. **Ask:**

- Were any of the sports that you read about the same as the ones you play or watch in the United States? If so, which ones? *(Possible answer: Yes, I play soccer and I watch ice skating and other winter sports on television.)*

- Were any of the sports that you read about different than the ones you play or watch in the United States? If so, which ones? *(Possible answer: I have never seen or played cricket or rugby.)* **ELL** Intrapersonal

V Visual Skills

Analyzing Charts Ask students to study the chart of European roots of English words. Have the students work in pairs to make flash cards of the word roots and their meanings. **Ask:** What new words can you make after knowing what these word roots mean? *(Students' answers will vary but should use the word roots and be actual words.)*

Make a class chart of the words that students brainstorm. Have them practice using the words in a sentence. **ELL** Verbal/ Linguistic

Content Background Knowledge

France's TGV (Train à Grande Vitesse, or "high-speed train") is the fastest train in Europe and one of the world's fastest trains. In 2007 it became the fastest train when it reached a speed of 357 miles per hour. However since then, Japan's magnetic levitation train, which does not connect with the rail, took the record for the fastest train of any kind. Its record speed is just slightly faster than the TGV.

ANSWERS, p. 354

CRITICAL THINKING
1. **telescope**—to see far; **telecast**—to send far
2. **microphone**—improving a small voice; **megaphone**—making a voice large

---

Daily Life

The most popular team sport across Western Europe is football— what Americans call soccer. Professional leagues have formed throughout Western Europe. In the United Kingdom, cricket and rugby are popular team sports. Switzerland and Austria's rugged Alps and plentiful winter snow make mountain climbing, skating, downhill skiing, and cross-country skiing popular in both countries.

Because so much of the population of Western Europe lives in cities, roads are crowded. Automobile traffic and pollution are extensive in parts of the region. In Switzerland, traffic congestion has created serious air pollution in the Alpine valleys. To relieve congestion and address problems with pollution, much of Europe turned to high-speed rail travel.

In many areas, tradition is part of their everyday lives. The people of Scotland and Wales, for example, take pride in their ancient languages—Scottish Gaelic in Scotland and Welsh in Wales. These languages are taught in schools to keep the old cultures alive.

Railways and Highways

Europeans first began riding high-speed rail lines in France in 1981. France went on to build a high-speed line connecting all of its major cities. These trains travel at speeds of up to 185 miles (298 km) per hour. In the 1990s, the French high-speed rail lines began connecting to other high-speed rail lines: from Paris to London via a tunnel beneath the English Channel, from Paris to the Netherlands, and from Paris to Brussels, Belgium.

CHART SKILLS >

ENGLISH WORDS FROM OTHER LANGUAGES

Many of the words we use every day are derived from French or German. Many words that are used in fields of science, law, and medicine have Greek or Latin roots.

French	German	Latin	Greek
ballet	kindergarten	a.m. /p.m.	atmosphere
denim	blitz	census	comedy
garage	poltergeist	millennium	democracy
infantry	noodle	lunar	geography
salon	hamster	solar	pediatrician
	pretzel		

▶ **CRITICAL THINKING**
1. ***Determining Word Meanings*** The word *telephone* is derived from the Greek prefix *tele* (far) and the suffix *phone* (voice). Determine the meaning of the words: *telescope* and *telecast.*
2. ***Determining Word Meanings*** Determine the meaning of the words: *microphone* and *megaphone.*

Here are other English words derived from other languages:

African: banana, cola, jazz, zebra

Arabic: algebra, chemistry

Spanish: breeze, canyon, mesa

Japanese: anime, tycoon, tsunami

Norwegian: fjord, ski, slalom

---

netw⚙rks   *Online Teaching Options*

MAP

Language: Western Europe

Analyze Maps Display the map of languages spoken in Western Europe. Ask students to look at the regions where similar languages are spoken and then compare those results to the charts that show European roots of English words. Ask them to write a paragraph to explain any connections. **BL** Visual/Spatial, Logical/ Mathematical

See page 331E for other online activities.

Life in Western Europe

A well-developed highway system also links Europe's major cities. Germany's superhighways, called autobahns, are among Europe's best roads. Many European countries are participating in the Forever Open Roads project. By combining efforts to develop innovative technology, the planners are working to transform the way roads are designed, built, and maintained in the twenty-first century.

The Louvre in Paris, France, is one of the world's great museums and the most-visited art museum in the world.

Education

Western Europe is one of the wealthiest, most urban, and well-educated regions in the world. In most of Western Europe, school is mandatory until students reach the age of 16, but many students then attend college.

Western Europe contains some of the oldest and most renowned universities. Oxford University in England and the University of Paris opened their doors to students before 1200. Many universities started at this time after Pope Gregory VII issued a ruling calling for the creation of schools of education for the clergy. Hundreds of secular colleges—those without religious affiliation—were established by the 1400s.

☑ **READING PROGRESS CHECK**

Describing In what ways do nations of Western Europe support art and culture?

Chapter 11 **355**

Buena Vista Images/The Image Bank/Getty Images

V Visual Skills

Analyzing Visuals Have students take a few minutes and study the picture in the text with their neighbor. Have them analyze the paintings shown and then ask volunteers to try to describe what era they may come from. Remind them of the Renaissance and the Enlightenment eras discussed in lesson 2. **Ask:**

• How does this famous painting, Mona Lisa by Leonardo da Vinci, which is housed in the Louvre museum illustrate the importance of art in French culture? *(Possible answer: It shows that art is extremely important to the French culture and that the French believe in sharing art and art history with visitors from around the world.)*

• Why do you think that the picture is protected and barriers have been put up to keep people from getting too close to the painting? *(Possible answer: The painting is very valuable and the museum wants to preserve and protect it.)* **Logical/Mathematical**

C Critical Thinking Skills

Comparing and Contrasting After students read about the section on education in Western Europe, **ask:** How is school for young people in Western Europe similar to school in the United States? *(In the United States, students are required to attend school until age 16, and in Western Europe they are required to attend school until age 16; Many students in both the United States and Western Europe attend college.)*

Invite students to share their examples of how the text shows things that are like those in their communities. **Verbal/Linguistic, Intrapersonal**

Content Background Knowledge

Share the following facts about the Mona Lisa with students:

• We still do not know who the woman in the painting was.

• Leonardo Da Vinci worked on and off for about four years painting the portrait.

• In 1911 the painting was stolen from the Louvre Museum. It was found 2 years later.

• In 1956 the painting was damaged when a man threw a rock at it.

IMAGE

360° View: The Louvre

Analyze Images Display the 360° image of the Louvre museum. Ask students if they have ever visited a museum like the one in the photograph. Invite students to compare and contrast the types of structures and items that they have seen in a museum with those in the image. They may do this orally or draw sketches. **ELL** **Visual/Spatial**

See page 331E for other online activities.

Peter Zelei/Vetta/Getty Images

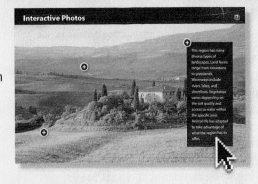

Interactive Photos

ANSWER, p. 355

☑ **READING PROGRESS CHECK** The governments support the arts. Museums and cultural institutions display the art of that country.

See page 331E for other online activities.

R Reading Skills

Citing Text Evidence Read the Guiding Question and first paragraph with students. Explain to them that citing text evidence to support a claim or argument is an important skill. Model for them how to cite text evidence. **Ask: What recent global event affected the economy of Western Europe?** *(Students' answers will vary.)*

Point out that students should go back into the text to find the answer and then to use the wording from the text in their response. Let students try out this skill on their own. **Ask: Which countries in Western Europe have the biggest economies?** *(France, Germany, and the United Kingdom have the biggest economies in Western Europe.)* **AL** Verbal/Linguistic

T Technology Skills

Making Presentations Have students work in small groups to present economic information on one nation in Western Europe. Students may use the Internet and other resources to do their research and computer presentation software for their final presentations.

Have students use the following question to guide their research: **What economic activities are most important to the nation?**

Remind students that using graphs and charts to show economic data is one way of communicating information as well as showing images. While each group is presenting, have students in the audience take notes. After all groups have presented, have students use their notes in a class discussion to compare and contrast the economic activities of the Western European nations presented by students. **BL** Verbal/Linguistic, Auditory/Musical

V Visual Skills

Analyzing Maps Have three small groups of students research one of the Western European empires as it existed in 1914. Have groups use their research and the map to explain each empire and how it controlled parts of the world at that time. Visual/Spatial

---

ANSWERS, p. 356

MAP SKILLS

1. the British empire
2. The world wars took a great toll on the British, French, and German empires. Germany was stripped of its colonies, and British and French colonies sought independence.

Current Challenges

GUIDING QUESTION *Why is Western Europe considered a postindustrial region?*

R France, Germany, and the United Kingdom are not the military giants they were in 1900, but they still have some of the biggest economies in the world. A global financial crisis, however, has hurt the entire region since the early 2000s.

Earning a Living

Since the Industrial Revolution, improvements in agriculture have made it possible for fewer people to cultivate larger areas of land. Today, more than half the population of Western Europe lives and works in cities. Even in France, Western Europe's leading agricultural nation, less than 4 percent of the workforce works in agriculture.

In the past few decades, the number of industrial workers has also declined. Only about 25 percent of Western Europeans work in the industrial, or secondary sector, of the economy. Many more people work in the tertiary sector, which is service industries. This sector includes government, education, health care, banking and financial services, retail, computing, and repair of mechanical equipment. The United Kingdom was the birthplace of modern industry. Yet today, only 18.2 percent of the workforce in the United Kingdom works in industry. **T**

MAP SKILLS

1. **THE GEOGRAPHER'S WORLD** Which empire controlled the largest territory?

2. **THE GEOGRAPHER'S WORLD** What effect do you think world wars had on the British, French, and German empires?

V **Western European Empires, 1914**

Legend:
- British Empire
- French Empire
- German Empire

0 — 2,000 miles
0 — 2,000 kilometers
Miller projection

---

netw⊕rks *Online Teaching Options*

MAP

Empires of Western Europe

Analyze Maps Display the map of the empires of Western Europe on the whiteboard. Have students take turns pointing out changes that they see in different areas of the map between 1914 and the present, such as new nations and boundaries. Ask them what key events may have caused these changes. Encourage students to write down their answers for comparison when chapters that discuss these countries are discussed. **AL** Visual/Spatial

When the economy of a country depends more on services than it does on industry, that country is said to be **postindustrial**. Every nation in Western Europe has a postindustrial economy.

Challenges

For hundreds of years, the nations of Western Europe were among the most powerful in the world. In 1900 Great Britain, France, and Germany ruled over empires that extended beyond Europe to Asia, Africa, the Americas, and the Pacific Islands. The 1900s was hard on Western Europe. The two world wars did extensive damage to nearly the entire region. Then the Cold War kept Western Europe on the brink of war for more than 40 years.

Even so, Germany, France, and the United Kingdom have been economically strong for a long time and remain among the seven biggest economies in the world. The cooperation made possible by the European Union helps Western European nations compete with larger economies, such as the United States, China, and Japan. For that to continue, the economies of all the EU member nations must be healthy. The global financial crisis of 2008, however, had an impact on all of Europe. Governments of the EU disagreed about how to deal with ongoing financial problems.

R

Immigration Brings Changes

The population of Western Europe is changing. Most population growth in Western Europe is caused by immigration. Many people come to Western Europe from Africa, Asia, and Eastern Europe looking for job opportunities or trying to escape political oppression. When they immigrate, they bring parts of their culture with them, including their religions. Germany, France, the Netherlands, and the United Kingdom each have large Muslim populations. The mix of European and immigrant cultures creates a richer, more **diverse** culture, but it also creates racial and religious tensions. To avoid these problems, some countries have attempted to restrict immigration.

W

Academic Vocabulary

diverse different from each other

Include this lesson's information in your Foldable®.

✓ **READING PROGRESS CHECK**

Determining Central Ideas What challenges do the nations of Western Europe face?

LESSON 3 REVIEW

Reviewing Vocabulary
1. Define *postindustrial* as it relates to industry and services.

Answering the Guiding Questions
2. ***Identifying*** Name one advantage and one disadvantage resulting from the creation of the European Union.

3. ***Analyzing*** How did the collapse of the Soviet Union affect the European Union?

4. ***Determining Central Ideas*** Why is Western Europe considered a postindustrial region?

5. ***Argument Writing*** Write an open letter to the nations of Western Europe explaining the need to form the European Union.

LESSON 3 REVIEW ANSWERS

Reviewing Vocabulary

1. An economy that depends more on services than on industry is called postindustrial.

Answering the Guiding Questions

2. **Identifying** One advantage of the European Union is in having a single monetary system. One disadvantage is the loss of each country's unique monetary system.

3. **Analyzing** West Germany was able to reunite with East Germany. Countries that were once under Soviet rule could join the EU.

4. **Determining Central Ideas** It is a postindustrial region because the economy of every nation in Western Europe depends more on services than it does industry.

5. **Argument** Responses should be in the form of a letter. Students' letters should include the following points: the more they cooperate, the less likely they will be to go to war. They need to combine their economic strength to compete with larger economies, such as those of the United States, China, and Japan.

R **Reading Skills**

Making Connections Have students connect the content of the section "Challenges" to the map on page 356. **Ask:** What besides the two world wars in the 1900s impacted the region of Western Europe? How did the Cold War affect Western Europe? *(the Cold War; it kept Western Europe on the brink of war for more than 40 years)* **AL** **Verbal/Linguistic**

W **Writing Skills**

Argument Review with students some of the challenges that Western Europe has had to face with increasing immigration. Some people think that there should be restrictions on immigration to the nations of Western Europe. Others think there should no limitations. Ask them to respond to this writing prompt: **Should the countries of Western Europe restrict immigration or continue to allow immigrants to arrive without any limitations?**

Provide time for students to do additional research to support their claim. Remind them to follow these guidelines when writing their essays.

- introduce your argument clearly
- support your argument with strong reasons and relevant evidence
- use credible sources and cite information correctly
- include a concluding statement and restate your argument

(Students' essays will vary but should provide a clear argument, offer supporting reasons and evidence, and include an introduction and conclusion.) **Verbal/Linguistic**

CLOSE & REFLECT

Making Connections To close this lesson, have students think about the world powers that have emerged from Western Europe and the economic unity the region's nations have fostered in recent years.

ANSWER, p. 357

✓ **READING PROGRESS CHECK** Western European nations have to compete with nations with larger economies. They were hurt in the financial crisis of 2008. Immigration has created tensions among the people.

ENGAGE

Bellringer Before students read the "What Do You Think?" feature, explain that this debate will center around the European Union's single currency, single market, joint plans for easier travel and marketing, and their economic benefits. **Ask:** Have you or your family members ever joined an organization or group to work together to achieve certain benefits and then it turned out that you had to make sacrifices that you never expected? *(Students' answers will vary but should include an understanding of membership in a group and working together for the good of the group, even when it means making sacrifices.)*

TEACH & ASSESS

R Reading Skills

Summarizing Have students identify the question that will be debated. Then ask them to summarize why the European Union's economic plan is an issue. Invite a few students to share their summaries with the class as a model. **Ask:** Why would a plan using a single currency benefit travelers and also businesses? *(Possible answer: Travelers would not have to exchange their money every time they entered a new country, which would encourage them to spend more money than if they had to exchange currency.)* **ELL**

C Critical Thinking Skills

Recognizing Bias Explain to students that different propaganda devices are used to persuade readers to agree with a writer's position. Inclusion, generalizations, or avoidance of facts can persuade a reader. "It is absolutely clear that nothing of that sort has happened" is a generalization that the writer uses to persuade the reader. Excluding specific data on inflation rates and the negative effects of creating the eurozone does not make the writer's argument as credible.

Stating opinions that are supported by hard facts that can be verified in credible sources can make an argument trustworthy. By citing and understanding the tools of persuasion, an informed judgment about the information and opinions presented can be made. **Ask:** What specific facts could Klaus have included to make his argument more credible? *(Sample answer: Klaus could have included specific data on inflation rates and the decline in economic growth of the EU member states after the creation of the eurozone.)* Verbal/Linguistic, Logical/Mathematical

---

What Do You Think?

Is the European Union an Effective Economic Union?

R The European Union was formed to build peace among its member states, but it also aims to build prosperity. In the 1990s, member states agreed to do away with trade barriers, create a single market, and make the euro their common currency. But the global financial crisis of 2008 hurt the EU greatly. Greece, Ireland, and Portugal needed bailouts to cover their huge debts. Italy and Spain struggled economically, too. EU leaders disagreed over how to respond to the crisis, and tensions still exist.

No!
PRIMARY SOURCE

C " The creation of the eurozone was presented as an unambiguous [clear] economic benefit to all the countries willing to give up their own currencies that had been in existence for decades or centuries. …[S]tudies promised that the euro would help accelerate economic growth and reduce inflation and stressed … that the member states of the eurozone would be protected against all kinds of unfavorable economic disruptions … It is absolutely clear that nothing of that sort has happened. After the establishment of the eurozone, the economic growth of its member states slowed down … Two distinct groups of countries have formed within the eurozone—one with a low inflation rate and one (Greece, Spain, Portugal, Ireland and some other countries) with a higher inflation rate. … [T]he economic performance of individual eurozone members diverged [went in different directions] and the negative effects of the 'straight-jacket' of a single currency over the individual member states have become visible. … [A]s a project that promised to be of considerable economic benefit to its members, the eurozone has failed." "

—Václav Klaus, president of the Czech Republic

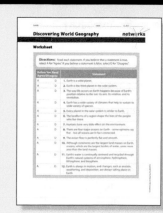

Italians protest their government's 2011 economic reforms and austerity measures.

TEXT: From "WHEN WILL THE EUROZONE COLLAPSE?" by Václav Klaus. Published May 26, 2010, Cato Institute Economic Bulletin No 14. Payable to the Cato Institute; PHOTO: Giorgio Cosulich/Getty Images News/Getty Images

358 Chapter 11

---

netwerks *Online Teaching Options*

WORKSHEET

How to Analyze a Primary Source

Analyzing Primary Sources Have students use the worksheet from the resource library to analyze the viewpoint and perspective in each primary source. Remind students to look for the bias shown in the arguments and to be aware of the persuasive tools the speakers use to appeal to their readers. **BL** Verbal/Linguistic

Cargo containers at Felixstowe in the United Kingdom are prepared for transfer to cargo ships.

Yes!
PRIMARY SOURCE

" [T]he single market has transformed for the better many aspects of European life. . . . People move freely across most borders. . . . Going to work in another Member State is much easier. . . . Goods are no longer delayed for hours or days at borders by heavy paperwork: this makes delivery times shorter, allowing manufacturers to save money and reduce prices for customers. . . . Consumer choice is vast: the range of products on sale across the EU is wider than ever and in most cases prices are easily compared thanks to the euro. Manufacturers have to keep prices down because they are selling into one huge competitive market. . . . Capital—the investment that businesses need to start and to grow—flows easily within the single market, sustaining companies and generating jobs. "

—The European Commission

What Do You Think? DBQ

1. **Determining Central Ideas** How has the EU's single market benefited travelers, workers, consumers, and manufacturers?

2. **Identifying Point of View** Why does Václav Klaus consider the EU's single currency to be a "straight-jacket"?

Critical Thinking

3. **Analyzing** Some people think the eurozone will dissolve. Others, including Václav Klaus, believe that it will survive, especially if new rules force member countries to behave responsibly. What factors might affect what happens in the future?

Chapter 11 **359**

WORKSHEET

Yes or No?

Defending Have students use the worksheet from the resource library to outline their own rebuttal to one of the writer's arguments. Students should make a claim to either agree or disagree with the writer and then list three details or reasons to support their claim. **AL** **ELL** Interpersonal

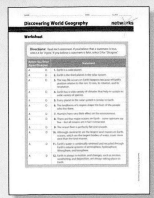

What Do You Think?

C Critical Thinking Skills

Recognizing Bias Have students read the opposing point of view on this page and identify examples of bias that the writer uses to sway readers. Explain that students need to evaluate text such as this, whether it is in print or in a speech, to understand that they are being manipulated. **Ask:** How does the writer's use of inclusion or avoidance of particular facts make you feel about the eurozone? Identify some examples of inclusion or avoidance of facts. *(Students' answers will vary but should demonstrate an understanding of propaganda techniques that include or exclude facts to persuade readers.)* Interpersonal, Verbal/Linguistic

W Writing Skills

Informative/Explanatory Have students write a paragraph that identifies a generalization and a fact used in the Yes! argument, and have them explain the difference between the two. Encourage students to tell how they can watch for this type of journalism and avoid being manipulated by others. *(Students' paragraphs should cite a generalization and a hard fact that can be proven. Students' answers should demonstrate the understanding of the use of propaganda techniques to influence readers and how to avoid being manipulated.)* Interpersonal, Verbal/Linguistic

CLOSE & REFLECT

Have students choose one side of the issue and divide the class into the two groups. Have each group give a three-minute summary of their side of the issue. After both sides have given their summary, have each side give a response to the other side's summary, challenging the points that they made. Remind students to be polite in their challenges and to focus as much as possible on facts rather than opinions.

ANSWERS, p. 359

DBQ What Do You Think?

1. Cross-border travel is easier; work and investment opportunities are greater; goods can be sold more cheaply and easily; consumers have more choices of products and can compare prices easily.
2. He thinks a single currency is too confining because member countries have different economic circumstances.
3. Possible answers: changes in EU policies; changes in political leadership; the cost of abandoning the euro; the resistance of stronger economies to helping weaker ones; developments in the global economic situation.

CHAPTER REVIEW ACTIVITY

Have students create a word web like the one below with "Western Europe" in the center circle. Tell students to complete the chart with examples about the region's physical geography, climate, natural resources, history, economy, culture, and challenges. *(Possible answers: **Geography:** low-lying plains, valleys, Pyrenees, Alps, North Sea, English Channel, Thames River, Danube River, Rhine River, Elbe River, Northern European Plain; **Climate:** mild, wet, Mediterranean area-dry; **Natural Resources:** Coal, soil, peat, oil, natural gas; **History:** Roman Empire, development of France and England, invaded by different groups, emergence of Christianity, Crusades, division of Christian Church, Enlightenment, French Revolution, Industrial Revolution, world wars, Cold War; **Economy:** EC, EU, economic cooperation, from agricultural to manufacturing to services economy **Culture:** Christianity is dominant but Judaism and Islam are also practiced, Bach, Beethoven, Schubert, Mozart, William Shakespeare, Bauhaus, football; **Challenges:** immigration, global financial crisis in early 2008)*

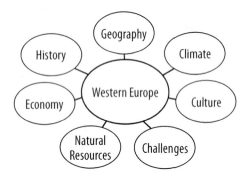

REVIEW THE ENDURING UNDERSTANDINGS

Review this chapter's Enduring Understandings with students:

• *People, places, and ideas change over time.*

Now pose the following questions in a class discussion to apply this to the chapter.

• How have the people benefitted from the region's geography and natural resources? *(Sample answers: They have used the natural resources in the region for agricultural and energy production. The geography of the region makes it easier for the countries to have closer economic ties, which has helped foster economic agreements.)*

• Why did many different countries form in Western Europe after the Roman civilization fell? *(Possible answer: Different groups such as the Visigoths, Franks, and Angles and Saxons came to the region and dominated small areas that later became individual countries such as England, France, and kingdoms in Prussia (later united to form Germany.)*

• What solutions would you suggest to the European Union as it deals with challenges resulting from the global financial crisis? *(Sample answer: Countries should work together and find solutions that will enable the weaker economies of EU member nations to grow stronger. This may negatively affect the stronger economies at least for a while, but in the long-term it will be better for the entire region.)*

Directions: Write your answers on a separate piece of paper.

1 Use your **FOLDABLES** to explore the Essential Question.
INFORMATIVE/EXPLANATORY WRITING Write an essay explaining how the physical geography and the climate of Western Europe influenced the development of agriculture in the region.

2 **21st Century Skills**
INTEGRATING VISUAL INFORMATION Working in small groups, choose any country in Western Europe and create a slide show depicting the country's landforms, waterways, and natural resources. Include images of the country's capital city. Describe at least one cultural tradition or holiday that is not familiar to you or to most Americans.

3 **Thinking Like a Geographer**
INTEGRATING VISUAL INFORMATION Fill in this graphic organizer to help you remember the climates of Western European countries.

Climate	Characteristics

4 **GEOGRAPHY ACTIVITY**

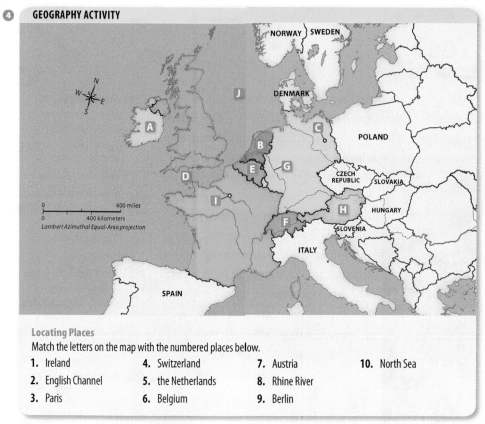

Locating Places
Match the letters on the map with the numbered places below.

1. Ireland
2. English Channel
3. Paris
4. Switzerland
5. the Netherlands
6. Belgium
7. Austria
8. Rhine River
9. Berlin
10. North Sea

ACTIVITIES ANSWERS
Determining Central Ideas

1 **INFORMATIVE/ EXPLANATORY WRITING** Students should make sure that they give facts, such as: the climate is mild and good for growing, but the land is somewhat rocky, so farms are generally small. France and Italy are noted for growing grapes and olives for wine and olive oils. Forests and grasslands are abundant, and there is a lot of dairy farming.

REVIEW THE GUIDING QUESTIONS

Directions: Choose the best answer for each question.

1 People in the Netherlands build dikes and reclaim land from the sea that they call
   A. peat bogs.
   B. estuaries.
   C. polders.
   D. reserves.

2 Which two mountain ranges separate Western Europe from Southern Europe?
   F. Alps and Urals
   G. Pyrenees and Alps
   H. Middle Rhine Highlands and Carpathians
   I. Tian Shan and Apennines

3 In which Western European country did the Industrial Revolution begin?
   A. Germany
   B. France
   C. the Netherlands
   D. Great Britain

4 The system of land ownership and farming during the Middle Ages was called
   F. pilgrimage.
   G. channeling.
   H. feudalism.
   I. slavery.

5 The Industrial Revolution resulted in
   A. a shortage of workers on farms.
   B. a great migration of people from rural areas to cities.
   C. more time for people to spend with their families.
   D. handmade goods.

6 Many Europeans now work in the tertiary sector, which includes
   F. factory work.
   G. construction.
   H. retail sales.
   I. mining.

Chapter 11 **361**

21st Century Skills

2 **INTEGRATING VISUAL INFORMATION** Students can obtain most of their slide shows from Internet sources. Tell them to verify the unfamiliar cultural tradition or holiday. Groups can present their slide shows for the rest of the class.

Thinking Like a Geographer

3 **INTEGRATING VISUAL INFORMATION** Marine West Coast characteristics: westerlies blow warm air from west to east, picking it up from the Gulf Stream and becoming the North Atlantic Current; warm moist air brings mild temperatures and rain throughout year; cool summers; mild winters; Mediterranean characteristics: summers hot and dry, winters mild and cool, most rainfall in spring and autumn

Geography Activity

4 **LOCATING PLACES**

1. A	**6.** E
2. D	**7.** H
3. I	**8.** G
4. F	**9.** C
5. B	**10.** J

ASSESSMENT ANSWERS

Review the Guiding Questions

1 **C** For this question, students will need to look for a word that is unique to the Netherlands. Peat bogs are unique to England and are a resource. An estuary is where the tide meets a river stream. Reserves would not be a sensible answer. They do not come from the sea, which makes answer choice C the only possible correct answer.

2 **G** Refer students to the chapter opener map so that they can identify the two mountain ranges, the Pyrenees and the Alps (answer choice G), as the ranges that separate Western and Southern Europe.

3 **D** To answer this question, students should think about the geography of the four countries listed as answer choice options. Logically, a country that is cut off from other nations might be motivated to produce its own manufactured goods. Of all the answer choices, Great Britain is the only island nation.

4 **H** Point out to students that they can eliminate answer choice G because the definition of the word relates to digging and producing a channel, which has nothing to do with land ownership. Answer choice F relates to a religious tradition, which rules it out as an option. Slavery is not mentioned in the chapter and deals with forcing people to do work without pay. Enslaved people have no land ownership. This makes answer choice H, feudalism, the only correct answer choice.

5 **B** Remind students that prior to the Industrial Revolution goods were handmade and most people lived in rural areas. During the Industrial Revolution people lived in cities and worked long hours. This will eliminate options C and D and focus on the correct answer B.

6 **H** Have students who do not answer correctly review the section "Earning a Living" in Lesson 3.

DBQ Analyzing Documents

7 **A** The passage says that Ireland owes its greenness to the fact that it has a more temperate climate than other lands at the same latitude, so it is warmer than expected.

8 **G** Agriculture benefits because the mild climate promotes plant growth; tourism benefits because Ireland's warm climate and green appearance helps attract visitors. Students should be able to eliminate the other choices because manufacturing, finance, and mining are not influenced by outside temperatures.

Short Response

9 The European Union was created with the purpose of promoting trade among European nations and as a way of reducing the likelihood that they would fight each other in another war.

10 Possible answer: World War II was so destructive, resulting in so many deaths and so much damage to cities and European nations' economies, that Europe's leaders became convinced they had to take strong steps to prevent another war from occurring.

Extended Response

11 Students' writing should reflect what they have learned from the text and other sources. An opinion about whether or not the European Union has been successful should also be clearly stated. Students should at least point out that the region has been comparatively peaceful since World War II, so in the matter of preventing conflict between nations the Union has had success. However, the region has had ongoing economic problems, so the Union has not been completely successful. Students' writing should also be grammatically correct and clearly organized.

DBQ ANALYZING DOCUMENTS

7 **DETERMINING CENTRAL IDEAS** Read the following passage:

"*Intense green vegetation . . . covers most of [Ireland]. . . . Ireland owes its greenness to moderate temperatures and moist air. The Atlantic Ocean, particularly the warm currents in the North Atlantic Drift, gives the country a more temperate climate than most others at the same latitude.*"

—from NASA, Earth Observatory Web Site (2011)

Based on this passage, what is unusual about Ireland's climate?

A. warmer than expected given its latitude

B. colder than expected given its nearness to the ocean

C. wetter than expected given that it is an island

D. drier than expected given its northerly location

8 **ANALYZING** Which economic activities in Ireland most likely benefit most from this climate?

F. manufacturing and transportation

G. agriculture and tourism

H. finance and retailing

I. mining and fishing

SHORT RESPONSE

"*The European Union [EU] . . . was created in the aftermath of the Second World War. The first steps were to foster economic cooperation: the idea being that countries who trade with one another become economically interdependent and so more likely to avoid conflict.*"

—from European Union, "Basic Information" (2012)

9 **IDENTIFYING** What was the original purpose of the European Union?

10 **CITING TEXT EVIDENCE** Why did World War II convince European leaders to form the European Union?

EXTENDED RESPONSE

11 **INFORMATIVE/EXPLANATORY WRITING** Explain why more countries have joined the European Union since its founding and whether you think it has been successful.

Need Extra Help?

If You've Missed Question	**1**	**2**	**3**	**4**	**5**	**6**	**7**	**8**	**9**	**10**	**11**
Review Lesson	1	1	2	2	2	3	1	3	3	3	3

http://europa.eu ©European Union, 1995-2012

networks *Online Teaching Options*

Remediation and Assessment

Evaluating The *Assess* tab in the online Teacher Lesson Center includes resources to help students improve their test-taking skills. It also contains many project-based rubrics to help you assess students' work.

CHAPTER 12

Northern and Southern Europe
Planner

UNDERSTANDING BY DESIGN®

Enduring Understandings
- *People, places, and ideas change over time.*
- *Countries have relationships with each other.*

Essential Questions
- *How do people adapt to their environment?*
- *Why do civilizations rise and fall?*
- *How do ideas change the way people live?*

Predictable Misunderstandings
- *Northern and Southern Europe have the same geographic landscapes as Western Europe.*
- *Northern and Southern Europeans share the same languages and cultures as Western Europeans.*

Assessment Evidence

Performance Tasks:
- *Project-Based Learning Digital Hands-On Chapter Project*
- *Project-Based Learning Hands-On Chapter Project*

Other Evidence:
- *Geography Skills Activity*
- *Cultural Geography Activity*
- *Participation in Interactive Whiteboard Activities*
- *Contribution to small-group activities*
- *Interpretation of slide show images and special purpose maps*
- *Participation in class discussions about physical geography topics*
- *Lesson Reviews*
- *Chapter Assessments*

SUGGESTED PACING GUIDE

Introducing the Chapter.............. 2 Days	Lesson 3 .... 2 Days
Lesson 1 .... 2 Days	Global Connections................. 3 Days
Lesson 2 .... 2 Days	Chapter Wrap-Up and Assessment..... 2 Days

TOTAL TIME   13 Days

Key for Using the Teacher Edition

SKILL-BASED ACTIVITIES

Types of skill activities found in the Teacher Edition.

* **V Visual Skills** require students to analyze maps, graphs, charts, and photos.

W Writing Skills provide writing opportunities to help students comprehend the text.

R Reading Skills help students practice reading skills and master vocabulary.

C Critical Thinking Skills help students apply and extend what they have learned.

T Technology Skills require students to use digital tools effectively.

*Letters are followed by a number when there is more than one of the same type of skill on the page.

DIFFERENTIATED INSTRUCTION

All activities are written for the on-level student unless otherwise marked with the leveled labels below.

BL Beyond Level
AL Approaching Level
ELL English Language Learners

All students benefit from activities that utilize different learning styles. Many activities are marked as below when a particular learning style is highlighted.

Intrapersonal	Naturalist
Logical/Mathematical	Kinesthetic
Visual/Spatial	Auditory/Musical
Verbal/Linguistic	Interpersonal

Indiana Academic Standards

Students will:

6.1.1 Summarize the rise, decline, and cultural achievements of ancient civilizations in Europe and Mesoamerica.

6.1.2 Describe and compare the beliefs, the spread and the influence of religions throughout Europe and Mesoamerica.

6.1.3 Explain the continuation and contributions of the Eastern Roman Empire after the fall of the Western Roman Empire.

6.1.4 Identify and explain the development and organization of political, cultural, social and economic systems in Europe and the Americas.

6.1.6 Identify trade routes and discuss their impact on the rise of cultural centers and trade cities in Europe and Mesoamerica.

6.1.8 Compare the diverse perspectives, ideas, interests and people that brought about the Renaissance in Europe.

6.1.9 Analyze the interconnections of people, places and events in the economic, scientific and cultural exchanges of the European Renaissance that led to the Scientific Revolution, voyages of discovery and imperial conquest.

6.1.12 Describe the Reformations and their effects on European and American society.

6.2.2 Explain how elements of Greek direct democracy and Roman representative democracy are present in modern systems of government.

6.3.1 Demonstrate a broad understanding of the countries and capitals of Europe and the Americas.

6.3.4 Describe and compare major cultural characteristics of regions in Europe and the Western Hemisphere.

6.3.7 Locate and describe the climate regions of Europe and the Americas and explain how and why they differ.

6.3.8 Identify major biomes of Europe and the Americas and explain how these are influenced by climate.

6.3.10 Explain the ways cultural diffusion, invention, and innovation change culture.

6.3.12 Compare the distribution and evaluate the importance of natural resources such as natural gas, oil, forests, uranium, minerals, coal, seafood and water in Europe and the Americas.

6.4.7 Identify economic connections between the local community and the countries of Europe or the Americas and identify job skills needed to be successful in the workplace.

CHAPTER OPENER PLANNER

Students will know:

- *that Northern and Southern Europe have a different geography than Western Europe.*
- *that Northern and Southern Europeans have different history and culture.*
- *that Northern and Southern Europe have different languages.*
- *that Northern and Southern Europe share similar modern struggles as Western Europe.*

Students will be able to:

- ***analyze*** *a world map to identify countries of Northern and Southern Europe.*
- ***use a time line*** *to discuss various events in the history of Northern and Southern Europe.*

UNDERSTANDING
BY DESIGN®

☑ *Print Teaching Options*

V Visual Skills

☐ **P. 364** Students use a map of Northern and Southern Europe to identify countries and capitals and compare and contrast countries. `AL`

☐ **P. 365** Students use a time line to answer questions about the sequence of events in the history of Northern and Southern Europe. Visual/Spatial

C Critical Thinking Skills

☐ **P. 365** Students infer how printed books affected society during the Renaissance. Verbal/Linguistic

☑ *Online Teaching Options*

☐ `MAP` **Reading a Map**—Students identify aspects of the region and locations on a map.

☐ `TIME LINE` **Reading a Time Line and Map**—Students learn where and when historical events occurred in Northern and Southern Europe. Visual/Spatial

☐ `MAP` **Interactive World Atlas**—Students use the interactive world atlas to identify the peninsulas of Northern and Southern Europe and describe their terrain.

☑ *Printable Digital Worksheets*

☐ `WORKSHEET` **Cultural Geography Activity: Scandinavian Culture**—Students compare and contrast daily life of Northern Europe to Southern Europe using a collaborative worksheet, and use a Venn diagram to visualize their comparisons. Verbal/Linguistic

☐ `WORKSHEET` **Geography Skills: Tourism in the Mediterranean**—Students use the worksheet to review the economic impact of tourism on the region.

Project-Based Learning

Hands-On

Create Picture Books

Students will work in small groups to create a picture book for young children, ages 7–9, to learn about the physical geography, climates, and history of Northern and Southern Europe. Each "chapter" of the book will highlight one of the categories. Chapters should include illustrations and descriptions using content vocabulary found in the Student Edition chapter. If possible, have students share their picture books with younger children at either your or a nearby school.

Digital Hands-On

Create Online Maps

Students will work in small groups to create online maps of Northern and Southern Europe. The online maps should include annotations that highlight the physical features of Northern and Southern Europe. Annotations might include text excerpts, embedded videos, or photos.

edtechteacher
21st Century Learning

Print Resources

ANCILLARY RESOURCES

These ancillaries are available for every chapter and lesson.

- **Reading Essentials and Study Guide Workbook** `AL` `ELL`
- **Chapter Tests and Lesson Quizzes Blackline Masters**

PRINTABLE DIGITAL WORKSHEETS

These printable digital worksheets are available for every chapter and lesson.

- **Hands-On Chapter Projects**
- **What Do You Know? Activities**
- **Chapter Summaries (English and Spanish)**
- **Vocabulary Builder Activities**
- **Quizzes and Tests**
- **Reading Essentials and Study Guide (English and Spanish)** `AL` `ELL`
- **Guided Reading Activities**

More Media Resources

SUGGESTED VIDEOS

NOTE: Be sure to preview videos to ensure they are age-appropriate.

- **GlobeRiders Iceland Adventure: A Motorcycle Tour of Iceland** (55 min.)
- **Cities of the World: Santorini, Greece** (58 min.)
- **The Danish Solution** (59 min.)

SUGGESTED READING

- ***Refusing to Crumble: The Danish Resistance in World War II,*** by Michael Burgan `BL`
- ***I Will Come Back for You: A Family in Hiding During World War II,*** by Marisabina Russo `AL`
- ***Vicious Vikings and Measly Middle Ages*** (Horrible Histories-2 books in 1), by Terry Deary

PHYSICAL GEOGRAPHY OF THE REGIONS

Students will know:
- that Northern and Southern Europe have a different geography than Western Europe.

Students will be able to:
- **identify** the different landforms and waterways in Northern and Southern Europe.
- **compare** and contrast the climates found in the region.
- **describe** important natural resources in the region.

UNDERSTANDING
BY DESIGN®

☑ Print Teaching Options

V Visual Skills

- ☐ **P. 366** Students use a political map to make comparisons between countries of Northern and Southern Europe. **ELL**

- ☐ **P. 367** Students identify the Pyrenees and the Alps on a physical map. **BL** Visual/Spatial

- ☐ **P. 368** Students illustrate a picture of what they imagine a fjord looks like. **ELL** **AL** Visual/Spatial

- ☐ **P. 369** Students create a Venn diagram comparing climates of Northern and Southern Europe. Visual/Spatial

W Writing Skills

- ☐ **P. 368** Students write a narrative describing the landscape as a tour guide through a fjord. **BL**

- ☐ **P. 370** Students write paragraphs on types of vegetation in Northern and Southern Europe. Naturalist

- ☐ **P. 371** Students write an argument on expanding "marine protected" areas in the Mediterranean Sea. **AL**

R Reading Skills

- ☐ **P. 367** Students determine the meaning of the word *tectonic* using context clues. Verbal/Linguistic

- ☐ **P. 368** Students summarize information about Northern and Southern Europe's waterways. Verbal/Linguistic

C Critical Thinking Skills

- ☐ **P. 367** Students make inferences about the way of life on the islands of Southern Europe. Logical/Mathematical

- ☐ **P. 369** Students determine how the Gulf Stream affects Northern Europe's climate. Verbal/Linguistic

- ☐ **P. 370** Students answer questions about the discovery of petroleum in the North Sea and its effects on Norway's economy. Logical/Mathematical, Verbal/Linguistic

T Technology Skills

- ☐ **P. 370** Students research and present findings on a country's natural resources. **BL** Naturalist, Visual/ Spatial

☑ Online Teaching Options

V Visual Skills

- ☐ **VIDEO** **Primary Geography—Arctic Lapland**—Students watch a video about the northern-most part of Northern Europe and share key facts with a partner. **AL** Verbal/Linguistic

- ☐ **ANIMATION** **How the Alps Formed**—Students watch the animation about the Alps and discuss its unique aspects. **BL** Visual/Spatial

- ☐ **DIAGRAM** **Hydroelectric, Wind, and Geothermal Power**—Students create and present a "How To" demonstration about hydroelectric power using only their bodies. **AL** **ELL** Kinesthetic, Logical/Mathematical

- ☐ **IMAGE** **360° View: The Alps**—Use the 360 photo of the Alps to further discuss this landform and the characteristics that these bring to Europe. Visual/Spatial

- ☐ **MAP** **Physical Geography: Northern and Southern Europe**—Students use the physical map to elaborate on the landforms and waterways of this region. Naturalist

- ☐ **MAP** **Climates: Northern and Southern Europe**—Students use the climate map to contrast the regional climates of Northern and Southern Europe.

- ☐ **MAP** **Resources: Northern and Southern Europe**—Students use the resources map to review the resources in this region. Naturalist

W Writing Skills

- ☐ **GRAPHIC ORGANIZER** **Landforms and Waterways of Northern and Southern Europe**—Students explain the characteristics of the various landforms and waterways of the regions.

R Reading Skills

- ☐ **VIDEO** **Fjords**—Students use the video of a fjord in Norway to elaborate on this vocabulary word.

- ☐ **GRAPHIC ORGANIZER** **Resources of Northern and Southern Europe**—Students use an interactive graphic organizer to review the resources of the region. Naturalist

C Critical Thinking Skills

- ☐ **MAP** **Comparing Climates**—Students use the map and corresponding images to compare and contrast the Mediterranean climate with other climates. Naturalist

- ☐ **CHART** **Biomes**—Students use the biomes chart to discuss how these climates regions are affected by weather.

T Technology Skills

- ☐ **ANIMATION** **Seasons on Earth**—Students can use the animation about Earth's tilt to discuss how this plays a role in climate in Europe.

- ☐ **ONLINE SELF-CHECK QUIZ** **Lesson 1**—Students receive instant feedback on their mastery of lesson content.

☑ Printable Digital Worksheets

W Writing Skills

- ☐ **WORKSHEET** **Geography Skills: Tourism in the Mediterranean**—Students use the worksheet to review the economic impact of tourism on the region.

HISTORY OF THE REGIONS

Students will know:
- Northern and Southern Europeans have different history and culture.
- Northern and Southern Europe share similar modern struggles as Western Europe.

Students will be able to:
- **discuss** the history of Northern and Southern Europe.
- **describe** the Renaissance and how it changed Northern and Southern Europe.
- **discuss** history in the modern era of Northern and Southern Europe.

UNDERSTANDING
BY DESIGN®

☑ *Print Teaching Options*

V Visual Skills

☐ **P. 373** Students calculate the size of Alexander's empire in 322 B.C. and the Roman Empire in A.D. 200 and compare each to the size of the United States. Visual/Spatial

☐ **P. 376** Students create a map showing where explorers traveled. Visual/Spatial

☐ **P. 377** Students create a T-chart of the relationships between countries in Northern and Southern Europe. AL Visual/Spatial

W Writing Skills

☐ **P. 373** Students prepare a speech to persuade listeners in favor of Athenian or Spartan government and society. Verbal/Linguistic

☐ **P. 374** Students summarize information on Viking culture. Verbal/Linguistic

R Reading Skills

☐ **P. 372** Students use context clues to find meaning and make connections. ELL AL Visual/Spatial

☐ **P. 374** Students discuss the terms *polytheism* and *monotheism* and words with the prefixes *poly-* and *mono-*. Verbal/Linguistic

C Critical Thinking Skills

☐ **P. 375** Students discuss why ancient Greek and Roman literature inspired Renaissance thinkers. BL Logical/Mathematical

☐ **P. 376** Students create a time line of events during the 1400s. AL Visual/Spatial, Logical/Mathematical

☐ **P. 376** Students discuss what caused kingdoms across Northern Europe to break from the Catholic church.

T Technology Skills

☐ **P. 373** Students make a presentation for an Athens Agora Achievements Fair. Verbal/Linguistic, Kinesthetic

☐ **P. 374** Students research Viking migration and trade routes and create a map based on their research. AL Visual/Spatial, Logical/Mathematical

☐ **P. 375** Students collaborate in groups to present thinkers, artists or scientists in a Renaissance Reality Show. BL Verbal/Linguistic, Kinesthetic

☑ *Online Teaching Options*

V Visual Skills

☐ **VIDEO** **Islam in Spain and the Alhambra**—Students watch a video about the history of Islam in Northern and Southern Europe and discuss its influence on modern-day civilizations. AL Visual/Spatial

☐ **MAP** **Greek and Roman Empires**—Students use the map to discuss the influences of the Greek and Roman Empires on early European culture. AL Logical/Mathematical

☐ **DIAGRAM** **Viking Longship**—Students use the diagram to discuss the Vikings and their explorations and write a paragraph about the Vikings and their legacy. BL

☐ **MAP** **Exploration to the New World**—Students use the chapter opener map with the layer about exploration to discuss Viking exploration. Verbal/Linguistic

☐ **MAP** **Silk Road**—Students can use the map of the Silk Road to discuss this aspect of exploration.

W Writing Skills

☐ **GRAPHIC ORGANIZER** **Exploration**—Students use a graphic organizer to begin to list and review the explorers from this area of Europe.

☐ **MAP** **Columbian Exchange**—Students use the Columbian Exchange map to discuss these other aspects of exploration. Verbal/Linguistic

☐ **MAP** **Three Religions in Europe, 1500s**—Students use the religion map to review how other religions affect this area of Europe. AL Visual/Spatial

R Reading Skills

☐ **LECTURE SLIDE** **Mythology**—Students use the lecture slide to review information about myth including Greek mythology, Roman mythology, and Norse Mythology. Verbal/Linguistic

☐ **LECTURE SLIDE** **Athens and Sparta**—Students can use the lecture slide that discusses Athens and Sparta to review the idea of the city-state and these two examples of this vocabulary term.

☐ **GAME** **Drag-and-Drop: Conflicts**—Students use the drag-and-drop game about conflicts in Northern and Southern Europe to discuss the changes in this region. Kinesthetic

C Critical Thinking Skills

☐ **SLIDE SHOW** **The Renaissance**—Using the interactive slideshow, students review the impact of Renaissance thinkers, artists, and scientists. AL Verbal/Linguistic

☐ **MAP** **Protestants in the 1500s**—Students analyze the map to determine how religions break apart. Students complete a Venn diagram comparing and contrasting the two religious splits. AL Visual/Spatial

T Technology Skills

☐ **ONLINE SELF-CHECK QUIZ** **Lesson 2**—Students receive instant feedback on their mastery of lesson content.

LIFE IN NORTHERN AND SOUTHERN EUROPE

Students will know:
- *that Northern and Southern Europe have different languages.*
- *that Northern and Southern Europe share modern struggles similar to Western Europe.*

Students will be able to:
- *describe* people and cultures of Northern and Southern Europe.
- *describe* ethnic and language groups in Northern and Southern Europe.
- *discuss* daily life in the region.
- *explain* current challenges facing Northern and Southern Europe.

UNDERSTANDING BY DESIGN®

☑ *Print Teaching Options*

V Visual Skills

☐ **P. 379** Pairs convert information into a circle graph. AL

☐ **P. 383** Students create and share a "Recreation Map" with icons and a legend of various recreational activities.

W Writing Skills

☐ **P. 383** Students write a "Daily Life" blog for people living in Northern and Southern Europe. Verbal/Linguistic

R Reading Skills

☐ **P. 378** Students define *infant mortality* through word parts. AL ELL Verbal/Linguistic

☐ **P. 380** Students determine the meaning of *homogeneous* through word parts. AL ELL Verbal/Linguistic

☐ **P. 381** Students summarize a paragraph about Renaissance art and architecture. AL Verbal/Linguistic

☐ **P. 382** Students review pronunciation of Scandinavian proper nouns. AL ELL Verbal/Linguistic

☐ **P. 385** Students connect the terms *recess* and *recession*. AL ELL Verbal/Linguistic

C Critical Thinking Skills

☐ **P. 379** Students convert Southern Europe's population percentages into fractions. BL Logical/Mathematical

☐ **P. 380** Students evaluate evidence to prove the success of the Protestant Reformation. Logical/Mathematical

☐ **P. 384** Students make predictions about issues for upcoming elections based on financial problems in Europe.

☐ **P. 384** Students consider how governments respond to economic hardships faced by their citizens. BL

T Technology Skills

☐ **P. 381** Students research and prepare a presentation about a specific architect of Northern or Southern Europe.

☐ **P. 382** Students research music or dances of a region, and present audio clips or videos. Auditory/Musical

☐ **P. 385** Students research and present a report on the current status of economies of countries in the European Union. BL Logical/Mathematical, Interpersonal

☑ *Online Teaching Options*

V Visual Skills

☐ **MAP** **Three Religions in Europe, 1500s**—Students use the religion map to discuss the three major religions and their impact on Northern and Southern Europe. AL

☐ **IMAGE** **LEGO Facts**—Students use the image to discuss Lego and create a time line to show key events in Lego's history. ELL

☐ **SLIDE SHOW** **Recreation in Northern and Southern Europe**—Students use the slide show to compare and contrast recreation activities. Verbal/Linguistic, Visual/Spatial

☐ **MAP** **Population: Northern and Southern Europe**—Students use the population map to discuss how populations are distributed in these countries.

☐ **MAP** **Geo Facts: Northern and Southern Europe**—Students use the Geo-Facts map to discuss unique aspects of city life in Northern and Southern European countries.

☐ **MAP** **The European Union**—Students use the map to discuss the impact of the EU and the financial crisis on the countries of this region. Logical/Mathematical, Interpersonal

W Writing Skills

☐ **VIDEO** **World's Wonders: Grand Canal of Venice**—Students watch a video about the Grand Canal of Venice and write a travel brochure. BL Verbal/Linguistic

R Reading Skills

☐ **GAME** **Drag-and-Drop: Capitals and Countries**—Students use a drag-and-drop activity to reinforce content. Kinesthetic

☐ **LECTURE SLIDE** **Defining: Periods in Art**—Students use this lecture slide to elaborate on what the Renaissance and Baroque period of art entailed and why they are different. Verbal/Linguistic

☐ **LECTURE SLIDE** **Popular Global Businesses**—Students use the lecture slide to discuss the influence of IKEA on culture and design in relation to the rise of LEGO as a global influence.

C Critical Thinking Skills

☐ **CHARTS** **Comparing Population Pyramids: Northern and Southern Europe**—Students use the population pyramids to discuss the aging of Europe's population and effects it might have on society. Logical/Mathematical

☐ **CHART** **Funding Higher Education**—Students discuss federal tax spending on education in different countries in Northern and Southern Europe and summarize information in the chart. BL

T Technology Skills

☐ **ONLINE SELF-CHECK QUIZ** **Lesson 3**—Students receive instant feedback on their mastery of lesson content.

☑ *Printable Digital Worksheets*

W Writing Skills

☐ **WORKSHEET** **Cultural Geography Activity: Scandinavian Culture**—Students compare and contrast daily life of Northern Europe to Southern Europe using a collaborative worksheet, and use a Venn diagram to visualize their comparisons. AL ELL

INTERVENTION AND REMEDIATION STRATEGIES

LESSON 1 Physical Geography of the Regions

Reading and Comprehension

Students may have trouble with the meaning and pronunciation of some of the content vocabulary words, such as *fjord*. Have students work in pairs to use each term correctly in a sentence. Circulate to provide corrective guidance if needed. Then have students collaborate to create one or two paragraphs using each content vocabulary term that demonstrates their understanding of landforms and waterways in Northern Europe and Southern Europe.

Text Evidence

Have students work in small groups to compare and contrast the climates of Northern Europe and Southern Europe. Tell students to use a graphic organizer, such as a Venn diagram, to visually depict the similarities and differences. After students have created their diagram, have them conduct additional research using reliable online sources to identify a recent climactic event that has occurred in Northern or Southern Europe. Tell students to summarize an analysis of their findings and present their diagrams to the class.

LESSON 2 History of the Regions

Reading and Comprehension

Have students scan the lesson to identify cause-and-effect relationships as they relate to the history of civilizations in Northern and Southern Europe. Tell students to look for signal words as they read. Remind students that words and phrases such as *because, since, as a result, due to, therefore, consequently, so, resulted in,* and *affected* all indicate cause or effect. Have students work with a partner to practice using these words to explain concepts and cause-and-effect relationships in this lesson.

Text Evidence

Have students work in pairs or small groups to research facts about one of the following topics discussed in this lesson: Ancient Greeks, Roman Empires, Vikings, the Renaissance, Religion, Conflict and War. Tell students to use information from the text and from their research to answer questions generated by their group as well as this lesson's essential question: Why do civilizations rise and fall? Have students present their findings to the class. Encourage students to use visual displays to enhance their presentations.

LESSON 3 Life in Northern and Southern Europe

Reading and Comprehension

To ensure comprehension of the concepts in this lesson, have students write a paragraph that explains how new ideas have changed the way people live in Northern and Southern Europe. Use the "It Matters Because" text as a launch point for students' paragraphs. Tell students to write a few sentences using at least one of the content vocabulary terms to explain how different ethnic and language groups in Northern and Southern Europe live.

Text Evidence

To help students make the connection between city life and rural communities in Northern and Southern Europe, have students work in pairs or small groups to create a visual representation of the issues facing cities discussed in this lesson. For example, students may choose to create a flow chart or diagram that shows the impact of population growth. Have students in each group work together to summarize how these issues impact daily life for people living in cities. Encourage students to use content vocabulary terms in their summaries.

Online Resources

Level Reader

Use this online lower-level text that corresponds directly to the text in the online Student Edition.

Guided Reading Activities

This resource uses graphic organizers and guiding questions to help students with comprehension.

What Do You Know?

Use these worksheets to pre-assess students' background knowledge before they read the chapter.

Reading Essentials and Study Guide Workbook

This resource offers writing and reading activities for the approaching-level student.

Self-Check Quizzes

This online assessment tool provides instant feedback for students to check their progress.

NORTHERN AND SOUTHERN EUROPE

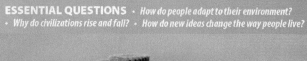

ESSENTIAL QUESTIONS · *How do people adapt to their environment?*
· *Why do civilizations rise and fall?* · *How do new ideas change the way people live?*

Christophe Boisvieux/age fotostock

Norwegian fisherman from a
Lofoten Island fishing village

networks
There's More Online about Northern and Southern Europe.

CHAPTER 12

Lesson 1
Physical Geography of the Regions

Lesson 2
History of the Regions

Lesson 3
Life in Northern and Southern Europe

The Story Matters...

The people of Northern Europe live in a land of cold, harsh winters. In contrast, the people of Southern Europe enjoy the warm Mediterranean climate. What do these people have in common? The countries in this subregion have long histories, dating back to the Vikings in the north and the ancient Greeks and Romans in the south. These ancient peoples influenced many aspects of culture—from exploration to philosophy to the discovery of new ideas.

FOLDABLES
Study Organizer

Go to the Foldables® library in the back of your book to make a Foldable™ that will help you take notes while reading this chapter.

363

ENGAGE

Bellringer Have students turn to the political map of Northern and Southern Europe in the Chapter Opener. Have students locate the countries in each part of Europe and have them consider how each region might be similar and different. Draw a Venn diagram on the board and write the labels *Northern Europe* and *Southern Europe* above the two circles. Call on volunteers to list similarities in the overlapping section. *(Examples: all have coastlines, all share long histories)* Then call on other volunteers to list features that are unique to each country in the appropriate side section. *(Examples for Northern Europe: colder climate; on Norwegian, North, or Baltic Sea. Examples for Southern Europe: warmer climate, on Atlantic Ocean, Mediterranean, Aegean, or Black Sea)*

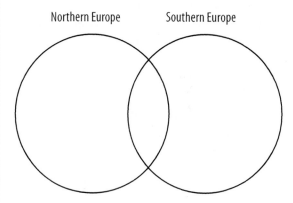

Northern Europe   Southern Europe

Ask students to read "The Story Matters..." and have them add new information to the Venn diagram. Point out the photograph. **Ask: How might the rich histories of Northern and Southern Europe affect the people and culture in these countries today?** *(Students may conclude that the countries in these regions have evolved with languages, cultures, clothing, and traditions that have been influenced by ancient Greeks and Romans. The rich histories may affect tourism and local economies.)*

Tell students that they will learn more about the features and cultures of countries in Northern and Southern Europe in this chapter.

Letter from the Author

Dear Geography Teacher,

This chapter offers a chance for comparative analysis. Half of the students should research about Northern Europe and the other half, Southern Europe. Groups might gather information about topics such as: culture, including historical evolution; resources, both human and natural; economic development; relationship to the European Union; and current or future challenges. Discuss their findings. Create a graphic organizer showing the differences and similarities between these two regions of Europe.

Richard G. Boehm

FOLDABLES
Study Organizer

Go to the Foldables® library for a cumulative chapter-based Foldable® activity that your students can use to help take notes and prepare for assessment.

TEACH & ASSESS

Step Into the Place

V Visual Skills

Reading a Map Have students read the introductory paragraph and look at the map. Explain that this map shows the countries in Northern and Southern Europe. Have students use the map to answer the Step Into the Place questions. **Ask:**

- Which Northern European countries share borders? *(Norway and Sweden, Norway and Finland, Sweden and Finland)*
- What do the capital cities of Norway, Sweden, and Finland have in common? *(They are all located near the water in the southern portion of their countries.)*
- How are the countries of Iceland and Cyprus similar? *(They are both island countries.)* How are they different? *(Iceland is much larger than Cyprus. Iceland is in Northern Europe, whereas Cyprus is in Southern Europe.)* **AL**

Content Background Knowledge

Here are some interesting historical facts about Northern and Southern Europe:

- The Vikings were ancient warriors known for their fierceness and seafaring abilities. They traveled extensively and invaded Northern Europe. Also known as Norsemen, the Vikings arrived first in Iceland about 500 years before Christopher Columbus travelled to the Americas.
- Ancient Greeks believed stories about a group of gods and heroes that had human emotions and characteristics. Zeus, the leader of all the gods, lived on Mount Olympus, the highest mountain in Greece. This ancient Greek religion is now referred to as mythology.
- Ruins of the Temple of Poseidon, the god of the sea and earthquakes, sit atop a hill in Soúnio, a town on the southern tip of Greece. The sacred site dates back to ancient times and is mentioned in the *Odyssey*, an epic poem thought to be written by Homer.

ANSWERS, p. 364

STEP INTO THE PLACE

1. **Northern Europe:** Scandinavian Peninsula is comprised of Norway and Sweden, Jutland Peninsula has most of Denmark; **Southern Europe:** Iberian Peninsula is comprised of Spain and Portugal, Italian Peninsula holds Italy, Greece is at bottom of the Balkan Peninsula
2. Students should realize that fishing is likely a part of all of the cultures and that seafood is a strong component of their diets.
3. Madrid, Rome, Oslo, Stockholm
4. **CRITICAL THINKING** Since Southern Europe is closer to the Equator, students should expect it to have a warmer climate than Northern Europe.

Chapter 12 NORTHERN AND SOUTHERN EUROPE

> **V** *Despite the distance between Northern and Southern Europe, many of the regions' countries are members of the European Union. Their histories show conflict, but today they are unified as members of the European continent, with similar economic goals.*

Step Into the Place

MAP FOCUS Use the map to answer the following questions.

1 **THE GEOGRAPHER'S WORLD** Northern and Southern Europe have several large peninsulas. Identify two peninsulas in Northern Europe and three in Southern Europe, and name the countries of each.

2 **PLACES AND REGIONS** With so many countries bordering water, such as the North Sea, the Atlantic Ocean, and the Mediterranean Sea, what activity would you expect to find in Northern and Southern Europe?

3 **PLACES AND REGIONS** Name the capital cities of Spain, Italy, Norway, and Sweden.

4 **CRITICAL THINKING**
Analyzing With the difference in latitude between Northern and Southern Europe, how would you expect their climates to differ?

A SOUTHERN COASTLINE Warm, bright sunshine floods the ruins of an ancient temple that overlooks the Mediterranean Sea in Greece.

B NORTHERN COASTLINE A red fox walks across rocks in a wilderness area of northern Finland. The rugged land in far northern areas of Europe was shaped by retreating glaciers at the end of the last Ice Age.

Step Into the Time

TIME LINE Choose an event from the time line and write a journal entry from the point of view of a teenager living during that time. Describe how that event has changed your perception of the world.

600 B.C. City-states dominate ancient Greece

509 B.C. Rome becomes a republic

c. 335 B.C. Greek philosopher Aristotle teaches in Athens

1000 A.D.

364 Chapter 12

(t to b) Philip Coblentz/Brand X Pictures/PictureQuest; FLPA/Harri Taavetti/FLPA/age fotostock; Dimitris Tavlikos/Alamy

Project-Based Learning

Hands-On

Creating a Picture Book
Students will work in small groups to create a picture book for young children, ages 7–9, to learn about the physical geography, climates, and history of Northern and Southern Europe. Each "chapter" of the book will highlight one of the categories. Chapters should include illustrations and descriptions using content vocabulary found in the Student Edition chapter. If possible, have students share their picture books with children at school.

Digital Hands-On

Creating an Online Map
Students will work in small groups to create online maps of Northern and Southern Europe. The online maps should include annotations that highlight the physical features of Northern and Southern Europe. Annotations might include text excerpts, embedded videos, or photos.

edtechteacher
21st Century Learning

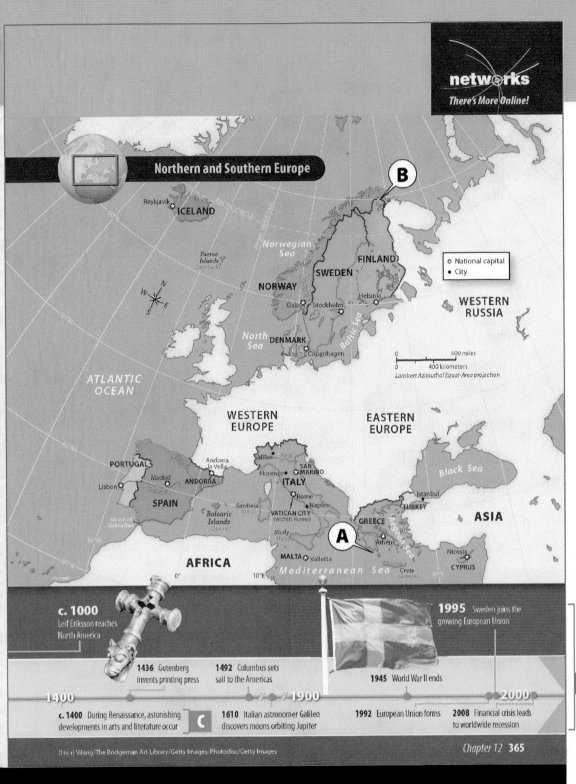

Northern and Southern Europe

Reykjavík
ICELAND

Norwegian Sea

FINLAND

SWEDEN

NORWAY

Oslo Stockholm

Helsinki

Faeroe Islands (Denmark)

North Sea **DENMARK**

Copenhagen

WESTERN RUSSIA

○ National capital
● City

ATLANTIC OCEAN

0   400 miles
0   400 kilometers
Lambert Azimuthal Equal-Area projection

WESTERN EUROPE

EASTERN EUROPE

PORTUGAL
Andorra la Vella
Lisbon Madrid **ANDORRA**
SPAIN

Milan
Florence **SAN MARINO**
ITALY
Rome Naples
Sardinia (Italy) **VATICAN CITY** (within Rome)
Balearic Islands (Spain)
Sicily (Italy)

AFRICA

MALTA ○ Valletta

Black Sea

Istanbul
TURKEY

GREECE
Athens

Aegean Sea

ASIA

Nicosia
CYPRUS

Mediterranean Sea Crete (Greece)

Ⓑ

Ⓐ

c. 1000
Leif Eriksson reaches North America

1436 Gutenberg invents printing press

1492 Columbus sets sail to the Americas

1945 World War II ends

1995 Sweden joins the growing European Union

1400

1900

2000

c. 1400 During Renaissance, astonishing developments in arts and literature occur Ⓒ

1610 Italian astronomer Galileo discovers moons orbiting Jupiter

1992 European Union forms

2008 Financial crisis leads to worldwide recession

(l to r) Viking/The Bridgeman Art Library/Getty Images; Photodisc/Getty Images

Chapter 12 **365**

Step Into the Time

Ⓥ Visual Skills

Reading a Time Line Have students review the time line and images. As a class, discuss its major points of interest. **Ask:**

- What Greek philosopher taught in Athens in 335 B.C.? *(Aristotle)*
- Approximately how many years after Rome became a republic did Leif Eriksson reach North America? *(almost 1500 years)*
- Did Galileo discover moons orbiting Jupiter before or after Columbus set sail to the Americas? *(after)*
- When did the European Union form, and when did Sweden join it? *(1992; 1995)* Visual/Spatial

Ⓒ Critical Thinking Skills

Making Connections Point out the word *Renaissance*, explaining that it means "rebirth." Tell students that the Renaissance is significant because of the impressive works of art and inventions created during this period in European history. Johannes Gutenberg, for example, developed a printing press using moveable type in 1448. This invention allowed people to have access to printed books. Before his invention, most books were written by hand, making them expensive so only the wealthy could afford them. **Ask: How do you think having printed books affected Europeans during the Renaissance?** *(Students should infer that having printed books allowed for people to gain knowledge and spread ideas. Printed books were probably less expensive, so more people could afford them. Literacy likely increased.)* Verbal/Linguistic

Ⓥ

CLOSE & REFLECT

Formulating Questions Have students generate a list of questions they have about Northern and Southern Europe based on the chapter introduction. Tell students to look for answers to these questions as they read the chapter.

INTERACTIVE TIME LINE

Reading a Time Line and Map

Display the time line and map on the whiteboard. Have volunteers read each event as it is revealed on the time line. Ask students to identify where on the map of Northern and Southern Europe each event took place. Visual/Spatial

See page 363B for other online activities.

ENGAGE

Bellringer Before students begin the lesson, have them think about how people adapt to their environment. **Ask:** How do you adapt, or what changes do you make, to adjust to a new season where you live or when visiting a different climate? *(Answers will vary but should include details about wearing warmer or lighter clothes or purchasing or using specific products such as umbrellas, raincoats, winter parkas, bug repellant, sun tan lotion, and so on.)*

Then read the Essential Question and the It Matters Because statement. Have students brainstorm the different challenges people who live in Northern and Southern Europe might face.

TEACH & ASSESS

C Critical Thinking Skills

Comparing and Contrasting Tell students that making comparisons between Northern and Southern Europe will help them understand their similarities and differences. As students read this lesson, have them note how physical features, such as landforms and waterways, in Northern and Southern Europe are similar and different. Suggest that they complete a Venn diagram or build on the one they started in the Chapter Opener to help them compare and contrast the two regions. **Visual/ Spatial**

V Visual Skills

Integrating Visual Information Have students reference the political map of Northern and Southern Europe in the Chapter Opener. Ask pairs to read the paragraph slowly and have students locate the individual countries on the map as their classmate reads each one. Have students make visual comparisons between each country by asking each other questions such as "Which country is bigger, Spain or Portugal?" *(Spain)*, or have students complete sentence starters, such as: "Denmark is south of _____ *(Norway)* and southwest of _____ *(Sweden)*" and so on. **ELL**
AL Interpersonal, Visual/Spatial

ANSWER, p. 366

Taking Notes Notes should include facts about each country's resources, such as: **Sweden:** copper, gold, zinc, lead, forest products, hydroelectric power from rivers; **Greece:** fishing, grapes, and olives; **Iceland:** fishing, geothermal energy, hydroelectric power from rivers, and so on.

networks

There's More Online!

☑ **ANIMATION** How the Alps Formed

☑ **VIDEO**

Reading **HELP**DESK

Academic Vocabulary

• **uniform**

Content Vocabulary

• **glaciation**
• **fjord**
• **tundra**
• **scrubland**
• **trawler**

TAKING NOTES: *Key Ideas and Details*

Identify Choose one of the countries in the region. List important resources of that country on a graphic organizer like the one below.

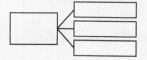
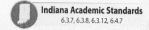

Indiana Academic Standards
6.3.7, 6.3.8, 6.3.12, 6.4.7

Lesson 1

Physical Geography of the Regions

ESSENTIAL QUESTION • *How do people adapt to their environment?*

IT MATTERS BECAUSE
Northern Europe and Southern Europe have different landforms, climates, and resources. The geography of the regions presents unique challenges to the people who live there.

Landforms and Waterways

C

GUIDING QUESTIONS *How are the landforms in Northern and Southern Europe similar? How are they different?*

Much of Northern Europe is a land of rugged mountains, rocky soils, and jagged coasts. A map of Northern Europe would show Denmark, Sweden, Norway, Finland, and Iceland. Together, these five far-northern lands are often called the Nordic countries.

The Mediterranean Sea dominates the coast of much of southern Europe, affecting the climate and the movement of people. Southern Europe is made up of Spain, Portugal, Italy, and Greece, as well as the tiny countries of Andorra, San Marino, and Vatican City. It also includes the island countries of Malta and Cyprus, the westernmost part of Turkey, and the tiny British territory of Gibraltar.

V

A Land of Peninsulas
A peninsula is an area of land surrounded on three sides by water. In the United States, Florida is a good example of a peninsula.

Two peninsulas make up most of Northern Europe. Jutland is a peninsula that extends northward from Germany and includes most of Denmark. The Scandinavian Peninsula is made up of Norway and Sweden. The large landmass east

(l to r) Maremagnum/Photographer's Choice/Getty Images; ©Doug Pearson/JAI/Corbis; Katja Kreder/age fotostock; Arnulf Husmo/Stone/Getty Images

---

netw⊕rks *Online Teaching Options*

VIDEO

Primary Geography—Arctic Lapland

Evaluating Use this video about geography and climate of Arctic Lapland, located in Northern Europe, to introduce the lesson. After watching the video, have students evaluate the information presented. Ask student partners to share one or two key facts they found interesting or surprising.
AL Verbal/Linguistic

See page 363C for other online activities.

BBC Motion Gallery Education

of Sweden is Finland. Much of the land of Norway, Sweden, and Finland lies north of 60° N latitude.

Northern Europe also includes many islands. Iceland is a large island in the northern Atlantic Ocean near the Arctic Circle. Denmark has about 400 islands. Its capital, Copenhagen, is on the largest of the islands.

Southern Europe also has several peninsulas. Spain and Portugal form the Iberian Peninsula. Most of Italy is the long, boot-shaped Italian peninsula. East of Italy, the larger Balkan Peninsula includes several Eastern European nations, with Greece at its southern tip.

In Southern Europe, the large Mediterranean islands of Sicily and Sardinia are part of Italy. The nearby islands of Malta form an independent country. The island of Crete is part of Greece. Farther east, the island of Cyprus contains the largely Greek but independent nation of Cyprus, as well as North Cyprus, a Turkish territory.

Mountains and Plains

The Scandinavian Peninsula has a spine of rugged mountains, formed when two tectonic plates collided. **Glaciation**, or the weathering and erosion caused by moving masses of ice called glaciers, carved the land into the mountains and plateaus we see today.

Iceland also has rugged terrain, but it formed from volcanic activity. The island is part of a mountain range, the Mid-Atlantic Ridge, which is mostly underwater. At Iceland, it rises above sea level. Iceland is home to more than 200 volcanoes and many hot springs, as well as Europe's largest glacier.

Part of the boundary between Western Europe and Southern Europe is formed by two mountain ranges, the Pyrenees and the Alps. The Pyrenees mark the boundary between southern France and the Iberian Peninsula. The Alps form the northern border of Italy and separate the Italian peninsula from the rest of Europe.

Hikers pass beneath steep rock formations in the Dolomites, a branch of the Alps in northeastern Italy.

▶ CRITICAL THINKING
Describing Describe the geographical relationship of the Alps to the Italian peninsula.

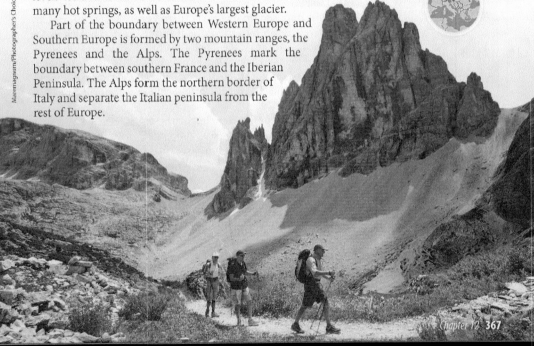

Maremagnum/Photographer's Choice/Getty Images

Chapter 12 367

C Critical Thinking Skills

Making Inferences Have students locate the islands referenced in the text on a political map of Southern Europe. Discuss what island life might be like, especially on the smaller islands. **Ask:** What might you infer about the way of life for people who live on the islands in Southern Europe? *(Students' answers will vary but might include that on the smaller islands, people may need to travel to the mainland for certain supplies or services, or they may have to pay more for products and services due to transportation costs.)* Logical/Mathematical

V

R Reading Skills

Determining Word Meanings Tell students that knowing the meaning of related words can help in understanding the meaning of unfamiliar ones. Point out the word *tectonic* and have students try to identify its meaning using context clues. *(formed, plates collided)* Point out that *tectonic* has more than one meaning. Its general definition is "having a large and important effect." **Ask:** What do you think *tectonic* means here as it relates to geography? *(relating to a big change in the Earth's surface)*

Have students look the word up in the dictionary to see if their definitions are correct. Tell students to use context clues to determine the meaning of unfamiliar words as they read. Verbal/Linguistic

V Visual Skills

Interpreting Have students identify two mountain ranges, the Pyrenees and the Alps, on a physical map of Northern and Southern Europe. **Ask:** What purpose do you think these landforms might have had for people who lived in the region years ago? *(The mountains might have served as a natural defense to protect people from conquest.)* BL Visual/Spatial

ANIMATION

How the Alps Formed

Discussing Use the animation about the Alps to discuss this landform and its role in Northern and Southern Europe. Guide students in understanding plate tectonics. Discuss unique aspects of this mountain range and information specific to the Alps, such as the fact that they are the highest mountain range in Europe. BL Visual/Spatial

See page 363C for other online activities.

ANSWER, p. 367

CRITICAL THINKING The Alps form the northern border of Italy and separate the Italian Peninsula from the rest of Europe.

Summarizing Tell students to read the section about Northern and Southern Europe's waterways and take turns summarizing the information. Remind students that summaries should only include the most important information. **Ask:**

- What is Southern Europe's most important body of water? *(the Mediterranean Sea)*
- What is an important river in Southern Europe and where is it located? *(the Po River; in Italy, running from the Alps to the Adriatic Sea)*
- Why is the Baltic Sea more likely to freeze than other bodies of salt water? *(It is shallow and has a low amount of salt.)* **Verbal/Linguistic**

Illustrating Tell students to close their books. Read aloud the definition of *fjord* and have students draw a picture of what they imagine a fjord looks like. Then have students open their books to this page and point out the visual and the vocabulary word *fjord*. Note that the word can also be spelled *fiord*. Explain that while the word is similar sounding to words like *board* and *chord*, it is pronounced *fēord*. Ask students to check if their illustrations are similar to the photograph. Tell students that visualizing a word's meaning can help them better understand the word. **ELL** **AL** **Visual/Spatial**

Narrative Have students use the photograph of the boat travelling along the fjord as a launch point for narrative writing. Have students write a script as if they are the tour guide on the boat describing the landscape to passengers on an excursion. Tell students to use precise words and descriptive details to tell passengers what they are seeing. As a further challenge, tell students to include descriptive language for those individuals who have never seen a fjord. **BL** **Verbal/Linguistic, Interpersonal**

ANSWER, p. 368

☑ **READING PROGRESS CHECK** Most of the land in Northern Europe is part of either peninsulas or islands. Mountains and rugged coastlines are also common.

Some countries of Southern Europe are mountainous. The Apennines extend along the length of Italy. They are volcanic and subject to earthquakes. Greece also has rugged highlands. The tallest and most famous of its mountains is Mount Olympus, which legend says was the home of the gods of Greek mythology.

Most of Spain lies on a plateau called the Meseta Central. It is a harsh landscape. To the north and south of the Meseta Central are mountain ranges, but its western side slopes gently toward the Atlantic Ocean. Valencia, along Spain's eastern coast, is a coastal plain of rolling hills.

Portugal is divided geographically by the Tagus River. South of the river, the landscape is characterized by extensive rolling plains. Throughout the area are abundant trees and plants, including evergreen oak trees, olive trees, figs, and vineyards. The northeastern coast features a landscape of wide valleys and steep hills.

The Mediterranean Sea

The most important body of water in Southern Europe is the Mediterranean Sea. It stretches about 2,500 miles (4,023 km) from the southern coast of Spain in the west to the coasts of Greece, Turkey, and various countries of Southwest Asia. The Mediterranean is almost completely surrounded by land. In the west, it connects to the Atlantic Ocean through the Strait of Gibraltar. At the Strait's narrowest point, just 8 miles (13 km) separates the southern tip of Spain from Africa.

Waterways

Among the important rivers of Southern Europe is Italy's Po. Many smaller rivers drain into the Po as it travels from the Alps to the Adriatic Sea. The Ebro is the longest river that lies entirely in Spain. It originates in the Cantabrian Mountains in the north and ends at Spain's Mediterranean coast. The longest river on the Iberian Peninsula is the Tagus, which crosses Spain and Portugal on its way to the Atlantic Ocean.

Northern Europe has few important rivers, but it has a long coastline, indented by many seas and bays. Norway is surrounded on three sides by water, and much of Norway's west coast is dotted by narrow, water-filled valleys called **fjords**.

The Baltic Sea borders Sweden's southern and southeastern coasts. Sweden has major ports on the Baltic, but the sea is more likely to freeze than other bodies of salt water. This is because the Baltic is shallow and has a fairly low concentration of salt. Finland also borders the Baltic Sea. Its interior is better known for its many lakes. Glaciers have carved as many as 56,000 lakes in Finland.

☑ **READING PROGRESS CHECK**

Analyzing Which landforms best characterize Northern Europe?

Visual Vocabulary

V

Fjord A fjord is a deep, narrow, sea-filled valley at the base of steep cliffs.

W

R

©Doug Pearson/JAI/Corbis

---

netw⊙rks *Online Teaching Options*

GRAPHIC ORGANIZER

Landforms and Waterways of Northern and Southern Europe

Explaining Display the interactive graphic organizer to review and discuss the various landforms and waterways of Northern and Southern Europe. Have students review and explain the characteristics of each feature as they are displayed in the interactive graphic organizer. **Visual/Spatial, Verbal/Linguistic**

See page 363C for other online activities.

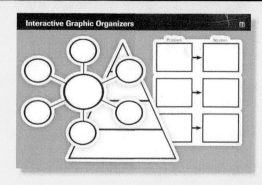

Interactive Graphic Organizers

Contrasting Climates

GUIDING QUESTION *How is the climate of Northern Europe different from the climate of Southern Europe?*

Northern Europe has a cool or cold climate. Yet, the conditions in some places are much harsher than in others. Landforms, distance from the sea, and ocean currents play a part in determining climate.

Chilly Northern Europe

The northern part of Norway is located as far north as Alaska, but it is not nearly as cold. The Norwegian Current, part of the Gulf Stream, flows past Norway carrying warm water from the tropics. As a result, western Norway has a marine climate, with mild winters and cool summers. The relatively mild climate does not extend far to the east. Mountains reduce the eastward flow of milder air. Eastern Norway thus has colder and snowier winters. Even so, the climate in eastern Norway and in Sweden is milder than in other parts of the world at the same latitude.

Finland's climate is considered continental because it receives little influence from the seas. It has cold winters and hot summers. Winters are harsh, especially north of the Arctic Circle. In the mountainous parts of northern Finland, the snow never melts. This land is mostly **tundra**, a region where subsoil is frozen and only plants such as lichens and mosses can survive.

The Gulf Stream brings warm water to the southern and western coasts of Iceland. This moderates the temperatures in these parts of the country. The effect does not reach northern Iceland, which just touches the Arctic Circle. There, drifting ice and fog are common in winter, and temperatures year-round are several degrees colder than they are in the southern and western parts of the country.

Warm Southern Europe

The most common climate in Southern Europe is Mediterranean. The climate features warm or hot summers and cool or mild winters. Spring and fall are rainy, but summers are dry. If you have ever been to the southern coast of California, you have experienced a Mediterranean climate.

Temperatures are not **uniform** across Southern Europe or even within countries. Northern Italy is nearer the Alps and has a cooler mountain climate, where winters are colder than in southern Italy and snow is heavy at higher elevations. The Meseta Central, a vast plateau in Spain, on the other hand, has a continental climate.

Katja Kreder/age fotostock

Academic Vocabulary

uniform the same or similar

Vacationers enjoy an attractive beach in Ibiza, one of the Balearic Islands. These scenic islands in the Mediterranean Sea are part of Spain.

▶ **CRITICAL THINKING**
Analyzing Why might many Northern Europeans vacation in Spain and other Mediterranean countries during the winter months?

CHAPTER 12, Lesson 1
Physical Geography of the Regions

V Visual Skills

Creating Visuals As they read this page, have students note how physical features in Northern and Southern Europe affect the climates of the regions. Tell students to create a Venn diagram or build on the one they started previously to compare and contrast the climates of Northern and Southern Europe. To reinforce understanding, have students turn to a partner and compare their diagrams. Then, **ask: What is the difference between a continental climate and a Mediterranean climate?** *(Places with a continental climate have cold winters and hot summers. A Mediterranean climate has warm or hot, dry summers and cool or mild winters, with rain in the spring and fall.)* **Visual/Spatial**

R Reading Skills

Using Context Clues Remind students that they can use words and phrases that surround an unfamiliar word to figure out its meaning. **Ask: What words in the text help you figure out the meaning of the word *tundra*?** *(frozen, no trees, only plants...and mosses can survive)*

Have students work in pairs to use context clues to define other unfamiliar words as they continue to read this page. **Verbal/Linguistic**

C Critical Thinking Skills

Determining Cause and Effect Discuss with students how the Gulf Stream in the Atlantic Ocean moderates the climate in Northern Europe. **Ask:**

- **How does the Gulf Stream affect Northern Europe's climate?** *(It brings warm water that moderates the temperatures on the southern and western coasts of Iceland.)*
- **Where in Northern Europe is the Gulf Stream not a factor? Why?** *(It does not affect northern Iceland because drifting ice and fog keep temperatures cooler year round.)* **Verbal/Linguistic**

MAP

Comparing Climates

Comparing and Contrasting Use the map and corresponding images to discuss the concept that "Mediterranean climate" occurs in other areas besides around the Mediterranean Sea. Explain that this climate occurs all over the world and that this term is used generally. Have students compare and contrast the Mediterranean climate with other climates. **Naturalist**

See page 363C for other online activities.

ANSWER, p. 369

CRITICAL THINKING Northern Europe is chilly during the winter months. Southern Europe, however, has a Mediterranean climate of mild winters, making the region ideal for vacations.

T Technology Skills

Researching on the Internet Assign student pairs one or more of the following regions in Northern and Southern Europe: Denmark, Sweden, Norway, Finland, Iceland, Spain, Portugal, Italy, Greece, Andorra, San Marino, Vatican City, Malta, Cyprus, the westernmost part of Turkey, and Gibraltar. Tell students they will expand on information in the text to research natural resources in their assigned country or region. Students' research should answer a self-generated question as well as the following: **What natural resources are available in this country or region? How does this area benefit from natural resources? How does it make up for a lack of certain resources?**

Have students use a software presentation program to present visuals and facts about their assigned region's natural resources. Encourage students to integrate technical information using visuals in their presentations such as flowcharts, diagrams, graphs, and tables. Students may wish to use the Taking Notes graphic organizer from the beginning of this lesson to organize their information. **BL** Naturalist, Visual/Spatial

W Writing Skills

Informative/Explanatory As students read this page, have them note the different types of vegetation in Northern and Southern Europe. Have students think about where certain products in their schools and homes come from. Tell students to write one or two paragraphs explaining how, or if they use, these types of vegetation. Tell students to use precise language and domain-specific vocabulary to elaborate on what types of vegetation they use most. Naturalist, Intrapersonal

C Critical Thinking Skills

Reasoning Have students read the section "Northern Minerals and Energy" independently. **Ask:**

- How does Norway make up for not being an "energy powerhouse"? *(The discovery of petroleum in the North Sea has allowed Norway to become Europe's biggest exporter of oil and a leading supplier of natural gas.)*

- How do you think this has affected Norway's economy? *(Norway's economy has likely improved because of income generated from petroleum.)* Logical/Mathematical, Verbal/Linguistic

---

ANSWERS, p. 370

☑ **READING PROGRESS CHECK** The climate of Norway's western coast is moderated by the warm waters of the Norwegian Current. Northern Italy has a colder mountain climate because it is near the Alps. Winters are colder and snowier than in the southern part of Italy.

CRITICAL THINKING Norway's main exports are petroleum and natural gas.

The area's high elevation and mountain barriers cause dry winds and drought conditions year-round. The dryness causes temperature extremes, with cold winters and hot summers.

☑ **READING PROGRESS CHECK**

Identifying How do landforms and waterways affect the climates of Norway and Italy?

Natural Resources

T GUIDING QUESTION *What natural resources are available to the people of Northern and Southern Europe?*

Northern and Southern Europe hold rich stores of resources. The sea also provides a variety of resources, from fish to oil and gas.

Vegetation

W Plants need to be drought resistant in order to survive the dry summers in a Mediterranean climate. Because of the dry climate and poor soils in Southern Europe, many areas are **scrubland**, or places where short grasses and shrubs are the dominant plants. Trees such as olive, fig, and cypress are common. Two of the most important crops throughout Southern Europe are grapes and olives. Wine, which is made from grapes, is an important export for Spain, Portugal, Italy, and Greece. Italy and Greece are also major exporters of olive oil.

The Sautso Dam in Norway spans northern Europe's largest canyon. The water reservoir behind the dam is 11.8 miles (19 km) long.
▶ **CRITICAL THINKING**
Identifying What are Norway's main exports?

In widely forested Northern Europe, the main plant resource is wood. Forests cover nearly three-fourths of Finland, and wood from these forests is Finland's most important natural resource. Finland exports birch, spruce, and pine wood and paper products to Western Europe. Sweden's forests produce timber, paper, wood pulp, and furniture.

Northern Minerals and Energy

C Norway might not be considered an energy powerhouse. But, thanks to the discovery of petroleum in the North Sea, Norway is now Europe's biggest exporter of oil and one of Europe's leading suppliers of natural gas.

Northern Europe also has rich mineral ore resources. With deposits of iron ore, copper, titanium, lead, nickel, and zinc, Norway remains one of the world's leading metal exporters. Sweden lacks fossil fuels, but it has rich mineral resources. These include iron ore, copper, gold, zinc, and lead.

Arnulf Husmo/Stone/Getty Images

370 *Chapter 12*

---

netw🌐rks   *Online Teaching Options*

ANIMATION

Hydroelectric, Wind, and Geothermal Power

Sequencing Use the animation about alternative energy sources to discuss how water is converted into energy. Have student groups integrate information from the diagram to create and present a "How To" demonstration using only their bodies. For example, one student might spin slowly acting as a turbine, one might raise his or her arm for a lever, and so on. Have one member of each group narrate the sequential process as other students in the group act it out. Remind narrators to use the sequence words *first, next, then,* and *last.* **AL** **ELL** Logical/Mathematical, Kinesthetic

See page 363C for other online activities.

Denmark has few natural mineral or energy resources. However, Denmark uses wind turbines to supply much of its electricity. Sweden and Norway get much of their electricity from hydroelectric power plants. Because of the volcanic nature of the island, Iceland has enormous reserves of geothermal energy. It provides energy for industries and all of the heating needs of Reykjavik, Iceland's major industrial area, as well as several other towns. Iceland's rivers also supply hydroelectric power.

Sea Resources

A rich variety of fish inhabit the North Sea, and the nations along its shores have long-standing fishing traditions. Norway has one of the biggest fishing industries in Europe. Some of the fish caught, such as sand eels and mackerel, are ground into fish meal, a powder that is used in animal feed and fertilizer. Today, fewer people work in the fishing industry. This is because ships that tow large nets behind them, called factory ships or **trawlers**, have increased catches.

At one time, whaling was an important industry for many countries by the sea, including Norway. Whales were hunted for their meat and oil, but by the mid-1900s, many of the largest species of whales were in danger of becoming extinct. Whaling is now limited to a few smaller species that are not believed to be endangered.

Spain and Portugal have extensive Atlantic Ocean coastlines, and fishing is an important industry in both countries. The cities of Vigo and La Coruña are Spain's biggest fishing ports. Spanish fishing fleets range far from their shores, however, leading to conflicts with other countries.

The Mediterranean Sea has long been an important fishing ground for the countries that border its shores, including Italy and Greece. However, overfishing and pollution have reduced fish populations. In addition, the Mediterranean Sea lacks the nutrients necessary to support large populations of fish. Commercial fisheries use fish hatcheries to cultivate and breed fish. After the fish mature, they are released into the sea. That way, they repopulate the fish population that has been overfished.

✔ **READING PROGRESS CHECK**

Analyzing How can a thriving fishing industry be a positive and a negative factor for a country?

Thinking Like a Geographer

A "Hot Water" Project

The building of the Sautso Dam and water plant sparked a heated debate in Norway when the original plans were presented. Opponents pointed out that the project threatened local villages of the indigenous Sami people, as well as an important river. Protests focused attention on the need to protect Sami culture and the environment. The dam was finally built, but the plans changed enough to meet many of the protesters' concerns.

W

FOLDABLES Study Organizer

Include this lesson's information in your Foldable®.

Northern and Southern Europe
Geography | History | Culture

LESSON 1 REVIEW

Reviewing Vocabulary
1. How does *glaciation* affect the landscape?

Answering the Guiding Questions
2. ***Describing*** How are the landforms of Northern and Southern Europe alike and different?

3. ***Describing*** How would the climate of Norway be different without the Norwegian Current?

4. ***Analyzing*** What kinds of problems does the fishing industry in Southern Europe face?

5. ***Informative/Explanatory*** Describe what is unique about the island of Iceland.

LESSON 1 REVIEW ANSWERS

Reviewing Vocabulary

1. Large masses of compacted ice and snow, or glaciers, wear away mountains, move dirt and rocks, and carve valleys into the landscape.

Answering the Guiding Questions

2. **Describing** Both are fairly mountainous; Southern Europe has more land area in large plateaus, plains, and rolling hills.

3. **Describing** The Norwegian Current is a warm current that flows along the western coast of Norway. Without it, western Norway would have much colder temperatures.

4. **Analyzing** Overfishing and pollution have decreased the populations of many types of fish in the Mediterranean Sea.

5. **Informative/Explanatory** Responses should mention that there are volcanoes on the island, that it rests on the Mid-Atlantic Ridge, that Iceland has geothermal energy reserves, and that the southern part of the island has a more moderate climate than the northern part because of a warm ocean current.

W Writing Skills

Argument Discuss the significance of the fishing industry in the Mediterranean Sea. Explain that Greece, for example, has many islands in the Mediterranean Sea, but overfishing and pollution have harmed the fish population, decreasing revenue. Italy has also seen a decline in fishing, even though it has over 4,700 miles (7,600 km) of coastline. Some environmentalists have criticized the use of large nets, widely used in the Mediterranean fishing industry. Some "driftnets" have been banned because of potential harm to marine life.

Oversized or illegal fishing vessels have also contributed to overfishing. According to a recent scientific study, areas that were once healthy ecosystems in the Mediterranean are now barren. The study found that designated marine reserves are now home to the healthiest marine life. Have students work in small groups to brainstorm the pros and cons of designating areas of the Mediterranean as marine reserves to protect its sea life.

Have students write a paragraph to answer the following prompt: **Should more areas in the Mediterranean Sea be designated as "marine protected"?** *(Students' arguments will vary but should include a clear claim either for or against designation of marine protected areas and at least two forms of evidence to support their claim.)* **AL** **Verbal/Linguistic**

Content Background Knowledge

Volcanic Activity In March 2010, an active volcano in southeast Iceland began erupting, shooting a huge plume of volcanic ash and smoke into the air. The smoke reached a height that caused commercial jets to be diverted away from Icelandic air space. Volcanic eruptions are common in Iceland, which has a sparse population, but a subsequent eruption on April 14 forced many of Europe's airports to close due to the enormous plume of volcanic ash.

CLOSE & REFLECT

To close this lesson, have students think about the challenges the physical geography of Northern and Southern Europe presents to the people who live there. Ask them to consider how the people have adapted to geographic issues that cannot be changed.

ANSWER, p. 371

✔ **READING PROGRESS CHECK** It can be positive because it creates jobs and boosts the economy as an export. It can be negative if overfishing causes fish populations to decline to dangerously low levels, limiting the livelihood of those in the industry.

History of the Regions

ENGAGE

Bellringer To introduce the lesson, have students draw a three-column chart in their notebooks labeled *What You Know, What You Want to Know,* and *What You Learned.* Ask students what comes to mind when you mention terms such as *Ancient Greece, the Roman Empire, the Vikings,* and *the Renaissance.* Elicit from students what they know about each topic as they fill in the first column. Then tell students to skim the chapter, looking at headings and images, and fill in the second column. Tell students that they will fill in the third column after they have completed the lesson.

TEACH & ASSESS

R Reading Skills

Determining Central Ideas Have students use context clues to figure out the meaning of the word *city-state (separate communities, independent, linked).* Note that while each city-state in ancient Greece was independent, groups of city-states often fought together against other groups of city-states.

To help students visualize the Greek groups of city-states, draw a web diagram on the board with the term city-state in each circle, connected by lines. Check students' understanding of the word city-state by having them explain the term to a partner.
ELL AL Visual/Spatial

Making Connections Tell students that just as today's countries compete for the opportunity to host the Olympic Games, ancient Greek city-states did, too. And just like today, the Olympic Games were held every four years, although modern games are held at both summer and winter Olympics.

Historians believe that the ancient Greek city-state of Elis was the first to hold the Olympic games in 776 B.C. Elis had a brief alliance with the city-state of Sparta but later chose to ally with the city-state of Athens. Elis managed to maintain neutrality as well as control of hosting the games even after Roman control of Greece, but the city-state eventually collapsed during the fall of the Roman Empire.

ANSWER, p. 372

Taking Notes Summary sentences should include important events in the selected country's history. Example of answers for Italy: joins the Triple Alliance with Germany and Austria; forms friendly relations with France and Great Britain and enters World War I on the side of the Allies; economy goes into a depression after World War I; Mussolini takes over the Italian government; joins forces with Nazi Germany; Italy's forces are defeated by the Allies, and they surrender in 1943.

---

netw⊕rks

There's More Online!

☑ **MAP** Greek and Roman Empires
☑ **SLIDE SHOW** The Renaissance
☑ **VIDEO**

Reading **HELP**DESK

Academic Vocabulary

- achievement
- convert
- rational

Content Vocabulary

- city-state
- longship
- pagan
- Renaissance

TAKING NOTES: *Key Ideas and Details*

Summarizing Choose one of the countries in the lesson. As you read, use a graphic organizer like the one below to describe three or more important events in that country's history.

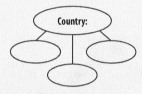

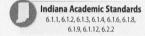
Country:

Indiana Academic Standards
6.1.1, 6.1.2, 6.1.3, 6.1.4, 6.1.6, 6.1.8, 6.1.9, 6.1.12, 6.2.2

Academic Vocabulary

achievement the result gained by a great or heroic deed

372

Lesson 2
History of the Regions

ESSENTIAL QUESTION • *Why do civilizations rise and fall?*

IT MATTERS BECAUSE
Some of the most influential civilizations in the world originated in these two regions. As you read, think about how the accomplishments of the past influence us today.

Early History of the Regions

GUIDING QUESTION *Why were early civilizations in Northern and Southern Europe important?*

Southern Europe produced two of the world's most influential civilizations: ancient Greece and ancient Rome. Greek and Roman, or classical, culture continue to affect our world. During the Middle Ages, the period between A.D. 500 and 1500, Christianity and other classical ideas helped build a new, orderly European civilization. But wars and invasions were still common. The Vikings of Northern Europe were seafarers and invaders. Their voyages changed the history of Western Europe and North America.

Ancient Greece

Greece's many mountains and seacoasts influenced the ancient Greeks to form separate communities called **city-states**. Each city-state was independent, but each one was linked to the other city-states by Greek language and culture. Powerful city-states, such as Athens and Sparta, were rivals, but they faced a common enemy to the east in mighty Persia. When the Persians invaded the Greek mainland in 490 B.C., the combined forces of Athens's navy and Sparta's army spent 40 years defeating them.

After the Persian Wars, Athens emerged as the most developed city-state. Its **achievements** were momentous. For

(l to r) Sigurgeir Jonasson/Nordic Photos/Getty Images; Salvator Barki/Flickr/Getty Images; Keystone-France/Gamma-Keystone/Getty Images

---

netw⊕rks   *Online Teaching Options*

VIDEO

Islam in Spain and the Alhambra

Discussing Use this video about the history of Islam in Spain to introduce the lesson. Ask students to share what they learned from the video and if anything surprised them. Guide a class discussion about the influence that Islamic, Greek, and Roman cultures have had on modern-day civilizations. Have students brainstorm everyday examples of this influence. **AL** Visual/Spatial

See page 363D for other online activities.

BBC Motion Gallery Education

example, the ideas of philosophers such as Socrates, Plato, and Aristotle are still studied. Greek art set a standard for beauty that later influenced the Romans and inspires people to this day. Athens was also the first known democracy. The free citizens of Athens enjoyed a way of life that was unique in ancient times.

Wars weakened the Greek city-states, and Macedon, a kingdom north of Greece, took advantage. The Macedonian king, Alexander the Great, extended his rule over not only Greece, but also Asia Minor (now the Asian part of Turkey), Persia, and Egypt. Even though Alexander died at the age of 33, he spread Greek culture throughout an empire that lasted another 300 years.

Roman Empires

While the Greek city-states were at their height, another group was slowly gaining power to the west on the Italian peninsula. A series of small settlements built on hills along the Tiber River eventually merged into a single city that became Rome. Later, the Romans put government into the hands of consuls, who were elected to office annually. This was the birth of the Roman Republic.

The Romans had a talent for warfare, and they set out to conquer their neighbors. By 275 B.C., they controlled the Italian peninsula, inspiring Rome to add even more territory.

Indiana CONNECTION

Democracy

Ancient Greek and Roman political practices live on today. Athens was a direct democracy in which citizens met to debate and vote on government matters. Today, many towns in New England hold meetings in which townspeople practice direct democracy. In the Roman Republic, citizens chose representatives to make laws and govern on their behalf. The United States today is a representative democracy, a republic in which citizens elect officials to government bodies such as the U.S. Senate, modeled in part on the ancient Roman Senate

MAP SKILLS

1 **PHYSICAL GEOGRAPHY** Why was Italy an ideal location to be the center of the Roman Empire?

2 **PLACES AND REGIONS** Which areas were part of Alexander's empire and later part of the Roman Empire?

Greek and Roman Empires

Alexander's empire in 322 B.C.
Roman Empire at its greatest extent, A.D. 200
Overlap between Alexander's empire and the Roman Empire

NORTH SEA
BRITANNIA
ATLANTIC OCEAN
GAUL
HISPANIA
Rome ITALY
Carthage
GREECE
Sparta Athens
Byzantium (Constantinople)
Black Sea
Caspian Sea
PERSIAN EMPIRE
INDIA
Babylon Persepolis
Mediterranean Sea
Alexandria
AFRICA
EGYPT
Thebes
ARABIA
Persian Gulf
TROPIC OF CANCER
Red Sea
INDIAN OCEAN

0 600 miles
0 600 kilometers
Lambert Azimuthal Equal-Area projection

MAP

Greek and Roman Empires

Determining Cause and Effect Use the interactive map of the rise, spread, and collapse of the Greek and Roman Empires to discuss the influences of these two empires on European culture in early history. As a class, discuss the cause and effect of the rise and fall of each empire. **AL** Logical/Mathematical

See page 363D for other online activities.

T Technology Skills

Collaborating and Making Presentations Tell students that the ancient Greek meeting place was known as the *agora*. Citizens met at the agora for social activities and to discuss religious and political business. The agora was also the marketplace and hosted dramatic performances. Organize students into five groups and assign each group one of the following: philosophy, plays/literature, government, art/sculpture, or architecture. Tell students that they will work together to make a presentation for an Athens Agora Achievements Fair in which they highlight aspects of ancient Greek accomplishments.

Direct students to research their topics using reliable online sources, such as .org or .edu sites. Then have groups present the information to the class. Encourage students to get creative with costumes, political speeches, skits, performances, and so on. **Verbal/Linguistic, Kinesthetic**

W Writing Skills

Argument Tell students to conduct online research about Athenian and Spartan society and government. Research should answer the following questions about both city-states: **Ask:**

- *How were citizens treated?*
- *Were all citizens free?*
- *How were women treated?*
- *What was the type of government?*

After students have had time to gather information and answer these questions, tell them to prepare a short speech from the point of view of an Athenian or Spartan political leader or citizen. Speeches should incorporate answers to the questions and persuade listeners to be in favor of either Athenian or Spartan government and society. **Verbal/Linguistic**

V Visual Skills

Reading a Map Have students work in small groups to calculate the size of Alexander's empire in 322 B.C. and the Roman Empire in A.D. 200. Tell students to use an online converting tool to calculate areas in both miles and kilometers. Challenge students to visualize the size of each empire by comparing it to the size of the United States. Then have students answer the Map Skills questions. **Logical/Mathematical, Visual/Spatial**

ANSWERS, p. 373

MAP SKILLS
1. It was located about midway in the Mediterranean area and was centrally located to govern a vast area from the Atlantic Ocean to the eastern Mediterranean Sea.
2. Greece, Asia Minor, Persia, and Egypt

Evaluating a Web Site Tell students that they will be interpreting information from two Web sites that present information about migration routes during the Viking Age. Suggest that students review Web sites affiliated with reputable publications such as *National Geographic* or museums such as the Smithsonian's National Museum of Natural History. Recommend search terms such as "Viking migration routes" or "Viking trade routes."

Students should take notes to assess the Web sites and determine if they present sound reasoning and relevant evidence to support their claims about Viking migration routes and raids. As homework, have students review other Web sites that present information about the Viking raids and determine if any irrelevant evidence is introduced. Based on their research, have students create a map depicting Viking migration routes and raids. **BL** Logical/Mathematical, Visual/Spatial

R Reading Skills

Determining Word Meanings Explain to students that the term *polytheism* refers to the belief in more than one god. The term *monotheism* refers to religions such as Christianity and Islam that ascribe to the belief in one god. To reinforce understanding, have students brainstorm other words that use the prefixes *poly-* and *mono-* (*polygon, monorail*). **Ask:** What religion did the Vikings follow? *(a pagan religion based on ancient myths with several gods)* Verbal/Linguistic

W Writing Skills

Informative/Explanatory Have students turn to a partner and summarize the information from the section on the Viking Age. For homework, direct students to read an online article about Viking culture, such as "The Amazing Vikings," published in *Time* magazine's May 8, 2000 issue. Have students write a summary of their findings. Verbal/Linguistic

---

ANSWER, p. 374

☑ READING PROGRESS CHECK The Greeks were able to defend themselves against more powerful empires by banding together in war. Eventually, though, war among the Greek city-states weakened them. Powerful Roman armies were able to conquer vast areas of Europe. Viking raids allowed the Vikings to reach other lands, and the people and beliefs in those places eventually changed the Vikings, turning them into Christians, explorers, and traders.

Thinking Like a Geographer

"Father of Geography"

Eratosthenes was a Greek scholar who closely estimated the circumference of Earth by measuring shadow lengths at different latitudes. Educated people of this time understood that Earth was round. Eratosthenes, who was born around 276 B.C., was the first person to use the term *geography*. He is often referred to as the father of geography.

T

Visual Vocabulary

Longship The Vikings raided and explored on sturdy ships that were 45 feet to 75 feet (14 m to 23 m) in length. These longships were made of oak and were powered by wind and up to 60 oarsmen. The square sails were sometimes brightly colored.

W

Academic Vocabulary

convert to bring about a change in beliefs

Spain, Sicily, Macedonia, Greece, and Asia Minor fell to Roman armies and were turned into Roman provinces. Eventually, a powerful military leader, Julius Caesar, seized control of Rome. After Caesar was assassinated, his great-nephew, Octavian, given the title Augustus, became the first of a series of emperors, and the Roman Republic was no more. The new Roman Empire expanded eastward to Egypt and westward to the British Isles.

In A.D. 330, Emperor Constantine moved the capital of the empire from Rome to the Greek city of Byzantium, in what is now Turkey. This location was closer to important trade routes to China and Southwest Asia. The new capital, renamed Constantinople, was also farther from the barbarians who were attacking the Roman Empire in the west. Repeated invasions continued to weaken the western empire. German invaders took control of Rome in A.D. 476. This was the end of the western Roman Empire. The eastern empire lasted for almost the next 1,000 years until it fell in 1453 to the Ottoman Turks. The Turks changed the name Constantinople to Istanbul.

The Viking Age

In the A.D. 700s, ships carrying warriors from Scandinavia began raiding the coasts of Western Europe. At home, these warriors were farmers or young men eager for adventure. At sea, they were pirates called Vikings, and they spread fear and destruction wherever their ships traveled. In A.D. 793, they raided and destroyed the abbey at Holy Island in northeastern England, killing and enslaving the monks. Later, the Vikings conquered other parts of Britain as well as Ireland and what is now Normandy in France.

The Vikings were excellent seafarers, and they sailed their **longships** great distances to explore and to trade. They sailed westward across the Atlantic, founding settlements in Iceland and Greenland. About the year A.D. 1000, Leif Eriksson led the Vikings to a land he named Vinland. Vinland was Newfoundland, in Canada. Eriksson became the first European known to have reached North America.

The Vikings followed a **pagan** religion, which was based on ancient myths and had a number of different gods. After about A.D. 1000, Viking groups throughout Scandinavia began to **convert** to Christianity. The Viking threat died out as more Scandinavians stayed home. They contributed to building the kingdoms of Norway, Sweden, and Denmark. However, traces of Viking culture—especially their epic tales of adventure and heroism—remained in the British Isles and other parts of Western Europe.

R

☑ READING PROGRESS CHECK
Determining Central Ideas How did warfare affect the civilizations of Greece, Rome, and the Vikings?

---

netw⊙rks   *Online Teaching Options*

DIAGRAM

Viking Longship

Analyzing Visuals Use the diagram of the Viking longship to discuss the Vikings and their explorations, along with the technologies they had to achieve to accomplish their early explorations. Have students write a paragraph about the Vikings and their legacy as seafaring warriors. **BL**

See page 363D for other online activities.

Interactive Charts/Tables/Diagrams

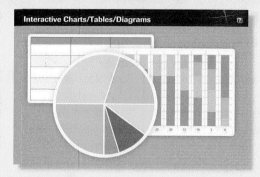

Discovery and "Rebirth"

GUIDING QUESTION *How did the Renaissance pave the way for voyages of discovery?*

During the long period known as the Middle Ages, many of the ancient achievements were forgotten. Important manuscripts were lost or destroyed. Many of the writings that survived ended up in the East, where scholars could still read classical Greek. Beginning in the 1300s, a curiosity for Greek and Roman learning took hold in the Italian city of Florence, where poets such as Dante and Petrarch were inspired by ancient literature. To them, these works were freer, more **rational**, and more joyous than the works of their world.

Renaissance

When the Byzantine Empire fell in 1453, many scholars traveled west with ancient Greek manuscripts. At the same time, a practical printing press was invented in Germany. Suddenly, it was possible to print many copies of manuscripts that until then had to be lettered by hand. People could now own and read books.

These breakthroughs resulted in a period of artistic and intellectual activity known as the **Renaissance**. The Italian city of Florence became a center of learning and culture. Architects drew inspiration from the ancients and created new architectural styles. Painters and sculptors, such as Leonardo da Vinci, looked to nature for inspiration.

Curiosity about the natural world also led to the birth of modern science. In 1609 Italian astronomer Galileo designed a telescope to observe the moon and the planets. Galileo's observations helped prove Copernicus's theory that the planets, including Earth, orbit the sun. The Renaissance began in Italy, but Galileo's work influenced scientists throughout Europe.

Empires and Exploration

By the 1400s, Europeans wanted to do more business with China and India, but overland routes were long and dangerous. Prince Henry of Portugal inspired sailors and navigators to find a sea route to Asia by sailing around Africa. In 1488 Portuguese sea captain Bartholomeu Dias reached the Cape of Good Hope at the southern tip of Africa.

Academic Vocabulary

rational based on reason or logic

Hagia Sophia (or "Holy Wisdom") in Istanbul, at first, was a Christian church. It later became a Muslim place of worship, and today it is a museum.

▶ **CRITICAL THINKING**

Identifying What was the name of the city of Istanbul when Hagia Sophia was built?

Chapter 12 **375**

C Critical Thinking Skills

Making Inferences Read aloud the Guiding Question. Then have students read the first paragraph on this page. Tell students that the period before the Renaissance is often referred to as the Dark Ages, which was a time of a lot of violence and little learning.

Have pairs of students discuss why Renaissance thinkers were inspired by Greek and Roman learning. **Ask:** What can be inferred about the literary works of the 1300s, knowing that ancient literature inspired poets such as Dante and Petrarch? *(Students' answers will vary but should include valid reasons as to why these poets might have been inspired by ancient literature. For example, the fact that they were inspired by these more "rational" works indicates that work during their time may have been irrational or illogical, which reflected the void of learning during the Dark Ages.)* **BL** Logical/Mathematical

T Technology Skills

Collaborating and Making Presentations Tell students to choose a person mentioned in the text who lived during the Renaissance, or to research other Renaissance philosophers, artists, and astronomers online. Have students use reliable online sources to research their chosen person and take notes about the contributions that person made to science, astronomy, philosophy, art, or literature.

Have students work in small groups to present a Renaissance Reality Show to the class featuring the people they have researched and learned about. You may wish to set up a scenario for the skit, such as a house on an Italian hillside where these people have gathered for the weekend. Tell students to say things that these Renaissance philosophers, artists, scientists, and astronomers would have said to each other based on their beliefs or field of work. Remind students to stay in character while performing their skits for the class.

BL Verbal/Linguistic, Kinesthetic

The Renaissance

Analyzing Use the interactive slide show on the Renaissance, Enlightenment, and the Byzantine Empire to discuss changes in European culture. Explain that new ways of thinking led to the birth of scientific methods and exploration. Guide students to understand the tremendous impact of Renaissance philosophers, artists, and scientists. **AL** Verbal/Linguistic

See page 363D for other online activities.

ANSWER, p. 375

CRITICAL THINKING Constantinople

V Visual Skills

Visualizing After students have read "Empires and Exploration," have them work in pairs to visualize the information presented in this section. Then have them work with their partners to create simple maps that show where the explorers traveled. Tell students to assign a different colored route for each explorer on their maps. Visual/Spatial

G₁ Critical Thinking Skills

Sequencing To help students understand the sequence of events and expeditions during the 1400s, have them read the information and create a time line with key dates and events from the text. **Ask:**

• Where did Bartholomeu Dias sail and when did he get there? *(the Cape of Good Hope at the southern tip of Africa in 1488)*

• Which explorer reached India, and in what year? *(Vasco da Gama, 1498)*

• Which country sponsored the voyage of Columbus? *(Spain)*

• Where did Columbus think he had landed in 1492? *(Asia)* **AL** Visual/Spatial, Logical/Mathematical

G₂ Critical Thinking Skills

Determining Cause and Effect Have students read the section, "Religion in the Regions," with a partner. Then **ask:**

• What caused kingdoms across Northern Europe to break from the Roman Catholic religion? *(New ideas by Martin Luther caused people to question their faith and seek religious freedom.)*

• What effect do you think this break from the Roman Catholic Church had on people in other parts of Europe? *(Students' answers may vary but might mention that Martin Luther's rebellion against certain Catholic practices, which led to a break from the Catholic church, likely caused other people in Europe to question the Catholic religious doctrine.)* Verbal/Linguistic

---

ANSWER, p. 376

✓ READING PROGRESS CHECK When the Roman Empire split, the Roman Catholic Church remained in the west and the Eastern Orthodox Church formed in the east. Christianity eventually spread through Western and Northern Europe. During the Renaissance, the new ideas of the Protestant Reformation reached into Northern Europe, and most of the people in that part of Europe eventually became Protestant.

376

Think Again ❓

Vatican City is the world's smallest country.

True. Vatican City is located within the city of Rome, but it is actually the world's smallest, fully independent country. In the mid-1800s, the Church began to lose the area known as the Papal States as Italy began to unite into a single country. The pope protested, and the Vatican refused to join with the rest of the country. In 1929 the Church reached an agreement with Italy. Vatican City became independent.

Ten years later, Vasco de Gama rounded the Cape and sailed to India. The Portuguese established sea trade with South Asia.

Christopher Columbus, an Italian navigator, had a different idea: Why not reach Asia via a westward sea route? Spain agreed to finance the expedition, and Columbus left Spain with three ships on August 3, 1492. Columbus underestimated the size of Earth and overestimated the size of Asia. When he finally saw land, he assumed he had reached Asia. In fact, it was a Caribbean island. Columbus, like Leif Eriksson before him, had landed in the Americas.

Through its expeditions to the Americas, Spain became the most powerful country in Europe. The Spanish built an empire in Mexico, Central America, and South America. They conquered the Aztec of Mexico and the Inca Empire in South America, and they enslaved the native peoples of the Caribbean.

Contact between Europe and the Americas also resulted in the exchange of goods. Europeans brought wheat, olives, bananas, coffee, sugar, horses, sheep, pigs, and cattle to the Americas. In exchange, the Europeans received tomatoes, corn (maize), potatoes, squash, cacao (the source of chocolate), and hot peppers. This commerce is known as the Columbian Exchange.

Religion in the Regions

Meanwhile, Christianity had become identified with Europe. Rome considered itself the seat of Christianity as early as the A.D. 100s. When the Roman Empire was split into eastern and western empires, Christianity in the empire also split into eastern and western branches. The western branch evolved into the Roman Catholic Church, which was dominant in Italy and Spain and throughout Western Europe. The eastern branch became the Eastern Orthodox Church, centered in Greece and parts of Eastern Europe.

The rise of the religion of Islam threatened the power of the Christian churches. The Moors were Muslims, followers of Islam, who invaded Spain from Northern Africa in the A.D. 700s and ruled most of Spain for more than 700 years. The Byzantine Empire fell to the Ottoman Turks, another Muslim people, in 1453. Under Ottoman rule, Greek Christians were free to practice their religion, but their rights were limited compared to those of Muslims. Over the next few centuries, Greek Christians struggled to preserve their traditions and beliefs. Today, the vast majority of people in Greece still belong to the Greek Orthodox Church.

During the 1520s, the ideas of Martin Luther contributed to the spread of the Protestant Reformation. Kingdoms across Northern Europe broke away from the Roman Catholic religion. The countries adopted some form of Protestantism as their official state religion.

✓ READING PROGRESS CHECK

Determining Central Ideas Why did Christianity change as it took hold in Southern and Northern Europe?

376 Chapter 12

---

netw⊙rks   *Online Teaching Options*

MAP

Protestants in the 1500s

Analyzing Maps Help students understand the significance of religion in Northern and Southern Europe by having them analyze a map about the religious split in the 1500s. Have students fill in a Venn diagram comparing and contrasting the two religious splits. **AL** Visual/Spatial

See page 363D for other online activities.

History in the Modern Era

GUIDING QUESTION *What has been the relationship between Northern Europe and Southern Europe over the last 200 years?*

The 1800s brought sweeping changes to the regions. The Scandinavian countries saw their military glory vanish, but they became prosperous democracies. Spain and Portugal lost much of their overseas empires, followed by conflicts at home. Greece won freedom from the Turks. Italy's separate territories, except for San Marino and what later became Vatican City, united in 1870.

Conflict and War

During the 1900s, Northern and Southern Europe were involved in both world wars. After fighting a civil war in the 1930s, Spain stayed out of World War II. However, Italy, ruled by dictator Benito Mussolini, sided with Nazi Germany in that conflict. The Italians were defeated by allied U.S. and British forces in 1943, a year and a half before the war in Europe ended.

The period following World War II brought even more political changes. Italy became a democracy and began to rebuild its economy. Greece suffered a brutal civil war between Communists and opponents of communism. Spain, Portugal, and Greece joined Italy as democracies.

The Modern Era

Since 1945, Scandinavia has enjoyed a high standard of living as well as political and social freedoms. Its leaders worked for world peace and economic growth in the world's new nations. Beginning in the 1990s, the nations of Northern and Southern Europe developed closer ties with each other and with other European countries as members of the European Union (EU).

☑ **READING PROGRESS CHECK**

Identifying What country did Italy side with during World War II?

Swedish troops helped Finland in that country's conflict with the Soviet Union during World War II.
▶ **CRITICAL THINKING**
Describing How was Southern Europe involved in World War II?

FOLDABLES
Study Organizer

Include this lesson's information in your Foldable®.

Northern and Southern Europe
Geography | History | Culture

LESSON 2 REVIEW

Reviewing Vocabulary
1. What changes did the *Renaissance* bring about in Europe?

Answering the Guiding Questions
2. *Identifying* Why were the ancient Greek and Roman civilizations important?

3. *Analyzing* How did the development of printing help promote voyages of discovery?

4. *Describing* How would you characterize the relationship among the countries of Northern Europe over the past 200 years?

5. *Argument Writing* Select a Renaissance thinker you believe was the most important. In a paragraph, explain why you believe this person's contributions were the most significant to the age and to people today.

Chapter 12 **377**

LESSON 2 REVIEW ANSWERS

Reviewing Vocabulary

1. People began to take new interest in the writings of ancient Greece and Rome. Painters and sculptors began to create new types of art. New styles of architecture developed. Modern science was born.

Answering the Guiding Questions

2. **Identifying** Responses should demonstrate students' understanding that Greek and Roman ideas about art, architecture, philosophy, and government are still influential today.

3. **Analyzing** People who read about foreign lands were eager to travel, which encouraged advances in navigation and allowed voyages that led to the discovery of new lands.

4. **Describing** Responses should note that there was often conflict among the countries, with many wars and invasions.

5. **Argument Writing** Accept any reasonable response that is supported by information about contributions and discoveries during the Renaissance.

V Visual Skills

Creating Charts Help students organize information about the changing relationships between countries in Northern Europe and Southern Europe. Have students create a two-column chart in which the left column is labeled with the countries or regions referenced in the paragraph. In the right column, have students note the change. **AL** Visual/Spatial

Scandinavia	military power decreased; wealthy democracies
Spain and Portugal	lost several overseas empires; endured conflicts at home
Greece	won freedom from Turks
Italy	territories united (except for San Marino and Vatican City)

Content Background Knowledge

The Eolie Islands (also referred to as the Aeolian Islands) are a group of small islands off the coast of Sicily in Italy. These volcanic islands were once home to ancient Greeks, who believed that Aeolus, god of the wind, lived on the islands, which is how the islands got their name. As with other regions in Southern Europe, the islands had their share of conflict. They were inhabited by the Greeks until the sixth century, when they were taken over by the Romans. Before World War II, political prisoners were sent to the Eolie Islands as a form of punishment. Ownership of the islands changed often during the 1300s, until they were officially united with Sicily in the late 1400s.

CLOSE & REFLECT

Categorizing Have students complete the charts they created at the beginning of the lesson by filling in the *What You Learned* column. Then guide a class discussion triggered by the Essential Question: *Why do civilizations rise and fall?*

ANSWERS, p. 377

CRITICAL THINKING Italy was the key southern European player in World War II. Under dictator Benito Mussolini, Italy joined forces with Nazi Germany against the Allies. Italian forces were defeated by Allied forces from the United States and Great Britain. Italy surrendered to the Allies in late 1943, a year and a half before Germany.
☑ **READING PROGRESS CHECK** Italy sided with Nazi Germany in World War II.

Keystone-France/Gamma-Keystone/Getty Images

ENGAGE

Bellringer Before students begin this lesson, ask them to think about the history of Northern and Southern Europe that they learned in the previous lesson. Have students consider the ideas and contributions made in these regions. Guide students to make connections to the Essential Question: *How do new ideas change the way people live?* **Ask:** How do you think ideas and contributions of the past have affected the people in the countries in Northern and Southern Europe? *(Possible answer: Ideas and art of the Renaissance led to countries like Italy becoming leaders in fashion and architecture.)*

TEACH & ASSESS

R Reading Skills

Determining Word Meanings Have students locate the phrase *infant mortality* in the text. Explain that the word *mortal* is from the Anglo-French *mortel, mortal;* and from the Latin *mortalis.* In French, the word *mort* means death. Ask anyone if they know what the word for death is in Spanish. *(muerte)* Explain the meaning of the prefix *im-,* meaning *not,* and write the word *immortal* on the board. **Ask:** The ancient Greeks believed their gods were immortal. What does this mean? *(They did not die.)* Then have students describe the meaning of *infant mortality* in their own words. **AL**
ELL Verbal/Linguistic

C Critical Thinking Skills

Making Inferences Tell students to read the information about where people live in Europe. Have them consider why people live where they do. **Ask:** Why do you think the population in rural areas of Southern Europe has decreased over the last 100 years? *(Students' answers will vary but may mention that more people have moved to cities in recent years due to employment opportunities, better public transportation, or cultural offerings.)*

Discuss the issues that might arise as a result of people moving to cities. *(overcrowding, pollution, crime, etc.)* Logical/Mathematical

---

ANSWER, p. 378

Taking Notes Notes should include several contributions, such as: for **Northern Europe:** classical composers Carl Nielsen (Denmark), Edvard Grieg (Norway), and Jean Sibelius (Finland), pop music performers ABBA (Sweden), Björk, Sigur Rós; **Southern Europe:** baroque painting, futurist painting, Giorgio di Chirico (all Italy), the guitar (Spain), Italian opera

---

netw⊕rks

There's More Online!

☑ **SLIDE SHOW** Recreation in Northern and Southern Europe

☑ **VIDEO**

Reading **HELP**DESK

Academic Vocabulary
• **contribution**

Content Vocabulary
• **homogeneous**
• **dialect**
• **welfare capitalism**
• **recession**

TAKING NOTES: *Key Ideas and Details*

Identify Use a graphic organizer like this one to list several artistic contributions of the countries of Northern and Southern Europe.

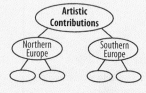

Artistic Contributions

Northern Europe   Southern Europe

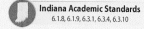

Indiana Academic Standards
6.1.8, 6.1.9, 6.3.1, 6.3.4, 6.3.10

378

Lesson 3
Life in Northern and Southern Europe

ESSENTIAL QUESTION · *How do new ideas change the way people live?*

IT MATTERS BECAUSE
The countries of Europe are experiencing changes that will affect the lives of the people who live there. These changes will alter the relationships of the countries to each other and to the rest of the world.

People and Places

GUIDING QUESTION *What is the distribution of the populations in Northern Europe and in Southern Europe?*

Aging Populations
In most places in Northern and Southern Europe, improvements in the standard of living have helped reduce infant mortality—the number of babies who die in their first year of life. Improvements in the standard of living have also helped people live longer. You might think this would mean that populations in European countries are growing more quickly than in the past. That is not the case. Birthrates have declined as Europeans decided to have fewer children, and population growth has slowed in the past few decades. Older people have become a larger percentage of the population. Therefore, the population is aging.

Where People Live
As in other parts of Europe, the proportion of people who live in the rural areas of Southern Europe has decreased over the last 100 years. In 1900 Italy's three largest cities—Rome, Milan, and Naples—each had about 500,000 residents. The combined metropolitan area population of the three cities is

---

netw⊕rks   *Online Teaching Options*

VIDEO

World's Wonders—Grand Canal of Venice

Analyzing Use this video about the Grand Canal of Venice to introduce the lesson. Have students write a travel brochure about the unique layout and architecture of Venice and the threat of rising sea levels to the life of the city.
BL Verbal/Linguistic

See page 363E for other online activities.

now about 10 million. About 60 percent of the population of Greece live in cities. In fact, 25 percent of the population live in the capital city of Athens. More than 75 percent of Spain's population live in cities and towns, making rugged rural areas such as the Meseta Central region seem nearly empty in comparison. Madrid, Spain's capital, has a population of more than 5 million, and the population density is 1,750 persons per square mile (675 per sq. km). Compare this to the population density for the country as a whole: 220 persons per square mile (85 per sq. km).

In Northern Europe, the population is even more concentrated in cities. Most people live in the southern parts of the countries because of the milder climates. More than half of Iceland's population lives in the capital city, Reykjavik. The capital cities of Northern European countries—Copenhagen (Denmark), Oslo (Norway), Stockholm (Sweden), and Helsinki (Finland)—have by far the largest populations of any cities in their countries. They are also their countries' primary cultural centers.

☑ READING PROGRESS CHECK

Analyzing Why is the population of Northern and Southern Europe growing older?

Bikers cross a historic square in the central area of Copenhagen, the capital of Denmark.

▶ **CRITICAL THINKING**
Describing What are major characteristics of capital cities in Northern European countries?

Life in Northern and Southern Europe

C Critical Thinking Skills

Synthesizing Review with students the steps to convert a percent into a fraction, using 50 percent as an example:

1. Write the percent divided by 100. *(50/100)*
2. If the percent is not a whole number, multiply the top and bottom by 10 (if one number follows the decimal point) or 100 (if two numbers follow the decimal point), and so on.
3. Simplify or reduce the fraction. *(50/100 = 5/10 = ½)*

Then have students convert the information about Southern Europe's population percentages into fractions. **Ask:**

- **What fraction of Greece's population lives in cities?** *(3/5)*
- **What fraction of Greece's population lives in Athens?** *(1/4)*
- **What fraction of Spain's population lives in cities and towns?** *(3/4)* **BL** Logical/Mathematical

V Visual Skills

Visualizing Have students work in pairs to convert the information given in the text about Northern Europe's population into a variety of circle graphs. You may want to encourage pairs to do additional research to make their circle graphs more accurate and complete. Have them give each of their circle graphs a title and label their circle graphs with the appropriate cities, countries, or regions of Northern Europe that they have chosen to represent. **Ask:**

- **Where does most of Northern Europe's population live?** *(in the southern part of its countries)* **Why?** *(The climate is milder.)*
- **What fraction of Iceland's population lives in the capital city?** *(more than half)*
- **Which cities in Northern Europe have the largest populations?** *(Copenhagen, Denmark; Oslo, Norway; Stockholm, Sweden; and Helsinki, Finland)*
- **Where would you like to live? Why?** *(Answers will vary but students should give reasons for their choices.)* **AL** Visual/Spatial, Logical/Mathematical, Intrapersonal

CHARTS

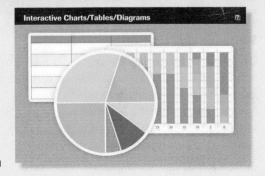

Interactive Charts/Tables/Diagrams

Comparing Population Pyramids: Northern and Southern Europe

Identifying Central Issues Use the population pyramids to discuss the aging of Europe's population. Ask students to consider the distribution across age and gender in Northern and Southern Europe and the impact it might have on future generations. Elicit from students some of the problems an aging population might have on society. *(Possible answers: increased need for health care facilities and in-home health care services, drop in work force, economic impact related to public pensions and social security, etc.)* Logical/Mathematical

See page 363E for other online activities.

ANSWERS, p. 379

☑ READING PROGRESS CHECK People are choosing to have fewer babies. At the same time, advances in medical technology allow people to live longer.

CRITICAL THINKING Most of Northern Europe's population is concentrated in cities, primarily capital cities, which are located in the southern parts of the Northern European countries, where the climate is milder. The capital cities are their countries' primary economic and cultural centers.

Dag Sundberg/Photographer's Choice/Getty Images

Life in Northern and Southern Europe

V Visual Skills

Diagramming Have students create a two-column chart with the labels *Country* and *Language*. As students read about the different ethnic and language groups, have them fill in their charts with languages that are spoken in various countries in Northern and Southern Europe. **Visual/Spatial**

Country	Language
Denmark	Danish
Sweden	Swedish
Norway	Norwegian
Finland	Finnish
Greece	Greek
Italy	Italian; northern Italy: German, French, Slovenian
Spain	Spanish (Castilian, Catalan, Galician)

R Reading Skills

Determining Word Meanings Have students locate the highlighted word *homogeneous* in the text. Guide students to break down the word into parts: *homo* = same; *gen* = birth, race, or produce; *-eous* = having the quality of, relating to. Have students work in pairs to brainstorm words they can think of using the word part *gen* (*generate, genesis, genetics, genealogy, pathogen, etc.*). Then have partners take turns using the word *homogeneous* in a sentence. **AL** **ELL** **Verbal/Linguistic**

C Critical Thinking Skills

Identifying Evidence Read the section "Religion and the Arts" to students. Then **ask:** What evidence proves the Protestant Reformation was a success in Northern Europe? *(More than three-quarters of all people living in Northern Europe belong to a Lutheran Church. This is evidence of the influence by Martin Luther, who initiated the Protestant Reformation.)* **Logical/Mathematical**

Content Background Knowledge

Share these fun facts about the Balearic Islands with students.

- The Balearic Islands are comprised of the islands of Ibiza, Formentera, Majorca, and Minorca. Pose the question, Which island do you think is bigger, Majorca or Minorca? Hint: look at the root words! (major/minor)
- The capital of Minorca is Mahon, where supposedly Mahon-esa was first made. According to legend, a French general brought the sauce back to France, where it became quite popular. Can you guess what this sauce is? That's right: mayonnaise!

Thinking Like a Geographer

The Euskera Language

The most unusual language in Spain is Euskera, an ancient language that is unrelated to other European languages. Euskera is spoken by the Basque people, who live near the Pyrenees mountains. The Basque are one of the oldest surviving ethnic groups in Europe. Today, most Basque people can also speak Spanish or French. Euskera is still widely spoken though, even in schools.

People and Cultures

V

GUIDING QUESTION *Why are most people in Northern Europe Protestant, whereas most people in Southern Europe are Catholic?*

Ethnic and Language Groups

The populations of the Northern European countries are relatively **homogeneous**, or alike, although they have some ethnic diversity due to immigration from Asia and Africa. The population of Norway is more than 90 percent Norwegian, and the population of Finland is more than 90 percent Finnish. Denmark and Sweden are similar. The original settlers of these lands were the Sami, or Lapps. Many of the Sami live by fishing and hunting, as they have for thousands of years. Most live in the northern parts of Sweden, Norway, and Finland. Iceland was first settled by Celts and later conquered by Norway. The bulk of the population in Iceland is a blend of the two ethnic groups.

R

The languages spoken in Denmark, Sweden, and Norway developed from a common German language base. Today, Danish, Swedish, and Norwegian are similar enough that the speakers can usually understand each other, even though each language is distinct. Finnish is unrelated to the other languages; it is closer to the Hungarian and Estonian languages.

The populations of the Southern European countries are relatively homogeneous but more diversified than it might seem at first. Spain is actually a nation of regions that constantly resist unifying pressures from the central government.

Greece also has small populations of Turks, Albanians, Macedonians, and Rom (gypsies). Most people speak Greek, which is closely related to the language spoken in ancient Greece. Most of Italy is ethnically Italian, but minority groups in northern Italy speak German, French, or Slovenian. The Italian language has many **dialects**, or regional variations, but most people speak and understand the Italian that originates around Florence and Rome. Most people in Spain speak a form of Spanish called Castilian. Other dialects are spoken in Spain as well. People in Catalonia, Valencia, and the Balearic Islands speak Catalan. Galicia is an area in northwestern Spain. People there speak Galician, which is closely related to Portuguese.

Religion and the Arts

C

The Protestant Reformation was successful in Northern Europe. To this day, more than three-quarters of all people living in Northern Europe belong to a Lutheran church. A small percentage are either Catholic or Muslim. In Finland, 15 percent of the people do not belong to any church.

---

networks   *Online Teaching Options*

WORKSHEET

Scandinavian Culture

Comparing and Contrasting Use a collaborative worksheet about the cultural geography in Scandinavia to launch a discussion about daily life in Northern and Southern Europe. Have students work together to compare and contrast the daily life of Northern Europe to Southern Europe. Suggest that students use a Venn diagram to visualize their comparisons. Guide a discussion about similarities and differences that students noted in their diagrams. **AL** **ELL**

See page 363E for other online activities.

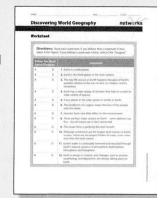

Sylvain Sonnet/Photographer's Choice/Getty Images

In Southern Europe, the Reformation had little lasting impact. Most people in Spain, Portugal, and Italy belong to the Roman Catholic Church. In Greece, nearly 98 percent of the population belongs to the Greek Orthodox Church. Immigrants from Muslim countries, however, have been slowly changing the religious makeup of Southern Europe.

As the birthplace of the Renaissance, Italy has made many contributions to painting, sculpture, and architecture. The Baroque artists who followed the Renaissance period also emerged from the Italian city-states. The genius of Renaissance and Baroque art can be seen in the palaces, churches, city squares, statues, and paintings of cities such as Rome and Florence. The art centers of Europe moved to Western Europe following the Baroque period—to countries such as France and the Netherlands. In the 1900s, the Italian futurist painters rebelled against traditional art. They painted scenes of modern life that celebrated the industrial age. Italy today is one of the world centers for architecture and fashion.

The Spanish Catalan architect Antoni Gaudí began to build the Sagrada Familia ("Holy Family") Church in Barcelona during the 1880s. This Roman Catholic place of worship, still being built, is due to be finished about 2026.

▶ CRITICAL THINKING

Analyzing Why are three different forms of Christianity practiced in Northern Europe and Southern Europe today?

R

Chapter 12 **381**

MAP

Three Religions in Europe, 1500s

Discussing Use the animated map to discuss the three major religions, the changes in Southern Europe, and their influences on the culture of Southern Europe. Guide a class discussion about the impact of these religions on the population and culture of Northern and Southern Europe.
AL Visual/Spatial, Verbal/Linguistic

See page 363E for other online activities.

T Technology Skills

Researching on the Internet Have students look at the photograph on this page. Explain that the influence of Renaissance and Baroque art and architecture can be seen throughout Europe in its great cathedrals, such as Barcelona's Sagrada Familia. Assign the following activity as a homework assignment:

Tell students they will act as tour guides for a group of American students studying architecture in Northern and Southern Europe. Using reliable online sources, have students research Antoni Gaudi and other architects of Northern and Southern Europe. To help narrow students' research efforts, recommend specific Web sites, such as: http://travel.nationalgeographic .com/travel/world-heritage/antoni-gaudi/ and http://www .artcyclopedia.com/ (with searches for specific architects, such as Filippo Brunelleschi, Michelangelo Buonarroti, Andrea Palladio, etc.)

Direct students to prepare a visual presentation of the architecture they are presenting, which could include photographs or drawn copies of the architect's work. Students' presentations should answer the following questions about each architect noted in their reports:

- **Where and when was the architect born?**
- **What style of architecture is the person known for, and how would you describe it?**
- **In which cities or towns can this person's architecture be found?**

Allow time for students to make their presentations, encouraging them to prepare a script to follow as if their classmates are the students studying architecture. For example, students might say, "Today, we'll visit Barcelona, Spain, where many examples of Antoni Gaudi's architecture can be found." Visual/Spatial, Verbal/Linguistic

R Reading Skills

Summarizing Have students summarize the paragraphs in the section "Religion and the Arts." Then, **Ask:**

- What country is considered the birthplace of the Renaissance? *(Italy)*
- How did Italian painting change in the 1900s? *(Works by Italian futurist painters reflected the fast-paced modern age.)*
AL Verbal/Linguistic

ANSWER, p. 381

CRITICAL THINKING After the Roman Empire divided, Christianity divided into western and eastern churches: Roman Catholic and Eastern Orthodox. Later, the Reformation movement divided the western church into Roman Catholic and Protestant branches. Today, in southern Europe, Greece is Eastern Orthodox, while Italy and Spain are mostly Roman Catholic. Protestant churches based on Luther's teachings are dominant in Northern Europe.

Life in Northern and Southern Europe

T Technology Skills

Making Presentations Organize students into small groups, assigning a different region or country to each group. Have students research composers and musical groups mentioned in the text that are from their assigned region. Students may also wish to research regional music or dances of countries in Northern and Southern Europe.

Have each group present audio clips or videos of the music and dances to the class. Encourage students who dance or play a musical instrument to perform a demonstration to clarify the information being conveyed. Discuss the characteristics of the cultural heritage in each group's assigned region.

After students have prepared and made their presentations, have them write a short paragraph summarizing the musical contributions in their assigned region. **Ask:** What do you consider the most important cultural or musical contribution in your assigned region? (Students' answers will vary but should reflect valid opinions about contributions made by musicians and composers in their region.) Interpersonal, Auditory/Musical

R Reading Skills

Applying Help students pronounce some of the proper nouns in the text that may have confusing spellings for some students. For example, point to the name *Björk* in the text and clarify its pronunciation *(Byork)*. Explain that the mark over the "o" is called an umlaut, which indicates a vowel sound that is different from how the letter without the symbol is pronounced. **Ask:** What vocabulary word from earlier in this chapter does the vowel sound in the word *Björk* sound like? *(fjord)*

Have students find other proper nouns in the text that may have confusing spellings or may be difficult to pronounce. Invite other students to help with the pronunciations. AL ELL Verbal/Linguistic

A bin is filled with toy blocks at a factory in Billund, Denmark.

Academic Vocabulary

contribution an important part played by a person, bringing about a significant result or advancement

The musical legacies of Northern and Southern Europe are rich and deep. Italian operas are among the most popular in the world. Operas are stage presentations that use music to tell a story. Among the masterworks of opera are *The Barber of Seville* by Rossini and *Tosca* by Puccini.

Spanish music has been influential all over Europe and the Americas. It was the Spanish, more than any other people, who advanced and promoted the guitar as a serious musical instrument. Northern European composers such as Jean Sibelius (Finland), Edvard Grieg (Norway), and Carl Nielsen (Denmark) made important **contributions** to the classical music tradition. Northern European pop music, such as that by the 1970s Swedish group ABBA, has also had an impact around the world. Iceland has produced original and critically acclaimed popular musicians, including Björk and Sigur Rós.

Denmark has made a major contribution to children's toys: the LEGO™. Based in the town of Billund, LEGO™ (a play on the Danish words for "play well") has been creating plastic building-block toys since the late 1940s. LEGO™ sets were introduced in the United States in the 1960s, and their popularity has remained strong.

382 Chapter 12

netw⦿rks *Online Teaching Options*

IMAGE

LEGO™ Facts

Creating Time Lines Use the interactive image about the history of LEGO™ to discuss this major corporation in Northern Europe and its global impact. Have student pairs work together to create a time line that shows key events in LEGO™'s history and where different LEGOland theme parks are located around the world. ELL

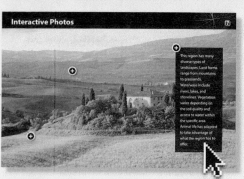

See page 363E for other online activities.

Daily Life

One of Northern Europe's most notable achievements is their literacy rate. In Norway, Sweden, and Denmark, the literacy rate is nearly 100 percent. The educational system in Northern European countries has strong support from the government, and most schooling is free. Northern European citizens pay relatively high taxes. In return, they receive a variety of public services and social welfare benefits. Every citizen is covered by health insurance.

Winter sports, such as skating and skiing, are popular in Northern Europe. Many people also enjoy skiing in the mountainous regions of Spain. Soccer (or, as it is known in Europe, football) is popular in Southern Europe. Spain, Portugal, Italy, and Greece have outstanding national soccer teams. Basketball is also common, especially in Spain and Greece. Bullfighting is still popular in Spain, although it is controversial because of the violence of the sport and cruelty to the bull.

Northern and Southern Europe are affected by the spread of popular culture, especially youth culture, from place to place. Young people throughout Europe are familiar with the same kinds of music. American fast-food chains, television programs, and films are popular throughout these regions.

☑ **READING PROGRESS CHECK**

Analyzing How is life in Southern Europe similar to life in the United States? How is it different?

W

V

Skiing is the most popular activity at a winter resort on Spain's side of the Pyrenees mountains.
▶ **CRITICAL THINKING**
Identifying Point of View Why does the sport of bullfighting arouse controversy?

AZAM Jean-Paul/hemis.fr/Getty Images

W Writing Skills

Informative/Explanatory Have students use the information in the text to write a "Daily Life" blog for people living in Northern and Southern Europe. Students may choose from the following topics: school, sports, music, food, or film, theater, and the arts. Blogs should include relevant facts about the topic, such as information about current athletes in the region, directions to stadiums or concert halls, and so on.

Encourage students to gather additional information about their topic using reliable online sources. Tell students that any quotes used from other sources should be put in a basic bibliography at the end of their blogs. Remind students that even though blogs can be less formal than other types of writing, they should still adhere to conventions of standard English and spelling. After students have written a rough draft of their blogs, have student pairs take turns doing a peer review, revising their work as needed. **Verbal/Linguistic**

V Visual Skills

Creating Visuals Display a political map of Northern and Southern Europe. Have students work with a partner to create a "Recreation Map" by creating icons and a legend using information in the text about various recreational activities. For example, students might draw a soccer ball in Spain, Portugal, Italy, and Greece to represent where soccer teams play. Have students share their recreation maps with the class, clarifying the meaning of icons. **Visual/Spatial, Interpersonal**

Content Background Knowledge

Share the names of some of the fast food restaurants that students know which are also in Europe: McDonald's, Burger King, Pizza Hut, Starbucks, Subway, Domino's Pizza, and KFC. Explain that in 2011, Subway surpassed McDonald's in the number of restaurants worldwide partly because its stores can be easily incorporated into gas stations, retail stores, and other outlets. However, McDonald's still leads as the fast food restaurant that makes the most money worldwide.

SLIDE SHOW

Recreation in Northern and Southern Europe

Comparing and Contrasting Use the interactive slide show about recreation activities in Northern and Southern Europe to compare and contrast the types of recreation activities people can enjoy if they travel to these countries. **Visual/Spatial, Verbal/Linguistic**

See page 363E for other online activities.

Slide Show

(l) ©Ocean/Corbis, ©Kryssia Campos/Getty Images,
(tr) Erica Simone Leeds, (br) ©JG Photography/Alamy

ANSWERS, p. 383

CRITICAL THINKING Bullfighting is controversial because of the violence of the sport and cruelty to the animal.

☑ **READING PROGRESS CHECK** Popular culture in Southern Europe is similar to popular culture in the United States. Young people hear a lot of the same music, see the same television programs and films, and eat at many of the same fast-food chains. One major difference is the popularity of bullfighting in Spain and Portugal.

C1 Critical Thinking Skills

Making Predictions Have students consider some of the financial problems that currently might be facing countries in Northern and Southern Europe. Ask them to consider recent stories in the news they may have read, heard, or seen. **Ask:** What do you predict will be a major issue in the next elections for some leaders of countries in Northern and Southern Europe? *(Students' answers will vary but should connect the struggling economies and financial problems to platforms of various European candidates.)* **BL** Logical/Mathematical

R Reading Skills

Using Context Clues and Determining Word Meanings Have students locate the term *welfare capitalism*. Ask them to consider nuances in the meaning of the word *welfare*. For example, ask students what it means to be "on welfare." *(to receive government assistance for food and housing)* Then ask students what context clues of nearby words help to determine the meaning of the word *capitalism*. *(government, ensure that all people have access)* Explain that capitalism is an economic system in which privately owned companies produce and distribute goods and services based on competition in a free market. To reinforce understanding, have students turn to a partner and use the term *capitalism* in a sentence. **Ask:** What is a capitalist country? *(a country with a market economy and private ownership)* Verbal/Linguistic

C2 Critical Thinking Skills

Predicting Consequences Discuss some of the economic challenges facing countries in Northern and Southern Europe today. Have students consider how governments respond to economic hardships faced by their citizens. **Ask:**

- What are some ways different governments might try to stimulate a country's economy? *(Students' answers may vary but might mention stimulus, spending more, cutting taxes, creating jobs, and so on.)*

- Why do you think most attempts by governments to stimulate economies in Southern Europe have failed? *(Students' answers may vary but might mention continued unemployment, stalled economic growth, increased debt, and so on.)*

- What consequences do countries in Northern and Southern Europe face due to lack of economic growth? *(Students' answers may vary but might mention the likelihood of an economic recession continuing or worsening.)* **BL** Logical/Mathematical

---

ANSWER, p. 384

CRITICAL THINKING Welfare capitalism ensures that people can obtain housing, medical care, and education regardless of their economic status.

Students relax in front of the Parliament building in Oslo, Norway's capital. The government in Northern Europe and Southern Europe are all democracies. Some, such as Norway and Spain, are constitutional monarchies, while others like Finland and Italy are republics.

▶ **CRITICAL THINKING**
Determining Central Ideas What is the purpose of welfare capitalism?

Issues in Northern and Southern Europe

GUIDING QUESTION *How do the financial problems of one country in Southern Europe affect other European countries?*

The natural resources of the North Sea are key to many people's employment in Norway. The petroleum resources in the North Sea provide the single most important industry.

Earning a Living

Many Northern Europeans work in service industries. The standard of living is high in these countries, but so are taxes. Northern Europeans practice a form of **welfare capitalism**, where the government uses tax money to provide a variety of services, such as health care and education, to all citizens. The intention of welfare capitalism is to ensure that all people have access to those aspects of life that are considered essential, even those people who might not otherwise be able to afford them.

Following World War II, Italy had one of the weakest economies in Europe. In the decades since, the country has built a strong industrial base. Still, the economy is much stronger in northern Italy. The government has tried to stimulate the economy in the south, but most attempts have failed.

Alexander Maximov/Alamy

384 *Chapter 12*

---

netw✦rks   *Online Teaching Options*

CHART

Funding Higher Education

Integrating Visual Information Use the chart that compares the amount of federal taxes spent on education in Italy, Norway, France, Britain, and the United States to discuss how the countries of Northern and Southern Europe spend their federal tax money. Have students turn to a partner and summarize the information presented in the chart. Circulate to provide corrective guidance. **BL**

See page 363E for other online activities.

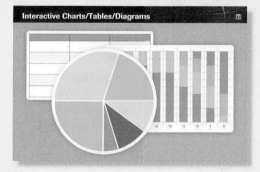

Interactive Charts/Tables/Diagrams

Making Connections

In 1992 a group of European countries signed a treaty creating the European Union (EU). The European Union is an attempt to provide common social, economic, and security policies throughout the continent. Today, 27 countries belong to the EU. Three Northern European countries are EU members: Denmark, Sweden, and Finland. In Southern Europe, Spain, Portugal, Italy, and Greece are members.

Meeting Challenges

Although the EU has helped ease conflicts among member countries, there have been many stumbling blocks to unifying the member nations. Immigration is one issue. Immigrants from many non-European countries bring their culture with them, creating a changing cultural landscape that can lead to conflict and violence. The EU promotes cooperation among member countries in easing conflicts, as well as preventing illegal immigration.

In 2008 a financial crisis swept the world. Europe experienced a **recession**, or a period of slow economic growth or decline. The three biggest banks in Iceland failed, forcing Iceland's prime minister to resign. The financial crisis hit Spain and Greece hard. Greece's inability to pay its skyrocketing debts became a threat to the economies of all the European countries.

Another issue surrounds two Northern European countries that are not members of the EU: Iceland and Norway. Whaling was an important industry in both countries. As populations of large whales began to shrink to near-extinction levels, a ban was placed on whaling. The ban has been lifted several times, but only to allow for hunting small, toothed whales. For now, the three remaining countries that hunt for whales—Norway, Iceland, and Japan—are under the watch of the International Whaling Commission.

FOLDABLES
Study Organizer

Include this lesson's information in your Foldable®.

☑ **READING PROGRESS CHECK**

Determining Central Ideas How does welfare capitalism work, and what advantages does it offer the people of Northern Europe?

LESSON 3 REVIEW

Reviewing Vocabulary

1. Why are the populations of Northern Europe considered *homogeneous*?

Answering the Guiding Questions

2. ***Determining Central Ideas*** Why do you think people in Northern and Southern Europe find living in cities more appealing than living in rural areas?

3. ***Analyzing*** Why do you think people in Norway, Denmark, and Sweden can easily understand each other's languages but find it more difficult to understand Icelandic?

4. ***Describing*** How has membership in the European Union changed the relationship among the countries of Northern and Southern Europe?

5. ***Informative/Explanatory*** Write a paragraph that compares the lives of people in Northern and Southern Europe.

Chapter 12 **385**

LESSON 3 REVIEW ANSWERS

Reviewing Vocabulary

1. Most of the people belong to the same ethnic group.

Answering the Guiding Questions

2. **Determining Central Ideas** Responses should include the awareness that there are more opportunities for jobs, housing, education, and cultural activities in cities than in rural areas.

3. **Analyzing** Danish, Swedish, and Norwegian are based on one language. These countries are also in close proximity to each other, so their people are in close contact and their languages developed similarly. Also, because of Iceland's isolation from the other countries, students should reason that its language developed differently from other Northern European countries.

4. **Describing** Students should understand that these relationships over past centuries have been marked by wars and other conflicts. The EU has forced all the nations of Europe to try to work together more closely for the common good.

5. **Informative/Explanatory Writing** Responses should mention the similar popular culture in both regions and the fact that most people live in or near cities. Responses might also describe the sports and other areas of lifestyle that are popular in both regions. Contrast should include the different terrains and climates in the two regions. Students could also contrast the economic activity in the two regions.

T Technology Skills

Collaborating and Making Presentations Discuss the current status of the European Union, particularly with regard to the economic situation in countries such as Spain and Greece. Assign the following activity as a homework assignment:

Have students work in pairs or small groups to research the current status of countries in the European Union. Remind students to use reliable online sources as they conduct their research to answer the following questions:

- **Which countries in the EU have the strongest economies? How do you know?**
- **Which countries in the EU have the weakest economies? What data tells you this?**
- **How have the economic struggles of countries in the EU affected the U.S. economy?**

Have each group present its report to the class with visuals such as graphs and charts to clarify information, emphasize specific points, and add interest. Reports should include a summary of the information and a bibliography of sources. After students have made their presentations, lead students to make connections to the Guiding Question: *How do the financial problems of one country in Southern Europe affect other European countries?* **BL** Logical/Mathematical, Visual/Spatial, Interpersonal

R Reading Skills

Determining Word Meanings Ask students what familiar word they see in the term *recession. (recess)* Guide students to make the connection between the term *recess* as it pertains to their lives *(a period to break or stop)* and an economic recession, a period of reduced economic activity. **AL** **ELL** Verbal/Linguistic

CLOSE & REFLECT

To close the lesson, ask students to think about life in Northern and Southern Europe. Encourage students to think about art, languages, religion, and where people live.

ANSWER, p. 385

☑ READING PROGRESS CHECK People pay higher taxes to make sure that everyone in those countries has access to services such as education and health care.

ENGAGE

Bellringer Before students read the Global Connections feature on Europe's aging population, explain that this feature in their text provides information and facts on a global issue, in this case a shift in the median population age of people in Europe. Have students suggest ways they interact with seniors within their family and community. Then **ask:**

- What do you think is meant by "an aging population"? *(Student answers will vary but should show an understanding that an aging population refers to individuals who usually are considered at or beyond retirement age.)*

- What might be some needs of an aging population? *(Student answers will vary but should include an awareness of health, housing, and financial changes, such as living on social security, that can create difficulties.)*

Direct students to the quote in the middle column on page 386. Have one student read it aloud and define what he or she understands as the definition of "retire." Have the class discuss the financial needs of adults who may be living alone or who may have age-related disabilities.

TEACH & ASSESS

C1 Critical Thinking Skills

Assessing Write a list of ages on the board. Circle the median number and explain the median age is the age that is in the middle of the entire list of ages from newborn to the oldest living person. **Ask:** What are the implications for Europe if the median age there is 40 while the median age for the world as a whole is 28.4? *(Answers will vary but should recognize that there are implications for the European workforce and health care system.)* **AL** Logical/Mathematical

R Reading Skills

Defining Have students define standard of living. **Ask:**

- What is meant by standard of living? *(the quality of one's life including health, housing, and opportunities)*

- What are the advantages of higher standard of living? *(people live longer, can work into their later years)*

- How have some European countries adjusted to individuals having improved health and living longer? *(raised age of retirement so people wait longer to receive government pensions)*

Have students create and share lists of what contributes to a higher standard of living. Logical/Mathematical

---

Aging of Europe's
Population

An aging population is defined as a population in which the number of elderly (65 years old and older) is increasing at a faster rate than younger age groups. Europe is the region with the highest proportion of older persons.

Median Age The median age of a population is the age that divides the population into two equal groups. In the world as a whole, the median age is 28.4 years old. For Europe, the median age is 40 years old. The median age of Europeans has continued to rise and is expected to increase to 46 years by 2050.

> "Some senior citizens continue working because they cannot afford to retire."

Living Longer As people live longer, many experience age-related health problems. That puts an added strain on the health care system and health care costs. Some senior citizens continue working because they cannot afford to retire.

Smaller Families Over the past 40 years, families in Europe have grown smaller. As a result, fewer young workers are entering the labor force, while the number of senior citizens continues to grow.

Age of Retirement Some European nations are seeking ways to cut costs. Several European nations have raised the age of retirement. Adjusting the retirement age upward means more people in the workforce and

fewer people depending on government pensions.

The Workforce European countries are trying to increase their workforce by attracting skilled workers from other countries. Some are trying to attract workers only from other parts of Europe. Some European nations will have to change their immigration laws if they want to attract immigrants from regions outside of Europe.

Standard of Living Europeans enjoy a higher standard of living than people in some of the other regions of the world. In general, Europeans are living longer thanks to improvements in health, diet, and preventive health care.

Hikers make their way on a trek through the Alps.

(l) Robert Harding Picture Library/SuperStock, (c) ©Charles O'Rear/Corbis, (r) Heath Korvola/Photodisc/Getty Images

---

netw⊕rks   *Online Teaching Options*

CHARTS

Population Pyramid of Europe Compared to the World

Interpreting Have students view the population pyramids and projections. Use these charts to help students understand the population projections compared to the actual population today in Europe and to the rest of the world. In small groups, have students research population pyramids for different countries. Then have groups compare and contrast what they learned with each other. **ELL** Logical/Mathematical

Interactive Charts/Tables/Diagrams

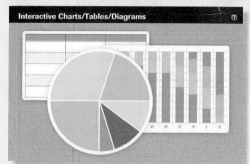

THERE'S MORE ONLINE

HEAR how the EU is funded • SEE a slide show on European health care • WATCH a video on immigration

Chapter 12 387

C2 Critical Thinking Skills

Comparing and Contrasting   Direct student attention to the photograph of the senior couple having breakfast on page 386. **Ask:**

• What types of opportunities might an aging population with a better standard of living have? *(time for leisure activities, such as dining out instead of going to work, or new interests and adventures)*

• What factors in Europe have led to a higher standard of living? *(improved health, diet, preventative care)* **Verbal/ Linguistic**

V

C3 Critical Thinking Skills

Formulating Questions   Direct student attention to the photograph of the young worker on page 386 carrying a tray of plants to be planted outdoors. **Ask:**

• Given an aging European population and possible work limitations of seniors, what questions regarding the workforce need to be addressed by European governments? *(How do we attract new workers? Where will workers come from to fill the labor needs of European industries?)*

• What question will European governments need to consider in order to expand their workforce? *(How do we change our country's immigration policies and laws to meet the demand for younger workers other than those from other European nations?)* **Visual/Spatial**

V Visual Skills

Interpreting   Have students spend a few minutes analyzing the photograph on this page. Then, have them write a few words describing what they see in the image. Have student volunteers share their descriptive words with the class. Then, **ask:**

• What recreational activities are enjoyed by seniors? *(Answers will vary but could include hiking, golf, boating, playing cards, community events.)*

• How might being retired free up an individual to experience new adventures? *(no work or family commitments)* **Visual/Spatial**

MAP

"Heat Map" of World's Population

Analyzing Maps   As a class, discuss the "heat map" of the world's average age of population in relation to Europe's population. Have students create "on the scene" scenarios where a news/camera team interviews seniors, some retired, some needing to work. Have students share their "interview" findings to discuss the opportunities and demands placed on both aging populations and on governments. **BL Interpersonal**

C Critical Thinking Skills

Making Inferences In pairs, have students discuss the data presented in one of the frames and share an inference they can make based on the data. List their inferences on the board as they are shared. **Ask:** What conclusion can we make based on our understanding of the aging population? *(Students should recognize that the trend toward an aging population in Europe, and its implications, is not a short term phenomenon but will continue for decades.)* Logical/Mathematical

R Reading Skills

Summarizing Review the statistics in the headings shown on the page. **Ask:** How can the data on this page and the impact of Europe's aging population be summarized? *(Students should state that the aging population will grow in percentage in comparison to younger age groups and that with that growth come greater strains on the health care, pension, and other systems of the government, while the low number of young people make up only 15% of the population.)* Logical/Mathematical

V Visual Skills

Interpreting Discuss any remaining questions students have about the statistics presented on this page, and have them compare the situation of the aging population in Europe to the aging of the baby boomers in the United States.

- What challenges do the people in Europe face in the future due to its decreasing population? *(economic challenges due to a reduction in a viable workforce)*
- What implications might an aging population in Europe have on the global economy? *(Accept all answers. Students should consider the importance of having a viable workforce to sustain the economy of a country.)* Logical/Mathematical

---

GLOBAL CONNECTIONS

C *These numbers and statistics highlight the problems associated with an aging population.*

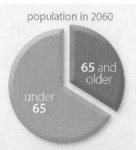

population in 2060

65 and older

under 65

R

Up to
30%

The share of the population aged 65 and over will rise from 17% in 2010 to 30% in 2060. The percentage of people aged 80 or older will more than double: from 5% in 2010 to 12% in 2060.

Seventy Five Years Old

Why is Europe's population growing older? People are living longer because of improved medical care and a better standard of living. In 1950 the average European lived to be 65. Today, the length of life is 75 years. At the same time, a decreasing birthrate means that there are fewer young people. In 2010 the birthrate—the number of births per 1,000 population—was half the birthrate in 1950.

65 and Older

V

Which countries have the highest percentage of residents who are 65 years old or older? Except for Japan, the world's 15 oldest countries are European countries. The five countries with the largest percentage of older citizens are: Japan and Italy, both at 19.5%, followed by Germany, 18.6%; Greece, 17.8%; and Sweden, 17.3%.

Life Expectancy at FIFTY

What problems are caused by an aging population? As the aging population grows and more people retire, great strain is put on the health care and pension systems. Life expectancy varies greatly, depending on the country or region. For example, a 50-year-old female can expect 10.4 more healthy life years in Estonia, but 24.1 more in Denmark. The life expectancy for a 50-year-old male is slightly less.

14 or younger

European countries have many more senior citizens than most other nations—and far fewer young people. More than one-quarter—26.3%—of the world's population is 14 years old or younger. In Europe, only 15% are in that age group.

(t) Janine Wiedel Photolibrary/Alamy: (b) ©Alex Masi/Corbis

388 *Chapter 12*

---

networks   *Online Teaching Options*

GRAPHIC ORGANIZER

Cause and Effect: Europe's Aging Population

Determining Cause and Effect Form small groups of students. Have students analyze the interactive graphic organizer on the causes and effects of decreased birthrates and an aging population of Europe. Have groups identify a set of "if-then" statements and then create visuals of the cause and effect relationships discussed. **BL** Visual/Spatial

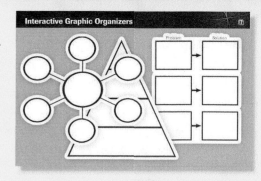

Interactive Graphic Organizers

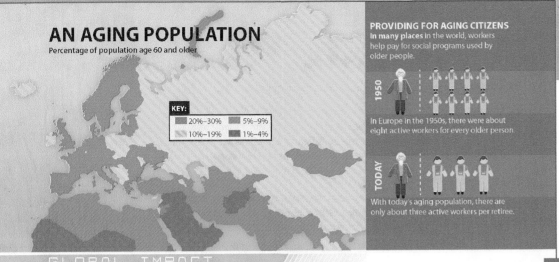

AN AGING POPULATION
Percentage of population age 60 and older

KEY:
- 20%–30%
- 10%–19%
- 5%–9%
- 1%–4%

PROVIDING FOR AGING CITIZENS
In many places in the world, workers help pay for social programs used by older people.

1950
In Europe in the 1950s, there were about eight active workers for every older person.

TODAY
With today's aging population, there are only about three active workers per retiree.

GLOBAL IMPACT

DEMOGRAPHIC TRENDS In many areas, the percentage of people who are older is increasing while the percentage of children is growing smaller.

The number of persons 60 years old and older has tripled between 1950 and 2000. By 2050, that number will more than triple again.

There is a higher proportion of older persons in Europe, but lower proportions in developing regions such as Africa. In 2050, 10 pecent of the population of Africa is projected to be 60 years old or older, up from 5 percent in 2000.

Europe, 2050

If projections hold, Europeans 60 years and older will comprise about 37 percent of the population by 2050. Persons younger than 15 will make up only about 14 percent of Europe's people.

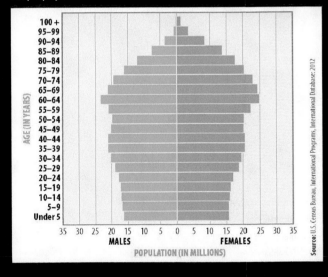

AGE (IN YEARS): 100+, 95–99, 90–94, 85–89, 80–84, 75–79, 70–74, 65–69, 60–64, 55–59, 50–54, 45–49, 40–44, 35–39, 30–34, 25–29, 20–24, 15–19, 10–14, 5–9, Under 5

MALES FEMALES
POPULATION (IN MILLIONS)
35 30 25 20 15 10 5 0 5 10 15 20 25 30 35

Source: U.S. Census Bureau, International Programs, International Database: 2012

Thinking like a Geographer

1. **Human Geography** Why is the percentage of elderly growing in Europe?

2. **Economic Geography** What kinds of businesses will grow in a place where the population is aging? What kinds of businesses will be in less demand?

3. **Human Geography** You and your classmates have been appointed by the mayor of a city to help companies find skilled workers from other countries. Prepare a PowerPoint presentation for the owners of those companies about ways to attract foreign workers.

Chapter 12 **389**

V Visual Skills

Interpreting Discuss the infographic at the top of the page. Have volunteers relate the key to the map in the top half and identify the areas of the world with the oldest populations. Then have other volunteers interpret the line graph in the bottom half of the infographic that applies specifically to the European population. **Ask:**

- How does the line graph support the information in the map and the information given on the previous pages of this feature? *(Answers will vary but should discuss how the dropping birthrate in Europe is shown in the line graph, which supports the higher percentage of older people in Europe shown in the map and which was previously discussed in the text of this feature.)*

- How does Europe's aging population compare to the United States? *(Europe's aging population makes up 20% to 30% of its population, while the United States' aging population makes up 10% to 19.9% of its population)* Visual/Spatial

CLOSE & REFLECT

Contact the local government or senior center and invite someone to visit the class to discuss the needs of an aging population. Have students prepare a list of questions to ask the individual prior to the visit regarding 1) the difficulties experienced by the local population of aging seniors and 2) the economic impact of later retirement on the aging population and on the community.

Following the visit, have students discuss how they can interact with the local community's aging population in positive and helpful ways.

ANSWER, p. 389

Thinking Like a Geographer

1. People in Europe are living longer, so there are more older people. Families are having fewer babies, so the percentage of younger people in the population is going down.

2. Businesses that serve older people such as medical care, drugs, medical equipment, recreational interests of the elderly such as golf, tennis, swimming, walking, and table games, suppliers of adaptive equipment for homes are some examples of businesses that would be in demand. Suppliers of toys, baby equipment, schools, school books, children's clothes, summer camps, and day-care centers might be in less demand.

3. Presentations should include efforts to help smooth the relations between the immigrants and the people who already live in the place. An important principle to convey is to allay fears about job loss and cultural conflict.

WORKSHEET

Services for an Aging Population

Creating Charts Working in small groups, have students evaluate products and advertisements targeting an aging population found in local news media, including ads by the insurance industry, banking industry, housing, medical facilities or products, and social/recreational activities using tips from the worksheet. Have each group create a poster presentation that discusses how these ads target this market. Have groups share their posters and discuss how an aging population has created a market focused on meeting their needs.

BL Visual/Spatial

CHAPTER REVIEW ACTIVITY

Have students create a four-column chart like the one below. Have students list *Physical Geography, Climate, History and Culture,* and *Daily Life* as column heads under headings for *Northern Europe* and *Southern Europe.* Tell students to complete the chart for each category with key information and examples from the text. *(Possible answers: **Physical Geography**—Alps are highest mountain range in Europe, Mediterranean Sea Southern Europe's most important body of water; **Climate**— Northern Europe is cold during winter months, Southern Europe has Mediterranean climate of mild winters; **History and Culture**—frequent conflict and wars among Northern European countries, strong influence of Greek and Roman Empires on European culture, new ideas and art and architecture flourished during Renaissance; **Daily Life**—people enjoy a wide range of recreational activities from skiing and skating in Northern Europe to soccer and basketball in countries such as Greece and Spain.)*

Northern Europe			
Physical Geography	Climate	History and Culture	Daily Life

Southern Europe			
Physical Geography	Climate	History and Culture	Daily Life

REVIEW THE ENDURING UNDERSTANDINGS

Review this chapter's Enduring Understanding with students:

- **People, places, and ideas change over time.**

Now pose the following questions in a class discussion to apply this to this chapter.

- Why can Northern and Southern Europe be described as a "land of peninsulas"? *(Most of Northern Europe is made up of two peninsulas—the Scandinavian Peninsula with Norway and Sweden, and Jutland, a peninsula that extends from Germany and includes most of Denmark. Southern Europe has several peninsulas, including the Iberian Peninsula, the Balkan Peninsula, and Italy's boot-shaped Italian peninsula.)*

- How did the ancient Greeks and Romans affect later civilizations in Southern Europe? *(Sample answer: Ancient Greek and Roman culture had a lasting impact on later civilizations as people embraced classical ideas during the Renaissance and beyond.)*

- Summarize the population concentrations in Northern and Southern Europe. *(Sample answer: The number of people in rural areas of Southern Europe has decreased over the last one hundred years as more people have moved to cities. The population of Northern Europe is even more concentrated in cities, such as in Iceland where more than half of that country's population lives in its capital city of Reykjavik.)*

Chapter 12 ACTIVITIES

Directions: Write your answers on a separate piece of paper.

① Use your **FOLDABLES** to explore the Essential Question.
INFORMATIVE/EXPLANATORY Students in Europe participate in sports that might not be as well-known where you live. Identify one of those sports. Then, write at least two paragraphs to answer this question: Is the popularity of the sport related to the physical geography of the region?

② **21st Century Skills**
ANALYZING The nations of Northern Europe have made progress in developing and using renewable energy sources. Work in small groups to choose a country in the region, and research that country's efforts to ensure that its people have adequate energy sources well into the future. Present your findings to the class in a slide show presentation.

③ **Thinking Like a Geographer**
DETERMINING CENTRAL ISSUES You have read that some locales in the regions are densely populated, but others are not. Identify the three major factors that affect population density.

④ **GEOGRAPHY ACTIVITY**

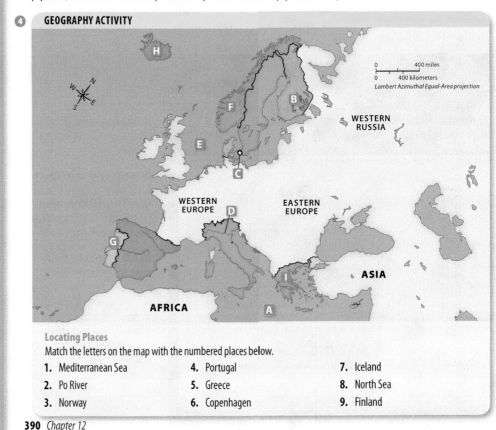

Locating Places
Match the letters on the map with the numbered places below.

1. Mediterranean Sea
2. Po River
3. Norway
4. Portugal
5. Greece
6. Copenhagen
7. Iceland
8. North Sea
9. Finland

390 *Chapter 12*

ACTIVITIES ANSWERS

Exploring the Essential Question

① **INFORMATIVE/EXPLANATORY** While each student's work will reflect personal interests, paragraphs should be well-organized, answer the question, and have correct spelling and grammar.

21st Century Skills

② **ANALYZING** Presentations or reports should reflect thorough research. They should be interesting, factual, well-organized and make use of charts, graphs, photos, or other visual materials to present their story.

REVIEW THE GUIDING QUESTIONS

Directions: Choose the best answer for each question.

1 What kind of energy heats all of the homes and most of the businesses in Reykjavík, Iceland?

A. nuclear
B. natural gas
C. geothermal
D. solar

2 Most of Southern Europe has a Mediterranean climate, which is much like the climate along the

F. southeastern coast of the United States.
G. Pacific northwest.
H. Chesapeake Bay.
I. coast of southern California.

3 What weakened Greece's city-states and eventually led to the fall of Greek civilization?

A. invasion by Vikings
B. years of war
C. Roman conquest
D. lack of trade routes

4 Who were the Scandinavian warriors and pirates who eventually became better known for exploring and trading?

F. Moors
G. Vikings
H. barbarians
I. Ottoman Turks

5 Most people in Northern and Southern Europe live in

A. rural areas.
B. small towns.
C. villages.
D. cities.

6 The Basques, one of the oldest minority groups in Europe, live in and around the Pyrenees mountains in

F. Spain and Portugal.
G. Italy and Greece.
H. France and Italy.
I. France and Portugal.

ASSESSMENT ANSWERS

Review the Guiding Questions

1 **C** For this question, knowing that Reykjavik, Iceland, has an abundance of geothermal energy due to the volcanic nature of the island will help students eliminate the other choices. If students answer incorrectly, have them reread the "Northern Minerals and Energy" section in Lesson 1 for help.

2 **I** To answer this question students need to remember that the most common climate in Southern Europe is the Mediterranean climate, with warm or hot summers and cool or mild winters. Choice F may confuse students, as the southeastern coast of the United States has a warm climate, but it does not always have cool winters. If students answer incorrectly, have them reread the "Warm Southern Europe" section in Lesson 1 for help.

3 **B** Students should recall that years of war eventually weakened Greek city-states. Choice C may mislead students; however, they should remember that the Roman Empire was only emerging as Greek city-states began to decline. If students answer incorrectly, have them reread the "Ancient Greece" section in Lesson 2 for help.

4 **G** To answer this question, students need to recall the information about the Vikings in Lesson 2. If students answer incorrectly, have them reread the "The Viking Age" section in Lesson 2 to help them recall the origin and seafaring expeditions of the Vikings to explore and set up trade routes. Remembering that Moors were an Arabic people who invaded Spain will eliminate choice F.

5 **D** Remembering that most people in the region live in cities will help eliminate choices A and C. If students answer incorrectly, have them reread the "Where People Live" section in Lesson 3 for help.

6 **F** The Basque people speak Euskera, a language in Spain, so this eliminates choices H and I. If students answer incorrectly, have them reread the "Mountains and Plains" section in Lesson 1 or the Thinking Like a Geographer feature in Lesson 3 for help.

Thinking Like a Geographer

3 **DETERMINING CENTRAL ISSUES** Factors include: physical environment such as climate and topography; proximity to water; or social, economic, and political development

Geography Activity

4 **LOCATING PLACES**

1. A
2. D
3. F
4. G
5. I
6. C
7. H
8. E
9. B

DBQ Document-Based Questions

7 **C** Davies states that Iberia fell under the control of Carthaginians, Romans, and Muslims at different times throughout history.

8 **G** With easy access to the Atlantic Ocean and with more of a focus on the Atlantic World than thoroughly Mediterranean lands like Greece and Italy, the nations of Iberia led the way in exploring the Atlantic Ocean, and Spain built the first colonial empire in the Americas.

Short Response

9 According to the text, Norway's private sector has been responsible for industrial expansion.

10 Some economic activities in Norway are managed by the private sector; others by the public sector. Thus, it is a mix of private and public ownership.

Extended Response

11 Student reports comparing the literacy rate and cost of education in Scandinavian countries with the literacy rate and cost of education in Southern Europe and the United States will vary, but the reports should be well-researched and organized using reliable sources. Grammar, spelling, and sentence construction should meet your high standards. Clear comparisons of both literacy rates and the cost of education should be included.

DBQ ANALYZING DOCUMENTS

7 **ANALYZING DOCUMENTS** Read the following passage about the Iberian Peninsula:

> "Its eastern seaboard forms part of the Mediterranean world, and in early times [it] was drawn successively [by turns] into the Carthaginian, Roman, and Muslim spheres. But much of the arid interior is drawn . . . towards the Atlantic."
>
> —from Norman Davies, *Europe: A History* (1998)

What statement about Iberia it true based on the passage?

A. Iberians defeated the Carthaginians.

B. Iberia was isolated from all other regions.

C. Iberia was often under the control of other empires.

D. Iberians invaded Rome.

8 **IDENTIFYING** What impact did Iberia's nearness to the Atlantic have on its history?

F. The area was often invaded by the British.

G. Iberian nations led the way in exploring the Atlantic.

H. Navies from the region could not fight Mediterranean navies.

I. Iberian nations were cut off from trade with Asia.

SHORT RESPONSE

> "The expansion of most industry in Norway has largely been governed by private property rights and the private sector. Nevertheless, some industrial activities are owned or run by the state."
>
> —from Aschehoug and Gyldendal's *Norwegian Encyclopedia*

9 **CITING TEXT EVIDENCE** Which economic sector, private or public, has been responsible for the expansion of most industry in Norway?

10 **ANALYZING** Why would economists label Norway's economy a "mixed economy"?

EXTENDED RESPONSE

11 **INFORMATIVE/EXPLANATORY WRITING** As you learned in your reading, the literacy rate in the Scandinavian countries is nearly 100 percent and education is free through college. How does that compare with literacy rates and the cost of education in Southern Europe and the United States? Research the issue, and report your findings.

Need Extra Help?

If You've Missed Question	**1**	**2**	**3**	**4**	**5**	**6**	**7**	**8**	**9**	**10**	**11**
Review Lesson	1	1	2	2	3	3	1	1	2	2	3

netwrks   *Online Teaching Options*

Practicing 21st Century Skills

Practicing Skills Your students can practice important 21st Century skills such as geography, reading, writing, and critical thinking by using resources found in the Skills Builder tab of the online Student Learning Center. Resources include templates, handbooks, and slide shows. These same resources are also available in the Resource Library of the Teacher Lesson Center.

CHAPTER 13

Eastern Europe and Western Russia
Planner

UNDERSTANDING BY DESIGN®

Enduring Understandings

- *People, places, and ideas change over time.*

Essential Questions

- *How does geography influence the way people live?*
- *How do governments change?*

Predictable Misunderstandings

- *Eastern Europe has more similarity to the other European nations.*
- *Western Russia has had no influence on the development of Eastern Europe.*
- *Eastern Europe and Western Russia have little cultural connection.*

Assessment Evidence

Performance Tasks:

- *Project-Based Learning Digital Hands-On Chapter Project*
- *Project-Based Learning Hands-On Chapter Project*

Other Evidence:

- *Critical Thinking Skills Activity*
- *Geography and History Activity*
- *Participation in Interactive Whiteboard Activities*
- *Contribution to small-group activities*
- *Interpretation of slide show images and special purpose maps*
- *Participation in class discussions about cultural and economic topics*
- *Lesson Reviews*
- *Chapter Assessments*

SUGGESTED PACING GUIDE

Introducing the Chapter.............. 2 Days	Lesson 3 .... 2 Days
Lesson 1 .... 2 Days	Chapter Wrap-Up and Assessment..... 2 Days
Lesson 2 .... 2 Days	

TOTAL TIME   10 Days

Key for Using the Teacher Edition

SKILL-BASED ACTIVITIES

Types of skill activities found in the Teacher Edition.

* **V Visual Skills** require students to analyze maps, graphs, charts, and photos.

W Writing Skills provide writing opportunities to help students comprehend the text.

R Reading Skills help students practice reading skills and master vocabulary.

C Critical Thinking Skills help students apply and extend what they have learned.

T Technology Skills require students to use digital tools effectively.

*Letters are followed by a number when there is more than one of the same type of skill on the page.

DIFFERENTIATED INSTRUCTION

All activities are written for the on-level student unless otherwise marked with the leveled labels below.

BL Beyond Level
AL Approaching Level
ELL English Language Learners

All students benefit from activities that utilize different learning styles. Many activities are marked as below when a particular learning style is highlighted.

Intrapersonal	Naturalist
Logical/Mathematical	Kinesthetic
Visual/Spatial	Auditory/Musical
Verbal/Linguistic	Interpersonal

Indiana Academic Standards

Students will:

6.1.8 Compare the diverse perspectives, ideas, interests and people that brought about the Renaissance in Europe.

6.1.15 Describe the impact of industrialization and urbanization on the lives of individuals and on trade and cultural exchange between Europe and the Americas and the rest of the world.

6.1.23 Identify issues related to an historical event in Europe or the Americas and give basic arguments for and against that issue utilizing the perspectives, interests and values of those involved.

6.2.5 Discuss the impact of major forms of government in Europe and the Americas on civil and human rights.

6.2.6 Identify and describe the functions of international political organizations in the world today.

6.2.7 Define and compare citizenship and the citizen's role throughout history in Europe and the Americas.

6.3.4 Describe and compare major cultural characteristics of regions in Europe and the Western Hemisphere.

6.3.5 Give examples and describe the formation of important river deltas, mountains and bodies of water in Europe and the Americas.

6.3.7 Locate and describe the climate regions of Europe and the Americas and explain how and why they differ.

6.3.10 Explain the ways cultural diffusion, invention, and innovation change culture.

6.3.12 Compare the distribution and evaluate the importance of natural resources such as natural gas, oil, forests, uranium, minerals, coal, seafood and water in Europe and the Americas.

6.4.6 Analyze current economic issues in the countries of Europe or the Americas using a variety of information resources.

6.4.7 Identify economic connections between the local community and the countries of Europe or the Americas and identify job skills needed to be successful in the workplace.

6.4.8 Identify ways that societies deal with helpful and harmful externalities (spillovers*) in Europe or the Americas.

CHAPTER OPENER PLANNER

Students will know:
- *that Eastern Europe and Western Russia share borders, landforms, and waterways.*
- *that Eastern Europe and Western Russia have had similar governments.*
- *that Eastern Europe and Western Russia share some cultural aspects.*
- *that Eastern Europe and Western Russia share similar climates.*
- *that Eastern Europe and Western Russia have similar economic issues.*

Students will be able to:
- ***analyze** a world map to identify countries of Eastern Europe and Western Russia.*
- ***use** a time line to discuss various events in the history of Eastern Europe and Western Russia.*

☑ *Print Teaching Options*

V **Visual Skills**

☐ **P. 394** Students use the map to reinforce map skills.

☐ **P. 395** Students review the time line and discuss its major points of interest. Visual/Spatial

W **Writing Skills**

☐ **P. 395** Students write paragraphs about how events on the time line contributed to the rise of communism in Russia and Eastern Europe. Logical/Mathematical, Verbal/Linguistic

T **Technology Skills**

☐ **P. 394** Students research photos of St. Sofia to present to the class and share their opinions of Byzantine architecture.

☑ *Online Teaching Options*

☐ **MAP** **Reading a Map**—Students identify aspects and locations of the region on a map.

☐ **TIME LINE** **Reading a Time Line and Map**—Students learn about when and where historical events occurred in Eastern Europe and Western Russia. **AL** **ELL** Visual/Spatial

☐ **MAP** **Interactive World Altas**—Students use the interactive world atlas to identify the Ural Mountains and describe its terrain.

☑ *Printable Digital Worksheets*

☐ **WORKSHEET** **Geography and History: Balkanization**—Students use the worksheet to review the concept of balkanization and its impact on the Balkan Peninsula.

☐ **WORKSHEET** **Critical Thinking Skills: Recognizing Bias—Serbia and Eastern Europe**—Students use the worksheet to understand and recognize bias.

Project-Based Learning

Hands-On

Write and Act Out a Skit

Students will work in small groups to write and act out short skits depicting a historical event from Eastern Europe or Western Russia. Students should research the event before they write the skit. The skit's dialogue must include information about why the event was important in this region's history. Have students present their skits to the class.

Digital Hands-On

Conduct Interviews

Have students work in small groups to conduct fictional interviews of a person who lived in Eastern Europe or Western Russia during a historical event in the region. The fictional interviews will be recorded as podcasts. Once the recording is complete, the podcasts can be uploaded and shared online, allowing the students to listen to each other's interviews.

Print Resources

ANCILLARY RESOURCES

These ancillaries are available for every chapter and lesson.

- **Reading Essentials and Study Guide Workbook** **AL** **ELL**
- **Chapter Tests and Lesson Quizzes Blackline Masters**

PRINTABLE DIGITAL WORKSHEETS

These printable digital worksheets are available for every chapter and lesson.

- **Hands-On Chapter Projects**
- **What Do You Know? Activities**
- **Chapter Summaries (English and Spanish)**
- **Vocabulary Builder Activities**
- **Quizzes and Tests**
- **Reading Essentials and Study Guide (English and Spanish)** **AL** **ELL**
- **Guided Reading Activities**

More Media Resources

SUGGESTED VIDEOS

NOTE: Be sure to preview videos to ensure they are age-appropriate.

- **Image Before My Eyes—A History of Jewish Life in Poland Before the Holocaust** (90 min.)
- **Secret Lives—Hidden Children and Their Rescuers During WWII** (90 min.)
- **St. Petersburg: Window on Europe** (56 min.)

SUGGESTED READING

- ***Catherine the Great: Empress of Russia (A Wicked History),*** by Zu Vincent
- ***Breaking Stalin's Nose,*** by Eugene Yelchin **BL**
- ***Russia: The Land, the People, the Culture*** (series of three books), by Greg Nickles

PHYSICAL GEOGRAPHY

Students will know:
- that Eastern Europe and Western Russia share borders, landforms, and waterways.
- that Eastern Europe and Western Russia share similar climates.

Students will be able to:
- **identify** the different landforms and waterways in Eastern Europe and Western Russia.
- **compare** and contrast the climates found in the region.
- **describe** important natural resources in the region.

UNDERSTANDING
BY DESIGN®

☑ *Print Teaching Options*

V Visual Skills

☐ **P. 396** Students use a map or globe to identify the Balkan Peninsula, and major landforms and waterways of Eastern Europe and Western Russia. **AL**

☐ **P. 397** Students locate landforms on a map and compare and contrast the vocabulary words *plain, upland, basin, steppe,* and *mountain* based on the context clues and landforms. **ELL** Visual/Spatial, Naturalist

☐ **P. 398** Students use a political map of Eastern Europe and Western Russia to identify seas, rivers, and lakes. **ELL**

W Writing Skills

☐ **P. 399** Students write a narrative paragraph explaining how the contents of their suitcases would be the same or different for a vacation to Albania or to Russia's far north.

R Reading Skills

☐ **P. 396** Students define the compound word *upland* by its root words and context clues. **AL** Verbal/Linguistic

☐ **P. 398** Students summarize the importance of rivers and lakes to Eastern Europe and Western Russia. Verbal

☐ **P. 399** Students calculate the difference between the low and high temperatures in Russia's far north.

C Critical Thinking Skills

☐ **P. 397** Students discuss how isolation results in cultural diversity and conflict among ethnic groups. **ELL**

☐ **P. 400** Students determine the effects of a lack of land suitable for agriculture on one of the largest countries of the world. Logical/Mathematical

☐ **P. 401** Students discuss challenges facing Russia's forestry industry. Naturalist

T Technology Skills

☐ **P. 397** Students research a point of interest in the Transylvanian Basin and present a travelogue about the area. Visual/Spatial, Verbal/Linguistic

☐ **P. 401** Students use the Internet to research different uses of sulfur. **AL** Visual/Spatial, Verbal/Linguistic

☑ *Online Teaching Options*

V Visual Skills

☐ **MAP** **How Landforms Create Boundaries**—Students write a paragraph telling about how landforms create political boundaries. **BL** Visual/Spatial, Verbal/Linguistic

☐ **SLIDE SHOW** **Adapting to Environments**—Students use the slide show to discuss how people, plants, and animals adapt to Arctic temperatures in Russia. Visual/Spatial, Naturalist

☐ **IMAGE** **The Ural Mountains**—Students use the interactive image about the Ural Mountains to discuss the interesting geographic features of the region.

☐ **MAP** **Physical Geography: Eastern Europe and Western Russia**—Students use the physical map to analyze how the physical landscape influences how people live and travel. **AL**

☐ **VIDEO** **The Black Sea**—Students use the video of the Black Sea to further connect the student to the region. Visual/Spatial, Verbal/Linguistic

☐ **MAP** **Resources: Eastern Europe and Western Russia**—Students use the resources map to review the resources of this region.

W Writing Skills

☐ **VIDEO** **World's Wonders—St. Petersburg**—Students watch the video about the city of St. Petersburg in Western Russia and write three questions they have about the city. **AL**

☐ **GRAPHIC ORGANIZER** **Resources of Eastern Europe and Western Russia**—Students use the interactive graphic organizer to review the content of this lesson.

R Reading Skills

☐ **GRAPHIC ORGANIZER** **Reviewing Political Borders**—Students use the interactive graphic organizer to review and discuss the various pieces of information about the region.

☐ **GRAPHIC ORGANIZER** **Landforms and Waterways of Eastern Europe and Western Russia**—Students use the interactive graphic organizer about landforms and waterways to review the physical geography of the region.

☐ **LECTURE SLIDE** **Defining: Climates**—Students use the lecture slide presentation about the climate definitions. Visual/Spatial, Verbal/Linguistic

C Critical Thinking Skills

☐ **CHART** **Using Resources**—Students make comparisons and contrasts between resources produced in the different countries in Eastern Europe and Western Russia. **AL**

☐ **MAP** **Comparing Climates**—Students use the climate map and compare the climate in this region to the climate in the Eastern United States.

T Technology Skills

☐ **ONLINE SELF-CHECK QUIZ** **Lesson 1**—Students receive instant feedback on their mastery of lesson content.

☑ *Printable Digital Worksheets*

W Writing Skills

☐ **WORKSHEET** **Geography and History: Balkanization**—Students use the worksheet to review the concept of balkanization and its impact on the Balkan Peninsula.

HISTORY OF THE REGIONS

Students will know:
- *Eastern Europe and Western Russia have had similar governments.*
- *Eastern Europe and Western Russia share some cultural aspects.*

Students will be able to:
- *discuss* the early history of Eastern Europe and Western Russia.
- *explain* the rise of communism.
- *discuss* the Cold War.

UNDERSTANDING
BY DESIGN®

☑ *Print Teaching Options*

V Visual Skills

☐ **P. 403** Students use the map to compare the Soviet Union and present-day Russia. Visual/Spatial

☐ **P. 408** Students determine the approximate distance between Cuba and the United States on a map to discuss the Cuban missile crisis. Visual/Spatial

W Writing Skills

☐ **P. 406** Students write a persuasive essay about whether life would be better under communist or democratic rule.

R Reading Skills

☐ **P. 403** Students cite text evidence as to why people of Kiev were able to organize the Slav communities into a loose union of city-states. Verbal/Linguistic

☐ **P. 403** Students determine the meaning of the word *imperial* and relate it to *imperial Russia*. ELL AL

☐ **P. 404** Students determine word meanings about the terms *serf* and *slave*. ELL AL Verbal/Linguistic

☐ **P. 406** Students determine the meaning of *communism* and *collectivization* from their Latin word roots. ELL

☐ **P. 407** Students describe the Cold War in their own words. AL Verbal/Linguistic

C Critical Thinking Skills

☐ **P. 405** Students make inferences about why food shortages would cause civilians to protest. Logical

☐ **P. 405** Students discuss why Turkey would deport Armenians to Syria and Mesopotamia during World War I.

☐ **P. 407** Students draw conclusions about the spread of communist government throughout the world. Logical

☐ **P. 407** Students infer possible outcomes of nuclear warfare. Logical/Mathematical

☐ **P. 408** Students compare and contrast the Solidarity movement in Poland to reforms in Czechoslovakia.

T Technology Skills

☐ **P. 407** Students work in small groups to research and orally report their findings on topics relating to NATO.

☐ **P. 409** Students use the Internet to gather images of the Berlin Wall over time and use presentation software to present their images and facts. Visual/Spatial

---

☑ *Online Teaching Options*

V Visual Skills

VIDEO **Communist Russia, A Great Economic Experiment**—After watching the video about the history of communism, students share what they learned about life under Soviet rule.

INFOGRAPHIC **Feudalism in Europe and Russia**—Students write a paragraph describing one benefit and one disadvantage of feudalism in Europe and Russia. BL Verbal/Linguistic

MAP **Russian Historical Changes: Modern History**—Students use the map of the expansion of Russia to discuss the expansion and collapse of Communism. BL Visual/Spatial

IMAGE **Ferdinand and Princip**—Student use the interactive image about Ferdinand and Princip to discuss these players in the assassination. Visual/Spatial

VIDEO **Cold War**—Students use the video on the Cold War to further elaborate on this idea.

IMAGE **Gorbachev**—Students use the interactive image of Gorbechev to discuss his role in the collapse of Soviet Russia. Visual/Spatial

W Writing Skills

GRAPHIC ORGANIZER **Organizing Information: Communism**—Extend this activity with an interactive graphic organizer for note-taking for reviewing information about communism. BL

GRAPHIC ORGANIZER **Organizing Information: Empires**—Extend this activity with a graphic organizer for note taking. Visual/Spatial

GRAPHIC ORGANIZER **USSR and Its Satellites**—Use the interactive graphic organizer to review the satellites of the USSR. Visual/Spatial

R Reading Skills

GAME **Drag-and-Drop: Empires**—Students can extend the lesson with a drag-and-drop game about empires. Kinesthetic

LECTURE SLIDE **Defining: Cold War**—Students use the lecture slide with the definition of "cold war" to discuss the term in the context of the chapter. Visual/Spatial

LECTURE SLIDE **NATO Countries**—Further extend the lesson with a discussion of NATO and the nations involved in that organization. Visual/Spatial

LECTURE SLIDE **Key Players: Modern Communism**—Extend the lesson with the lecture slide about the major players from the Cold War to the present day. Visual/Spatial

C Critical Thinking Skills

MAP **Russian Historical Changes: Early History**—Students use the map to discuss the early history in Russia and theorize how these changes helped to make Russia a powerful country in the world. Visual/Spatial, Verbal/Linguistic

MAP **Alliances in Europe During WWI**—Students discuss the "domino effect" of an alliance system using this map.

CHART **Sequencing: Cold War Events**—Students use the sequencing flow chart to write about events that led to the collapse of the Cold War.

T Technology Skills

ONLINE SELF-CHECK QUIZ **Lesson 2**—Students receive instant feedback on their mastery of lesson content.

LIFE IN EASTERN EUROPE AND WESTERN RUSSIA

Students will know:
- *Eastern Europe and Western Russia have had similar governments.*
- *Eastern Europe and Western Russia share some cultural aspects.*
- *Eastern Europe and Western Russia have similar economic issues.*

Students will be able to:
- *discuss social and economic changes in Russia after the fall of the Soviet Union.*
- *describe people and cultures in the region.*
- *explore religion, the arts, and daily life in the region.*
- *examine economic issues in Eastern Europe and Western Russia.*

UNDERSTANDING
BY DESIGN®

☑ *Print Teaching Options*

V Visual Skills

☐ **P. 411** Students compare and contrast features of cities in Western Russia and Eastern Europe. Visual/Spatial

W Writing Skills

☐ **P. 412** Small groups discuss a government imposing travel restrictions and write a persuasive essay to discuss whether restrictions are ever justified. Verbal/Linguistic

☐ **P. 415** Students write about how traditions are kept alive when they are publicly forbidden. Intrapersonal

R Reading Skills

☐ **P. 414** Students name some of the major contributors of cultural works in Russia during the 1800s and early 1900s.

☐ **P. 417** Students explain the benefits of being a member of the European Union. AL Verbal/Linguistic

C Critical Thinking Skills

☐ **P. 410** Students make generalizations about the transfer of industry to private ownership and its effects on people.

☐ **P. 411** Students draw conclusions about Russia's response to the separatist movement in Chechnya. Logical

☐ **P. 412** Students compare the text and the map about the various Slavic people from Eastern Europe. Logical

☐ **P. 413** Students infer why religious faith was strengthened under Soviet repression. AL Logical

☐ **P. 415** Students discuss how the generation gap affects the opinions and attitudes of different generations in Eastern Europe and Western Russia. Logical

☐ **P. 417** Students make a chart of the ways Russian culture has been influenced by both Europe and Asia. Visual

T Technology Skills

☐ **P. 414** Small groups use the Internet and presentation software to give a short biographical sketch of an artist from Eastern Europe or Western Russia. BL

☐ **P. 416** Students list and research the natural resources Russia supplies to other countries. Verbal/Linguistic

☑ *Online Teaching Options*

V Visual Skills

☐ **MAP** **Slavic Settlement in Eastern Europe and Western Russia**—Students identify three Slavic groups and discuss what each group may have in common. AL ELL Visual/Spatial

☐ **IMAGES** **A Visual Tour of Eastern Europe's Capital Cities**—Students use images of the cities of Eastern Europe to analyze these cities. Visual/Spatial

☐ **MAP** **Population: Eastern Europe and Western Russia**—Students use the population map to review the population distribution of this region. Visual/Spatial

☐ **MAP** **Slavic Languages**—Students use the language map of the Slavic languages to discuss the languages that are used in the Slavic groups. Verbal/Linguistic

☐ **MAP** **Resources: Eastern Europe and Western Russia**—Students use the resources map to review the resources in this region. Naturalist

W Writing Skills

☐ **VIDEO** **Russia Concerned Over Shrinking Population**—Students write a narrative paragraph about one aspect of the video that surprised or interested them. AL Visual

☐ **TIME LINE** **Post-Cold War Leaders**—Students use the interactive time line to discuss the changes each Post-Cold war leader faced in Russia. Verbal/Linguistic

R Reading Skills

☐ **GAME** **Drag-and-Drop: Cities of Eastern Europe and Western Russia**—Students take turns matching the capital cities in Eastern Europe with their countries. AL ELL Kinesthetic

☐ **GRAPHIC ORGANIZER** **Russia and the Arts**—Students discuss the importance of the arts in Russia using the interactive graphic organizer.

C Critical Thinking Skills

☐ **CHART** **Russia's Population**—Students discuss the changes in Russia's populations after WWII and write a paragraph about what they think the causes were.

☐ **GRAPHIC ORGANIZER** **Cause and Effect: Generation Gap in Post-Soviet Russia**—Students analyze the effects of the end of the Soviet system on modern Russia and the influence of Western culture and write a paragraph detailing three things they learned.

☐ **SLIDE SHOW** **Russia's Role Between Europe and Asia**—Students use the slide show showing Russia's role between Europe and Asia to analyze this relationship.

T Technology Skills

☐ **ONLINE SELF-CHECK QUIZ** **Lesson 3**—Students receive instant feedback on their mastery of lesson content.

☑ *Printable Digital Worksheets*

W Writing Skills

☐ **WORKSHEET** **Critical Thinking Skills: Recognizing Bias—Serbia and Eastern Europe**—Students use the worksheet to understand and recognize bias.

INTERVENTION AND REMEDIATION STRATEGIES

LESSON 1 Physical Geography

Reading and Comprehension

Organize students into six groups. Assign one of the three academic vocabulary words or one of the three content vocabulary words to each group. Challenge students in each group to write a paragraph, using the term they have been assigned, to explain a concept in the lesson. After groups have completed their paragraphs, ask a volunteer from each group to read the paragraph. Provide guidance as needed, ensuring that students have used each term correctly and that they demonstrate a thorough understanding of lesson concepts.

Text Evidence

Have students review the lesson and use the headings and subheadings to create an outline to better comprehend lesson concepts. Have students write key words and phrases in their notebooks to remind them about important content under each heading and subheading. Then have students conduct a peer review by switching outlines with a partner. After students have reviewed each other's outlines, have them take back their own outline and make revisions and additions as needed.

LESSON 2 History of the Regions

Reading and Comprehension

To ensure comprehension of the academic and content vocabulary words in this lesson, have students work in mixed-ability pairs to review each word. Have students say each word while their partner writes down a definition based on context clues in the text. Have partners quiz each other on the terms, clarifying meanings by locating the definitions in a dictionary. Circulate to help students with potentially tricky multisyllabic words such as *inevitable* and *collectivization*.

Text Evidence

Have students work in pairs or small groups to look up the term *imperial* in an online or print dictionary. Have partners create a list of synonyms that relate to the word, and use the word *imperial* in a sentence. Then have students work with their partner to write a paragraph discussing why the adjective *imperial* is used to describe Russia in this lesson. Tell students to cite specific evidence from the text to support their reasoning.

LESSON 3 Life in Eastern Europe and Western Russia

Reading and Comprehension

To ensure comprehension of the concepts explained in this lesson, have students work in small groups and take turns acting as the teacher. Tell students the assignment to teach is titled "Changes and Challenges in Eastern Europe and Western Russia." Students should choose a concept, place, or vocabulary word from the lesson and explain it to the rest of their group. Tell students they may use the board to draw diagrams or charts to better explain their concept, place, or term.

Text Evidence

Have students work in pairs or small groups to create a visual representation of an aspect of life in Eastern Europe and Western Russia discussed in this lesson. Assign groups the following topics to depict in their visual displays: Social and Economic Changes, Where People Live, Ethnic and Language Groups, Religion, the Arts, and Daily Life. Students may choose to create a poster, a graphic organizer, or diagram and use photographs they find online to enhance their displays. Have students present their displays to the class.

Online Resources

Level Reader

Use this online lower-level text that corresponds directly to the text in the online Student Edition.

Guided Reading Activities

This resource uses graphic organizers and guiding questions to help students with comprehension.

What Do You Know?

Use these worksheets to pre-assess students' background knowledge before they read the chapter.

Reading Essentials and Study Guide Workbook

This resource offers writing and reading activities for the approaching-level student.

Self-Check Quizzes

This online assessment tool provides instant feedback for students to check their progress.

EASTERN EUROPE AND WESTERN RUSSIA

net w rks
There's More Online about Eastern Europe
and Western Russia.

CHAPTER 13

ESSENTIAL QUESTIONS · *How does geography influence the way people live?*
· *How do governments change?*

Dancers with Moscow's
world-famous Bolshoi Ballet
rehearse for an upcoming
performance.

Dmitry Kostyukov/AFP/Getty Images

Lesson 1
Physical Geography

Lesson 2
History of the Regions

Lesson 3
*Life in Eastern Europe and
Western Russia*

The Story Matters...

The people of Eastern Europe and
Western Russia share an
agricultural background, which
has been important in their
history. Over the centuries,
however, the people in this
subregion have faced many
political, ethnic, and economic
challenges. The rise and fall of
communism in Russia has had a
tremendous impact on the
countries of Eastern Europe.

FOLDABLES
Study Organizer

Go to the Foldables®
library in the back of
your book to make a
Foldable® that will
help you take notes
while reading this
chapter.

393

ENGAGE

Think-Pair-Share Have students brainstorm a list of
characteristics they as students share and economic
challenges they face. Students may cite common ages, goals,
and social backgrounds as shared characteristics and not having
enough money to buy what they want or being unable to get a
job as economic challenges. Have students share their lists.
Then have students read "The Story Matters..." about the
people of Eastern Europe and Western Russia.

Discuss with the class what it means to face political, ethnic,
and economic challenges and the following questions. If people
are unhappy with their government, how might a change of
power occur? What problems may surface when people of
different ethnic backgrounds live near each other? How might a
poor economy affect people's morale? Tell students that in this
chapter, they will learn about the subregions of Eastern Europe
and Western Russia and the challenges they face.

Making Connections Have students look at the picture and
read the caption about ballet. **Ask:** What do you know about
ballet? Have you ever seen a ballet performed?

After students respond, explain that ballet began in Italy during
the Renaissance in the 15th century. It began as a dance
performance given between the courses of a banquet. The action
in the ballet was related to the food on the menu. The French
further developed this form of dance in the 16th century where it
was mainly performed before nobility in the royal courts. The
Ballets Russes from Russia performed in Paris in 1909. Vaslav
Nijinsky and Anna Pavlova performed with the company. Nijinsky
amazed audiences with gravity-defying leaps. He is considered
one of the most gifted male dancers in history.

Have volunteers use the Internet to research famous Russian
ballet dancers, both male and female. Ask them to show photos
or video clips, if possible, of the dancers' performances and tell
the class two or three interesting facts about the
dancers. Visual/Spatial, Verbal/Linguistic

Letter from the Author

Dear Geography Teacher,

Satellite data from the American National Snow and Ice Data
Center show that Arctic ice has shrunk far below the long-term
range. It is expected that this melting will reveal mineral
deposits along the Canadian and Russian continental shelves. The
melting ice will also help Russia develop its Arctic shipping
lanes. Development of Russia's Northern Sea Route will reduce the
shipping distance between Europe and Asia. This route will allow
Russia to send its Arctic resources to Asian markets more easily.

Richard H. Boehm

FOLDABLES
Study Organizer

Go to the Foldables® library for a
cumulative chapter-based
Foldable® activity that your
students can use to help take
notes and prepare for assessment.

TEACH & ASSESS

Step Into the Place

T Technology Skills

Researching on the Internet Direct students to image A of St. Sofia Cathedral in the city of Kiev, Ukraine. Tell students that since its founding in 1037, the cathedral has been damaged and restored numerous times due to many fires and destruction during periods of civil unrest. The interior walls, pillars, and vaults are decorated with mosaics and frescos, their purpose being to inspire the people inside the church and to act as a window to the spiritual world. Many princes of Kiev are buried inside the cathedral. Have students use the Internet to research photos of St. Sofia to present to the class. Ask students to evaluate and share their opinions of Byzantine architecture.
Visual/Spatial, Verbal Linguistic, Logical/Mathematical

V1 Visual Skills

Reading a Map Use the following questions to reinforce students' map skills. **Ask:**

- In what latitude range is most of this subregion? *(between 40°N and 70°N)*
- Based on this latitude range, what conclusion can you draw about the climate of the area? *(Possible answer: The southern areas have a Mediterranean climate with hot summers and mild winters. The northern areas have a subarctic climate with very cold winters.)*
- On which continent does Western Russia lie? *(Europe)*

Content Background Knowledge

The Volga River begins in the Valday Hills northwest of Moscow and flows southeast to the Caspian Sea. The river provides transportation, hydroelectric power, and water for irrigation for Russia. The Russian people lovingly refer to the river as "Mother Volga." A series of reservoirs, dams, and locks make navigation possible and control flooding. However, industrialization has affected the river's water quality. Most species of sturgeon, which make their home in the river and are the source for caviar, are either threatened or endangered because of poaching.

ANSWERS, p. 394

STEP INTO THE PLACE
1. Estonia
2. Dnieper River
3. Answers may include the Czech Republic, Hungary, Serbia, Kosovo, Macedonia, Moldova, Belarus, and Slovakia.
4. CRITICAL THINKING It would make sense to ship the crops from the Black Sea (which connects to the Mediterranean Sea). The fastest method might be to move the crops by water on the Dnieper River, which empties into the Black Sea.

Rolling hills and fertile soil blanket much of Eastern Europe and Western Russia, two regions that merge just south of the Baltic Sea and north of the Black Sea and the Caspian Sea. As you study the map of Eastern Europe and Western Russia, look for geographic features that make this area unique.

Step Into the Place

MAP FOCUS Use the map to answer the following questions.

1 **THE GEOGRAPHER'S WORLD** Which Eastern European country bordering Russia is located farthest north?

2 **PLACES AND REGIONS** Which river runs across the border of Russia and Eastern Europe?

3 **THE GEOGRAPHER'S WORLD** Name four landlocked countries in Eastern Europe.

4 **CRITICAL THINKING**
Analyzing If you were a farmer in Belarus who needed to ship crops overseas, from which sea would you transport your crops? How would you get them to that sea?

A

CHURCH ARCHITECTURE St. Sophia Cathedral, with its 13 domes, is one of the oldest churches in Ukraine. It was built in 1037 to rival the church of the same name in Constantinople.

B

EUROPE'S LONGEST RIVER Boats line the Volga River, which flows about 2,300 miles (3,701 km) through west central Russia.

Step Into the Time

TIME LINE Using events on the time line, write a paragraph explaining how these events contributed to the rise of communism in Russia and Eastern Europe.

1762 Catherine the Great becomes empress of Russia

1700

1721 Peter the Great founds the Russian Empire

394 *Chapter 13*

(t to b) ©MORANDI Bruno/Hemis/Corbis; Tim Makins/Lonely Planet Images/Getty Images; GL Archive/Alamy

Project-Based Learning ✋

Hands-On

Creating a Short Skit
Students will work in small groups to write and act out short skits depicting a historical event from Eastern Europe or Western Russia. Students should research the event before they write the skit. The skit's dialogue must include information about why the event was important in this region's history. Have students present their skits to the class.

Digital Hands-On

Conducting a Fictional Interview
Have students work in small groups to conduct fictional interviews of a person who lived in Eastern Europe or Western Russia during a historical event in the region. The fictional interviews will be recorded as podcasts and uploaded and shared online, allowing the students to listen to each other's interviews.

edtechteacher
21st Century Learning

Eastern Europe and Western Russia

o National capital
• City

1917 Czarist government overthrown in Russia

1920 The Communist Party gains absolute power in Russia

1939 Germany invades Poland and World War II begins

1945 Josip Broz Tito leads postwar Yugoslavia

1980 Lech Walesa founds the labor union Solidarity in Poland

1987 Gorbachev introduces reforms in USSR

1991 Baltic states declare their independence

1991 The Soviet Union breaks up into 15 independent states

(l to r) RIA Novosti/Alamy; Peter Horree/Alamy

Chapter 13 **395**

Step Into the Time

V₂ Visual Skills

Reading a Time Line Have students review the time line and as a class, discuss its major points of interest. **Ask:**

- What period of time is shown on the time line? *(from 1700 to 2000)*
- Which events happened during the same year? What was the year? *(In 1991, the Baltic states declared their independence and the Soviet Union broke up into 15 independent states.)*
- When did Russia stop being ruled by czars? *(1917)*
- Which event happened first—Lech Walesa founding a labor union in Poland or Gorbachev introducing reforms in the USSR? *(Lech Walesa founding a labor union in Poland)*

Ask students to list some historical events that could be added to the time line. *(Student answers will vary but should include accurate event placement.)* Visual/Spatial, Verbal/Linguistic

W Writing Skills

Informative/Explanatory Read aloud the activity described at the beginning of the time line. Before students write their paragraphs, have them brainstorm ideas about how the events on the time line contributed to the rise of communism in Western Russia and Eastern Europe. Then have students write and share their paragraphs with the class. Logical/Mathematical, Verbal/Linguistic

V₂

CLOSE & REFLECT

Making Inferences Have students use the events on the time line to make an inference about why the Soviet Union broke up in 1991. *(Possible answer: The people in the Soviet Union did not like the Communist form of government and rebelled against it.)* **Ask:** Why did Russia have such a great influence and control over the governments of Eastern Europe? *(Possible answer: Since Russia is bigger and stronger than the countries in Eastern Europe, it could use its military power to control other countries' governments.)* Verbal/Linguistic, Logical/Mathematical

---

TIME LINE

Reading a Time Line and Map

Integrating Visual Information Display the time line and map on the whiteboard. Have volunteers read each event as it is revealed on the time line. Ask students to identify where in the world the event took place and find its location on the map. ELL AL Visual/Spatial

See page 393B for other online activities.

ENGAGE

Bellringer Before students begin the lesson, have them visualize the Great Plains in the United States. **Ask:**

- What characteristics describe the Great Plains? *(Possible answers: flat or rolling terrain; few trees; fertile soil; grasslands)*
- How does the landscape of the Great Plains influence how people live? *(Possible answer: Many people are farmers, ranchers, or work in jobs in agriculture.)*

Then read the Essential Question and the "It Matters Because" statement. Have students brainstorm occupations people in this subregion might pursue and how the rugged mountains might hamper people's travels.

TEACH & ASSESS

V Visual Skills

Reading a Map Have students reference a physical or political map of Europe and Asia. Ask volunteers to locate the following major landforms and waterways: Baltic Sea, Barents Sea, Caucasus Mountains, Adriatic Sea, Black Sea, Caspian Sea, Ural Mountains. **Ask:** What is a peninsula? *(a piece of land surrounded by water on three sides)*

Then, using the Chapter Opener map for Eastern Europe and Western Russia, have volunteers identify and locate the 10 Eastern European countries on the Balkan Peninsula and identify the surrounding bodies of water. *(Slovenia, Croatia, Bosnia and Herzegovina, Serbia, Kosovo, Montenegro, Macedonia, Albania, Bulgaria, Romania; Adriatic Sea, Black Sea)*

Continue by having volunteers identify and locate the 11 countries in the northern part of Eastern Europe: Estonia, Latvia, Lithuania, Poland, Czech Republic, Slovakia, Hungary, Maldova, Ukraine, Belarus, and Georgia. **AL** Visual/Spatial

R Reading Skills

Determining Word Meanings Have students define the word *upland* using the meanings of the two smaller words in it. *(ground or land that is up or high)* Then have students find its definition using context clues. *(an area of high elevation)* **Ask:** What would an area of low elevation be called? *(lowland)* Remind students to add vocabulary words to the lists in their notebooks. Verbal/Linguistic

---

ANSWER, p. 396

Taking Notes Answers include agricultural goods (grains), forests, coal, oil, natural gas, and fish.

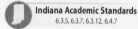

Reading **HELP**DESK

Academic Vocabulary

- impact
- extract

Content Vocabulary

- upland
- steppe
- balkanization
- brackish
- reserves

TAKING NOTES: *Key Ideas and Details*

Identify On a web diagram like this one, list at least four natural resources found in Eastern Europe and Western Russia.

Natural Resources

I **Indiana Academic Standards**
6.3.5, 6.3.7, 6.3.12, 6.4.7

Lesson 1
Physical Geography

ESSENTIAL QUESTION • *How does geography influence the way people live?*

IT MATTERS BECAUSE
Both the rugged mountains and the gentle plains of Eastern Europe and Western Russia have shaped the cultures of the people living there.

Landforms and Waterways

GUIDING QUESTION *In what way have the landforms in the Balkan Peninsula shaped the cultures of that region?*

You can locate Eastern Europe and Western Russia on a map or a globe by identifying physical characteristics that border the regions. To the north are the Baltic and Barents Seas. The southern border is defined by the Caucasus Mountains and the Adriatic, Black, and Caspian Seas. The regions extend eastward to the Ural Mountains. Eastern Europe includes 10 countries in the north and 11 on the Balkan Peninsula. Russia is a huge country, extending through Europe and Asia and covering 11 time zones. Western Russia is the part of Russia that lies within Europe. Western Russia and Eastern Europe share characteristics of physical and human geography that unite them into a single region.

Vast Plains

Eastern Europe and Western Russia rest mostly on a group of plains. The largest plain is the Russian Plain, which begins in Belarus and Ukraine and stretches east about 1,000 miles (1,609 km) from Russia's western borders. In central European Russia, the Russian Plain rises to form the central Russian **upland**. An upland is an area of high elevation. To the east are the Ural Mountains, and beyond that, the west Siberian Plain.

(l to r) ©Serguei Fomine/Global Look/Corbis; ©Dallas and John Heaton/Corbis; Bloomberg/Getty Images

---

netw**o**rks *Online Teaching Options*

VIDEO

World's Wonders—St. Petersburg

Formulating Questions Use this video about the city of St. Petersburg to introduce the lesson. Discuss some of the information mentioned in the video about how the city was constructed and why. Ask students to write three questions they have about this city after watching the video. Collect the questions and discuss them as a class after the lesson. **AL** Visual/Spatial, Verbal/Linguistic

See page 393C for other online activities.

BBC Motion Gallery Education

The Northern European Plain includes Poland in Eastern Europe, but it also extends into parts of Western Europe. South and southeast of the Northern European Plain is the Hungarian Plain, which includes parts of many different countries. Within Romania is the Transylvanian basin. A basin is an area of land that slopes gently downward from the surrounding land. Much of Ukraine is **steppe**, or vast, level areas of land that support only low-growing, vegetation-like grasses.

Bordering Mountains

To the south of the Russian Plain are two chains of mountains that make up the Greater and Lesser Caucasus Mountains. They extend from the northwest to the southeast with a valley between.

East of the Russian Plain, the Ural Mountains form a boundary between Europe and Asia. The Urals are up to 250 million years old. The northern mountains are covered in forests and some glaciers. Grasslands cover the southern Urals.

The Carpathian Mountains are much younger. On a map, the Carpathians appear almost as an eastward extension of the Alps. The Vienna basin in Austria separates the two mountain ranges.

The Balkan Peninsula is a mountainous region. In fact, *balkan* is a Turkish word for mountain. The Carpathian Mountains run through the peninsula's north and are linked to the Balkan Mountains. The region is so mountainous that human settlements are isolated from one another. This isolation results in cultural diversity among the people, but it is also the source of conflict among ethnic groups. Conflict among ethnic groups within a state, a country, or a region is known as **balkanization**.

C

Russia's Komi region borders the Urals and other mountain ranges. It is rich in coal, oil, natural gas, diamonds, gold, and timber.
▶ CRITICAL THINKING
Describing What characteristic of the Ural Mountains makes them unique?

©Serguei Fomine/Global Look/Corbis

Chapter 13 **397**

How Landforms Create Political Boundaries

Explaining Using the animated map, display the various landforms, beginning with the Ural Mountains, that show how mountain chains, rivers, and lakes create natural physical and political borders. Discuss with students why landforms make good boundaries. Then have students write a paragraph telling three things they learned about how landforms create political boundaries.
BL Visual/Spatial, Verbal/Linguistic

See page 393C for other online activities.

Integrating Visual Information Display a physical map of the world or of Eastern Europe and Western Russia. As students read about the various plains and chains of mountains in this region, have them locate the landforms on the map. Have students consult their lists of vocabulary words, identify context clues in the text, or use dictionaries to understand how a *plain*, *upland*, *basin*, *steppe*, and *mountain* are alike or different.
ELL Visual/Spatial, Naturalist

T Technology Skills

Making Presentations Transylvania is a real place, not a myth created by Hollywood for vampire movies. The Transylvanian Basin is located in central Romania and is surrounded by the arc of the Carpathian mountain chain. About 5 million people live in its 34,177 square miles. *Transylvania* means "land beyond the forest." The area has many towns with well-preserved medieval architecture including castles, churches, and traditional villages.

Have students work in small groups and use the Internet to research a point of interest in the Transylvanian Basin. Using presentation software, have groups present a travelogue to the class about the area. Visual/Spatial, Verbal/Linguistic

C Critical Thinking Skills

Making Inferences Remind students that when people are isolated, they are alone or apart from others. **Ask:** How might being isolated result in cultural diversity and conflict among ethnic groups? *(Students' answers will vary but should demonstrate an understanding about how limited or no contact among groups can cause fear and distrust of outsiders and prevent the exchange of ideas.)* **ELL** Verbal/Linguistic, Logical/Mathematical

Content Background Knowledge

Near the city of Brasov in Transylvania is Bran Castle, also known as Dracula's Castle. It was built in the fourteenth century as a fortress to protect the Hungarian king from the Ottomans and other enemies. In 1897 an Irish novelist, Bram Stoker, wrote a story about Count Dracula, based on the real life of Vlad Tepes, also known as Vlad the Impaler. The castle is supposed to be Dracula's house. In reality, Vlad the Impaler only stayed there as a guest for a short time. However, the people in the area keep the vampire legend alive because the castle attracts many tourists.

ANSWER, p. 397

CRITICAL THINKING The Urals form a boundary between Europe and Asia.

Physical Geography

V Visual Skills

Integrating Visual Information Display a political map of the world or have students reference the Chapter Opener map of Eastern Europe and Western Russia. As students read about the seas in this region, have them locate them on the map. Tell students that the Caspian Sea is actually the world's largest lake. The Romans called it a sea because they found its water salty and the name has never been changed. Continue the activity by having volunteers locate the rivers and lakes mentioned in the next section. **ELL** Visual/Spatial

R Reading Skills

Summarizing Have students summarize what they learned about the importance of rivers and lakes to Eastern Europe and Western Russia. *(Possible answer: Rivers, canals, lakes, and reservoirs provide the region with transportation routes, hydroelectric power, irrigation for farmlands, water to relieve shortages, and fishing.)* Logical/Mathematical, Verbal/Linguistic

Content Background Knowledge

Facts about the Black Sea:

- The Black Sea is surrounded by six countries: Turkey, Romania, Ukraine, Bulgaria, Russia, and Georgia.
- It is believed that during the Middle Ages, the Turks named this body of water the Black Sea.
- Its lower layers of water are anoxic, meaning they contain absolutely no oxygen.
- Because there's no oxygen in the lower water layers, remains of shipwrecks—including humans and cargo—can be found on the seabed with little or no decomposition after hundreds of years.
- There are no high or low tides, so the sea is always calm and quiet on the surface.
- The Black Sea is connected to the Mediterranean Sea through the Bosporus Strait, the Sea of Marmara, and the Dardanelles.

Bulgaria, located in the Balkan Peninsula, has a mild climate and sandy beaches along its Black Sea coast.
▶ **CRITICAL THINKING**
Identifying What seas other than the Black Sea border the Balkan Peninsula?

Surrounding Seas

The Baltic Sea lies northwest of Russia and Eastern Europe. The Baltic is shallow and **brackish**, or somewhat salty, because it is seawater mixed with river water. In the southwest, the Adriatic, Ionian, and Black seas surround the Balkan Peninsula on three sides. The Black Sea borders the southern coast of Ukraine and southwestern Russia. The sea also separates Turkey from Ukraine and the Balkan Peninsula. At Europe's most southeastern point is the Caspian Sea. The Caspian Sea is the world's largest inland body of water, covering an area larger than Japan.

Rivers and Lakes

A vast number of rivers, canals, lakes, and reservoirs are found in Eastern Europe and Western Russia. The Volga River is the longest river in Europe and Russia's most important waterway. Originating northwest of Moscow, the Volga and its many tributaries carry more freight and passenger traffic than any other river in Russia. It provides hydroelectric power and water to many parts of Russia.

The Dnieper River also originates in Russia. It flows through Belarus and Ukraine before emptying into the Black Sea. Dams and reservoirs southeast of Kiev provide hydroelectric power. They also irrigate farmlands and help relieve water shortages in parts of Ukraine. Originating in the Carpathian Mountains and emptying into the Black Sea, the Dniester River is the second-longest river in Ukraine. The Dniester carries freight and passenger ships, and it serves as an important route to the Black Sea.

From its origins in southwestern Germany, the Danube flows toward the east through several countries before emptying into the Black Sea. The Danube provides transportation, hydroelectric power, fishing, and water for irrigation. Historically, the river transported traders as well as invading armies. Today, many cities are located along its banks, including three capital cities: Vienna, Austria; Budapest, Hungary; and Belgrade, Serbia. The Main River became connected to the Danube via the Main-Danube Canal, which linked the North Sea with the Black Sea.

☑ **READING PROGRESS CHECK**

Analyzing How is the location of the Black Sea strategic to the region?

©Dallas and John Heaton/Corbis

---

net**w**rks *Online Teaching Options*

MAP

Physical Geography: Eastern Europe and Western Russia

Analyzing Display the physical geography layer of the Chapter Opener map. Have students discuss and analyze the geographic landscapes of the region. **Ask:** How does the physical landscape influence where people live and how they travel? *(Students' answers will vary but should include relevant details about how landforms and waterways influence how people live and travel.)* **AL** Visual/Spatial, Verbal/Linguistic

See page 393C for other online activities.

ANSWERS, p. 398

CRITICAL THINKING The Adriatic and Ionian Seas, along with the Black Sea, border the Balkan Peninsula.

☑ READING PROGRESS CHECK The Black Sea borders the southern coasts of Ukraine and Russia and separates Turkey from Ukraine and the Balkan Peninsula. The Black Sea is an important transportation route between Europe and Asia.

Climates

GUIDING QUESTION *How does climate affect plants that are grown and harvested in Eastern Europe and Western Russia?*

Several different types of climate are found in Eastern Europe and Western Russia, from the hot summers and rainy winters in Albania to the cold, polar reaches of northern Russia.

Humid Continental Climates

Much of Eastern Europe and Western Russia have a humid continental climate. These areas experience mild or warm summers and long, cold winters. Farther south, in places such as Croatia, Serbia, and Bulgaria, summers are hotter, and winter weather is similar to that of areas farther north.

Albania and Macedonia experience a more Mediterranean climate, especially in the western areas. Summers tend to be hot and dry, and winters are mild to cool and rainy.

W

Russia's Far North

North of 60°N latitude, Western Russia has a subarctic climate. Winters are very cold, with temperatures as low as −40°F (−40°C). The summers are short and cool, though temperatures can range from 50°F (10°C) to 86°F (30°C).

R

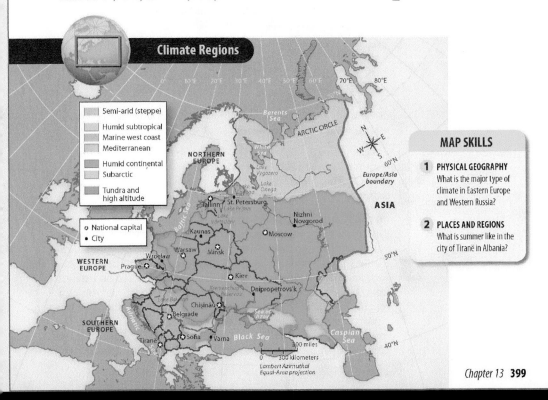

Climate Regions

Legend:
- Semi-arid (steppe)
- Humid subtropical
- Marine west coast
- Mediterranean
- Humid continental
- Subarctic
- Tundra and high altitude

○ National capital
● City

Lambert Azimuthal Equal-Area projection

MAP SKILLS

1 PHYSICAL GEOGRAPHY
What is the major type of climate in Eastern Europe and Western Russia?

2 PLACES AND REGIONS
What is summer like in the city of Tiranë in Albania?

W Writing Skills

Narrative Have small groups of students brainstorm what they might pack for a summer vacation in Albania and for a trip during the same time of year to Russia's far north. Then have students write a narrative paragraph explaining how the contents of their suitcases would be the same or different for a vacation to Albania or to Russia's far north. *(Students' paragraphs may vary but should include an understanding of the differences in climates between the two places. For example, shorts and swimsuits would be suitable in Albania because of its Mediterranean climate with hot and dry summers. Shorts may be worn during the summer in Russia's far north on days when the temperatures are warmer, but jeans, sweaters, and light jackets would be the preferred clothing to pack.)* Verbal/Linguistic, Intrapersonal

R Reading Skills

Calculating Encourage students to use the statistics given in the text to make calculations that have more meaning to them and to which they can relate. **Ask:** What is the temperature range between the low and high temperatures in Russia's far north? *(126°F/70°C)* Logical/Mathematical

Content Background Knowledge

Hypothermia, an abnormally low core body temperature that can be life threatening, is a real danger in Arctic climates. Normal human core body temperature is 98.6°F. Hypothermia begins to occur when a person's body temperature drops to 94°F and is usually fatal when the body temperature reaches 85°F.

To protect against hypothermia, people should wear insulated clothing and limit outdoor activities to when the temperatures are warmer. In some Arctic cultures, huddling and sleeping together in family groups cuts down on heat loss. Shivering is also the body's natural response to low temperatures. It increases muscle activity and produces some heat.

SLIDE SHOW

Adapting to Environments

Discussing Present the photo slide show about adaptation and discuss with students how the people, plants, and animals adapt to the Arctic temperatures in Russia. **Ask:** What adaptations would people need to make in their living conditions and clothing to be able to survive the Arctic temperatures? What adaptations would plants and animals need to make? *(Students' answers may vary but should demonstrate an understanding of extremely cold temperatures, short growing seasons, and many months of no sunlight.)* Visual/Spatial, Naturalist

See page 393C for other online activities.

Slide Show

ANSWERS, p. 399

MAP SKILLS

1. humid continental climate (mild or warm summers and long, cold winters)
2. Summer is typically hot and dry in Tiranë, Albania.

Physical Geography

C1 Critical Thinking Skills

Reasoning Review with students what they already have learned about the relationship of abundant natural resources and the economy of a region. **Ask:** How might abundant mineral resources, dense forests, fertile farmlands, and rich fishing grounds help the economy of a region? *(Students' answers will vary but should demonstrate an understanding of how abundant supplies of natural resources provide wealth and products, especially if the demand for the resources or products is high.)* Logical/Mathematical, Verbal/Linguistic

C2 Critical Thinking Skills

Determining Cause and Effect Discuss with students the importance of looking for cause and effect relationships in any text they read so that they understand why things happen and the effects that these things cause. **Ask:** What might be the effect of having only about one-sixth of the land being suitable for agriculture in one of the largest countries in the world? *(Possible answer: It may not be possible to produce enough food to feed all the people, which would then result in the need to import food products from other countries.)* Logical/ Mathematical

Content Background Knowledge

The Arctic archipelago of Novaya Zemlya is an extension of the Ural Mountains. The northern island is half covered permanently with ice while the other half is totally bare Arctic desert. The southern island is covered by Arctic tundra (no trees or bushes) and is partially inhabited by a small number of reindeer herders and trappers. Polar bears, Arctic foxes, lemmings, seals, walruses, and a variety of birds can be found on the southern island. A Russian scientific station has been operating on the island since 1896. Between 1955 and 1990, the Soviets conducted 224 nuclear tests on the islands.

ANSWERS, p. 400

CRITICAL THINKING Sulfur, aluminum, copper, lead, and zinc

☑ **READING PROGRESS CHECK** Students in the northern United States will most likely compare their climate to the humid continental climates of Latvia, Lithuania, Estonia, Poland, the Czech Republic, northern Romania, Slovakia, Belarus, Moldova, and most of Hungary and Ukraine. Students living farther south may compare their climate to that found in Croatia, Serbia, Bulgaria, as well as southern Romania, Hungary and Ukraine. Students along the California coast will more likely identify with the Mediterranean climate found in Albania and Macedonia.

A miner watches as the arm of a drill machine draws out coal from a mine in southern Poland.
▶ **CRITICAL THINKING**
Identifying What other minerals are important to Poland's economy?

Farther north is Novaya Zemlya, an archipelago consisting of two large islands and several small islands. The climate here is polar, and a large part of Novaya Zemlya is covered in ice year-round. Only the southern island is inhabited by a small number of the indigenous Nenets, who are herders and fishers.

☑ **READING PROGRESS CHECK**

Identifying What area in Eastern Europe or Western Russia has a climate most similar to where you live?

Natural Resources

GUIDING QUESTION *What are three important challenges to the development of resources in Eastern Europe and Western Russia?*

C1 Eastern Europe and Western Russia have abundant mineral resources, as well as dense forests, fertile farmlands, and rich fishing grounds. These resources play a vital role in people's lives and in the economy of the countries in which they live.

Forests and Agriculture

C2 Russia is a vast country—by far the largest in the world. However, only about one-sixth of Russia's land is suitable for agriculture. Farmers grow a number of crops, including grains such as wheat, oats, and barley. Most agricultural land is in an area that extends from the western shores of the Baltic Sea to the Black Sea, forming a roughly triangular shape. This area is known as the fertile triangle.

More than one-fifth of the world's forests are in Russia. They cover an area almost the size of the continental United States. Lumber, paper, and cardboard are important products of the forestry

Bloomberg/Getty Images

---

netw⊙rks *Online Teaching Options*

IMAGE/CHART

Using Resources

Reading a Chart Display the interactive image to launch the chart about the production of resources throughout Eastern Europe and Western Russia. Have volunteers identify the information presented on the chart and have students make comparisons and contrasts between resources produced in the different countries. **AL**
Visual/Spatial, Verbal/Linguistic

See page 393C for other online activities.

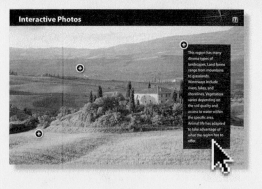

Interactive Photos

Peter Zelei/Vetta/Getty Images

industry. The long, cold winters of Western Russia's continental climate, however, cause forests to grow slowly. The intense harvesting of forests and the slow rates of growth threaten the forests and the forestry industry.

In 2010 Russia experienced the hottest summer in 130 years, with drought conditions and temperatures reaching 104°F (40°C). That summer, wildfires destroyed 37 million acres (about 15 million ha) of forests, agricultural crops, and other vegetation. The **impact** of these fires was tremendous, taking lives, destroying homes, and damaging Russia's forestry and agricultural industries.

C

Academic Vocabulary

impact a dramatic or forceful effect or influence on something

Energy and Minerals

Most of Russia's vast coal, oil, and natural gas **reserves** are in Siberia. Reserves are the estimated total amount of a resource in a certain area. Russia's coal and rich deposits of iron ore fuel the country's steel industry. Machines made from steel are used to build Russia's automobiles, railroads, ships, and many consumer products.

Poland's important mineral resources include aluminum, coal, copper, lead, and zinc. Poland is one of the world's major sources of sulfur. Romania has rich deposits of coal, and it **extracts** oil from the Black Sea. Hydroelectric and thermal power plants also support Romania's energy needs. Other important mineral resources include copper and bauxite, the raw material for aluminum.

T

Academic Vocabulary

extract to draw or pull out

Fishing Industry

Russia's fishing industry is an important part of the country's economy. Salmon, cod, herring, and pollack are among the most important commercial fish in Russia. Many of Russia's lakes and rivers are also used for freshwater fishing.

Romania's fishing industry is concentrated in the southeastern area of that country. The Danube River and lakes and rivers near the Black Sea provide much of the fish. The European Union's restrictions on overfishing has hurt Romania somewhat, but fishing remains important to the country's economy.

FOLDABLES
Study Organizer

Include this lesson's information in your Foldable®.

☑ **READING PROGRESS CHECK**

Analyzing Why are Russia's mineral industries so important to its economy?

LESSON 1 REVIEW

Reviewing Vocabulary
1. What caused the *balkanization* on the Balkan Peninsula?

Answering the Guiding Questions
2. *Describing* In what way have the landforms in the Balkan Peninsula shaped the cultures of the region?

3. *Analyzing* Why do few people live on the archipelago of Novaya Zemlya?

4. *Identifying* What are two important challenges to Russia's forestry industry?

5. *Informative/Explanatory Writing* Explain how the mineral resources in Russia are important to its industry.

Chapter 13 **401**

LESSON 1 REVIEW ANSWERS

Reviewing Vocabulary

1. Geographic isolation due to the mountainous region led to the great cultural diversity and balkanization of the people in the region.

Answering the Guiding Questions

2. **Describing** The region is so mountainous that communities became isolated from each other. This isolation resulted in great cultural diversity among the people who live there.

3. **Analyzing** The area's polar climate and ice-covered land make it difficult for humans to live there.

4. **Identifying** Long, cold winters mean trees take longer to grow. Intense tree farming threatens the forests and forestry industry. Dryness and heat waves create the danger of wildfires.

5. **Informative/Explanatory Writing** Students' responses should mention that iron ore deposits and abundant coal deposits are the basis of the Russian steel industry. The steel provides material for Russia's machine-building industry, which makes most of the machinery used in Russia.

C Critical Thinking Skills

Determining Cause and Effect Again remind students of the importance of understanding cause and effect relationships. **Ask:**

• What effect does Western Russia's continental climate have on the forestry industry? *(Forests grow slowly.)*

• What causes Russia's forests to be at risk? *(intense harvesting and the slow rates of growth of forests)* Naturalist, Logical/Mathematical

T Technology Skills

Researching on the Internet Sulfur is a nonmetallic chemical element that is tasteless, odorless, and pale yellow in color. However, sulfur compounds, such as hydrogen sulfide, are especially "stinky," smelling like rotting eggs. Most sulfur is converted to sulfuric acid and is used in industry. Have small groups use the Internet to research different uses of sulfur and report their findings to the class. **AL** Verbal/Linguistic, Visual/Spatial

Content Background Knowledge

Caviar is an expensive delicacy that consists of the roe, or fish eggs, of sturgeon. Four species of sturgeon found in the Caspian Sea produce roe that is considered of the highest quality and flavor. Roe from these sturgeons tastes salty with a subtle buttery taste. The most expensive caviar comes from the Iranian Beluga sturgeon that swims in the southern Caspian Sea where the water is less polluted. People have paid over $34,000 for a little over 2 pounds of this "black gold." It is important for those who serve or eat caviar to not use any kind of metal plates or utensils, as metal gives the roe a bad flavor. When eating, many people prefer to roll the eggs around in their mouths and then pop them to release their flavor.

CLOSE & REFLECT

Formatting Questions To close this lesson, have students write questions based on the information presented in this lesson about landforms and waterways, climates, and natural resources. Collect the questions and answer them as a class. Post the questions that still need answers and add responses as students continue increasing their knowledge of the region. Have volunteers do research to add responses to any unanswered questions.

ANSWER, p. 401

☑ **READING PROGRESS CHECK** The iron deposits are the raw material for Russia's steel industry, and coal fuels that industry. The steel is important to Russia's machine-building industry.

ENGAGE

Bellringer The Founders of the United States drafted the Constitution in 1787 to provide a new government for the United States of America. The democracy has lasted over 200 years, and the basic framework for the government has remained essentially unchanged to this day. Have students brainstorm a list of benefits of living in a stable democracy. Students might cite guaranteed freedoms that citizens have or peaceful and safe living conditions. Then make a connection to the Essential Question: *How do governments change?* **Ask:** How do we change our government? *(Possible answers: through free, democratic elections; amendments to the Constitution)*

TEACH & ASSESS

C Critical Thinking Skills

Drawing Conclusions Work with students to complete the section "Early Slavic States." Have them refer to the maps in the lesson to clarify where the Slavic states are located. Then, **ask:**

- What conclusions might you draw after learning that Slavs include Poles, Serbs, Ukrainians, and other eastern Europeans? *(Students' answers will vary but should be based on knowing that Slavs include people from many cultural and ethnic backgrounds. This diversity might cause differences in beliefs that could lead to conflict, such as where borders lie.)*

- What might have caused the early Slavs to migrate from Asia to Eastern Europe and Western Russia? *(Possible answer: They might have been seeking better hunting grounds, fertile land for farming, or freedom from harsh rule.)* **Verbal/Linguistic, Logical/Mathematical**

Content Background Knowledge

The origin of the name *Slav* is unclear. Some scholars suggest that the name comes from the Slavic word *slovo*, meaning "word." Others suggest the name is related to the Slavic word *slava*, meaning "glory" or to the Latin word *sclavus*, meaning "slave."

networks

There's More Online!

☑ **ANIMATION** Russian Historical Changes

☑ **VIDEO**

Reading **HELP**DESK

Academic Vocabulary

- **strategy**
- **inevitable**

Content Vocabulary

- **czar**
- **serf**
- **genocide**
- **communism**
- **collectivization**

TAKING NOTES: *Key Ideas and Details*

Identify Use a graphic organizer like the one shown here to identify two ways that Joseph Stalin fashioned the Soviet Union into a communist dictatorship.

How Stalin Created Communist Dictatorship

Indiana Academic Standards
6.1.15, 6.1.23, 6.2.5, 6.2.6, 6.2.7

402

Lesson 2
History of the Regions

ESSENTIAL QUESTION · *How do governments change?*

IT MATTERS BECAUSE
For most of the late 1900s, the USSR was one of the two most powerful countries in the world. The Soviets ruled Russia, nearly all of Eastern Europe, and much of Central Asia.

Early History

GUIDING QUESTION *How did Peter I and Catherine II change Russia?*

For the last 1,000 years, the people of Eastern Europe and Western Russia have been part of great empires that struggled against each other—and sometimes against their own people.

Early Slavic States

Many different ethnic groups settled in the regions of Eastern Europe and Western Russia long before modern national borders were set. Most of the people in the region are Slavs. Slavs are an ethnic group that includes Poles, Serbs, Ukrainians, and other Eastern Europeans.

Early Slavs migrated from Asia and settled in the area that now includes Ukraine and Poland. In the A.D. 400s and A.D. 500s, Slavs moved westward and southward, coming into contact with migrating Celtic and Germanic groups.

In the A.D. 800s, Slavic groups in the present-day Czech Republic formed Great Moravia, an empire covering much of central Europe. Other Slav people settled in the Balkans, eventually coming under the rule of the Ottoman Empire.

Another early Slav group settled in the forest and plains of present-day Ukraine and Belarus. The people of a settlement called Kiev organized the Slav communities into a union of city-states known as Kievan Rus. The leaders controlled the area's trade, using Russia's western rivers as a link between the

(l to r) DEA/A. DAGLI ORTI/De Agostini Picture Library/Getty Images; ©Dean Conger/Corbis; ©Peter Turnley/Corbis

---

networks *Online Teaching Options*

VIDEO

Communist Russia, a Great Economic Experiment

Interpreting Use this video about the history and collapse of communism to introduce the lesson. Ask students to share what they learned from the video about life under Soviet rule. Ask students if anything surprised them. **AL**
Visual/Spatial, Verbal/Linguistic

See page 393D for other online activities.

BBC Motion Gallery Education

ANSWER, p. 402

Taking Notes Possible answers: Stalin used terror and brute force to put all aspects of society under strict control of the Communist Party. Stalin forced the collectivization of all agriculture.

Baltic Sea and the Black Sea. Kievan Rus prospered from trade with the Mediterranean world and Western Europe. Later, non-Slavic people also settled in the region. Besides ethnic Russians who make up the majority of the population today, there are Hungary's Magyars, Romanians, Slavs, Ukrainians, and many others.

Throughout Russia's history, the Russian Slavs have dominated the country's politics and culture. Most Slavs practice Eastern Orthodoxy, a form of Christianity brought to Russia from the eastern Mediterranean area. By the A.D. 1000s, the ruler and people of Kievan Rus had accepted Eastern Orthodox Christianity. It remains Russia's largest religion today.

R1

Imperial Russia

R2
During the later 1200s, the warrior armies of the Mongols of Central Asia invaded Russia. For the next 250 years, they controlled most of Russia. Near the end of the Mongol reign, the princes of Muscovy (now the city of Moscow) rose to power.

MAP SKILLS

1 HUMAN GEOGRAPHY
Why did early Slav communities develop in the area of Western Russia?

2 PLACES AND REGIONS
In what time period did Russia gain control of the area around the Baltic Sea?

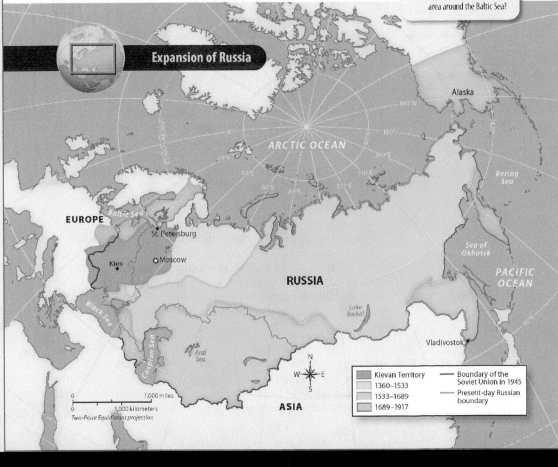

Expansion of Russia

Kievan Territory	—— Boundary of the Soviet Union in 1945
1360–1533	
1533–1689	—— Present-day Russian boundary
1689–1917	

R1 Reading Skills

Citing Text Evidence Have students use text evidence from the previous page and this page to answer the following question. **Ask:** What might be one reason why the people of Kiev were able to organize the Slav communities into a loose union of city-states? *(Their leaders controlled a prosperous trading route and that control gave them power.)* Verbal/Linguistic, Logical/Mathematical

R2 Reading Skills

Determining Word Meanings Explain to students that the word *imperial* means "relating to an empire or emperor." An emperor is a ruler, as is a king, but is considered to have more power than a king—a king usually rules only one country, but an emperor rules the many countries that make up the empire. The term *imperial Russia* refers to the time in history when Russia was an empire ruled by an emperor, or czar. **ELL** **AL** Verbal/Linguistic

V

V Visual Skills

Reading a Map Before students answer the map skills questions, have them identify the information given in the map key and connect it to the different colored areas and lines on the map. **Ask:**

- What does this map show? *(how the country of Russia expanded its territory)*
- What color is represented by the years 1533–1689? *(green)*
- What does the red line represent? *(present-day Russian boundary)*
- What North American state used to be owned by the Soviet Union? *(Alaska)*
- Was the Soviet Union larger or smaller than present-day Russia? *(larger)* Then have students answer the map skills questions. Visual/Spatial

MAP

Russian Historical Changes—Early History

Integrating Visual Information Display the animated map that shows the expansion of Russia from the Ottoman Empire to the rise of Communism. Discuss the changes in Russia over time. Have students theorize about how these changes helped to make Russia one of the most powerful countries in the world. **BL** Visual/Spatial, Verbal/Linguistic

See page 393D for other online activities.

ANSWERS, p. 403

MAP SKILLS
1. Western Russia's rivers provided a link between the Baltic and Black Seas, encouraging the rise of a prosperous trading route.
2. 1689–1917

R Reading Skills

Determining Word Meanings Explain to students the difference between the terms *serf* and *slave*: A serf was required by law to work and to stay on the land where he was born. He could not travel freely without permission from his lord, the landowner. However, he was free to do as he pleased in his daily life. On the other hand, a slave was the property of his master and had to do as he was told at all times. Slaves were bought and sold as goods. Neither a serf nor a slave had any legal rights.

Ask: Why might ex-serfs working in industries in the city work long hours for low wages? *(Students' answers will vary but should include an understanding that serfs could not read or write and had few skills so they were not prepared to do anything but menial work. They were also accustomed to working long hours on farms for little compensation so the switch into long hours doing factory work was something they could easily accept and being able to move off the farm gave them a little more freedom.)* **ELL** **AL** Logical/Mathematical, Verbal/Linguistic

Content Background Knowledge

When Peter the Great began his rule in 1696, Russia was severely underdeveloped and lacked the modernization found in many European countries. Peter initiated extensive reforms to once again make Russia a great nation. He built a strong navy; restructured his army, modeling it after those in Western countries; made schools public; took control of the Orthodox Church; and reorganized the country's administrative procedures. Peter made science a priority and focused on strengthening commerce and industry. He also modernized the Russian alphabet, adopted the Julian calendar, and established the first Russian newspaper.

Through his leadership, Russia took possession of parts of Estonia, Latvia, Finland, and Sweden. He moved the capital from Moscow to a location he called St. Petersburg. But, for all the "great" things he accomplished, he was also considered a cruel and tyrannical ruler. When citizens revolted against his high taxes, they were immediately crushed. He also secretly executed his eldest son for treason.

ANSWER, p. 404

CRITICAL THINKING Monarchs needed nobles and lords for military protection during the constant warfare, so they gave them land in exchange for their service. Serfs farmed the land because the nobles and lords were off fighting.

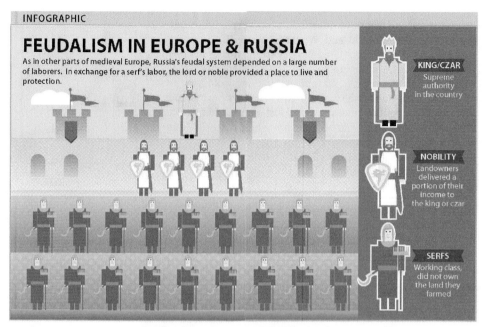

INFOGRAPHIC

FEUDALISM IN EUROPE & RUSSIA

As in other parts of medieval Europe, Russia's feudal system depended on a large number of laborers. In exchange for a serf's labor, the lord or noble provided a place to live and protection.

KING/CZAR Supreme authority in the country

NOBILITY Landowners delivered a portion of their income to the king or czar

SERFS Working class, did not own the land they farmed

Under feudalism, monarchs gave land to nobles and lords in exchange for military protection. Serfs farmed the land of the nobles in exchange for the use of the land and protection.

▶ **CRITICAL THINKING**
Explaining How did constant warfare lead to the development of feudalism?

The most powerful of these princes, Ivan IV, defeated the Mongols and declared himself the **czar** of Russia. *Czar* is Russian for Caesar, or powerful ruler. The Russian nobility, dissatisfied with the czars who ruled after Ivan, looked for a young noble to lead the country. In 1613 they elected 16-year-old Michael Romanov as czar. The Romanovs ruled for the next 300 years.

Powerful Czars

Later, a czar now known as Peter the Great attempted to turn Russia into a major power. After Peter's death in 1725, Russia endured a string of weak czars. During the late 1700s, Empress Catherine the Great came to power. Catherine encouraged the development of Russian education, journalism, architecture, and theater. During her reign, Russia expanded its empire and took possession of the entire northern coast of the Black Sea.

Plight of the Serfs

R The czars and nobles enjoyed rich, comfortable lives. At the bottom of society, however, were the great masses of people. Most were **serfs**, or farm laborers who could be bought and sold along with the land. These people lived hard lives. In 1861 Czar Alexander II abolished serfdom. The new law, however, did little to help the serfs.

netw⊕rks   *Online Teaching Options*

INFOGRAPHIC

Feudalism in Europe and Russia

Interpreting Visual Information Display the interactive infographic. Use the labor pyramid to explain feudalism in Europe and Russia and to discuss this older way of farming and working the land. Have students write a paragraph telling one benefit and one disadvantage of this social system. **BL** Visual/Spatial, Verbal/Linguistic

See page 393D for other online activities.

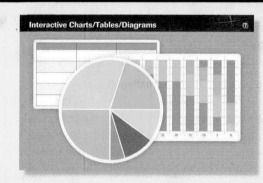

Interactive Charts/Tables/Diagrams

They had no education and few ways to earn a living. Industrialization drew some serfs to cities, where they worked long hours for low wages.

☑ READING PROGRESS CHECK

Describing How did Catherine the Great expand the Russian Empire?

Conflict and Communism

GUIDING QUESTION *How did the Russian Communist Party plan to transform Russia into an industrial giant?*

In the early 1900s, discontent with the rule of the czars spilled into the streets. Strikes and demonstrations in 1905 nearly ended the reign of Czar Nicholas II. One event, called Bloody Sunday, began with workers marching toward the czar's palace in St. Petersburg to demand better working conditions. The march ended when soldiers fired into the marchers, killing nearly 1,000 people. Another much larger conflict was brewing—one that would involve millions of people, military and civilian.

Wars and Revolution

The threat of war in Europe had been brewing for many years. The major powers had already formed alliances. Austria-Hungary, Germany, and the Ottoman Empire made up the Central Powers. Great Britain, France, and Russia were called the Allies. An assassination triggered World War I. A Bosnian terrorist named Gavrilo Princip assassinated Archduke Francis Ferdinand of Austria-Hungary on June 28, 1914, in Bosnia. By August, nearly all of Europe was at war.

At first, the Russian people supported the war effort, but as military failures, high casualties, and food shortages began mounting, public opinion turned against the war and against the czar. Russia encouraged Armenians in Turkish-controlled lands to fight alongside them. The Turks responded by deporting 1.75 million Armenians to Syria and Mesopotamia. During this mass deportation, about 600,000 Armenians starved or were murdered by Turkish soldiers and police. The mass murder of vast numbers of an ethnic or cultural group is called **genocide**.

In 1917 food shortages in Russia triggered riots in the capital. Soldiers began deserting, joining civilians in their protests against the war. Even though the Allies won the war, Russia emerged as a weakened nation. **C₂**

The killing of Archduke Ferdinand, heir to Austria-Hungary's throne, lit the fuse of World War I.

▶ **CRITICAL THINKING**
Determining Central Ideas Why did this killing lead to a war involving many nations?

DEA/A. DAGLI ORTI/De Agostini Picture Library/Getty Images

C₁ Critical Thinking Skills

Problem-Solving Before World War I broke out, Russia controlled the eastern part of Armenia, and Turkey controlled the western part of the country. During the war, the Russians and the Turks fought brutal and violent battles against each other for control of Armenia. **Ask:** Why would Turkey deport Armenians to Syria and Mesopotamia during World War I? *(Students' answers will vary but should demonstrate an understanding of Turkey's strategy of removing the threat of a group of people fighting against Turkey and possibly being successful.)* Logical/Mathematical

C₂ Critical Thinking Skills

Making Inferences Have students read the section "Wars and Revolution" with a partner. Then **ask:** Why might food shortages cause civilians to protest against the war and soldiers to desert the army? *(Students' answers may vary but should include the understanding of the importance of food to people's well-being and how the lack of food can induce negative feelings toward a ruler or government.)* Logical/Mathematical, Verbal/Linguistic

Content Background Knowledge

In March 1917, Russian workers in the largest factory in St. Petersburg demanded more money so they could buy food. They were denied an increase in wages so they went on strike and were subsequently locked out of work. The workers persuaded others to join them on strike and demonstrate against Czar Nicholas and his government. Riots ensued. The Russian Parliament wanted the Czar to release emergency food supplies, but instead, the Czar ordered the riots squashed. People were killed and the rioters became more angry. As some of the soldiers joined the rioters, the Czar tried to shut down the Parliament. Instead, the Parliament formed a temporary government to replace the Czar and eventually forced the Czar to give up his throne. This was the first time since 1480 that Russia was not ruled by a czar.

MAP

Alliances in Europe During WWI

Determining Cause and Effect Display the layer of the Chapter Opener map about the alliances in Europe during WWI. Discuss the idea of "domino effect"—that an event that affects one country then directly affects all the other countries within an alliance system. Visual/Spatial, Verbal/Linguistic

See page 393D for other online activities.

ANSWERS, p. 405

☑ READING PROGRESS CHECK Russia took control of the northern coast of the Black Sea.

CRITICAL THINKING A system of alliances bound the major powers of Europe to fight on either one side or the other.

R Reading Skills

Determining Word Meanings Remind students that knowing the meaning of Greek and Latin roots can help them understand the meanings of unfamiliar words. Point out that *commun*, meaning "common," is the Latin root of the word *communism*. **Ask:** How can knowing the meaning of *commun* help you understand the meaning of *communism*? *(Possible answer: Communism is an economic system built on the idea of <u>common</u> property belonging to the government.)*

Continue this teaching in the second paragraph for the word *collectivization*, from the Latin root *collect*, meaning "gathered together." Stalin forced all farmland to be gathered together and controlled by the government. **ELL** Logical/Mathematical

W Writing Skills

Argument Explain to students that Karl Marx based Communism on the idea of common ownership of property and the belief that all people were equal and deserved equal rights and opportunities. His economic system was a classless society that did not allow private ownership of property and one in which a group of people held the power to make all the decisions. This ruling group could decide on the activities of the public and could even interfere in people's public lives. The group also controlled all production and the distribution of goods and resources.

Ask: What is *democracy*? *(Democracy is a political system based on rule of the people and by the people with elected representatives carrying out the wishes of society. Free enterprise and private ownership of property and businesses are allowed in a democracy—both of which can lead to rich and poor classes. People are considered equal under the law and have certain freedoms and liberties protected by a constitution.)*

Have students write a persuasive essay to answer the question: **Would life under communist rule be better than life under democratic rule?** *(Students' arguments should make a claim and present at least three supporting ideas or facts. Their arguments should show evidence of sound reasoning.)* Verbal/Linguistic, Logical/Mathematical

Czar Nicholas was forced to step down. A new government was installed, but it could not maintain power. By the end of 1917, a group of revolutionaries known as the Bolsheviks had seized control of the government.

Rise of Communism

The Bolsheviks had strong support all over Russia. Inspired by the writings of Karl Marx, they remade Russia into a communist state. **Communism** is an economic system built on the idea that all property should belong to the community or the state, not to private individuals. The Bolsheviks, who had become the Russian Communist Party, took control of all land and industry. Their leader, Vladimir Lenin, became the first premier of the new Union of Soviet Socialist Republics (also known as the Soviet Union).

When Lenin died in 1924, the secretary of the Central Committee of the Communist Party, Joseph Stalin, became leader of the Soviet Union. Stalin used terror and brute force to fashion the Soviet Union into a communist dictatorship. He forced the **collectivization** of all agriculture, so that all farmland was owned and controlled by the government. Peasants and landowners protested, especially in Ukraine. The clash between agricultural workers and the government resulted in a famine that killed millions.

May Day was an official holiday in the Soviet Union and Soviet satellite countries. Held on May 1, celebrations, like this one in Moscow, typically included military parades.

networks *Online Teaching Options*

Organizing Information: Communism

Discussing Display the interactive graphic organizer and discuss its content with students. Use the interactive graphic organizer as you proceed through the next few pages of the lesson to review the information about Communism, the leaders involved in its development, and the concepts behind collectivization. Encourage students to copy down the graphic organizer for later use. **BL** Visual/Spatial, Verbal/Linguistic

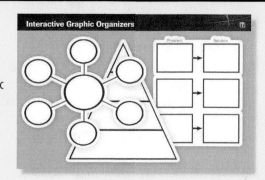

Interactive Graphic Organizers

See page 393D for other online activities.

By the early 1930s, the Soviet Union was on its way to becoming one of the world's industrial giants. Stalin wanted something more, however. His vision was to spread a Soviet-style communist government throughout the world.

The USSR and Its Satellites

In 1941 Nazi Germany invaded the Soviet Union, drawing the country into World War II. During the conflict, the Soviets joined with Great Britain and the United States to defeat the Germans. At the end of World War II, the fate of Europe was left to the victors—the United States, Great Britain, and the USSR. The Soviet army already occupied Czechoslovakia, Poland, Romania, Hungary, and Bulgaria. Stalin agreed to allow elections in those countries but soon installed communist governments. Germany was split in two. The United States, Great Britain, and their allies set up West Germany as a democracy under their guidance, and East Germany became a communist state. Countries under Soviet rule came to be known as satellite countries, meaning they were under the economic and political domination of a more powerful country.

☑ READING PROGRESS CHECK

Analyzing How did the USSR come to control most of Eastern Europe?

The Regions in the Modern Era

GUIDING QUESTION *How is a "cold war" different from other kinds of war?*

After World War II, the Soviet Union shared superpower status with the United States. Both superpowers possessed weapons of unimaginable destructive force. Would they dare to use those weapons against each other?

The Cold War

The Cold War was the rivalry and conflict between the USSR and the United States and their allies. During the next four decades, the Soviet Union and the United States engaged in a struggle for world influence and power.

Although both superpowers built destructive weapons, they also used other **strategies**, such as the threat of force and providing military and financial aid to their allies. At times, however, an outcome of nuclear warfare seemed **inevitable**.

The United States and its allies created the North Atlantic Treaty Organization (NATO) in 1949. Any attack on a member country would be considered an attack on all of them, and NATO countries agreed to respond as a group. The original NATO countries included many of the non-Eastern European nations. When NATO admitted West Germany in 1955, the USSR responded by creating the Warsaw Pact. Member countries were Albania, Bulgaria, Czechoslovakia, East Germany, Hungary, Poland, Romania, and the USSR.

Academic Vocabulary

strategy a plan to solve a problem

inevitable sure to happen

Chapter 13 **407**

MAP

Russian Historical Changes—Modern History

Discussing Display the animated map of the expansion of Russia. Discuss with students the expansion of Communism through Russia (1917–1945) and the expansion to Eastern Europe (1945–1973). Continue to use the expansion map to discuss the collapse of Communism up to the fall of the Berlin Wall and the opening of the Eastern Bloc. Visual/Spatial, Verbal/Linguistic

See page 393D for other online activities.

Ⓒ₁ Critical Thinking Skills

Drawing Conclusions Read the section "The USSR and Its Satellites" to students. **Ask:** What might you conclude after knowing that the satellite countries were under the economic and political domination of Stalin and the Soviets? *(Students' answers will vary but should include relevant details to support conclusions such as Stalin's vision was to spread a Soviet-style communist government throughout the world.)* Verbal/Linguistic, Logical/Mathematical

Ⓡ Reading Skills

Paraphrasing Remind students that paraphrasing is a good way to check that they understand what they are reading. Have students use their own words to describe the Cold War. *(Possible answer: Both the United States and the Soviet Union wanted to be the dominant or most superior country in the world, but they did not want to use destructive weapons to achieve that status.)* ᴬᴸ Verbal/Linguistic

Ⓒ₂ Critical Thinking Skills

Making Inferences Have students analyze the word *inevitable* from the text, in the context of nuclear warfare. Have students refer to dictionaries or the glossary in the text to figure out the definition of *inevitable*. **Ask:** What might be an outcome of nuclear warfare? *(Students' answers will vary but should demonstrate an understanding of the total devastation and destruction caused by nuclear bombs and the resultant radiation fallout.)* Logical/Mathematical

Ⓣ Technology Skills

Researching on the Internet The North Atlantic Treaty Organization was established on April 4, 1949, when the treaty was officially signed. Divide students into small groups and assign each group a topic about NATO to research on the Internet, such as the three purposes the Alliance was to serve, the names of the original member countries and those countries who joined later, the intention of the strategic doctrine of "Massive Retaliation," and the origin of the NATO emblem and motto. Have groups report their findings orally to the class. Suggest that they use visuals when appropriate. Interpersonal, Visual/Spatial

---

ANSWER, p. 407

☑ READING PROGRESS CHECK Ukraine and Belarus were part of the original USSR. Moldova, Estonia, Lithuania, and Latvia were added in 1940. At the end of World War II, Great Britain, the United States, and the Soviet Union decided the fates of European countries. It was agreed to let the Soviets stay in the countries where they already had troops: Czechoslovakia, Poland, Romania, Hungary, and Bulgaria.

Eastern Bloc

(1949) Date joined Soviet Union/Eastern Bloc
— Border of the Soviet Union
— Border of the Eastern Bloc states

RUSSIA

ESTONIA *(1940)*
LATVIA *(1940)*
LITHUANIA *(1940)*
EAST GERMANY *(1949)*
POLAND *(1947)*
BELARUS *(1922)*
CZECHOSLOVAKIA *(1948)*
UKRAINE *(1922)*
HUNGARY *(1947)*
MOLDOVA *(1940)*
ROMANIA *(1947)*
YUGOSLAVIA *(1945)*
BULGARIA *(1946)*
ALBANIA *(1945)*

Barents Sea
Baltic Sea
Black Sea
Caspian Sea

0   600 miles
0   600 kilometers
Lambert Azimuthal Equal-Area projection

V Visual Skills

Integrating Visual Information Display a map of the world or have students use the Reference Atlas map of the United States in the front of their student editions. Have a volunteer locate Cuba on the map. Have students use the map key to determine the approximate number of miles between Cuba and the United States. **Ask:**

- How might Soviet missiles in Cuba be a threat to the United States? *(Students' answers will vary but should demonstrate an understanding of how close Cuba is to the border of the United States and that a nuclear missile could easily reach the United States.)*

- What might have happened if the Soviet premier had not agreed to stop shipping missiles to Cuba? *(Possible answer: World War III could have started because members of NATO, who were aligned with the United States, and members of the Warsaw Pact, who were aligned with the Soviet Union, would all have considered any attack as personal.)* Logical/Mathematical, Verbal/Linguistic

C1 Critical Thinking Skills

Analyzing Have students independently read the section "Unrest in the Soviet Satellites." Then, **ask:** Why were the sweeping reforms in Czechoslovakia put down by the Soviets? *(Students' answers may vary but should demonstrate an understanding of the absolute control the Soviets held over the Czech people and their government and how the Soviets did not tolerate any reforms that threatened the idea of Communism.)* Verbal/Linguistic, Logical/Mathematical

C2 Critical Thinking Skills

Comparing and Contrasting Then have students read the section "Changes Under Gorbachev" aloud. **Ask:** How was the Polish Solidarity movement similar to and different from the reforms in Czechoslovakia? *(Possible answer: Both movements wanted reforms that would benefit the citizens of the countries. The reforms in Czechoslovakia were stopped by an invasion of Soviet troops. The Solidarity movement was stopped by the Polish government.)* Verbal/Linguistic, Logical/Mathematical

MAP SKILLS

1 HUMAN GEOGRAPHY
What countries became tied to the Soviet Union during the early part of World War II?

2 PHYSICAL GEOGRAPHY
What about the location of Eastern Europe made this region important to the Soviet Union?

The two superpowers came close to war during the Cuban Missile Crisis. In October 1962, after learning that the Soviets were sending missiles to Cuba, the U.S. set up a naval blockade around Cuba to prevent the shipment of missiles. Both sides seemed prepared to go to war. As tensions grew, Soviet premier Nikita Khrushchev agreed to stop shipping the missiles to Cuba. Another crisis was brewing, however. The Soviet satellite countries in Eastern Europe began to rebel against Soviet control.

Unrest in the Soviet Satellites

In 1968 Czechoslovakia's leader Alexander Dubček announced sweeping reforms. He wanted to give the press more freedom and to guarantee citizens' civil rights. The Czech people welcomed the reforms, but the Soviets removed Dubček from power.

In 1980 dozens of Polish trade unions joined together to form Solidarity. Solidarity used strikes to put pressure on the government. The Polish government responded by declaring Solidarity illegal and putting its leaders in jail. Solidarity became an underground, or secret, organization.

Changes Under Gorbachev

Then in the 1980s, a new Soviet leader, Mikhail Gorbachev, came to power and implemented new policies. *Glasnost*, which means "openness," was an attempt to allow the people in the USSR and its

408 *Chapter 13*

netw⊚rks   *Online Teaching Options*

CHART

Sequencing: Cold War Events

Sequencing Display the sequencing flow chart of Cold War events on the Interactive Whiteboard. Discuss with students the events that led to the collapse of the Cold War. Have students write a short paragraph explaining which event they think was most influential in ending the Cold War. **AL** Visual/Spatial, Verbal/Linguistic

See page 393D for other online activities.

Interactive Charts/Tables/Diagrams

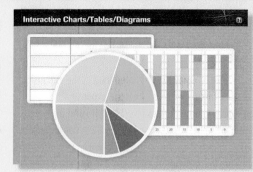

ANSWERS, p. 408

MAP SKILLS
1. Estonia, Latvia, Lithuania, and Moldova
2. Eastern Europe was located between the Soviet Union and non-Communist Western Europe. The Soviet Union could use Eastern Europe either as a shield to ward off any threat from Western Europe or as a base to expand westward.

R satellite countries to have more social and political freedoms. *Perestroika,* which means "restructuring," was an attempt to reform the Soviet economy.

Change came quickly in Eastern Europe. Solidarity was legalized in Poland in 1989, then the Communists were voted out of power. By 1990, Hungary, Czechoslovakia, Bulgaria, and Romania had new governments. In Germany, the Berlin Wall that separated West and **T** East Berlin was torn down. By the next year, East and West Germany were reunited. Soviet control of Eastern Europe was broken.

In 1991 a group of Soviet officials, who thought Gorbachev's policies meant the downfall of the Soviet Union, staged a coup and arrested Gorbachev. Gorbachev's allies resisted, the people protested, and the military turned against the coup leaders. Gorbachev was released, and the coup leaders were arrested. Communist control of the USSR was at an end. By the end of 1991, the Soviet Union was dissolved, and all the republics had become independent countries.

Divisions and Conflict

When Eastern Europe shook free of Soviet domination in 1989, ethnic tensions flared in the Balkan Peninsula. The former Yugoslav republics used to be one large country called Yugoslavia. In the early 1990s, disputes among ethnic groups tore the country apart. Croatia, Slovenia, Macedonia, and Bosnia and Herzegovina broke free of Yugoslavia and became separate countries. Serbia and Montenegro each became its own country in 2006.

Kosovo, which was considered part of Serbia, has a mostly Albanian Muslim population. When Yugoslavia broke apart, many people in Kosovo decided they wanted to break free of Serbian control. When the Kosovo Liberation Army began an armed rebellion in 1998, Serbs responded with military force. NATO intervened to end the bloodshed, and the United Nations began governing Kosovo. Finally, in 2008 Kosovo declared itself independent, though Serbia, Russia, and other countries refused to recognize this.

☑ READING PROGRESS CHECK

Determining Central Ideas How did glasnost and perestroika affect the USSR?

©Peter Turnley/Corbis

Soviet leader Mikhail Gorbachev worked to improve the Soviet Union's relations with the United States and other Western countries.
▶ **CRITICAL THINKING**
Citing Text Evidence How did Gorbachev's policy of glasnost affect Eastern Europe?

FOLDABLES
Study Organizer

Include this lesson's information in your Foldable®.

LESSON 2 REVIEW

Reviewing Vocabulary
1. Why did landowners protest *collectivization* of agriculture?

Answering the Guiding Questions
2. *Describing* How did Peter I and Catherine II change Russia?

3. *Determining Central Ideas* What were Stalin's main goals for the Soviet Union?

4. *Analyzing* How is a "cold war" different from other kinds of war?

5. *Argument Writing* Write a speech encouraging Czar Alexander II to abolish serfdom and to grant rights and liberties to all peasants.

Chapter 13 **409**

LESSON 2 REVIEW ANSWERS

Reviewing Vocabulary

1. *Collectivization* took ownership and control of farmland away from the peasants and landowners and gave it to the government.

Answering the Guiding Questions

2. **Describing** Peter: improved education, modernized the army, created a navy, and turned Russia into a major European power. Catherine: encouraged the development of Russian education, journalism, architecture, and theater. During her reign, Russia defeated the Ottoman Turks and took possession of the northern coast of the Black Sea.

3. **Determining Central Ideas** Stalin wanted to make the Soviet Union an industrial power and spread communist governments throughout the world.

4. **Analyzing** A cold war never erupts into open war. The threat of destruction is so great that neither side wants to fight, but they remain hostile to each other anyway and continue to build powerful weapons.

5. **Argument Writing** Speeches will vary, but students should cite information from the text about serfdom and peasants.

ENGAGE

Bellringer Before students begin the lesson, ask them to think about how they face change. It may be a change in schools or homes, in schedules, or in family rules. **Ask:** How do changes influence your life? Are you able to accept changes and move forward, or do changes upset you and hold you back from being happy or reaching your goals? Explain. *(Students' answers will vary but should include specific details about changes they have personally faced and how they dealt with them.)* Then have students make a connection to the Essential Question: *How does geography influence the way people live?*

TEACH & ASSESS

C1 Critical Thinking Skills

Giving Examples Have students give examples of military hardware and heavy industrial machinery that might have been produced by the communist government before the collapse of the USSR. *(Possible answers: weapons, airplanes, tanks, ships, electronics, turbines, engines, generators, tractors)* **Ask:** What kinds of consumer products would appeal to the buying public? *(Possible answers: personal computers, televisions, clothing, home accessories)* Verbal/Linguistic, Logical/Mathematical

C2 Critical Thinking Skills

Making Generalizations Have students read the section "Economic Changes" with a partner. Encourage students to write down questions that were not answered in the reading and address those questions as needed. **Ask:** What generalization could you make about how the transfer of industry to private ownership was handled? Was it a great deal for the wealthy individuals who had connections in government and did these changes improve the living conditions for most Russians? *(Possible answer: The wealthy benefited from the collapse of the USSR and the change from communism to a free market system, but most Russians still faced economic hardships.)* Logical/Mathematical, Verbal/Linguistic

---

ANSWER, p. 410

Taking Notes Any three of these four: Relations among countries are challenging. Russia still has boundary disputes with former republics. Russia still has problems with rebel forces in Chechnya. The 2008 financial crisis hurt the economies of these countries.

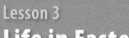

networks

There's More Online!

☑ **CHART/GRAPH** Russia's Population

☑ **MAP** Slavic Settlements

☑ **VIDEO**

Reading **HELP**DESK

Academic Vocabulary
- decline
- unique
- factor

Content Vocabulary
- inflation
- oligarch
- devolution

TAKING NOTES: *Key Ideas and Details*

Identify Use a graphic organizer like this one to identify three challenges faced by Russia and the countries of Eastern Europe.

Challenges for Russia and Eastern Europe Today

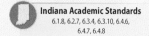

Indiana Academic Standards
6.1.8, 6.2.7, 6.3.4, 6.3.10, 6.4.6, 6.4.7, 6.4.8

410

Lesson 3

Life in Eastern Europe and Western Russia

ESSENTIAL QUESTION • *How does geography influence the way people live?*

IT MATTERS BECAUSE

It has been more than 20 years since the collapse of the USSR. The countries that the USSR once ruled in Eastern Europe have all moved forward, some more easily than others.

People and Places

GUIDING QUESTION *What were some of the challenges Russia faced after the fall of the Soviet Union?*

Life has changed in Eastern Europe and Western Russia. Some people have benefited from the changes; others have not. The attempt to change from a communist state to a free market economy has not been easy or particularly successful.

Economic Changes

Russia faced enormous challenges following the collapse of the USSR. The economy that was centrally controlled by the communist government had been in **decline** for years. Most of its industry had centered on military hardware and heavy industrial machinery. The country was not prepared to transform into a producer of consumer products that are the real engine of free market economies.

Inflation, or the rise in prices for goods and services, increased, while production slowed. The transfer of industry to private ownership was a great deal for wealthy individuals who had connections in government. However, these changes did not improve the living conditions for most Russians. People refer to the new owners of industrial Russia as **oligarchs**. An oligarch is one of a small group of people who control the government and use it to further their own goals.

(l to r) ©Caro/Alamy; Dallas and John Heato/age fotostock; Bruce Yuanyue Bi/Lonely Planet Images/Getty Images; ©Shepard Sherbell/Corbis SABA

---

networks **Online Teaching Options**

VIDEO

Russia Concerned Over Shrinking Population

Narrative Use this video about Russia's shrinking population and the government's concern over this trend to introduce the lesson. Have students write a paragraph about one aspect of the video that was interesting or surprising to them. **AL** Visual/Spatial, Verbal/Linguistic

See page 393E for other online activities.

BBC Motion Gallery Education

Social and Political Changes

When the Soviet Union existed, the central government kept tight control over its many ethnic groups. Some groups wanted to form their own countries. Among them are the Chechens, who live in Chechnya near the Caspian Sea and Caucasus Mountains in southern Russia. The region has many oil reserves, and its oil pipelines transport fuel to major Russian cities. Russian troops fought Chechen rebels to keep Chechnya a part of Russia. When Russia finally pulled out in 1996, the Chechen rebellion was still not over. President Boris Yeltsin was widely blamed for being unable to solve these problems.

At the end of 1999, Yeltsin resigned and was replaced by Vladimir Putin, who was elected president in 2000. Putin, a former officer in the KGB, the country's secret police, was viewed as someone who wanted to keep a tight rein on government power. Putin launched reforms to reduce the power of the oligarchs and encouraged economic development. Although Putin helped stabilize the Russian economy, he dealt harshly with those who opposed him.

He was reelected for a second term in 2004. In 2008 Dmitry Medvedev was elected president, and he appointed Putin to be prime minister. In 2012 Putin ran for the presidency a third time and won. Soon after, new restrictive laws were passed strengthening penalties against demonstrators, blocking some Internet sites, and restricting free speech.

Where People Live

The two largest cities in Western Russia are Moscow and St. Petersburg. In addition to being the political capital of Russia, Moscow is the cultural, educational, and scientific capital. It has also been the spiritual home of the Russian Orthodox Church for more than 600 years. St. Petersburg was founded by Peter the Great in 1703.

The biggest population centers in Eastern Europe are the capital cities, such as Kiev, Ukraine; Minsk, Belarus; Budapest, Hungary; Warsaw, Poland; and Prague in the Czech Republic. Each of these cities is a center of national culture.

At one time, most Eastern Europeans lived in rural areas. Now more people live in urban areas. The urban population of Albania, Macedonia, and Croatia, for example, is above 50 percent. In some countries, urbanization is even higher. In Poland and Montenegro, the urban population is about 60 percent. In Hungary, the Czech Republic, and Belarus, urbanization is 70 percent or more.

Academic Vocabulary

decline a gradual deterioration into a weakened condition

A family sits in front of its farmhouse in Senj, a seaside town in Croatia. Although parts of Eastern Europe remain rural, most people now live in urban areas.

©Caro/Alamy

Chapter 13 **411**

C Critical Thinking Skills

Making Generalizations Discuss with students the content of the section "Social and Political Changes," focusing on the fighting in Chechnya. **Ask:**

- Why did Russia want Chechnya to remain a part of Russia? *(Possible answer: Chechnya has valuable oil reserves and Russia wanted to control them.)*
- Is this something worth fighting over? *(Students' opinions will vary but should demonstrate an awareness of how valuable oil reserves are.)*

Then discuss the election of Vladimir Putin and his history as a political leader. Be sure to discuss his reelection in 2012 and the new laws restricting free speech. Have students compare these restrictions to the guaranteed protections of free speech in the United States. Then **ask:** How might you describe the presidency of Vladimir Putin? *(Possible answers: Putin governs like a dictator by limiting personal freedoms and restricting free speech.)* **Logical/Mathematical, Verbal/Linguistic**

V Visual Skills

Reading a Map As students read about the population centers in Western Russia and Eastern Europe, have them locate these cities on a map: Moscow, St. Petersburg, Kiev, Minsk, Budapest, Warsaw, and Prague. Have volunteers find pictures of these cities on the Internet and present a slide show to the class. Have students compare and contrast the architecture and other features seen in the pictures. **Visual/Spatial**

Content Background Knowledge

The Committee for State Security, or KGB, was the world's largest secret police organization, charged with state security, internal and external intelligence, counterintelligence, and espionage in the old Soviet Union. Created in 1954 and dismantled in 1991, the agency was feared by both Russian citizens and people throughout the world for its ruthless and harsh tactics.

Agents visited schools to indoctrinate students politically and deliver propaganda about the "bad" Western countries, especially the United States. The KGB censored literature and other media. Writers and artists were routinely harassed or expelled from their jobs for expressing unfavorable views of the Soviets.

GAME

Drag-and-Drop: Cities of Eastern Europe and Western Russia

Identifying Display the drag-and-drop game on the Interactive Whiteboard. Have students take turns matching the cities in Eastern Europe and Western Russia with their countries. Discuss and review wrong answers by looking at a map or researching on the Internet. **AL**
ELL Visual/Spatial, Kinesthetic

See page 393E for other online activities.

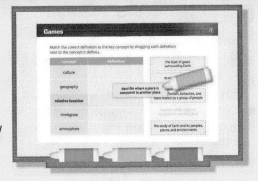

Life in Eastern Europe and Western Russia

W Writing Skills

Argument Have students gather in small groups to brainstorm reasons why a government might have travel restrictions for its citizens. **Ask:** What does it mean when a country places travel restrictions on its citizens? *(Students' answers will vary but should demonstrate an understanding that the restrictions would prevent free movement to places of people's choosing.)* Have each student write a persuasive essay explaining their thoughts to answer the question: ***Are government travel restrictions ever justified?*** Interpersonal, Logical/Mathematical, Verbal/Linguistic

C Critical Thinking Skills

Identifying Problems Review with students the content of the section "Ethnic and Language Groups." Make comparisons with students between the topic discussed in the text and the visual representation of the material in the map on the corresponding page. **Ask:** What problems might have occurred when Slavic people from different parts of Eastern Europe tried to communicate or live near each other? *(Students' answers may vary but should demonstrate an understanding of the different languages and cultural traditions practiced by different groups of Slavic people.)* Logical/ Mathematical, Verbal/Linguistic

Content Background Knowledge

Along with economic and political domination, the Soviet Union exerted control over the people at home and in its satellite countries by placing strict travel restrictions on people's movements. The Soviet government was afraid that any of its citizens traveling to western countries would see a higher standard of living and learn of the freedoms that foreigners enjoyed. This would then prompt criticism of the Soviet government and unfavorable comparisons to be made between communism and capitalism. Foreign travelers might return home with new, radical ideas or maybe not even return at all. Additionally, the Soviet government wanted its citizens to stay home and to spend their money within their countries' borders to boost the economy. The Soviet government made obtaining passports almost impossible with high fees and lengthy delays. Sometimes passport applications were simply ignored.

ANSWERS, p. 412

☑ READING PROGRESS CHECK to escape political oppression and to seek better economic opportunities
GRAPH SKILLS
CRITICAL THINKING
1. 1950 through 1990
2. the high loss of life during World War II

W During the industrial age, people began moving from Eastern Europe to Western Europe and North America; that trend continues. Eastern Europeans have moved to escape political oppression and to seek better economic opportunities. Countries such as Romania have lost population since the lifting of Soviet travel restrictions.

☑ **READING PROGRESS CHECK**

Determining Central Ideas Why have so many Eastern Europeans emigrated to other parts of Europe or to the United States?

People and Cultures

GUIDING QUESTION *How did geographical barriers affect the development of Slavic culture in Eastern Europe?*

The history of Western Russia and Eastern Europe has created a rich mix of cultures and people. People take great pride in their folk and religious traditions, most of which were frowned upon by Soviet authorities.

Ethnic and Language Groups

At one time, a single Slavic language, understood by most Slavic people, was spoken. As Slavic people settled in different parts of Eastern Europe, geographical barriers separated and isolated them. These groups developed distinct languages and cultures.

C Slavs generally belong to one of three categories. East Slavs are represented by the Slavic ethnic groups in Russia, Ukraine, and Belarus. West Slavs include ethnic Slavs in Poland, the Czech Republic, Slovakia, and parts of eastern Germany. The most diverse group are the South Slavs, who live in Bulgaria and other countries

GRAPH SKILLS >

POPULATION OF RUSSIA
The graph shows the changes in the population of Russia from 1940 to 2010.

▶ **CRITICAL THINKING**
1. **Describing** In what decades did the population of Russia increase?
2. **Analyzing** What is a possible explanation for Russia's sharp drop in population during the 1940s?

412 Chapter 13

---

netw⊕rks *Online Teaching Options*

CHART

Russia's Population

Integrating Visual Information Display the interactive chart about Russia's population. Have volunteers identify the information shown on the chart. Have students discuss the changes in Russia's populations after WWII. Ask students to write a paragraph about what they think caused the changes in population. Visual/Spatial, Logical/Mathematical

See page 393E for other online activities.

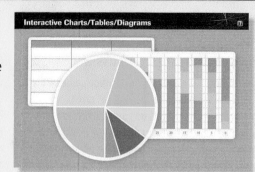
Interactive Charts/Tables/Diagrams

Slavic Settlement

East Slavs
West Slavs
South Slavs

300 miles
300 kilometers
Lambert Azimuthal
Equal-Area projection

of the Balkans. Each of these groups speaks its own language. Russia is made up of more than 120 ethnic groups, although almost 80 percent of the population is ethnic Russian.

The people of Albania are a distinct ethnic group that has been living in that region for about 4,000 years. Albanian is the last surviving language of an entire Indo-European language group. It is the ancestor of the language spoken by present-day Albanians, and it has survived thousands of years of conquest and cultural change.

Religion

For most of the 1900s, religious practice was strongly discouraged throughout Eastern Europe and Western Russia. In some countries in Eastern Europe, a sizable percentage of the population does not practice any religion. Less than half the population of the Czech Republic belongs to any church. In the Baltic region, nearly two-thirds of Latvians and one-third of Estonians are not affiliated with any church. In most of Eastern Europe, however, Soviet repression strengthened religious faith. The dominant religion in most of these countries is the Eastern Orthodox Church. Many different churches exist within the Orthodox faith.

Most of these churches are affiliated with a specific ethnic group or country. The majority of people in Belarus, Bulgaria, Moldova, Montenegro, Romania, Serbia, and Ukraine worship at an Eastern Orthodox Church. The majority of people in Croatia, Hungary, Lithuania, Poland, Slovakia, and Slovenia are Roman Catholics. Most of these countries also support minority populations of

Chapter 13 **413**

MAP SKILLS

1 HUMAN GEOGRAPHY
What three large divisions make up the Slavic people of Eastern Europe and Western Russia?

2 PLACES AND REGIONS
What countries in the region do not have majority Slavic populations?

MAP

Slavic Settlement in Eastern Europe and Western Russia

Discussing Display the map showing the three Slavic groups. Have volunteers identify the location of each group. Have students discuss which Slavic group is located in which area. Discuss with students what the groups may have in common. Encourage students to find more information using the Internet. **AL** **ELL**
Visual/Spatial, Verbal/Linguistic

See page 393E for other online activities.

V Visual Skills

Reading a Map Have students study the map and use the title and the map key to explain what the map shows before they answer the Map Skills questions. Have students explain how the map shows what they have been reading about concerning the ethnic and language groups of the Slavs. Then discuss the areas of the map that are not in color and discuss why these areas may not have been influenced or settled by the Slavs. **Ask:** Why might the people of Albania have strong cultural ties to the past? *(Students' answers will vary but should include the understanding of the uniqueness of having an ethnic group and a language that has survived for 4,000 years in the same area.)* Visual/Spatial, Logical/Mathematical

C Critical Thinking Skills

Making Inferences Discuss with students times they have been told not to do something that has made them want to do the thing even more. Build on these previous experiences of students to discuss why the Soviet's repression of religion might have had an opposite effect on people. **Ask:** What might you infer about why religious faith was strengthened under Soviet repression? *(Possible answer: I would infer that most people who had religious beliefs would not have wanted to be told by the government that they could no longer practice their religion. Therefore, it was strengthened.)* **AL** Logical/Mathematical, Verbal/Linguistic

Content Background Knowledge

Karl Marx once said, "Religion is the opium of the people." Both Vladamir Lenin and Joseph Stalin adopted Marx's opposition to religious beliefs. Communist governments followed an anti-religion policy and promoted the Godless League. Under Soviet rule, many churches were demolished or converted to other uses. The government openly ridiculed and belittled religious beliefs and practices. The education of new religious leaders and religious education of children was forbidden. This led to new generations being schooled using Marx's ideas, rationalism, and scientific inquiry. Today, religious organizations hold little influence in Russia.

ANSWERS, p. 413

MAP SKILLS
1. East Slavs, West Slavs, and South Slavs
2. Estonia, Latvia, Lithuania, Hungary, Romania, Moldova, and Albania

R Reading Skills

Naming After students are finished reading the section on the arts, discuss the contributions of the artists and the ones students are most likely familiar with, such as Tchaikovsky's Nutcracker Suite. Play this music for students, if possible, or selections from other composers. **Ask:**

- Who were some of the major contributors of cultural works in Russia during the 1800s and early 1900s? *(Dostoyevsky, Mussorgsky, Rimsky-Korsakov, Tolstoy, Tchaikovsky, Gogol, and Chekhov)*
- Why would the people of Eastern Europe still be proud of these artists today? *(Their works are considered classics and still highly regarded today. Also the works often portray their national character.)* Visual/Spatial, Auditory/Musical

T Technology Skills

Making Presentations Divide students into small groups. Tell students that, as a group, they will need to choose an artistic contribution made before 1991 by someone from Eastern Europe or Western Russia. The chosen contribution can come from a writer of novels, short stories, or plays; a classical or popular composer or musician; or a filmmaker. Using reliable resources on the Internet, have students research their artists. Then have them use presentation software to give a short biographical sketch of the artist and show samples of the artist's work to the class. **BL** Visual/Spatial, Verbal/Linguistic, Logical/Mathematical

Content Background Knowledge

Many students may be familiar with going to see *The Nutcracker* ballet, which is often an annual winter holiday tradition. The ballet is based on the novelette, *The Nutcracker and the Mouse King* by E.T.A. Hoffman. In 1891 Tchaikovsky was commissioned to compose the music for the ballet. Nearly 50 years later in 1940, Americans heard the music for the first time when the Ballet Russe gave a performance of *The Nutcracker* ballet in New York City.

Shoppers walk along the boulevard past a mall in Plovdiv, Bulgaria. Plovdiv is the country's second-largest city. Only the capital city of Sofia is larger.

Muslims, Roman Catholics, Eastern Orthodox, Protestants, and Jews. Nearly 70 percent of Albanians are Muslim, as are a sizable number of people in Bosnia and Herzegovina.

The Arts

R In the 1800s and early 1900s, Russians produced some of the most important cultural works in all of Europe. The novels of Tolstoy and Dostoyevsky; the music of Mussorgsky, Tchaikovsky, and Rimsky-Korsakov; and the plays and short stories of Chekhov and Gogol are still considered among the world's finest.

People in the countries of Eastern Europe are proud of the great art produced by their people. In many cases, those works are an important symbol of their national character. Although a small amount of literary work was written in the Czech language, Czech literature did not became internationally important until Czechoslovakia became an independent country in 1918. Karel Čapek was a Czech writer who was famous for his plays and novels.

T His most well-known contribution to world literature is a word he coined—*robot*—in his 1921 play *R.U.R.* Eastern European composers, such as Béla Bartók and Zoltán Kodály, celebrated the traditional music of Hungary and Romania by using it in their compositions. Bulgaria also has a rich tradition in folk and choir music.

©Dallas and John Heato/age fotostock

net·works · *Online Teaching Options*

GRAPHIC ORGANIZER

Russia and the Arts

Discussing Display the interactive graphic organizer about the arts in Russia. Have volunteers identify the information presented. Discuss with students the importance of the artists, writers, and musicians to the region. Visual/Spatial, Verbal/Linguistic

See page 393E for other online activities.

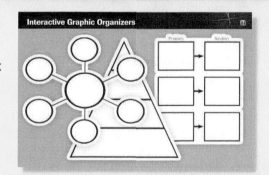

Interactive Graphic Organizers

Western popular culture has had a huge impact on the art of Eastern Europe and Western Russia. Russian and Polish filmmakers can follow their national traditions, but they also can see how well-liked and influential American films and television are. Rock and pop music from the United States and Western Europe are extremely popular. Young artists in this part of the world are creating international popular culture while trying to bring something uniquely Eastern European to it.

Daily Life

For much of the 1900s, the people of Eastern Europe and Western Russia lived under communist governments that attempted to control their private lives. The collapse of the USSR brought about **devolution** in Russian government and in governments throughout Eastern Europe. Devolution occurs when a strong central government surrenders its powers to more local authorities.

One of the results of this change is the return of national traditions and identity. Most of these countries have strong cultural and religious traditions. These traditions were never really lost, but the lack of strong Soviet control has made it possible for people to live and speak more freely about their beliefs and interests. Such freedoms emphasize **unique** aspects of these countries and their people.

The other result of the loss of Soviet control is the rising influence of international popular culture. Soviet authorities did not trust the music, films, and television programs coming from capitalist countries such as the United States, but they could not effectively outlaw them. Young Russians and Eastern Europeans are now having the same cultural experiences that young people are having in the rest of Europe and in the Americas. This shared culture emphasizes those things that all these people have in common with each other.

One issue in Russia is the generation gap that exists between people who grew up in communist USSR or are old enough to remember it, and those people who have lived most or all of their lives in the post-Soviet era. One big question is how to teach the history of the USSR to young people who never experienced life under the Soviet system.

W

Academic Vocabulary

unique unusual or distinctive

Teenagers stroll on the main street of Minsk, the capital and largest city of Belarus.
▶ **CRITICAL THINKING**
Analyzing How has the end of Communist rule affected young people in Eastern Europe and Western Russia?

C

Bruce Yuanyue Bi/Lonely Planet Images/Getty Images

Chapter 13 415

W Writing Skills

Informative/Explanatory Have students consider how they would feel and what they would do if they were forbidden to practice family traditions that they enjoy and that are important to them. **Ask:** How might you keep traditions alive when you are forbidden to practice them openly? *(Possible answer: pass them down orally from generation to generation and practice them in secret)*

Then have students write about a personal tradition that has been practiced in their family for years and what they would do if they were forbidden to practice this tradition. Students may want to talk to family members about how long some of these traditions have been practiced in their family. **Intrapersonal, Verbal/ Linguistic**

C Critical Thinking Skills

Making Inferences Explain that a generation gap is a difference in outlook and opinions between people born at different times. For example, grandparents, parents, and children are three different generations.

Have students think about how their lives are different from their parents' or grandparents' lives. They might cite technology use and say their grandparents used typewriters instead of computers in school; their parents used computers and cell phones that were not as sophisticated as those on today's market. **Ask:**

- How would the opinions and general attitude toward life of adults who grew up in communist USSR be different from Russian young people growing up in the post-Soviet era? *(Students' answers will vary but should demonstrate an understanding of the freedoms and western influences that today's young people have that Russia's adults did not have.)*

- How do music, films, and television influence what you do and what you think? How do you think American music, films, and television will influence young Russians and Eastern Europeans? *(Students' answers will vary but should include relevant details and specific examples of how music, films, and television influence people's actions and thoughts.)* **Interpersonal, Verbal/Linguistic Logical/Mathematical**

GRAPHIC ORGANIZER

Cause and Effect: Generation Gap in Post-Soviet Russia

Analyzing Guide students in analyzing the effects of the end of the Soviet system on modern Russia using the cause-and-effect interactive graphic organizer. Have students consider how the region's younger population is being influenced by Western culture and the effects this has on the relations between the generations there. Then have students write a paragraph telling three things they learned about the cultural changes in post-Soviet Russia. **Visual/Spatial, Verbal/Linguistic**

See page 393E for other online activities.

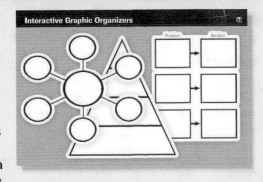

Interactive Graphic Organizers

ANSWERS, p. 415

CRITICAL THINKING The end of Communist rule has meant the rising influence of international popular culture. Young Russians and Eastern Europeans now have the same cultural experiences that young people have in the rest of Europe and in the Americas.

C Critical Thinking Skills

Giving Examples After students have read the section, "Earning a Living," have students compare and contrast the economic sectors of the three regions of Europe that they have read about in Chapters 11, 12, and 13. Have them look back to the other chapters as needed and make a chart of the different kinds of jobs or careers that are primarily done in each region. Then, **ask:** What kinds of jobs or careers are considered to be in the field of agriculture? *(Possible answers: agricultural education teacher, animal scientist, beef producer, crop consultant, ecologist, farmer, farm manager, geneticist, nutritionist, soil conservationist)* Logical/Mathematical, Verbal/Linguistic

T Technology Skills

Researching Begin this activity by asking students: What natural resources does Russia supply to other countries? *(oil, natural gas, iron ore and other metals, raw timber)* Have students research the amount of oil produced and exported by Russia, and write a paragraph summarizing their research. Verbal/Linguistic

V Visual Skills

Interpreting Photographs Challenge students to cover the caption before they read it and to interpret what the photograph shows. Discuss what the people are doing standing outside and what their expressions tell about them. Have students speculate why the shelves in the store are so empty and compare these shelves to the ones they see in grocery stores in their community. Then have students uncover the caption and compare their interpretation of the photograph to the information given in the caption. Visual/Spatial

Content Background Knowledge

In July 2012, Russia joined the World Trade Organization, a place where member governments try to solve trade problems between member countries. Membership in the organization allows Russia to export raw timber to Finland at a lower cost and to import Finnish paper products at lower prices. Finland benefits because it will gain greater access to the Russian market.

ANSWERS, p. 416

☑ READING PROGRESS CHECK Folk and religious traditions are no longer frowned upon. People have increased access to international popular culture, such as movies, television, and popular music.

CRITICAL THINKING Many Eastern European countries have joined the European Union (EU). The EU has sought to protect employment, improve workers' living and work conditions, and create a strong European trading bloc.

In the 1990s, historians took a critical look at the Russian Revolution, the leadership of Lenin and Stalin, and the excesses of the Soviet government. They took a more positive approach when looking back at the era of the Romanov czars.

☑ **READING PROGRESS CHECK**

Determining Central Ideas How has daily life changed in Russia since the fall of the USSR?

Academic Vocabulary

factor something that actively contributes to a result

During Communist rule and shortly after its end, shoppers in Eastern Europe had to wait in long lines outside of stores. Food and other products often were in short supply and had to be rationed, or divided equally.
▶ **CRITICAL THINKING**
Describing What benefit has come to Eastern European workers in recent years?

Issues in Eastern Europe and Western Russia

GUIDING QUESTION *What are the economic advantages and disadvantages of Eastern Europe's location between continents?*

Eastern Europe and Western Russia are still in the process of change. They are trying to modernize their industries and governments during difficult economic times.

Earning a Living

Western Russia and the countries of Eastern Europe cover a vast area. The landforms, the soil, the mineral resources, the climate, the economies, and the national traditions are different throughout the region. These **factors** combine to determine how people earn a living in these places. Nearly half the working population in Albania is employed in agriculture. Romania, Serbia, and Bosnia and Herzegovina also have many people employed in agriculture.

Russia is one of the world's leading suppliers of oil and natural gas. Most of it comes from western Siberia or the region between the Volga River and the Ural Mountains. Pipelines link these regions to the rest of the country. Russia supplies oil as well as natural gas to European countries, especially the countries in Eastern Europe.

Russia is also a major supplier of iron ore and other metals. About 1 million people work in Russia's forestry industry. The majority of people in Russia and in most of Eastern Europe now work in the service industries, or businesses that provide services to individuals as well as other businesses.

Many of the industries in Eastern Europe fell on hard times after the collapse of the Soviet Union. Many industries suffered big losses, leading to high unemployment, especially in the

416 *Chapter 13*

---

netw⊚rks   *Online Teaching Options*

SLIDE SHOW

Russia's Role Between Europe and Asia

Analyzing Ask student volunteers to read each slide aloud. After students view the slide show, discuss the types of effects trade had on the Slavic culture. Have students write a paragraph describing the pros and cons of each effect. Visual/Spatial

See page 393E for other online activities.

Slide Show

Balkans. One positive move is the number of Eastern European countries that have joined the European Union. Since 2004, the following countries have joined the EU: the Czech Republic, Hungary, Latvia, Lithuania, Poland, Slovakia, Slovenia, Bulgaria, and Romania. The EU has sought to protect employment, improve workers' living and working conditions, and create a strong European trading bloc that can compete effectively with the United States.

R

Connections: Europe and Asia

Developments in Europe and Asia have affected Russia. Russians lived under Mongol rulers for centuries and later were next door to the Ottoman Turks, one of the most powerful Islamic empires to exist. Russia was influenced by developments in Europe, and, in turn, made contributions to European culture. Russian culture has always been a mix of European and Asian influences.

Today, oil and natural gas extracted from the Siberian oil fields in Central Asia are delivered via pipeline to all of Russia, Eastern Europe, and as far west as Italy and Germany. Geographically and culturally, Russia plays a key role in the relationship between Europe and Asia.

C

Addressing Challenges

Russia and countries that were formerly part of the Soviet republic continue to discuss agreements on the borders of the countries. The countries involved are Estonia, Latvia, Lithuania, Ukraine, and Kazakhstan (in Central Asia). Even though fighting died down in Chechnya, occasional outbreaks of violence still occur in that republic, and rebels continue to call for independence.

The 2008 financial crisis hit Eastern Europe hard. The countries there struggled as they transformed into free market economies. Joining the EU should have been a great benefit to the economies of its new members, but all members of the EU have suffered as a result of the financial crisis.

T

☑ **READING PROGRESS CHECK**

What have been two setbacks in the economies of Eastern Europe since the collapse of the USSR?

FOLDABLES
Study Organizer

Include this lesson's information in your Foldable®.

LESSON 3 REVIEW

Reviewing Vocabulary
1. Why were the *oligarchs* unpopular with some Russians?

Answering the Guiding Questions
2. *Analyzing* How did the rebellion in Chechnya affect the presidency of Boris Yeltsin?

3. *Describing* How did geographical barriers affect the development of Slavic culture in Eastern Europe?

4. *Determining Central Ideas* What are the economic advantages and disadvantages of Eastern Europe's location between continents?

5. *Narrative Writing* Imagine that you live in an Eastern European country and are writing a letter to your cousin who has lived in the United States for many years. Try to get your cousin to come visit you. Be sure to remind him or her of all the positive changes that have occurred since the collapse of the Soviet Union.

Chapter 13 **417**

LESSON 3 REVIEW ANSWERS

Reviewing Vocabulary

1. The oligarchs used their connections in government to further their own selfish aims.

Answering the Guiding Questions

2. **Analyzing** Yeltsin was blamed when Russian troops went in to Chechnya to put down the rebellion but could not stop the violence. Yeltsin then resigned.

3. **Describing** The Slavs developed many distinct languages and cultures. Isolation from each other sometimes made them enemies.

4. **Determining Central Ideas** Students' responses will vary, but students should recognize that being close to Russia and Asian countries gives Eastern European countries access to Russian industry and

energy resources. It also provides the opportunity to have a closer relationship to Asian markets. Closeness to Western Europe provides access to a higher standard of living than Eastern Europeans are used to. One disadvantage is that these countries have been dominated by a much more powerful Russia in the past, and many still do not trust Russia.

5. **Narrative Writing** Students' letters will vary but should include information from the text about changes that have occurred in Russia since the collapse of communism and the Soviet Union.

R Reading Skills

Explaining Remind students that the European Union has been discussed in Chapters 11 and 12. Ask students if they remember the nations already in the European Union. Call on participants and have students copy down the countries as they are recited. **Ask:** *What are the benefits of being a member of the European Union? (reduced barriers to individuals seeking employment among member nations, elimination of tariffs and trade barriers among members, better benefits and improved working and living conditions for workers, increased market force to compete with countries like the United States, China, India, and Japan)* **Verbal/Linguistic**

C Critical Thinking Skills

Interpreting After students have read the section, "Connections: Europe and Asia," have them make a chart of the ways Europe has influenced Russia and the ways Asia has influenced Russia. Then, **ask:** *Why do you think that Russian culture has always been a mix of European and Asian influences? (Students' answers will vary but should demonstrate the understanding that geographically Russia extends across both continents and its population is diverse culturally, Russia was ruled by Asian Mongol rulers for hundreds of years, was influenced by their neighbor, the Ottoman Turks, and was also influenced by the Enlightenment in Europe.)* **Logical/Mathematical, Verbal/Linguistic**

T Technology Skills

Researching Have students research on the Internet to find newspaper or magazine articles about how the financial crisis of 2008 has impacted Eastern Europe. **Ask:** *Why do you think that Eastern Europe was so negatively affected by the 2008 financial crisis? (Possible answers: The economic crisis hit just as many Eastern European countries were changing to free market economies.)* **Logical/Mathematical, Verbal/Linguistic**

CLOSE & REFLECT

Formatting Questions To close this lesson, have each student think of a question about the challenges that Yugoslavia and some former countries that were once part of the Soviet Union may still be facing. Write all of the questions on paper and post them for everyone to see. Discuss any breaking news they hear or read.

ANSWER, p. 417

☑ **READING PROGRESS CHECK** The challenge of changing from a central-government-based economy to a free-market economy resulted in big losses and high unemployment. The 2008 financial crisis hurt Eastern European economies.

CHAPTER REVIEW ACTIVITY

Have students create a three-column chart like the one below about Eastern Europe and Western Russia. Have students list *Landforms and Waterways, Climates,* and *Natural Resources* as column heads. Tell students to complete the chart for each category with information and examples from the text. *(Possible answers:* **Landforms and Waterways**—*vast plains including the Russian Plain, Siberian Plain, and Nothern European Plain; Ural Mountains, Greater and Lesser Caucacus Mountains, and Carpathian Mountains; Baltic Sea, Black Sea, and Caspian Sea; Volga River, Dneiper River, Dniester River, Danube River;* **Climates**—*most of region is humid continental; Albania and Macedonia experience a Mediterranean climate; Western Russia is subarctic, and north of that is polar;* **Natural Resources**—*minerals, forests, good soil, fish)* Visual/Spatial, Logical/Mathematical

Eastern Europe and Western Russia		
Landforms and Waterways	Climates	Natural Resources

REVIEW THE ENDURING UNDERSTANDING

Review this chapter's Enduring Understanding with students:

- *People, places, and ideas change over time.*

Now pose the following questions in a class discussion to apply this to this chapter.

- How did mountains hurt trade between people in Eastern Europe and Western Russia? *(Possible answer: Mountains made travel between areas difficult or prevented it. Mountains caused people to be isolated from one another.)*

- The czars were powerful rulers in imperial Russia. What were some of the benefits of their rule and some of the disadvantages? *(Sample answer: Benefits included an expanded Russian empire, educational opportunities, and support for the arts. Disadvantages included serfdom and a big gap in lifestyles between the czars and nobles and the greater masses of people.)*

- How do you think the teaching of history changed in the countries that once comprised the USSR after its collapse? *(Sample answer: When the Soviet Union existed, the communist government controlled what was taught and censored information from the West and the United States much like China and North Korea do today. After the collapse, students were introduced to western ideas of government and history.)*

Chapter 13 ACTIVITIES

Directions: Write your answers on a separate piece of paper.

1 Use your FOLDABLES to explore the Essential Question.
INFORMATIVE/EXPLANATORY WRITING Explain the meaning of the word *balkanization* and how it acquired its meaning.

2 21st Century Skills
ANALYZING With a partner, research to find one primary source and one secondary source about the Cuban missile crisis. Then, discuss and answer these questions: Which source provided a clearer picture of the event? Why? Did either source seem to support or favor one side over the other?

City	Country
Moscow, St. Petersburg	Russia
Kiev	Ukraine

3 Thinking Like a Geographer
IDENTIFYING On a chart like the one shown, list the most populous cities of Western Russia and Eastern Europe with their countries.

4 GEOGRAPHY ACTIVITY

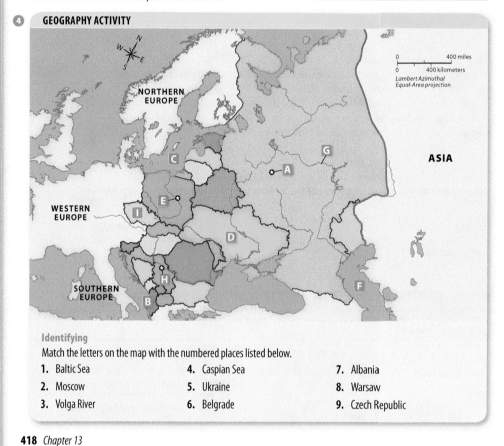

Identifying
Match the letters on the map with the numbered places listed below.

1. Baltic Sea
2. Moscow
3. Volga River
4. Caspian Sea
5. Ukraine
6. Belgrade
7. Albania
8. Warsaw
9. Czech Republic

ACTIVITIES ANSWERS

Exploring the Essential Question

1 **INFORMATIVE/EXPLANATORY WRITING** Students' explanations will vary but should refer to the Balkan Peninsula and the Carpathian and Balkan Mountains that isolate groups of people from one another. Isolation has led to cultural diversity, feuds, invasions, and wars. The word *balkanization* is often used to describe this type of cultural hostility.

21st Century Skills

2 **ANALYZING** Students' answers will vary, but should make note that the primary source better enables the reader to get as close as possible to what actually happened during a historical event or time period. Secondary sources might provide a better overview of the event.

REVIEW THE GUIDING QUESTIONS

Directions: Choose the best answer for each question.

❶ Which mountains form a boundary between Europe and Asia?

A. the Carpathians

B. the Urals

C. the Balkans

D. the Alps

❷ Although Russia is the largest country in the world, it has a relatively small percentage of land available for farming. Its main crop is

F. tobacco.

G. sunflowers.

H. grains.

I. lavender.

❸ What did Czar Alexander II abolish in Russia in 1861?

A. the Russian Orthodox Church

B. diamond mining

C. the Russian army and navy

D. serfdom

❹ The North Atlantic Treaty Organization (NATO), created in 1949, is an alliance of which countries?

F. the Balkan states

G. Western Russia and Eastern Europe

H. the United States and its allies

I. the USSR and Cuba

❺ The dominant religion in most of Eastern Europe and Western Russia is

A. Islam.

B. Eastern Orthodox.

C. Protestantism.

D. Moldavan.

❻ The difference in experience and viewpoints between those who grew up in the Communist USSR and Russians of the post-Soviet era is referred to as

F. a generation gap.

G. the diaspora.

H. cultural dissonance.

I. capitalism.

Chapter 13 **419**

Thinking Like a Geographer

❸ IDENTIFYING

City	Country
Minsk	Belarus
Budapest	Hungary
Warsaw	Poland
Prague	Czech Republic

Geography Activity

❹ LOCATING PLACES

1. C

2. A

3. G

4. F

5. D

6. H

7. B

8. E

9. I

ASSESSMENT ANSWERS

Review the Guiding Questions

❶ B To answer this question, students need to visualize where each mountain chain is located. Knowing that the Carpathian Mountains are in the Balkan Peninsula's northern region, the Balkan Mountains are linked to the Carpathians, and the Alps are mainly in Western Europe, will help them eliminate choices A, C, and D. Refer students to Lesson 1 for help.

❷ H Using logic will help students eliminate choices F, G, and I. The purpose of farmland is to grow food to feed the people. Tobacco, sunflowers, and lavender would not help feed a large population. Grains are used to make food, including bread, pasta, oatmeal, and cereals. Thus, grains would be a main crop grown in Russia. Refer students to Lesson 1 for help.

❸ D The word *abolish* in the question gives a clue to the answer. Knowing that *abolish* means "to put an end to or to get rid of" helps eliminate choices A, B, and C. The Czar would not want to get rid of a "good" thing. That leaves *serfdom*, which was bad for the common people. Refer students to Lesson 2 for help.

❹ H The word *Atlantic* in the organization's name gives a clue to the answer. Knowing that the Balkan states, Western Russia, Eastern Europe, and the USSR are not near the Atlantic Ocean helps eliminate choices F, G, and I. Knowing that the Atlantic Ocean is between the United States and Western Europe, confirms H as the correct choice. Refer students to Lesson 2 for help.

❺ B Knowing that Moldavan is not a religion helps to eliminate choice D. Remembering that the dominant religion in this region is the Eastern Orthodox Church helps to eliminate choices A and C. Refer students to Lesson 3 for help if they cannot figure out the correct answer.

❻ F To answer this question, students need to remember what a *generation gap* is. Also knowing the meanings of the other choices will help eliminate the wrong answers. Refer students to Lesson 3 for help if they cannot figure out the answer.

Assessment Answers

DBQ Analyzing Documents

7 **C** Contact with Western cultures comes as a result of movement of people, technology, and ideas between Russia and parts of Europe with Western culture.

8 **F** Russia is a large country with a cold climate that is not easy to farm. Much of it is covered by flat plains and is far from neighboring people, so vast space is the most likely influence from its natural surroundings.

Short Response

9 The physical geography of the Balkans leads to divisions as mountains separate groups of people from each other and make movement from one place to another difficult. In addition, the people of the Balkans have different ethnic identities, languages, cultures, and religions, which further separate them.

10 Possible answer: One way for people of different groups to connect is to find common ground by appealing to aspects of culture or history that are shared or by focusing on common concerns or desires.

Extended Response

11 The attempt to restructure the Russian economy got off to a rocky start. It was imposed from the top down at Premier Gorbachev's urging. Many government officials did not want economic changes, and the people did not trust the government to put a new system into place. The privatization of industry was a bonus for people who had ties to the government and could step into ownership—these people were called oligarchs—but ordinary people continued to live in the same conditions. There was not enough organization to make a smooth transition to producing consumer goods, so production declined and inflation rose. The country also suffered economic losses in the 2008 global financial downturn. Most of Russia's economic power today is from its oil production. On the whole, however, it has not been easy to rid the system of the corruption to which it has long been victim, so the economy is still not a free-market system.

DBQ ANALYZING DOCUMENTS

7 **IDENTIFYING** Read the following passage about Russian culture:

"*As one looks at the history of Russian culture, it may be helpful to think of the forces rather than the forms behind it. Three in particular—the natural surroundings, the Christian heritage, and the Western contacts of Russia—hover bigger than life.*"

—from James H. Billington, *The Icon and the Axe* (1970)

Which theme of geography is represented by the influence of Western contacts on Russia?

A. human-environment interaction   C. movement

B. location   D. place

8 **ANALYZING** Which of these aspects of natural surroundings is most likely to have affected Russian culture?

F. sense of vast space

G. warm climate

H. fertile farmland

I. nearness to neighbors

SHORT RESPONSE

"*The southern half of Eastern Europe is referred to as the Balkans or Balkan Peninsula, after the name of a mountain range in Bulgaria. Balkanization [means] the recurrent division and fragmentation of this part of Eastern Europe, and it is now applied to any place where such processes take place.*"

—from H.J. de Blij and Peter O. Muller, *Geography* (2006)

9 **ANALYZING** What characteristics of the Balkans and the people who live there led to these frequent divisions?

10 **IDENTIFYING POINT OF VIEW** If you were a leader of one of the peoples of the Balkans, how would you try to bridge the divisions separating your group from others?

EXTENDED RESPONSE

11 **INFORMATIVE/EXPLANATORY WRITING** In the 1990s, Russia began to make a transition from a communist economy to a more capitalistic economy. Discuss how this transition has worked so far. What are some of the positive and negative factors in the change? You will want to examine some outside sources to explain this economic transition.

Need Extra Help?

If You've Missed Question	**1**	**2**	**3**	**4**	**5**	**6**	**7**	**8**	**9**	**10**	**11**
Review Lesson	1	1	2	2	3	3	3	1	3	3	3

---

netw**o**rks   *Online Teaching Options*

Evaluation and Assessment

Assessing Use eAssessment to create your own tests from hundreds of available questions. eAssessment helps you design assessments that meet the needs of different types of learners.

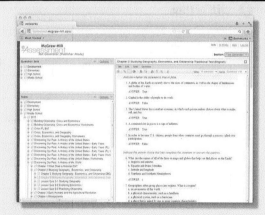

Using **FOLDABLES** is a great way to organize notes, remember information, and prepare for tests. Follow these easy directions to create a Foldable® for the chapter you are studying.

CHAPTER 1: WHAT IS GEOGRAPHY?

Describing   Make this Foldable and label the top *Geographer's View* and the bottom *Geographer's Tools*. Under the top fold, describe three ways you experience geography every day. Under the bottom fold, list and describe the tools of geography and explain how a map is a tool. In your mind, form an image of a map of the world. Sketch and label what you visualize on the back of your shutter fold.

Step 1
Bend a sheet of paper in half to find the midpoint.

Step 2
Fold the outer edges of the paper to meet at the midpoint.

CHAPTER 2: EARTH'S PHYSICAL GEOGRAPHY

Identifying   Make this Foldable and label the four tabs *Processes*, *Forces*, *Land*, and *Water*. Under *Processes*, identify and describe the processes that operate above and below Earth's surface. Include specific examples. Under *Forces*, give examples of how forces are changing Earth's surface where you live. Finally, under *Land* and *Water*, identify land and water features within 100 miles (161 km) of your community and explain how they influence your life.

Step 1
Fold the outer edges of the paper to meet at the midpoint. Crease well.

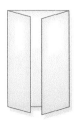

Step 2
Fold the paper in half from side to side.

Step 3
Open and cut along the inside fold lines to form four tabs.

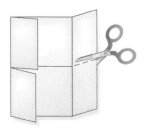

Step 4
Label the tabs as shown.

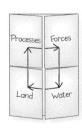

CHAPTER 3: EARTH'S PEOPLE

Analyzing Create this Foldable, and then label the tabs *Adaptations*, *Cultural Views*, and *Basic Needs*. Under *Adaptations*, describe how humans have adapted to life in two different geographic regions and describe population trends in each. Under *Cultural Views*, analyze what makes two different cultures unique. Finally, under *Basic Needs*, describe how your basic needs might be met in two different economic systems.

Step 1
Fold a sheet of paper in half, leaving a ½-inch tab along one edge.

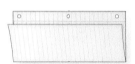

Step 2
Then fold the paper into three equal sections.

Step 3
Cut along the folds on the top sheet of paper to create three tabs.

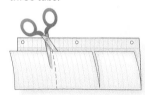

Step 4
Label your Foldable as shown.

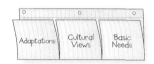

CHAPTER 4: THE UNITED STATES EAST OF THE MISSISSIPPI

Organizing After you create the Foldable below, write the chapter title on the cover tab and label the three small tabs *East and West*, *Geographic Barriers*, and *Diversity*. Under *East and West*, sketch an outline of the United States and draw the Mississippi River. Then list facts about the region. Under *Geographic Barriers*, give examples of physical features that were barriers to westward expansion. Under *Diversity*, explain how cultural diversity makes the United States East of the Mississippi a unique region.

Step 1
Stack two sheets of paper so that the back sheet is 1 inch higher than the front sheet.

Step 2
Fold the paper to form four equal tabs.

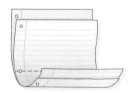

Step 3
When all tabs are an equal distance apart, fold the papers and crease well.

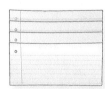

Step 4
Open the papers, and then glue or staple them along the fold.

CHAPTER 5: THE UNITED STATES WEST OF THE MISSISSIPPI

Identifying Make a three-tab book with three columns. Label the columns *Geography*, *History*, and *Economy*. Under each column heading, write: *Know* and *Learned*. Use the book to record what you know and what you learn about the western region of the United States.

Step 1
Fold a sheet of paper in half, leaving a ½-inch tab along one edge.

Step 2
Then fold the paper into three equal sections.

Step 3
Cut along the folds on the top sheet of paper to create three tabs.

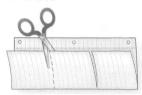

Step 4
Label your Foldable as shown.

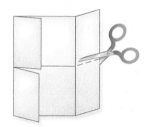

CHAPTER 6: CANADA

Identifying Follow the steps below, and then label the four tabs *North*, *South*, *Past and Present*, and *World Relations*. Describe and give examples of the geography of the northern and southern regions of Canada under either the *North* or the *South* tab. Under *Past and Present*, identify important people, places, and events from Canada's history. Explain Canada's relations with other countries under the *World Relations* tab.

Step 1
Fold the outer edges of the paper to meet at the midpoint. Crease well.

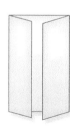

Step 2
Fold the paper in half from side to side.

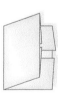

Step 3
Open and cut along the inside fold lines to form four tabs.

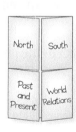

Step 4
Label the tabs as shown.

CHAPTER 7: MEXICO, CENTRAL AMERICA, AND THE CARIBBEAN ISLANDS

Analyzing   Make the Foldable below. Write the chapter title on the cover tab, and label the three small tabs *Gulf of Mexico*, *Civilizations*, and *Trade and Commerce*. Under *Gulf of Mexico*, explain how the gulf has affected life in the region. Include information on weather, tourism, and the economy. Under *Civilizations*, sequence and describe the major civilizations that developed in this region and their cultural influences. Finally, under *Trade and Commerce*, compare and contrast trade events that are important to the economy of the region.

Step 1
Stack two sheets of paper so that the back sheet is 1 inch higher than the front sheet.

Step 2
Fold the paper to form four equal tabs.

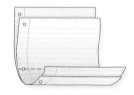

Step 3
When all tabs are an equal distance apart, fold the papers and crease well.

Step 4
Open the papers, and glue or staple them along the fold.

Trade and Commerce
Civilizations
Gulf of Mexico
Mexico, Central America, and the Caribbean Islands

CHAPTER 8: BRAZIL

Organizing   Create the Foldable below. On the back, write the chapter title and sketch a map of Brazil. Label the two front tabs *Valuable Natural Resources* and *Urban Population*. On your sketch, label Brazil's major geographic features. Under *Valuable Natural Resources*, outline when and where valuable natural resources were discovered and how the discoveries affected the native and colonial populations. Under *Urban Population*, discuss the impact of the population distribution.

Step 1
Bend a sheet of paper in half to find the midpoint.

Step 2
Fold the outer edges of the paper to meet at the midpoint.

Valuable Natural Resources
Urban Population

CHAPTER 9: THE TROPICAL NORTH

Identifying Create the Foldable below. Label the cover *The Tropical North* and the layers *Geography*, *Foreign Influences and Resources*, and *Trade*. Under *Geography*, explain how geography and resources affect the countries and people of the region. Under *Foreign Influences and Resources*, explain how resources and foreign countries have impacted the Tropical North. Under *Trade*, explain how countries in the region are trying to expand trade and why.

Step 1
Stack two sheets of paper so that the back sheet is 1 inch higher than the front sheet.

Step 2
Fold the paper to form four equal tabs.

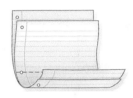

Step 3
When all tabs are an equal distance apart, fold the papers and crease well.

Step 4
Open the papers, and then glue or staple them along the fold.

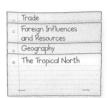

CHAPTER 10: ANDES AND MIDLATITUDE COUNTRIES

Describing Make the Foldable below, and then label the top of the sections *Geography*, *Culture*, and *Economy*. Under *Geography*, explain how the Andes Mountains affect the lives of the people who live near or around them. Under *Culture*, describe the rise and fall of the Inca Empire and what it tells about the history of the region. Finally, under *Economy*, explain how the terrain and the resources available affect the way people live.

Step 1
Fold a sheet of paper into thirds to form three equal columns.

Step 2
Label your Foldable as shown.

CHAPTER 11: WESTERN EUROPE

Analyzing Follow the steps below to create a Foldable. Then sketch an outline of Western Europe on the back. Label important geographic features in the region. On the front, label the tabs as illustrated. Under *Waterways—Landforms*, explain how waterways and landforms have influenced the development of Western Europe. Under *Early Civilizations—Industrial Revolution*, sequence the cultural and technological changes that occurred. Finally, under *War—Post-War*, summarize the effects of war on the region and explain why the EU was formed.

Step 1
Fold the outer edges of the paper to meet at the midpoint. Crease well.

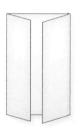

Step 2
Open and cut three equal tabs from the outer edge to the crease on each side.

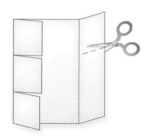

Step 3
Label the tabs as shown.

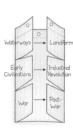

CHAPTER 12: NORTHERN AND SOUTHERN EUROPE

Describing Create the Foldable below, and label the anchor tab *Northern and Southern Europe*. Label the front of the tabs *Geography*, *History*, and *Culture*. Under *Geography*, describe how geography has influenced the lifestyles and economies in the region. Under *History*, explain the importance of the Silk Road and how trade with China influenced the people of the region. Finally, under *Culture*, identify different culture groups in each region.

Step 1
Fold a sheet of paper in half, leaving a ½-inch tab along one edge.

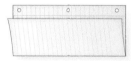

Step 2
Then fold the paper into three equal sections.

Step 3
Cut along the folds on the top sheet of paper to create three tabs.

Step 4
Label your Foldable as shown.

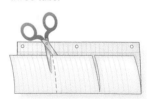

CHAPTER 13: EASTERN EUROPE AND WESTERN RUSSIA

Organizing Create this Foldable, and then sketch and label Eastern Europe, Western Russia, and the Ural Mountains on the back. On the front, label the top-left tab *Eastern Europe* and the top-right tab *Western Russia*. Under the tabs, describe landforms and natural resources found in each area. Label the two bottom tabs *Empires* and *Populations*. List the empires that once controlled this region and one important event from each. Finally, explain why populations are declining.

Step 1
Fold the outer edges of the paper to meet at the midpoint. Crease well.

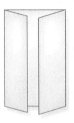

Step 2
Fold the paper in half from side to side.

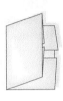

Step 3
Open and cut along the inside fold lines to form four tabs.

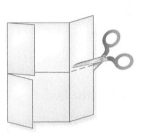

Step 4
Label the tabs as shown.

Foldables® Library

Gazetteer

A gazetteer (ga·zuh·TIHR) is a geographic index or dictionary. It shows latitude and longitude for cities and certain other places. Latitude and longitude are shown in this way: 48°N 2°E, or 48 degrees north latitude and two degrees east longitude. This Gazetteer lists many important geographic features and most of the world's largest independent countries and their capitals. The page numbers tell where each entry can be found on a map in this book. As an aid to pronunciation, most entries are spelled phonetically.

A

Abidjan [AH·BEE·JAHN] Capital of Côte d'Ivoire. 5°N 4°W (p. RA22)

Abu Dhabi [AH·BOO DAH·bee] Capital of the United Arab Emirates. 24°N 54°E (p. RA24)

Abuja [ah·BOO·jah] Capital of Nigeria. 8°N 9°E (p. RA22)

Accra [ah·KRUH] Capital of Ghana. 6°N 0° longitude (p. RA22)

Addis Ababa [AHD·dihs AH·bah·BAH] Capital of Ethiopia. 9°N 39°E (p. RA22)

Adriatic [AY·dree·A·tihk] **Sea** Arm of the Mediterranean Sea between the Balkan Peninsula and Italy. (p. RA20)

Afghanistan [af·GA·nuh·STAN] Central Asian country west of Pakistan. (p. RA25)

Albania [al·BAY·nee·uh] Country on the Adriatic Sea, south of Serbia. (p. RA18)

Algeria [al·JIHR·ee·uh] North African country east of Morocco. (p. RA22)

Algiers [al·JIHRZ] Capital of Algeria. 37°N 3°E (p. RA22)

Alps [ALPS] Mountain ranges extending through central Europe. (p. RA20)

Amazon [A·muh·ZAHN] **River** Largest river in the world by volume and second-largest in length. (p. RA17)

Amman [a·MAHN] Capital of Jordan. 32°N 36°E (p. RA24)

Amsterdam [AHM·stuhr·DAHM] Capital of the Netherlands. 52°N 5°E (p. RA18)

Andes [AN·DEEZ] Mountain system extending north and south along the western side of South America. (p. RA17)

Andorra [an·DAWR·uh] Small country in southern Europe between France and Spain. 43°N 2°E (p. RA18)

Angola [ang·GOH·luh] Southern African country north of Namibia. (p. RA22)

Ankara [AHNG·kuh·ruh] Capital of Turkey. 40°N 33°E (p. RA24)

Antananarivo [AHN·tah·NAH·nah·REE·voh] Capital of Madagascar. 19°S 48°E (p. RA22)

Arabian [uh·RAY·bee·uhn] **Peninsula** Large peninsula extending into the Arabian Sea. (p. RA25)

Argentina [AHR·juhn·TEE·nuh] South American country east of Chile. (p. RA16)

Armenia [ahr·MEE·nee·uh] European-Asian country between the Black and Caspian Seas. 40°N 45°E (p. RA26)

Ashkhabad [AHSH·gah·BAHD] Capital of Turkmenistan. 38°N 58°E (p. RA25)

Asmara [az·MAHR·uh] Capital of Eritrea. 16°N 39°E (p. RA22)

Astana Capital of Kazakhstan. 51°N 72°E (p. RA26)

Asunción [ah·SOON·see·OHN] Capital of Paraguay. 25°S 58°W (p. RA16)

Athens Capital of Greece. 38°N 24°E (p. RA19)

Atlas [AT·luhs] **Mountains** Mountain range on the northern edge of the Sahara. (p. RA23)

Australia [aw·STRAYL·yuh] Country and continent in Southern Hemisphere. (p. RA30)

Austria [AWS·tree·uh] Western European country east of Switzerland and south of Germany and the Czech Republic. (p. RA18)

Azerbaijan [A·zuhr·BY·JAHN] European-Asian country on the Caspian Sea. (p. RA25)

B

Baghdad Capital of Iraq. 33°N 44°E (p. RA25)

Bahamas [buh·HAH·muhz] Country made up of many islands between Cuba and the United States. (p. RA15)

Bahrain [bah·RAYN] Country located on the Persian Gulf. 26°N 51°E (p. RA25)

Baku [bah·KOO] Capital of Azerbaijan. 40°N 50°E (p. RA25)

Balkan [BAWL·kuhn] **Peninsula** Peninsula in southeastern Europe. (p. RA21)

Baltic [BAWL·tihk] **Sea** Sea in northern Europe that is connected to the North Sea. (p. RA20)

Bamako [BAH·mah·KOH] Capital of Mali. 13°N 8°W (p. RA22)

Bangkok [BANG·KAHK] Capital of Thailand. 14°N 100°E (p. RA27)

Bangladesh [BAHNG·gluh·DEHSH] South Asian country bordered by India and Myanmar. (p. RA27)

Bangui [BAHNG·GEE] Capital of the Central African Republic. 4°N 19°E (p. RA22)

Banjul [BAHN·JOOL] Capital of Gambia. 13°N 17°W (p. RA22)

Barbados [bahr·BAY·duhs] Island country between the Atlantic Ocean and the Caribbean Sea. 14°N 59°W (p. RA15)

Beijing [BAY·JIHNG] Capital of China. 40°N 116°E (p. RA27)

Beirut [bay·ROOT] Capital of Lebanon. 34°N 36°E (p. RA24)

Belarus [BEE•luh•ROOS] Eastern European country west of Russia. 54°N 28°E (p. RA19)

Belgium [BEHL•juhm] Western European country south of the Netherlands. (p. RA18)

Belgrade [BEHL•GRAYD] Capital of Serbia. 45°N 21°E (p. RA19)

Belize [buh•LEEZ] Central American country east of Guatemala. (p. RA14)

Belmopan [BEHL•moh•PAHN] Capital of Belize. 17°N 89°W (p. RA14)

Benin [buh•NEEN] West African country west of Nigeria. (p. RA22)

Berlin [behr•LEEN] Capital of Germany. 53°N 13°E (p. RA18)

Bern Capital of Switzerland. 47°N 7°E (p. RA18)

Bhutan [boo•TAHN] South Asian country northeast of India. (p. RA27)

Bishkek [bihsh•KEHK] Capital of Kyrgyzstan. 43°N 75°E (p. RA26)

Bissau [bihs•SOW] Capital of Guinea-Bissau. 12°N 16°W (p. RA22)

Black Sea Large sea between Europe and Asia. (p. RA21)

Bloemfontein [BLOOM•FAHN•TAYN] Judicial capital of South Africa. 26°E 29°S (p. RA22)

Bogotá [BOH•GOH•TAH] Capital of Colombia. 5°N 74°W (p. RA16)

Bolivia [buh•LIHV•ee•uh] Country in the central part of South America, north of Argentina. (p. RA16)

Bosnia and Herzegovina [BAHZ•nee•uh HEHRT•seh•GAW•vee•nuh] Southeastern European country bordered by Croatia, Serbia, and Montenegro. (p. RA18)

Botswana [bawt•SWAH•nah] Southern African country north of the Republic of South Africa. (p. RA22)

Brasília [brah•ZEEL•yuh] Capital of Brazil. 16°S 48°W (p. RA16)

Bratislava [BRAH•tih•SLAH•vuh] Capital of Slovakia. 48°N 17°E (p. RA18)

Brazil [bruh•ZIHL] Largest country in South America. (p. RA16)

Brazzaville [BRAH•zuh•VEEL] Capital of Congo. 4°S 15°E (p. RA22)

Brunei [bru•NY] Southeast Asian country on northern coast of the island of Borneo. (p. RA27)

Brussels [BRUH•suhlz] Capital of Belgium. 51°N 4°E (p. RA18)

Bucharest [BOO•kuh•REHST] Capital of Romania. 44°N 26°E (p. RA19)

Budapest [BOO•duh•PEHST] Capital of Hungary. 48°N 19°E (p. RA18)

Buenos Aires [BWAY•nuhs AR•eez] Capital of Argentina. 34°S 58°W (p. RA16)

Bujumbura [BOO•juhm•BUR•uh] Capital of Burundi. 3°S 29°E (p. RA22)

Bulgaria [BUHL•GAR•ee•uh] Southeastern European country south of Romania. (p. RA19)

Burkina Faso [bur•KEE•nuh FAH•soh] West African country south of Mali. (p. RA22)

Burundi [bu•ROON•dee] East African country at the northern end of Lake Tanganyika. 3°S 30°E (p. RA22)

C

Cairo [KY•roh] Capital of Egypt. 31°N 32°E (p. RA24)

Cambodia [kam•BOH•dee•uh] Southeast Asian country south of Thailand and Laos. (p. RA27)

Cameroon [KA•muh•ROON] Central African country on the northeast shore of the Gulf of Guinea. (p. RA22)

Canada [KA•nuh•duh] Northernmost country in North America. (p. RA6)

Canberra [KAN•BEHR•uh] Capital of Australia. 35°S 149°E (p. RA30)

Cape Town Legislative capital of the Republic of South Africa. 34°S 18°E (p. RA22)

Cape Verde [VUHRD] Island country off the coast of western Africa in the Atlantic Ocean. 15°N 24°W (p. RA22)

Caracas [kah•RAH•kahs] Capital of Venezuela. 11°N 67°W (p. RA16)

Caribbean [KAR•uh•BEE•uhn] **Islands** Islands in the Caribbean Sea between North America and South America, also known as West Indies. (p. RA15)

Caribbean Sea Part of the Atlantic Ocean bordered by the West Indies, South America, and Central America. (p. RA15)

Caspian [KAS•pee•uhn] **Sea** Salt lake between Europe and Asia that is the world's largest inland body of water. (p. RA21)

Caucasus [KAW•kuh•suhs] **Mountains** Mountain range between the Black and Caspian Seas. (p. RA21)

Central African Republic Central African country south of Chad. (p. RA22)

Chad [CHAD] Country west of Sudan in the African Sahel. (p. RA22)

Chang Jiang [CHAHNG jee•AHNG] Principal river of China that begins in Tibet and flows into the East China Sea near Shanghai; also known as the Yangtze River. (p. RA29)

Chile [CHEE•lay] South American country west of Argentina. (p. RA16)

China [CHY•nuh] Country in eastern and central Asia, known officially as the People's Republic of China. (p. RA27)

Chişinău [KEE•shee•NOW] Capital of Moldova. 47°N 29°E (p. RA19)

Colombia [kuh•LUHM•bee•uh] South American country west of Venezuela. (p. RA16)

Colombo [kuh•LUHM•boh] Capital of Sri Lanka. 7°N 80°E (p. RA26)

Comoros [KAH•muh•ROHZ] Small island country in Indian Ocean between the island of Madagascar and the southeast African mainland. 13°S 43°E (p. RA22)

Conakry [KAH•nuh•kree] Capital of Guinea. 10°N 14°W (p. RA22)

Congo [KAHNG•goh] Central African country east of the Democratic Republic of the Congo. 3°S 14°E (p. RA22)

Congo, Democratic Republic of the Central African country north of Zambia and Angola. 1°S 22°E (p. RA22)

Copenhagen [KOH•puhn•HAY•guhn] Capital of Denmark. 56°N 12°E (p. RA18)

Costa Rica [KAWS•tah REE•kah] Central American country south of Nicaragua. (p. RA15)

Côte d'Ivoire [KOHT dee•VWAHR] West African country south of Mali. (p. RA22)

Croatia [kroh•AY•shuh] Southeastern European country on the Adriatic Sea. (p. RA18)

Cuba [KYOO•buh] Island country in the Caribbean Sea. (p. RA15)

Cyprus [SY•pruhs] Island country in the eastern Mediterranean Sea, south of Turkey. (p. RA19)

Czech [CHEHK] **Republic** Eastern European country north of Austria. (p. RA18)

D

Dakar [dah•KAHR] Capital of Senegal. 15°N 17°W (p. RA22)

Damascus [duh•MAS•kuhs] Capital of Syria. 34°N 36°E (p. RA24)

Dar es Salaam [DAHR EHS sah•LAHM] Commercial capital of Tanzania. 7°S 39°E (p. RA22)

Denmark Northern European country between the Baltic and North Seas. (p. RA18)

Dhaka [DA•kuh] Capital of Bangladesh. 24°N 90°E (p. RA27)

Djibouti [jih•BOO•tee] East African country on the Gulf of Aden. 12°N 43°E (p. RA22)

Dodoma [doh•DOH•mah] Political capital of Tanzania. 6°S 36°E (p. RA22)

Doha [DOH•huh] Capital of Qatar. 25°N 51°E (p. RA25)

Dominican [duh•MIH•nih•kuhn] **Republic** Country in the Caribbean Sea on the eastern part of the island of Hispaniola. (p. RA15)

Dublin [DUH•blihn] Capital of Ireland. 53°N 6°W (p. RA18)

Dushanbe [doo•SHAM•buh] Capital of Tajikistan. 39°N 69°E (p. RA25)

E

East Timor [TEE•MOHR] Previous province of Indonesia, now under UN administration. 10°S 127°E (p. RA27)

Ecuador [EH•kwuh•dawr] South American country southwest of Colombia. (p. RA16)

Egypt [EE•jihpt] North African country on the Mediterranean Sea. (p. RA24)

El Salvador [ehl SAL•vuh•dawr] Central American country southwest of Honduras. (p. RA14)

Equatorial Guinea [EE•kwuh•TOHR•ee•uhl GIH•nee] Central African country south of Cameroon. (p. RA22)

Eritrea [EHR•uh•TREE•uh] East African country north of Ethiopia. (p. RA22)

Estonia [eh•STOH•nee•uh] Eastern European country on the Baltic Sea. (p. RA19)

Ethiopia [EE•thee•OH•pee•uh] East African country north of Somalia and Kenya. (p. RA22)

Euphrates [yu•FRAY•teez] **River** River in southwestern Asia that flows through Syria and Iraq and joins the Tigris River. (p. RA25)

F

Fiji [FEE•jee] **Islands** Country comprised of an island group in the southwest Pacific Ocean. 19°S 175°E (p. RA30)

Finland [FIHN•luhnd] Northern European country east of Sweden. (p. RA19)

France [FRANS] Western European country south of the United Kingdom. (p. RA18)

Freetown Capital of Sierra Leone. (p. RA22)

French Guiana [gee•A•nuh] French-owned territory in northern South America. (p. RA16)

G

Gabon [ga•BOHN] Central African country on the Atlantic Ocean. (p. RA22)

Gaborone [GAH•boh•ROH•nay] Capital of Botswana. (p. RA22)

Gambia [GAM•bee•uh] West African country along the Gambia River. (p. RA22)

Georgetown [JAWRJ•town] Capital of Guyana. 8°N 58°W (p. RA16)

Georgia [JAWR•juh] European-Asian country bordering the Black Sea south of Russia. (p. RA26)

Germany [JUHR•muh•nee] Western European country south of Denmark, officially called the Federal Republic of Germany. (p. RA18)

Ghana [GAH•nuh] West African country on the Gulf of Guinea. (p. RA22)

Great Plains The continental slope extending through the United States and Canada. (p. RA7)

Greece [GREES] Southern European country on the Balkan Peninsula. (p. RA19)

Greenland [GREEN•luhnd] Island in northwestern Atlantic Ocean and the largest island in the world. (p. RA6)

Guatemala [GWAH•tay•MAH•lah] Central American country south of Mexico. (p. RA14)

Guatemala Capital of Guatemala. 15°N 91°W (p. RA14)

Guinea [GIH•nee] West African country on the Atlantic coast. (p. RA22)

Guinea-Bissau [GIH•nee bih•SOW] West African country on the Atlantic coast. (p. RA22)

Gulf of Mexico Gulf on part of the southern coast of North America. (p. RA7)

Guyana [gy•AH•nuh] South American country between Venezuela and Suriname. (p. RA16)

H

Haiti [HAY•tee] Country in the Caribbean Sea on the western part of the island of Hispaniola. (p. RA15)

Hanoi [ha•NOY] Capital of Vietnam. 21°N 106°E (p. RA27)

Harare [hah•RAH•RAY] Capital of Zimbabwe. 18°S 31°E (p. RA22)

Havana [huh•VA•nuh] Capital of Cuba. 23°N 82°W (p. RA15)

Helsinki [HEHL•SIHNG•kee] Capital of Finland. 60°N 24°E (p. RA19)

Himalaya [HI•muh•LAY•uh] Mountain ranges in southern Asia, bordering the Indian subcontinent on the north. (p. RA28)

Honduras [hahn•DUR•uhs] Central American country on the Caribbean Sea. (p. RA14)

Hong Kong Port and industrial center in southern China. 22°N 115°E (p. RA27)

Huang He [HWAHNG HUH] River in northern and eastern China, also known as the Yellow River. (p. RA29)

Hungary [HUHNG•guh•ree] Eastern European country south of Slovakia. (p. RA18)

I

Iberian [eye•BIHR•ee•uhn] Peninsula Peninsula in southwest Europe, occupied by Spain and Portugal. (p. RA20)

Iceland Island country between the North Atlantic and Arctic Oceans. (p. RA18)

India [IHN•dee•uh] South Asian country south of China and Nepal. (p. RA26)

Indonesia [IHN•duh•NEE•zhuh] Southeast Asian island country known as the Republic of Indonesia. (p. RA27)

Indus [IHN•duhs] River River in Asia that begins in Tibet and flows through Pakistan to the Arabian Sea. (p. RA28)

Iran [ih•RAN] Southwest Asian country that was formerly named Persia. (p. RA25)

Iraq [ih•RAHK] Southwest Asian country west of Iran. (p. RA25)

Ireland [EYER•luhnd] Island west of Great Britain occupied by the Republic of Ireland and Northern Ireland. (p. RA18)

Islamabad [ihs•LAH•muh•BAHD] Capital of Pakistan. 34°N 73°E (p. RA26)

Israel [IHZ•ree•uhl] Southwest Asian country south of Lebanon. (p. RA24)

Italy [IHT•uhl•ee] Southern European country south of Switzerland and east of France. (p. RA18)

J

Jakarta [juh•KAHR•tuh] Capital of Indonesia. 6°S 107°E (p. RA27)

Jamaica [juh•MAY•kuh] Island country in the Caribbean Sea. (p. RA15)

Japan [juh•PAN] East Asian country consisting of the four large islands of Hokkaido, Honshu, Shikoku, and Kyushu, plus thousands of small islands. (p. RA27)

Jerusalem [juh•ROO•suh•luhm] Capital of Israel and a holy city for Christians, Jews, and Muslims. 32°N 35°E (p. RA24)

Jordan [JAWRD•uhn] Southwest Asian country south of Syria. (p. RA24)

Juba [JU•buh] Capital of South Sudan. 5°N 31°E (p. RA22)

K

Kabul [KAH•buhl] Capital of Afghanistan. 35°N 69°E (p. RA25)

Kampala [kahm•PAH•lah] Capital of Uganda. 0° latitude 32°E (p. RA22)

Kathmandu [KAT•MAN•DOO] Capital of Nepal. 28°N 85°E (p. RA26)

Kazakhstan [kuh•ZAHK•STAHN] Large Asian country south of Russia and bordering the Caspian Sea. (p. RA26)

Kenya [KEHN•yuh] East African country south of Ethiopia. (p. RA22)

Khartoum [kahr•TOOM] Capital of Sudan. 16°N 33°E (p. RA22)

Kigali [kee•GAH•lee] Capital of Rwanda. 2°S 30°E (p. RA22)

Kingston [KIHNG•stuhn] Capital of Jamaica. 18°N 77°W (p. RA15)

Kinshasa [kihn•SHAH•suh] Capital of the Democratic Republic of the Congo. 4°S 15°E (p. RA22)

Kuala Lumpur [KWAH•luh LUM•PUR] Capital of Malaysia. 3°N 102°E (p. RA27)

Kuwait [ku•WAYT] Country on the Persian Gulf between Saudi Arabia and Iraq. (p. RA25)

Kyiv (Kiev) [KEE•ihf] Capital of Ukraine. 50°N 31°E (p. RA19)

Kyrgyzstan [s•gih•STAN] Central Asian country on China's western border. (p. RA26)

L

Laos [LOWS] Southeast Asian country south of China and west of Vietnam. (p. RA27)

La Paz [lah PAHS] Administrative capital of Bolivia, and the highest capital in the world. 17°S 68°W (p. RA16)

Latvia [LAT•vee•uh] Eastern European country west of Russia on the Baltic Sea. (p. RA19)

Lebanon [LEH•buh•nuhn] Country south of Syria on the Mediterranean Sea. (p. RA24)

Lesotho [luh•SOH•TOH] Southern African country within the borders of the Republic of South Africa. (p. RA22)

Liberia [ly•BIHR•ee•uh] West African country south of Guinea. (p. RA22)

Libreville [LEE•bruh•VIHL] Capital of Gabon. 1°N 9°E (p. RA22)

Libya [LIH•bee•uh] North African country west of Egypt on the Mediterranean Sea. (p. RA22)

Liechtenstein [LIHKT•uhn•SHTYN] Small country in central Europe between Switzerland and Austria. 47°N 10°E (p. RA18)

Lilongwe [lih•LAWNG•GWAY] Capital of Malawi. 14°S 34°E (p. RA22)

Lima [LEE•mah] Capital of Peru. 12°S 77°W (p. RA16)

Lisbon [LIHZ•buhn] Capital of Portugal. 39°N 9°W (p. RA18)

Lithuania [LIH•thuh•WAY•nee•uh] Eastern European country northwest of Belarus on the Baltic Sea. (p. RA21)

Ljubljana [lee•oo•blee•AH•nuh] Capital of Slovenia. 46°N 14°E (p. RA18)

Lomé [loh•MAY] Capital of Togo. 6°N 1°E (p. RA22)

London Capital of the United Kingdom, on the Thames River. 52°N 0° longitude (p. RA18)

Luanda [lu•AHN•duh] Capital of Angola. 9°S 13°E (p. RA22)

Lusaka [loo•SAH•kah] Capital of Zambia. 15°S 28°E (p. RA22)

Luxembourg [LUHK•suhm•BUHRG] Small European country bordered by France, Belgium, and Germany. 50°N 7°E (p. RA18)

M

Macao [muh•KOW] Port in southern China. 22°N 113°E (p. RA27)

Macedonia [ma•suh•DOH•nee•uh] Southeastern European country north of Greece. (p. RA19). Macedonia also refers to a geographic region covering northern Greece, the country Macedonia, and part of Bulgaria.

Madagascar [MA•duh•GAS•kuhr] Island in the Indian Ocean off the southeastern coast of Africa. (p. RA22)

Madrid Capital of Spain. 41°N 4°W (p. RA18)

Malabo [mah•LAH•boh] Capital of Equatorial Guinea. 4°N 9°E (p. RA22)

Malawi [mah•LAH•wee] Southern African country south of Tanzania and east of Zambia. (p. RA22)

Malaysia [muh•LAY•zhuh] Southeast Asian country with land on the Malay Peninsula and on the island of Borneo. (p. RA27)

Maldives [MAWL•DEEVZ] Island country southwest of India in the Indian Ocean. (p. RA26)

Mali [MAH•lee] West African country east of Mauritania. (p. RA22)

Managua [mah•NAH•gwah] Capital of Nicaragua. (p. RA15)

Manila [muh•NIH•luh] Capital of the Philippines. 15°N 121°E (p. RA27)

Maputo [mah•POO•toh] Capital of Mozambique. 26°S 33°E (p. RA22)

Maseru [MA•zuh•ROO] Capital of Lesotho. 29°S 27°E (p. RA22)

Masqat [MUHS•KAHT] Capital of Oman. 23°N 59°E (p. RA25)

Mauritania [MAWR•uh•TAY•nee•uh] West African country north of Senegal. (p. RA22)

Mauritius [maw•RIH•shuhs] Island country in the Indian Ocean east of Madagascar. 21°S 58°E (p. RA3)

Mbabane [uhm•bah•BAH•nay] Capital of Swaziland. 26°S 31°E (p. RA22)

Mediterranean [MEH•duh•tuh•RAY•nee•uhn] **Sea** Large inland sea surrounded by Europe, Asia, and Africa. (p. RA20)

Mekong [MAY•KAWNG] **River** River in southeastern Asia that begins in Tibet and empties into the South China Sea. (p. RA29)

Mexico [MEHK•sih•KOH] North American country south of the United States. (p. RA14)

Mexico City Capital of Mexico. 19°N 99°W (p. RA14)

Minsk [MIHNSK] Capital of Belarus. 54°N 28°E (p. RA19)

Mississippi [MIH•suh•SIH•pee] **River** Large river system in the central United States that flows southward into the Gulf of Mexico. (p. RA11)

Mogadishu [MOH•guh•DEE•shoo] Capital of Somalia. 2°N 45°E (p. RA22)

Moldova [mawl•DAW•vuh] Small European country between Ukraine and Romania. (p. RA19)

Monaco [MAH•nuh•KOH] Small country in southern Europe on the French Mediterranean coast. 44°N 8°E (p. RA18)

Mongolia [mahn•GOHL•yuh] Country in Asia between Russia and China. (p. RA23)

Monrovia [muhn•ROH•vee•uh] Capital of Liberia. 6°N 11°W (p. RA22)

Montenegro [MAHN•tuh•NEE•groh] Eastern European country. (p. RA18)

Montevideo [MAHN•tuh•vuh•DAY•oh] Capital of Uruguay. 35°S 56°W (p. RA16)

Morocco [muh•RAH•KOH] North African country on the Mediterranean Sea and the Atlantic Ocean. (p. RA22)

Moscow [MAHS•KOW] Capital of Russia. 56°N 38°E (p. RA19)

Mount Everest [EHV•ruhst] Highest mountain in the world, in the Himalaya between Nepal and Tibet. (p. RA28)

Mozambique [MOH•zahm•BEEK] Southern African country south of Tanzania. (p. RA22)

Myanmar [MYAHN•MAHR] Southeast Asian country south of China and India, formerly called Burma. (p. RA27)

N

Nairobi [ny•ROH•bee] Capital of Kenya. 1°S 37°E (p. RA22)

Namibia [nuh•MIH•bee•uh] Southern African country south of Angola on the Atlantic Ocean. 20°S 16°E (p. RA22)

Nassau [NA•SAW] Capital of the Bahamas. 25°N 77°W (p. RA15)

N'Djamena [uhn•jah•MAY•nah] Capital of Chad. 12°N 15°E (p. RA22)

Nepal [NAY•PAHL] Mountain country between India and China. (p. RA26)

Netherlands [NEH•thuhr•lundz] Western European country north of Belgium. (p. RA18)

New Delhi [NOO DEH•lee] Capital of India. 29°N 77°E (p. RA26)

New Zealand [NOO ZEE•luhnd] Major island country southeast of Australia in the South Pacific. (p. RA30)

Niamey [nee•AHM•ay] Capital of Niger. 14°N 2°E (p. RA22)

Nicaragua [NIH•kuh•RAH•gwuh] Central American country south of Honduras. (p. RA15)

Nicosia [NIH•kuh•SEE•uh] Capital of Cyprus. 35°N 33°E (p. RA19)

Niger [NY•juhr] West African country north of Nigeria. (p. RA22)

Nigeria [ny•JIHR•ee•uh] West African country along the Gulf of Guinea. (p. RA22)

Nile [NYL] **River** Longest river in the world, flowing north through eastern Africa. (p. RA23)

North Korea [kuh•REE•uh] East Asian country in the northernmost part of the Korean Peninsula. (p. RA27)

Norway [NAWR•way] Northern European country on the Scandinavian Peninsula. (p. RA18)

Nouakchott [nu•AHK•SHAHT] Capital of Mauritania. 18°N 16°W (p. RA22)

O

Oman [oh•MAHN] Country on the Arabian Sea and the Gulf of Oman. (p. RA25)

Oslo [AHZ•loh] Capital of Norway. 60°N 11°E (p. RA18)

Ottawa [AH•tuh•wuh] Capital of Canada. 45°N 76°W (p. RA13)

Ouagadougou [WAH•gah•DOO•goo] Capital of Burkina Faso. 12°N 2°W (p. RA22)

P

Pakistan [PA•kih•STAN] South Asian country northwest of India on the Arabian Sea. (p. RA26)

Palau [puh•LOW) Island country in the Pacific Ocean. 7°N 135°E (p. RA30)

Panama [PA•nuh•MAH] Central American country on the Isthmus of Panama. (p. RA15)

Panama Capital of Panama. 9°N 79°W (p. RA15)

Papua New Guinea [PA•pyu•wuh NOO GIH•nee] Island country in the Pacific Ocean north of Australia. 7°S 142°E (p. RA30)

Paraguay [PAR•uh•GWY] South American country northeast of Argentina. (p. RA16)

Paramaribo [PAH•rah•MAH•ree•boh] Capital of Suriname. 6°N 55°W (p. RA16)

Paris Capital of France. 49°N 2°E (p. RA18)

Persian [PUHR•zhuhn] **Gulf** Arm of the Arabian Sea between Iran and Saudi Arabia. (p. RA25)

Peru [puh•ROO] South American country south of Ecuador and Colombia. (p. RA16)

Philippines [FIH•luh•PEENZ] Island country in the Pacific Ocean southeast of China. (p. RA27)

Phnom Penh [puh•NAWM PEHN] Capital of Cambodia. 12°N 106°E (p. RA27)

Poland [POH•luhnd] Eastern European country on the Baltic Sea. (p. RA18)

Port-au-Prince [POHRT•oh•PRIHNS] Capital of Haiti. 19°N 72°W (p. RA15)

Port Moresby [MOHRZ•bee] Capital of Papua New Guinea. 10°S 147°E (p. RA30)

Port-of-Spain [SPAYN] Capital of Trinidad and Tobago. 11°N 62°W (p. RA15)

Porto-Novo [POHR•toh•NOH•voh] Capital of Benin. 7°N 3°E (p. RA22)

Portugal [POHR•chih•guhl] Country west of Spain on the Iberian Peninsula. (p. RA18)

Prague [PRAHG] Capital of the Czech Republic. 51°N 15°E (p. RA18)

Puerto Rico [PWEHR•toh REE•koh] Island in the Caribbean Sea; U.S. Commonwealth. (p. RA15)

P'yǒngyang [pee•AWNG•YAHNG] Capital of North Korea. 39°N 126°E (p. RA27)

Q

Qatar [KAH•tuhr] Country on the southwestern shore of the Persian Gulf. (p. RA25)

Quito [KEE•toh] Capital of Ecuador. 0° latitude 79°W (p. RA16)

R

Rabat [ruh•BAHT] Capital of Morocco. 34°N 7°W (p. RA22)

Reykjavík [RAY•kyah•VEEK] Capital of Iceland. 64°N 22°W (p. RA18)

Rhine [RYN] **River** River in western Europe that flows into the North Sea. (p. RA20)

Riga [REE•guh] Capital of Latvia. 57°N 24°E (p. RA19)

Rio Grande [REE•oh GRAND] River that forms part of the boundary between the United States and Mexico. (p. RA10)

Riyadh [ree•YAHD] Capital of Saudi Arabia. 25°N 47°E (p. RA25)

Rocky Mountains Mountain system in western North America. (p. RA7)

Romania [ru•MAY•nee•uh] Eastern European country east of Hungary. (p. RA19)

Rome Capital of Italy. 42°N 13°E (p. RA18)

Russia [RUH•shuh] Largest country in the world, covering parts of Europe and Asia. (pp. RA19, RA27)

Rwanda [ruh•WAHN•duh] East African country south of Uganda. 2°S 30°E (p. RA22)

S

Sahara [suh•HAR•uh] Desert region in northern Africa that is the largest hot desert in the world. (p. RA23)

Saint Lawrence [LAWR•uhns] River River that flows from Lake Ontario to the Atlantic Ocean and forms part of the boundary between the United States and Canada. (p. RA13)

Sanaa [sahn•AH] Capital of Yemen. 15°N 44°E (p. RA25)

San José [SAN hoh•ZAY] Capital of Costa Rica. 10°N 84°W (p. RA15)

San Marino [SAN muh•REE•noh] Small European country located on the Italian Peninsula. 44°N 13°E (p. RA18)

San Salvador [SAN SAL•vuh•DAWR] Capital of El Salvador. 14°N 89°W (p. RA14)

Santiago [SAN•tee•AH•goh] Capital of Chile. 33°S 71°W (p. RA16)

Santo Domingo [SAN•toh duh•MIHNG•goh] Capital of the Dominican Republic. 19°N 70°W (p. RA15)

São Tomé and Príncipe [sow too•MAY PREEN•see•pee] Small island country in the Gulf of Guinea off the coast of central Africa. 1°N 7°E (p. RA22)

Sarajevo [SAR•uh•YAY•voh] Capital of Bosnia and Herzegovina. 43°N 18°E (p. RA18)

Saudi Arabia [SOW•dee uh•RAY•bee•uh] Country on the Arabian Peninsula. (p. RA25)

Senegal [SEH•nih•GAWL] West African country on the Atlantic coast. (p. RA22)

Seoul [SOHL] Capital of South Korea. 38°N 127°E (p. RA27)

Serbia [SUHR•bee•uh] Eastern European country south of Hungary. (p. RA18)

Seychelles [say•SHEHL] Small island country in the Indian Ocean off eastern Africa. 6°S 56°E (p. RA22)

Sierra Leone [see•EHR•uh lee•OHN] West African country south of Guinea. (p. RA22)

Singapore [SIHNG•uh•POHR] Southeast Asian island country near tip of the Malay Peninsula. (p. RA27)

Skopje [SKAW•PYAY] Capital of the country of Macedonia. 42°N 21°E (p. RA19)

Slovakia [sloh•VAH•kee•uh] Eastern European country south of Poland. (p. RA18)

Slovenia [sloh•VEE•nee•uh] Southeastern European country south of Austria on the Adriatic Sea. (p. RA18)

Sofia [SOH•fee•uh] Capital of Bulgaria. 43°N 23°E (p. RA19)

Solomon [SAH•luh•muhn] Islands Island country in the Pacific Ocean northeast of Australia. (p. RA30)

Somalia [soh•MAH•lee•uh] East African country on the Gulf of Aden and the Indian Ocean. (p. RA22)

South Africa [A•frih•kuh] Country at the southern tip of Africa, officially the Republic of South Africa. (p. RA22)

South Korea [kuh•REE•uh] East Asian country on the Korean Peninsula between the Yellow Sea and the Sea of Japan. (p. RA27)

South Sudan [soo•DAN] East African country south of Sudan. (p. RA22)

Spain [SPAYN] Southern European country on the Iberian Peninsula. (p. RA18)

Sri Lanka [SREE LAHNG•kuh] Country in the Indian Ocean south of India, formerly called Ceylon. (p. RA26)

Stockholm [STAHK•HOHLM] Capital of Sweden. 59°N 18°E (p. RA18)

Sucre [SOO•kray] Constitutional capital of Bolivia. 19°S 65°W (p. RA16)

Sudan [soo•DAN] East African country south of Egypt. (p. RA22)

Suriname [SUR•uh•NAH•muh] South American country between Guyana and French Guiana. (p. RA16)

Suva [SOO•vah] Capital of the Fiji Islands. 18°S 177°E (p. RA30)

Swaziland [SWAH•zee•land] Southern African country west of Mozambique, almost entirely within the Republic of South Africa. (p. RA22)

Sweden Northern European country on the eastern side of the Scandinavian Peninsula. (p. RA18)

Switzerland [SWIHT•suhr•luhnd] European country in the Alps south of Germany. (p. RA18)

Syria [SIHR•ee•uh] Southwest Asian country on the east side of the Mediterranean Sea. (p. RA24)

T

Taipei [TY•PAY] Capital of Taiwan. 25°N 122°E (p. RA27)

Taiwan [TY•WAHN] Island country off the southeast coast of China; the seat of the Chinese Nationalist government. (p. RA27)

Tajikistan [tah•JIH•kih•STAN] Central Asian country east of Turkmenistan. (p. RA26)

Tallinn [TA•luhn] Capital of Estonia. 59°N 25°E (p. RA19)

Tanzania [TAN•zuh•NEE•uh] East African country south of Kenya. (p. RA22)

Tashkent [tash•KEHNT] Capital of Uzbekistan. 41°N 69°E (p. RA26)

Tbilisi [tuh•bih•LEE•see] Capital of the Republic of Georgia. 42°N 45°E (p. RA26)

Tegucigalpa [tay•GOO•see•GAHL•pah] Capital of Honduras. 14°N 87°W (p. RA14)

Tehran [TAY•uh•RAN] Capital of Iran. 36°N 52°E (p. RA25)

Thailand [TY•LAND] Southeast Asian country east of Myanmar. 17°N 101°E (p. RA27)

Thimphu [thihm•POO] Capital of Bhutan. 28°N 90°E (p. RA27)

Tigris [TY•gruhs] **River** River in southeastern Turkey and Iraq that merges with the Euphrates River. (p. RA25)

Tiranë [tih•RAH•nuh] Capital of Albania. 42°N 20°E (p. RA18)

Togo [TOH•goh] West African country between Benin and Ghana on the Gulf of Guinea. (p. RA22)

Tokyo [TOH•kee•OH] Capital of Japan. 36°N 140°E (p. RA27)

Trinidad and Tobago [TRIH•nuh•DAD tuh•BAY•goh] Island country near Venezuela between the Atlantic Ocean and the Caribbean Sea. (p. RA15)

Tripoli [TRIH•puh•lee] Capital of Libya. 33°N 13°E (p. RA22)

Tshwane [ch•WAH•nay] Executive capital of South Africa. 26°S 28°E (p. RA22)

Tunis [TOO•nuhs] Capital of Tunisia. 37°N 10°E (p. RA22)

Tunisia [too•NEE•zhuh] North African country on the Mediterranean Sea between Libya and Algeria. (p. RA22)

Turkey [TUHR•kee] Country in southeastern Europe and western Asia. (p. RA24)

Turkmenistan [tuhrk•MEH•nuh•STAN] Central Asian country on the Caspian Sea. (p. RA25)

U

Uganda [yoo•GAHN•dah] East African country south of Sudan. (p. RA22)

Ukraine [yoo•KRAYN] Eastern European country west of Russia on the Black Sea. (p. RA25)

Ulaanbaatar [oo•LAHN•BAH•TAWR] Capital of Mongolia. 48°N 107°E (p. RA27)

United Arab Emirates [EH•muh•ruhts] Country made up of seven states on the eastern side of the Arabian Peninsula. (p. RA25)

United Kingdom Western European island country made up of England, Scotland, Wales, and Northern Ireland. (p. RA18)

United States of America Country in North America made up of 50 states, mostly between Canada and Mexico. (p. RA8)

Uruguay [YUR•uh•GWAY] South American country south of Brazil on the Atlantic Ocean. (p. RA16)

Uzbekistan [uz•BEH•kih•STAN] Central Asian country south of Kazakhstan. (p. RA25)

V

Vanuatu [VAN•WAH•TOO] Country made up of islands in the Pacific Ocean east of Australia. (p. RA30)

Vatican [VA•tih•kuhn] **City** Headquarters of the Roman Catholic Church, located in the city of Rome in Italy. 42°N 13°E (p. RA18)

Venezuela [VEH•nuh•ZWAY•luh] South American country on the Caribbean Sea between Colombia and Guyana. (p. RA16)

Vienna [vee•EH•nuh] Capital of Austria. 48°N 16°E (p. RA18)

Vientiane [vyehn•TYAHN] Capital of Laos. 18°N 103°E (p. RA27)

Vietnam [vee•EHT•NAHM] Southeast Asian country east of Laos and Cambodia. (p. RA27)

Vilnius [VIL•nee•uhs] Capital of Lithuania. 55°N 25°E (p. RA19)

W

Warsaw Capital of Poland. 52°N 21°E (p. RA19)

Washington, D.C. Capital of the United States, in the District of Columbia. 39°N 77°W (p. RA8)

Wellington [WEH•lihng•tuhn] Capital of New Zealand. 41°S 175°E (p. RA30)

West Indies Caribbean islands between North America and South America. (p. RA15)

Windhoek [VIHNT•HUK] Capital of Namibia. 22°S 17°E (p. RA22)

Y

Yamoussoukro [YAH•MOO•SOO•kroh] Second capital of Côte d'Ivoire. 7°N 6°W (p. RA22)

Yangon [YAHNG•GOHN] City in Myanmar; formerly called Rangoon. 17°N 96°E (p. RA27)

Yaoundé [yown•DAY] Capital of Cameroon. 4°N 12°E (p. RA22)

Yemen [YEH•muhn] Country south of Saudi Arabia on the Arabian Peninsula. (p. RA25)

Yerevan [YEHR•uh•VAHN] Capital of Armenia. 40°N 44°E (p. RA25)

Z

Zagreb [ZAH•GREHB] Capital of Croatia. 46°N 16°E (p. RA18)

Zambia [ZAM•bee•uh] Southern African country north of Zimbabwe. (p. RA22)

Zimbabwe [zihm•BAH•bway] Southern African country northeast of Botswana. (p. RA22)

GLOSSARY/GLOSARIO

- Content vocabulary words are words that relate to world geography content.
- Words that have an asterisk (*) are academic vocabulary. They help you understand your school subjects.
- All vocabulary words are **boldfaced** or **highlighted in yellow** in your textbook.

aboriginal • autonomy

ENGLISH — A — ESPAÑOL

ENGLISH	ESPAÑOL
aboriginal a native people (p. 184)	**aborigen** persona nativa (pág. 184)
absolute location the exact location of something (p. 21)	**localización absoluta** ubicación exacta de algo (pág. 21)
*access a way to reach a distant area (p. 183)	***acceso** vía para llegar a un lugar distante (pág. 183)
*accurate without mistakes or errors (p. 44)	***exacto** sin faltas o errores (pág. 44)
*achievement a great accomplishment due to hard work (pp. 372–73)	***logro** consecución importante que resulta de un trabajo arduo (págs. 372–73)
acid rain rain that contains harmful amounts of poisons due to pollution (p. 65)	**lluvia ácida** lluvia que contiene cantidades nocivas de venenos debido a la polución (pág. 65)
*adapt to change a trait in order to survive (p. 336)	***adaptar** cambiar un rasgo para sobrevivir (pág. 336)
aerospace the industry that makes vehicles that travel in the air and in outer space (p. 170)	**aeroespacial** industria que construye vehículos que viajan por el aire y el espacio exterior (pág. 170)
agribusiness an industry based on huge farms that rely on machines and mass-production methods (p. 170)	**agronegocio** industria basada en granjas extensas que dependen de máquinas y técnicas de producción masiva (pág. 170)
agriculture the practice of growing crops and raising livestock (p. 129)	**agricultura** actividad que consiste en cultivar la tierra y criar ganado (pág. 129)
altiplano the high plains (p. 299)	**altiplano** meseta elevada (pág. 299)
altitude the height above sea level (p. 301)	**altitud** altura sobre el nivel del mar (pág. 301)
annex to declare ownership of an area (p. 159)	**anexionar** declarar la propiedad de un territorio (pág. 159)
*annual yearly or each year (p. 165)	***anual** cada año (pág. 165)
archipelago a group of islands (p. 181)	**archipiélago** grupo de islas (pág. 181)
*area a geographic location (p. 241)	***área** territorio geográfico (pág. 241)
atmosphere the layer of gases surrounding Earth (p. 44)	**atmósfera** capa de gases que rodea la Tierra (pág. 44)
autonomy having independence from another country (p. 194)	**soberanía** independencia respecto de otro país (pág. 194)

axis an imaginary line that runs through Earth's center from the North Pole to the South Pole (p. 42)

eje línea imaginaria que atraviesa el centro de la Tierra desde el Polo Norte hasta el Polo Sur (pág. 42)

B

balkanization to break a country up into smaller units that are often hostile to one another (p. 397)

balcanizar fragmentar un país en partes más pequeñas, con frecuencia hostiles entre sí (pág. 397)

basin an area of land that is drained by a river and its tributaries (p. 241)

cuenca área de terreno drenada por un río y sus afluentes (pág. 241)

bauxite the mineral that is used to make aluminum (p. 206)

bauxita mineral metalífero que se utiliza para producir aluminio (pág. 206)

*behalf in the interest of (p. 87)

*a favor de en beneficio de (pág. 87)

*benefit an advantage (p. 203)

*beneficio ventaja (pág. 203)

bilingual able to use two languages (p. 191)

bilingüe que habla dos idiomas (pág. 191)

birthrate the number of babies born compared to the total number of people in a population at a given time (p. 72)

tasa de natalidad número de nacimientos comparado con el número total de habitantes de una población en un tiempo determinado (pág. 72)

brackish water that is somewhat salty (p. 398)

salobre agua algo salada (pág. 398)

C

canopy the umbrella-like covering formed by the tops of trees in a rain forest (p. 241)

manto cubierta en forma de sombrilla formada por las copas de los árboles en una selva tropical (pág. 241)

cash crop a farm product grown for sale (p. 213)

cultivo comercial producto agrícola que se cultiva para la venta (pág. 213)

caudillo a person who often ruled a Latin American country as a dictator and was generally a high-ranking military officer or a rich man (p. 213)

caudillo persona que gobernaba un país latinoamericano como dictador; por lo general, era un oficial de alto rango o un hombre pudiente (pág. 213)

central city the densely populated center of a metropolitan area (p. 257)

ciudad central centro densamente poblado de un área metropolitana (pág. 257)

chinook a dry wind that sometimes blows over the Great Plains in winter (p. 154)

chinook viento seco que sopla a veces sobre las Grandes Llanuras en invierno (pág. 154)

*circumstances conditions (p. 217)

*circunstancias condiciones (pág. 217)

city-state an independent political unit that includes a city and the surrounding area (p. 372)

ciudad-Estado unidad política independiente que incluye una ciudad y el área circundante (pág. 372)

civil rights the basic rights that belong to all citizens (p. 137)

derechos civiles los derechos fundamentales de todos los ciudadanos (pág. 137)

Glossary/Glosario

climate the average weather in an area over a long period of time (p. 23)

clima tiempo atmosférico promedio en una zona durante un periodo largo (pág. 23)

coastal plain the flat, lowland area along a coast (p. 121)

llanura litoral planicie de baja altitud que bordea la costa (pág. 121)

collectivization a system in which small farms were combined into huge, state-run enterprises with work done by mechanized techniques in the hopes of making farming more efficient and reducing the need for farmworkers (p. 406)

colectivización sistema en el cual pequeños granjeros se integran a empresas gigantescas administradas por el Estado, en las que el trabajo se realiza mediante métodos técnicos con la esperanza de hacer más eficiente la agricultura y reducir la demanda de trabajadores agrícolas (pág. 406)

colonialism a policy based on control of one country by another (p. 212)

colonialismo política que se basa en el control o dominio de un país sobre otro (pág. 212)

colonist a person sent to live in a new place and claim land for his or her home country (p. 126)

colonizador persona enviada a establecerse en un nuevo lugar y reclamar territorios para su país de origen (pág. 126)

Columbian Exchange the transfer of plants, animals, and people between Europe, Asia, and Africa on one side and the Americas on the other (p. 214)

intercambio colombino traslado de plantas, animales y personas entre Europa, Asia y África, de un lado, y América, del otro (pág. 214)

command economy an economy in which the means of production are publicly owned (p. 96)

economía planificada sistema económico en el que los medios de producción son de propiedad pública (pág. 96)

communism a system of government in which the government controls the ways of producing goods (p. 406)

comunismo forma de gobierno en la que el gobierno controla los modos de producción de los bienes (pág. 406)

compass rose the feature on a map that shows direction (p. 28)

rosa de los vientos convención de un mapa que señala la dirección (pág. 28)

*component a part of something (p. 23)

*componente parte de algo (pág. 23)

*comprise to make up (p. 179)

*incluir integrar (pág. 179)

compulsory mandatory; enforced (p. 255)

compulsivo obligatorio; forzoso (pág. 255)

condensation the result of water vapor changing to a liquid or a solid state (p. 64)

condensación cambio del vapor de agua a un estado líquido o sólido (pág. 64)

*conflict a serious disagreement (p. 283)

*conflicto desacuerdo grave (pág. 283)

coniferous describing evergreen trees that produce cones to hold seeds and that have needles instead of leaves (p. 179)

coníferas árboles perennes que producen conos para contener las semillas y tienen agujas en vez de hojas (pág. 179)

conquistador a Spanish explorer of the early Americas (p. 211)

conquistador explorador español de América en sus inicios (pág. 211)

*contemporary of the present time; modern (p. 315)

*contemporáneo perteneciente al tiempo presente; moderno (pág. 315)

contiguous joined together inside a common boundary (p. 149)

contiguo unido dentro de un límite común (pág. 149)

continent a large, unbroken mass of land (p. 52)

continente extensión de tierra grande e ininterrumpida (pág. 52)

Continental Divide an imaginary line through the Rocky Mountains that separates rivers that flow west from rivers that flow east (p. 152)

divisoria continental línea imaginaria que atraviesa las montañas Rocosas para separar los ríos que fluyen hacia el oeste de los que fluyen hacia el este (pág. 152)

continental shelf the part of a continent that extends into the ocean in a plateau, then drops sharply to the ocean floor (p. 60)

plataforma continental parte de un continente que se adentra en el océano en forma de meseta y luego desciende abruptamente hasta el fondo oceánico (pág. 60)

*contribution something that is given (p. 382)

*contribución algo que se entrega (pág. 382)

*convert to change from one thing to another (p. 27)

*convertir cambiar de una cosa a otra (pág. 27)

*cooperate to work together (pp. 350–51)

*cooperar trabajar en unión (págs. 350–51)

cordillera a region of parallel mountain chains (pp. 149, 299)

cordillera región de cadenas montañosas paralelas (págs. 149, 299)

coup an action in which a group of individuals seize control of a government (p. 311)

golpe (de Estado) acción mediante la cual un grupo de individuos se apodera del control de un gobierno (pág. 311)

*create to make (p. 151)

*crear hacer (pág. 151)

Creole a group of languages developed by enslaved people on colonial plantations that is a mixture of French, Spanish, and African (p. 289)

Criollo grupo de lenguas desarrollado por las personas esclavizadas en las plantaciones colonials, que consiste en una mezcla de francés, espanol y africano (pág. 289)

cultural region a geographic area in which people have certain traits in common (p. 86)

región cultural área geográfica donde las personas tienen ciertos rasgos comunes (pág. 86)

culture the set of beliefs, behaviors, and traits shared by a group of people (p. 82)

cultura conjunto de creencias, comportamientos y rasgos compartidos por un grupo de personas (pág. 82)

*currency the paper money and coins in circulation (p. 101)

*moneda dinero en billetes y monedas en circulación (pág. 101)

czar the title given to an emperor of Russia's past (p. 403)

zar título dado a un emperador de Rusia en el pasado (pág. 403)

D

*data information (p. 158)

*dato información (pág. 158)

death rate the number of deaths compared to the total number of people in a population at a given time (p. 72)

tasa de mortalidad número de defunciones comparado con el número total de habitantes de una población en un tiempo determinado (pág. 72)

deciduous describing trees that shed their leaves in the autumn (p. 179)

caducifolios árboles que pierden sus hojas en el otoño (pág. 179)

*decline to reduce in number (p. 170)

*declinar reducirse en número (pág. 170)

delta an area where sand, silt, clay, or gravel is dropped at the mouth of a river (p. 62)

delta área donde se deposita arena, sedimento, lodo o gravilla en la desembocadura de un río (pág. 62)

democracy a type of government run by the people (p. 86)

democracia tipo de gobierno dirigido por el pueblo (pág. 86)

dependence too much reliance (p. 218)

desalinization a process that makes salt water safe to drink (p. 61)

*despite in spite of (p. 276)

devolution the process by which a large, centralized government gives power away to smaller, local governments (p. 415)

dialect a regional variety of a language with unique features, such as vocabulary, grammar, or pronunciation (p. 83)

dictatorship a form of government in which one person has absolute power to rule and control the government, the people, and the economy (p. 87)

dike a large barrier built to keep out water (p. 336)

*distort to change something so it is no longer accurate (p. 27)

*diverse composed of many distinct and different parts (p. 256)

dormant still capable of erupting but showing no signs of activity (p. 208)

doubling time the number of years it takes a population to double in size based on its current growth rate (p. 73)

Dust Bowl the southern Great Plains during the severe drought of the 1930s (p. 167)

*dynamic always changing (p. 20)

dependencia confianza excesiva (pág. 218)

desalinización proceso que elimina la sal del agua para hacerla potable (pág. 61)

*a pesar de no obstante (pág. 276)

autonomía proceso mediante el cual un gran gobierno centralizado cede poder a gobiernos locales menores (pág. 415)

dialecto variedad regional de una lengua con características únicas, como vocabulario, gramática o pronunciación (pág. 83)

dictadura forma de gobierno en la que una persona detenta el poder absoluto para mandar y controlar al gobierno, el pueblo y la economía (pág. 87)

dique barrera grande construida para no dejar pasar el agua (pág. 336)

*distorsionar cambiar algo de modo que ya no es correcto (pág. 27)

*diverso compuesto de muchas partes distintivas y diferentes (pág. 256)

inactivo que aún es capaz de entrar en erupción pero no muestra señales de actividad (pág. 208)

tiempo de duplicación número de años que le toma a una población doblar su tamaño con base en la tasa de crecimiento actual (pág. 73)

Dust Bowl las Grandes Llanuras meridionales durante la fuerte sequía de la década de 1930 (pág. 167)

*dinámico en permanente cambio (pág. 20)

E

earthquake an event in which the ground shakes or trembles, brought about by the collision of tectonic plates (p. 54)

economic system how a society decides on the ownership and distribution of its economic resources (p. 96)

elevation the measurement of how much above or below sea level a place is (p. 29)

emancipate to make free (p. 254)

terremoto suceso en el cual el suelo se agita o tiembla como consecuencia de la colisión de placas tectónicas (pág. 54)

sistema económico la forma en que una sociedad decide la propiedad y distribución de sus recursos económicos (pág. 96)

elevación medida de cuánto más alto o más bajo está un lugar respecto del nivel del mar (pág. 29)

emancipar liberar (pág. 254)

emigrate to leave one's home to live in another place (p. 78)

encomienda the Spanish system of enslaving Native Americans and making them practice Christianity (p. 281)

environment the natural surroundings of a place (p. 23)

Equator a line of latitude that runs around the middle of Earth (p. 21)

equinox one of two days each year when the sun is directly overhead at the Equator (p. 46)

erosion the process by which weathered bits of rock are moved elsewhere by water, wind, or ice (p. 55)

escarpment a steep cliff at the edge of a plateau with a lowland area below (p. 242)

*establish to start (p. 157)

estuary an area where river currents and the ocean tide meet (p. 301)

ethanol a liquid fuel made in part from plants (p. 155)

ethnic group a group of people with a common racial, national, tribal, religious, or cultural background (p. 83)

evaporation the change of liquid water to water vapor (p. 63)

*eventually at a later time (p. 185)

*exceed to go beyond a limit (pp. 274–75)

export to send a product produced in one country to another country (p. 99)

extinct describing a particular kind of plant or animal that has disappeared completely from Earth (p. 160); describing a volcano that is no longer able to erupt (p. 208)

*extract to remove or take out (p. 249)

emigrar abandonar el hogar propio para vivir en otro lugar (pág. 78)

encomienda sistema español de esclavizar a los indígenas americanos y obligarlos a profesar el cristianismo (pág. 281)

medioambiente entorno natural de un lugar (pág. 23)

ecuador línea de latitud que atraviesa la mitad de la Tierra (pág. 21)

equinoccio uno de dos días al año cuando el sol se halla situado directamente sobre el ecuador (pág. 46)

erosión proceso por el cual fragmentos desgastados de rocas son llevados a otra parte por acción del agua, el viento o el hielo (pág. 55)

escarpado acantilado pendiente, al borde de una meseta, que tiene debajo un área de tierras bajas (pág. 242)

*establecer comenzar (pág. 157)

estuario área donde convergen corrientes fluviales y la marea oceánica (pág. 301)

etanol combustible líquido que se fabrica a partir de vegetales (pág. 155)

grupo étnico grupo de personas con un antecedente racial, nacional, tribal, religioso o cultural común (pág. 83)

evaporación cambio del agua en estado líquido a vapor (pág. 63)

*finalmente en un tiempo posterior (pág. 185)

*exceder traspasar un límite (págs. 274–75)

exportar enviar un bien producido en un país a otro país (pág. 99)

extinto espécimen específico de una planta o un animal que ha desaparecido por completo de la Tierra (pág. 160); volcán que ya no puede entrar en erupción (pág. 208)

*extraer remover o sacar (pág. 249)

F

*factor a cause (p. 416)

*factor causa (pág. 416)

Glossary/Glosario

fall line the area where waterfalls flow from higher to lower ground (p. 122)

línea de descenso área donde las cascadas fluyen de un terreno más alto a uno más bajo (pág. 122)

fault a place where two tectonic plates grind against each other (p. 54)

falla lugar donde dos placas tectónicas chocan entre sí (pág. 54)

favela an overcrowded city slum in Brazil (p. 257)

favela tugurio urbano superpoblado de Brasil (pág. 257)

*feature a noteworthy characteristic (pp. 210–11)

*rasgo característica notable (págs. 210–11)

feudalism the political and social system in which kings gave land to nobles in exchange for the nobles' promise to serve them; those nobles provided military service as knights for the king (p. 343)

feudalismo sistema social y político en el cual los reyes entregaban tierras a los nobles, que a cambio prometían servirles; estos nobles proveían de servicio militar al rey como caballeros (pág. 343)

fishery an area where fish come to feed in huge numbers (p. 182)

pesquería zona donde los peces llegan a alimentarse en gran número (pág. 182)

fjord a narrow, U-shaped coastal valley with steep sides formed by the action of glaciers (p. 368)

fiordo valle costero estrecho, en forma de U con laderas escarpadas, formado por la acción de glaciares (pág. 368)

free trade arrangement whereby a group of countries decides to set little or no tariffs or quotas (p. 100)

libre comercio acuerdo por el cual un grupo de países decide imponer aranceles bajos a las cuotas o no fija ningún arancel (pág. 100)

free-trade zone an area where trade barriers between countries are relaxed or lowered (p. 219)

zona de libre comercio área donde las barreras comerciales entre los países se distienden o reducen (pág. 219)

frontier a region just beyond the edge of a settled area (p. 158)

frontera región inmediatamente posterior al borde de un área poblada (pág. 158)

G

genocide the mass murder of people from a particular ethnic group (p. 405)

genocidio asesinato masivo de personas de un grupo étnico específico (pág. 405)

geography the study of Earth and its people, places, and environments (p. 18)

geografía estudio de la Tierra y de sus gentes, lugares y entornos (pág. 18)

glaciation the process of becoming covered by glaciers (p. 367)

glaciación proceso en el cual los glaciares cubren zonas amplias del planeta (pág. 367)

glacier a large body of ice that moves slowly across land (p. 56)

glaciar masa de hielo enorme que se mueve lentamente sobre la tierra (pág. 56)

globalization the process by which nations, cultures, and economies become mixed (p. 89)

globalización proceso mediante el cual naciones, culturas y economías se integran (pág. 89)

granary a building used to store harvested grain (p. 188)

granero edificación en la cual se almacena el grano cosechado (pág. 188)

gross domestic product (GDP) the total dollar value of all final goods and services produced in a country during a single year (p. 98)

producto interno bruto (PIB) valor total en dólares de todos los bienes y servicios finales producidos en un país durante un año (pág. 98)

groundwater the water contained inside Earth's crust (p. 61)

agua subterránea agua contenida en el interior de la corteza terrestre (pág. 61)

guerrilla a member of a small, defensive force of irregular soldiers (p. 309)

guerrillero miembro de una fuerza pequeña y defensiva de soldados irregulares (pág. 309)

H

hacienda a large estate (p. 281)

hacienda gran propiedad rural (pág. 281)

hemisphere each half of Earth (p. 26)

hemisferio cada mitad de la Tierra (pág. 26)

*hierarchy a ruling body arranged by rank or class (p. 307)

*jerarquía cuerpo de gobierno organizado por rango o clase (pág. 307)

hinterland an inland area that is remote from the urban areas of a country (p. 256)

hinterland zona interior distante de las áreas urbanas de un país (pág. 256)

Holocaust the mass killing of 6 million European Jews by Germany's Nazi leaders during World War II (p. 348)

Holocausto exterminio masivo de 6 millones de judíos europeos ejecutado por los líderes nazis de Alemania durante la Segunda Guerra Mundial (pág. 348)

homogeneous made up of many things that are the same (p. 380)

homogéneo compuesto por muchas cosas iguales (pág. 380)

human rights the rights belonging to all individuals (p. 87)

derechos humanos los derechos que tienen todos los individuos (pág. 87)

hurricane a storm with strong winds and heavy rains (p. 122)

huracán tormenta con vientos fuertes y lluvias copiosas (pág. 122)

I

immigrate to enter and live in a new country (p. 78)

inmigrar entrar a un nuevo país y vivir allí (pág. 78)

immunity the ability to resist infection by a particular disease (p. 281)

inmunidad capacidad de resistir la infección provocada por una enfermedad específica (pág. 281)

*impact the effect or influence (pp. 312–13)

*impacto efecto o influencia (págs. 312–13)

import when a country brings in a product from another country (p. 99)

importación cuando un país ingresa un producto de otro país (pág. 99)

indigenous living or existing naturally in a particular place (p. 125)

nativo que vive o existe de modo natural en un lugar específico (pág. 125)

Glossary/Glosario

industrialized describing a country in which manufacturing is a primary economic activity (p. 346)

industry the manufacturing and making of products to sell (p. 130)

***inevitable** sure to happen (p. 407)

inflation a sharp increase in the price of goods, sometimes caused by a shortage of goods (p. 410)

***initiate** to begin (p. 218)

***intense** strong (p. 54)

irrigation the process of collecting water and using it to water crops (p. 153)

***isolate** to make separate from others (p. 125)

isthmus a narrow strip of land that connects two larger land areas (p. 59)

industrializado país en el cual la manufactura es la principal actividad económica (pág. 346)

industria manufactura y fabricación de bienes para la venta (pág. 130)

***inevitable** que sucederá con certeza (pág. 407)

inflación incremento drástico en el precio de los bienes, a veces ocasionado por su escasez (pág. 410)

***iniciar** comenzar (pág. 218)

***intenso** poderoso (pág. 54)

irrigación proceso de recolección del agua para regar los cultivos (pág. 153)

***aislar** separar de otros (pág. 125)

istmo franja estrecha de tierra que conecta dos áreas de tierra más grandes (pág. 59)

K

key the feature on a map that explains the symbols, colors, and lines used on the map (p. 28)

clave elemento de un mapa que explica los símbolos, colores y líneas usados en este (pág. 28)

L

landform a natural feature found on land (p. 23)

landscape the portions of Earth's surface that can be viewed at one time from a location (p. 19)

latitude the lines on a map that run east to west (p. 21)

levee a raised riverbank used to control flooding (p. 120)

lock a gated passageway used to raise or lower boats in a waterway (p. 119)

longitude the lines on a map that run north to south (p. 21)

longship a ship with oars and a sail used by the Vikings (p. 374)

accidente geográfico formación natural que se encuentra sobre la tierra (pág. 23)

paisaje partes de la superficie terrestre que se pueden observar a un mismo tiempo desde una ubicación (pág. 19)

latitud líneas sobre un mapa que van de este a oeste (pág. 21)

dique ribera elevada que sirve para controlar las inundaciones (pág. 120)

esclusa compartimento con puertas que se utiliza para subir o bajar los barcos en un canal (pág. 119)

longitud líneas sobre un mapa que van de norte a sur (pág. 21)

drakkar barco con remos y velas que utilizaban los vikingos (pág. 374)

M

Manifest Destiny the idea that it was the right of Americans to expand westward to the Pacific Ocean (p. 158)

Destino Manifiesto ideología según la cual los estadounidenses tenían derecho a expandirse al oeste hacia el océano Pacífico (pág. 158)

map projection one of several systems used to represent the round Earth on a flat map (p. 28)

proyección cartográfica uno de los varios sistemas que se usan para representar la esfera terrestre en un mapa plano (pág. 28)

maquiladora a foreign-owned factory where workers assemble parts (p. 216)

maquiladora fábrica de propiedad extranjera donde los obreros ensamblan partes (pág. 216)

market economy an economy in which most of the means of production are privately owned (p. 96)

economía de mercado economía en la cual la mayoría de los medios de producción son de propiedad privada (pág. 96)

*mature fully grown and developed as an adult; also refers to older adults (p. 72)

*maduro adulto plenamente crecido y desarrollado; también se refiere a los adultos mayores (pág. 72)

megalopolis a huge city or cluster of cities with an extremely large population (p. 80)

megalópolis ciudad enorme o cúmulo de ciudades que tienen una población extremadamente grande (pág. 80)

Métis the child of a French person and a native person (p. 187)

métis hijo de un francés y una indígena (pág. 187)

metropolitan having to do with a large city (p. 132); an area that includes a city and its surrounding suburbs (pp. 190; 257)

metropolitano(a) relativo a una ciudad grande (pág. 132); área que incluye una ciudad y los suburbios que la rodean (págs. 190; 257)

Middle Ages the period in European history from about A.D. 500 to about 1450 (p. 343)

Edad Media periodo de la historia europea que abarca aproximadamente del año 500 al 1450 (pág. 343)

*migrate to move to an area to settle (pp. 185; 288)

*migrar trasladarse a un lugar para establecerse allí (págs. 185; 288)

mission a Catholic-based community in the west (p. 157)

misión comunidad católica del Oeste (pág. 157)

mixed economy an economy in which parts of the economy are privately owned and parts are owned by the government (p. 96)

economía mixta economía en la cual unos sectores son de propiedad privada y otros son de propiedad del gobierno (pág. 96)

monarchy the system of government in which a country is ruled by a king or queen (p. 87)

monarquía sistema de gobierno en el que un rey o una reina gobiernan un país (pág. 87)

Mormon a member of the Church of Jesus Christ of Latter Day Saints (p. 167)

mormón miembro de la Iglesia de Jesucristo de los Santos de los Últimos Días (pág. 167)

multinational a company that has locations in more than one country (p. 310)

multinacional compañía que tiene oficinas en más de un país (pág. 310)

mural a large painting on a wall (p. 217)

mural pintura de gran tamaño hecha sobre un muro (pág. 217)

Glossary/Glosario

N

national park a park that has been set aside for the public to enjoy for its great natural beauty (p. 155)

nomadic describes a way of life in which a person or group lives by moving from place to place (p. 156)

nonrenewable resources the resources that cannot be totally replaced (p. 95)

parque nacional parque destinado al público para que disfrute sus grandes bellezas naturales (pág. 155)

nómada forma de vida en la que una persona o grupo vive trasladándose de un lugar a otro (pág. 156)

recursos no renovables recursos que no se pueden reponer por completo (pág. 95)

O

*occupy to settle in a place (p. 184)

*occur to happen or take place (p. 244)

oligarch a member of a small ruling group that holds great power (p. 410)

orbit to circle around something (p. 42)

*ocupar establecerse en un lugar (pág. 184)

*ocurrir suceder o acontecer (pág. 244)

oligarca miembro de un pequeño grupo gobernante que detenta gran poder (pág. 410)

orbitar moverse en círculo alrededor de algo (pág. 42)

P

pagan someone who believes in more than one god or someone who has little or no religious belief (p. 374)

pampas the treeless grassland of Argentina and Uruguay (p. 242)

*parallel running side by side with something; following the same general course and direction (p. 121)

Parliament the national legislature of England (now the United Kingdom), consisting of the House of Lords and the House of Commons (p. 345)

peacekeeping sending trained members of the military to crisis spots to maintain peace and order (p. 193)

pilgrimage a journey to a sacred place (p. 343)

plain a large expanse of land that can be flat or have a gentle roll (p. 58)

plantation a large farm (p. 213)

plateau a flat area that rises above the surrounding land (p. 58)

pagano persona que cree en más de un dios o cuya creencia religiosa es escasa o nula (pág. 374)

pampas praderas sin árboles de Argentina y Uruguay (pág. 242)

*paralelo que corre lado a lado con algo; que sigue el mismo curso y dirección generales (pág. 121)

Parlamento asamblea legislativa nacional de Inglaterra (hoy Reino Unido) integrada por la Cámara de los Lores y la Cámara de los Comunes (pág. 345)

pacificación envío de miembros entrenados de las fuerzas armadas a sitios críticos para mantener la paz y el orden (pág. 193)

peregrinación viaje a un lugar sagrado (pág. 343)

llanura gran extensión de tierra plana o con ligeras ondulaciones (pág. 58)

plantación granja grande (pág. 213)

meseta área plana que se eleva por encima del terreno circundante (pág. 58)

polder the land reclaimed from building dikes and then draining the water from the land (p. 336)

pólder terreno ganado al mar a partir de la construcción de diques y el posterior desecado de la tierra (pág. 336)

population density the average number of people living within a square mile or a square kilometer (p. 76)

densidad de población número promedio de personas que habitan en una milla cuadrada o un kilómetro cuadrado (pág. 76)

population distribution the geographic pattern of where people live (p. 76)

distribución de la población patrón geográfico que muestra dónde habita la gente (pág. 76)

postindustrial describing an economy that is based on providing services rather than manufacturing (p. 357)

posindustrial economía que se basa en la prestación de servicios, no en la manufacturación (pág. 357)

precipitation the water that falls on the ground as rain, snow, sleet, hail, or mist (p. 48)

precipitación agua que cae al suelo en forma de lluvia, nieve, aguanieve, granizo o rocío (pág. 48)

Prime Meridian the starting point for measuring longitude (p. 21)

primer meridiano punto de partida para medir la longitud (pág. 21)

productivity the measurement of what is produced and what is required to produce it (p. 98)

productividad medición de lo que se produce y lo que se requiere para producirlo (pág. 98)

province an administrative unit similar to a state (p. 178)

provincia unidad administrativa similar a un estado (pág. 178)

pueblo a town built by the Pueblo people in the American Southwest (p. 156)

pueblo poblado construido por las tribus pueblo del sudeste estadounidense (pág. 156)

pueblo jóven shantytown with poor housing and little or no infrastructure built outside a large metropolitan area (p. 313)

pueblo jóven barrio marginal con viviendas precarias y poca o ninguna infraestructura, construido en las afueras de una gran área metropolitana (pág. 313)

R

rain forest a dense stand of trees and other vegetation that receives a great deal of precipitation each year (p. 241)

selva tropical formación densa de árboles y otra vegetación que recibe una gran cantidad de precipitación todos los años (pág. 241)

rain shadow an area that receives reduced rainfall because it is on the side of a mountain facing away from the ocean (p. 49)

sombra pluviométrica zona que recibe pocas precipitaciones porque se halla en la ladera de una montaña que está en el lado contrario al océano (pág. 49)

*ratio the relationship in amount or size between two or more things (p. 286)

*ratio relación en cantidad o tamaño entre dos o más cosas (pág. 286)

*rational reasonable (p. 375)

*racional razonable (pág. 375)

recession a time when many businesses close and people lose their jobs (p. 385)

recesión época en que muchos negocios cierran y las personas pierden sus empleos (pág. 385)

refugee a person who flees a country because of violence, war, persecution, or disaster (p. 78)

refugiado persona que huye de un país por la violencia, una guerra, una persecución o un desastre (pág. 78)

reggae a traditional Jamaican style of music that uses complex drum rhythms (p. 221)

reggae género musical tradicional de Jamaica que utiliza complejos ritmos de tambor (pág. 221)

region a group of places that are close to one another and that share some characteristics (p. 22)

región agrupación de lugares cercanos que comparten algunas características (pág. 22)

*regulate to control something (p. 351)

*regular controlar algo (pág. 351)

relative location the location of one place compared to another place (p. 20)

localización relativa la ubicación de un lugar comparada con la de otro (pág. 20)

relief the difference between the elevation of one feature and the elevation of another feature near it (p. 29)

relieve diferencia entre la elevación de una formación y la de otra formación cercana (pág. 29)

remittance the money sent back to the homeland by people who have gone somewhere else to work (p. 221)

remesa dinero enviado al país de origen por personas que se han ido a trabajar a otro lugar (pág. 221)

remote sensing the method of getting information from far away, such as deep below the ground (p. 32)

detección remota método para obtener información muy lejana, como de las profundidades del subsuelo (pág. 32)

Renaissance the period in Europe that began in Italy in the 1300s and lasted into the 1600s, during which art and learning flourished (p. 375)

Renacimiento periodo de Europa que comenzó en Italia en el siglo XII y finalizó en el siglo XV, durante el cual florecieron el arte y la cultura (pág. 375)

renewable resources a resource that can be totally replaced or is always available naturally (p. 95)

recursos renovables recursos que pueden reponerse totalmente o siempre se encuentran disponibles en la naturaleza (pág. 95)

representative democracy a form of democracy in which citizens elect government leaders to represent the people (p. 87)

democracia representativa forma de democracia en la que los ciudadanos eligen líderes de gobierno para que representen al pueblo (pág. 87)

reservation an area of land that has been set aside for Native Americans (p. 161)

reservación territorio que ha sido destinado a los indígenas americanos (pág. 161)

reserves a large amount of a resource that has not yet been tapped (p. 401)

reservas gran cantidad de un recurso que aún no ha sido explotada (pág. 401)

resource a material that can be used to produce crops or other products (p. 23)

recurso materia prima que se puede utilizar para obtener cultivos u otros productos (pág. 23)

*revenue the income generated by a business (p. 133)

*renta ingresos generados por un negocio (pág. 133)

revolution a complete trip of Earth around the sun (p. 42); a period of violent and sweeping change (p. 212)

revolución recorrido completo de la Tierra alrededor del Sol (pág. 42); periodo de cambio violento y radical (pág. 212)

Ring of Fire a long, narrow band of volcanoes surrounding the Pacific Ocean (p. 54)

Cinturón de Fuego banda larga y estrecha de volcanes que rodean el océano Pacífico (pág. 54)

rural describes an area that is lightly populated (p. 77)

rural área poco poblada (pág. 77)

Rust Belt the area of the Midwest, Mid-Atlantic, and New England where many factories closed during the 1980s (p. 139)

Rust Belt zona del Medio Oeste, Atlántico Medio y Nueva Inglaterra donde muchas fábricas se cerraron durante la década de 1980 (pág. 139)

Glossary/Glosario

S

scale the relationship between distances on the map and on Earth (p. 29)

scale bar the feature on a map that tells how a measured space on the map relates to the actual distance on Earth (p. 28)

scrubland land that is dry and hot in the summer and cool and wet in the winter (p. 370)

separatists a group that wants to break away from control by a dominant group (p. 194)

serf a farm laborer who could be bought and sold along with the land (p. 404)

service industry a type of business that provides services rather than products (p. 139)

shield a large area of relatively flat land made up of ancient, hard rock (p. 179)

*significant important (p. 151)

*similar having qualities in common (p. 203)

slash-and-burn agriculture a method of farming that involves cutting down trees and underbrush and burning the area to create a field for crops (p. 249)

smallpox an often-fatal disease that causes a rash and leaves marks on the skin (p. 308)

smelting the process of refining ore to create metal (p. 342)

solstice one of two days of the year when the sun reaches its northernmost or southernmost point (p. 45)

spatial Earth's features in terms of their places, shapes, and relationships to one another (p. 18)

*sphere a round shape like a ball (p. 26)

*stable staying in the same condition; not likely to change or fail (p. 285)

standard of living the level at which a person, group, or nation lives as measured by the extent to which it meets its needs (p. 98)

escala relación entre distancias en un mapa y en la Tierra (pág. 29)

escala numérica elemento cartográfico que muestra la relación entre un espacio medido sobre el mapa y la distancia real sobre la Tierra (pág. 28)

chaparral territorio seco y caliente en el verano, y frío y húmedo en el invierno (pág. 370)

separatista grupo que quiere sustraerse del control de un grupo dominante (pág. 194)

siervo trabajador agrícola que podía comprarse y venderse junto con la tierra (pág. 404)

industria de servicios tipo de negocio que provee servicios en vez de productos (pág. 139)

escudo extensa área de terreno relativamente plano formado por rocas duras y antiguas (pág. 179)

*significativo importante (pág. 151)

*similar que tiene cualidades en común (pág. 203)

agricultura de tala y quema método agrícola que consiste en talar árboles y rastrojos y quemar el área despejada para crear un campo de cultivo (pág. 249)

viruela enfermedad, por lo general mortal, que causa sarpullido y deja marcas en la piel (pág. 308)

fundición proceso mediante el cual se refinan minerales para producir metales (pág. 342)

solsticio uno de dos días al año cuando el sol alcanza su máxima declinación norte o sur (pág. 45)

espaciales características de la Tierra en cuanto a sus lugares, formas y relaciones entre sí (pág. 18)

*esfera figura redonda como una pelota (pág. 26)

*estable que permanece en la misma condición; algo que es improbable que cambie o decaiga (pág. 285)

estándar de vida nivel en que vive una persona, grupo o nación, medido según la capacidad de satisfacer sus necesidades (pág. 98)

staple a food that is eaten regularly (p. 210)

alimento básico alimento que se consume habitualmente (pág. 210)

steppe a partly dry grassland often found on the edge of a desert (p. 397)

estepa pradera parcialmente seca que se encuentra con frecuencia al borde de un desierto (pág. 397)

*__strategy__ a plan to solve a problem (p. 407)

*__estrategia__ plan para resolver un problema (pág. 407)

subregion a smaller part of a region (p. 116)

subregión parte más pequeña de una región (pág. 116)

surplus extra; more than needed (p. 210)

excedente sobrante; más de lo que se necesita (pág. 210)

sustainability the economic principle by which a country works to create conditions where all the natural resources for meeting the needs of society are available (p. 101)

sostenibilidad principio económico según el cual un país crea condiciones para que estén disponibles todos los recursos naturales que satisfacen las necesidades de la sociedad (pág. 101)

T

tariff a tax added to the price of goods that are imported (p. 290)

arancel impuesto añadido al precio de los productos importados (pág. 290)

technology any way that scientific discoveries are applied to practical use (p. 30)

tecnología cualquier forma en que los descubrimientos científicos se aplican para un uso práctico (pág. 30)

tectonic plate one of the 16 pieces of Earth's crust (p. 53)

placa tectónica uno de las 16 partes de la corteza terrestre (pág. 53)

territory the land administered by the national government (p. 178)

territorio tierra administrada por el gobierno nacional (pág. 178)

thematic map a map that shows specialized information (p. 30)

mapa temático mapa que muestra información especializada (pág. 30)

*__theory__ an explanation of why or how something happens (p. 345)

*__teoría__ explicación de por qué o cómo ocurre algo (pág. 345)

tierra caliente the warmest climate zone, located at lower elevations (p. 205)

tierra caliente la zona climática más cálida, ubicada en elevaciones bajas (pág. 205)

tierra fría a colder climate zone, located at higher elevations (p. 205)

tierra fría zona climática fría, ubicada entre elevaciones altas (pág. 205)

tierra templada a temperate climate zone, located at mid-level elevations (p. 205)

tierra templada zona de clima templado, ubicada entre elevaciones medias (pág. 205)

timberline the elevation above which it is too cold for trees to grow (p. 149)

límite forestal elevación por encima de la cual hace demasiado frío para que los árboles prosperen (pág. 149)

topsoil the fertile soil that crops depend on to grow (p. 168)

mantillo suelo fértil del cual dependen las plantas para crecer (pág. 168)

tourism the industry that provides services to people who are traveling for enjoyment (p. 133)

turismo industria que presta servicios a las personas que viajan por placer (pág. 133)

Glossary/Glosario

trade winds the winds that blow regularly in the Tropics (p. 277)

traditional economy an economy where resources are distributed mainly through families (p. 96)

transcontinental describing something that crosses a continent (p. 187)

*****transform** to change something completely (p. 64)

trawler a large fishing boat (p. 371)

trench a long, narrow, steep-sided cut on the ocean floor (p. 60)

tributary a small river that flows into a larger river (p. 119)

Tropics an area between the Tropic of Cancer and the Tropic of Capricorn that has generally warm temperatures because it receives the direct rays of the sun for much of the year (p. 243)

tsunami a giant ocean wave caused by volcanic eruptions or movement of the earth under the ocean floor (p. 54)

tundra a flat, treeless plain with permanently frozen ground (pp. 181; 369)

vientos alisios vientos que soplan regularmente en los trópicos (pág. 277)

economía tradicional economía en la que los recursos se distribuyen principalmente entre las familias (pág. 96)

transcontinental que atraviesa un continente (pág. 187)

*****transformar** cambiar algo por completo (pág. 64)

trainera barco pesquero grande (pág. 371)

fosa depresión larga, estrecha y profunda del fondo oceánico (pág. 60)

tributario río pequeño que desemboca en uno más grande (pág. 119)

trópicos zona entre el trópico de Cáncer y el trópico de Capricornio que generalmente tiene temperaturas cálidas porque recibe los rayos directos del sol la mayor parte del año (pág. 243)

tsunami gigantesca ola oceánica provocada por erupciones volcánicas o movimientos de la tierra bajo el lecho oceánico (pág. 54)

tundra llanura plana y sin vegetación cuyo suelo permanece helado (págs. 181; 369)

U

*****uniform** not varying across several parts (p. 369)

*****unique** unusual (p. 259)

upland the high land away from the coast of a country (p. 396)

urban describes an area that is densely populated (p. 77)

urbanization when a city grows larger and spreads into nearby areas (p. 80)

*****uniforme** que no cambia en varias partes (pág. 369)

*****único** inusual (pág. 259)

tierra alta tierra elevada de un país, alejada de la costa (pág. 396)

urbana área densamente poblada (pág. 77)

urbanización cuando una ciudad crece y se expande hacia las áreas adyacentes (pág. 80)

V

*****vary** to show differences between things (p. 191)

*****via** on the way through (pp. 190–91)

*****variar** mostrar diferencias entre cosas (pág. 191)

*****vía** en el camino hacia (págs. 190–91)

Glossary/Glosario

W

water cycle the process in which water is used and reused on Earth, including precipitation, collection, evaporation, and condensation (p. 63)

ciclo del agua proceso en el cual el agua se usa y reutiliza en la Tierra; incluye la precipitación, recolección, evaporación y condensación (pág. 63)

weathering the process by which Earth's surface is worn away by natural forces (p. 55)

meteorización proceso mediante el cual la superficie terrestre se deteriora por la acción de fuerzas naturales (pág. 55)

welfare capitalism a system in which the government is the main provider of support for the sick, the needy, and the retired (p. 384)

capitalismo de bienestar sistema en el cual el gobierno es el principal proveedor de ayuda para los enfermos, necesitados y jubilados (pág. 384)

Westerlies strong winds that blow from west to east (p. 338)

Vientos del oeste vientos fuertes que soplan de oeste a este (pág. 338)

Glossary/Glosario

Index

Index

Index

Index

Index

petroleum: in United States west of the Mississippi, 155
Phoenix, Arizona, 165
physical geography, 39–68; changing Earth, 52–57; land, 58–60; planet Earth, 42–51; water, 60–65. *See also entries for individual regions*
physical map, 29
physical systems, *c24*; Earth's, 44
Pico de Aneto, 335
pilgrimage, 343
Pinochet, Augusto (Chilean dictator), 311
Pisgah National Forest: waterfall in, *p122*
Pizarro, Francisco, 307, *p308*
place, *c24*; characteristics of, 19–20; as geography theme, 22
plains, 58; creation of, 56
Plains people, 157
plantation agriculture, 213, 252
plant life: in salt water, 61
plateau: defined, 58, 241; in western United States, 150
plate movements, 53–54
plate tectonics, Pacific coast mountains and, 149
Plato, 373
Platte River, 152
Plovdiv, Bulgaria: boulevard in, *p414*
Plymouth, Massachusetts, 126
Poland, 397, *m395*; as EU member, 417; mineral resources in, 401; miner in southern, *p400*; religion in, 413; Solidarity union in, 395, 408; Soviet army occupation of, 407; urban population of, 411; in Warsaw Pact, 407. *See also* Eastern Europe
polar climate, 49–50
polar ice caps, 61
polders, 336
political map, 29
pollution: air, in Mexico, 217; effects on Earth, 57; of lakes and rivers, *p65*; population growth and, 74–75
Popocateptl Volcano, *p204*
population. *See* **entries for specific regions**
population centers, 134
population changes, 77–81
population density, 76
population distribution, 76
population growth, 72–75; causes of, 72–73; challenges of, 74; effects on environment, 74; rates of, 73, 75
population movement, 77–81
population pyramid, *g73*
Po River, 368
Portland, Oregon, as Pacific port, 151

Portugal: conquest of Brazil, 250–51; as democracy, 377; as EU member, 385; soccer teams, 383; Tagus River in, 368; Treaty of Tordesillas and, 248. *See also* Southern Europe
Portuguese Empire, Rio de Janeiro as capital of, 253
Portuguese language, 259
postindustrial, 357
poverty: in Mexico, 218; population growth and, 74–75
Prague, Czech Republic, 411
Prairie Provinces, Canada, 180, 189
precipitation: defined, 48; evaporation and, 64
primate city, 81
Prime Meridian, 21, *c21*, 26, *c27*
Prince Edward Island, Canada, 179
Princip, Gavrilo, 405
productivity, 98
Protestant Reformation, 345, 352, 376, 380
provinces, 178
Provo, Utah, 165
Ptolemy, *p16*
Puccini, 382
pueblo, 156; ancient, near Taos, new Mexico, *p157*
Pueblo people, 156
Pueblos jóvenes, 313
Puerto Rico, 207, 208, *m201*; independence of, 215; Spanish colonies in, 214. *See also* Caribbean Islands
Puig, Manuel, 315
Push-pull factors for migration, 78–79
Putin, Vladimir, 411
Pyrenees mountains, 335, 367; skiing in Spain's, *p383*
Quebec, Canada, 179; in Dominion of Canada, 186; French settlement in, 185; Montreal and Quebec in province of, 191; rally against independence for, *p194*
Quebec Act, 186
Quechua language, 314
Quechuan family, *p318*
Queens (New York borough), 133
Quinn, Arthur, *q198*
quipu, 307, *p307*
Quito, Ecuador, 281, 288
Quitu people, 280
railroad: from the Mississippi to the Pacific, 160; Transcontinental, 187; Western Europe, 354–55
rainfall. *See* monsoon
rain forest, 264–67, *m267*; as biome, 50; climate and, 51; defined, 241. *See also* Amazon rain forest; tropical rain forest
rain shadow, 49, *c48*
rainwater, 64
recession, 385
refugees: defined, 78; Libyan, *p79*
reggae music, 221

region, 22, *c24*
relative location, 20–21
relief, on physical maps, 29
religion: Brazil, 259–60; Christian missions in colonial U.S., 157; culture and, 84; Eastern Europe and Western Russia, 413–14; eastern United States, 138; major world, *c84*; pagan, 374; population growth and, 75; Tropical North, 289; Western Europe, 352; west of the Mississippi River, 167. *See also entries for individual religions*
remittance, 221
remote sensing, 32
Renaissance: defined, 375; Italy as birthplace of, 381
renewable resources, 95
representative democracy, 87
reservations, Native American, 161
reserves, energy and mineral, 401
resources: defined, 23; nonrenewable, 95; renewable, 95; wants and, 94–95. *See also* mineral resources
revolution, 212; of Earth around the sun, 42–43
Revolutionary Armed Forces of Colombia (FARC), 291
Revolutionary War (U.S.), 127, 186
Reykjavík, Iceland, 371, 379
Rhine River, 337
Rhode Island: in New England subregion, 117, *m117*. *See also* United States, east of the Mississippi River
Rimsky-Korsakov, 414
Ring of Fire, *m40–41*; Andes mountains in, 299; defined, 54; Mexico and Central America in, 203, 208
Rio Bravo, 204, *p205*
Rio de Janeiro, Brazil, 243, 245, 253; Carnival in, 260; "Christ the Redeemer" statue, *p238*; favelas in, 257–58; Sugarloaf Mountain and Copacabana Beach in, *p257*
Río de la Plata, 301
Rio Grande River, 152, 204; Spanish settlements along, 157. *See also* Rio Bravo
rivers: freshwater, 62; liquid water in, 61; mouth of, 62; as natural boundaries, 120; in western United States, 152. *See also entries for individual rivers*
Riverside, California, 165
Robinho (Brazilian soccer player), *p237*
Rocky Mountains, 149, 152; Oregon Trail over, 159; resources in, 155; as vacation spot, 163. *See also* Canadian Rockies
Roman Catholic Church: Black Death and, 345; in Brazil, 259; in Eastern Europe, 413–14. *See also* Catholic Church
Roman Catholicism, 22
Romance languages, 352

Index

Index

McGraw-Hill Networks™ meets you anywhere—takes you everywhere. Go online at MHEonline.com.

Circle the globe, travel across time. How do you access networks?

1. Log on to the internet and go to MHEonline.com
2. Get your User Name and Password from your teacher and enter them.
3. Click on your networks book.
4. Select your chapter and lesson. Start networking.